P9-CKR-860

MyAccountingLab

Save Time.

Improve Results.

More than 3 million students have used a Pearson MyLab product to get a better grade.

MyAccountingLab is an all-in-one learning and testing environment for accounting. This easy-to-navigate site provides students with a variety of resources including:

- An interactive Pearson eText
- Audio and video material to view or listen to, whatever your learning style
- Personalized learning opportunities—YOU choose what, where, and when you want to study
- Self-assessment tests that create a personalized study plan to guide you on making the most efficient use of study time

To take advantage of all that *MyAccountingLab* has to offer, you will need an access code. If you do not already have an access code, you can buy one online at:

www.myaccountinglab.com

MyAccountingLab

Improve Your Grade

It's easy to prepare wisely with practice quizzes and tutorials.

MyAccountingLab helps you focus your efforts where they are needed. Know your strengths and weaknesses before your first in-class exam.

Go to www.myaccountinglab.com and follow the simple registration instructions on the Student Access Code Card provided with this text. Your unique access code is hidden there.

Save Time. Improve Results. www.myaccountinglab.com

Pearson eText

Pearson eText gives students access to the text whenever and wherever they have access to the internet. eText pages look exactly like the printed text, offering powerful new functionality for students and instructors.

Users can create notes, highlight text in different colours, create bookmarks, zoom, click hyperlinked words and phrases to view definitions, and choose single-page or two-page view.

Pearson eText allows for quick navigation using a table of contents and provides full-text search. The eText may also offer links to associated media files, enabling users to access videos, animations, or other activities as they read the text.

Personalized Learning!

In *MyAccountingLab* you are treated as an individual with specific learning needs.

The study and assessment resources that come with your textbook allow you to review content and develop what you need to know, on your own time, and at your own pace.

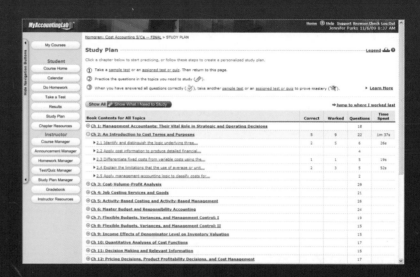

MyAccountingLab provides

- Quizzes with immediate grades
- A personalized study plan that tells you where to study based on your results
- A gradebook where you can find your grades to see your progress as the term unfolds
- Exercises and problems that correspond to those found in your text
- Help Me Solve This – a step-by-step tutorial tool that helps work through the problem material
- Animations that illustrate important text concepts including the Accounting Cycle
- Animated Demo Doc examples that guide you through specific examples
- Acadia/Pearson Business Insider Videos that contain interviews with industry executives featured in the text
- A section in your study plan for math review, covering the basics to help you in your accounting course
- A multimedia library containing your eText, Audio Chapter Summaries, Glossary Flashcards, Student PowerPoint Slides, Excel templates, and more

Save Time. Improve Results. www.myaccountinglab.com

ACCOUNTING

CANADIAN EIGHTH EDITION

CHARLES T. HORNGREN STANFORD UNIVERSITY

WALTER T. HARRISON, JR. BAYLOR UNIVERSITY

M. SUZANNE OLIVER NORTHWEST FLORIDA STATE COLLEGE

PETER R. NORWOOD LANGARA COLLEGE

JO-ANN L. JOHNSTON BRITISH COLUMBIA INSTITUTE OF TECHNOLOGY

Pearson Canada
Toronto

VOLUME ONE

Library and Archives Canada Cataloguing in Publication

Accounting / Charles T. Horngren ... [et al.]. — Canadian 8th ed.
  Canadian ed. published under title: Accounting / Charles T. Horngren,
  Walter T. Harrison, W. Morley Lemon; with Carol E. Dilworth.

Includes index.

ISBN 978-0-13-815601-5 (v. 1)—ISBN 978-0-13-815602-2 (v. 2).

  1. Accounting—Textbooks. 2. Managerial accounting—Textbooks.
I. Horngren, Charles T., 1926- II. Horngren, Charles T., 1926-. Accounting.

HF5636.A32 2011   657'.044   C2009-906520-7

Copyright © 2011, 2007, 2005, 2002, 1999, 1996, 1993, 1991 Pearson Canada Inc., Toronto, Ontario.

Pearson Prentice Hall. All rights reserved. This publication is protected by copyright and permission should be obtained from the publisher prior to any prohibited reproduction, storage in a retrieval system, or transmission in any form or by any means, electronic, mechanical, photocopying, recording, or likewise. For information regarding permission, write to the Permissions Department.

Original edition published by Pearson Education, Inc., Upper Saddle River, New Jersey, USA. Copyright © 2009 Pearson Education, Inc. This edition is authorized for sale only in Canada.

ISBN: 978-0-13-815601-5

Vice-President, Editorial Director: Gary Bennett
Editor-in-Chief: Nicole Lukach
Executive Marketing Manager: Cas Shields
Developmental Editor: Anita Smale
Production Editor: Lila Campbell
Copy Editor: Marg Bukta
Proofreader: Tom Gamblin
Production Coordinator: Andrea Falkenberg
Compositor: MPS Limited, A Macmillan Company
Photo and Permissions Researcher: Sandy Cooke
Art Director: Julia Hall
Cover and Interior Designer: Anthony Leung
Cover Image: Veer.com

1 2 3 4 5   14 13 12 11 10

Printed and bound in United States of America.

Photo Credits

1 Jupiter Unlimited; **51** AP Photo/Lisa Poole; **107** CP Photo/Larry MacDougal;
164 CP Photo/Darryl Dyck; **224** Shutterstock; **300** CP Photo/Larry MacDougal;
342 Photo by Ryan Nunn; **402** © Jim Craigmyle/Corbis; **450** Courtesy of Canadian Tire;
499 CP Photo/Larry MacDougal; **549** CP Photo/Jacques Boissinot

BRIEF Contents

Contents

*In each chapter, Assignment Material includes Questions, Starters, Exercises (including Serial and Challenge Exercises), Beyond the Numbers, an Ethical Issue, and Problems (Group A and B, and Challenge Problems).
**Extending Your Knowledge includes Decision Problems and Financial Statement Cases.

About the Authors

CHARLES T. HORNGREN is the Edmund W. Littlefield Professor of Accounting, Emeritus, at Stanford University. A graduate of Marquette University, he received his MBA from Harvard University and his PhD from the University of Chicago. He is also the recipient of honorary doctorates from Marquette University and DePaul University.

A Certified Public Accountant, Horngren served on the Accounting Principles Board for six years, the Financial Accounting Standards Board Advisory Council for five years, and the Council of the American Institute of Certified Public Accountants for three years. For six years, he served as a trustee of the Financial Accounting Foundation, which oversees the Financial Accounting Standards Board and the Government Accounting Standards Board.

Horngren is a member of the Accounting Hall of Fame.

A member of the American Accounting Association, Horngren has been its President and its Director of Research. He received its first annual Outstanding Accounting Educator Award.

The California Certified Public Accountants Foundation gave Horngren its Faculty Excellence Award and its Distinguished Professor Award. He is the first person to have received both awards.

The American Institute of Certified Public Accountants presented its first Outstanding Educator Award to Horngren.

Horngren was named Accountant of the Year, in Education, by the national professional accounting fraternity, Beta Alpha Psi.

Professor Horngren is also a member of the Institute of Management Accountants, from whom he has received its Distinguished Service Award. He was a member of the Institute's Board of Regents, which administers the Certified Management Accountant examinations.

Horngren is the author of other accounting books published by Pearson Prentice Hall: *Cost Accounting: A Managerial Emphasis*, Thirteenth Edition, 2008 (with Srikant Datar and George Foster); *Introduction to Financial Accounting*, Ninth Edition, 2006 (with Gary L. Sundem and John A. Elliott); *Introduction to Management Accounting*, Fourteenth Edition, 2008 (with Gary L. Sundem and William Stratton); *Financial Accounting*, Seventh Edition, 2008 (with Walter T. Harrison, Jr.).

Horngren is the Consulting Editor for Pearson Prentice Hall's Charles T. Horngren Series in Accounting.

WALTER T. HARRISON, JR. is Professor Emeritus of Accounting at the Hankamer School of Business, Baylor University. He received his BBA degree from Baylor University, his MS from Oklahoma State University, and his PhD from Michigan State University.

Professor Harrison, recipient of numerous teaching awards from student groups as well as from university administrators, has also taught at Cleveland State Community College, Michigan State University, the University of Texas, and Stanford University.

A member of the American Accounting Association and the American Institute of Certified Public Accountants, Professor Harrison has served as Chairman of the Financial Accounting Standards Committee of the American Accounting Association, on the Teaching/Curriculum Development Award Committee, on the Program Advisory Committee for Accounting Education and Teaching, and on the Notable Contributions to Accounting Literature Committee.

Professor Harrison has lectured in several foreign countries and published articles in numerous journals, including *Journal of Accounting Research, Journal of Accountancy, Journal of Accounting and Public Policy, Economic Consequences of Financial*

Accounting Standards, Accounting Horizons, Issues in Accounting Education, and *Journal of Law and Commerce*.

He is co-author of *Financial Accounting*, Seventh Edition, 2008 (with Charles T. Horngren), published by Pearson Prentice Hall. Professor Harrison has received scholarships, fellowships, and research grants or awards from PriceWaterhouse Coopers, Deloitte & Touche, the Ernst & Young Foundation, and the KPMG Foundation.

M. SUZANNE OLIVER is an associate professor of accounting at Northwest Florida State College in Niceville, Florida. She received her B.A. in Accounting Information Systems and her Masters in Accountancy from the University of West Florida.

Professor Oliver began her career in accounting in the tax department of a regional accounting firm, specializing in benefit plan administration. She has served as a software analyst for a national software development firm (CPASoftware) and as the Oracle fixed assets analyst for Spirit Energy, formerly part of Union Oil of California (Unocal). A Certified Public Accountant, Oliver is a member of the Florida Institute of Certified Public Accountants.

Professor Oliver has taught financial accounting, managerial accounting, intermediate accounting, tax accounting, accounting software applications, payroll accounting, auditing, accounting systems, advanced accounting, managerial finance, business math, and supervision. She has also taught pension continuing education classes for CPAs, and has developed and instructed online courses using MyAccountingLab, WebCT, and other proprietary software.

Professor Oliver lives in Niceville where she is a member of the First United Methodist Church with her husband Greg and son C.J.

PETER R. NORWOOD is an instructor in accounting and the chair of the Langara School of Management at Langara College in Vancouver. A graduate of the University of Alberta, he received his MBA from the University of Western Ontario. He is a Chartered Accountant, a Fellow of the Institute of Chartered Accountants of British Columbia, a Certified Management Accountant, and a Fellow of the Society of Management Accountants of Canada.

Before entering the academic community, Mr. Norwood worked in public practice and industry for over fifteen years. He is First Vice-President of the Institute of Chartered Accountants of British Columbia (President in 2010–2011) and a member of the board of the Chartered Accountants School of Business (CASB). He is chair of the Chartered Accountants Education Foundation for the British Columbia Institute of Chartered Accountants, for whom he has served on a variety of committees. Mr. Norwood is a past member of the Board of Evaluators of the Canadian Institute of Chartered Accountants. Mr. Norwood is also a sessional instructor in the Sauder School of Business, University of British Columbia. He is a past chair of the Langara College Foundation.

JO-ANN L. JOHNSTON is an instructor in accounting and financial planning in the Financial Management Department at the British Columbia Institute of Technology (BCIT). She obtained her Bachelor in Administrative Studies from British Columbia Open University, her Diploma of Technology in Financial Management from BCIT, and her MBA from Simon Fraser University. She is also a Certified General Accountant and recently completed the Canadian Securities Course.

Prior to entering the field of education, Mrs. Johnston worked in public practice and industry for over 10 years. She is a past member of the Board of Governors of the Certified General Accountants Association of British Columbia and has served on various committees for the Association. She was also a member of the Board of Directors for the BCIT Faculty and Staff Association, and served as Treasurer during that tenure. She currently serves as chair of the CGA Student Advisory Group and is a member of CGA-BC Education Foundation and the Strategic Planning Committee for the Certified General Accountants Association of British Columbia.

In addition to teaching duties and committee work for the British Columbia Institute of Technology, Mrs. Johnston is the financial officer for a family-owned business.

A Letter to Students

Students will "Get It" Anytime, Anywhere with *Accounting's* Student Learning System

Welcome to your introductory accounting course! Accounting is the language of business. Whether you intend to be an accountant or not, you owe it to yourself to develop your skills with this language so that you can give yourself a winning edge in your career.

As instructors, we know that you want to ace your accounting course, and we also know that the volume of material covered in introductory accounting can be overwhelming. To help you develop your skills and understanding of accounting principles—to help you "get it"—we created the *Accounting* **Student Learning System.** All the features of the **student textbook, study resources,** and **online homework system** are designed to work together to provide you with more "I get it!" moments inside the classroom and especially outside the classroom, when you don't have access to your instructor.

We first had to create a really solid textbook, one that covered the material in a way that makes new and possibly intimidating topics easier to understand. To make sure we were on the right track, we held focus groups with first-year accounting students like you. Many of the changes made to the textbook and many of the new study resources were a direct result of suggestions from these students.

We have also created a number of tools and resources to support you, and your portal to these resources is MyAccountingLab. In intro accounting, sometimes the only way to "get it" is to do it—to practise similar questions many times until the concepts are clear, and MyAccountingLab allows you to do this. Sometimes seeing the basics of accounting presented in a slightly different, interactive way will help you "get it," and the Accounting Cycle Tutorials and the Demo Docs in MyAccountingLab help you do this. The tools and the features of MyAccountingLab appear in the fold-out at the front of this book. The tools and the features of this textbook are described in detail in the tour, Helping You "Get" Accounting, which is presented over the next few pages. And reminders appear in Chapter 1 to describe how each feature in the text can help you to master accounting.

Best of luck with your course, and much success!

Peter Norwood
Jo-Ann Johnston

Helping You "Get" Accounting

Each chapter of *Accounting* includes a number of tools and features designed to guide you through the process of developing your skills and understanding of key accounting concepts. Please read through the next few pages to learn more about these tools and the many ways in which they will help you learn, understand, and apply accounting concepts.

Learning Objectives are listed on the first page of each chapter. This "roadmap" shows you what will be covered and what is especially important. Each Learning Objective is repeated in the margin where the material is first covered. The Learning Objectives are summarized at the end of the chapter. Notice that the final Learning Objective deals with International Financial Reporting Standards (IFRS).

Chapter openers present a story about a real company or a real business situation, and show why the topics in the chapter are important to real companies. Some of the companies you'll read about include WestJet Airlines, Bombardier Recreational Products Inc., Canadian Tire, and The Forzani Group. Students tell us that using real companies makes it easier for them to learn and remember accounting concepts.

Key questions appear at the beginning of each chapter to highlight the important issues and questions that will be answered in the chapter. Once you read these questions, they will remain in the back of your mind. As you work through the chapter, you'll discover the answers and see why the chapter topics really are important.

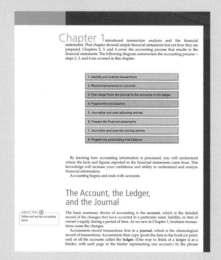

Learning Objectives in the margin visually signal the beginning of the section that covers the objective topic. Look for this feature when you are studying and want to review a particular topic.

Exhibits are provided in full colour to make the concepts easier to understand and easier to remember.

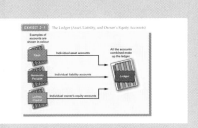

Learning Tips in the margin are suggestions for learning or remembering concepts that you might find difficult.

Key Points in the margin highlight important details from the text. These are good review tools for when you prepare for tests or exams.

Real World Examples show how real companies make use of the concepts just discussed in the text. Linking concepts to real companies makes them easier to understand and remember.

Did You Get It? boxes appear at the end of each Learning Objective. The questions allow you to slow down for a moment and test your mastery of the material just covered in the Learning Objective before moving on in the chapter. These serve as an excellent way to check your progress because the answers are provided on MyAccountingLab. Notice the MyAccountingLab reminder!

Decision Guidelines show how the accounting concepts covered in the chapter are used by business people to make business decisions. This feature shows why accounting principles and concepts are important in a broader business context, not just to accountants. The Decision Guidelines also serve as an excellent summary of the chapter topics.

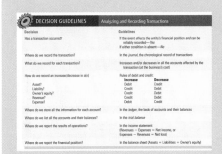

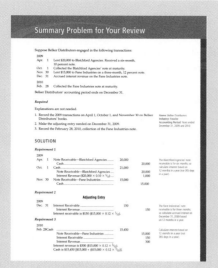

Summary Problem for Your Review pulls together the chapter concepts with an extensive and challenging review problem. Full worked solutions are given so that you can check your progress. Red notes in the margin or in the solution give you hints for how to tackle the solution, reminders of things to watch for, and further explanations about the solutions.

Summary appears at the end of each chapter. It gives a concise description of the material covered in the chapter and is organized by objective. Use this summary as a starting point for organizing your review when studying for a test or exam.

Self-Study Questions are multiple-choice questions that allow you to test your understanding of the chapter on your own. Page references are given so that you can review a section quickly if you miss an answer.

Answers to Self-Study Questions appear immediately (but upside down!) so you can check your progress.

Accounting Vocabulary lists all the terms that were defined and appeared in bold type in the chapter. The page references are given so you can review the meanings of the terms. These terms are also collected and defined in the Glossary at the end of the text.

Similar Accounting Terms link the accounting terms used in the chapter to similar terms you might have heard outside your accounting class, in the media, in other courses, or in day-to-day business dealings. Knowing similar terms should make it easier to remember the accounting terms.

While practice may not make you perfect, it is still the best way to make sure you grasp new accounting concepts and procedures. Working through the end of chapter exercises and problems will help you confirm your understanding of accounting concepts and develop your accounting skills. These review and practice materials are described in the following pages.

Questions require short, written answers or short calculations, often on a single topic.

Starters serve as warm-ups and confidence builders at the beginning of the assignment material. They address a single topic from the chapter. A brief description, the learning objectives covered, and **Check figures** appear in the margin beside each Starter. All of the Starters appear on MyAccountingLab in book-match form and algorithmic form (where applicable).

Exercises on a single or a few topics require you to "do the accounting" and, often, to consider the implications of the results in the same way that real companies would. **Check figures** appear in the margin beside each Exercise. All of the Exercises appear on MyAccountingLab in book-match form and algorithmic form (where applicable).

Excel Spreadsheet Template icons appear beside selected Exercises and Problems to remind you that Excel spreadsheets have been created to answer these questions. You can find these spreadsheets on MyAccountingLab. You don't have to use the spreadsheets to answer the questions, but you may find they save you time.

Serial Exercise in each chapter in Volume 1 and Volume 2 follows one company and builds in complexity with each chapter, providing an excellent way to see the big picture and to see how the accounting topics build off one another. Each Serial Exercises appears on MyAccountingLab in book-match form and algorithmic form (where applicable).

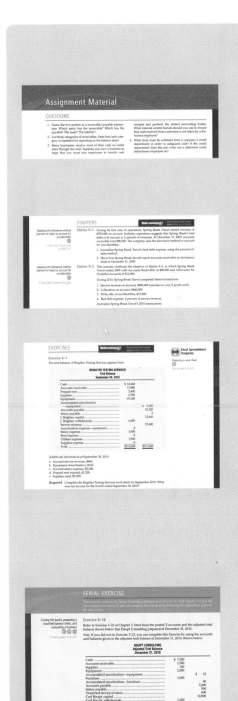

Challenge Exercises provide a challenge for those students who have mastered the Exercises, and appear on MyAccountingLab in book-match form and algorithmic form (where applicable).

Beyond the Numbers exercises require analytical thinking and written responses about the topics presented in the chapter.

Ethical Issues are thought-provoking situations that help you recognize when ethics should affect an accounting decision.

Problems are presented in two groups that mirror each other, "A" and "B." Many instructors work through problems from Group A in class to demonstrate accounting concepts, then assign problems from Group B for homework or extra practice. **Check figures** are included for the **"A" Problems only** to make sure you're on the right track. Each Problem appears on MyAccountingLab in book-match form and algorithmic form (where applicable).

Challenge Problems encourage you to consider the effect of accounting information and apply it to decision situations.

Decision Problems allow you to prepare and interpret accounting information and then make recommendations to a business based on this information.

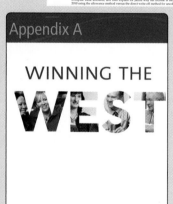

Appendix A

WINNING THE WEST

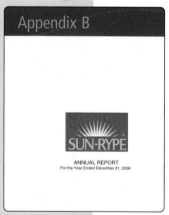

Appendix B

SUN-RYPE

ANNUAL REPORT
For the Year Ended December 31, 2008

Financial Statement Cases allow you to use real financial information from a service company and a manufacturer/merchandiser. Canadian Western Bank is Canada's largest publicly traded Schedule I bank headquartered in Western Canada. Sun-Rype Products Ltd. is a leading Canadian manufacturer and marketer of juice-based beverages and fruit-based snacks. Selected financial information from each company's 2008 Annual Report appear in Appendix A and Appendix B of Volume 1 and Volume 2 of *Accounting*. The full annual reports appear on MyAccountingLab.

Comprehensive Problem appears at the end of each part of Volume 1 and Volume 2. It covers the content addressed in the book so far. This is a relatively long problem that provides an excellent review of all of the topics covered in the chapters in that part. See your instructor for the solution to this problem.

Working Papers are available for purchase, and are a set of tear-out forms that you can use to solve all the exercises and problems in Volume I. Because the forms you need have already been created, you avoid time-consuming set-up and can focus on the accounting right away.

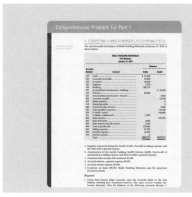

MyAccountingLab Online Homework and Assessment Manager

Experiencing the Power of Practice with MyAccountingLab:
www.myaccountinglab.com

MyAccountingLab is an online homework system that gives students more "I get it!" moments through the power of practice. The power of repetition when you "get it" means learning happens. With MyAccountingLab students can:

- Work on the exact end-of-chapter material and/or similar problems assigned by the instructor.
- Use the Study Plan for self-assessment and customized study outlines.
- Use the Help Me Solve This tool for a step-by-step tutorial.
- View the Demo Docs Example to see an animated demonstration of where the numbers came from.
- View the Flash Animations to understand important text concepts
- Watch a Video to see additional information pertaining to the lecture.
- Open Textbook Pages to find the material they need to get help on specific problems.

Multimedia Library

The **Multimedia Library** provides direct links to all media assets for this course, the eText, Audio Chapter Summaries, Glossary Flashcards, Demo Docs, Accounting Cycle Tutorial, Animations, Excel Templates, Student PowerPoint Slides, Solutions to Did You Get It? Questions, and Acadia Videos.

Multiple Pathways to Learning

Pearson Canada's **Multiple Pathways to Learning Assessment** helps you discover your own personal learning style, including identifying your personal strengths and weaknesses. After completing the survey, you can refer to the "Mapping Guide" to learn which features of your textbook or MyAccountingLab will be most effective for your learning style, ultimately enabling you to develop productive and effective study practices.

StudyLife

Studying can be lonely and difficult—**StudyLife** can help by matching you with your ideal study partner. Using **StudyLife** is simple. It works much like facebook.com or MySpace®. Once you complete our profile, **StudyLife** will match you with ideal study partners—other students taking the same subject with complementary learning styles, study techniques, and skills. They could be your classmates or they could be students on the other side of the country.

To the Instructor

Welcome to *Accounting*! Instructors have told us that their greatest challenges are effectively teaching students with very different business and accounting backgrounds, and motivating students to give accounting the study time and attention it deserves. Add to this an accounting environment that is changing like never before, with new generally accepted accounting principles (GAAP) for private enterprises and new International Financial Reporting Standards (IFRS), and you have teaching challenges like never before. *Accounting*'s approach and features were designed to help you address and overcome these challenges.

Accounting's Approach

With all the changes in the accounting environment, we gave serious thought to all the options before selecting the best approach for presenting the material in *Accounting*. We have chosen **GAAP for private enterprises as the basis for this textbook.** This allows us to base all discussions on the conceptual framework of GAAP for private enterprises, a framework shared in large part with IFRS. GAAP for private enterprises also streamlines some of the material to reduce complexity at the introductory level. One example is the number of categories of investments is reduced, which streamlines recording by focusing on the nature of the investment and its accounting treatment, rather than its label and specific accounting treatment.

We also gave serious thought to **our approach to IFRS.** IFRS will be in effect for all publicly accountable enterprises beginning January 1, 2011, with comparative IFRS figures for 2010 required as well. Given the number of Canadian companies that will have to report results according to IFRS, we thought it was vital for students to be exposed to IFRS and have some understanding of them, even in Introductory Accounting. We thought the "Wait until Intermediate Accounting" approach was *not* an option. However, students can't learn two sets of accounting standards in one introductory-accounting course—many find one set of standards a challenge.

*Accounting***'s approach is to include the description and implications of IFRS as the final Learning Objective in each chapter.** It has been designed to stand out from all the other Learning Objectives, but like all the others, it ends with Did You Get It? questions for students and, where applicable, has related Starters, Exercises, or Problems in the end-of-chapter assignment material. While it is integrated with the rest of the chapter's content, its position at the end of the chapter and its self-contained nature make the IFRS Learning Objective "skippable" for those instructors who choose to cover IFRS elsewhere or at another time.

Additional IFRS support materials and updates will be available in the Instructor's section of MyAccountingLab.

A Student-Friendly Textbook Integrated with MyAccountingLab

Instructors have told us that if students miss an accounting class, they must be able to keep up by reading the text. An accounting textbook must help students prepare for class or, should they miss a session, catch up without being overwhelmed. We've taken a two-pronged approach to ensure *Accounting* makes this happen: created a student-friendly textbook and integrated it with a powerful, robust MyAccountingLab.

The biggest change we made to the textbook pedagogy is the introduction of Did You Get It? questions at the end of each Learning Objective. Students have the opportunity to pause at the end of a Learning Objective and check whether they grasped its concepts before moving on to the next Learning Objective. The solutions are provided in MyAccountingLab so students can check their progress immediately and take action if necessary.

We also added examples of documents, such as invoices, cheques, and deposit slips, in Chapter 2. They serve as the source documents for the transactions described there, but they also ensure that all students have the basics covered regardless of their real-life business experience.

The textbook continues to reflect the changes made in previous editions that were well-received by students and that helped them to keep up or catch up if they missed a class:

- The **book design** is colourful, open, and inviting. Bulleted points and more art highlight key ideas and make the layout of explanations less imposing. Features in the margins—Key Points, Learning Tips, and Real World Examples—help students when they study. Artwork is positioned to reduce page flipping. In all, the textbook's design makes it easier to use and makes the concepts more clear. That is encouraging for students.

- **Highlights in Chapter 1** describe each feature of the text and explain how the feature can help students study and learn. A feature can't be effective unless students understand it and use it.

- **Did You Get It?** questions at the end of each Learning Objective, described above, encourage students to be active in their learning.

- We added new **International Financial Reporting Standards (IFRS)** material as the final Learning Objective in every chapter.

- **Worked solutions** for the Summary Problem for Your Review include the full solution as well as red notes in the margin to give students hints for how to tackle the solution, reminders of things to watch for, and further explanations about the solutions. These should help students overcome the "How do I start?" dilemma, as well as the "Why did they do that?" questions that can arise even when a full solution is given.

- **Check figures** in the margins for the Starters, Exercises, and the "A" set of Problems so students can make sure they are on track when they are working on their own. We have not provided check figures for the "B" set of Problems so that they can be assigned for homework or testing. The "B" Problems solutions are available to instructors on MyAccountingLab.

- **Examples from real Canadian** companies enliven the material, make difficult concepts easier to grasp, and illustrate the role of accounting in business. For that reason, we continue to include the **annual reports of two Canadian companies** in the text and on MyAccountingLab—in this edition, we are pleased to present data from the Canadian Western Bank and Sun-Rype Products Ltd. 2008 annual reports.

In those situations where "live" data drawn from real companies would complicate the material for introductory students, we illustrate the accounting with realistic examples from generic companies to give students the clearest examples possible.

- **MyAccountingLab icons and references** appear in the margins or in the headings to remind students of additional materials or resources available on MyAccountingLab, including the solutions to the Did You Get It? questions, reminders of relevant Accounting Cycle Tutorials topics, reminders of Excel Template Spreadsheets to help answer questions, and, of course, opportunities to practise end-of-chapter questions. Seeing a topic presented in a consistent but other, interactive way may help students understand it more fully. MyAccountingLab also includes a complete Study Guide and links to the Acadia Videos, as well as all the material described in the MyAccountingLab spread at the beginning of this book and in the student section of the preface.

Accuracy

As instructors, we know that **accuracy in problems and solutions** is every bit as important as clear writing and effective pedagogy. Tremendous effort has been made to ensure that the solutions to problem materials in *Accounting*, Canadian Eighth Edition are correct.

- The **authors** have developed their own problem and solutions materials.
- Our **Developmental Editor,** Anita Smale, CA, reviewed all problems and solutions.

- As a final stage, **technical checkers** have reviewed all problems and solutions.

We have made every effort to bring you the most accurate text possible. However, if you discover something that is inaccurate, please let us know so we can fix it as soon as possible.

Supplements for Instructors

The primary goal of the Instructor Resources is to help instructors deliver their course with ease, using any delivery method—traditional, self-paced, or online.

www.myaccountinglab.com

MyAccountingLab is web-based tutorial and assessment software for accounting that not only gives students more "I get it!" moments, but also provides instructors the flexibility to make technology an integral part of their course or a supplementary resource for students. And, because practice makes perfect, MyAccountingLab offers exactly the same end-of-chapter material found in the text along with algorithmic options that can be assigned for homework, all auto-graded for unlimited practice. MyAccountingLab also features the same look and feel for exercises and problems so that students are familiar and comfortable working with the material.

It also provides students with rich media assets that are closely integrated with the text including Audio Chapter Summaries, Glossary Flashcards, Demo Docs, Accounting Cycle Tutorial, Animations, Excel Templates, Student Power-Point Slides, Solutions to Did You Get It? Questions, Acadia Videos, and the eText.

Instructor's Resource CD-ROM or http://vig.pearsoned.ca/

This CD-ROM and password-protected site provide a collection of resources to help you with lecture preparation, presentation, and assessment. It contains the following supplements:

- **Instructor's Solutions Manual** Now provided in both Adobe PDF and MS Word format for ease of use.
- **Instructor's Resource Manual** Also provided in both Adobe PDF and MS Word format, the Instructor's Resource Manual includes Chapter Overviews and Outlines, Assignment Grids, Ten-Minute Quizzes, and other valuable teaching resources including how to integrate MyAccountingLab in your course. In addition there is a new section describing all the supplements that come with *Accounting*, along with suggestions for how and when they can be used, written by an instructor who has used them all!
- **TestGen** This powerful and user-friendly computerized test bank includes well over 100 questions per chapter, ranging from True False, Multiple-Choice, and Matching to Problems and Critical Thinking Exercises.
- **PowerPoint Teaching Transparencies** For flexibility of use, we provide two sets of transparencies: a brief set with six to eight slides per chapter, and a comprehensive set with 40 to 50 slides per chapter.
- **Exhibits** We are pleased to provide the exhibits from the text in GIF format for use in the classroom and easy conversion to acetate format.
- **Adapting Your Lecture Notes** These detailed transition notes, including comparison of tables of content, chapter objectives, and chapter content, will facilitate your course preparation if you make the switch to *Accounting* from another introductory accounting text.
- **Personal Response Systems (PRS) Questions** For classrooms that use PRS, an exciting new wireless polling technology that makes classrooms even more interactive by enabling instructors to pose questions to the students, record results, and display those results instantly.

Other items include:

- **Group Projects**
- **Solutions to Group Projects**
- **Check Figures**
- **Excel Spreadsheet Templates**
- **Accounting Cycle Tutorials**
- **Canadian Western Bank 2008 Annual Report**
- **Sun-Rype Products Ltd. 2008 Annual Report**

Finally, we want to draw your attention to a great service offered by Pearson to further enhance the use of *Accounting* in your course:

Pearson Custom Publishing We know that not every instructor follows the exact order of a course text. Some may not even cover all the material in a given volume. Pearson Custom Publishing provides the flexibility to select the chapters you need, presented in the order you want, to tailor fit your text to your course and your students' needs. Contact your Pearson Education Canada Sales and Editorial Representative to learn more.

We hope you enjoy *Accounting*!

Peter Norwood
Jo-Ann Johnston

Acknowledgements for the Canadian Eighth Edition

We would like to thank Charles Horngren and Tom Harrison for their encouragement and support.

Thanks are due to the following instructors for reviewing the previous edition of this text during the planning and development of this new edition, and for their excellent suggestions and ideas:

Rod Comrie, *Douglas College*
Vincent Durant, *St. Lawrence College*
Kim Dyke, *Red River College*
Elizabeth Hicks, *Douglas College*
Paul Hurley, *Durham College*
Glen Stanger, *Douglas College*
Selina Tang, *Douglas College*
Richard Wright, *Fanshawe College*

We would also like to thank the following instructors for participating in our accounting focus groups. Your excellent suggestions and feedback helped to shape the development of this textbook and its accompanying MyAccountingLab:

Anita Braaksma, *Kwantlen University College*
Liang Chen, *University of Toronto Scarborough*
Ann Clarke-Okah, *Carleton University*
Douglas Cliff, *Comosun College*
Rod Comrie, *Douglas College*
Cheryl Dyson, *Ryerson University*
Tim Edwards, *British Columbia Institute of Technology*
Erin Egeland, *Comosun College*
Gunter Eisenberg, *Douglas College*
George Fisher, *Douglas College*
Vern Gibson, *British Columbia Institute of Technology*
Elizabeth Hicks, *Douglas College*
Amy Hoggard, *Comosun College*
Gordon Holyer, *Vancouver Island University*
Paul Jeyakumar, *British Columbia Institute of Technology*
Barb Katz, *Kwantlen University College*
Jack Lin, *Douglas College*
Ho Yee Low, *Kwantlen University College*
Carol Meissner, *Georgian College*
Sally Mitzel, *Sheridan College*
Randy Murie, *British Columbia Institute of Technology*
Joe Pidutti, *Durham College*
George Robertson, *Douglas College*
Pat Sauve, *Durham College*
Catherine Seguin, *University of Toronto*
Dave Scott, *Niagara College*
Glen Stanger, *Douglas College*
Carol Stewart, *Kwantlen University College*
Agatha Thalheimer, *Comosun College*
Barry Tober, *Niagara College*
Helen Vallee, *Kwantlen University College*
Victor Waese, *British Columbia Institute of Technology*
Elizabeth Zaleschuk, *Douglas College*

We would like to acknowledge and thank the students who attended focus groups at Douglas College and Kwantlen University College, whose feedback and suggestions helped guide this new edition.

Scott Allen
Karen Fisher

Bradley Head
Matthew Gregory Hunter
Susan Kennedy
Eunji Lee
Kristana Sampang
Nasim Sarafraz-Shekari
Abby Tumak
Marc Andre Villeneuve

These students took the time to give us feedback on what we have been doing well and what we could improve upon with this new edition. As a result of their feedback, many changes were incorporated into the revision. For example, we "chunked" the material in each chapter by inserting Did You Get It? questions at the end of each Learning Objective, giving students the opportunity to check their understanding before moving on in the chapter. New materials have been added to MyAccountingLab as a direct result of these students' suggestions, including animations of important accounting concepts (the links among financial statements; the process of journalizing and posting; creating an accounting work sheet); a business math review; and instructions on using financial calculators. Several students asked for a new design with a fresh and open feel, and we have redesigned this new edition with this in mind.

Thanks are extended to Canadian Western Bank and Sun-Rype Products Ltd. for permission to use their annual reports in Volumes I and II of this text. Thanks are extended to JVC Canada Inc. for permission to use its invoice in Chapter 5. We acknowledge the support provided by *The Globe and Mail's Report on Business*, the *Financial Post*, the websites of various news organizations, and by the annual reports of a large number of public companies.

The Canadian Institute of Chartered Accountants, as the official promulgator of generally accepted accounting principles in Canada, and the *CICA Handbook*, are vital to the conduct of business and accounting in Canada. We have made every effort to incorporate the most current *Handbook* recommendations in this new edition of *Accounting* for both private enterprises and for publicly accountable enterprises subject to international financial reporting standards (IFRS).

We would like to give special thanks to Amy Lam, CA, Senior Director of Member Services, Institute of Chartered Accountants of British Columbia, for her guidance and technical support during this time of great changes in the accounting-standards environment. Her willingness to review and discuss portions of the manuscript was very generous and insightful, and it is gratefully acknowledged.

We would like to acknowledge the people of Pearson Education Canada, in particular President Steve O'Hearn, V-P Editorial Director Gary Bennett, Editor-in-Chief Nicole Lukach, and Marketing Manager Cas Shields. Special thanks to Production Editors Mary Ann Blair and Lila Campbell, Production Coordinator Andrea Falkenberg, and their teams for their superior efforts in guiding this edition through the various phases of preparation and production. We would also like to acknowledge the editorial and technical support of Anita Smale, CA.

I would like to thank my wife, Helen, and my family very much for their support, assistance, and encouragement.

Peter R. Norwood

I would like to thank my husband Bill and my family for their encouragement and support.

Jo-Ann L. Johnston

The accounting profession offers exciting career opportunities because every organization uses accounting. The corner grocery store keeps accounting records to measure its success in selling groceries. The largest corporations need accounting to monitor their locations and transactions. And the dot.coms must account for their transactions. Why is accounting so important? Because it helps an organization understand its business in the same way a model helps an architect construct a building. Accounting helps a manager understand the organization as a whole without drowning in its details.

The Work of Accountants

Positions in the field of accounting may be divided into several areas. Two general classifications are *public accounting* and *private accounting*.

In Canada, most accountants, both public and private, belong to one of three accounting bodies, which set the standards for admission of members and deal with matters like the rules of professional conduct followed by their members: The Canadian Institute of Chartered Accountants (CICA), whose members are called *Chartered Accountants (CA)*; the Certified General Accountants Association of Canada (CGAAC), whose members are called *Certified General Accountants (CGA)*; and the Society of Management Accountants of Canada (SMAC), whose members are called *Certified Management Accountants (CMA)*. The role and activities of each of these bodies are discussed below.

Private accountants work for a single business, such as a local department store, the St-Hubert restaurant chain, or McCain Foods Ltd. Charitable organizations, educational institutions, and government agencies also employ private accountants. The chief accounting officer usually has the title of controller, treasurer, or chief financial officer. Whatever the title, this person often carries the status of vice-president.

Public accountants are those who serve the general public and collect professional fees for their work, much as doctors and lawyers do. Their work includes auditing, income tax planning and preparation of returns, management consulting, and various accounting services. These specialized accounting services are discussed in the next section. Public accountants represent about a quarter of all professional accountants.

Some public accountants pool their talents and work together within a single firm. Public accounting firms are called CA firms, CGA firms, or CMA firms, depending on the accounting body from which the partners of the firm come. Public accounting firms vary greatly in size. Some are small businesses, and others are medium-sized partnerships. The largest firms are worldwide partnerships with over 2,000 partners. There are four large, international accounting firms:

Deloitte & Touche LLP	KPMG LLP
Ernst & Young LLP	PricewaterhouseCoopers LLP

Although these firms employ less than 25 percent of the more than 60,000 CAs in Canada, they audit most of the 1,000 largest corporations in Canada. The top partners in large accounting firms earn about the same amount as the top managers of other large businesses.

Exhibit 1 shows the accounting positions within public accounting firms and other organizations. Of special interest in the exhibit is the upward movement of accounting personnel, as the arrows show. In particular, note how accountants may move from positions in public accounting firms to similar or higher positions

EXHIBIT 1   Accounting Position within Organizations

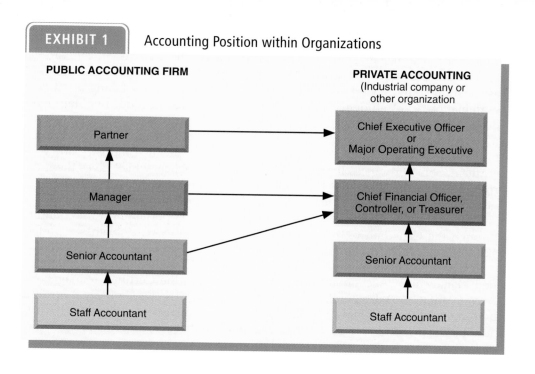

in industry and government. This is a frequently travelled career path. Because accounting deals with all facets of an organization—such as purchasing, manufacturing, marketing, and distribution—it provides an excellent basis for gaining broad business experience.

Accounting Organizations and Designations

The position of accounting in today's business world has created the need for control over the professional, educational, and ethical standards of accountants. Through statutes passed by provincial legislatures, the three accounting organizations in Canada have received the authority to set educational requirements and professional standards for their members and to discipline members who fail to adhere to their codes of conduct. The acts make them self-regulating bodies, just as provincial associations of doctors and lawyers are.

The *Canadian Institute of Chartered Accountants (CICA)*, whose members are chartered accountants or CAs, is the oldest accounting organization in Canada. Experience and education requirements for becoming a CA vary among the provinces. Generally, the educational requirement includes a university degree. All the provincial institutes require that an individual, to qualify as a CA, pass a national three-day uniform examination administered by the CICA and meet experience requirements. The provincial institutes grant the right to use the professional designation CA.

The practical-experience requirements for CAs require that a student be employed by an approved training office. Most of these approved offices are in public accounting, but CAs can now accumulate their experience outside of public practice as well.

CAs belong to a provincial institute (*Ordre* in Quebec) and through that body to the CICA. The provincial institutes have the responsibility for developing and enforcing the code of professional conduct that guides the actions of the CAs in that province.

The CICA publishes a monthly professional journal entitled *CA Magazine*.

The *Certified General Accountants Association of Canada (CGAAC)* is also regulated by provincial law. The experience and education requirements for becoming a CGA vary from province to province, but in all provinces the individual must either pass national examinations administered by the CGAAC in the various subject areas or gain exemption by taking specified university, college, and association courses. Certain subjects may only be passed by taking a national examination. CGA students require a university degree in order to obtain their designation; they do not need to have the degree to enroll as a student.

CGAs may gain their practical experience through work in public accounting, industry, or government. They are employed in public practice, industry, and government. Some provinces license CGAs in public practice, which gives them the right to conduct audits and issue opinions on financial statements, while some other provinces do not require a licence for them to perform audits.

The association supports research in various areas pertaining to accounting through the Canadian CGA Research Foundation. CGAAC publishes a professional journal entitled *CGA Magazine*.

The *Society of Management Accountants of Canada (SMAC)* administers the Certified Management Accountant program that leads to the Certified Management Accountant (CMA) designation. The use of this designation is similarly controlled by provincial law. Students generally must have a university degree. The SMAC administers an admission or entrance examination that students must pass before embarking on a two-year professional program and completing two years of required work experience. After completing the professional program and the work experience, they write a final examination and make a presentation to a SMAC committee, based on the professional program administered by the SMAC, in order to obtain the CMA designation. The SMAC also administers the professional program and the final examination. CMAs earn their practical experience in industry or government, and are generally employed in industry or government, although some CMAs are in public accounting. The Society issues standards relating to management accounting through the SMAC. The SMAC conducts and publishes research relating primarily to management accounting. The SMAC publishes a professional journal entitled *Cost and Management*.

The *Financial Executives Institute (FEI)* is an organization composed of senior financial executives from many of the large corporations in Canada, who meet on a regular basis with a view to sharing information on how they can better manage their organizations. Most of these executives have one of the three designations just discussed. The FEI supports and publishes research relating to management accounting. The FEI also publishes a journal, the *Financial Executive*.

The *Institute of Internal Auditors (IIA)* is a world-wide organization of internal auditors. It administers the examinations leading to and grants the Certified Internal Auditor (CIA) designation. Internal auditors are employees of an organization whose job is to review the operations, including financial operations, of the organization with a view to making it more economical, efficient, and effective. Many Canadian internal auditors are members of Canadian chapters of the IIA. The IIA supports and publishes research and conducts courses related to internal auditing. The IIA journal is *The Internal Auditor*.

The *Canadian Academic Accounting Association (CAAA)* directs its attention toward the academic and research aspects of accounting. A high percentage of its members are professors. The CAAA publishes a journal devoted to research in accounting and auditing, *Contemporary Accounting Research*.

While it is not an accounting organization or designation, *Canada Revenue Agency (CRA)* enforces the tax laws and collects the revenue needed to finance the federal government.

Specialized Accounting Services

As accounting affects so many people in so many different fields, public accounting and private accounting include specialized services.

Public Accounting

Auditing is one of the accounting profession's most significant services to the public. An audit is the independent examination that ensures the reliability of the reports that management prepares and submits to investors, creditors, and others outside the business. In carrying out an audit, public accountants from outside a business examine the business's financial statements. If the public accountants believe that these documents are a fair presentation of the business's operations, they offer a professional opinion stating that the firm's financial statements have been prepared in accordance with generally accepted accounting principles, or, if generally accepted accounting principles are not applicable, with an appropriate disclosed basis of accounting. Why is the audit so important? Creditors considering loans want assurance that the facts and figures the borrower submits are reliable. Shareholders, who have invested in the business, need to know that the financial picture management shows them is complete. Government agencies need information from businesses. All want information that is unbiased.

Tax accounting has two aims: complying with the tax laws and minimizing taxes to be paid. Because combined federal and provincial income tax rates range as high as 53 percent for individuals and 46 percent for corporations, reducing income tax is an important management consideration. Tax work by accountants consists of preparing tax returns and planning business transactions to minimize taxes. In addition, since the imposition of the Goods and Services Tax (GST), public accountants have been involved in advising their clients how to properly collect and account for GST. Public accountants advise individuals on what types of investments to make, and on how to structure their transactions. Accountants in corporations provide tax planning and preparation services as well.

Management consulting is the term that describes the wide scope of advice public accountants provide to help managers run a business. As they conduct audits, public accountants look deep into a business's operations. With the insight they gain, they often make suggestions for improvements in the business's management structure and accounting systems. The *Sarbanes-Oxley Act of 2002* has created the need for auditors to help their clients ensure the clients have complied with the Act. This includes ensuring that proper and effective internal controls are in place. However, Sarbanes-Oxley has also limited the management consulting services that auditors can supply to their audit clients.

Accounting services is also a catchall term used to describe the wide range of services related to accounting provided by public accountants. These services include bookkeeping and preparation of financial statements on a monthly or annual basis. Some small companies have all their accounting done by a public accounting firm.

Private Accounting

Cost accounting analyzes a business's costs to help managers control expenses or set selling prices. Good cost accounting records guide managers in pricing their products to achieve greater profits. Also, cost accounting information shows management when a product is not profitable and should be dropped from a product line.

Budgeting sets sales and profit goals, and develops detailed plans—called budgets—for achieving those goals. Some of the most successful companies in Canada have been pioneers in the field of budgeting.

Information systems design identifies the organization's information needs, both internal and external. Using flow charts and manuals, designers develop and implement the system to meet those needs.

Internal auditing is performed by a business's own audit staff. Many large organizations, Ontario Power Generation Inc., Hudson's Bay Co., and The Bank of Nova Scotia among them, maintain a staff of internal auditors. These accountants evaluate the firm's own accounting and management systems to improve operating efficiency, and to ensure that employees follow management's policies.

Internal auditors also help to ensure that organizations comply with Sarbanes-Oxley by documenting and assessing internal controls, and by implementing checklists of items prescribed by the Act. Organizations are increasingly hiring outside, freelance accountants to help their own accountants ensure compliance with Sarbanes-Oxley.

Exhibit 2 summarizes these accounting specializations.

As you work through Accounting you will learn how to use accounting to make business decisions. With the exciting career opportunities accounting offers, consider a career in accounting.

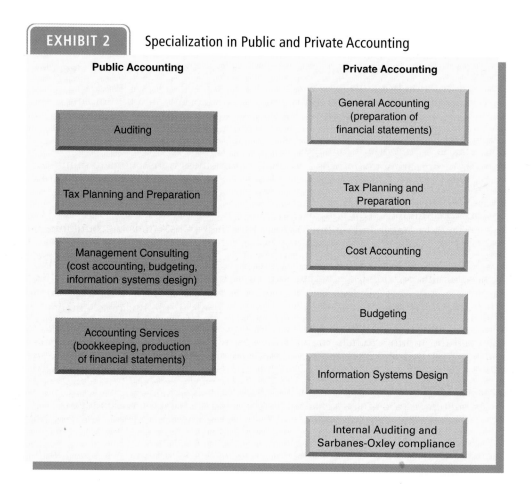

EXHIBIT 2   Specialization in Public and Private Accounting

Public Accounting

- Auditing
- Tax Planning and Preparation
- Management Consulting (cost accounting, budgeting, information systems design)
- Accounting Services (bookkeeping, production of financial statements)

Private Accounting

- General Accounting (preparation of financial statements)
- Tax Planning and Preparation
- Cost Accounting
- Budgeting
- Information Systems Design
- Internal Auditing and Sarbanes-Oxley compliance

Each chapter opens with questions about why the chapter is important. The questions are answered throughout the chapter and summarized in the Decision Guidelines at the end of the chapter.

1 Accounting and the Business Environment

Why are accounting and the business environment important? How do we organize a business?

How much do we record for assets and liabilities? How do we measure profits and losses?

How do we determine where a business stands financially?

These questions and others will be answered throughout this chapter. The Decision Guidelines at the end of this chapter will provide the answers in a useful summary.

LEARNING OBJECTIVES

1. Define accounting, and describe the users of accounting information

2. Explain why ethics and rules of conduct are crucial in accounting and business

3. Describe and discuss the forms of business organizations

4. Explain the development of accounting standards, and describe the concepts and principles

5. Describe and use the accounting equation to analyze business transactions

6. Prepare and evaluate the financial statements

7. Explain the development of international financial reporting standards (IFRS)

Learning Objectives are a "roadmap" showing what will be covered and what is especially important in each chapter.

A chapter-opening story shows why the topics in the chapter are important to real companies and business people. We refer to this story throughout the chapter.

Shawn Tran is a university student. During his first year at university, Shawn started looking for opportunities for summer employment. Shawn approached several companies but became intrigued by an offer to stage promotional events for a local brewery, which would mean starting his own company. The brewery would pay Shawn a fee for each event he staged, but Shawn would have to cover all expenses associated with the event. Thus, Shawn's income would be determined by his ability to successfully operate his own business. Overnight, Shawn became an entrepreneur. He had to develop a marketing strategy, hire staff to run the events, set up an office, and learn some basic bookkeeping. To keep track of the revenues and expenses earned from staging these events, Shawn started a proprietorship that he called Milestone Promotions. By the time the second term of school had ended in April, Shawn had developed a plan to put on seven events over the summer, hired staff for the events, and purchased a truck to transport supplies and promotional material.

At the end of the summer, Shawn had earned enough income from his company to cover his tuition and living expenses for the next school year. "It was a very busy summer for me, but I had lots of fun. The events were energizing but a lot of work. I learned that you need to have a good plan and you have to watch your finances. Costs can get out of control in a hurry. My profit margin was much higher on the last event compared to the first."

What role does accounting play in Shawn Tran's situation? Tran had to decide how to organize his company. He set up his business as a proprietorship—a single-owner company—with himself as the owner. If he decides to run the business again, he may decide to expand it by taking on a partner. He might also choose to incorporate—that is, to form a corporation. In this chapter, we discuss all three forms of business organization: proprietorships, partnerships, and corporations.

You may already know various accounting terms and relationships, because accounting affects people's behaviour in many ways. This first accounting course will sharpen your focus by explaining how accounting works. As you progress through this course, you will see how accounting helps people like Shawn Tran—and you—achieve business goals.

Accounting: The Language of Business

Boldfaced words are new terms that are explained here and defined in the Glossary at the end of the book.

┌ OBJECTIVE ①
Define accounting, and describe the users of accounting information

Learning Objectives in the margin signal the beginning of the section that covers the learning-objective topic. Look for the Objective when you want to review this topic.

Accounting is the information system that measures business financial activities, processes that information into reports, and communicates the results to decision makers. For this reason it is called "the language of business." The better you understand the language, the better your decisions will be, and the better you can manage financial information. A recent survey indicates that business managers believe it is more important for university students to learn accounting than any other business subject. Decisions concerning personal financial planning, education expenses, loans, car payments, income taxes, and investments are based on the *information system* that we call accounting.

Financial statements are a key product of an accounting system and provide information that helps people make informed business decisions. **Financial statements** report on a business in monetary terms. Is my business making a profit? Should I hire assistants? Am I earning enough money to expand my business? Answering business questions like these requires a knowledge of financial statements.

Students sometimes mistake bookkeeping for accounting. *Bookkeeping* is a procedural element of accounting, just as arithmetic is a procedural element of mathematics. Increasingly, people are using computers to do detailed bookkeeping—in households, businesses, and organizations of all types. Exhibit 1–1 illustrates the role of accounting in business. The process starts and ends with people making decisions.

Decision Makers: The Users of Accounting Information

Decision makers need information. The more important the decision, the greater the need for information. Virtually all businesses and most individuals keep accounting records to aid decision making. Here are some decision makers who use accounting information.

EXHIBIT 1–1   The Accounting System: The Flow of Information

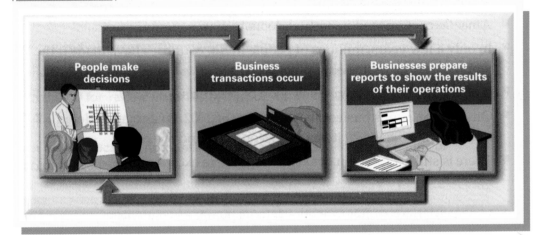

Exhibits summarize key ideas in a visual way.

Individuals People use accounting information in day-to-day affairs to manage bank accounts, evaluate job prospects, make investments, and decide whether to lease or buy a new car.

Businesses Business owners and managers use accounting information to set goals for their organizations. They evaluate their progress toward those goals, and they take corrective action when it is necessary. For example, Shawn Tran makes decisions based on accounting information. He knows the revenue that will be earned, since he and the brewery agreed on a fee per event. He needs to determine how many staff to hire for each event, how much to spend on promotional materials, and how much to spend on supplies and accessories for each event. He needs to make sure that his costs do not exceed the fee he will receive from the brewery if he wants to make sure that he meets his goal of earning enough to pay for his next school year.

Investors Outside investors often provide the money a business needs to begin operations. To decide whether to invest, potential investors predict the amount of income to be earned on their investment. This evaluation means analyzing the financial statements of the business and keeping up with developments in the business press, for example, *The Financial Post* (a part of *The National Post*) and *Report on Business,* published by *The Globe and Mail.*

Creditors Before lending money, creditors (lenders) such as banks evaluate the borrower's ability to make scheduled payments. This evaluation includes a report of the borrower's financial position and a prediction of future operations, both of which are based on accounting information.

Government Regulatory Agencies Most organizations face government regulation. For example, the provincial securities commissions, such as the British Columbia Securities Commission and the Ontario Securities Commission, dictate that businesses selling their shares to and borrowing money from the public disclose certain financial information to the investing public.

Taxing Authorities Provincial and federal governments levy taxes on individuals and businesses. Income tax is calculated using accounting information. Businesses use their accounting records to help them determine their goods and services tax and sales tax.

Not-for-profit Organizations Not-for-profit organizations such as churches, hospitals, government agencies, universities, and colleges, which operate for purposes other than to earn a profit, use accounting information in much the same way that profit-oriented businesses do.

Other Users Employees and labour unions may make wage demands based on the accounting information that shows their employer's reported income. Consumer groups and the general public are also interested in the amount of income that businesses earn. And newspapers may report "an improved profit picture" of a major company as it emerges from economic difficulties. Such news, based on accounting information, relates to the company's health.

Financial Accounting and Management Accounting

Users of accounting information are a diverse population, but they may be grouped as external users or internal users. This distinction allows us to classify accounting into two fields—financial accounting and management accounting.

Financial accounting provides information to people outside the company. Creditors and outside investors, for example, are not part of the day-to-day management of the company. Likewise, government agencies and the general public are external users of a company's accounting information. Chapters 2 through 18 in Volumes I and II of this book deal primarily with financial accounting.

Management accounting generates information for internal decision makers, such as company executives, department heads, university deans, and hospital administrators. Chapters 19 through 26 in Volume III of this book cover management accounting.

Exhibit 1–2 shows how financial accounting and management accounting are used by Milestone Promotions' internal and external decision makers.

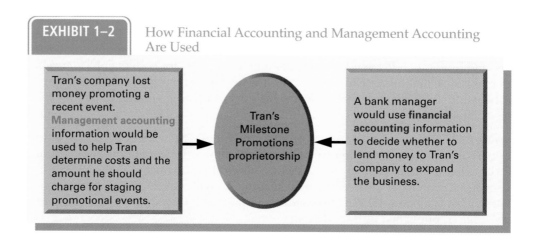

EXHIBIT 1–2 How Financial Accounting and Management Accounting Are Used

The History and Development of Accounting

Accounting has a long history. Some scholars claim that writing arose in order to record accounting information. Accounting records date back to the ancient civilizations of China, Babylonia, Greece, and Egypt. The rulers of these civilizations used accounting to keep track of the cost of labour and materials used in building structures like the great pyramids. The need for accounting has existed as long as there has been business activity.

Accounting developed further as a result of the information needs of merchants in the city-states of Italy during the 1400s. In that busy commercial climate, the monk Luca Pacioli, a mathematician and friend of Leonardo da Vinci's, published the first known description of double-entry bookkeeping in 1494.

In the Industrial Revolution of the 19th century, the growth of corporations spurred the development of accounting. The corporation owners—the shareholders—were no longer necessarily the managers of their business. Managers had to create accounting systems to report to the owners and government how well their businesses were doing. Because managers want their performance to look good, society needs a way to ensure that the business information provided is reliable. To meet this need, generally accepted accounting principles were developed. These will be discussed in more detail shortly.

As required in other segments of society, accounting must be practised in an ethical manner. We look next at the ethical dimension of accounting.

DID YOU GET IT?

To check your understanding of the material in this Learning Objective, complete these questions. The solutions appear on MyAccountingLab so you can check your progress.

1. What is accounting?
2. Name three decision makers that rely on financial information, and briefly describe how they use it.
3. What is the difference between management accounting and financial accounting?

Did You Get It? questions appear at the end of each Learning Objective, allowing you to test your mastery of the concepts in this Learning Objective before moving on to the next one. The solutions appear on MyAccountingLab.

Ethical Considerations in Accounting and Business

Ethical considerations affect all areas of accounting and business. Investors, creditors, and regulatory bodies need relevant and reliable information about a company. Naturally, companies want to make themselves look as good as possible to attract investors, so there is a potential for conflict. An **audit** is a financial examination. Audits are conducted by independent accountants who express an opinion on whether or not the financial statements fairly reflect the economic events that occurred during the accounting period. It is vital that companies and their auditors behave in an ethical manner. Exhibit 1–3 illustrates the relationship among accounting and business entities that are public companies (companies that sell shares of stock to investors).

OBJECTIVE 2
Explain why ethics and rules of conduct are crucial in accounting and business

EXHIBIT 1–3   Relationship among Accounting and Business Entities

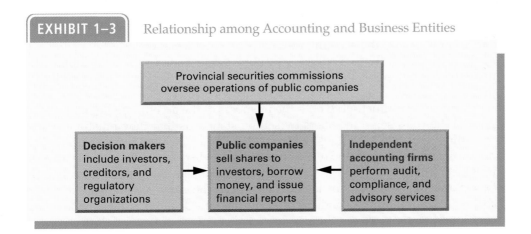

Unfortunately for the accounting profession, accounting scandals involving both public companies and their auditors have made the headlines in recent years. Enron Corporation, which was the seventh-largest company in the United States, allegedly issued misleading financial statements that reported fewer debts than the company really owed. Enron was forced into bankruptcy and its auditors were forced out of business (although on May 31, 2005, the U.S. Supreme Court overturned the conviction of accounting firm Arthur Andersen). The impact of the Enron bankruptcy was felt by many different parties, including Enron shareholders, who saw their investments become worthless; employees who lost their jobs and their pensions; and the accounting profession, which lost some of its integrity and reputation as gatekeepers and stewards for the investing public. Scandals like this shocked the business community and hurt investor confidence.

In response to the scandals, the *Sarbanes-Oxley Act of 2002* was introduced. It is landmark legislation designed to make U.S. public companies more transparent in their financial reporting and more proactive in sharing material information with other participants in the financial reporting chain, including auditors, audit committees, analysts, and investors. If Canadian companies are registered in the United States, they must follow the rules of the *Sarbanes-Oxley Act*. Nortel Networks Corporation, the Canadian communication-networks company, was forced to comply with these rules and, as a result, restated its December 31, 2004, financial statements.

Rather than move toward U.S. standards, Canada is adopting International Financial Reporting Standards (IFRS) for publicly accountable enterprises residing in Canada. The new standards for these companies will be effective starting the 2011 fiscal year. The role of these international standards will be discussed more thoroughly in Learning Objective 7, later in this chapter.

Companies that are not publicly accountable have a choice. They may choose to adopt IFRS, or they may choose to follow Canadian standards for private enterprises, which are designed to simplify financial reporting for most Canadian businesses. In this book, we will primarily follow the Canadian standards for private companies, although each chapter will also provide information about international standards for publicly accountable companies.

The Professional Accounting Bodies and Their Standards of Professional Conduct

Chartered Accountants (CAs), Certified General Accountants (CGAs), and Certified Management Accountants (CMAs) are all governed by rules of conduct created by their respective organizations. Many of the rules apply whether the members are public accountants working in public practice or private accountants working in industry or government. These rules concern the confidentiality of information the accountant is privy to, maintenance of the reputation of the profession, the need to perform accountancy work with integrity and due care, competence, refusal to be associated with false or misleading information, and compliance by the accountant with professional standards. Other rules are applicable only to those members in public practice, and deal with things like the need for independence, and how to advertise, seek clients, and conduct a practice.

The rules of conduct serve both the members of the accounting bodies and the public. The rules serve members by setting standards that they must meet, and providing a benchmark against which they will be measured by their peers. The public is served because the rules of conduct provide it with a list of the standards to which the members of the body adhere. This helps the public determine its expectations of members' behaviour. However, the rules of conduct should be considered a minimum standard of performance; ideally, the members should continually strive to exceed them.

Throughout this book, we provide several problems that allow you to consider ethical dilemmas. Consider them carefully. The perception that accountants follow the highest standard of professional conduct must also be the reality. In today's business climate, behaving in an ethical manner is crucial.

Codes of Business Conduct of Companies

Many companies have codes of conduct that apply to their employees in their dealings with each other and with the companies' suppliers and customers. Some of these companies mention their code in their annual report or on their website. For example, Vancouver City Savings Credit Union states on its website:

Our Values

Integrity: We act with courage, consistency and respect to do what is honest, fair and trustworthy.

Innovation: We anticipate and respond to challenges and changing needs with creativity, enthusiasm and determination.

Responsibility: We are accountable to our members, employees, colleagues and communities for the results of our decisions and actions.

Source: From Vancouver City Savings Credit Union's website, www.vancity.com (accessed May 28, 2009).

The company indicates to its employees and to the general public how management expects employees to behave.

DID YOU GET IT?

MyAccountingLab

To check your understanding of the material in this Learning Objective, complete these questions. The solutions appear on MyAccountingLab so you can check your progress.

4. What is an audit, and why is it important that it be performed by independent accountants?

5. Why do the professional accounting bodies establish rules of professional conduct for their members?

6. Refer to the Student Policies, Bylaws, and Codes of Conduct of your college or university. Why do these policies exist?

Forms of Business Organizations

A business can be organized as a

> Key Points highlight important details from the text and are good tools for reviewing concepts.

- Proprietorship
- Partnership
- Corporation

You should understand the differences among the three.

Proprietorship   A **proprietorship** has a single owner, called the proprietor, who often manages the business. Proprietorships tend to be small retail stores and individual professional businesses, such as those of physicians, lawyers, and accountants, but also can be very large. From the accounting viewpoint, each proprietorship is distinct from its owner. Thus, the accounting records of the proprietorship do *not* include the proprietor's personal accounting records. However, from a legal perspective, the business *is* the proprietor. In this book, we start with a proprietorship because many students organize their first business that way.

Partnership   A **partnership** joins two or more individuals together as co-owners. Each owner is a partner. Many retail stores and professional organizations of physicians, lawyers, and accountants are partnerships. Most partnerships are small and medium-sized, but some are quite large; there are public accounting firms in Canada with more than 500 partners and law firms with more than 100 partners. Accounting treats the partnership as a separate organization distinct from the personal affairs of each partner. But again, from a legal perspective, a partnership *is* the partners in a manner similar to a proprietorship.

OBJECTIVE ③
Describe and discuss the forms of business organizations

A proprietorship and a partnership (Ch. 12) are not legal entities separate from their owners, so the income from proprietorships and partnerships is taxable to their owners, not to the business. But in accounting, the owner and the business are considered separate entities, and separate records are kept for each. A corporation (Ch. 13) is a separate legal entity. The corporation is taxed on its income, and the owners are taxed on any income they receive from the corporation.

EXHIBIT 1–4

The Formation
and Ownership
of a Corporation

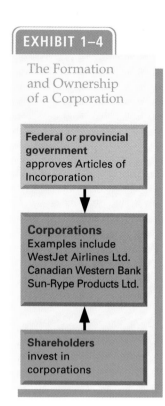

Corporation   A **corporation** is a business owned by **shareholders**. These are the people or other corporations who own shares of ownership in the business. The corporation is the dominant form of business organization in Canada. Although proprietorships and partnerships are more numerous, corporations engage in more business and are generally larger in terms of total assets, income, and number of employees. In Canada, generally, corporations must have *Ltd.* or *Limited*, *Inc.* or *Incorporated*, or *Corp.* or *Corporation* in their legal name to indicate that they are incorporated. Corporations need not be large; a business with only a few assets and employees could be organized as a corporation.

From a legal perspective, a corporation is formed when the federal government or a provincial government approves its articles of incorporation. Unlike a proprietorship or a partnership, a corporation is a legal entity distinct from its owners. The corporation operates as an "artificial person" that exists apart from its owners and that conducts business in its own name. The corporation has many of the rights that a person has. For example, a corporation may buy, own, and sell property. The corporation may enter into contracts and sue and be sued.

Since corporations are entities separate from their owners, they will prepare financial reports separate from their owners. As mentioned previously, these corporations may choose to follow international financial reporting standards (IFRS) when preparing their financial reports, or, if they are not publicly accountable companies, they may choose to follow Canadian accounting standards for private companies.

Corporations differ significantly from proprietorships and partnerships in another way. If a proprietorship or partnership cannot pay its debts, lenders can take the owners' personal assets—cash and belongings—to satisfy the business's obligations. But if a corporation goes bankrupt, lenders cannot take the personal assets of the shareholders. This *limited personal liability* of shareholders for corporate debts explains why corporations are so popular compared to proprietorships and partnerships. Exhibit 1–4 shows the formation and ownership of a corporation.

Another factor for corporations is the division of ownership into individual shares. Companies such as WestJet, Canadian Imperial Bank of Commerce, and Canadian Tire Corporation, Limited, have issued millions of shares of stock and have tens of thousands of shareholders. An investor with no personal relationship either to the corporation or to any other shareholder can become an owner by buying 30, 100, 5,000, or any number of shares of its stock. For most corporations, the investor may sell the shares at any time. It is usually harder to sell one's investment in a proprietorship or a partnership than to sell one's investment in a corporation.

Limited-Liability Partnership (LLP) and Limited-Liability Company (LLC)   A **limited-liability partnership (LLP)** is a partnership in which one partner cannot create a large liability for the other partners. Each partner is liable only for his or her own

EXHIBIT 1–5   Comparison of the Three Forms of Business Organization

	Proprietorship	Partnership	Corporation
1. Owner(s)	Proprietor—one owner	Partners—two or more owners	Shareholders—generally many owners
2. Life of organization	Limited by owner's choice or death	Limited by owners' choices or death	Indefinite
3. Personal liability of owner(s) for business debts	Proprietor is personally liable*	Partners are personally liable**	Shareholders are not personally liable
4. Legal status	The proprietorship is the proprietor*	The partnership is the partners**	The corporation is separate from the shareholders (owners)

*Unless it is a limited-liability company (LLC)

**Unless it is a limited-liability partnership (LLP)

actions and those actions under his or her control. A proprietorship can be organized as a **limited-liability company (LLC)**, where the company and not the proprietor is liable for the company's debts. Today, most proprietorships and partnerships are organized as LLCs and LLPs. The limited-liability aspect gives these organizations one of the chief advantages of a corporation.

Exhibit 1–5 summarizes the differences between proprietorships, partnerships, and corporations.

Accounting for corporations includes some unique complexities. For this reason, we initially focus on proprietorships. We cover partnerships in Chapter 12 and begin our discussion of corporations in Chapter 13.

DID YOU GET IT?

MyAccountingLab

To check your understanding of the material in this Learning Objective, complete these questions. The solutions appear on MyAccountingLab so you can check your progress.

7. How does a partnership differ from a proprietorship?

8. How does a corporation differ from either a proprietorship or a partnership?

9. List two advantages of the corporate form of business over a proprietorship.

Accounting Concepts

Accounting practices follow certain guidelines. The rules that govern how accountants measure, process, and communicate financial information fall under the heading GAAP, which stands for **generally accepted accounting principles**. The *Accounting Standards Board* (*AcSB*), an independent body with the authority to develop and establish standards and guidance governing financial accounting and reporting in Canada, is responsible for creating GAAP. The AcSB consists of a maximum of nine members from a variety of backgrounds. Members are chosen so that the AcSB has an appropriate balance of competencies and expertise to set accounting standards. The federal and provincial legislatures through the various companies acts and the various provincial securities commissions have given the standards or GAAP issued by the AcSB and collected in the Canadian Institute of Chartered Accountants (CICA) *Handbook* their legal status.

Accounting principles draw their authority from their acceptance in the business community. They are generally accepted by those people and organizations who need guidelines in accounting for their financial undertakings.

Currently, GAAP in Canada are based on the *CICA Handbook,* Section 1000, Financial Statement Concepts, and Section 1100, Generally Accepted Accounting Principles. Section 1100 lists the sources of GAAP in Canada, which include accounting sections in the *CICA Handbook* and other guidelines, abstracts, and background information issued by the Accounting Standards Board and its committees. Section 1100 states that standards can change over time to reflect changes in economic and social conditions. Section 1100 also states that the *Handbook* cannot (and is not intended to) address every possible financial transaction or situation. When a transaction or situation is not addressed specifically in the *Handbook* or other primary sources of GAAP listed in Section 1100, then accountants should refer to Section 1000 and apply their professional judgment.

Exhibit 1–6 summarizes the financial statement concepts described in *Handbook* Section 1000. Level 1 in Exhibit 1–6 shows that the primary objective of financial statements is to provide information useful for making resource-allocation decisions (helping people decide where to invest their money) and for assessing management's stewardship (judging whether managers are running a company well).

OBJECTIVE ④
Explain the development of accounting standards, and describe the concepts and principles

EXHIBIT 1–6   A Hierarchy of Financial-Statement Concepts

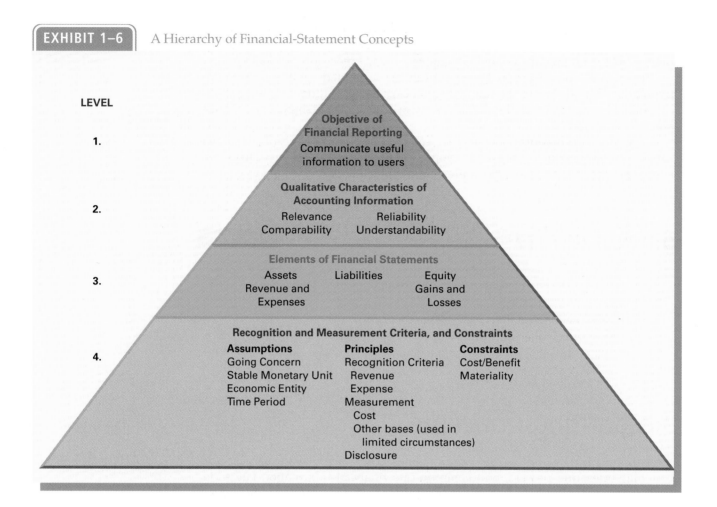

LEVEL

1.

Objective of
Financial Reporting
Communicate useful
information to users

2.

Qualitative Characteristics of
Accounting Information
Relevance   Reliability
Comparability   Understandability

3.

Elements of Financial Statements
Assets   Liabilities   Equity
Revenue and   Gains and
Expenses   Losses

4.

Recognition and Measurement Criteria, and Constraints

Assumptions	Principles	Constraints
Going Concern	Recognition Criteria	Cost/Benefit
Stable Monetary Unit	Revenue	Materiality
Economic Entity	Expense	
Time Period	Measurement	
	Cost	
	Other bases (used in	
	limited circumstances)	
	Disclosure	

The qualitative characteristics that increase the value of accounting information appear in Level 2 of Exhibit 1–6.

To be useful, information must be *understandable, relevant,* and *reliable,* as well as *comparable.* The information must be *understandable* to users if they are to be able to use it. *Relevant* information influences decisions and is useful for making predictions and for evaluating past performance. *Reliable* information is free from error and the bias of a particular viewpoint; it is in agreement with the underlying events and transactions. *Comparable* information is information that is produced by organizations using the same accounting principles and policies, and that allows comparison between the organizations. Comparability also allows comparisons over time or at two points in time.

There are two constraints to providing information to users that is understandable, relevant, reliable, and comparable. They are shown in Level 4 of Exhibit 1–6. The first constraint is that the benefits of the information produced should exceed the costs of producing the information, as stated in Paragraph 1000.16 in the *CICA Handbook.* The second constraint is *materiality,* as stated in Paragraph 1000.17; a piece of information is material if it would affect a decision maker's decision. Materiality is not defined in the standards but is a matter of the information preparer's judgment. For example, information about inventory is important to users of Canadian Tire's financial statements, since a change in inventory could change a decision maker's decision about investing in Canadian Tire or selling products to Canadian Tire. Thus, such information would be provided to decision makers. However, information about the supplies inventory at Coast Capital Savings Credit Union would not likely change the investment decision of a member of the credit union, so details of such information are not provided.

Level 3 in Exhibit 1–6 shows the standard elements of the financial statements. We will learn more about these items later in this chapter. In addition to the constraints described above, Level 4 in Exhibit 1–6 also contains the recognition and measurement criteria that form the basis of GAAP.

Exhibit 1–6 summarizes the key points of *Handbook* Section 1000: For any financial transaction or situation, the GAAP in Level 4 are used as guidelines for classifying the transaction's financial data into the standard financial-statement elements shown in Level 3. If these elements meet the Level-2 qualitative characteristics of accounting information, they are combined into financial statements that meet the Level-1 objective of reporting financial information useful for users.

This course will expose you to the generally accepted methods of accounting. We begin the discussion of GAAP in this section and introduce additional assumptions and principles as needed throughout the book.

Appendix C at the end of Volumes I and II summarizes the major elements of generally accepted accounting principles.

The Economic-Entity Assumption

The most basic assumption in accounting is that of the **entity**. An accounting entity is an organization or a section of an organization that stands apart from other organizations and individuals as a separate economic unit. From an accounting perspective, sharp boundaries are drawn around each entity so as not to confuse its affairs with those of other entities.

Suppose you decide to tutor other students, so you start a proprietorship and deposit all the money you earn in a bank account. After the first year, you have $2,000 in your bank account. Suppose only $1,000 of that amount came from your business's operation. The other $1,000 was a gift from your parents. If you follow the entity concept, you will keep separate the money generated by the business— one economic unit—from the money generated by the gift from your family—a second economic unit. This separation makes it possible to view the business's cash clearly; otherwise, you might be misled into believing that the business produced more cash than it did.

KEY POINT

The economic-entity assumption requires that the transactions of each entity be accounted for separately from the transactions of all other organizations and persons.

The economic-entity assumption also applies to not-for-profit organizations such as churches, synagogues, and government agencies. A hospital, for example, may have an emergency room, a pediatrics unit, and a surgery unit. The accounting system of the hospital should account for each separately to allow the managers to evaluate the progress of each unit.

In summary, the transactions of different entities making up the whole organization should not be accounted for together. Each entity should be accounted for separately, and then later, the results of each entity can be combined to create results for the whole organization.

The Reliability Characteristic

Accounting records and statements are based on the most reliable data available so that they will be as accurate and useful as possible. This guideline is the **reliability characteristic**. Reliable data are verifiable. They may be confirmed by any independent observer. For example, a purchase of supplies can be supported by paid invoices. A paid invoice is objective evidence of the cost of the supplies. Ideally, accounting records are based on information that flows from activities that are documented using objective evidence. Without the reliability characteristic, accounting records might be based on whims and opinions and would be subject to dispute.

Suppose you want to open a music store. To have a place for operations, you transfer a small building to the business. You believe the building is worth $200,000. Two real-estate professionals appraise the building at $190,000. Is $200,000 or $190,000 the more reliable estimate of the building's value? The real-estate appraisal of $190,000 is, because it is supported by independent, objective observations. The business should record the building at a cost of $190,000.

Measurement

Measurement is the process of determining the amount at which an item is recognized in the financial statements. There are a number of bases on which an amount can be measured. Financial statements are prepared primarily using the historical-cost basis of measurement, commonly called the *cost principle*. The **cost principle of measurement** states that acquired assets and services should be recorded at their actual cost (also called *historical cost*). Even though the purchaser may believe the price paid is a bargain, the item is recorded at the price actually paid and not at the "expected" cost. Suppose your music store purchased some compact discs from a supplier who was going out of business. Assume you got a good deal on this purchase and paid only $5,000 for merchandise that would have cost you $8,000 elsewhere. The cost principle of measurement requires you to record this merchandise at its actual cost of $5,000, not the $8,000 that you believe the compact discs to be worth.

The cost principle of measurement also holds that the accounting records should continue reporting the historical cost of an asset for as long as the business holds the asset. Why? Because cost is a reliable measure. Suppose your store holds the compact discs for three months. During that time, compact disc prices increase, and the compact discs can be sold for $9,000. Should their accounting value—the figure "on the books"—be the actual cost of $5,000 or the current market value of $9,000? According to the cost principle of measurement, the accounting value of the compact discs remains at actual cost of $5,000. There are some exceptions that will be discussed at various times throughout this book.

The Going-Concern Assumption

Another reason for measuring assets at historical cost is the **going-concern assumption**, which assumes that the entity will remain in operation for the foreseeable future. Most assets—that is, the firm's resources, such as supplies, land, buildings, automobiles, and equipment—are acquired to use rather than to sell. Under the going-concern assumption, accountants assume the business will remain in operation long enough to use existing assets for their intended purpose.

To understand the going-concern assumption, assume a business bought a delivery van for $5,000 and it is now worth $3,000. The going-concern assumption ensures that proper accounting procedures are followed, as if the business is going to continue operating indefinitely. For a going concern, the delivery van is valued at its cost of $5,000 in the accounting records. However, if the business is holding a Going-out-of-Business Sale, it would want to value the delivery van at $3,000 in the accounting records because that is the amount the business could sell it for today, on its final day of business. Accountants assume a business will operate indefinitely.

The Stable-Monetary-Unit Assumption

We think of the cost of a loaf of bread and a month's apartment rent in terms of their dollar value. In Canada, accountants record transactions in dollars because the dollar is the medium of exchange. French and German transactions are measured in euros. The Japanese record transactions in yen.

Unlike a litre, a kilometre, or a tonne, the value of a dollar or a euro changes over time. A rise in the general level of prices is called *inflation*. During inflation a dollar will purchase less milk, less toothpaste, and less of other goods over time. When prices are relatively stable—when there is little inflation—the purchasing power of money is also stable.

Accountants assume that the dollar's purchasing power is relatively stable. The **stable-monetary-unit assumption** is the basis for ignoring the effect of inflation in the accounting records. It allows accountants to add and subtract dollar amounts as though each dollar has the same purchasing power as any other dollar at any other time. In certain countries in South America, where inflation rates are often high, accountants make adjustments to report monetary amounts in units of current buying power—a very different concept.

DID YOU GET IT?

MyAccountingLab

To check your understanding of the material in this Learning Objective, complete these questions. The solutions appear on MyAccountingLab so you can check your progress.

10. Explain why financial information must be both relevant and reliable.

11. Suppose you are considering the purchase of land for future expansion. The seller is asking $100,000 for land that cost her $70,000. An appraisal shows the land has a value of $94,000. You first offer $80,000. The seller counteroffers with $96,000. Finally, you and the seller agree on a price of $92,000. What dollar amount for this land is reported on your financial statements? Which accounting assumption or principle guides your answer?

12. Suppose you own a company that delivers newspapers. The company owns two trucks that are used for delivering the papers. You have decided that you need a new car for mainly personal purposes but you want the company to buy it for you. Is this appropriate? Name the assumption or principle that must be considered.

The Accounting Equation

Financial statements tell us how a business is performing and where it stands. They are the final product of the accounting process. But how do we arrive at the items and amounts that make up the financial statements? The most basic tool of the accountant is the **accounting equation**. It measures the resources of a business and the claims to those resources.

OBJECTIVE 5
Describe and use the accounting equation to analyze business transactions

Assets and Liabilities

Assets are economic resources controlled by an entity that are expected to benefit the business in the future. Cash, office supplies, merchandise inventory, furniture, land, and buildings are examples of assets.

Claims to those assets come from two sources. **Liabilities** are debts that are payable to outsiders. These *outside* parties are called *creditors*. For example, a creditor who has lent money to a business has a claim—a legal right—to a part of the assets until the business pays the debt. Many liabilities have the word *payable* in their titles. Examples include Accounts Payable, Notes Payable, and Salaries Payable. *Insider* claims to the business assets are owners' claims called **owner's equity** or **capital**. An owner's claim to some of the entity's assets begins when the owner invests in the business.

The accounting equation in Exhibit 1–7 shows how assets, liabilities, and owner's equity are related. Assets appear on the left side of the equation. The legal and economic claims against the assets—the liabilities and owner's equity—appear on the right side of the equation. As Exhibit 1–7 shows, *the two sides must be equal*:

EXHIBIT 1–7

The Accounting Equation

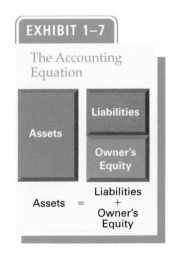

Economic Resources   Claims to Economic Resources

(Outsiders)   (Insiders)

Assets   =   Liabilities + Owner's Equity

KEY POINT

Increases in cash are not always revenues. Cash also increases when a company borrows money, but borrowing money creates a liability—not a revenue. Revenue results from rendering a service or selling a product, not necessarily from the receipt of cash.

KEY POINT

Decreases in cash are not always expenses. Cash decreases when land is purchased, for example, but the purchase also increases the asset Land, which is not an expense. Expenses result from using goods or services in the course of earning revenue, not necessarily from the payment of cash.

Owner's Equity

Owner's equity is the amount of an entity's assets that remains after the liabilities are subtracted. For this reason, owner's equity is often referred to as *net assets,* and the accounting equation can be written to show this:

$$\textbf{Assets} - \textbf{Liabilities} = \textbf{Owner's Equity}$$

The purpose of business is to increase owner's equity through **revenues,** which are amounts earned by delivering goods or services to customers. Revenues increase owner's equity because they increase the business's assets but not its liabilities. As a result, the owner's share of business assets increases. Examples of revenue include sales revenue from selling goods, service revenue from selling services, interest revenue from saving money in a bank, and dividend revenue from investing in shares of stock. Exhibit 1–8 shows that owner investments and revenues increase the owner's equity of the business.

Exhibit 1–8 also shows that owner withdrawals and expenses decrease owner's equity. **Owner withdrawals** are those amounts or resources removed from the business by the owner. Withdrawals are the opposite of owner investments. **Expenses** are decreases in owner's equity that occur from using or consuming assets or increasing liabilities in the course of delivering goods and services to customers. Expenses are the cost of doing business and are the opposite of revenues. Expenses include the cost of office rent; interest payments; salaries of employees; insurance; advertisements; property taxes; utility payments for water; electricity; gas; and so forth.

EXHIBIT 1–8 | Transactions that Increase and Decrease Owner's Equity

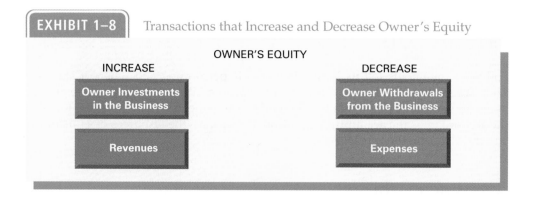

Accounting for Business Transactions

Accounting is based on transactions, not opinions or desires. A **transaction** is any event that affects the financial position of the business entity *and* can be measured reliably. Many events may affect a company, including elections and economic booms. Accountants do not record the effects of these events because they cannot be measured reliably. An accountant records as transactions only events with dollar amounts that can be measured reliably, such as purchases and sales of merchandise inventory, payment of rent, and collection of cash from customers. In Exhibit 1–1 on page 3, transactions are the middle step in the flow of information in an accounting system.

KEY POINT

A transaction is an event that must always satisfy these two conditions:

1. It affects the financial position of a business entity, and
2. It can be reliably recorded in the accounting records.

To illustrate accounting for business transactions, let's assume that John Ladner opens an environmental consulting business, Ladner Environmental Services (LES). We will now consider 11 events and analyze each in terms of its effect on the accounting equation of LES. *Remember that the accounting equation must always remain in balance.* Transaction analysis is the essence of accounting.

Transaction 1: Starting the Business   Ladner invests $250,000 of his money to start the business. Specifically, he deposits $250,000 in a bank account entitled Ladner Environmental Services.

The effect of this transaction on the accounting equation of the LES business entity is

	Assets	=	Liabilities	+	Owner's Equity	Type of Owner's Equity Transaction
	Cash				John Ladner, Capital	
(1)	+250,000				+250,000	*Owner investment*

For every transaction, the amount on the left side of the equation must equal the amount on the right side. The first transaction increases both the assets (in this case, Cash) and the owner's equity of the business (John Ladner, Capital). The transaction involves no liabilities of the business because it creates no obligation for LES to pay an outside party. The Assets and Liabilities elements of the accounting equation will be expanded to show the specific accounts affected by a transaction, but Owner's Equity will not be expanded. Therefore, to the right of the transaction, we write "owner investment" to keep track of the reason for the effect on Owner's Equity.

Transaction 2: Purchase of Land   LES purchases land for a future office location, paying cash of $100,000. The effect of this transaction on the accounting equation is

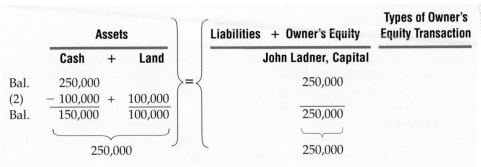

LEARNING TIPS

Note that the sums of balances (which we abbreviate Bal.) on both sides of the equation are equal. This equality must always exist.

Learning Tips are suggestions for learning or remembering important concepts.

The cash purchase of land increases one asset, Land, and decreases another asset, Cash, by the same amount. After the transaction is completed, LES has cash of $150,000, land of $100,000, no liabilities, and owner's equity of $250,000.

Transaction 3: Purchase of Office Supplies   LES buys stationery and other office supplies, agreeing to pay $5,000 within 30 days. This transaction increases both the assets and the liabilities of the company, as follows:

		Assets				=	Liabilities	+	Owner's Equity
	Cash	+	Office Supplies	+	Land		Accounts Payable	+	John Ladner, Capital
Bal.	150,000				100,000				250,000
(3)			+ 5,000				+ 5,000		
Bal.	150,000		5,000		100,000		5,000		250,000
			255,000					255,000	

The asset affected is Office Supplies, and the liability is called an **account payable**. A *payable is always a liability.* Because LES is obligated to pay $5,000 in the future but signs no formal promissory note, we record the liability as an Account Payable. (If a promissory note had been signed, we would have recorded the liability as a **Note Payable**.)

Transaction 4: Earning of Service Revenue LES earns service revenue by providing environmental consulting services for clients. Assume the business earns $20,000 and collects this amount in cash. The effect on the accounting equation is an increase in the asset Cash and an increase in John Ladner, Capital, as follows:

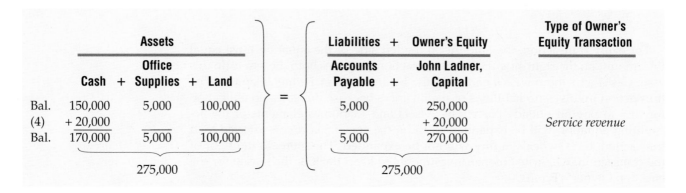

A revenue transaction causes the business to grow, as shown by the increase in total assets and in the sum of total liabilities plus owner's equity. A company like Home Hardware or The Bay that sells goods to customers is a merchandising business. Its revenue is called *sales revenue.* In contrast, LES performs services for clients. LES's revenue is called *service revenue.*

KEY POINT

All receivables are assets. All payables are liabilities.

Transaction 5: Earning of Service Revenue on Account LES performs consulting services for clients who do not pay immediately. In return for the services, LES issues an invoice and the clients will pay the $15,000 amount within one month. This debt is an asset to LES, an **account receivable** because the business expects to collect the cash in the future. In accounting, we say that LES performed this service *on account* and earned the revenue. Performing the service, not collecting the cash, earns the revenue. This $15,000 of service revenue is as real an increase in the wealth of LES's business as the $20,000 of revenue that was collected immediately in Transaction 4. LES records an increase in the asset Accounts Receivable and an increase in Service Revenue, which increases John Ladner, Capital, as follows:

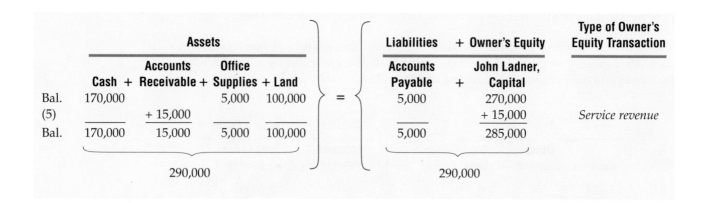

Transaction 6: Payment of Expenses During the month, LES pays $7,500 in cash expenses: office rent, $3,000 (LES purchased land to build an office in the future (transaction 2), but the company is renting office space in the meantime);

employee salary, $3,500 (for a full-time assistant); and total utilities, $1,000. The effects on the accounting equation are

		Assets					Liabilities	+ Owner's Equity	Type of Owner's Equity Transaction
	Cash	+ Accounts Receivable	+ Office Supplies	+ Land		=	Accounts Payable	+ John Ladner, Capital	
Bal.	170,000	15,000	5,000	100,000			5,000	285,000	
(6)	−3,000							−3,000	Rent expense
	−3,500							−3,500	Salary expense
	−1,000							−1,000	Utilities expense
Bal.	162,500	15,000	5,000	100,000			5,000	277,500	

282,500 = 282,500

Expenses have the opposite effect of revenues. Expenses cause the business to shrink, as shown by the decreased balances of total assets and owner's equity.

Each expense should be recorded in a separate transaction. Here, for simplicity, the expenses are listed together. Alternatively, we could record the cash payment in a single amount for the sum of those three expenses, $7,500 ($3,000 + $3,500 + $1,000). In either case, the "balance" of the equation holds, as we know it must.

Transaction 7: Payment on Account LES pays $4,000 to the store from which it purchased $5,000 worth of office supplies in Transaction 3. In accounting, we say that the business pays $4,000 *on account*. The effect on the accounting equation is a decrease in the asset Cash and a decrease in the liability Accounts Payable as follows:

		Assets					Liabilities	+ Owner's Equity
	Cash	+ Accounts Receivable	+ Office Supplies	+ Land		=	Accounts Payable	+ John Ladner, Capital
Bal.	162,500	15,000	5,000	100,000			5,000	277,500
(7)	−4,000						−4,000	
Bal.	158,500	15,000	5,000	100,000			1,000	277,500

278,500 = 278,500

The payment of cash on account has no effect on the asset Office Supplies because the payment does not increase or decrease the supplies available to the business. Likewise, the payment on account does not affect expenses. LES was paying off a liability, not an expense.

Transaction 8: Personal Transaction Ladner remodels his home at a cost of $30,000, paying cash from personal funds. This event is *not* a transaction of LES. It has no effect on LES's business affairs and therefore is not recorded by the business. It is a transaction of the Ladner *personal* entity, not the LES business entity. We are focusing now solely on the *business* entity, and this event does not affect it. This transaction illustrates the *economic-entity assumption*.

Transaction 9: Collection on Account In Transaction 5, LES performed consulting services for clients on account. The business now collects $11,000 from a client. We say that it collects the cash *on account*. It will record an increase in the asset Cash and a decrease in the asset Accounts Receivable. Should it also record an increase in service revenue? No, because LES already recorded the revenue when it performed the service in Transaction 5. The effect on the accounting equation is

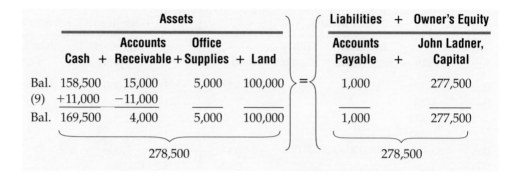

Total assets are unchanged from the preceding transaction's total. Why? Because LES merely exchanged one asset for another.

Transaction 10: Sale of Land   Ladner sells 50% of the land purchased in Transaction 2. The sale price of $50,000 is equal to LES's cost of the land. LES sells the land and receives $50,000 cash, and the effect on the accounting equation is

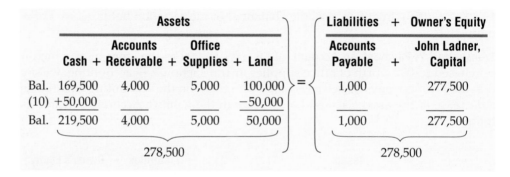

Transaction 11: Withdrawing of Cash   Ladner withdraws $5,500 cash for his personal use. The effect on the accounting equation is

	Assets					Liabilities	+	Owner's Equity	Type of Owner's Equity Transaction
	Cash +	Accounts Receivable +	Office Supplies +	Land		Accounts Payable	+	John Ladner, Capital	
Bal.	219,500	4,000	5,000	50,000	=	1,000		277,500	
	−5,500							−5,500	*Owner withdrawal*
Bal.	214,000	4,000	5,000	50,000		1,000		272,000	
		273,000					273,000		

Ladner's withdrawal of $5,500 cash decreases the asset Cash and also the owner's equity of the business.

Owner withdrawals do not represent a business expense because the cash is used for the owner's personal affairs unrelated to the business. We record this decrease in owner's equity as Withdrawals or Drawings. The double underlines below each column indicate a final total after the last transaction.

Evaluating Business Transactions

MyAccountingLab | Accounting Cycle Tutorial
1. Balance Sheet Accounts and Transactions pages 1–12
2. Income Statement Accounts and Transactions pages 1–6

Exhibit 1–9 summarizes the 11 preceding transactions. Panel A of the exhibit lists the details of the transactions, and Panel B presents the analysis. As you study the exhibit, note that every transaction maintains the equality of the equation

Assets = Liabilities + Owner's Equity

These references to MyAccountingLab are reminders that you can review these topics using the Accounting Cycle Tutorials on MyAccountingLab.

EXHIBIT 1–9	Analysis of Transactions of Ladner Environmental Services

PANEL A: DETAILS OF TRANSACTIONS

(1) The business recorded the $250,000 cash investment made by Ladner.
(2) Paid $100,000 cash for land.
(3) Bought $5,000 of office supplies on account.
(4) Received $20,000 cash from clients for service revenue earned.
(5) Performed services for clients on account, $15,000.
(6) Paid cash expenses: rent, $3,000; employee salary, $3,500; utilities, $1,000.
(7) Paid $4,000 on the account payable created in Transaction 3.
(8) Remodelled Ladner's personal residence. This is *not* a transaction of the business.
(9) Collected $11,000 on the account receivable created in Transaction 5.
(10) Sold land for cash equal to its cost of $50,000.
(11) The business paid $5,500 cash to Ladner as a withdrawal.

PANEL B: ANALYSIS OF TRANSACTIONS

	Assets				=	Liabilities	+ Owner's Equity	Type of Owner's Equity Transaction
	Cash +	Accounts Receivable +	Office Supplies +	Land		Accounts Payable +	John Ladner, Capital	
(1)	+250,000						+250,000	Owner investment
Bal.	250,000						250,000	
(2)	−100,000			+ 100,000				
Bal.	150,000			100,000			250,000	
(3)			+5,000			+5,000		
Bal.	150,000		5,000	100,000		5,000	250,000	
(4)	+20,000						+20,000	Service revenue
Bal.	170,000		5,000	100,000		5,000	270,000	
(5)		+15,000					+15,000	Service revenue
Bal.	170,000	15,000	5,000	100,000		5,000	285,000	
(6)	−3,000						−3,000	Rent expense
	−3,500						−3,500	Salary expense
	−1,000						−1,000	Utilities expense
Bal.	162,500	15,000	5,000	100,000		5,000	277,500	
(7)	−4,000					−4,000		
Bal.	158,500	15,000	5,000	100,000		1,000	277,500	
(8)	Not a transaction of the business							
(9)	+11,000	−11,000						
Bal.	169,500	4,000	5,000	100,000		1,000	277,500	
(10)	+50,000			−50,000				
Bal.	219,500	4,000	5,000	50,000		1,000	277,500	
(11)	−5,500						−5,500	Owner withdrawal
Bal.	214,000	4,000	5,000	50,000		1,000	272,000	

273,000   273,000

To check your understanding of the material in this Learning Objective, complete these questions. The solutions appear on MyAccountingLab so you can check your progress.

13. a. If the assets of a business are $50,000 and the liabilities total $45,000, how much is the owner's equity?

 b. If the owner's equity in a business is $40,000 and the liabilities are $10,000, how much are the assets?

14. Indicate whether each account listed below is a(n) asset (A), liability (L), owner's equity (OE), revenue (R), or expense (E) account.

Accounts Receivable	_____	Salary Expense	_____
Computer Equipment	_____	Consulting Service Revenue	_____
S. Scott, Capital	_____	Cash	_____
Rent Expense	_____	Notes Payable	_____
Supplies	_____	Supplies Expense	_____
S. Scott, Withdrawals	_____	Accounts Payable	_____

15. A customer pays a deposit of $25,000 to your company for a service that you will begin to provide six months from now. How do you account for this transaction?

The Financial Statements

OBJECTIVE 6

Prepare and evaluate the financial statements

Once the analysis of the transactions is complete, what is the next step in the accounting process? How does a business present the results of the transactions? We now look at the *financial statements,* which are the formal reports of an entity's financial information. The primary financial statements are the:

- Income statement
- Statement of owner's equity
- Balance sheet
- Cash flow statement

Income Statement   The **income statement** presents a summary of the *revenues* and *expenses* of an entity for a specific period of time, such as a month or a year. The income statement, also called the **statement of earnings** or **statement of operations**, is like a video of the entity's operations—a moving financial picture of business operations during the period. The income statement holds perhaps the most important single piece of information about a business—its *net income or net loss.* Business people run their businesses with the objective of having more revenues than expenses. An excess of total revenues over total expenses is called **net income**, **net earnings**, or **net profit**. If total expenses exceed total revenues, the result is called a **net loss**.

Statement of Owner's Equity   The **statement of owner's equity** presents a summary of the changes that occurred in the entity's *owner's equity* during a specific period of time, such as a month or a year.

 Increases in owner's equity arise from:

- Owner investments
- Net income (revenues exceed expenses)

 Decreases in owner's equity arise from:

- Owner withdrawals
- Net loss (expenses exceed revenues)

 Net income or net loss comes directly from the income statement. Owner investments and withdrawals are capital transactions between the business and its owner, so they do not affect the income statement.

Balance Sheet   The **balance sheet** lists all the assets, liabilities, and owner's equity of an entity as of a specific date, usually the end of a month or a year. The balance sheet is like a snapshot of the entity. For this reason, it is also called the **statement of financial position**.

Cash Flow Statement The **cash flow statement** reports the cash coming in (*cash receipts*) and the cash going out (*cash payments* or *disbursements*) during a period. Business activities result in a net cash inflow (receipts greater than payments) or a net cash outflow (payments greater than receipts). The cash flow statement shows the net increase or decrease in cash during the period and the cash balance at the end of the period. We focus on the cash flow statement in Chapter 17.

Computers and software programs have had a significant impact on the preparation of the financial statements. Financial statements can be produced instantaneously after the data from the financial records are entered into the computer. Of course, in manual *and* computerized accounting systems, any errors that occur in the financial records will be passed on to the financial statements. For this reason, the person responsible for analyzing the accounting data is critical to the accuracy of the financial statements.

Financial Statement Headings

Each financial statement has a heading, which gives three pieces of data:

- The proper name of the business (in our discussion Ladner Environmental Services)
- The full name of the particular statement
- The date or time period covered by the statement

A balance sheet taken at the end of year 2010 would be dated December 31, 2010. A balance sheet prepared at the end of March 2011 is dated March 31, 2011.

An income statement or a statement of owner's equity covering a year ending on December 31, 2010, is dated "For the Year Ended December 31, 2010." A monthly income statement or statement of owner's equity for September 2011 has in its heading "For the Month Ended September 30, 2011" or simply "For the Month of September 2011." Income *must* be identified with a particular time period. This is because if December 31, 2010, appeared in the heading of these statements, you would not know whether the net income amount was good or bad unless you knew the time period covered by the statements. The net income amount could be good if the time period were one day, but it could be bad if the time period were one year.

Relationships among the Financial Statements

Exhibit 1–10 on page 22 illustrates all four financial statements. Their data come from the transaction analysis in Exhibit 1–9. We are assuming the transactions occurred during the month of April 2010. Study the exhibit carefully, because it shows the relationships among the four financial statements.

Observe the following in Exhibit 1–10:

1. The *income statement* for the month ended April 30, 2010,
   a. Reports all *revenues* and all *expenses* during the period. Expenses are often listed alphabetically, but can also be listed in decreasing order of amount, with the largest expense first.
   b. Reports *net income* of the period if total revenues exceed total expenses, as in the case of LES's operations for April. If total expenses exceed total revenues, a *net loss* is reported instead.

2. The *statement of owner's equity* for the month ended April 30, 2010,
   a. Opens with the owner's capital balance at the beginning of the period.
   b. Adds *investment by the owner* and adds *net income* (or subtracts *net loss,* as the case may be). Net income (or net loss) comes directly from the income statement (see arrow 1 in Exhibit 1–10).

EXHIBIT 1–10   Financial Statements of Ladner Environmental Services

LADNER ENVIRONMENTAL SERVICES
Income Statement
For the Month Ended April 30, 2010

Revenue:		
Service revenue...		$35,000
Expenses:		
Rent expense	$3,000	
Salary expense	3,500	
Utilities expense	1,000	
Total expenses...		7,500
Net income		$27,500

LADNER ENVIRONMENTAL SERVICES
Statement of Owner's Equity
For the Month Ended April 30, 2010

John Ladner, capital, April 1, 2010...	$ 0
Add: Investment by owner..	250,000
Net income for the month...	27,500
	277,500
Less: Withdrawals by owner	(5,500)
John Ladner, capital, April 30, 2010..	$272,000

1

LADNER ENVIRONMENTAL SERVICES
Balance Sheet
April 30, 2010

2

Assets		Liabilities	
Cash..	$214,000	Accounts payable	$ 1,000
Accounts receivable	4,000	**Owner's Equity**	
Office supplies	5,000	John Ladner, capital	272,000
Land	50,000		
		Total liabilities and	
Total assets	$273,000	owner's equity..................	$273,000

LADNER ENVIRONMENTAL SERVICES
Cash Flow Statement*
For the Month Ended April 30, 2010

3

Cash flows from operating activities		
Cash collections from customers**		$ 31,000
Cash payments to suppliers***	$ (8,000)	
Cash payments to employees..	(3,500)	(11,500)
Net cash inflow from operating activities		19,500
Cash flows from investing activities		
Acquisition of land	$(100,000)	
Proceeds from sale of land	50,000	
Net cash outflow from investing activities		(50,000)
Cash flows from financing activities		
Investment by owner..	$ 250,000	
Withdrawal by owner	(5,500)	
Net cash inflow from financing activities		244,500
Net increase in cash		$214,000
Cash balance, April 1, 2010..		0
Cash balance, April 30, 2010..		$214,000

*Chapter 17 explains how to prepare this statement.
**$20,000 + $11,000 = $31,000
***$3,000 + $1,000 + $4,000 = $8,000

c. Subtracts *withdrawals by the owner.* The parentheses around an amount indicate a subtraction.

d. Ends with the owner's capital balance at the end of the period.

3. The *balance sheet* at April 30, 2010, the end of the period,

a. Reports all *assets,* all *liabilities,* and *owner's equity* of the business at the end of the period.

b. Reports that total assets equal the sum of total liabilities plus total owner's equity.

c. Reports the owner's ending capital balance, taken directly from the statement of owner's equity (see arrow 2).

4. The *cash flow statement* for the month ended April 30, 2010,

a. Reports cash flows from three types of business activities (*operating, investing,* and *financing* activities) during the month. Each category of cash-flow activities includes both cash receipts, which are positive amounts, and cash payments, which are negative amounts (denoted by parentheses). Each category results in a net cash inflow or a net cash outflow for the period. We discuss these categories in detail in Chapter 17.

b. Reports a net increase in cash (or a net decrease, as the case may be) during the month and ends with the cash balance at April 30, 2010. This is the amount of cash to report on the balance sheet (see arrow 3).

DID YOU GET IT?

MyAccountingLab

To check your understanding of the material in this Learning Objective, complete these questions. The solutions appear on MyAccountingLab so you can check your progress.

16. Indicate whether each account listed below appears on the balance sheet (B), income statement (I), statement of owner's equity (OE), or cash flow statement (CF). Some items appear on more than one statement.

Accounts Receivable	_____	Salary Expense	_____
Computer Equipment	_____	Consulting Service Revenue	_____
S. Scott, Capital	_____	Cash	_____
Rent Expense	_____	Notes Payable	_____
Supplies	_____	Supplies Expense	_____
S. Scott, Withdrawals	_____	Accounts Payable	_____

17. Study Exhibit 1–10, which gives the financial statements for Ladner Environmental Services (LES) at April 30, 2010, the end of the first month of operations. Answer these questions about LES to evaluate the business's results.

a. What was the business's result of operations for the month of April—a net income (profit) or a net loss, and how much? Which financial statement provides this information?

b. How much owner capital did the company have at the beginning of April? At the end of April? Identify all the items that changed owner's capital during the month, along with their amounts. Which financial statement provides this information?

c. How much cash does the company have as it moves into the next month—that is, May 2010? Which financial statement provides this information?

d. How much do clients owe LES at April 30? Is this an asset or a liability for the business? What does the business call this item?

e. How much does the business owe outsiders at April 30? Is this an asset or a liability for the business? What does the business call this item?

International Financial Reporting Standards: Recognizing the Globalization of Accounting

OBJECTIVE ⑦

Explain the development of international financial reporting standards (IFRS)

The final Learning Objective in each chapter addresses international financial reporting standards (IFRS) as they relate to the topics discussed in that chapter. When appropriate, Did You Get It? questions and end-of-chapter material related to this Learning Objective are provided.

The accounting concepts and principles described earlier in this chapter have been developed in response to the accounting and economic environment in Canada. The Accounting Standards Board and its predecessor committees have been charged with the task of creating accounting standards for most of the past century.

The fact that most countries in the world developed their own set of accounting standards was not seen as problematic until recently. International accounting associations have always exchanged ideas on standards, and most countries have followed approximately the same standards. However, differences have arisen over the years due primarily to unique legal, regulatory, and cultural issues. For example, the standards followed in the United States would be seen to be more "rules-based." In a rules-based environment, accountants are provided "rules" for how to account for nearly every transaction. In part, this approach is in response to the concerns of the securities regulator, the Securities and Exchange Commission (SEC), and to the accounting scandals of recent years. In other countries, such as Canada, the accounting standards have followed a "principles-based" approach, where accountants use professional judgment combined with an understanding of the conceptual framework for accounting to determine the proper accounting treatment for various transactions.

As globalization has become more common over the past decade, with many companies doing business internationally and selling ownership in their companies worldwide, the use of different accounting standards in different countries has become more problematic. For example, suppose you were interested in investing in shares of Australia and New Zealand Banking Group Limited (ANZ), which has its head office in Melbourne, Australia. Its shares trade on the Australian Securities Exchange, which performs the same function in Australia as the Toronto Stock Exchange does in Canada. You could accomplish this goal quite quickly, as you or a stockbroker working on your behalf could readily purchase the shares. However, what if you were unsure of whether to buy shares in ANZ or Royal Bank of Canada? To help you decide which banking group to buy shares in, you might review the financial statements of each company and try to compare financial performance. While you would have confidence in your understanding of how Royal Bank's financial statements were prepared (following Canadian GAAP), ANZ's financial statements have been prepared using the standards incorporated in the *Australian Corporations Act of 2001*. While many of the accounting standards are the same, many are different. Even the presentation of the financial information is quite different from that followed in the Canadian model.

To address the concerns of international investors, regulatory groups, and other interested parties, international financial reporting standards (IFRS) issued by the International Accounting Standards Board have been adopted by most of the industrialized countries of the world. Publicly accountable companies in Canada will begin using IFRS in 2011, while private enterprises in Canada will have the option of using IFRS or following Canadian GAAP for private enterprises. After Canada's adoption of IFRS, the only major country not following IFRS for publicly accountable companies will be the United States.

While the focus in this textbook will be on Canadian GAAP for private enterprises, each relevant chapter will include a separate Learning Objective where the impact of IFRS will be discussed.

DID YOU GET IT?

To check your understanding of the material in this Learning Objective, complete this question. The solution appears on MyAccountingLab so you can check your progress.

18. Canadian public companies sell their shares to the public through Canadian stock exchanges. Why is it important for Canadian public companies to follow accounting principles that are being followed in most industrialized countries in the world?

As we conclude this chapter, we return to our opening question: Why are accounting and the business environment important? The Decision Guidelines feature below summarizes the chapter by examining examples of business decisions that are made. The chapter-opening questions are answered here. A Decision Guidelines feature appears in each chapter of this book. The Decision Guidelines serve as useful summaries of the decision-making process and its foundation in accounting information.

> Decision Guidelines show why accounting principles and concepts are important to business people, not just accountants. They are also an excellent summary of the chapter topic.

DECISION GUIDELINES — Major Business Decisions

Decision	Guidelines
How should we organize a business?	If a single owner, but not incorporated—a *proprietorship*. If two or more owners, but not incorporated—a *partnership*. If the business issues shares to shareholders—a *corporation*.
What should we account for?	Account for the business, which is a separate entity apart from its owner (*Economic-entity assumption*). Account for transactions and events that affect the business *and* can be measured objectively (*Reliability characteristic*).
How much should we record for assets and liabilities?	Actual historical amount (*Measurement—historical cost basis*).
How do we analyze a transaction?	Use accounting equation: Assets = Liabilities + Owner's Equity Note: Owner's equity is called shareholders' equity if the entity is a corporation.
How do we measure profits and losses?	Income statement: Revenues − Expenses = Net Income (or Net Loss)
Did owner's equity increase or decrease?	Statement of owner's equity: Beginning capital + Owner investments + Net income (or − Net loss) − Owner withdrawals = Ending capital
Where does the business stand financially?	Balance sheet (accounting equation): Assets = Liabilities + Owner's Equity Income statement
How did the owner's investment change over the period?	Statement of owner's equity
Where did the business's cash come from? Where did the cash go?	Cash flow statement: *Operating activities:* Net cash inflow (or outflow) + *Investing activities:* Net cash inflow (or outflow) + *Financing activities:* Net cash inflow (or outflow) = Net increase (decrease) in cash

Summary Problem for Your Review

The Summary Problem for Your Review is an extensive, challenging review problem that pulls together the chapter concepts.

Lynn Raffan opens a home design business in Hamilton. She is the sole owner of the proprietorship, which she names Premier Home Design. During the first month of operations, July 2010, the following transactions occurred:

a. Raffan invests $50,000 of personal funds to start the business.

b. The business purchases, on account, office supplies costing $1,200.

c. Premier Home Design pays cash of $35,000 to acquire a parcel of land. The business intends to use the land as a future building site for its business office.

d. The business provides services for clients and receives cash of $6,000.

e. The business pays $900 on the account payable created in Transaction (b).

f. Raffan pays $4,000 of personal funds for a vacation for her family.

g. The business pays cash expenses for office rent, $1,500, and utilities, $400.

h. The business returns to the supplier office supplies that cost $200. The wrong supplies were shipped.

i. Raffan withdraws $2,000 cash for personal use.

Required

Name: Premier Home Design
Industry: Home design consulting
Fiscal Period: Month of July 2010

1. Analyze the preceding transactions in terms of their effects on the accounting equation of Premier Home Design. Use Exhibit 1–9 on page 19 as a guide but show balances only after the last transaction.

2. Prepare the income statement, statement of owner's equity, and balance sheet of Premier Home Design after recording the transactions. Use Exhibit 1–10 on page 22 as a guide.

SOLUTION

As you review the details of each transaction, think of the names of the accounts that will be affected.

1. Panel A: Details of Transactions

a. Raffan invested $50,000 cash to start the business.

The worked solution provides a full solution so you can check your progress, as well as reminders and hints for how to find the solution.

b. Purchased $1,200 in office supplies on account.

c. Paid $35,000 to acquire land as a future building site.

d. Earned service revenue and received cash of $6,000.

e. Paid $900 on account.

f. Paid for a personal vacation, which is not a transaction of the business.

g. Paid cash expenses for rent, $1,500, and utilities, $400.

h. Returned office supplies that cost $200.

i. Withdrew $2,000 cash for personal use.

Panel B: Analysis of Transactions

	Assets						Liabilities	+	Owner's Equity	Type of Owner's Equity Transaction
	Cash	+	Office Supplies	+	Land		Accounts Payable	+	Lynn Raffan, Capital	
(a)	+ 50,000								+50,000	Owner investment
(b)			+1,200				+1,200			
(c)	− 35,000				+35,000					
(d)	+ 6,000								+ 6,000	Service revenue
(e)	− 900					=	− 900			
(f)	Not a business transaction									
(g)	− 1,500								− 1,500	Rent expense
	− 400								− 400	Utilities expense
(h)			− 200				− 200			
(i)	− 2,000								− 2,000	Owner withdrawal
Bal.	16,200		1,000		35,000		100		52,100	

Assets total: 52,200

Liabilities + Owner's Equity total: 52,200

For each transaction, make sure the accounting equation Assets = Liabilities + Owner's Equity balances before going on to the next transaction.

2. Financial Statements of Premier Home Design

PREMIER HOME DESIGN
Income Statement
For the Month Ended July 31, 2010

Revenue:		
Service revenue...		$ 6,000
Expenses:		
Rent expense	$1,500	
Utilities expense	400	
Total expenses		1,900
Net Income		$ 4,100

The title must include the name of the company, "Income Statement," and the specific period of time covered. It is critical that the time period be defined.

Gather all the revenue and expense account names and amounts from Panel B. They appear in the Lynn Raffan, Capital column.
- List the revenue account first.
- List the expense accounts next. Expenses are usually listed in alphabetical order.

PREMIER HOME DESIGN
Statement of Owner's Equity
For the Month Ended July 31, 2010

Lynn Raffan, capital, July 1, 2010...	$ 0
Add: Investment by owner	50,000
Net income for July	4,100
	54,100
Less: Withdrawal by owner	2,000
Lynn Raffan, capital, July 31, 2010...	$ 52,100

The title must include the name of the company, "Statement of Owner's Equity," and the specific period of time covered. It is critical that the time period be defined.

The net income amount (or net loss amount) is transferred from the income statement.

The withdrawal amount is found in Panel B in the Lynn Raffan, Capital column.

PREMIER HOME DESIGN
Balance Sheet
July 31, 2010

Assets		Liabilities	
Cash...............................	$16,200	Accounts payable	$ 100
Office supplies..........................	1,000		
Land..	35,000	**Owner's Equity**	
		Lynn Raffan, capital	52,100
		Total liabilities and	
Total assets.................................	$52,200	owner's equity	$52,200

The title must include the name of the company, "Balance Sheet," and the date of the balance sheet. It shows the financial position on one specific date.

Gather all the asset and liability accounts and Bal. amounts from Panel B. List assets first, then liabilities. The owner's equity amount is transferred from the statement of owner's equity.

It is vital that Total Assets = Total Liabilities + Owner's Equity

Summary

The Summary gives a concise description of the material covered in the chapter. It is organized by Learning Objective.

1. **Define accounting, and describe the users of accounting information.** Accounting is an information system for measuring, processing, and communicating financial information. As the "language of business," accounting helps a wide range of users make business decisions. Examples of users include individual investors, businesses, government agencies, and lenders.

2. **Explain why ethics and rules of conduct are crucial in accounting and business.** Ethical considerations affect all areas of accounting and business. Users need relevant and reliable information about companies to make decisions. The professional accounting groups in Canada have codes of ethics and rules of conduct to assure society that accountants behave ethically.

3. **Describe and discuss the forms of business organizations.** The three basic forms of business organizations are the proprietorship, the partnership, and the corporation. A summary and comparison of the three forms are given in Exhibit 1–5 on page 8. Limited-liability partnerships (LLPs) and limited-liability companies (LLCs) are special forms of partnerships and proprietorships.

4. **Explain the development of accounting standards, and describe the concepts and principles.** *Generally accepted accounting principles (GAAP)* for private enterprises guide accountants in their work. They are developed by the *Accounting Standards Board (AcSB)* and published in the *CICA Handbook*. For example, accountants use the *economic-entity assumption* to keep the business's records separate from the records of other economic units. Other important guidelines or standards are the *reliability characteristic*, the *cost principle*, the *going-concern assumption*, and the *stable-monetary-unit assumption*.

5. **Describe and use the accounting equation to analyze business transactions.** In its most common form, the accounting equation is

    Assets = Liabilities + Owner's Equity

    A transaction is an event that affects the financial position of an entity *and* can be reliably recorded. Transactions affect a business's assets, liabilities, and owner's equity. Therefore, transactions are often analyzed in terms of their effect on the accounting equation.

6. **Prepare and evaluate the financial statements.** The *financial statements* communicate information for decision making by users of the entity's financial information, including managers, owners, and creditors. The *income statement* summarizes the entity's operations in terms of revenues earned and expenses incurred during a specific period of time. Total revenues minus total expenses equal net income. The *statement of owner's equity* reports the changes in owner's equity during the period. The *balance sheet* lists the entity's assets, liabilities, and owner's equity at a specific date. The *cash flow statement* reports the changes in cash during the period.

    High net income indicates success in business; a net loss indicates a lack of success in business.

7. **Explain the development of international financial reporting standards (IFRS).** International financial reporting standards (IFRS) will become the basis for financial reporting for publicly accountable companies beginning in 2011. These standards are generally the same as for private-enterprise Canadian companies but allow for great comparability with other companies from around the world. We will discuss major differences between GAAP for private enterprises and IFRS at various points throughout the text.

Test your understanding with these multiple-choice questions. Page references are given if you need review, and the answers are given after Self-Study Question 12.

SELF-STUDY QUESTIONS

Test your understanding of the chapter by marking the correct answer for each of the following questions:

1. The organization that formulates generally accepted accounting principles is the (*p. 9*)
    a. Ontario Securities Commission
    b. Public Accountants Council of Canada
    c. Accounting Standards Board (AcSB)
    d. Canada Revenue Agency (CRA)

2. Which of the following forms of business organization is an "artificial person" and must obtain legal approval from the federal government or a province to conduct business? (*p. 8*)
    a. Law firm   c. Partnership
    b. Proprietorship   d. Corporation

3. You have purchased some T-shirts for $2,000 and can sell them immediately for $3,000. What accounting assumption or principle governs the amount at which to record the goods you purchased? (*p. 12*)
    a. Economic-entity assumption
    b. Reliability characteristic
    c. Cost principle
    d. Going-concern assumption

4. The economic resources of a business are called (*p. 13*)
    a. Assets   c. Owner's equity
    b. Liabilities   d. Accounts payable

5. If the assets of a business are $187,500 and the liabilities are $89,000, how much is the owner's equity? (*p. 14*)
    a. $276,500   c. $187,500
    b. $98,500   d. $89,000

6. A business has assets of $80,000 and liabilities of $120,000. How much is its owner's equity? (*p. 14*)
   a. $0
   b. ($40,000)
   c. $80,000
   d. $200,000

7. If the owner's equity in a business is $66,000 and the liabilities are $36,000, how much are the assets? (*p. 13*)
   a. $30,000
   b. $66,000
   c. $102,000
   d. $36,000

8. Purchasing office supplies on account will (*p. 15*)
   a. Increase an asset and increase a liability
   b. Increase an asset and increase owner's equity
   c. Increase one asset and decrease another asset
   d. Increase an asset and decrease a liability

9. Performing a service for a customer or client and the immediate receiving of cash will (*p. 16*)
   a. Increase one asset and decrease another asset
   b. Increase an asset and increase owner's equity
   c. Decrease an asset and decrease a liability
   d. Increase an asset and increase a liability

10. Paying an account payable will (*p. 17*)
    a. Increase one asset and decrease another asset
    b. Decrease an asset and decrease owner's equity
    c. Decrease an asset and decrease a liability
    d. Increase an asset and increase a liability

11. The financial statement that summarizes assets, liabilities, and owner's equity is called the (*p. 20*)
    a. Cash flow statement
    b. Balance sheet
    c. Income statement
    d. Statement of owner's equity

12. The financial statements that are dated for a time period (rather than for a specific point in time) are the (*pp. 21–22*)
    a. Balance sheet and income statement
    b. Balance sheet and statement of owner's equity
    c. Income statement, statement of owner's equity, and cash flow statement
    d. All financial statements are dated for a time period.

Answers to Self-Study Questions

| 1. c | 3. c | 5. b | 6. b | 4. a | 2. d |
| 11. b | 9. b | 7. c | 8. a | 10. c | 12. c |

Check how well you answered the Self-Study Questions.

Accounting Vocabulary lists all the new boldfaced terms that were explained in the chapter and are defined in the Glossary. Page references help you to review the terms.

ACCOUNTING VOCABULARY

Like many other subjects, accounting has a special vocabulary. It is important that you understand the following terms. They are explained in the chapter and also in the glossary at the end of the book.

Account payable (*p. 16*)
Account receivable (*p. 16*)
Accounting (*p. 2*)
Accounting equation (*p. 13*)
Asset (*p. 13*)
Audit (*p. 5*)
Balance sheet (*p. 20*)
Capital (*p. 13*)
Cash flow statement (*p. 21*)
Corporation (*p. 8*)
Cost principle of measurement (*p. 12*)
Entity (*p. 11*)
Expense (*p. 14*)
Financial accounting (*p. 4*)
Financial statements (*p. 2*)
Generally accepted accounting principles (GAAP) (*p. 9*)
Going-concern assumption (*p. 12*)
Income statement (*p. 20*)
Liability (*p. 13*)

Limited-liability company (LLC) (*p. 9*)
Limited-liability partnership (LLP) (*p. 8*)
Management accounting (*p. 4*)
Measurement (*p. 12*)
Net earnings (*p. 20*)
Net income (*p. 20*)
Net loss (*p. 20*)
Net profit (*p. 20*)
Note payable (*p. 16*)
Owner's equity (*p. 13*)
Owner withdrawals (*p. 14*)
Partnership (*p. 7*)
Proprietorship (*p. 7*)
Reliability characteristic (*p. 11*)
Revenue (*p. 14*)
Shareholder (*p. 8*)
Stable-monetary-unit assumption (*p. 12*)
Statement of earnings (*p. 20*)
Statement of financial position (*p. 20*)
Statement of operations (*p. 20*)
Statement of owner's equity (*p. 20*)
Transaction (*p. 14*)

SIMILAR ACCOUNTING TERMS

Accounting equation	Assets = Liabilities + Owner's Equity
Balance Sheet	Statement of Financial Position
Income Statement	Statement of Operations; Statement of Earnings
Net income	Net earnings; Net profit

> Similar Accounting Terms are a link between the terms used in this book and similar terms you might have heard outside your accounting class in the media or your day-to-day business dealings.

Assignment Material

QUESTIONS

1. Distinguish between accounting and bookkeeping.
2. Identify five users of accounting information and explain how they use it.
3. Name two important historical reasons for the development of accounting.
4. Name three professional designations of accountants. Also give their abbreviations.
5. What organization formulates generally accepted accounting principles? Is this organization a government agency?
6. Identify the owner(s) of a proprietorship, a partnership, and a corporation.
7. Why do ethical standards exist in accounting? Which professional organizations direct their standards more toward independent auditors? Which organizations direct their standards more toward management accountants?
8. Why is the economic-entity assumption so important to accounting?
9. Give four examples of types of accounting entities.
10. Briefly describe the reliability characteristic.
11. What role does the cost principle of measurement play in accounting?
12. If assets = liabilities + owner's equity, then how can liabilities be expressed?

13. Explain the difference between an account receivable and an account payable.
14. What role do transactions play in accounting?
15. A company reported monthly revenues of $92,000 and expenses of $96,400. What is the result of operations for the month?
16. Give a more descriptive title for the balance sheet.
17. What feature of the balance sheet gives this financial statement its name?
18. Give another title for the income statement.
19. Which financial statement is like a snapshot of the entity at a specific time? Which financial statement is like a video of the entity's operation during a period of time?
20. What information does the statement of owner's equity report?
21. Give another term for the owner's equity of a proprietorship.
22. What piece of information flows from the income statement to the statement of owner's equity? What information flows from the statement of owner's equity to the balance sheet? What balance sheet item is explained by the cash flow statement?

> A brief description and the Learning Objectives covered appear beside each Starter, Exercise, and Problem.

STARTERS

MyAccountingLab All questions in this section appear in MyAccountingLab.

Explaining revenues and expenses

Starter 1–1 Sherman Lawn Service has been open for one year, and Hannah Sherman, the owner, wants to know whether the business earned a net income or a net loss for the year. First, she must identify the revenues earned and the expenses incurred during the year. What are *revenues* and *expenses*?

Users of financial information

Starter 1–2 Suppose you need a bank loan to purchase music equipment for Greg's Groovy Tunes, a company you manage. In evaluating your loan request, the banker asks about the assets and liabilities of your business. In particular, the banker wants to know the amount of the business's owner's equity.

Required

1. Is the banker considered an internal or an external user of financial information?

2. Which financial statement would provide the best information to answer the banker's questions?

Starter 1-3 Claire Hunter plans to open Claire Hunter Floral Designs. She is considering the various types of business organizations and wishes to organize her business with unlimited life and limited liability features. Which type of business organization will meet Hunter's needs best?

Forms of business organizations

Starter 1-4 Wendy Craven is the proprietor of a property management company near the campus of a local university. The business has cash of $6,000 and furniture that cost $12,000 and has a market value of $16,000. Debts include accounts payable of $5,000. Craven's personal home is valued at $350,000 and her personal bank account contains $9,000.

Applying accounting concepts and principles

④

Required

1. Consider the accounting concepts and principles discussed in the chapter and define the principle that best matches each of the following situations:
   a. Craven's personal assets are not recorded on the property management company's balance sheet.
   b. Craven records furniture at its cost of $12,000, not the market value of $16,000.
   c. Craven does not make adjustments for inflation.
   d. The account payable of $5,000 is documented by a statement from the furniture company showing the property management company still owes $5,000 on the furniture. Craven's friend thinks the property management company should only owe about $4,000. The account payable is recorded at $5,000.

2. How much is the owner's equity of the property management company?

Starter 1-5 Snail Creek Kennel earns service revenue by caring for the pets of customers. Snail Creek's main expense is the salary paid to an employee. Write the accounting equation for (a) the receipt of $420 cash for service revenue earned, and (b) the payment of $1,350 for salary expense.

Using the accounting equation

Starter 1-6 Awesome Adventures Travel recorded revenues of $2,400 earned on account by providing travel service for clients.

Analyzing transactions

Required

1. How much are the business's cash and total assets, assuming this is the only transaction?

2. Name the business asset that was increased as a result of this transaction.

Starter 1-7 Match the assumption, principle, or constraint description with the appropriate term by placing a, b, c, d, e, and f on the appropriate line.

Describing accounting concepts, principles, and constraints

④

   a. Cost principle of measurement   _____ Benefits of the information produced by an accounting system must be greater than the costs

   b. Going-concern assumption   _____ Amounts may be ignored if the effect on a decision maker's decision is not significant

   c. Stable-monetary-unit assumption   _____ Transactions are recorded based on the cash amount received or paid

   d. Economic-entity assumption   _____ Transactions are expressed using units of money

   e. Cost/benefit constraint   _____ Assumes that a business is going to continue operations indefinitely

   f. Materiality constraint   _____ Business must keep its accounting records separate from its owner's accounting records

Starter 1-8 Suppose Alexis Andrews Kayaks rents kayaks to tourists. The company purchased a storage building for the kayaks for $150,000 and financed the

Using the accounting equation

purchase with a loan of $85,000 and an investment by the owner for the remainder. Use the accounting equation to calculate the owner's equity amount.

Defining transactions

Starter 1–9 A potential customer is extremely interested in renting a number of kayaks from Alexis Andrews Kayaks and emails his intention to rent kayaks in the summer. Would an accountant consider this event a transaction to be recorded in the accounting records? Explain.

Examples of financial statements

Starter 1–10 What four main financial statements are provided in a company's annual report? Examples of two companies' annual reports are provided in Appendix A and Appendix B at the back of this textbook.

Preparing the income statement

Net income, $47,100

Starter 1–11 Party Planners Extraordinaire has just completed operations for the year ended December 31, 2010. This is the third year of operations for the company. As the owner, you want to know how well the company performed during the year. To address this question, you have assembled the data below. Use these data to prepare the income statement of Party Planners Extraordinaire for the year ended December 31, 2010.

Check figures appear in the margin when applicable to help you make sure you are "on track."

Insurance Expense	$ 3,000	Salary Expense	$44,000
Service Revenue	109,000	Accounts Payable	7,700
Supplies Expense	900	Supplies	2,400
Rent Expense	14,000	Withdrawals	40,000

Evaluating business performance

Starter 1–12 Review the income statement prepared in Starter 1-11. Evaluate the results of 2010 operations for Party Planners Extraordinaire. Was it a good year or a bad year?

EXERCISES

 All questions in this section appear in MyAccountingLab.

Using accounting vocabulary

Exercise 1–1

Match each of the following accounting terms with its correct definition:

TERMS:

1. Accounting equation
2. Asset
3. Balance sheet
4. Expense
5. Income statement
6. Liability
7. Net income
8. Net loss
9. Revenue
10. Cash flow statement
11. Statement of owner's equity

DEFINITIONS:

A. An economic resource that is expected to be of benefit in the future

B. An economic obligation (a debt) payable to an individual or an organization outside the business

C. Excess of total expenses over total revenues

D. Excess of total revenues over total expenses

E. The basic tool of accounting, stated as Assets = Liabilities + Owner's Equity

F. Decrease in equity that occurs from using assets or increasing liabilities in the course of delivering goods or services to customers

G. Amounts earned by delivering goods or services to customers

H. Report of cash receipts and cash payments during a period

I. Report of an entity's assets, liabilities, and owner's equity as of a specific date

J. Report of an entity's revenues, expenses, and net income or net loss for a period of time

K. Report that shows the changes in owner's equity for a period of time

Exercise 1–2

Jack and Virginia Swadden want to open a restaurant. In need of cash, they ask TD Canada Trust for a loan. With little knowledge of finance, the Swaddens don't know how the lending process works. Explain to them the information provided to the bank by the income statement (statement of operations) and the balance sheet (statement of financial position). Indicate why a lender would require this information.

Users of financial statements, explaining the income statement and the balance sheet

Exercise 1–3

The accounting records of Jackman Consulting Services contain the following accounts:

Classifying accounts, working with financial statements

Supplies Expense
Accounts Receivable
J. Jackman, Capital
Salary Expense
Computer Equipment
Consulting Service Revenue

Accounts Payable
Rent Expense
Cash
J. Jackman, Withdrawals
Supplies
Notes Payable

Required

1. Indicate whether each account listed is a(n) asset (A), liability (L), owner's equity (OE), revenue (R), or expense (E) account.

2. Indicate whether each account listed appears on the balance sheet (B), income statement (I), statement of owner's equity (SOE), or cash flow statement (CF). Some accounts can appear on more than one statement.

Exercise 1–4

Give an example of a business transaction that has each of the following effects on the accounting equation:

Business transactions

a. Increases an asset and increases a liability.

b. Increases one asset and decreases another asset.

c. Decreases an asset and decreases owner's equity.

d. Decreases an asset and decreases a liability.

e. Increases an asset and increases owner's equity.

Exercise 1–5

Skeena Enterprises, a business owned by Sophie Chang, experienced the following events. State whether each event (1) increased, (2) decreased, or (3) had no effect on the *total assets* of the business. Identify any specific asset affected.

Transaction analysis

a. Chang increased her cash investment in the business.

b. Paid cash on accounts payable.

c. Purchased office equipment; signed a note payable in payment.

d. Performed service for a customer on account.

e. Chang withdrew cash for personal expenses.

f. Received cash from a customer on account receivable.

g. Chang used personal funds to purchase a swimming pool for her home.

h. Sold undesirable land for a price equal to the cost of the land; received cash.

i. Borrowed money from the bank.

j. Cash purchase of desirable land for a future building site.

Exercise 1–6

Select financial information for three proprietorships follows:

Characteristics of a proprietorship, accounting concepts and principles, using the accounting equation

	Assets	Liabilities	Owner's Equity
Nice Cuts	$?	$90,000	$30,000
Love Dry Cleaners	76,000	?	40,000
Hudson Gift and Cards	110,000	84,000	?

Love Dry Cleaners liabilities, $36,000

Required

1. Compute the missing amount in the accounting equation for each entity.
2. Which accounting concept or principle tells us that the three companies will cease to exist if the owners die?

Exercise 1–7

Using the accounting equation

Owner's equity $16,000

Janice Iverson owns Common Grounds Coffee House, near the campus of Western Community College. The company has cash of $16,000 and furniture that cost $36,000. Debts include accounts payable of $10,000 and a $26,000 note payable. Write the accounting equation of Common Grounds Coffee House. What is the owner's equity of the company?

Exercise 1–8

Using the accounting equation, evaluating business performance

1. Increase in owner's equity $4,000

Eager Beaver began 2010 with total assets of $24,000 and total liabilities of $11,000. At the end of 2010, the business's total assets were $34,000 and total liabilities were $17,000.

Required

1. Did the owner's equity of Eager Beaver increase or decrease during 2010? By how much?
2. Identify two possible reasons for the change in owner's equity of Eager Beaver during the year.

Exercise 1–9

Transaction analysis

Indicate the effects of the following business transactions on the accounting equation of a proprietorship. Transaction *a* is answered as a guide.

a. Received $40,000 cash from the owner.

   Answer: Increase asset (Cash)

           Increase owner's equity (Owner, Capital)

b. Paid the current month's office rent of $3,000.

c. Paid $3,100 cash to purchase office supplies.

d. Performed engineering service for a client on account, $5,000.

e. Purchased on account office furniture at a cost of $4,000.

f. Received cash on account, $4,000.

g. Paid cash on account, $2,000.

h. Sold land for $45,000, which was the business's cost of the land.

i. Performed engineering services for a client and received cash of $7,000.

Exercise 1–10

Excel Spreadsheet Template

Transaction analysis, accounting equation

Total assets $211,950

Don Hill, M.D., opens a medical clinic. During his first month of operation, January, the clinic, entitled Forest Heights Clinic, experienced the following events:

Jan.	6	Hill invested $200,000 in the clinic by opening a bank account in the name of Forest Heights Clinic.
	9	Forest Heights Clinic paid cash for land costing $140,000. There are plans to build a clinic on the land. Until then, the business will rent an office.
	12	The clinic purchased medical supplies for $7,000 on account.
	15	On January 15, Forest Heights Clinic officially opened for business.
	15–31	During the rest of the month, the clinic earned professional fees of $17,000 and received cash immediately.
	15–31	The clinic paid cash expenses: employee salaries, $5,000; office rent, $3,100; utilities, $450.
	28	The clinic sold supplies to another clinic at cost for $800.
	31	The clinic paid $3,500 on the account from Jan. 12.

Required Analyze the effects of these events on the accounting equation of Forest Heights Clinic. Use a format similar to that of Exhibit 1–9, Panel B, on page 19 with headings for: Cash; Medical Supplies; Land; Accounts Payable; and Don Hill, Capital.

Exercise 1–11

The analysis of the transactions that Ace Equipment Rental engaged in during its first month of operations follows. The business buys electronic equipment that it rents out to earn rental revenue. The owner of the business, Steve Mitchell, made only one investment to start the business and made no withdrawals from Ace Equipment Rental.

Business organizations, transactions, net income

2. Net income $3,500

	Cash	+	Accounts Receivable	+	Rental Equipment	=	Accounts Payable	+	S. Mitchell, Capital
a.	+ 30,000								+ 30,000
b.	+ 500								+ 500
c.					+ 60,000		+ 60,000		
d.			+ 600						+ 600
e.	− 1,800								− 1,800
f.	+ 4,200								+ 4,200
g.	+ 125		− 125						
h.	− 6,000						− 6,000		

Required

1. Describe each transaction of Ace Equipment Rental.
2. If these transactions fully describe the operations of Ace Equipment Rental during the month, what was the amount of net income or net loss?

Exercise 1–12

Presented below are the balances of the assets and liabilities of Riverbend Consulting Services as of September 30, 2010. Also included are the revenue and expense account balances of the business for September. Linda Hall, the owner, invested $40,000 when the business was formed.

Business organization, balance sheet

2. Total assets $134,750

Consulting Service Revenue	$55,500	Computer Equipment	$82,500
Accounts Receivable	41,000	Supplies	6,000
Accounts Payable	14,250	Note Payable	40,000
Salary Expense	8,000	Rent Expense	4,500
L. Hall, Capital	?	Cash	5,250

Required

1. What type of business entity or organization is Riverbend Consulting Services? How can you tell?
2. Prepare the balance sheet of Riverbend Consulting Services as of September 30, 2010.
3. What does the balance sheet report—financial position or operating results? Which financial statement reports the other information?

Exercise 1–13

Examine Exhibit 1–9 on page 19. The exhibit summarizes the transactions of Ladner Environmental Services for the month of April 2010. Suppose the business completed transactions 1 to 7 and needed a bank loan on April 21, 2010. The vice-president of the bank requires financial statements to support all loan requests.

Preparing the financial statements

Total assets $278,500

Required   Prepare the income statement, statement of owner's equity, and balance sheet that Ladner Environmental Services would present to the banker on April 21, 2010, after completing the first seven transactions. Exhibit 1–10, page 22, shows the format of these financial statements.

Excel Spreadsheet Template

This symbol reminds you that an Excel template is available in MyAccountingLab to help you answer this question.

Income statement for a proprietorship

1. Net income $70,600

Exercise 1–14

The assets, liabilities, owner's equity, revenue and expenses of Hollins Company, a proprietorship, have the following final balances at December 31, 2010, the end of its first year of business. During the year, the proprietor, Gary Hollins, invested $55,000 in the business.

Note Payable	$ 45,000	Office Furniture	$ 75,000
Utilities Expense	16,000	Rent Expense	36,000
Accounts Payable	12,800	Cash	14,600
G. Hollins, Capital	75,000	Office Supplies	14,800
Service Revenue	581,200	Salary Expense	410,000
Accounts Receivable	35,000	Salary Payable	6,000
Supplies Expense	24,000	Research Expense	24,600
Equipment	70,000		

Required

1. Prepare the income statement of Hollins Company for the year ended December 31, 2010. What is Hollins Company's net income or net loss for 2010? (Hint: Ignore balance sheet items.)

2. What was the total amount of Hollins's withdrawals during the year?

Reasons for following international financial reporting standards (IFRS)

Exercise 1–15

Publicly accountable enterprises in Canada must start using international financial reporting standards (IFRS) beginning in 2011. Provide two reasons why Canada is switching to these standards.

SERIAL EXERCISE

The Serial Exercise involves a company that will be revisited throughout relevant chapters in Volume 1 and Volume 2. It begins as a proprietorship in Volume 1, and then grows to a partnership and then a corporation in Volume 2. You can complete the Serial Exercises using MyAccountingLab.

Transaction analysis, accounting equation, financial statements

2. Net income $1,300

Exercise 1–16

Haupt Consulting began operations and completed the following transactions during the first half of December 2010.

Dec.	2	Received $10,000 cash from owner Carl Haupt. The business gave owner's equity in the business to Haupt.
	2	Paid monthly office rent, $1,000.
	3	Paid cash for a Dell computer, $2,000. The computer is expected to remain in service for five years.
	4	Purchased office furniture on account, $3,600. The furniture should last for five years.
	5	Purchased supplies on account, $300.
	9	Performed consulting services for a client on account, $1,700.
	12	Paid utility expenses, $200.
	18	Performed consulting services for a client and received cash of $800.

Required

1. Analyze the effects of Haupt Consulting's transactions on the accounting equation. Use the format of Exhibit 1–9, Panel B, on page 19, and use these headings: Cash; Accounts Receivable; Supplies; Equipment; Furniture; Accounts Payable; and Carl Haupt, Capital.

2. Prepare the income statement of Haupt Consulting for the period of December 1 to 18, 2010. List expenses in decreasing order of amount.

3. Prepare the statement of owner's equity of Haupt Consulting for the period of December 1 to 18, 2010.

4. Prepare the balance sheet of Haupt Consulting at December 18, 2010.

In Chapter 2, we will account for these same transactions in a different way—as the accounting is actually performed in practice.

CHALLENGE EXERCISE

Exercise 1–17

Compute the missing amounts for each of the following businesses.

Using the financial statements
⑤ ⑥

Net income:
Yew Co. $180,000
Ash Co. $135,000
Arbutus Co. $150,000

	Yew Co.	Ash Co.	Arbutus Co.
Beginning:			
Assets	$330,000	$150,000	$270,000
Liabilities	150,000	60,000	180,000
Ending:			
Assets	$480,000	$210,000	$?
Liabilities	210,000	105,000	240,000
Owner's equity:			
Investments by owner	$?	$ 0	$ 20,000
Withdrawals by owner	330,000	120,000	210,000
Income Statement:			
Revenues	$660,000	$315,000	$600,000
Expenses	480,000	?	450,000

Exercise 1–18

Worldwide Travel Company's balance sheet data are shown below.

Using the accounting equation, preparing the statement of owner's equity
⑤ ⑥

1. Net loss, $10,000

	January 1, 2010	December 31, 2010
Total assets	$210,000	$312,000
Total liabilities	175,000	235,000

Required

1. Compute the amount of net income or net loss for the company during the year ended December 31, 2010, if the owner invested $62,000 in the business and withdrew $10,000 during the year. Show all calculations.

2. Prepare the statement of owner's equity for Sam Pratt, the owner of Worldwide Travel Company, for the year ended December 31, 2010. Use the format shown in Exhibit 1–10 on page 22.

BEYOND THE NUMBERS

Beyond the Numbers 1–1

As an analyst for Royal Bank, it is your job to write recommendations to the bank's loan committee. Kettle Engineering Co., a client of the bank, has submitted these summary data to support the company's request for a $200,000 loan:

Analyzing a loan request
① ⑥

Income Statement Data	2010	2009	2008
Total revenues	$534,000	$498,000	$492,000
Total expenses	384,000	342,000	324,000
Net income	$150,000	$156,000	$168,000

Statement of Owner's Equity Data	2010	2009	2008
Beginning capital	$228,000	$240,000	$234,000
Add: Net income	150,000	156,000	168,000
	$378,000	$396,000	$402,000
Less: Withdrawals	(174,000)	(168,000)	(162,000)
Ending capital	$204,000	$228,000	$240,000

Balance Sheet Data	2010	2009	2008
Total assets......................................	$438,000	$432,000	$396,000
Total liabilities	$234,000	$204,000	$156,000
Total owner's equity	204,000	228,000	240,000
Total liabilities and owner's equity	$438,000	$432,000	$396,000

Required Analyze these financial statement data to decide whether the bank should lend $200,000 to Kettle Engineering Co. Consider the trends in net income and owner's equity and the change in total liabilities in making your decision. Write a one-paragraph recommendation to the bank's loan committee.

Transaction analysis, effects on financial statements

Beyond the Numbers 1–2

Shining Star Camp conducts summer camps for children with physical challenges. Because of the nature of its business, Shining Star Camp experiences many unusual transactions. Evaluate each of the following transactions in terms of its effect on Shining Star Camp's income statement and balance sheet.

a. A camper suffered a dental injury that was not covered by insurance. Shining Star Camp paid $500 for the child's dental care. How does this transaction affect the income statement and the balance sheet?

b. One camper's mother is a physician. Shining Star Camp allows this child to attend camp in return for the mother's serving part-time in the camp infirmary for the two-week term. The standard fee for a camp term is $1,000. The physician's salary for this part-time work would be $1,000. How should Shining Star Camp account for this arrangement?

c. Lightning during a storm damaged the camp dining hall. The cost to repair the damage will be $8,000 over and above what the insurance company will pay.

ETHICAL ISSUES

Ethical Issue 1

The following excerpt was taken from the President's letter to the shareholders in CV Technology's 2007 Annual Report:

> In the fall of 2006, encouraged by enthusiasm from American retailers, we launched COLD-fX® in the U.S. In the face of unexpectedly high return rates from U.S. retailers, we announced on April 11, 2007 that we would restate our financial results, due to a reconsideration of the way we apply our revenue recognition policy. As a result of our announcement, Securities Commissions in Alberta, British Columbia, and Ontario issued interim trading halts on our shares. After restated financials were released, trading in the shares resumed on July 11, 2007.

Required

1. Why is it important that this type of information be disclosed?

2. Suppose you are the chief financial officer (CFO) responsible for the financial statements of CV Technologies. What ethical issues would you face as you consider what to report in the 2007 Annual Report?

3. What are the negative consequences to CV Technologies of not telling the truth? What are the negative consequences to CV Technologies of telling the truth?

Ethical Issue 2

The board of directors of Cloutier Inc. is meeting to discuss the past year's results before releasing financial statements to the public. The discussion includes this exchange:

> Sue Cloutier, company president: "Well, this has not been a good year! Revenue is down and expenses are up—way up. If we don't do some fancy stepping, we'll

report a loss for the third year in a row. I can temporarily transfer some land that I own into the company's name, and that will beef up our balance sheet. Rob, can you shave $500,000 from expenses? Then we can probably get the bank loan that we need."

Rob Samuels, company chief accountant: "Sue, you are asking too much. Generally accepted accounting principles are designed to keep this sort of thing from happening."

Required

1. What is the fundamental ethical issue in this situation?
2. Discuss how Cloutier's proposals violate generally accepted accounting principles. Identify the specific concept(s) or principle(s) involved.

PROBLEMS (GROUP A)

 All questions in this section appear in MyAccountingLab.

Problem 1–1A

Entity concept, transaction analysis, accounting equation

2. Total assets $29,600

Janice McLean was a civil engineer and partner in a large firm, a partnership, for five years after graduating from university. Recently she resigned her position to open her own consultancy practice, which she operates as a proprietorship. The name of the new company is McLean Consultants.

McLean recorded the following events during the organizing phase of her new business and its first month of operations. Some of the events were personal and did not affect the consultancy practice. Others were business transactions and should be accounted for by the business.

July	4	McLean received $90,000 cash from her former partners in the firm from which she resigned.
	5	McLean invested $20,000 cash in her business, McLean Consultants.
	5	The business paid office rent expense for the month of July, $2,400.
	6	The business paid $600 cash for letterhead stationery for the office.
	7	The business purchased office furniture for the office and will pay the account payable, $5,000, within six months.
	10	McLean sold 2,000 shares of WestJet stock, which she had owned for several years, receiving $25,000 cash from her stockbroker.
	11	McLean deposited the $25,000 cash from sale of the Westjet shares in her personal bank account.
	12	A representative of a large construction company telephoned McLean and told her of the company's intention to transfer its consulting business to McLean Consultants.
	29	The business finished an assessment for a client and submitted the bill for services, $10,000. The business expected to collect from this client within two weeks.
	31	McLean withdrew $3,000 cash from the business.

Required

1. Classify each of the preceding events as one of the following (list each date, then choose a, b, or c):

   a. A business transaction to be accounted for by the business, McLean Consultants.

   b. A business-related event but not a transaction to be accounted for by McLean Consultants.

   c. A personal transaction not to be accounted for by McLean Consultants.

2. Analyze the effects of the above events on the accounting equation of McLean Consultants. Use a format similar to Exhibit 1–9, Panel B, on page 19.

Problem 1–2A

Trevor Michaels is a realtor. He buys and sells properties on his own, and he also earns commission revenue as a real estate agent. He organized his business as a sole proprietorship on November 15, 2010. Consider the following facts as of November 30, 2010:

a. Michaels owed $20,000 on a note payable for some undeveloped land. This land had been acquired by the business for a total price of $40,000.

b. Michaels's business had spent $10,000 for a Re/Max Ltd. real estate franchise, which entitled him to represent himself as a Re/Max agent. Re/Max is a national affiliation of independent real estate agents. This franchise is a business asset.

c. Michaels owed $300,000 on a personal mortgage on his personal residence, which he acquired in 2001 for a total price of $550,000.

d. Michaels had $30,000 in his personal bank account and $7,000 in his business bank account.

e. Michaels owed $2,000 on a personal charge account with The Bay.

f. The business acquired business furniture for $7,000 on November 25. Of this amount, the company owed $2,000 on account at November 30.

g. The real estate office had $500 worth of office supplies on hand on November 30.

Required

1. Michaels is concerned about liability exposure. Which proprietorship feature, if any, limits his personal liability?

2. Prepare the balance sheet of the real estate business of Trevor Michaels, Realtor, at November 30, 2010.

3. Identify the personal items given in the preceding facts that would not be reported in the financial records of the business.

Problem 1–3A

Tofino Suppliers was recently formed as a proprietorship. The balance of each item in the business's accounting equation is shown below for June 21 and for each of the nine following business days.

		Cash	Accounts Receivable	Supplies	Land	Accounts Payable	Owner's Equity
June	21	$18,000	$ 9,000	$3,000	$18,000	$ 9,000	$39,000
	22	25,000	9,000	3,000	18,000	9,000	46,000
	23	15,000	9,000	3,000	28,000	9,000	46,000
	24	15,000	9,000	6,000	28,000	12,000	46,000
	25	11,000	9,000	6,000	28,000	8,000	46,000
	26	14,000	6,000	6,000	28,000	8,000	46,000
	27	21,000	6,000	6,000	28,000	8,000	53,000
	28	16,000	6,000	6,000	28,000	3,000	53,000
	29	13,000	6,000	9,000	28,000	3,000	53,000
	30	3,000	6,000	9,000	28,000	3,000	43,000

Required Assuming that a single transaction took place on each day, describe briefly the transaction that was most likely to have occurred. Begin with June 22 and complete up to June 30. Indicate which accounts were affected and by what amount. No revenue or expense transactions occurred on these dates.

Problem 1–4A

Presented below are the amounts of (a) the assets and liabilities of Superior Sounds as of December 31, 2010, and (b) the revenues and expenses of the company for the year ended December 31, 2010. The items are listed in alphabetical order.

Accounts Payable	$ 38,000	Insurance Expense	$ 3,000
Accounts Receivable	24,000	Interest Expense	10,000
Advertising Expense	19,000	Land	25,000
Building	200,000	Note Payable	130,000
Cash	10,000	Salary Expense	160,000
Consultant Expense	18,000	Salary Payable	15,000
Electronic Equipment	110,000	Service Revenue	300,000
Furniture	30,000	Supplies	5,000

The opening balance of owner's equity was $200,000. At year end, after the calculation of net income, the owner, Susan Chan, withdrew $69,000.

Required

1. Prepare the business's income statement for the year ended December 31, 2010.
2. Prepare the statement of owner's equity of the business for the year ended December 31, 2010.
3. Prepare the balance sheet of the business at December 31, 2010.
4. Answer these questions about the business:

   a. Was the result of operations for the year a profit or a loss? How much was it?

   b. Did the business's owner's equity increase or decrease during the year? How would this affect the business's ability to borrow money from a bank in the future?

   c. How much in total economic resources does the business have at December 31, 2010, as it moves into the new year? How much does the business owe? What is the dollar amount of the owner's portion of the business at December 31, 2010?

Problem 1–5A

The bookkeeper of Enderby Services Co., a proprietorship, prepared the balance sheet of the company while the accountant was ill. The balance sheet is not correct. The bookkeeper knew that the balance sheet should balance, so he "plugged in" the owner's equity amount needed to achieve this balance. The owner's equity amount, however, is not correct. All other amounts are accurate except the "Total assets" amount.

Balance sheet for a
proprietorship

1. Total assets $330,000

ENDERBY SERVICES CO.
Balance Sheet
For the Month Ended July 31, 2010

Assets		Liabilities	
Cash	$ 66,000	Service revenue	$216,000
Office supplies	3,000	Note payable	48,000
Land	132,000	Accounts payable	54,000
Advertising expense	8,000		
Office furniture	60,000		
Accounts receivable	69,000	**Owner's Equity**	
Rent expense	24,000	J. Enderby, capital	44,000
		Total liabilities and	
Total assets	$362,000	owner's equity	$362,000

Required

1. Prepare the corrected balance sheet, and date it correctly. Compute total assets, total liabilities, and owner's equity.
2. Consider the original balance sheet as presented and the corrected balance sheet you prepared for Requirement 1. Did the total assets presented in your corrected balance sheet increase, decrease, or stay the same compared to the original balance sheet? Why?

Problem 1–6A

Phyllis Baines is the proprietor of a career counselling and employee search business, Baines Personnel Services. The following amounts summarize the financial position of the business on August 31, 2010:

Transaction analysis, accounting
equation, financial statements

2. Net income $63,000

	Assets			=	Liabilities	+	Owner's Equity
			Furniture				
	Accounts		and		Accounts		P. Baines,
Cash +	Receivable +	Supplies +	Computers	=	Payable	+	Capital
Bal. 30,000	32,000		96,000		52,000		106,000

During September 2010, the following company transactions occurred:

a. Baines deposited $120,000 cash in the business bank account.

b. Performed services for a client and received cash of $7,000.

c. Paid off the August 31, 2010, balance of accounts payable.

d. Purchased supplies on account, $8,000.

e. Collected cash from a customer on account, $10,000.

f. Consulted on a large downsizing by a major corporation and billed the client for services rendered, $64,000.

g. Recorded the following business expenses for the month:
   (1) Paid office rent for September 2010—$6,000.
   (2) Paid advertising—$2,000.

h. Sold supplies to another business for $1,000 cash, which was the cost of the supplies.

i. Baines withdrew $32,000 cash.

Required

1. Analyze the effects of the above transactions on the accounting equation of Baines Personnel Services. Adapt the format of Exhibit 1–9, Panel B, on page 19.

2. Prepare the income statement of Baines Personnel Services for the month ended September 30, 2010. List expenses in decreasing order of amount.

3. Prepare the business's statement of owner's equity for the month ended September 30, 2010.

4. Prepare the balance sheet of Baines Personnel Services at September 30, 2010.

Accounting concepts/principles

④

Problem 1–7A

Barry Melrose had been operating his law practice in Mississauga under the name Barry Melrose, Lawyer, for two years and had the following business assets and liabilities (at their historical costs) on April 30, 2010:

Cash	$27,000
Accounts Receivable	15,000
Supplies	2,000
Furniture and Computers	63,000
Accounts Payable	15,000

The following business transactions took place during the month of May 2010:

May	1	Melrose deposited $30,000 cash into the business bank account.
	3	Melrose completed legal work for a home builder. He charged the builder $4,000, not the $6,000 the work was worth, in order to promote business from the builder.
	5	The business bought furniture from Arthur Frame for $6,000, paying $2,000 cash and promising to pay $1,000 per month at the beginning of each month starting June 1, 2010, for four months. Melrose would like to expense the entire amount to reduce net income for tax reasons.
	10	The company signed a lease to rent additional space at a cost of $2,000 per month. Melrose will occupy the premises effective June 1, 2010.
	18	Determining that the business would need more cash in June, Melrose went to the bank and borrowed $10,000 on a personal loan and transferred the money to the company.
	25	Melrose purchased a painting for his home from one of his clients. He paid for the $2,000 purchase with his personal credit card.
	28	Melrose withdrew $6,000 from the business. He used $2,000 of the money to repay a portion of the loan arranged on May 18.
	31	The business did legal work with a value of $8,000 for Apex Computers Ltd. Apex paid for the work by giving the company computer equipment with a selling price of $10,000.

Required
Identify the accounting characteristic, assumption, or principle that would be applicable to each of the transactions and discuss the effects it would have on the financial statements of Barry Melrose, Lawyer.

Problem 1-8A

Bieksa Board Rentals was started on January 1, 2010, by Harvey Bieksa with an investment of $100,000 cash. The company rents out snowboards and related gear from a small store. During the first 11 months, Bieksa made additional investments of $25,000 and borrowed $50,000 from the bank. He did not withdraw any funds. The balance sheet accounts at November 30, 2010, are as follows:

Cash...	$25,000
Accounts Receivable	15,000
Rental Gear..	52,000
Rental Snowboards	48,000
Store Equipment..................................	26,000
Accounts Payable	24,000
Note Payable	16,000

Accounting concepts/principles, transaction analysis, accounting equation, financial statements, evaluation

④ ⑤ ⑥

3. Net income $113,000

The following transactions took place during the month of December 2010:

Dec.	1	Bieksa borrowed $30,000 from his family and invested $24,000 in the business. The other $6,000 was intended for Bieksa's living expenses.
	1	The business paid $6,000 for the month's rent on the store space.
	4	The business signed a one-year lease for the rental of additional store space at a cost of $4,000 per month. The lease is effective January 1. The business will pay the first month's rent in January.
	6	Rental fees for the week were: Gear, $6,000; Boards, $12,000. 75% of the fees were paid in cash and the rest on account.
	10	The business paid the accounts payable from November 30, 2010.
	12	The business purchased gear for $9,000 and boards for $16,000, all on account.
	13	Rental fees for the week were: Gear, $14,000; Boards, $26,000. All the fees were paid in cash.
	15	The company received payment for the accounts receivable owing at November 30, 2010.
	18	The company purchased store equipment for $10,000 by paying $2,000 cash with the balance due in 60 days.
	20	Rental fees for the week were: Gear, $11,000; Boards, $22,000. Half the fees were paid in cash and half on account.
	24	The company paid the balance owing for the purchases made on December 12.
	27	Rental fees for the week were: Gear, $8,000; Boards, $20,000. All the fees were paid in cash.
	27	The company received payment for rental fees on account from December 6.

Required

1. What is the total net income earned by the business over the period of January 1, 2010 to November 30, 2010?

2. Analyze the effects of the December 2010 transactions on the accounting equation of Bieksa Board Rentals. Include the account balances from November 30, 2010.

3. Prepare the income statement for Bieksa Board Rentals for the month ended December 31, 2010.

4. Prepare the statement of owner's equity for Bieksa Board Rentals for the month ended December 31, 2010.

5. Prepare the balance sheet for Bieksa Board Rentals at December 31, 2010.

6. Bieksa has expressed concern that although the business seems to be profitable and growing, he constantly seems to be investing additional money into it and has been unable to make any withdrawals for the work he has put into it. Prepare a reply to his concerns.

PROBLEMS (GROUP B)

MyAccountingLab All questions in this section appear in MyAccountingLab.

Problem 1-1B

Diana Rose is an architect and was a partner with a large firm, a partnership, for 10 years after graduating from university. Recently she resigned her position to open her own architecture office, which she operates as a proprietorship. The name of the new entity is Rose Design.

Entity concept, transaction analysis, accounting equation

④ ⑤

Rose recorded the following events during the organizing phase of her new business and its first month of operations. Some of the events were personal and did not affect the practice of architecture. Others were business transactions and should be accounted for by the business.

July	1	Rose sold 1,000 shares of Royal Bank stock, which she had owned for several years, receiving $30,000 cash from her stockbroker.
	2	Rose deposited the $30,000 cash from sale of the Royal Bank shares in her personal bank account.
	3	Rose received $80,000 cash from her former partners in the architecture firm from which she resigned.
	5	Rose deposited $60,000 into a bank account in the name of Rose Design.
	5	Rose Design paid office rent for the month of July, $3,000.
	6	A representative of a large real estate company telephoned Diana Rose and told her of the company's intention to transfer its design business to her business, Rose Design.
	7	Rose Design paid $500 cash for letterhead stationery.
	9	Rose Design purchased office furniture for the office, on account, for $6,000, promising to pay in three months.
	23	Rose Design finished design work for a client and submitted the bill for design services, $8,000. It expects to collect from this client within one month.
	31	Rose withdrew $3,000 for personal use.

Required

1. Classify each of the preceding events as one of the following (list each date and then choose a, b, or c):
   a. A business transaction to be accounted for by the business, Rose Design.
   b. A business-related event but not a transaction to be accounted for by Rose Design.
   c. A personal transaction not to be accounted for by Rose Design.

2. Analyze the effects of the above events on the accounting equation of Rose Design. Use a format similar to Exhibit 1–9, Panel B, on page 19.

Balance sheet, entity concept

Problem 1–2B

Hayley Wilson is a realtor. She buys and sells properties on her own, and she also earns commission revenue as a real estate agent. She invested $50,000 on March 10, 2010, in the business, Hayley Wilson Realty. Consider the following facts as of March 31, 2010:

a. Wilson had $15,000 in her personal bank account and $75,000 in the business bank account.
b. The real estate office had $12,000 of office supplies on hand on March 31, 2010.
c. Hayley Wilson Realty had spent $24,000 for a Realty World Canada franchise, which entitled the company to represent itself as a Realty World Canada member firm. This franchise is a business asset.
d. The company owed $110,000 on a note payable for some undeveloped land that had been acquired by the company for a total price of $156,000.
e. Wilson owed $185,000 on a personal mortgage on her personal residence, which she acquired in 2001 for a total price of $320,000.
f. Wilson owed $2,000 on a personal charge account with Sears.
g. The company acquired business furniture for $24,000 on March 26. Of this amount, Hayley Wilson Realty owed $20,000 on account at March 31, 2010.

Required

1. Wilson is concerned about liability exposure. Which proprietorship feature, if any, limits her personal liability?

2. Prepare the balance sheet of the real estate business of Hayley Wilson Realty at March 31, 2010.

3. Identify the personal items given in the preceding facts that would not be reported on the balance sheet of the business.

Problem 1–3B

Business transactions and analysis

Recently, Michelle Hopkins formed a management accounting practice as a proprietorship. The balance of each item in the proprietorship accounting equation follows for November 16 and for each of the eight following business days.

	Cash	Accounts Receivable	Office Supplies	Furniture	Accounts Payable	Owner's Equity
Nov. 16	$1,000	$3,000	$ 500	$6,000	$3,000	$7,500
17	2,000	2,000	500	6,000	3,000	7,500
18	1,000	2,000	500	6,000	2,000	7,500
19	1,000	2,000	800	6,000	2,300	7,500
20	3,000	2,000	800	6,000	2,300	9,500
23	2,200	2,000	800	6,000	1,500	9,500
24	4,200	2,000	800	4,000	1,500	9,500
25	4,000	2,000	1,000	4,000	1,500	9,500
26	3,000	2,000	1,000	4,000	1,500	8,500

Required   Assuming that a single transaction took place on each day, describe briefly the transaction that was most likely to have occurred. Begin with November 17 and complete up to November 26. Indicate which accounts were affected and by what amount. Assume that no revenue or expense transactions occurred on these dates.

Problem 1–4B

Excel Spreadsheet Template

Income statement, statement of owner's equity, balance sheet

The amounts of (a) the assets and liabilities of Morishita Office Cleaning as of December 31, 2010, and (b) the revenues and expenses of the company for the year ended on December 31, 2010, appear below. The items are listed in alphabetical order.

Accounts Payable	$ 75,000	Land	$140,000
Accounts Receivable	25,000	Notes Payable	180,000
Building	250,000	Property Tax Expense	10,000
Cash	5,000	Repairs Expense	40,000
Equipment	105,000	Salary Expense	220,000
Interest Expense	9,000	Service Revenue	550,000
Interest Payable	3,000	Supplies	10,000
Furniture	11,000	Utilities Expense	15,000

The beginning amount of owner's equity was $110,000. During the year, the owner, Brandon Morishita, withdrew $78,000.

Required

1. Prepare the income statement of Morishita Office Cleaning for the year ended December 31, 2010.

2. Prepare the statement of owner's equity of the business for the year ended December 31, 2010.

3. Prepare the balance sheet of the business at December 31, 2010.

4. Answer these questions about Morishita Office Cleaning.
   a. Was the result of operations for the year a profit or a loss? How much was it?
   b. Did the business's owner's equity increase or decrease during the year? How would this affect the business's ability to borrow money from a bank in the future?
   c. How much in total economic resources does the company have at December 31, 2010, as it moves into the new year? How much does the company owe? What is the dollar amount of the owner's portion of the business at December 31, 2010?

Problem 1–5B

Balance sheet

The bookkeeper of Campbell Insurance Agency prepared the balance sheet of the company while the accountant was ill. The balance sheet contains errors. In particular, the bookkeeper knew that the balance sheet should balance, so she "plugged in" the owner's equity amount needed to achieve this balance. The owner's equity amount, however, is not correct. All other amounts are accurate except the "Total assets" amount.

CAMPBELL INSURANCE AGENCY
Balance Sheet
For the Month Ended October 31, 2010

Assets		Liabilities	
Cash..	$12,000	Premium revenue........................	$26,500
Insurance expense	1,000	Accounts payable	11,500
Rent expense	3,000	Note payable................................	20,000
Salary expense..........................	4,000		
Office furniture	10,000		
Accounts receivable	11,000	**Owner's Equity**	
Utilities expense.......................	1,000	C. Campbell, capital....................	(4,000)
Notes receivable.......................	12,000	Total liabilities and	
Total assets	$54,000	owner's equity......................	$54,000

Required

1. Prepare the corrected balance sheet, and date it correctly. Compute total assets, total liabilities, and owner's equity.

2. Identify the accounts listed above that should *not* be presented on the balance sheet and state why you excluded them from the corrected balance sheet you prepared for Requirement 1.

Transaction analysis, accounting equation, financial statements
5 6

Problem 1–6B

Jan Robertson operates an interior design studio called Robertson Design Studio. The following amounts summarize the financial position of the business on April 30, 2010:

	Assets			=	Liabilities	+	Owner's Equity
		Accounts				Accounts		J. Robertson,
Cash +	Receivable +	Supplies +	Land	=	Payable	+	Capital
Bal. 13,500	13,000		51,000		16,500		61,000

During May 2010 the company did the following:

a. Robertson received $15,000 as a gift and deposited the cash in the business bank account.

b. Paid the beginning balance of accounts payable.

c. Performed services for a client and received cash of $2,500.

d. Collected cash from a customer on account, $2.000.

e. Purchased supplies on account, $1,400.

f. Consulted on the interior design of a major office building and billed the client for services rendered, $8,000.

g. Recorded the following business expenses for the month:

(1) Paid office rent for May 2010—$3,000.

(2) Paid advertising—$2,100.

h. Sold supplies to another interior designer for $500 cash, which was the cost of the supplies.
i. Robertson withdrew $3,500 cash for personal use.

Required

1. Analyze the effects of the above transactions on the accounting equation of Robertson Design Studio. Adapt the format of Exhibit 1–9, Panel B, on page 19.

2. Prepare the income statement of Robertson Design Studio for the month ended May 31, 2010. List expenses in decreasing order of amount.

3. Prepare the statement of owner's equity of Robertson Design Studio for the month ended May 31, 2010.

4. Prepare the balance sheet of Robertson Design Studio at May 31, 2010.

Problem 1–7B

John Bridges has been operating a plumbing business as a proprietorship (John Bridges Plumbing) for four years and had the following business assets and liabilities (at their historical costs) on May 31, 2010:

Cash	$45,000
Accounts Receivable	22,500
Shop Supplies	9,000
Shop Equipment	67,500
Accounts Payable	18,000

The following events took place during the month of June 2010:

June	1	John's brother, Mark, had been in a similar business in the same city and moved to Halifax. He sold John his equipment for $25,000. The equipment had cost $45,000 and had a replacement cost of $33,000.
	3	The business did some plumbing repairs for a customer. The business would normally have charged $800 for the work, but had agreed to do it for $500 cash in order to encourage more business from the client.
	10	The business signed a lease to rent additional shop space for the business at a cost of $2,500 per month. The business will occupy the premises effective July 1, 2010.
	18	Finding he was low on cash, John Bridges went to the bank and borrowed $7,000 on a personal loan.
	22	Inflation has caused the value of the shop equipment to double to $80,000. John Bridges does not understand why accountants ignore the effect of inflation in the accounting records.
	28	John Bridges withdrew $8,000 from the business and used $7,000 to repay the personal bank loan of June 18.

Required   Identify the accounting assumption, principle, or characteristic that would be applicable to each of the events, and discuss the effects it would have on the financial statements of John Bridges Plumbing.

Problem 1–8B

Armstrong Marketing Consulting, a proprietorship owned by Jody Armstrong, was started on January 1, 2009, with an investment of $30,000 cash. The company prepares marketing plans for clients. It has been operating for two years. Business was quite slow in the first year of operations but has steadily increased. Armstrong has made additional investments of $28,000 but has not made any withdrawals. The general ledger showed the following balances as of December 31, 2009:

Cash	$20,000
Accounts Receivable	19,000
Software	18,000
Office Furniture	14,000
Computer Equipment	21,000
Accounts Payable	18,000
J. Armstrong, Capital	74,000

The following transactions took place during the month of January 2010:

Jan.	2	Armstrong invested $15,000 in the business.
	2	The business paid $3,000 for the month's rent on the office space.
	4	The business signed a lease for the rental of additional office space at a cost of $2,000 per month. The lease is effective February 1. The business will pay the first month's rent in February.
	6	The business developed a systems design for Fleming Ltd. and received $8,000 now plus additional $6,000 payments to be received on the 15th of the month for the next three months.
	10	The business paid $1,000 to a courier service.
	12	Armstrong signed an agreement to provide design work to Smith Inc. for $20,000 to be paid upon completion of the work.
	14	The company purchased $6,000 of software that will be required for the Smith assignment. The company paid $3,000 and promised to pay the balance by the end of the month.

Jan.	15	The company received $6,000 as the monthly payment from Fleming Ltd. of January 6.
	18	The company purchased computer equipment for $12,000 by paying $4,000 cash with the balance due in 60 days.
	23	The company completed a network design for Wong Ltd., which promised to pay $10,000 by the end of the month.
	29	The company paid the balance owing for the software purchased on January 14.

Required

1. What is the total net income earned by the business over the period of January 1, 2009, to December 31, 2009?

2. Analyze the effects of the January 2010 transactions on the accounting equation of Armstrong Marketing Consulting. Be sure to include the account balances from December 31, 2009.

3. Prepare the income statement for Armstrong Marketing Consulting for the month ended January 31, 2010.

4. Prepare the statement of owner's equity for Armstrong Marketing Consulting for the month ended January 31, 2010.

5. Prepare the balance sheet for Armstrong Marketing Consulting at January 31, 2010.

6. Armstrong has expressed concern that although the business seems to be profitable and growing, she constantly seems to be investing additional money into it and has been unable to make any withdrawals for the work she has put into it. Prepare a reply to her concerns.

CHALLENGE PROBLEMS

Understanding the going-concern assumption

Problem 1–1C

The going-concern assumption is becoming an increasing source of concern for users of financial statements. There are instances of companies filing for bankruptcy several months after issuing their annual audited financial statements. The question is: why didn't the financial statements predict the problem?

A friend has just arrived on your doorstep; you realize she is very angry. After calming her down, you ask what the problem is. She tells you that she had inherited $40,000 from an uncle and invested the money in the common shares of Always Good Yogourt Corp. She had carefully examined Always Good Yogourt's financial statements for the latest year end and had concluded that the company was financially sound. This morning, she had read in the local paper that the company had gone bankrupt and her investment was worthless. She asks you why the financial statements valued the assets at values that are in excess of those the Trustee in Bankruptcy expects to realize from liquidating the assets. Why have the assets suddenly lost so much of the value they had six months ago?

Required Explain to your friend why assets are valued on a going-concern basis in the financial statements and why they are usually worth less when the company goes out of business. Use inventory and accounts receivable as examples.

Accounting for business transactions

Problem 1–2C

You and three friends have decided to go into the lawn-care business for the summer to earn money to pay for your schooling in the fall. Your first step was to sign up customers to satisfy yourselves that the business had the potential to be profitable. Next, you planned to go to the bank to borrow money to buy the equipment you would need.

After considerable effort, your group obtained contracts from customers for 200 lawns for the summer. One of your partners wants to prepare a balance sheet showing the value of the contracts as an asset. She is sure that you will have no trouble with borrowing the necessary funds from the bank on the basis of the proposed balance sheet.

Required Explain to your friend why the commitments (signed contracts) from customers cannot be recognized as assets. What suggestions do you have that might assist your group in borrowing the necessary funds?

Extending Your Knowledge

DECISION PROBLEMS

Decision Problem 1

Using financial statements to evaluate a request for a loan

Two businesses, Tyler's Bicycle Centre and Ryan's Catering, have sought business loans from you. To decide whether to make the loans, you have requested their balance sheets.

TYLER'S BICYCLE CENTRE
Balance Sheet
December 31, 2010

Assets		Liabilities	
Cash...	$ 13,500	Accounts payable	$ 18,000
Accounts receivable	21,000	Notes payable	177,000
Merchandise inventory............	127,500	Total liabilities...........................	195,000
Store supplies...........................	750		
Furniture and fixtures..............	13,500	**Owner's Equity**	
Building	123,000	T. Jones, capital	125,250
Land...	21,000	Total liabilities and	
Total assets	$320,250	owner's equity	$320,250

RYAN'S CATERING
Balance Sheet
December 31, 2010

Assets		Liabilities	
Cash...	$ 15,000	Accounts payable	$ 4,500
Accounts receivable	6,000	Note payable	102,000
Office supplies	3,000	Total liabilities...........................	106,500
Inventory	30,000		
Office furniture	7,500	**Owner's Equity**	
Investments*.............................	300,000	R. Smith, capital.........................	255,000
		Total liabilities and	
Total assets	$361,500	owner's equity	$361,500

*The investments of $300,000 can be sold today for $380,000.

Required

1. Based solely on these balance sheets, which entity would you be more comfortable lending money to? Explain fully, citing specific items and amounts from the balance sheets.
2. In addition to the balance sheet data, what other financial statement information would you require? Be specific.

Decision Problem 2

Using accounting information

A friend learns that you are taking an accounting course. Knowing that you do not plan a career in accounting, the friend asks why you are "wasting your time." Explain to the friend:

1. Why you are taking the course.
2. How accounting information is used or will be used:
   a. In your personal life.
   b. In the business life of your friend, who plans to be a farmer.
   c. In the business life of another friend, who plans a career in sales.

FINANCIAL STATEMENT CASES

These and similar problems in later chapters focus on the financial statements of two real Canadian companies—Canadian Western Bank and Sun-Rype Products Ltd. Canadian Western Bank (CWB) was created in 1984 by a group of determined western Canadians with the goal of servicing a western niche. The West responded well, and the little bank grew steadily with double-digit growth, acquisitions, and amalgamations to become the largest publicly traded Schedule I bank headquartered in Western Canada. CWB consists of 36 bank branches, 7 trust locations, 2 insurance call centres, and 1 investment management office, with combined assets of over $10 billion. Sun-Rype Products Ltd. is a leading manufacturer and marketer of juice-based beverages and fruit-based snacks located in the fruit-growing district of British Columbia but with sales across Canada. As you study each financial statement problem using these two companies, you will gradually build the confidence to understand and use actual financial statements.

Identifying items from a company's financial statements

October 31, 2008, net income $102,019 thousand

Financial Statement Case 1

Refer to the CWB financial statements located in Appendix A at the end of this book. Notice that the amounts reported are in thousands of dollars.

Required

1. How much cash, short-term deposits, and items in transit did CWB have at October 31, 2008?
2. What were total assets at October 31, 2008? At October 31, 2007?
3. Write the company's accounting equation at October 31, 2008, by filling in the dollar amounts:

Assets = Liabilities + Shareholders' Equity

4. Identify total revenue for the year ended October 31, 2008. Do the same for the year ended October 31, 2007. Did revenue increase or decrease in fiscal 2008?
5. How much net income or net loss did CWB experience for the year ended October 31, 2008? Was 2008 a good year or bad year compared to 2007?

Identifying items from a company's financial statements

5. Dec. 31, 2008, net loss ($11,673 thousand)

Financial Statement Case 2

Refer to the Sun-Rype Products Ltd. financial statements located in Appendix B at the end of this book. Notice that the amounts reported in Sun-Rype's financial statements are in thousands of dollars.

Required

1. How much cash and cash equivalents did Sun-Rype have at December 31, 2008?
2. What were total assets at December 31, 2008? At December 31, 2007?
3. Write the company's accounting equation at December 31, 2008, by filling in the dollar amounts:

Assets = Liabilities + Shareholders' Equity

4. Identify total sales revenue for the year ended December 31, 2008, and the year ended December 31, 2007. Did revenue increase or decrease during 2008?
5. How much net income or net loss did Sun-Rype experience for the year ended December 31, 2008? Was 2008 a good year or bad year compared to 2007?

2 Recording Business Transactions

Why is recording business transactions important?
How do we know if a transaction has occurred?

If a transaction has occurred, where do we record it and what amount do we record?
How do we record the increases and decreases

in various types of accounts?
How do we report a business's results of operations and financial position?

These questions and others will be answered throughout this chapter. The Decision Guidelines at the end of this chapter will provide the answers in a useful summary.

LEARNING OBJECTIVES

1 Define and use key accounting terms

2 Apply the rules of debit and credit

3 Analyze and record transactions in the journal

4 Post from the journal to the ledger

5 Prepare and use a trial balance

6 Apply international financial reporting standards (IFRS) to recording business transactions

What is your favourite snack food? If you are like many people, it may be Doritos, Earth Chips, or plain potato chips. All these are Frito-Lay Canada products. Year in and year out, Frito-Lay Canada is one of the leaders in the prepared snack-food industry. How does this company deliver fresh quantities of chips to thousands of stores every day of the year?

One of Frito-Lay Canada's great advantages is its accounting system. Route managers use hand-held computers to record how many products are sold each day. The data are relayed to company headquarters, and managers can see instantly which products are selling, and where. Suppose Doritos are selling well and potato chips are currently out of favour. Frito-Lay Canada managers know they should buy more corn for Doritos and fewer potatoes for chips. The company avoids waste by buying only what it needs to meet consumer demand.

The result? Frito-Lay Canada is very profitable. This chapter shows how Frito-Lay Canada and other companies record their business transactions. The procedures outlined in this chapter are followed by entities ranging from giants like Frito-Lay Canada to a local environmental consulting firm such as Ladner Environmental Services.

Chapter 1 introduced transaction analysis and the financial statements.

That chapter showed simple financial statements but not how they are prepared. Chapters 2, 3, and 4 cover the accounting process that results in the financial statements. The following diagram summarizes the accounting process—steps 2, 3, and 4 are covered in this chapter.

> 1. Identify and analyze transactions
>
> 2. Record transactions in a journal
>
> 3. Post (copy) from the journal to the accounts in the ledger
>
> 4. Prepare the trial balance
>
> 5. Journalize and post adjusting entries
>
> 6. Prepare the financial statements
>
> 7. Journalize and post the closing entries
>
> 8. Prepare the postclosing trial balance

By learning how accounting information is processed, you will understand where the facts and figures reported in the financial statements come from. This knowledge will increase your confidence and ability to understand and analyze financial information.

Accounting begins and ends with accounts.

The Account, the Ledger, and the Journal

OBJECTIVE ①

Define and use key accounting terms

The basic summary device of accounting is the **account**, which is the detailed record of the changes that have occurred in a particular asset, liability, or item of owner's equity during a period of time. As we saw in Chapter 1, business transactions cause the changes.

Accountants record transactions first in a **journal**, which is the chronological record of transactions. Accountants then copy (post) the data to a book (or printout) of all the accounts called the **ledger**. (One way to think of a ledger is as a binder, with each page in the binder representing one account.) In the phrase "keeping the books," *books* refers to the ledger. A list of all the ledger accounts and their balances is called a **trial balance**.

Accounts are grouped in three broad categories, according to the accounting equation:

ASSETS = LIABILITIES + OWNER'S EQUITY

Recall that in Chapter 1, page 13, we learned that the accounting equation is the basic tool of accounting. It measures assets and claims to those assets.

Exhibit 2–1 shows how asset, liability, and owner's equity accounts can be grouped into the ledger.

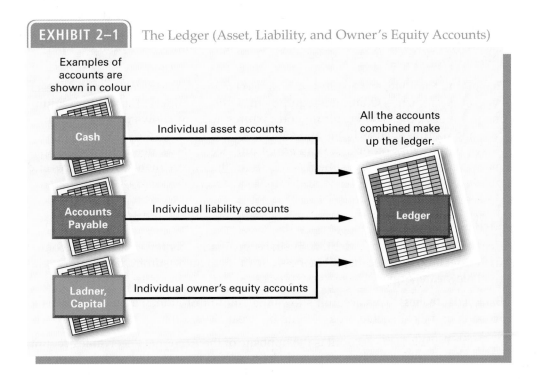

EXHIBIT 2–1 The Ledger (Asset, Liability, and Owner's Equity Accounts)

Assets

Assets are economic resources that will benefit the business in the future. Most firms use the following asset accounts.

Cash The Cash account shows the changes in cash from a business's transactions. Cash means money and any medium of exchange that a bank accepts at face value, such as bank account balances, paper currency, coins, certificates of deposit, and cheques. Successful companies such as Frito-Lay Canada usually have plenty of cash. Most business failures result from a shortage of cash.

Accounts Receivable A business may sell its goods or services in exchange for an oral or implied promise of future cash receipts. Such sales are made on credit ("on account") to customers that buy a business's products or services. They are often known as *trade accounts*. The Accounts Receivable account contains these amounts.

A receivable is always an asset. A payable is always a liability.

Notes Receivable A business may sell its goods or services in exchange for a *promissory note*, which is a written pledge that the customer will pay the business a fixed amount of money by a certain date. The Notes Receivable account is a record of the promissory notes that the business expects to collect in cash. A **note receivable** offers more security for collection than an account receivable does and it can require the customer to pay interest on the amount the customer owes.

Notes Receivable, Interest Receivable, and Rent Receivable are *not* the same as Accounts Receivable.

Prepaid Expenses A business often pays certain expenses in advance. A *prepaid expense* is an asset because it provides future benefits to the business. The business avoids having to pay cash in the future for the specified expense. The ledger holds a separate asset account for each prepaid expense. Prepaid Rent, Prepaid Insurance, and Office Supplies are accounted for as prepaid expenses.

Land The Land account is a record of the cost of land a business owns and uses in its operations. Land held for sale is accounted for separately—in an investment account.

Building The cost of a business's buildings—office, warehouse, garage, and the like—appears in the Building account. Buildings held for sale are separate assets accounted for as investments. Intrawest Corporation is a Canadian developer and operator of ski and golf resorts. Intrawest's Whistler ski lodge would appear in its Buildings account. However, the condominiums that Intrawest builds at its resorts and sells would *not* be included in the Building account; they would be a part of inventory, discussed in Chapter 5.

Equipment, Furniture, and Fixtures A business has a separate asset account for each type of equipment—Computer Equipment, Office Equipment, and Store Equipment, for example. The Furniture and Fixtures account shows the costs of furniture and fixtures such as lights and signs.

We will discuss other asset categories and accounts as needed. For example, many businesses have investment accounts for their investments in the shares and bonds of other companies.

Liabilities

Recall that a *liability* is a debt. A business generally has fewer liability accounts than asset accounts because a business's liabilities can be summarized under relatively few categories.

Bank Indebtedness This account shows the amount of money a business owes to its bank that it expects to repay within one year.

Accounts Payable This account is the opposite of the Accounts Receivable account. The oral or implied promise to pay off debts arising from credit purchases appears in the Accounts Payable account. Such purchases are said to be made on account, and Accounts Payable are usually amounts owed to a business's suppliers for goods or services purchased. Most companies, including Frito-Lay Canada, have accounts payable.

Notes Payable The Notes Payable account is the opposite of the Notes Receivable account. Notes Payable represents the amounts that the business must pay because it signed a promissory note to borrow money to purchase goods or services. Notes payable can require the business to pay interest on the amount it borrowed.

Accrued Liabilities Liability categories and accounts are added as needed. Taxes Payable, Interest Payable, and Salaries Payable are accrued liability accounts used by most companies for expenses that have been incurred but not yet paid in cash.

Owner's Equity

The owner's claims to the assets of a business are called *owner's equity.* In a proprietorship, like that of Shawn Tran or John Ladner, described in Chapter 1, or a partnership, owner's equity is split into separate accounts for the owner's Capital balance and for the owner's Withdrawals. In a partnership, each partner would have a separate Capital account and a separate Withdrawals account.

Capital The Capital account shows the owner's claim to the assets of the business, whether it is Shawn Tran or John Ladner of Ladner Environmental Services.

Amounts received from the owner's investment in the business are recorded directly in the Capital account. The Capital balance equals the owner's investments in the business plus net income, minus net losses and owner withdrawals over the life of the business.

Withdrawals When John Ladner withdraws cash or other assets from Ladner Environmental Services for personal use, the business's assets and owner's equity decrease. The amounts taken out of the business appear in a separate account entitled John Ladner, Withdrawals, or John Ladner, Drawings. If withdrawals were recorded directly in the Capital account, the amount of owner withdrawals would *not* be highlighted and decision making would be more difficult.

Revenues The increase in owner's equity created by delivering goods or services to customers or clients is called *revenue*. The ledger contains as many revenue accounts as needed. Ladner Environmental Services would have a Service Revenue account for amounts earned by providing services for clients. If a business lends money to an outsider, it will need an Interest Revenue account for the interest earned on the loan. If the business rents a building to a tenant, it will need a Rent Revenue account.

Expenses Expenses use up assets or create liabilities in the course of operating a business. Expenses have the opposite effect of revenues; they decrease owner's equity. A business needs a separate account for each type of expense, such as Salaries Expense, Office Supplies Expense, Rent Expense, Advertising Expense, and Utilities Expense. Businesses strive to minimize their expenses in order to maximize net income, whether they are Shawn Tran, Ladner Environmental Services, or Frito-Lay Canada.

Exhibit 2–2 shows the effect on the Capital account of the owner's equity items described above.

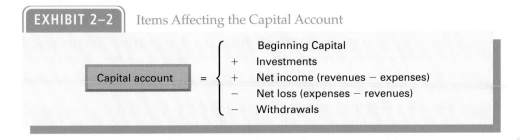

EXHIBIT 2–2 Items Affecting the Capital Account

Chart of Accounts

The ledger contains the accounts grouped under these headings:

- Assets, Liabilities, and Owner's Equity
- Revenues and Expenses

Companies use a **chart of accounts** to list all their accounts along with the account numbers. Account numbers are just shorthand versions of the account names. One number equals one account name—just like your social insurance number is unique to you. This numbering system makes it easy to locate individual accounts in the ledger.

Accounts are identified by account numbers with two or more digits. Assets are often numbered beginning with 1, liabilities with 2, owner's equity with 3, revenues with 4, and expenses with 5. The second, third, and higher digits in an account number indicate the position of the individual account within the category. For example, if Ladner Environmental Services is using four-digit account numbers, Cash might be account number 1100, which is the first asset account. Accounts Receivable may be account number 1200, the second asset account. Accounts Payable may be number 2100, the first liability account. All accounts are numbered by this system. Many numbers remain between 1100 and 1200 in case new accounts with new account numbers are added later. This company chose to use a four-digit numbering system. However, each company chooses its own account-numbering system.

The chart of accounts for Ladner Environmental Services appears in Exhibit 2–3. Notice the gap in account numbers between 1200 and 1400. John Ladner realizes that at some later date the business may need to add another category of receivables—for example, Notes Receivable—to be numbered 1210.

EXHIBIT 2–3 Chart of Accounts—Ladner Environmental Services

Balance Sheet Accounts:

Assets		Liabilities		Owner's Equity	
1100	Cash	2100	Accounts Payable	3000	John Ladner, Capital
1200	Accounts Receivable	2300	Notes Payable	3100	John Ladner,
1400	Office Supplies				Withdrawals
1500	Furniture				
1900	Land				

**Income Statement Accounts
(part of Owner's Equity)**

Revenues		Expenses	
4000	Service Revenue	5100	Rent Expense
		5200	Salary Expense
		5300	Utilities Expense

Appendix D at the end of the book gives three expanded charts of accounts that you will find helpful as you work through this course. The first chart lists the typical accounts of a large *service* proprietorship, along with those of a service partnership. The second chart is for a *merchandising* corporation, one that sells a product rather than a service. The third chart lists some accounts a *manufacturing* company uses. These accounts will be used in connection with Chapters 19–26.

The expense accounts are listed in alphabetical order throughout this chapter. Many businesses follow such a scheme for their records and financial statements since computer programs often list accounts alphabetically. The other system of ordering is by liquidity or size, with the accounts that are most readily converted to cash listed first. The service, merchandising, and manufacturing accounts shown in Appendix D are taken from the financial statements of real companies and are listed in the order used by those companies.

DID YOU GET IT?

MyAccountingLab

To check your understanding of the material in this Learning Objective, complete these questions. The solutions appear on MyAccountingLab so you can check your progress.

1. Suppose you bought a Honda Civic for $28,000 and had to borrow $18,000 to pay for the car. Write your personal accounting equation for this transaction.

2. Indicate whether each account listed below is a(n) asset (A), liability (L), owner's equity (OE), revenue (R), or expense (E) account.

Salary Payable	_____	Salary Expense	_____
Land	_____	Rent Revenue	_____
L. Graham, Capital	_____	Computer Equipment	_____
Rent Expense	_____	Notes Payable	_____
Supplies	_____	Prepaid Rent	_____
Accounts Payable	_____	L. Graham, Withdrawals	_____

3. Create a chart of accounts by matching each of the following account names with its account number. Assume this company uses a system similar to that described in the chapter, with asset numbers beginning with 1 and expense numbers beginning with 5.

Accounts Payable	30200
Rent Expense	10100
Furniture and Fixtures	50600
Service Revenue	20100
L. Starks, Capital	40100
Accounts Receivable	10400
Cash	30100
Income Taxes Payable	20500
L. Starks, Withdrawals	10200

Double-Entry Accounting

Each business transaction has at least two effects:

- The receiving side
- The giving side

OBJECTIVE ② Apply the rules of debit and credit

For example, in the $250,000 cash receipt by Ladner Environmental Services, the business

- Received cash of $250,000
- Gave John Ladner $250,000 of owner's equity in the business.

Accounting uses the *double-entry system*, which means that we record the dual, or two, effects of each transaction. As a result, *every transaction affects at least two accounts*. It would be incomplete to record only the giving side, or only the receiving side, of a transaction.

Consider a cash purchase of supplies. What are the dual effects of this transaction? A cash purchase of supplies

1. Increases supplies (the business *received* supplies)
2. Decreases cash (the business *gave* cash)

Similarly, a credit purchase of a truck (a purchase made with a bank loan)

1. Increases vehicles (the business *received* the truck)
2. Increases the bank loan payable (the business *gave* a promise to pay in the future)

The T-Account

How do we record transactions? The form of account used for most illustrations in this book is called the *T-account* because it takes the form of the capital letter "T."

The vertical line divides the account into its left and right sides, with the account title at the top. For example, the Cash account appears in the following T-account format:

KEY POINT

A T-account is a quick way to show the effect of transactions on a particular account—a useful shortcut or tool used in accounting.

Cash

(Left side)	(Right side)
Debit	*Credit*

KEY POINT

The accounting equation must balance after every transaction; however, verifying that total assets = total liabilities + owner's equity is no longer necessary after every transaction. The equation will balance as long as the debits in each transaction equal the credits in the transaction.

The left side of the account is called the **debit** side, and the right side is called the **credit** side. The words *debit* and *credit* can be confusing because they are new. To become comfortable using them, simply remember this:

Debit = Left	Credit = Right

Even though *left side* and *right side* may be more convenient, *debit* and *credit* are deeply entrenched in business.[1] Debit and credit are abbreviated as follows:

Dr = Debit	Cr = Credit

Increases and Decreases in the Accounts

In everyday conversation, we may praise someone by saying, "She deserves credit for her good work." In your study of accounting, forget this general usage because accounting uses this term in a specialized way. Remember that *debit means left side* and *credit means right side*. Debits are not "good" or "bad." Neither are credits. Debits are not always increases or decreases—neither are credits.

The type of an account (asset, liability, equity) determines how we record increases and decreases. For any given type of account, all increases are recorded on one side, and all decreases are recorded on the other side. Increases in *assets* are recorded in the left (debit) side of the account. Decreases in assets are recorded in the right (credit) side of the account. Conversely, increases in *liabilities* and *owner's equity* are recorded by *credits*. Decreases in liabilities and owner's equity are recorded by *debits*. These are the *rules of debit and credit*, and can be summarized as follows:

Assets		Liabilities and Owner's Equity	
Increase = Debit	Decrease = Credit	Decrease = Debit	Increase = Credit

This pattern of recording debits and credits is based on the accounting equation:

ASSETS = LIABILITIES + OWNER'S EQUITY

DEBITS = CREDITS

Assets are on the opposite side of the accounting equation from liabilities and owner's equity. Therefore, increases and decreases in assets are recorded in the opposite manner from increases and decreases in liabilities and owner's equity. Liabilities and owner's equity are on the same side of the equal sign, so they are treated in the same way. Exhibit 2–4 shows the relationship between the accounting equation and the rules of debit and credit.

In a computerized accounting system, the computer interprets debits and credits as increases or decreases, based on the account type. For example, a computer reads a debit to Cash as an increase, because it is an asset account. The computer reads a debit to Accounts Payable as a decrease, because it is a liability account.

---

[1] The words *debit* and *credit* abbreviate the Latin terms *debitum* and *creditum*. Luca Pacioli, the Italian monk who wrote about accounting in the 15th century, used these terms.

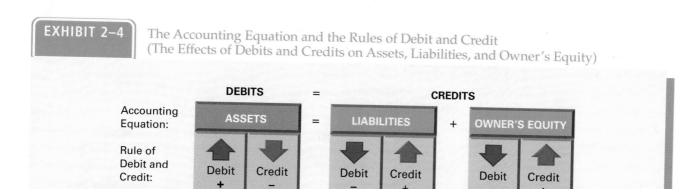

To illustrate the ideas diagrammed in Exhibit 2–4, reconsider Transaction 1 from Chapter 1. John Ladner invested $250,000 cash to begin the environmental consulting firm. The company received $250,000 cash from Ladner and gave him the owner's equity. We are accounting for the business entity, Ladner Environmental Services (LES). What accounts of LES are affected? By what amounts? On what side (debit or credit)? The answer is that Assets and Capital would increase by $250,000, as the following T-accounts show:

ASSETS = LIABILITIES + OWNER'S EQUITY

Cash		John Ladner, Capital	
Debit for increase, 250,000			Credit for increase, 250,000

The amount remaining in an account is called its *balance.* Transaction 1 gives Cash a $250,000 debit balance, and John Ladner, Capital a $250,000 credit balance. Notice that Assets = Liabilities + Owner's Equity *and* that total debit amounts = total credit amounts. Exhibit 2–5, on page 60, illustrates the accounting equation and LES's first two transactions.

LEARNING TIPS

In each transaction, total debits must equal total credits.

Transaction 2 is a $100,000 cash purchase of land. This transaction affects two assets: Cash and Land. It decreases (credits) Cash and increases (debits) Land, as shown in the T-accounts:

ASSETS = LIABILITIES + OWNER'S EQUITY

Cash		John Ladner, Capital	
Balance 250,000	Credit for decrease, 100,000		Balance 250,000
Balance 150,000			

Land	
Debit for increase, 100,000	
Balance 100,000	

After this transaction, Cash has a $150,000 debit balance ($250,000 debit balance reduced by the $100,000 credit amount), Land has a debit balance of $100,000, and John Ladner, Capital has a $250,000 credit balance as shown in the section of Exhibit 2–5 labelled Transaction 2.

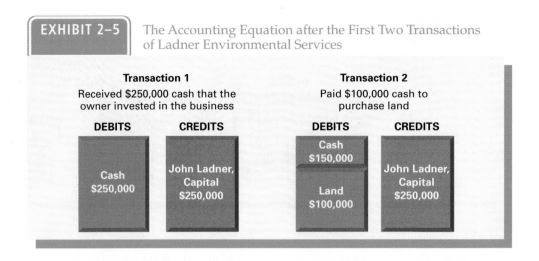

We create accounts as they are needed. The process of creating a new account in preparation for recording a transaction is called *opening the account*. For Transaction 1, we opened the Cash account and the John Ladner, Capital account. For Transaction 2, we opened the Land account.

Expanding the Rules of Debit and Credit: Revenues and Expenses

Owner's equity includes revenues and expenses because revenues and expenses make up net income or net loss, which flows into owner's equity. As we have discussed, *revenues* are increases in owner's equity from providing goods and services to customers. *Expenses* are decreases in owner's equity from using assets or increasing liabilities in the course of operating the business. Therefore, we must expand the accounting equation. Exhibit 2–6 shows revenues and expenses under equity because they directly affect owner's equity.

EXHIBIT 2-6   Expansion of the Accounting Equation to Include Revenues and Expenses

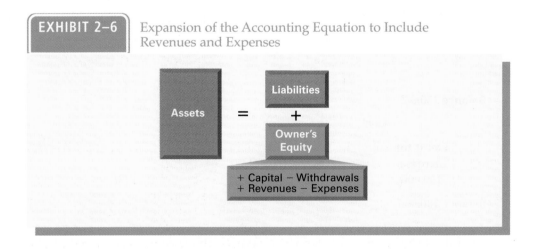

We can now express the rules of debit and credit in final form as shown in Exhibit 2–7.

EXHIBIT 2–7 | Final Rules of Debit and Credit

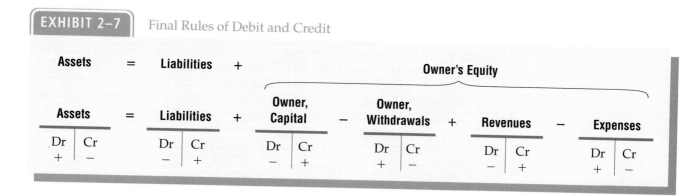

Assets	=	Liabilities	+	Owner's Equity					

Assets	=	Liabilities	+	Owner, Capital	−	Owner, Withdrawals	+	Revenues	−	Expenses
Dr +	Cr −		Dr −	Cr +		Dr −	Cr +		Dr +	Cr −		Dr −	Cr +		Dr +	Cr −

Normal Balance of an Account

An account's **normal balance** appears on the side of the account—debit or credit—where *increases* are recorded. For example, Cash and other assets usually have a debit balance, so the normal balance of assets is on the debit side, and assets are called *debit-balance accounts.* Conversely, liabilities and owner's equity usually have a credit balance, so their normal balances are on the credit side, and they are called *credit-balance accounts.* Exhibit 2–8 illustrates the normal balances of assets, liabilities, and equity accounts.

KEY POINT

The normal balance of an account is the side on which increases are recorded.

EXHIBIT 2–8 | Normal Balances of the Accounts

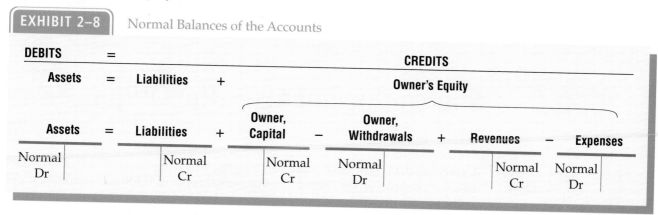

DEBITS	=			CREDITS					
Assets	=	Liabilities	+	Owner's Equity					

Assets	=	Liabilities	+	Owner, Capital	−	Owner, Withdrawals	+	Revenues	−	Expenses
Normal Dr		Normal Cr		Normal Cr		Normal Dr		Normal Cr		Normal Dr

As we have seen, owner's equity includes

John Ladner, Capital—a credit-balance account

John Ladner, Withdrawals—a debit-balance account

The sum of these two accounts should be a credit, for example,

John Ladner, Capital	John Ladner, Withdrawals
250,000	5,500

Owner's Equity = $244,500, a credit

Revenues increase equity, so a revenue's normal balance is a credit. Expenses decrease equity, so an expense's normal balance is a debit.

An account that normally has a debit balance may occasionally have a credit balance, which indicates a negative amount of the item. For example, Cash will have a credit balance if the entity overdraws its bank account. Similarly, the liability Accounts Payable—normally a credit-balance account—will have a debit balance if the entity overpays its accounts payable. In other instances, the shift of a balance amount away from its normal column may indicate an accounting error. For example, a credit balance in Office Supplies, Furniture, or Buildings is an error because negative amounts of these assets cannot exist.

DID YOU GET IT?

MyAccountingLab

To check your understanding of the material in this Learning Objective, complete these questions. The solutions appear on MyAccountingLab so you can check your progress.

4. Indicate whether each account listed below is a(n) asset (A), liability (L), owner's equity (OE), revenue (R), or expense (E) account. Next to each answer, indicate whether the account's normal balance is a debit (Dr) or a credit (Cr).

Accounts Payable	___ ; ___	Cash	___ ; ___
Service Revenue	___ ; ___	Rent Expense	___ ; ___
K. Lockyer, Withdrawals	___ ; ___	Vehicles	___ ; ___
Rent Revenue	___ ; ___	Notes Payable	___ ; ___
Accounts Receivable	___ ; ___	Land	___ ; ___
Insurance Expense	___ ; ___	K. Lockyer, Capital	___ ; ___

5. Indicate on which side of these accounts—debit (Dr) or credit (Cr)—you would record an increase.

_____ Accounts Receivable	_____ Salary Expense
_____ Accounts Payable	_____ Building
_____ Equipment	_____ Supplies Expense
_____ John Ladner, Capital	_____ Interest Payable
_____ Service Revenue	_____ Furniture

6. Indicate on which side of these accounts—debit (Dr) or credit (Cr)—you would record a decrease.

_____ Notes Payable	_____ Land
_____ Accounts Receivable	_____ Travel Expense
_____ Cash	_____ Supplies
_____ John Ladner, Withdrawals	_____ Accounts Payable
_____ Income Tax Payable	_____ Income Tax Expense

Source Documents—The Origin of Transactions

OBJECTIVE 3
Analyze and record transactions in the journal

Accounting data come from source documents, which are the evidence of a transaction. For example, when Ladner Environmental Services (LES) receives cash, it deposits the cash into its bank account. The *bank deposit slip* is the document that shows the amount of cash received by the business and deposited in its bank account. Based on this document, the company can record this transaction in the accounting records.

When LES buys supplies on account, the vendor sends LES an invoice requesting payment. The *purchase invoice* is the source document that tells the business to pay the vendor. The invoice shows what LES purchased and how much it cost, giving LES the information it needs to record the transaction.

LES may pay the account payable with a *bank cheque*, another source document. The cheque and the purchase invoice give the business the information it needs to record the cash payment accurately.

When LES provides environmental consulting services to a client, LES faxes a sales invoice to the client. LES's *sales invoice* is the source document that gives LES the amount of revenue to record.

There are many different types of source documents in business. Later in this chapter, we illustrate some of the more common types of documents that LES uses in its business.

Recording Transactions in the Journal

We could record all transactions directly in the accounts as we have shown for the first two transactions. However, that way of accounting does not leave a clear record of each transaction. You may have to search through all the accounts to find both sides of a particular transaction. To save time, accountants first keep a record of each transaction in a *journal*, the chronological (by date) record of the entity's transactions. They then transfer this information from the journal into the accounts.

The process of journalizing transactions follows four steps:

1. Identify the transactions from source documents, such as bank deposit slips, sales invoices, and cheque stubs (described above).
2. Identify each account affected by the transaction and its type (asset, liability, owner's equity, revenue, or expense).
3. Determine whether each account is increased or decreased by the transaction. Using the rules of debit and credit, determine whether to debit or credit the account to record its increase or decrease.
4. Record the transaction in the journal, including a brief explanation for the journal entry. The debit side of the entry is entered first and the credit side last. Total debits must always equal total credits. This step is also called "making the journal entry" or "journalizing the transaction."

These four steps are completed in a computerized accounting system as well as in a manual system. In step 4, however, the computerized journal entry is generally entered into the computer by account number, and the account name then appears automatically. Most computer programs replace the explanation in the journal entry with some other means of tracing the entry back to its source documents.

Let's apply the four steps to journalize Transaction 1 of Ladner Environmental Services (LES)—the business's receipt of John Ladner's $250,000 cash investment in the business.

Step 1. The source documents are LES's bank deposit slip and the $250,000 cheque, which is deposited in the business bank account.

Step 2. The accounts affected by the transaction are Cash and John Ladner, Capital. Cash is an asset account, and John Ladner, Capital is an owner's equity account.

Step 3. Both accounts increase by $250,000. Therefore, Cash, the asset account, is increased (debited), and John Ladner, Capital, the owner's equity account, is increased (credited).

Step 4. The journal entry is

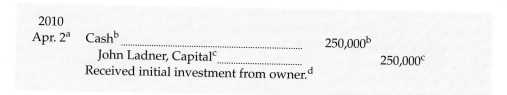

2010			
Apr. 2[a]	Cash[b]	250,000[b]	
	John Ladner, Capital[c]		250,000[c]
	Received initial investment from owner.[d]		

KEY POINT

In a journal entry, such as Exhibit 2–9 on the next page, the account debited is always written first (not indented). The account credited is indented on the line below, and the explanation is on the next line, and not indented. Journal entries should always be recorded in this format.

The journal entry includes the

a. date of the transaction
b. title of the account debited (placed flush left), along with the dollar amount
c. title of the account credited (indented slightly), along with the dollar amount
d. short explanation of the transaction.

Dollar signs are omitted in the money columns because it is understood that the amounts are in dollars.

The journal offers detailed information that the ledger accounts do not provide. Each journal entry shows the complete effect of a business transaction. Consider Ladner's initial investment. The Cash account shows the $250,000 debit. We know that every transaction has a credit, so the corresponding $250,000 credit is in the Capital account. But imagine the difficulties you would face trying to link debits and credits for hundreds of daily transactions—without a separate record of each transaction. The journal solves this problem and presents the full story for each transaction. Exhibit 2–9 shows how Journal page 1 looks after the first transaction is recorded.

Regardless of the accounting system in use, an accountant must analyze every business transaction in the manner we are presenting in these opening chapters.

EXHIBIT 2–9 The Journal

				Page 1
	Journal			
Date	**Account Titles and Explanations**	**Post. Ref.**	**Debit**	**Credit**
2010 Apr. 2	Cash		250,000	
	John Ladner, Capital			250,000
	Received initial investment from owner.			

3. The Journal and the Ledger pages 1–6

Once the transaction has been analyzed, a computerized accounting package performs the same actions as accountants do in a manual system. For example, when a sales clerk keys in your transaction and runs your VISA card through the credit-card reader, the underlying accounting system records the store's sales revenue and receivable from VISA. The computer automatically records the transaction as a journal entry, but an accountant had to program the computer to do so. A computer's ability to perform routine tasks and mathematical operations quickly and without error frees accountants for decision making.

DID YOU GET IT?

To check your understanding of the material in this Learning Objective, complete these questions. The solutions appear on MyAccountingLab so you can check your progress.

7. For each of the following transactions, select the source document that provides the best evidence of the transaction. Choose from these source documents: bank deposit slip, bank cheque, invoice received from a vendor, or invoice sent to a customer.

   a. A company purchases supplies on account.
   b. A company pays for the supplies it purchased in transaction a.
   c. A company performs services on account for a community college.
   d. The community college pays the company for the services performed in transaction c.
   e. A customer pays the company immediately for services performed.
   f. The company hires a student to provide office support during the summer.

8. Analyze the following transactions of Peterson Engineering in the manner shown for the December 1 transaction.

   Sept. 1   Paid monthly utilities expense of $140.
              (Analysis: The expense, utilities expense, is increased; therefore, debit Utilities Expense. The asset, cash, is decreased; therefore, credit Cash.)
        4   Borrowed $10,000 cash, signing a note payable.
        8   Performed service on account for a customer, $3,000.
      12   Purchased equipment on account, $2,000.
      24   Purchased supplies for $600 and paid cash.
      27   Paid the liability created on September 12.

9. Refer to the Peterson Engineering transactions in the previous question. Record each transaction on page 1 of the journal. Include an explanation for each journal entry.

Posting (Transferring Information) from the Journal to the Ledger

OBJECTIVE 4
Post from the journal to the ledger

Journalizing a transaction records the data only in the journal—but not in the ledger. To appear in the ledger, the data must be copied or transferred to the ledger. The process of transferring data from the journal to the ledger is called **posting**. We *post* from the journal to the ledger.

Debits in the journal are posted as debits in the ledger, and credits in the journal are posted as credits in the ledger—there are no exceptions. The first transaction of Ladner Environmental Services is posted to the ledger as shown in Exhibit 2–10. Computers perform this tedious task quickly and without error. The details for posting from the journal to the ledger will be presented later in this chapter.

EXHIBIT 2–10 | Making a Journal Entry and Posting to the Ledger

Panel A—Journal Entry

	Journal			Page 1
Date	**Accounts Titles and Explanations**	**Post. Ref.**	**Debit**	**Credit**
2010 Apr. 2	Cash		250,000	
	John Ladner, Capital...................................			250,000
	Received initial investment from owner.			

Panel B—Posting to the Ledger

Account: **Cash**					Account No. **1100**
Date	**Item**	**Jrnl. Ref.**	**Debit**	**Credit**	**Balance**
2010					
Apr. 2			250,000		250,000 Dr

Account: **John Ladner, Capital**					Account No. **3000**
Date	**Item**	**Jrnl. Ref.**	**Debit**	**Credit**	**Balance**
2010					
Apr. 2				250,000	250,000 Cr

The Flow of Accounting Data

Exhibit 2–11 summarizes the flow of accounting data from the business transaction all the way through the accounting system to the ledger. In the pages that follow, we record the early transactions of Ladner Environmental Services (LES). Keep in

EXHIBIT 2–11 | Flow of Accounting Data

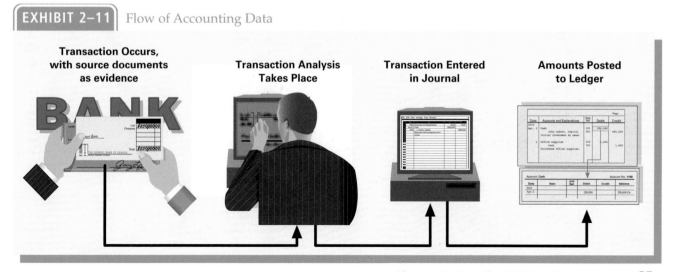

mind that we are accounting for the business entity, Ladner Environmental Services. We are *not* accounting for John Ladner's *personal* transactions. We temporarily ignore the date of each transaction in order to focus on the accounts and their dollar amounts. We will also post the transactions to T-accounts instead of ledger accounts for the same reason.

When analyzing a transaction, first determine whether it is a transaction, then pinpoint the obvious effects on the accounts. For example, cash effects are easy to identify. Did cash increase or decrease? Then find the effect on other accounts.

Transaction Analysis, Journalizing, and Posting to the Ledger

> 1. *Transaction:* John Ladner invested $250,000 cash to begin his environmental consulting business, Ladner Environmental Services. The money was deposited in the company's bank account, as shown by the following deposit ticket:

CREDIT ACCOUNT OF:
LADNER ENVIRONMENTAL SERVICES
10300 004 06000303600

BUSINESS ACCOUNT DEPOSIT SLIP

BANK OF THE PEOPLE
SHOPPING CONCOURSE BRANCH
DOMINION CENTRE
WINNIPEG, MANITOBA R5W 2X1

CREDIT ACCOUNT OF:
LADNER ENVIRONMENTAL SERVICES
10300 004 06000303600

DATE		
DAY 02	MONTH 04	YEAR 10

LIST OF CHEQUES
PLEASE LIST FOREIGN CHEQUES ON SEPARATE DEPOSIT SLIP

CHEQUE IDENTIFICATION

1 John Ladner	250,000	0	0
2			
3			
4			
5			
6			
7			
8			
9			
10			
11			
12			
13			
14			
15			
16			
17			
18			
CHEQUE SUBTOTAL	$ 250,000	0	0

DATE			INITIALS	
DAY 02	MONTH 04	YEAR 10	DEPOSITORS *jl*	TELLERS *sm*

CASH COUNT

× 5
× 10
× 20
× 50
× 100
× $ 2 COIN
× $ 1 COIN

COIN

CASH SUBTOTAL	0

DEPOSIT

ENTER CREDIT CARD VOUCHER TOTAL			0
CASH SUBTOTAL			0
CHEQUE SUBTOTAL	250,000	0	0
U.S. CASH			0
RATE			0
U.S. CHQS.			0
RATE			0
DEPOSIT TOTAL	$ 250,000	0	0

10300 004 0090 0303600

| *Analysis:* | Ladner's investment in Ladner Environmental Services increased its asset cash; to record this increase, debit Cash. The investment also increased its owner's equity; to record this increase, credit John Ladner, Capital. |

Accounting Equation:

ASSETS	=	LIABILITIES	+	OWNER'S EQUITY
Cash				John Ladner, Capital
+250,000	=	0	+	250,000

The journal entry records the same information that you learned by using the accounting equation in Chapter 1. Both accounts—Cash and Ladner, Capital—increased because the business received $250,000 cash and gave Ladner $250,000 of capital (owner's equity) in the business.

Journal Entry:

Cash... 250,000
    John Ladner, Capital.................... 250,000
Received initial investment from owner.

Ledger Accounts:

Cash		John Ladner, Capital	
(1) 250,000			(1) 250,000

---

2. Transaction: Ladner Environmental Services paid $100,000 cash for land as a future office location.

Analysis: The purchase decreased cash; therefore, credit Cash. The purchase increased the entity's asset, land; to record this increase, debit Land.

Accounting Equation:

ASSETS		=	LIABILITIES	+	OWNER'S EQUITY
Cash	Land				
−100,000	+100,000	=	0	+	0

This transaction increased one asset, land, and decreased another asset, cash. The net effect on the business's total assets was zero, and there was no effect on liabilities or owner's equity. We use the term *net* in business to mean an amount after a subtraction.

Journal Entry:

Land... 100,000
    Cash... 100,000
Paid cash for land.

Ledger Accounts:

Cash		Land	
(1) 250,000	(2) 100,000	(2) 100,000	

---

3. Transaction: The business purchased office supplies for $5,000 on account, as shown by the purchase invoice on the next page.

Analysis: The credit purchase of office supplies increased this asset, so we debit Office Supplies. The purchase also increased a liability; to record this increase, credit Accounts Payable.

Accounting Equation:

ASSETS	=	LIABILITIES	+	OWNER'S EQUITY
Office Supplies		Accounts Payable		
+5,000	=	+5,000	+	0

Journal Entry:

Office Supplies 5,000
    Accounts Payable......................... 5,000
Purchased office supplies on account.

Ledger Accounts:

Office Supplies		Accounts Payable	
(3) 5,000			(3) 5,000

INVOICE (purchase)

WHOLESALE OFFICE SUPPLY
500 HENDERSON ROAD
WINNIPEG, MANITOBA R5W 5Y6

Date: April 3, 2010
Terms: 30 days
Sold to: **Ladner Environmental Services**
281 Wave Avenue
Winnipeg, Manitoba R5W 9C8

Quantity	Item	Price	Total
380	Laser paper	$10	$3,800.00
80	Desk calendars	15	1,200.00

Total amount due: **$5,000.00**

---

4. *Transaction:* The business provided environmental consulting services for clients and received $20,000 cash. The source document is Ladner Environmental Services' sales invoice shown below.

INVOICE (sale)

Ladner Environmental Services
281 Wave Avenue
Winnipeg, Manitoba R5W 9C8

Date: April 8, 2010
Sold to: **Allied Energy Corporation**
325 Brooks Street
Winnipeg, Manitoba

PAID

Invoice No: **0001**
Service: 1000 DVD0503 service for all locations

Total amount due: $20,000

All accounts are due and payable within 30 days.

Analysis: The asset, cash, is increased; therefore, debit Cash. The revenue account, service revenue, is increased; credit Service Revenue.

Accounting Equation:

ASSETS	=	LIABILITIES	+	OWNER'S EQUITY
			+	REVENUES
Cash				Service Revenue
+20,000	=	0	+	20,000

Journal Entry:

Cash 20,000
   Service Revenue   20,000
Performed service and received cash.

Ledger Accounts:

Cash				Service Revenue	
(1)	250,000	(2)	100,000		
(4)	20,000			(4)	20,000

5. *Transaction*: The business provided environmental consulting services of $15,000 to clients who will pay for the services within one month.

Analysis: The asset, accounts receivable, is increased; therefore, debit Accounts Receivable. Service revenue is increased; credit Service Revenue.

Accounting Equation:

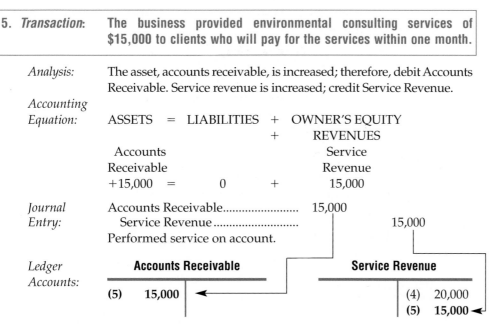

ASSETS = LIABILITIES + OWNER'S EQUITY
$\qquad\qquad\qquad\qquad\qquad\qquad$ + $\qquad\qquad$ REVENUES
$\quad$ Accounts $\qquad\qquad\qquad\qquad\qquad$ Service
$\quad$ Receivable $\qquad\qquad\qquad\qquad\quad$ Revenue
$\quad$ +15,000 $\quad$ = $\qquad$ 0 $\qquad$ + $\qquad\qquad$ 15,000

Journal Entry:

Accounts Receivable........................ 15,000
$\quad$ Service Revenue .... $\qquad\qquad\qquad$ 15,000
Performed service on account.

Ledger Accounts:

Accounts Receivable		Service Revenue	
(5) **15,000**			**(4)** 20,000
			(5) **15,000**

Notice the differences and the similarities between Transactions 4 and 5. In both transactions, Service Revenue was increased because in both cases the company earned revenue. However, in Transaction 4, the company was paid at the time of service. In Transaction 5, the company will receive cash later (Accounts Receivable). This is key, because the amount of earnings is not determined by when the company receives cash. Earnings (revenue) are recorded when the company does the work, or earns revenue.

6. *Transaction*: The business paid the following cash expenses: office rent, $3,000; employee salary, $3,500; and utilities, $1,000.

Analysis: The asset cash is decreased; therefore, credit Cash for each of the three expense amounts. The following expenses are increased: Rent Expense, Salary Expense, and Utilities Expense. Each should be debited for the appropriate amount.

Accounting Equation:

ASSETS = LIABILITIES + OWNER'S EQUITY
$\qquad\qquad\qquad\qquad\qquad\qquad\qquad$ − $\qquad\qquad$ EXPENSES
$\qquad\qquad\qquad\qquad\qquad\qquad\qquad\qquad\quad$ Rent $\qquad$ Salary $\quad$ Utilities
$\quad$ Cash $\qquad\qquad\qquad\qquad\qquad\qquad$ Expense $\;$ Expense $\;$ Expense
$\quad$ −7,500 $\quad$ = $\qquad$ 0 $\qquad\qquad\qquad$ −3,000 $\;$ −3,500 $\;$ −1,000

Journal Entry:

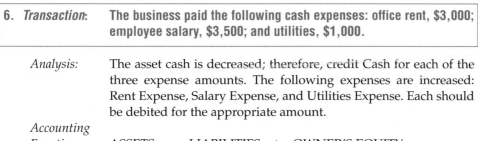

Rent Expense 3,000
Salary Expense 3,500
Utilities Expense 1,000
$\quad$ Cash .... $\qquad\qquad\qquad$ 7,500
Issued three cheques to pay cash for expenses.

Ledger Accounts:

Cash				Rent Expense	
(1) 250,000	**(2)** 100,000			**(6)** **3,000**	
(4) 20,000	**(6)** **7,500**				

Salary Expense				Utilities Expense	
(6) **3,500**				**(6)** **1,000**	

Note: *In practice, the business would record these three transactions separately since they are all paid with separate cheques. To save space, we can record them together to illustrate a compound journal entry.* No matter how many accounts a compound entry affects—there may be any number—total debits must equal total credits.

| 7. *Transaction:* | The business paid $4,000 on the account payable created in Transaction 3. The paid cheque is Ladner Environmental Services' source document, or proof, for this transaction. |

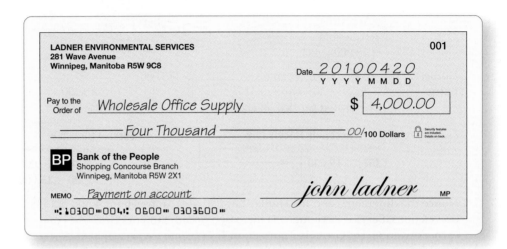

Analysis: The payment decreased the asset cash; therefore, credit Cash. The payment also decreased the liability accounts payable, so we debit Accounts Payable.

Accounting Equation:

ASSETS	=	LIABILITIES	+	OWNER'S EQUITY
Cash		Accounts Payable		
−4,000	=	−4,000	+	0

Journal Entry:

Accounts Payable............................ 4,000
    Cash 4,000
Paid cash on account.

Ledger Accounts:

Cash				Accounts Payable			
(1)	250,000	(2)	100,000	(7)	4,000	(3)	5,000
(4)	20,000	(6)	7,500				
		(7)	4,000				

| 8. *Transaction:* | John Ladner remodelled his personal residence with personal funds. This is not a business transaction of the environmental consulting business, so no journal entry is made. |

| 9. *Transaction:* | The business received $11,000 cash from one of the clients discussed in Transaction 5. |

Analysis: The asset cash is increased; therefore, debit Cash. The asset accounts receivable is decreased; therefore, credit Accounts Receivable.

Accounting Equation:

ASSETS		=	LIABILITIES	+	OWNER'S EQUITY
	Accounts				
Cash	Receivable				
+11,000	−11,000	=	0	+	0

Journal	Cash	11,000	
Entry:	Accounts Receivable.....................		11,000
	Received cash on account.		

Note: This transaction has no effect on revenue; the related revenue is accounted for in Transaction 5.

Ledger Accounts:

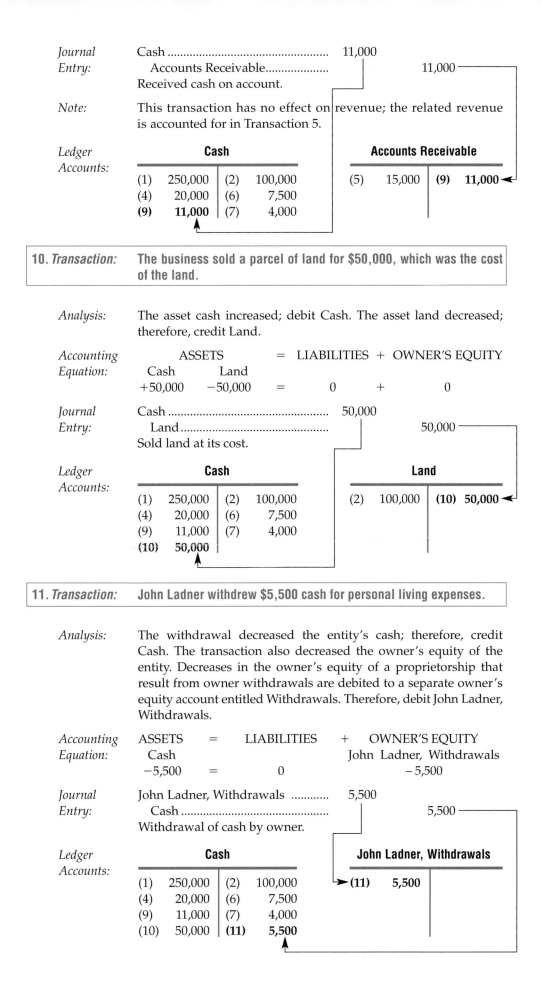

Cash			
(1)	250,000	(2)	100,000
(4)	20,000	(6)	7,500
(9)	**11,000**	(7)	4,000

Accounts Receivable			
(5)	15,000	**(9)**	**11,000**

---

10. *Transaction:* **The business sold a parcel of land for $50,000, which was the cost of the land.**

Analysis: The asset cash increased; debit Cash. The asset land decreased; therefore, credit Land.

Accounting Equation:

ASSETS		=	LIABILITIES	+	OWNER'S EQUITY
Cash	Land				
+50,000	−50,000	=	0	+	0

Journal	Cash	50,000	
Entry:	Land..		50,000
	Sold land at its cost.		

Ledger Accounts:

Cash			
(1)	250,000	(2)	100,000
(4)	20,000	(6)	7,500
(9)	11,000	(7)	4,000
(10)	**50,000**		

Land			
(2)	100,000	**(10)**	**50,000**

---

11. *Transaction:* **John Ladner withdrew $5,500 cash for personal living expenses.**

Analysis: The withdrawal decreased the entity's cash; therefore, credit Cash. The transaction also decreased the owner's equity of the entity. Decreases in the owner's equity of a proprietorship that result from owner withdrawals are debited to a separate owner's equity account entitled Withdrawals. Therefore, debit John Ladner, Withdrawals.

Accounting Equation:

ASSETS	=	LIABILITIES	+	OWNER'S EQUITY
Cash				John Ladner, Withdrawals
−5,500	=	0		− 5,500

Journal	John Ladner, Withdrawals	5,500	
Entry:	Cash...		5,500
	Withdrawal of cash by owner.		

Ledger Accounts:

Cash			
(1)	250,000	(2)	100,000
(4)	20,000	(6)	7,500
(9)	11,000	(7)	4,000
(10)	50,000	**(11)**	**5,500**

John Ladner, Withdrawals			
(11)	**5,500**		

Each journal entry posted to the T-accounts (representing the ledger) is identified by date or by transaction number (in this example, the transaction numbers have been in brackets). In this way any transaction can be traced from the journal to the ledger, and, if need be, back to the journal. This helps to locate efficiently any information you may need.

The T-Accounts after Posting

We next show the accounts of Ladner Environmental Services after posting. The account numbers are shown for each T-account. The accounts are grouped under the accounting equation's headings in Exhibit 2–12.

EXHIBIT 2–12 | Ladner Environmental Services' Ledger Accounts after Posting

| ASSETS | = | LIABILITIES | + | OWNER'S EQUITY |

Cash #1100

(1) 250,000	(2) 100,000
(4) 20,000	(6) 7,500
(9) 11,000	(7) 4,000
(10) 50,000	(11) 5,500
Bal. 214,000	

Accounts Payable #2100

| (7) 4,000 | (3) 5,000 |
| | Bal. 1,000 |

John Ladner, Capital #3000

| | (1) 250,000 |
| | Bal. 250,000 |

Accounts Receivable #1200

| (5) 15,000 | (9) 11,000 |
| Bal. 4,000 | |

John Ladner, Withdrawals #3100

| (11) 5,500 | |
| Bal. 5,500 | |

Office Supplies #1400

| (3) 5,000 | |
| Bal. 5,000 | |

REVENUE

Service Revenue #4000

	(4) 20,000
	(5) 15,000
	Bal. 35,000

Land #1900

| (2) 100,000 | (10) 50,000 |
| Bal. 50,000 | |

EXPENSES

Rent Expense #5100

| (6) 3,000 | |
| Bal. 3,000 | |

Salary Expense #5200

| (6) 3,500 | |
| Bal. 3,500 | |

Utilities Expense #5300

| (6) 1,000 | |
| Bal. 1,000 | |

Each account has a balance, denoted as *Bal.* This amount is the difference between the account's total debits and its total credits. For example, the $214,000 balance in the Cash account is the difference between

- Total debits, $331,000 ($250,000 + $20,000 + $11,000 + $50,000)
- Total credits, $117,000 ($100,000 + $7,500 + $4,000 + $5,500)

We set a balance apart by a horizontal line. The final figure in an account below the horizontal line is the balance of the account after the transactions have been posted.

If the sum of an account's debits is greater than the sum of its credits, that account has a debit balance, as the Cash account does here. If the sum of its credits is greater, that account has a credit balance, as Accounts Payable does.

KEY POINT

If an account has only one entry, you can total the account and label its balance, but you do not have to since the balance is obvious.

DID YOU GET IT?

MyAccountingLab

To check your understanding of the material in this Learning Objective, complete these questions. The solutions appear on MyAccountingLab so you can check your progress.

10. Refer to Did You Get It? Question 8 on page 64 for the transactions of Peterson Engineering.

Required

1. Create the following T-accounts with their September 1 balances: Cash #101, debit balance $3,000; Accounts Receivable #103 $0; Supplies #105, $0; Equipment #107 $0; Land #110, debit balance $29,000; Accounts Payable #201 $0; Notes Payable #205 $0; R. Peterson, Capital #301, credit balance $32,000; Service Revenue #401 $0; Utilities Expense #501 $0.

2. Record the transactions of Did You Get It? Question 8 directly in the T-accounts affected. Use dates as posting references in the T-accounts. Start with September 1 or (1). Journal entries are not required.

3. Compute the September 30 balance for each account, then add the balances to prove that total debits equal total credits.

11. Compute the missing amount represented by X in each account:

(1) Cash			(2) Accounts Payable			(3) R. Glennie, Capital		
Bal. 10,000	13,000		X	Bal. 12,800		22,000	Bal.	X
20,000				45,600			56,000	
Bal. X				Bal. 23,500			15,000	
							Bal. 73,000	

The Trial Balance

A *trial balance* summarizes the ledger by listing all accounts with their balances—assets first, followed by liabilities and then owner's equity. Before computers, the trial balance provided an accuracy check by showing whether the total debits equalled the total credits. The trial balance is still useful as a summary of all the accounts and their balances. A trial balance may be taken at any time the postings are up to date. The most common time is at the end of the accounting period. Exhibit 2–13 is the trial balance of Ladner Environmental Services at April 30, 2010, the end of the first month of operations. Most trial balances include the account numbers from the chart of accounts. Accounts with zero balances typically are not listed on the trial balance.

OBJECTIVE 5
Prepare and use a trial balance

Details of Journals and Ledgers

In practice, the journal and the ledger provide additional details that create a "trail" through the accounting records for future reference. For example, suppose a supplier bills us twice for the same item we purchased on account. To prove we have already paid the bill, we must prove that we made our payment. To do this, we trace the payment using the journal and the ledger.

MyAccountingLab | Accounting Cycle Tutorials

3. The Journal and the Ledger pages 7–11

EXHIBIT 2–13 | Trial Balance

LADNER ENVIRONMENTAL SERVICES
Trial Balance
April 30, 2010

Account Number	Account	Balance Debit	Balance Credit
1100	Cash	$214,000	
1200	Accounts receivable...	4,000	
1400	Office supplies...	5,000	
1900	Land..	50,000	
2100	Accounts payable...		$ 1,000
3000	John Ladner, capital...		250,000
3100	John Ladner, withdrawals	5,500	
4000	Service revenue		35,000
5100	Rent expense...	3,000	
5200	Salary expense...	3,500	
5300	Utilities expense..	1,000	
	Total..	$286,000	$286,000

Note: Do not confuse the trial balance with the balance sheet. A trial balance is an internal document seen only by the company's owners, managers, and accountants. The company reports its financial position—both inside the business and to the public—on the balance sheet, a formal financial statement. And remember that the financial statements are the focal point of the accounting process. The trial balance is merely a step in the preparation of the financial statements.

Details in the Journal Exhibit 2–14, Panel A, describes two transactions, and Panel B presents a widely used journal format. The journal page number appears in the upper-right corner. As the column headings indicate, the *journal* displays the following information:

1. The *date,* which indicates when the transaction occurred. The year appears directly under the Date heading at the top of each journal page or when the year has changed. The date of the transaction is recorded for every transaction
2. The *account titles* and *explanations* of the transaction, as in Exhibit 2–9
3. The *posting reference,* abbreviated Post. Ref. (or sometimes PR). How this column helps the accountant will become clear when we discuss the details of posting
4. The *debit* column, which shows the amount debited
5. The *credit* column, which shows the amount credited

Details in the Ledger Exhibit 2–14, Panel C, presents the *ledger* in the three-column format. The first two amount columns are for the debit and credit amounts posted from the journal. The third amount column is for the account's balance. This three-column format keeps a running balance for the account. The balance can be followed by the letters Dr or Cr (indicating a debit or credit, respectively); however, this is not always required. Each account has its own record in the illustrative ledger. Our example shows Ladner Environmental Services' Cash account; Land account; and John Ladner, Capital account. Each account in the ledger has its own identification number, from the chart of accounts.

KEY POINT

Notice that the three-column ledger account is a more formal version of the T-account. (See the yellow T-account in the John Ladner, Capital ledger account in Exhibit 2–14.)

EXHIBIT 2-14 Details of Journalizing and Posting

Panel A: Two of Ladner Environmental Services' Transactions

Date	Transaction
Apr. 2, 2010	John Ladner invested $250,000 in the business. The business received cash and gave Ladner owner's equity in the business.
Apr. 3, 2010	Paid $100,000 cash for land.

Panel B: The Journal

Page 1

Date	Account Titles and Explanations	Post. Ref.	Debit	Credit
2010				
Apr. 2	Cash	1100	250,000	
	John Ladner, Capital	3000		250,000
	Received initial investment from owner.			
3	Land	1900	100,000	
	Cash	1100		100,000
	Purchased land.			

① ② ③ ④

Panel C: The Ledger

Account: **Cash**   Account No. **1100**

Date	Item	Jrnl. Ref.	Debit	Credit	Balance
2010					
Apr. 2		J1	250,000		250,000 Dr
Apr. 3		J1		100,000	150,000 Dr

1 Transfer the date of the transaction from the journal to the ledger.

2 Transfer the page number from the journal to the journal reference column of the ledger. "J1" signifies Journal page 1.

3 Post the debit figure from the journal as a debit figure in the ledger account.

4 Enter the account number in the posting reference column of the journal once the figure has been posted to the ledger.

Account: **Land**   Account No. **1900**

Date	Item	Jrnl. Ref.	Debit	Credit	Balance
2010					
Apr. 3		J1	100,000		100,000 Dr

Account: **John Ladner, Capital**   Account No. **3000**

Date	Item	Jrnl. Ref.	Debit	Credit	Balance
2010					
Apr. 2		J1		250,000	250,000 Cr

KEY POINT

The Item column is often left blank because special notations are rarely used. Typically, the only item notation used is an indication of an opening balance or a balance brought forward from a previous period.

The column headings identify the ledger account's features:

1. The date
2. The item column. This space is used for any special notation. An example is "Beginning balance"
3. The journal reference column, abbreviated Jrnl. Ref. (or sometimes JR). The importance of this column will become clear when we discuss the mechanics of posting
4. The debit column, with the amount debited
5. The credit column, with the amount credited
6. The balance column, with the debit or credit running balance

Posting from the Journal to the Ledger

We know that posting means transferring information from the journal to the ledger accounts. But how do we handle the additional details that appear in the journal and the ledger formats that we have just seen? Exhibit 2–14 illustrates the steps in full detail. Panel A lists the first two transactions of Ladner Environmental Services; Panel B presents the journal; and Panel C shows the ledger. The posting process includes four steps:

After recording the transaction in the journal:

Arrow ①—Post the transaction date from the journal to the ledger.

Arrow ②—Post the journal page number from the journal to the ledger. We use these abbreviations:

Jrnl. Ref. means Journal Reference. J1 refers to Journal page 1.

This step indicates where the information in the ledger came from: Journal page 1.

Arrow ③—Post the dollar amount of the debit ($250,000) from the journal as a debit to the same account (Cash) in the ledger. Likewise, post the dollar amount of the credit (also $250,000) from the journal to the appropriate account in the ledger. Now the ledger accounts have their correct amounts.

Arrow ④—Copy (post) the account number (1100) from the ledger back to the journal. This step indicates that the $250,000 debit to Cash has been posted to the Cash account in the ledger. Also, copy the account number (3000) for John Ladner, Capital back to the journal to show that the $250,000 amount of the credit has been posted to the ledger. As mentioned earlier, the account numbers come from the chart of accounts, as shown in Exhibit 2–3 on page 56.

Post. Ref. is the abbreviation for Posting Reference, and the posting reference is the account number.

After posting, you should prepare the trial balance, as we discussed earlier.

Correcting Trial Balance Errors

Throughout the accounting process, total debits should always equal total credits. If they are not equal, then accounting errors exist. Computerized accounting systems eliminate many errors because most software will not let you make a journal entry that doesn't balance. But computers cannot *eliminate* all errors because humans sometimes input the wrong data or input data to the wrong accounts.

Some errors can be detected by computing the difference between total debits and total credits on the trial balance. Then perform one or more of the following actions:

1. Search the trial balance for a missing account. For example, suppose the accountant omitted John Ladner, Withdrawals from the trial balance in Exhibit 2–13 on page 74. Total debits would then be $280,500 ($286,000 − $5,500) and total credits would be $286,000, a difference of $5,500. Trace each account and its balance from the ledger to the trial balance, and you will locate the missing account.

Accounting Cycle Tutorials

1. Balance Sheet Accounts and Transactions
2. Income Statement Accounts and Transactions
3. The Journal and the Ledger

2. Search the journal for the amount of the difference. For example, suppose the total credits on Ladner Environmental Services' trial balance equal $286,000 and total debits equal $285,000. A $1,000 transaction may have been posted incorrectly to the ledger by omitting the debit entry. Search the journal for a $1,000 transaction and check its posting to the ledger.

3. Divide the difference between total debits and total credits by 2. A debit treated as a credit, or vice versa, doubles the amount of error. Suppose the accountant paid $1,000 cash for the utilities expenses. This transaction was recorded correctly in the journal, but was posted as a debit to Cash and a debit to Utilities Expense. Thus, $2,000 appears on the debit side of the trial balance, and there is nothing on the credit side relating to this transaction. The out-of-balance amount is $2,000, and dividing by 2 reveals that the relevant transaction may have had a value of $1,000. Search the journal for a $1,000 transaction and check the posting to the ledger.

4. Divide the out-of-balance amount by 9. If the result is evenly divisible by 9, the error may be a *slide,* which is adding or deleting one or several zeros in a figure (example: writing $61 as $610), or a *transposition* (example: treating $61 as $16). Suppose the accountant listed the $5,500 balance in John Ladner, Withdrawals as $55,000 on the trial balance—a slide-type error. Total debits would differ from total credits by $ 49,500 (i.e., $55,000 − $5,500 = $49,500). Dividing $49,500 by 9 yields $5,500, the correct amount of the withdrawals. Trace this amount through the ledger until you reach the John Ladner, Withdrawals account with a balance of $5,500. Dividing by 9 can give the correct transaction amount for a slide, but not for a transposition.

DID YOU GET IT?

MyAccountingLab

To check your understanding of the material in this Learning Objective, complete these questions. The solutions appear on MyAccountingLab so you can check your progress.

12. On July 2, 2010, Efficient Energy Services performed an energy audit for an industrial client and earned $4,000 of revenue on account. On July 14, 2010, the company received a cheque for the entire amount.

Required

   1. Journalize the two transactions for Efficient Energy Services on page 6 of the journal. Include an explanation for each transaction.

   2. Create the Service Revenue three-column ledger account and post the two transactions. The account number for Service Revenue is #40010.

13. Shiny Floor Cleaning's accounting records reported the following data on December 31, 2010. Accounts appear in no particular order.

Supplies	$ 7,500	S. Shaw, Withdrawals	$ 5,000
Equipment	2,000	Cash	13,000
Accounts Payable	1,000	Supplies Expense	6,000
S. Shaw, Capital	15,000	Accounts Receivable	12,500
Cleaning Revenue	30,000		

   Prepare the trial balance of Shiny Floor Cleaning at December 31, 2010. List the accounts in proper order, as shown on page 74.

14. Refer to the trial balance for Shiny Floor Cleaning created in the question above. Suppose Susan Shaw, the owner, accidentally listed equipment as $200 instead of the correct amount of $2,000. Compute the incorrect trial balance totals for debits and credits. Then show how to correct this error, which is called a *slide.*

Recording Business Transactions Under International Financial Reporting Standards (IFRS)

OBJECTIVE ⑥

Apply international financial reporting standards (IFRS) to recording business transactions

In this chapter, the focus has been on identifying and recording business transactions. The procedures described in this chapter are followed by companies that report their results using international financial reporting standards (IFRS). These companies still need to ensure that the debits and the credits are equal for every transaction. Under certain circumstances, the accounts used to record the transaction may differ. We will describe these differences as they appear in future chapters.

As we conclude this chapter, we return to our opening question: Why is recording business transactions important? By recording business transactions, posting to the ledger accounts, and preparing a trial balance, we have the process we need to assess the results of operations and financial position. The Decision Guidelines feature summarizes all our chapter-opening questions.

DECISION GUIDELINES — Analyzing and Recording Transactions

Decision	Guidelines
Has a transaction occurred?	If the event affects the entity's financial position *and* can be reliably recorded—*Yes* If either condition is absent—*No*
Where do we record the transaction?	In the *journal*, the chronological record of transactions
What do we record for each transaction?	Increases and/or decreases in all the accounts affected by the transaction (at the business's cost)
How do we record an increase/decrease in a(n)	Rules of debit and credit:

	Increase	Decrease
Asset?	Debit	Credit
Liability?	Credit	Debit
Owner's equity?	Credit	Debit
Revenue?	Credit	Debit
Expense?	Debit	Credit

Decision	Guidelines
Where do we store all the information for each account?	In the *ledger*, the book of accounts and their balances
Where do we list all the accounts and their balances?	In the *trial balance*
Where do we report the results of operations?	In the income statement (Revenues − Expenses = Net income, or Expenses − Revenues = Net loss)
Where do we report the financial position?	In the balance sheet (Assets = Liabilities + Owner's equity)

The trial balance of Aylmer Service Centre on March 1, 2010, lists the company's assets, liabilities, and owner's equity on that date.

AYLMER SERVICE CENTRE
Trial Balance
March 1, 2010

Account Number	Account Title	Debit	Credit
1100	Cash..	$26,000	
1200	Accounts receivable	4,500	
2100	Accounts payable		$ 2,000
3100	Jim Aylmer, capital...		28,500
	Total..	$82,400	$82,400

During March the business engaged in the following transactions:

a. Borrowed $45,000 from the bank and signed a note payable in the name of the business.

b. Paid cash of $40,000 to a real estate company to acquire land.

c. Performed service for a customer and received cash of $5,000.

d. Purchased supplies on account, $300.

e. Performed customer service and earned revenue on account, $2,600.

f. Paid $1,200 of the Accounts Payable from the March 1, 2010, trial balance.

g. Paid the following cash expenses: salaries, $3,000; rent, $1,500; and interest, $400.

h. Received $3,100 of the Accounts Receivable balance from the March 1, 2010, trial balance.

i. Received a $200 utility bill that will be paid next week.

j. Aylmer withdrew $1,800 for personal use.

Name: Aylmer Service Centre
Industry: Services proprietorship
Fiscal Period: Month of March 2010
Key Fact: An existing, ongoing business

Required

1. Open the following accounts, with the balances indicated, in the ledger of Aylmer Service Centre. Use the three-column ledger format.

   Assets: Cash, #1100, $26,000; Accounts Receivable, #1200, $4,500; Supplies, #1400, no balance; Land, #1900, no balance
   Liabilities: Accounts Payable, #2100, $2,000; Notes Payable, #2300, no balance
   Owner's Equity: Jim Aylmer, Capital, #3000, $28,500; Jim Aylmer, Withdrawals, #3100, no balance
   Revenues: Service Revenue, #4000, no balance
   Expenses: Interest Expense, #5100; Rent Expense, #5200; Salaries Expense, #5300; Utilities Expense, #5400 (none have balances)

2. Journalize the preceding transactions. Identify journal entries by their transaction letter.

3. Post to the ledger.

4. Prepare the trial balance of Aylmer Service Centre at March 31, 2010.

5. Compute the net income or net loss of the entity during the month of March by producing an income statement. List expenses in alphabetical order.

Prepare a ledger account for each account name. Place the opening balance in the ledger account, remembering that the normal balance in an asset account is a debit, in a liability or equity account is a credit, in a revenue account is a credit, and in an expense account is a debit.

For each transaction, ensure that Assets = Liabilities + Owner's equity.

Refer to the rules of debit and credit shown in Exhibit 2–7 on page 61.

SOLUTION

Requirement 1 is combined with Requirement 3

Requirement 2

Ensure total debits equal total credits in each journal entry. Selected journal entries are explained more fully.

When a transaction involves cash, always first decide whether cash increased or decreased. An increase is a debit to Cash. A decrease is a credit to Cash. Then decide which other accounts are affected.

"On account" means no cash was used in the transaction. Therefore, use Accounts Payable or Accounts Receivable since cash will be paid or collected in the future.

"Paid" means a cheque was written, so Cash is credited.

This transaction could also have been recorded with three journal entries, with a debit to the expense and a credit to Cash for each of the expenses.

Receiving a bill indicates an amount is owed for goods or services received. Increase the liability Accounts Payable, since cash will be paid for the utility bill in the future.

To make sure all the beginning account balances have been entered correctly, trace each ledger account's beginning balance back to the March 1, 2010, trial balance given on the previous page.

	Account Titles and Explanations	Post. Ref.	Debit	Page 1 Credit
a.	Cash	1100	45,000	
	Notes Payable	2300		45,000
	Borrowed cash on note payable.			
b.	Land	1900	40,000	
	Cash	1100		40,000
	Purchased land for cash.			
c.	Cash	1100	5,000	
	Service Revenue	4000		5,000
	Performed service and received cash.			
d.	Supplies	1400	300	
	Accounts Payable	2100		300
	Purchased supplies on account.			
e.	Accounts Receivable	1200	2,600	
	Service Revenue	4000		2,600
	Performed service on account.			
f.	Accounts Payable	2100	1,200	
	Cash	1100		1,200
	Paid cash to reduce accounts payable.			
g.	Salary Expense	5300	3,000	
	Rent Expense	5200	1,500	
	Interest Expense	5100	400	
	Cash	1100		4,900
	Issued three cheques to pay cash expenses.			
h.	Cash	1100	3,100	
	Accounts Receivable	1200		3,100
	Received cash on account.			
i.	Utilities Expense	5400	200	
	Accounts Payable	2100		200
	Received utility bill.			
j.	Jim Aylmer, Withdrawals	3100	1,800	
	Cash	1100		1,800
	Withdrew cash for personal use.			

Requirements 1 and 3

Account: Cash Account No. **1100**

Date	Item	Jrnl. Ref.	Debit	Credit	Balance
	Beginning balance				26,000 Dr.
a.		J1	45,000		71,000 Dr.
b.		J1		40,000	31,000 Dr.
c.		J1	5,000		36,000 Dr.
f.		J1		1,200	34,800 Dr.
g.		J1		4,900	29,900 Dr.
h.		J1	3,100		33,000 Dr.
j.		J1		1,800	31,200 Dr.

Account: **Accounts Receivable** Account No. **1200**

Date	Item	Jrnl. Ref.	Debit	Credit	Balance
	Beginning balance				4,500 Dr.
e.		J1	2,600		7,100 Dr.
h.		J1		3,100	4,000 Dr.

Account: **Supplies** Account No. **1400**

Date	Item	Jrnl. Ref.	Debit	Credit	Balance
d.		J1	300		300 Dr.

Account: **Land** Account No. **1900**

Date	Item	Jrnl. Ref.	Debit	Credit	Balance
b.		J1	40,000		40,000 Dr.

Account: **Accounts Payable** Account No. **2100**

Date	Item	Jrnl. Ref.	Debit	Credit	Balance
	Beginning balance				2,000 Cr.
d.		J1		300	2,300 Cr.
f.		J1	1,200		1,100 Cr.
i.		J1		200	1,300 Cr.

Account: **Notes Payable** Account No. **2300**

Date	Item	Jrnl. Ref.	Debit	Credit	Balance
a.		J1		45,000	45,000 Cr.

Account: **Jim Aylmer, Capital** Account No. **3000**

Date	Item	Jrnl. Ref.	Debit	Credit	Balance
	Beginning balance				28,500 Cr.

Account: **Jim Aylmer, Withdrawals** Account No. **3100**

Date	Item	Jrnl. Ref.	Debit	Credit	Balance
j.		J1	1,800		1,800 Dr.

Transfer amounts from the journal entries in Requirement 2 into the ledger accounts here. Write the letter of each transaction in the Date column in the ledger account.

Make sure each transaction is posted to the proper ledger account, and make sure no transactions were missed. Make sure that Assets = Liabilities + Owner's Equity for each transaction before going to the next transaction.

Account: Service Revenue					Account No. 4000
Date	Item	Jrnl. Ref.	Debit	Credit	Balance
c.		J1		5,000	5,000 Cr.
e.		J1		2,600	7,600 Cr.

Account: Interest Expense					Account No. 5100
Date	Item	Jrnl. Ref.	Debit	Credit	Balance
g.		J1	400		400 Dr.

Account: Rent Expense					Account No. 5200
Date	Item	Jrnl. Ref.	Debit	Credit	Balance
g.		J1	1,500		1,500 Dr.

Account: Salary Expense					Account No. 5300
Date	Item	Jrnl. Ref.	Debit	Credit	Balance
g.		J1	3,000		3,000 Dr.

Account: Utilities Expense					Account No. 5400
Date	Item	Jrnl. Ref.	Debit	Credit	Balance
i.		J1	200		200 Dr.

Requirement 4

AYLMER SERVICE CENTRE
Trial Balance
March 31, 2010

Account Number*	Account Title	Balance Debit	Balance Credit
1100	Cash	$31,200	
1200	Accounts receivable	4,000	
1400	Supplies	300	
1900	Land	40,000	
2100	Accounts payable		$ 1,300
2300	Notes payable		45,000
3000	Jim Aylmer, capital		28,500
3100	Jim Aylmer, withdrawals	1,800	
4000	Service revenue		7,600
5100	Interest expense	400	
5200	Rent expense	1,500	
5300	Salary expense	3,000	
5400	Utilities expense	200	
	Total	$82,400	$82,400

The title must include the name of the company, "Trial Balance," and the date of the trial balance. It shows the account balances on one specific date.

List all the accounts that have a balance in their ledger accounts. Accounts with a zero balance typically are not listed on the trial balance. Write the final balance amount for each account from Requirement 3 into the debit or credit column of the trial balance. Make sure that the total of the Debit column equals the total of the Credit column. Double underline the totals to show that the columns have been added and the totals are final.

* Note: Listing the account numbers is optional.

Requirement 5

AYLMER SERVICE CENTRE
Income Statement
For the Month Ended March 31, 2010

Revenues:		
Service revenue		$7,600
Expenses:		
Interest expense	$ 400	
Rent expense	1,500	
Salary expense	3,000	
Utilities expense	200	
Total expenses		5,100
Net income		$2,500

The title must include the name of the company, "Income Statement," and the specific period of time covered. It is critical that the time period be defined.

Prepare the income statement by listing the revenue accounts first, then the expense account names in alphabetical order from the trial balance. Then transfer the amounts from the trial balance to the income statement, and calculate net income or net loss.

Summary

1. **Define and use key accounting terms.** *Accounts* can be viewed either in the form of the letter "T" or in the three-column format shown in Exhibit 2–14 on page 75. The left side of each T-account is its *debit* side. The right side is its *credit* side. The first amount column in a three-column ledger account is the *debit* column, the second is the *credit* column, and the third is the *balance* column. The *ledger,* which contains a record for each account, groups and numbers accounts by category in the following order: assets, liabilities, and owner's equity (and its subparts, revenues and expenses). A *chart of accounts* lists all the accounts in the ledger and their account numbers.

2. **Apply the rules of debit and credit.** *Assets* and *expenses* are increased by debits and decreased by credits. *Liabilities, owner's equity,* and *revenues* are increased by credits and decreased by debits. An account's *normal balance* is the side of the account—debit or credit—in which increases are recorded. Thus, the normal balance of assets and expenses is a debit, and the normal balance of liabilities, owner's equity, and revenues is a credit. The Withdrawals account, which decreases owner's equity, normally has a debit balance. *Revenues,* which are increases in owner's equity, have a normal credit balance. *Expenses,* which are decreases in owner's equity, have a normal debit balance.

3. **Analyze and record transactions in the journal.** The accountant begins the recording process by analyzing the transaction, deciding if it is a transaction, and then entering the transaction's information in the *journal,* a chronological list of all the entity's transactions.

4. **Post from the journal to the ledger.** *Posting* means transferring to the *ledger* accounts. Posting references are used to trace amounts back and forth between the journal and the ledger.

5. **Prepare and use a trial balance.** The *trial balance* is a summary of all the non-zero account balances in the ledger. When *double-entry accounting* has been done correctly, the total debits and the total credits in the trial balance are equal.

6. **Apply international financial reporting standards (IFRS) to recording business transactions.** The procedures to identify and record business transactions are the same for private enterprises in Canada and for companies that report their results using international financial reporting standards (IFRS). IFRS companies still need to ensure that the debits and the credits are equal for every transaction.

We can now trace the flow of accounting information through these steps:

Business Transaction → Source Documents → Journal Entry → Posting to Ledger Accounts → Trial Balance

SELF-STUDY QUESTIONS

Test your understanding of the chapter by marking the correct answer for each of the following questions:

1. A T-account has two sides called the *(p. 57)*
   a. Debit and credit
   b. Asset and liability
   c. Revenue and expense
   d. Journal and ledger

2. Increases in liabilities are recorded by *(p. 57)*
   a. Debits
   b. Credits

3. Why do accountants record transactions in the journal? *(p. 62)*
   a. To ensure that all transactions are posted to the ledger
   b. To ensure that total debits equal total credits
   c. To have a chronological record of all transactions
   d. To help prepare the financial statements

4. Posting is the process of transferring information from the *(p. 64)*
   a. Journal to the trial balance
   b. Ledger to the trial balance
   c. Ledger to the financial statements
   d. Journal to the ledger

5. The purchase of land for cash is recorded by a *(p. 67)*
   a. Debit to Cash and a credit to Land
   b. Debit to Cash and a debit to Land
   c. Debit to Land and a credit to Cash
   d. Credit to Cash and a credit to Land

6. The purpose of the trial balance is to *(p. 73)*
   a. List all accounts with their balances
   b. Ensure that all transactions have been recorded
   c. Speed the collection of cash receipts from customers
   d. Increase assets and owner's equity

7. What is the normal balance of the Accounts Receivable, Office Supplies, and Rent Expense accounts? *(p. 61)*
   a. Debit
   b. Credit

8. A business has Cash of $3,000, Notes Payable of $2,500, Accounts Payable of $4,300, Service Revenue of $7,000, and Rent Expense of $2,400. Based on these data, how much are its total liabilities? *(p. 54)*
   a. $4,600
   b. $6,800
   c. $9,800
   d. $13,800

9. Smale Transport earned revenue on account. The earning of revenue on account is recorded by a (p. 69)
   a. Debit to Cash and a credit to Revenue
   b. Debit to Accounts Receivable and a credit to Revenue
   c. Debit to Accounts Payable and a credit to Revenue
   d. Debit to Revenue and a credit to Accounts Receivable

10. The account credited for a receipt of cash on account is (p. 70)
   a. Cash
   b. Accounts Payable
   c. Service Revenue
   d. Accounts Receivable

Answers to Self-Study Questions

1. a	3. c	5. c	7. a	9. b
2. b	4. d	6. a	8. b ($6,800 = $2,500 + $4,300)	10. d

ACCOUNTING VOCABULARY

Account (p. 52)
Chart of accounts (p. 55)
Credit (p. 58)
Debit (p. 58)
Journal (p. 52)

Ledger (p. 52)
Normal balance (p. 61)
Note receivable (p. 53)
Posting (p. 64)
Trial balance (p. 53)

SIMILAR ACCOUNTING TERMS

Cr	Credit; right
Dr	Debit; left
The Journal	A general journal; a book of original entry
The Ledger	The Books; the General Ledger
Entering the transaction in a journal	Making the journal entry; journalizing the transaction
Withdrawals by owner(s)	In a proprietorship or partnership, distributions from a company to its owner(s); Drawings
Open the accounts	Set up the accounts; create the ledger accounts

Assignment Material

QUESTIONS

1. Name the basic shortcut device or tool used in accounting. What letter of the alphabet does it resemble? Name its two sides.

2. Is the following statement true or false? Debit means decrease and credit means increase. Explain your answer.

3. Write two sentences that use the term *debit* differently.

4. What are the three *basic* types of accounts? Name two additional types of accounts. To which one of the three basic types are these two additional types of accounts most closely related?

5. Suppose you are the accountant for Smith Courier Service. Keeping in mind double-entry bookkeeping, identify the *dual effects* of Mary Smith's investment of $10,000 cash in her business.

6. Briefly describe the flow of accounting information using the accounting cycle.

7. To what does the *normal balance* of an account refer?

8. Indicate the normal balance of the five types of accounts.

Account Type	Normal Balance
Assets	_____
Liabilities	_____
Owner's equity	_____
Revenues	_____
Expenses	_____

9. What does posting accomplish? Why is it important? Does it come before or after journalizing?

10. Label each of the following transactions as increasing owner's equity (+), decreasing owner's equity (−), or having no effect on owner's equity (0). Write the appropriate symbol in the space provided.

_____ Investment by owner

_____ Invoice customer for services

_____ Purchase of supplies on credit

_____ Pay expenses

_____ Cash payment on account

_____ Withdrawal by owner

_____ Borrowing money on a note payable

_____ Sale of services on account

11. What four steps does the posting process include? Which step is the fundamental purpose of posting?

12. Rearrange the following accounts in their logical sequence in the chart of accounts:

Note Payable   Cash
Accounts Receivable Jane East, Capital
Sales Revenue   Salary Expense

13. What is the meaning of the statement "Accounts Payable has a credit balance of $1,700"?

14. Campus Cleaners launders the shirts of customer Bobby Baylor, who has a charge account at the cleaners. When Baylor picks up his clothes and is short of cash, he charges it. Later, when he receives his monthly statement from the cleaners, Baylor writes a cheque on his bank account and mails the cheque to the cleaners. Identify the two business transactions described here. Which transaction increases the business's owner's equity? Which transaction increases Campus Cleaners' cash?

15. Explain the difference between the ledger and the chart of accounts.

16. Why do accountants prepare a trial balance?

17. What is a compound journal entry?

18. The accountant for Bower Construction mistakenly recorded a $500 purchase of supplies on account as $5,000. He debited Supplies and credited Accounts Payable for $5,000. Does this error cause the trial balance to be out of balance? Explain your answer.

19. What is the effect on total assets of collecting cash on account from customers?

20. Briefly summarize the similarities and differences between manual and computer-based accounting systems in terms of journalizing, posting, and preparing a trial balance.

STARTERS

MyAccountingLab | All questions in this section appear in MyAccountingLab.

Using accounting terms
(1)

Starter 2–1 Review basic accounting definitions by completing the following crossword puzzle.

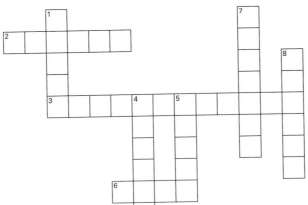

Across:

2. Records an increase in a liability
3. List of accounts with their balances
6. Another word for liability

Down:

1. Left side of an account
4. Book of accounts
5. An economic resource
7. Record of transactions
8. Normal balance of a revenue

Using accounting terms

(1)

Starter 2–2 Fill in the blanks to review some key definitions.

Rita Bowden is describing the accounting process for a friend who is a philosophy major. Rita states, "The basic summary device in accounting is the _____. The left side is called the _____ side, and the right side is called the _____ side. We record transactions first in a _____. Then we post (copy the data) to the _____. It is helpful to list all the accounts with their balances on a _____."

Starter 2–3 Accounting has its own vocabulary and basic relationships. Match the accounting terms at left with the corresponding definitions at right.

Using accounting terms
①

_____ 1. Posting   A. Record of transactions
_____ 2. Normal balance   B. Always an asset
_____ 3. Payable   C. Right side of an account
_____ 4. Journal   D. Side of an account where increases are recorded
_____ 5. Receivable   E. Copying data from the journal to the ledger
_____ 6. Capital   F. Increases in equity from providing goods and services
_____ 7. Credit   G. Always a liability
_____ 8. Revenue   H. Revenues – Expenses
_____ 9. Net loss   I. Grouping of accounts
_____ 10. Ledger   J. Owner's equity in the business

Starter 2–4 Allison Franklin is tutoring Blaine McCormick, who is taking introductory accounting. Allison explains to Blaine that *debits* are used to record increases in accounts and *credits* record decreases. Blaine is confused and seeks your advice.

Explaining the rules of debit and credit
②

- When are credits increases? When are credits decreases?
- When are debits increases? When are debits decreases?

Starter 2–5 The accounting records of all businesses include three basic categories of accounts: assets, liabilities, and owner's equity. In turn, owner's equity holds the following categories: capital, withdrawals, revenues, and expenses. Identify which categories of all the accounts—including the subparts of owner's equity—have a normal debit balance and which categories have a normal credit balance.

Normal account balances
②

Starter 2–6 Liana Garcia opened a veterinary practice. Record the following transactions in the journal of Liana Garcia, Veterinarian. Include an explanation with each journal entry.

Recording transactions
③

Sept. 1 Garcia invested $32,000 cash in a business bank account to start her practice. The business received the cash and gave Garcia owner's equity in the business.
      2 Purchased medical supplies on account, $8,000.
      2 Paid monthly office rent of $4,100.
      3 Recorded $6,000 revenue for service rendered to patients on account.

Starter 2–7 After operating for a month, Liana Garcia, Veterinarian, completed the following transactions during the latter part of October:

Recording transactions
③

Oct. 22 Performed service for patients on account, $6,000.
     30 Received cash on account from patients, $3,000.
     31 Received a utility bill, $150, which will be paid during November.
     31 Paid monthly salary to nurse, $2,000.
     31 Paid advertising expense of $700.

Journalize the transactions of Liana Garcia, Veterinarian. Include an explanation with each journal entry.

Starter 2–8 Nancy Carpenter Optical Dispensary bought supplies on account for $10,000. Two weeks later, the company paid half on account.

Journalizing transactions; posting
③ ④

1. Journalize the two transactions for Nancy Carpenter Optical Dispensary. Include an explanation for each transaction.
2. Open the Accounts Payable T-account and post to Accounts Payable. Compute the balance, and denote it as *Bal.*

Starter 2–9 Tina Serelio performed legal services for a client who could not pay immediately. The business expected to collect the $12,000 the following month. Later, the business received $5,500 cash from the client.

Journalizing transactions; posting
③ ④

3. a. Earned $12,000

1. Record the two transactions for Tina Serelio, Lawyer. Include an explanation for each transaction.
2. Open these T-accounts: Cash; Accounts Receivable; Service Revenue. Post to all three accounts. Compute each account's balance, and denote it as *Bal.*

3. Answer these questions based on your analysis:
   a. How much did the business earn? Which account shows this amount?
   b. How much in total assets did the business acquire as a result of the two transactions? Identify each asset and show its amount.

Note: Starter 2–10 should be used in connection with Starter 2–6.

Posting, preparing
a trial balance

3. Trial bal. total $46,000

Starter 2–10 Use the September transaction data for Liana Garcia, Veterinarian, given in Starter 2–6.

1. Open the following T-accounts: Cash; Accounts Receivable; Medical Supplies; Accounts Payable; Liana Garcia, Capital; Service Revenue, Rent Expense.
2. After making the journal entries in Starter 2–6, post to the T-accounts. No dates or posting references are required. Compute the balance of each account, and denote it as *Bal.*
3. Prepare the trial balance, complete with a proper heading, at September 3, 2010.

Preparing a trial balance

Trial bal. total $75,000

Starter 2–11 Redwing Floor Covering reported the following summarized data at December 31, 2010. Accounts appear in no particular order.

Revenue	$32,000	Other Liabilities	$17,000
Equipment	43,000	Cash	6,000
Accounts Payable	1,000	Expenses	26,000
Capital	25,000		

Prepare the trial balance of Redwing Floor Covering at December 31, 2010. List the accounts in proper order, as on page 74.

Correcting a trial balance

Incorrect trial bal. total debits
$536,000

Starter 2–12 Ladner Environmental Services prepared its trial balance on page 74. Suppose John Ladner made an error: He erroneously listed his Capital balance of $250,000 as a debit rather than a credit.

Compute the incorrect trial balance totals for debits and credits. Then refer to the discussion of correcting errors on pages 76 and 77 and show how to correct this error.

Correcting a trial balance

Incorrect trial bal. total debits
$285,100

Starter 2–13 Return to Ladner Environmental Services' trial balance on page 74. Assume that John Ladner accidentally listed his utilities expense as $100 instead of the correct amount of $1,000. Compute the incorrect trial balance totals for debits and credits. Then show how to correct this error, which is called a *slide.*

EXERCISES

MyAccountingLab | All questions in this section appear in MyAccountingLab.

Exercise 2–1

Using accounting vocabulary

Your employer, Prairie Tours, has just hired an office manager who does not understand accounting. The Prairie Tours trial balance lists Cash of $57,800. Write a short memo to the office manager, explaining the accounting process that produced this listing on the trial balance. Mention *debits, credits, journal, ledger, posting,* and *trial balance.*

Exercise 2–2

Using accounting vocabulary

Review accounting terms by completing the following crossword puzzle.

Across:

2. Amount collectible from a customer
3. Statement of financial position
5. Copy data from the journal to the ledger
6. Records a decrease in an asset

Down:

1. Records a decrease in a liability
4. "Bottom line" of an income statement
7. Revenue – Net income = _____

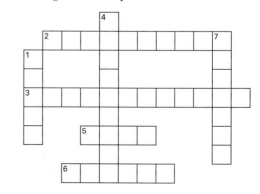

Exercise 2–3

Refer to the Summary Problem for Your Review, specifically the trial balance on page 83.

Using debits and credits with the accounting equation

2. Net income $2,500

Required

1. Write the company's accounting equation, and label each element as a·debit amount or a credit amount. If you use $28,500 for the owner's equity, why is the accounting equation out of balance?

2. Write the equation to compute Aylmer Service Centre's net income or net loss for March 2010. Indicate which element is a debit amount and which element is a credit amount. Does net income represent a net debit or a net credit? Does net loss represent a net debit or a net credit?

3. How much did the owner, Jim Aylmer, withdraw during March 2010? Did the withdrawal represent a debit amount or a credit amount?

4. Considering both the net income (or net loss) and withdrawal for March 2010, by how much did the company's owner's equity increase or decrease? Was the change in owner's equity a debit amount or a credit amount?

Exercise 2–4

Analyze the following transactions of Ryan Jackson Engineering in the manner shown for the December 1 transaction. Also, record each transaction in the journal.

Analyzing and journalizing transactions

| Dec. | 1 | Paid monthly utilities expense of $200. |
| | | (Analysis: The expense, utilities expense, is increased; therefore, debit Utilities Expense. The asset, cash, is decreased; therefore, credit Cash.) |

	1	Utilities Expense 200
		Cash 200
	4	Borrowed $20,000 cash, signing a note payable.
	8	Purchased equipment on account, $4,000.
	12	Performed service on account for a customer, $6,000.
	19	Sold for $24,000 land that had cost this same amount.
	22	Purchased supplies for $1,200 and paid cash.
	27	Paid the liability created on December 8.

Exercise 2–5

Refer to Exercise 2–4 for the transactions of Ryan Jackson Engineering.

Posting transactions using T-accounts

3. Total debits $61,000

Required

1. Open the following T-accounts with their December 1 balances: Cash, debit balance $6,000; Accounts Receivable $0; Supplies, $0; Equipment $0; Land, debit balance $24,000; Accounts Payable $0; Notes Payable $0; R. Jackson, Capital, credit balance $35,000; Service Revenue $0; Utilities Expense $0.

2. Record the transactions of Exercise 2–4 directly in the T-accounts affected. Use dates as posting references in the T-accounts. Start with December 1. Journal entries are not required.

3. Compute the December 31 balance for each account, and prove that total debits equal total credits.

Exercise 2–6

Yula's Yoga engaged in the following transactions during March 2010, its first month of operations:

Excel Spreadsheet Template

Journalizing transactions

Mar.	1	The business received a $15,000 cash investment from Yula Gregore to start Yula's Yoga.
	1	Paid $4,000 cash to rent a yoga studio for the month of March.
	4	Purchased studio supplies for $4,000 on account.
	6	Presented a wellness seminar for a corporate customer and received cash, $3,000.
	9	Paid $1,000 on accounts payable.
	17	Taught yoga classes for customers on account, $800.

Mar. 23 Received $200 cash from a customer on account.
31 Paid the following expenses: utilities, $420; cell phone, $150.

Required

Record the preceding transactions in the journal of Yula's Yoga. Identify transactions by their date and include an explanation for each entry, as illustrated in the chapter. Use the following accounts: Cash; Accounts Receivable; Studio Supplies; Accounts Payable; Yula Gregore, Capital; Service Revenue; Rent Expense; Utilities Expense; Cellphone Expense.

Posting transactions using
T-accounts, preparing a
trial balance

2. Trial bal. total $21,800

Exercise 2–7

Refer to Exercise 2–6 for the transactions of Yula's Yoga.

Required

1. After journalizing the transactions of Exercise 2–6, post the entries to T-accounts. Identify transactions by their date. Date the ending balance of each account Mar. 31.

2. Prepare the trial balance of Yula's Yoga at March 31, 2010.

Describing transactions, posting
using T-accounts

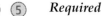

4. Trial bal. total $7,784

Exercise 2–8

The journal of Alert Defensive Driving for October 2010 is below.

Journal				Page 5
Date 2010	**Account Titles and Explanations**	**Post. Ref.**	**Debit**	**Credit**
Oct. 2	Cash..		5,600	
	Tom Marshall, Capital................			5,600
9	Supplies......................................		54	
	Accounts Payable.......................			54
11	Accounts Receivable..................		1,620	
	Service Revenue.........................			1,620
14	Rent Expense..............................		1,400	
	Cash..			1,400
22	Cash..		280	
	Accounts Receivable..................			280
25	Advertising Expense..................		570	
	Cash..			570
27	Accounts Payable........................		54	
	Cash..			54
31	Fuel Expense...............................		564	
	Accounts Payable.......................			564

Required

1. Describe each transaction.

2. Set up T-accounts using the following account numbers: Cash, #1000; Accounts Receivable, #1200; Supplies, #1400; Accounts Payable, #2000; Tom Marshall, Capital, #3000; Service Revenue, #4000; Advertising Expense, #5100; Rent Expense, #5600; Fuel Expense, #5800.

3. Post to the T-accounts. Identify each transaction by date. You may write the account numbers as posting references directly in the journal in your book unless directed otherwise by your instructor. Compute the balance in each account after posting.

4. Prepare Alert Defensive Driving's trial balance at October 31, 2010.

Journalizing transactions

Exercise 2–9

The first five transactions of Dash Carter Hockey School have been posted to the company's accounts as shown on the next page:

Cash				Supplies		Hockey Equipment	
(1)	7,500	(3)	5,250	(2)	75	(5)	1,500
(4)	1,375	(5)	1,500				

Land		Accounts Payable		Note Payable	
(3)	5,250	(2)	75	(4)	1,375

D. Carter, Capital	
(1)	7,500

Required Prepare the journal entries that served as the sources for posting the five transactions. Date each entry April 30, 2010, and include an explanation for each entry as illustrated in the chapter.

Exercise 2–10

Prepare the trial balance of Dash Carter Hockey School at April 30, 2010, using the account data from Exercise 2–9.

Preparing a trial balance

5

Trial bal. total $8,950

Exercise 2–11

The accounts of Western Consulting are listed below with their normal balances at October 31, 2010. The accounts are listed in no particular order.

Excel Spreadsheet Template

Preparing a trial balance

5

Trial bal. total $760,600

Account	Balance
T. Western, capital	$292,800
Advertising expense	9,900
Accounts payable	33,800
Service revenue	164,000
Land	174,000
Notes payable	270,000
Cash	30,000
Salary expense	36,000
Building	390,000
Computer rental expense	42,000
T. Western, withdrawals	36,000
Utilities expense	2,400
Accounts receivable	35,000
Supplies expense	3,800
Supplies	1,500

Required Prepare the company's trial balance at October 31, 2010, listing accounts in the sequence illustrated in the chapter. Supplies comes before Building and Land. List the expenses alphabetically.

Exercise 2–12

Open the following three-column ledger accounts for Yarrow Strategic Consulting at May 1, 2010: Cash, #1100; Accounts Receivable, #1300; Office Supplies, #1500; Office Furniture, #1800; Accounts Payable, #2100; Florence Yarrow, Capital, #3100; Florence Yarrow, Withdrawals, #3200; Consulting Revenue, #4100; Rent Expense, #5500; Salary Expense, #5600.

Journalize the following May 2010 transactions on page 9 of the journal, and then post to the ledger accounts. Use the dates to identify the transactions.

Journalizing and posting transactions

May	2	Florence Yarrow opened a strategic consulting firm by investing $39,200 cash and office furniture valued at $16,200.
	2	Paid monthly rent of $2,500.
	2	Purchased office supplies on account, $1,800.
	15	Paid employee salary, $4,000.
	17	Paid $1,200 of the account payable from May 2.
	19	Performed consulting service on account, $69,000.
	30	Withdrew $8,000 for personal use.

Exercise 2–13

After recording the transactions in Exercise 2–12, prepare the trial balance of Yarrow Strategic Consulting at May 31, 2010.

Exercise 2–14

The trial balance of Zoom Travel at February 28, 2010, does not balance.

Cash	$ 3,100	
Accounts receivable	1,900	
Supplies	700	
Land	26,100	
Accounts payable		$ 11,400
D. Tudin, capital		11,900
Service revenue		9,600
Rent expense	900	
Salary expense	1,600	
Utilities expense	500	
Total	$34,800	$32,900

Investigation of the accounting records reveals that the bookkeeper

a. Recorded a $400 cash revenue transaction by debiting Accounts Receivable. The credit entry was correct.

b. Posted a $2,000 credit to Accounts Payable as $200.

c. Did not record utilities expense or the related account payable in the amount of $500.

d. Understated D. Tudin, Capital by $100.

Required Prepare the corrected trial balance at February 28, 2010, complete with a heading. Journal entries are not required.

SERIAL EXERCISE

Exercise 2–15

Exercise 2–15 continues with the consulting business of Carl Haupt, begun in Serial Exercise 1-16. Here you will account for Haupt Consulting's transactions as it is actually done in practice.

Haupt Consulting completed the following transactions during early December 2010:

Dec.	2	Received $10,000 cash from owner Carl Haupt. The business gave owner's equity in the business to Haupt.
	2	Paid monthly office rent, $1,000.
	3	Paid cash for a Dell computer, $2,000. The computer is expected to remain in service for five years.
	4	Purchased office furniture on account, $3,600. The furniture should last for five years.
	5	Purchased supplies on account, $300.
	9	Performed consulting services for a client on account, $1,700.
	12	Paid utility expenses, $200.
	18	Performed consulting services for a client and received cash of $800.

Required

1. Open T-accounts in the ledger: Cash; Accounts Receivable; Supplies; Equipment; Furniture; Accounts Payable; Carl Haupt, Capital; Carl Haupt, Withdrawals; Service Revenue; Rent Expense; Salaries Expense; and Utilities Expense. (Some of these T-accounts will be used in later chapters.)

2. Journalize the transactions. Explanations are not required.

3. Post to the T-accounts. Identify all items by date, and label an account balance as *Bal.* Formal posting references are not required.

4. Prepare a trial balance at December 18, 2010. (In the Serial Exercise of Chapter 3, we will add transactions for the remainder of December and will require a trial balance at December 31, 2010.)

CHALLENGE EXERCISES

Exercise 2–16

Computing financial statement amounts

b. Cash paid $10,880

The owner of Fergus Technical Services is an architect with little understanding of accounting. She needs to compute the following summary information from the accounting records:

a. Net income for the month of March
b. Total cash paid during March
c. Cash collections from customers during March
d. Payments on account during March

The quickest way to compute these amounts is to analyze the following accounts:

	Balance		Additional Information for the Month of March
Account	Feb. 28	Mar. 31	
a. B. Fergus, Capital	$1,440	$2,400	Withdrawals, $640
b. Cash...	1,800	1,640	Cash receipts, $10,720
c. Accounts Receivable	3,840	6,160	Sales on account, $12,160
d. Accounts Payable	2,080	2,560	Purchases on account, $508

The net income for March can be computed as follows:

B. Fergus, Capital

March Withdrawals	640	Feb. 28 Bal.	1,440	
		March Net Income	x	= $1,600
		March 31 Bal.	2,400	

Use a similar approach to compute the other three items.

Exercise 2–17

Analyzing accounting errors

Bridget Battle has trouble keeping her debits and credits equal. During a recent month, Bridget made the following errors:

a. In preparing the trial balance, Bridget omitted a $5,000 note payable.

b. Bridget posted a $1,000 utility expense as $100. The credit to Cash was correct.

c. In recording a $200 payment on account, Bridget debited Supplies instead of Accounts Payable.

d. In journalizing a receipt of cash from service revenue, Bridget debited Cash for $50 instead of the correct amount of $500. The credit was correct.

e. Bridget recorded a $340 purchase of supplies on account by debiting Supplies and crediting Accounts Payable for $430.

Required

1. For each of these errors, state whether the total debits equal total credits on the trial balance.

2. Identify each account that has an incorrect balance, and indicate the amount and direction of the error (such as "Accounts Receivable $500 too high").

BEYOND THE NUMBERS

Beyond the Numbers 2–1

Jake Fissel asks your advice in setting up the accounting records for his new business, Jake's Photo Shop. The business will be a photography studio and will operate in a rented building. Jake's Photo Shop will need office equipment and cameras. The business will borrow money using a note payable to buy the needed equipment. Jake's Photo Shop will purchase on account photographic supplies and office supplies. Each asset has a related expense account, some of which have not yet been discussed. For example, equipment wears out (amortizes) and thus needs an amortization account. As supplies are used up, the business must record a supplies expense.

The business will need an office manager. This person will be paid a weekly salary of $1,800. Other expenses will include advertising and insurance. Since Jake's Photo Shop will want to know which aspects of the business generate the most and the least revenue, it will use separate service revenue accounts for portraits, school pictures, and weddings. Jake's Photo Shop's better customers will be allowed to open accounts with the business.

Required List all the accounts Jake's Photo Shop will need, starting with the assets and ending with the expenses. Indicate which accounts will be reported on the balance sheet and which accounts will appear on the income statement.

ETHICAL ISSUE

Associated Charities Inc., a charitable organization in Brandon, Manitoba, has a standing agreement with Prairie Trust. The agreement allows Associated Charities Inc. to overdraw its cash balance at the bank when donations are running low. In the past, Associated Charities Inc. managed funds wisely and rarely used this privilege. Greg Glowa has recently become the president of Associated Charities Inc. To expand operations, Glowa is acquiring office equipment and spending large amounts for fund-raising. During his presidency, Associated Charities Inc. has maintained a negative bank balance (a credit Cash balance) of approximately $28,000.

Required What is the ethical issue in this situation? State why you approve or disapprove of Glowa's management of Associated Charities Inc.'s funds.

PROBLEMS (GROUP A)

MyAccountingLab All questions in this section appear in MyAccountingLab.

Problem 2–1A

Analyzing a trial balance

Net income $55,000

The owner of Archer Communications, Nancy Archer, is selling the business. She offers the trial balance shown below to prospective buyers.

ARCHER COMMUNICATIONS **Trial Balance** **December 31, 2010**		
Cash..	$ 28,000	
Accounts receivable	30,500	
Prepaid expenses....................................	6,000	
Land	64,000	
Accounts payable....................................		$ 62,500
Note payable..		38,000
N. Archer, capital.....................................		45,000
N. Archer, withdrawals	72,000	
Service revenue.......................................		151,000
Advertising expense	4,500	
Rent expense..	39,000	
Supplies expense.....................................	10,500	
Wages expense	42,000	
Totals..	$296,500	$296,500

Your best friend is considering buying Archer Communications. He seeks your advice in interpreting this information. Specifically, he asks whether this trial balance is the same as a balance sheet and an income statement. He also wonders whether Archer Communications is a sound company because all the accounts are in balance.

Required Write a short note to answer your friend's questions. To aid his decision, state how he can use the information on the trial balance to compute Archer Communications' net income or net loss for the current period. State the amount of net income or net loss in your note.

Problem 2–2A

Analyzing and journalizing transactions

Party Time Amusements Company owns movie theatres. Party Time engaged in the following transactions in November 2010:

Nov.	1	Darrell Palusky invested $350,000 personal cash in the business by depositing that amount in a bank account titled Party Time Amusements Company. The business gave capital to Palusky.
	1	Paid monthly rent on a theatre building, $6,000.
	2	Paid $320,000 cash to purchase land for a theatre site.
	5	Borrowed $220,000 from the bank to finance the first phase of construction of the new theatre. Palusky signed a note payable to the bank in the name of Party Time.
	10	Purchased theatre supplies on account, $1,000.
	15	Paid $600 on account.
	15	Paid property tax expense on the land for the new theatre, $1,400.
	16	Paid employees' salaries of $2,900.
	28	Palusky withdrew $8,000.
	30	Received $20,000 cash from service revenue and deposited that amount in the bank.

Party Time uses the following accounts: Cash; Supplies; Land; Accounts Payable; Notes Payable; Darrell Palusky, Capital; Darrell Palusky, Withdrawals; Service Revenue; Property Tax Expense; Rent Expense; Salary Expense.

Required

1. Prepare an analysis of each business transaction of Party Time as shown for the November 1 transaction:

    Nov. 1   The asset Cash is increased. Increases in assets are recorded by debits; therefore, debit Cash. The owner's equity of the entity is increased. Increases in owner's equity are recorded by credits; therefore, credit Darrell Palusky, Capital.

2. Record each transaction in the journal, using the account titles given. Identify each transaction by its date. Explanations are not required.

Problem 2–3A

Harry Lawson opened a renovation business called Lawson Renovations on September 3, 2010. During the first month of operations, the business completed the following transactions:

Journalizing transactions, posting to T-accounts, preparing a trial balance

3. Trial bal. total $41,500

Sept.	3	Lawson deposited his cheque for $36,000 into the business bank account to start the business.
	4	Purchased supplies, $300, and furniture, $2,200, on account.
	5	Paid September rent expense, $750.
	6	Performed design services for a client and received $1,200 cash.
	7	Paid $22,000 cash to acquire land for a future office site.
	10	Designed a bathroom for a client, billed the client, and received her promise to pay the $700 within one week.
	14	Paid for the furniture purchased September 4 on account.
	15	Paid assistant's salary, $470.
	17	Received cash on account, $700.
	20	Prepared a recreation room design for a client on account, $800.
	28	Received $2,500 cash from a client for renovation of a cottage.
	30	Paid assistant's salary, $470.
	30	Lawson withdrew $2,800 for personal use.

Required

Open the following T-accounts: Cash; Accounts Receivable; Supplies; Furniture; Land; Accounts Payable; H. Lawson, Capital; H. Lawson, Withdrawals; Service Revenue; Rent Expense; Salary Expense.

1. Record each transaction in the journal, using the account titles given. Identify each transaction by date. Explanations are not required.

2. Post the transactions to the T-accounts, using transaction dates as posting references in the T-accounts. Label the balance of each account *Bal.,* as shown in the chapter.

3. Prepare the trial balance of Lawson Renovations at September 30, 2010.

Problem 2–4A

Journalizing transactions, posting to ledger accounts, preparing a trial balance

3. Trial bal. total $75,400

The trial balance of Thomson Engineering is dated February 28, 2010. During March, Thomson Engineering completed the following transactions:

March		
	4	Collected $600 cash from a client on account.
	8	Designed a system for a client on account, $580.
	13	Paid for items purchased on account, $320.
	18	Purchased supplies on account, $120.
	20	R. Thomson withdrew $200 for personal use.
	21	Received a verbal promise of a $2,000 contract.
	22	Received cash of $620 for consulting work just completed.
	31	Paid employees' salaries, $1,300.

THOMSON ENGINEERING
Trial Balance
February 28, 2010

Account Number	Account	Debit	Credit
1100	Cash	$ 4,000	
1200	Accounts receivable	16,000	
1300	Supplies	3,600	
1600	Automobile	37,200	
2000	Accounts payable		$ 8,000
3000	R. Thomson, Capital		50,000
3100	R. Thomson, Withdrawals	4,400	
5000	Service revenue		16,400
6100	Rent expense	2,000	
6200	Salary expense	7,200	
	Total	$74,400	$74,400

Required

1. Record the March transactions in *Page 3* of the journal. Include an explanation for each entry.

2. Open three-column ledger accounts for the accounts listed in the trial balance, together with their balances at February 28. Enter *Bal.* (for previous balance) in the Item column, and place a check mark (✓) in the journal reference column for the February 28 balance in each account.

    Post the transactions to the ledger, using dates, account numbers, journal references, and posting references.

3. Prepare the trial balance of Thomson Engineering at March 31, 2010.

Problem 2–5A

Recording transactions, using three-column ledger accounts, preparing a trial balance

4. Trial bal. total $95,500

Jane Frideris started an investment counselling business, Frideris Consulting, in Montreal on June 1, 2010. During the first month of operations, the business completed the following selected transactions:

a. Frideris began the business with an investment of $20,000 cash, land valued at $20,000, and a building valued at $40,000. The business gave Frideris owner's equity in the business for the value of the cash, land, and building.

b. Purchased office supplies on account, $2,600.

c. Paid $15,000 for office furniture.

d. Paid employee salary, $2,200.

e. Performed consulting service on account for client, $6,100.

f. Paid $800 of the account payable created in transaction b.

g. Received a $2,000 bill for advertising expense that will be paid in the near future.

h. Performed consulting services for customers and received cash, $5,600.

i. Received cash on account, $2,400.

j. Paid the following cash expenses:

   (1) Rent of photocopier, $1,200.

   (2) Utilities, $400.

k. Frideris withdrew $2,500 for personal use.

Required

1. Record each transaction in the journal. Use the letters to identify the transactions.

2. Open the following three-column ledger accounts: Cash, #1100; Accounts Receivable, #1300; Office Supplies, #1400; Office Furniture, #1500; Building, #1700; Land, #1800; Accounts Payable, #2100; Jane Frideris, Capital, #3100; Jane Frideris, Withdrawals, #3200; Service Revenue, #4100; Advertising Expense, #5100; Equipment Rental Expense, #5300; Salary Expense, #5500; Utilities Expense, #5700.

3. Post to the accounts and keep a running balance for each account.

4. Prepare the trial balance of Frideris Consulting at June 30, 2010.

Problem 2–6A

Refer to Problem 2–5A. After completing the trial balance in Problem 2–5A, prepare the following financial statements for Frideris Consulting:

Preparing the financial statements

1. Net income $5,900

1. Income statement for the month ended June 30, 2010.

2. Statement of owner's equity for the month ended June 30, 2010.

3. Balance sheet at June 30, 2010.

Draw arrows linking the financial statements. If needed, use Exhibit 1–10, page 22, as a guide for preparing the financial statements.

Problem 2–7A

The following trial balance does not balance:

Correcting errors in a trial balance

Trial bal. total $70,000

MINTER LANDSCAPE CONSULTING
Trial Balance
June 30, 2010

	Debit	Credit
Cash	$ 1,600	
Accounts receivable	10,000	
Supplies	900	
Office furniture	3,600	
Land	46,600	
Accounts payable		$ 3,800
Notes payable		23,000
R. Minter, capital		31,600
R. Minter, withdrawals	2,000	
Consulting service revenue		7,300
Advertising expense	400	
Rent expense	1,000	
Salary expense	2,100	
Utilities expense	410	
Total	$68,610	$65,700

The following errors were detected:

a. The cash balance is understated by $1,300.

b. The cost of the land was $44,600, not $46,600.

c. A $400 purchase of supplies on account was neither journalized nor posted.

d. A $3,000 credit to Consulting Service Revenue was not posted.

e. Rent Expense of $200 was posted as a credit rather than a debit.

f. The balance of Advertising Expense is $600, but it was listed as $400 on the trial balance.

g. A $300 debit to Accounts Receivable was posted as $30. The credit to Consulting Service Revenue was correct.

h. The balance of Utilities Expense is overstated by $80.

i. A $900 debit to the R. Minter, Withdrawals account was posted as a debit to R. Minter, Capital.

Required Prepare the corrected trial balance at June 30, 2010. Journal entries are not required.

Problem 2–8A

Applying the rules of debit and credit, recording transactions in the journal

Ken Suzuki operates a fishing charter business, Pacific Charters. The business had the following transactions in September 2010:

Sept.	1	Suzuki invested $15,000 cash and his 10-metre power boat in the charter business. The business gave Suzuki owner's equity in the business. The boat had originally cost him $60,000, but had a fair market value of $37,500 on September 1, 2010.
	3	Purchased a new boat by paying $10,500 cash and promising to pay another $26,000 in one week. Suzuki felt that this was an excellent bargain as the boat had a catalogue price of $45,000 and he knew it was worth at least $37,500.
	4	Paid moorage fees of $1,200 for the month of September. These fees covered two moorage slips—one for each charter boat.
	5	Hired a deckhand at a rate of $500 per week.
	9	Took clients out on a charter for $1,950. They paid $1,000 and promised to pay the balance in 30 days.
	10	Paid $2,000 of the amount owing on the boat purchased on September 3. Signed a promissory note for the balance, as the company was unable to pay the full amount that day.
	15	Purchased $2,000 of equipment from a supplier. To pay for the equipment, Pacific Charters took the supplier and her employees out on a day charter and also paid the supplier $500 cash.
	20	Received $950 from the clients of September 9 as payment on the charter.
	26	Paid the deckhand for three weeks' work.
	29	A client chartered the two boats for two days for $6,000. In payment, the client, the owner of a service station, provided Pacific Charters with $3,000 of repair parts that can be used on the boats, and cash.
	30	Used $800 of repair parts on one boat (a boat operating expense).

Required Record each transaction in the journal. Identify each transaction by date. Explanations are not required.

Problem 2–9A

Applying the rules of debit and credit, recording transactions

CrossCountry Movers had the following account balances, in random order, on December 15, 2010 (all accounts have their "normal" balances):

Moving fees earned	$261,600	Cash	$ 7,200
Accounts receivable	17,400	Storage fees earned	57,900
Rent expense	47,100	Notes receivable	45,000
H. Martinez, capital	150,000	Utilities expense	2,400
Office supplies expense	2,100	Office supplies	9,600
Mortgage payable	39,000	Accounts payable	33,000
Salaries expense	161,100	Office equipment	12,300
Insurance expense	6,300	Moving equipment	32,200

The following events took place during the final days of the year:

Dec.   16   The accountant discovered that an error had been made in posting an entry to the Moving Fees Earned account. The entry was correctly journalized but $2,400 was accidentally posted as $4,200 in the account.

17   Moved a customer's goods to CrossCountry's rented warehouse for storage. The moving fees were $4,000. Storage fees are $600 per month. The customer was billed for one month's storage and the moving fees.

18   Collected a $15,000 note owed to CrossCountry Movers and collected interest of $1,800.

19   Used a company cheque to pay for Martinez's hydro bill in the amount of $400.

21   Purchased storage racks for $12,000. Paid $3,600, provided moving services for $1,500, and promised to pay the balance in 60 days.

23   Collected $3,000; $2,600 of this was for moving goods on December 15 (recorded as an account receivable at that time) and the balance was for storage fees for the period of December 16 to 23.

24   CrossCountry Movers paid $18,000 owing on the mortgage.

27   Martinez withdrew $5,000 for personal use.

29   Provided moving services to a lawyer for $2,400. The lawyer paid CrossCountry Movers $1,500 and provided legal work for the balance.

31   Martinez, the owner of CrossCountry Movers, sold 2,000 shares he held in Brandon Haulage Inc. for $12,000.

Required Where appropriate, record each transaction from December 16 to 31 in the journal. Explanations are not required.

PROBLEMS (GROUP B)

MyAccountingLab All questions in this section appear in MyAccountingLab.

Problem 2–1B

Joan Simpson, the owner of Simpson Designs, is selling the business. She offers the trial balance below to prospective buyers.

Analyzing a trial balance

Your best friend is considering buying Simpson Designs. She seeks your advice in interpreting this information. Specifically, she asks whether this trial balance is the same as a balance sheet and an income statement. She also wonders whether Simpson Designs is a sound company. She thinks it must be because the accounts are in balance.

Required Write a short note to answer your friend's questions. To aid her decision, state how she can use the information on the trial balance to compute the Simpson Designs net income or net loss for the current period. State the amount of net income or net loss in your note.

SIMPSON DESIGNS
Trial Balance
December 31, 2010

Cash	$ 36,000	
Accounts receivable	10,000	
Prepaid expenses	4,000	
Land	78,000	
Accounts payable		$ 72,000
Note payable		44,000
Joan Simpson, capital		76,000
Joan Simpson, withdrawals	30,000	
Service revenue		120,000
Advertising expense	16,000	
Rent expense	24,000	
Supplies expense	18,000	
Wage expense	96,000	
Total	$312,000	$312,000

Problem 2–2B

Analyzing and journalizing transactions

Gladys Yu practises civil engineering under the business title Gladys Yu Consulting. During April 2010 the company engaged in the following transactions:

April	1	Yu deposited $40,000 cash in the business bank account. The business gave Yu owner's equity in the business.
	5	Paid monthly rent on drafting equipment, $200.
	9	Paid $25,000 cash to purchase land for an office site.
	10	Purchased supplies on account, $600.
	19	Paid $100 on account for supplies purchased on April 10.
	22	Borrowed $15,000 from the bank for business use. Yu signed a note payable to the bank in the name of the business.
	30	Revenues earned during the month included $1,300 cash and $2,400 on account.
	30	Paid employee salaries of $2,000, office rent of $900, and utilities of $180.
	30	Yu withdrew $1,200 from the business for personal use.

Gladys Yu Consulting uses the following accounts: Cash; Accounts Receivable; Supplies; Land; Accounts Payable; Notes Payable; G. Yu, Capital; G. Yu, Withdrawals; Service Revenue; Rent Expense; Salaries Expense; Utilities Expense.

Required

1. Prepare an analysis of each business transaction of Gladys Yu Consulting, as shown for the April 1 transaction:

   Apr. 1 The asset cash is increased. Increases in assets are recorded by debits; therefore, debit Cash. The owner's equity is increased. Increases in owner's equity are recorded by credits; therefore, credit G. Yu, Capital.

2. Record each transaction in the journal, using the dates and account titles given. Explanations are not required.

Problem 2–3B

Journalizing transactions, posting to T-accounts, preparing a trial balance

Scott Jameson opened a translation business on January 2, 2010. During the first month of operations, the business completed the following transactions:

Jan.	2	The business received $60,000 cash from Jameson, which was deposited in a business bank account entitled Jameson Translation Service.
	3	Purchased supplies, $750, and furniture, $2,800, on account.
	3	Paid January rent expense, $1,100.
	4	Performed translation services for a client and received cash, $2,250.
	7	Paid $38,000 cash to acquire land for a future office site.
	11	Translated a brochure for a client and billed the client $1,200.
	15	Paid secretary salary, $975.
	16	Paid for the furniture purchased January 3 on account.
	18	Received partial payment from a client on account, $600.
	19	Translated legal documents for a client on account, $11,350.
	22	Paid the water and electricity bills, $300.
	29	Received $2,700 cash for translation for a client in an overseas business transaction.
	31	Paid secretary salary, $975.
	31	Jameson withdrew $12,000 for personal use.

Required

Open the following T-accounts: Cash; Accounts Receivable; Supplies; Furniture; Land; Accounts Payable; Scott Jameson, Capital; Scott Jameson, Withdrawals; Translation Revenue; Rent Expense; Salary Expense; Utilities Expense.

1. Record each transaction in the journal, using the account titles given. Key each transaction by date. Explanations are not required.
2. Post the transactions to the ledger using T-accounts, using transaction dates in the ledger. Label the balance of each account *Bal.*, as shown in the chapter.
3. Prepare the trial balance of Jameson Translation Service at January 31, 2010.
4. How will what you have learned in this problem help you manage a business?

Problem 2–4B

The trial balance of the desktop publishing business of Doug Foster at November 15, 2010, is shown below.

Journalizing transactions, posting to three-column ledger accounts, preparing a trial balance

FOSTER PUBLISHING
Trial Balance
November 15, 2010

Account Number	Account	Debit	Credit
1100	Cash..	$ 16,000	
1200	Accounts receivable	16,000	
1300	Supplies..	1,200	
1900	Equipment..	70,000	
2100	Accounts payable		$ 9,200
4000	D. Foster, Capital.............................		90,000
4100	D. Foster, Withdrawals	4,600	
5000	Service revenue................................		14,200
6000	Rent expense	2,000	
6100	Salaries expense..............................	3,600	
	Total...	$113,400	$113,400

During the remainder of November, the business completed the following transactions:

Nov.	16	Collected $4,000 cash from a client on account.
	17	Performed publishing services for a client on account, $2,100.
	21	Paid on account, $2,600.
	22	Purchased supplies on account, $10,600.
	23	Foster withdrew $2,100 for personal use.
	24	Was advised that Desk Top Inc. was prepared to buy all of Foster Publishing for $60,000.
	26	Received $11,900 cash for design work just completed.
	30	Paid employees' salaries, $2,400.

Required

1. Record the transactions that occurred during November 16 through 30 in *Page 6* of the journal. Include an explanation for each entry.
2. Post the transactions to three-column accounts in the ledger, using dates, account numbers, journal references, and posting references. Open the ledger accounts listed in the trial balance together with their balances at November 15. Enter *Bal.* (for previous balance) in the Item column, and place a check mark (✓) in the journal reference column for the November 15 balance of each account.
3. Prepare the trial balance of Foster Publishing at November 30, 2010.

Problem 2–5B

Bill Ronalds started a catering service called Blue Ribbon Catering. During the first month of operations, January 2010, the business completed the following selected transactions:

Recording transactions, using three-column ledger accounts, preparing a trial balance

a. Ronalds began the company with an investment of $50,000 cash and a van (automobile) valued at $26,000. The business gave Ronalds owner's equity in the business.

b. Paid $8,000 for food service equipment.

c. Purchased supplies on account, $14,800.

d. Paid employee salary, $12,600.

e. Received $4,000 for a catering job.

f. Performed services at a wedding on account, $8,600.

g. Paid $12,000 of the account payable created in transaction c.

h. Received a $1,600 bill for advertising expense that will be paid in the near future.

i. Received cash on account, $2,200.

j. Paid the following cash expenses:

   (1) Rent, $3,000.

   (2) Insurance, $1,600.

k. Ronalds withdrew $12,000 for personal use.

Required

1. Record the transactions in the journal. Use the letters to identify the transactions.

2. Open the following three-column ledger accounts: Cash, #1100; Accounts Receivable, #1300; Supplies, #1500; Food Service Equipment, #1600; Automobile, #1700; Accounts Payable, #2100; B. Ronalds, Capital, #3100; B. Ronalds, Withdrawals, #3200; Service Revenue, #4100; Advertising Expense, #5100; Insurance Expense, #5500; Rent Expense, #5700; Salary Expense, #5800.

3. Post to the accounts and keep a running balance for each account.

4. Prepare the trial balance of Blue Ribbon Catering at January 31, 2010.

Problem 2–6B

Preparing the financial statements ⑤

Refer to Problem 2–5B. After completing the trial balance in Problem 2–5B, prepare the following financial statements for Blue Ribbon Catering.

1. Income statement for the month ended January 31, 2010.

2. Statement of owner's equity for the month ended January 31, 2010.

3. Balance sheet at January 31, 2010.

Draw arrows linking the financial statements. If needed, use Exhibit 1–10, page 22, as a guide for preparing the financial statements.

Problem 2–7B

Correcting errors in a trial balance ② ⑤

The trial balance for Delainey Fitness, shown below, does not balance. The following errors were detected:

a. The cash balance is overstated by $6,000.

b. Rent expense of $3,000 was posted as a credit rather than a debit.

c. The balance of Advertising Expense is $4,500, but it is listed as $6,000 on the trial balance.

d. A $9,000 debit to Accounts Receivable was posted as $900.

e. The balance of Utilities Expense is understated by $900.

f. A $19,500 debit to the E. Delainey, Withdrawals account was posted as a debit to E. Delainey, Capital.

g. A $1,500 purchase of supplies on account was neither journalized nor posted.

h. An $87,000 credit to Service Revenue was not posted.

i. Office furniture should be listed in the amount of $19,500.

DELAINEY FITNESS
Trial Balance
October 31, 2010

Cash	$ 47,000	
Accounts receivable	30,000	
Supplies	7,500	
Office furniture	34,500	
Fitness equipment	710,000	
Accounts payable		$ 30,000
Notes payable		294,500
E. Delainey, Capital		442,500
E. Delainey, Withdrawals	55,500	
Service revenue		73,500
Salary expense	32,500	
Rent expense	9,000	
Advertising expense	6,000	
Utilities expense	3,000	
Total	$935,000	$840,500

Required Prepare the corrected trial balance at October 31, 2010. Journal entries are not required.

Problem 2–8B

Applying the rules of debit and credit, recording transactions in the journal

Ryan Kessler operates a heavy equipment transport company, Kessler Transport. The company had the following transactions for the month of August 2010:

Aug. 1   Kessler Transport received $20,000 cash and a truck and trailer from Kessler. The truck had originally cost Kessler $300,000, but had a fair market value of $230,000 on August 1. The trailer had a fair market value of $30,000.

3   Purchased a new trailer by paying $10,000 cash and promising to pay another $20,000 in one week. The trailer had a list price of $40,000 and Kessler knew it was worth at least $35,000.

4   Paid parking space rental fees of $400 for the month of August. These fees covered three spaces—two for the trailers and one for the truck.

5   Hired an assistant at a rate of $750 per week.

9   Transported equipment for clients for $3,200. They paid $1,600 and promised to pay the balance in 30 days.

10   Paid $6,000 of the amount owing on the trailer purchase on August 3. Signed a promissory note for the balance, as the company was unable to pay the full amount that day.

15   Paid Kessler's personal telephone bill for $110. Treat this as a withdrawal.

20   Received $1,600 from the clients of August 9 as payment on the haulage.

26   Paid the assistant for three weeks' work.

29   Billed a client $6,000 for hauling equipment from Prince Albert to Saskatoon. The client, who was the owner of a service station, paid the bill by providing the company with $6,000 of repair parts that can be used on the truck.

30   Used $60 of repair parts on the truck (a truck operating expense).

Required Record each transaction in the journal. Identify each transaction by its date. Explanations are not required.

Problem 2–9B

Applying the rules of debit and credit, recording transactions

Maquina Lodge, owned by Bob Palmiter, had the following account balances, in random order, on December 15, 2010 (all accounts have their "normal" balances):

Guest revenue	$209,000	Furniture	$57,800
Accounts receivable	8,800	Cash	3,800
Equipment rental expense	11,800	Notes receivable	26,000
B. Palmiter, capital	93,800	Utilities expense	1,000
Supplies expense	2,800	Supplies inventory	5,800
Mortgage payable	30,000	Accounts payable	12,000
Salaries expense	81,000	Office equipment	10,200
Insurance expense	6,800	Boating equipment	96,800

The following events also took place during the final days of the year:

Dec. 16   The accountant discovered that an error had been made in posting an entry to the Guest Revenue account. The entry was correctly journalized but $4,200 was accidentally posted as $2,400 in the account.

17   Signed an agreement to let a retired professor move in, in the off season for a long stay, beginning today. The monthly rate is $3,200 payable in advance.

18   Collected an $18,000 note owed to Maquina and collected interest of $2,400.

21   Purchased boating equipment for $14,000 from Boats Unlimited. Maquina Lodge paid $5,000, provided room rentals for $1,600 to Boats Unlimited, and promised to pay the balance in 60 days.

23   Collected $2,800 for rooms for a conference held from December 16 to 23.

24   Maquina Lodge paid $2,000 owing on the mortgage.

27   Palmiter withdrew $14,000 for personal use.

29   Provided meeting rooms to a lawyer for $2,000. The lawyer paid Maquina Lodge $1,100 and provided legal work for the balance.

Required Where appropriate, record each transaction from December 16 to 29 in the journal. Explanations are not required.

CHALLENGE PROBLEMS

Problem 2–1C

Understanding the rules of debit and credit

Some individuals, for whatever reason, do not pay income tax or pay less than they should. Often their business transactions are cash transactions, so there is no paper trail to prove how much or how little they actually earned. Canada Revenue Agency, however, has a way of dealing with these individuals; they use a model (based on the accounting equation) to calculate how much the individual must have earned.

Canada Revenue Agency is about to audit Donna Wynn for the period January 1, 2010, to December 31, 2010. Wynn buys and sells used cars for cash; the purchaser is responsible for having the car certified so it can be licensed and insured. Wynn had $8,000 cash and no other assets or liabilities at January 1, 2010.

Required

1. Use the accounting equation (specifically owners' equity) to explain how the Canada Revenue Agency model will be used to audit Donna.

2. What do you think are the accounting concepts underlying the model?

Problem 2–2C

Using a formal accounting system

Over the years you have become friendly with a farmer, Jack Russell, who raises crops, which he sells, and has small herds of beef cattle and sheep. Russell maintains his basic herds and markets the calves and lambs each fall. His accounting system is quite simple; all his transactions are in cash. Russell pays tax each year on his income, which he estimates. He indicated to you once that he must be doing it right because Canada Revenue Agency audited him recently and assessed no additional tax.

You are taking your first accounting course and are quite impressed with the information one can gain from a formal accounting system.

Required Explain to Russell why it would be to his advantage to have a more formal accounting system with accounts, ledgers, and journals.

Problem 2–3C

Understanding the rules of debit and credit, preparing a trial balance

Trial bal. total $14,681

Cash	$2,840	Notes Payable	$1,200
Accounts Receivable	3,331	Fees Earned	2,380
Supplies	800	Salary Expense	3,400
Equipment	3,000	Office Expense	910
Accounts Payable	2,666		

Each of the above accounts has a normal balance in the ledger of Thomas Services at December 31, 2010. An examination of the ledger and journal reveals the following errors:

a. Cash received from a customer on account was debited for $570 and Accounts Receivable was credited for the same amount. The actual collection was for $750.

b. The purchase of a computer monitor on account for $480 was recorded as a debit to Supplies for $480 and a credit to Accounts Payable for $480.

c. Services were performed on account for a client for $890. Accounts Receivable was debited for $890 and Fees Earned was credited for $89.

d. A debit posting to Salaries Expense of $600 was omitted.

e. A payment on account for $206 was credited to Cash for $206 and credited to Accounts Payable for $260.

f. The withdrawal of $600 cash for Pete Thomas's personal use was debited to Salaries Expense for $600 and credited to Cash for $600.

Required

1. For each item above, describe how a correction would be made, either by giving a correcting journal entry or by describing how a posting error would be corrected in the ledger.

2. Prepare the trial balance for Thomas Services after the corrections are made.

Extending Your Knowledge

DECISION PROBLEMS

Decision Problem 1

Your friend, Amin Akmali, has asked your advice about the effects that certain business transactions will have on his business. His business, Car Finders, finds the best deals on automobiles for clients. Time is short, so you cannot journalize transactions. Instead, you must analyze the transactions and post them directly to T-accounts. Akmali will continue in the business only if he can expect to earn monthly net income of $8,000. The business had the following transactions during March 2010:

Recording transactions directly in the ledger, preparing a trial balance, measuring net income or loss

3. Trial bal. total $86,100

a. Akmali deposited $50,000 cash in a business bank account.

b. The business borrowed $8,000 cash from the bank and issued a note payable due within one year.

c. Paid $1,600 cash for supplies.

d. Paid cash for advertising in the local newspaper, $1,200.

e. Paid the following cash expenses for one month: commission, $12,400; office rent, $800; utilities, $600; interest, $200.

f. Earned revenue on account, $20,600.

g. Earned $7,500 revenue and received cash.

h. Collected cash from customers on account, $2,400.

Required

1. Open the following T-accounts: Cash; Accounts Receivable; Supplies; Notes Payable; Amin Akmali, Capital; Service Revenue; Advertising Expense; Interest Expense; Rent Expense; Commission Expense; Utilities Expense.

2. Record the transactions directly in the T-accounts without using a journal. Identify each transaction by its letter.

3. Prepare a trial balance at March 31, 2010. List expenses alphabetically.

4. Compute the amount of net income or net loss for this first month of operations. Would you recommend Akmali continue in business?

Decision Problem 2

Although all the following questions deal with the accounting equation, they are not related:

Using the accounting equation
②

1. Explain the advantages of double-entry bookkeeping to a friend who is opening a used-book store.

2. When you deposit money in your bank account, the bank credits your account. Is the bank misusing the word *credit* in this context? Why does the bank use the term *credit* to refer to your deposit, and not *debit*?

3. Your friend asks, "When revenues increase assets and expenses decrease assets, why are revenues credits and expenses debits and not the other way around?" Explain to your friend why revenues are credits and expenses are debits.

FINANCIAL STATEMENT CASES

Financial Statement Case 1

Banks provide a unique set of financial statements to their users. Refer to the Canadian Western Bank (CWB) financial statements in Appendix A and answer the following questions.

Applying the rules of debit and credit, journalizing transactions
② ③

1. Why would loans be considered an asset on CWB's balance sheet?

2. Why are deposits considered to be a liability on CWB's balance sheet?

3. What is CWB's main source of income?

4. What is CWB's largest expense? Explain how this expense occurs.

5. Do the same laws of debit and credit apply to banks? Why is a credit to your bank account good for you as a customer and a debit to your bank account bad for you as a customer?

Financial Statement Case 2

Journalizing transactions

This problem helps to develop journalizing skills by using an actual company's account titles. Refer to the Sun-Rype Products Ltd. financial statements in Appendix B at the back of the book. Assume Sun-Rype completed the following selected transactions during December 2008. All amounts are in thousands of dollars.

a. Made sales on account, $4,435.

b. Paid cash for advertising (selling, general, and administrative expenses), $13,613.

c. Paid interest expense of $879.

d. Collected accounts receivable of $7,567.

e. Paid cash for inventory, $3,330.

f. Purchased equipment on account for $5,000.

g. Paid cash for annual rent (selling, general, and administrative expenses), $15,440.

Required

1. Set up T-accounts for Cash (debit balance of $26,230); Accounts Receivable (debit balance of $14,962); Inventory (debit balance of $24,448); Property, Plant, and Equipment (debit balance of $20,130); Accounts Payable (credit balance of $10,229); Sales Revenue (credit balance of $120,933); Selling, General, and Administrative Expenses ($0 balance); Interest Expense ($0 balance).

2. Journalize Sun-Rype's transactions a to g. Explanations are not required.

3. Post to the T-accounts and compute the balance for each account. Identify each posting by its transaction letter.

4. For each of the accounts, compare your balances to Sun-Rype's actual balances as shown on the December 31, 2008, balance sheet and income statement in Appendix B. All your amounts should agree with the actual figures rounded to the nearest thousand.

   Cash
   Accounts receivable
   Inventories
   Property, plant, and equipment
   Accounts payable and accrued liabilities
   Net sales
   Selling, general, and administrative expenses
   Interest expense

5. Balance sheet and income statement accounts listed are really categories representing summarized account balances. List three accounts that would be reflected in the following categories:
   a) Property, plant, and equipment,
   b) Accounts payable and accrued liabilities, and
   c) Selling, general, and administrative expenses.

3 Measuring Business Income: The Adjusting Process

What is the adjusting process and why is it important?
Why can't we record only the transactions that affect cash?

How many categories of adjusting entries are there?
How do adjusting entries differ from other journal entries?

Why is the adjusted trial balance used to determine a business's results of operations and financial position?

These questions and others will be answered throughout this chapter. The Decision Guidelines at the end of this chapter will provide the answers in a useful summary.

LEARNING OBJECTIVES

1. Distinguish accrual-basis accounting from cash-basis accounting
2. Apply the recognition criteria for revenues and expenses
3. Make adjusting entries
4. Prepare an adjusted trial balance
5. Prepare the financial statements from the adjusted trial balance
6. Describe the adjusting-process implications of international financial reporting standards (IFRS)

CHAPTER 3 APPENDIX

A1. Account for a prepaid expense recorded initially as an expense
A2. Account for an unearned (deferred) revenue recorded initially as a revenue

WestJet is Canada's leading high-value low-cost airline offering scheduled service throughout its 55-city North American and Caribbean network. Named one of Canada's most admired corporate cultures in 2005, 2006, 2007 and 2008, WestJet pioneered low-cost flying in Canada. WestJet has a modern fleet of 77 Boeing Next-Generation 737 aircraft. With future confirmed deliveries for an additional 44 aircraft, bringing its fleet to 121 by 2013, WestJet strives to be the number one choice for travellers.[1]

WestJet Airlines Ltd. has grown significantly from its creation in 1996 by four Calgary entrepreneurs, beginning with 220 employees and three aircraft. Its initial routes were solely in Western Canada, stretching from Vancouver to Winnipeg. The 1999 merger of Canadian Airlines with Air Canada provided WestJet with the opportunity to add routes to several Eastern-Canadian cities. Since that time, the company has continued to expand its operations and maintain its profitability.

The global economy changed significantly in the last half of 2008. How did that affect the financial strength of WestJet? In the year ending December 31, 2008, the company earned a profit of over $178 million on sales revenue of over $2.5 billion. In its 2008 Annual Report, the company stated:

"We remain confident we will be able to effectively manage through the economic challenges as they are presented in 2009. We are well-positioned to adapt our capacity during this period . . . our WestJet brand has remained strong as we continue focusing on gaining market share by capitalizing on our lower-cost structure, maintaining a strong balance sheet, and delivering high-value service to our guests. With our airline's healthy underlying fundamentals, enviable corporate culture and people providing an award-winning guest experience, we believe that 2009 will be another successful and profitable year for WestJet."[2]

---

[1] *Source:* February 24, 2009, press release filed online at SEDAR.com; accessed on June 23, 2009.
[2] *Source:* Management Discussion & Analysis (from the 2008 Annual Report), posted online at SEDAR.com on February 11, 2009; accessed on June 23, 2009.

What do we mean when we say that WestJet earned $178 million in the year ended December 31, 2008?

The business earned net income, or profit, of $178 million for the year as reported on its income statement. WestJet's revenues consist of passenger and other revenues of $2.5 billion. What are WestJet's expenses? They include advertising, salaries, costs of running the aircraft including fuel, administrative and other office costs, maintenance, and many others. WestJet operates in much the same way, except on a much larger scale, as Ladner Environmental Services, the business we studied in Chapters 1 and 2.

Whether the business is WestJet Airlines Ltd. or Ladner Environmental Services, the profit motive increases the owners' drive to carry on the business. As you study this chapter, consider how important net income is to a business.

At the end of each accounting period, the entity prepares its financial statements. The period may be one month, three months, six months, or a full year. WestJet is typical. The company reports internally on a monthly basis. As a public company, it reports externally on a quarterly basis—at the end of every three months—with audited financial statements at the end of its year.

Whatever the length of the period, the end accounting product is the set of financial statements. And one of the most important single amounts in these statements is the net income or net loss for the period. Net income or net loss captures much information: total revenues minus total expenses for the period. A business that consistently earns net income adds value to its owners, its employees, its customers, and society.

An important step in financial statement preparation is the trial balance. The trial balance, introduced in Chapter 2 on page 73, lists the ledger accounts and their balances. The account balances in the trial balance include the effects of the transactions that occurred during the period—cash collections, purchases of assets, payments of bills, sales of assets, and so on. To measure its income, however, a business must do some additional accounting at the end of the period to bring the records up to date before preparing the financial statements. This process is called *adjusting the books* and it consists of making special entries called *adjusting entries*. This chapter focuses on these adjusting entries to show how to measure business income. This is Step 5 of the accounting cycle shown in the margin.

The accounting profession has concepts and principles to guide the measurement of business income. Chief among these are

- Accrual-basis accounting versus cash-basis accounting
- The accounting period
- The recognition principle for revenues and expenses (including the matching of costs with revenues)

In this chapter, we apply these (and other) concepts and principles to measure the income and prepare the financial statements of Ladner Environmental Services (LES) for the month of April. All other companies follow the same principles.

Accounting Cycle

1. Identify and analyze transactions

2. Record transactions in a journal

3. Post (copy) from the journal to the accounts in the ledger

4. Prepare the trial balance

5. Journalize and post adjusting entries

6. Prepare the financial statements

7. Journalize and post the closing entries

8. Prepare the postclosing trial balance

Accrual-Basis Accounting versus Cash-Basis Accounting

There are two ways to do accounting:

- **Accrual-basis accounting**, frequently called simply *accrual accounting*, records the effect of every business transaction as it occurs, no matter when cash receipts and cash payments occur. Most businesses use the accrual basis, and that is the method covered in this book. The Canada Revenue Agency (CRA) requires accrual accounting for income tax purposes except in special cases.

- **Cash-basis accounting** records transactions only when cash receipts and cash payments occur. It ignores receivables, payables, and amortization. Only very small businesses tend to use cash-basis accounting.

OBJECTIVE ①
Distinguish accrual-basis accounting from cash-basis accounting

Suppose LES purchased $4,000 of supplies on account. On the accrual basis, LES records the asset Supplies and the liability Accounts Payable as follows:

Supplies...	4,000	
Accounts Payable		4,000
Purchased supplies on account.		

Under the accrual basis, LES's balance sheet reports the asset Supplies and the liability Accounts Payable.

In contrast, cash-basis accounting ignores this transaction because LES paid no cash. The cash basis records only cash receipts and cash payments.

- Most cash receipts are treated as revenues.

- Most cash payments are handled as expenses.

Therefore, under the cash basis, LES would record the transaction only when the cash is paid for the supplies, and the $4,000 cash payment is recorded as an expense rather than as an asset. This is faulty accounting: LES acquired supplies, which are assets.

Now let's see how differently the accrual basis and the cash basis account for a revenue. Suppose LES performed service and earned revenue but collected no cash. Under the accrual basis, LES records $15,000 of revenue on account as follows:

Accounts Receivable	15,000	
Service Revenue....................................		15,000
Earned revenue on account.		

The balance sheet then reports the asset Accounts Receivable, and the income statement reports Service Revenue. We have a complete picture of the transaction.

Under the cash basis, LES would record no revenue because there is no cash receipt. Instead, it would wait until cash is received and then record the cash as revenue. As a result, cash-basis accounting never reports accounts receivable from customers. Cash-basis accounting shows the revenue in the wrong accounting period if cash is *received* in a period different from the one in which it is *earned*. Revenue should be recorded when it is earned, and that is how the accrual basis operates.

Exhibit 3–1 illustrates the difference between the accrual basis and the cash basis for a flower shop. Keep in mind that the accrual basis is the correct way to do accounting.

As we saw in Exhibit 1–6 on page 10, the objective of financial statements is to communicate information that is useful to users. Clearly, accrual-basis accounting provides more complete information than does cash-basis accounting. This difference is important because the more complete the data, the better equipped decision makers are to reach accurate conclusions about the firm's financial health and future prospects. Three concepts used in accrual accounting are the accounting period, the recognition principle, and the time-period assumption.

LEARNING TIPS

You can distinguish cash-basis and accrual-basis accounting this way:

Cash basis: Record revenue when you receive cash, regardless of when the service was performed or the sale made. Record expenses when you pay cash, regardless of when the expense was incurred or the item used. There are no accounts receivable and no accounts payable.

Accrual basis: Forget cash flow. Record revenue when you make a sale or perform a service. Record expenses when the business uses goods or services. Revenues and expenses may not coincide with cash flows.

EXHIBIT 3–1 Accrual-Basis Accounting versus Cash-Basis Accounting

ACCOUNTING FOR REVENUE

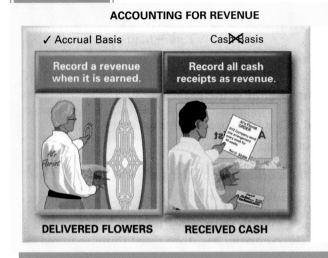

✓ Accrual Basis   Cash Basis

| Record a revenue when it is earned. | Record all cash receipts as revenue. |

DELIVERED FLOWERS   RECEIVED CASH

ACCOUNTING FOR EXPENSE

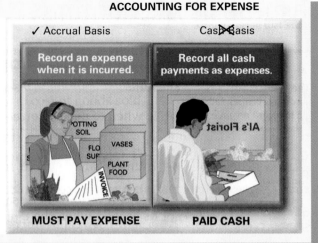

✓ Accrual Basis   Cash Basis

| Record an expense when it is incurred. | Record all cash payments as expenses. |

MUST PAY EXPENSE   PAID CASH

The Accounting Period

LES will know for certain how well it has operated only after it sells all its assets, pays the liabilities, and returns any leftover cash to the owner. This process, called *liquidation,* is the same as going out of business. Obviously, it is not practical for accountants to measure business income in this manner because businesses need periodic reports on their progress. Accountants slice time into small segments and prepare financial statements for specific periods.

The most basic accounting period is one year, and virtually all businesses prepare annual financial statements. For most companies, the annual accounting period is the calendar year from January 1 through December 31. Other companies use a *fiscal year* ending on some date other than December 31. The year-end date is usually the low point in business activity for the year. Retailers are a notable example. Traditionally, their fiscal year ends on or around January 31, because the low point in their business activity has followed the after-Christmas sales in January; for the Forzani Group Ltd., which operates a chain of sporting goods stores across Canada, its fiscal year ends on the first Sunday after January 31.

Managers and investors cannot wait until the end of the year to gauge a company's progress. Companies therefore prepare financial statements for *interim* periods, which are less than a year. Managers want financial information more often, so monthly financial statements are common. A series of monthly statements can be combined for quarterly and semiannual periods. Most of the discussions in this book are based on an annual accounting period, but the procedures and statements can be applied to interim periods as well.

DID YOU GET IT?

MyAccountingLab

To check your understanding of the material in this Learning Objective, complete these questions. The solutions appear on MyAccountingLab so you can check your progress.

1. All parts of the financial statements are important in describing the financial condition of a business. Which financial statement would be most helpful to WestJet's management in evaluating the company's performance for 2008?

2. Suppose LES collects $6,000 from customers on January 1. The company will earn the $6,000 evenly during January, February, and March. How much service revenue will LES report each month under (a) accrual-basis accounting and (b) cash-basis accounting?

3. Suppose LES prepays $1,500 for TV advertising on October 1. The ads will run during October, November, and December. How much advertising expense will LES report each month under (a) accrual-basis accounting and (b) cash-basis accounting?

Recognition Criteria for Revenues and Expenses

Section 1000 of the *CICA Handbook* discusses financial-statement concepts. A significant part of the section relates to recognition criteria. Recognition is the process of including an item in the financial statements of a business. There are two parts to consider. First, we will discuss the recognition of revenue; then, we will discuss the recognition of expenses.

OBJECTIVE 2

Apply the recognition criteria for revenues and expenses

Revenue Recognition

The **recognition criteria for revenues** tell accountants

- *When* to record revenue—that is, when to make a journal entry for a revenue transaction.
- The *amount* of revenue to record.

Revenue, defined in Chapter 1, page 14, is the increase in owner's equity from delivering goods and services to customers in the course of operating a business. When we speak of "recording" something in accounting, we mean to make an entry in the journal. That is where the accounting process starts.

When to Record Revenue   Revenue-recognition criteria state that revenue should be recorded when it has been earned—but not before. In *most* cases, revenue is earned when the business has delivered a completed good or service to the customer. The business has done everything required by the agreement, including transferring the item to the customer.

Exhibit 3–2 shows two situations that provide guidance on when to record revenue. The first situation illustrates when *not* to record revenue, because the client merely states her plans. Situation 2 illustrates when revenue should be recorded—after LES has performed the service for the client.

EXHIBIT 3–2   Recording Revenue: The Recognition Criteria for Revenues

The Amount of Revenue to Record   The general principle is to record revenue equal to the cash value of the goods or the service transferred to the customer. Suppose that, in order to obtain a new client, LES performs environmental assessment services for the price of $5,000. Ordinarily, the business would have charged $7,000 for this service. How much revenue should the business record? The answer is $5,000 because that was the cash value of the transaction. LES will not receive the full value of $7,000, so that is not the amount of revenue to record. The business will receive only $5,000 cash, and that pinpoints the amount of revenue earned.

Recognition Criteria for Expenses

Just as we have criteria that help us determine when to recognize revenue and how much revenue we should record, we also have criteria to help us determine when to recognize expenses. A key criterion is commonly referred to as the **matching objective**. Recall that expenses—such as utilities, advertising, and amortization—are the costs of assets and services that are consumed in the earning of revenue. The matching objective directs accountants to

1. Identify all expenses incurred during the accounting period.
2. Measure the expenses.
3. Match the expenses against the revenues earned during that period.

To match expenses against revenues means to subtract the related expenses from the revenues in order to compute net income or net loss. Exhibit 3–3 illustrates the matching objective.

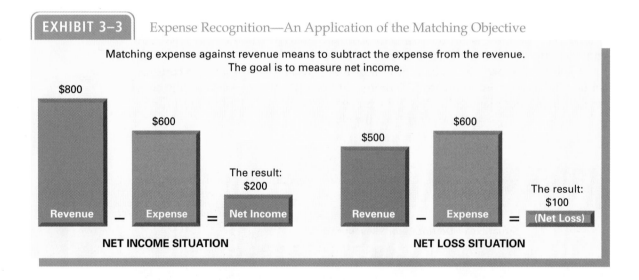

EXHIBIT 3–3 Expense Recognition—An Application of the Matching Objective

Matching expense against revenue means to subtract the expense from the revenue. The goal is to measure net income.

$800 Revenue − $600 Expense = Net Income The result: $200

NET INCOME SITUATION

$500 Revenue − $600 Expense = (Net Loss) The result: $100

NET LOSS SITUATION

There is a natural link between some expenses and revenues. Accountants follow the matching objective by first identifying the revenues of a period and then the expenses that can be linked to particular revenues. For example, a business that pays sales commissions to its salespeople will have commission expense if the employees make sales. If they make no sales, the business has no commission expense.

Other expenses are not so easy to link with particular sales. LES's monthly rent expense occurs, for example, regardless of the revenues earned during the period. The matching objective directs accountants to identify these types of expenses with a particular time period, such as a month or a year. If LES employs a secretary at a monthly salary of $2,500, the business will record salary expense of $2,500 each month.

How does LES bring its accounts up to date for preparing the financial statements? To address this question, accountants use the time-period assumption.

Time-Period Assumption

Managers, investors, and creditors make decisions daily and need periodic readings on the business's progress. Therefore, accountants prepare financial statements at regular intervals.

The **time-period assumption** ensures that accounting information is reported at regular intervals. This principle defines the accounting period, and interacts with the revenue- and expense-recognition criteria to underlie the use of accruals. To measure income accurately, companies update the revenue and expense accounts immediately prior to the end of the period. Royal Bank provides a real example of an expense accrual. Royal Bank has an October 31 year end. When October 31 falls during a pay period—say on a Tuesday—and Royal Bank pays its employees bi-weekly on Fridays, the company must record the employee compensation owed for unpaid services performed up to and including October 31. Assume weekly salary and wages expense for Royal Bank's B.C. Division is $5,000,000 and assume that the previous pay period ended on Friday, February 27; the entry to accrue the expense would be ($\frac{2}{5} \times \$5,000,000 = \$2,000,000$):

Oct. 31	Salary and Wages Expense.....................................	2,000,000	
	Salary and Wages Payable................................		2,000,000
	Accrued salary and wages expense for October 30 and 31.		

This entry serves two purposes. First, it assigns the expense to the proper period. Without the accrual entry at October 31, total expenses for the year would be understated, and, as a result, net income would be overstated. Incorrectly, the expense would fall in the following fiscal year when Royal Bank makes the next payroll disbursement. Second, the accrual entry also records the liability for reporting on the balance sheet at October 31. Without the accrual entry, total liabilities would be understated.

At the end of the accounting period, companies also accrue revenues that have been earned but not collected. The remainder of the chapter discusses how to make the adjusting entries to bring the accounts up to date.

DID YOU GET IT?

MyAccountingLab

To check your understanding of the material in this Learning Objective, complete these questions. The solutions appear on MyAccountingLab so you can check your progress.

4. Why is it important to have recognition criteria for both revenues and expenses?

5. On December 20, 2010, Shiloh Company receives an order for $5,000 from Windsor Company. The order will not be shipped until January 5, 2011. Shiloh wants to record the revenue on December 20 so it can include it in the current year's financial statements. As Shiloh's accountant, you object to this accounting treatment. Why?

6. On December 20, 2010, Shiloh Company receives an order for $5,000 from Windsor Company. The order is shipped immediately. The company pays a commission of 5 percent of the selling price to its sales representative who received the order. This commission will not be paid until January 2011. Shiloh's fiscal year end is December 31. How should the company account for the sales commission?

Adjusting the Accounts

At the end of the period, the accountant prepares the financial statements. This end-of-the-period process begins with the trial balance that lists the accounts and their balances after the period's transactions have been recorded in the journal and posted to the accounts in the ledger. We prepared trial balances in Chapter 2.

OBJECTIVE ③
Make adjusting entries

Exhibit 3–4 is the trial balance of LES at April 30, 2010. (Account numbers are not shown. Some accounts and balances differ from those in Chapter 2. Assume the company had a few more transactions since Chapter 2.) This *unadjusted trial balance* includes some new accounts that will be explained here. It lists most, but not all, of the revenue accounts and the expenses of the company for the month of April. These trial balance amounts are incomplete because they omit certain revenue and expense transactions that affect more than one accounting period. That is why the trial balance is *unadjusted*. In most cases, however, we refer to it simply as the trial balance, without the label "unadjusted."

EXHIBIT 3–4 Unadjusted Trial Balance

LADNER ENVIRONMENTAL SERVICES
Unadjusted Trial Balance
April 30, 2010

Cash	$ 31,000	
Accounts receivable	14,000	
Office supplies	1,500	
Prepaid insurance	3,600	
Land	50,000	
Furniture	45,000	
Accounts payable		$ 12,000
Unearned service revenue		3,000
John Ladner, capital		120,100
John Ladner, withdrawals	6,000	
Service revenue		24,000
Rent expense	3,000	
Salary expense	4,000	
Utilities expense	1,000	
Total	$159,100	$159,100

Accrual-basis accounting requires adjusting entries at the end of the period in order to produce correct balances for the financial statements. To see why, consider the Office supplies account in Exhibit 3–4.

KEY POINT

When an asset is used up, it becomes an expense.

LES uses supplies (an asset) in providing consulting services for clients during the month. This use reduces the supplies on hand and creates an expense, just like salary expense or rent expense. It is not worth the effort to record supplies expense each time supplies are used. But by the end of the month, the Office supplies balance of $1,500 on the unadjusted trial balance (Exhibit 3–4) is not correct. So how does the business account for supplies expense? LES must adjust the accounts at April 30.

Adjusting entries assign revenues to the period in which they are earned and expenses to the period in which they are incurred. Adjusting entries also update the asset and liability accounts. They are needed to

1. Measure properly the period's income on the income statement.
2. Bring related asset and liability accounts to correct balances for the balance sheet.

The end-of-the-period process of updating the accounts is called *adjusting the accounts, making the adjusting entries,* or *adjusting the books.* This chapter shows the adjusting process as it moves from the trial balance to the adjusted trial balance.

Prepaids (Deferrals) and Accruals

Two basic types of adjustments are *prepaids* and *accruals*. In a *prepaid*-type adjustment, the cash transaction occurs before the related expense or revenue is recorded. Prepaids are also called *deferrals* because the recording of the expense or the revenue is deferred to periods after cash is paid or received. *Accrual*-type adjustments are the opposite of prepaids. For accruals we record the expense or revenue before the related cash is paid or received.

Adjusting entries can be further divided into five categories:

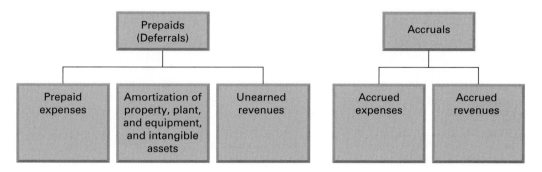

The core of this chapter is the discussion of these five types of adjusting entries on pages 115–121. Study this material carefully because it is the most challenging topic in all of introductory accounting.

Prepaid Expenses

Prepaid expenses are advance payments of expense. The category includes miscellaneous assets that typically expire or are used up in the near future. Prepaid rent and prepaid insurance are examples of prepaid expenses. They are called "prepaid" expenses because they are expenses that are paid in advance. Salary expense and utilities expense, among others, are typically *not* prepaid expenses because they are not paid in advance. All companies, large and small, must make adjustments regarding prepaid expenses. For example, Swiss Chalet makes prepayments for rent, packaging supplies, and insurance. Prepaid expenses are assets, not expenses, since they represent a potential future economic benefit.

Prepaid expenses are assets, not expenses.

Prepaid Insurance   Automobile insurance is usually paid in advance. This prepayment creates an asset for the policyholder, because that person has purchased the future benefit of insurance protection. Suppose LES purchases insurance on April 1, 2010, for two automobiles. The cost of the insurance is $3,600. The entry to record the payment is a debit to the asset account, Prepaid Insurance, as follows:

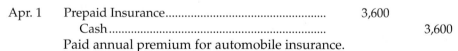

Apr. 1	Prepaid Insurance..	3,600	
	Cash..		3,600
	Paid annual premium for automobile insurance.		

After posting, Prepaid Insurance appears as follows:

ASSETS
Prepaid Insurance

Apr. 1	3,600	

The trial balance at April 30, 2010, lists Prepaid Insurance as an asset with a debit balance of $3,600. Throughout April, the Prepaid Insurance account maintains this beginning balance, as shown in Exhibit 3–4 (page 114). But $3,600 is *not* the amount of Prepaid Insurance for LES's balance sheet at April 30. Why?

At April 30, Prepaid Insurance should be adjusted to remove from its balance the amount of insurance that has been used up, which is one month's worth of the prepayment. By definition, the amount of an asset that has been used, or has expired, is an *expense*. The adjusting entry transfers one-twelfth, or $300 ($3,600 × $\frac{1}{12}$), of the debit balance from Prepaid Insurance to Insurance Expense. The debit side of the entry records an increase in Insurance Expense and the credit records a decrease in the asset Prepaid Insurance.

Apr. 30	Insurance Expense...	300	
	Prepaid Insurance...		300
	To record insurance expense ($3,600 × $\frac{1}{12}$).		

After posting, Prepaid Insurance and Insurance Expense show correct ending balances as follows:

ASSETS					EXPENSES		
Prepaid Insurance					**Insurance Expense**		
Apr. 1	3,600	**Apr. 30**	**300**		**Apr. 30**	**300**	
Bal.	3,300				Bal.	300	

Correct asset amount, $3,300	→	**Total accounted for, $3,600**	←	**Correct expense amount, $300**	

The full $3,600 has been accounted for. Eleven-twelfths measures the asset, and one-twelfth measures the expense. Recording this expense illustrates the matching objective.

The same analysis applies to a prepayment of 12 months' rent. The only difference is in the account titles, which would be Prepaid Rent and Rent Expense instead of Prepaid Insurance and Insurance Expense. In a computerized system, the adjusting entry crediting the prepaid account and debiting the expense account could be established to recur automatically in each subsequent accounting period until the prepaid account has a zero balance.

The chapter appendix shows an alternative treatment of prepaid expenses. The end result on the financial statements is the same as that for the method given here.

Supplies Supplies are accounted for in the same way as prepaid expenses. On April 2, LES paid cash of $1,500 for office supplies.

Apr. 2	Office supplies	1,500	
	Cash...		1,500
	Paid cash for office supplies.		

Assume that the business purchased no additional supplies during April. The April 30 trial balance, therefore, lists Office supplies with a $1,500 debit balance as shown in Exhibit 3–4. But LES's April 30 balance sheet should *not* report supplies of $1,500. Why?

During April, LES used supplies in performing services for clients. The cost of the supplies used is the measure of *supplies expense* for the month. To measure LES's supplies expense during April, John Ladner counts the supplies on hand at the end of the month. This is the amount of the asset still available to the business. Assume the count indicates that supplies costing $1,000 remain. Subtracting the entity's $1,000 of supplies on hand at the end of April from the cost of supplies available during April ($1,500) measures supplies expense during the month ($500).

Cost of asset available during the period	−	Cost of asset on hand at the end of the period	=	Cost of asset used (expense) during the period
$1,500	−	$1,000	=	$500

The April 30 adjusting entry updates the Office supplies account and records the supplies expense for April as follows:

Apr. 30   Supplies Expense...   500
               Office supplies   500
               To record supplies expense ($1,500 − $1,000).

After posting, the Office supplies and Supplies Expense accounts hold correct ending balances:

	ASSETS					EXPENSES		
	Office Supplies					**Supplies Expense**		
Apr. 2	1,500	**Apr. 30**	**500**	⟶	**Apr. 30**	**500**	
Bal.	1,000				Bal.	500	

Correct asset amount, $1,000	→	Total accounted for, $1,500	←	Correct expense amount, $500

The Office supplies account enters the month of May with a $1,000 balance, and the adjustment process is repeated each month.

Amortization of Property, Plant, and Equipment, and Intangible Assets

The logic of the accrual basis of accounting is best illustrated by how businesses account for capital assets. **Property, plant, and equipment** are identifiable *tangible* assets, such as land, buildings, furniture, machinery, and equipment. All of these tangible assets except land decline in usefulness as they age. This decline is an *expense* to the business. Accountants systematically spread the cost of each type of property, plant, and equipment, except land, over the years of its useful life. The *CICA Handbook* calls this process of allocating the cost of property, plant, and equipment to an expense account over its life **amortization**. (Another term for amortization in common usage is *depreciation*.) Land is the exception. We record no amortization for land.

Many companies also acquire or use *intangible* assets, such as patents and trademarks, in their business. A recognized intangible asset should be amortized over its useful life. This topic will be discussed in more detail in Chapter 10.

LEARNING TIPS

An expense is recorded whenever a good or service is used. As plant and equipment are used, the portion of the cost that is used during the period is an expense called *amortization*.

Similarity to Prepaid Expenses   The concept of accounting for plant and equipment and amortization expense is the same as for prepaid expenses. In a sense, plant and equipment are large prepaid expenses that expire over a number of periods. For both prepaid expenses and plant and equipment, the business purchases an asset that wears out or is used up. As the asset is used, more and more of its cost is transferred from the asset account to the expense account. The major difference between prepaid expenses and capital assets is the length of time it takes for the asset to lose its usefulness (or expire). Prepaid expenses usually expire within a year, whereas plant and equipment assets remain useful for a number of years.

Consider LES's operations. Suppose that, on April 3, the business purchased furniture for $45,000 and made this journal entry:

Apr. 3   Furniture...   45,000
           Cash..   45,000
           Purchased office furniture.

After posting, the Furniture account appears as follows:

ASSETS	
Furniture	
Apr. 3 45,000	

In accrual-basis accounting, an asset is recorded when the furniture is acquired. Then, a portion of the asset's cost is transferred from the asset account to Amortization Expense each period that the asset is used. This method matches the asset's expense to the revenue of the period, which is an application of the matching objective. In many computerized systems, the adjusting entry for amortization is programmed to occur automatically each month for the duration of the asset's life.

John Ladner believes the furniture will remain useful for five years and be virtually worthless at the end of its life. One way to compute the amount of amortization for each year is to divide the cost of the asset ($45,000 in our example) by its useful life (5 years). This procedure—called the straight-line method—gives annual amortization of $9,000 ($45,000 ÷ 5 years = $9,000 per year). Amortization for the month of April is $750 ($9,000 ÷ 12 months = $750 per month). Amortization expense for April is recorded by the following entry:

Apr. 30	Amortization Expense—Furniture	750
	Accumulated Amortization—Furniture	750
	To record monthly amortization expense on furniture.	

KEY POINT

Use a separate Amortization Expense account and Accumulated Amortization account for each major type of tangible asset. (Amortization Expense—Furniture, Amortization Expense—Buildings, and so on). You must know the amount of amortization recorded for each asset. All Accumulated Amortization accounts may or may not be combined on the balance sheet and all Amortization Expense accounts may or may not be combined on the income statement. It depends on the company and its financial-statement presentation.

The Accumulated Amortization Account   Accumulated Amortization is credited—not Furniture—because the original cost of any property, plant, and equipment acquisition should remain in the asset account as long as the business uses the asset. Accountants and managers may refer to the Furniture account to see how much the asset cost. This information is useful in a decision about whether to replace the furniture and the amount to pay. Accountants use the **Accumulated Amortization** account to show the cumulative sum of all amortization expense from the date of acquiring the tangible capital asset. Therefore, the balance in this account increases over the life of the asset—the account balance continues to "accumulate" over the life of the asset.

Accumulated Amortization is a *contra asset* account, which means an asset account with a normal credit balance. (Recall from Chapter 2, page 61, that the normal balance on an account marks the side of the account where increases are recorded.) A **contra account** has two main characteristics:

- A contra account has a companion account.
- A contra account's normal balance (debit or credit) is the opposite of the companion account's normal balance.

In this case, Accumulated Amortization—Furniture is the contra account that accompanies Furniture. It appears in the ledger directly after Furniture. Furniture has a debit balance, and therefore Accumulated Amortization—Furniture, a contra asset, has a credit balance. *All contra asset accounts have credit balances.*

A business carries an accumulated amortization or depreciation account for each depreciable tangible asset. If a business has a building and a machine, for example, it will carry the accounts Accumulated Amortization—Building, and Accumulated Amortization—Machine.

After posting the amortization, the Furniture, Accumulated Amortization—Furniture, and Amortization Expense—Furniture accounts of LES are as follows:

ASSETS Furniture		CONTRA ASSET Accumulated Amortization—Furniture		EXPENSES Amortization Expense—Furniture	
Apr. 3 45,000			Apr. 30 750	Apr. 30 750	
Bal. 45,000			Bal. 750	Bal. 750	

Carrying Value   The balance sheet reports both Furniture and Accumulated Amortization—Furniture. Because it is a contra account, the balance of Accumulated Amortization—Furniture is subtracted from the balance of Furniture. This net amount (cost minus accumulated amortization) of a capital asset is called its **carrying value,** or *net carrying value*, or *book value*, as shown for Furniture:

Furniture	$45,000
Less: Accumulated Amortization—Furniture	750
Carrying value..	$44,250

Suppose LES owns a building that cost $120,000, on which annual amortization is $6,000. The amount of amortization for one month would be $500 ($6,000 ÷ 12), and the following entry records amortization for April.

Apr. 30	Amortization Expense—Building.........................	500	
	Accumulated Amortization—Building..........		500
	To record monthly amortization on building.		

The balance sheet at April 30 would report LES's property, plant, and equipment as shown in Exhibit 3–5.

EXHIBIT 3–5 Property, Plant, and Equipment on the Balance Sheet of Ladner Environmental Services (April 30)

Property, Plant, and Equipment

Furniture	$ 45,000	
Less: Accumulated amortization—furniture	750	$ 44,250
Building	120,000	
Less: Accumulated amortization—building	500	119,500
Property, Plant, and Equipment, Net		$163,750

Exhibit 3–6 shows information about Sun-Rype Products Ltd., the company whose financial statements are in Appendix B of this text. In its 2008 financial statements, the balance sheet reports Property, Plant, and Equipment of $25,130 (amount in thousands) and Note 5 of the financial statements shows the details. The first column shows the cost, the middle column shows the accumulated amortization, and the third column shows the net book value (carrying value) for each type of capital asset.

EXHIBIT 3–6 Sun-Rype Products Ltd. Reporting of Property, Plant, and Equipment (Amounts in Thousands)

From Note 5 of the financial statements:

	Cost	Accumulated Amortization	Net Book Value
Land	$ 170	$ —	$ 170
Building	16,643	13,293	3,350
Processing equipment	51,860	32,229	19,631
Other equipment	8,522	6,543	1,979
Total	$77,195	$52,065	$25,130

Let's now return to LES's situation.

KEY POINT

A prepaid expense is paid first and expensed later. An accrued expense is expensed first and paid later. Prepaid expenses and accrued expenses are opposites.

Accrued Expenses

Businesses incur many expenses before they pay cash. Payment is not due until later. Consider an employee's salary. The employer's salary expense and salary payable grow as the employee works, so the liability is said to *accrue*. Another example is interest expense on a note payable. Interest accrues as time passes. The term **accrued expense** refers to an expense that the business has incurred but has not yet recorded. An accrued expense always creates a liability. Therefore, accrued expenses can be viewed as the opposite of prepaid expenses.

It is time-consuming to make hourly, daily, or even weekly journal entries to accrue expenses. Consequently, the accountant waits until the end of the period. Then an adjusting entry brings each expense (and related liability) up to date just before the financial statements are prepared.

Accruing Salary Expense Most companies pay their employees at predetermined times. Suppose LES pays its two employees a monthly salary of $8,000 in total, half on the 15th and half on the last day of the month. Here is a calendar for April with the two paydays circled:

			APRIL			
S	M	T	W	T	F	S
					1	2
3	4	5	6	7	8	9
10	11	12	13	14	(15)	16
17	18	19	20	21	22	23
24	25	26	27	28	29	(30)

Assume that, if either payday falls on a weekend, LES pays the employees on the following Monday. During April, LES paid its employees' first half-month salary of $4,000 on Friday, April 15, and recorded the following entry:

Apr. 15	Salary Expense..	4,000	
	Cash...		4,000
	To pay salary.		

After posting, the Salary Expense account is

EXPENSES
Salary Expense

Apr. 15	4,000

The trial balance at April 30 (Exhibit 3–4, page 114) includes Salary Expense, with its debit balance of $4,000. Because April 30, the second payday of the month, falls on a Saturday, the second half-month amount of $4,000 will be paid on Monday, May 2. Without an adjusting entry, this second $4,000 amount is not included in the April 30 trial balance amount for Salary Expense, even though the expense has been incurred. Therefore, at April 30, the business adjusts for additional *salary expense* and *salary payable* of $4,000 by recording an increase in each of these accounts as follows:

Apr. 30	Salary Expense..	4,000	
	Salary Payable..		4,000
	To accrue salary expense.		

After posting, the Salary Expense and Salary Payable accounts are updated to April 30:

EXPENSES
Salary Expense

Apr. 15	4,000	
Apr. 30	**4,000**	
Bal.	8,000	

LIABILITIES
Salary Payable

	Apr. 30	**4,000**
	Bal.	4,000

The accounts at April 30 now contain the complete salary information for the month of April. The expense account has a full month's salary, and the liability account shows the portion that the business still owes at April 30. LES will record the payment of this liability on Monday, May 2.

This payment entry does not affect April or May expenses because the April expense was recorded on April 15 and April 30. May expense will be recorded in a like manner, starting on May 15. All accrued expenses are recorded with similar entries—a debit to the appropriate expense account and a credit to the related liability account.

(In reality, most companies pay their employees on the last business day *before* the end of the period, to allow employees to make rent and other payments due at the beginning of the month. In such a situation, no accrual for Salary Expense would be made.)

Accrued Revenues

As we have just seen, expenses can occur before the cash payment, and that creates an accrued expense. Likewise, businesses often earn revenue before they collect the cash. Collection occurs later. Revenue that has been earned but not yet collected is called an **accrued revenue**.

Assume LES is hired on April 15 by Rock Creek Development to provide environmental consulting services on a monthly basis. Under this agreement, Rock Creek will pay LES $3,000 monthly, with the first payment on May 15. During April, LES will earn half a month's fee, $1,500, for work performed April 15 through April 30. On April 30, LES makes the following adjusting entry to record an increase in Accounts Receivable and Service Revenue:

Apr. 30   Accounts Receivable 1,500
              Service Revenue... 1,500
          To accrue service revenue ($3,000 × $^1/_2$).

We see from the unadjusted trial balance in Exhibit 3–4 (page 114) that Accounts Receivable has an unadjusted balance of $14,000. The Service Revenue unadjusted balance is $24,000. Posting the April 30 adjustment has the following effects on these two accounts:

ASSETS Accounts Receivable		REVENUES Service Revenue	
14,000			24,000
Apr. 30 1,500			Apr. 30 1,500
Bal. 15,500			Bal. 25,500

This adjusting entry illustrates the concept of revenue recognition. Without the adjustment, LES's financial statements would be misleading—they would understate Accounts Receivable and Service Revenue by $1,500 each. All accrued revenues are accounted for similarly: debit a receivable and credit a revenue.

We now turn to a different category of adjusting entries.

Unearned Revenues

Some businesses collect cash from customers in advance of doing work for them. Receiving cash in advance creates a liability called **unearned revenue** or **deferred revenue**. The company owes a product or service to the customer. Only when the job is completed will the business have earned the revenue.

Suppose a real estate developer engages LES to provide consulting services, agreeing to pay $3,000 monthly in advance beginning immediately. Suppose LES

KEY POINT

An unearned revenue is a liability, not a revenue. With all unearned revenue, cash is received before the work is performed or the goods are delivered.

receives in advance the first payment on April 20. LES records the cash receipt and the related increase in the business's liabilities as follows:

Apr. 20	Cash...	3,000	
	Unearned Service Revenue.............................		3,000
	Received revenue in advance.		

After posting, the liability account appears as follows:

LIABILITIES
Unearned Service Revenue

| | Apr. 20 | 3,000 |

Unearned Service Revenue is a liability because it represents LES's obligation to perform service for the client. The April 30 unadjusted trial balance (Exhibit 3–4) lists Unearned Service Revenue with a $3,000 credit balance prior to the adjusting entries. During the last 10 days of the month—April 21 through April 30—LES will have *earned* one-third (10 days divided by April's total 30 days) of the $3,000, or $1,000. Therefore, the accountant makes the following adjustment to decrease the liability, Unearned Service Revenue, and to record an increase in Service Revenue as follows:

Apr. 30	Unearned Service Revenue....................................	1,000	
	Service Revenue...		1,000
	To record service revenue that was collected in advance ($3,000 × $\frac{1}{3}$).		

This adjusting entry shifts $1,000 of the total amount of unearned service revenue from the liability account to the revenue account. After posting, the balance of Service Revenue is increased by $1,000 and the balance of Unearned Service Revenue has been reduced by $1,000 to $2,000. Now, both accounts have their correct balances at April 30, as follows:

| **LIABILITIES** | | | | **REVENUES** | |
Unearned Service Revenue				**Service Revenue**	
Apr. 30 **1,000**	Apr. 20	3,000			24,000
	Bal.	2,000		Apr. 30	1,500
				Apr. 30	**1,000**
				Bal.	26,500

Correct liability amount, $2,000 → Total accounted for, $3,000 ← Correct revenue amount, $1,000

All types of revenues that are collected in advance are accounted for similarly. Remember, an unearned revenue is a liability, not a revenue.

An unearned revenue to one company is a prepaid expense to the company that made the payment. Consider the real estate developer in the preceding example. The real estate developer had prepaid for consulting services—an asset. LES had unearned consulting revenue—a liability.

Exhibit 3–7 diagrams the timing of prepaid-type and accrual-type adjusting entries. The chapter appendix shows an alternative treatment of unearned revenues and prepaid expenses.

Summary of the Adjusting Process

The adjusting process has two purposes:

1. Accurately measure net income or net loss on the *income statement*. Every adjusting entry affects either a *Revenue* or an *Expense*.

2. Update the *balance sheet*. Every adjusting entry affects either an *Asset* or a *Liability*.

EXHIBIT 3–7 Prepaid-Type and Accrual-Type Adjustments* (Examples and amounts are from pages 115–122)

PREPAIDS—The cash transaction occurs initially. (The expense is incurred or the revenue is earned later.)

	Initially	Later

Prepaid expenses	Pay expense in advance and record an asset:
	Prepaid Expense (e.g., Insurance).. 3,600
	    Cash 3,600
		→ Record the expense later and decrease the asset:
		Expense (e.g., Insurance).................... 300
		    Prepaid Expense (e.g., Insurance) ... 300

Unearned revenues	Receive cash in advance and
	  record unearned revenue (a liability):
	Cash.. 3,000
	      Unearned Revenue (e.g., Consulting) 3,000
		→ Record the revenue later and
		  decrease unearned revenue:
		Unearned Revenue (e.g., Consulting) .. 1,000
		    Revenue (e.g., Consulting Service) .. 1,000

ACCRUALS—The cash transaction occurs later. (The expense is incurred or the revenue is earned first.)

	Initially	Later

Accrued expenses	Record (accrue) an expense first and
	  the related payable:
	Expense (e.g., Salary)...................... 4,000
	      Payable (e.g., Salary) 4,000
		→ Pay the liability later.
		
		Payable (e.g., Salary) 4,000
		    Cash 4,000

Accrued revenues	Record (accrue) a revenue first and
	  the related receivable:
	Receivable (e.g. from customer) ... 1,500
	      Revenue (e.g., Consulting Service).. 1,500
		→ Collect cash later:
		
		Cash 1,500
		    Receivable (e.g., from customer)..... 1,500

The authors thank Darrel Davis and Alfonso Oddo for suggesting this exhibit.
*See the Appendix of this chapter for an alternative treatment of accounting for prepaid expenses and accruals.

No adjusting entry debits or credits Cash because the cash transactions are recorded at other times. (The exception to this rule is an adjusting entry that is made to correct an error involving Cash.)

Exhibit 3–8 summarizes the adjusting entries. Exhibit 3–9 summarizes the adjusting entries of LES at April 30. The adjustments are identified by their letter.

- Panel A of the exhibit briefly describes the data for each adjustment.
- Panel B gives the adjusting entries.
- Panel C shows the accounts after they have been posted.

EXHIBIT 3–8 Summary of Adjusting Entries

Category of Adjusting Entry	Type of Account	
	Debited	**Credited**
Prepaid expense	Expense	Asset
Amortization	Expense	Contra asset
Accrued expense	Expense	Liability
Accrued revenue	Asset	Revenue
Unearned revenue	Liability	Revenue

Adapted from material provided by Beverly Terry.

PANEL A: Information for Adjustments at April 30, 2010

a. Prepaid insurance expired during April, $300.
b. Supplies remaining on hand at April 30, 2010, $1,000.
c. Amortization on furniture for the month of April, $750.
d. Accrued salary expense, $4,000.
e. Accrued service revenue, $1,500.
f. Amount of unearned service revenue that was earned during April, $1,000.

PANEL B: Adjusting Entries

a. Insurance Expense	300	
Prepaid Insurance		300
To record insurance expense.		
b. Supplies Expense	500	
Office Supplies		500
To record supplies used.		
c. Amortization Expense—Furniture	750	
Accumulated Amortization—Furniture...		750
To record amortization on furniture.		
d. Salary Expense	4,000	
Salary Payable		4,000
To accrue salary expense.		
e. Accounts Receivable	1,500	
Service Revenue...		1,500
To accrue service revenue.		
f. Unearned Service Revenue	1,000	
Service Revenue...		1,000
To record unearned revenue that has been earned.		

PANEL C: Amounts Posted to T-Accounts

ASSETS

Cash	
Bal. 31,000	

Accounts Receivable	
Bal. 14,000	
(e) 1,500	
Bal. 15,500	

Office Supplies	
Bal. 1,500	(b) 500
Bal. 1,000	

Prepaid Insurance	
Bal. 3,600	(a) 300
Bal. 3,300	

Land	
Bal. 50,000	

Furniture	
Bal. 45,000	

Accumulated Amortization—Furniture	
	(c) 750

LIABILITIES

Accounts Payable	
	Bal. 12,000

Salary Payable	
	(d) 4,000
	Bal. 4,000

Unearned Service Revenue	
(f) 1,000	Bal. 3,000
	Bal. 2,000

OWNER'S EQUITY

John Ladner, Capital	
	Bal. 120,100

John Ladner, Withdrawals	
Bal. 6,000	

REVENUES

Service Revenue	
	Bal. 24,000
	(e) 1,500
	(f) 1,000
	Bal. 26,500

EXPENSES

Amortization Expense—Furniture	
(c) 750	
Bal. 750	

Insurance Expense	
(a) 300	
Bal. 300	

Rent Expense	
Bal. 3,000	

Salary Expense	
Bal. 4,000	
(d) 4,000	
Bal. 8,000	

Supplies Expense	
(b) 500	
Bal. 500	

Utilities Expense	
Bal. 1,000	

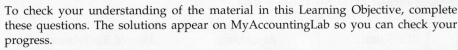
To check your understanding of the material in this Learning Objective, complete these questions. The solutions appear on MyAccountingLab so you can check your progress.

7. At the beginning of the month, Supplies were $500. During the month, the company purchased $600 of supplies. At month's end, $400 of supplies were still on hand.

   a. What was the cost of supplies used during the month? Where is this item reported?

   b. What is the ending balance of Supplies? Where is this item reported?

   c. Make the adjusting entry to update the Supplies account at the end of the month.

8. Suppose Ladner Environmental Services (LES) holds a note receivable from a client. At the end of April, LES has earned $500 of interest revenue on the note.

   a. Which accounts need to be adjusted at April 30?

   b. Make the adjusting entry.

9. In which, if any, of the five categories of adjusting entries would the following transactions fall?

   (1) Paid one year's insurance in advance.

   (2) Recorded part of a building's cost as an expense for the current period.

   (3) Recorded revenue from renting a building before receiving cash.

   (4) Paid a bill for maintenance of company automobiles.

The Adjusted Trial Balance

This chapter began with the trial balance before any adjusting entries—the unadjusted trial balance (Exhibit 3–4). After the adjustments are journalized and posted, the accounts appear as shown in Exhibit 3–9, Panel C. A useful step in preparing the financial statements is to list the accounts, along with their adjusted balances, on an **adjusted trial balance**. This document has the advantage of listing all the accounts and their adjusted balances in a single place. Exhibit 3–10 shows the preparation of the adjusted trial balance.

Exhibit 3–10 shows the first six columns of a *work sheet*. We will consider the complete work sheet in Chapter 4. For now, simply note how clearly this format presents the data. The information in the Account Title column and in the Trial Balance columns is drawn directly from the ledger (in our example, from the T-accounts in Exhibit 3–9). The two Adjustments columns list the debit and credit adjustments directly across from the appropriate account title. Each adjusting debit and credit is identified by a letter in parentheses that refers to the adjusting entry in Exhibit 3–9. For example, the debit labelled (a) on the work sheet refers to the debit adjusting entry of $300 to Insurance Expense in Panel B of Exhibit 3–9. The corresponding credit—labelled (a)—refers to the $300 credit to Prepaid Insurance.

The Adjusted Trial Balance columns give the adjusted account balances. Each amount on the adjusted trial balance of Exhibit 3–10 is computed by combining the amounts from the unadjusted trial balance plus or minus the adjustments. For example, Accounts Receivable starts with a debit balance of $14,000. Adding the $1,500 debit amount from adjusting entry (e) gives Accounts Receivable an adjusted balance of $15,500. Supplies begins with a debit balance of $1,500. After the $500 credit adjustment, its adjusted balance is $1,000. More than one entry may affect a single account, as is the case for Service Revenue. If an account is unaffected by the adjustments, it will show the same amount on both the adjusted

OBJECTIVE ④

Prepare an adjusted trial balance

K E Y   P O I N T

The differences between the amounts in the trial balance in Exhibit 3–4 and in the adjusted trial balance of Exhibit 3–10 result from the adjusting entries. If the adjusting entries were not given, you could determine them by computing the differences between the adjusted and unadjusted amounts.

Accounting Cycle Tutorials

4. Adjustments pages 1–17

EXHIBIT 3–10 | Preparation of the Adjusted Trial Balance

LADNER ENVIRONMENTAL SERVICES
Preparation of Adjusted Trial Balance
April 30, 2010

Account Title	Trial Balance Debit	Trial Balance Credit	Adjustments Debit		Adjustments Credit		Adjusted Trial Balance Debit	Adjusted Trial Balance Credit	
Cash	31,000						31,000		Balance Sheet (Exhibit 3–13)
Accounts receivable	14,000		(e)	1,500			15,500		
Supplies	1,500				(b)	500	1,000		
Prepaid insurance	3,600				(a)	300	3,300		
Furniture	45,000						45,000		
Accumulated amortization —furniture		0			(c)	750		750	
Land	50,000						50,000		
Accounts payable		12,000						12,000	
Salary payable		0			(d)	4,000		4,000	Statement of Owner's Equity (Exhibit 3–12)
Unearned service revenue		3,000	(f)	1,000				2,000	
John Ladner, capital		120,100						120,100	
John Ladner, withdrawals	6,000						6,000		
Service revenue		24,000			(e)	1,500		26,500	Income Statement (Exhibit 3–11)
					(f)	1,000			
Amortization expense	0		(c)	750			750		
Insurance expense	0		(a)	300			300		
Rent expense	3,000						3,000		
Salary expense	4,000		(d)	4,000			8,000		
Supplies expense	0		(b)	500			500		
Utilities expense	1,000						1,000		
	159,100	159,100	8,050		8,050		165,350	165,350	

and unadjusted trial balances. This is true for the Cash, Furniture, Accounts Payable, and John Ladner, Withdrawals accounts, to name a few.

A large company would use accounting software to print out a trial balance. For example, at Nexen Inc., a multi-divisional company that locates, produces, and transports oil and natural gas, each division has accounting software that prints a monthly trial balance. The accountants then analyze the amounts on the trial balance. This analysis results in the adjusting entries. Nexen posts the adjusting entries to update its ledger accounts. The trial balance has now become the company's *adjusted* trial balance. At Nexen, the adjusted trial balances from all divisions are consolidated, or grouped.

DID YOU GET IT?

MyAccountingLab

To check your understanding of the material in this Learning Objective, complete these questions. The solutions appear on MyAccountingLab so you can check your progress.

10. The following information was taken from Swift Company's unadjusted trial balance and shows a few related adjusting entries from the company's journal. Calculate the adjusted trial balance amounts for each account shown.

Account Title	Trial Balance		Adjustments		Adjusted Trial Balance	
	Debit	Credit	Debit	Credit	Debit	Credit
Cash	2,900					
Supplies	4,000			3,000		
Prepaid insurance	4,800			1,600		
Truck	40,000					
Accumulated amortization—truck		24,800		8,000		
Unearned revenue		2,500	1,000			

11. The following information was taken from Shirley Company's unadjusted trial balance and adjusted trial balance. Calculate the adjustment amounts for each account shown. Only one adjustment affected each account.

Account Title	Trial Balance		Adjustments		Adjusted Trial Balance	
	Debit	Credit	Debit	Credit	Debit	Credit
Supplies	6,000				2,000	
Prepaid insurance	3,200				1,600	
Unearned revenue		5,500				1,500
Service revenue		55,000				59,000
Insurance expense	0				1,600	
Supplies expense	2,900				6,900	

Preparing the Financial Statements from the Adjusted Trial Balance

The April financial statements of Ladner Environmental Services (LES) can be prepared from the adjusted trial balance in Exhibit 3–10. The right margin shows how the accounts are distributed from the adjusted trial balance to three of the four main financial statements.

OBJECTIVE 5
Prepare the financial statements from the adjusted trial balance

- The income statement (Exhibit 3–11) comes from the revenue and expense accounts.
- The statement of owner's equity (Exhibit 3–12) shows the reasons for the change in the owner's capital account during the period.
- The balance sheet (Exhibit 3–13) reports the assets, liabilities, and owner's equity.

The financial statements are best prepared in the order shown: the income statement first, followed by the statement of owner's equity, and then the balance sheet. The essential features of all financial statements are as follows:

Heading:

- Name of the entity
- Title of the statement
- Date of the statement, or period covered by the statement

Body of the statement
Many large companies list expenses in descending order of amount, as shown in Exhibit 3–11; many small and medium-sized companies list expenses in alphabetical order. However, Miscellaneous Expense, a catch-all account for expenses that do not fit in another category, is usually reported last. Miscellaneous Expense should be a relatively low dollar amount. If it is not, new expense accounts should be created.

Relationships among the Three Financial Statements

MyAccountingLab | Accounting Cycle Tutorials

5. Financial Statements
   pages 1–10

The arrows in Exhibits 3–11, 3–12, and 3–13 illustrate the relationships among the income statement, the statement of owner's equity, and the balance sheet. (The relationships among the financial statements were introduced in Chapter 1, page 20.) Consider why the income statement is prepared first and the balance sheet last.

EXHIBIT 3–11 | Income Statement

LADNER ENVIRONMENTAL SERVICES
Income Statement
For the Month Ended April 30, 2010

Revenue:		
Service revenue		$ 26,500
Expenses:		
Salary expense	$ 8,000	
Rent expense	3,000	
Utilities expense	1,000	
Amortization expense	750	
Supplies expense	500	
Insurance expense	300	
Total expenses		13,550
Net income		$ 12,950

EXHIBIT 3–12 | Statement of Owner's Equity

LADNER ENVIRONMENTAL SERVICES
Statement of Owner's Equity
For the Month Ended April 30, 2010

John Ladner, capital, April 1, 2010	$120,100
Add: Net income	12,950
	133,050
Less: Withdrawals	6,000
John Ladner, capital, April 30, 2008	$127,050

①

EXHIBIT 3–13 | Balance Sheet

LADNER ENVIRONMENTAL SERVICES
Balance Sheet
April 30, 2010

Assets			Liabilities		
Cash		$ 31,000	Accounts payable		$ 12,000
Accounts receivable		15,500	Salary payable		4,000
Supplies		1,000	Unearned service		
Prepaid insurance		3,300	revenue		2,000
Furniture	$45,000		Total liabilities		18,000
Less: Accumulated					
amortization—furniture	750	44,250	**Owner's Equity**		
Land		50,000	John Ladner, capital		127,050
			Total liabilities and		
Total assets		$145,050	owner's equity		$145,050

②

1. The income statement reports net income or net loss, calculated by subtracting expenses from revenues. Because revenues and expenses are owner's equity accounts, their net figure is then transferred to the statement of owner's equity. Note that net income in Exhibit 3–11, $12,950, increases owner's equity in Exhibit 3–12. A net loss would decrease owner's equity.

2. Capital is a balance sheet account, so the ending balance in the statement of owner's equity is transferred to the balance sheet. This amount is the final balancing element of the balance sheet. To solidify your understanding of this relationship, trace the $127,050 figure from Exhibit 3–12 to Exhibit 3–13.

You may be wondering why the total assets on the balance sheet ($145,050 in Exhibit 3–13) do not equal the total debits on the adjusted trial balance ($165,350 in Exhibit 3–10). Likewise, the total liabilities and owner's equity do not equal the total credits on the adjusted trial balance ($165,350 in Exhibit 3–10). One reason for these differences is that Accumulated Amortization—Furniture and John Ladner, Withdrawals are contra accounts. Recall that contra accounts are *subtracted* from their companion accounts on the balance sheet. However, on the adjusted trial balance, contra accounts are *added* as a debit or credit in their respective columns.

Ethical Issues in Accrual Accounting

Like most other aspects of life, accounting poses ethical challenges. At the most basic level, accountants must be honest in their work. Only with honest and complete information, including accounting data, can people expect to make wise decisions. An example will illustrate the importance of ethics in accrual accounting.

Ladner Environmental Services (LES) has been quite successful and so John Ladner decides to open a second office. He needs to borrow $50,000. Suppose LES understated expenses purposely in order to inflate net income as reported on the company's income statement. A banker could be tricked into lending money to LES. Then if LES could not repay the loan, the bank might lose money if Ladner cannot repay LES's loan himself—all because the banker relied on incorrect accounting information.

Accrual accounting provides several opportunities for unethical accounting. Recall from earlier in this chapter that amortization expense is an estimated figure. No business can foresee exactly how long its buildings and equipment will last, so accountants must estimate these assets' useful lives. Accountants then record amortization on capital assets over their *estimated* useful lives. A dishonest proprietor could buy a five-year asset and amortize it over 10 years. For each of the first five years, the company will report less amortization expense, and more net income, than it should. Or a dishonest business owner could overlook amortization expense altogether. Failing to record amortization would overstate net income. In both these situations, people who rely on the company's financial statements, such as bank lenders, can be deceived into doing business with the company. Accounting information must be honest and complete—completely ethical—to serve its intended purpose. As you progress through introductory accounting, you will see other situations that challenge the ethics of accountants.

The cash basis of accounting poses fewer ethical challenges because cash is not an estimated figure. Either the company has the cash, or it does not. Therefore, the amount of cash a company reports is rarely disputed. By contrast, adjusting entries for accrued expenses, accrued revenues, and amortization must often be estimated. Whenever there is an estimate, the accountant must often deal with pressure from managers or owners of the business to use the adjusting process to make the company look different from its true condition. The rules of conduct of the various professional accounting associations (discussed in Chapter 1) prohibit accountants from being associated with false or misleading financial information. Even with added ethical challenges, the accrual basis provides more complete accounting information than the cash basis. That is why accounting rests on the accrual basis.

DID YOU GET IT?

MyAccountingLab

To check your understanding of the material in this Learning Objective, complete these questions. The solutions appear on MyAccountingLab so you can check your progress.

12. Examine LES's adjusted trial balance in Exhibit 3–10. Use the information from the trial balance to create LES's income statement for the month ended April 30, 2010. Present the expenses in alphabetical order.

13. Examine LES's adjusted trial balance in Exhibit 3–10. Suppose the accountant forgot to record the $4,000 accrual of salary expense at April 30. What net income would LES have reported for April? What total assets, total liabilities, and total owner's equity would the balance sheet have reported at April 30?

OBJECTIVE 6

Describe the adjusting-process implications of international financial reporting standards (IFRS)

Adjusting-Process Implications of International Financial Reporting Standards (IFRS)

The concept of accrual accounting is accepted around the world. The accounting guidelines for all countries recommend the use of accrual accounting. Consequently, the adjustment process that has been described in this chapter is applicable in all developed countries that provide standards for the preparation of financial statements.

The adoption, in 2011, of international financial reporting standards (IFRS) for publicly accountable enterprises in Canada will have no direct impact on the adjusting process for Canadian companies. However, as we will see in future chapters, there may be an impact on the way the financial statements are presented. This topic will be discussed in Chapter 4.

The adoption of IFRS in Canada has caused some change in the way private companies (those that do not have to follow IFRS) record and report transactions. These companies will be allowed to follow Canadian guidelines for financial statement preparation, which may make it less complex to record and disclose some transactions. We will follow this topic through the rest of the textbook as well.

DID YOU GET IT?

To check your understanding of the material in this Learning Objective, complete this question. The solution appears on MyAccountingLab so you can check your progress.

14. Will the adoption, in 2011, of international financial reporting standards (IFRS) for publicly accountable enterprises in Canada have an impact on the adjusting process for Canadian companies?

As we conclude this chapter, we return to our opening question: What is the adjusting process and why is it important? It all comes down to the advantages of accrual-basis accounting over cash-basis accounting. The Decision Guidelines feature summarizes all of our chapter-opening questions and provides a map of the adjusting process that leads up to the adjusted trial balance.

DECISION GUIDELINES — Measuring Business Income: The Adjusting Process

Decision	Guidelines
Which basis of accounting better measures income (Revenues – Expenses)?	*Accrual basis,* because it provides more complete reports of operating performance
How do you measure Revenues? Expenses?	Recognition criteria for revenues Matching objective
Where do you start when you want to measure income at the end of the period?	Unadjusted trial balance, usually referred to simply as the *trial balance*
How do you update the accounts for preparation of the financial statements?	*Adjusting entries* at the end of the accounting period
What are the categories of adjusting entries?	Prepaid expenses Amortization of property, plant, and equipment, and intangible assets Accrued expenses Accrued revenues Unearned revenues
How do the adjusting entries differ from other journal entries?	1. Adjusting entries are usually made at the end of the accounting period. 2. Adjusting entries never affect cash (except to correct errors). 3. All adjusting entries debit or credit • At least one *income statement* account (a **Revenue** or an **Expense**) and • At least one *balance sheet* account (an **Asset** or a **Liability**)
Which statement summarizes the accounts with their adjusted balances?	*Adjusted trial balance,* which becomes the basis for preparing the financial statements

The trial balance of Potter Employment Services pertains to December 31, 2010, which is the end of its year-long accounting period.

POTTER EMPLOYMENT SERVICES
Trial Balance
December 31, 2010

Cash	$ 13,800	
Accounts receivable	10,000	
Supplies	2,000	
Furniture	20,000	
Accumulated amortization—furniture		$ 8,000
Building	100,000	
Accumulated amortization—building		60,000
Land	44,000	
Accounts payable		4,000
Salary payable		0
Unearned service revenue		16,000
Rick Potter, capital		64,000
Rick Potter, withdrawals	50,000	
Service revenue		120,000
Salary expense	32,000	
Supplies expense	0	
Amortization expense—furniture	0	
Amortization expense—building	0	
Miscellaneous expense	200	
Total	$272,000	$272,000

Data needed for the adjusting entries include:

a. A count of supplies shows $400 of unused supplies on hand on December 31.
b. Amortization for the year on furniture, $4,000.
c. Amortization for the year on building, $2,000.
d. Salary owed but not yet paid, $1,000.
e. Accrued service revenue, $2,600.
f. Of the $16,000 balance of unearned service revenue, $6,000 was earned during the year.

Required

1. Open the ledger accounts with their unadjusted balances using T-account format.
2. Journalize Potter Employment Services' adjusting entries at December 31, 2010. Identify entries by their letter as in Exhibit 3–9 (page 124).
3. Write the trial balance on a form as shown in Exhibit 3–10 (page 126), enter the adjusting entries, and prepare an adjusted trial balance on this form.
4. Prepare the income statement, the statement of owner's equity, and the balance sheet. Draw the arrows linking these three statements.
5. Post the adjusting entries into the T-accounts.

Name: Potter Employment Services
Industry: Service proprietorship
Fiscal Period: Year ended December 31, 2010
Key Fact: Existing, ongoing business

SOLUTION

Requirements 1 and 5

For Requirement 1, create a T-account for each account name listed in the December 31, 2010, trial balance on the previous page. Insert the opening balances into the T-accounts from the trial balance, ensuring debit and credit balances on the trial balance are debit and credit balances in the T-accounts.

To make sure all the account balances have been entered correctly, trace each T-account's balance back to the December 31, 2010, trial balance.

For Requirement 5, make sure each transaction is posted to the proper T-account, and make sure no transactions were missed.

ASSETS

Cash

Bal. 13,800	

Accounts Receivable

Bal. 10,000	
(e) 2,600	
Bal. 12,600	

Supplies

Bal. 2,000	(a) 1,600
Bal. 400	

Furniture

Bal. 20,000	

Accumulated Amortization—Furniture

	Bal. 8,000
	(b) 4,000
	Bal. 12,000

Building

Bal. 100,000	

Accumulated Amortization—Building

	Bal. 60,000
	(c) 2,000
	Bal. 62,000

Land

Bal. 44,000	

LIABILITIES

Accounts Payable

	Bal. 4,000

Salary Payable

	(d) 1,000
	Bal. 1,000

Unearned Service Revenue

(f) 6,000	Bal. 16,000
	Bal. 10,000

OWNER'S EQUITY

Rick Potter, Capital

	Bal. 64,000

Rick Potter, Withdrawals

Bal. 50,000	

REVENUE

Service Revenue

	Bal. 120,000
	(e) 2,600
	(f) 6,000
	Bal. 128,600

EXPENSES

Salary Expense

Bal. 32,000	
(d) 1,000	
Bal. 33,000	

Supplies Expense

(a) 1,600	
Bal. 1,600	

Amortization Expense—Furniture

(b) 4,000	
Bal. 4,000	

Amortization Expense—Building

(c) 2,000	
Bal. 2,000	

Miscellaneous Expense

Bal. 200	

Requirement 2

2010

a. Dec. 31   Supplies Expense 1,600
          Supplies.. 1,600
        To record supplies used ($2,000 – $400).

b. Dec. 31   Amortization Expense—Furniture................. 4,000
          Accumulated Amortization—Furniture ... 4,000
        To record amortization expense on furniture.

c. Dec. 31   Amortization Expense—Building 2,000
          Accumulated Amortization—Building..... 2,000
        To record amortization expense on building.

d. Dec. 31   Salary Expense 1,000
          Salary Payable... 1,000
        To accrue salary expense.

e. Dec. 31   Accounts Receivable... 2,600
          Service Revenue... 2,600
        To accrue service revenue.

f. Dec. 31   Unearned Service Revenue 6,000
          Service Revenue... 6,000
        To record unearned service revenue that has been earned.

Refer to the rules of debit and credit shown in Chapter 2, Exhibit 2–7, on page 61.

Make sure that Assets = Liabilities + Owner's equity for each transaction before going to the next transaction.

Selected transactions are explained more fully:

a. On the December 31, 2010, trial balance, Supplies has a balance of $2,000. If the supplies on hand at year end are $400, then make an adjusting entry for the $1,600 of supplies that were used ($2,000 – $400). Increase Supplies Expense (expense) and decrease Supplies (assets).

The remaining transactions do not require further calculations to determine the amounts of the adjustments.

Requirement 3

Write the account balances from the December 31, 2010, trial balance in the first two columns (the Trial Balance columns). Write the adjustment amounts from Requirement 2 in the next two columns. For each account name, add across (or subtract) the amounts in the first four columns to fill in the Adjusted Trial Balance columns. Ensure total debits equal total credits for each pair of columns, then double underline the totals to show they are final.

POTTER EMPLOYMENT SERVICES
Preparation of Adjusted Trial Balance
December 31, 2010

Account Title	Trial Balance Debit	Trial Balance Credit	Adjustments Debit	Adjustments Credit	Adjusted Trial Balance Debit	Adjusted Trial Balance Credit
Cash	13,800				13,800	
Accounts receivable	10,000		(e) 2,600		12,600	
Supplies	2,000			(a) 1,600	400	
Furniture	20,000				20,000	
Accumulated amortization —furniture		8,000		(b) 4,000		12,000
Building	100,000				100,000	
Accumulated amortization —building		60,000		(c) 2,000		62,000
Land	44,000				44,000	
Accounts payable		4,000				4,000
Salary payable		0		(d) 1,000		1,000
Unearned service revenue		16,000	(f) 6,000			10,000
Rick Potter, capital		64,000				64,000
Rick Potter, withdrawals	50,000				50,000	
Service revenue		120,000		(e) 2,600 (f) 6,000		128,600
Salary expense	32,000		(d) 1,000		33,000	
Supplies expense	0		(a) 1,600		1,600	
Amortization expense —furniture	0		(b) 4,000		4,000	
Amortization expense —building	0		(c) 2,000		2,000	
Miscellaneous expense	200				200	
	272,000	272,000	17,200	17,200	281,600	281,600

Requirement 4

POTTER EMPLOYMENT SERVICES
Income Statement
For the Year Ended December 31, 2010

Revenues:		
Service revenue		$128,600
Expenses:		
Salary expense	$33,000	
Amortization expense—furniture	4,000	
Amortization expense—building	2,000	
Supplies expense	1,600	
Miscellaneous expense	200	
Total expenses		40,800
Net income		$ 87,800

The title must include the name of the company, "Income Statement," and the specific period of time covered. It is critical that the time period be defined.

Gather all the revenue and expense account names and amounts from the Adjusted Trial Balance columns of the work sheet.

Expenses are listed here from highest to lowest dollar amount, with Miscellaneous Expense always listed as the final expense item. They could also be listed alphabetically.

POTTER EMPLOYMENT SERVICES
Statement of Owner's Equity
For the Year Ended December 31, 2010

R. Potter, capital, January 1, 2010	$ 64,000
Add: Net income	87,800
	151,800
Less: Withdrawals	50,000
R. Potter, capital, December 31, 2010	$101,800

(1)

The title must include the name of the company, "Statement of Owner's Equity," and the specific period of time covered. It is critical that the time period be defined.

Beginning owner's equity and withdrawals are from the Adjusted Trial Balance columns of the work sheet.

The net income amount is transferred from the income statement.

POTTER EMPLOYMENT SERVICES
Balance Sheet
December 31, 2010

(2)

Assets			Liabilities		
Cash		$ 13,800	Accounts payable		$ 4,000
Accounts			Salary payable		1,000
receivable		12,600	Unearned service		
Supplies		400	revenue		10,000
Furniture	$ 20,000		Total liabilities		15,000
Less: Accumulated					
amortization	12,000	8,000	**Owner's Equity**		
Building	100,000		R. Potter, capital		101,800
Less: Accumulated					
amortization	62,000	38,000			
Land		44,000			
			Total liabilities and		
Total assets		$116,800	owner's equity		$116,800

The title must include the name of the company, "Balance Sheet," and the date of the balance sheet. It shows the financial position on one specific date.

Gather all the asset and liability accounts and amounts from the Adjusted Trial Balance columns of the form. The owner's equity amount is transferred from the statement of owner's equity.

It is vital that Total assets = Total liabilities + Owner's equity.

Summary

1. **Distinguish accrual-basis accounting from cash-basis accounting.** In *accrual-basis accounting*, business events are recorded as they occur. In *cash-basis accounting*, only those events that affect cash are recorded. The cash basis omits important events such as purchases and sales of assets on account. It also distorts the financial statements by labelling as expenses those cash payments that have long-term effects, such as the purchases of buildings and equipment. The generally accepted method of accounting is the accrual basis.

2. **Apply the recognition criteria for revenues and expenses.** Businesses divide time into definite periods—such as a month, a quarter, and a year—to report the entity's financial statements. The year is the basic *accounting period*, but companies prepare financial statements as often as they need the information. Accountants have developed the *recognition criteria for revenues* to determine when to record revenue and the amount of revenue to record. The *matching objective* guides the accounting for expenses. It directs accountants to match expenses against the revenues earned during a particular period of time.

3. **Make adjusting entries.** *Adjusting entries* are a result of the accrual basis of accounting. Made at the end of the period, these entries update the accounts for preparation of the financial statements. Adjusting entries can be divided into five categories: *prepaid expenses, amortization, accrued expenses, accrued revenues,* and *unearned revenues.*

4. **Prepare an adjusted trial balance.** To prepare the *adjusted trial balance* using a form with columns, enter the adjusting entries next to the *unadjusted trial balance* and compute each account's balance by adding or subtracting horizontally.

5. **Prepare the financial statements from the adjusted trial balance.** The adjusted trial balance can be used to prepare the financial statements. The three financial statements are related as follows: Income, shown on the *income statement*, increases the owner's capital, which also appears on the *statement of owner's equity*. The ending balance of capital is the last amount reported on the *balance sheet*.

6. **Describe the adjusting-process implications of international financial reporting standards (IFRS).** The introduction of international financial reporting standards (IFRS) will have no significant impact on the adjusting process, as accrual accounting is still necessary.

CHAPTER 3 APPENDIX

Alternative Treatment of Accounting for Prepaid Expenses and Unearned Revenues

OBJECTIVE **A1**
Account for a prepaid expense recorded initially as an expense

Chapters 1 through 3 illustrate the most popular way to account for prepaid expenses and unearned revenues. This appendix illustrates an alternative—and equally appropriate—approach to handling prepaid expenses and unearned revenues.

Prepaid Expenses

Prepaid expenses are advance payments of expenses. Prepaid Insurance, Prepaid Rent, Prepaid Advertising, and Prepaid Legal Cost are prepaid expenses. Supplies that will be used up in the current period or within one year are also accounted for as prepaid expenses.

When a business prepays an expense—insurance, for example—it can debit an *asset* account (Prepaid Insurance) as illustrated on page 115 as follows:

Aug. 1	Prepaid Insurance	3,600	
	Cash		3,600

Alternatively, it can debit an *expense* account in the entry to record this cash payment:

Aug. 1	Insurance Expense	3,600	
	Cash		3,600

Regardless of the account debited, the business must adjust the accounts at the end of the period to report the correct amounts of the expense and the asset.

Prepaid Expense Recorded Initially as an Expense

Prepaying an expense creates an asset, as explained under the "Prepaid Insurance" heading on page 115. However, the asset may be so short-lived that it will expire in the current accounting period—within one year or less. Thus the accountant may decide to debit the prepayment to an expense account at the time of payment. A $4,800 cash payment for an advertising contract (for one year, in advance) on August 1, 2010, may be debited to Advertising Expense:

2010

Aug. 1	Advertising Expense	4,800	
	Cash		4,800
	Bought a 12-month advertising contract.		

At December 31, 2010, only five months' prepayment has expired, leaving seven months' advertising still prepaid. In this case, the accountant must transfer $7/12$ of the original prepayment of $4,800, or $2,800, to Prepaid Advertising. At December 31, 2010, the business still has the benefit of the prepayment for January through July of 2011. The December 31, 2010, adjusting entry is as follows:

Adjusting Entries

2010

Dec. 31	Prepaid Advertising................................	2,800	
	Advertising Expense		2,800
	Prepaid advertising of $2,800 ($4,800 × $7/12$).		

After posting, the two accounts appear as follows:

ASSETS	EXPENSES
Prepaid Advertising	**Advertising Expense**

2010		2010	2010
Dec. 31 Adj. 2,800		Aug. 1 Payment 4,800	Dec. 31 Adj. 2,800
Dec. 31 Bal. 2,800		Dec. 31 Bal. 2,000	

7 months remaining	**5 months expired**

The balance sheet for 2010 reports Prepaid Advertising of $2,800, and the income statement for 2010 reports Advertising Expense of $2,000, regardless of whether the business initially debits the prepayment to an asset account or to an expense account.

Unearned (Deferred) Revenues

Unearned (deferred) revenues arise when a business collects cash in advance of earning the revenue. The recognition of revenue is *deferred* until later when it is earned. Unearned revenues are liabilities because the business that receives cash owes the other party goods or services to be delivered later.

Unearned (Deferred) Revenue Recorded Initially as a Revenue

OBJECTIVE A2

Account for an unearned (deferred) revenue recorded initially as a revenue

Receipt of cash in advance of earning the revenue creates a liability, as discussed on page 121. Another way to account for the initial receipt of cash is to credit a *revenue* account when the business receives the cash. If the business then earns all the revenue within the period during which it received the cash, no adjusting entry is needed at the end of the period. However, if the business earns only a part of the revenue during the period, it must make adjusting entries.

Suppose on October 1, 2010, a consulting firm records as consulting revenue the receipt of $18,000 cash for revenue to be earned over nine months. The cash receipt entry is

2010			
Oct. 1	Cash..	18,000	
	Consulting Revenue...........................		18,000
	Received revenue to be earned over nine months.		

At December 31 the firm has earned only $3/9$ of the $18,000, or $6,000. Accordingly, the firm makes an adjusting entry, to transfer the unearned portion ($6/9$ of $18,000, or $12,000) from the revenue account to a liability account as follows:

Adjusting Entries

2010			
Dec. 31	Consulting Revenue	12,000	
	Unearned Consulting Revenue		12,000
	Adjust for consulting revenue still to be earned.		

The adjusting entry moves the unearned portion ($6/9$, or $12,000) of the original amount into the liability account because the consulting firm still owes consulting service to the client during January through June of 2011. After posting, the total amount ($18,000) is properly divided between the liability account ($12,000) and the revenue account ($6,000), as follows:

KEY POINT

The required adjusting entry depends on the way the transaction was originally recorded.

(1) If the receipt of cash is recorded as a liability before it is earned, what adjusting entry is required?

(2) If the receipt of cash is originally recorded as revenue, what adjusting entry is required?

A:

(1)

Unearned Revenue   XX
    Revenue   XX

(2)

Revenue   XX
    Unearned Revenue   XX

These entries are not interchangeable.

LIABILITIES		**REVENUE**	
Unearned Consulting Revenue		**Consulting Revenue**	
	2010	2010	2010
	Dec. 31 Adj. 12,000	Dec. 31 Adj. 12,000	Oct. 1 Receipt 18,000
	Dec. 31 Bal. 12,000		Dec. 31 Bal. 6,000

$2/3$ of the balance is still unearned. $1/3$ of the balance is earned.

The firm's 2010 income statement reports consulting revenue of $6,000, and the balance sheet at December 31, 2010, reports as a liability the unearned consulting revenue of $12,000, regardless of whether the business initially credits a liability account or a revenue account.

SELF-STUDY QUESTIONS

Test your understanding of the chapter by marking the correct answer for each of the following questions:

1. Accrual-basis accounting (*p. 109*)
   a. Results in higher income than cash-basis accounting
   b. Leads to the reporting of more complete information than does cash-basis accounting
   c. Is not acceptable under GAAP
   d. Omits adjusting entries at the end of the period

2. Under the recognition criteria for revenues, revenue is recorded (*pp. 111–112*)
   a. At the earliest acceptable time
   b. At the latest acceptable time
   c. After it has been earned, but not before
   d. At the end of the accounting period

3. The matching objective provides guidance in accounting for (p. 112)
   a. Expenses
   b. Owner's equity
   c. Assets
   d. Liabilities

4. Adjusting entries (p. 114)
   a. Assign revenues to the period in which they are earned
   b. Help to properly measure the period's net income or net loss
   c. Bring asset and liability accounts to correct balances
   d. Do all of the above

5. A building-cleaning firm began November with supplies of $210. During the month, the firm purchased supplies of $290. At November 30, supplies on hand total $160. Supplies expense for the period is (pp. 116–117)
   a. $160
   b. $340
   c. $290
   d. $500

6. A building that cost $120,000 has accumulated amortization of $70,000. The carrying value of the building is (pp. 118–119)
   a. $70,000
   b. $50,000
   c. $120,000
   d. $190,000

7. The adjusting entry to accrue salary expense (pp. 120–121)
   a. Debits Salary Expense and credits Cash
   b. Debits Salaries Payable and credits Salary Expense
   c. Debits Salaries Payable and credits Cash
   d. Debits Salary Expense and credits Salaries Payable

8. A business received cash of $3,000 in advance for service that will be provided later. The cash receipt entry debited Cash and credited Unearned Revenue for $3,000. At the end of the period, $1,100 is still unearned. The adjusting entry for this situation will (pp. 121–122)
   a. Debit Unearned Revenue and credit Revenue for $1,900
   b. Debit Unearned Revenue and credit Revenue for $1,100
   c. Debit Revenue and credit Unearned Revenue for $1,900
   d. Debit Revenue and credit Unearned Revenue for $1,100

9. The links among the financial statements are (pp. 128–129)
   a. Net income from the income statement to the statement of owner's equity
   b. Ending capital from the statement of owner's equity to the balance sheet
   c. Net income from the balance sheet to the income statement.
   d. Both a and b above

10. Accumulated Amortization is reported on (p. 129)
    a. The balance sheet
    b. The income statement
    c. The statement of owner's equity
    d. Both a and b

Answers to Self-Study Questions

1. b
2. c
3. a
4. d

5. b ($210 + $290 − $160 = $340)
6. b ($120,000 − $70,000 = $50,000)
7. d
8. a ($3,000 received − $1,100 unearned = $1,900 earned)

9. d
10. a

ACCOUNTING VOCABULARY

Accrual-basis accounting   (p. 109)
Accrued expense   (p. 120)
Accrued revenue   (p. 121)
Accumulated amortization   (p. 118)
Adjusted trial balance   (p. 125)
Adjusting entry   (p. 114)
Amortization   (p. 117)
Carrying value (of property, plant, and equipment)   (p. 119)
Cash-basis accounting   (p. 109)

Contra account   (p. 118)
Deferred revenue   (p. 121)
Matching objective   (p. 112)
Prepaid expense   (p. 115)
Property, plant, and equipment   (p. 117)
Recognition criteria for revenues   (p. 111)
Time-period assumption   (p. 113)
Unearned revenue   (p. 121)

SIMILAR ACCOUNTING TERMS

Accrual-basis accounting	Accrual accounting
Adjusting the accounts	Making the adjusting entries; adjusting the books
Amortization	Depreciation; depletion
Carrying value	Book value
Deferred	Unearned
Property, plant, and equipment	Capital asset; plant asset; fixed asset; tangible capital asset

Assignment Material

QUESTIONS

1. Distinguish accrual-basis accounting from cash-basis accounting.

2. How long is the basic accounting period? What is a fiscal year? What is an interim period?

3. What two questions do the recognition criteria for revenues help answer?

4. Briefly explain the matching objective.

5. What is the purpose of making adjusting entries?

6. Why are adjusting entries usually made at the end of the accounting period, not during the period?

7. Name five categories of adjusting entries and give an example of each.

8. Do all adjusting entries affect the net income or net loss of the period? Include the definition of an adjusting entry.

9. Why must the balance of Supplies be adjusted at the end of the period?

10. Manning Supply Company pays $3,600 for an insurance policy that covers three years. At the end of the first year, the balance of its Prepaid Insurance account contains two elements. What are the two elements, and what is the correct amount of each?

11. The title Prepaid Expense suggests that this type of account is an expense. If it is, explain why. If it is not, what type of account is it?

12. What is a contra account? Identify the contra account introduced in this chapter, along with the account's normal balance.

13. The manager of Quickie-Pickie, a convenience store, presents the company's balance sheet to a banker to obtain a loan. The balance sheet reports that the company's property, plant, and equipment have a carrying value of $135,000 and accumulated amortization of $65,000. What does *carrying value* of property, plant, and equipment mean? What was the cost of the property, plant, and equipment?

14. Give the entry to record accrued interest revenue of $500.

15. Why is unearned revenue a liability? Give an example.

16. Identify the types of accounts (assets, liabilities, and so on) debited and credited for each of the five types of adjusting entries.

17. What purposes does the adjusted trial balance serve?

18. Explain the relationships among the income statement, the statement of owner's equity, and the balance sheet.

19. Bellevue Company failed to record the following adjusting entries at December 31, the end of its fiscal year: (a) accrued expenses, $1,000; (b) accrued revenues, $1,700; and (c) amortization, $2,000. Did these omissions cause net income for the year to be understated or overstated and by what overall amount?

*20. A company pays $6,000 on February 1 to rent its office for February, March, and April. Make journal entries dated February 1 to illustrate the two ways this company can record its prepayment of rent.

*21. *Swim World Magazine* received $3,000 for magazine subscriptions in advance and recorded the cash receipt as Subscription Revenue. At the end of the year, only $1,400 of this revenue has been earned. What is the required year-end adjusting entry?

STARTERS

MyAccountingLab All questions in this section appear in MyAccountingLab.

Comparing accrual-basis accounting and cash-basis accounting

Service revenue:
Cash basis $600

Starter 3–1 Suppose you work summers house-sitting for people while they are away on vacation. Most of your customers pay you immediately after you finish a job. A few ask you to send them a bill. It is now June 30 and you have collected $600 from cash-paying customers. Your remaining customers owe you $1,400. How much service revenue would you have under the (a) cash basis and (b) accrual basis of accounting? Which method of accounting provides more information about your house-sitting business? Explain your answer.

Accrual-basis accounting versus cash-basis accounting for expenses

Starter 3–2 Smith Barnes Chartered Accountants uses a client database. Suppose the company paid $3,000 for a Dell computer. Describe how the company would account for the $3,000 expenditure under (a) the cash basis and (b) the accrual basis. State in your own words why the accrual basis is more realistic for this situation.

*These Questions cover Chapter 3 Appendix topics.

Starter 3-3 *Sports Unlimited* sells annual subscriptions for the 12 monthly magazines mailed to customers each year. The company collects cash in advance and then mails out the magazines to subscribers each month. Suppose the company collected $80,000 for subscriptions for January to December.

Apply the recognition criteria for revenues to determine (1) when the company should record revenue for this situation and (2) the amount of revenue the company should record for the January through March mailings.

Applying the recognition criteria for revenues

Starter 3-4 On April 1, 2010, you prepaid six months of rent, for a total of $12,000. Give your adjusting entry to record rent expense at April 30, 2010. Include the date of the entry and an explanation. Then, using T-accounts, post to the two accounts involved, and show their balances at April 30, 2010.

Adjusting prepaid expenses

Starter 3-5 On May 1, your company paid cash of $27,000 for computers that are expected to remain useful for three years. At the end of three years, the value of the computers is expected to be zero.

Make journal entries to record (a) purchase of the computers on May 1 and (b) amortization on May 31. Include dates and explanations, and use the following accounts: Computer Equipment; Accumulated Amortization—Computer Equipment; and Amortization Expense—Computer Equipment.

Recording amortization

(b) Amort. Expense $750

Starter 3-6 Refer to the data in Starter 3-5.

1. Using T-accounts, post to the accounts listed in Starter 3-5, and show their balances at May 31.
2. What is the computer equipment's carrying value at May 31?

Recording amortization

2. Carrying value $26,250

Starter 3-7 Suppose Ladner Environmental Services (LES) borrowed $50,000 on October 1 by signing a note payable to Royal Bank. LES's interest expense for the remainder of the year (October through December) is $600.

1. Make LES's adjusting entry to accrue interest expense at December 31. Date the entry and include its explanation.
2. Using T-accounts, post to the two accounts affected by the adjustment.

Accruing and paying interest expense

2. Interest Payable at Dec. 31 $600

Starter 3-8 *The Big Clipper Magazine* collects cash from subscribers in advance and then mails the magazines to subscribers over a one-year period. Give the adjusting entry that the company makes to record the earning of $10,000 of Subscription Revenue that was collected in advance. Include an explanation for the entry, as illustrated in the chapter.

Accounting for unearned revenues

Starter 3-9 Scissors Hair Stylists has begun the preparation of its adjusted trial balance as follows:

Preparing an adjusted trial balance

Adjusted trial bal. total $24,300

SCISSORS HAIR STYLISTS
Preparation of Adjusted Trial Balance
December 31, 2010

Account Title	Trial Balance Debit	Trial Balance Credit	Adjustments Debit	Adjustments Credit	Adjusted Trial Balance Debit	Adjusted Trial Balance Credit
Cash	600					
Supplies	800					
Equipment	16,200					
Accumulated amortization —equipment		1,100				
Accounts payable		500				
Interest payable		0				
Note payable		2,900				
Suzanne Byrd, capital		5,300				
Service revenue		13,000				
Rent expense	4,800					
Supplies expense	0					
Amortization expense	0					
Interest expense	400					
	22,800	22,800				

Year-end data:

a. Supplies remaining on hand, $200
b. Amortization, $1,100
c. Accrued interest expense, $400

Complete the company's adjusted trial balance. Identify each adjustment by its letter. To save time, you may write your answer in the spaces provided on the adjusted trial balance.

Note: Starters 3–10 and 3–11 should be used only after completing Starter 3–9.

Computing net income

Starter 3–10 Refer to the data in Starter 3–9. Compute Scissors Hair Stylists' net income for the year ended December 31, 2010.

Computing total assets

Total assets $14,800

Starter 3–11 Refer to the data in Starter 3–9. Compute Scissors Hair Stylists' total assets at December 31, 2010. Remember that Accumulated Amortization is a contra asset.

EXERCISES

Accrual-basis accounting

Exercise 3–1

Sorento Lodge had the following selected transactions during January:

Jan. 1 Paid cash for rent for January, February, and March, $4,200.
5 Paid electricity expenses, $600.
9 Received cash for the day's room rentals, $1,800.
14 Paid cash for six television sets, $6,000. They will last three years.
23 Served a banquet on account, $1,800.
31 Made an adjusting entry for January's rent (from January 1).
31 Accrued salary expense for January, $1,500.

Show how each transaction would be handled using the accrual basis of accounting. Give the amount of revenue or expense for January. Journal entries are not required. Use the following format for your answer, and show your computations:

Sorento Lodge—Amount of Revenue or Expense for January		
Date	Revenue (Expense)	Accrual-Basis Amount

Applying accounting assumptions, criteria, and objectives

Exercise 3–2

Identify the accounting assumption, criteria, or objective that gives the most direction on how to account for each of the following situations:

a. The owner of a business desires monthly financial statements to measure the financial progress of the entity on an ongoing basis.

b. Expenses of the period total $6,000. This amount should be subtracted from revenue to compute the period's income.

c. Expenses of $3,000 must be accrued at the end of the period to measure income properly.

d. A customer states her intention to switch travel agencies. Should the new travel agency record revenue based on this intention? Give the reason for your answer.

Applying the recognition criteria for revenues and the matching objective, accrual basis versus cash basis

1. Net income $8.6 million

Exercise 3–3

Dominion Storage operates approximately 300 mini-warehouses across Canada. The company's headquarters are in Medicine Hat, Alberta. During 2010, Dominion earned rental revenue of $26.0 million and collected cash of $23.6 million from customers. Total expenses for 2010 were $17.4 million, of which Dominion paid $15.9 million.

Required

1. Apply the recognition criteria for revenues and the matching objective to compute Dominion Storage's net income for 2010.
2. Identify the information that you did not use to compute Dominion Storage's net income. Give the reason for not using the information.

Exercise 3–4

Applying accounting concepts
②

Write a memo to your supervisor explaining in your own words the concept of amortization as it is used in accounting. Use the following format:

Date:	(fill in)
To:	Supervisor
From:	(Student Name)
Subject:	The concept of amortization

Exercise 3–5

 Excel Spreadsheet Template

Compute the amounts indicated by question marks for each of the following Prepaid Insurance situations. For situations A and B, make the needed journal entry. Consider each situation separately.

Allocating prepaid expense to asset and expense

A. Insurance Expense $6,000

	Situation			
	A	**B**	**C**	**D**
Beginning Prepaid Insurance	$ 4,200	$ 6,000	$16,800	$ 6,800
Payments for Prepaid Insurance during the year	19,800	?	13,200	?
Total amount to account for	?	?	30,000	15,600
Ending Prepaid Insurance	18,000	6,000	?	6,000
Insurance Expense	?	$12,000	$25,000	$ 9,600

Exercise 3–6

Journalize the entries for the following adjustments at January 31, the end of the accounting period:

Journalizing adjusting entries
② ③

a. Amortization, $5,000.

b. Prepaid insurance expired, $500.

c. Interest expense accrued, $400.

d. Employee salaries owed for Monday through Thursday of a five-day workweek; weekly payroll, $16,000.

e. Unearned service revenue that becomes earned, $2,000.

Exercise 3–7

Suppose the adjustments required in Exercise 3–6 were not made. Compute the overall overstatement or understatement of net income as a result of the omission of these adjustments.

Analyzing the effects of adjustments on net income
③

Exercise 3–8

Journalize the adjusting entry needed at December 31 for each of the following independent situations.

Journalizing adjusting entries
③

a. On July 1, when we collected $48,000 rent in advance, we debited Cash and credited Unearned Rent Revenue. The tenant was paying for one year's rent in advance. At December 31, we must account for the amount of rent we have earned.

b. The business owes interest expense of $7,200 that it will pay early in the next period.

c. Interest revenue of $2,400 has been earned but not yet received on a $60,000 note receivable held by the business.

d. Salary expense is $7,500 per day—Monday through Friday—and the business pays employees each Friday. This year December 31 falls on a Wednesday.

e. The unadjusted balance of the Supplies account is $13,500. The total cost of supplies remaining on hand on December 31 is $4,500.

f. Equipment was purchased last year at a cost of $200,000. The equipment's useful life is four years. It will have no value after four years. Record the year's amortization.

g. On September 1, when we paid $6,000 for a one-year insurance policy, we debited Prepaid Insurance and credited Cash.

Exercise 3–9

Recording adjustments in T-accounts

Service Revenue bal. $91,000

The accounting records of Event Planners include the following unadjusted balances at March 31: Accounts Receivable, $5,400; Supplies, $2,700; Salary Payable, $0; Unearned Service Revenue, $3,000; Service Revenue, $88,000; Salary Expense, $22,000; Rent Expense, $18,000, Utilities Expense, $12,000; and Supplies Expense, $0.

The company's accountant develops the following data for the March 31 adjusting entries:

a. Service revenue accrued, $2,000

b. Unearned service revenue that has been earned, $1,000

c. Supplies on hand, $700

d. Salary owed to employee, $2,000

Open T-accounts as needed and record the adjustments directly in the accounts, identifying each adjustment amount by its letter. Show each account's adjusted balance. Journal entries are not required.

Exercise 3–10

Explaining unearned revenues

Write a paragraph to explain why unearned revenues are liabilities rather than revenues. In your explanation use the following actual example: *Maclean's Magazine* collects cash from subscribers in advance and later mails the magazines to subscribers over a one-year period. Explain what happens to the unearned subscription revenue over the course of a year as the magazines are mailed to subscribers. Into what other account does the unearned subscription revenue go? Give the adjusting entry that *Maclean's Magazine* would make to record the earning of $75,000 of subscription revenue. Include an explanation for the entry.

Exercise 3–11

Preparing an adjusted trial balance

Adjusted trial balance total $75,200

Valley Cleaners, a cleaning service, started the preparation of its adjusted trial balance as follows:

	VALLEY CLEANERS Preparation of Adjusted Trial Balance June 30, 2010					
	Trial Balance		Adjustments		Adjusted Trial Balance	
Account Title	Debit	Credit	Debit	Credit	Debit	Credit
Cash	2,400					
Supplies	4,000					
Prepaid insurance	1,800					
Equipment	40,000					
Accumulated amortization —equipment		6,000				
Accounts payable		4,000				
Salary payable		0				
Unearned service revenue		1,200				
Les Valley, capital		17,000				
Les Valley, withdrawals	8,000					
Service revenue		44,000				
Salary expense	16,000					
Supplies expense	0					
Amortization expense	0					
Insurance expense	0					
	72,200	72,200				

During the six months ended June 30, 2010, Valley Cleaners

a. Used supplies of $500.

b. Used up prepaid insurance of $900.

c. Used up $2,000 of the equipment through amortization.

d. Accrued salary expense of $1,000 that still must be paid.

e. Earned $600 of the unearned service revenue.

Complete the adjusted trial balance. Identify each adjustment by its letter. To save time, you may write your answers directly in the spaces provided.

Note: Exercises 3-12 and 3–13 should be used only in conjunction with Exercise 3–11.

Exercise 3–12

Refer to the data in Exercise 3–11. Journalize the five adjustments, all dated June 30, 2010. Explanations are not required.

Exercise 3–13

Refer to the data in Exercise 3–11.

a. Compute Valley Cleaners' net income for the period ended June 30, 2010.

b. Compute Valley Cleaners' total assets at June 30, 2010.

Exercise 3–14

The adjusted trial balance below of Cleary Consulting is incomplete. Enter the adjustment amounts directly in the adjustment columns of the text. Service Revenue is the only account affected by more than one adjustment.

CLEARY CONSULTING
Preparation of Adjusted Trial Balance
May 31, 2010

Account Title	Trial Balance Debit	Trial Balance Credit	Adjustments Debit	Adjustments Credit	Adjusted Trial Balance Debit	Adjusted Trial Balance Credit
Cash	27,000				27,000	
Accounts receivable	57,000				62,600	
Supplies	8,000				6,400	
Office furniture	160,000				160,000	
Accumulated amortization		108,000				112,000
Salary payable		0				7,000
Unearned revenue		12,500				6,000
J. Cleary, capital		141,000				141,000
J. Cleary, withdrawals	65,000				65,000	
Service revenue		108,000				120,100
Salary expense	34,500				41,500	
Rent expense	18,000				18,000	
Amortization expense	0				4,000	
Supplies expense	0				1,600	
	369,500	369,500			386,100	386,100

Exercise 3–15

Make journal entries for the adjustments that would complete the preparation of the adjusted trial balance in Exercise 3–14. Date the entries and include explanations.

Exercise 3–16

Write a business memorandum to your supervisor explaining the difference between the unadjusted amounts and the adjusted amounts in Exhibit 3–10, page 126. Use Accounts Receivable in your explanation. If necessary, refer back to the discussion of Accrued Revenues on page 121.

Using an adjusted trial balance

Computing net income

a. Net income $24,200

 Excel Spreadsheet Template

Adjusting the accounts

Adjustments total $24,700

Journalizing adjustments

Explaining the adjusted trial balance

Business memos are formatted as follows:

Date:	(fill in)
To:	Supervisor
From:	(Student Name)
Subject:	Difference between the *unadjusted* and the *adjusted* amounts on an adjusted trial balance

Excel Spreadsheet Template

Preparing the financial statements
⑤

Net income $55,000
Preparing the income statement
⑤
1. Net income $469,250

Exercise 3–17

Refer to the adjusted trial balance in Exercise 3–14. Prepare Cleary Consulting's income statement and statement of owner's equity for the month ended May 31, 2010, and its balance sheet on that date. Draw the arrows linking the three statements.

Exercise 3–18

The accountant for Sandra Storm's business, Storm Technologies, has posted adjusting entries (a) through (e) to the accounts at December 31, 2010. Selected balance sheet accounts and all the revenues and expenses of the entity follow in T-account form:

Accounts Receivable

	103,500		
(e)	40,500		

Supplies

	18,000	(a)	4,500

Accumulated Amortization— Furniture

			22,500
		(b)	19,000

Accumulated Amortization— Electronic Equipment

			148,500
(c)	22,500		

Salary Payable

		(d)	6,750

Service Revenue

			607,500
		(e)	40,500

Salary Expense

	126,000		
(d)	6,750		

Supplies Expense

(a)	4,500		

Amortization Expense— Furniture

(b)	19,000		

Amortization Expense— Electronic Equipment

(c)	22,500		

Required

1. Prepare the income statement of Storm Technologies for the year ended December 31, 2010. List expenses in order from the largest to the smallest.
2. Were the company's 2010 operations successful? Give a reason for your answer.

Preparing the statement of owner's equity
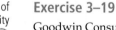⑤
1. Owner's equity, Dec. 31, 2010 $106,000

Exercise 3–19

Goodwin Consulting began the year on January 1, 2010, with capital of $65,000. On July 12, 2010, Eric Goodwin (the owner) invested $16,000 cash in the business. On September 26, 2010, he transferred to the company land valued at $70,000. The income statement for the year ended December 31, 2010, reported a net loss of $21,000. During this fiscal year, Goodwin withdrew $2,000 monthly for personal use.

Required

1. Prepare the company's statement of owner's equity for the year ended December 31, 2010.
2. Did the owner's equity of the business increase or decrease during the year? What caused this change?

Recording supplies transactions in two ways
Ⓐ①
Supplies Expense bal., $12,200

*Exercise 3–20

At the beginning of the year, supplies of $4,800 were on hand. During the year, the business paid $10,800 for more supplies. At the end of the year, the count of supplies indicates supplies of $3,400 on hand.

*These Exercises cover Chapter 3 Appendix topics.

Required

1. Assume that the business records supplies by initially debiting an *asset* account. Therefore, place the beginning balance in the Supplies T-account, and record the above entries directly in the accounts without using a journal.

2. Assume that the business records supplies by initially debiting an *expense* account. Therefore, place the beginning balance in the Supplies Expense T-account, and record the above entries directly in the accounts without using a journal.

3. Compare the ending account balances under both approaches. Are they the same? Explain.

*Exercise 3–21

Recording unearned revenues in two ways

Unearned Service Revenue bal. $3,500

At the beginning of the year, a business had a liability to customers of $7,500 for unearned service revenue collected in advance. During the year, the business received advance cash receipts of $20,000. At year end, the company's liability to customers was $3,500 for unearned service revenue collected in advance.

Required

1. Assume that the company records unearned revenues by initially crediting a *liability* account. Open T-accounts for Unearned Service Revenue and Service Revenue, and place the beginning balance in Unearned Service Revenue. Journalize the cash collection and adjusting entries, and post their dollar amounts. As references in the T-accounts, label the balance, the cash receipt, and the adjustment.

2. Assume that the company records unearned revenues by initially crediting a *revenue* account. Open T-accounts for Unearned Service Revenue and Service Revenue, and place the beginning balance in Service Revenue. Journalize the cash collection and adjusting entries, and post their dollar amounts. As references in the T-accounts, label the balance, the cash receipt, and the adjustment.

3. Compare the ending balances in the two accounts. Explain why they are the same or different.

*Exercise 3–22

Recording prepaids as expenses and unearned revenues as revenues, adjusting entries

Supplies Expense Cr $700

Fort Services initially records all prepaid expenses as expenses and all unearned revenues as revenues. Given the following information, prepare the necessary adjusting entries at December 31, 2010, the company's year end.

a. On January 3, 2010, the company's first day of operations, $2,500 of supplies were purchased. A physical count revealed $700 of supplies still on hand at December 31, 2010.

b. On January 4, 2010, a $15,000 payment for insurance was made to an insurance agency for a 30-month policy.

c. On June 30, 2010, Fort Services received nine months' rent totalling $13,500 in advance from a tenant.

SERIAL EXERCISE

Exercise 3–23 continues the Haupt Consulting situation from Exercise 2–15 of Chapter 2. If you did not complete Exercise 2–15 you can complete Exercise 3–23 by following the instructions in the note below.

Exercise 3–23

Adjusting the accounts, preparing an adjusted trial balance, preparing the financial statements

6. Adjusted trial balance total $17,993
7. Net income $1,207
Total assets $14,307

Refer to Exercise 2–15 of Chapter 2. Start from the trial balance and the posted T-accounts that Haupt Consulting prepared at December 18. Make sure the account balances in your trial balance and T-accounts match those in the trial balance at December 18, 2010, shown on the next page.

---

*These Exercises cover Chapter 3 Appendix topics.

Note: If you did not do Exercise 2–15, you can complete this Exercise by creating T-accounts for the accounts and balances given in the trial balance at December 18, 2010, shown below.

HAUPT CONSULTING Trial Balance December 18, 2010		
Cash	$ 7,600	
Accounts receivable	1,700	
Supplies	300	
Equipment	2,000	
Furniture	3,600	
Accounts payable		$ 3,900
Carl Haupt, capital		10,000
Carl Haupt, withdrawals	0	
Service revenue		2,500
Rent expense	1,000	
Utilities expense	200	
Salaries expense	0	
Total	$16,400	$16,400

Later in December, the business completed these transactions:

Dec. 21   Received $900 in advance for client service to be performed evenly over the next 30 days.

21   Hired a part-time secretary to be paid $1,500 salary on the 20th day of each month. The secretary begins work immediately.

26   Paid $300 for the supplies purchased on December 5.

28   Collected $600 from the consulting client of December 18.

30   Carl Haupt withdrew $1,600 cash for personal use.

Required

1. Open these T-accounts: Accumulated Amortization—Equipment; Accumulated Amortization—Furniture; Salaries Payable; Unearned Service Revenue; Amortization Expense—Equipment; Amortization Expense—Furniture; Supplies Expense.

2. Journalize the transactions of December 21 through 30.

3. Post to the T-accounts, identifying all items by date.

4. Prepare a trial balance at December 31. Also set up columns for the adjustments and for the adjusted trial balance, as illustrated in Exhibit 3–10 on page 126.

5. At December 31, the company gathers the following information for the adjusting entries:

   a. Accrued service revenue, $400.
   b. Earned $300 of the service revenue collected in advance on December 21.
   c. Supplies remaining on hand at December 31, $100.
   d. Amortization expense—equipment, $33; furniture, $60.
   e. Accrued $500 expense for the secretary's salary.

   Make these adjustments directly in the adjustments columns, and complete the adjusted trial balance at December 31.

6. Journalize and post the adjusting entries into the T-accounts. Label each adjusting amount as *Adj.* and an account balance as *Bal.*

7. Prepare the income statement and statement of owner's equity of Haupt Consulting for the month ended December 31, 2010, and prepare the balance sheet at that date.

CHALLENGE EXERCISE

Computing the financial statement

Supplies expense $10,000
Salary expense $91,000
Service revenue $166,000

Exercise 3–24

The adjusted trial balances of Pacific Services at December 31, 2010, and December 31, 2009 include these amounts:

	2010	2009
Supplies	$ 4,000	$ 2,000
Salary payable	5,000	8,000
Unearned service revenue	26,000	32,000

Analysis of the accounts at December 31, 2010, reveals these transactions for 2010:

Cash payment for supplies................................	$ 12,000
Cash payment for salaries	94,000
Cash receipts in advance for service revenue.	160,000

Compute the amount of supplies expense, salary expense, and service revenue to report on the Pacific Services income statement for 2010.

BEYOND THE NUMBERS

Beyond the Numbers 3–1

Suppose a new management team is in charge of Alpine Waters Inc., a micro-brewery. Assume Alpine Waters Inc.'s new top executives rose through the company ranks in the sales and marketing departments and have little appreciation for the details of accounting. Consider the following conversation between two executives:

John Ramsay, President: "I want to avoid the hassle of adjusting the books every time we need financial statements. Sooner or later we receive cash for all our revenues, and we pay cash for all our expenses. I can understand cash transactions, but all these accruals confuse me. If I cannot understand *our own* accounting, I'm fairly certain the average person who invests in our company cannot understand it either. Let's start recording only our cash transactions. I bet it won't make any difference to anyone."

Kate McNamara, Chief Financial Officer: "Sounds good to me. This will save me lots of headaches. I'll implement the new policy immediately."

Write a business memo to the company president giving your response to the new policy. Identify at least five individual items (such as specific accounts) in the financial statements that will be reported incorrectly. Will outside investors care? Use the format of a business memo given with Exercise 3–16 on page 146.

ETHICAL ISSUE

The net income of Corcorran's, a specialty store, decreased sharply during 2010. Mary Corcorran, owner of the store, anticipates the need for a bank loan in 2011. Late in 2010, she instructs the accountant to record a $35,000 sale of furniture to the Corcorran family, even though the goods will not be shipped from the manufacturer until January 2011. Corcorran also tells the accountant not to make the following December 31, 2010, adjusting entries:

Salaries owed to employees	$27,000
Prepaid insurance that has expired..................	1,500

Required

1. Compute the overall effect of these transactions on the store's reported income for 2010.

2. Why did Corcorran take this action? Is this action ethical? Give your reason, identifying the parties helped and the parties harmed by Corcorran's action.

3. As a personal friend, what advice would you give *the accountant*?

MyAccountingLab | All questions in this section appear in MyAccountingLab.

Applying accounting assumptions, criteria, and objectives

Problem 3–1A

As the controller of Best Security Systems, you have hired a new bookkeeper, whom you must train. She objects to making an adjusting entry for accrued salaries at the end of the period. She reasons, "We will pay the salaries soon. Why not wait until payment to record the expense? In the end, the result will be the same." Write a business memo to explain to the bookkeeper why the adjusting entry for accrued salary expense is needed.

This is the format of the business memo:

Date:	(fill in)
To:	New Bookkeeper
From:	(Student Name)
Subject:	Why the adjusting entry for salary expense is needed

Cash-basis versus accrual-basis accounting

2. Net income $2,200

Problem 3–2A

Kerr Office Design had the following transactions during January:

Jan.	1	Paid for insurance for January through March, $2,400.
	4	Performed design service on account, $7,000.
	5	Purchased office furniture on account, $2,100.
	8	Paid advertising expense, $1,800.
	15	Purchased office equipment for cash, $4,500.
	19	Performed design services and received cash, $5,000.
	24	Collected $3,500 on account for the January 4 service.
	26	Paid account payable from January 5.
	29	Paid salary expense, $7,200.
	31	Recorded adjusting entry for January insurance expense (see January 1).

Required

1. Show how each transaction would be accounted for using the accrual basis of accounting. Use the format below for your answer, and show your computations. Give the amount of revenue or expense for January. Journal entries are not required.

Amount of Revenue or Expense for January

Date	Revenue/Expense	Accrual-Basis Amount

2. Compute January net income or net loss under the accrual basis of accounting.

3. State why the accrual basis of accounting is preferable to the cash basis.

Journalizing adjusting entries

c. Supplies Expense $10,200

Problem 3–3A

Journalize the adjusting entry needed on December 31, the company's year end, for each of the following independent cases affecting Eagle Communications:

a. Each Friday the company pays its employees for the current week's work. The amount of the payroll is $12,000 for a five-day workweek. The current accounting period ends on Wednesday.

b. Eagle has received notes receivable from some clients for professional services. During the current year, Eagle has earned interest revenue of $800, which will be received next year.

c. The beginning balance of Supplies was $5,800. During the year the company purchased supplies costing $7,600, and at December 31 the inventory of supplies remaining on hand is $3,200.

d. The company is developing a wireless communication system for a large company, and the client paid Eagle $120,000 at the start of the project. Eagle recorded this amount as Unearned Consulting Revenue. The development will take several months to complete. Eagle executives estimate that the company has earned three-fourths of the total fee during the current year.

e. Amortization for the current year includes: Office Furniture, $9,600, and Design Equipment, $16,000. Make a compound entry.

f. Details of Prepaid Insurance are shown in the account:

Prepaid Insurance

Jan. 2 Bal. 6,000	

Eagle Communications prepays a full year's insurance on January 2. Record insurance expense for the year ended December 31.

Problem 3–4A

The trial balance of Kaplan Printing at December 31, 2010, appears below. The data needed for the month-end adjustments follow the trial balance.

Journalizing and posting adjustments to T-accounts, preparing and using the adjusted trial balance

(3) (4)

3. Adjusted trial bal. total $73,435

KAPLAN PRINTING
Trial Balance
December 31, 2010

Cash..	$ 5,400	
Accounts receivable..........................	18,600	
Prepaid rent	4,500	
Supplies	1,200	
Furniture and equipment	19,200	
Accumulated amortization—		
furniture and equipment		$ 5,760
Accounts payable..............................		3,400
Salary payable		0
Unearned printing revenue...............		2,400
S. Kaplan, capital.............................		23,140
S. Kaplan, withdrawals	6,000	
Printing revenue...............................		36,500
Salary expense	12,500	
Rent expense.....................................	0	
Amortization expense—		
furniture and equipment	0	
Advertising expense..........................	3,600	
Supplies expense...............................	0	
Miscellaneous expense......................	200	
Total	$71,200	$71,200

Adjustment data:

a. Unearned printing revenue still remaining to be earned at December 31, $800.
b. Prepaid rent still available at December 31, $3,000.
c. Supplies used during the month, $450.
d. Amortization for the month, $160.
e. Accrued miscellaneous expense at December 31, $200. (Credit Accounts Payable.)
f. Accrued salary expense at December 31, $1,875.

Required

1. Open T-accounts for the accounts listed in the trial balance, inserting their December 31 unadjusted balances.

2. Journalize the adjusting entries on December 31, and post them to the T-accounts. Identify the journal entries and posted amounts by their letter.

3. Prepare the adjusted trial balance.

4. How will the company use the adjusted trial balance?

Problem 3–5A

Wolcott Consulting's unadjusted and adjusted trial balances at December 31, 2010, follow:

	WOLCOTT CONSULTING			
	Unadjusted and Adjusted Trial Balances			
	December 31, 2010			
	Trial Balance		Adjusted Trial Balance	
Account Title	**Debit**	**Credit**	**Debit**	**Credit**
Cash	11,000		11,000	
Accounts receivable	8,500		14,100	
Supplies	1,100		300	
Prepaid insurance	3,600		2,400	
Furniture	22,500		22,500	
Accumulated amortization—furniture		9,000		11,250
Accounts payable		6,400		6,400
Salary payable		0		2,800
Interest payable		0		500
Note payable		15,000		15,000
Unearned consulting revenue		3,600		1,800
S. Wolcott, capital		33,550		33,550
S. Wolcott, withdrawals	28,000		28,000	
Consulting revenue		74,000		81,400
Amortization expense—furniture	0		2,250	
Supplies expense	0		800	
Utilities expense	4,600		4,600	
Salary expense	32,000		34,800	
Rent expense	30,000		30,000	
Interest expense	250		750	
Insurance expense	0		1,200	
	141,550	141,550	152,700	152,700

Required Journalize the adjusting entries that account for the differences between the two trial balances.

Excel Spreadsheet Template

Problem 3–6A

The adjusted trial balance of Cook Antique Auctioneers at the end of its year, December 31, 2010, is shown on the next page.

Required

1. Prepare Cook Antique Auctioneers' 2010 income statement, statement of owner's equity, and balance sheet. List expenses in decreasing-balance order on the income statement and show total liabilities on the balance sheet. If your three financial statements appear on one page, draw the arrows linking the three financial statements. If they are on separate pages, write a short paragraph describing how the three financial statements are linked. How will what you have learned in this problem help you manage a business?

2. a. Which financial statement reports Cook's results of operations? Were 2010 operations successful? Cite specifics from the financial statements to support your evaluation.

   b. Which statement reports the company's financial position? Does Cook's financial position look strong or weak? Give the reason for your evaluation.

COOK ANTIQUE AUCTIONEERS
Adjusted Trial Balance
December 31, 2010

Cash	$ 9,400	
Accounts receivable	166,000	
Prepaid rent	8,000	
Supplies	4,200	
Equipment	468,420	
Accumulated amortization—equipment		$ 72,000
Office furniture	96,000	
Accumulated amortization—office furniture		38,400
Accounts payable		56,000
Unearned service revenue		8,000
Interest payable		1,100
Salary payable		4,200
Notes payable		220,000
A. Cook, capital		129,520
A. Cook, withdrawals	92,000	
Service revenue		780,000
Amortization expense—equipment	36,000	
Amortization expense—office furniture	9,600	
Salary expense	320,000	
Rent expense	48,000	
Interest expense	13,200	
Utilities expense	21,600	
Insurance expense	13,200	
Supplies expense	3,600	
Total	$1,309,220	$1,309,220

Problem 3–7A

Consider the unadjusted trial balance of Burrows Landscaping at December 31, 2010, and the related month-end adjustment data.

Preparing an adjusted trial balance and the financial statements

2. Net income $6,050

BURROWS LANDSCAPING
Trial Balance
December 31, 2010

Cash	$ 24,500	
Accounts receivable	22,000	
Prepaid rent	9,000	
Supplies	1,500	
Equipment	66,000	
Accumulated amortization—equipment		$ 12,650
Accounts payable		7,200
Salary payable		0
A. Burrows, capital		122,700
A. Burrows, withdrawals	25,000	
Landscaping design revenue		126,000
Salary expense	82,000	
Rent expense	22,500	
Utilities expense	6,000	
Amortization expense—equipment	6,050	
Supplies expense	4,000	
Total	$268,550	$268,550

The following adjustments need to be made before the financial statements for the year can be prepared:

Adjustment data:

a. Accrued landscaping design revenue at December 31, $6,000.
b. Some of the prepaid rent had expired during the month. The unadjusted prepaid balance of $9,000 relates to the period December 1, 2010, through March 31, 2011.
c. Supplies remaining on hand at December 31, $900.
d. Amortization on equipment for the month of December. The equipment's expected useful life is 10 years; it will have no value at the end of its useful life, and the straight-line method of amortization is used.
e. Accrued salary expense at December 31 should be for one day only. The five-day weekly payroll is $10,000.

Required

1. Recopy the trial balance using the format in Exhibit 3–10 (page 126), and prepare the adjusted trial balance of Burrows Landscaping at December 31, 2010. Identify each adjusting entry by its letter.

2. Prepare the income statement and the statement of owner's equity for the year ended December 31, 2010, and the balance sheet at December 31, 2010. Draw the arrows linking the three financial statements, or write a short description of how they are linked.

Applying the recognition criteria for revenues and the matching objective, making adjusting entries, preparing an adjusted trial balance and income statement

2. Adjusted trial bal. total
$863,650

Problem 3–8A

Kessler Employment Counsellors provides counselling services to employees of companies that are downsizing. On December 31, 2010, the end of its first year of operations, the business had the following account balances (in alphabetical order):

Accounts payable	$ 93,600
Accounts receivable	23,200
Accumulated amortization—building	0
Accumulated amortization—computer equipment	0
Building	288,000
Cash	9,000
Computer equipment	69,000
Counselling revenue	367,000
R. Kessler, capital	330,000
R. Kessler, withdrawals	79,000
Land	144,000
Prepaid advertising	11,500
Salaries expense	120,000
Supplies	5,000
Supplies expense	24,500
Utilities expense	17,400

The following information was available on December 31, 2010:

a. A physical count shows $7,600 of supplies remaining on hand on December 31.
b. The building has an expected useful life of eight years, with no expected value after eight years. The building was purchased on January 2, and the straight-line method of amortization is used.
c. The computer equipment, purchased on January 2, is expected to be used for four years with no expected value after four years. The straight-line method of amortization is used.
d. On November 1, the company hired a marketing consultant and agreed to pay her $2,875 per month. The company paid her for four months' advertising, in advance.
e. The company's Managing Director, who earns $800 per day, worked the last six days of the year and will be paid on January 4, 2011.
f. On December 29, the company provided counselling services to a customer for $15,000, to be paid in 30 days.

Required

1. Journalize the adjusting entries required on December 31, 2010.

2. Prepare, with accounts in the correct sequence and expenses in alphabetical order, an adjusted trial balance on December 31, 2010.

3. Prepare an income statement for the year ended December 31, 2010.

*Problem 3–9A

Park Sales and Service completed the following transactions during 2010:

Aug. 31 Paid $15,000 store rent covering the six-month period ending February 28, 2011.

Dec. 1 Collected $8,000 cash in advance from customers. The service revenue earned will be $1,600 each month over the four-month period ending March 31, 2011.

Recording prepaid rent and service revenue collected in advance in two ways

Rent Expense bal. $10,000

Required

1. Journalize these entries by debiting an asset account for Prepaid Rent and by crediting a liability account for Unearned Service Revenue. Explanations are not required.

2. Journalize the related adjustments at December 31, 2010.

3. Post the entries to T-accounts, and show their balances at December 31, 2010. Posting references are not required.

4. Repeat Requirements 1 through 3. This time debit Rent Expense for the rent payment and credit Service Revenue for the collection of revenue in advance.

5. Compare the account balances in Requirements 3 and 4. They should be equal.

*Problem 3–10A

Sedin Consulting develops custom software for clients in the construction business. Sedin Consulting had the following information available at the close of its first year of business, June 30, 2010:

1. Insurance payments during the year were debited to Insurance Expense. An examination of the policies showed the following:
   - Policy 1: a two-year policy purchased on March 31, 2010, for $9,600.
   - Policy 2: a one-year policy purchased on July 2, 2009, for $3,600.

2. On July 2, 2009, the company purchased $2,000 of supplies and recorded the purchase as a debit to Supplies Expense. Throughout the year the company purchased additional supplies for $4,800, recording the purchase in the same way. An inventory count on June 30, 2010, showed that $3,200 of supplies remained on hand.

3. Computer equipment was purchased on January 2, 2010, for $48,000. The equipment was expected to be used for four years and then discarded.

4. The six employees each earn an average of $400 per day for a five-day week and are paid each Friday. June 30, 2010, is a Wednesday.

5. An examination of the contracts signed with clients showed the following:
   - Customer A signed a contract on September 1, 2009, and paid $48,000 to Sedin Consulting. The contract was for software that was to be completed in 12 months from the date of signing.
   - Customer B signed a contract on October 30, 2009, and was to make progress payments of $2,500 each month commencing November 1. The contract was for 30 months. Revenue was recognized on a monthly basis.

All money received to date on the two contracts was credited to Development Fees Earned. Any change to the contract amount will be made at the end of the contract.

Applying the recognition criteria for revenues and the matching objective, making adjusting entries, accounting for prepaid expenses recorded initially as an expense, accounting for unearned revenue recorded initially as a revenue

1. Insurance Expense adj. $8,400 Cr

Required

1. Journalize the adjusting entries on June 30, 2010.

2. Give the journal entry required to record the payment of wages on July 2, 2010. Since all employees are paid for the July 1 holiday, each was paid for five working days on July 2.

3. Calculate the *total effects* of the adjusting entries (parts 1 to 5) on each of the:
   a. Income statement
   b. Balance sheet

---

*These Problems cover Chapter 3 Appendix topics.

Applying accounting assumptions, criteria, and objectives

Problem 3–1B

Write a business memo to a new bookkeeper to explain the difference between the cash basis of accounting and the accrual basis. Mention the roles of the recognition criteria for revenues and the matching objective in accrual-basis accounting.

This is the format of a business memo:

Date:	(fill in)
To:	New Bookkeeper
From:	(Student Name)
Subject:	Difference between cash-basis and accrual-basis accounting

Accrual-basis accounting

Problem 3–2B

Khalil Speech and Hearing Clinic experienced the following selected transactions during October:

Oct.		
	1	Paid for insurance for October through December, $6,000.
	4	Paid utility invoice, $1,200.
	5	Performed services on account, $5,000.
	9	Purchased office equipment for cash, $8,000.
	12	Received cash for services performed, $4,400.
	14	Purchased office equipment on account, $2,400.
	28	Collected $3,000 on account from October 5.
	31	Paid salary expense, $4,400.
	31	Paid account payable from October 14.
	31	Recorded adjusting entry for October insurance expense (see October 1).

Required

1. Show how each transaction would be accounted for using the accrual basis of accounting. Use the format below for your answer, and show your computations. Give the amount of revenue or expense for October. Journal entries are not required.

Amount of Revenue or Expense for October		
Date	Revenue (Expense)	Accrual-Basis Amount

2. Compute October net income or net loss under the accrual basis of accounting.
3. Why is the accrual basis of accounting preferable to the cash basis?

Journalizing adjusting entries

Problem 3–3B

Journalize the adjusting entry needed on December 31, the company's year end, for each of the following independent cases affecting East Coast Contractors:

a. Details of Prepaid Rent are shown in the account:

Prepaid Rent		
Jan. 1	Bal.	4,500
Mar. 31		9,000
Sept. 30		9,000

East Coast Contractors pays office rent semiannually on March 31 and September 30. At December 31, part of the last payment is still available to cover January to March of the next year. No rent expense was recorded during the year.

b. East Coast Contractors pays its employees each Friday. The amount of the weekly payroll is $10,000 for a five-day workweek, and the daily salary amounts are equal. The current accounting period ends on Wednesday.

c. East Coast Contractors has lent money to help employees find housing, receiving notes receivable in return. During the current year the entity has earned interest revenue of $2,400 from employees' loans, which it will receive next year.

d. The beginning balance of Supplies was $5,100. During the year the company purchased supplies costing $18,500, and at December 31 the inventory of supplies remaining on hand is $5,500.

e. East Coast Contractors is installing cable in a large building, and the owner of the building paid East Coast Contractors $42,000 as the annual service fee. East Coast Contractors recorded this amount as Unearned Service Revenue. Robin Zweig, the general manager, estimates that the company has earned one-fourth of the total fee during the current year.

f. Amortization for the current year includes: Equipment, $11,500; and Trucks, $33,000. Make a compound entry.

Problem 3–4B

The trial balance of Wellwood Realty at December 31, 2010, appears below. The data needed for the month-end adjustments follow the trial balance.

Journalizing and posting adjustments to T-accounts, preparing the adjusted trial balance

WELLWOOD REALTY Trial Balance December 31, 2010		
Cash	$ 24,180	
Accounts receivable	44,500	
Prepaid rent	8,800	
Supplies	2,100	
Furniture	69,000	
Accumulated amortization—furniture		$ 34,500
Accounts payable		5,800
Salary payable		0
Unearned commission revenue		6,400
K. Wellwood, capital		75,180
K. Wellwood, withdrawals	12,000	
Commission revenue		48,000
Salary expense	7,200	
Rent expense	0	
Amortization expense—furniture	0	
Advertising expense	2,100	
Supplies expense	0	
Total	$169,880	$169,880

Adjustment data at December 31:

a. Prepaid rent still available at December 31, $6,600.

b. Supplies used during the month, $1,800.

c. Amortization on furniture for the month, $575.

d. Accrued salary expense at December 31, $600.

e. Unearned commission revenue still remaining to be earned at December 31, $2,500.

Required

1. Open T-accounts for the accounts listed in the trial balance, inserting their December 31 unadjusted balances.

2. Journalize the adjusting entries and post them to the T-accounts. Key the journal entries and the posted amounts by letter. Show the ending balance of each account.

3. Prepare the adjusted trial balance.

4. How will the company use the adjusted trial balance?

Problem 3–5B

Ohlund Construction's unadjusted and adjusted trial balances at April 30, 2010, are shown on the next page.

Analyzing and journalizing adjustments

OHLUND CONSTRUCTION
Adjusted Trial Balance
April 30, 2010

Account Title	Trial Balance		Adjusted Trial Balance	
	Debit	Credit	Debit	Credit
Cash	24,800		24,800	
Accounts receivable	25,600		29,200	
Supplies	4,900		1,100	
Prepaid rent	9,200		4,600	
Equipment	272,000		272,000	
Accumulated amortization—equipment		81,600		108,800
Accounts payable		29,000		29,000
Wages payable		0		4,200
Unearned service revenue		3,800		800
M.Ohlund, capital		124,100		124,100
M. Ohlund, withdrawals	53,000		53,000	
Service revenue		179,000		185,600
Wages expense	22,000		26,200	
Rent expense	0		4,600	
Amortization expense—equipment	0		27,200	
Supplies expense	0		3,800	
Utilities expense	6,000		6,000	
	417,500	417,500	452,500	452,500

Required Journalize the adjusting entries that account for the differences between the two trial balances.

Excel Spreadsheet Template

Preparing the financial statements from an adjusted trial balance

Problem 3–6B

The adjusted trial balance of Barnes Systems at December 31, 2010, is shown below.

BARNES SYSTEMS
Adjusted Trial Balance
December 31, 2010

Cash	$ 4,200	
Accounts receivable	28,500	
Supplies	5,200	
Prepaid rent	7,500	
Equipment	152,000	
Accumulated amortization—equipment		$ 38,000
Office furniture	60,000	
Accumulated amortization—office furniture		36,000
Accounts payable		14,800
Interest payable		500
Unearned service revenue		13,800
Notes payable		50,000
J. Barnes, capital		29,300
J. Barnes, withdrawals	77,000	
Service revenue		391,000
Amortization expense—equipment	19,000	
Amortization expense—office furniture	6,000	
Salary expense	145,000	
Rent expense	45,000	
Interest expense	3,500	
Utilities expense	7,200	
Insurance expense	4,800	
Supplies expense	8,500	
Total	$573,400	$573,400

Required

1. Prepare Barnes Systems' 2010 income statement, statement of owner's equity, and balance sheet. List expenses in decreasing-balance order on the income statement and show total liabilities on the balance sheet. If your three financial statements appear on one page, draw the arrows linking the three financial statements. If they are on separate pages, write a short paragraph describing how the three financial statements are linked. How will what you have learned in this problem help you manage a business?

2. a. Which financial statement reports Barnes Systems' results of operations? Were operations successful during 2010? Cite specifics from the financial statements to support your evaluation.

   b. Which statement reports the company's financial position? Does Barnes Systems' financial position look strong or weak? Give the reason for your evaluation.

Problem 3–7B

Preparing an adjusted trial balance and the financial statements

The unadjusted trial balance of LaBarbara Data at December 31, 2010, appears below. Adjustments had been made until November, but no adjustments for December have been made.

LABARBARA DATA
Trial Balance
December 31, 2010

Cash	$ 24,200	
Accounts receivable	38,500	
Prepaid rent	12,000	
Supplies	2,400	
Furniture	72,000	
Accumulated amortization—furniture		$ 13,800
Accounts payable		18,400
Salary payable		0
J. LaBarbara, capital		125,000
J. LaBarbara, withdrawals	46,000	
Consulting revenue		121,500
Salary expense	32,000	
Rent expense	33,000	
Utilities expense	12,000	
Amortization expense—furniture	6,600	
Supplies expense	0	
Total	$278,700	$278,700

Adjustment data:

a. Accrued consulting revenue at December 31, $3,300.

b. Prepaid rent had expired during the month. The unadjusted prepaid balance of $12,000 relates to the period December 2010 through March 2011.

c. Supplies remaining on hand at December 31, $900.

d. Amortization on furniture for the month. The estimated useful life of the furniture is 10 years, it will have no value at the end of the 10 years, and the straight-line method of amortization is used. Amortization expense had been taken for the first 11 months.

e. Accrued salary expense at December 31 for two days. The five-day weekly payroll is $6,000.

Required

1. Using Exhibit 3–10 (page 126) as an example, recopy the trial balance and prepare the adjusted trial balance of LaBarbara Data at December 31, 2010. Key each adjusting entry by letter.

2. Prepare the income statement and the statement of owner's equity for the month ended December 31, 2010, and the balance sheet at December 31, 2010. Draw the arrows linking the three financial statements, or write a short description of how they are linked.

Applying the recognition criteria
for revenues and the matching
objective, making adjusting
entries, preparing an adjusted
trial balance and income
statement

Problem 3–8B

Hilton Communications provides telecommunications consulting services. On December 31, 2010, the end of its first year of operations, the business had the following account balances (in alphabetical order):

Accounts payable	$ 18,000
Accounts receivable	17,100
Accumulated amortization—equipment	0
Accumulated amortization—furniture	0
Cash	9,000
Computer equipment	54,000
Consulting revenue	276,800
Furniture	120,000
H. Hilton, capital	96,000
H. Hilton, withdrawals	45,000
Prepaid advertising	11,000
Salaries expense	82,500
Supplies	3,900
Supplies expense	16,200
Travel expense	32,100

The following information was available on December 31, 2010:

a. A physical count shows $5,100 of supplies remaining on hand on December 31.
b. The computer equipment has an expected useful life of four years, with no expected value after four years. The computers were purchased on January 2, and the straight-line method of amortization is used.
c. The furniture, purchased on January 2, is expected to be used for eight years, with no expected value after eight years. The straight-line method of amortization is used.
d. On October 1, Hilton hired an advertising firm to prepare a marketing plan and agreed to pay the firm $2,200 per month. The business paid for five months' work in advance and has made no adjusting entries for this during 2010.
e. The company's office manager, who earns $400 per day, worked the last five days of the year and will be paid on January 5, 2011.
f. On December 30, Hilton provided consulting for a client for $5,000 to be paid in 30 days.

Required

1. Journalize the adjusting entries required on December 31, 2010. Identify the journal entries by their letter.

2. Prepare, with accounts in the correct sequence and expenses in alphabetical order, an adjusted trial balance on December 31, 2010.

3. Prepare an income statement for the year ended December 31, 2010. List expenses in alphabetical order.

Recording prepaid advertising
and flight travel revenue
collected in advance in two ways

*Problem 3–9B

Connect Air completed the following transactions during 2010:

Oct. 15 Paid $10,000 for advertising and promotional material covering the four-month period ending February 15, 2011.

Nov. 1 Received $15,600 payment in advance for a series of charter flights. Revenue of $2,600 will be earned each month over the six-month period ending April 30, 2011.

Required

1. Open T-accounts for Advertising Expense, Prepaid Advertising, Unearned Flight Revenue, and Flight Revenue.

2. Journalize these entries by debiting an asset account for Prepaid Advertising and by crediting a liability account for Unearned Flight Revenue. Explanations are not required.

3. Journalize the related adjustments at December 31, 2010.

4. Post the entries to the T-accounts, and show their balances at December 31, 2010. Posting references are not required.

5. Repeat requirements 1 through 4. This time debit Advertising Expense instead of Prepaid Advertising, and credit Flight Revenue instead of Unearned Flight Revenue.

6. Compare the account balances in requirements 4 and 5. They should be equal.

---

*These Problems cover Chapter 3 Appendix topics.

*Problem 3–10B

Applying the recognition criteria for revenues and the matching objective, making adjusting entries, accounting for prepaid expenses recorded initially as an expense, accounting for unearned revenue recorded initially as a revenue

O'Brien Construction specializes in industrial and commercial renovations. O'Brien had the following information available at the close of its first year of business, March 31, 2010:

1. On April 1, 2009, the company purchased $4,000 of supplies and recorded the purchase as a debit to Supplies Expense. Throughout the year, the company purchased additional supplies for $4,800, recording the purchases in the same way. An inventory count on March 31, 2010, showed that $2,400 of supplies remained on hand.

2. The 12 employees each earn an average of $420 per day for a five-day week and are paid each Friday. March 31, 2010, is a Wednesday.

3. An examination of the contracts signed with clients showed the following:
   • Customer A signed a contract on September 1, 2009, and paid $80,000 to O'Brien Construction. The contract was for a building renovation that was to be completed in eight months from the date of signing.
   • Customer B signed a contract on July 31, 2009, and was to make progress payments of $3,000 each month commencing August 1. The contract was for 60 months. The company has received three payments.

   All money received to date on the two contracts was credited to Construction Revenue. Any change to the contract amount will be made at the end of the contract.

4. Equipment was purchased on October 1, 2009, for $96,000. The equipment was expected to be used for eight years and then discarded.

5. Insurance payments during the year were debited to Insurance Expense. An examination of the policies showed the following:
   • Policy 1: a two-year policy purchased on December 31, 2009, for $9,600.
   • Policy 2: a three-year policy purchased on April 2, 2009, for $2,400.

Required

1. Journalize the adjusting entries on March 31, 2010.
2. Give the journal entry required to record the payment of wages on April 2, 2010.
3. Calculate the total effects of the adjusting entries (parts 1 to 5) on each of the
   a. Income statement
   b. Balance sheet

CHALLENGE PROBLEMS

Problem 3–1C

The basic accounting period is one year and all organizations report on an annual basis. It is common for large companies to report on a semiannual basis, and some even report monthly. Interim reporting has a cost, however.

You are working part-time as an accounting clerk for Paradise Corp. The company was private and prepared only annual financial statements for its shareholders. Paradise has gone public and now must report quarterly. Samantha Fleming, your supervisor in the accounting department, is concerned about all the additional work that will be required to produce the quarterly statements.

Required What does Fleming mean when she talks about "additional work"?

Problem 3–2C

The matching objective is well established as a basis for recording expenses.

Required

1. New accountants sometimes state the objective as matching revenues against expenses. Explain to a new accountant why matching revenues against expenses is incorrect.

2. It has been suggested that not-for-profit organizations, such as churches and hospitals, should flip their income statements and show revenues as a deduction from expenses. Why do you think that the suggestion has been made?

---

*These Problems cover Chapter 3 Appendix topics.

Extending Your Knowledge

DECISION PROBLEMS

Valuing a business on the basis of its net income

Decision Problem 1

Cameron Masson has owned and operated Alberta Biotech, a management consulting firm, since its beginning 10 years ago. From all appearances the business has prospered. Masson lives in the fast lane—flashy car, home located in an expensive suburb, frequent trips abroad, and other signs of wealth. In the past few years, you have become friends with him through weekly rounds of golf at the country club. Recently, he mentioned that he has lost his zest for the business and would consider selling it for the right price. He claims that his clientele is firmly established, and that the business "runs on its own." According to Masson, the consulting procedures are fairly simple, and anyone could perform the work.

Assume you are interested in buying this business. You obtain its most recent monthly trial balance, which follows. Assume that revenues and expenses vary little from month to month and April is a typical month.

Your investigation reveals that the trial balance does not include the effects of monthly revenues of $3,300 and expenses totalling $6,300. If you were to buy Alberta Biotech, you would hire a manager so you could devote your time to other duties. Assume that this person would require a monthly salary of $6,000.

ALBERTA BIOTECH Trial Balance April 30, 2010		
Cash	$ 29,100	
Accounts receivable	44,700	
Prepaid expenses	7,800	
Property, plant, and equipment	723,900	
Accumulated amortization—property, plant, and equipment		$568,800
Land	144,000	
Accounts payable		41,400
Salaries payable		0
Unearned consulting revenue		170,100
C. Masson, capital		172,200
C. Masson, withdrawals	27,000	
Consulting revenue		36,900
Salary expense	10,200	
Rent expense	0	
Utilities expense	2,700	
Amortization expense	0	
Supplies expense	0	
Total	$989,400	$989,400

Required

1. Is this an unadjusted or an adjusted trial balance? How can you tell?

2. Assume that the most you would pay for the business is 40 times the monthly net income you could expect to earn from it. Compute this possible price.

3. Masson states that the lowest price he will accept for the business is $450,000 plus the balance in owner's equity on April 30. Compute this amount.

4. Under these conditions, how much should you offer Masson? Give your reasons.

Decision Problem 2

The following independent questions relate to the accrual basis of accounting:

Understanding the concepts underlying the accrual basis of accounting

1. It has been said that the only time a company's financial position is known for certain is when the company is wound up and its only asset is cash. Why is this statement true?

2. A friend suggests that the purpose of adjusting entries is to correct errors in the accounts. Is your friend's statement true? What is the purpose of adjusting entries if the statement is wrong?

3. The text suggested that furniture (and each other property, plant, and equipment asset that is amortized) is a form of prepaid expense. Do you agree? Why do you think some accountants view property, plant, and equipment this way?

FINANCIAL STATEMENT CASES

Financial Statement Case 1

Explaining the effects of accruals and deferrals on the financial statements

During the year ended October 31, 2008, Canadian Western Bank (CWB) experienced numerous accruals and deferrals. As a long-term employee of CWB's accounting and financial staff, it is your job to explain the effects of accruals and deferrals on CWB's 2008 financial statements. (CWB's 2008 financial statements appear in Appendix A.) Suppose the following questions were raised at the shareholders' meeting in January 2009 (all amounts are in thousands of dollars):

1. "Prepaid expenses" in the amount of $3,520 thousand are listed on the October 31, 2008, balance sheet. What items could be included in this balance, and why is this account listed as a balance-sheet account instead of an expense account? (*Hint:* Refer to Note 12 for this balance.)

2. The balance sheet lists an account called Accrued Interest Receivable in the amount of $40,241 thousand at October 31, 2008. What would be included in this balance, and how would this amount normally be calculated?

3. Refer to Note 15 and "unearned premiums." How would this account have been created?

4. Refer to Note 16. "Accrued interest payable" is shown on the balance sheet in the amount of $101,584 thousand. Define an accrued liability and give an example of items to be included in this liability.

5. What is amortization, and how much amortization would have been recorded for the year ended October 31, 2008? (*Hint:* Refer to Note 8 for this amount.)

Financial Statement Case 2

Explaining the effects of accruals and deferrals on the financial statements

During the year ended December 31, 2008, Sun-Rype Products Ltd. experienced numerous accruals and deferrals. As a long-term employee of Sun-Rype's accounting and financial staff, it is your job to explain the effects of accruals and deferrals on Sun-Rype's 2008 financial statements. (Sun-Rype's 2008 financial statements appear in Appendix B.) Suppose the following questions were raised at the shareholders' meeting in February 2009 (all amounts are in thousands of dollars):

1. "Prepaid expenses" in the amount of $554 thousand are listed on the December 31, 2008, balance sheet. What items would be included in this balance, and why is this account listed as a balance-sheet account instead of an expense account?

2. Accounts payable and accrued liabilities are shown on the balance sheet in the amount of $15,229 thousand. Define an accrued liability.

3. What is amortization, and how much amortization would have been recorded for the year ended December 31, 2008?

4 Completing the Accounting Cycle

How do you complete the accounting cycle, and why is it important?

What are closing entries? How do closing entries differ from other journal entries?

Why are some types of accounts closed? How do decision makers evaluate a company?

These questions and others will be answered throughout this chapter. The Decision Guidelines at the end of this chapter will provide the answers in a useful summary.

LEARNING OBJECTIVES

1. Prepare an accounting work sheet
2. Use the work sheet to complete the accounting cycle
3. Close the revenue, expense, and withdrawal accounts
4. Correct typical accounting errors
5. Classify assets and liabilities as current or long-term, and prepare a classified balance sheet
6. Use the current ratio and the debt ratio to evaluate a company
7. Describe the accounting-cycle and financial-reporting implications of international financial reporting standards (IFRS)

CHAPTER 4 APPENDIX

A1. Describe and prepare reversing entries

It's a beautiful day in late spring in Vancouver, but you are still immersed in hockey as you watch the Vancouver Canucks play the Toronto Maple Leafs in the sixth game of the Stanley Cup Championship. The teams are playing a best-of-seven series and the Leafs lead the series three games to two. The Canucks need to win this game or Toronto will win the Stanley Cup.

The game is tied 1–1 at the end of the second period. Toronto scores early in the third period to take a 2–1 lead. The Canucks fight back and score the tying goal with two minutes to go. There is no more scoring in regulation time and the final result will be decided in overtime.

The game goes back and forth in overtime, before the Canucks finally score to force a seventh game back in Toronto.

When the teams return to Toronto to play the seventh game, what will the scoreboard say at the start of the game? Will it be 3–2 to carry over the score from the previous game or will the scoreboard be set back to zero? The answer is obvious: After a game is completed, the scoreboard is always set back to zero.

In the same way, the accounting process sets the scoreboard back to zero at the end of each fiscal year. The process is called "closing the books," and that is the main topic in this chapter. The logic behind the closing process in accounting is the same as setting the scoreboard back to zero after a game. The final step in the accounting process is preparing the financial statements.

Thus far, we have prepared the financial statements from an adjusted trial balance. That approach works well for quick decision making, but organizations of all sizes take the accounting process a step further. Whether it's General Motors or Ladner Environmental Services, the closing process follows the basic pattern outlined in this chapter. It marks the end of the *accounting cycle* for a given period, as shown in the margin.

The accounting process often uses a document known as the accountant's *work sheet*. Work sheets are useful because they summarize a lot of data, allow for changes, and aid decision making.

The Accounting Cycle

The **accounting cycle** is the process by which companies produce their financial statements for a specific period of time. For a new business, the cycle begins with setting up (opening) the ledger accounts. John Ladner started Ladner Environmental Services (LES) on April 2, 2010, so the first step in the cycle was to plan and open the accounts. After a business has operated for one period, such as for one month, the account balances carry over from period to period until the accounting cycle is complete, for example, at the end of one year. Therefore, the accounting cycle usually starts with the account balances at the beginning of the period. Exhibit 4–1 outlines the complete accounting cycle and shows examples of data and documents you see at each step. The work-sheet part of Step 5, and Steps 7 and 8, are the new steps that we will be discussing in this chapter.

The accounting cycle includes work performed at two different times:

- During the period—Journalizing transactions
  Posting to the ledger
- End of the period—Adjusting the accounts
  Preparing the financial statements
  Closing the accounts

The end-of-period work also readies the accounts for the next period. In Chapters 3 and 4, we cover the end-of-period accounting for a service business such as LES. Chapter 5 will show how a merchandising entity adjusts and closes its books.

Companies prepare financial statements on a monthly or a quarterly basis, and steps 1 to 6 in Exhibit 4–1 are adequate for statement preparation. Steps 7 and 8 can be performed monthly or quarterly but are necessary only at the end of the year.

1. Identify and analyze transactions

2. Record transactions in a journal

3. Post (copy) from the journal to the accounts in the ledger

4. Prepare the trial balance

5. Journalize and post adjusting entries

6. Prepare the financial statements

7. Journalize and post the closing entries

8. Prepare the postclosing trial balance

KEY POINT

The accounting cycle is repeated each accounting period. The goal of the cycle is the financial statements.

EXHIBIT 4–1   The Accounting Cycle

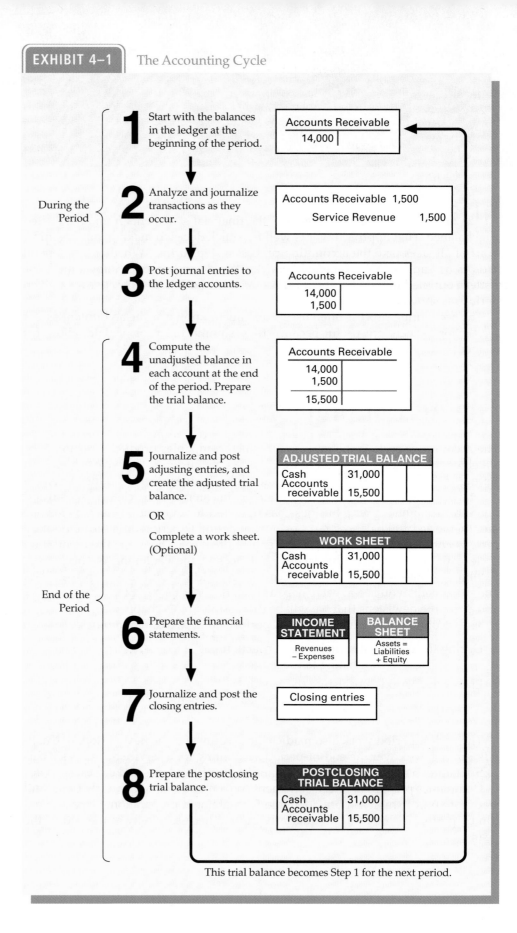

During the Period

1 Start with the balances in the ledger at the beginning of the period.

Accounts Receivable	
14,000	

2 Analyze and journalize transactions as they occur.

Accounts Receivable	1,500	
Service Revenue		1,500

3 Post journal entries to the ledger accounts.

Accounts Receivable	
14,000	
1,500	

End of the Period

4 Compute the unadjusted balance in each account at the end of the period. Prepare the trial balance.

Accounts Receivable	
14,000	
1,500	
15,500	

5 Journalize and post adjusting entries, and create the adjusted trial balance.

ADJUSTED TRIAL BALANCE			
Cash	31,000		
Accounts receivable	15,500		

OR

Complete a work sheet. (Optional)

WORK SHEET			
Cash	31,000		
Accounts receivable	15,500		

6 Prepare the financial statements.

INCOME STATEMENT	BALANCE SHEET
Revenues – Expenses	Assets = Liabilities + Equity

7 Journalize and post the closing entries.

Closing entries

8 Prepare the postclosing trial balance.

POSTCLOSING TRIAL BALANCE		
Cash	31,000	
Accounts receivable	15,500	

This trial balance becomes Step 1 for the next period.

The Work Sheet

OBJECTIVE ①
Prepare an accounting
work sheet

Accountants often use a **work sheet**, a document with many columns, to help summarize data for the financial statements. Listing all the accounts and their unadjusted balances helps identify the accounts that need adjustment. The work sheet aids the closing process by listing the ending adjusted balances of all the accounts.

The work sheet is not part of the journal or the ledger, nor is it a financial statement. Therefore, it is not part of the formal accounting system. Instead, it is a summary device that exists for the accountant's convenience. An Excel spreadsheet works well for an accounting work sheet.

Exhibits 4–2 through 4–6 illustrate the development of a typical work sheet for Ladner Environmental Services. The heading at the top displays the

- Name of the business (Ladner Environmental Services)
- Title of the document (Accounting Work Sheet)
- Period covered by the work sheet (For the Month Ended April 30, 2010)

A step-by-step description of its preparation follows, with all amounts given in Exhibits 4–2 through 4–6. Simply turn the acetate pages to follow from exhibit to exhibit.

Exhibit 4–2 *1. Print the account titles and their unadjusted ending balances in the Trial Balance columns of the work sheet, and total the amounts.* The account titles and balances come directly from the ledger accounts before any adjusting entries are prepared. Accounts are grouped on the work sheet by category (assets, liabilities, owner's equity, revenues, expenses) and are usually listed in the order in which they appear in the ledger (Cash first, Accounts Receivable second, and so on). Total debits must equal total credits.

Accounts may have zero balances (for example, Amortization Expense). All accounts are listed on the trial balance because they appear in the ledger. Electronically prepared work sheets list all the accounts, not just those with a balance.

Exhibit 4–3 *2. Enter the adjusting entries in the Adjustments columns, and total the amounts.* Exhibit 4–3 includes the April adjusting entries that we made in Chapter 3 to prepare the adjusted trial balance.

KEY POINT

Cash needs no adjusting entry
unless there is an error that needs
to be corrected. An error in cash is
a rare occurrence.

We can identify the accounts that need to be adjusted by scanning the trial balance. Cash needs no adjustment because all cash transactions are recorded as they occur during the period. Consequently, Cash's balance is up to date.

Accounts Receivable is listed next. Has Ladner Environmental Services earned revenue that it has not yet recorded? The answer is yes. At April 30, the business has earned $1,500, which must be accrued because the cash will be received during May. Ladner Environmental Services debits Accounts Receivable and credits Service Revenue on the work sheet in Exhibit 4–3. A letter is used to link the debit and the credit of each adjusting entry ("(e)" in this case).

By moving down the trial balance, the accountant identifies other accounts that need adjustment, such as Office Supplies. The business has used supplies during April, so it debits Supplies Expense and credits Office Supplies. The other adjustments are analyzed and entered on the work sheet as you learned in Chapter 3. After the adjustments are entered on the work sheet, the amount columns are totalled. Total debits equal total credits.

Listing all the accounts in their proper sequence aids the process of identifying accounts that need to be adjusted. But suppose that one or more accounts are omitted from the trial balance. Such accounts can always be written below the first column totals—$159,100. Assume that Supplies Expense was accidentally omitted and thus did not appear on the trial balance. When the accountant identifies the need to update the Office Supplies account, he or she knows that the debit in the adjusting entry is to Supplies Expense. In this case, the accountant can write Supplies Expense on the line beneath the amount totals and enter the debit adjustment—$500—on the Supplies Expense line. Keep in mind that the work sheet is not the finished version of the financial statements, so the order of the accounts on the work sheet is not critical. Supplies Expense should preferably be listed in its proper sequence on the income statement.

EXHIBIT 4–2 Trial Balance

LADNER ENVIRONMENTAL SERVICES
Accounting Work Sheet
For the Month Ended April 30, 2010

Account Title	Trial Balance Dr.	Trial Balance Cr.	Adjustments Dr.	Adjustments Cr.	Adjusted Trial Balance Dr.	Adjusted Trial Balance Cr.	Income Statement Dr.	Income Statement Cr.	Balance Sheet Dr.	Balance Sheet Cr.
Cash	31,000									
Accounts receivable	14,000									
Supplies	1,500									
Prepaid insurance	3,600									
Furniture	45,000									
Accumulated amortization —furniture		0								
Land	50,000									
Accounts payable		12,000								
Salary payable		0								
Unearned service revenue		3,000								
John Ladner, capital		120,100								
John Ladner, withdrawals	6,000									
Service revenue		24,000								
Amortization expense	0									
Insurance expense	0									
Rent expense	3,000									
Salary expense	4,000									
Supplies expense	0									
Utilities expense	1,000									
	159,100	159,100								
Net income										

Print the account titles and their unadjusted ending balances in the Trial Balance columns of the work sheet. Total the amounts.

Exhibit 4–4 *3. Compute each account's adjusted balance by combining the trial balance and the adjustment figures. Enter the adjusted amounts in the Adjusted Trial Balance columns.* Exhibit 4–4 shows the work sheet with the Adjusted Trial Balance columns completed. Accountants perform this step as illustrated in Chapter 3. For example, Cash is up to date, so it receives no adjustment. Accounts Receivable's adjusted balance of $15,500 is computed by adding the $1,500 debit adjustment to the trial balance debit amount of $14,000. Office Supplies' adjusted balance of $1,000 is determined by subtracting the $500 credit adjustment from the unadjusted debit balance of $1,500. An account may receive more than one adjustment, as does Service Revenue. In the Adjusted Trial Balance columns, total debits equal total credits.

Steps 1, 2, and 3 were introduced in Chapter 3 to prepare the adjusted trial balance. Steps 4 and 5 are introduced in this chapter.

Exhibit 4–5 *4. Extend (that is, transfer) the asset, liability, and owner's equity amounts from the Adjusted Trial Balance to the Balance Sheet columns. Extend the revenue and expense amounts to the Income Statement columns. Total the statement columns.* Every account is either a balance sheet account or an income statement account. The asset, liability, and owner's equity accounts go to the balance sheet, and the revenues and expenses go to the income statement. Debits on the adjusted trial balance remain debits in the statement columns, and credits remain credits. Generally, each account's adjusted balance should appear in only one statement column, as shown in Exhibit 4–5.

Total the *Income Statement* columns first, as follows:

Income Statement

- Debits (Dr)   Total expenses   = $13,550 ⎫ Difference = $12,950,
- Credits (Cr)   Total revenues   = $26,500 ⎬ a net income
                                                because revenues
                                                exceed expenses

Then total the *Balance Sheet* columns:

Balance Sheet

- Debits (Dr)   Total assets and   = $151,800 ⎫
                 withdrawals   ⎪ Difference = $12,950,
                                                    ⎪ a net income
- Credits (Cr)   Total accumulated   ⎬ because total debits
                 amortization, liabilities,   ⎪ are greater
                 and owner's equity   = $138,850 ⎭

Exhibit 4–6 *5. On the income statement, compute net income or net loss as the difference between total revenues and total expenses. Enter net income as a debit balancing amount on the income statement. Also add net income as a credit balancing amount on the balance sheet. Then total the financial statement columns.* Exhibit 4–6 completes the accounting work sheet, which shows net income of $12,950, computed as follows:

Revenue (total *credits* on the income statement) $26,500
Expenses (total *debits* on the income statement) 13,550
Net income $12,950

KEY POINT

Net income is the difference between the debit and credit Income Statement columns.

Net Income   Net income of $12,950 is entered as a "plug figure" in the Income Statement debit column. This brings total debits up to total credits on the income statement. Net income is also entered as a "plug figure" in the Balance Sheet credit column because an excess of revenues over expenses increases Capital, and increases in Capital are recorded by a credit. In the closing process, net income will find its way into the Capital account, as we shall soon see. After completion, total debits equal total credits in the Income Statement columns and in the Balance Sheet columns. The Balance Sheet columns are totalled at $151,800. This process is shown on the next page:

LADNER ENVIRONMENTAL SERVICES
Accounting Work Sheet
For the Month Ended April 30, 2010

	Trial Balance		Adjustments		Adjusted Trial Balance		Income Statement		Balance Sheet	
	Dr	Cr	Dr	Cr	Dr	Cr	Dr	Cr	Dr	Cr
Cash	31,000				31,000				31,000	
Accounts receivable	14,000		(e) 1,500		15,500				15,500	
Supplies expense	0		(b) 500		500				500	
Utilities expense	1,000				1,000				1,000	
	159,100	159,100	8,050	8,050	165,350	165,350	13,550	26,500	151,800	138,850
Net income							12,950			12,950
							26,500	26,500	151,800	151,800

Net Loss If expenses exceed revenues, the result is a net loss. In that event, *Net loss* is printed on the work sheet. The net loss amount should be entered in the *credit* column of the income statement (to balance out) and in the *debit* column of the balance sheet (to balance out). This is because an excess of expenses over revenue decreases capital, and decreases in capital are recorded by a debit. After completion, total debits equal total credits in the Income Statement columns and in the Balance Sheet columns, as shown here (amounts are assumed):

LADNER ENVIRONMENTAL SERVICES
Accounting Work Sheet
For the Month Ended April 30, 2010

	Trial Balance		Adjustments		Adjusted Trial Balance		Income Statement		Balance Sheet	
	Dr	Cr	Dr	Cr	Dr	Cr	Dr	Cr	Dr	Cr
Cash	31,000				31,000				31,000	
Accounts receivable	14,000		(e) 1,500		15,500				15,500	
Supplies expense	0		(b) 500		500				500	
Utilities expense	1,000				1,000				1,000	
	186,100	186,100	4,250	4,250	189,100	189,100	19,100	15,000	170,000	174,100
Net loss								4,100	4,100	
							19,100	19,100	174,100	174,100

DID YOU GET IT?

To check your understanding of the material in this Learning Objective, complete these questions. The solutions appear on MyAccountingLab so you can check your progress.

1. In a work sheet, where is each of the following accounts extended—Income Statement, debit column; Income Statement, credit column; Balance Sheet, debit column; or Balance Sheet, credit column?

a. Cash
b. Supplies
c. Supplies Expense

d. Unearned Revenue
e. Service Revenue
f. Owner's Equity

2. The trial balance of Curry's Service Company at December 31, 2010, the end of its fiscal year, is presented below.

CURRY'S SERVICE COMPANY
Trial Balance
December 31, 2010

Cash..	$ 6,000	
Accounts receivable	5,000	
Supplies	1,000	
Furniture...	10,000	
Accumulated amortization—furniture..............		$ 4,000
Building...	60,000	
Accumulated amortization—building................		30,000
Land	20,000	
Accounts payable...		2,000
Salary payable...		0
Unearned service revenue		8,000
Bill Curry, capital..		40,000
Bill Curry, withdrawals.....................................	25,000	
Service revenues..		60,000
Salary expense	16,000	
Supplies expense...	0	
Amortization expense—furniture......................	0	
Amortization expense—building	0	
Miscellaneous expense.......................................	1,000	
Total	$144,000	$144,000

Data needed for the adjusting entries are as follows:

a. Supplies remaining on hand at year end, $200.

b. Amortization on furniture, $2,000.

c. Amortization on building, $1,000.

d. Salary owed but not yet paid, $500.

e. Service revenues to be accrued, $1,300.

f. Of the $8,000 balance of Unearned Service Revenue, $3,000 was earned during 2010.

To plan your work sheet, check the adjusting entries data to see if the same account is affected more than once. If it is, leave 1 or 2 blank lines under the account name. Do this for Service Revenues on this work sheet.

Required

1. Prepare the work sheet of Curry's Service Company for the year ended December 31, 2010. Identify each adjusting entry by the letter corresponding to the data given.

2. If the company neglected to accrue a bonus of $50,000 in the Salary Expense account, what would the effect on the work sheet be?

Completing the Accounting Cycle

The work sheet helps organize accounting data and compute the net income or net loss for the period. It also helps accountants prepare the financial statements, record the adjusting entries, and close the accounts.

OBJECTIVE ②
Use the work sheet to complete the accounting cycle

Preparing the Financial Statements

The work sheet shows the amount of net income or net loss for the period, but it is still necessary to prepare the financial statements. (The financial statements can be prepared directly from the adjusted trial balance; see page 126. This is why completion of the work sheet is optional.) The sorting of accounts to the balance sheet and income statement eases the preparation of the statements. The work sheet also provides the data for the statement of owner's equity. Exhibit 4–7 presents the April financial statements for Ladner Environmental Services (based on the data from the work sheet in Exhibit 4–6). We can prepare LES's financial statements immediately after completing the work sheet.

EXHIBIT 4–7 April 2010 Financial Statements of Ladner Environmental Services

LADNER ENVIRONMENTAL SERVICES
Income Statement
For the Month Ended April 30, 2010

Revenues:		
Service revenue		$26,500
Expenses:		
Salary expense	$8,000	
Rent expense	3,000	
Utilities expense	1,000	
Amortization expense—furniture	750	
Supplies expense	500	
Insurance expense	300	
Total expenses		13,550
Net income		$12,950

LADNER ENVIRONMENTAL SERVICES
Statement of Owner's Equity
For the Month Ended April 30, 2010

John Ladner, capital, April 1, 2010	$120,100
Add: Net income	12,950
	133,050
Less: Withdrawals	6,000
John Ladner, capital, April 30, 2010	$127,050

LADNER ENVIRONMENTAL SERVICES
Balance Sheet
April 30, 2010

Assets			Liabilities		
Cash		$ 31,000	Accounts payable		$ 12,000
Accounts receivable		15,500	Salary payable		4,000
Supplies		1,000	Unearned service revenue		2,000
Prepaid insurance		3,300	Total liabilities		18,000
Furniture	$45,000				
Less: Accumulated			**Owner's Equity**		
amortization—			John Ladner, capital		127,050
furniture	750	44,250			
Land		50,000			
			Total liabilities and		
Total assets		$145,050	owner's equity		$145,050

Recording the Adjusting Entries

The adjusting entries are a key element of accrual-basis accounting. The work sheet helps identify the accounts that need adjustments. But, actual adjustment of the accounts requires journal entries that are posted to the ledger accounts. Panel A of Exhibit 4–8 repeats the LES adjusting entries that we journalized in Chapter 3. Panel B shows the postings to the T-accounts, with "Adj." denoting an amount posted from an adjusting entry. Only the revenue and expense accounts are presented in the exhibit in order to focus on the closing process, which is discussed in the next section. T-accounts, instead of ledger accounts, are used for demonstration purposes.

The adjusting entries can be recorded in the journal as they are entered on the work sheet, but it is not necessary to journalize them at the same time. Most accountants prepare the financial statements immediately after completing the work sheet. They can wait to journalize and post the adjusting entries before they make the closing entries.

Delaying the journalizing and posting of the adjusting entries illustrates another use of the work sheet. Many companies journalize and post the adjusting entries—as in Exhibit 4–8—only at the end of the year. The need for monthly and

KEY POINT

Adjusting entries must be journalized and posted prior to closing the accounts.

EXHIBIT 4–8   Journalizing and Posting the Adjusting Entries

Panel A: Journalizing Adjusting Entries   Page 4

Apr. 30	Insurance Expense	300	
	Prepaid Insurance		300
30	Supplies Expense	500	
	Office Supplies		500
30	Amortization Expense—Furniture	750	
	Accumulated Amortization—Furniture		750
30	Salary Expense	4,000	
	Salaries Payable		4,000
30	Accounts Receivable	1,500	
	Service Revenue		1,500
30	Unearned Service Revenue	1,000	
	Service Revenue		1,000

Panel B: Posting the Adjustments to the Revenue and Expense T-Accounts

REVENUE

Service Revenue

	24,000
	Adj. 1,500
	Adj. 1,000
	Bal. 26,500

EXPENSES

Rent Expense

3,000	
Bal. 3,000	

Salary Expense

4,000	
Adj. 4,000	
Bal. 8,000	

Amortization Expense—Furniture

Adj. 750	
Bal. 750	

Utilities Expense

1,000	
Bal. 1,000	

Supplies Expense

Adj. 500	
Bal. 500	

Insurance Expense

Adj. 300	
Bal. 300	

Adj. = Amount posted from an adjusting entry
Bal. = Balance

quarterly financial statements, however, requires a tool like the work sheet. The entity can use the work sheet to aid in preparing interim statements without journalizing and posting the adjusting entries.

DID YOU GET IT?

MyAccountingLab

To check your understanding of the material in this Learning Objective, complete these questions. The solutions appear on MyAccountingLab so you can check your progress.

3. Using the work sheet created in Did You Get It? Question 2, prepare the financial statements of Curry's Service Company.
4. Using the work sheet created in Did You Get It? Question 2, journalize and post using T-accounts the adjusting entries for Curry's Service Company.

We are now ready to move to the last step—closing the accounts.

Closing the Accounts

OBJECTIVE 3
Close the revenue, expense, and withdrawal accounts

Closing the accounts occurs at the end of the period. Closing prepares the accounts for recording the transactions of the next period and consists of journalizing and posting the closing entries. Closing results in the balances of the revenue and expense accounts becoming zero in order to clearly measure the net income of each period separately from all other periods. We also close the owner's withdrawals account to reset its balance to zero. The example regarding the hockey playoff game discussed at the beginning of this chapter illustrates this concept.

Recall that the income statement reports net income for a specific period. For example, net income for Molson Breweries for the year ended March 31, 2010, relates exclusively to the 12 months ended on that date. At March 31, 2010, Molson accountants close the company's revenue and expense accounts for that year. Because these accounts' balances relate to a particular accounting period (2010 in this case) and are therefore closed at the end of the period (March 31, 2010), the revenue and expense accounts are called **temporary (nominal) accounts**. For example, assume LES's year end is April 30, 2010. The balance of Service Revenue at April 30, 2010, is $26,500. This balance relates exclusively to the month of April and must be zeroed out before LES records revenue for May.

The Withdrawals account—although not a revenue or an expense—is also a temporary account, because it measures withdrawals taken during a specific period. The Withdrawals account is also closed at the end of the period. The closing process applies only to temporary accounts.

To better understand the closing process, contrast the nature of the temporary accounts with the nature of the **permanent (real) accounts**—the assets, liabilities, and owner's capital. The asset, liability, and owner's capital accounts are *not* closed at the end of the period because their balances are not used to measure income. Consider Cash, Accounts Receivable, Office Supplies, Buildings, Accounts Payable, Notes Payable, and John Ladner, Capital. These accounts do not represent *business activity* for a single period, as do revenues and expenses, which relate exclusively to one accounting period. Instead, the permanent accounts represent assets, liabilities, and capital that are on hand at a specific time. This is why their balances at the end of one accounting period carry over to become the beginning balances of the next period. For example, the Cash balance at December 31, 2010, is also the beginning Cash balance for 2011.

Closing entries transfer the revenue, expense, and withdrawal balances from their respective accounts to the Capital account. Recall that

REVENUES	*increase*	owner's equity
EXPENSES and WITHDRAWALS	*decrease*	owner's equity

It is when we post the closing entries that the Capital account absorbs the impact of the balances in the temporary accounts.

As an intermediate step, however, the revenues and the expenses are transferred first to an account entitled **Income Summary**. This temporary account collects in one place the sum of all the expenses (a debit) and the sum of all the revenues (a credit). The Income Summary account is like a temporary "holding tank" that is used only in the closing process. The balance of the Income Summary account is then transferred to the Capital account. Exhibit 4–9 summarizes the closing process. Start with Revenues at the far right and Expenses at the left. Work toward the middle and then down. Owner, Capital is the final account in the closing process.

EXHIBIT 4–9 The Closing Process

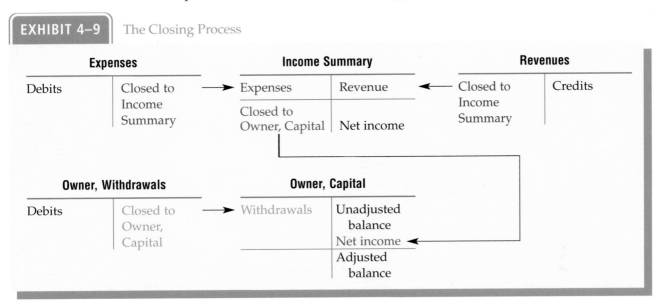

Closing a Net Income The steps in closing the accounts of a company like LES that has a net income are as follows (the circled numbers are keyed to Exhibit 4–10 on page 174):

1. Debit each *revenue* account for the amount of its credit balance. Credit Income Summary for the sum of the revenues.

   This closing entry transfers the sum of the revenues to the *credit* side of the Income Summary.

2. Credit each *expense* account for the amount of its debit balance. Debit Income Summary for the sum of the expenses.

   This closing entry transfers the sum of the expenses to the *debit* side of the Income Summary. It is not necessary to make a separate closing entry for each expense. In one closing entry, record one debit to Income Summary and a separate credit to each expense account.

3. The Income Summary account now holds the net income of the period, but only for a moment. To close net income, debit Income Summary for the amount of its *credit balance* (*net income* equals revenues minus expenses) and credit the Capital account.

   This closing entry transfers the net income from Income Summary to the Capital account.

4. Credit the *Withdrawals* account for the amount of its debit balance. Debit the Capital account.

   This entry transfers the Withdrawals amount to the *debit* side of the Capital account. Withdrawals are not expenses and do not affect net income or net loss.

KEY POINT

There is no account for Net Income, which is the net result of all revenue and expense accounts. The Income Summary combines all revenue and expense amounts into one account, and its balance should equal net income.

EXHIBIT 4-10 Journalizing and Posting the Closing Entries

Panel A: Journalizing

Closing Entries   **Page 5**

① Apr. 30   Service Revenue   26,500
                  Income Summary   26,500
                  To close the revenue account and create the
                  Income Summary account.

② 30   Income Summary   13,550
                  Amortization Expense—Furniture   750
                  Insurance Expense..   300
                  Rent Expense   3,000
                  Salary Expense   8,000
                  Supplies Expense...   500
                  Utilities Expense   1,000
                  To close the expense accounts.

③ 30   Income Summary   12,950
                  John Ladner, Capital   12,950
                  To close the Income Summary account and
                  transfer net income to the Capital account.
                  (Income Summary balance = $26,500 − $13,550).

④ 30   John Ladner, Capital..   6,000
                  John Ladner, Withdrawals   6,000
                  To close the Withdrawals account and transfer
                  the Withdrawals amount to the Capital account.

Panel B: Posting

Amortization Expense—Furniture

Adj.	750		
Bal.	750	Clo.	750

Insurance Expense

Adj.	300		
Bal.	300	Clo.	300

Rent Expense

Adj.	3,000		
Bal.	3,000	Clo.	3,000

Salary Expense

	4,000		
Adj.	4,000		
Bal.	8,000	Clo.	8,000

Supplies Expense

Adj.	500		
Bal.	500	Clo.	500

Utilities Expense

	1,000		
Bal.	1,000	Clo.	1,000

Service Revenue

			24,000
		Adj.	1,500
		Adj.	1,000
Clo.	26,500	Bal.	26,500

②

①

Income Summary

Clo.	13,550	Clo.	26,500
Clo.	12,950	Bal.	12,950

③

John Ladner, Withdrawals

Bal.	6,000	Clo.	6,000

④

John Ladner, Capital

Clo.	6,000		120,100
		Clo.	12,950
		Bal.	127,050

Adj. = Amount posted from an adjusting entry; Clo. = Amount posted from a closing entry; Bal. = Balance

These steps are best illustrated with an example. Suppose LES closes the books at the end of April. Exhibit 4–10 presents the complete closing process for the business. Panel A gives the closing journal entries, and Panel B shows the accounts after the closing entries have been posted.

The amount in the debit side of each expense account is its adjusted balance. For example, Insurance Expense has a $300 debit balance. Also note that Service Revenue has a credit balance of $26,500 before closing. These amounts come directly from the adjusted balances in Exhibit 4–8, Panel B.

- Closing entry ①, denoted in the Service Revenue account by *Clo.*, transfers Service Revenue's balance to the Income Summary account.
- Closing entry ② zeroes out the expenses and moves their total ($13,550) to the debit side of Income Summary. Income Summary's balance is the month's net income ($12,950).
- Closing entry ③ closes the Income Summary account by transferring net income to the credit side of John Ladner, Capital.
- The last closing entry, ④, moves the owner withdrawals to the debit side of John Ladner, Capital, leaving a zero balance in the John Ladner, Withdrawals account.

The closing entries set all the revenues, the expenses, and the Withdrawals account back to zero. Now the Capital account includes the full effects of the April revenues, expenses, and withdrawals. These amounts, combined with the beginning Capital's balance, give John Ladner, Capital an ending balance of $127,050. Trace this ending Capital balance to the statement of owner's equity and also to the balance sheet in Exhibit 4–7 on page 170.

Closing a Net Loss What would the closing entries be if LES had suffered a net *loss* during April? Suppose April expenses totalled $27,500 and all other factors were unchanged. Only closing entries ② and ③ would change. Closing entry ② would transfer expenses of $27,500 to Income Summary, as follows:

Income Summary

Clo.	27,500	Clo.	26,500
Bal.	1,000		

Closing entry ③ would then credit Income Summary to close its debit balance and to transfer the net loss to John Ladner, Capital:

③ Apr. 30 John Ladner, Capital 1,000
            Income Summary 1,000

After posting, these two accounts would appear as follows:

Income Summary					**John Ladner, Capital**		
Clo.	27,500	Clo.	26,500	Clo.	1,000		120,100
Bal.	1,000	Clo.	1,000				

Finally, the Withdrawals balance would be closed to Capital, as before. The double underline in a T-account means that the account has a final balance, which is zero in this case; nothing more will be posted to it in the current period.

The closing process is fundamentally mechanical and is completely automated in a computerized system. Accounts are identified as either temporary or permanent. The temporary accounts are closed automatically by selecting that option from the software's menu. Posting also occurs automatically. Many accounting programs allow for the beginning of a new period prior to closing the previous period. The reason for this is because time is needed to accumulate the information to properly adjust and close the accounts, but companies do not want to hold up the processing of the next period's transactions.

Postclosing Trial Balance

 Accounting Cycle Tutorials

6. Adjusting and Closing Entries pages 1–13

The accounting cycle can end with the **postclosing trial balance** (Exhibit 4–11). The postclosing trial balance is the final check on the accuracy of journalizing and posting the adjusting and closing entries. It lists the ledger's accounts and their adjusted balances after closing, and it is dated as of the end of the period for which the statements have been prepared.

EXHIBIT 4–11 | Postclosing Trial Balance

LADNER ENVIRONMENTAL SERVICES
Postclosing Trial Balance
April 30, 2010

Cash	$ 31,000	
Accounts receivable	15,500	
Office supplies	1,000	
Prepaid insurance	3,300	
Furniture	45,000	
Accumulated amortization—furniture		$ 750
Land	50,000	
Accounts payable		12,000
Salary payable		4,000
Unearned service revenue		2,000
John Ladner, Capital		127,050
Total	$145,800	$145,800

The postclosing trial balance resembles the balance sheet. It contains the ending balances of the permanent accounts—the balance sheet accounts: the assets, liabilities, and owner's equity. No temporary accounts—revenues, expenses, or withdrawal accounts—are included because their balances have been closed. The ledger is up to date and ready for the next period's transactions.

DID YOU GET IT?

MyAccountingLab

To check your understanding of the material in this Learning Objective, complete these questions. The solutions appear on MyAccountingLab so you can check your progress.

5. Would the Income Summary have a debit or a credit balance if a company suffers a net loss? In the event of a loss, how is Income Summary closed?
6. Using the work sheet created in Did You Get It? Question 2, journalize and post using T-accounts the closing entries for Curry's Service Company at December 31, 2010. (Each T-account should carry its balance as shown in the adjusted trial balance.) Provide an explanation for each journal entry.
7. Prepare the postclosing trial balance for Curry's Service Company at December 31, 2010.

Correcting Journal Entries

OBJECTIVE 4
Correct typical accounting errors

In Chapter 2 we discussed errors that affect the trial balance: treating a debit as a credit and vice versa; transpositions; and slides. Here we show how to correct errors in journal entries.

When a journal entry contains an error and the error is detected before posting, the entry can be corrected.

When a journal entry contains an error and the error is detected after posting, the accountant makes a *correcting entry*. Correcting entries can appear on the work sheet with the adjusting entries at the end of a period, but they can be journalized and posted as soon as the error is detected. Knowing how to detect and correct errors is a very important function in the preparation of accurate financial statements.

Suppose LES paid $10,000 cash for furniture and, in error, debited Office Supplies as follows:

Incorrect Entry

May 13	Office Supplies..	10,000	
	Cash...		10,000
	Bought supplies.		

The debit to Office Supplies is incorrect, so it is necessary to make the following correcting entry:

Correcting Entry

May 15	Furniture..	10,000	
	Office Supplies...		10,000
	To correct May 13 entry. Furniture was purchased.		

The credit to Office Supplies in the second entry offsets the incorrect debit of the first entry. The debit to Furniture in the correcting entry places the furniture's cost in the correct account. Now both Office Supplies and Furniture are correct. Cash was unaffected by the error because Cash was credited correctly in the entry on May 13. Most correcting entries will normally not involve cash since the cash balance is constantly compared with the cash balance in the company's bank account.

DID YOU GET IT?

MyAccountingLab

To check your understanding of the material in this Learning Objective, complete these questions. The solutions appear on MyAccountingLab so you can check your progress.

8. Suppose a company purchased $200 of supplies on account but in error debited Accounts Receivable for $200. Make the journal entry to correct this error.
9. Suppose the company from the previous question made the following journal entry to pay for the supplies purchased:

Accounts Receivable	200	
Cash		200
To pay for supplies purchased on account.		

   Is this an error? If so, make the journal entry to correct the error.
10. Suppose a company made the following journal entry to close its revenue accounts:

Income Summary..	60,000	
Service Revenue...		55,000
Other Revenue		5,000
To close the revenue accounts.		

   Make the journal entry to correct this error.

Classifying Assets and Liabilities

On the balance sheet, assets and liabilities are classified as either *current* or *long-term* to show their relative liquidity. **Liquidity** is a measure of how quickly an item can be converted to cash. Cash is the most liquid asset. Accounts receivable is a relatively liquid asset because the business expects to collect the amount in cash in the near future. Supplies are less liquid than accounts receivable, and furniture and buildings are even less so.

Users of financial statements are interested in liquidity because business difficulties often arise from a shortage of cash. How quickly can the business convert an asset to cash and pay a debt? How soon must a liability be paid? These are questions of liquidity. A classified balance sheet lists assets and liabilities in the order of their relative liquidity.

Assets

Current Assets **Current assets** are assets that are expected to be converted to cash, sold, or consumed during the next 12 months or within the business's normal operating cycle if longer than a year. The **operating cycle** is the time span during which

1. Cash is used to acquire goods and services.
2. Those goods and services are sold to customers.
3. The business collects cash from those customers.

For most businesses, the operating cycle is a few months. A few types of business have operating cycles longer than a year. Cash, Accounts Receivable, Notes Receivable due within a year or less, Supplies, and Prepaid Expenses are all current assets. Merchandising entities such as The Bay and Canadian Tire and manufacturing entities such as Magna International Inc. and Bombardier Inc. have an additional current asset, Inventory. This account shows the cost of goods that are held for sale to customers.

Long-Term Assets **Long-term assets** are all assets not classified as current assets. Long-term assets include property, plant, and equipment; goodwill; and intangible assets. **Property, plant, and equipment** includes the accounts Land, Buildings, Furniture and Fixtures, and Equipment. Of these, LES has only Furniture and Land.

Other categories of long-term assets are Long-Term Investments and Other Assets (a catch-all category for assets that are not classified more precisely). We discuss these categories in more detail in later chapters.

Liabilities

Financial statement users (such as creditors) are interested in the due dates of an entity's liabilities. Liabilities that must be paid the soonest create the greatest strain on cash. Therefore, the balance sheet lists liabilities in the order they are due to be paid. Balance sheets usually have at least two liability classifications, *current liabilities* and *long-term liabilities*. Knowing how many of a business's liabilities are current and how many are long-term helps creditors assess the likelihood of collecting from the entity.

Current Liabilities **Current liabilities** are debts that are due to be paid with cash or with goods and services within one year or the entity's operating cycle if the cycle is longer than a year. Accounts Payable, Notes Payable due within one year, Salaries Payable, Goods and Services Tax Payable, Interest Payable, and Unearned Revenue are all current liabilities.

Long-Term Liabilities All liabilities that are not current are classified as **long-term liabilities**. Many notes payable are long-term—payable after the longer of one year or the entity's operating cycle. Some notes are paid in instalments, with the first instalment due within one year, the second instalment due the second year, and so on. The first instalment would be a current liability and the remainder long-term liabilities. For example, a $100,000 note payable to be paid $10,000 per year over 10 years would include:

- A current liability of $10,000 for next year's payment, and
- A long-term liability of $90,000.

The Classified Balance Sheet

Thus far in this book we have presented the *unclassified* balance sheet of LES. Our purpose was to focus on the main points of assets, liabilities, and owner's equity without the details of *current* assets, *current* liabilities, and so on. Exhibit 4–12 presents LES's classified balance sheet. (Notice that LES has no long-term liabilities. Suppose the company had incurred a debt for its furniture and the debt would not be repaid during the coming year. This debt would have appeared as a long-term liability on the balance sheet.)

EXHIBIT 4–12 Classified Balance Sheet of Ladner Environmental Services in Account Format

LADNER ENVIRONMENTAL SERVICES
Balance Sheet
April 30, 2010

Assets		Liabilities	
Current assets:		Current liabilities:	
Cash	$ 31,000	Accounts payable	$ 12,000
Accounts receivable	15,500	Salary payable	4,000
Supplies	1,000	Unearned service revenue	2,000
Prepaid insurance	3,300	Total current liabilities	18,000
Total current assets	50,800		
		Owner's Equity	
Property, plant, and equipment:		John Ladner, capital	127,050
Furniture $45,000			
Less: Accumulated			
amortization 750	44,250		
Land	50,000		
Total property, plant, and equipment	94,250	Total liabilities and	
Total assets	$145,050	owner's equity	$145,050

Compare LES's *classified* balance sheet in Exhibit 4–12 with the *unclassified* balance sheet in Exhibit 4–7. The classified balance sheet reports totals for current assets and current liabilities, which do not appear on the unclassified balance sheet. Also, LES has no long-term liabilities, so there are none to report on either balance sheet.

The classified balance sheet of Ivaco Products Company, a fictitious company, is shown in Exhibit 4–13. It shows how a company with many different accounts could present its data on a classified balance sheet.

IVACO PRODUCTS COMPANY
Balance Sheet
June 30, 2010

Assets

Current assets:

Cash..	$ 26,400	
Short-term investments.................................	57,000	
Accounts receivable.......................................	235,000	
Interest receivable	26,800	
Current portion of note receivable	51,600	
Inventory	847,800	
Supplies	5,200	
Prepaid insurance	24,600	
Prepaid rent..	27,000	
Total current assets		$1,301,400

Other assets:

Note receivable..	100,000	
Less: Current portion of note receivable ...	51,600	
Total other assets..		48,400

Property, plant, and equipment:

Equipment...	$ 60,000		
Less: accumulated amortization	18,000	42,000	
Furniture and fixtures	70,000		
Less: accumulated amortization	30,000	40,000	
Buildings..	240,000		
Less: accumulated amortization	160,000	80,000	
Land		70,000	
Total property, plant, and equipment........			232,000
Total assets			$1,581,800

Liabilities

Current liabilities:

Accounts payable..	$357,000	
Salaries and wages payable............................	22,400	
Interest payable	24,600	
Current portion of notes payable	60,000	
Goods and services tax payable......................	64,600	
Current portion of mortgage payable............	72,200	
Other current liabilities	23,600	
Total current liabilities		$ 624,400

Long-term liabilities:

Notes payable	$340,000		
Less current portion of notes payable........	60,000	280,000	
Mortgage payable	220,000		
Less current portion of mortgage payable	72,200	147,800	
Total long-term liabilities............................			427,800
Total liabilities			1,052,200

Owner's Equity

Ivan Hanley, capital		529,600
Total liabilities and owner's equity.................		$1,581,800

Formats of Balance Sheets

The balance sheets of Ivaco Products Company shown in Exhibit 4–13 and of LES shown in Exhibit 4–14 list the assets at the top, with the liabilities and owner's equity below. This is the *report format*. LES's balance sheet in Exhibit 4–12 lists the assets at the left, with the liabilities and the owner's equity at the right. That is the *account* (or *equation*) *format*.

Either format is acceptable. The report format is more extensively used by Canadian companies.

5. Financial Statements
   pages 12–14

| **EXHIBIT 4–14** | Classified Balance Sheet of Ladner Environmental Services in Report Format |

LADNER ENVIRONMENTAL SERVICES
Balance Sheet
April 30, 2010

Assets

Current assets:

Cash..		$ 31,000
Accounts receivable...		15,500
Supplies		1,000
Prepaid insurance		3,300
Total current assets		50,800

Property, plant, and equipment:

Furniture...	$45,000	
Less: Accumulated amortization	750	44,250
Land		50,000
Total property, plant, and equipment.........................		94,250
Total assets..		$145,050

Liabilities

Current liabilities:

Accounts payable...		$ 12,000
Salary payable		4,000
Unearned service revenue		2,000
Total current liabilities		18,000

Owner's Equity

John Ladner, capital..		127,050
Total liabilities and owner's equity		$145,050

DID YOU GET IT?

To check your understanding of the material in this Learning Objective, complete these questions. The solutions appear on MyAccountingLab so you can check your progress.

11. Why is the classified balance sheet in Exhibit 4–12 more useful than an unclassified balance sheet (Exhibit 4–7) to a banker considering whether to lend $10,000 to LES?

12. Some of the accounts from the December 31, 2010, trial balance of Mark Wearing Engineers appear here. All accounts have their normal balances.

Mark Wearing, Capital	$14,160	Salaries Payable	$ 1,400
Cash	23,600	Accumulated Amortization—	
Furniture	11,200	Furniture	240
Accounts Payable	11,200	Mortgage Payable (current)	1,000
Accumulated Amortization—		Unearned Service Revenue	2,400
Equipment	200	Supplies	200
Accounts Receivable	7,600	Mortgage Payable (current	
Equipment	7,000	and long-term)	20,000

Identify the assets (including contra assets) and liabilities, and identify whether each asset and liability is current or long-term.

13. Refer to the previous question. Create the classified balance sheet in report format for Mark Wearing Engineers at December 31, 2010.

Accounting Ratios

OBJECTIVE 6
Use the current ratio and the debt ratio to evaluate a company

The purpose of accounting is to provide information for decision making. Chief users of accounting information include managers, investors, and creditors. A creditor considering lending money must predict whether the borrower can repay the loan. If the borrower already has a large amount of debt, the probability of repayment is lower than if the borrower has a small amount of debt. To assess financial position, decision makers use ratios they compute from a company's financial statements. Two of the most widely used decision aids in business are the current ratio and the debt ratio.

Current Ratio

One of the most common ratios is the **current ratio**, which is the ratio of an entity's current assets to its current liabilities:

$$\textbf{Current Ratio} = \frac{\textbf{Total current assets}}{\textbf{Total current liabilities}}$$

The current ratio measures the ability to pay current liabilities with current assets. A company prefers a high current ratio, which means the business has sufficient current assets to pay current liabilities when they come due, plus a cushion of additional current assets. An increasing current ratio from period to period generally indicates improvement in ability to pay current debts.

A general rule: A strong current ratio would be in the range of 2.00, which indicates that the company has approximately $2.00 in current assets for every $1.00 in current liabilities. Such a company would probably have little trouble paying its current liabilities and could probably borrow money on better terms, such as at a lower rate of interest. Most successful businesses operate with current ratios between 1.30 and 2.00. A current ratio of 1.00 is considered quite low.

Let's examine LES's current ratio, using the company's balance sheet in Exhibit 4–14.

$$\text{Current ratio} = \frac{\text{Total current assets}}{\text{Total current liabilities}} = \frac{\$50,800}{\$18,000} = 2.82$$

LES has $2.82 in current assets for every dollar the company owes in current liabilities. LES's current ratio is very high, which is not risky and makes the business look safe.

Debt Ratio

A second aid to decision making is the **debt ratio**, which is the ratio of total liabilities to total assets:

$$\text{Debt Ratio} = \frac{\text{Total liabilities}}{\text{Total assets}}$$

The debt ratio indicates the proportion of a company's assets that are financed with debt, as opposed to the proportion financed by the owner(s) of the company. This ratio measures a company's ability to pay both current and long-term debts—total liabilities.

A *low* debt ratio is safer than a high debt ratio. Why? Because a company with low liabilities has low required payments. Such a company is unlikely to get into financial difficulty. A rule of thumb: A debt ratio below 0.60, or 60 percent, is considered safe for most businesses. A debt ratio above 0.80, or 80 percent, borders on high risk. Most companies have debt ratios in the range of 0.60 to 0.80.

Let's examine LES's debt ratio, using the company's balance sheet in Exhibit 4–14.

$$\text{Debt ratio} = \frac{\text{Total liabilities}}{\text{Total assets}} = \frac{\$18,000}{\$145,050} = 0.12, \text{ or } 12\%$$

The percentage of LES's total assets that is financed with debt is 12 percent. A debt ratio of 12 percent is very safe.

Managing Both the Current Ratio and the Debt Ratio   In general, a *high* current ratio is preferred over a low current ratio. *Increases* in the current ratio indicate improving financial position. By contrast, a *low* debt ratio is preferred over a high debt ratio. Improvement is indicated by a *decrease* in the debt ratio.

Financial ratios are an important aid to decision makers. However, it is unwise to place too much confidence in a single ratio or group of ratios. For example, a company may have a high current ratio, which indicates financial strength, and it may also have a high debt ratio, which suggests weakness. Which ratio gives the more reliable signal about the company? Experienced managers, lenders, and investors evaluate a company by examining a large number of ratios over several years to spot trends and turning points. These people also consider other facts, such as the company's cash position and its trend in net income. No single ratio gives the whole picture about a company.

As you progress through the study of accounting, we will introduce key ratios used for decision making. Chapter 18 (in Volume 2) then summarizes all the ratios discussed in this book and provides a good overview of ratios used in decision making.

DID YOU GET IT?

MyAccountingLab

To check your understanding of the material in this Learning Objective, complete these questions. The solutions appear on MyAccountingLab so you can check your progress.

14. A company has current assets of $100,000 and current liabilities of $50,000. How will the payment of a $10,000 account payable affect the current ratio?

15. Using the work sheet created in Did You Get It? Question 2, prepare a classified balance sheet for Curry's Service Company at December 31, 2010.

16. Refer to the previous question. Compute the current ratio and the debt ratio for Curry's Service Company. Evaluate these ratios.

Accounting-Cycle and Financial-Reporting Implications of IFRS

OBJECTIVE ⑦

Describe the accounting-cycle and financial-reporting implications of international financial reporting standards (IFRS)

The accounting cycle for companies following international financial reporting standards (IFRS) is the same approach as that for companies following Canadian GAAP for private enterprises that we have studied in Chapters 1 to 4. While the approach to recording these transactions has been essentially the same under both reporting systems, the presentation of the information may be quite different. Under Canadian GAAP, companies provide the following financial statements:

* The balance sheet
* The income statement
* The statement of owner's equity (the statement of retained earnings for a corporation)
* The cash flow statement
* Notes, including significant accounting policies and explanatory information

Companies that prepare and report financial information under IFRS must provide the following financial statements:

* Statement of financial position (the balance sheet)
* Statement of comprehensive income
* Statement of changes in equity
* Statement of cash flows
* Notes, including significant accounting policies and explanatory information

In this chapter, we will concentrate on the differences in the balance sheet and the statement of financial position.

The balance sheet described in this chapter shows the typical presentation under Canadian GAAP for private enterprises. Under IFRS, companies have a choice in their method of presentation. Many companies, such as BMW (a company with its head office in Germany) and British Airways (a company with its head office in the United Kingdom) present balance-sheet information in a different order than most North American companies. On the asset side of the balance sheet, many IFRS companies present the long-term assets first, followed by the current assets. On the liability and equity side of the balance sheet, many IFRS companies present the equity section, then the long-term liabilities, followed by the current liabilities. Canadian companies reporting under IFRS have the option of following this approach for balance-sheet presentation or staying with the traditional approach that has been followed in Canada and described in this chapter.

DID YOU GET IT?

MyAccountingLab

To check your understanding of the material in this Learning Objective, complete this question. The solution appears on MyAccountingLab so you can check your progress.

17. Why would a Canadian company reporting under IFRS choose to follow the traditional approach for its balance-sheet presentation rather than the IFRS approach?

As we conclude this chapter, we return to our opening questions: How do you complete the accounting cycle and why is it important? What are closing entries? Closing the books is a necessary process so that the accounting cycle can begin anew in the next accounting period, ensuring the results of the next accounting period will be measured accurately. The Decision Guidelines feature summarizes all of our chapter-opening questions, highlighting the final steps in the accounting cycle and the topics covered in this chapter.

DECISION GUIDELINES · Completing the Accounting Cycle

Decision	Guidelines
What document summarizes the effects of all the company's transactions and adjustments throughout the period?	Accountant's *work sheet* with columns for: • Trial balance • Adjustments • Adjusted trial balance • Income statement • Balance sheet
What is the last *major* step in the accounting cycle?	*Closing entries* for the *temporary accounts:* Revenues $\Big\}$ Income statement accounts Expenses Owner's withdrawals
Why close revenues, expenses, and owner's withdrawals?	The *temporary accounts* have balances that relate only to one accounting period (fiscal year) and do *not* carry over to the next accounting period (fiscal year).
Which accounts do not get closed?	*Permanent (balance sheet) accounts:* • Assets • Liabilities • Owner's capital The balances of these accounts *do* carry over to the next accounting period.
How do businesses classify their assets and liabilities for reporting on the balance sheet?	*Current* (within one year or the company's operating cycle if longer than a year) or *Long-term* (not current).
How do decision makers evaluate a company?	There are many ways, such as the company's net income or net loss on the income statement and the trend of net income from year to year. Another way to evaluate a company is based on the company's *financial ratios.* Two key ratios: $$\text{Current ratio} = \frac{\text{Total current assets}}{\text{Total current liabilities}}$$ The current ratio measures the ability to pay current liabilities with current assets. $$\text{Debt ratio} = \frac{\text{Total liabilities}}{\text{Total assets}}$$ The debt ratio measures the overall ability to pay liabilities. The debt ratio shows the proportion of the entity's assets that are financed with debt.

Summary Problem for Your Review

The trial balance of Cloud Break Consulting at June 30, 2010, the end of its fiscal year, is presented below.

CLOUD BREAK CONSULTING
Trial Balance
June 30, 2010

Cash	$ 131,000	
Accounts receivable	104,000	
Supplies	4,000	
Prepaid rent	27,000	
Building	300,000	
Accumulated amortization—building		$155,000
Land	45,000	
Accounts payable		159,000
Salary payable		0
Unearned service revenue		40,000
Michael Moe, capital		102,000
Michael Moe, withdrawals	7,000	
Service revenue		450,000
Salary expense	255,000	
Supplies expense	0	
Rent expense	25,000	
Amortization expense—building	0	
Miscellaneous expense	8,000	
Total	$ 906,000	$906,000

Name: Cloud Break Consulting
Industry: Service proprietorship
Fiscal Period: Year ended June 30, 2010
Key Fact: Existing, ongoing business

Data needed for the adjusting entries include:

a. Supplies remaining on hand at year end, $1,000.

b. Nine months of rent ($27,000) were paid in advance on April 1, 2010. No rent expense has been recorded since that date.

c. Amortization expense has not been recorded on the building for the 2010 fiscal year. Amortization is $12,000 per year on the building.

d. Employees work Monday through Friday. The weekly payroll is $5,000 and is paid every Friday. June 30, 2010, is a Wednesday.

e. Service revenue of $15,000 must be accrued.

f. Cloud Break Consulting received $40,000 in advance for consulting services to be provided evenly from January 1, 2010, through August 31, 2010. None of the revenue from this client has been recorded.

To plan your work sheet, check the adjusting entries data to see if the same account is affected more than once. If it is, leave one or two blank lines under the account name. Do this for Service Revenues on this work sheet.

Required

1. Prepare the work sheet of Cloud Break Consulting for the year ended June 30, 2010. Identify each adjusting entry by the letter corresponding to the data given.

2. Journalize the adjusting entries and post them to T-accounts. (Before posting to the T-accounts, enter into each T-account its balance as shown in the trial balance. For example, enter the $104,000 balance in the Accounts Receivable account before posting its adjusting entry.) Identify adjusting entries by *letter*. You can take the adjusting entries straight from the work sheet from Requirement 1. Explanations are not required. Find the ending balances of the permanent accounts.

3. Journalize and post the closing entries. (Each T-account should carry its balance as shown in the adjusted trial balance.) Provide explanations. To distinguish closing entries from adjusting entries, identify the closing entries by *number*. Draw the arrows to illustrate the flow of data, as shown in Exhibit 4–10, page 174. Indicate the balance of the Capital account after the closing entries are posted.

4. Prepare the income statement for the year ended June 30, 2010. List Miscellaneous Expense last among the expenses, a common practice.

5. Prepare the statement of owner's equity for the year ended June 30, 2010. Draw the arrow that links the income statement to the statement of owner's equity, if both statements are on the same page. Otherwise, explain how they are linked.

6. Prepare the classified balance sheet at June 30, 2010. Use the report format. All liabilities are current. Draw the arrow that links the statement of owner's equity to the balance sheet, if both statements are on the same page. Otherwise, explain how they are linked.

Selected adjusting entries are explained below, under the work sheet.

SOLUTION

Requirement 1

Using the trial balance given, write the account titles in the first column of the work sheet and the amounts in the "Trial Balance" columns, ensuring debit and credit balances on the trial balance are debit and credit balances on the work sheet. To make sure all the account balances have been entered correctly, trace each work-sheet balance back to the June 30, 2010, trial balance.

When calculating the Adjusted Trial Balance amounts, remember to add and subtract the adjustments properly. For assets, withdrawals, and expenses, add debits and subtract credits. For contra assets, liabilities, owner's equity, and revenues, add credits and subtract debits.

CLOUD BREAK CONSULTING
Work Sheet
For the Year Ended June 30, 2010

Account Title	Trial Balance Debit	Trial Balance Credit	Adjustments Debit	Adjustments Credit	Adjusted Trial Balance Debit	Adjusted Trial Balance Credit	Income Statement Debit	Income Statement Credit	Balance Sheet Debit	Balance Sheet Credit
Cash	131,000				131,000				131,000	
Accounts receivable	104,000		(e) 15,000		119,000				119,000	
Supplies	4,000			(a) 3,000	1,000				1,000	
Prepaid rent	27,000			(b) 9,000	18,000				18,000	
Building	300,000				300,000				300,000	
Accum. amort.—building		155,000		(c) 12,000		167,000				167,000
Land	45,000				45,000				45,000	
Accounts payable		159,000				159,000				159,000
Salary payable		0		(d) 4,000		4,000				4,000
Unearned service revenue		40,000	(f) 30,000			10,000				10,000
Michael Moe, capital		102,000				102,000				102,000
Michael Moe, withdrawals	7,000				7,000				7,000	
Service revenue		450,000		(e) 15,000		495,000		495,000		
				(f) 30,000						
Salary expense	255,000		(d) 4,000		259,000		259,000			
Supplies expense	0		(a) 3,000		3,000		3,000			
Rent expense	25,000		(b) 9,000		34,000		34,000			
Amort. exp.—bldg	0		(c) 12,000		12,000		12,000			
Miscellaneous expense	8,000				8,000		8,000			
	906,000	906,000	73,000	73,000	937,000	937,000	316,000	495,000	621,000	442,000
Net income							179,000			179,000
							495,000	495,000	621,000	621,000

The same "plug figure" must make the final Income Statement column totals equal and the final Balance Sheet column totals equal.
Selected adjusting entries are explained further:
(a) Supplies on hand ($4,000) – Supplies still on hand ($1,000) = $3,000 adjustment
(b) Of the $27,000 rent paid for 9 months (or $3,000 per month), $9,000 should be recorded as rent expense for April, May, and June.

(f) Unearned Service Revenue ($40,000) – Service revenue earned ($30,000, the portion for January to June) = $10,000 of service revenue still to be earned, which is a liability.
Refer to the Adjustments columns of the work sheet. Make journal entries for all the transactions in the Adjustments columns.

Requirement 2

a. Jun. 30	Supplies Expense	3,000	
	Supplies...		3,000
b. Jun. 30	Rent Expense	9,000	
	Prepaid Rent...		9,000
c. Jun. 30	Amortization Expense—Building	12,000	
	Accumulated Amortization—Building		12,000
d. Jun. 30	Salary Expense	4,000	
	Salary Payable..		4,000
e. Jun. 30	Accounts Receivable..	15,000	
	Service Revenue...		15,000
f. Jun. 30	Unearned Service Revenue	30,000	
	Service Revenue...		30,000

Create T-accounts only for the accounts affected by the adjusting entries.

Remember that the beginning balance in each of these T-accounts is the amount from the Trial Balance columns of the work sheet.

When you post the adjusting entries, use the letters a to f to identify each adjustment.

Find the balance of each T-account.

Accounts Receivable

	104,000	
(e)	15,000	
Bal.	119,000	

Supplies

	4,000	(a)	3,000
Bal.	1,000		

Prepaid Rent

	27,000		
		(b)	9,000
Bal.	18,000		

Accumulated Amortization—Building

		155,000
		(c)	12,000
		Bal.	167,000

Salary Payable

		(d)	4,000
		Bal.	4,000

Unearned Service Revenue

(f)	30,000		40,000
		Bal.	10,000

Service Revenue

		450,000
		(e)	15,000
		(f)	30,000
		Bal.	495,000

Salary Expense

	255,000	
(d)	4,000	
Bal.	259,000	

Supplies Expense

(a)	3,000	
Bal.	3,000	

Rent Expense

	25,000	
(b)	9,000	
Bal.	34,000	

Amortization Expense—Building

(c)	12,000	
Bal.	12,000	

Requirement 3

1. Jun. 30	Service Revenue...	495,000	
	Income Summary...		495,000
	To close the revenue account and create the		
	Income Summary account.		
2. Jun. 30	Income Summary...	316,000	
	Salary Expense		259,000
	Supplies Expense		3,000
	Rent Expense		34,000
	Amortization Expense—Building		12,000
	Miscellaneous Expense		8,000
	To close the expense accounts.		
3. Jun. 30	Income Summary...	179,000	
	Michael Moe, Capital		179,000
	To close the Income Summary account.		
	(Income Summary balance = $495,000 – $316,000).		
4. Jun. 30	Michael Moe, Capital	7,000	
	Michael Moe, Withdrawals		7,000
	To close the Withdrawals account and		
	transfer the Withdrawals amount to the		
	Capital account.		

Recall that all the temporary accounts are closed at the end of the period, namely the revenue, expense, and withdrawals accounts.

To close revenue accounts, debit each revenue account for the amount reported in the Income Statement column of the work sheet. Credit Income Summary for the total of the debits.

To close expense accounts, credit each expense account for the amount reported in the Income Statement column of the work sheet. Debit Income Summary for the total of the credits.

To close the Income Summary account, calculate the difference between the total debits and total credits in the Income Summary account. This should match the net income or net loss amount on the work sheet. In this case, Income Summary has a credit balance. Therefore, debit Income Summary to close it and credit the Capital account. Using an Income Summary T-account may help you close Income Summary more easily.

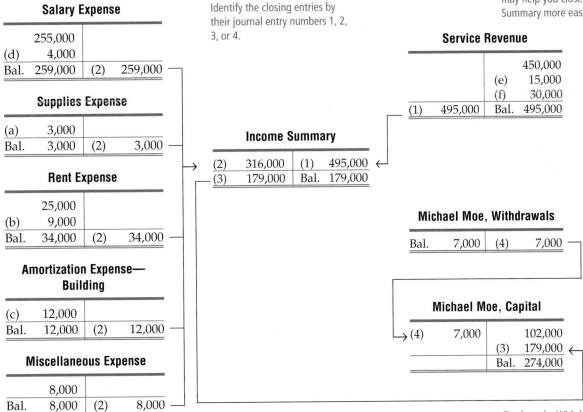

Identify the closing entries by their journal entry numbers 1, 2, 3, or 4.

To close the Withdrawals account, credit the Withdrawals account for the amounts reported in the Balance Sheet columns of the work sheet, and debit the Capital account.

Requirement 4

The title must include the name of the company, "Income Statement," and the specific period of time covered. It is critical that the time period be defined.

Gather all the revenue and expense account names and amounts from the Income Statement columns of the work sheet.

CLOUD BREAK CONSULTING
Income Statement
For the Year Ended June 30, 2010

Revenues:		
Service revenue...		$495,000
Expenses:		
Salary expense	$259,000	
Rent expense	34,000	
Amortization expense—building..................................	12,000	
Supplies expense	3,000	
Miscellaneous expense	8,000	
Total expenses		316,000
Net income		$179,000

Requirement 5

The title must include the name of company, "Statement of Owner's Equity," and the specific period of time covered. It is critical that the time period be defined.

Beginning owner's equity and withdrawals are from the Balance Sheet columns of the work sheet.

The net income amount is transferred from the income statement.

CLOUD BREAK CONSULTING
Statement of Owner's Equity
For the Year Ended June 30, 2010

Michael Moe, Capital, July 1, 2009...	$102,000
Add: Net income...	179,000
	281,000
Less: Withdrawals...	7,000
Michael Moe, Capital, June 30, 2010	$274,000

Requirement 6

The title must include the name of the company, "Balance Sheet," and the date of the balance sheet. It shows the financial position on one specific date.

The classified balance sheet uses the accounts and balances that appear in the Balance Sheet columns of the work sheet on page 187.

For a classified balance sheet, separate current assets (assets expected to be converted to cash within one year) from other assets.

Separate current liabilities (liabilities expected to be paid or settled within one year) from other liabilities.

CLOUD BREAK CONSULTING
Balance Sheet
June 30, 2010

Assets		
Current assets:		
Cash		$131,000
Accounts receivable...		119,000
Supplies		1,000
Prepaid rent		18,000
Total current assets		269,000
Property, plant, and equipment:		
Building...	$300,000	
Less: Accumulated amortization	167,000	133,000
Land..		45,000
Total property, plant, and equipment......................		178,000
Total assets		$447,000
Liabilities		
Current liabilities:		
Accounts payable...		$159,000
Salary payable		4,000
Unearned service revenue..		10,000
Total current liabilities..		173,000
Owner's Equity		
Michael Moe, capital		274,000
Total liabilities and owner's equity		$447,000

Summary

1. **Prepare an accounting work sheet.** The *accounting cycle* is the process by which accountants produce the financial statements for a specific period of time. The cycle starts with the beginning account balances. During the period, the business journalizes transactions and posts them to the ledger accounts. At the end of the period, the trial balance is prepared, and the accounts are adjusted in order to measure the period's net income or net loss. Completion of the accounting cycle is aided by the use of a *work sheet*. This multi-columned document summarizes the effects of all the period's activity.

2. **Use the work sheet to complete the accounting cycle.** The work sheet is neither a journal nor a ledger but merely a convenient device for completing the accounting cycle. It has columns for the trial balance, the adjustments, the adjusted trial balance, the income statement, and the balance sheet. It aids the adjusting process, and it is the place where the period's net income or net loss is first computed. The work sheet also provides the data for the financial statements and the *closing entries*. It is not, however, a necessity. The accounting cycle can be completed from the less elaborate adjusted trial balance.

3. **Close the revenue, expense, and withdrawal accounts.** Revenues, expenses, and owner withdrawals represent increases and decreases in the Capital account for a specific period. At the end of the period, their balances are closed out to zero, and, for this reason, they are called *temporary accounts*. Assets, liabilities, and capital accounts are not closed out to zero because they are the *permanent accounts*. Their balances at the end of one period become the beginning balances of the next period. The final accuracy check of the period is the *post-closing trial balance*.

4. **Correct typical accounting errors.** Accountants correct errors by making correcting journal entries.

5. **Classify assets and liabilities as current or long-term, and prepare a classified balance sheet.** The balance sheet reports *current* and *long-term assets* and *current* and *long-term liabilities*. It can be presented in *report format* or *account* format.

6. **Use the current ratio and the debt ratio to evaluate a company.** Two decision-making aids are the *current ratio* (total current assets divided by total current liabilities) and the *debt ratio* (total liabilities divided by total assets).

7. **Describe the accounting-cycle and financial-reporting implications of international financial reporting standards (IFRS).** The accounting cycle for companies following international financial reporting standards (IFRS) is the same approach as that for companies following Canadian GAAP for private enterprises. Canadian companies reporting under IFRS can present their balance sheet in the traditional format described in this chapter or in reverse order of liquidity—the choice is theirs.

CHAPTER 4 APPENDIX

Reversing Entries: An Optional Step

OBJECTIVE **A1**
Describe and prepare reversing entries

Reversing entries are special types of entries that ease the burden of accounting after adjusting and closing entries have been made at the end of a period. Reversing entries are used most often in conjunction with accrual-type adjustments such as accrued salary expense and accrued service revenue. Reversing entries are *not* used for adjustments to record amortization and prepayments. *GAAP do not require reversing entries. They are used only for convenience and to save time.*

KEY POINT

Reversing entries are most frequently used for accrued revenue and accrued expense items.

Accounting for Accrued Expenses To see how reversing entries work, return to LES's unadjusted trial balance at April 30, 2010 (Exhibit 4–2, page 166a).

Salary Expense has a debit balance of $4,000 from salaries paid during April. At April 30, the company owes employees an additional $4,000 for the last part of the month.

Assume for this illustration that on May 5, the next payroll date, LES will pay $4,000 of accrued salary plus $200 in salary that the employee has earned in the first few days of May. LES's next payroll payment will be $4,200 ($4,000 + $200). But LES must include the $4,000 in salary expense for April. To do so, LES makes the following adjusting entry on April 30:

Adjusting Entries

Apr. 30	Salary Expense...	4,000	
	Salary Payable		4,000

After posting, the Salary Payable and Salary Expense accounts appear as follows:

Salary Payable

	Apr. 30 Adj.[1] 4,000
	Apr. 30 Bal. 4,000

Salary Expense

Paid during	
Apr. CP 4,000	
Apr. 30 Adj. 4,000	
Apr. 30 Bal. 8,000	

After the adjusting entry,

- The April income statement reports salary expense of $8,000.
- The April 30 balance sheet reports salary payable of $4,000.

The $8,000 debit balance of Salary Expense is eliminated by this closing entry at April 30, 2010, as follows:

Closing Entries

Apr. 30	Income Summary...	8,000	
	Salary Expense		8,000

After posting, Salary Expense has a zero balance as follows:

Salary Expense

Paid during	
Apr. CP 4,000	
Apr. 30 Adj. 4,000	
Bal. 8,000	Clo. 8,000

Accounting without a Reversing Entry On May 5, the next payday, LES pays the payroll of $4,200 and makes this journal entry:

May 5	Salary Payable	4,000	
	Salary Expense...	200	
	Cash		4,200

This method of recording the cash payment is correct. However, it wastes time because the company's accountant must refer to the adjusting entries of April 30. Otherwise, LES does not know the amount of the debit to Salary Payable (in this example, $4,000). Searching the preceding period's adjusting entries takes time and, in business, time is money. To save time, accountants use reversing entries, which eliminates the need to search the preceding period's adjusting entries.

Making a Reversing Entry A **reversing entry** switches the debit and the credit of a previous adjusting entry. *A reversing entry, then, is the exact opposite of a prior adjusting*

---

[1] Entry explanations used throughout this discussion are
   Adj. = Adjusting entry; CP = Cash payment entry—includes a credit to Cash
   Bal. = Balance; CR = Cash receipt entry—includes a debit to Cash
   Clo. = Closing entry; Rev. = Reversing entry

entry. The reversing entry is dated the first day of the period following the adjusting entry.

To illustrate reversing entries, recall that on April 30, 2010, LES made the following adjusting entry to accrue Salary Payable:

Adjusting Entries

Apr. 30	Salary Expense..	4,000	
	Salary Payable		4,000

The reversing entry simply reverses the position of the debit and the credit:

Reversing Entries

May 1	Salary Payable	4,000	
	Salary Expense		4,000

Observe that the reversing entry is dated the first day of the new period. It is the exact opposite of the April 30 adjusting entry. Ordinarily, the accountant who makes the adjusting entry also prepares the reversing entry at the same time. LES dates the reversing entry as of the first day of the next period, however, so that it affects only the new period. Note how the accounts appear after the company posts the reversing entry:

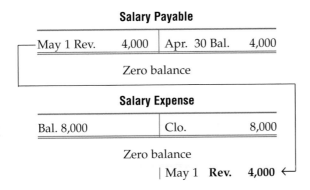

The arrow shows the transfer of the $4,000 credit balance from Salary Payable to Salary Expense. This credit balance in Salary Expense does not mean that the entity has negative salary expense, as you might think. Instead, the odd credit balance is merely a temporary result of the reversing entry. The credit balance is eliminated on May 5 when the $4,200 cash payment for salaries is debited to Salary Expense in the customary manner:

May 5	Salary Expense..	4,200	
	Cash		4,200

Then this cash payment entry is posted to Salary Expense as follows:

Salary Expense

May 5 CP	4,200	May 1 Rev.	4,000
May 5 Bal.	200		

Now Salary Expense has its correct debit balance of $200, which is the amount of salary expense incurred thus far in May.

Exhibit 4–A1 shows these transactions side by side to highlight the differences and show that the results are the same whether or not reversing entries are used.

6. Adjusting and Closing Entries
pages 16–17

EXHIBIT 4–A1 Reversing Entries for Accrued Expenses

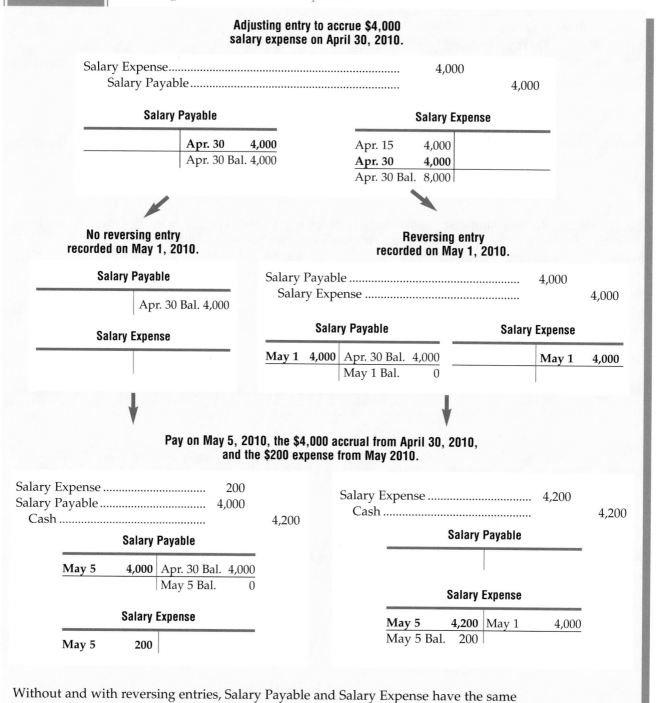

Adjusting entry to accrue $4,000 salary expense on April 30, 2010.

Salary Expense.. 4,000
    Salary Payable... 4,000

Salary Payable		
	Apr. 30	**4,000**
	Apr. 30 Bal.	4,000

Salary Expense		
Apr. 15	4,000	
Apr. 30	**4,000**	
Apr. 30 Bal.	8,000	

No reversing entry recorded on May 1, 2010.

Salary Payable	
	Apr. 30 Bal. 4,000

Salary Expense	

Reversing entry recorded on May 1, 2010.

Salary Payable 4,000
    Salary Expense 4,000

Salary Payable		
May 1	**4,000**	Apr. 30 Bal. 4,000
		May 1 Bal. 0

Salary Expense		
		May 1 4,000

Pay on May 5, 2010, the $4,000 accrual from April 30, 2010, and the $200 expense from May 2010.

Salary Expense 200
Salary Payable 4,000
    Cash 4,200

Salary Payable		
May 5	**4,000**	Apr. 30 Bal. 4,000
		May 5 Bal. 0

Salary Expense	
May 5	200

Salary Expense 4,200
    Cash 4,200

Salary Payable	

Salary Expense		
May 5	**4,200**	May 1 4,000
May 5 Bal.	200	

Without and with reversing entries, Salary Payable and Salary Expense have the same May 5, 2010, balances after the May 5 payment of salary.

Accounting for Accrued Revenues While most reversing entries are made to accrue expenses, reversing entries may be made to accrue revenues. For example, if LES had completed some consulting work for a client, an entry would be made to debit Accounts Receivable and credit Service Revenue at April 30, 2010. Service Revenue would be closed to the Income Summary in the usual way. A reversing entry on May 1, 2010, would reduce Accounts Receivable and temporarily create a debit balance in Service Revenue. When the payment is received, the accountant would debit Cash and credit Service Revenue.

SELF-STUDY QUESTIONS

Test your understanding of the chapter by marking the correct answer to each of the following questions:

1. The focal point of the accounting cycle is the (p. 165)
   a. Financial statements
   b. Trial balance
   c. Adjusted trial balance
   d. Work sheet

2. Arrange the following accounting cycle steps in their proper order assuming a work sheet is used. (p. 166)
   a. Complete the work sheet
   b. Journalize and post adjusting entries
   c. Prepare the postclosing trial balance
   d. Journalize and post cash transactions
   e. Prepare the financial statements
   f. Journalize and post closing entries

3. The work sheet is a (p. 166)
   a. Journal
   b. Ledger
   c. Financial statement
   d. Convenient device for completing the accounting cycle

4. The usefulness of the work sheet is (pp. 166–168)
   a. Identifying the accounts that need to be adjusted
   b. Summarizing the effects of all the transactions of the period
   c. Aiding the preparation of the financial statements
   d. All of the above

5. Which of the following accounts is not closed? (p. 172)
   a. Supplies Expense
   b. Prepaid Insurance
   c. Interest Revenue
   d. Withdrawals

6. The closing entry for Salary Expense, with a balance of $322,000, is (p. 173)

   a. Salary Expense   322,000
       Income Summary   322,000

   b. Salary Expense   322,000
       Salary Payable   322,000

   c. Income Summary   322,000
       Salary Expense   322,000

   d. Salary Payable   322,000
       Salary Expense   322,000

7. The purpose of the postclosing trial balance is to (p. 176)
   a. Provide the account balances for preparation of the balance sheet
   b. Ensure that the ledger is in balance for the start of the next period
   c. Aid the journalizing and posting of the closing entries
   d. Ensure that the ledger is in balance for completion of the work sheet

8. A $500 payment on account was recorded by debiting Supplies and crediting Cash. This entry was posted. The correcting entry is (pp. 176–177)

   a. Accounts Payable   500
       Supplies   500

   b. Supplies   500
       Accounts Payable   500

   c. Cash   500
       Accounts Payable   500

   d. Cash   500
       Supplies   500

9. The classification of assets and liabilities as current or long-term depends on (pp. 178–179)
   a. Their order of listing in the ledger
   b. Whether they appear on the balance sheet or the income statement
   c. The relative liquidity of the item
   d. The format of the balance sheet—account format or report format

10. Suppose in 2010, LES debited Amortization Expense for the cost of a computer used in the business. For 2010, this error (pp. 176–177)
    a. Overstated net income
    b. Understated net income
    c. Did either a or b, depending on the circumstances
    d. Had no effect on net income

Answers to Self-Study Questions

1. a 2. d, a, e, b, f, c 3. d 4. d 5. b 6. c 7. b 8. a 9. c 10. b

ACCOUNTING VOCABULARY

Accounting cycle   (p. 165)
Closing entry   (p. 172)
Closing the accounts   (p. 172)
Current asset   (p. 178)
Current liability   (p. 178)
Current ratio   (p. 182)
Debt ratio   (p. 183)
Income Summary   (p. 173)
Liquidity   (p. 178)
Long-term asset   (p. 178)

Long-term liability   (p. 179)
Nominal account   (p. 172)
Operating cycle   (p. 178)
Permanent account   (p. 172)
Postclosing trial balance   (p. 176)
Property, plant, and equipment   (p. 178)
Real account   (p. 172)
Reversing entry   (p. 191)
Temporary account   (p. 172)
Work sheet   (p. 166a)

Property, plant, and equipment	Fixed assets, Plant and equipment, Plant assets
Current ratio	Working capital ratio
Permanent account	Real account
Temporary account	Nominal account

Assignment Material

QUESTIONS

1. Identify the steps in the accounting cycle, distinguishing those that occur during the period from those that are performed at the end of the period.

2. Why is the work sheet a valuable accounting tool?

3. Name two advantages the work sheet has over the adjusted trial balance.

4. Why must the adjusting entries be journalized and posted if they have already been entered on the work sheet?

5. Why should the adjusting entries be journalized and posted before the closing entries are made?

6. Which types of accounts are closed?

7. What purpose is served by closing the accounts?

8. State how the work sheet helps with recording the closing entries.

9. Distinguish between permanent accounts and temporary accounts, indicating which type is closed at the end of the period. Give five examples of each type of account.

10. Is Income Summary a permanent account or a temporary account? When and how is it used?

11. Is net income a permanent account, a temporary account, or something else? Explain.

12. Give the closing entries for the following accounts (balances in parentheses): Service Revenue ($4,700), Salary Expense ($1,100), Income Summary (credit balance of $2,000), Withdrawals ($2,300).

13. Why are assets classified as current or long-term? On what basis are they classified? Where do the classified amounts appear?

14. Indicate which of the following accounts are current assets and which are long-term assets: Prepaid Rent, Building, Furniture, Accounts Receivable, Merchandise Inventory, Cash, Note Receivable (due within one year), Note Receivable (due after one year).

15. In what order are assets and liabilities listed on the balance sheet?

16. Name an outside party that is interested in whether a liability is current or long-term. Why would this party be interested in this information?

17. A friend tells you that the difference between a current liability and a long-term liability is that they are payable to different types of creditors. Is your friend correct? Include in your answer the definitions of these two categories of liabilities.

18. Show how to compute the current ratio and the debt ratio. Indicate what ability each ratio measures, and state whether a high value or a low value is safer for each.

19. Capp Company purchased supplies of $120 on account. The accountant debited Inventory and credited Accounts Payable for $120. A week later, after this entry has been posted to the ledger, the accountant discovers the error. How should the accountant correct the error?

*20. Why are reversing entries used?

STARTERS

MyAccountingLab All questions in this section appear in MyAccountingLab.

Explaining items on the work sheet

Starter 4–1 Explain why the following accounts must be adjusted:

a. Salary Payable
b. Unearned Service Revenue
c. Supplies

d. Prepaid Rent
e. Accumulated Amortization

*This Question covers Chapter 4 Appendix topics.

Starter 4–2 Explain what the following terms mean:

a. Accounts receivable
b. Supplies
c. Prepaid rent
d. Furniture
e. Accumulated amortization

f. Accounts payable
g. Unearned service revenue
h. Service revenue
i. Rent expense

Explaining items on the work sheet

Starter 4–3 Answer the following questions:

1. What type of balance does the Owner, Capital account have—debit or credit?
2. Which income statement account has the same type of balance as the Capital account?
3. Which type of income statement account has the opposite type of balance as the Capital account?
4. What do we call the difference between total debits and total credits on the income statement? Into what account is the difference figure closed at the end of the period?

Using the work sheet

Starter 4–4 It is December 31, 2010, and time to close the books. Journalize the following closing entries for Kaufman Services:

a. Service revenue, $11,000
b. A compound closing entry for all the expenses: Salaries, $3,500; Rent, $2,000; Advertising, $1,500
c. Income Summary
d. Owner, Withdrawals, $3,000. Brett Kaufman is the owner.

Journalizing closing entries

Starter 4–5 This exercise should be used in conjunction with Starter 4–4.

1. Set up all the T–accounts in Starter 4–4 and insert their adjusted balances (denote as *Bal.*) at December 31, 2010. Also set up a T-account for Brett Kaufman, Capital, $12,500, and for Income Summary. Post the closing entries to the accounts, denoting posted amounts as *Clo.*
2. Compute the ending balance of Brett Kaufman, Capital.

Analyzing the overall effect of the closing entries on the owner's Capital account

2. B. Kaufman, Capital $13,500

Starter 4–6 Lipsky Insurance Agency reported the following items at May 31:

Sales and Marketing Expense..	$1,600	Cash	$1,000
Other Assets................................	500	Service Revenue.........	4,200
Amortization Expense	700	Accounts Payable.......	300
Long-Term Liabilities................	400	Accounts Receivable...	1,200

Make Lipsky Insurance Agency's closing entries, as needed, for these accounts.

Making closing entries

Starter 4–7 This exercise should be used in conjunction with Starter 4–6. Use the data in Starter 4–6 to set up T-accounts for those accounts that Lipsky Insurance Agency closed on May 31. Insert their account balances prior to closing, post the closing entries to these accounts, and show each account's ending balance after closing. Also show the Income Summary T-account. Label a balance as *Bal.* and a closing entry amount as *Clo.*

Posting closing entries

Income Summary Credit bal. $1,900

Starter 4–8 After closing its accounts at March 31, 2010, Watts Home Services had the following balances:

Long-Term Liabilities................	$1,000	Equipment	$8,000
Other Assets................................	1,600	Cash	600
Accounts Receivable	4,000	Service Revenue.........	0
Total Expenses............................	0	Will Watts, Capital.....	8,800
Accounts Payable.......................	1,800	Supplies........................	200
Unearned Service Revenue	800	Accumulated Amortization	
		—Equipment	2,000

Prepare Watts Home Services' postclosing trial balance at March 31, 2010. List accounts in proper order, as shown in Exhibit 4–11 on page 176.

Preparing a postclosing trial balance

Trial bal. total $14,400

Starter 4–9 Assume that there is only one transposition error in the following trial balance. Identify the incorrect amount, and correct the trial balance.

Identifying errors

FISHER SERVICES
Trial Balance
December 31, 2010

Cash	$ 2,500	
Accounts receivable	4,150	
Supplies	375	
Accounts payable		$3,850
R. Fisher, capital		1,025
R. Fisher, withdrawals	500	
Service fees earned		5,000
Insurance expense	475	
Salaries expense	3,100	
Utilities expense	575	
Total	$11,675	$9,875

Classifying assets and liabilities
as current or long-term

Starter 4–10 Ink Jet Printing reported the following (amounts in thousands):

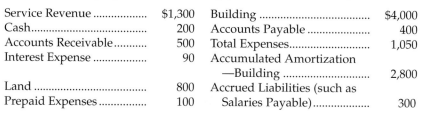

Service Revenue	$1,300	Building	$4,000
Cash	200	Accounts Payable	400
Accounts Receivable	500	Total Expenses	1,050
Interest Expense	90	Accumulated Amortization	
		—Building	2,800
Land	800	Accrued Liabilities (such as	
Prepaid Expenses	100	Salaries Payable)	300

1. Identify the assets (including contra assets) and liabilities.
2. Classify each asset and each liability as current or long-term.

Classifying assets and liabilities
as current or long-term

Starter 4–11 This exercise should be used in conjunction with Starter 4–10. Examine Ink Jet Printing's account balances in Starter 4–10. Identify or compute the following amounts for Ink Jet Printing:

a. Total current assets
b. Book value of the building
c. Total current liabilities
d. Total long-term liabilities

Computing the current ratio
and the debt ratio

6

Current ratio 2.00

Starter 4–12 Belleville Services has these account balances at December 31, 2010:

Accounts Payable	$ 8,000	Note Payable, Long-term	$18,000
Accounts Receivable	12,000	Prepaid Rent	4,000
Cash	6,000	Salary Payable	4,000
Accum. Amortization—			
Equipment	8,000	Service Revenue	62,000
Equipment	24,000	Supplies	2,000

Compute Belleville Services' current ratio and debt ratio.

Computing and using the
current ratio and the debt ratio

1. $2.00

Starter 4–13 This exercise should be used in conjunction with Starter 4–12.

1. How much in *current* assets does Belleville Services have for every dollar of *current* liabilities that it owes? What ratio measures this relationship?
2. What percentage of Belleville Services total assets are financed with debt? What is the name of this ratio?
3. What percentage of Belleville Services total assets does the owner of the company actually own?

EXERCISES

Exercise 4–1

The trial balance of Brighter Testing Services appears here.

Excel Spreadsheet Template

Preparing a work sheet

Net income $12,620

BRIGHTER TESTING SERVICES
Trial Balance
September 30, 2010

Cash...	$ 14,240	
Accounts receivable...	11,880	
Prepaid rent	2,400	
Supplies	6,780	
Equipment...	65,200	
Accumulated amortization		
—equipment		$ 5,680
Accounts payable..		10,320
Salary payable		0
J. Brighter, capital..		72,060
J. Brighter, withdrawals	6,000	
Service revenue		23,600
Amortization expense—equipment.................	0	
Salary expense..	3,600	
Rent expense...	0	
Utilities expense...	1,560	
Supplies expense..	0	
Total	$111,660	$111,660

Additional information at September 30, 2010:

a. Accrued service revenue, $840.
b. Equipment Amortization, $160.
c. Accrued salary expense, $2,000.
d. Prepaid rent expired, $1,200.
e. Supplies used, $3,300.

Required Complete the Brighter Testing Services work sheet for September 2010. What was net income for the month ended September 30, 2010?

Exercise 4–2

Journalize the adjusting and closing entries for the company in Exercise 4–1.

Journalizing adjusting and closing entries

Exercise 4–3

Set up T-accounts for only those accounts affected by the adjusting and closing entries in Exercise 4–1. Post the adjusting and closing entries from Exercise 4–2 to the accounts, identifying adjustment amounts as *Adj.*, closing amounts as *Clo.*, and balances as *Bal.* Double underline the accounts with zero balances after you close them and show the ending balance in each account.

Posting adjusting and closing entries

J. Brighter, Capital bal. $78,680

Exercise 4–4

After completing Exercises 4–2 and 4–3, prepare the postclosing trial balance for Brighter Testing Services at September 30, 2010.

Preparing a postclosing trial balance

Trial bal. total $96,840

Exercise 4–5

Husky Systems, a transportation company, reported the following items in a recent financial report:

Identifying and journalizing closing entries

Cash and Term Deposits	$ 2,917	Amortization Expense—	
		Equipment.............................	$1,090
Revenues.....................................	29,452	Equipment	8,043
Accounts Payable	6,866	Interest Expense........................	726
Accounts Receivable	1,684	Long-term Liabilities................	5,666

Prepare Husky Systems' closing entries for the above accounts.

Exercise 4–6

Identifying and journalizing closing entries

Dan Viera, Capital bal. $235,600

Viera Printers reported the following selected accounts in its June 30, 2010, annual financial statements. Prepare the company's closing entries.

Dan Viera, Capital	$118,400	Interest Expense	$ 8,800
Service Revenue	356,400	Accounts Receivable	56,000
Unearned Revenues	5,400	Salaries Payable	3,400
Salary Expense	70,000	Amortization Expense	40,800
Accumulated Amortization	140,000	Rent Expense	23,600
Supplies Expense	11,800	Dan Viera, Withdrawals	90,000
Interest Revenue	5,800	Supplies	5,600

Prepare a T-account for Dan Viera, Capital. What is the ending Capital balance at June 30, 2010?

Exercise 4–7

Identifying and journalizing closing entries

2. B. Decker, Capital bal. $109,550

The accountant for Decker Environmental Consulting has posted adjusting entries (a) through (e) to the accounts at December 31, 2010. All the revenue, expense, and owner's equity accounts of the entity are listed here in T-account form.

Required

1. Journalize Decker Environmental Consulting's closing entries at December 31, 2010.
2. Determine Decker Environmental Consulting's ending Capital balance at December 31, 2010.

Accounts Receivable

	39,000	
(a)	7,250	

Supplies

6,000		(b)	3,000

Accumulated Amortization— Furniture

		9,000
	(c)	1,650

Accumulated Amortization— Building

		49,500
(d)	6,000	

Salaries Payable

	(e)	1,050

B. Decker, Capital

	108,600

B. Decker, Withdrawals

122,100	

Service Revenue

		166,500
	(a)	7,250

Salary Expense

	36,000	
(e)	1,050	

Supplies Expense

(b)	6,000	

Amortization Expense— Furniture

(c)	1,650	

Amortization Expense— Building

(d)	6,000	

Exercise 4–8

Preparing a statement of owner's equity

J. Howser, Capital bal. $23,500

From the following accounts of Howser Consulting, prepare the entity's statement of owner's equity for the year ended December 31, 2010.

J. Howser, Capital

Dec. 31	16,000	Jan. 1	18,000
		Dec. 31	21,500

J. Howser, Withdrawals

Mar. 31	2,250	Dec. 31	16,000
Jun. 30	3,500		
Sept. 30	4,500		
Dec. 31	3,500		

Income Summary

Dec. 31	42,500	Dec. 31	64,000
Dec. 31	21,500		

Exercise 4–9

The adjusted trial balance from the March work sheet of O'Neill Systems follows:

Making closing entries

2. Net loss $5,800

Account Title	Adjusted Trial Balance	
	Debit	Credit
Cash...	27,600	
Supplies	7,000	
Prepaid rent	3,600	
Office equipment..	170,400	
Accumulated amortization—office equipment		26,000
Accounts payable..		28,400
Salaries payable..		3,200
Unearned service revenue		17,600
P. O'Neill, capital...		153,200
P. O'Neill, withdrawals................................	14,000	
Service revenue		62,000
Salary expense..	45,200	
Rent expense...	15,600	
Amortization expense—office equipment	1,200	
Supplies expense..	2,600	
Utilities expense	3,200	
	290,400	290,400

Required

1. Journalize the closing entries of O'Neill Systems at March 31, 2010.

2. How much net income or net loss did O'Neill Systems earn for March 2010? How can you tell?

Exercise 4–10

Refer to Exercise 4–9.

Preparing a classified balance sheet

1. Total assets $182,600

Required

1. After solving Exercise 4–9, use the data in that exercise to prepare O'Neill Systems' classified balance sheet at March 31, 2010. Use the report format. You must compute the ending balance of P. O'Neill, Capital.

2. Compute O'Neill Systems' current ratio and debt ratio at March 31, 2010. One year ago, the current ratio was 1.20 and the debt ratio was 0.30. Indicate whether O'Neill Systems' ability to pay its debts has improved or deteriorated during the current year.

Exercise 4–11

1. Suppose LES paid an account payable of $2,400 and erroneously debited Supplies. Make the journal entry to correct this error.

Making correcting entries

2. Suppose LES made the following adjusting entry to record amortization at April 30:
   Amortization Expense—Furniture........... 4,000
      Furniture   4,000

   Make the journal entry to correct this error.

3. Suppose, in closing the books to a profitable year, LES made this closing entry:
   Income Summary....................................... 59,200
      Service Revenue..................................   59,200

   Make the journal entry to correct this error.

Exercise 4–12

Correcting accounting errors

Prepare a correcting entry for each of the following accounting errors:

a. Debited Supplies and credited Accounts Payable for a $9,000 purchase of office equipment on account.

b. Accrued interest revenue of $3,000 by a debit to Accounts Receivable and a credit to Interest Revenue.

c. Adjusted prepaid rent by debiting Prepaid Rent and crediting Rent Expense for $4,000. This adjusting entry should have debited Rent Expense and credited Prepaid Rent for $4,000.

d. Debited Salary Expense and credited Accounts Payable to accrue salary expense of $12,000.

e. Recorded the earning of $7,800 service revenue collected in advance by debiting Accounts Receivable and crediting Service Revenue.

Exercise 4–13

Balance-sheet presentation implications of international financial reporting standards (IFRS)

Shown below are extracts from the balance sheets of two airlines. WestJet Airlines Ltd. is a Canadian corporation and reported its results under Canadian GAAP. British Airways is a British airline that reported its results under IFRS.

Review each balance sheet and describe at least three differences in the way the balance-sheet information is presented.

WestJet Airlines Ltd.
(thousands of Canadian dollars)

Assets

Current assets		
Cash	$820,214	
Accounts receivable	16,837	
Future income tax	4,196	
Prepaid expenses	67,693	
Inventory	17,054	
Total current assets		$ 925,994
Property and equipment		2,281,850
Other assets		71,005
Total assets		$3,278,849

Liabilities and shareholders' equity

Current liabilities		
Accounts payable	$249,354	
Advance ticket sales	251,354	
Non-refundable guest credits	73,020	
Current portion of long-term debt	165,721	
Current portion of obligations under capital lease	395	
Total current liabilities		$ 739,844
Long-term debt		1,186,182
Obligations under capital leases		713
Other liabilities		24,233
Future income tax		241,740
Total liabilities		2,192,712

Shareholders' equity

Share capital	452,885	
Contributed surplus	60,193	
Accumulated other comprehensive loss	(38,112)	
Retained earnings	611,171	
Total shareholders' equity		1,086,137
Total liabilities and shareholders' equity		$3,278,849

British Airways
(millions of pounds)

Non-current assets

Property, plant & equipment

Fleet	5,996	
Property	971	
Equipment	266	
	7,233	

Intangibles

Goodwill	40	
Landing rights	205	
Software	22	
	267	
Investments in associates	209	
Available-for-sale financial assets	65	
Employee benefit assets	340	
Derivative financial instruments.........................	3	
Prepayments and accrued income	25	
Total non-current assets		**8,142**

Current assets and receivables

Inventories...	127	
Trade receivables	530	
Other current assets	268	
Derivative financial instruments.........................	40	
Other current interest-bearing deposits..............	979	
Cash and cash equivalents..................................	402	
Total current assets and receivables		**2,346**
Total assets..		**10,488**

Shareholders' equity

Issued share capital..	288	
Share premium	937	
Investment in own shares	(9)	
Other reserves..	430	
Total shareholders' equity.............................		**1,646**
Minority interest..	200	
Total equity..		**1,846**

Non-current liabilities

Interest-bearing long-term borrowings...............	3,074	
Employee benefit obligations	191	
Provisions for deferred tax.................................	652	
Other provisions..	256	
Derivative financial instruments.........................	123	
Other long-term liabilities..................................	204	
Total non-current liabilities..........................		**4,500**

Current liabilities

Current portion of long-term borrowings	689	
Trade and other payables....................................	2,796	
Derivative financial instruments.........................	471	
Current tax payable..	4	
Short-term provisions...	182	
Total current liabilities.................................		**4,142**
Total equity and liabilities		**10,488**

*Exercise 4–14

On December 31, 2010, Tristar Industries recorded an adjusting entry for $10,000 of accrued interest revenue. On January 15, 2011, the company received interest payments in the amount of $22,000. Assuming Tristar Industries uses reversing entries, prepare the 2010 and 2011 journal entries for these interest transactions.

Journalizing reversing entries

*Exercise 4–15

On September 30, 2010, its fiscal year end, Slolam Services recorded an adjusting entry for $2,000 of interest it owes at year end and will include as part of its payment on October 31, 2010. On October 31, 2010, the company paid interest in the amount of $3,000. Assuming Slolam Services uses reversing entries, prepare the journal entries for these interest transactions.

Journalizing reversing entries

---

*These Exercises cover Chapter 4 Appendix topics.

SERIAL EXERCISE

This exercise continues the Haupt Consulting situation from Exercise 3–23 of Chapter 3. If you did not complete Exercise 3–23, you can complete Exercise 4–16 by following the instructions given in the note below.

Exercise 4–16

Closing the books, preparing a classified balance sheet, evaluating a business

③ ⑤ ⑥

2. Total assets $14,307

Refer to Exercise 3–23 of Chapter 3. Start from the posted T-accounts and the adjusted trial balance shown below that Haupt Consulting prepared at December 31, 2010.

Note: If you did not do Exercise 3–23, you can complete this Exercise by using the accounts and balances given in the adjusted trial balance at December 31, 2010, shown below.

HAUPT CONSULTING
Adjusted Trial Balance
December 31, 2010

Cash	$ 7,200	
Accounts receivable	1,500	
Supplies	100	
Equipment	2,000	
Accumulated amortization—equipment		$ 33
Furniture	3,600	
Accumulated amortization—furniture		60
Accounts payable		3,600
Salary payable		500
Unearned service revenue		600
Carl Haupt, capital		10,000
Carl Haupt, withdrawals	1,600	
Service revenue		3,200
Rent expense	1,000	
Utilities expense	200	
Salary expense	500	
Amortization expense—equipment	33	
Amortization expense—furniture	60	
Supplies expense	200	
Total	$17,993	$17,993

Required

1. Journalize and post to T-accounts the closing entries at December 31, 2010. Denote each closing amount as *Clo.* and account balance as *Bal.*
2. Prepare a classified balance sheet in report format at December 31, 2010.
3. Compute the current ratio and the debt ratio of Haupt Consulting and evaluate these ratio values as indicative of a strong or weak financial position.
4. If your instructor assigns it, complete the accounting work sheet at December 31, 2010.

CHALLENGE EXERCISE

Exercise 4–17

Computing financial statement amounts

② ⑤

1. Net income $50,000

The unadjusted account balances of Stinson Consulting follow:

Cash	$ 1,900	Unearned Service Revenue	$ 5,300
Accounts Receivable	7,200	Scott Stinson, Capital	90,200
Supplies	2,100	Scott Stinson, Withdrawals	46,200
Prepaid Insurance	3,200	Service Revenue	90,600
Furniture	8,400	Salary Expense	32,700
Accumulated Amortization—		Amortization Expense—	
Furniture	1,300	Furniture	0
Building	53,800	Amortization Expense—	
Accumulated Amortization—		Building	0
Building	14,900	Supplies Expense	0
Land	51,200	Insurance Expense	0
Accounts Payable	7,100	Utilities Expense	2,700
Salaries Payable	0		

Adjusting data at the end of the year included the following:

a. Unearned service revenue that has been earned, $4,600.

b. Accrued service revenue, $2,700.

c. Supplies used in operations, $1,900.

d. Accrued salary expense, $2,400.

e. Insurance expense, $2,800.

f. Amortization expense—furniture, $2,300; building, $3,100.

Scott Stinson, the proprietor of Stinson Consulting, has received an offer to sell his company. He needs to know the following information as soon as possible:

1. Net income for the year covered by these data.

2. Total assets.

3. Total liabilities.

4. Total owner's equity.

5. Proof that total assets equal total liabilities plus total owner's equity after all items are updated.

Required Without opening any accounts, making any journal entries, or using a work sheet, provide Scott Stinson with the requested information. Show all computations.

*Exercise 4–18

Refer to Exercise 4–17. Which adjusting entries (a, b, c, d, e, and/or f) can be reversed with reversing journal entries?

Reversing entries

Exercise 4–19

The Adjusted Trial Balance columns on the work sheet have total debits of $110,000 and total credits of $128,000. Show how the following errors would create this imbalance. How would you correct each error?

Correcting accounting errors

a. A $6,000 debit adjustment to Prepaid Insurance was incorrectly subtracted on the work sheet and appears as a $6,000 credit. The Prepaid Insurance account balance after the error is $8,000.

b. A $2,000 credit (accrual) to Fees Earned was subtracted from the Fees Earned credit balance. The Fees Earned account balance after the error is $6,000.

c. A $5,000 debit adjustment to Wages Expense was subtracted from the Wages Expense debit balance. Wages Expense had a zero balance after the error.

ETHICAL ISSUE

Discount Hardware wishes to expand its business and has borrowed $200,000 from Royal Bank. As a condition for making this loan, the bank required Discount Hardware to maintain a current ratio of at least 1.50 and a debt ratio of no more than 0.50, and to submit annual financial statements to the bank.

Business during the third year has been good but not great. Expansion costs have brought the current ratio down to 1.40 and the debt ratio up to 0.51 at December 15. The managers of Discount Hardware are considering the implication of reporting this current ratio to Royal Bank. One course of action that the managers are considering is to record in December of the third year some revenue on account that Discount Hardware will earn in January of next year. The contract for this job has been signed, and Discount Hardware will deliver the materials during January.

Required

1. Journalize the revenue transaction using your own numbers, and indicate how recording this revenue in December would affect the current ratio and the debt ratio.

---

* This Exercise covers Chapter 4 Appendix topics.

2. State whether it is ethical to record the revenue transaction in December. Identify the accounting criteria relevant to this situation.

3. Propose an ethical course of action for Discount Hardware.

PROBLEMS (GROUP A)

MyAccountingLab All questions in this section appear in MyAccountingLab.

Problem 4–1A

Preparing a work sheet

Net income $111,760

The trial balance of Brentwood Construction at July 31, 2010, appears below.

BRENTWOOD CONSTRUCTION
Trial Balance
July 31, 2010

Cash	$ 127,200	
Accounts receivable	226,920	
Supplies	105,960	
Prepaid insurance	23,800	
Equipment	196,140	
Accumulated amortization—equipment		$ 157,440
Building	257,340	
Accumulated amortization—building		63,000
Land	179,800	
Accounts payable		136,140
Interest payable		0
Wages payable		0
Unearned service revenue		63,360
Notes payable, long-term		134,400
T. Jackson, capital		474,780
T. Jackson, withdrawals	25,200	
Service revenue		141,140
Amortization expense—equipment	0	
Amortization expense—building	0	
Wages expense	19,200	
Insurance expense	0	
Interest expense	0	
Utilities expense	6,660	
Advertising expense	2,040	
Supplies expense	0	
Total	$1,170,260	$1,170,260

Additional data at July 31, 2010:

a. Amortization: equipment, $2,040; building, $4,220.

b. Accrued wages expense, $3,440.

c. A count of supplies showed that unused supplies amounted to $88,440.

d. During July, $7,000 of prepaid insurance coverage expired.

e. Accrued interest expense, $1,080.

f. Of the $63,360 balance of Unearned Service Revenue, $29,820 was earned during July.

g. Accrued advertising expense, $2,600. (Credit Accounts Payable.)

h. Accrued service revenue, $6,600.

Preparing financial statements from an adjusted trial balance, journalizing adjusting and closing entries, evaluating a business

2. Net income $48,778

Required Complete Brentwood Construction's work sheet for July. Identify each adjusting entry by its letter.

Problem 4–2A

The *adjusted* trial balance of Alan Wood Design at June 30, 2010, the end of the company's fiscal year, appears on the following page.

ALAN WOOD DESIGN
Adjusted Trial Balance
June 30, 2010

Cash	$ 12,610	
Accounts receivable	15,882	
Supplies	18,774	
Prepaid insurance	1,920	
Equipment	33,480	
Accumulated amortization—equipment		$ 9,888
Building	68,940	
Accumulated amortization—building		10,110
Land	18,000	
Accounts payable		25,040
Interest payable		1,894
Wages payable		1,462
Unearned service revenue		1,380
Notes payable, long-term		58,200
Alan Wood, capital		41,034
Alan Wood, withdrawals	28,180	
Service revenue		83,916
Amortization expense—equipment	4,380	
Amortization expense—building	2,382	
Wages expense	13,882	
Insurance expense	1,860	
Interest expense	7,906	
Utilities expense	2,580	
Supplies expense	2,148	
Total	$232,924	$232,924

Adjusting data at June 30, 2010, which *have been incorporated* into the trial balance figures, consist of the following:

a. Amortization for the year: equipment, $4,380; building, $2,382.

b. Supplies used during the year, $2,148.

c. During the year, $1,860 of prepaid insurance coverage expired.

d. Accrued interest expense, $1,414.

e. Accrued service revenue, $564.

f. Of the balance of Unearned Service Revenue at the beginning of the year, $4,674 was earned during the year.

g. Accrued wages expense, $1,462.

Required

1. Journalize the adjusting entries that would lead to the adjusted trial balance shown above. Also journalize the closing entries.

2. Prepare the income statement and statement of owner's equity for the year ended June 30, 2010, and the classified balance sheet on that date. Use the account format for the balance sheet.

3. Compute Alan Wood Design's current ratio and debt ratio at June 30, 2010. One year ago, the current ratio stood at 1.01, and the debt ratio was 0.71. Did Alan Wood Design's ability to pay debts improve or deteriorate during the fiscal year?

Problem 4–3A

The unadjusted T-accounts of Byford Systems at December 31, 2010, and the related year-end adjustment data are given on the next page.

Taking the accounting cycle through the closing entries and the classified balance sheet

2. Net income $87,000

Cash			Accounts Receivable			Supplies	
Bal. 7,500			Bal. 54,000			Bal. 13,500	

Equipment			Accumulated Amortization—Equipment			Accounts Payable	
Bal. 148,500				Bal. 54,000			Bal. 9,000

Salary Payable			Unearned Service Revenue			Note Payable, Long-term	
	0			Bal. 7,500			Bal. 90,000

T. Byford, Capital			T. Byford, Withdrawals			Service Revenue	
	Bal. 54,000		Bal. 93,000				Bal. 223,500

Salary Expense			Supplies Expense			Rent Expense	
Bal. 79,500			0			Bal. 22,500	

Amortization Expense—Equipment			Interest Expense			Insurance Expense	
0			Bal. 9,000			Bal. 10,500	

Adjustment data at December 31, 2010, include the following:

a. Of the $7,500 balance of Unearned Service Revenue at the beginning of the year, all of it was earned during the year.
b. Supplies still unused at year end, $3,000.
c. Amortization for the year, $13,500.
d. Accrued salary expense, $3,000.
e. Accrued service revenue, $4,500.

Required

1. Write the account data in the Trial Balance columns of a work sheet, and complete the work sheet. Identify each adjusting entry by the letter corresponding to the data given.
2. Prepare the income statement, the statement of owner's equity, and the classified balance sheet in account format.
3. Journalize the adjusting and closing entries.
4. Did Byford Systems have a profitable year or a bad year during 2010? Give the reason for your answer.

Problem 4–4A

Completing the accounting cycle

2. Trial bal. total $217,500

This problem should be used only in conjunction with Problem 4–3A. It completes the accounting cycle by posting to T-accounts and preparing the postclosing trial balance.

Required

1. Using the Problem 4–3A data, post the adjusting and closing entries to the T-accounts, identifying adjusting amounts as *Adj.*, closing amounts as *Clo.*, and account balances as *Bal.*, as shown in Exhibit 4–10 (page 174). Double underline all accounts with a zero ending balance.
2. Prepare the postclosing trial balance.

Problem 4–5A

The trial balance of Goldman Insurance Agency at August 31, 2010, appears below. The data needed for the month-end adjustments follow.

Excel Spreadsheet Template

Completing the accounting cycle

②③⑤

3. Net income $148,500

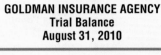

GOLDMAN INSURANCE AGENCY
Trial Balance
August 31, 2010

Acct.		
110 Cash..	$142,800	
120 Accounts receivable.......................	83,360	
130 Prepaid rent....................................	7,740	
140 Supplies	5,400	
150 Furniture..	92,100	
151 Accumulated amortization—furniture....		$ 76,800
170 Building	449,400	
171 Accumulated amortization—building.....		161,600
180 Land	80,000	
210 Accounts payable............................		25,440
220 Salaries payable..............................		0
230 Unearned commission revenue		53,400
300 O. Goldman, capital.........................		421,520
330 O. Goldman, withdrawals	28,800	
400 Commission revenue.......................		163,800
510 Salary expense	6,600	
520 Rent expense	0	
530 Utilities expense	2,460	
540 Amortization expense—furniture	0	
550 Amortization expense—building	0	
560 Advertising expense........................	3,900	
570 Supplies expense............................	0	
Total	$902,560	$902,560

Adjustment data:

a. Commission revenue received in advance that had not been earned at August 31, $40,500.

b. Rent still prepaid at August 31, $2,300.

c. Supplies used during the month, $2,040.

d. Amortization on furniture for the month, $2,220.

e. Amortization on building for the month, $2,780.

f. Accrued salary expense at August 31, $2,760.

Required

1. Open ledger accounts for the accounts listed in the trial balance and insert their August 31 unadjusted balances. Also open the Income Summary account (account #340). Date the balances of the following accounts as of August 1: Prepaid Rent, Supplies, Furniture, Accumulated Amortization—Furniture, Building, Accumulated Amortization—Building, Unearned Commission Revenue, and O. Goldman, Capital.

2. Write the trial balance on a work sheet and complete the work sheet of Goldman Insurance Agency for the month ended August 31, 2010.

3. Using the completed work sheet, prepare the income statement, the statement of owner's equity, and the classified balance sheet in account format.

4. Using the work-sheet data, journalize and post the adjusting and closing entries. Use dates and posting references. Use page 7 as the number of the journal page.

5. Prepare a postclosing trial balance.

Preparing a classified balance
sheet in report format,
evaluating a business

1. Total assets $393,900

Problem 4–6A

The accounts of Bolton Travel at December 31, 2010, are listed in alphabetical order:

Accounts Payable........................	$ 15,300	Interest Payable........................	$ 4,300
Accounts Receivable...................	19,800	Interest Receivable....................	600
Accumulated Amortization—		Land...	62,500
Building.....................................	113,400	Notes Payable, Long-Term......	88,400
Accumulated Amortization		Notes Receivable, Long-Term..	12,000
—Furniture...............................	34,800	Other Assets	13,300
Advertising Expense..................	6,600	Other Current Liabilities	14,100
Amortization Expense...............	3,900	Prepaid Insurance....................	3,300
Building	313,200	Prepaid Rent............................	19,800
Cash...	22,000	Salary Expense	73,800
Commission Revenue.................	280,500	Salary Payable..........................	11,700
E. Bolton, Capital........................	209,400	Supplies....................................	7,500
E. Bolton, Withdrawals...............	142,200	Supplies Expense.....................	17,100
Furniture.....................................	68,100	Unearned Commission	
Insurance Expense	2,400	Revenue	16,200

Required

1. *All adjustments have been journalized and posted, but the closing entries have not yet been made.* Prepare the company's classified balance sheet in report format at December 31, 2010.

2. Compute Bolton Travel's current ratio and debt ratio at December 31, 2010. At December 31, 2009, the current ratio was 1.52 and the debt ratio was 0.37. Did Bolton Travel's ability to pay both current and total debts improve or deteriorate during 2010?

Problem 4–7A

Analyzing and journalizing
corrections, adjustments, and
closing entries

d. Net income overstated
by $4,380

Accountants for Mainland Catering Service encountered the following situations while adjusting and closing the books at December 31. Consider each situation independently.

a. The company bookkeeper made the following entry to record a $4,500 credit purchase of office equipment:

Nov. 12	Office Supplies...................................	4,500	
	Accounts Payable		4,500

Prepare the correcting entry, dated December 31.

b. A $9,000 credit to Accounts Receivable was posted as a debit.
   (1) At what stage of the accounting cycle will this error be detected?
   (2) Describe the technique for identifying the amount of the error.

c. The $88,500 balance of Equipment was entered as $8,850 on the trial balance.
   (1) What is the name of this type of error?
   (2) Assume this is the only error in the trial balance. Which will be greater, the total debits or the total credits, and by how much?
   (3) How can this type of error be identified?

d. The accountant failed to make the following adjusting entries at December 31:
   (1) Accrued property tax expense, $2,400.
   (2) Supplies expense, $13,080.
   (3) Accrued interest revenue on a note receivable, $7,800.
   (4) Amortization of equipment, $12,000.
   (5) Earned service revenue that had been collected in advance, $15,300.

   Compute the overall net income effect of these omissions.

e. Record each of the adjusting entries identified in item d.

f. The revenue and expense accounts, *after* the adjusting entries had been posted, were Service Revenue, $115,200; Interest Revenue, $9,000; Salary Expense, $25,380; Rent Expense, $7,650; and Amortization Expense, $12,320. Two balances prior to closing were S. Jones, Capital, $72,900, and S. Jones, Withdrawals, $45,000. Journalize the closing entries.

Problem 4–8A

Slee Truck Services performs overhauls and repairs to trucks. The company's trial balance for the year ended March 31, 2010, is shown here.

Preparing a work sheet, journalizing the adjustments, closing the accounts

① ③

4. Trial bal. total $357,000

SLEE TRUCK SERVICES
Trial Balance
March 31, 2010

Cash..	$ 5,100	
Accounts receivable..	21,800	
Repair supplies...	13,350	
Prepaid insurance	5,850	
Equipment...	105,000	
Accumulated amortization—equipment.........		$ 42,000
Building..	121,000	
Accumulated amortization—building.............		28,200
Land	97,500	
Accounts payable..		10,800
Unearned repair revenues		2,250
Employee withholdings payable		3,000
Notes payable, long-term...............................		12,000
Mortgage payable		70,000
J. Slee, capital		133,550
J. Slee, withdrawals..	13,500	
Repair fees earned..		121,450
Wages expense	27,100	
Utilities expense	1,650	
Travel expense..	11,400	
Total	$423,250	$423,250

Additional information:

a. On March 31, repair supplies costing $3,900 were still on hand.

b. An examination of the insurance policies showed $3,150 of insurance coverage had expired during the year ended March 31, 2010.

c. An examination of the equipment and the building showed the following:

	Equipment	Building
Estimated useful life	5 years	10 years
Estimated value at the end of the useful life	$0	$0

Amortization is calculated on a straight-line basis over the asset's life.

d. The company had performed $1,200 of services for a client who had paid $2,250 in advance.

e. Accrued interest on the mortgage at March 31, $1,800.

f. Accrued wages at March 31 for 10 employees for one day. Each employee earned $13.50 per hour and worked a 10-hour day.

Required

1. Complete a work sheet for the year ended March 31, 2010.

2. Journalize the adjusting entries required on March 31, 2010.

3. Journalize the closing entries that would be required on March 31, 2010.

4. Prepare a postclosing trial balance at March 31, 2010.

Problem 4–9A

Len Thomas, the accountant for Lancaster Consulting, prepared the work sheet shown on the next page on a computer spreadsheet but has lost much of the data. The only particular item Thomas can recall is that there was an adjustment made to correct an error made where $600 of supplies, purchased on credit, had been incorrectly recorded as $600 of equipment.

Preparing a work sheet, closing the accounts, classifying the assets and liabilities, evaluating the current and debt ratios

① ③ ④ ⑤ ⑥

3. Total assets $205,600

LANCASTER CONSULTING
Work Sheet
For the Year Ended December 31, 2010

Account Title	Trial Balance Debit	Trial Balance Credit	Adjustments Debit	Adjustments Credit	Adjusted Trial Balance Debit	Adjusted Trial Balance Credit	Income Statement Debit	Income Statement Credit	Balance Sheet Debit	Balance Sheet Credit
Cash	19,000				19,000					
Accounts receivable	20,400				20,700					
Supplies	2,850			(b) 1,200						
Prepaid insurance	3,000				2,400					
Equipment	41,250				40,650					
Accum. amort.—equip.		3,600				5,400				
Building	90,000				90,000					
Accum. amort.—bldg.		6,000		(e) 3,000						
Land	45,000				45,000					
Accounts payable		7,500								
Interest payable		4,500								
Wages payable		1,800		(f) 900						
Unearned consulting fees		5,250	(g) 750							
Mortgage payable		75,000				75,000				
L. Lancaster, capital		61,500				61,500				
L. Lancaster, withdrawals	9,000				9,000				9,000	
Consulting fees earned		127,450				128,500				
Wages expense	50,250				51,150					
Insurance expense	6,600									
Interest expense	4,500									
Utilities expense	750				750					
Supplies expense			(b) 1,200		1,200					
Amort. exp.—equip.			(d) 1,800		1,800					
Amort. exp.—bldg.										
Totals	292,600	292,600								

Required

1. Complete the work sheet by filling in the missing data.
2. Journalize the closing entries that would be required on December 31, 2010.
3. Prepare the company's classified balance sheet at December 31, 2010.
4. Compute Lancaster Consulting's current ratio and debt ratio for December 31, 2010. On December 31, 2009, the current ratio was 2.14 and the debt ratio was 0.47. Comment on the changes in the ratios.

*Problem 4–10A

Refer to the data in Problem 4–5A, page 209.

Using reversing entries

Required

1. Open ledger accounts for Salaries Payable and Salary Expense. Insert their unadjusted balances at August 31, 2010.
2. Journalize adjusting entry f and the closing entry for Salary Expense at August 31. Post to the accounts.
3. On September 5, Goldman Insurance Agency paid the next payroll amount of $3,480. Journalize this cash payment, and post to the accounts. Show the balance in each account.
4. Repeat Requirements 1 through 3 using a reversing entry. Compare the balances of Salaries Payable and Salary Expense computed by using a reversing entry with those balances computed without using a reversing entry (as they appear in your answer to Requirement 3).

PROBLEMS (GROUP B)

MyAccountingLab | All questions in this section appear in MyAccountingLab.

Problem 4–1B

The trial balance of Denise Arami Design at May 31, 2010, is shown here.

Preparing a work sheet
①

DENISE ARAMI DESIGN
Trial Balance
May 31, 2010

Cash	$ 18,670	
Notes receivable	10,340	
Interest receivable	0	
Supplies	560	
Prepaid insurance	5,790	
Furniture	27,410	
Accumulated amortization—furniture		$ 1,480
Building	53,900	
Accumulated amortization—building		34,560
Land	43,700	
Accounts payable		34,730
Interest payable		0
Salary payable		0
Unearned design services revenue		8,800
Notes payable, long-term		18,700
Denise Arami, capital		44,290
Denise Arami, withdrawals	3,800	
Design services revenue		26,970
Interest revenue	0	
Amortization expense—furniture	0	
Amortization expense—building	0	
Salary expense	3,170	
Insurance expense	0	
Interest expense	0	
Utilities expense	1,130	
Advertising expense	1,060	
Supplies expense	0	
Total	$169,530	$169,530
Net income	$20,220	

---

*This Problem covers Chapter 4 Appendix topics.

Additional data at May 31, 2010:

a. Amortization: furniture, $480; building, $460.

b. Accrued salary expense, $1,200.

c. A count of supplies showed that unused supplies amounted to $410.

d. During May, $1,390 of prepaid insurance coverage expired.

e. Accrued interest expense, $220.

f. Of the $8,800 balance of Unearned Design Services Revenue, $4,400 was earned during May.

g. Accrued advertising expense, $2,060. (Credit Accounts Payable.)

h. Accrued interest revenue, $170.

Required Complete Denise Arami Design's work sheet for May 2010. Identify each adjusting entry by its letter.

Problem 4–2B

Preparing financial statements from an adjusted trial balance, journalizing adjusting and closing entries, evaluating a business

The adjusted trial balance of Musquem Golf School at April 30, 2010, the end of the company's fiscal year, is shown here.

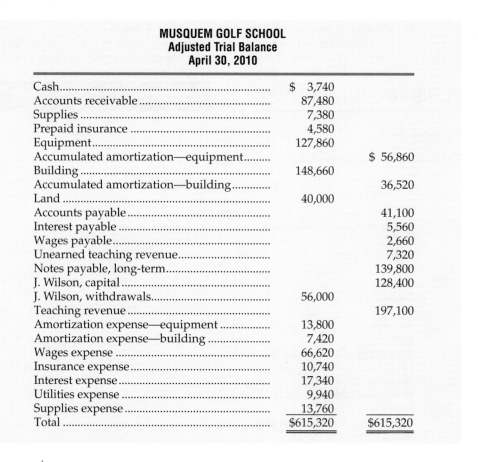

MUSQUEM GOLF SCHOOL
Adjusted Trial Balance
April 30, 2010

Cash	$ 3,740	
Accounts receivable	87,480	
Supplies	7,380	
Prepaid insurance	4,580	
Equipment	127,860	
Accumulated amortization—equipment		$ 56,860
Building	148,660	
Accumulated amortization—building		36,520
Land	40,000	
Accounts payable		41,100
Interest payable		5,560
Wages payable		2,660
Unearned teaching revenue		7,320
Notes payable, long-term		139,800
J. Wilson, capital		128,400
J. Wilson, withdrawals	56,000	
Teaching revenue		197,100
Amortization expense—equipment	13,800	
Amortization expense—building	7,420	
Wages expense	66,620	
Insurance expense	10,740	
Interest expense	17,340	
Utilities expense	9,940	
Supplies expense	13,760	
Total	$615,320	$615,320

Adjusting data at April 30, 2010, which have all been incorporated into the trial balance figures, consist of the following:

a. Of the balance of Unearned Teaching Revenue at the beginning of the year, $8,360 was earned during the year.

b. Supplies used during the year, $11,760.

c. During the year, $10,740 of prepaid insurance coverage expired.

d. Accrued interest expense, $3,560.

e. Accrued teaching revenue, $4,400.

f. Amortization for the year: equipment, $13,800; building, $7,420.

g. Accrued wages expense, $2,660.

Required

1. Journalize the adjusting entries that would lead to the adjusted trial balance shown here. Also journalize the closing entries.

2. Prepare Musquem Golf School's income statement and statement of owner's equity for the year ended April 30, 2010, and the classified balance sheet on that date. Use the account format for the balance sheet.

3. Compute Musquem Golf School's current ratio and debt ratio at April 30, 2010. One year ago, the current ratio stood at 1.21, and the debt ratio was 0.82. Did Musquem Golf School's ability to pay debts improve or deteriorate during 2010?

Problem 4–3B

Taking the accounting cycle through the closing entries

The unadjusted T-accounts of Super Media at December 31, 2010, are shown here. The related year-end adjustment data appear below them.

Cash		Accounts Receivable		Supplies	
Bal. 87,000		Bal. 132,000		Bal. 18,000	

Equipment		Accumulated Amortization—Equipment		Accounts Payable	
Bal. 171,000			Bal. 36,000		Bal. 48,000

Salary Payable		Unearned Service Revenue		Notes Payable, Long-Term	
	0		Bal. 6,000		Bal. 120,000

W. Super, Capital		W. Super, Withdrawals		Service Revenue	
	Bal. 123,000	Bal. 162,000			Bal. 390,000

Supplies Expense		Salary Expense		Insurance Expense	
0		Bal. 108,000		Bal. 30,000	

Amortization Expense—Equipment		Interest Expense	
0		Bal. 15,000	

Adjustment data at December 31, 2010, include the following:

a. Amortization for the year, $7,500.
b. Supplies still unused at the year end, $10,000.
c. Accrued service revenue, $12,000.
d. Of the $6,000 balance of Unearned Service Revenue at the beginning of the year, $3,000 was earned during the year.
e. Accrued salary expense, $8,000.

Required

1. Write the account data in the Trial Balance columns of a work sheet and complete the work sheet. Identify each adjusting entry by the letter corresponding to the data given.

2. Prepare the income statement, the statement of owner's equity, and the classified balance sheet in account format.

3. Journalize the adjusting and closing entries.

4. Did Super Media have a profitable year or a bad year during 2010? Give the reason for your answer.

Problem 4–4B

This problem should be used only in conjunction with Problem 4–3B. It completes the accounting cycle by posting to T-accounts and preparing the postclosing trial balance.

Completing the accounting cycle

Required

1. Using the Problem 4–3B data, post the adjusting and closing entries to the T-accounts, identifying adjusting amounts as *Adj.,* closing amounts as *Clo.,* and account balances as *Bal.,* as shown in Exhibit 4–10 (page 174). Double underline all accounts with a zero ending balance.

2. Prepare the postclosing trial balance.

Excel Spreadsheet Template

Completing the accounting cycle

Problem 4–5B

The trial balance of Stone Environmental Services at October 31, 2010, and the data needed for the month-end adjustments, are shown below.

STONE ENVIRONMENTAL SERVICES
Trial Balance
October 31, 2010

Acct.		
110 Cash	$ 32,050	
120 Accounts receivable	63,895	
130 Prepaid rent	9,900	
140 Supplies	3,780	
150 Furniture	140,735	
151 Accumulated amortization—furniture		$ 25,300
160 Building	307,350	
161 Accumulated amortization—building		49,450
180 Land	76,000	
210 Accounts payable		32,805
220 Salary payable		0
230 Unearned consulting revenue		23,850
300 K. Stone, capital		476,205
330 K. Stone, withdrawals	17,550	
400 Consulting revenue		56,520
510 Salary expense	8,280	
520 Rent expense	0	
530 Utilities expense	4,590	
540 Amortization expense—furniture	0	
550 Amortization expense—building	0	
570 Supplies expense	0	
Total	$664,130	$664,130

The data needed for the month-end adjustments are as follows:

a. Unearned consulting revenue that still had not been earned at October 31, $22,050.
b. Rent still prepaid at October 31, $7,000.
c. Supplies used during the month, $3,465.
d. Amortization on furniture for the month, $11,125.
e. Amortization on building for the month, $1,610.
f. Accrued salary expense at October 31, $2,395.

Required

1. Open ledgers for the accounts listed in the trial balance, inserting their October 31 unadjusted balances. Also open the Income Summary account (account #340). Date the balances of the following accounts October 1: Prepaid Rent, Supplies, Furniture, Accumulated Amortization—Furniture, Building, Accumulated Amortization—Building, Unearned Consulting Revenue, and K. Stone, Capital.

2. Write the trial balance on a work sheet and complete the work sheet of Stone Environmental Services for the month ended October 31, 2010.

3. Using the completed work sheet, prepare the income statement, the statement of owner's equity, and the classified balance sheet in account format.

4. Using the work-sheet data, journalize and post the adjusting and closing entries. Use dates and posting references. Use 12 as the number of the journal page.

5. Prepare a postclosing trial balance.

Problem 4–6B

Preparing a classified balance sheet in report format, evaluating a business

The accounts of Wang Financial Services at March 31, 2010, are listed in alphabetical order here.

Accounts Payable..........................	$21,760	Interest Receivable.....................	$ 720
Accounts Receivable....................	9,200	Land..	23,000
Accumulated Amortization—		Notes Payable, Long-Term......	22,560
Building	37,840	Notes Receivable, Long-Term ..	5,520
Accumulated Amortization—		Other Assets	16,840
Furniture..................................	6,160	Other Current Liabilities	880
Advertising Expense..................	720	Prepaid Insurance....................	480
Amortization Expense...............	1,520	Prepaid Rent.............................	3,760
A. Wang, Capital	40,560	Salary Expense..........................	14,240
A. Wang, Withdrawals	24,960	Salary Payable..........................	11,920
Building	44,720	Service Revenue........................	56,880
Cash..	17,720	Supplies.....................................	3,040
Furniture....................................	34,560	Supplies Expense......................	3,680
Insurance Expense	480	Unearned Service Revenue.....	1,360
Interest Payable	5,240		

Required

1. *All adjustments have been journalized and posted, but the closing entries have not yet been made.* Prepare the company's classified balance sheet in report format at March 31, 2010. Use captions for total assets, total liabilities, and total liabilities and owner's equity.

2. Compute Wang Financial Services' current ratio and debt ratio at March 31, 2010. At March 31, 2009, the current ratio was 1.28, and the debt ratio was 0.32. Did Wang Financial Services' ability to pay both current and total debts improve or deteriorate during fiscal 2010?

Problem 4–7B

Analyzing and journalizing corrections, adjustments, and closing entries

The auditors of Cohen Logistics encountered the following situations while adjusting and closing the books at February 28. Consider each situation independently.

a. The company bookkeeper made the following entry to record a $2,480 credit purchase of supplies:

| Feb. 26 | Equipment... | 2,480 | |
| | Accounts Payable .... | | 2,480 |

Prepare the correcting entry, dated February 28.

b. A $540 debit to Accounts Receivable was posted as $450.
(1) At what stage of the accounting cycle will this error be detected?
(2) Describe the technique for identifying the amount of the error.

c. The $3,480 balance of Utilities Expense was entered as $34,800 on the trial balance.
(1) What is the name of this type of error?
(2) Assume this is the only error in the trial balance. Which will be greater, the total debits or the total credits, and by how much?
(3) How can this type of error be identified?

d. The accountant failed to make the following adjusting entries at February 28:
(1) Accrued service revenue, $10,800.
(2) Insurance expense that had been prepaid, $2,160.
(3) Accrued interest expense on a note payable, $6,240.
(4) Amortization of equipment, $22,200.
(5) Earned service revenue that had been collected in advance, $8,100.

Compute the overall net income effect of these five omissions.

e. Record each of the adjusting entries identified in item d.

f. The revenue and expense accounts *after* the adjusting entries had been posted were Service Revenue, $199,995; Wages Expense, $78,325; Amortization Expense, $30,540; and Insurance Expense, $1,860. Two balances prior to closing were N. Cohen, Capital, $137,725, and N. Cohen, Withdrawals, $111,000. Journalize the closing entries.

Problem 4–8B

Preparing a work sheet, journalizing adjustments and closing entries, closing the accounts

Glen Eagle Marina performs overhauls and repairs to boats and motors at the marina and at the customer's location. The company's trial balance for the year ended June 30, 2010, follows.

GLEN EAGLE MARINA
Trial Balance
June 30, 2010

Cash	$ 16,900	
Accounts receivable	36,600	
Repair supplies	59,400	
Prepaid insurance	14,100	
Equipment	28,000	
Accumulated amortization—equipment		$ 12,000
Building	264,000	
Accumulated amortization—building		52,800
Land	165,000	
Accounts payable		19,500
Unearned repair revenues		6,000
Property taxes payable		13,000
Notes payable, long-term		27,000
Mortgage payable		138,000
J. Alexander, capital		172,800
J. Alexander, withdrawals	51,000	
Repair fees earned		377,500
Wages expense	133,800	
Utilities expense	2,400	
Travel expense	47,400	
Total	$ 818,600	$ 818,600

Additional information:

a. On June 30, repair supplies costing $16,600 were still on hand.

b. An examination of the insurance policies showed $8,700 of insurance coverage had expired in the year ended June 30, 2010.

c. An examination of the equipment and the building showed the following:

	Equipment	Building
Estimated useful life	10 years	10 years
Estimated value at the end of the useful life	$0	$0

Amortization is calculated on a straight-line basis over the asset's life.

d. The company had performed $3,000 of services for a client who had paid $6,000 in advance.

e. Accrued interest on the mortgage at June 30, $14,800.

f. Accrued wages at June 30 were for 60 employees for one day at a rate of $60 per day per employee.

Required

1. Complete a work sheet for the year ended June 30, 2010.
2. Journalize the adjusting entries required on June 30, 2010.
3. Journalize the closing entries that would be required on June 30, 2010.
4. Prepare a postclosing trial balance for June 30, 2010.

Problem 4–9B

Preparing a work sheet, journalizing the adjustments, closing the accounts

Mark Hanson, the accountant for Glenn Graphics, had prepared the work sheet shown on the next page on a computer spreadsheet but has lost much of the data. The only particular item the accountant can recall is that an adjustment was made to correct an error made where $900 of supplies, purchased on credit, had been incorrectly recorded as $9,000 of equipment.

Account Title	Trial Balance Dr	Trial Balance Cr	Adjustments Dr	Adjustments Cr	Adjusted Trial Balance Dr	Adjusted Trial Balance Cr	Income Statement Dr	Income Statement Cr	Balance Sheet Dr	Balance Sheet Cr
Cash	18,000				18,000					
Accounts receivable	34,050				34,200					
Supplies	2,100			(b) 1,050	2,100					
Prepaid insurance	2,400									
Equipment	39,000				30,000					
Accum. amort.—equip.		4,500				6,750				
Building	129,000				129,000					
Accum. amort.—bldg.		36,900		(e) 3,450						
Land	36,000				36,000					
Accounts payable		24,000			15,900					
Wages payable		1,350								
Interest payable		3,000		(f) 600						
Unearned revenues		4,050	(g) 600							
Mortgage payable		60,000				60,000				
W. Glenn, capital		118,500				118,500				
W. Glenn, withdrawals	37,000				37,000				37,000	
Graphics fees earned		147,650				148,400				
Wages expense	85,050				85,650					
Insurance expense	3,300									
Interest expense	13,000									
Utilities expense	1,050				1,050					
Supplies expense			(b) 1,050		1,050					
Amort. exp.—equip.			(d) 2,250		2,250					
Amort. exp.—bldg.										
Totals	399,950	399,950								

Required

1. Complete the work sheet by filling in the missing data.
2. Journalize the closing entries that would be required on December 31, 2010.
3. Prepare the company's classified balance sheet as of December 31, 2010.
4. Compute Glenn Graphics' current ratio and debt ratio for December 31, 2010. On December 31, 2009, the current ratio was 2.25 and the debt ratio was 0.41. Comment on the changes in the ratios.

*Problem 4–10B

Using reversing entries

Refer to the data in Problem 4–3B on page 215.

Required

1. Open ledger accounts for Accounts Receivable and Service Revenue. Insert their unadjusted balances at December 31, 2010.
2. Journalize the adjusting entry c only and the resulting closing entry for Service Revenue at December 31, 2010. Post to the accounts.
3. On January 10, 2011, Super Media received a payment of $12,000 in settlement of this invoice. Journalize this cash receipt, and post to the accounts. Show the balance in each account.
4. Repeat Requirements 1 through 3 using a reversing entry. Compare the balances of Accounts Receivable and Service Revenue computed by using a reversing entry with those balances computed without using a reversing entry (as they appear in your answer to Requirement 3).

CHALLENGE PROBLEMS

Problem 4–1C

Identifying and correcting errors

(4)

The following errors were made by Classy Catering's new bookkeeper:

a. A debit of $3,000 was recorded as an account receivable instead of a note receivable.
b. A salary expense accrual in the amount of $10,000 was overlooked when the work sheet was prepared.
c. A catering service revenue accrual of $10,000 was not recorded.

How would you correct these errors if they occurred

1. After completing the work sheet, but before the financial statements were prepared (the accounts have not yet been closed)?
2. After closing entries were completed?

Problem 4–2C

Understanding the current ratio

(6)

It is July 15, 2010. A friend, who works in the office of a local company that has four fast-food restaurants, has come to you with a question. She knows you are studying accounting and asks if you could help her sort something out. She acknowledges that although she has worked for the company for three years as a general clerk, she really does not understand the accounting work she is doing.

   The company has a large bank loan and, as your friend understands it, the company has agreed with the bank to maintain a current ratio (she thinks that is what it is called) of 1.8 to 1 (1.8:1). The company's year end is June 30. The owner came to her on July 7, 2010, and asked her to issue a batch of cheques to suppliers but to date them June 30. Your friend recognizes that the cheques will have an effect on the June 30, 2010, financial statements but doesn't think the effect will be too serious.

Required

Explain to your friend what the effect of paying invoices after June 30 but dating the cheques prior to June 30 has on the current ratio. Provide an example to illustrate your explanation.

---

*This Problem covers Chapter 4 Appendix topics.

Extending Your Knowledge

Decision Problem 1

One year ago, your friend Don Jenner founded Jenner Consulting Services. The business has prospered. Jenner, who remembers that you took an accounting course while in university, comes to you for advice. He wishes to know how much net income his business earned during the past year. He also wants to know what the entity's total assets, liabilities, and owner's equity are. The accounting records consist of the T-accounts of the company's ledger, which were prepared by a bookkeeper who moved to another city. The ledger at December 31, 2010 appears as follows:

Completing the accounting cycle to develop the information for a bank loan

Net income $65,110
Ending owner's equity $42,480

Cash			Accounts Receivable			Prepaid Rent	
Dec. 31	8,745		Dec. 31	18,540		Jan. 2	9,200

Supplies			Computer Equipment			Accumulated Amortization—Equipment	
Jan. 2	7,800		Jan. 2	65,400			0

Accounts Payable			Unearned Service Revenue			Salaries Payable	
	Dec. 31	27,810		Dec. 31	11,195		0

D. Jenner, Capital			D. Jenner, Withdrawals			Service Revenue	
	Jan. 2	42,500	Dec. 31	65,130		Dec. 31	121,110

Amortization Expense—Equipment			Salary Expense			Supplies Expense	
0			Dec. 31	25,500		0	

Rent Expense			Utilities Expense	
0			Dec. 31	2,300

Jenner indicates that at the year's end customers owe the company $4,800 accrued service revenue, which he expects to collect early next year. These revenues have not been recorded. During the year, the company collected $11,195 service revenue in advance from customers, but the company earned only $1,800 of that amount. Rent expense for the year was $7,200, and the company used up $6,300 in supplies. Jenner estimates that amortization on the equipment was $17,700 for the year. At December 31, Jenner Consulting owes an employee $3,600 accrued salary.

Jenner expresses concern that his withdrawals during the year might have exceeded the business's net income. To get a loan to expand the business, Jenner must show the bank that Jenner Consulting's owner's equity has grown from its original $42,500 balance. Has it? You and Jenner agree that you will meet again in one week. You perform the analysis and prepare the financial statements to answer his questions.

Decision Problem 2

You are preparing the financial statements for the year ended October 31, 2010, for Cusik Publishing Company, a weekly newspaper. You began with the trial balance of the ledger, which balanced, and then made the required adjusting entries. To save time, you omitted preparing an adjusted trial balance. After making the adjustments on the work sheet, you extended the balances from the trial balance, adjusted for the adjusting entries, and computed amounts for the Income Statement and Balance Sheet columns.

Finding an error in the work sheets

a. When you added the debits and credits in the Income Statement columns, you found that the credits exceeded the debits by $15,000. According to your finding, did Cusik Publishing Company have a profit or a loss?

b. You took the balancing amount from the Income Statement columns to the Balance Sheet debit column and found that the total debits exceeded the total credits in the balance sheet. The difference between the total debits and the total credits on the balance sheet is $30,000, which is two times the amount of the difference you calculated for the Income Statement columns. What is the cause of this difference? (Except for these errors, everything else is correct.)

FINANCIAL STATEMENT CASES

Financial Statement Case 1

Using an actual balance sheet and other information

This case, based on Canadian Western Bank's balance sheet in Appendix A, will familiarize you with some of the assets and liabilities of this actual company. Answer these questions, using the bank's balance sheet and other information, as shown.

Required

1. Compare Canadian Western Bank's balance sheet to the balance sheet in Exhibit 4–13 on page 180. What differences in style do you notice between these two balance sheets? Describe these differences.

   Questions 2, 3, 4, and 6 refer to the liquidity data shown below.

Table 15—Liquid Assets
($ thousands)

	2008	2007	Change from 2007
Cash	$ 8,988	$ 6,446	$ 2,542
Deposits with regulated financial institutions	464,193	405,122	59,071
Cheques and other items in transit	18,992	1,122	17,870
Total Cash Resources	492,173	412,960	79,483
Securities purchased under resale agreements	77,000	206,925	(129,925)
Government of Canada treasury bills	214,482	332,358	(117,876)
Government of Canada, provincial and municipal bonds, term to maturity 1 year or less	167,683	332,721	(165,038)
Government of Canada, provincial and municipal bonds, term to maturity more than 1 year	417,657	216,735	200,922
Preferred shares	256,232	221,878	34,354
Other marketable securities	171,671	236,256	(64,585)
Total Securities Purchased Under Resale Agreements and Marketable Securities	1,304,725	1,546,873	(242,148)
Total Liquid Assets	$ 1,796,898	$ 1,959,563	$ (162,665)
Total Assets	$ 10,600,732	$ 9,525,040	$ 1,075,692
Liquid Assets as a Percentage of Total Assets	17%	21%	(4)%
Total Deposit Liabilities	$ 9,245,719	$ 8,256,918	$ 988,801
Liquid Assets as a Percentage of Total Deposit Liabilities	19%	24%	(5)%

2. What is the value of Canadian Western Bank's total liquid assets for 2008? For 2007? What was the dollar amount of the change from 2007 to 2008?

3. What is the value of the total deposit liabilities for 2008? For 2007? What was the dollar amount of the change from 2007 to 2008?

4. What was the percentage of liquid assets compared to total deposit liabilities for 2008? For 2007?

5. What was the value of total assets for 2008?

6. Based on the amounts calculated in Questions 2 to 5, does Canadian Western Bank appear to have a strong liquidity position?

7. What is the main purpose of the notes to the financial statements?

Financial Statement Case 2

This case, based on Sun-Rype Products Ltd.'s balance sheet in Appendix B, will familiarize you with some of the assets and liabilities of this actual company. Answer these questions, using Sun-Rype's balance sheet.

Using an actual balance sheet

⑤ ⑥

6. Dec. 31, 2008 current
ratio 1.627

Required

1. Compare Sun-Rype's balance sheet to the balance sheet in Exhibit 4–13 on page 180. What differences in style do you notice between these two balance sheets? Describe these differences.

2. What is Sun-Rype's largest current asset in 2008? In 2007?

3. What is the company's largest current liability in 2008? In 2007?

4. What were the total current assets in 2008? In 2007?

5. What were the total current liabilities in 2008? In 2007?

6. Compute Sun-Rype's current ratio at December 31, 2008, and at December 31, 2007. Did the ratio values improve or deteriorate during the year?

7. Compute Sun-Rype's debt ratio at December 31, 2008, and at December 31, 2007. Did the ratio values improve or deteriorate during the year?

8. Many items on the balance sheet refer to notes that accompany the financial statements. Refer to the property, plant and equipment Note 5, and calculate the total cost of the assets, the accumulated amortization (depreciation), and the book value at December 31, 2008.

9. What is the main purpose of the notes to the financial statements?

5 Merchandising Operations and the Accounting Cycle

How do merchandising operations differ from service operations, and why is it important?

What are inventory and cost of goods sold? What types of inventory systems are there?

How do decision makers evaluate a company's inventory operations?

These questions and others will be answered throughout this chapter, and the Decision Guidelines at the end of this chapter will provide the answers in a useful summary.

LEARNING OBJECTIVES

1. Use sales and gross margin to evaluate a company

2. Account for the purchase and sale of inventory under the perpetual inventory system

3. Adjust and close the accounts of a merchandising business under the perpetual inventory system

4. Prepare a merchandiser's financial statements under the perpetual inventory system

5. Use the gross margin percentage and the inventory turnover ratio to evaluate a business

6. Describe the merchandising-operations effects of international financial reporting standards (IFRS)

CHAPTER 5 APPENDIX A

7. Account for the purchase and sale of inventory under the periodic inventory system

8. Compute the cost of goods sold under the periodic inventory system

9. Adjust and close the accounts of a merchandising business under the periodic inventory system

10. Prepare a merchandiser's financial statements under the periodic inventory system

CHAPTER 5 APPENDIX B

11. Compare the perpetual and periodic inventory systems

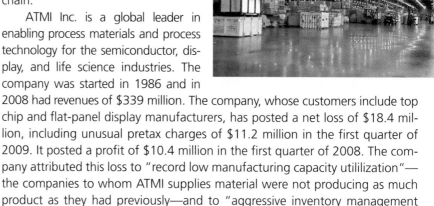

In its first quarter of 2009, semiconductor material supplier ATMI Inc. slipped to a quarterly loss, hurt by unusual charges as well as low manufacturing-capacity utilization and tight inventory management throughout the semiconductor supply chain.

ATMI Inc. is a global leader in enabling process materials and process technology for the semiconductor, display, and life science industries. The company was started in 1986 and in 2008 had revenues of $339 million. The company, whose customers include top chip and flat-panel display manufacturers, has posted a net loss of $18.4 million, including unusual pretax charges of $11.2 million in the first quarter of 2009. It posted a profit of $10.4 million in the first quarter of 2008. The company attributed this loss to "record low manufacturing capacity utillization"—the companies to whom ATMI supplies material were not producing as much product as they had previously—and to "aggressive inventory management throughout the entire semiconductor supply chain." In other words, ATMI's customers were not ordering any more material from ATMI than they absolutely needed to.

"While we have recently seen increased customer activity turn into order rate increases for several of our consumable materials, we do not yet feel confident that a sustainable and meaningful recovery is underway," Chief Financial Officer Tim Carlson said in a statement.

ATMI's situation is not unique. Many companies produce inventory in hopes of selling it to their customers. As their customers' needs decline, the producing company must monitor and probably reduce its own production in order to manage its business profitably.

Source: "ATMI Reports First Quarter 2009 Financial Results," April 22, 2009 (Globe-Newswire via COMTEX News Network), cited on the company's website, atmi.com. Accessed July 9, 2009.

What comes to mind when you think of *merchandising?* You are familiar with Canadian retailers who sell you the clothing you purchase at a clothing store, the bread you buy at the grocery store, or the gas you purchase at your local service station. Merchandisers include Zellers, The Bay, Canadian Tire, Petro-Canada, Shoppers Drug Mart, and Dell Computers (although most of these merchandisers also provide services, such as tire installation and repair services). In addition to these retailers, many companies, such as ATMI Inc., sell products or parts to companies that manufacture products that are, in turn, sold to retail stores.

How do the operations of Zellers, Canadian Tire, and other merchandisers differ from those of the businesses we have studied so far? In the first four chapters, Ladner Environmental Services provided an illustration of a business that earns revenue by selling its services. Service enterprises include Fairmont Hotels, West-Jet, physicians, lawyers, public accountants, the Calgary Flames hockey club, and the 12-year-old who cuts lawns in your neighbourhood. A *merchandising entity* earns its revenue by selling products, called *merchandise inventory* or, simply, *inventory*.

This chapter demonstrates the central role of inventory in a business, such as Zellers or ATMI Inc., that sells merchandise. **Inventory** includes all goods that the company owns and expects to sell to customers in the normal course of operations. Some businesses, such as Wal-Mart department stores, Esso gas stations, and Safeway grocery stores, buy their inventory in finished form ready for sale to customers. Others, such as Big Rock Breweries and Dell Inc., manufacture their own products. Both groups sell products rather than services.

Chapter 5 introduces merchandising. We show how to account for the purchase and sale of inventory. We feature a small electronics store, and we use an actual business document to illustrate transactions.

Before launching into merchandising, let's compare service entities, with which you are familiar, with merchandising companies. Exhibit 5–1 shows how the financial statements of a service entity (on the left) differ from those of a merchandiser (on the right).

What Are Merchandising Operations?

Merchandising consists of buying and selling products rather than services. Merchandisers have some new balance sheet and income statement items.

OBJECTIVE 1
Use sales and gross margin to evaluate a company

Balance Sheet
- Inventory, an asset

Income Statement
- Sales revenue
- Cost of goods sold, an expense
- Gross margin

These items are highlighted in Exhibit 5–1 for Merchandising Co. and explained further here.

The selling price of merchandise sold by a business is called **sales revenue**, often abbreviated as **sales**. (**Net sales** equals sales revenue minus any sales returns

EXHIBIT 5–1

SERVICE CO.*		
Income Statement		
For the Year Ended June 30, 2010		
Service revenue		$XXX
Expenses		
Salary expense	X	
Amortization expense	X	
Net income		$ X

MERCHANDISING CO.**		
Income Statement		
For the Year Ended June 30, 2010		
Sales revenue		$XXX
Cost of goods sold		X
Gross margin		XX
Operating expenses		
Salary expense		X
Amortization expense		X
Rent expense		X
Net income		$ X

SERVICE CO.	
Balance Sheet	
June 30, 2010	
Assets	
Current assets:	
Cash	$X
Held-for-trading investments	X
Accounts receivable, net	X
Prepaid expenses	X

MERCHANDISING CO.	
Balance Sheet	
June 30, 2010	
Assets	
Current assets:	
Cash	$X
Held-for-trading investments	X
Accounts receivable, net	X
Inventory	X
Prepaid expenses	X

*Such as Ladner Environmental Services

**Such as Austin Sound Centre, a small electronics store in Winnipeg, Manitoba.

and sales discounts.) The major revenue of a merchandising entity, sales revenue, results in an increase in capital from delivering inventory to customers.

The major expense of a merchandiser is **cost of goods sold**, also called **cost of sales**. It represents the entity's cost of the goods (the inventory) it sold to customers. While inventory is held by a business, it is an asset because the goods are an economic resource with future value to the company. When the inventory is sold, however, its cost becomes an expense to the seller because the goods are no longer available.

Net sales minus cost of goods sold is called **gross margin** or **gross profit**.

Gross margin is a measure of business success. A sufficiently high gross margin is vital to a merchandiser, since all other expenses of the company are deducted from this gross margin.

The following example will clarify the nature of gross margin. Consider Danier Leather Inc., the company that sells leather clothing and accessories across Canada. Suppose Danier Leather's cost for a certain jacket is $300 and Danier sells the jacket to a customer in Edmonton for $600. Danier's gross margin on the jacket is $300 ($600 − $300). The gross margin reported on Danier's year-end income statement is the sum of the gross margins on all the products the company sold during its fiscal year.

What Goes into Inventory Cost?

The cost of inventory on a merchandiser's balance sheet represents all the costs incurred to bring the merchandise to the point of sale. Suppose Danier Leather

Inc. purchases handbags from a manufacturer in Asia. Danier's cost of a handbag would include

- Cost of the handbag—say $50.00 per handbag.
- Customs duties paid to the Canadian government in order to import the handbags—say $5.00, added to the cost of each handbag.
- Shipping cost from the manufacturer in Asia to one of Danier's stores. This cost is called *freight* or *freight in*. Assume freight adds $2.50 of cost to each handbag.
- Insurance on the handbags while in transit—say $1.50 per handbag.

In total, Danier Leather's cost of this handbag totals $59.00 ($50.00 + $5.00 + $2.50 + $1.50). The cost principle of measurement applies to all assets, as follows:

**The cost of any asset is the sum of all the costs
incurred to bring the asset to its intended use.**

For merchandise inventory, the intended use is readiness for sale. After the goods are ready for sale, then other costs, such as advertising, display, and sales commissions, are expensed. These costs are *not* included as the cost of inventory.

The Operating Cycle for a Merchandising Business

Some merchandising entities buy inventory, sell the inventory to their customers, and use the cash to purchase more inventory to repeat the cycle. Other merchandisers, like Lake Breeze Winery in the Okanagan Valley or the Ford Motor Company, manufacture their products and sell them to customers. The balance of this chapter considers the first group of merchandisers, which buy products and resell them. Exhibit 5–2 diagrams the operating cycle for *cash sales* and for *sales on account*. For a cash sale—Panel A—the cycle is from cash to inventory, which is purchased for resale, and back to cash. For a sale on account—Panel B—the cycle is from cash to inventory to accounts receivable and back to cash. In all lines of business, managers strive to shorten the cycle in order to keep assets active. The faster the sale of inventory and the collection of cash, the higher the profits, assuming cost and selling price stay the same.

EXHIBIT 5–2 | Operating Cycle of a Merchandiser

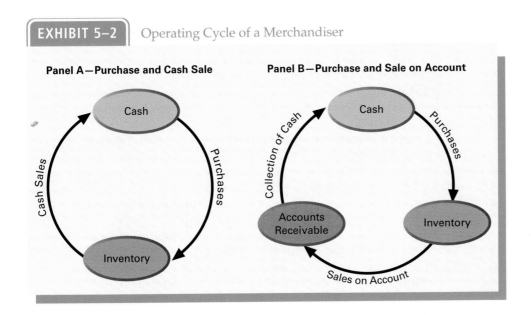

Now let's see how companies account for their inventory. We begin with journal entries, post to the ledger accounts, and prepare the financial statements.

Inventory Systems: Perpetual and Periodic

There are two main types of inventory accounting systems:

- Periodic system
- Perpetual system

The **periodic inventory system** is used by businesses that sell relatively inexpensive goods. A very small grocery store without optical-scanning point-of-sale equipment to read UPC codes does not keep a daily running record of every loaf of bread and litre of milk that it buys and sells. The cost of record keeping would be overwhelming. Instead, it counts its inventory periodically—at least once a year—to determine the quantities on hand. The inventory amounts are used to prepare the annual financial statements. Businesses such as restaurants and small retail stores also use the periodic inventory system.

Once the cost of the goods remaining in inventory at the end of the period (ending inventory) is determined by the inventory count, then we can calculate the cost of the inventory sold during the period. To do this, follow these steps:

1. Determine the cost of the goods that were in inventory at the beginning of the period, which is beginning inventory. This is the same amount as the prior period's ending inventory.

2. Add the cost of goods purchased during the period. Adding beginning inventory and purchases will give the cost of the goods available for sale during the period.

3. Subtract the cost of the goods on hand at the end of the period (ending inventory, based on the inventory count).

The formula for cost of goods sold is demonstrated in the graphic below:

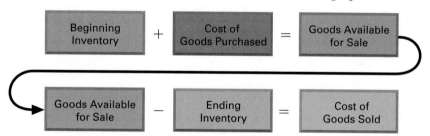

The resulting cost of goods sold amount, a merchandiser's major expense, is included on the income statement for the period.

Appendix A of this chapter (page 255) covers the periodic inventory system. This system is being used less and less since most businesses have computerized their inventory records.

Under the **perpetual inventory system**, the business keeps a running record of inventory and cost of goods sold. Cost of goods sold is *not* calculated at the end of the period as it is with the periodic system; cost of goods sold is recorded every time a sale is made. The perpetual system achieves control over the inventory, especially expensive goods such as automobiles, jewellery, and furniture. The low cost of automated information systems has increased the use of perpetual systems. This technology reduces the time required to manage inventory and thus increases a company's ability to control its merchandise. But even under a perpetual system the business counts the inventory on hand at least once a year. The physical count establishes the correct amount of ending inventory for the financial statements (which may have been affected by theft or spoilage) and serves as a check on the perpetual records.

The following chart compares the perpetual and periodic systems:

Perpetual Inventory System	Periodic Inventory System
• Keeps a running record of all inventory as it is bought and sold (units and price) • Inventory counted at least once a year	• Does *not* keep a running record of all goods bought and sold • Inventory counted at least once a year

Automated Perpetual Inventory Systems

A modern automated perpetual inventory system records

- Units purchased
- Units sold
- The quantity of inventory on hand

Inventory systems are often integrated with accounts receivable and sales. The computer can keep up-to-the-minute records, so managers can call up current inventory information at any time. For example, in their perpetual system the point-of-sale equipment at IKEA or Home Depot is a computer terminal that records sales and also updates the inventory records. Bar codes, such as the one shown here, are scanned by a laser. The lines of the bar code represent inventory and cost data that keep track of each item. Most businesses use bar codes, so we focus our inventory discussions on the perpetual system.

Bar code

DID YOU GET IT?

To check your understanding of the material in this Learning Objective, complete these questions. The solutions appear on MyAccountingLab so you can check your progress.

1. a. What is the gross margin if net sales are $200,000 and cost of goods sold is $120,000?

   b. If gross margin is $20,000 and cost of goods sold is $60,000, what were net sales?

   c. If net sales are $75,000 and gross margin is $15,000, what was cost of goods sold?

   d. If net sales are 100 percent and gross margin is 15 percent of net sales, what is the percentage of net sales represented by cost of goods sold?

2. Which of the following costs would be included in the cost of inventory?

   - Purchase price of an item for resale
   - Advertising cost
   - Insurance on an item for resale
   - Customs duties paid to import an item for resale
   - Freight in
   - Freight out
   - Sales commission
   - Cost to display an item for resale

3. Supply the missing inventory amounts in each of the following situations:

Beginning Inventory	Cost of Goods Purchased	Goods Available for Sale	Ending Inventory	Cost of Goods Sold
$21,000	$15,000	$ (a)	$12,000	$24,000
(b)	25,000	35,000	20,000	15,000
45,000	(c)	55,000	(d)	20,000
(e)	10,000	65,000	35,000	(f)

Accounting for Inventory in the Perpetual Inventory System

OBJECTIVE 2
Account for the purchase and sale of inventory under the perpetual inventory system

The cycle of a merchandising entity begins with the purchase of inventory, as Exhibit 5–2 shows. For example, a menswear store records the purchase of sweaters, shirts, and other items of inventory acquired for resale by debiting the Inventory account. A $30,000 purchase on account is recorded as follows:

May 14	Inventory..	30,000	
	Accounts Payable		30,000
	Purchased inventory on account.		

The Inventory account should be used only for purchases of merchandise for resale. Purchases of any other assets are recorded in a different asset account. For example, the purchase of supplies is debited to Supplies, not to Inventory. Inventory is an asset until it is sold.

The Purchase Invoice: A Basic Business Document

Business documents are the tangible evidence of transactions. In this section, we trace the steps that Austin Sound Centre, a small electronics store in Winnipeg, Manitoba, takes to order, receive, and pay for inventory. Many companies buy and sell their goods electronically—with no invoices, no cheques, and so on. Here we use actual documents to illustrate what takes place behind the scenes.

1. Suppose Austin Sound Centre wants to stock JVC-brand Camcorders, home theatre systems, flat-screen televisions, and speakers. Austin prepares a *purchase order* and transmits it to JVC Canada Inc.

2. On receipt of the purchase order, JVC searches its warehouse for the inventory that Austin Sound Centre has ordered. JVC ships the equipment and sends the invoice to Austin Sound on the same day. The **invoice** is the seller's request for payment from the purchaser. It is also called the *bill*.

3. Often the purchaser receives the invoice before the inventory arrives. Austin Sound does not pay immediately. Instead, Austin Sound waits until the inventory arrives in order to ensure that it is the correct type and quantity ordered, and that it arrives in good condition. After the inventory is inspected and approved, Austin Sound pays JVC the invoice amount according to the terms of payment previously negotiated.

Exhibit 5–3 is a copy of an invoice from JVC Canada Inc. to Austin Sound Centre.

Discounts from Purchase Prices

There are two major types of discounts from purchase prices: quantity discounts and cash discounts (called *purchase discounts*).

Quantity Discounts A *quantity discount* works this way: The larger the quantity purchased, the lower the price per item. For example, JVC may offer no quantity discount for the purchase of only one Camcorder, and charge the *list* price—the full price—of $475 per unit. However, JVC may offer the following quantity discount terms in order to persuade customers to order more Camcorders:

Quantity	Quantity Discount	Net Price per Unit
Minimum quantity, 2 Camcorders	5%	$451.25 [$475 – 0.05($475)]
4–9 Camcorders	10%	$427.50 [$475 – 0.10($475)]
More than 9 Camcorders	20%	$380.00 [$475 – 0.20($475)]

EXHIBIT 5–3   Purchase Invoice

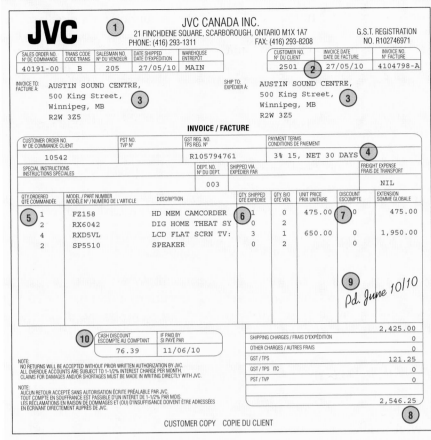

① The seller is JVC Canada Inc.

② The invoice date is needed to determine whether the purchaser gets a discount for prompt payment (see 4).

③ The purchaser. This inventory is invoiced (billed) and shipped to the same address.

④ Credit terms of the transaction: If Austin Sound pays within 15 days of the invoice date, it may deduct 3% of the total amount. Otherwise, the full amount—net—is due in 30 days.*

⑤ Austin ordered 1 HD Memory Camcorder, 2 Digital Home Theatre Systems, 4 LCD Flat-Screen Televisions, and 2 sets of speakers.

⑥ JVC shipped 1 HD Memory Camcorder, no Digital Home Theatre Systems, 3 LCD Flat-Screen Televisions, and no speakers.

⑦ Quantity discount offered by JVC.

⑧ Total invoice amount (Austin's purchases are PST exempt).

⑨ Austin's payment date. How much did Austin pay? (See 10.)

⑩ Payment occurred 14 days after the invoice date—within the discount period—so Austin paid $2,469.86 ($2,546.25 – 3% discount). We will disregard GST for now.

*A full discussion of discounts appears below.

Suppose Austin Sound Centre purchases five Camcorders from JVC. The cost of each Camcorder is, therefore, $427.50. Purchase of five units on account would be recorded by debiting Inventory and crediting Accounts Payable for the total price of $2,137.50 ($427.50 per unit × 5 items purchased).

There is no Quantity Discount account and no special accounting entry for a quantity discount. Instead, all accounting entries are based on the net price of a purchase after the quantity discount has been subtracted, as shown on the invoice.

Purchase Discounts   Many businesses also offer purchase discounts to their customers. A purchase discount is totally different from a quantity or volume discount. A *purchase discount* (also referred to as a *cash discount*) is a reward for prompt payment. If a quantity discount is also offered, the purchase discount is computed on the net purchase amount after the quantity discount has been subtracted, further reducing the cost of the inventory to the purchaser.

JVC's credit terms of "3% 15, net 30 days" can also be expressed as "3/15, n/30." This means that Austin Sound Centre may deduct 3 percent of the total amount due if Austin pays within 15 days of the invoice date. Otherwise, the full amount—net—is due in 30 days.

Terms of "n/30" indicate that no discount is offered, and payment is due 30 days after the invoice date. Terms of *eom* mean that payment is due by the end of the current month. However, a purchase after the 25th of the current month on terms of *eom* can be paid at the end of the next month.

A computerized accounting system is typically programmed to flag invoices as the date for taking the discount approaches so the business can take advantage of the purchase discount.

Let's use the Exhibit 5–3 transaction to illustrate accounting for a purchase discount. For the moment, disregard GST and use the invoice total of $2,546.25 when recording purchases and purchase discounts. (Normally, the purchase amount and purchase discount would be taken on the balance before GST.) GST is discussed on page 238. Austin Sound Centre records the purchase on account as follows:

May 27	Inventory...	2,546.25	
	Accounts Payable		2,546.25
	Purchased inventory on account.		

Austin paid within the discount period of 15 days, so its cash payment entry is

Jun. 10	Accounts Payable	2,546.25	
	Cash...		2,469.86
	Inventory..		76.39
	Paid on account within discount period.		
	The discount is $76.39 ($2,546.25 × 0.03).		

The discount is credited to Inventory. After Austin Sound has taken its discount, Austin Sound must adjust the Inventory account to reflect its true cost of the goods. In effect, this inventory cost Austin Sound $2,469.86 ($2,546.25 minus the purchase discount of $76.39) as shown in the following Inventory account:

Inventory

May 27	2,546.25	Jun. 10	76.39
Bal.	2,469.86		

However, if Austin Sound pays this invoice after the discount period, it must pay the full invoice amount. In this case, the payment entry is

Jun. 25	Accounts Payable	2,546.25	
	Cash...		2,546.25
	Paid on account after discount period.		

Without the discount, Austin Sound's cost of the inventory is the full amount of $2,546.25, as shown in the following T-account:

Inventory

May 27	2,546.25	

Purchase Returns and Allowances

Most businesses allow their customers to *return* merchandise that is defective, damaged in shipment, or otherwise unsuitable. Or, if the buyer chooses to keep damaged goods, the seller may deduct an *allowance* from the amount the buyer owes. Both purchase returns and purchase allowances decrease the amount that the buyer must pay the seller.

Suppose the $475.00 Camcorder (model FZ158) purchased by Austin Sound Centre (in Exhibit 5–3) was not the Camcorder ordered. Austin Sound returns the merchandise to the seller and records the purchase return as follows:

Jun. 3	Accounts Payable	475.00	
	Inventory..		475.00
	Returned inventory to seller.		

Now assume that one of the JVC Flat-Screen Televisions was damaged in shipment to Austin Sound Centre. The damage is minor, and Austin decides to keep the television in exchange for a $75.00 allowance from JVC. To record this purchase allowance, Austin Sound Centre makes this entry:

Jun. 4 Accounts Payable 75.00
            Inventory... 75.00
            Received a purchase allowance.

The return and the allowance had two effects:

1. They decreased Austin Sound's liability, which is why we debit Accounts Payable.

2. They decreased the net cost of the inventory, which is why we credit Inventory.

Assume that Austin Sound has not yet paid its liability to JVC. After these return ($475.00) and allowance ($75.00) transactions are posted, Austin Sound's accounts will show these balances:

Inventory					Accounts Payable			
May 27	2,546.25	Jun. 3	475.00		Jun. 3	475.00	May 27	2,546.25
		Jun. 4	75.00		Jun. 4	75.00		
Bal.	1,996.25						Bal.	1,996.25

Austin Sound's cost of *inventory* is $1,996.25, and Austin Sound owes JVC $1,996.25 on *account payable*. If Austin Sound pays within the discount period, 3 percent will be deducted from these balances.

Transportation Costs: Who Pays?

The transportation cost of moving inventory from seller to buyer can be significant. Someone must pay this cost. The purchase agreement specifies FOB (*free on board*) terms to indicate who pays the shipping charges. FOB governs

1. When legal title passes from the seller to buyer.

2. Who pays the freight.

- Under FOB *shipping point* terms, title passes when the inventory leaves the seller's place of business—the shipping point. The buyer owns the goods while they are in transit, and therefore the buyer pays the transportation cost, or freight.

- Under FOB *destination* terms, title passes when the goods reach the destination, so the seller pays the freight.

Exhibit 5–4 summarizes FOB.

EXHIBIT 5–4 FOB Terms Determine Who Pays the Freight

Freight costs are either freight in or freight out.

- *Freight in* is the transportation cost on *purchased goods.*
- *Freight out* is the transportation cost on *goods sold.*

Freight In   FOB shipping point terms are the most common. The buyer owns the goods while they are in transit, so the buyer pays the freight. In accounting, the cost of an asset includes all costs incurred to bring the asset to its intended use. For inventory, cost therefore includes the

- *Net cost* after all discounts, returns, and allowances have been subtracted, plus
- *Freight in*

To record the payment for freight in, the buyer debits Inventory and credits Cash or Accounts Payable for the amount. Suppose Austin Sound receives a $100.00 shipping bill directly from the freight company. Austin's entry to record payment of the freight charge is as follows:

Jun.	1	Inventory..	100.00	
		Cash		100.00
		Paid a freight bill.		

The freight charge increases the cost of the inventory to $2,096.25 as follows:

Inventory

(Purchase)	May 27	2,546.25	Jun. 3	475.00	(Return)
(Freight)	Jun. 1	100.00	Jun. 4	75.00	(Allowance)
(Net cost)	Bal.	2,096.25			

Any discounts would be computed only on the account payable to the seller, not on the transportation costs, because the discount was offered by the seller, not the freight company. The freight company usually offers no discount.

Under FOB shipping point, the seller sometimes prepays the transportation cost as a convenience and adds this cost on the invoice. The buyer can debit Inventory for the combined cost of the inventory and the shipping cost because both costs apply to the merchandise. A $10,000 purchase of goods, coupled with a related freight charge of $800, would be recorded as follows:

Mar.	12	Inventory..	10,800.00	
		Accounts Payable		10,800.00
		Purchased inventory on account, including freight of $800.		

If the buyer pays within the discount period, the discount will be computed on the $10,000 merchandise cost, not on the $10,800. No discount is offered on transportation cost.

Freight Out   The seller may pay freight charges to ship goods to customers. This is called *freight out*. Freight out is a delivery expense. Delivery expense is a selling expense, an operating expense for the seller. It is debited to the Delivery Expense account.

Summary of Purchase Returns and Allowances, Discounts, and Transportation Costs
Suppose Austin Sound Centre buys $50,000 of audio/video inventory, takes a discount, and returns some of the goods. Austin Sound also pays some freight in. The following summary shows Austin Sound's net purchases of this inventory. All amounts are assumed for this illustration.

Inventory

Purchases of inventory	50,000	Purchase ret. & allow.	2,000
Freight in	2,500	Purchase discounts	1,000
Balance	49,500		

Purchases of Inventory										
Inventory	−	Purchase Returns and Allowances	−	Purchase Discounts	+	Freight in	=	Net Purchases of Inventory		
$50,000	−	$2,000	−	$1,000	+	$2,500	=	$49,500		

Selling Inventory and Recording Cost of Goods Sold

After a company buys inventory, the next step in the operating cycle is to sell the goods. We shift now to the selling side and follow Austin Sound Centre through a sequence of selling transactions. A sale earns a reward, Sales Revenue. A sale also requires a sacrifice in the form of an expense, Cost of Goods Sold, as the seller gives up the asset Inventory.

After making a sale on account, Austin Sound Centre may experience any of the following:

- A sales return: The customer may return goods to Austin Sound.
- A sales allowance: For one reason or another, Austin Sound may grant a sales allowance to reduce the amount of cash to be collected from the customer.
- A sales discount: If the customer pays within the discount period—under terms such as 2/10, n/30—Austin Sound collects the discounted (reduced) amount.
- Freight out: Austin Sound may have to pay Delivery Expense to transport the goods to the buyer's location.

The sale of inventory may be for cash or on account, as Exhibit 5–2 shows. Let's begin with a cash sale.

Cash Sale   Assume that Austin Sound Centre has $60,000 of inventory on hand on January 2. Sales by retailers, such as Austin Sound Centre, grocery stores, and restaurants, are often for cash. Cash sales of $10,000 would be recorded by debiting Cash and crediting Sales Revenue as follows:

Jan.	9	Cash	10,000
		Sales Revenue	10,000
		Cash sales.	

To update the inventory records for the goods sold, the business also must decrease the Inventory balance. Suppose these goods cost the seller $6,000. An accompanying entry is needed to transfer the $6,000 cost of the goods—*not their selling price of $10,000*—from the Inventory account to the Cost of Goods Sold account as follows:

Jan.	9	Cost of Goods Sold	6,000
		Inventory	6,000
		Recorded the cost of goods sold.	

Cost of goods sold (also called cost of sales) is the largest single expense of most businesses that sell merchandise, such as Best Buy, JVC, and Austin Sound Centre. It is the cost of the inventory that the business has sold to customers. The Cost of Goods Sold account keeps a current balance as transactions are journalized and posted.

After posting, the Cost of Goods Sold account holds the cost of the merchandise sold ($6,000 in this case):

KEY POINT

The recording of cost of goods sold along with sales revenue is an example of the matching objective (Chapter 3, page 112)—matching expense against revenue to measure net income.

Inventory		Cost of Goods Sold	
Jan. 2 Bal. 60,000	Jan. 9 6,000	Jan. 9 6,000	

The cashier scans the bar code on the product and the computer automatically records the cost of goods sold entry.

Sale on Account   A large amount of sales in Canada are made on account (on credit), using either the seller's credit facility or a credit card such as Visa or MasterCard. To simplify the discussion, we will assume the seller records the receivable as a regular account receivable rather than a special receivable from the credit-card company. A

$12,000 sale on account is recorded by a debit to Accounts Receivable and a credit to Sales Revenue, as follows:

Jan.	2	Accounts Receivable	12,000	
		Sales Revenue.......................................		12,000
		Sale on account.		

If we assume that these goods cost the seller $7,200, the accompanying cost of goods sold and inventory entry is

Jan.	2	Cost of Goods Sold	7,200	
		Inventory...		7,200
		Recorded the cost of goods sold.		

When the cash is received, the seller records the cash receipt on account as follows:

Jan.	10	Cash...	12,000	
		Accounts Receivable		12,000
		Collection on account.		

Why is there no January 10 entry to Sales Revenue, Cost of Goods Sold, or Inventory? This is because on January 10 the seller merely receives one asset—Cash—in place of another asset—Accounts Receivable. The sales revenue, the related cost of goods sold, and the decrease in inventory for the goods sold were recorded on January 2.

Offering Sales Discounts and Sales Returns and Allowances

We saw that purchase discounts and purchase returns and allowances decrease the cost of inventory purchases. In the same way, **sales discounts** and **sales returns and allowances** decrease the revenue earned on sales. Sales Discounts and Sales Returns and Allowances are contra accounts to Sales Revenue.

KEY POINT

A contra account always has a companion account with the opposite balance. Thus, both Sales Discounts and Sales Returns and Allowances (debit balances) are reported with Sales Revenue (credit balance) on the income statement.

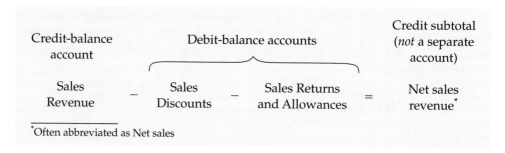

This equation calculates net sales. Sales discounts can be given on both goods and services.

Companies keep close watch on their customers' paying habits and on their own sales of defective and unsuitable merchandise. They maintain separate accounts for Sales Discounts and Sales Returns and Allowances. Let's examine a sequence of JVC sale transactions. Assume JVC is selling to Austin Sound Centre.

On July 7, JVC sells stereo components for $24,000 on credit terms of 3/15, n/30. These goods cost JVC $14,400. JVC's entries to record this credit sale and the related cost of goods sold are as follows:

Jul.	7	Accounts Receivable	24,000	
		Sales Revenue.......................................		24,000
		Sale on account.		
	7	Cost of Goods Sold	14,400	
		Inventory...		14,400
		Recorded the cost of goods sold.		

Sales Returns Assume the buyer, Austin Sound Centre, returns goods that were sold by JVC for $3,000. These goods are not damaged and can be resold. JVC, the seller, records the sales return and the related decrease in Accounts Receivable as follows:

KEY POINT

The sale of inventory and the return of goods by customers require two separate journal entries.

Jul. 12	Sales Returns and Allowances	3,000	
	Accounts Receivable		3,000
	Received returned goods.		

JVC receives the returned merchandise and updates the inventory records. JVC must also decrease cost of goods sold as follows (the returned goods cost JVC $1,800):

Jul. 12	Inventory	1,800	
	Cost of Goods Sold		1,800
	Returned goods to inventory.		

Sales Allowances Suppose JVC grants to the buyer a $500 sales allowance for damaged goods. Austin Sound then subtracts $500 from the amount it will pay JVC. JVC journalizes this transaction by debiting Sales Returns and Allowances and crediting Accounts Receivable as follows:

Jul. 15	Sales Returns and Allowances	500	
	Accounts Receivable		500
	Granted a sales allowance for damaged goods.		

No inventory entry is needed for a sales allowance transaction because the seller, JVC, receives no returned goods from the customer. Instead, JVC will simply receive less cash from the customer.

After the preceding entries are posted, all the accounts have up-to-date balances. JVC's Accounts Receivable has a $20,500 debit balance, as follows:

Accounts Receivable

(Sale)	Jul. 7	24,000	Jul. 12	3,000	(Return)
			Jul. 15	500	(Allowance)
	Bal.	20,500			

On July 22, the last day of the discount period, JVC collects $15,500 of this accounts receivable. Assume JVC allows customers to take discounts on all amounts JVC receives within the discount period (some companies allow purchasers to only take a discount if the invoice is paid in full). JVC's cash receipt is $15,035 [calculated as $15,500 − (0.03 × $15,500)], and the collection entry is as follows:

Jul. 22	Cash	15,035	
	Sales Discounts	465	
	Accounts Receivable		15,500
	Cash collection within the discount period.		
	Sales discount is $465 (0.03 × $15,500).		

Suppose JVC collects the remaining amount outstanding of $5,000 on July 28. That date is after the discount period, so there is no sales discount. To record this collection on account, JVC debits Cash and credits Accounts Receivable for the same amount, as follows:

Jul. 28	Cash	5,000	
	Accounts Receivable		5,000
	Cash collection after the discount period.		

Now, JVC's Accounts Receivable balance is zero:

Accounts Receivable

(Sale)	Jul. 7	24,000	Jul. 12	3,000	(Return)
			Jul. 15	500	(Allowance)
			Jul. 22	15,500	(collection)
			Jul. 28	5,000	(collection)
	Bal.	0			

Goods and Services Tax

This topic is introduced here to make you aware of the Goods and Services Tax (GST) because most goods and services sold today in Canada have the GST levied on them by the federal government at the time of sale. However, it was decided to omit consideration of the GST from the discussion and examples in the early chapters to avoid making the material overly complicated. The following discussion provides a brief introduction to the topic; GST is dealt with more fully in Chapter 11.

The manufacturer, wholesaler, and retailer pay the GST on the cost of their purchases and then pass it on to the next link in the economic chain by charging and collecting it on their respective sales. The consumer, the last link in the chain, pays the final tax. Each entity that collects the GST remits the net tax collected to the Receiver General at the Canada Revenue Agency (CRA).

The GST is designed to be a consumption tax and, as was suggested above, the entity ultimately paying the tax is the final purchaser of the product or service. Earlier links in the chain (for example, the retailer) pay tax on their purchases, but are then allowed to deduct (or recover) the tax on their purchases from the tax they themselves collect on their sales. Therefore, the GST paid on purchases does not really affect the cost of the purchase. For example, Austin Sound Centre paid the GST of 5 percent, or $121.25 ($2,425 × 0.05), on the items purchased in Exhibit 5–3. The entry to record the purchase, in summary form, of these items would have been as follows:

May 27	Inventory	2,425.00	
	GST Recoverable	121.25	
	Accounts Payable		2,546.25
	Purchased various inventory items on account.		

Assume Austin Sound did not return it to JVC but instead sold the FZ158 Camcorder for $650.00 to a customer; the GST on the sale would be $32.50 ($650.00 × 0.05). The entry to record the sale would be as follows:

Jun. 10	Cash	682.50	
	GST Payable		32.50
	Sales		650.00
	Sold JVC FZ158 Camcorder for cash.		

Subsequently, Austin Sound would have to remit to the Receiver General at the CRA the difference between the GST paid and the GST collected, the net GST. Assume that for the month of July, Austin Sound collected $10,000 in GST from its customers and paid $8,000 to its suppliers. The entry would be as follows:

Jul. 31	GST Payable	10,000	
	GST Recoverable		8,000
	Cash		2,000
	Payment of GST collected net of GST paid		
	(recoverable) on purchases ($10,000 − 8,000).		

The discussion of GST above is greatly simplified for the purposes of this text. The actual GST is more complicated than as presented for two major reasons:

1. Supplies and services are divided into three classes and each class is taxed differently. The three classes are (1) Taxable supplies and services; (2) Zero-rated supplies and services; (3) Exempt supplies and services.

2. Some provinces (Nova Scotia, New Brunswick, and Newfoundland and Labrador, along with perhaps Ontario and British Columbia in the future) have harmonized, or combined, their provincial sales tax with the GST.

As well, the GST rate can be changed by the Parliament of Canada. Since July 1, 2006, the GST rate has dropped from 7 percent to 5 percent. The rate may change again in the future. Any more advanced discussion of the GST is beyond the scope of this chapter.

DID YOU GET IT?

MyAccountingLab

To check your understanding of the material in this Learning Objective, complete these questions. The solutions appear on MyAccountingLab so you can check your progress.

4. Oak Sales Company engaged in the following transactions during September 2010, the first month of the company's fiscal year. Assume the company had no inventory on hand prior to September 3. Journalize the transactions and include any calculations in the journal-entry explanations.

Sept. 3 Purchased inventory costing $7,000 on credit terms of 1/10, net eom. The goods were shipped FOB Oak's warehouse.

9 Returned 10 percent of the inventory purchased on September 3. It was defective.

12 Sold goods for cash, $6,000 (cost, $3,000).

15 Purchased inventory of $15,400, less a $400 quantity discount. Credit terms were 3/15, n/30. The goods were shipped FOB the supplier's warehouse.

16 Paid a $1,200 freight bill on the inventory purchased on September 15.

18 Sold inventory for $9,000 on credit terms of 2/10, n/30 (cost, $4,500).

22 Received merchandise returned from the customer from the September 18 sale, $2,000 (cost, $1,000). Merchandise was the wrong size.

24 Borrowed exactly enough money from the bank to pay for the September 15 purchase in time to take advantage of the discount offered. Signed a note payable to the bank for the net amount.

24 Paid supplier for goods purchased on September 15, less all returns and discounts.

28 Received cash in full settlement of the account from the customer who purchased inventory on September 18, less the return on September 22 and less the discount.

29 Paid the amount owed on account from the purchase of September 3, less the September 9 return.

30 Purchased inventory for cash, $4,640, less a quantity discount of $140.

5. Refer to the Oak Sales Company journal entries in the previous question. Set up T-accounts and post the journal entries to show the ending balances in the Inventory and Cost of Goods Sold accounts.

6. Refer to the Oak Sales Company journal entries in Question 4 above. Assume that the note payable signed on September 24 requires the payment of $380 interest expense. Was the decision to borrow funds to take advantage of the cash discount wise or unwise?

Adjusting and Closing the Accounts of a Merchandising Business

A merchandising business adjusts and closes the accounts the same way a service entity does. If a work sheet is used, the trial balance is entered and the work sheet is completed to determine net income or net loss. The work sheet provides the data for journalizing the adjusting and closing entries, and for preparing the financial statements.

OBJECTIVE 3
Adjust and close the accounts of a merchandising business under the perpetual inventory system

Adjusting Inventory Based on a Physical Count

In theory, the Inventory account remains up to date at all times. However, the actual amount of inventory on hand may differ from what the books show. Losses due to theft and damage can be significant. Also, accounting errors can cause Inventory's balance to need adjustment either upward or, more often, downward. For this reason, virtually all merchandising businesses take a physical count of inventory at least once each year. The most common time for a business to count its inventory is at the end of the fiscal year, before the financial statements are prepared. The business then adjusts the Inventory account to the correct amount based on the physical count.

At year end, Austin Sound Centre's Inventory account shows an unadjusted balance of $174,000.

Inventory

Dec. 31	174,000		

With no shrinkage—due to theft or error—the business should have on hand inventory costing $174,000. But on December 31, Steve Austin, the owner of Austin Sound, counts the merchandise in the store, and the total cost of the goods on hand comes to only $168,000.

KEY POINT

If book inventory exceeds physical inventory, book inventory is adjusted downward. As a result of this inventory adjustment, cost of goods sold is higher and gross margin is lower. The cost associated with buying the missing units is not accompanied by the revenue from a sale. Therefore, gross margin shrinks by the amount of this cost.

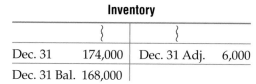

Inventory Balance Before Adjustment	−	Actual Inventory on Hand	=	Adjusting Entry to Inventory
$174,000	−	$168,000	=	Credit of $6,000

Austin Sound would record the inventory shrinkage of $6,000 (which is $174,000 − $168,000) with this adjusting entry:

Dec. 31	Cost of Goods Sold..	6,000	
	Inventory		6,000
	Adjustment for inventory shrinkage.		

This entry brings Inventory to its correct balance.[1]

Inventory

Dec. 31	174,000	Dec. 31 Adj.	6,000
Dec. 31 Bal.	168,000		

The physical count can indicate that more inventory is present than the books show. A search of the records may reveal that Austin Sound received inventory but did not record the corresponding purchase entry. This would be entered the standard way: debit Inventory and credit Cash or Accounts Payable. If the reason for the excess inventory cannot be identified, the business adjusts the accounts by debiting Inventory and crediting Cost of Goods Sold.

Closing the Accounts of a Merchandising Business

LEARNING TIPS

The closing entries here are very similar to those discussed in Chapter 4, pages 172–176. The closing entries also clear the Cost of Goods Sold expense account for accumulating costs in the next period.

Exhibit 5–5 presents Austin Sound Centre's closing entries, which are similar to those you have seen previously, except for the new accounts highlighted with bold text.

The first closing entry

- Debits the revenue accounts for their credit balances.
- Credits Income Summary for total revenues ($780,000).

The second closing entry

- Debits Income Summary for total expenses plus the contra revenues ($648,000).

---

[1] Some companies record the inventory shrinkage of $6,000 with this adjusting entry:

Dec. 31	Loss on Inventory	6,000	
	Inventory..		6,000

This is done to highlight the shrinkage so it can be monitored and to identify it as a loss.

EXHIBIT 5–5 Closing Entries for a Merchandiser

Journal

Closing Entries

1. Dec. 31	**Sales Revenue**	**777,000**	
	Interest Revenue	3,000	
	Income Summary		780,000
2. Dec. 31	Income Summary	648,000	
	Cost of Goods Sold		**427,000**
	Sales Discounts		**7,500**
	Sales Returns and Allowances		**8,000**
	Wages Expense		142,000
	Rent Expense		48,000
	Amortization Expense		6,000
	Insurance Expense...................................		4,000
	Supplies Expense		1,000
	Interest Expense.......................................		4,500
3. Dec. 31	Income Summary ($780,000 – $648,000)...	132,000	
	Steve Austin, Capital		132,000
4. Dec. 31	Steve Austin, Capital..................................	65,000	
	Steve Austin, Withdrawals....................		65,000

Income Summary					Steve Austin, Withdrawals				
Closing	648,000	Closing	780,000		Bal.	65,000	Closing	65,000
Closing	132,000	Balance	132,000					

Steve Austin, Capital			
Closing	65,000	Balance	90,000
		(assumed)	
		Closing	132,000
		Balance	157,000

- Credits the contra revenues (Sales Discounts and Sales Returns and Allowances) and all the expenses, including Cost of Goods Sold, for their debit balances.

The last two closing entries

- Close net income from Income Summary to the Capital account.
- Close the owner withdrawals into the Capital account.

DID YOU GET IT?

MyAccountingLab

To check your understanding of the material in this Learning Objective, complete these questions. The solutions appear on MyAccountingLab so you can check your progress.

7. At December 31, 2010, a merchandising company's year end, the accounting records show a balance of $250,000 in the Inventory account. Suppose a physical count of the goods in the warehouse shows inventory on hand costing $245,000. What journal entry would bring the Inventory account to its correct balance?

8. At December 31, 2010, a merchandising company's year end, the accounting records show a balance of $150,000 in the Inventory account. Suppose a physical count of the goods in the warehouse shows inventory on hand costing $153,000. What journal entry would bring the Inventory account to its correct balance?

9. Refer to Exhibit 5–5. Using the accounts and balances listed in Exhibit 5–5, calculate the following amounts:
   a. Net sales
   b. Gross margin

Preparing a Merchandiser's Financial Statements

OBJECTIVE ④

Prepare a merchandiser's financial statements under the perpetual inventory system

Exhibit 5–6 presents Austin Sound Centre's financial statements (prepared after all year-end adjusting entries have been entered).

Income Statement   The income statement reports **operating expenses**, which are those expenses other than cost of goods sold incurred in the entity's major line of business—merchandising. Austin Sound's operating expenses include wages, rent, insurance, amortization of furniture and fixtures, and supplies.

Many companies report their operating expenses in two categories:

- *Selling expenses* are those expenses related to marketing the company's products—sales salaries; sales commissions; advertising; amortization, rent, utilities, and property taxes on store buildings; amortization on store furniture; delivery expense; and so on.

- *General expenses* include office expenses, such as the salaries of the executives and office employees; amortization, rent, utilities, property taxes on the home office building; and office supplies.

Gross margin minus operating expenses equals **income from operations**, or **operating income**. Many people view operating income as an important indicator of a business's performance because it measures the results of the entity's major ongoing activities.

The last section of Austin Sound's income statement is **other revenue and expense**. This category reports revenues and expenses that are outside the main operations of the business. Examples include gains and losses on the sale of long-term assets like property, plant, and equipment (not inventory), and gains and losses on lawsuits. Accountants have traditionally viewed Interest Revenue and Interest Expense as "other" items, because they arise from lending money and borrowing money. These are financing activities that are outside the operating scope of selling merchandise.

The bottom line of the income statement is net income:

Net income = Total revenues and gains − Total expenses and losses

We often hear the term *bottom line* used to refer to a final result. *Bottom line* originated from the position of net income on the income statement.

Statement of Owner's Equity   A merchandiser's statement of owner's equity looks exactly like that of a service business. In fact, you cannot determine whether the entity sells merchandise or services from looking at the statement of owner's equity.

Balance Sheet   If the business is a merchandiser, the balance sheet shows inventory as a current asset. In contrast, service businesses usually have no inventory at all or minor amounts of inventory.

An adjusting entry for inventory shrinkage is unique to merchandisers, who have inventory. All other adjusting entries are the same for service entities and merchandisers, and they were described in Chapter 4.

Work Sheet for a Merchandising Business

The work sheet of a merchandiser is similar to the work sheet for a service business. The main new account is the Inventory account, which must be adjusted based on a physical count, as discussed on page 240. Also, the merchandiser's work sheet carries the other new merchandising accounts (Sales Revenue, Cost of Goods Sold, and so on).

Austin Sound Centre's work sheet for the year ended December 31, 2010, appears in Exhibit 5–7. The year-end adjustments reflected on the worksheet are:

a. Interest revenue that has been earned but not yet collected, $1,000.

b. Inventory on hand based on a physical count of inventory, $168,000.

EXHIBIT 5–6 Financial Statements of Austin Sound Centre

AUSTIN SOUND CENTRE
Income Statement
For the Year Ended December 31, 2010

Sales revenue		$777,000
Less: Sales discounts	$ 7,500	
Sales returns and allowances	8,000	15,500
Net sales revenue		761,500
Cost of goods sold		427,000
Gross margin		334,500
Operating expenses:		
Wages expense	142,000	
Rent expense	48,000	
Amortization expense	6,000	
Insurance expense	4,000	
Supplies expense	1,000	201,000
Income from operations		133,500
Other revenue and (expense):		
Interest revenue	3,000	
Interest expense	(4,500)	(1,500)
Net income		$132,000

AUSTIN SOUND CENTRE
Statement of Owner's Equity
For the Year Ended December 31, 2010

Steve Austin, capital, January 1, 2010	$ 90,000
Add: Net income	132,000
	222,000
Less: Withdrawals	65,000
Steve Austin, capital, December 31, 2010	$157,000

AUSTIN SOUND CENTRE
Balance Sheet
December 31, 2010

Assets			Liabilities		
Current assets:			Current liabilities:		
Cash		$ 6,000	Accounts payable		$ 128,000
Accounts receivable		24,000	Unearned sales revenue		1,500
Note receivable		32,000	Wages payable		3,000
Interest receivable		1,000	Interest payable		500
Inventory		168,000	Total current liabilities		133,000
Prepaid insurance		600			
Supplies		500	Long-term liability:		
Total current assets		232,100	Note payable		44,100
Property, plant, and equipment:			Total liabilities		177,100
Furniture and					
fixtures	$120,000		**Owner's Equity**		
Less: Accumulated			S. Austin, capital		157,000
amortization	18,000	102,000			
			Total liabilities and		
Total assets		$334,100	owner's equity		$334,100

c. Supplies on hand, $500.

d. Prepaid insurance expired during the year, $4,000.

e. Amortization, $6,000.

f. Unearned sales revenue earned during the year, $2,600.

g. Accrued wages expense, $3,000.

h. Accrued interest expense, $500.

The Exhibit 5–7 work sheet is similar to the work sheets we have seen so far, but there are a few differences. This work sheet does not include Adjusted Trial Balance columns. In most accounting systems, a single operation combines trial balance amounts with the adjustments and extends the adjusted balances directly to the Income Statement and Balance Sheet columns. Therefore, to reduce clutter, the Adjusted Trial Balance columns are omitted so that the work sheet contains four pairs of columns, not five.

Account Title Column   The trial balance on a work sheet lists a number of accounts without balances. Ordinarily, these accounts are affected by the adjusting process. Examples include Interest Receivable, Wages Payable, and Amortization Expense. The accounts are listed in order by account number, the order in which they appear in the ledger. If additional accounts are needed, they can be written in at the bottom of the work sheet above the net income amount.

EXHIBIT 5–7   Work Sheet for a Merchandiser

AUSTIN SOUND CENTRE
Work Sheet
For the Year Ended December 31, 2010

Account Title	Trial Balance Dr	Trial Balance Cr	Adjustments Dr	Adjustments Cr	Income Statement Dr	Income Statement Cr	Balance Sheet Dr	Balance Sheet Cr
Cash	6,000						6,000	
Accounts receivable	24,000						24,000	
Note receivable, current	32,000						32,000	
Interest receivable	0		(a) 1,000				1,000	
Inventory	174,000			(b) 6,000			168,000	
Supplies	1,500			(c) 1,000			500	
Prepaid insurance	4,600			(d) 4,000			600	
Furniture and fixtures	120,000						120,000	
Accumulated amortization		12,000		(e) 6,000				18,000
Accounts payable		128,000						128,000
Unearned sales revenue		4,100	(f) 2,600					1,500
Wages payable		0		(g) 3,000				3,000
Interest payable		0		(h) 500				500
Note payable, long-term		44,100						44,100
Steve Austin, capital		90,000						90,000
Steve Austin, withdrawals	65,000						65,000	
Sales revenue		774,400		(f) 2,600		777,000		
Sales discounts	7,500				7,500			
Sales returns and allowances	8,000				8,000			
Interest revenue		2,000		(a) 1,000		3,000		
Cost of goods sold	421,000		(b) 6,000		427,000			
Wages expense	139,000		(g) 3,000		142,000			
Rent expense	48,000				48,000			
Amortization expense	0		(e) 6,000		6,000			
Insurance expense	0		(d) 4,000		4,000			
Supplies expense	0		(c) 1,000		1,000			
Interest expense	4,000		(h) 500		4,500			
	1,054,600	1,054,600	24,100	24,100	648,000	780,000	417,100	285,100
Net income					132,000			132,000
					780,000	780,000	417,100	417,100

Trial Balance Columns   Examine the Inventory account in the trial balance. Inventory has a balance of $174,000 before the physical count at the end of the year. Cost of Goods Sold's balance is $421,000 before any adjustment based on the physical count. We shall assume that any difference between the Inventory amount on the trial balance ($174,000) and the correct amount based on the physical count ($168,000) is unexplained and should be debited or credited directly to Cost of Goods Sold.

Adjustments Columns   The adjustments are similar to those discussed in Chapters 3 and 4. They may be entered in any order desired. The debit amount of each entry should equal the credit amount, and total debits should equal total credits. You should review the adjusting data in Exhibit 5–7 to reassure yourself that the adjustments are correct.

KEY POINT

If you were preparing a work sheet, you could omit the Adjusted Trial Balance columns. Once you understand the mechanics of the work sheet, you can take a trial balance amount, add or subtract the adjustments, and extend the new amount to either the Income Statement or the Balance Sheet column.

Income Statement Columns   The Income Statement columns contain adjusted amounts for the revenues and expenses. Sales Revenue, for example, has an adjusted balance of $777,000.

The *Income Statement* column subtotals indicate whether the business had a net income or a net loss.

- Net income: Total credits > Total debits
- Net loss: Total debits > Total credits

Austin Sound's total credits of $780,000 exceed the total debits of $648,000, so the company earned a net income.

Insert the net *income* amount in the debit column to bring total debits into agreement with total credits. Insert a net *loss* amount in the credit column to equalize total debits and total credits. Net income or net loss is then extended to the opposite column of the balance sheet, so that total debits equal total credits.

Balance Sheet Columns   The only new item on the balance sheet, compared to previous chapters, is Inventory. The balance listed in Exhibit 5–7 is the ending amount of $168,000, as determined by the physical count of goods on hand at the end of the period.

Income Statement Formats: Multi-Step and Single-Step

As we saw in Chapter 4, the balance sheet appears in two formats:

- The report format (assets on top, owner's equity at the bottom)
- The account format (assets at left, liabilities and owner's equity at right).

For a review of balance sheet formats, see Chapter 4, page 181.
There are also two basic formats for the income statement:

- The multi-step format
- The single-step format

The multi-step format is the most popular.

Multi-Step Income Statement

A **multi-step income statement** shows subtotals to highlight significant relationships. In addition to net income, it also presents gross margin and operating income, or income from operations. This format communicates a merchandiser's results of operations especially well, because gross margin and income from operations are two key measures of operating performance. The income statements presented thus far in this chapter have been multi-step income statements. Austin Sound Centre's multi-step income statement appears in Exhibit 5–6 on page 243.

Single-Step Income Statement

The **single-step income statement** groups all revenues together, and then lists and deducts all expenses together without drawing any subtotals. Maple Leaf Foods Inc. uses this format. The single-step format has the advantage of listing all revenues together and all expenses together. Thus it clearly distinguishes revenues from expenses. The income statements in Chapters 1 through 4 were single-step. This format works well for service entities, because they have no gross margin to report, and for companies that have several types of revenues. Exhibit 5–8 shows a single-step income statement for Austin Sound Centre.

EXHIBIT 5–8 Single-Step Income Statement

AUSTIN SOUND CENTRE
Income Statement
For the Year Ended December 31, 2010

Revenues:		
Sales revenue		$777,000
Less: Sales discounts	$7,500	
Sales returns and allowances	8,000	15,500
Net sales revenue		761,500
Interest revenue		3,000
Total revenues		764,500
Expenses:		
Cost of goods sold		427,000
Wages expense		142,000
Rent expense		48,000
Amortization expense		6,000
Interest expense		4,500
Insurance expense		4,000
Supplies expense		1,000
Total expenses		632,500
Net income		$132,000

Most published financial statements are highly condensed. Appendix A at the end of the book gives the income statements for Canadian Western Bank, and Appendix B gives the income statement for Sun-Rype Products Ltd. Of course, condensed statements can be supplemented with desired details in the notes to the financial statements.

DID YOU GET IT?

To check your understanding of the material in this Learning Objective, complete these questions. The solutions appear on MyAccountingLab so you can check your progress.

10. The adjusted trial balance of Patti's Party Supplies for the year ended December 31, 2010, appears on the next page. Use this information to prepare the company's single-step income statement for the year ended December 31, 2010.

PATTI'S PARTY SUPPLIES
Adjusted Trial Balance
December 31, 2010

Cash..	$ 5,600	
Accounts receivable	21,900	
Inventory..	25,800	
Supplies	1,300	
Prepaid rent..	1,000	
Furniture...	26,500	
Accumulated amortization—furniture............		$ 23,800
Accounts payable...		6,300
Salaries payable...		2,000
Interest payable		600
Unearned sales revenue		2,400
Note payable, long-term		35,000
Patti Grandy, capital		22,200
Patti Grandy, withdrawals...............................	48,000	
Sales revenue		244,000
Interest revenue...		2,000
Sales discounts..	10,000	
Sales returns and allowances..........................	8,000	
Cost of goods sold...	81,000	
Salaries expense...	72,700	
Rent expense	7,700	
Amortization expense—furniture	2,700	
Utilities expense	17,400	
Supplies expense..	5,800	
Interest expense...	2,900	
Total...	$338,300	$338,300

11. Refer to the Patti's Party Supplies adjusted trial balance in the previous question. Use that information to prepare the company's multi-step income statement for the year ended December 31, 2010.
12. Refer to the Patti's Party Supplies adjusted trial balance in Question 10. What type of business is Patti's Party Supplies? Which accounts in the adjusted trial balance are unique to this type of business and support your answer?

Two Ratios for Decision Making

Inventory is the most important asset to a merchandising business because it captures the essence of the entity. To manage the business, owners and managers focus on the best way to sell the inventory. They use several ratios to evaluate operations, among them *gross margin percentage* and *rate of inventory turnover*.

The Gross Margin Percentage

Gross margin (gross profit) is net sales minus cost of goods sold. Merchandisers strive to increase the **gross margin percentage**, which is computed as follows:

For Austin Sound Centre
(Exhibit 5–6)

$$\text{Gross margin percentage} = \frac{\text{Gross margin}}{\text{Net sales revenue}} = \frac{\$334,500}{\$761,500} = 0.439, \text{ or } 43.9\%$$

A 43.9 percent gross margin means that each dollar of sales generates almost 44 cents of gross profit. On average, the goods cost the seller 56 cents. The gross margin percentage (also called the *gross profit percentage*) is one of the most carefully

EXHIBIT 5–9

Gross Margin on
$1.00 of Sales for
Two Merchandisers

watched measures of profitability. A small increase in the gross margin percentage may signal an important rise in income, and vice versa for a decrease.

Many businesses use the gross margin percentage (also known as the markup percentage) as a means of determining how well inventory is selling. If too much inventory is purchased and it must be marked down, the gross margin percentage will decline. By monitoring the gross margin percentage, a business can correct problems quickly.

Exhibit 5–9 compares Austin Sound Centre's gross margin to Wal-Mart's gross margin.

The Rate of Inventory Turnover

Owners and managers strive to sell inventory as quickly as possible. This is because there is a cost to carrying inventory. If a company purchases inventory on credit (creating an account payable), there is a risk it may buy too much inventory and be unable to sell it before having to pay for the inventory. If this happens, the company either has to borrow funds to pay for the inventory and incur interest expense, or use cash that could have been in a bank earning interest. For example, Dell Inc., the computer manufacturer and merchandiser, carries only *two hours* of parts inventory. Why? Prices of parts are continually declining, and Dell does not want to have any more inventory on hand than is absolutely necessary.

Dell is in a unique position in that it sells directly to customers and does not have to keep an inventory of computers on hand. Most retailers, such as Austin Sound Centre, must keep inventory on hand for customers. Successful merchandisers purchase carefully to keep goods moving through the business at a rapid pace. **Inventory turnover**, the ratio of cost of goods sold to average inventory, indicates how rapidly inventory is sold. Its computation follows:

**For Austin Sound Centre
(Exhibit 5–6)**

$$\text{Inventory turnover} = \frac{\text{Cost of goods sold}}{\text{Average inventory}} = \frac{\text{Cost of goods sold}}{(\text{Beginning inventory}^* + \text{ending inventory})/2} = \frac{\$427,000}{(\$158,400 + \$168,000)/2}$$

= 2.6 times per year
(about every 140 days**)

*Taken from the balance sheet at the end of the preceding period.
**Calculation: 365 days ÷ 2.6 times = approximately 140 days

Inventory turnover is usually computed for an annual period, and the relevant cost of goods sold figure is the amount from the entire year. Average inventory is computed from the beginning and ending balances of the annual period. Austin Sound Centre's beginning inventory would be taken from the business's balance sheet at the end of the preceding year. The resulting inventory turnover statistic shows how many times the average level of inventory was sold during the year. A high rate of turnover is preferable to a low turnover rate. An increase in turnover rate usually means higher profits but may sometimes lead to a shortage of inventory to sell.

Inventory turnover varies from industry to industry. Grocery stores, for example, turn their goods over faster than automobile dealers do. Drug stores have a higher turnover than furniture stores do. Retailers of electronic products, such as Austin Sound Centre, have an average turnover of 3.6 times per year. Exhibit 5–10 compares the inventory turnover rate of Austin Sound and Wal-Mart Stores, Inc.

Exhibits 5–9 and 5–10 tell an interesting story. Wal-Mart sells lots of inventory at a relatively low gross profit margin. Wal-Mart earns its profits by turning its inventory over rapidly—7.0 times during the year. Austin Sound Centre, a small business, prices inventory to earn a higher gross margin on each dollar of sales and only turns over its inventory 2.6 times during the year.

Gross margin percentage and rate of inventory turnover do not provide enough information to yield an overall conclusion about a merchandiser, but this example shows how owners and managers may use accounting information to evaluate a company.

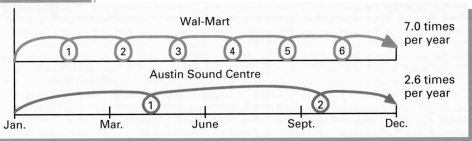

EXHIBIT 5-10 Rate of Inventory Turnover for Two Merchandisers

DID YOU GET IT?

MyAccountingLab

To check your understanding of the material in this Learning Objective, complete these questions. The solutions appear on MyAccountingLab so you can check your progress.

13. Refer to the Patti's Party Supplies adjusted trial balance in Did You Get It? Question 10 on pages 246 and 247 and the multi-step income statement you created in Did You Get It? Question 11. Calculate the gross margin percentage of this company.

14. Refer to the Patti's Party Supplies adjusted trial balance in Did You Get It? Question 10 on pages 246 and 247 and the multi-step income statement you created in Did You Get It? Question 11. Ending inventory at December 31, 2009, was $24,000. Calculate the inventory turnover of this company.

Accounting-Cycle and Financial-Reporting Implications of IFRS

The procedures that have been explained in this chapter also apply to companies that report under international financial reporting standards (IFRS). Two concepts from earlier chapters remain important. The first relates to the recognition of revenue. There are guidelines that merchandising companies must follow before they can recognize a sale. The most important of these is that the goods have been delivered and the likelihood of the goods being returned is small. Some companies do provide generous return policies. If these companies are unable to properly estimate the amount of inventory that might be returned, the recognition of revenue (and the corresponding cost of goods sold) should be delayed until the end of the return period. While this policy is explicitly stated in the IFRS guidelines, it applies equally to private enterprises that report under Canadian GAAP.

┌─ OBJECTIVE ⑥
Describe the merchandising-operations effects of international financial reporting standards (IFRS)

The second concept involves the matching of the cost of the goods sold and all other expenses related to the sale with the revenue earned. The purpose is to ensure that the gross margin earned by a company can be properly determined so that the readers of the financial statements will be able to properly evaluate the profitability of the company. Again, this approach is similar in all aspects to the policies followed by private enterprises that report under Canadian GAAP.

As we conclude this chapter, we return to our opening questions: How do merchandising operations differ from service operations, and why is it important? What are inventory and cost of goods sold? What types of inventory systems are there? How do decision makers evaluate a company's inventory operations? The Decision Guidelines feature summarizes all our chapter-opening questions and highlights inventory, the item that makes merchandisers different from service entities.

DID YOU GET IT?

MyAccountingLab

To check your understanding of the material in this Learning Objective, complete this question. The solution appears on MyAccountingLab so you can check your progress.

15. What are two key criteria that merchandisers who report under IFRS must follow? Do these criteria differ from those followed by companies that report under Canadian GAAP for private enterprises?

Decision

How do merchandising operations differ from service operations?

Guidelines

- Merchandisers, such as Austin Sound Centre, buy and sell *merchandise inventory* (often called inventory, or goods).
- Service entities, such as Ladner Environmental Services, perform a *service*.

How do a merchandiser's financial statements differ from the financial statements of a service business?
Balance sheet:
Merchandiser has *Inventory*, an asset.

Service business has no inventory.

Income statement (assumed amounts):

Merchandiser

Sales revenue	$1,000
− Cost of goods sold	500
= Gross margin	500
− Operating expenses	300
= Net income	$ 200

Service Business

Service revenue	$1,000
− Operating expenses	700
= Net income	$ 300

Statements of owner's equity:

No difference

What types of inventory systems are there?

- *Perpetual system* shows the amount of inventory on hand (the asset) and the cost of goods sold (the expense) at all times.
- *Periodic system* shows the correct balances of inventory and cost of goods sold only after a count of the inventory and adjustment of the books to reflect that count, which occurs at least once each year.

Use the *cost of goods sold formula* for the periodic system (assumed amounts):

Beginning inventory	$100
+ Net purchases and freight in	800
= Cost of goods available	900
− Ending inventory	200
= Cost of goods sold	$700

Cost of goods sold is computed continuously in the perpetual inventory system.

How do the adjusting and closing processes of merchandisers and service entities differ?

Very little.
The merchandiser
- Adjusts Inventory for shrinkage
- Closes Cost of Goods Sold and the contra revenue accounts

How can you format the merchandiser's income statement?

Multi-step format (assumed amounts)

Sales revenue	$1,000
− Cost of goods sold	500
= Gross margin	500
− Operating expenses	300
= Income from operations	200
+ Other revenues	30
− Other expenses	(50)
= Net income	$ 180

Single-step format (assumed amounts)

Revenues:

Sales revenue	$1,000
Other revenues	30
Total revenues	1,030

Expenses:

Cost of goods sold	500
Operating expenses	300
Other expenses	50
Total expenses	850
Net income	$ 180

How can you evaluate merchandising operations?

Two ratios:

$$\frac{\text{Gross margin}}{\text{percentage}}^* = \frac{\text{Gross margin}}{\text{Net sales revenue}} \qquad \frac{\text{Inventory}}{\text{turnover}}^* = \frac{\text{Cost of goods sold}}{\text{Average inventory}}$$

*In most cases—the higher, the better

Summary Problem for Your Review

The following trial balance and additional data are related to Sierra Distributing Company for the year ended December 31, 2010.

SIERRA DISTRIBUTING COMPANY
Trial Balance
December 31, 2010

Cash	$ 17,010	
Accounts receivable	111,300	
Inventory	181,500	
Supplies	11,790	
Prepaid rent	18,000	
Furniture	79,500	
Accumulated amortization—furniture		$ 63,600
Accounts payable		139,020
Salaries payable		0
Interest payable		0
Unearned sales revenue		10,500
Notes payable, long-term		105,000
Susan Sierra, capital		71,040
Susan Sierra, withdrawals	144,000	
Sales revenue		1,040,100
Sales discounts	30,900	
Sales returns and allowances	24,600	
Cost of goods sold	515,310	
Salaries expense	248,250	
Rent expense	21,000	
Amortization expense—furniture	0	
Utilities expense	17,400	
Supplies expense	0	
Interest expense	8,700	
Total	$1,429,260	$1,429,260

Additional data at December 31, 2010:

a. Supplies used during the year, $7,740.

b. Prepaid rent remaining in force, $3,000.

c. Unearned sales revenue still not earned, $7,200. The company expects to earn this amount during the next few months.

d. Amortization. The furniture's estimated useful life is 10 years, and it is expected to have no value when it is retired from service.

e. Accrued salaries, $3,900.

f. Accrued interest expense, $1,800.

g. Inventory still remaining on hand, $179,200.

Required

1. Enter the trial balance on a work sheet and complete the work sheet.

2. Journalize the adjusting and closing entries at December 31, 2010. Post to the Income Summary account as an accuracy check on the entries affecting that account. The credit balance closed out of Income Summary should equal net income computed on the work sheet.

Name: Sierra Distributing Company
Industry: Merchandising
Fiscal Period: Year ended December 31, 2010
Key Fact: Merchandiser uses the perpetual inventory system

3. Prepare the company's multi-step income statement, statement of owner's equity, and balance sheet in account format. Draw arrows connecting the statements, or state how the statements are linked.

4. Compute the inventory turnover for 2010. Inventory at December 31, 2009, was $168,400. Turnover for 2009 was 2.1 times. Would you expect Sierra Distributing Company to be more or less profitable in 2010 than in 2009? Give your reason.

SOLUTION

Requirement 1

Notice that this work sheet has eliminated the two Adjusted Trial Balance columns, as shown in the chapter.

Adjustments a. through f. are similar to the adjustments you made in Chapter 4. For adjustment g., the only new adjustment, compare the amount of inventory remaining on hand with the Inventory amount on the trial balance. If inventory on hand is lower, then record inventory shrinkage. If inventory on hand is higher, record a correction to increase the Inventory account.

SIERRA DISTRIBUTING COMPANY
Work Sheet
For the Year Ended December 31, 2010

Account Title	Trial Balance Dr	Trial Balance Cr	Adjustments Dr	Adjustments Cr	Income Statement Dr	Income Statement Cr	Balance Sheet Dr	Balance Sheet Cr
Cash	17,010						17,010	
Accounts receivable	111,300						111,300	
Inventory	181,500			(g) 2,300			179,200	
Supplies	11,790			(a) 7,740			4,050	
Prepaid rent	18,000			(b) 15,000			3,000	
Furniture	79,500						79,500	
Accum. amort.—furniture		63,600		(d) 7,950				71,550
Accounts payable		139,020						139,020
Salaries payable		0		(e) 3,900				3,900
Interest payable		0		(f) 1,800				1,800
Unearned sales revenue		10,500	(c) 3,300					7,200
Notes payable, long-term		105,000						105,000
Susan Sierra, capital		71,040						71,040
Susan Sierra, withdrawals	144,000						144,000	
Sales revenue		1,040,100		(c) 3,300		1,043,400		
Sales discounts	30,900				30,900			
Sales ret. and allow.	24,600				24,600			
Cost of goods sold	515,310		(g) 2,300		517,610			
Salaries expense	248,250		(e) 3,900		252,150			
Rent expense	21,000		(b) 15,000		36,000			
Amort. exp.—furniture	0		(d) 7,950		7,950			
Utilities expense	17,400				17,400			
Supplies expense	0		(a) 7,740		7,740			
Interest expense	8,700		(f) 1,800		10,500			
	1,429,260	1,429,260	41,990	41,990	904,850	1,043,400	538,060	399,510
Net income					138,550			138,550
					1,043,400	1,043,400	538,060	538,060

Requirement 2

Adjusting entries

2010

a. Dec. 31	Supplies Expense..	7,740		
	Supplies..		7,740	
b. Dec. 31	Rent Expense ($18,000 – $3,000)	15,000		
	Prepaid Rent...		15,000	
c. Dec. 31	Unearned Sales Revenue ($10,500 – $7,200)	3,300		
	Sales Revenue...		3,300	
d. Dec. 31	Amortization Expense—Furniture ($79,500/10)..	7,950		
	Accumulated Amortization—Furniture........		7,950	
e. Dec. 31	Salaries Expense..	3,900		
	Salaries Payable		3,900	
f. Dec. 31	Interest Expense..	1,800		
	Interest Payable..		1,800	
g. Dec. 31	Cost of Goods Sold ($181,500 – $179,200)	2,300*		
	Inventory..		2,300	

Adjustment g. The amount of inventory remaining on hand is lower than the Inventory amount on the trial balance. This indicates shrinkage, so reduce the Inventory account balance.

Closing entries

2010

Dec. 31	Sales Revenue..	1,043,400	
	Income Summary...		1,043,400
Dec. 31	Income Summary..	904,850	
	Sales Discounts		30,900
	Sales Returns and Allowances.........................		24,600
	Cost of Goods Sold		517,610
	Salaries Expense...		252,150
	Rent Expense..		36,000
	Amortization Expense—Furniture...................		7,950
	Utilities Expense		17,400
	Supplies Expense..		7,740
	Interest Expense...		10,500
Dec. 31	Income Summary ($1,043,000 – $904,850)..........	138,550	
	Susan Sierra, Capital		138,550
Dec. 31	Susan Sierra, Capital	144,000	
	Susan Sierra, Withdrawals		144,000

The merchandiser's accounts Cost of Goods Sold, Sales Discounts, and Sales Returns and Allowances are all expenses. They are temporary accounts that are closed just like other expense accounts.

All other closing entries are the same for service entities and for merchandisers that use the perpetual inventory system.

Income Summary

Clo.	904,850	Clo.	1,043,400
Clo.	138,550	Bal.	138,550

The T-account balance of $138,550 matches the net income amount on the work sheet.

---

*Adjustment of inventory to reflect physical count. This adjustment brings Inventory to its correct balance.

Requirement 3

The title must include the name of the company, "Income Statement," and the specific period of time covered. It is critical that the time period be defined.

Present the calculation of net sales revenue on a merchandiser's multi-step income statement.

SIERRA DISTRIBUTING COMPANY
Income Statement
For the Year Ended December 31, 2010

Sales revenue..		$1,043,400
Less: Sales discounts	$ 30,900	
Sales returns and allowances	24,600	55,500
Net sales revenue..		987,900
Cost of goods sold..		517,610
Gross margin..		470,290
Operating expenses:		
Salaries expense	252,150	
Rent expense...	36,000	
Utilities expense...	17,400	
Amortization expense—furniture	7,950	
Supplies expense..	7,740	321,240
Income from operations		149,050
Other expense:		
Interest expense...		10,500
Net income		$ 138,550

The title must include the name of company, "Statement of Owner's Equity," and the specific period of time covered. It is critical that the time period be defined.

The statement of owner's equity is the same for service entities and merchandisers.

SIERRA DISTRIBUTING COMPANY
Statement of Owner's Equity
For the Year Ended December 31, 2010

Susan Sierra, capital, January 1, 2010	$ 71,040
Add: Net income...	138,550
	209,590
Less: Withdrawals..	144,000
Susan Sierra, capital, December 31, 2010	$ 65,590

The title must include the name of the company, "Balance Sheet," and the date of the balance sheet. It shows the financial position on one specific date.

This is a classified balance sheet with Inventory listed among the current assets.

The Inventory balance is the cost of the inventory on hand based on the inventory count.

SIERRA DISTRIBUTING COMPANY
Balance Sheet
December 31, 2010

Assets			Liabilities		
Current assets:			Current liabilities:		
Cash..................................	$ 17,010		Accounts payable................	$139,020	
Accounts receivable.....	111,300		Salaries payable..................	3,900	
Inventory........................	179,200		Interest payable	1,800	
Supplies..........................	4,050		Unearned sales revenue.....	7,200	
Prepaid rent	3,000		Total current liabilities....	151,920	
Total current assets....	314,560		Long-term liabilities		
Property, plant, and			Notes payable......................	105,000	
equipment:			Total liabilities..................	256,920	
Furniture........................	$79,500				
Less: Accumulated			**Owner's Equity**		
amortization..............	71,550	7,950	Susan Sierra, capital	65,590	
			Total liabilities and		
Total assets......................		$322,510	owner's equity	$322,510	

Requirement 4

Refer to page 248 for the inventory turnover formula. Generally, the higher the inventory turnover is, the better.

$$\frac{\text{Inventory}}{\text{turnover}} = \frac{\text{Cost of goods sold}}{\text{Average inventory}} = \frac{\$517,610}{(\$168,400 + \$179,200)/2} = 2.98 \text{ times}$$

The increase in the rate of inventory turnover from 2.1 to 2.98 *suggests* higher profits in 2010 than in 2009. However, gross margin and expenses for both years must be checked to verify this suggestion.

CHAPTER 5 APPENDIX A
Accounting for Merchandise in a Periodic Inventory System

Purchasing Merchandise in the Periodic Inventory System

Some businesses find it too expensive to invest in a computerized (perpetual) inventory system that keeps up-to-the-minute records of merchandise on hand and the cost of the goods sold. Sometimes the nature of the inventory makes the perpetual inventory system impractical. For example, most baked goods in a local bake shop don't carry bar codes, so only their prices are recorded during a sale, not their cost as well. These businesses use the periodic inventory system.

┌ OBJECTIVE ⑦
Account for the purchase and sale of inventory under the periodic inventory system

Recording Purchases of Inventory

All inventory systems use the Inventory account. But in a periodic inventory system, purchases, purchase discounts, purchase returns and allowances, and transportation costs are recorded in separate expense accounts bearing these titles. Let's account for Austin Sound Centre's purchase of the JVC goods shown in Exhibit 5–3 on page 231. For the moment, disregard GST and use the invoice total of $2,425.00 when recording purchases and purchase discounts. GST is discussed on page 238. The following entries record the purchase and payment on account within the discount period:

May	27	Purchases....................................	2,425.00	
		Accounts Payable..............................		2,425.00
		Purchased inventory on account.		
Jun.	10	Accounts Payable...................................	2,425.00	
		Cash...		2,352.25
		Purchase Discounts............................		72.75
		Paid for inventory on account within discount period.		
		The discount is $72.75 [$2,425.00 × 0.03].		

Recording Purchase Returns and Allowances

Suppose instead that prior to payment, Austin Sound returned to JVC goods costing $475.00 and also received from JVC a purchase allowance of $75.00. Austin Sound would record these transactions as follows:

Jun.	3	Accounts Payable...................................	475.00	
		Purchase Returns and Allowances ...		475.00
		Returned inventory to seller.		
Jun.	4	Accounts Payable...................................	75.00	
		Purchase Returns and Allowances ...		75.00
		Received a purchase allowance.		

During the period, the business records the cost of all inventory bought in the Purchases account. The balance of Purchases is a *gross* amount because it does not include subtractions for purchase discounts, returns, or allowances. **Net purchases** is the remainder computed by subtracting the contra accounts from Purchases:

> **Purchase** (*debit* balance account)
> – **Purchase Discounts** (*credit* balance account)
> – **Purchase Returns and Allowances** (*credit* balance account)
> = **Net purchases** (a *debit* subtotal, not a separate account)

KEY POINT

A contra account always has a companion account with the opposite balance. Thus, both Purchase Discounts and Purchase Returns and Allowances (credit balances) are reported with Purchases (debit balance) on the income statement.

Recording Transportation Costs

Under the periodic system, costs to transport purchased inventory from seller to buyer are debited to a separate expense account, as shown for payment of a $100.00 freight bill:

Jun.	1	Freight In	100.00	
		Cash		100.00
		Paid a freight bill.		

Recording Sales of Inventory

Recording sales is streamlined in the periodic system. With no running record of inventory to maintain, we can record a $5,000 credit sale as follows:

Jun.	5	Accounts Receivable	5,000	
		Sales Revenue		5,000
		Sale on account.		

No accompanying entry to Inventory and Cost of Goods Sold is required in the periodic system.

Accounting for sales discounts and sales returns and allowances is the same as in the perpetual inventory system (pages 236–237) except that there are no entries to Inventory and Cost of Goods Sold.

DID YOU GET IT?

MyAccountingLab

To check your understanding of the material in this Learning Objective, complete this question. The solution appears on MyAccountingLab so you can check your progress.

16. Refer to the Oak Sales Company transactions in Did You Get It? Question 4 on page 239. Oak Sales Company engaged in those transactions during September 2010, the first month of the company's fiscal year. Assume the company uses a periodic inventory system and had no inventory on hand prior to September 3. Journalize the transactions and include any calculations in the journal-entry explanations.

Cost of Goods Sold

OBJECTIVE 8

Compute the cost of goods sold under the periodic inventory system

Cost of goods sold (also called **cost of sales**) is the largest single expense of most businesses that sell merchandise, such as ATMI Inc., Zellers, and Austin Sound Centre. It is the cost of the inventory that the business has sold to customers. In a periodic system, cost of goods sold must be computed as shown in Exhibit 5A–1 and is *not* a ledger account. It is the residual left when we subtract ending inventory from the cost of goods available for sale. Exhibit 5A–1 is an expansion of the cost of goods sold formula introduced on page 228.

EXHIBIT 5A–1 Measuring Cost of Goods Sold in the Periodic Inventory System

Panel A

Beginning inventory
+ Net purchases
+ Freight in

= Cost of goods available for sale
– Ending inventory

= Cost of goods sold

Purchases of inventory
– Purchase discounts
– Purchase returns and allowances

= Net purchases

Panel B

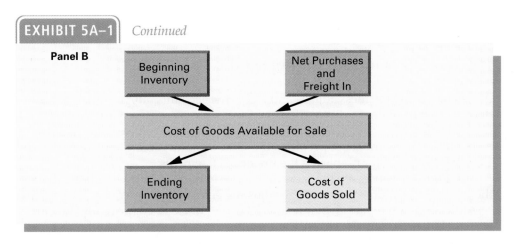

Exhibit 5A–2 shows Austin Sound Centre's net sales revenue; cost of goods sold, including net purchases and freight in; and gross margin on the income statement for the periodic system. (All amounts are assumed.)

EXHIBIT 5A–2 | Partial Income Statement

AUSTIN SOUND CENTRE
Income Statement
For the Year Ended December 31, 2010

PANEL A—Detailed Gross Margin Section—Often Required by Management

Sales revenue		$777,000
Less: Sales discounts	$ 7,500	
Sales returns and allowances	8,000	15,500
Net sales		761,500
Cost of goods sold:		
Beginning inventory..	158,400	
Purchases	$422,600	
Less: Purchase discounts	12,000	
Purchase returns and allowances.........................	5,000	
Net purchases..	405,600	
Freight in...	31,000	
Cost of goods available for sale................................	595,000	
Less: Ending inventory	168,000	
Cost of goods sold..		427,000
Gross margin...		$334,500

PANEL B—Summary Gross Margin Section—Most Common in Annual Reports to Outsiders

Net sales..........................	$761,500
Cost of goods sold	427,000
Gross margin	$334,500

DID YOU GET IT?

To check your understanding of the material in this Learning Objective, complete this question. The solution appears on MyAccountingLab so you can check your progress.

17. Refer to the Oak Sales Company journal entries created in Did You Get It? Question 16 on page 256. The inventory count at the end of September 2010 showed $20,050 of inventory on hand. Using this information and the amounts from the journal entries, compute the cost of goods sold under the periodic inventory system for Oak Sales Company for the month ended September 30, 2010.

Adjusting and Closing the Accounts in a Periodic Inventory System

OBJECTIVE (9)

Adjust and close the accounts of a merchandising business under the periodic inventory system

KEY POINT

Recall that Purchases (not Inventory) was debited for merchandise purchased. In the periodic system, no entries are made to the Inventory account for purchases or sales. Beginning inventory remains on the books and on the trial balance until ending inventory replaces it at the end of the period.

A merchandising business adjusts and closes the accounts much as a service entity does. The steps of this end-of-period process are the same: If a work sheet is used, the trial balance is entered and the work sheet completed to determine net income or net loss. The work sheet provides the data for journalizing the adjusting and closing entries and for preparing the financial statements.

The adjusting entries are the same for service entities and merchandisers that use the periodic inventory system. These adjusting entries were described in Chapter 4.

At the end of the period, before any adjusting or closing entries, the Inventory account balance is still the cost of the inventory that was on hand at the end of the preceding period. It is necessary to remove this beginning balance and replace it with the cost of the inventory on hand at the end of the period, based on the inventory count. Closing entries bring the inventory records up to date.

To illustrate a merchandiser's closing process under the periodic inventory system, let's use Austin Sound's December 31, 2010, adjusted trial balance in Exhibit 5A–3. All the new accounts—Inventory, Purchases, Freight In, and the

EXHIBIT 5A–3 Adjusted Trial Balance

AUSTIN SOUND CENTRE
Trial Balance
December 31, 2010

Cash	$ 6,000	
Accounts receivable	24,000	
Note receivable, current	32,000	
Interest receivable	1,000	
Inventory	**158,400**	
Supplies	500	
Prepaid insurance	600	
Furniture and fixtures	120,000	
Accumulated amortization—furniture and fixtures		$ 18,000
Accounts payable		128,000
Unearned sales revenue		1,500
Wages payable		3,000
Interest payable		500
Note payable, long-term		44,100
Steve Austin, capital		90,000
Steve Austin, withdrawals	65,000	
Sales revenue		777,000
Sales discounts	7,500	
Sales returns and allowances	8,000	
Interest revenue		3,000
Purchases	**422,600**	
Purchase discounts		**12,000**
Purchase returns and allowances		**5,000**
Freight in	**31,000**	
Wages expense	142,000	
Rent expense	48,000	
Amortization expense—furniture and fixtures	6,000	
Insurance expense	4,000	
Supplies expense	1,000	
Interest expense	4,500	
Total	$1,082,100	$1,082,100

contra accounts—are highlighted for emphasis. Inventory is the only account that is affected by the new closing procedures. The physical count of inventory gives the ending inventory figure of $160,800.

Journalizing the Closing Entries in the Periodic Inventory System

Exhibit 5A–4 gives Austin Sound's closing entries.

Closing entry 1

- Debits the revenue accounts and the contra expenses (Purchase Discounts and Purchase Returns and Allowances) for their credit balances.
- Credits Income Summary for the total revenues plus the contra expenses ($797,000).

Closing entry 2

- Debits Income Summary for total expenses ($674,600).
- Credits the contra revenues (Sales Discounts, and Sales Returns and Allowances) and all the expenses, including Purchases and Freight In, for their debit balances.

Closing entries 3 and 4 are new. Closing entry 3

- Debits Income Summary for the amount of the beginning balance of the Inventory account ($158,400).
- Credits Inventory for its debit balance.

Closing entries for a merchandising company accomplish the same tasks as in Chapter 4 and also replace beginning Inventory with the ending Inventory balance. The debit and credit to Income Summary match the Income Statement column totals from the work sheet.

Here is an easy way to remember the closing process.

1. Debit all income statement accounts that have a credit balance. Credit Income Summary for the sum of all these debits.

2. Credit all income statement accounts that have a debit balance. Debit Income Summary for the sum of all these credits.

3. Credit the inventory account for the amount of opening inventory and debit Income Summary for the same amount.

4. Debit Inventory for the amount of ending inventory obtained from the year-end physical count and credit Income Summary for the same amount.

5. Calculate the balance in the Income Summary account. If the account has a debit balance, there is a net loss; credit Income Summary for that amount, and debit Capital. If Income Summary has a credit balance, there is a net income for the period; debit Income Summary for that amount, and credit Capital.

6. Look at the debit balance of Withdrawals in the balance-sheet column. Credit Withdrawals for its balance, and debit Capital for the same amount.

| EXHIBIT 5A–4 | Closing Entries for the Periodic Inventory System |

Journal

Closing Entries

1.	Dec. 31	Sales Revenue	777,000	
		Interest Revenue	3,000	
		Purchase Discounts	12,000	
		Purchase Returns and Allowances	5,000	
		Income Summary		797,000
2.	Dec. 31	Income Summary	674,600	
		Sales Discounts		7,500
		Sales Returns and Allowances		8,000
		Purchases		422,600
		Freight In		31,000
		Wages Expense		142,000
		Rent Expense		48,000
		Amortization Expense		6,000
		Insurance Expense		4,000
		Supplies Expense		1,000
		Interest Expense		4,500
3.	Dec. 31	Income Summary	158,400	
		Inventory (beginning balance)		158,400
4.	Dec. 31	Inventory (ending balance)	168,000	
		Income Summary		168,000
5.	Dec. 31	Income Summary ($797,000 − $674,600 − $158,400 + $168,000)	132,000	
		Steve Austin, Capital		132,000
6.	Dec. 31	Steve Austin, Capital	65,000	
		Steve Austin, Withdrawals		65,000

Closing entry 4

- Debits Inventory for its ending balance, which was determined by the count of inventory at the end of the period ($168,000).
- Credits Income Summary for the amount of the ending balance of the Inventory account.

Closing entries 5 and 6

- Closes net income from Income Summary to the Capital account.
- Closes the Withdrawals balance into the Capital account.

Now Inventory has its correct ending balance as shown below.

Inventory

Jan. 1	Bal. 158,400	Dec. 31	Clo. 158,400
Dec. 31	Clo. 168,000		
Dec. 31	Bal. 168,000		

The entries to the Inventory account deserve additional explanation. Recall that before the closing process Inventory still has the period's beginning balance. At the end of the period, this balance is one year old and must be replaced with the ending balance in order to prepare the financial statements at December 31, 2010. The closing entries give Inventory its correct ending balance of $168,000.

DID YOU GET IT?

MyAccountingLab

To check your understanding of the material in this Learning Objective, complete this question. The solution appears on MyAccountingLab so you can check your progress.

18. Refer to the Oak Sales Company journal entries created in Did You Get It? Question 16 on page 256. The inventory count at the end of September 2010 showed $20,050 of inventory on hand. Using this information and the amounts from the journal entries, prepare the closing entries under the periodic inventory system for Oak Sales Company for the month ended September 30, 2010. Assume no other transactions took place during September 2010.

Preparing the Financial Statements of a Merchandiser

OBJECTIVE (10)
Prepare a merchandiser's financial statements under the periodic inventory system

Exhibit 5A–5 presents Austin Sound Centre's financial statements. The *income statement* through gross margin repeats Exhibit 5A–2. This information is followed by the **operating expenses**, expenses other than cost of goods sold that are incurred in the entity's major line of business—merchandising. Wages expense is Austin Sound's cost of employing workers. Rent is the cost of obtaining store space. Insurance helps to protect the inventory. Store furniture and fixtures wear out over time; the expense is amortization. Supplies expense is the cost of stationery, mailing, and the like, used in operations.

Many companies report their operating expenses in two categories.

- *Selling expenses* are those expenses related to marketing the company's products—sales salaries; sales commissions; advertising; amortization, rent, utilities, and property taxes on store buildings; amortization on store furniture; delivery expense; and so on.
- *General expenses* include office expenses, such as the salaries of office employees and amortization, rent, utilities, and property taxes on the head office building.

AUSTIN SOUND CENTRE
Income Statement
For the Year Ended December 31, 2010

Sales revenue			$777,000
Less: Sales discounts		$ 7,500	
Sales returns and allowances		8,000	15,500
Net sales revenue			761,500
Cost of goods sold:			
Beginning inventory		158,400	
Purchases	$422,600		
Less: Purchase discounts	12,000		
Purchase returns and allowances	5,000		
Net purchases		405,600	
Freight in		31,000	
Cost of goods available for sale		595,000	
Less: Ending inventory		168,000	
Cost of goods sold			427,000
Gross margin			334,500
Operating expenses:			
Wages expense		142,000	
Rent expense		48,000	
Amortization expense		6,000	
Insurance expense		4,000	
Supplies expense		1,000	201,000
Income from operations			133,500
Other revenue and (expense):			
Interest revenue		3,000	
Interest expense		(4,500)	(1,500)
Net income			$132,000

AUSTIN SOUND CENTRE
Statement of Owner's Equity
For the Year Ended December 31, 2010

Steve Austin, capital, January 1, 2010	$ 90,000
Add: Net income	132,000
	222,000
Less: Withdrawals	65,000
Steve Austin, capital, December 31, 2010	$157,000

AUSTIN SOUND CENTRE
Balance Sheet
December 31, 2010

Assets			Liabilities		
Current assets:			Current liabilities:		
Cash	$ 6,000		Accounts payable	$128,000	
Accounts receivable	24,000		Unearned sales revenue	1,500	
Note receivable	32,000		Wages payable	3,000	
Interest receivable	1,000		Interest payable	500	
Inventory	168,000		Total current liabilities	133,000	
Prepaid insurance	600		Long-term liability:		
Supplies	500		Note payable	44,100	
Total current assets	232,100		Total liabilities	177,100	
Property, plant and equipment:					
Furniture and fixtures	$120,000		**Owner's Equity**		
Less: Accumulated			S. Austin, capital	157,000	
amortization	18,000	102,000			
			Total liabilities and		
Total assets		$334,100	owner's equity		$334,100

Gross margin minus operating expenses plus any other operating revenues equals **operating income**, or **income from operations**. Many business people view operating income as the most reliable indicator of a business's success because it measures the entity's major ongoing activities.

The last section of Austin Sound's income statement is **other revenue and expenses**, which is handled in the same way in both inventory systems. This category reports revenues and expenses that are outside the company's main line of business.

Net sales, cost of goods sold, operating income, and net income are unaffected by the choice of inventory system. You can prove this by comparing Austin Sound's financial statements given in Exhibit 5A–5 with the corresponding statements in Exhibit 5–6 on page 243. The only differences appear in the cost-of-goods-sold section of the income statement, and those differences are unimportant. In fact, virtually all companies report cost of goods sold in streamlined fashion, as shown for Austin Sound in Exhibit 5–6.

Preparing and Using the Work Sheet in a Periodic Inventory System

The Exhibit 5A–6 work sheet on page 263 is similar to the work sheets we have seen so far, but a few differences appear. This work sheet is slightly different from the one you saw in Chapter 4; it does not include Adjusted Trial Balance columns. In most accounting systems, a single operation combines trial-balance amounts with the adjustments and extends the adjusted balances directly to the Income Statement and Balance Sheet columns. Therefore, to reduce clutter, the Adjusted Trial Balance columns are omitted so that the work sheet contains four pairs of columns, not five. The differences from the merchandiser's work sheet for the perpetual inventory system (page 244) are highlighted here.

Trial Balance Columns   Examine the Inventory account, $158,400 in the trial balance. This $158,400 is the cost of the beginning inventory. The work sheet is designed to replace this outdated amount with the new ending balance, which in our example is $168,000 [additional data item (h)]. As we saw, this task is accomplished in the columns for the income statement and the balance sheet during the closing process.

Income Statement Columns   The Income Statement columns contain adjusted amounts for the revenues and the expenses. Recall why the two inventory amounts appear in the Income Statement columns. The reason is that both beginning inventory and ending inventory enter the computation of cost of goods sold. *Placement of beginning inventory ($158,400) in the work sheet's Income Statement debit column has the effect of adding beginning inventory in computing cost of goods sold. Placing ending inventory ($168,000) in the credit column decreases cost of goods sold.*

Purchases and Freight In appear in the debit column because they are added in computing cost of goods sold. Purchase Discounts and Purchase Returns and Allowances appear as credits because they are subtracted in computing cost of goods sold.

The Income Statement column subtotals on the work sheet indicate whether the business earned a net income or incurred a net loss. If total credits are greater, the result is net income, as shown in Exhibit 5A–6. If total debits are greater, a net loss has occurred.

Balance Sheet Columns   The only new item on the balance sheet is inventory. The balance listed is the ending amount of $168,000, which is determined by a physical count of inventory on hand at the end of the period.

KEY POINT

If you were preparing a work sheet, you could omit the Adjusted Trial Balance columns. Once you understand the mechanics of the work sheet, you can take a trial balance amount, add or subtract the adjustment(s), and extend the new amount to either the Income Statement or the Balance Sheet column.

AUSTIN SOUND CENTRE
Work Sheet
For the Year Ended December 31, 2010

Account Title	Trial Balance Dr	Trial Balance Cr	Adjustments Dr	Adjustments Cr	Income Statement Dr	Income Statement Cr	Balance Sheet Dr	Balance Sheet Cr
Cash	6,000						6,000	
Accounts receivable	24,000						24,000	
Note receivable, current	32,000						32,000	
Interest receivable	0		(a) 1,000				1,000	
Inventory	**158,400**				158,400	168,000	168,000	
Supplies	1,500			(b) 1,000			500	
Prepaid insurance	4,600			(c) 4,000			600	
Furniture and fixtures	120,000						120,000	
Accum. amort.—furn. and fixt.		12,000		(d) 6,000				18,000
Accounts payable		128,000						128,000
Unearned sales revenue		4,100	(e) 2,600					1,500
Wages payable		0		(f) 3,000				3,000
Interest payable		0		(g) 500				500
Note payable, long-term		44,100						44,100
Steve Austin, capital		90,000						90,000
Steve Austin, withdrawals	65,000						65,000	
Sales revenue		774,400		(e) 2,600		777,000		
Sales discounts	7,500				7,500			
Sales returns and allowances	8,000				8,000			
Interest revenue		2,000		(a) 1,000		3,000		
Purchases	**422,600**				422,600			
Purchase discounts		12,000				12,000		
Purchase returns and allowances		5,000				5,000		
Freight in	31,000				31,000			
Wages expense	139,000		(f) 3,000		142,000			
Rent expense	48,000				48,000			
Amort. expense—furn. and fixt.	0		(d) 6,000		6,000			
Insurance expense	0		(c) 4,000		4,000			
Supplies expense	0		(b) 1,000		1,000			
Interest expense	4,000		(g) 500		4,500			
	1,071,600	1,071,600	18,100	18,100	833,000	965,000	417,100	285,100
Net income					132,000			132,000
					965,000	965,000	417,100	417,100

Additional data at December 31, 2010

a. Interest revenue earned but not yet collected, $1,000.
b. Supplies on hand, $500.
c. Prepaid insurance expired during the year, $4,000.
d. Amortization for the year, $6,000.
e. Unearned sales revenue earned during the year, $2,600.
f. Accrued wages expense, $3,000.
g. Accrued interest expense, $500.
h. Inventory on hand based on inventory count, $168,000.

The following trial balance pertains to Sierra Distributing Company.

The Summary Problem for Your Review on pages 251–254 was for a merchandiser using the perpetual inventory system. This Summary Problem uses the same data for the same company, but this time the company uses the periodic inventory system. The only differences are that this problem includes purchase discounts and purchase returns and allowances.

SIERRA DISTRIBUTING COMPANY
Trial Balance
December 31, 2010

Cash	$ 17,010	
Accounts receivable..	111,300	
Inventory...	168,400	
Supplies...	11,790	
Prepaid rent	18,000	
Furniture	79,500	
Accumulated amortization—furniture............................		$ 63,600
Accounts payable..		139,020
Salaries payable..		0
Interest payable..		0
Unearned sales revenue..		10,500
Notes payable, long-term...		105,000
Susan Sierra, capital		71,040
Susan Sierra, withdrawals...	144,000	
Sales revenue...		1,040,100
Sales discounts	30,900	
Sales returns and allowances..	24,600	
Purchases	540,800	
Purchase discounts...		18,000
Purchase returns and allowances..................................		22,290
Freight in...	27,900	
Salaries expense	248,250	
Rent expense..	21,000	
Amortization expense—furniture..................................	0	
Utilities expense...	17,400	
Supplies expense..	0	
Interest expense...	8,700	
Total	$1,469,550	$1,469,550

Name: Sierra Distributing Company
Industry: Merchandising
Fiscal Period: Year ended December 31, 2010
Key Fact: Merchandiser uses the periodic inventory system

Additional data at December 31, 2010:

a. Supplies used during the year, $7,740.
b. Prepaid rent remaining in force, $3,000.
c. Unearned sales revenue still not earned, $7,200. The company expects to earn this amount during the next few months.
d. Amortization. The furniture's estimated useful life is 10 years, and it is expected to have no value when it is retired from service.
e. Accrued salaries, $3,900.
f. Accrued interest expense, $1,800.
g. Inventory on hand based on an inventory count, $179,200.

Required

1. Enter the trial balance on a work sheet and complete the work sheet.
2. Journalize the adjusting and closing entries at December 31, 2010. Post to the Income Summary account as an accuracy check on the entries affecting that account. The credit balance closed out of Income Summary should equal net income computed on the work sheet.

3. Prepare the company's multi-step income statement, statement of owner's equity, and balance sheet in account format. Draw arrows connecting the statements, or state how the statements are linked.

4. Compute the inventory turnover for 2010. Turnover for 2009 was 2.1 times. Would you expect Sierra Distributing Company to be more or less profitable in 2010 than in 2009? Give your reason.

SOLUTION

Requirement 1

Notice that this work sheet has eliminated the two Adjusted Trial Balance columns, as shown in the chapter.
   Adjustments a. through f. are similar to the adjustments you made on page 252. Use additional data item g. when you create the closing entries.

SIERRA DISTRIBUTING COMPANY
Work Sheet
For the Year Ended December 31, 2010

Account Title	Trial Balance Dr	Trial Balance Cr	Adjustments Dr	Adjustments Cr	Income Statement Dr	Income Statement Cr	Balance Sheet Dr	Balance Sheet Cr
Cash	17,010						17,010	
Accounts receivable	111,300						111,300	
Inventory	168,400				168,400	179,200	179,200	
Supplies	11,790			(a) 7,740			4,050	
Prepaid rent	18,000			(b) 15,000		3,000		
Furniture	79,500						79,500	
Accum. amort.—furn.		63,600		(d) 7,950				71,550
Accounts payable		139,020						139,020
Salaries payable		0		(e) 3,900				3,900
Interest payable		0		(f) 1,800				1,800
Unearned sales revenue		10,500	(c) 3,300					7,200
Notes payable, long-term		105,000						105,000
Susan Sierra, capital		71,040						71,040
Susan Sierra, withdrawals	144,000						144,000	
Sales revenue		1,040,100		(c) 3,300		1,043,400		
Sales discounts	30,900				30,900			
Sales returns and allowances	24,600				24,600			
Purchases	540,800				540,800			
Purchase discounts		18,000				18,000		
Purchase returns and allowances		22,290				22,290		
Freight in	27,900				27,900			
Salaries expense	248,250		(e) 3,900		252,150			
Rent expense	21,000		(b) 15,000		36,000			
Amort. exp.—furniture	0		(d) 7,950		7,950			
Utilities expense	17,400				17,400			
Supplies expense	0		(a) 7,740		7,740			
Interest expense	8,700		(f) 1,800		10,500			
	1,469,550	1,469,550	39,690	39,690	1,124,340	1,262,890	538,060	399,510
Net income					138,550			138,550
					1,262,890	1,262,890	538,060	538,060

Requirement 2

These adjusting entries are the same as adjusting entries a. to f. on page 253.

Adjusting Entries

2010

			Debit	Credit
a.	Dec. 31	Supplies Expense	7,740	
		Supplies...		7,740
b.	Dec. 31	Rent Expense ($18,000 – $3,000)......................	15,000	
		Prepaid Rent...		15,000
c.	Dec. 31	Unearned Sales Revenue ($10,500 – $7,200)...	3,300	
		Sales Revenue..		3,300
d.	Dec. 31	Amortization Expense—Furniture ($79,500/10)	7,950	
		Accumulated Amortization—Furniture ...		7,950
e.	Dec. 31	Salaries Expense..	3,900	
		Salaries Payable		3,900
f.	Dec. 31	Interest Expense	1,800	
		Interest Payable..		1,800

Closing Entries

2010

The contra accounts Purchase Discounts and Purchase Returns and Allowances are temporary accounts closed at the same time as the revenue accounts.

Sales Discounts, Sales Returns and Allowances, Purchases, and Freight In are all expenses. They are temporary accounts that are closed just like other expense accounts.

The beginning balance of Inventory is first closed to Income Summary, then the ending balance of Inventory is debited and Income Summary is credited.

All other closing entries are the same for service entities and for merchandisers that use the periodic or the perpetual inventory system.

		Debit	Credit
Dec. 31	Sales Revenue	1,043,400	
	Purchase Discounts	18,000	
	Purchase Returns and Allowances..................	22,290	
	Income Summary..		1,083,690
31	Income Summary...	955,940	
	Sales Discounts		30,900
	Sales Returns and Allowances....................		24,600
	Purchases		540,800
	Freight In		27,900
	Salaries Expense		252,150
	Rent Expense...		36,000
	Amortization Expense—Furniture		7,950
	Utilities Expense		17,400
	Supplies Expense..		7,740
	Interest Expense...		10,500
31	Income Summary...	168,400	
	Inventory (beginning balance)....................		168,400
31	Inventory (ending balance)	179,200	
	Income Summary..		179,200
31	Income Summary ($1,083,690 – $955,940 – $168,400 + $179,200)...	138,550	
	Susan Sierra, Capital		138,550
31	Susan Sierra, Capital	144,000	
	Susan Sierra, Withdrawals		144,000

The T-account balance of $138,550 matches the net income amount on the work sheet.

Income Summary

Clo.	955,940	Clo.	1,083,690
Clo.	168,400	Clo.	179,200
Clo.	138,550	Bal.	138,550

Requirement 3

SIERRA DISTRIBUTING COMPANY
Income Statement
For the Year Ended December 31, 2010

Sales revenue		$1,043,400
Less: Sales discounts	$ 30,900	
Sales returns and allowances	24,600	55,500
Net sales revenue		987,900
Cost of goods sold:		
Beginning inventory		168,400
Purchases	$540,800	
Less: Purchase discounts	18,000	
Purchase returns and allowances	22,290	
Net purchases		500,510
Freight in		27,900
Cost of goods available for sale		696,810
Less: Ending inventory		179,200
Cost of goods sold		517,610
Gross margin		470,290
Operating expenses:		
Salaries expense	252,150	
Rent expense	36,000	
Utilities expense	17,400	
Amortization expense—furniture	7,950	
Supplies expense	7,740	321,240
Income from operations		149,050
Other expenses:		
Interest expense		10,500
Net income		$ 138,550

SIERRA DISTRIBUTING COMPANY
Statement of Owner's Equity
For the Year Ended December 31, 2010

Susan Sierra, capital, January 1, 2010	$ 71,040
Add: Net income	138,550
	209,590
Less: Withdrawals	144,000
Susan Sierra, capital, December 31, 2010	$ 65,590

SIERRA DISTRIBUTING COMPANY
Balance Sheet
December 31, 2010 Assets

Assets			Liabilities	
Current assets:			Current liabilities:	
Cash	$ 17,010		Accounts payable	$139,020
Accounts receivable	111,300		Salaries payable	3,900
Inventory	179,200		Interest payable	1,800
Supplies	4,050		Unearned sales revenue	7,200
Prepaid rent	3,000		Total current liabilities	151,920
Total current assets		314,560	Long-term liabilities:	
Property, plant, and equipment:			Notes payable	105,000
Furniture	$79,500		Total liabilities	256,920
Less: Accumulated amortization	71,550	7,950	**Owner's Equity**	
			Susan Sierra, capital	65,590
			Total liabilities and	
Total assets		$322,510	owner's equity	$322,510

The title must include the name of the company, "Income Statement," and the specific period of time covered. It is critical that the time period be defined.

Cost of goods sold is a *calculation* on the income statement under the periodic inventory system. (It is an *account balance* under the perpetual inventory system.) If the income statement is prepared for a company's external users, only the final cost of goods sold balance is typically presented, and then the income statement is the same regardless of the inventory system used.

The title must include the name of the company, "Statement of Owner's Equity," and the specific period of time covered. It is critical that the time period be defined.

The statement of owner's equity is the same for service entities and merchandisers using either of the inventory systems.

The title must include the name of the company, "Balance Sheet," and the date of the balance sheet. It shows the financial position on one specific date.

This is a classified balance sheet with Inventory listed among the current assets.

The Inventory balance is the cost of the inventory on hand based on the inventory count, and it is the same regardless of the inventory system used.

Requirement 4

$$\text{Inventory turnover} = \frac{\text{Cost of goods sold}}{\text{Average inventory}} = \frac{\$517,610}{(\$168,400 + \$179,200)/2} = 2.98 \text{ times}$$

The increase in the rate of inventory turnover from 2.1 to 2.98 times *suggests* higher profits in 2010 than in 2009. However, gross margin and expenses for both years must be checked to verify this suggestion.

CHAPTER 5 APPENDIX B

Comparing the Perpetual and Periodic Inventory Systems

OBJECTIVE 11
Compare the perpetual and periodic inventory systems

Exhibit 5B–1 provides a side-by-side comparison of the two inventory-accounting systems. It gives the journal entries, the T-accounts, and all financial-statement effects of both inventory systems.

In the periodic system, the purchase of inventory is *not* recorded in the Inventory account. Instead, purchases are recorded in the Purchases account, which is an expense (see transaction 1 in the exhibit, right column). A sale transaction includes *no* cost of goods sold entry (transaction 2). How, then, does the business record inventory and cost of goods sold?

Transactions 3a and 3b give the end-of-period entries to update the Inventory account. Transaction 3c closes the Purchases account into Income Summary to complete the periodic process.

Panel B of the exhibit shows the financial statements under both systems.

Panel A—Recording in the Journal and Posting to the Accounts

Perpetual System	Periodic System

1. Credit purchases of $600,000:

Inventory 600,000
    Accounts Payable.................... 600,000

2. Credit sales of $1,000,000 (cost $550,000):

Accounts Receivable.................... 1,000,000
    Sales Revenue 1,000,000

Cost of Goods Sold....................... 550,000
    Inventory 550,000

3. End-of-period entries:

No entries required. Both Inventory and Cost of Goods Sold are up-to-date.

---

1. Credit purchases of $600,000:

Purchases 600,000
    Accounts Payable...................... 600,000

2. Credit sales of $1,000,000:

Accounts Receivable 1,000,000
    Sales Revenue............................ 1,000,000

3. End-of-period entries to update Inventory:

   a. Transfer the cost of beginning inventory ($100,000) to Income Summary:

   Income Summary........................... 100,000
      Inventory (beginning balance) .. 100,000

   b. Record the cost of ending inventory ($150,000) based on a physical count:

   Inventory (ending balance).......... 150,000
      Income Summary...................... 150,000

   c. Transfer the cost of purchases to Income Summary:

   Income Summary........................... 600,000
      Purchases 600,000

INVENTORY AND COST OF GOODS SOLD ACCOUNTS

Inventory		Cost of Goods Sold	
100,000*	550,000	550,000	
600,000			
150,000			

*Beginning inventory was $100,000.

INVENTORY AND INCOME SUMMARY ACCOUNTS

Inventory		Income Summary	
100,000**	100,000	100,000	150,000
150,000		600,000	
150,000		550,000	

**Beginning inventory was $100,000.

Panel B—Reporting in the Financial Statements

Perpetual System	Periodic System

Income Statement (partial)

Perpetual System:

Sales revenue $1,000,000
Cost of goods sold   550,000
Gross margin............................... $ 450,000

Periodic System:

Sales revenue................................. $1,000,000
Cost of goods sold:
  Beginning inventory $100,000
  Purchases................................... 600,000
  Cost of goods available for sale 700,000
  Less: Ending inventory............ (150,000)
  Cost of goods sold....................   550,000
Gross margin .... $ 450,000

Balance Sheet (partial)

Perpetual System:

Current assets:
  Cash.. $ XXX
  Accounts receivable XXX
  Inventory 150,000

Periodic System:

Current assets:
  Cash... $ XXX
  Accounts receivable XXX
  Inventory 150,000

Summary

1. **Use sales and gross margin to evaluate a company.** The major revenue of a merchandising business is *sales revenue*, or *net sales*. The major expense is *cost of goods sold*. Net sales minus cost of goods sold is called *gross margin*, or *gross profit*. This amount measures the business's success or failure in selling its products at a higher price than it paid for them. The cost of goods sold formula is: Beginning inventory + Purchases − Ending inventory = Cost of goods sold

2. **Account for the purchase and sale of inventory under the perpetual inventory system.** The merchandiser's major asset is *inventory*. In a merchandising entity the accounting cycle is from cash to inventory as the inventory is purchased for resale, and back to cash as the inventory is sold. The *invoice* is the business document generated by a purchase or sale transaction. Most merchandising entities offer *purchase returns* to their customers to allow them to return unsuitable merchandise. They also grant *allowances* for damaged goods that the buyer chooses to keep. Sales Discounts and Sales Returns and Allowances are contra accounts to Sales Revenue. Some suppliers offer merchandising entities (their customers) *purchase discounts* to encourage them to pay their invoice promptly within the discount period.

3. **Adjust and close the accounts of a merchandising business under the perpetual inventory system.** The end-of-period adjusting and closing process of a merchandising business is similar to that of a service business. In addition, a merchandiser adjusts inventory for theft losses, damage, and accounting errors.

4. **Prepare a merchandiser's financial statements under the perpetual inventory system.** The income statement may appear in the *single-step format* or the *multi-step format*. A single-step income statement has only two sections—one for revenues and the other for expenses—and a single income amount for net income. A multi-step income statement has subtotals for gross margin and income from operations. The multi-step format is the most widely used format.

5. **Use the gross margin percentage and the inventory turnover ratio to evaluate a business.** Two key decision aids for a merchandiser are the *gross margin percentage* (Gross margin ÷ Net sales revenue) and the *rate of inventory turnover* (Cost of goods sold ÷ Average inventory). Increases in these measures usually signal an increase in profits.

6. **Describe the merchandising-operations effects of international financial reporting standards (IFRS).** The preparation of the income statement for a merchandising company that is following IFRS is not significantly different from the approach used by companies following GAAP for private enterprises in Canada. Revenue is recognized in the same way at the same time, and cost of goods sold and other selling expenses are matched against their related sales revenues in the same way under both reporting systems.

7. **Account for the purchase and sale of inventory under the periodic inventory system.** Under the periodic system, purchases of inventory are recorded in the Purchases account, and purchase discounts and purchase returns and allowances are recorded in separate contra accounts. The Inventory account is *not* used to record inventory purchases. Sales are recorded in the normal way but no entry is made to record the cost of the goods sold (as is done under the perpetual system).

8. **Compute the cost of goods sold under the periodic inventory system.** Cost of goods sold is computed at the end of the period using an expansion of the cost of goods sold formula. The physical inventory count gives the amount of ending inventory that is required by the cost of goods sold formula. There is *no* Cost of Goods Sold account in the chart of accounts, as there is under the perpetual inventory system.

9. **Adjust and close the accounts of a merchandising business under the periodic inventory system.** The closing entries for the periodic system are more complicated than the corresponding entries for the perpetual system. The Purchases, Purchase Returns and Allowances, and Freight In accounts are all closed to the Income Summary. As well, the opening inventory is closed to Income Summary and replaced by the ending inventory balance, which is credited to Income Summary. The result of these income summary transactions related to inventory is the cost of the goods sold amount appearing on the income statement.

10. **Prepare a merchandiser's financial statements under the periodic inventory system.** The financial statements report the same results regardless of whether the merchandiser uses the periodic inventory system or the perpetual inventory system. The only difference is on the income statement, where the cost of goods sold amount is a calculation under the periodic system as compared to an account balance under the perpetual system.

11. **Compare the perpetual and periodic inventory systems.** In the perpetual system, inventory purchases are recorded in the Inventory account; in the periodic system, they are recorded in the Purchases account, an expense. In the perpetual system, each sale is accompanied by a transaction that records the cost of the sale and reduces inventory, giving the current amount of inventory on hand. In the periodic system, only the sale is recorded; the cost of goods sold is calculated at the end of the period. Both inventory systems require a physical count of inventory at least once per year, usually at the end of the period. Both inventory systems report the same financial results at the end of the period since both adjust Inventory to match the amount based on the physical count.

SELF-STUDY QUESTIONS

Test your understanding of the chapter by marking the correct answer for each of the following questions:

1. The major expense of a merchandising business is (*p. 226*)
   a. Cost of goods sold   c. Rent
   b. Amortization   d. Interest

2. Sales total $890,000, cost of goods sold is $440,000, and operating expenses are $350,000. How much is gross margin? (*p. 226*)
   a. $890,000   c. $540,000
   b. $450,000   d. $100,000

3. If a merchandiser's beginning inventory was $120,000, it purchased $250,000 during the period and a count shows $100,000 of inventory on hand at the end of the period, what was the cost of the goods sold? (*p. 256*)
   a. $220,000   c. $270,000
   b. $370,000   d. $150,000

4. A purchase discount results from (*p. 231*)
   a. Returning goods to the seller
   b. Receiving a purchase allowance from the seller
   c. Buying a large enough quantity of merchandise to get the discount
   d. Paying within the discount period

5. Which of the following is *not* an account? (*p. 236*)
   a. Sales Revenue
   b. Net Sales
   c. Inventory
   d. Supplies Expense

6. Which account causes the main difference between a merchandiser's adjusting and closing process and that of a service business? (*pp. 240–241*)
   a. Advertising Expense   c. Cost of Goods Sold
   b. Interest Revenue   d. Accounts Receivable

7. The closing entry for Sales Discounts includes (*pp. 240–241*)
   a. Sales Discounts
         Income Summary
   b. Sales Discounts
         Sales Revenue
   c. Income Summary
         Sales Discounts
   d. Not used: Sales Discounts is a permanent account, which is not closed.

8. Which income statement format reports income from operations? (*p. 245*)
   a. Account format   c. Single-step format
   b. Report format   d. Multi-step format

9. A company has sales of $750,000, cost of goods sold of $450,000, average inventory during the year of $150,000, and ending inventory of $180,000. The company's inventory turnover for the year is (*p. 248*)
   a. 5.00 times   c. 2.50 times
   b. 3.00 times   d. 4.17 times

10. Refer to Self-Study Question 9. About how many days does it take the inventory to turn over? (*p. 248*)
    a. 122   c. 73
    b. 146   d. 88

Answers to Self-Study Questions

1. a
2. b ($890,000 − $440,000 = $450,000)
3. c ($120,000 + $250,000 − $100,000 = $270,000)
4. d
5. b
6. c
7. c
8. d
9. b ($450,000 ÷ $150,000 = 3.00 times)
10. a (365 days ÷ 3.00 times = 122 days)

ACCOUNTING VOCABULARY

Cost of goods sold   (*pp. 226, 256*)
Cost of sales   (*pp. 226, 256*)
Gross margin   (*p. 226*)
Gross margin percentage   (*p. 247*)
Gross profit   (*p. 226*)
Income from operations   (*pp. 242, 262*)
Inventory   (*p. 225*)
Inventory turnover   (*p. 248*)
Invoice   (*p. 230*)
Multi-step income statement   (*p. 245*)
Net purchases   (*p. 255*)
Net sales   (*p. 225*)

Operating expense   (*pp. 242, 260*)
Operating income   (*pp. 242, 262*)
Other expense   (*pp. 242, 262*)
Other revenue   (*pp. 242, 262*)
Periodic inventory system   (*p. 228*)
Perpetual inventory system   (*p. 228*)
Sales   (*p. 225*)
Sales discounts   (*p. 236*)
Sales returns and allowances   (*p. 236*)
Sales revenue   (*p. 225*)
Single-step income statement   (*p. 246*)

SIMILAR ACCOUNTING TERMS

Freight in	Freight; Transportation in; Transportation costs
Gross margin	Gross profit
Income from operations	Operating income
Invoice	Bill
List price	Full price; Price with no discounts deducted
Purchase discount	Cash discount; Discount given to reward prompt payment
Quantity discount	Volume discount; Discount given to reward purchase of more than one of a particular item
Sales revenue	Sales
Cost of goods sold	Cost of sales

Assignment Material

QUESTIONS

1. Gross margin is often mentioned in the business press as an important measure of success. What does gross margin measure, and why is it important?

2. Describe the operating cycle for (a) the purchase and cash sale of inventory, and (b) the purchase and sale of inventory on account.

3. Identify 10 items of information on an invoice.

4. Indicate which accounts are debited and credited under the perpetual inventory system for (a) a credit purchase of inventory and the subsequent cash payment, and (b) a credit sale of inventory and the subsequent cash collection. Assume no discounts, returns, allowances, or freight.

5. Inventory costing $4,000 is purchased and invoiced on July 28 under terms of 3/10, n/30. Compute the payment amount on August 6. How much would the payment be on August 9? What explains the difference? What is the latest acceptable payment date under the terms of sale?

6. Inventory listed at $80,000 is sold subject to a quantity discount of $6,000 and under payment terms of 2/15, n/45. What is the net sales revenue on this sale if the customer pays within 15 days?

7. Name the new contra accounts introduced in this chapter.

8. Briefly discuss the similarity in computing supplies expense and computing cost of goods sold under the periodic inventory system using the formula shown on page 228.

9. Why is the title of Cost of Goods Sold especially descriptive? What type of account is Cost of Goods Sold?

10. Beginning inventory is $10,000, net purchases total $55,000, and freight in is $2,000. If ending inventory is $14,000, what is cost of goods sold?

11. You are evaluating two companies as possible investments. One entity sells its services; the other entity is a merchandiser. How can you identify the merchandiser by examining the two entities' balance sheets and income statements?

12. You are beginning the adjusting and closing process at the end of your company's fiscal year. Does the trial balance carry the final ending amount of inventory if your company uses the perpetual inventory system? Why or why not?

13. Give the adjusting entry for inventory if shrinkage is $11,000.

14. What is the identifying characteristic of the "other" category of revenues and expenses? Give an example of each.

15. Name and describe two formats for the income statement, and identify the type of business to which each format best applies.

16. List eight different operating expenses.

17. Which financial statement reports sales discounts and sales returns and allowances? Show how they are reported, using any reasonable amounts in your illustration.

18. Does a merchandiser prefer a high or a low rate of inventory turnover? Explain.

19. In general, what does a decreasing gross margin percentage, coupled with an increasing rate of inventory turnover, suggest about a business's pricing strategy?

*20. In the periodic inventory system, what is meant by the term "cost of goods available for sale"?

---

*This Question covers Chapter 5 Appendix A or B topics.

*21. In a periodic inventory system, why must inventory be physically counted to determine cost of goods sold?

*22. Why do accountants use a Purchases account when inventory items are acquired in a periodic inventory system?

*23. How are purchase discounts accounted for in a periodic inventory system?

*24. Suppose you are starting a new retail business. What factors would you consider in determining whether to implement a periodic or a perpetual inventory system?

STARTERS

MyAccountingLab All questions in this section appear in MyAccountingLab.

Starter 5-1 Ending inventory of the previous period was $300,000, and net purchases this period were $1,500,000. If ending inventory this period is $200,000, what is cost of goods sold?

Using the cost of goods sold formula

Starter 5-2 Suppose Gap purchased T-shirts on account for $15,000. Credit terms are 2/10, n/30. Gap paid for the purchase a week later. Journalize the following transactions for Gap:

a. Purchase of inventory.
b. Payment on account.

Recording purchase and cash payment transactions—perpetual

b. Credit Cash $14,700

Starter 5-3 Suppose Toys Unlimited buys $200,000 of LEGO® toys on credit terms of 3/15, n/45. Some of the goods are damaged in shipment, so Toys Unlimited returns $25,000 of the merchandise to LEGO®. How much must Toys Unlimited pay LEGO®

a. After the discount period?
b. Within the discount period?

Accounting for the purchase of inventory, purchase discount—perpetual

b. $169,750

Starter 5-4 Refer to the Toys Unlimited situation in Starter 5-3 and journalize the following transactions on the books of Toys Unlimited. Explanations are not required.

a. Purchase of the goods on July 8, 2010.
b. Return of the damaged goods on July 12, 2010.
c. Payment on July 15, 2010.
d. In the end, how much did the inventory cost Toys Unlimited?

Recording purchase, purchase return, and cash payment transactions—perpetual

c. Credit Cash $169,750

Starter 5-5 Suppose The Bay purchases $80,000 of women's sportswear on account from Liz Claiborne, Inc., on August 1, 2010. Credit terms are 2/10, net 30. The Bay pays electronically, and Liz Claiborne receives the money on August 10, 2010.

Journalize The Bay's (a) purchase, and (b) payment transactions. What was The Bay's net cost of this inventory?

Note: Starter 5-6 covers this same situation for the seller.

Recording purchase transactions—perpetual

(b) Net inventory cost $78,400

Starter 5-6 Liz Claiborne, Inc., sells $80,000 of women's sportswear to The Bay under credit terms of 2/10, net 30 on August 1, 2010. Liz Claiborne's cost of the goods is $38,000, and Liz Claiborne receives the appropriate amount of cash from The Bay on August 10, 2010. Assume Liz Claiborne, Inc., uses the perpetual inventory system.

Journalize Liz Claiborne's transactions for August 1, 2010, and August 10, 2010.

Note: Starter 5-5 covers the same situation for the buyer.

Recording sales, cost of goods sold, and cash collections—perpetual

Cash receipt $78,400

Starter 5-7 Suppose Pearson Education, the publisher, sells 1,000 books on account for $75 each (cost of these books is $50,000) on October 10, 2010. The customer discovered that 100 of these books were the wrong edition, so Pearson later received these books as sales returns on October 13, 2010. Then the customer paid the balance on October 22, 2010. Credit terms were 2/15, net 30.

Journalize Pearson's October 2010 transactions.

Recording sales, sales return, and collection entries—perpetual

Cash receipt $66,150

Starter 5-8 Use the data in Starter 5-7 to compute Pearson Education's

a. Net sales revenue
b. Gross margin

Computing net sales and gross margin—perpetual

b. Gross margin $21,150

Starter 5-9 Patio Furniture's Inventory account at year end showed a debit balance of $75,000. A physical count of inventory showed goods on hand of $73,500. Journalize the adjusting entry.

Adjusting inventory for shrinkage—perpetual

*These Questions cover Chapter 5 Appendix A or B topics.

Making closing entries—
perpetual

Starter 5–10 Chandler RV Accessories' accounting records include the following accounts at December 31, 2010:

Cost of Goods Sold	$410,000	Accumulated Amortization	$300,000
Accounts Payable	24,000	Cash	20,000
Advertising Expense	20,000	Sales Revenue	720,000
Building	500,000	Amortization Expense	50,000
C. Chandler, Capital	455,000	C. Chandler, Withdrawals	60,000
Inventory	380,000	Sales Discounts	17,000
Land	100,000	Accounts Receivable	45,000
Selling Expenses	27,000		

Journalize the required closing entries for Chandler RV Accessories at December 31, 2010.

Preparing a merchandiser's
income statement—perpetual

Net income $3,000

Starter 5–11 Suppose Northern Communications reported these figures in its December 31, 2010, financial statements:

Cash	$ 7,600
Total operating expenses	7,000
Accounts payable	8,000
Owner, capital	8,400
Long-term notes payable	1,800
Inventory	800
Cost of goods sold	40,000
Equipment, net	7,400
Accrued liabilities	3,200
Net sales revenue	50,000
Accounts receivable	5,600

Preparing a merchandiser's
balance sheet—perpetual

Prepare Northern Communications' multi-step income statement for the year ended December 31, 2010.

Starter 5–12 Use the data in Starter 5–11 to prepare Northern Communications' classified balance sheet at December 31, 2010. Use the report format with all headings.

Computing the gross margin
percentage and the rate of
inventory turnover

Starter 5–13 Refer to the Northern Communications situation in Starters 5–11 and 5–12. Compute the gross margin percentage and rate of inventory turnover for 2010. One year earlier, at December 31, 2009, Northern's inventory balance was $600.

Recording purchase and cash
payment transactions—periodic
system

⑦

b. $169,750

*Starter 5–14** Suppose Toys Unlimited buys $200,000 of LEGO® toys on credit terms of 3/15, n/45. Some of the goods are damaged in shipment, so Toys Unlimited returns $25,000 of the merchandise to LEGO®. Assuming Toys Unlimited uses a periodic inventory system, how much must Toys Unlimited pay LEGO®

a. After the discount period?
b. Within the discount period?
c. Journalize the purchase of the goods. An explanation is not required.
d. Journalize the return of the damaged goods. An explanation is not required.

Recording sales and cash
collections—periodic system

⑦

Cash receipt $78,400

*Starter 5–15** Liz Claiborne, Inc., sells $80,000 of women's sportswear to The Bay under credit terms of 2/10, net 30 on August 1, 2010. Liz Claiborne's cost of goods sold is $38,000, and Liz Claiborne receives the appropriate amount of cash from The Bay on August 10, 2010. Assume Liz Claiborne, Inc., uses a periodic inventory system.

Journalize Liz Claiborne's transactions for August 1, 2010, and August 10, 2010.

Computing cost of goods
sold—periodic system

⑧

*Starter 5–16** Minit Company began the year with inventory of $8,000. During the year, Minit purchased $90,000 of goods and returned $6,000 due to damage. Minit also paid freight charges of $1,000 on inventory purchases. At year end, Minit's inventory based on the physical inventory count stood at $11,000. Minit uses the periodic inventory system.

Compute Minit Company's cost of goods sold for the year.

Comparing periodic and
perpetual inventory systems

⑪

*Starter 5–17** Suppose Ronny's Clothing purchased T-shirts on account for $18,130. Credit terms are 1/15, n/45. Ronny's Clothing paid within the discount period.

*These Starters cover Chapter 5 Appendix A or B topics.

a. If Ronny's Clothing uses a periodic inventory system, when will the purchase of inventory be recorded as an expense—when it is purchased or when it is sold?

b. If Ronny's Clothing uses a perpetual inventory system, when will the purchase of inventory be recorded as an expense—when it is purchased or when it is sold?

EXERCISES

MyAccountingLab All questions in this section appear in MyAccountingLab.

Exercise 5–1

The following characteristics are related to either periodic inventory or perpetual inventory systems.

A. Purchases of inventory are journalized to an asset account at the time of purchase.
B. Purchases of inventory are journalized to an expense account at the time of purchase.
C. Inventory records are constantly updated.
D. Sales made require a second entry to be journalized to record cost of goods sold.
E. Bar code scanners that record sales transactions are most often associated with this inventory system.
F. A physical count of goods on hand at year end is performed.

Identify each characteristic as one of the following:

a. Periodic inventory system
b. Perpetual inventory system
c. Both periodic and perpetual inventory systems
d. Neither periodic nor perpetual inventory system

Describing periodic and perpetual inventory systems

Exercise 5–2

The Electronics Store reported the information shown below.

Evaluating a company's revenues, gross margin, operating income, and net income

2. Gross margin 2010 $2,700 thousands

THE ELECTRONICS STORE
Income Statement
(Dollars in thousands)

	Fiscal Year Ended	
	January 31, 2010	January 31, 2009
Net sales	$9,000	$8,550
Costs and expenses:		
Cost of goods sold	6,300	6,030
Selling, advertising, general, and administrative	1,830	1,710
Amortization	186	173
Other expenses	54	355
Interest expense	90	94
Other income (expenses)	(17)	(17)
	8,443	8,345
Net earnings	$ 557	$ 205

THE ELECTRONICS STORE
Balance Sheet (partial)
(Dollars in thousands)

	January 31, 2010	January 31, 2009
Assets		
Current assets:		
Cash	$ 690	$ 185
Accounts and other receivables	130	208
Inventory	1,990	1,800
Prepaid expenses and other current assets	40	80
Total current assets	$2,850	$2,273

Required

1. Is The Electronics Store a merchandising entity, a service business, or both? How can you tell? List the items in The Electronics Store financial statements that influence your answer.

2. Compute The Electronics Store's gross margin for fiscal years 2010 and 2009. Did the gross margin increase or decrease in 2010? Is this a good sign or a bad sign about the company?

3. Write a brief memo to the owner advising her of The Electronics Store's trend of sales, gross margin, and net income. Indicate whether the outlook for The Electronics Store is favourable or unfavourable, based on this trend. Use the following memo format:

Date:	_____
To:	The Owner
From:	Student Name
Subject:	Trend of sales, gross margin, and net income for The Electronics Store

Exercise 5–3

The Wholesale Company began the year with inventory of $12,000. During the year, the company purchased $136,000 of goods and returned $9,000 due to damage. At year end, the Inventory balance was $17,000. The Wholesale Company uses the periodic inventory system.
Compute The Wholesale Company's cost of goods sold for the year.

Exercise 5–4

Suppose SportChek reported cost of goods sold totalling $750 million. Ending inventory was $325 million, and beginning inventory was $290 million. How much inventory did SportChek purchase during the year?

Exercise 5–5

Suppose The Bay purchases $600,000 of sporting goods on account from Nike on April 10, 2010. Credit terms are 2/10, net 30. The Bay pays electronically, and Nike receives the money on April 20, 2010.
Journalize The Bay's (a) purchase and (b) cash payment transactions. What was The Bay's net cost of this inventory?

Note: Exercise 5–6 covers this same situation for the seller.

Exercise 5–6

Nike sells $600,000 of sporting goods to The Bay under credit terms of 2/10, net 30 on April 10, 2010. Nike's cost of the goods is $420,000, and it receives the appropriate amount of cash from The Bay on April 20, 2010.
Journalize Nike's transactions on April 10, 2010, and April 20, 2010. How much gross margin did Nike earn on this sale?

Note: Exercise 5–5 covers the same situation for the buyer.

Exercise 5–7

Journalize, without explanations, the following transactions of Current Fashion Distributors, a wholesaler, during the month of June 2010:

Jun. 3   Purchased $14,500 of inventory from a manufacturer under terms of 2/10, n/eom and FOB shipping point.

7   Returned $2,700 of defective merchandise purchased on June 3.

9   Paid freight bill of $750 on June 3 purchase.

10   Sold inventory for $11,500 to a retail store, collecting cash of $2,400. Payment terms on the remainder were 2/15, n/30. The goods cost Current Fashion Distributors $6,900.

12   Paid amount owed on credit purchase of June 3.

16   Granted a sales allowance of $1,200 on the portion of the June 10 sale that was on account.

23   Received cash from June 10 customer in full settlement of the debt.

Exercise 5–8

As the proprietor of Willow Auto Service, you receive the invoice on the next page from a supplier (GST has been disregarded).

Margin notes (left column):

Using the cost of goods sold formula in a periodic inventory system

Computing inventory purchases

Purchase $785 million

Recording sales, cost of goods sold, and cash collections under the perpetual inventory system

Net inventory cost $588,000

Recording purchase transactions under the perpetual inventory system

Gross margin $168,000

Journalizing purchase and sale transactions under the perpetual inventory system

June 23 cash receipt $7,742

Journalizing transactions from a purchase invoice under the perpetual inventory system

3. Net cash paid $2,175.60

```
                    ABC AUTO PARTS WHOLESALE DISTRIBUTORS
                              2600 Victoria Avenue
                         Saskatoon, Saskatchewan S4P 1B3

    Invoice date: May 14, 2010              Payment terms: 2/10, n/30


    Sold to: Willow Auto Service
             4219 Cumberland Avenue
             Prince Albert, SK S7M 1X3


    Quantity                              Quantity
    Ordered           Description         Shipped        Price        Amount

       6         P135-X4 Radials.........    6          $90.00        $540.00
       8         L912 Belted-bias........    8          100.00         800.00
      14         R39 Truck tires.........   14          120.00       1,680.00


                 Total.....................................$3,020.00


    Due date:                          Amount:
      May 24, 2010                       $2,959.60
      May 25 through June 13, 2010       $3,020.00

    Paid:
```

Required

1. Journalize the transaction required on May 14, 2010.

2. The L912 Belted-bias tires were ordered by mistake and therefore were returned to ABC. Journalize the return on May 19, 2010.

3. Journalize the payment on May 22, 2010, to ABC Auto Parts.

Exercise 5–9

On April 30, 2010, Duncan Jewellers purchased inventory of $45,000 on account from Northern Gems Ltd., a jewellery importer. Terms were 3/15, n/45. On receiving the goods Duncan checked the order and found $5,500 worth of items that were not ordered. Therefore, Duncan returned this amount of merchandise to Northern on May 4. On May 14, Duncan paid Northern.

Required Journalize all necessary transactions for Duncan Jewellers. Explanations are not required.

Journalizing purchase transactions under the perpetual inventory system

May 14 cash paid $38,315

Exercise 5–10

Refer to the business situation in Exercise 5–9. Journalize the transactions of Northern Gems Ltd. Northern's gross margin is 45 percent, so cost of goods sold is 55 percent of sales. Explanations are not required.

Journalizing sale transactions under the perpetual inventory system

May 14 cash receipt $38,315

Exercise 5–11

Supply the missing income statement amounts in each of the following situations:

Computing inventory and cost of goods sold amounts

f. $74,600; g. $71,100

Sales	Sales Discounts	Net Sales	Cost of Goods Sold	Gross Margin
$94,500	$2,200	$92,300	$56,700	(a)
99,500	(b)	95,520	(c)	$36,000
68,700	2,100	(d)	37,700	(e)
(f)	3,500	(g)	52,500	18,600

Exercise 5–12

Making closing entries under a
perpetual inventory system

③

2. J. McClelland, Capital bal.
$44,100

McClelland Hardware Store's accounting records (partial) carried the following accounts at December 31, 2010:

Accounts Receivable	$ 39,500	Selling Expenses....................	$ 351,000
Interest Revenue	1,400	Sales Revenue........................	1,600,400
Accounts Payable..................	99,000	Interest Expense	12,000
Other Expense	64,500	Inventory................................	220,500
Cost of Goods Sold	880,200	General and Administrative	
J. McClelland, Withdrawals ...	84,000	Expenses.............................	220,000

Required Note: For simplicity, all operating expenses have been summarized in the accounts Selling Expenses and General and Administrative Expenses.

1. Journalize all of this company's closing entries at December 31, 2010.
2. Set up T-accounts for the Income Summary account and the J. McClelland, Capital account. Post to these accounts and calculate their ending balances. One year earlier, at December 31, 2009, the Capital balance was $54,000.

Exercise 5–13

Adjusting and closing entries
under the perpetual inventory
system, computing gross margin

① ③

c. Gross margin $26,900

Just Candy's accounts at December 31, 2010, included these unadjusted balances:

Inventory...	$ 7,800
Cost of Goods Sold	62,400
Sales Revenue..	93,600
Sales Discounts..	1,500
Sales Returns and Allowances.....................	2,400

The physical count of inventory showed $7,400 of inventory on hand. This is the only adjustment needed.

Required

a. Journalize the adjustment for inventory shrinkage. Include an explanation.
b. Journalize the closing entries for the appropriate accounts.
c. Compute the gross margin.

Exercise 5–14

Using work-sheet data to make
the closing entries under the
perpetual inventory system

③

Net income $83,700

The Trial Balance and Adjustments columns of the work sheet of Wells Decorating Centre include these accounts and balances at December 31, 2010.

Account Title	Trial Balance		Adjustments	
	Debit	Credit	Debit	Credit
Cash...	17,000			
Accounts receivable	27,500		(a) 2,200	
Inventory	63,500			(b) 1,400
Supplies..	8,600			(c) 6,400
Store fixtures	70,000			
Accumulated amortization		35,000		(d) 7,000
Accounts payable		21,200		
Salary payable...................................		0		(e) 3,800
Note payable, long-term		12,500		
B. Wells, capital................................		41,800		
B. Wells, withdrawals	24,000			
Sales revenue....................................		421,400		(a) 2,200
Sales discounts.................................	4,300			
Cost of goods sold............................	244,400		(b) 1,400	
Selling expenses...............................	42,800		(c) 5,200	
			(e) 3,800	
General expenses.............................	28,700		(c) 1,200	
			(d) 7,000	
Interest expense	1,100			
Total	531,900	531,900	20,800	20,800

Required Compute the adjusted balance for each account that must be closed. Then journalize Wells Decorating Centre's closing entries at December 31, 2010. How much was Wells Decorating Centre's net income or net loss?

Exercise 5–15

Use the data in Exercise 5–14 to prepare the multi-step income statement of Wells Decorating Centre for the year ended December 31, 2010.

Exercise 5–16

Refer to Exercise 5–15. After completing Wells Decorating Centre's income statement for the year ended December 31, 2010, compute these ratios to evaluate Wells Decorating Centre's performance:

- Gross margin percentage
- Inventory turnover (ending inventory one year earlier, at December 31, 2009, was $54,500)

Compare your figures with the 2009 gross margin percentage of 40 percent and the inventory turnover rate of 3.82 times. Does the two-year trend suggest that Wells Decorating Centre's profits are increasing or decreasing?

Exercise 5–17

Selected amounts from the accounting records of Vallarta Video Sales for the year ended December 31, 2010, follow:

Journal Entries

Dec.	31	Sales Revenue	281,400	
		Interest Revenue	1,800	
		Income Summary		283,200
	31	Income Summary	254,400	
		Cost of Goods Sold		141,200
		Sales Discounts		12,600
		Sales Returns and Allowances		6,900
		Selling Expenses		57,800
		General Expenses		35,900
	31	Income Summary	28,800	
		B. Vallarta, Capital		28,800
	31	B. Vallarta, Capital	25,000	
		B. Vallarta, Withdrawals		25,000

Required

1. Prepare the business's multi-step income statement for the year ended December 31, 2010.

2. Compute the rate of inventory turnover for the year. The inventory balance on December 31, 2009, was $25,400 and on December 31, 2010, was $28,600. Last year the turnover rate was 5.42 times. Does this two-year trend suggest improvement or deterioration in inventory turnover?

Exercise 5–18

Prepare Vallarta Video Sales' single-step income statement for 2010, using the data from Exercise 5–17. Compute the gross margin percentage, and compare it with last year's value of 49 percent for Vallarta Video. Does this two-year trend suggest better or worse profitability during the current year?

Exercise 5–19

Networking Systems earned sales revenue of $66 million in 2010. Cost of goods sold was $35 million, and net income reached $8 million, Networking's highest ever. Total current assets included inventory of $7.0 million at December 31, 2010. Last year's ending inventory was $6.6 million. The managers of Networking Systems need to know the company's gross margin percentage and rate of inventory turnover for 2010. Compute these amounts.

Preparing a multi-step income statement under the perpetual inventory system

Gross margin $173,500

Using the gross margin percentage and the rate of inventory turnover to evaluate profitability

Gross margin 41.4%

 Excel Spreadsheet Template

Preparing a merchandiser's multi-step income statement under the perpetual inventory system to evaluate the business

1. Net income $28,800

 Excel Spreadsheet Template

Preparing a single-step income statement for a merchandising business under the perpetual inventory system

Net income $28,800

Computing gross margin percentage and inventory turnover

Gross margin 47.0%

Journalizing purchase and sale
transactions under the periodic
inventory system

June 23 cash receipt $17,248

Journalize, without explanations, the following transactions of McBride Auto Parts, a
distributor, during the month of June 2010:

Jun. 3   Purchased $16,800 of inventory under terms of 2/10, n/eom and FOB
          shipping point.
       7   Returned $1,600 of defective merchandise purchased on June 3.
       9   Paid freight bill of $350 on June 3 purchase.
      10   Sold inventory for $22,400, collecting cash of $3,600. Payment terms on the
          remainder were 2/15, n/30.
      12   Paid amount owed on credit purchase of June 3.
      16   Granted a sales allowance of $1,200 on the June 10 sale.
      23   Received cash from June 10 customer in full settlement of the debt.

*Exercise 5–21

Journalizing transactions from a
purchase invoice under the
periodic inventory system

3. May 22 payment $2,175.60

As the proprietor of OK Auto Repair, you receive this invoice from a supplier (GST has
been disregarded).

ABC AUTO PARTS WHOLESALE DISTRIBUTORS
2600 Victoria Avenue
Saskatoon, Saskatchewan S4P 1B3

Invoice date: May 14, 2010   **Payment terms:** 2/10, n/30

Sold to: OK Auto Repair
4245 Cumberland Avenue
Prince Albert, SK S7M 1X3

Quantity Ordered	Description	Quantity Shipped	Price	Amount
6	P135-X4 Radials.........	6	$90.00	$540.00
8	L912 Belted-bias........	8	100.00	800.00
14	R39 Truck tires.........	14	120.00	1,680.00
	Total..$3,020.00			

Due date:	Amount:
May 24, 2010	$2,959.60
May 25 through June 13, 2010	$3,020.00
Paid:	

Required

1. Journalize the transaction required on May 14, 2010.

2. The L912 belted-bias tires were ordered by mistake and therefore were returned to ABC.
   Journalize the return on May 19, 2010.

3. Journalize the payment on May 22, 2010, to ABC Auto Parts.

*Exercise 5–22

Journalizing purchase transactions under the periodic
inventory system

May 14 cash paid $38,315

On April 30, 2010, Duncan Jewellers purchased inventory of $45,000 on account from
Northern Gems Ltd., a jewellery importer. Terms were 3/15, net 45. On receiving the goods,
Duncan checked the order and found $5,500 of unsuitable merchandise. Therefore, Duncan
returned the merchandise to Northern on May 4, 2010.

On May 14, 2010, Duncan Jewellers paid the net amount owed from April 30.

Required Record the required transactions in the journal of Duncan Jewellers. Use the
periodic inventory system. Explanations are not required.

---

*These Exercises cover Chapter 5 Appendix A topics.

*Exercise 5–23

Refer to the business situation in Exercise 5–22. Journalize the transactions of Northern Gems Ltd., which uses the periodic inventory system. Explanations are not required.

*Exercise 5–24

The periodic inventory records of Vallarta Video Sales include these accounts at December 31, 2010:

Purchases	$152,500
Purchase Discounts	6,800
Purchase Returns and Allowances..............	8,600
Freight In..	7,300
Inventory, December 31, 2009.....................	25,400
Inventory, December 31, 2010.....................	28,600

Required Compute Vallarta Video's cost of goods sold for 2010. (Note: Your answer should be the same as the amount given in Exercise 5–17.)

*Exercise 5–25

Supply the missing income statement amounts in each of the following situations:

Sales	Sales Discounts	Net Sales	Beginning Inventory	Net Purchases	Ending Inventory	Cost of Goods Sold	Gross Margin
$24,100	(a)	$23,400	$8,800	$16,700	$9,900	(b)	$7,800
20,600	$500	(c)	6,400	10,800	(d)	$11,100	(e)
23,400	400	23,000	(f)	11,200	5,700	14,900	(g)
(h)	800	(i)	10,100	(j)	12,100	18,100	9,700

*Exercise 5–26

For the year ended December 31, 2010, Home Distributors, a retailer of home-related products, reported net sales of $859,000 and cost of goods sold of $450,000. The company's balance sheet at December 31, 2009 and 2010, reported inventories of $346,000 and $335,000, respectively. What were Home Distributors' net purchases during 2010?

*Exercise 5–27

Rees Distributors uses the periodic inventory system. Rees reported these amounts at May 31, 2010:

Inventory, May 31, 2009........	$29,000	Freight In.................................	$ 4,000
Inventory, May 31, 2010........	31,000	Sales Revenue.........................	190,000
Purchases (of inventory).......	92,000	Sales Discounts......................	3,000
Purchase Discounts	2,000	Sales Returns	5,000
Purchase Returns	3,000		

Compute Rees Distributors'

a. Net sales revenue
b. Cost of goods sold
c. Gross margin

SERIAL EXERCISE

This exercise continues the Haupt Consulting situation from Exercise 4–16 of Chapter 4. If you did not complete Exercise 4–16 you can still complete Exercise 5–28 as it is presented.

Exercise 5–28

Haupt Consulting performs systems consulting. Haupt Consulting has also begun selling accounting software. During January 2011, the business completed these transactions:

Jan.	2	Completed a consulting engagement and received cash of $7,200.
	2	Prepaid three months' office rent, $3,000.

_____
*These Exercises cover Chapter 5 Appendix A topics.

Side notes (right margin):

Journalizing sale transactions under the periodic inventory system

May 14 cash received $38,315

Computing cost of goods sold in a periodic inventory system

Cost of goods sold $141,200

Computing inventory and cost of goods sold under the periodic inventory system

a. $700 f. $9,400 j. $20,100

Computing cost of goods sold under the periodic inventory system

Net purchases $439,000

Cost of goods sold in a periodic inventory system

c. Gross margin $93,000

Accounting for both merchandising and service transactions under the perpetual inventory system

4. Net income $7,167

Chapter 5 Merchandising Operations and the Accounting Cycle **281**

Jan.	7	Purchased 100 units of software inventory on account, $1,900, plus freight in, $100.
	16	Paid employee salary, $1,400.
	18	Sold 70 software units on account, $3,100 (cost $1,400).
	19	Consulted with a client for a fee of $900 on account.
	21	Paid on account, $2,000.
	22	Purchased 200 units of software inventory on account, $4,600.
	24	Paid utilities, $300.
	28	Sold 100 units of software for cash, $4,000 (cost $2,210).
	31	Recorded the following adjusting entries:

           Accrued salary expense, $1,400.

           Prepaid rent expired, $1,000.

           Amortization of office furniture, $60, and of equipment, $33.

           Physical count of inventory, 120 units, $2,760.

Required

1. Open the following selected T-accounts in the ledger with their normal opening balances as shown: Cash, $7,200; Accounts Receivable, $1,500; Software Inventory; Prepaid Rent; Accumulated Amortization—Equipment, $33; Accumulated Amortization—Office Furniture, $60; Accounts Payable, $3,600; Salaries Payable, $500; Carl Haupt, Capital, $9,607; Income Summary; Service Revenue; Sales Revenue; Cost of Goods Sold; Salaries Expense; Rent Expense; Utilities Expense; Amortization Expense—Equipment; and Amortization Expense—Office Furniture.

2. Journalize and post to the T-accounts the January transactions. Key all items by date. Compute each account balance, and denote the balance as *Bal*.

3. Journalize and post the closing entries. Denote each closing amount as *Clo*.

4. Prepare the January 2011 income statement of Haupt Consulting. Use the multi-step format.

BEYOND THE NUMBERS

Beyond the Numbers 5–1

Evaluating a company's profitability

①⑤

Gross margin in 2010 27%

Wilson Distributors is a provider of automotive products. The company recently reported the following:

WILSON DISTRIBUTORS
Consolidated Statements of Operations (Adapted)
For the Years Ended July 31, 2010 and 2009

	2010	2009
Sales	$1,320,000	$984,000
Cost of sales	960,000	732,000
Gross margin	360,000	252,000
Cost and expenses:		
Selling, general, and administrative	264,000	204,000
Amortization	24,000	11,000
Restructuring charges	84,000	—
	372,000	215,000
Operating income (loss)	(12,000)	37,000
Other items (summarized)	(7,000)	(16,000)
Net income (loss)	$ (19,000)	$ 21,000

Required   Evaluate Wilson Distributors' operations during 2010 in comparison with 2009. Consider sales, gross margin, operating income, and net income. Track the gross margin percentage and inventory turnover in both years. Wilson Distributors' inventories at December 31, 2010, 2009, and 2008, were $92,000, $145,000, and $122,000, respectively. In the annual report, management describes the restructuring charges in 2010, the costs of downsizing the company, as a one-time event. How does this additional information affect your evaluation?

ETHICAL ISSUE

Parkhurst Bearing Company makes all sales of industrial bearings under terms of FOB shipping point. The company usually receives orders for sales approximately one week before shipping inventory to customers. For orders received late in December, Bob Parkhurst, the owner, decides when to ship the goods. If profits are already at an acceptable level, the company delays shipment until January. If profits are lagging behind expectations, the company ships the goods during December.

Required

1. Under Parkhurst Bearing Company's FOB policy, when should the company record a sale?
2. Do you approve or disapprove of Parkhurst Bearing Company's means of deciding when to ship goods to customers? If you approve, give your reason. If you disapprove, identify a better way to decide when to ship goods. (There is no accounting rule against Parkhurst Bearing Company's practice.)

PROBLEMS (GROUP A)

 All questions in this section appear in MyAccountingLab.

Problem 5–1A

Canadian Tire is one of the largest retailers in Canada. The hardware department of Canadian Tire purchases tools from many well-known manufacturers. Canadian Tire uses a sophisticated perpetual inventory system.

Explaining the perpetual inventory system

Required

You are the manager of a Canadian Tire store. Write a memo to a new employee in the hardware department that explains how the company accounts for the purchase and sale of merchandise inventory.

Use the following heading for your memo:

Date:	_____
To:	New Employee
From:	Store Manager
Subject:	Canadian Tire's accounting system for inventories

Problem 5–2A

The following transactions occurred between King Pharmaceuticals and Hall's Drug Store during February of the current year. Both companies use the perpetual inventory system.

Accounting for the purchase and sale of inventory under the perpetual inventory system

Feb. 27 Cash amount $31,000

Feb. 6   Hall purchased $60,000 of merchandise from King on credit terms of 2/10, n/30, FOB shipping point. Separately, Hall paid a $1,000 bill for freight in. King invoiced Hall for $60,000 (these goods cost King $36,000).

    10   Hall returned $5,000 of the merchandise purchased on February 6. King issued a credit memo for this amount and returned the goods to inventory (cost, $3,000).

    15   Hall paid $24,000 of the invoice amount owed to King for the February 6 purchase. King allows its customers to take the cash discount on partial payments.

    27   Hall paid the remaining amount owed to King for the February 6 purchase.

Required   Journalize these transactions, first on the books of Hall Drug Store and second on the books of King Pharmaceuticals.

Problem 5–3A

Singh Distributing Company engaged in the following transactions during May of the current year:

May	3	Purchased office supplies for cash, $5,500.
	7	Purchased inventory on credit terms of 3/10, net eom, $38,000.
	8	Returned 25 percent of the inventory purchased on May 7. It was not the inventory ordered.
	10	Sold goods for cash, $8,500 (cost, $5,100).
	13	Sold inventory on credit terms of 2/15, n/45, for $75,400, less $7,540 quantity discount offered to customers who purchased in large quantities (cost, $45,240).
	16	Paid the amount owed on account from the purchase of May 7, less the discount and the return.
	17	Received wrong-sized inventory as a sales return from May 13 sale, $6,200, which is the net amount after the quantity discount. Singh's cost of the inventory received was $3,720.
	18	Purchased inventory of $82,000 on account. Payment terms were 2/10, net 30.
	26	Paid supplier for goods purchased on May 18.
	28	Received cash in full settlement of the account from the customer who purchased inventory on May 13.
	29	Purchased inventory for cash, $42,000, less a quantity discount of $4,200, plus freight charges of $1,100.

Required Journalize the preceding transactions on the books of Singh Distributing Company.

Problem 5–4A

The trial balance of Stuart's Fine Gems pertains to December 31, 2010, and is shown below.

STUART'S FINE GEMS
Trial Balance
December 31, 2010

Cash	$ 3,100	
Accounts receivable	28,500	
Inventory	177,400	
Prepaid rent	14,000	
Equipment	54,000	
Accumulated amortization—equipment		$ 21,600
Accounts payable		21,600
Salary payable		0
Interest payable		0
Note payable, long-term		43,500
J. Stuart, capital		135,000
J. Stuart, withdrawals	76,500	
Sales revenue		417,700
Cost of goods sold	164,000	
Salary expense	59,300	
Rent expense	22,000	
Advertising expense	10,800	
Utilities expense	15,400	
Amortization expense—equipment	0	
Insurance expense	6,600	
Interest expense	1,300	
Miscellaneous expense	6,500	
Total	$639,400	$639,400

Additional data at December 31, 2010:

a. Rent expense for the year, $24,000.

b. The equipment has an estimated useful life of 10 years and is expected to have no value when it is retired from service.

c. Accrued salaries at December 31, $3,500.

d. Accrued interest expense at December 31, $1,300.

e. Inventory based on the inventory count on December 31, $175,600.

Required Complete Stuart's Fine Gems' work sheet for the year ended December 31, 2010.

Problem 5–5A

Refer to the data in Problem 5–4A.

Required

1. Journalize the adjusting and closing entries.

2. Determine the December 31, 2010, Capital balance for Stuart's Fine Gems.

Journalizing the adjusting and closing entries of a merchandising business under the perpetual inventory system

2. Dec. 31, 2010, Capital bal. $176,300

Problem 5–6A

Items from the accounts of Powell Distributors at May 31, 2010, follow, listed in alphabetical order. The General Expenses account summarizes all operating expenses.

 Excel Spreadsheet Template

Preparing a single-step income statement and a classified balance sheet under the perpetual inventory system

1. Net income $259,600

Accounts Payable	$ 51,000	Interest Payable	$ 2,800	
Accounts Receivable	127,500	Interest Revenue	600	
Accumulated Amortization		Inventory May 31, 2010	167,100	
—Equipment	96,900	Notes Payable, Long-Term	114,800	
C. Powell, Capital	147,800	Salaries Payable	7,200	
C. Powell, Withdrawals	46,900	Sales Discounts	26,500	
Cash	19,900	Sales Returns and Allowances	45,900	
Cost of Goods Sold	986,900	Sales Revenue	1,991,500	
Equipment	340,800	Selling Expenses	357,200	
General Expenses	306,800	Supplies	13,100	
Interest Expense	9,200	Unearned Sales Revenue	35,200	

Required

1. Prepare the business's single-step income statement for the year ended May 31, 2010.

2. Prepare Powell Distributors' statement of owner's equity at May 31, 2010.

3. Prepare Powell Distributors' classified balance sheet in *report format* at May 31, 2010.

Problem 5–7A

1. Use the data of Problem 5–6A to prepare Powell Distributors' *multi-step* income statement for the year ended May 31, 2010.

2. Corry Powell, owner of the company, strives to earn a gross margin of at least 50 percent and a net income of 20 percent (Net income percentage = Net income ÷ Net sales revenue). Did Powell Distributors achieve these goals? Show your calculations.

Preparing a multi-step income statement and calculating gross margin percentage under the perpetual inventory system

1. Net income $259,600

Problem 5–8A

The adjusted trial balance of Propp Products at November 30, 2010, is shown on the next page.

Required

1. Journalize Propp Products' closing entries.

2. Compute the gross margin percentage and the rate of inventory turnover for 2010. Inventory on hand one year ago was $21,400. For 2009, Propp Products' gross margin was 32 percent, and inventory turnover was 4.9 times during the year. Does the two-year trend in these ratios suggest improvement or deterioration in profitability?

Making closing entries, computing gross margin percentage and inventory turnover under the perpetual inventory system

2. Gross margin percentage for 2010 38.4%

Account Title	Adjusted Trial Balance	
	Debit	Credit
Cash	8,000	
Accounts receivable..	48,500	
Inventory...	27,400	
Supplies...	1,400	
Furniture	40,000	
Accumulated amortization—furniture.......		24,000
Accounts payable..		14,500
Salary payable		2,200
Unearned sales revenue.................................		7,200
Note payable, long-term................................		45,000
A. Propp, capital		41,300
A. Propp, withdrawals....................................	36,000	
Sales revenue...		225,000
Sales returns	6,000	
Cost of goods sold	135,000	
Selling expenses	33,700	
General expenses	21,000	
Interest expense..	2,200	
Total	359,200	359,200

Under the perpetual inventory system, accounting for the purchase and sale of inventory, computing cost of goods sold and gross margin, using the gross margin percentage to evaluate a business

3. Gross margin $96,920

Problem 5–9A

Esposito Distributors uses the perpetual inventory system to track its inventory purchases and sales. All sales that result in a return, allowance, or discount are tracked in separate accounts in order to give management the proper information to control operations. The following information is available for the month of November 2010:

Nov. 1 Inventory on hand at the beginning of the month was $165,600.

2 Purchased $60,000 of merchandise from Smith Ltd., terms 2/10, n/30. The goods were expected to be resold for $132,000.

4 Sold merchandise for $84,000 to Coast Ltd., terms 2/10, n/60. The goods had a cost of $48,000 to Esposito Distributors.

6 Esposito Distributors returned $9,000 of defective merchandise purchased from Smith Ltd. on November 2.

8 Sold merchandise for $96,000 on account; the goods had a cost of $72,000.

9 Purchased $108,000 of merchandise from Goodwin Inc., terms 2/10, n/30.

10 Esposito Distributors paid the balance owing to Smith Ltd.

12 Esposito Distributors accepted the return of half of the merchandise sold on November 8 as it was not compatible with the customer's needs. The goods were returned to inventory and Esposito reduced the receivable from the customer.

18 Paid the balance owing to Goodwin Inc. from the purchase of November 9.

20 Sold merchandise for $60,000 to Prairie Ltd., terms 2/10, n/60. The goods had cost $36,000.

22 Prairie Ltd. complained about the quality of goods it received, and Esposito Distributors gave an allowance of $6,000.

25 Purchased $72,000 of merchandise for cash and paid $4,000 for freight.

29 Esposito Distributors sold merchandise for $70,000 to Atlantic Inc., terms 2/10, n/30. The goods had cost $38,000. The terms of the sale were FOB shipping point, but, as a convenience, Esposito prepaid $2,200 of freight for Atlantic Inc.

30 Collected the balance owing from Prairie Ltd.

Required

1. Record any journal entries required for the above transactions.

2. What is the inventory balance on November 30, 2010?

3. Prepare a multi-step income statement, to the point of gross margin, for the month of November 2010.

4. The average gross margin percentage for the industry is 50 percent. How does Esposito Distributors compare with the industry?

Problem 5–10A

Extreme Adventures has the following account balances (in alphabetical order) on July 31, 2010:

Accounts Payable...	$ 10,800
Accounts Receivable..	11,600
Accumulated Amortization—Equipment	32,300
Cash..	4,200
Cost of Goods Sold	343,500
E. Buono, Capital	201,000
E. Buono, Withdrawals..	46,000
Equipment...	90,000
Interest Earned	2,000
Inventory...	71,500
Operating Expenses..	177,500
Sales Discounts...	5,150
Sales Returns and Allowances.......................................	16,450
Sales Revenue...	522,600
Supplies	7,300
Unearned Sales Revenue	4,500

Note: For simplicity, all operating expenses have been summarized in the account Operating Expenses.

Additional data at July 31, 2010:

a. A physical count of items showed $1,500 of supplies on hand.

b. An inventory count showed inventory on hand at July 31, 2010, of $68,400.

c. The equipment has an estimated useful life of eight years and is expected to have no value at the end of its life.

d. Unearned sales revenue of $2,800 was earned by July 31, 2010.

Required

1. Record all adjustments and closing entries that would be required on July 31, 2010.

2. Prepare the financial statements of Extreme Adventures for the year ended July 31, 2010.

Under the perpetual inventory system, computing cost of goods sold and gross margin, adjusting and closing the accounts of a merchandising company, preparing a merchandiser's financial statements

③ ④ ⑤

2. Net loss $35,350

*Problem 5–11A

The following transactions occurred between King Pharmaceuticals and Hall Drug Store during February of the current year.

Accounting for the purchase and sale of inventory under the periodic system

Feb. 6   Hall purchased $50,000 of merchandise from King on credit terms 2/10, n/30, FOB shipping point. Separately, Hall paid a $2,000 bill for freight in. King invoiced Hall for $50,000.

10   Hall returned $7,000 of the merchandise purchased on February 6. King issued a credit memo for this amount.

15   Hall paid $24,000 of the invoice amount owed to King for the February 6 purchase. This payment included none of the freight charge.

27   Hall paid the remaining amount owed to King for the February 6 purchase.

Required Journalize these transactions, first on the books of Hall Drug Store and second on the books of King Pharmaceuticals. Assume both companies use the periodic inventory system.

*Problem 5–12A

Singh Distributing Company engaged in the following transactions during May of the current year:

Journalizing purchase and sale transactions under the periodic inventory system

May 3   Purchased office supplies for cash, $5,500.

7   Purchased inventory on credit terms of 3/10, net eom, $40,000.

---

*These Problems cover Chapter 5 Appendix A topics.

May 8   Returned 10 percent of the inventory purchased on May 7. It was not the inventory ordered.

     10   Sold goods for cash, $9,100.

     13   Sold inventory on credit terms of 2/15, n/45 for $60,300, less $8,800 quantity discount offered to customers who purchased in large quantities.

     16   Paid the amount owed on account from the purchase of May 7.

     17   Received wrong-sized inventory returned from May 13 sale, $3,200, which is the net amount after the quantity discount.

     18   Purchased inventory of $76,000 on account. Payment terms were 2/10, net 30.

     26   Paid supplier for goods purchased on May 18.

     28   Received cash in full settlement of the account from the customer who purchased inventory on May 13.

     29   Purchased inventory for cash, $26,000, less a quantity discount of $2,200, and paid freight charges of $600.

Required   Journalize the preceding transactions on the books of Singh Distributing Company.

*Problem 5–13A

Preparing a merchandiser's work sheet under the periodic inventory system

Net income $117,800

The trial balance of Stuart's Fine Gems pertains to December 31, 2010, and is shown here.

STUART'S FINE GEMS
Trial Balance
December 31, 2010

Cash..	$ 3,100	
Accounts receivable.....................................	28,500	
Inventory...	172,500	
Prepaid rent...	14,000	
Equipment...	54,000	
Accumulated amortization—equipment.........		$ 21,600
Accounts payable...		21,600
Salary payable..		0
Interest payable...		0
Note payable, long-term...............................		43,500
J. Stuart, capital..		135,000
J. Stuart, withdrawals..................................	76,500	
Sales revenue...		417,700
Purchases...	168,900	
Salary expense...	59,300	
Rent expense..	22,000	
Advertising expense.....................................	10,800	
Utilities expense..	15,400	
Amortization expense—equipment...............	0	
Insurance expense.......................................	6,600	
Interest expense..	1,300	
Miscellaneous expense.................................	6,500	
Total..	$639,400	$639,400

Additional data at December 31, 2010:

a. Rent expense for the year, $24,000.

b. The equipment has an estimated useful life of 10 years and is expected to have no value when it is retired from service.

c. Accrued salaries at December 31, $3,500.

d. Accrued interest expense at December 31, $1,300.

e. Inventory based on the inventory count on December 31, 2010, $175,600.

Required   Complete Stuart's Fine Gems' work sheet for the year ended December 31, 2010.

---

*This Problem covers Chapter 5 Appendix A topics.

*Problem 5–14A

Refer to the data in Problem 5–13A.

Required

1. Journalize the adjusting and closing entries.
2. Determine the December 31, 2010, balance of Capital for Stuart's Fine Gems.

Journalizing the adjusting and closing entries of a merchandising business under the periodic inventory system

Dec. 31, 2009, Capital bal. $176,300

*Problem 5–15A

Items from the accounts of Powell Distributors at May 31, 2010, follow, listed in alphabetical order. The General Expenses account summarizes all operating expenses.

Preparing a single-step income statement and a classified balance sheet under the periodic inventory system

1. Net income $259,600

Accounts Payable...................	$ 51,000	Interest Revenue	$ 600
Accounts Receivable	127,500	Inventory May 31, 2009	151,800
Accumulated Amortization		Notes Payable, Long-Term...	114,800
—Equipment	96,900	Purchases	1,002,200
C. Powell, Capital	147,800	Salaries Payable.....................	7,200
C. Powell, Withdrawals	46,900	Sales Discounts......................	26,500
Cash	19,900	Sales Returns and Allowances	45,900
Equipment	340,800	Sales Revenue.........................	1,991,500
General Expenses..................	306,800	Selling Expenses....................	357,200
Interest Expense....................	9,200	Supplies..................................	13,100
Interest Payable.....................	2,800	Unearned Sales Revenue......	35,200

Required

1. Prepare the business's single-step income statement for the year ended May 31, 2010. A physical count of inventory on May 31, 2010, valued it at $167,100.
2. Prepare Powell Distributors' statement of owner's equity at May 31, 2010.
3. Prepare Powell Distributors' classified balance sheet in *report format* at May 31, 2010.

*Problem 5–16A

1. Use the data of Problem 5–15A to prepare Powell Distributors' *multi-step* income statement for the year ended May 31, 2010.

2. Corry Powell, owner of the company, strives to earn a gross margin of at least 50 percent and a net income of 20 percent (Net income percentage = Net income ÷ Net sales revenue). Did Powell Distributors achieve these goals? Show your calculations.

Preparing a multi-step income statement and calculating gross margin percentage under the periodic inventory system

1. Net income $259,600

*Problem 5–17A

Selected accounts from the accounting records of Boggio Security had the balances shown below at November 30, 2010.

Computing cost of goods sold and gross margin in a periodic inventory system, evaluating the business

1. Gross margin $43,600

Purchases..	$ 160,000
Selling Expenses..	10,000
Furniture and Fixtures	40,000
Purchase Returns and Allowances...................................	1,000
Salaries Payable...	1,500
Sales Revenue..	205,000
Sales Returns and Allowances	1,900
Inventory: November 30, 2009...	36,000
November 30, 2010....................................	37,000
Accounts Payable..	9,000
Accounts Receivable...	15,000
Cash..	3,500
Freight In	1,400
Accumulated Amortization—Furniture and Fixtures.....	16,000
Purchase Discounts..	1,500
Sales Discounts...	1,600
General Expenses..	22,000
Amortization Expense—Furniture and Fixtures...........	4,000
L. Boggio, Capital...	81,900
L. Boggio, Withdrawals..	20,500

*These Problems cover Chapter 5 Appendix A topics.

Required

1. Show the computation of Boggio Security's net sales, cost of goods sold, and gross margin for the year ended November 30, 2010.
2. Len Boggio, the proprietor of Boggio Security, strives to earn a gross margin percentage of 25 percent. Did he achieve this goal?
3. Did the rate of inventory turnover reach the industry average of 3.8 times per year?

PROBLEMS (GROUP B)

All questions in this section appear in *MyAccountingLab*.

Problem 5–1B

Explaining the perpetual inventory system

Iris Optical is a regional chain of optical shops. The company offers a large selection of eyeglass frames, and Iris Optical stores provide while-you-wait service. Iris Optical has launched a vigorous advertising campaign promoting its two-for-the-price-of-one frame sale.

Required   Iris Optical expects to grow rapidly and increase its level of inventory. As chief accountant of the company, you wish to install a perpetual inventory system. Write a memo to the company president to explain how the system would work.

Use the following heading for your memo:

> Date : _____
>
> To: Company President
> From: Chief Accountant
> Subject: How a perpetual inventory system works

Problem 5–2B

Accounting for the purchase and sale of inventory under the perpetual inventory system

The following transactions occurred between Gerson Pharmaceuticals and Arnold Drug Stores during June of the current year.

Jun. 8   Arnold purchased $29,400 of merchandise from Gerson on credit terms 2/10, n/30, FOB shipping point. Separately, Arnold paid freight in of $600. Gerson invoiced Arnold for $29,400. These goods cost Gerson $12,600.

11   Arnold returned $3,600 of the merchandise purchased on June 8. Gerson issued a credit memo for this amount and returned the goods, in excellent condition, to inventory (cost $1,500).

17   Arnold paid $12,000 of the invoice amount owed to Gerson for the June 8 purchase. This payment included none of the freight charge. Arnold took the purchase discount on the partial payment.

26   Arnold paid the remaining amount owed to Gerson for the June 8 purchase.

Required   Journalize these transactions, first on the books of Arnold Drug Stores, and second on the books of Gerson Pharmaceuticals.

Problem 5–3B

Journalizing purchase and sale transactions under the perpetual inventory system

Coburn Furniture Company engaged in the following transactions during July of the current year:

Jul. 2   Purchased inventory for cash, $6,400, less a quantity discount of $900.

5   Purchased store supplies on credit terms of net eom, $1,700.

8   Purchased inventory of $27,000 less a quantity discount of 10 percent, plus freight charges of $1,100. Credit terms are 3/15, n/30.

9   Sold goods for cash, $10,800. Coburn's cost of these goods was $6,500.

11   Returned $1,000 (net amount after the quantity discount) of the inventory purchased on July 8. It was damaged in shipment.

12   Purchased inventory on credit terms of 3/10, n/30, $30,000.

14   Sold inventory on credit terms of 2/10, n/30, for $69,200, less a $6,920 quantity discount (cost, $41,500).

Jul. 16   Received and paid the electricity bill, $1,600.
     20   Received returned inventory from the July 14 sale, $2,500 (net amount after the
            quantity discount). Coburn shipped the wrong goods by mistake. Coburn's
            cost of the inventory received was $1,500.
     21   Paid supplier for goods purchased on July 8 less the discount and the return.
     23   Received $43,120 cash in partial settlement of the account from the customer
            who purchased inventory on July 14. Granted the customer a 2 percent
            discount and credited his account receivable for $44,000.
     30   Paid for the store supplies purchased on July 5.

Required Journalize the preceding transactions on the books of Coburn Furniture
         Company.

Problem 5–4B

Cozelis Produce Company's trial balance below pertains to December 31, 2010.

**Excel Spreadsheet
Template**

Preparing a merchandiser's
work sheet under the perpetual
inventory system

COZELIS PRODUCE COMPANY
Trial Balance
December 31, 2010

Cash	$ 22,150	
Accounts receivable	129,600	
Inventory	119,600	
Store supplies	8,800	
Prepaid insurance	18,000	
Store fixtures	270,000	
Accumulated amortization—store fixtures		$ 162,000
Accounts payable		89,900
Salaries payable		0
Interest payable		0
Notes payable, long-term		47,000
F. Cozelis, capital		99,000
F. Cozelis, withdrawals	52,000	
Sales revenue		1,290,500
Cost of goods sold	706,600	
Salaries expense	258,600	
Rent expense	72,000	
Utilities expense	16,200	
Amortization expense—store fixtures	0	
Insurance expense	6,000	
Store supplies expense	0	
Interest expense	2,350	
Miscellaneous expense	6,500	
Total	$1,688,400	$1,688,400

Additional data at December 31, 2010:

a. Insurance expense for the year should total $21,600.

b. Store fixtures have an estimated useful life of 10 years and are expected to have no value
   when they are retired from service.

c. Accrued salaries at December 31, $5,500.

d. Accrued interest expense at December 31, $1,600.

e. Store supplies on hand at December 31, $3,800.

f. Inventory based on the inventory count on December 31, $116,500.

Required Complete Cozelis Produce Company's work sheet for the year ended
         December 31, 2010. Key adjustments by letter.

Problem 5–5B

Refer to the data in Problem 5–4B.

Journalizing the adjusting and
closing entries of a merchandising business under the perpetual
inventory system

Required

1. Journalize the adjusting and closing entries of Cozelis Produce Company.
2. Determine the December 31, 2010, balance in the Capital account.

Problem 5–6B

Excel Spreadsheet Template

Preparing a single-step income statement and a classified balance sheet under the perpetual inventory system

Selected accounts of Hilton Building Supplies, at July 31, 2010, are listed in alphabetical order below. For simplicity, all operating expenses are summarized in the accounts Selling Expenses and General Expenses.

Accounts Payable.................	$ 51,000	Inventory: July 31, 2010	$262,500
Accounts Receivable	58,500	Notes Payable, Long-Term ...	250,000
Accumulated Amortization		Salaries Payable.....................	11,500
—Store Equipment	30,750	Sales Discounts......................	12,500
B. Hilton, Capital	431,700	Sales Returns and	
B. Hilton, Withdrawals	21,150	Allowances	26,400
Cash	23,100	Sales Revenue........................	945,600
Cost of Goods Sold...............	783,000	Selling Expenses....................	158,625
General Expenses..................	142,125	Store Equipment	242,000
Interest Expense...................	5,100	Supplies.................................	8,100
Interest Payable....................	4,400	Unearned Sales Revenue......	17,400
Interest Revenue	750		

Required

1. Prepare Hilton Building Supplies' single-step income statement for the year ended July 31, 2010.
2. Prepare Hilton Building Supplies' statement of owner's equity.
3. Prepare Hilton Building Supplies' classified balance sheet in *report format*.

Problem 5–7B

Preparing a multi-step income statement and calculating gross margin percentage under the perpetual inventory system

1. Use the data of Problem 5–6A to prepare Hilton Building Supplies' *multi-step* income statement for the year ended July 31, 2010.

2. Bev Hilton, owner of the company, strives to earn a gross margin of at least 50 percent and a net income of 20 percent (Net income percentage = Net income ÷ Net sales revenue). Did Hilton Building Supplies achieve these goals? Show your calculations.

Problem 5–8B

Making closing entries and computing gross margin percentage and inventory turnover under the perpetual inventory system

The adjusted trial balance of Harrison Trading Company at September 30, 2010, appears below.

	Adjusted Trial Balance	
Account Title	**Debit**	**Credit**
Cash	14,000	
Accounts receivable...........................	9,000	
Inventory..	42,000	
Supplies..	3,000	
Building..	280,000	
Accumulated amortization—building		196,000
Land..	70,000	
Accounts payable...............................		11,000
Salary payable		2,400
Unearned sales revenue.....................		1,600
Note payable, long-term....................		80,000
B. Harrison, capital............................		70,900
B. Harrison, withdrawals	55,000	
Sales revenue.....................................		355,000
Sales returns	14,000	
Cost of goods sold	167,000	
Selling expenses	36,500	
General expenses	22,400	
Interest expense.................................	4,000	
Total	716,900	716,900

Required

1. Journalize Harrison Trading Company's closing entries.

2. Compute the gross margin percentage and the rate of inventory turnover for 2010. Inventory on hand at September 30, 2009, was $40,000. For 2009, Harrison Trading Company's gross margin percentage was 34.8 percent and the inventory turnover rate was 3.9 times. Does the two-year trend in these ratios suggest improvement or deterioration in profitability?

Problem 5–9B

Ralph Distributors uses the perpetual inventory system to track its inventory purchases and sales. All sales that result in a return, allowance, or discount are tracked in separate accounts in order to give management the proper information to control operations. The following information is available for the month of April 2010:

Under the perpetual inventory system, accounting for the purchase and sale of inventory, computing cost of goods sold and gross margin, using the gross margin percentage to evaluate a business
② ⑤

Apr.	1	The balance of inventory on hand at the beginning of the month was $169,500.
	2	Purchased $36,000 of merchandise from Grier Corp., terms 2/10, n/30. The goods were expected to be resold for $75,000.
	4	Sold merchandise for $54,000 to Armstrong Ltd., terms 2/10, n/60. The goods had a cost of $27,000 to Ralph.
	6	Ralph returned $9,000 of defective merchandise purchased from Grier Corp. on April 2.
	8	Sold merchandise for $81,000 cash; the goods had a cost of $54,000.
	9	Purchased $72,000 of merchandise from Robson Corp., terms 2/10, n/30.
	10	Ralph paid the balance owing to Grier Corp.
	12	Ralph accepted the return of one-quarter of the merchandise sold on April 8 as it was not compatible with the customer's needs. The goods were returned to stock and a cash refund paid.
	18	Paid the balance owing to Robson Corp. for the purchase of April 9.
	20	Sold merchandise for $45,000 to Clearbrook Ltd., terms 2/10, n/60. The goods had a cost of $31,500.
	22	Clearbrook Ltd. complained about the quality of goods it received, and Ralph gave an allowance of $5,400.
	25	Purchased $62,000 of merchandise for cash and paid $2,500 for freight.
	29	Ralph sold merchandise for $45,000 to Golden Ltd., terms 2/10, n/30. The goods had a cost of $22,500. The terms of the sale were FOB shipping point, but, as a convenience, Ralph prepaid $950 of freight for Golden Ltd. and included the charge on its invoice.
	30	Collected the balance owing from Clearbrook Ltd.

Required

1. Record any journal entries required for the above transactions.

2. What is the Inventory balance on April 30, 2010?

3. Prepare a multi-step income statement, to the point of gross margin, for the month of April 2010.

4. The average gross margin percentage for the industry is 48 percent. How does Ralph Distributors compare to the industry?

Problem 5–10B

Rees Sports Products has the following account balances (in alphabetical order) on August 31, 2010:

Under the perpetual inventory system, computing cost of goods sold and gross margin, adjusting and closing the accounts of a merchandising company, preparing a merchandiser's financial statements
③ ④ ⑤

Accounts Payable	$ 41,500
Accounts Receivable	44,700
Accumulated Amortization—Equipment	124,000
Cash	14,400
C. Rees, Capital	305,100
C. Rees, Withdrawals	42,400
Cost of Goods Sold	789,900
Equipment	336,000
Interest Earned	2,600

Inventory	$ 248,400
Operating Expenses	561,200
Sales Discounts	16,200
Sales Returns and Allowances	48,600
Sales Revenue	1,620,000
Supplies	27,600
Unearned Sales Revenue	36,200

Note: For simplicity, all operating expenses have been summarized in the account Operating Expenses.

Additional data at August 31, 2010:

a. A physical count of items showed $14,200 of supplies were on hand.

b. An inventory count showed inventory on hand at August 31, 2010, of $247,400.

c. The equipment is expected to last five years and to have no value at the end of this time.

d. Unearned sales of $9,600 were earned by August 31, 2010.

Required

1. Record all adjusting and closing entries required on August 31, 2010.

2. Prepare the financial statements of Rees Sports Products for the year ended August 31, 2010.

*Problem 5–11B

Accounting for the purchase and sale of inventory under the periodic system

The following transactions occurred between Gerson Pharmaceuticals and Arnold Drug Stores during June of the current year.

Jun. 6   Arnold purchased $29,400 of merchandise from Gerson on credit terms 2/10, n/30, FOB shipping point. Separately, Arnold paid freight in of $300. Gerson invoiced Arnold for $29,400.

    10   Arnold returned $3,600 of the merchandise purchased on June 6. Gerson issued a credit memo for this amount.

    15   Arnold paid $12,000 of the invoice amount owed to Gerson for the June 6 purchase. This payment included none of the freight charge.

    27   Arnold paid the remaining amount owed to Gerson for the June 6 purchase.

Required   Journalize these transactions, first on the books of Arnold Drug Stores and second on the books of Gerson Pharmaceuticals. Assume both companies use the periodic inventory system.

*Problem 5–12B

Journalizing purchase and sale transactions under the periodic inventory system

Coburn Furniture Company, which uses a periodic inventory system, engaged in the following transactions during July of the current year:

Jul. 2   Purchased inventory for cash, $6,400, less a quantity discount of $900.

    5   Purchased store supplies on credit terms of net eom, $1,700.

    8   Purchased inventory of $27,000, less a quantity discount of 10 percent, plus freight charges of $1,100. Credit terms are 3/15, n/30.

    9   Sold goods for cash, $10,800.

    11   Returned $1,000 (net amount after the quantity discount) of the inventory purchased on July 8. It was damaged in shipment.

    12   Purchased inventory on credit terms of 3/10, n/30, for $30,000.

    14   Sold inventory on credit terms of 2/10, n/30, for $69,200, less a $6,920 quantity discount.

    16   Received and paid the electricity bill, $1,600.

    20   Received returned inventory from the July 14 sale, $2,500 (net amount after the quantity discount). Coburn shipped the wrong goods by mistake.

    21   Paid supplier for goods purchased on July 8.

---

*These Problems cover Chapter 5 Appendix A topics.

Jul. 23 Received $43,120 cash in partial settlement of the account from the customer who purchased inventory on July 14. Granted the customer a 2 percent discount and credited his account receivable for $44,000.

30 Paid for the store supplies purchased on July 5.

Required Journalize the preceding transactions on the books of Coburn Furniture Company.

*Problem 5–13B

Cozelis Produce Company's trial balance below pertains to December 31, 2010.

Preparing a merchandiser's work sheet under the periodic inventory system

10

COZELIS PRODUCE COMPANY
Trial Balance
December 31, 2010

Cash..	$ 22,150	
Accounts receivable..	129,600	
Inventory...	108,300	
Store supplies..	8,800	
Prepaid insurance	18,000	
Store fixtures...	270,000	
Accumulated amortization—store fixtures.....		$ 162,000
Accounts payable..		89,900
Salaries payable..		0
Interest payable		0
Notes payable, long-term		47,000
F. Cozelis, capital		99,000
F. Cozelis, withdrawals.................................	52,000	
Sales revenue		1,290,500
Purchases...	717,900	
Salaries expense..	258,600	
Rent expense..	72,000	
Utilities expense	16,200	
Amortization expense—store fixtures	0	
Insurance expense...	6,000	
Store supplies expense	0	
Interest expense..	2,350	
Miscellaneous expense...................................	6,500	
Total..	$1,688,400	$1,688,400

Additional data at December 31, 2010:

a. Insurance expense for the year should total $21,600.

b. Store fixtures have an estimated useful life of 10 years and are expected to have no value when they are retired from service.

c. Accrued salaries at December 31, $5,500.

d. Accrued interest expense at December 31, $1,600.

e. Store supplies on hand at December 31, $3,800.

f. Inventory based on the inventory count on December 31, $116,500.

Required Complete Cozelis Produce Company's work sheet for the year ended December 31, 2010. Key adjustments by letter.

*Problem 5–14B

Refer to the data in Problem 5–13B.

Journalizing the adjusting and closing entries of a merchandising business under the periodic inventory system

9

Required

1. Journalize the adjusting and closing entries of Cozelis Produce Company.

2. Determine the December 31, 2010, balance in the Capital account.

---

*These Problems cover Chapter 5 Appendix A topics.

*Problem 5–15B

Preparing a single-step income
statement and a classified
balance sheet under the periodic
inventory system

Selected accounts of Hilton Building Supplies, at July 31, 2010, are listed in alphabetical order below. For simplicity, all operating expenses are summarized in the accounts Selling Expenses and General Expenses.

Accounts Payable	$51,000	Inventory: July 31, 2009	$365,000
Accounts Receivable	58,500	Inventory: July 31, 2010	262,500
Accumulated Amortization		Notes Payable, Long-Term	250,000
—Equipment	30,750	Purchases	680,500
B. Hilton, Capital	431,700	Salaries Payable	11,500
B. Hilton, Withdrawals	21,150	Sales Discounts	12,500
Cash	23,100	Sales Returns and Allowances	26,400
Equipment	242,000	Sales Revenue	945,600
General Expenses	142,125	Selling Expenses	158,625
Interest Expense	5,100	Supplies	8,100
Interest Payable	4,400	Unearned Sales Revenue	17,400
Interest Revenue	750		

Required

1. Prepare the business's single-step income statement for the year ended July 31, 2010.

2. Prepare Hilton Building Supplies' statement of owner's equity at July 31, 2010.

3. Prepare Hilton Building Supplies' classified balance sheet in *report format* at July 31, 2010.

*Problem 5–16B

Preparing a multi-step income
statement and calculating gross
margin percentage under the
periodic inventory system

1. Use the data of Problem 5–15B to prepare Hilton Building Supplies' *multi-step* income statement for the year ended July 31, 2010.

2. Bev Hilton, owner of the company, strives to earn a gross margin percentage of at least 50 percent and a net income percentage of 20 percent (Net income percentage = Net income ÷ Net sales revenue). Did Hilton Building Supplies achieve these goals? Show your calculations.

*Problem 5–17B

Computing cost of goods sold
and gross margin in a periodic
system, evaluating the business

Selected accounts from the accounting records of Burke Imports at September 30, 2010, are shown below.

Cash	$ 14,300
Purchases	103,100
Freight In	3,100
Sales Revenue	188,200
Purchases Returns and Allowances	1,600
Salaries Payable	2,200
Glen Burke, Capital	33,400
Sales Returns and Allowances	5,300
Inventory: September 30, 2009	13,100
September 30, 2010	15,700
Selling Expense	34,200
Equipment	48,000
Purchase Discounts	1,365
Accumulated Amortization—Equipment	9,600
Sales Discounts	3,600
General Expenses	18,500
Accounts Payable	14,700
Accounts Receivable	17,200

---

*These Problems cover Chapter 5 Appendix A topics.

Required

1. Show the computation of Burke Imports' net sales, cost of goods sold, and gross margin for the year ended September 30, 2010.

2. Glen Burke, owner of Burke Imports, strives to earn a gross margin percentage of 40 percent. Did he achieve this goal?

3. Did the rate of inventory turnover reach the industry average of 3.4 times per year?

CHALLENGE PROBLEMS

Problem 5–1C

Understanding purchasing and gross margin

You have been hired recently as an accountant by One Cellular, a small chain of stores that sells wireless products. One of your first activities is to review the accounting system for One Cellular.

In your review, you discover that the company determines selling prices by adding a standard markup on cost of 10 percent (i.e., cost plus 10 percent of cost) to the cost of all products. The company uses a perpetual inventory system. You also discover that your predecessor, a bookkeeper, had set up the accounting system so that all purchase discounts and purchase returns and allowances were accumulated in an account that was treated as "other income" for financial statement purposes because he believed that they were financing items and not related to operations.

Megan Wilson, owner of One Cellular, uses modern decision-making techniques in running One Cellular. Two ratios she particularly favours are the gross margin percentage and inventory turnover ratio.

Required

1. What is a possible effect of the accounting system described on the pricing of products and thus operations of One Cellular stores?

2. What is the effect of the accounting system instituted by your predecessor on the two ratios Ms. Wilson favours?

Problem 5–2C

Using an inventory system for control

Michael Clarke is concerned about theft by shoplifters in his chain of three discount stores and has come to your public accounting firm for advice. Specifically, he has several questions he would like you to answer.

a. He wonders if there is any inventory system he can use that will allow him to keep track of products that leave his stores as legitimate sales and will also allow him to determine if inventory has been lost or stolen.

b. He realizes that carrying inventory is expensive. He wants to know if you have any suggestions as to how he can keep close tabs on his inventory at the three stores so he can be sure that the stores don't run out of product or have too much on hand.

c. The space in the stores is limited. Michael wants to install an inventory system that will tell him when a product is slow-moving or obsolete so he can clear it out and replace it with a potentially faster-moving product.

Required Indicate whether a perpetual inventory system or a periodic inventory system will provide Michael with answers to the three questions he has asked. Explain how the inventory system indicated will provide the specific information he has requested.

Extending Your Knowledge

DECISION PROBLEMS

Using financial statements to decide on a business expansion

Net income $125,100

Decision Problem 1

Mitch Hopkins owns the Happy Valley Drug Store, which has prospered during its second year of operation. To help Hopkins decide whether to open another pharmacy in the area, his bookkeeper has prepared the current income statement of the business.

HAPPY VALLEY DRUG STORE
Income Statement
For the Year Ended December 31, 2010

Sales revenue		$720,000
Interest revenue		30,000
Total revenue		750,000
Cost of goods sold		348,000
Gross margin		402,000
Operating expenses:		
Salary expense	$107,000	
Rent expense	32,000	
Amortization expense	24,500	
Interest expense	10,500	
Utilities expense	6,800	
Supplies expense	4,000	
Total operating expenses		184,800
Income from operations		217,200
Other revenues:		
Sales discounts ($11,000) and returns ($24,000)		35,000
Net income		$252,200

Hopkins recently read in an industry trade journal that a successful two-year-old pharmacy meets these criteria:

a. Gross margin is at least 50 percent.

b. Net income is at least $150,000.

Basing his opinion on the entity's income statement data, Hopkins believes the business meets both criteria. He plans to go ahead with the expansion plan, and asks your advice on preparing the pharmacy's income statement in accordance with generally accepted accounting principles. When you point out that the income statement includes errors, Hopkins assures you that all amounts are correct.

Required   Prepare a correct multi-step income statement and make a recommendation about whether to undertake the expansion at this time.

Decision Problem 2

Understanding the operating cycle of a merchandiser

Jeremy Chan has come to you for advice. Earlier this year, he opened a video store in a plaza near the university he had attended. The store rents movies on DVD at very low prices and on special credit for students. Many of the students at the university are co-op students who alternate school and work terms. Chan allows co-op students to buy on credit while they are on a school term, with the understanding that they will pay their account shortly after starting a work term.

Business has been very good. Chan is sure it is because of his competitive prices and the unique credit terms he offers. His problem is that he is short of cash, and his loan with the bank has grown significantly. The bank manager has indicated that he wishes to reduce Chan's line of credit because she is worried that he will get into financial difficulties.

Required

1. Explain to Chan why he, in your opinion, is short of cash.

2. Chan has asked you to explain his problem to the bank manager and to assist in asking for more credit. What might you say to the bank manager to assist Chan?

Decision Problem 3

The employees of Olford Furniture Company made an error when they performed the periodic inventory count at year end, October 31, 2010. Part of one warehouse was not counted and therefore was not included in inventory. (Assume the error is not material, so the October 31, 2010, financial statements were not corrected.)

Correcting an inventory error

Required

1. Indicate the effect of the inventory error on cost of goods sold, gross margin, and net income for the year ended October 31, 2010.

2. Will the error affect cost of goods sold, gross margin, and net income in 2011? If so, what will be the effect?

FINANCIAL STATEMENT PROBLEM

This problem uses both the income statement (statement of earnings) and the balance sheet of Sun-Rype Products Ltd. in Appendix B. It will aid your understanding of the closing process of a business that has inventory.

Closing entries for a corporation that sells merchandise, evaluating ratio data

3. 2008 Inventory $27,778,000

1. Journalize Sun-Rype's closing entries for the year ended December 31, 2008, to the line Earnings (loss) before income taxes. You will be unfamiliar with certain revenues and expenses, but you should treat them all similarly. Instead of closing to a Capital account, close to the Retained Earnings account (since Sun-Rype is a corporation, not a proprietorship).

2. What amount was closed to Retained Earnings? What were dividends in 2008?

3. Sun-Rype Products Ltd. is a manufacturer and distributor of juice-based beverages and fruit-based snacks. On the balance sheet, the company reports an inventory figure and the detail is provided in the notes to the financial statements. What amounts are shown on the balance sheets for the Inventory account for December 31, 2008, and December 31, 2007? Of these amounts, how much is raw materials in 2007 and 2008? How much is finished goods in 2007 and 2008?

6 Accounting for Merchandise Inventory

Which inventory system should a merchandiser use, and why is it important?

What are the different inventory costing methods?

How do they differ? Which methods can be used for income tax purposes?

Which inventory costing method should a merchandiser choose?

How can merchandisers estimate the cost of inventory destroyed in a fire or some other disaster?

These questions and others will be answered throughout this chapter. The Decision Guidelines at the end of this chapter will provide the answers in a useful summary.

LEARNING OBJECTIVES

1. Account for perpetual inventory under the specific-unit-cost, FIFO, and moving-weighted-average-cost methods

2. Compare the effects of the FIFO and moving-weighted-average-cost methods

3. Account for periodic inventory under the FIFO and weighted-average-cost methods

4. Apply the lower-of-cost-and-net-realizable-value rule to inventory

5. Measure the effects of inventory errors

6. Estimate ending inventory by the gross margin method and the retail method

7. Assess the inventory recording and reporting impacts of international financial reporting standards (IFRS)

The Forzani Group Ltd. (Forzani) is Canada's largest and only national retailer of sporting goods, apparel, and footwear. There are currently 337 operating corporate stores from coast to coast and 227 franchise stores primarily in the province of Quebec.

Forzani conducts its business through two distinct operating segments: corporate and franchise. The corporate banners include Sport Chek, Sport Mart, Coast Mountain Sports, National Sports, Athletes World, and Hockey Experts. The franchise banners include Sports Experts, Intersport, Atmosphere, Nevada Bob's Golf, Hockey Experts, The Fitness Source, Pegasus, RnR, S3, Tech Shop, and Econosports.

By far the largest asset on Forzani's balance sheet is inventory. In 2009, the company's year-end balance was over $291 million. For the company to be successful, it must manage its inventory very well. It has to understand the wants and needs of its customers. If it guesses wrong, it may end up with too much inventory (or too much of the wrong items). If it has too little inventory, customers may look elsewhere for items they require.

Forzani recognizes this risk. Not only do successful retail companies like Forzani need to understand trends in their industry, but they also need to be aware of economic factors such as consumer spending and debt levels, and the state of the overall economy. For Forzani, the fiscal year ended February 1, 2009, was a difficult year because of the economic recession that started in the fall of 2008. The chairman of the board stated the following in Forzani's 2009 annual report:

In my 35 years in this business, I thought I had seen it all; the ebbs and flows of retail that make it so interesting. But nothing compares to the environment that we find ourselves in today. These increasingly uncertain times cause even the most optimistic to be concerned . . . . the worst possible scenario for consumer optimism. And yet, for those companies that are strong and looking to increase market share, or reduce costs in a deflationary environment, it provides opportunities.[1]

---

[1] The Forzani Group Limited 2009 Annual Report, page 9.

Chapter 5

introduced the accounting for merchandise inventory. It showed how Austin Sound Centre, a music store, recorded the purchase and sale of its inventory. Amazon.com, The Bay, and The Forzani Group Ltd. are other merchandising companies. This chapter completes the accounting for merchandise inventory.

SportChek, one of The Forzani Group Ltd.'s chains of stores, sells running shoes (among many other items) for men, women, and children. SportChek, like all other companies, may select from several different methods of accounting for its inventory. Inventory is the first area in which a company must pick the accounting method it will use and it is a key decision for a merchandiser. We will use a SportChek store to illustrate the different inventory accounting methods.

This chapter will introduce a new vocabulary, including the term FIFO. By the end of this chapter, you will also be prepared to decide which accounting method is most appropriate if you ever start your own business.

First let's review the balance sheet and the income statement, because the financial statements show how merchandise inventory affects a company. Exhibit 6–1 gives the merchandising section of The Forzani Group Ltd.'s balance sheet and income statement. Inventories, cost of goods sold, and gross margin are labelled A, B, and C, respectively, to indicate that, throughout the chapter, we will be computing them using various accounting methods.

EXHIBIT 6–1	The Forzani Group Ltd. Merchandising Section of the Financial Statements

THE FORZANI GROUP LTD.
Balance Sheet (partial; adapted)
February 1, 2009

Assets:	(thousands)
Current assets:	
Cash	$ 3,474
Accounts receivable	84,455
Inventories	291,497 (**A**)
Prepaid expenses	2,827

THE FORZANI GROUP LTD.
Income Statement (partial; adapted)
For the Year Ended February 1, 2009

	(thousands)
Net sales	$1,346,758
Cost of goods sold	863,239 (**B**)
Gross margin	$ 483,519 (**C**)

As you can see in Exhibit 6–1, inventory is the most significant current asset for The Forzani Group Ltd., as it is for most retail companies. Companies like Forzani want to make sure that they carry enough inventory to meet customer demand. At the same time, if companies carry too much inventory, they risk "tying up" too much of the company's assets in inventory.

The remainder of the chapter explores how to compute these amounts:

- Ending inventory on the balance sheet
- Cost of goods sold and gross margin on the income statement

We turn now to the different inventory costing methods.

Inventory Costing Methods

OBJECTIVE ①

Account for perpetual inventory under the specific-unit-cost, FIFO, and moving-weighted-average-cost methods

As we saw in Chapter 5,

$$\text{Ending inventory} = \text{Number of units } on \text{ } hand \times \text{Unit cost}$$
$$\text{Cost of goods sold} = \text{Number of units } sold \times \text{Unit cost}$$

Companies determine the number of units from perpetual inventory records that are verified by a physical count. The cost of each unit of inventory is

$$\text{Unit cost} = \text{Purchase price} - \text{Purchase discounts} - \text{Quantity discounts}$$
$$+ \text{ Any costs necessary to put the unit in a saleable}$$
$$\text{condition, such as freight in, customs duties,}$$
$$\text{and insurance}$$

Exhibit 6–2 gives the inventory data for a line of running shoes carried by SportChek.

EXHIBIT 6–2   Perpetual Inventory Record—Quantities Only

Item: Running Shoes, Model XL

Date	Quantity Purchased	Quantity Sold	Quantity on Hand
Nov. 1			10
5	60		70
15		40	30
26	70		100
30		80	20
Totals	130	120	20

In this illustration, SportChek began November with 10 pairs of running shoes on hand. After buying and selling, SportChek had 20 pairs at the end of the month. Assume that SportChek's unit cost of each pair is $60. In this case,

$$\text{Ending inventory} = \textbf{Number of units } \textit{on hand} \textbf{ (Exhibit 6–2)} \times \textbf{Unit cost}$$
$$= \quad\quad 20 \quad\quad\quad \times \quad \$60$$
$$= \$1,200$$

$$\text{Cost of goods sold} = \textbf{Number of units } \textit{sold} \textbf{ (Exhibit 6–2)} \times \textbf{Unit cost}$$
$$= \quad\quad 120 \quad\quad\quad \times \quad \$60$$
$$= \$7,200$$

What would SportChek's ending inventory and cost of goods sold be if the cost of these running shoes increased from $60 to $65 or $70 during the period? Companies face price increases like these all the time. To determine inventory costs, the accounting profession has developed several costing methods.

Measuring inventory cost is easy when prices are constant. However, in reality, the unit cost often changes. A pair of running shoes that cost SportChek $60 in January may cost $65 in April. Suppose SportChek sells 10,000 pairs of these running shoes in November. How many of the shoes cost $60? How many cost $65? To compute ending inventory and cost of goods sold, SportChek must assign a unit cost to each item. The three costing methods that GAAP allow are

1. Specific-unit cost
2. Weighted-average cost
3. First-in, first-out (FIFO) cost

KEY POINT

The three inventory costing methods affect the cost of inventory and, consequently, the cost of goods sold. The method used does *not* have to match the physical flow of goods.

A company can use any of these methods to account for its inventory. The method chosen does *not* have to match the physical flow of goods. Once it is chosen, however, the company should use this method going forward for consistency and comparability. Any of these methods are allowed for income tax purposes in Canada.

The **specific-unit-cost method**, also called the **specific identification method**, uses the specific cost of each unit of inventory for items that have a distinctive identity. Some businesses deal in items that differ from unit to unit, such as automobiles, jewels, and real estate. For instance, a Toyota dealer may have two vehicles—a model with vehicle identification number (VIN) 010 that costs $21,000 and a model with VIN 020 that costs $27,000. If the dealer sells the model with VIN 020, cost of goods sold is $27,000, the cost of the specific unit. Suppose the model with VIN 010 is the only unit left in inventory at the end of the period; ending inventory is $21,000, the dealer's cost of that particular car.

Amazon.com uses the specific-unit-cost method to account for its inventory. But very few other companies use this method, and so we shift to the more popular inventory costing methods. These methods are *cost-flow assumptions* that do not have to match the actual flow of inventory costs. Exhibit 6–3 illustrates how each method works.

EXHIBIT 6–3

Cost Flows for the Most Popular Inventory Methods

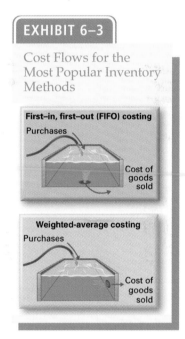

- Under the first-in, first-out (FIFO) method, the cost of goods sold is based on the oldest purchases. This is illustrated by the cost of goods sold coming from the *bottom* of the container.

- Under the weighted-average-cost method, the cost of goods sold is based on an average cost for the period. This is illustrated by the cost of goods sold coming from the *middle* of the container.

Now let's see how to compute inventory amounts under the FIFO and weighted-average-cost methods. We use the following transaction data for all the illustrations:

Running Shoes, Model XL	Number of Units	Unit Cost
Nov. 1 Beginning inventory	10	$60
5 Purchase	60	65
15 Sale	40	
26 Purchase	70	70
30 Sale	80	

We begin with inventory costing in a perpetual system.

KEY POINT

Remember that the term *FIFO* describes which goods are sold, *not* which goods are left. FIFO assumes that goods in first are sold first; therefore, the last goods purchased are left in ending inventory.

Inventory Costing in a Perpetual System

The inventory costing methods produce different amounts for:

- Ending inventory
- Cost of goods sold

First-in, First-out Method

Many companies use the **first-in, first-out (FIFO) method** to account for their inventory. FIFO costing is consistent with the physical movement of inventory for most companies. That is, they sell their oldest inventory first.

Under FIFO costing, the first costs incurred by SportChek each period are the first costs assigned to cost of goods sold. FIFO leaves in ending inventory the last—the most recent—costs incurred during the period. This is illustrated in the FIFO perpetual inventory record in Exhibit 6–4.

EXHIBIT 6–4 Perpetual Inventory Record—FIFO Cost for SportChek

Running Shoes, Model XL

Date	Purchases Qty.	Purchases Unit Cost	Purchases Total Cost	Cost of Goods Sold Qty.	Cost of Goods Sold Unit Cost	Cost of Goods Sold Total Cost	Inventory on Hand Qty.	Inventory on Hand Unit Cost	Inventory on Hand Total Cost
Nov. 1							10	$60	$ 600
5	60	$65	$3,900				10	60	600
							60	65	3,900
15				10	$60	$ 600			
				30	65	1,950	30	65	1,950
26	70	70	4,900				30	65	1,950
							70	70	4,900
30				30	65	1,950			
				50	70	3,500	20	70	1,400
30	130		$8,800	120		$8,000	20		$1,400

SportChek began November with 10 pairs of running shoes that cost $60. After the November 5 purchase, the inventory on hand consists of 70 units.

$$\text{70 units on hand} \begin{cases} 10 @ \$60 = \$ 600 \\ 60 @ \$65 = 3,900 \end{cases}$$
$$\text{Inventory on hand} = \underline{\underline{\$4,500}}$$

On November 15, SportChek sold 40 units. Under FIFO costing, the first 10 units sold are costed at the oldest cost ($60 per unit). The next 30 units sold come from the group that cost $65 per unit. That leaves 30 units in inventory on hand, and those units cost $65 each. The remainder of the inventory record follows that same pattern.

The FIFO monthly summary at November 30 is

- Cost of goods sold: 120 units that cost a total of $8,000
- Ending inventory: 20 units that cost a total of $1,400

If SportChek used the FIFO method, it would measure cost of goods sold and inventory in this manner to prepare its financial statements.

Notice that you can use the familiar cost of goods sold model to check the accuracy of the inventory record, as follows:

Beginning inventory	$ 600
+ Net purchases	8,800
= Cost of goods available for sale	9,400
− Ending inventory	**(1,400)**
= Cost of goods sold	**$ 8,000**

Journal Entries Under FIFO

The journal entries under FIFO costing for the perpetual inventory system follow the data in Exhibit 6–4. For example, on November 5, SportChek purchased $3,900 of inventory and made the first journal entry. On November 15, SportChek sold 40 pairs of running shoes for the sale price of $100 each. SportChek recorded the sale ($4,000) and the cost of goods sold ($2,550). The remaining journal entries (November 26 and 30) follow the inventory data in Exhibit 6–4.

FIFO Journal Entries: (All purchases and sales on account. The sale price of a pair of running shoes is $100 per unit.)

Nov.	5	Inventory	3,900	
		Accounts Payable..		3,900
		Purchased inventory on account (60 × $65 = $3,900).		
	15	Accounts Receivable..	4,000	
		Sales Revenue		4,000
		Sale on account (40 × $100 = $4,000).		
	15	Cost of Goods Sold	2,550	
		Inventory		2,550
		Cost of goods sold ($600 + $1,950 = $2,550).		
	26	Inventory	4,900	
		Accounts Payable..		4,900
		Purchased inventory on account. (70 × $70 = $4,900).		
	30	Accounts Receivable..	8,000	
		Sales Revenue		8,000
		Sale on account (80 × $100 = $8,000).		
	30	Cost of Goods Sold	5,450	
		Inventory		5,450
		Cost of goods sold ($1,950 + $3,500 = $5,450).		

Moving-Weighted-Average-Cost Method

Suppose SportChek uses the **moving-weighted-average-cost method** to account for its inventory of running shoes. With this method, the business computes a new weighted-average cost per unit after each purchase. Ending inventory and cost of goods sold are then based on the same most recent weighted-average cost per unit. Exhibit 6–5 shows a perpetual inventory record for the moving-weighted-average-cost method. We round average unit cost to the nearest cent and total cost to the nearest dollar.

After each purchase, SportChek computes a new average cost per unit. For example, on November 5, the new weighted-average unit cost is

Total cost of inventory on hand	÷	Number of units on hand	=	Average cost per unit
Nov. 5 $600 + $3,900 = $4,500	÷	70 units	=	$64.29

Running Shoes Model XL

Date	Purchases Qty.	Purchases Unit Cost	Purchases Total Cost	Cost of Goods Sold Qty.	Cost of Goods Sold Unit Cost	Cost of Goods Sold Total Cost	Inventory on Hand Qty.	Inventory on Hand Unit Cost	Inventory on Hand Total Cost
Nov. 1							10	$60.00	$ 600
5	60	$65	$3,900				70	64.29	4,500
15				40	$64.29	$2,572	30	64.29	1,928
26	70	70	4,900				100	68.28	6,828
30				80	68.28	5,462	20	68.28	1,366
30	130		$8,800	120		$8,034	20		$1,366

The goods sold on November 15 are then costed at $64.29 per unit. SportChek computes a new average cost after the November 26 purchase, which is why it is called a "moving" weighted-average cost.

The moving-weighted-average-cost summary at November 30 is

- Cost of goods sold: 120 units that cost a total of $8,034

- Ending inventory: 20 units that cost a total of $1,366

If SportChek used the moving-weighted-average-cost method, it would measure cost of goods sold and inventory in this manner to prepare its financial statements.

Journal Entries Under Moving-Weighted-Average Costing

The journal entries under moving-weighted-average costing follow the data in Exhibit 6–5. On November 5, SportChek purchased $3,900 of inventory and made the first journal entry. On November 15, SportChek sold 40 pairs of running shoes for $100 each. SportChek recorded the sale ($4,000) and the cost of goods sold ($2,572). The remaining journal entries (November 26 and 30) follow the data in Exhibit 6–5.

Moving-Weighted-Average-Cost Journal Entries: (All purchases and sales on account. The sale price of a pair of running shoes is $100 per unit.)

Nov. 5	Inventory		3,900	
	Accounts Payable			3,900
	Purchased inventory on account (60 × $65 = $3,900).			
15	Accounts Receivable		4,000	
	Sales Revenue			4,000
	Sale on account (40 × $100 = $4,000).			
15	Cost of Goods Sold		2,572	
	Inventory			2,572
	Cost of goods sold (40 × $64.29 = $2,572).			
26	Inventory		4,900	
	Accounts Payable			4,900
	Purchased inventory on account (70 × $70 = $4,900).			

Nov. 30	Accounts Receivable..	8,000	
	Sales Revenue		8,000
	Sale on account (80 × $100 = $8,000).		
30	Cost of Goods Sold	5,462	
	Inventory..		5,462
	Cost of goods sold, calculated as:		
	Cost of inventory on hand: $1,928 + $4,900 = $6,828		
	Moving-weighted-average cost per unit: $6,828 ÷ 100 = $68.28		
	Cost of goods sold = 80 × $68.28 = $5,462		

DID YOU GET IT?

MyAccountingLab

To check your understanding of the material in this Learning Objective, complete these questions. The solutions appear on MyAccountingLab so you can check your progress.

1. Examine Exhibit 6–4 (FIFO costing) and Exhibit 6–5 (moving-weighted-average costing). Focus on the sale of goods on November 15. Why is cost of goods sold different between FIFO costing and moving-weighted-average costing? Explain.

2. The Watch Shop carries only watches. Assume The Watch Shop began June with an inventory of 20 wristwatches that cost $60 each. The Watch Shop sells those watches for $100 each. During June, The Watch Shop bought and sold inventory as follows:

   Jun.   3   Sold 16 units for $100 each.

         16   Purchased 20 units at $65 each.

         23   Sold 16 units for $100 each.

   Prepare a perpetual inventory record for The Watch Shop under each method.
   - FIFO
   - Moving-weighted-average cost

3. Refer to The Watch Shop data given in the previous question. Journalize all of The Watch Shop's inventory transactions for June for the FIFO and moving-weighted-average-cost methods.

Comparing FIFO and Moving-Weighted-Average Cost

What leads SportChek to select the moving-weighted-average-cost method and Celestica Inc. to use FIFO? The different methods have different benefits.

Exhibit 6–6 summarizes the results for the two inventory methods for SportChek. It shows sales revenue (assumed), cost of goods sold, and gross margin for FIFO and moving-weighted-average costing. All data (except for sales revenue) come from Exhibits 6–4 and 6–5.

Exhibit 6–6 also shows that, when inventory costs are increasing, FIFO costing produces the lowest cost of goods sold and the highest gross margin. Net income is also the highest under FIFO costing when inventory costs are rising. Many companies prefer high income to attract investors and borrow money on favourable terms. In an environment of increasing costs, FIFO costing offers this benefit.

OBJECTIVE ②
Compare the effects of the FIFO and moving-weighted-average-cost methods

| EXHIBIT 6–6 | Comparative Results for FIFO and Moving-Weighted-Average Cost |

	FIFO	Moving-Weighted-Average
Sales revenue (assumed)	$12,000	$12,000
Cost of goods sold	8,000	8,034
Gross margin	$ 4,000	$ 3,966
	(from Exhibit 6–4)	(from Exhibit 6–5)

The moving-weighted-average-cost method generates a gross margin that will be lower than the gross margin generated under FIFO costing when prices are rising. The opposite is true when inventory purchase prices are falling—the moving-weighted-average-cost method would generate a higher gross margin than FIFO costing.

DID YOU GET IT?

MyAccountingLab

To check your understanding of the material in this Learning Objective, complete these questions. The solutions appear on MyAccountingLab so you can check your progress.

4. Refer to the information in Did You Get It? Question 2 on page 307 and your journal entries created in Did You Get It? Question 3 on page 307. Use that information to show the computation of gross margin for the FIFO and moving-weighted-average-costing methods for The Watch Shop.

5. Refer to Question 4. Which method maximizes net income? Which method minimizes income taxes?

6. How would your answer to Question 5 change if inventory purchase prices were falling during June?

Inventory Costing in a Periodic System

OBJECTIVE 3

Account for periodic inventory under the FIFO and weighted-average-cost methods

We described the periodic inventory system in Chapter 5. Accounting is simpler in a periodic system because the company keeps no daily running record of inventory on hand. The only way to determine the ending inventory and cost of goods sold in a periodic system is to count the goods—usually at the end of the year. The periodic system works well for a small business where the owner can control inventory by visual inspection. Appendix A in Chapter 5 illustrates how the periodic system works.

Cost of goods sold in a periodic inventory system is computed by the following formula (using assumed amounts for this illustration):

Beginning inventory	
(the inventory on hand at the end of the preceding period)........	$ 5,000
Net purchases (often abbreviated as Purchases)	20,000*
Cost of goods available for sale	25,000
Less: Ending inventory	
(the inventory on hand at the end of the current period)	(7,000)
Cost of goods sold...	$18,000

*The Net purchases amount is determined as follows (all amounts assumed):	
Purchases	$21,000
Less: Purchase discounts	(2,000)
Purchase returns and allowances...........................	(5,000)
Add: Freight in...	6,000
Net purchases..	$20,000

The application of the FIFO and weighted-average-costing methods in a periodic inventory system follows the pattern illustrated earlier for the perpetual system. To show how the periodic inventory system works, we use the same SportChek data that we used for the perpetual system, as follows:

Running Shoes, Model XL	Number of Units	Unit Cost
Nov. 1 Beginning inventory	10	$60
5 Purchase	60	$65
15 Sale	40	
26 Purchase	70	$70
30 Sale	80	

First-in, First-out (FIFO) Method

SportChek could use the FIFO costing method with a periodic inventory system. The FIFO computations follow:

Beginning inventory (10 units at $60)	$ 600
Purchases (60 units at $65 + 70 units at $70)..............................	8,800
Cost of goods available for sale (140 units)................................	9,400
Less: Ending inventory (20 units at $70)....................................	(1,400)
Cost of goods sold (120 units)	$8,000

The cost of goods available is always the sum of beginning inventory plus purchases. Under FIFO costing, the ending inventory comes from the latest—the most recent—purchases, which cost $70 per unit. Ending inventory is therefore $1,400, and cost of goods sold is $8,000. These amounts will always be the same as the amounts calculated under the perpetual system.

There are fewer journal entries in the periodic system because SportChek would record a sale with only a single entry. For example, SportChek's sale of 40 pairs of running shoes for $100 each is recorded as follows:

Nov. 15	Accounts Receivable (40 × $100)	4000	
	Sales Revenue...		4000

There is no cost-of-goods-sold entry in the periodic system.

Weighted-Average-Cost Method

In the **weighted-average-cost method**, we compute a single weighted-average cost per unit for the entire period as follows:

Cost of goods available for sale	÷	Number of units available for sale	=	Average cost per unit for the entire period
$9,400	÷	140 units	=	$67.14

This average cost per unit is then used to compute the ending inventory and cost of goods sold as follows:

Beginning inventory (10 units at $60)	$ 600
Purchases (60 units at $65 + 70 units at $70).............................	8,800
Cost of goods available for sale	
(140 units at weighted-average cost of $67.14)	9,400
Less: Ending inventory (20 units at $67.14)...............................	(1,343)
Cost of goods sold (120 units at $67.14).....................................	$8,057

Using the weighted-average-cost method, ending inventory and cost of goods sold under the periodic system differ from the amounts in a perpetual system. Why? Because under the perpetual system, a new average cost is computed after each purchase (it is a "moving" weighted-average cost). But the periodic system uses a single average cost that is determined at the end of the period.

Accounting Principles and Inventories

Several accounting concepts have special relevance to inventories. Among them are consistency, disclosure, materiality, and accounting conservatism.

Consistency

The characteristic of **consistency** states that businesses should use the same accounting methods and procedures from period to period. Consistency helps investors compare a company's financial statements from one period to the next.

Suppose you are analyzing a company's net income pattern over a two-year period. The company switched from moving-weighted-average to FIFO costing during that time. Its net income increased dramatically, but only as a result of the change in inventory method. If you did not know of the change, you might believe that the company's income increased because of improved operations. Therefore, companies must report any changes in the accounting methods they use. Investors need this information in order to make wise decisions about the company.

Disclosure Principle

The **disclosure principle** holds that a company's financial statements should report enough information for outsiders to make knowledgeable decisions about the company. In short, the company should report *relevant*, *reliable*, and *comparable* information about itself. This means disclosing the method or methods used to value inventories. Suppose a banker is comparing two companies—one using weighted-average costing and the other using FIFO. The FIFO company reports higher net income, but only because it uses the FIFO inventory method. Without knowledge of these accounting methods, the banker could lend money to the wrong business. In addition, different categories of inventory should be disclosed, such as raw materials, work-in-process, and finished goods inventories.

Materiality Concept

The **materiality concept** states that a company must perform strictly proper accounting *only* for items that are significant to the business's financial statements. Information is significant—or, in accounting terminology, *material*—when its presentation in the financial statements would cause someone to change a decision. The materiality concept frees accountants from having to report every item in strict accordance with GAAP. For inventory, this means immaterial items can be expensed rather than included in inventory. For example, if freight for an inventory item is immaterial, then it could be expensed immediately, even if the inventory item is sold in a later period.

Accounting Conservatism

Conservatism in accounting means reporting items in the financial statements at amounts that lead to the most cautious immediate results. Conservatism appears in accounting guidelines such as

- "Anticipate no gains, but provide for all probable losses."
- "If in doubt, record an asset at the lowest reasonable amount and a liability at the highest reasonable amount."
- "When there's a question, record an expense rather than an asset."

The goal is for financial statements to report realistic figures. However, do not deliberately understate assets, revenues, and gains, nor deliberately overstate liabilities, expenses, and losses.

To check your understanding of the material in this Learning Objective, complete these questions. The solutions appear on MyAccountingLab so you can check your progress.

7. Pemberton Company began May with 20 units of inventory that cost a total of $800. During May, Pemberton purchased and sold goods as follows:

May	8	Purchase: 30 units at $25
	14	Sale: 25 units at $50
	22	Purchase: 20 units at $30
	27	Sale: 30 units at $60

Calculate the gross margin amount using the FIFO method, assuming Pemberton uses a periodic inventory system.

8. Refer to the Pemberton Company data in the previous question. Calculate the gross margin amount using the weighted-average method, assuming Pemberton uses a periodic inventory system.

Other Inventory Issues

In addition to the FIFO and weighted-average inventory costing methods, accountants face other inventory issues. This section covers

- The lower-of-cost-and-net-realizable-value rule
- Effects of inventory errors
- Ethical issues
- Estimating ending inventory

> **OBJECTIVE ④**
> Apply the lower-of-cost-and-net-realizable-value rule to inventory

Lower-of-Cost-and-Net-Realizable-Value Rule

The **lower-of-cost-and-net-realizable-value rule** (abbreviated as **LCNRV**) shows accounting conservatism in action. LCNRV requires that inventory be reported in the financial statements at whichever is lower:

- The historical cost of the inventory
- The net realizable value (market value) of the inventory

For inventories, *net realizable value* generally means the expected selling price (that is, the amount the business could get if it sold the inventory less the costs of selling it).

If the net realizable value of inventory falls below its historical cost, the business must write down the value of its goods. This situation may arise if inventory has become damaged or if it has become obsolete. On the balance sheet, the business reports ending inventory at its LCNRV.

At each year end, a new assessment of the net realizable value is made. If the circumstances that caused inventories to be written down below cost no longer exist, the amount of the write-down is reversed, up to the original cost of the inventory in question. However, inventory is *never* written up to an amount greater than its original cost, since this would violate LCNRV.

Suppose SportChek paid $6,000 for inventory on September 26. By December 31, the inventory can only be sold for $5,000, and the decline in value appears permanent. Net realizable value is below FIFO cost, and the entry to write down the inventory to LCNRV follows:

LEARNING TIPS

| Costs of Goods Sold | 1,000 | |
| Inventory | | 1,000 |

To write down inventory to net realizable value.
(cost, $6,000 − net realizable value, $5,000)

Note that the matching objective of the measurement principle is applied to ending inventory with LCNRV. The reduction in the value of the inventory is shown in the year the inventory declines in value, *not* in the year the inventory is sold.

In this case, The Forzani Group Ltd.'s balance sheet would report this inventory as follows:

Balance Sheet

Current assets:
    Inventory, at market $5,000
        (which is lower than $6,000 cost)

Companies often disclose LCNRV in notes to their financial statements, as shown here for The Forzani Group Ltd., SportChek's parent company:

> NOTE 2: SIGNIFICANT ACCOUNTING POLICIES
> (b) *Inventory valuation*
> Inventory is valued at the lower of laid-down cost and net realizable value. Laid-down cost is determined using the weighted average cost method and includes invoice cost, duties, freight, and distribution costs. Net realizable value is defined as the expected selling price. . . .

DID YOU GET IT?

MyAccountingLab

To check your understanding of the material in this Learning Objective, complete these questions. The solutions appear on MyAccountingLab so you can check your progress.

9. Suppose Indy Computers paid $10,000 for inventory. By its year end, the company had sold 60 percent of the inventory but determined that the remaining inventory could be sold for only 50 percent of its original cost. The company anticipated that this decline was permanent. At what amount would inventory be reported on the year-end balance sheet?

10. Refer to the inventory data in the previous question. Suppose, one month later, a worldwide shortage of this inventory now gives it a net realizable value of $5,000. At what amount would this inventory be reported on the balance sheet one month later?

Effects of Inventory Errors

OBJECTIVE 5
Measure the effects of inventory errors

Businesses count their inventories at the end of the period. For the financial statements to be accurate, it is important to get a correct count of ending inventory. This can be difficult for a company with inventory in many locations.

An error in ending inventory creates a whole string of errors. To illustrate, suppose SportChek accidentally counted too much ending inventory. Therefore, ending inventory is overstated on the balance sheet. The following diagram shows how an overstatement of ending inventory affects cost of goods sold, gross margin, and net income:

	Ending Inventory Overstated
Sales revenue...	Correct
Cost of goods sold:	
Beginning inventory	Correct
Net purchases	Correct
Cost of goods available for sale	Correct
Ending inventory	**ERROR: Overstated**
Cost of goods sold..	**Understated**
Gross margin...	**Overstated**
Operating expenses...	Correct
Net income	**Overstated**

Understating the ending inventory—reporting the inventory too low—has the opposite effect, as shown here:

	Ending Inventory Understated
Sales revenue	Correct
Cost of goods sold:	
Beginning inventory	Correct
Net purchases	Correct
Cost of goods available for sale	Correct
Ending inventory	**ERROR: Understated**
Cost of goods sold	**Overstated**
Gross margin	**Understated**
Operating expenses	Correct
Net income	**Understated**

Recall that one period's ending inventory is the next period's beginning inventory. Thus, an error in ending inventory carries over into the next period. Exhibit 6–7 illustrates the effect of an inventory error. Period 1's ending inventory is overstated by $10,000. The error carries over to Period 2. Period 3 is correct. In fact, both Period 1 and Period 2 should look like Period 3.

EXHIBIT 6–7   Inventory Errors: An Example

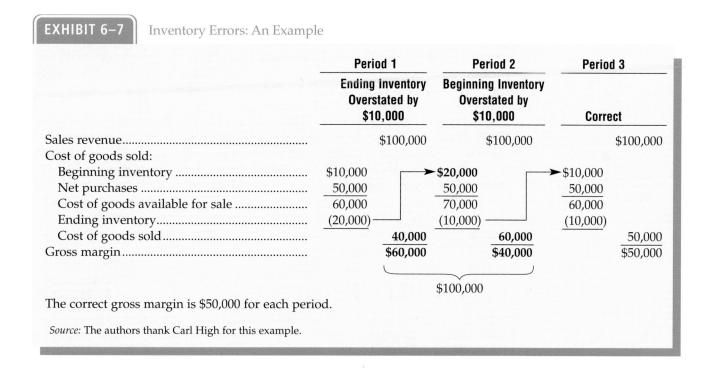

	Period 1 Ending Inventory Overstated by $10,000		Period 2 Beginning Inventory Overstated by $10,000		Period 3 Correct	
Sales revenue		$100,000		$100,000		$100,000
Cost of goods sold:						
Beginning inventory	$10,000		$20,000		$10,000	
Net purchases	50,000		50,000		50,000	
Cost of goods available for sale	60,000		70,000		60,000	
Ending inventory	(20,000)		(10,000)		(10,000)	
Cost of goods sold		40,000		60,000		50,000
Gross margin		$60,000		$40,000		$50,000

$100,000

The correct gross margin is $50,000 for each period.

Source: The authors thank Carl High for this example.

Ending inventory is *subtracted* in computing cost of goods sold in one period and the same amount is *added* as beginning inventory the next period. Therefore, an inventory error cancels out after two periods. The overstatement of cost of goods sold in Period 2 counterbalances the understatement for Period 1. Thus, the total gross margin for the two periods combined is correct. These effects are summarized in Exhibit 6–8.

EXHIBIT 6–8 Effects of Inventory Errors

	Period 1		Period 2	
Inventory Error	Cost of Goods Sold	Gross Margin and Net Income	Cost of Goods Sold	Gross Margin and Net Income
Period 1 ending inventory *overstated*	Understated	Overstated	Overstated	Understated
Period 1 ending inventory *understated*	Overstated	Understated	Understated	Overstated

KEY POINT

Recognize that a dollar change in ending inventory means a dollar change in income. This is one reason auditors examine the ending inventory so carefully. An income statement may be manipulated by altering the amount of ending inventory.

Ethical Issues

No area of accounting has a deeper ethical dimension than inventory. Companies whose profits do not meet expectations can be tempted to "cook the books" to increase reported income. The increase in reported income will make the business look more successful than it really is.

There are two main schemes for using inventory to increase reported income. The easier, and the more obvious, is to overstate ending inventory. In Exhibit 6–8, we see how an error in ending inventory affects net income.

The second way of using inventory to increase reported income involves sales. Sales schemes are more complex than simple inventory overstatements. Datapoint Corporation and MiniScribe, both computer-related companies, were charged with creating fictitious sales to boost reported profits.

Datapoint is alleged to have hired drivers to transport its inventory around the city so that the goods could *not* be counted. Datapoint's plan was to create the impression that the inventory must have been sold. This scheme broke down when the trucks returned the goods to the warehouse. The sales returns were much too high to be realistic, and the sales proved to be phony.

MiniScribe is alleged to have "cooked its books" by shipping boxes of bricks labelled as computer parts to its distributors right before year end. The distributors refused to accept the goods and returned them to MiniScribe—but in the next accounting period. The scheme affected MiniScribe's reported year-end assets and equity: sales and net income were overstated and inventories were understated by millions of dollars—but only temporarily. The offsetting effect of the scheme occurred in the next accounting period when MiniScribe had to record the sales returns. In virtually every area, accounting imposes a discipline that brings out the facts sooner or later.

DID YOU GET IT?

MyAccountingLab

To check your understanding of the material in this Learning Objective, complete these questions. The solutions appear on MyAccountingLab so you can check your progress.

11. Leena's Craft Shop uses a periodic inventory system. The inventory data for the year ended December 31, 2010, follow.

Sales revenue	$120,000
Cost of goods sold:	
Beginning inventory	22,000
Net purchases	90,000
Cost of goods available for sale	112,000
Less: Ending inventory	(24,000)
Cost of goods sold	88,000
Gross margin	$ 32,000

Suppose it was discovered after the year end that $4,000 of craft supplies had dried up in their packages and should have been destroyed before year end. These supplies had been counted and recorded as ending inventory. What effects did these obsolete craft supplies have on the accounting information above?

12. Refer to the Leena's Craft Shop data in the previous question. What effects will the obsolete craft supplies have on the accounting information for the following year?

Estimating Ending Inventory

OBJECTIVE 6
Estimate ending inventory by the gross margin method and the retail method

Often a business must *estimate* the value of its ending inventory. Suppose the company suffers a fire loss and must estimate the value of the inventory destroyed. Or suppose a company needs monthly financial statements.

The **gross margin method** (also known as the **gross profit method**) provides a way to estimate inventory using the cost of goods sold model (amounts are assumed for illustration):

	Beginning inventory	$ 20
+	Net purchases	100
=	Cost of goods available for sale	120
−	**Ending inventory**	(40)
=	**Cost of goods sold**	$ 80

Rearranging *ending inventory* and *cost of goods sold* makes the model useful for estimating ending inventory (amounts are assumed for illustration):

	Beginning inventory	$ 20
+	Purchases	100
=	Cost of goods available for sale	120
−	**Cost of goods sold**	(80)
=	**Ending inventory**	$ 40

Suppose a fire destroys your inventory. To collect insurance, you must estimate the cost of the ending inventory. Using your normal *gross margin percent* (that is, gross margin divided by net sales revenue), you can estimate cost of goods sold. Then subtract cost of goods sold from cost of goods available to estimate ending inventory. Exhibit 6–9 illustrates the gross margin method using assumed amounts.

EXHIBIT 6–9 Gross Margin Method of Estimating Inventory (amounts assumed)

Beginning inventory		$ 14,000
Purchases		66,000
Cost of goods available for sale		80,000
Estimate cost of goods sold:		
Sales revenue	$100,000	
Less: Estimated gross margin of 40%	(40,000)	
Estimated cost of goods sold		(60,000)
Estimated cost of *ending inventory*		$ 20,000

LEARNING TIPS

Remember that the gross margin % + the cost of goods sold % = 100%. If gross margin is 35% of sales, then cost of goods sold is 65% of sales.

Retail Method The **retail method** of estimating the cost of ending inventory is often used by retail establishments that use the periodic inventory system. This is because it is often easier for retail establishments to calculate the selling price, or retail price, of a wide range of items rather than to look at all the individual invoices to find the costs of each of those items.

Like the gross margin method, the retail method is based on the familiar cost of goods sold model, rearranged to calculate ending inventory:

$$
\begin{array}{rl}
& \text{Beginning inventory} \\
+ & \text{Net purchases} \\
\hline
= & \text{Cost of goods available for sale} \\
- & \text{Cost of goods sold} \\
\hline
= & \text{Ending inventory}
\end{array}
$$

However, to use the retail method, a business must know both the total cost and the total selling price of its opening inventory, as well as both the total cost and the total selling price of its net purchases. Total selling price is determined by counting each item of inventory and multiplying it by the item's retail selling price (the price given on the price tag). By summing the costs and selling prices of beginning inventory and net purchases, the business knows the cost and retail selling price of the goods it has available for sale.

REAL WORLD EXAMPLE

The gross margin and retail methods are also used to estimate inventory for interim periods when it is impractical to take a physical inventory.

The business can calculate the total selling price of its sales because this is the sum of the amounts recorded on the cash register when sales are made. The total of sales at retail is deducted from the total selling price of the goods available for sale to give the total selling price of ending inventory. To convert ending inventory at selling price to ending inventory at cost, the business multiplies the ending inventory at selling price by the *retail ratio*. The retail ratio is the ratio of the cost of goods available for sale at *cost* to the cost of goods available for sale at *selling price*. It is usually expressed as a percent. Exhibit 6–10 illustrates the retail method.

EXHIBIT 6–10 Retail Method of Estimating Inventory (amounts assumed)

	Cost	Selling Price
Beginning inventory	$151,200	$216,000
Purchases	504,000	720,000
Goods available for sale	655,200	936,000
Net sales, at selling price (retail)		696,000
Ending inventory, at selling price (retail)		$240,000
Ending inventory, at cost ($240,000 × *70%)	$168,000	

*Retail ratio = ($655,200 ÷ 936,000) × 100% = 70%

The retail method can be used to estimate inventory at any point in time, and it is acceptable to use the retail method to calculate year-end inventory cost for financial statement and income tax purposes, although an inventory count must be done at least once per year.

DID YOU GET IT?

MyAccountingLab

To check your understanding of the material in this Learning Objective, complete these questions. The solutions appear on MyAccountingLab so you can check your progress.

13. Beginning inventory is $90,000, net purchases total $320,000, and net sales are $500,000. The normal gross margin is 40 percent of sales. Use the gross margin method to calculate ending inventory.

14. A beachwear shop needs to estimate the cost of its ending inventory for insurance purposes, and since it is summer, it cannot close for a physical count of inventory. The insurance company will accept an estimate using the retail method. The shop's owner knows the cost of opening inventory was $50,000 from the previous year end's physical count and its selling price was $120,000. From invoices, the owner knows the cost of purchases was $200,000 and their retail selling prices totalled $480,000. Cash register receipts show that sales from the beginning of the year totalled $500,000. Calculate the cost of ending inventory for the insurance company.

Accounting-Cycle and Financial-Reporting Implications of IFRS

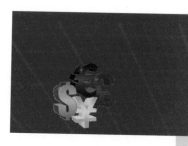

The treatment of inventories under Canadian GAAP for private enterprises is significantly the same as the treatment for companies reporting under international financial reporting standards (IFRS). There are three basic issues surrounding inventory reporting: the costs to include in inventory, the inventory costing methods that are available, and the rules for recording and reporting inventory that has a value lower than its original cost.

Costs included in the determination of inventory are the same for IFRS-reporting companies as they are for Canadian private enterprises. The main categories are purchase cost, conversion costs, and other inventoriable costs, such as freight costs to get the product to the company's facility, to make the inventory ready for sale.

The same three inventory costing methods that are permitted under Canadian GAAP are allowed under IFRS—specific identification, FIFO, and weighted average. As with Canadian GAAP, companies are free to choose whichever method they wish, but once chosen, it is expected that that method will be used on a consistent basis into the future.

Finally, both Canadian GAAP for private enterprises and IFRS require companies to reduce the value of items or categories of inventory if those items can only be sold for an amount lower than their original cost to the company. Companies must use net realizable value to determine the appropriate value of the inventory. When the circumstances that previously caused the inventories to be written down no longer exist, the amount of the write-down is reversed. Under no circumstances can inventory ever be valued higher than the lower of cost or net realizable value.

OBJECTIVE (7)
Assess the inventory recording and reporting impacts of international financial reporting standards (IFRS)

DID YOU GET IT?

MyAccountingLab

To check your understanding of the material in this Learning Objective, complete this question. The solution appears on MyAccountingLab so you can check your progress.

15. Why are standard setters, including those setting IFRS, interested in ensuring that companies use the same inventory costing method from one year to the next?

As we conclude this chapter, we return to our opening questions: Which inventory system should a merchandiser use, and why is it important? What are the different inventory costing methods? How do they differ? Which methods can be used for income tax purposes? Which inventory costing method should a merchandiser choose? How can merchandisers estimate the cost of inventory destroyed in a fire or other disaster? The Decision Guidelines feature summarizes all of our chapter-opening questions and gives guidelines that are helpful for managing a business's inventory operations.

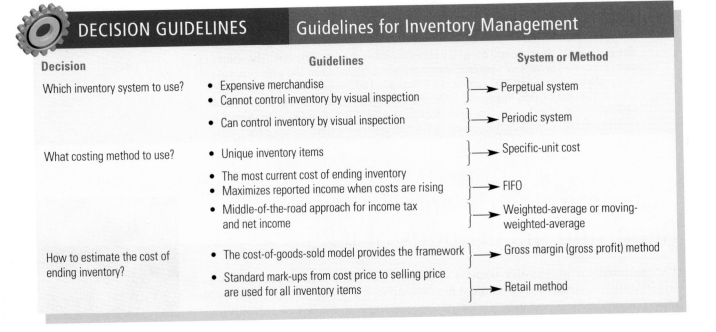

Decision	Guidelines	System or Method
Which inventory system to use?	• Expensive merchandise • Cannot control inventory by visual inspection	→ Perpetual system
	• Can control inventory by visual inspection	→ Periodic system
What costing method to use?	• Unique inventory items	→ Specific-unit cost
	• The most current cost of ending inventory • Maximizes reported income when costs are rising	→ FIFO
	• Middle-of-the-road approach for income tax and net income	→ Weighted-average or moving-weighted-average
How to estimate the cost of ending inventory?	• The cost-of-goods-sold model provides the framework	→ Gross margin (gross profit) method
	• Standard mark-ups from cost price to selling price are used for all inventory items	→ Retail method

Summary Problem for Your Review

Suppose a division of Regal Computer Sales that handles computer parts uses the periodic inventory system and has these inventory records for December 2010.

Name: Computer Parts Division, Regal Computer Sales
Industry: Retailer
Fiscal Period: Month of December 2010
Key Fact: Periodic inventory system

Date		Item	Quantity	Unit Cost	Sale Price
Dec.	1	Beginning inventory	100 units	$16	
	10	Purchase	60 units	18	
	15	Sale	70 units		$40
	21	Purchase	100 units	20	
	30	Sale	90 units		50

Company accounting records reveal that operating expenses for January were $4,000.

Required

Prepare the December 2010 income statement in multi-step format. Show amounts for FIFO cost and weighted-average cost. Label the bottom line "Operating income." (Round the average cost per unit to three decimal places and all other figures to whole-dollar amounts.) Show your computations, and use the periodic inventory model from pages 308–309 to compute cost of goods sold.

SOLUTION

<table>
<tr><th colspan="3">REGAL COMPUTER SALES
Income Statement for Computer Parts Division
For the Month Ended December 31, 2010</th></tr>
<tr><th></th><th>FIFO</th><th>WEIGHTED-AVERAGE</th></tr>
<tr><td>Sales revenue...</td><td>$7,300</td><td>$7,300</td></tr>
<tr><td>Cost of goods sold:</td><td></td><td></td></tr>
<tr><td> Beginning inventory .... $1,600</td><td></td><td>$ 1,600</td></tr>
<tr><td> Net purchases .... 3,080</td><td></td><td>3,080</td></tr>
<tr><td> Cost of goods available for sale .... 4,680</td><td></td><td>4,680</td></tr>
<tr><td> Ending inventory .... (2,000)</td><td></td><td>(1,800)</td></tr>
<tr><td> Cost of goods sold...</td><td>2,680</td><td>2,880</td></tr>
<tr><td>Gross margin...</td><td>4,620</td><td>4,420</td></tr>
<tr><td>Operating expenses..</td><td>4,000</td><td>4,000</td></tr>
<tr><td>Operating income...</td><td>$ 620</td><td>$ 420</td></tr>
</table>

Computations

Sales revenue:	$(70 \times \$40) + (90 \times \$50)$	$= \$7,300$
Beginning inventory:	$100 \times \$16$	$= \$1,600$
Purchases:	$(60 \times \$18) + (100 \times \$20)$	$= \$3,080$
Ending inventory:		
FIFO:	$100^* \times \$20$	$= \$2,000$
Average cost:	$100^* \times \$18^{**}$	$= \$1,800$

*Number of units in ending inventory $= 100 + 60 - 70 + 100 - 90 = 100$
**Average cost per unit $= \$4,680/260^\dagger$ units $= \$18$
†Number of units available $= 100 + 60 + 100 = 260$

The best approach to this solution is an organized one. One approach is to complete one income statement line before going to the next, until "Ending inventory." Notice that the amounts for sales revenue, beginning inventory, net purchases, and operating expenses are the same for the two inventory costing methods.

Summary

1. **Account for perpetual inventory under the specific-unit-cost, FIFO, and moving-weighted-average-cost methods.** In a perpetual inventory system, the business keeps a continuous record for each inventory item to show the inventory on hand at all times. Inventory is debited immediately at cost when an item is purchased and inventory is credited immediately at cost when an item is sold. Businesses multiply the quantity of inventory items by their unit cost to determine inventory cost. To compute ending inventory and cost of goods sold, a cost is assigned to each inventory item. The specific-unit-cost method is typically used for unique or expensive items. Two methods of assigning costs to similar items are: *first-in, first-out (FIFO)* and *moving-weighted-average*. FIFO costing reports ending inventory at the most current cost, and moving-weighted-average costing reports

ending inventory at the average cost at the time of the sale.

2. **Compare the effects of the FIFO and moving-weighted-average-cost methods.** FIFO costing reports ending inventory at the most current cost. Moving-weighted-average costing reports ending inventory and cost of goods sold at an average amount determined by the value of all relevant units in inventory at the time of the sale. When prices are rising, moving-weighted-average costing produces the higher cost of goods sold and the lower income. When prices are rising, FIFO costing produces the higher income.

3. **Account for periodic inventory under the FIFO and weighted-average-cost methods.** In a periodic inventory system, the business does not keep an up-to-date balance for ending inventory. Instead, at the end of the

period, the business counts the inventory on hand and updates its records. To compute ending inventory and cost of goods sold, a cost is assigned to each inventory item. Two methods of assigning costs to similar items are: *first-in, first-out (FIFO)* and *weighted-average*. FIFO costing produces identical balances for ending inventory and cost of goods sold under the periodic and perpetual inventory systems, but the weighted-average method produces a different result under the periodic and perpetual systems.

4. **Apply the lower-of-cost-and-net-realizable-value rule to inventory.** The *lower-of-cost-and-net-realizable-value (LCNRV) rule*—an example of accounting *conservatism*—requires that businesses report inventory on the balance sheet at the lower of its cost and net realizable value or current replacement. Companies disclose their definition of "net realizable value" for purposes of applying LCNRV in notes to their financial statements.

5. **Measure the effects of inventory errors.** Although inventory overstatements in one period are counterbalanced by inventory understatements in the next period,

effective decision making depends on accurate inventory information.

6. **Estimate ending inventory by the gross margin method and the retail method.** The *gross margin method* and the *retail method* are techniques for estimating the cost of ending inventory. They are useful for preparing interim financial statements and for estimating the cost of inventory destroyed by fire or other disasters.

7. **Assess the inventory recording and reporting impacts of international financial reporting standards (IFRS).** The principles of accounting for inventories under Canadian GAAP for private enterprises and under IFRS are essentially the same. The three main issues for inventory are the costs to include in inventory, the inventory costing method to use, and accounting for inventory whose market value has fallen below its cost. The Canadian practice and IFRS rules are essentially the same.

SELF-STUDY QUESTIONS

Test your understanding of the chapter by marking the correct answer to each of the following questions:

1. Suppose a store made sales of $1,000,000 and ended the year with inventories totalling $100,000. Cost of goods sold was $600,000. Total operating expenses were $270,000. How much net income did the chain store earn for the year? (*pp. 301–302*)

   a. $130,000   c. $400,000
   b. $900,000   d. $630,000

2. Which inventory costing method assigns to ending inventory the latest—the most recent—costs incurred during the period? (*p. 304*)

   a. Specific-unit cost   c. Average cost
   b. First-in, first-out (FIFO)   d. None of the above

3. Assume Lauder Company began June with 10 units of inventory that cost a total of $760. During June, Lauder purchased and sold goods as follows:

Jun.	8	Purchase:	30 units at $80
	14	Sale:	25 units at $160
	22	Purchase:	20 units at $88
	27	Sale:	30 units at $160

   Assume Lauder uses the FIFO inventory method and the perpetual inventory system. How much is Lauder's cost of goods sold for the transaction on June 14? (*p. 304*)

   a. $3,160   c. $2,000
   b. $4,000   d. $1,960

4. After the purchase on June 22 in question 3, what is Lauder's cost of the inventory on hand if the company is using the FIFO inventory costing method? (*p. 304*)

   a. $1,200   c. $2,960
   b. $1,760   d. $2,880

5. Lauder's journal entry (entries) on June 14 is (are) (*p. 305*)

a.	Accounts Receivable.........	1,960	
	Inventory		1,960
b.	Accounts Receivable.........	4,000	
	Sales Revenue		4,000
c.	Cost of Goods Sold	1,960	
	Inventory		1,960

   d. Both b and c

6. Which inventory costing method results in the lowest net income during a period of rising inventory costs? (*pp. 307–308*)

   a. Specific-unit cost
   b. First-in, first out (FIFO)
   c. Weighted-average cost
   d. None of the above

7. Suppose Lauder Company used the weighted-average-cost method and the periodic inventory system. Use the Lauder data in question 3 to compute the cost of the company's inventory on hand at June 30. Round unit cost to the nearest cent. (*p. 309*)

   a. $410.00
   b. $420.80
   c. $820.00
   d. $841.60

8. Which of the following is most closely linked to accounting conservatism? (*p. 311*)

   a. Consistency principle
   b. Disclosure principle
   c. Materiality concept
   d. Lower-of-cost-and-net-realizable-value rule

9. At December 31, 2010, McAdam Company understated ending inventory by $20,000. How does this error affect cost of goods sold and net income for 2010? (*pp. 312–314*)

   a. Overstates cost of goods sold, understates income
   b. Understates cost of goods sold, overstates net income
   c. Overstates both cost of goods sold and net income
   d. Leaves both cost of goods sold and net income correct because the errors cancel each other

10. Suppose a SportChek location suffered a fire loss and needs to estimate the cost of the goods destroyed. Beginning inventory was $200,000, net purchases totalled $1,200,000, and sales came to $2,000,000. SportChek's normal gross margin is 45 percent. Use the gross margin method to estimate the cost of the inventory lost in the fire. (*p. 315*)

    a. $600,000
    b. $500,000
    c. $300,000
    d. $700,000

Answers to Self-Study Questions

1. a ($1,000,000 − $600,000 − $270,000 = $130,000)
2. b
3. d (10 × $76) + (15 × $80) = $1,960
4. c (15 × $80) + (20 × $88) = $2,960
5. d
6. c
7. a Cost of goods available = $760 + $2,400 + $1,760 = $4,920
   Number of units available = 10 + 30 + 20 = 60
   $4,920/60 units = $82; $82 × 5 = $410
8. d
9. a
10. c $200,000 + $1,200,000 = $1,400,000
    $2,000,000 − (0.45 × $2,000,000) = $1,100,000
    $1,400,000 − $1,100,000 = $300,000

ACCOUNTING VOCABULARY

Conservatism   (*p. 310*)
Consistency characteristic   (*p. 310*)
Disclosure principle   (*p. 310*)
First-in, first-out (FIFO) method   (*p. 304*)
Gross margin method   (*p. 315*)
Gross profit method   (*p. 315*)
Lower-of-cost-and-net-realizable-value
   (LCNRV) rule   (*p. 311*)

Materiality concept   (*p. 310*)
Moving-weighted-average-cost method   (*p. 305*)
Retail method   (*p. 316*)
Specific identification method   (*p. 303*)
Specific-unit-cost method   (*p. 303*)
Weighted-average-cost method   (*p. 309*)

SIMILAR ACCOUNTING TERMS

Cost of goods sold	Cost of sales
Gross margin method	Gross profit method
Weighted-average-cost method	Average-cost method

Assignment Material

QUESTIONS

1. Why is merchandise inventory so important to a retailer or wholesaler?

2. Suppose your business deals in expensive jewellery. Which inventory system should you use to achieve good internal control over the inventory? If your business is a hardware store that sells low-cost goods, which inventory system would you be likely to use? Why would you choose this system?

3. Identify the accounts debited and credited in the standard purchase and sale entries under (a) the perpetual inventory system, and (b) the periodic inventory system.

4. What is the role of the physical count of inventory in (a) the perpetual inventory system and, (b) the periodic inventory system?

5. If beginning inventory is $120,000, purchases total $270,000, and ending inventory is $125,000, how much is cost of goods sold?

6. If beginning inventory is $88,000, purchases total $218,000, and cost of goods sold is $230,000, how much is ending inventory?

7. What two items determine the cost of ending inventory?

8. Briefly describe the two generally accepted inventory costing methods. During a period of rising prices, which method produces the higher reported income? Which produces the lower reported income?

9. Which inventory costing method produces the ending inventory valued at the most current cost?

10. Describe the impact on cost of goods sold of using the FIFO method as opposed to the weighted-average-cost method of valuing ending inventory when the price of inventory purchases is rising. Which method provides a more accurate value of the goods remaining in ending inventory at the end of an accounting period?

11. Your accounting instructor tells you that companies should use the specific identification method to most accurately value items that have been sold and transferred to cost of goods sold, yet most companies do not use this method. Why not?

12. How does the consistency characteristic affect accounting for inventory?

13. Briefly describe the influence that the concept of conservatism has on accounting for inventory.

14. Manley Company's inventory has a cost of $54,000 at the end of the year, and the net realizable value of the inventory is $65,000. At which amount should the company report the inventory on its balance sheet? Suppose the net realizable value of the inventory is $51,000 instead of $65,000. At which amount should Manley Company report the inventory? What rule governs your answers to these questions?

15. Gabriel Products accidentally overstated its ending inventory by $10,000 at the end of Period 1. Is the gross margin of Period 1 overstated or understated? Is the gross margin of Period 2 overstated, understated, or unaffected by the Period 1 error? Is the total gross margin for the two periods overstated, understated, or correct? Give the reason for your answers.

16. Identify two important methods of estimating inventory amounts.

17. A fire destroyed the inventory of Bronk Supplies, but the accounting records were saved. The beginning inventory was $63,000, purchases for the period were $136,500, and sales were $240,000. Bronk's customary gross margin is 40 percent of sales. Use the gross margin method to estimate the cost of the inventory destroyed by the fire.

18. The retail method of estimating inventory seems simple but in reality can be difficult to apply. Why is this so?

STARTERS

MyAccountingLab All questions in this section appear in MyAccountingLab.

Computing ending inventory—
specific-unit-cost method

(1)

Ending inventory $62,900

Starter 6–1 Fairhill Company has the following items in its inventory on August 1:

Serial Number	Cost
661	$18,200
665	18,600
668	17,400
675	21,900

The company uses the specific-unit-cost method for costing inventory. During August, it sold units 661 and 668 for $30,000 each, and purchased unit 676 for $22,400. What is the value of the ending inventory at August 31?

Computing gross margin—
specific-unit-cost method

(1)

Gross margin $24,400

Starter 6–2 Refer to the information in Starter 6–1. Calculate the gross margin for the month of August.

Perpetual inventory
record—FIFO

(1)

Ending inventory $1,000

Starter 6–3 Casio Cycles uses the FIFO inventory method. Casio started June with 10 bicycles that cost $190 each. On June 16, Casio bought 20 bicycles at $200 each. On June 30, Casio sold 25 bicycles. Prepare Casio's perpetual inventory record.

Recording inventory
transactions—FIFO

(1)

c. COGS $4,900

Starter 6–4 Use the Casio Cycles data in Starter 6–3 to journalize

a. The June 16 purchase of inventory on account.
b. The June 30 sale of inventory on account. Casio sold each bicycle for $240.
c. Cost of goods sold under FIFO.

Starter 6–5 Use the Casio Cycles' data in Starter 6–3 to prepare a perpetual inventory record for the moving-weighted-average-cost method. Round average cost per unit to the nearest cent and all other amounts to the nearest dollar.

Perpetual inventory record—moving-weighted-average cost

Ending inventory $983

Starter 6–6 Use the Casio Cycles data in Starter 6–3 to journalize

   a. The June 16 purchase of inventory on account.

   b. The June 30 sale of inventory on account. Casio sold each bicycle for $240.

   c. Cost of goods sold under the moving-weighted-average-cost method.

Recording inventory transactions—moving-weighted-average method

c. COGS $4,917

Starter 6–7 Answer these questions in your own words:

   1. Why does FIFO produce the lower cost of goods sold during a period of rising prices?

   2. Why does moving-weighted-average costing produce the higher cost of goods sold during a period of rising prices?

   3. Which inventory costing method—FIFO or moving-weighted-average—results in the higher, and the lower, cost of ending inventory? Prices are rising. Exhibits 6–4 and 6–5, on pages 304 and 306, provide the needed information.

Comparing cost of goods sold and ending inventory under FIFO and moving-weighted-average-cost methods

Starter 6–8 Park Dry Goods uses a periodic inventory system. Park completed the following inventory transactions during April, its first month of operations:

Computing FIFO and weighted-average amounts in a periodic system

Gross margin FIFO $250

Apr.	1	Purchased 10 shirts at $50 each
	7	Sold 6 shirts for $80 each
	13	Purchased 3 shirts for $55 each
	21	Sold 2 shirts at $85 each

Compute Park's ending inventory and cost of goods sold under FIFO costing. Then compute ending inventory and cost of goods sold under the weighted-average-cost method. Round average unit cost to the nearest cent. Compute gross margin under both methods. Which method results in the higher gross margin?

Starter 6–9 Van Dyke Cycles uses a periodic inventory system. The inventory data for the year ended December 31, 2010, follow.

Effect of an inventory error—one year only

Sales revenue..	$150,000
Cost of goods sold:	
Beginning inventory	22,000
Net purchases	80,000
Cost of goods available for sale	102,000
Less: Ending inventory...	(24,000)
Cost of goods sold..	78,000
Gross margin...	$ 72,000

Assume that the ending inventory was accidentally overstated by $2,000. What are the correct amounts of cost of goods sold and gross margin?

Starter 6–10 Refer back to the Van Dyke Cycles' inventory data in Starter 6–9. The ending inventory balance is stated correctly at the end of 2011. What would be the effect on cost of goods sold and gross margin for the year ended December 31, 2011?

Next year's effect of an inventory error

Starter 6–11 Dream Carpets began the year with inventory of $700,000. Inventory purchases for the year totalled $3,200,000. Sales revenue for the year was $7,000,000 and the gross margin was 50 percent. How much is Dream Carpets' estimated cost of ending inventory? Use the gross margin method.

Estimating ending inventory by the gross margin method

Ending inventory $400,000

Starter 6–12 Thorne Industries began the year with inventory of $80,000 and purchased $350,000 of goods during the year. Sales for the year are $600,000, and Thorne Industries' gross margin is 55 percent of sales. Compute the estimated cost of ending inventory by the gross margin method.

Estimating ending inventory by the gross margin method

Est. cost of ending inventory $160,000

EXERCISES

MyAccountingLab | All questions in this section appear in MyAccountingLab.

Exercise 6–1

Computing gross margin—specific-unit-cost method

2. Gross margin $34,100

Reguly Company buys transformers from manufacturers and sells them to utility companies. The units are costly, and the company keeps track of them by using serial numbers. On April 1, the company had two transformers in stock:

Serial Number	Unit Cost
2010901	$27,500
2010905	29,600

During the month, the company purchased the following two transformers:

Serial Number	Unit Cost
20101001	$25,500
20101002	28,400

Reguly Company sold two transformers—serial numbers 2010901 and 20101002—during the month of April. The selling price of the transformers was $45,000 per unit.

Required

1. Reguly Company uses the specific-unit-cost method for costing inventory. Why would the company prefer to use this method?
2. Compute the gross margin for Reguly Company for the month of April.

Exercise 6–2

Measuring ending inventory and cost of goods sold in a perpetual system—FIFO

Cost of goods sold $5,190

The Music Store carries a large inventory of guitars and other musical instruments. The store uses the FIFO method and a perpetual inventory system. Company records indicate the following for a particular line of guitars:

Date		Item	Quantity	Unit Cost
May	1	Balance	5	$450
	6	Sale...	3	
	8	Purchase..	10	420
	17	Sale...	4	
	30	Sale...	5	

Required Prepare a perpetual inventory record for the guitars. Then determine the amounts The Music Store should report for ending inventory and cost of goods sold by the FIFO method.

Exercise 6–3

Recording perpetual inventory transactions

Applying the moving-weighted-average-cost method in a perpetual inventory system

Cost of goods sold $5,175

Calculating gross margin under FIFO and the moving-weighted-average-cost method in a perpetual inventory system

Gross margin: Moving-weighted-average-cost method, $4,425

After preparing the FIFO perpetual inventory record in Exercise 6–2, journalize The Music Store's May 8 purchase of inventory on account and the cash sale on May 17 (sale price of each guitar was $800).

Exercise 6–4

Refer to The Music Store inventory data in Exercise 6–2. Assume that the store uses the moving-weighted-average-cost method. Prepare The Music Store's perpetual inventory record for the guitars on the moving-weighted-average-cost basis. Round average cost per unit to the nearest cent and all other amounts to the nearest dollar.

Exercise 6–5

Use your results from Exercises 6–2 and 6–4 to calculate the gross margin for The Music Store under both the FIFO and the moving-weighted-average-cost methods. Explain why the gross margin is higher under the moving-weighted-average-cost method.

Exercise 6–6

Carson Tackle Shop's accounting records yield the following data for the year ended December 31, 2010.

Inventory: January 1, 2010	$ 24,000
Purchases of inventory (on account)	147,000
Sales of inventory—80 percent on account, 20 percent for cash (cost $123,000)	225,000
Inventory at FIFO cost December 31, 2010	?

Recording perpetual inventory transactions

2. Gross margin $102,000

Required

1. Journalize Carson Tackle Shop's inventory transactions for the year in the perpetual system.
2. Report ending inventory, sales, cost of goods sold, and gross margin on the appropriate financial statement.

Exercise 6–7

Refer to the Carson Tackle Shop data in Exercise 6–6. Assume that Carson is using a periodic inventory system. Inventory on hand at December 31, 2010, was $48,000, based on the physical count.

Recording periodic inventory transactions

2. Gross margin $102,000

Required

1. Journalize Carson Tackle Shop's inventory transactions for the year in the periodic system.
2. Report ending inventory, sales, cost of goods sold, and gross margin on the appropriate financial statement. How do these amounts compare to the same amounts in the perpetual inventory system calculated in Exercise 6–6, Requirement 2?

Exercise 6–8

Balkin Office Products markets the ink used in inkjet printers. Balkin started the year with 10,000 containers of ink (moving-weighted-average cost of $9 each; FIFO cost of $8 each). During the year, Balkin purchased 80,000 containers of ink at $11 on the first day of its fiscal year and sold 70,000 units for $23 each, with all transactions on account. Balkin paid operating expenses throughout the year, a total of $500,000.

Journalize Balkin's purchases, sales, and operating expense transactions under the following format. Balkin uses the perpetual inventory system to account for inkjet printer ink.

Applying the moving-weighted-average and FIFO methods in a perpetual inventory system

Cost of goods sold: Moving-weighted-average cost $754,600

DEBIT/CREDIT AMOUNTS

Accounts	Moving-Weighted-Average*	FIFO

*Round moving-weighted-average unit cost to the nearest cent.

Exercise 6–9

Kelso Electrical's inventory records for industrial switches indicate the following at November 30, 2010:

Nov.			
	1	Beginning inventory	14 units at $80
	8	Purchase..	4 units at $85
	15	Purchase..	11 units at $90
	26	Purchase..	5 units at $95

The physical count of inventory at November 30, 2010, indicates that six units remain in ending inventory, and the company owns them.

Excel Spreadsheet Template

Computing ending inventory by applying four inventory costing methods in a periodic inventory system

3. FIFO cost of goods sold $2,360

Required Compute ending inventory and cost of goods sold using each of the following methods, assuming the periodic inventory system:

1. Specific-unit cost, assuming three $85 units and three $90 units are on hand on November 30, 2010.
2. Weighted-average cost.
3. First-in, first-out (FIFO).

Exercise 6–10

1. Supply the missing income statement amounts for each of the following companies for the year ended December 31, 2010:

Company	Net Sales	Beginning Inventory	Net Purchases	Ending Inventory	Cost of Goods Sold	Gross Margin
Arc Co.	$ 46,500	$ 6,300	$31,400	$ 9,700	(a)	$18,500
Bell Co.	(b)	13,700	46,500	(c)	$47,000	26,300
Court Co.	47,000	(d)	27,900	11,300	28,700	(e)
Dolan Co.	51,200	5,400	(f)	4,100	(g)	23,700

2. Prepare the income statement for Dolan Co., which uses the periodic inventory system. Dolan's operating expenses for the year were $8,700.

Exercise 6–11

This exercise tests your understanding of the three inventory methods. In the space provided, write the name of the inventory method that best fits the description. Assume that the cost of inventory is rising.

_____ a. Provides the same result for ending inventory in a periodic and in a perpetual inventory system.

_____ b. Maximizes reported net income when inventory purchase prices are falling.

_____ c. Results in a cost of ending inventory that is close to the current cost of replacing the inventory.

_____ d. Maximizes reported net income when inventory purchase prices are rising.

_____ e. Used to account for automobiles, jewellery, and art objects.

_____ f. Provides a smoother measure of ending inventory and cost of goods sold over time.

Exercise 6–12

Applying the lower-of-cost-and-
net-realizable-value rule to
inventories: perpetual system

(1) (4)

Robertson Garden Supplies, which uses a perpetual inventory system and the FIFO method, has these account balances at December 31, 2010, prior to releasing the financial statements for the year:

Inventory		Cost of Goods Sold		Sales Revenue	
Beg. bal. 50,000					
End. bal. 84,000		Bal. 500,000			Bal. 940,000

The company has determined that the net realizable value of the December 31, 2010, ending inventory is $70,000.

Required Prepare Robertson Garden Supplies' balance sheet at December 31, 2010, to show how Robertson would apply the lower-of-cost-and-net-realizable-value rule to inventories. Include a complete heading for the statement.

Exercise 6–13

**Excel Spreadsheet
Template**

Applying the lower-of-cost-
and-net-realizable-value rule to
inventories: periodic system

Gross margin $94,100

Valley Tool Company's income statement for the month ended August 31, 2010, reported the following data:

Income Statement

Sales revenue		$320,000
Cost of goods sold:		
Beginning inventory...	$ 62,000	
Net purchases..	243,700	
Cost of goods available for sale..........................	305,700	
Ending inventory...	85,700	
Cost of goods sold		220,000
Gross margin		$100,000

Before the financial statements were released, it was discovered that the current net realizable value of ending inventory was $79,800. Adjust the preceding income statement to apply the lower-of-cost-and-net-realizable-value rule to Valley Tool Company's inventory. Also, show the relevant portion of Valley Tool Company's balance sheet. The net realizable value of the beginning inventory was $85,000.

Exercise 6–14

Provence Bakery reported sales revenue of $128,000 and cost of goods sold of $71,000. Compute Provence Bakery's correct gross margin if the company made each of the following accounting errors. Show your work.

a. Ending inventory is overstated by $3,000.

b. Ending inventory is understated by $3,000.

Measuring the effect of an inventory error

a. Gross margin $54,000

Exercise 6–15

Maple Bay Marine Supply reported the comparative income statement for the years ended September 30, 2010 and 2009, shown below.

Correcting an inventory error

Net income before taxes 2009 $34,000

MAPLE BAY MARINE SUPPLY
Income Statement
For the Years Ended September 30, 2010 and 2009

	2010		2009	
Sales revenue......................................		$165,000		$146,000
Cost of goods sold:				
Beginning inventory..................	$ 16,500		$15,400	
Net purchases............................	91,000		78,000	
Cost of goods available..............	107,500		93,400	
Ending inventory.......................	23,600		16,500	
Cost of goods sold		83,500		76,900
Gross margin		81,100		69,100
Operating expenses......................		36,400		31,500
Net income before taxes		$ 44,500		$ 37,600

During 2010, accountants for the company discovered that ending 2009 inventory was overstated by $3,600. Prepare the corrected comparative income statement for the two-year period, complete with a heading for the statement. What was the effect of the error on net income for the two years combined? Explain your answer.

Exercise 6–16

Janet Klein, accountant of Portage Electronics Ltd., learned that Portage Electronics' $24 million cost of inventory at the end of last year was overstated by $3.6 million. She notified the company president, Eric Moffat, of the accounting error and the need to alert the company's lenders that last year's reported net income was incorrect. Moffat explained to Klein that there is no need to report the error to lenders because the error will counterbalance this year. This year's error will affect this year's net income in the opposite direction of last year's error. Even with no correction, Moffat reasons, net income for both years combined will be the same whether or not Portage Electronics Ltd. corrects its errors.

Assessing the effect of an inventory error on two years' statements

Required

1. Was last year's reported net income of $37.0 million overstated, understated, or correct? What was the correct amount of net income last year?

2. Is this year's net income of $41 million overstated, understated, or correct? What is the correct amount of net income for the current year?

3. Whose perspective is better, Klein's or Moffat's? Give your reason. Consider the trend of reported net income both without the correction and with the correction.

Exercise 6–17

Determine whether each of the actions on the next page in buying, selling, and accounting for inventories is ethical or unethical. Give your reason for each answer.

Ethical implications of inventory actions

1. Spartan Corporation knowingly overstated purchases to produce a high figure for cost of goods sold (low amount of net income). The real reason was to decrease the company's income tax payments to the government.

2. In applying the lower-of-cost-and-net-realizable-value rule to inventories, Kerr Industries recorded an excessively low realizable value for ending inventory. This allowed the company to pay no income tax for the year.

3. In a period of decreasing prices, Sparrow Distributors purchased lots of inventory shortly before year end to decrease the moving-weighted-average cost of goods sold and increase reported income for the year to reach the level of profit demanded by the company's investors.

4. During a period of rising prices, Callais Electrical Products delayed the purchase of inventory until after December 31, 2010, in order to keep 2010's moving-weighted-average cost of goods sold from growing too large. The delay in purchasing inventory helped net income of 2010 to reach the level of profit demanded by the company's investors.

5. Lacombe Sales Company deliberately overstated ending inventory in order to report higher profits (net income).

Exercise 6–18

Estimating inventory by the gross margin method

Est. inventory cost $260,000

Bathurst Company began April with inventory of $200,000. The business made net purchases of $600,000 and had net sales of $900,000 before a fire destroyed the company's inventory. For the past several years, Bathurst Company's gross margin on sales has been 40 percent. Estimate the cost of the inventory destroyed by the fire. Identify another reason owners and managers use the gross margin method to estimate inventory on a regular basis.

Exercise 6–19

Estimating inventory by the retail method

6

Est. ending inventory cost, Teenage line $125,000

Tanya's Designs has three lines of women's sportswear: Teenage, Young Woman, and Mature. The selling price of each item is double its cost price. On May 18, 2010, Tanya's Designs had a fire that destroyed the entire inventory. Sales for the period January 1 to May 18 were: Teenage, $420,000; Young Woman, $560,000; and Mature, $750,000. Inventory at January 1, 2010, was: Teenage, $95,000; Young Woman, $130,000; and Mature, $170,000. Purchases made from January 1 to May 18, at cost, were: Teenage, $240,000; Young Woman, $220,000; and Mature, $310,000.

Use the retail method to calculate the cost of the inventory lost in the fire.

SERIAL EXERCISE

This exercise continues the Haupt Consulting situation from Exercise 5–28 of Chapter 5. If you did not complete Exercise 5–28, you can still complete Exercise 6–20 as it is presented.

Exercise 6–20

Accounting for both merchandising and service transactions under the perpetual inventory system

1 2

1. Cost of goods sold $3,887

Consider the January 2011 transactions for Haupt Consulting Company that were presented in Chapter 5.

Jan.	2	Completed a consulting engagement and received cash of $7,200.
	2	Prepaid three months' office rent, $3,000.
	7	Purchased 100 units of software inventory on account, $1,900, plus freight in, $100.
	16	Paid employee salary, $1,400.
	18	Sold 70 software units on account, $3,100.
	19	Consulted with a client for a fee of $900 on account.
	21	Paid on account, $2,000.
	22	Purchased 200 units of software inventory on account, $4,600.
	24	Paid utilities, $300.
	28	Sold 100 units of software for cash, $4,000.
	31	Recorded the following adjusting entries:

        Accrued salary expense, $1,400.
        Prepaid rent expired, $1,000.
        Amortization of office furniture, $60, and of equipment, $33.
        Physical count of inventory, 120 units

Required

1. Prepare perpetual inventory records for January for Haupt Consulting Company using the moving-weighted-average perpetual method. Round average cost per unit to the nearest cent and all other amounts to the nearest dollar. (Note: You must calculate cost for the January 18, 22, 28, and 31 transactions.)

2. Journalize and post to T-accounts the January transactions using the perpetual inventory record created in Requirement 1. Key all items by date. Use the opening balances given in Serial Exercise 5-28 on page 282. Compute each account balance, and denote the balance as *Bal*.

3. Journalize and post to T-accounts the adjusting entries. Denote each adjusting amount as *Adj*. After posting all adjusting entries, prove the equality of debits and credits in the ledger.

CHALLENGE EXERCISES

Exercise 6–21

For each of the following situations, identify the inventory method that you are using or would prefer to use, or, given the use of a particular method, state the strategy that you would follow to accomplish your goal.

Inventory policy decisions

a. Inventory costs are increasing. Your business uses the FIFO method and is having an unexpectedly good year. It is near year end, and you need to keep net income from increasing too much.

b. Inventory costs have been stable for several years, and you expect costs to remain stable for the indefinite future. (Give your reason for your choice of method.)

c. Inventory costs are decreasing, and you want to maximize income.

d. Company management prefers an inventory policy that avoids extremes.

e. Your inventory turns over very rapidly, and the business uses a perpetual inventory system. Inventory costs are increasing, and the business prefers to report high income.

Exercise 6–22

Central Glass Products Ltd. is a leading provider of bottles for the brewing industry. Suppose the company recently reported these figures.

Evaluating a company's profitability

CENTRAL GLASS PRODUCTS LTD.
Income Statement
For the Years Ended December 31, 2010 and 2009 (amounts in thousands)

	2010	2009
Sales	$135,000	$103,000
Cost of sales	97,200	77,700
Gross margin	37,800	25,300
Cost and expenses		
Selling, general and administrative	27,800	21,100
Amortization	2,750	1,170
Restructuring charges	9,050	—
	39,600	22,270
Operating income (loss)	(1,800)	3,030
Other items (summarized)	(800)	(1,700)
Net income (loss)	$ (2,600)	$ 1,330

Required Evaluate Central Glass's operations during 2010 in comparison with 2009. Consider sales, gross margin, operating income, and net income. In the annual report, Central Glass's management describes the restructuring charges in 2010 as a one-time event that is not expected to recur. How does this additional information affect your evaluation?

BEYOND THE NUMBERS

Assessing the impact of the inventory costing method on the financial statements

The inventory costing method chosen by a company can affect the financial statements and thus the decisions of the users of those statements.

Required

1. A leading accounting researcher stated that one inventory costing method reports the more recent costs in the income statement, while another method reports the more recent costs in the balance sheet. In this person's opinion, this results in one or the other of the statements being "inaccurate" when prices are rising. What did the researcher mean?

2. Conservatism is an accepted accounting concept. Would you want management to be conservative in accounting for inventory if you were (a) a shareholder, and (b) a prospective shareholder? Give your reason.

3. Premier Cycle Shoppe follows conservative accounting and writes the value of its inventory of bicycles down to net realizable value, which has declined below cost. The following year, an unexpected cycling craze results in a demand for bicycles that far exceeds supply, and the net realizable value increases well above the previous cost. What effect will conservatism have on the income of Premier Cycle Shoppe over the two years?

ETHICAL ISSUE

During 2009, Bryant Electronics changed to the weighted-average-cost method of accounting for inventory. Suppose that during 2010, Bryant Electronics changes back to the FIFO method, and in the following year switches back to the weighted-average-cost method again.

Required

1. What would you think of a company's ethics if it changed accounting methods every year?
2. What accounting principle would changing methods every year violate?
3. Who can be harmed when a company changes its accounting methods too often? How?

PROBLEMS (GROUP A)

MyAccountingLab | All questions in this section appear in MyAccountingLab.

Problem 6–1A

Using the perpetual inventory system—FIFO

2. Cost of goods sold $9,280

Markham Leather, a distributor of leather products, uses the FIFO method for valuing inventories. It began August with 50 units of an inventory item that cost $80 each. During August, the store completed these inventory transactions:

			Units	Unit Cost	Unit Sale Price
Aug.	3	Sale	40		$140
	8	Purchase	80	$88	
	21	Sale	70		150
	30	Purchase	10	96	

Required

1. Prepare a perpetual inventory record for this item.
2. Determine the store's cost of goods sold for August.
3. Compute gross margin for August.

Problem 6–2A

Accounting for inventory using the perpetual system—FIFO

1. Cost of goods sold $38,350

Acme Distributors purchases inventory in crates of merchandise.

Assume the company began January with an inventory of 20 units that cost $300 each. During the month, the company purchased and sold merchandise on account as shown.

Jan.	10	Purchased 30 units at $320.
	15	Sold 40 units at $600.
	22	Purchased 70 units at $350.
	29	Sold 75 units at $700.

Assume Acme Distributors uses the FIFO cost method for valuing inventories. The company uses a perpetual inventory system.

Cash payments on account totalled $20,000. Company operating expenses for the month were $15,000. The company paid two-thirds in cash, with the rest accrued as Accounts Payable.

Required

1. Prepare a perpetual inventory record, at FIFO cost, for this merchandise.
2. Make journal entries to record the company's transactions.

Problem 6–3A

Refer to the Acme Distributors situation in Problem 6–2A. Keep all the data unchanged, except assume that Acme uses the moving-weighted-average-cost method.

Accounting for inventory in a perpetual system—moving-weighted-average cost

1. Cost of goods sold $38,374

Required

1. Prepared a perpetual inventory record at moving-weighted-average cost. Round the average unit cost to the nearest cent and all other amounts to the nearest dollar.
2. Prepare a multi-step income statement for Acme Distributors for the month of January.

Problem 6–4A

Prairie Hardware operates a store in Red Deer, Alberta. The company began 2010 with an inventory of 50 power nailers that cost $4,000 in total. During the year, the company purchased merchandise on account as follows:

Accounting for inventory in a perpetual system—FIFO

3. Gross margin $16,420

March (60 units at $85)	$ 5,100
August (40 units at $87)	3,480
October (180 units at $90)	16,200
Total purchases	$24,780

Cash payments on account during the year totalled $22,000.

During November 2010, the company sold 300 units of merchandise for $42,500, of which $26,000 was for cash and the balance was on account. Prairie uses the FIFO method for inventories.

Required

1. Make summary journal entries to record the company's transactions for the year ended December 31, 2010. The company uses a perpetual inventory system.
2. Determine the FIFO cost of the company's ending inventory at December 31, 2010. Use a T-account.
3. Calculate Prairie Hardware's gross margin for the year ended December 31, 2010.

Problem 6–5A

Sharpe Framing Co. began March with 73 units of inventory that cost $50 each. During the month, Sharpe made the following purchases:

Computing inventory by two methods—periodic system

2. Gross margin: Weighted-avg. $10,471

Mar.	4	113 units at $48
	12	81 units at $49
	19	167 units at $52
	25	44 units at $54

The company uses the periodic inventory system, and the physical count at March 31 includes 51 units of inventory on hand.

Required

1. Determine the ending inventory and cost-of-goods-sold amounts for the March financial statements under (a) weighted-average cost, and (b) FIFO cost. Round average cost per unit to the nearest cent and all other amounts to the nearest dollar.
2. Sales revenue for March totalled $32,000. Compute Sharpe's gross margin for March under each method.
3. Which method will result in the lowest income taxes for Sharpe? Why?
4. Which method will result in the highest net income for Sharpe? Why?

Problem 6–6A

Using the periodic inventory system—weighted-average and FIFO

③

2. Cost of goods sold, weighted average $274,260

Rupert Products, which uses a periodic inventory system, began 2010 with 6,000 units of inventory that cost a total of $90,000. During 2010, Rupert Products purchased merchandise on account as follows:

Purchase 1 (10,000 units at $14 per unit)................................ $140,000
Purchase 2 (20,000 units at $12 per unit)................................ 240,000

At year end, the physical count indicated 15,000 units of inventory on hand.

Required

1. How many units did Rupert Products sell during the year? The sale price per unit was $28. Determine Rupert's sales revenue for the year.

2. Compute cost of goods sold by the weighted-average method. Round average cost per unit to the nearest cent and all other amounts to the nearest dollar. Then determine gross margin for the year.

3. Compute cost of goods sold by the FIFO method. Then determine gross margin for the year.

4. Compare the gross margins you calculated for each inventory method in Requirements 2 and 3. What conclusions can you draw when the purchase prices for inventory are falling?

Problem 6–7A

Using the perpetual and periodic inventory systems

① ③

3. Gross margin $4,100

Thunder Performance Tire began June with 50 units of inventory that cost $132 each. During June, Thunder Performance Tire completed these inventory transactions:

			Unit	Unit Cost	Unit Selling Price
Jun.	2	Purchase	12	$135	
	8	Sale	27	132	$180
	13	Sale	23	132	180
		Sale	3	135	185
	17	Purchase	24	135	
	22	Sale	31	135	185
	29	Purchase	24	140	

Required

1. The above data are taken from Thunder Performance Tire's perpetual inventory records. Which cost method does Thunder Performance Tire use?

2. Compute Thunder Performance Tire's cost of goods sold for June under the

   a. Perpetual inventory system

   b. Periodic inventory system

3. Compute gross margin for June.

Problem 6–8A

Applying the lower-of-cost-and-net-realizable-value rule to inventories

④

Cost of goods sold $66,300,000

Chesley Home Furniture has recently been plagued with lacklustre sales. The rate of inventory turnover has dropped, and some of the business's merchandise is gathering dust. At the same time, competition has forced the business to lower the selling prices of its inventory. It is now December 31, 2010. Assume the net realizable value of a Chesley Home Furniture store's ending inventory is $1,100,000 below what Chesley Home Furniture paid for the goods, which was $10,300,000. Before any adjustments at the end of the period, assume the store's Cost of Goods Sold account has a balance of $65,200,000.

Required

a. What action should Chesley Home Furniture take in this situation, if any?

b. Give any journal entry required.

c. At what amount should Chesley Home Furniture report Inventory on the balance sheet?

d. At what amount should the business report cost of goods sold on the income statement?

e. Discuss the accounting principle or concept that is most relevant to this situation.

Problem 6–9A

The accounting records of Webb Music Stores show these data (in thousands):

Correcting inventory errors over a three-year period

1. Net income 2010 $30 thou.

	2010	2009	2008
Net sales revenue.........................	$426	$366	$378
Cost of goods sold:			
Beginning inventory................	$ 36	$ 60	$ 96
Net purchases...........................	276	240	216
Cost of goods available...........	312	300	312
Less ending inventory.............	72	36	60
Cost of goods sold	240	264	252
Gross margin	186	102	126
Operating expenses	148	92	110
Net income.................................	$ 38	$ 10	$ 16

In early 2011, a team of auditors discovered that the ending inventory of 2008 had been understated by $10 thousand. Also, the ending inventory for 2010 had been overstated by $8 thousand. The ending inventory at December 31, 2009, was correct.

Required

1. Show corrected comparative income statements for the three years.

2. State whether each year's net income as reported here and the related owner's equity amounts are understated or overstated. For each incorrect figure, indicate the amount of the understatement or overstatement.

Problem 6–10A

Sweeney Stores estimates its inventory by the gross margin method when preparing monthly financial statements (Sweeney Stores uses the periodic method otherwise). For the past two years, gross margin has averaged 30 percent of net sales. The business's inventory records for its stores reveal the following data:

 **Excel Spreadsheet Template**

Estimating inventory by the gross margin method, preparing the income statement

2. Gross margin $3,337,500

Inventory: July 1, 2010...	$ 240,000
Transactions during July:	
Purchases...	7,890,000
Purchases returns...	230,000
Sales..	11,250,000
Sales returns...	125,000

Required

1. Estimate the July 31, 2010, inventory using the gross margin method.
2. Prepare the July 2010 income statement through gross margin for Sweeney Stores.

Problem 6–11A

Burrows Shoe Company has a periodic inventory system and uses the gross margin method of estimating inventories for interim financial statements. The company had the following account balances for the fiscal year ended August 31, 2010:

Accounting for inventory by the periodic system, estimating inventory by the gross margin method

1. Est. inventory, Aug. 31, 2010 $105,000

Inventory: Sept. 1, 2009	$ 195,000
Purchases..	1,157,000
Purchases Returns and Allowances	23,000
Freight In	11,000
Sales..	1,922,000
Sales Returns and Allowances...	22,000

Required

1. Use the gross margin method to estimate the cost of the business's ending inventory, assuming the business has an average gross margin rate of 35 percent.

2. The business has done a physical count of the inventory on hand on August 31, 2010. For convenience, this inventory was calculated using the retail selling prices marked on the goods, which amounted to $152,000. Use the information from Requirement 1 to calculate the cost of the inventory counted.

3. What is the cost of the business's estimated inventory overage or shrinkage?

4. Give the summary journal entries required at August 31, 2010. Also record any overage or shrinkage.

Problem 6–12A

Computing ending inventory by applying two inventory costing methods in a periodic inventory system

③

2. Gross margin (a) $238,033

Sherman Office Supplies distributes office furniture. The company's fiscal year ends on December 31, 2010. On September 30, 2010, one department in the company had in inventory 20 office suites that cost $1,800 each. During the quarter, the department purchased merchandise on account as follows:

	Units	Unit Cost	Total
October	60	$1,850	$111,000
November	40	1,900	76,000
December	30	1,950	58,500

Sales for each month in the quarter were as follows:

	Units	Selling Price	Total
October	50	$3,600	$180,000
November	20	3,700	74,000
December	60	3,800	228,000

Operating expenses in the quarter were $210,000.

Required

1. Determine the cost of the department's ending inventory at January 31, 2010, under (a) weighted-average costing, and (b) FIFO costing. Assume the company uses the periodic inventory system and determines cost of goods sold at the end of each quarter.

2. Prepare the department's income statement for the quarter ended December 31, 2010, under each method described in Requirement 1. Show gross margin and operating income.

Problem 6–13A

Computing ending inventory by applying two inventory costing methods in a perpetual inventory system

①

2. Gross margin (a) $238,540

Refer to the information in Problem 6–12A. Assume that the company uses a perpetual inventory system. Also assume that monthly purchases of inventory occur on the first day of each month.

Required

1. Determine the cost of the department's ending inventory at December 31, 2010, under (a) moving-weighted-average costing, and (b) FIFO costing.

2. Prepare the department's income statement for the quarter ended December 31, 2010, under each method described in Requirement 1. Show gross margin and operating income.

Problem 6–14A

Accounting for inventory by the perpetual inventory system, applying the moving-weighted-average and FIFO costing methods, estimating inventory by the gross margin method

① ⑤ ⑥

1. Cost of goods sold (a) Moving avg. $676,170

Toffler Auto Parts uses the perpetual inventory system for the purchase and sale of inventory and had the following information available on November 30, 2010:

Purchases and Sales		Number of Units	Cost or Selling Price per Unit
Nov.	1 Balance of inventory	3,900	$20
	7 Purchased	6,000	28
	8 Sold	4,500	38
	12 Purchased	7,500	26
	16 Sold	9,000	42
	21 Purchased	4,500	26
	25 Purchased	10,500	24
	29 Sold	13,500	42

Required

1. Calculate the cost of goods sold and the cost of the ending inventory for November under each of the following inventory costing methods: (a) moving-weighted-average cost, and (b) FIFO cost.

2. Prepare the journal entries required to record the transactions using the perpetual inventory system with FIFO costing.

3. An internal audit has discovered that a new employee—an accounting clerk—had been stealing merchandise and covering up the shortage by changing the inventory records. For example, if 120 units were purchased at $20 per unit, he would record it as 100 units purchased at $24 per unit and then steal the other 20 units.

    The external auditors examined the accounting records prior to the employment of the individual and noted that the company has an average gross margin rate of 40 percent. They estimate that 95 percent of the incorrectly costed units have been sold.

    Use the gross margin method to estimate the cost of the inventory shortage (under the FIFO costing method) and give the journal entry required to correct it.

4. What would be the effect on the net income for the year ending November 30, 2010, if the inventory shortage had not been discovered? For the year ending November 30, 2011?

PROBLEMS (GROUP B)

 MyAccountingLab | All questions in this section appear in MyAccountingLab.

Problem 6–1B

Ferrell Lawn Supply, which uses the FIFO method, began March with 200 units of inventory that cost $20 each. During March, Ferrell completed these inventory transactions:

Using the perpetual inventory system—FIFO

(1)

			Units	Unit Cost	Unit Sale Price
Mar.	2	Purchase	48	$25	
	8	Sale	160		$72
	17	Purchase	96	30	
	22	Sale	124		80

Required

1. Prepare a perpetual inventory record for the lawn supply merchandise.
2. Determine Ferrell's cost of goods sold for March.
3. Compute gross margin for March.

Problem 6–2B

Pierce Imports is a furniture distributor. The following information is for one item of inventory, kitchen chairs, for the month of February. The store purchased and sold merchandise on account as follows:

Accounting for inventory in a perpetual system—FIFO

(1)

Feb.	1	Opening inventory	50 chairs at $ 50
	3	Purchase	60 chairs at $ 55
	10	Sale	100 chairs at $100
	22	Purchase	90 chairs at $ 60
	24	Sale	70 chairs at $120

Assume that Pierce Imports uses the FIFO cost method. All sales were made on account. Operating expenses were $12,400, with two-thirds paid in cash and the rest accrued in Accounts Payable.

Required

1. Prepare a perpetual inventory record, at FIFO cost, for this merchandise.
2. Make journal entries to record the company's transactions.

Problem 6–3B

Refer to the Pierce Imports situation in Problem 6–2B. Keep all the data unchanged, except that Pierce uses the moving-weighted-average-cost method.

Accounting for inventory in a perpetual system—moving-weighted-average cost

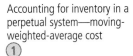

Required

1. Prepare a perpetual inventory record at moving-weighted-average cost. Round the average unit cost to the nearest cent and all other amounts to the nearest dollar.

2. Prepare a multi-step income statement for Pierce Imports for the month of February.

Problem 6–4B

Accounting for inventory in a perpetual system—FIFO

(1)

Chen Hardware Store purchases inventory in crates of merchandise, so each unit of inventory is a crate of tools or building supplies. Assume you are dealing with a single department in the store. Assume the department began the year with an inventory of 40 units that cost a total of $6,000. During the year, the department purchased merchandise on account as follows:

April 30 (60 units at $145)	$ 8,700
July 31 (100 units at $145)	14,500
October 31 (200 units at $140)	28,000
Total purchases	$51,200

Cash payments on account during the year totalled $38,000.

During the year, the department sold 380 units of merchandise for $115,000, as follows:

March 31:	30 units
June 30:	50 units
September 30:	90 units
December 31:	210 units

Of the sales revenue, $103,000 was from cash sales and the balance was on account. Assume Chen uses the FIFO method for inventories. Department operating expenses for the year were $56,000. The department paid two-thirds of the operating expenses in cash and accrued the rest.

Required

1. Make summary journal entries to record the department transactions for the year ended December 31, 2010. Chen uses a perpetual inventory system.

2. Determine the FIFO cost of the store's ending inventory at December 31, 2010. Use a T-account.

3. Prepare the department's income statement for the year ended December 31, 2010. Include a complete heading, and show totals for the gross margin and net income.

Problem 6–5B

Computing inventory by two methods—periodic system

(3)

Comet Appliances and Supply began December with 280 units of inventory that cost $180 each. During December, the store made the following purchases:

Dec.	3	430 units at $182
	12	190 units at $184
	18	420 units at $186
	24	426 units at $184

The store uses the periodic inventory system, and the physical count at December 31 indicates that 458 units of inventory are on hand.

Required

1. Determine the ending inventory and cost-of-goods-sold amounts for the December financial statements under the weighted-average-cost and FIFO methods. Round the average cost per unit to the nearest cent and all other amounts to the nearest dollar.

2. Sales revenue for December totalled $384,000. Compute Comet Appliances and Supply's gross margin for December under each method.

3. Which method will result in the lower income taxes for Comet? Why? Which method will result in the higher net income for Comet? Why?

Problem 6–6B

Ball Hardware Company, which uses a periodic inventory system, began 2010 with 9,000 units of inventory that cost a total of $45,000. During 2010, Ball purchased merchandise on account as follows:

Using the periodic inventory system—FIFO and weighted average

Purchase 1 (15,000 units)	$ 90,000
Purchase 2 (30,000 units)	210,000

At year end, the physical count indicated 10,000 units of inventory on hand.

Required

1. How many units did Ball sell during the year? The sale price per unit was $14. Determine Ball's sales revenue for the year.
2. Compute cost of goods sold by both the FIFO and the weighted-average-cost method. Then determine gross margin for the year under each method.

Problem 6–7B

The Canvas Company (TCC) began August 2010 with 100 units of inventory that cost $60 each. The sale price of each of those units was $120. During August, TCC completed these inventory transactions:

Using the perpetual and periodic inventory systems

			Units	Unit Cost	Units Sales Price
Aug.	3	Sale	32	$60	$120
	8	Purchase	160	62	124
	11	Sale	68	60	120
	19	Sale	18	62	124
	24	Sale	70	62	124
	30	Purchase	36	64	126
	31	Sale	12	62	124

Required

1. The above data are taken from TCC's perpetual inventory records. Which cost method does the company use?
2. Compute TCC's cost of goods sold for August 2010 under the
   a. Perpetual inventory system
   b. Periodic inventory system
3. Compute the gross margin for August 2010.

Problem 6–8B

Deck Building Supplies has recently been plagued with declining sales. The rate of inventory turnover has dropped, and some of the company's merchandise is gathering dust. At the same time, competition has forced Deck Building Supplies to lower the selling prices of its inventory. It is now December 31, 2010, and the net realizable value of Deck Building Supplies' ending inventory is $1,092,000 below what the business actually paid for the goods, which was $7,644,000. Before any adjustments at the end of the period, Deck Building Supplies' Cost of Goods Sold account has a balance of $44,928,000.

Applying the lower-of-cost-and-net-realizable-value rule to inventories

What action should Deck Building Supplies take in this situation, if any? Give any journal entry required. At what amount should Deck Building Supplies report Inventory on the balance sheet? At what amount should the company report Cost of Goods Sold on the income statement? Discuss the accounting principle or concept that is most relevant to this situation.

Problem 6–9B

Correcting inventory errors over a three-year period

(5)

The books of Hayes Windows and Siding show these data (in thousands):

	2010	2009	2008
Net sales revenue.........................	$270	$205	$180
Cost of goods sold:			
Beginning inventory................	$ 49	$ 41	$ 52
Net purchases..........................	146	101	98
Cost of goods available...........	195	142	150
Less ending inventory.............	52	49	41
Cost of goods sold..................	143	93	109
Gross margin	127	112	71
Operating expenses	89	82	54
Net income...................................	$ 38	$ 30	$ 17

In early 2011, a team of Canada Revenue Agency auditors discovered that the ending inventory of 2008 had been overstated by $9 thousand. Also, the ending inventory for 2010 had been understated by $4 thousand. The ending inventory at December 31, 2009, was correct.

Required

1. Show corrected comparative income statements for the three years.

2. State whether each year's net income as reported here and the related owner's equity amounts are understated or overstated. For each incorrect figure, indicate the amount of the understatement or overstatement.

Problem 6–10B

Excel Spreadsheet Template

Estimating ending inventory by the gross margin method, preparing the income statement

(7)

Assume Falcon Linen Stores estimates its inventory by the gross margin method when preparing monthly financial statements (it uses the periodic method otherwise). For the past two years, the gross margin has averaged 40 percent of net sales. Assume further that the company's inventory records for its stores reveal the following data:

Inventory: June 1, 2010	$ 240,000
Transactions during June:	
Purchases	2,460,000
Sales	4,180,000

Required

1. Estimate the June 30, 2010, inventory using the gross margin method.

2. Prepare the June income statement through gross margin for Falcon Linen Stores.

Problem 6–11B

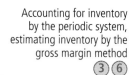

Accounting for inventory by the periodic system, estimating inventory by the gross margin method

(3) (6)

Kenora Supplies has a periodic inventory system and uses the gross margin method of estimating inventories for interim financial statements. The business had the following account balances for the fiscal year ended August 31, 2010:

Inventory: September 1, 2009	$ 68,000
Purchases	590,000
Purchases Returns and Allowances	18,000
Freight In..	12,000
Sales	1,050,000
Sales Returns and Allowances	25,000

Required

1. Use the gross margin method to estimate the cost of the business's ending inventory, assuming the business has an average gross margin rate of 45 percent.

2. The business has done a physical count of the inventory on hand on August 31, 2010. For convenience, this inventory was calculated using the retail selling prices marked on the goods, which amounted to $84,750. Use the information from Requirement 1 to calculate the cost of the inventory counted.

3. What is the cost of the business's estimated inventory shortage?

4. Give the summary journal entries required at August 31, 2010, and the adjustment required for the shortage.

5. Of what other use would the information in Requirement 4 be to the business?

Problem 6–12B

Pinton Industrial Supplies distributes industrial equipment. The company's fiscal year ends on December 31, 2010. One department in the company had 50 items that cost $540 each on hand at October 1, 2010. During the quarter, the department purchased merchandise on account as shown here.

Computing ending inventory by applying two inventory costing methods in a periodic inventory system

	Units	Unit Cost	Total
October	120	$585	$70,200
November	24	360	8,640
December	48	450	21,600

Sales for each month in the quarter were as follows:

	Units	Selling Price	Total
October	36	$1,260	$ 45,360
November	108	1,080	116,640
December	60	990	59,400

Operating expenses in the quarter were $60,000.

Required

1. Determine the cost of the department's ending inventory at December 31, 2010, under (a) the weighted-average-cost method, and (b) the FIFO method. Assume the company uses the periodic inventory system and determines cost of goods sold at the end of the quarter.

2. Prepare the department's income statement for the quarter ended December 31, 2010, under each method described in Requirement 1. Show totals for gross margin and operating income.

Problem 6–13B

Refer to the information in Problem 6–12B. Assume that the company uses a perpetual inventory system. Also assume that monthly purchases of inventory occur on the first day of each month.

Computing ending inventory by applying two inventory costing methods in a perpetual inventory system

Required

1. Determine the cost of the department's ending inventory at December 31, 2010, under (a) moving-weighted-average cost, and (b) FIFO cost.

2. Prepare the department's income statement for the quarter ended December 31, 2010, under each method described in Requirement 1. Show totals for gross margin and operating income.

Problem 6–14B

Booth Sales uses the perpetual inventory system for the purchase and sale of inventory and had the following information available on August 31, 2010:

Accounting for inventory by the perpetual inventory system, applying the moving-weighted-average and FIFO costing methods estimating inventory by the gross margin method

Purchases and Sales		Number of Units	Cost or Selling Price per Unit
Aug.	1 Balance of inventory	810	$15
	7 Purchased	2,250	14
	8 Sold	1,800	25
	12 Purchased	1,575	15
	16 Sold	2,600	26
	21 Purchased	1,800	17
	25 Purchased	2,700	19
	29 Sold	3,600	27

Required

1. Calculate the cost of goods sold and the cost of the ending inventory for August under each of the following inventory costing methods: (a) moving-weighted-average cost, and (b) FIFO cost.

2. Prepare the journal entries required to record the August transactions using the perpetual inventory system with FIFO costing.

3. An internal audit has discovered that two new employees—an accounting clerk and an employee from the purchasing department—have been stealing merchandise and covering up the shortage by changing the inventory records. For example, if 130 units were purchased at $10 per unit, they would record it as 100 units purchased at $13 per unit and then steal the other 30 units.

   The external auditors examined the accounting records prior to the employment of the two individuals and noted that the company had an average gross margin rate of 50 percent. They estimate that 90 percent of the incorrectly costed units have been sold.

   Use the gross margin method to estimate the cost of the inventory shortage (under the FIFO costing method) and give the journal entry required to correct it.

4. What would be the effect on the net income for the year ending August 31, 2010, if the inventory shortage had not been discovered? For the year ending August 31, 2011?

CHALLENGE PROBLEMS

Problem 6–1C

Inventory measurement and income

An anonymous source advised Canada Revenue Agency (CRA) that Jim Chaney, owner of Chaney Grocery Store, has been filing fraudulent tax returns for the past several years. You, a tax auditor with CRA, are in the process of auditing Chaney Grocery Store for the year ended December 31, 2010. The tax returns for the past five years show a decreasing value for ending inventory from 2006, when Williams bought the business, to 2009; the return for 2010 shows the same sort of decrease. You have performed a quick survey of the large store and the attached warehouse and observed that both seemed very well stocked.

Required Does the information set forth above suggest anything to you that might confirm the anonymous tip? What would you do to confirm or deny your suspicions?

Problem 6–2C

Estimating inventory from incomplete records

It is Monday morning. You heard on the morning news that a client of your public accounting firm, Mainland Electronics, had a fire the previous Friday night that destroyed its office and warehouse, and you concluded that inventory records as well as inventory probably perished in the fire. Since you had been at Mainland Electronics on the previous Friday preparing the monthly income statement for the previous month that ended on Thursday, you realize you probably have the only current financial information available for Mainland Electronics.

Upon arrival at your firm's office, you meet your partner who confirms your suspicions. Mainland Electronics lost its entire inventory and its records. She tells you that the company wants your firm to prepare information for a fire loss claim for Mainland Electronics' insurance company for the inventory.

You know the audit file for the fiscal year that ended three months earlier contains a complete section dealing with inventory and the four product lines Mainland Electronics carried, including the most recent gross margin rate for each line. The file will show total inventory and how much inventory there was by product line at the year end. You also recall that the file contains an analysis of sales by product line for the past several years and that Mainland Electronics used a periodic inventory system.

Required Explain how you would use the information available to you to calculate the fire loss by product line.

Extending Your Knowledge

DECISION PROBLEM

Alpine Camping Supplies is nearing the end of its first year of operations. The company uses the periodic inventory method and made inventory purchases of $176,250 during the year as follows:

January	150	units at $165	=	$ 24,750
July	600	units at $195	=	117,000
November	150	units at $230	=	34,500
Totals	900			$176,250

Sales for the year will be 750 units for $290,000 revenue. Expenses other than cost of goods sold will be $65,000. The owner of the company is undecided about whether to adopt FIFO or weighted-average costing as the company's method.

The company has storage capacity for 600 additional units of inventory. Inventory prices are expected to stay at $230 per unit for the next few months. The president is considering purchasing 150 additional units of inventory at $230 each before the end of the year. He wishes to know how the purchase would affect net income before taxes under both the FIFO and weighted-average-costing methods.

Required

1. To help the owner make the decision, prepare income statements under FIFO costing and under weighted-average costing, both without and with the year-end purchase of 150 units of inventory at $230 per unit.

2. Compare net income before taxes under FIFO costing without and with the year-end purchase. Make the same comparison under weighted-average costing. Under which method does the year-end purchase have the greater effect on net income before taxes?

3. If the company wanted to manipulate net income for the year, is one method more manipulative than the other?

Assessing the impact of a year-end purchase of inventory—periodic system

1. Without purchase:
FIFO gross margin $116,250
Weighted-average gross margin $108,000

FINANCIAL STATEMENT CASE

The notes are an important part of a company's financial statements, giving valuable details that would clutter the tabular data presented in the statements. This problem will help you learn to use a company's inventory notes. Refer to the Sun-Rype Products Ltd. financial statements and the related notes in Appendix B. Answer the following questions:

1. What types of inventory does Sun-Rype have? What was the value of each category at December 31, 2008? At December 31, 2007?

2. What valuation method does Sun-Rype use for valuing each category of inventory? *Hint:* Refer to the significant accounting policies in Note 1.

3. What costs are included in the calculation of finished goods inventory?

Inventories

7 Accounting Information Systems

What is an accounting information system, and why is it important?

What are the differences between manual and computerized accounting systems?

How can special journals be used to combine similar transactions and speed the accounting process?

These questions and others will be answered throughout this chapter. The Decision Guidelines at the end of this chapter will provide the answers in a useful summary.

LEARNING OBJECTIVES

1. Describe an effective accounting information system

2. Understand the elements of computerized and manual accounting systems

3. Journalize and post transactions using the sales journal, the cash receipts journal, and the accounts receivable subsidiary ledger

4. Journalize and post transactions using the purchases journal, the cash payments journal, and the accounts payable subsidiary ledger

5. Balance the ledgers

6. Use special journals to record and post transactions with sales taxes

7. Assess the impact on accounting information systems of international financial reporting standards (IFRS)

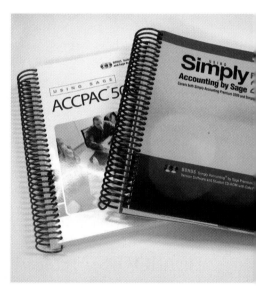

Wayne Cahill, CGA, has been in public practice for 24 years. Client accounting records have changed significantly during that time. In today's fast-paced environment, Wayne helps his clients develop strong accounting systems to ensure that financial statements are provided on a timely basis with consistently reliable information. Strong systems are imperative, he feels:

"There is a clear correlation between the success of the business and the strength of the accounting system. Accurate, timely information allows the business owner to have confidence when making key decisions that may significantly impact the operations. In addition, when the owner has taken the time to build solid accounting systems, you can bet that he or she has most likely developed excellent systems around the operations side of the business that keep things running smoothly."

"The computerized accounting packages have become very user friendly. Most of my clients can use these packages without extensive training in the fundamentals of accounting. The program will help them manage accounts receivable and accounts payable, and will provide the company with preliminary financial statements. I can then review the statements and make the adjustments necessary to finalize them. It is a real value-added approach. It allows the clients to do their own data entry, and they only pay me for my accounting knowledge, rather than my bookkeeping skills. I can concentrate on analyzing their businesses and advising them on significant accounting and tax issues."

Every organization needs an accounting system. An **accounting information system** is the combination of personnel, records, and procedures that a business uses to meet its needs for financial data. The system collects information, processes it, and produces reports that meet users' needs. We have already been using the records portion of an accounting information system in this text. It consists of two basic input components:

- A general journal
- A general ledger

Every accounting system has these components, but this simple system can efficiently handle only a few transactions per accounting period. Businesses cope with heavy transaction loads in two ways: computerization and specialization. We *computerize* to do the accounting faster and more reliably. *Specialization* combines similar transactions to speed the process. The second half of this chapter covers special journals that can be used for repetitive transactions.

Effective Accounting Information Systems

Good personnel are critical to success. Employees must be both competent and honest. Good design features also make an accounting system run smoothly. An effective system—whether computerized or manual—provides

OBJECTIVE (1)
Describe an effective accounting information system

- Control
- Compatibility
- Flexibility
- Reports that meet users' needs
- A favourable cost/benefit relationship

Features

Control Owners and managers must *control* the business. *Internal controls* safeguard assets and eliminate waste. They are the methods and procedures used to authorize transactions, to ensure adherence to management policy, to safeguard assets and records, to prevent and detect error and fraud, to provide security by limiting access to assets and records, and to ensure that information produced is relevant, accurate, and timely.

For example, in companies such as Sun-Rype Products Ltd. and Canadian National Railway Company (CN), managers control cash payments to avoid theft through unauthorized payments. VISA, MasterCard, American Express, and other credit-card companies keep accurate records of their accounts receivable to ensure that customers are billed and collections are received on time.

Compatibility A *compatible* system is one that works smoothly with the business's operations, personnel, and organizational structure. An example is The Bank of Nova Scotia, which is organized as a network of branch offices. The bank's top managers want to know how much revenue was generated in each region where the bank does business. They also want to analyze the bank's loans in different geographic regions. If revenues and loans in Alberta or Nova Scotia are lagging, the managers can concentrate their collection efforts in that region. They may relocate some branch offices, open new branches, or hire new personnel to increase their revenues and net income. A compatible accounting *information* system conforms to the particular needs of the business.

Flexibility   Organizations evolve. They develop new products, sell off unprofitable operations and acquire new ones, adjust employee pay scales, and decide to "go green." Changes in the business often call for changes in the accounting system. A well-designed system is *flexible* if it accommodates changes without needing a complete overhaul. Consider Bombardier's acquisition of Canadair, the aircraft manufacturer. Bombardier's accounting system had the flexibility to fold Canadair's financial statements into those of Bombardier Inc., the parent company.

Reports that Meet Users' Needs   If the accounting system processes the information collected but does not produce reports that are usable, then the accounting system is lacking. Suppose a company purchases a computerized accounting package that cannot be modified to produce the special reports the company used to produce with its old system. To make comparisons to historical financial data, the company has to create spreadsheets outside the new accounting package to produce the reports it needs. This is a problem. Some accounting packages, such as ACCPAC®, allow users to program user preferences for financial statement presentation; however, some accounting packages do not allow this.

Favourable Cost/Benefit Relationship   Achieving control, compatibility, and flexibility costs money. Managers strive for a system that offers maximum benefits at a minimum cost—that is, a favourable *cost/benefit relationship.* Most small companies, such as Steveston Marine and Hardware, an independent hardware store near Vancouver, use off-the-shelf computerized accounting packages. Examples of such packages are ACCPAC®, Simply Accounting®, and QuickBooks®. Less-expensive accounting software may have limited flexibility and limited capabilities. The very smallest businesses might not computerize at all. But large companies, such as the brokerage firm ScotiaMcLeod, have specialized needs for information. For them, customized programming is a must because the benefits—in terms of information tailored to the company's needs—far outweigh the cost of the system. The result? Better decisions.

All these features are needed whether the accounting system is computerized or manual. Let's begin with a computerized system.

Components of a Computerized Accounting System

A computerized accounting system has two basic components in addition to the personnel and procedures to operate it:

- Hardware
- Software

Hardware is the electronic equipment that includes computers, monitors, printers, and the network that connects them. Most systems require a **network** to link computers. In a networked system, a **server** stores the program and the data. With its network, a KPMG auditor in Calgary can access the data of a client located in Tokyo, Japan. The result is a speedier audit for the client, often at lower cost than if the auditor had to perform all the work on site in Tokyo.

Software is the set of programs that drives the computer. Accounting software reads, edits, and stores transaction data. It also generates the reports you can use to run the business. Many software packages are flexible. For example, a company that is only partly computerized may use the computer to account for employee payroll, and sales and accounts receivable. The other parts of the accounting system may be manual.

For large enterprises, such as Molson Canada and Royal Bank of Canada, the accounting software is integrated into the company **database**, or computerized storehouse of information. Many business databases, or *management information systems*, include both accounting and nonaccounting data. For example, VIA Rail, in negotiating a union contract, often needs to examine the relationship between the employment history and salary levels of company employees. VIA's database provides the data that managers need to negotiate effectively with their labour unions. During negotiations, both parties carry laptops so that they can access the database and analyze data on the spot.

Personnel who operate the system must be properly trained. Properly trained staff are critical to the success of any accounting information system. Modern accounting systems give nonaccounting personnel access to parts (but not all) of the system. For example, a Frito-Lay Canada marketing manager (a non-accountant) may use a computer to access regional sales data (accounting information) to identify the territory that needs a promotional campaign. Management of a computerized accounting system requires careful consideration of data security and screening of the people in the organization who will have access to the data. Security is usually achieved with *passwords*, codes that restrict access to computerized records.

REAL WORLD EXAMPLE

Access to computer information must be strictly controlled. At a Bay store, it would be risky for all employees to gain access to customer accounts. An unauthorized employee could change a customer's account balance or learn confidential information about the customer. Hence, access codes limit access to certain information. Source documents should support all sensitive changes to computer files.

DID YOU GET IT?

MyAccountingLab

To check your understanding of the material in this Learning Objective, complete these questions. The solutions appear on MyAccountingLab so you can check your progress.

1. Why does every business need an accounting information system? Give several reasons.

2. Suppose you are the controller for a small industrial ventilation company that wants to change accounting systems. The new system you are considering will not accept the current alpha characters in the job-order numbers. Each job is assigned a number, and then, as extras are added to the job, an alpha character is added to the job-order number, for example, job 1645a. Which feature of a good accounting system is being compromised, and what could you do to solve this dilemma?

3. How might a business such as Zellers save money with a computerized information system? How might a business such as McDonald's save money with a computerized information system?

How Computerized and Manual Accounting Systems Work

Computerized accounting systems have replaced manual systems in many organizations—even small businesses such as Steveston Marine and Hardware. As we discuss the stages of data processing, observe the differences between a computerized system and a manual system. The relationship among the three stages of data processing—inputs, processing, and outputs—is shown in Exhibit 7–1.

OBJECTIVE ②
Understand the elements of computerized and manual accounting systems

| EXHIBIT 7–1 | The Three Stages of Data Processing |

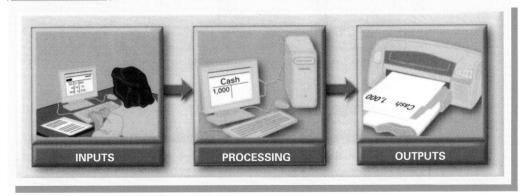

INPUTS   PROCESSING   OUTPUTS

KEY POINT

The output (financial reports) can only be as reliable as the input. If the input is incorrect or incomplete, the output will be flawed.

REAL WORLD EXAMPLE

Often, a cash register doubles as a computer terminal, called a point-of-sale terminal. The cashier passes the Universal Product Code (UPC) of merchandise over the scanner, which identifies the merchandise to the computer. The scanner eliminates errors in recording sales and automatically updates inventory records (costs and units) in a perpetual inventory system, as discussed in Chapter 5.

Inputs   Inputs come from source documents, such as orders received from customers, sales receipts, and bank deposit slips. Inputs are usually grouped by type. For example, a firm would enter cash sales separately from credit sales and purchases.

Processing   In a manual system, *processing* includes journalizing transactions, posting to the accounts, and preparing the financial statements. A computerized system also processes transactions, but without the intermediate steps (journal, ledger, and trial balance). The initial data entered will be posted automatically to the ledger and then processed into reports and financial statements.

Outputs   *Outputs* are the reports used for decision making, including the financial statements. Business owners can make better decisions with the reports produced by a good accounting system. In a computerized accounting system, a trial balance is a report (an output). But a manual system would treat the trial balance as a *processing* step leading to the preparation of financial statements. Exhibit 7–2 is an overview of a computerized accounting system. Start with data inputs in the lower-left corner.

EXHIBIT 7–2   Overview of a Computerized Accounting System

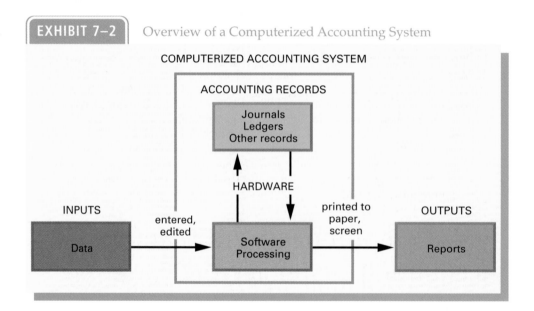

Designing an Accounting System: The Chart of Accounts

An accounting system begins with the chart of accounts. Recall from Chapter 2, page 55, that the chart of accounts lists all accounts in the general ledger and their account numbers. In the accounting system of most companies, the account *numbers* take on added importance. It is efficient to represent a complex account title, such as Accumulated Amortization—Photographic Equipment, with a concise account number (for example, 16570).

Recall that asset accounts generally begin with the digit 1, liabilities with the digit 2, owner's equity accounts with the digit 3, revenues with 4, and expenses with 5. Exhibit 7–3 diagrams one structure for computerized accounts. Assets in this case are divided into current assets; property, plant, and equipment; and other assets. Among the current assets we illustrate only three general ledger accounts: Cash (Account No. 111), Accounts Receivable (No. 115), and Inventory (No. 120)—there are others that are not shown. Accounts Receivable holds the *total* dollar amount receivable from customers A, B, C, and D.

EXHIBIT 7–3 Structure for Computerized Accounts

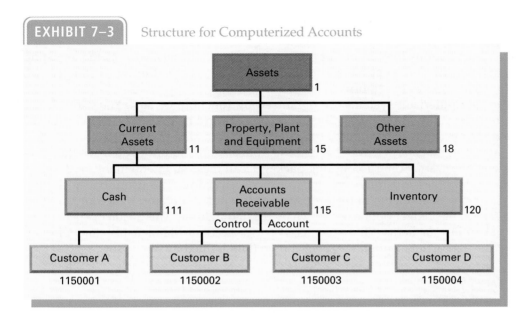

The account numbers in Exhibit 7–3 get longer and more detailed as you move from top to bottom. For example, Customer A's account number is 1150001, in which 115 represents Accounts Receivable and 0001 refers to Customer A. Many computer systems have account numbers of fixed length, such as 100000 for Assets, 110000 for Current Assets, 111000 for Cash, and so on.

The importance of a well-structured chart of accounts cannot be over-emphasized. This is because the reporting component of a computerized accounting system relies on *account number ranges* to translate accounts and their balances into properly organized financial statements and other reports. For example, the accounts numbered 101–399 (assets, liabilities, and owner's equity) are sorted to the balance sheet, and the accounts numbered 401–599 (revenues and expenses) go to the income statement. As another example, reports can be generated based on account numbers if the account numbers are detailed enough to include departments, locations, or divisions of the company. For example, account numbers for the housewares department might end with the digit 2. Thus, a departmental income statement could easily be prepared for the housewares department by selecting all revenue and expense accounts that end in "2." It is crucial to leave room for future accounts and account numbers when designing a chart of accounts.

Processing Transactions: Manual and Menu-Driven Accounting Systems

Recording transactions in an actual accounting system requires an additional step that we have skipped thus far. A business of any size *classifies transactions by type* for efficient handling. In an expanded manual system, credit sales, purchases on account, cash receipts, and cash payments are treated as four separate categories. Each category of transactions has its own special journal. (We discuss these journals in detail later in this chapter.) For example:

Sales Journal	Cash Receipts Journal	Purchases Journal	Cash Payments Journal	General Journal
For recording credit sales	For recording cash receipts	For recording credit purchases	For recording cash payments	For transactions *not* in special journals

KEY POINT

Computerized systems reduce both time and personnel costs. They free employees from processing large numbers of transactions manually with the related repetitive bookkeeping, providing time for decision making and reducing the number of errors. Since data are only entered once, the entire process is more accurate.

Payroll payments are another category of transactions and are recorded in the *payroll journal*.

Transactions that do not fit any of the special journals, such as the adjusting and closing entries at the end of the period, are recorded in the *general journal*, which serves as the "journal of last resort."

Computerized systems are organized by function, or task. You can select a function, such as recording sales on account, from a menu. A **menu** is a list of options for choosing computer functions. In such a *menu-driven* system, you first access the *main menu*. You then choose from a submenu until you reach the function you want. Some accounting packages call these submenu items **modules**.

Exhibit 7–4 illustrates one type of menu structure. The menu bar at the top gives the main menu. In the diagram, the computer operator (or accountant) had chosen the Ledger option, as shown by the highlighting. This action opened a submenu of four items—Transactions, Posting, Account Maintenance, and Closing. The Transactions option was then chosen (highlighted by the cursor).

EXHIBIT 7–4 Main Menu of a Computerized Accounting System

Posting in a computerized system can be performed continuously (**online** or **real-time processing**) or later for a group of similar transactions (**batch processing**). The posting then updates the account balances automatically. Outputs—accounting reports—are the final stage of data processing. In a computerized system, the financial statements can be printed automatically. Spreadsheets can be linked to accounting packages to help prepare more complex reports.

Exhibit 7–5 summarizes the accounting cycle in a computerized system and in a manual system. As you study the exhibit, compare and contrast the two types of systems.

Enterprise Resource Planning Systems

Many small businesses use QuickBooks® or Simply Accounting®. But larger companies like Nova Scotia Power and Eastlink Telephone are using **enterprise resource planning (ERP)** systems to manage their data. ERP systems such as SAP®, Oracle®, and PeopleSoft® (now owned by Oracle) can integrate all company data into a single data warehouse. ERP feeds the data into software for all company activities—from purchasing to production and customer service.

Advantages of ERP systems include the following:

- A centralized ERP system can save lots of money in the long run by allowing integration of data and systems.

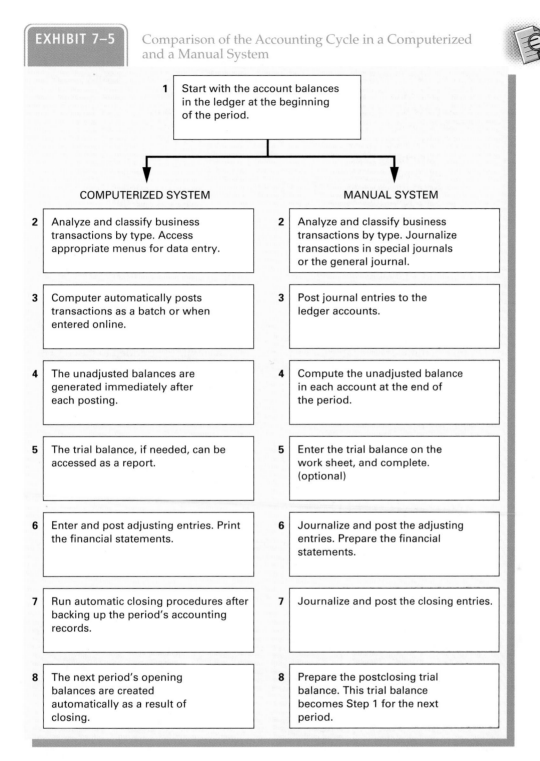

KEY POINT

You may think a computer skips steps when data are entered because the computer performs some of the steps internally. However, a computerized accounting system performs all the steps a manual system does, except for the work sheet. Even if you never keep a manual set of books, you still need to understand the entire accounting system.

1 Start with the account balances in the ledger at the beginning of the period.

COMPUTERIZED SYSTEM

2 Analyze and classify business transactions by type. Access appropriate menus for data entry.

3 Computer automatically posts transactions as a batch or when entered online.

4 The unadjusted balances are generated immediately after each posting.

5 The trial balance, if needed, can be accessed as a report.

6 Enter and post adjusting entries. Print the financial statements.

7 Run automatic closing procedures after backing up the period's accounting records.

8 The next period's opening balances are created automatically as a result of closing.

MANUAL SYSTEM

2 Analyze and classify business transactions by type. Journalize transactions in special journals or the general journal.

3 Post journal entries to the ledger accounts.

4 Compute the unadjusted balance in each account at the end of the period.

5 Enter the trial balance on the work sheet, and complete. (optional)

6 Journalize and post the adjusting entries. Prepare the financial statements.

7 Journalize and post the closing entries.

8 Prepare the postclosing trial balance. This trial balance becomes Step 1 for the next period.

- ERP helps companies adjust to changes. A change in sales ripples through the purchasing, shipping, and accounting systems.
- An ERP system can replace separate software systems, such as sales and payroll systems.

ERP is expensive in the short run. Major installations can cost millions of dollars. Implementation also requires a large commitment of time and people. For example, Hershey Foods Corporation tried to shrink a four-year ERP project into two-and-a-half years. The result? The software did not map into Hershey's operations, and the resulting disrupted deliveries decreased profits in the critical Halloween candy-buying season.

DID YOU GET IT?

MyAccountingLab

To check your understanding of the material in this Learning Objective, complete these questions. The solutions appear on MyAccountingLab so you can check your progress.

4. Create a chart of accounts by matching the account name with the most appropriate account number. Assume the company lists its accounts in the chart of accounts in this order: assets, liabilities, owner's equity, revenues, expenses.

T. Pioneer, Capital	11001
Advertising Expense	12001
Building	17001
Accounts Payable	18001
Sales Revenue	21001
Miscellaneous Expenses	25001
Cash	30001
T. Pioneer, Withdrawals	31001
Land	41001
Notes Payable	51001
Accounts Receivable	54001
Salaries Expense	59001

5. Refer to the information in the previous question. Suppose you needed to add the accounts listed below to the chart of accounts in the previous question. Specify the range of numbers available for each of the new accounts to be added to the chart of accounts. Assume expenses are listed alphabetically in this chart of accounts.

Notes Receivable
Automobile
Supplies
Supplies Expense
Unearned Revenue
Service Revenue

KEY POINT

Special journals are labour-saving devices: They are not mandatory, but serve a very useful purpose by summarizing similar transactions. However, a business need not use *any* special journals.

Special Journals

Exhibit 7–6 diagrams a typical accounting system for a merchandising business. The remainder of this chapter describes how this system works.

EXHIBIT 7–6 Overview of an Accounting System with Special Journals for a Merchandising Business

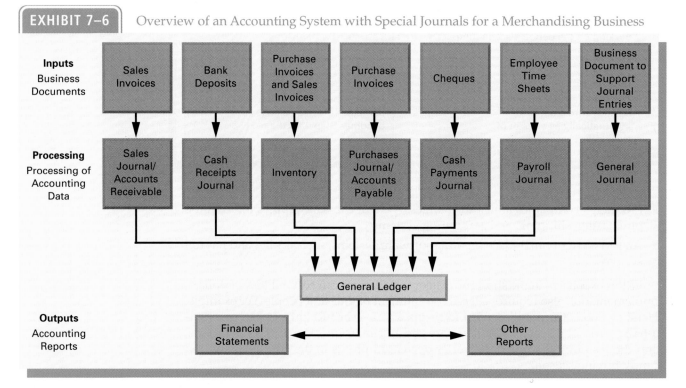

Special Journals in a Manual System

The journal entries illustrated so far have been made in the **general journal**. It is not efficient to record all transactions in the general journal, so we use special journals. A **special journal** is an accounting journal designed to record one specific type of transaction.

Most transactions fall into one of five categories, so accountants use five different journals. This system saves time and money, as we will see. The five types of transactions, the special journals, and the posting abbreviations are as follows:

Transaction	Special Journal	Posting Abbreviation
1. Sale of merchandise on account	Sales journal	S
2. Cash receipt	Cash receipts journal	CR
3. Purchase on account	Purchases journal	P
4. Cash payment*	Cash payments journal	CP
5. All others	General journal	G

*Some companies also use a Payroll Journal for payroll transactions, which is a part of the companies' payroll system. Payroll systems are covered in Chapter 11.

Transactions are recorded in either the general journal or a special journal, but not both.

You may be wondering why we cover manual accounting systems, since many businesses have computerized accounting systems. There are four main reasons:

1. Learning a manual system will equip you to work with both manual and electronic systems. The accounting is the same regardless of the system.

2. Few small businesses have computerized all their accounting. Even companies that use QuickBooks or Simply Accounting keep some manual accounting records. For businesses that use manual systems, these systems follow the principles and procedures that we illustrate in this chapter.

3. Learning a manual system will help you master accounting. One of the authors of this book has a friend who uses QuickBooks for his business. This man knows only which keys to punch. If he knew the accounting, he could better manage his business.

4. Learning a manual system will help you recognize a computer system that is not set up properly or is not working as intended.

KEY POINT

Transactions are recorded in either the general journal or a special journal, but not in both.

The Sales Journal

Most merchandisers sell inventory on account. These *credit sales* are recorded in the **sales journal**. Credit sales of assets other than inventory—for example, buildings—occur infrequently and may be recorded in the general journal.

Exhibit 7–7 illustrates a sales journal (Panel A) and the related posting to the ledgers (Panel B) of Austin Sound Centre, the small electronics shop we introduced in Chapter 5. Each entry in the Accounts Receivable Dr/Sales Revenue Cr column of the sales journal in Exhibit 7–7 is a debit (Dr) to Accounts Receivable and a credit (Cr) to Sales Revenue, as the heading above this column indicates. For each transaction, the accountant enters the

- Date
- Invoice number

OBJECTIVE 3

Journalize and post transactions using the sales journal, the cash receipts journal, and the accounts receivable subsidiary ledger

Panel A: Sales Journal

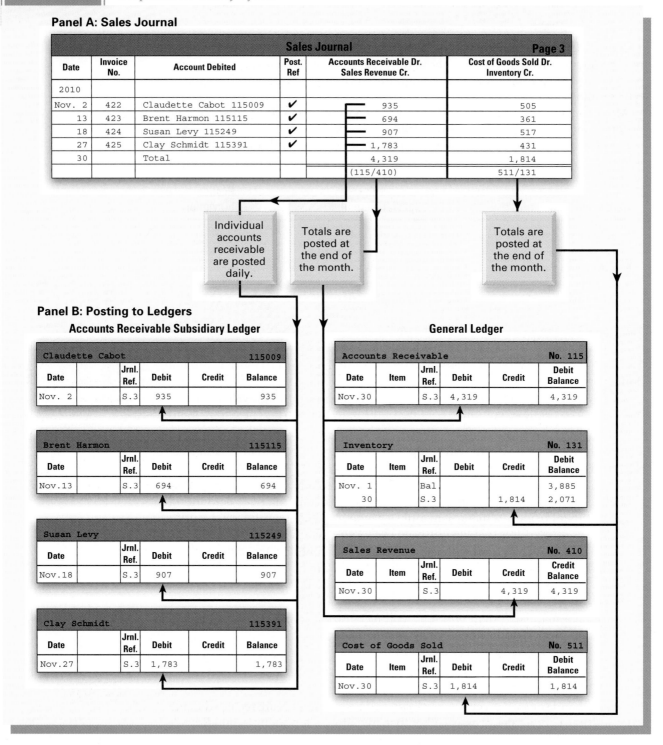

Sales Journal					Page 3
Date	Invoice No.	Account Debited	Post. Ref	Accounts Receivable Dr. Sales Revenue Cr.	Cost of Goods Sold Dr. Inventory Cr.
2010					
Nov. 2	422	Claudette Cabot 115009	✔	935	505
13	423	Brent Harmon 115115	✔	694	361
18	424	Susan Levy 115249	✔	907	517
27	425	Clay Schmidt 115391	✔	1,783	431
30		Total		4,319	1,814
				(115/410)	511/131

Individual accounts receivable are posted daily.

Totals are posted at the end of the month.

Totals are posted at the end of the month.

Panel B: Posting to Ledgers

Accounts Receivable Subsidiary Ledger

Claudette Cabot 115009

Date		Jrnl. Ref.	Debit	Credit	Balance
Nov. 2		S.3	935		935

Brent Harmon 115115

Date		Jrnl. Ref.	Debit	Credit	Balance
Nov.13		S.3	694		694

Susan Levy 115249

Date		Jrnl. Ref.	Debit	Credit	Balance
Nov.18		S.3	907		907

Clay Schmidt 115391

Date		Jrnl. Ref.	Debit	Credit	Balance
Nov.27		S.3	1,783		1,783

General Ledger

Accounts Receivable   No. 115

Date	Item	Jrnl. Ref.	Debit	Credit	Debit Balance
Nov.30		S.3	4,319		4,319

Inventory   No. 131

Date	Item	Jrnl. Ref.	Debit	Credit	Debit Balance
Nov. 1		Bal.			3,885
30		S.3		1,814	2,071

Sales Revenue   No. 410

Date	Item	Jrnl. Ref.	Debit	Credit	Credit Balance
Nov.30		S.3		4,319	4,319

Cost of Goods Sold   No. 511

Date	Item	Jrnl. Ref.	Debit	Credit	Debit Balance
Nov.30		S.3	1,814		1,814

KEY POINT

Only credit sales of merchandise are recorded in the sales journal.

- Customer name and number
- Transaction amount

This streamlined way of recording sales on account saves a vast amount of time that, in a manual system, would be spent entering account titles and dollar amounts in the general journal.

In recording credit sales in the previous chapters, we did not record the names of credit-sale customers. In practice, the business must know the amount receivable from each customer. How else can the company identify who owes it money, when payment is due, and how much?

Consider the first transaction in Panel A. On November 2, 2010, Austin Sound sold stereo equipment on account to Claudette Cabot for $935. The invoice number is 422. All this information appears on a single line in the sales journal. No explanation is necessary. The transaction's presence in the sales journal means that it is a credit sale, debited to Accounts Receivable—Claudette Cabot and credited to Sales Revenue. To gain any additional information about the transaction, we would look at the actual invoice.

Recall from Chapter 5 that Austin Sound uses a *perpetual* inventory system. When recording the sale, Austin Sound also records the cost of goods sold and the decrease in inventory.

Computerized accounting systems can read both the sales amount and the cost of goods sold from the bar code on the package of the item sold. The far-right column of the sales journal records the cost of goods sold and inventory amount—$505 for the goods sold to Claudette Cabot. If Austin Sound used a *periodic* inventory system, it would not record cost of goods sold or the decrease in inventory at the time of sale. The sales journal would need only one column to debit Accounts Receivable and to credit Sales Revenue for the amount of the sale.

Additional data can be recorded in the sales journal. For example, a company may add a column to record sale terms, such as 2/10, n/30. The design of the journal depends on the managers' needs for information. Special journals are flexible—they can be tailored to meet any special needs of a business.

Posting to the General Ledger   The only ledger we have used so far is the **general ledger**, which holds the accounts reported in the financial statements. We will soon introduce other ledgers.

The accounts debited and credited are the same whether or not the accounting system uses special journals. However, the debits and credits are grouped together and totalled in a special journal system.

Posting from the sales journal to the general ledger can be done at any time, but for efficiency, most companies post only once each month. In Exhibit 7–7 (Panel A), November's credit sales total $4,319. This column has two headings, Accounts Receivable and Sales Revenue. In a manual system, when the $4,319 is posted to Accounts Receivable and Sales Revenue in the general ledger, you can print their account numbers beneath the total in the sales journal. In Panel B of Exhibit 7–7, you can see that the account number for Accounts Receivable is 115 and the account number for Sales Revenue is 410. Printing these account numbers beneath the credit sales total in the sales journal shows that the $4,319 has been posted to those two accounts.

In a perpetual inventory system, the debit to Cost of Goods Sold (account number 511) and the credit to Inventory (account number 131) for the monthly total of $1,814 is normally posted at the end of the month. After posting, these account numbers are written beneath the total to show that Cost of Goods Sold and Inventory have been updated. No such posting would be necessary if Austin Sound used a periodic inventory system.

Posting to the Accounts Receivable Subsidiary Ledger   The $4,319 debit to Accounts Receivable does not identify the amount receivable from any specific customer. A business may have many customers. For example, *Maclean's Magazine* has a customer account for each of its thousands of subscribers.

Businesses must create an account for each customer in a subsidiary ledger called the accounts receivable subsidiary ledger. A **subsidiary ledger** is a book or file of the individual accounts that make up a total for a general ledger account. The customer accounts in the subsidiary ledger are usually arranged in alphabetical order and often have a customer number.

Amounts in the sales journal are posted to the subsidiary ledger *daily* to keep a current record of the amount receivable from each customer. The amounts are

The purpose of a subsidiary ledger account is to provide detail of a customer's account to facilitate billing and collection. The accounts receivable subsidiary ledger should show all sales to, and collections from, the customer—the customer's credit history. However, the subsidiary ledger is *not* part of the general ledger and the subsidiary accounts will *not* appear on the trial balance.

Chapter 7 Accounting Information Systems   **353**

KEY POINT

You may think that posting to the subsidiary ledger and to the general ledger is double posting. However, the subsidiary ledger is *not* part of the general ledger and the subsidiary accounts will *not* appear on the trial balance. Posting to both the subsidiary ledger and the general ledger is necessary to keep the two in balance.

KEY POINT

After *all* postings, the balance in the control account should equal the sum of all the subsidiary accounts.

debits. Daily posting allows the business to answer customer inquiries promptly. Suppose Claudette Cabot telephones Austin Sound on November 11 to ask how much money she owes. The subsidiary ledger readily provides that information, $935 in Exhibit 7–7, Panel B.

When each transaction amount is posted to the subsidiary ledger in a manual system, a check mark or some other notation is printed in the posting reference column of the sales journal (see Exhibit 7–7, Panel A). This is because subsidiary ledger accounts are not part of the general ledger and, thus, have no general ledger account numbers.

Journal References in the Ledgers   As you post to the ledgers, print the journal page number in the account to identify the source of the data. All transaction data in Exhibit 7–7 originated on page 3 of the sales journal, so all posting references in the ledger accounts are S.3. "S" indicates sales journal.

Trace all the postings in Exhibit 7–7. The way to learn about accounting systems and special journals is to study the flow of data.

Balancing the Ledgers   The arrows in Exhibit 7–7 indicate the direction of the information. The arrows show the links between the individual customer accounts in the subsidiary ledger and the Accounts Receivable account. (The arrows are for illustration only—they do not appear in the accounting records.) The Accounts Receivable debit balance in the general ledger should equal the sum of the individual customer balances in the subsidiary ledger, as follows. This is called balancing the ledgers.

Accounts Receivable debit balance in the general ledger:

Accounts Receivable... $4,319 ◄

Data from the Accounts Receivable Subsidiary Ledger

AUSTIN SOUND CENTRE
Schedule of Accounts Receivable
November 30, 2010

115009 Claudette Cabot	$ 935
115115 Brent Harmon..	694
115249 Susan Levy..	907
115391 Clay Schmidt	1,783
Total accounts receivable..................................	$4,319 ◄

Accounts Receivable in the general ledger is an example of a **control account**. A control account's balance equals the sum of the balances of a group of related accounts in a subsidiary ledger. The individual customer accounts are subsidiary accounts and are listed in a *schedule*. They are said to be "controlled" by the Accounts Receivable account in the general ledger.

The Cash Receipts Journal

Cash transactions are common in most businesses because cash receipts from customers are the lifeblood of business. To record a large number of cash receipt transactions, accountants use the **cash receipts journal**.

Exhibit 7–8, Panel A, illustrates the cash receipts journal. The related posting to the ledgers is shown in Panel B. The exhibit illustrates November 2010 transactions for Austin Sound Centre.

Every transaction recorded in this journal is a cash receipt, so the first column is for debits to the Cash account. The next column is for debits to Sales Discounts on

EXHIBIT 7–8 Cash Receipts Journal (Panel A) and Posting to the Ledgers (Panel B) under the Perpetual Inventory System

Panel A: Cash Receipts Journal

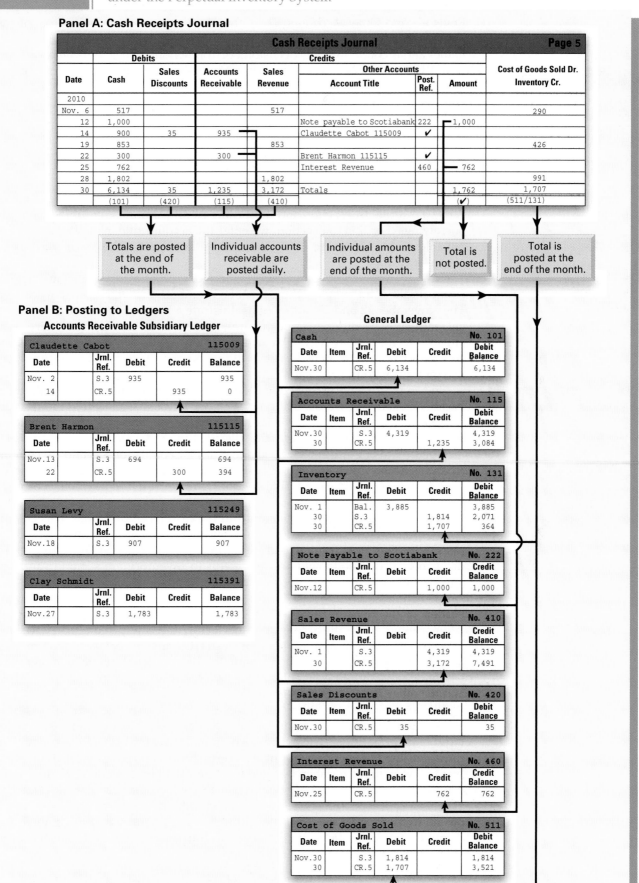

	Debits		Credits					Cost of Goods Sold Dr.
Date	Cash	Sales Discounts	Accounts Receivable	Sales Revenue	Other Accounts			Inventory Cr.
					Account Title	Post. Ref.	Amount	
2010								
Nov. 6	517			517				290
12	1,000				Note payable to Scotiabank	222	1,000	
14	900	35	935		Claudette Cabot 115009	✔		
19	853			853				426
22	300		300		Brent Harmon 115115	✔		
25	762				Interest Revenue	460	762	
28	1,802			1,802				991
30	6,134	35	1,235	3,172	Totals		1,762	1,707
	(101)	(420)	(115)	(410)			(✔)	(511/131)

Totals are posted at the end of the month.

Individual accounts receivable are posted daily.

Individual amounts are posted at the end of the month.

Total is not posted.

Total is posted at the end of the month.

Panel B: Posting to Ledgers

Accounts Receivable Subsidiary Ledger

Claudette Cabot   115009

Date		Jrnl. Ref.	Debit	Credit	Balance
Nov. 2		S.3	935		935
14		CR.5		935	0

Brent Harmon   115115

Date		Jrnl. Ref.	Debit	Credit	Balance
Nov.13		S.3	694		694
22		CR.5		300	394

Susan Levy   115249

Date		Jrnl. Ref.	Debit	Credit	Balance
Nov.18		S.3	907		907

Clay Schmidt   115391

Date		Jrnl. Ref.	Debit	Credit	Balance
Nov.27		S.3	1,783		1,783

General Ledger

Cash   No. 101

Date	Item	Jrnl. Ref.	Debit	Credit	Debit Balance
Nov.30		CR.5	6,134		6,134

Accounts Receivable   No. 115

Date	Item	Jrnl. Ref.	Debit	Credit	Debit Balance
Nov.30		S.3	4,319		4,319
30		CR.5		1,235	3,084

Inventory   No. 131

Date	Item	Jrnl. Ref.	Debit	Credit	Debit Balance
Nov. 1		Bal.	3,885		3,885
30		S.3		1,814	2,071
30		CR.5		1,707	364

Note Payable to Scotiabank   No. 222

Date	Item	Jrnl. Ref.	Debit	Credit	Credit Balance
Nov.12		CR.5		1,000	1,000

Sales Revenue   No. 410

Date	Item	Jrnl. Ref.	Debit	Credit	Credit Balance
Nov. 1		S.3		4,319	4,319
30		CR.5		3,172	7,491

Sales Discounts   No. 420

Date	Item	Jrnl. Ref.	Debit	Credit	Debit Balance
Nov.30		CR.5	35		35

Interest Revenue   No. 460

Date	Item	Jrnl. Ref.	Debit	Credit	Credit Balance
Nov.25		CR.5		762	762

Cost of Goods Sold   No. 511

Date	Item	Jrnl. Ref.	Debit	Credit	Debit Balance
Nov.30		S.3	1,814		1,814
30		CR.5	1,707		3,521

collections from customers. In a typical merchandising business, the main sources of cash are collections on account and cash sales.

The cash receipts journal has credit columns for Accounts Receivable, Sales Revenue, and Other Accounts. The Other Accounts columns list sources of cash other than cash sales and collections on account, and are also used to record the names and account numbers of customers from whom cash is received on account.

In Exhibit 7–8, cash sales occurred on November 6, 19, and 28. Observe the debits to Cash and the credits to Sales Revenue ($517, $853, and $1,802). Each sale entry is accompanied by an entry that debits Cost of Goods Sold and credits Inventory for the cost of the merchandise sold, since the perpetual inventory system is being used. The column for this entry is at the far-right side of the cash receipts journal. No such entry would be made if Austin Sound used a periodic inventory system.

On November 12, Austin Sound borrowed $1,000 from Scotiabank. Cash is debited, and Note Payable to Scotiabank is credited in the Other Accounts column because it is a rare transaction and no specific credit column is set up to account for borrowings. For this transaction, we enter the account title, Note Payable to Scotiabank, in the Other Accounts/Account Title column. This entry records the source of cash.

On November 25, Austin Sound collected $762 of interest revenue. The account credited, Interest Revenue, must be written in the Other Accounts column. The November 12 and 25 transactions illustrate a key fact about business. Different entities have different types of transactions, and they design their special journals to meet their particular needs for information. In this case, the Other Accounts Credit column is the catch-all that is used to record all nonroutine cash receipt transactions.

On November 14, Austin Sound collected $900 from Claudette Cabot. Referring back to Exhibit 7–7, we see that on November 2 Austin Sound sold merchandise for $935 to Claudette Cabot. The terms of sale allowed a $35 discount for prompt payment and she paid within the discount period. Austin's cash receipt is recorded by debiting Cash for $900 and Sales Discounts for $35 and by crediting Accounts Receivable for $935. The customer's name and account number appear in the Other Accounts/Account Title column to make sure the payment received is posted to the subsidiary ledger.

Total debits must equal total credits in the cash receipts journal. This equality holds for each transaction and for the monthly totals. For the month, total debits ($6,134 + $35 = $6,169) equal total credits ($1,235 + $3,172 + $1,762 = $6,169). The debit to Cost of Goods Sold and the credit to Inventory are separate, and only apply to the perpetual inventory system.

Posting to the General Ledger The column totals are usually posted monthly. After posting, write the account number below the column total in the cash receipts journal. The account number for Cash (101) appears below the column total $6,134, and likewise for the other column totals posted to the general ledger (Sales Discounts, Accounts Receivable, and Sales Revenue). Trace the posting to Cash and the other accounts in the general ledger.

The column total for Other Accounts is *not* posted. Instead, these credits are posted individually. In Exhibit 7–8, the November 12 transaction reads "Note Payable to Scotiabank." This account's number (222) in the Post. Ref. column indicates that the transaction amount was posted individually. The check mark, instead of an account number, below the column total means that the column total was not posted because individual items above were posted. The November 25 collection of interest revenue is also posted individually. These amounts can be posted to the general ledger at the end of the month. But their date in the ledger accounts should be their actual date in the journal to make it easy to trace each amount back to the cash receipts journal.

KEY POINT

Every entry in the cash receipts journal includes a debit to Cash. Cash sales are recorded here rather than in the sales journal. (Credit sales are recorded in the sales journal.)

REAL WORLD EXAMPLE

Accountants call the process of totalling the columns *footing* (adding down). *Cross-foot* means to add debits and subtract credits across the page. A special journal or spreadsheet that foots and cross-foots has numbers that add down correctly and add across so that debits equal credits. Users must always evaluate the reasonableness and correctness of amounts or they may make bad decisions.

Posting to the Subsidiary Ledger Amounts from the cash receipts journal are posted to the accounts receivable subsidiary ledger daily to keep the individual balances up to date. The postings to the accounts receivable ledger are credits. Trace the $935 credit to Claudette Cabot's account. It reduces the balance in her account to zero. The $300 receipt from Brent Harmon reduces his accounts receivable balance to $394.

Balancing the Ledgers After posting, the sum of the individual balances that remain in the accounts receivable subsidiary ledger equals the general ledger balance in Accounts Receivable.

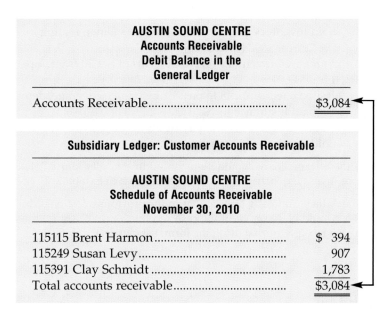

AUSTIN SOUND CENTRE
Accounts Receivable
Debit Balance in the
General Ledger

Accounts Receivable..	$3,084

Subsidiary Ledger: Customer Accounts Receivable

AUSTIN SOUND CENTRE
Schedule of Accounts Receivable
November 30, 2010

115115 Brent Harmon...	$ 394
115249 Susan Levy..	907
115391 Clay Schmidt	1,783
Total accounts receivable...................................	$3,084

Austin Sound's list of account balances from the subsidiary ledger helps it follow up on slow-paying customers. Good accounts receivable records help a business manage its cash.

DID YOU GET IT?

To check your understanding of the material in this Learning Objective, complete these questions. The solutions appear on MyAccountingLab so you can check your progress.

6. Refer to the Austin Sound Centre information given in this chapter. Suppose you worked in the accounting department of the company. If Austin Sound did not use an accounts receivable subsidiary ledger and Claudette Cabot asked you for her account balance, could you answer her?

7. Sidney Company experienced the following transactions during February 2010.

Feb. 2 Issued invoice no. 291 for a sale on account to Limpert Design Ltd., $400. Sidney's cost of this inventory was $240.

3 Purchased inventory on credit terms of 1/10, n/30 from Dunning Co., $2,600.

4 Sold inventory for cash, $300 (cost, $204).

5 Issued cheque no. 45 to Office Depot to purchase office furniture for cash, $1,400.

Feb. 8 Received payment on account, $200. The discount period had expired.

10 Purchased inventory from Mega Corp. for cash, $1,300, issuing cheque no. 46.

13 Received $400 cash from Limpert Design Ltd. in full settlement of its account receivable.

13 Issued cheque no. 47 to pay Delwood Co. the net amount owed from February 3.

14 Purchased supplies on account from Office Corp., $500. Payment is due in 30 days.

15 Sold inventory on account to Frankie's Diner, issuing invoice no. 292 for $800 (cost, $550).

20 Purchased inventory on credit terms of net 30 from Super Sales Ltd., $1,600.

22 Issued cheque no. 48 to pay for insurance coverage, debiting Prepaid Insurance for $2,000.

25 Issued cheque no. 49 to pay utilities, $450.

28 Sold goods for $550 cash (cost, $325).

Which of these transactions would be recorded in the sales journal? Record those transactions in a sales journal using the format shown in Exhibit 7–7.

8. Refer to the Sidney Company transactions in the previous question. Which of those transactions would be recorded in the cash receipts journal? Record those transactions in a cash receipts journal using the format shown in Exhibit 7–8.

The Purchases Journal

OBJECTIVE 4

Journalize and post transactions using the purchases journal, the cash payments journal, and the accounts payable subsidiary ledger

KEY POINT

The source document for entries in the purchases journal is the supplier's (creditor's) invoice or bill.

A merchandising business such as Austin Sound Centre purchases inventory and supplies frequently. Such purchases are usually made on account. The **purchases journal** is designed to account for all purchases of inventory, supplies, and other assets *on account*. It can also be used to record expenses incurred *on account*. Cash purchases are recorded in the cash payments journal.

Exhibit 7–9 illustrates Austin Sound's purchases journal (Panel A) and posting to the ledgers (Panel B).[1] The purchases journal in Exhibit 7–9 has amount columns for

- Credits to Accounts Payable
- Debits to Inventory, Supplies, and Other Accounts.

A periodic inventory system would replace the Inventory column with a column entitled "Purchases." The Other Accounts columns record purchases of assets other than inventory and supplies. Each business designs its purchases journal to meet its own needs for information and efficiency. Accounts Payable is credited for all transactions recorded in the purchases journal.

On November 2, Austin Sound purchased stereo inventory costing $700 from JVC Canada Inc. The supplier's name (JVC Canada Inc.) and account number is entered in the Supplier Account Credited column. The purchase terms of 3/15, n/30 are also entered to help identify the due date and the discount available. Accounts Payable is credited and Inventory is debited for the transaction amount. On November 19, a purchase of supplies on account is entered as a debit to Supplies and a credit to Accounts Payable.

---

[1] This is the only special journal that we illustrate with the credit column usually placed to the left and the debit columns to the right. This arrangement of columns focuses on Accounts Payable, which is credited for each entry to this journal, and on the individual supplier to be paid.

Panel A: Purchases Journal

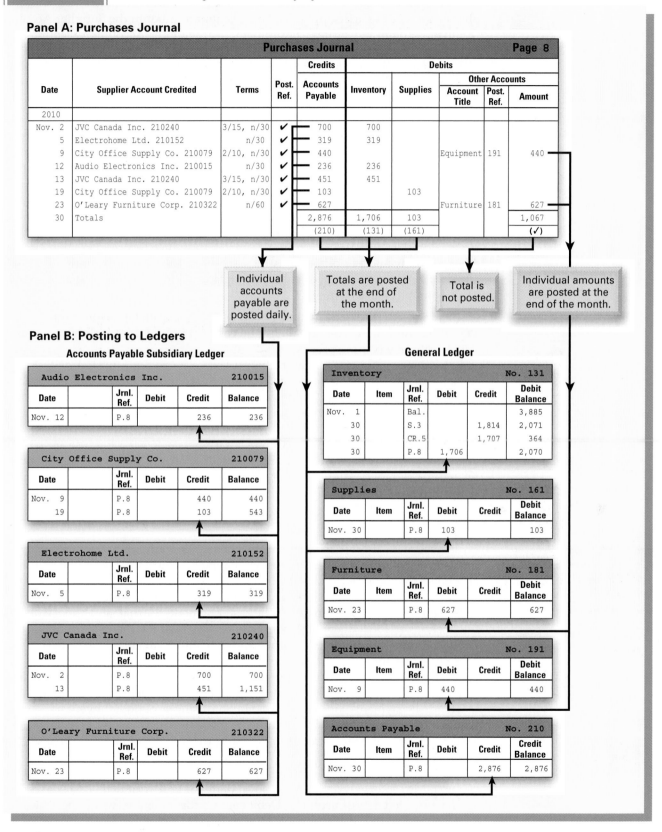

				Credits	Debits				
								Other Accounts	
Date	Supplier Account Credited	Terms	Post. Ref.	Accounts Payable	Inventory	Supplies	Account Title	Post. Ref.	Amount
2010									
Nov. 2	JVC Canada Inc. 210240	3/15, n/30	✔	700	700				
5	Electrohome Ltd. 210152	n/30	✔	319	319				
9	City Office Supply Co. 210079	2/10, n/30	✔	440			Equipment	191	440
12	Audio Electronics Inc. 210015	n/30	✔	236	236				
13	JVC Canada Inc. 210240	3/15, n/30	✔	451	451				
19	City Office Supply Co. 210079	2/10, n/30	✔	103		103			
23	O'Leary Furniture Corp. 210322	n/60	✔	627			Furniture	181	627
30	Totals			2,876	1,706	103			1,067
				(210)	(131)	(161)			(✓)

Purchases Journal — Page 8

Individual accounts payable are posted daily.

Totals are posted at the end of the month.

Total is not posted.

Individual amounts are posted at the end of the month.

Panel B: Posting to Ledgers

Accounts Payable Subsidiary Ledger

Audio Electronics Inc.   210015

Date		Jrnl. Ref.	Debit	Credit	Balance
Nov. 12		P.8		236	236

City Office Supply Co.   210079

Date		Jrnl. Ref.	Debit	Credit	Balance
Nov. 9		P.8		440	440
19		P.8		103	543

Electrohome Ltd.   210152

Date		Jrnl. Ref.	Debit	Credit	Balance
Nov. 5		P.8		319	319

JVC Canada Inc.   210240

Date		Jrnl. Ref.	Debit	Credit	Balance
Nov. 2		P.8		700	700
13		P.8		451	1,151

O'Leary Furniture Corp.   210322

Date		Jrnl. Ref.	Debit	Credit	Balance
Nov. 23		P.8		627	627

General Ledger

Inventory   No. 131

Date	Item	Jrnl. Ref.	Debit	Credit	Debit Balance
Nov. 1		Bal.			3,885
30		S.3		1,814	2,071
30		CR.5		1,707	364
30		P.8	1,706		2,070

Supplies   No. 161

Date	Item	Jrnl. Ref.	Debit	Credit	Debit Balance
Nov. 30		P.8	103		103

Furniture   No. 181

Date	Item	Jrnl. Ref.	Debit	Credit	Debit Balance
Nov. 23		P.8	627		627

Equipment   No. 191

Date	Item	Jrnl. Ref.	Debit	Credit	Debit Balance
Nov. 9		P.8	440		440

Accounts Payable   No. 210

Date	Item	Jrnl. Ref.	Debit	Credit	Credit Balance
Nov. 30		P.8		2,876	2,876

Note the November 9 purchase of equipment from City Office Supply Co. The purchases journal contains no column for Equipment, so the Other Accounts debit column is used. Because this was a credit purchase, the accountant enters the supplier name (City Office Supply Co.) and account number in the Supplier Account Credited column and writes "Equipment" in the Other Accounts/Account Title column.

The total credits in the purchases journal ($2,876) must equal the total debits ($1,706 + $103 + $1,067 = $2,876). This equality proves the accuracy of the entries in the purchases journal.

REAL WORLD EXAMPLE

Companies design journals to meet their special needs. A repair service might not use a Supplies column but might need a Small Tools column for frequent purchases of tools.

Accounts Payable Subsidiary Ledger   To pay debts on time, a company must know how much it owes each supplier. The Accounts Payable account in the general ledger shows only a single total for the amount owed on account. It does not indicate the amount owed to each supplier. Companies keep an accounts payable subsidiary ledger that is similar to the accounts receivable subsidiary ledger.

The accounts payable subsidiary ledger lists suppliers in alphabetical order, often by account number, along with the amounts owed to them. Exhibit 7–9, Panel B, shows Austin Sound's accounts payable subsidiary ledger, which includes accounts for Audio Electronics Inc., City Office Supply Co., and others. After the daily and period-end postings are done, the total of the individual balances in the subsidiary ledger equals the balance in the Accounts Payable control account in the general ledger.

Posting from the Purchases Journal   Posting from the purchases journal is similar to posting from the sales journal and the cash receipts journal. Exhibit 7–9, Panel B, illustrates the posting process.

Individual accounts payable in the purchases journal are posted daily to the *accounts payable subsidiary ledger*, and column totals and other amounts are usually posted to the *general ledger* at the end of the month. The column total for *Other Accounts* is not posted. Each account's number in the Post. Ref. column indicates that the transaction amount was posted individually. The check mark below the column total indicates that the column total was *not* posted because individual items in the column were posted. In the ledger accounts, in the Jrnl. Ref. (journal reference) column, P. 8 indicates the source of the posted amounts—that is, page 8 of the purchases journal.

The Cash Payments Journal

REAL WORLD EXAMPLE

Businesses make most cash payments by cheque to control their cash. Imagine the confusion and the opportunity for theft if all employees could take cash from the cash register to pay for purchases.

Businesses make most cash payments by cheque for control purposes, and all payments by cheque are recorded in the **cash payments journal**. This special journal is also called the *cheque register* or the *cash disbursements journal*. Like the other special journals, it has multiple columns for recording cash payments that occur frequently.

Exhibit 7–10, Panel A, illustrates the cash payments journal, and Panel B shows the postings to the ledgers of Austin Sound. This cash payments journal has two debit columns—for Other Accounts and Accounts Payable. It has two credit columns—one for purchase discounts, which are credited to the Inventory account in a perpetual inventory system, and one for Cash. This special journal also has columns for the date, cheque number, and payee of each cash payment.

The cash payments journal for a company using a periodic inventory system would have the same two debit columns as those shown in Exhibit 7–10, Panel A— Other Accounts and Accounts Payable—and two credit columns—Purchase Discounts and Cash.

Suppose a business makes numerous cash purchases of inventory and uses the perpetual inventory system. What additional column would its cash payments journal need to be most useful? A Debit column for Inventory would be added.

All entries in the cash payments journal include a credit to Cash. Payments on account are debits to Accounts Payable. On November 15, Austin Sound paid JVC Canada Inc. on account, with credit terms of 3/15, n/30 (for details, see the first transaction in Exhibit 7–9). Therefore, Austin took the 3 percent discount and paid $679 ($700 less the $21 discount). The discount is credited to the Inventory account.

EXHIBIT 7–10 Cash Payments Journal (Panel A) and Posting to the Ledgers (Panel B) under the Perpetual Inventory System

Panel A: Cash Payments Journal

					Debits		Credits	
Date	Ch. No.	Payee	Account Debited	Post. Ref.	Other Accounts	Accounts Payable	Inventory	Cash
2010								
Nov. 3	101	R. Landis Ltd.	Rent Expense	541	1,200			1,200
8	102	Grand and Toy	Supplies	161	61			61
15	103	JVC Canada Inc.	JVC Canada Inc. 210240	✔		700	21	679
20	104	Electrohome Ltd.	Electrohome Ltd. 210152	✔		119		119
26	105	Yu Supplies Ltd.	Inventory	131	2,200			2,200
30			Totals		3,461	819	21	4,259
					(✔)	(210)	(131)	(101)

Total is not posted.

Totals are posted at the end of the month.

Individual accounts payable are posted daily.

Panel B: Posting to Ledgers

Individual amounts are posted at the end of the month.

Accounts Payable Subsidiary Ledger

Audio Electronics Inc.   210015

Date		Jrnl. Ref.	Debit	Credit	Balance
Nov.12		P.8		236	236

City Office Supply Co.   210079

Date		Jrnl. Ref.	Debit	Credit	Balance
Nov. 9		P.8		440	440
19		P.8		103	543

Electrohome Ltd.   210152

Date		Jrnl. Ref.	Debit	Credit	Balance
Nov. 5		P.8		319	319
20		CP.6	119		200

JVC Canada Inc.   210240

Date		Jrnl. Ref.	Debit	Credit	Balance
Nov. 2		P.8		700	700
13		P.8		451	1,151
15		CP.6	700		451

O'Leary Furniture Co.   210322

Date		Jrnl. Ref.	Debit	Credit	Balance
Nov.23		P.8		627	627

General Ledger

Cash   No. 101

Date		Jrnl. Ref.	Debit	Credit	Debit Balance
Nov.30		CR.5	6,134		6,134
30		CP.6		4,259	1,875

Inventory   No. 131

Date	Item	Jrnl. Ref.	Debit	Credit	Debit Balance
Nov. 1		Bal.			3,885
30		S.3		1,814	2,071
30		CR.5		1,707	364
30		P.8	1,706		2,070
26		CP.6	2,200		4,270
30		CP.6		21	4,249

Supplies   No. 161

Date		Jrnl. Ref.	Debit	Credit	Debit Balance
Nov.30		P.8	103		103
8		CP.6	61		164

Accounts Payable   No. 210

Date		Jrnl. Ref.	Debit	Credit	Credit Balance
Nov.30		P.8		2,876	2,876
30		CP.6	819		2,057

Rent Expense   No. 541

Date		Jrnl. Ref.	Debit	Credit	Debit Balance
Nov. 3		CP.6	1,200		1,200

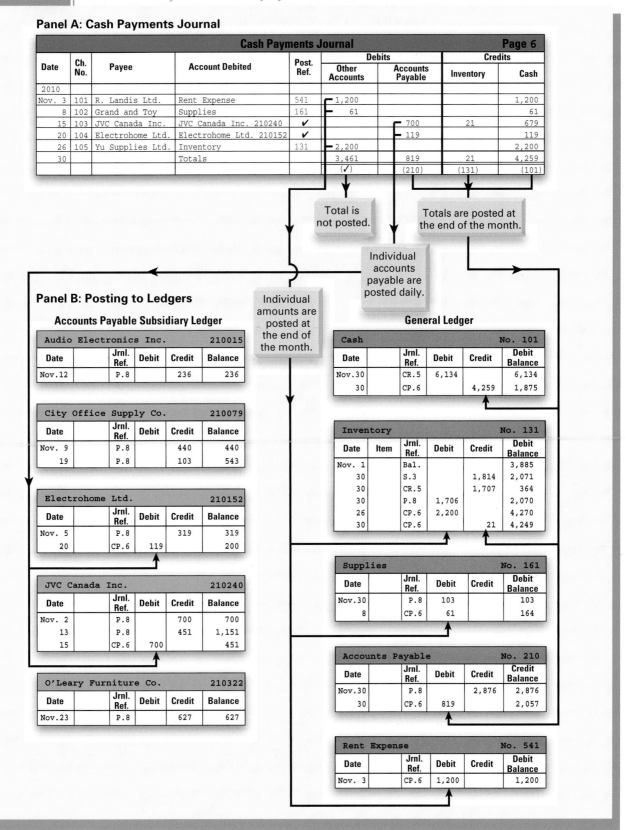

The Other Accounts column is used to record debits to accounts for which no special column exists. For example, on November 3, Austin Sound paid rent expense of $1,200.

As with all the other journals, the total debits ($3,461 + $819 = $4,280) must equal the total credits ($21 + $4,259 = $4,280).

Posting from the Cash Payments Journal   Posting from the cash payments journal is similar to posting from the cash receipts journal. Individual creditor amounts are posted daily. Column totals and Other Accounts are usually posted at the end of the month. Exhibit 7–10, Panel B, illustrates the posting process.

Observe the effect of posting to the Accounts Payable account in the general ledger. The first posted amount in the Accounts Payable account (credit $2,876) originated in the purchases journal, page 8 (P. 8). The second posted amount (debit $819) came from the cash payments journal, page 6 (CP. 6). The resulting credit balance in Accounts Payable is $2,057. Also, see the Cash account. After posting, its debit balance is $1,875.

Amounts in the Other Accounts column are posted individually (for example, Rent Expense—debit $1,200). When each Other Accounts amount is posted to the general ledger, the account number is written in the Post. Ref. column of the journal. The check mark below the column total signifies that the total is *not* posted.

To review their accounts payable, companies list the individual supplier balances in the accounts payable subsidiary ledger:

From the general ledger

Accounts Payable (control account)................... $2,057 ◀

From the Accounts Payable Subsidiary Ledger:
AUSTIN SOUND CENTRE
Schedule of Accounts Payable
November 30, 2010

210015 Audio Electronics Inc.	$ 236
210079 City Office Supply Co.	543
210152 Electrohome Ltd...................................	200
210240 JVC Canada Inc.	451
210322 O'Leary Furniture Co.	627
Total accounts payable.....................................	$2,057 ◀

This total agrees with the Accounts Payable balance in Exhibit 7–10. Agreement of the two amounts indicates that the resulting account balances are correct.

The payroll register is a special form of cash payments journal and is discussed in Chapter 11.

The Role of the General Journal

Special journals save much time in recording repetitive transactions and posting to the ledgers. But some transactions do not fit into any of the special journals. Examples include adjustments such as the amortization of buildings and equipment, the expiration of prepaid insurance, and the accrual of salary payable at the end of the period.

Even the most sophisticated accounting system needs a general journal. The adjusting entries and the closing entries that we illustrated in Chapters 3 through 5 are recorded in the general journal, along with other non-routine transactions.

Many companies also use the general journal for sales returns and allowances and purchase returns and allowances. Let's turn now to sales returns and allowances, and the related business document, the *credit memo*.

The Credit Memo—The Document for Recording Sales Returns and Allowances

As we saw in Chapter 5, customers sometimes return merchandise to the seller, and sellers grant sales allowances to customers because of product defects and for other reasons. The effect of sales returns and sales allowances is the same—they decrease net sales and accounts receivable in the same way a sales discount does. The document issued by the seller for a credit to the customer's Account Receivable is called a **credit memo**, because the company gives the customer credit for the returned merchandise. When a company issues a credit memo, it debits Sales Returns and Allowances and credits Accounts Receivable.

On November 27, Austin Sound sold four stereo speakers for $1,783 on account to Clay Schmidt. Later, Schmidt discovered a defect and returned the speakers. Austin Sound then issued to Schmidt a credit memo like the one in Exhibit 7–11.

KEY POINT

The *originator* of the credit memo is "crediting" Accounts Receivable. The *receiver* of the credit memo debits Accounts Payable.

EXHIBIT 7–11 Credit Memo

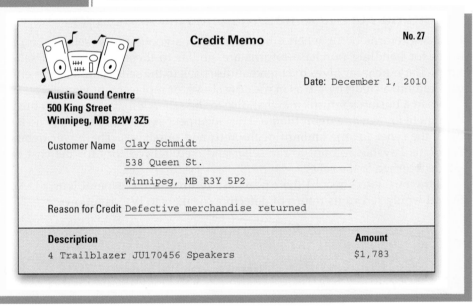

To record the *sale return* and receipt of the defective speakers from customer Clay Schmidt, Austin Sound would make the following entries in the general journal:

	General Journal			Page 9
Date 2010	Accounts	Post Ref.	Debit	Credit
Dec. 1	Sales Returns and Allowances	430	1,783	
	Accounts Receivable—Clay Schmidt 115391	115/✓		1,783
	Credit memo no. 27.			
Dec. 1	Inventory	131	431	
	Cost of Goods Sold	511		431
	Received defective goods from customer.			

KEY POINT

Two posting are needed for Accounts Receivable because the control account and the customer account must both be updated. This is noted in the general journal on the same line.

Focus on the first entry. The debit side of the entry is posted to Sales Returns and Allowances. After posting, its account number (430) is written in the Posting Reference column. The credit side of the entry requires two $1,783 postings, one to Accounts Receivable, the *control account* in the general ledger (account number 115), and the other to Clay Schmidt's *individual account* in the accounts receivable subsidiary ledger, account number 115391. These credit postings explain why the document is called a *credit memo*.

Observe that the posting reference of the credit includes two notations. The account number (115) denotes the posting to Accounts Receivable in the general ledger. The check mark (✓) denotes the posting to Schmidt's account in the subsidiary ledger. It doesn't have specially designed columns, so it is necessary to write both posting references on the same line, and a (✓) is sufficient.

A business with a high volume of sales returns, such as a department store chain, may use a special journal for sales returns and allowances.

The second general-journal entry records Austin Sound's receipt of the defective inventory from the customer. The speakers cost Austin Sound $431, and Austin Sound, like all other merchandisers, records its inventory at cost. Now let's see how Austin Sound records the return of the defective speakers to JVC, from which Austin Sound purchased them.

The Debit Memo—The Business Document for Recording Purchase Returns and Allowances

Purchase returns occur when a business returns goods to the seller. The procedures for handling purchase returns are similar to those dealing with sales returns. The purchaser gives the merchandise back to the seller and receives either a cash refund, a credit memo as in the case above, or replacement goods.

When a business returns merchandise to the seller, it may also send a business document known as a **debit memo**. This document states that the buyer no longer owes the seller for the amount of the returned purchases. The buyer debits the Accounts Payable account to the seller and credits Inventory for the cost of the goods returned to the seller.

Many businesses record their purchase returns in the general journal. Austin Sound would record its return of defective speakers to JVC as follows:

General Journal					Page 9
Date 2010	Accounts		Post Ref.	Debit	Credit
Dec. 2	Accounts Payable—JVC Corp. 210240.......................		210/✓	431	
	Inventory		131		431
	Debit memo no. 16.				

When using a perpetual inventory system, Inventory must be kept up to date for returns of goods to the seller. Therefore, Inventory is credited, because the items are no longer on hand. When using a periodic inventory system, the Purchase Returns and Allowances account will be credited so that cost of goods sold can be calculated properly.

When you first learn about special journals, it may be confusing to remember which special journal to use for a transaction. Exhibit 7–12 summarizes a process you can follow to choose the special journal to use for a transaction.

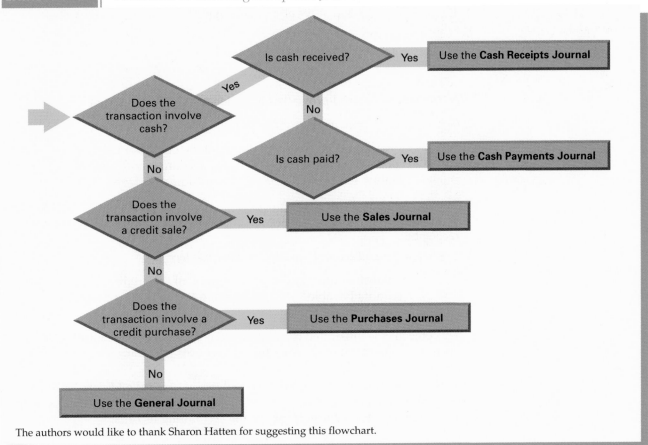

The authors would like to thank Sharon Hatten for suggesting this flowchart.

DID YOU GET IT?

MyAccountingLab

To check your understanding of the material in this Learning Objective, complete these questions. The solutions appear on MyAccountingLab so you can check your progress.

9. In which journal would you record each transaction?

    (1) Building rent paid in cash
    (2) Sale of land
    (3) Bank lends a business cash
    (4) Business purchases a personal computer for cash
    (5) Purchase of supplies on credit
    (6) Accrue salary payable

10. Refer to the Sidney Company transactions in Did You Get It? Question 7 on page 357–358. Which of those transactions would be recorded in the purchases journal? Record those transactions in a purchases journal using the format shown in Exhibit 7–9.

11. Refer to the Sidney Company transactions in Did You Get It? Question 7 on page 357–358. Which of those transactions would be recorded in the cash payments journal? Record those transactions in a cash payments journal using the format shown in Exhibit 7–10.

Balancing the Ledgers

At the end of the period, after all postings have been made, equality should exist as follows:

1. *General ledger:*

$$\text{Total debits} = \text{Total credits}$$

A trial balance would prove that total debits equal total credits.

2. *General ledger and accounts receivable subsidiary ledger:*

$$\begin{array}{ccc}\text{Balance of the} & & \text{Sum of all the customer balances} \\ \text{Accounts Receivable} & = & \text{in the accounts receivable} \\ \text{control account} & & \text{subsidiary ledger}\end{array}$$

This objective is illustrated on page 357. The comparison shows that the general ledger control account balance equals the total of the schedule of accounts receivable.

3. *General ledger and accounts payable subsidiary ledger:*

$$\begin{array}{ccc}\text{Balance of the} & & \text{Sum of all the creditor} \\ \text{Accounts Payable} & = & \text{balances in the accounts payable} \\ \text{control account} & & \text{subsidiary ledger}\end{array}$$

This objective is illustrated on page 362. The general ledger control account balance equals the total of the schedule of accounts payable.

This process of ensuring that these equalities exist is called *balancing the ledgers, reconciling the ledgers,* or *proving the ledgers.* It is an important control procedure because it helps ensure the accuracy of the accounting records.

Special Journals and Sales Taxes

In Chapter 5, the federal Goods and Services Tax (GST) was introduced; recall that the GST is collected at each level of transaction right down to the consumer, the final level. The discussion that follows relates to consumption or sales taxes levied by all the provinces except Alberta. The Yukon, the Northwest Territories, and Nunavut also do not have a sales tax. Sellers must add the tax to the sale amount, then pay or remit the tax to the provincial government. In most jurisdictions except Quebec, sales tax is levied only on final consumers, so retail businesses usually do not pay sales tax on the goods they purchase for resale. For example, Austin Sound Centre would not pay sales tax on a purchase of equipment from JVC Canada Inc., a wholesaler. However, when retailers like Austin Sound Centre make sales, they must collect sales tax from the consumer. In effect, retailers serve as collecting agents for the taxing authorities. The amount of tax depends on the total sales and the provincial tax rate.

Retailers set up procedures to collect the sales tax, account for it, and pay it on time. Invoices may be preprinted with a place for entering the sales tax amount, and the general ledger has a liability account entitled Sales Tax Payable. Special journals may include a special column for sales tax, such as those illustrated in Exhibit 7–13. The sales tax rate in the exhibit is 7 percent, the rate of sales tax in Manitoba and British Columbia, and the GST rate is 5 percent, the rate in effect at the time of printing.

In the sales journal in Exhibit 7–13, note that the amount debited to Accounts Receivable ($3,717.28) is the sum of the credits to Sales Tax Payable ($232.33), GST Payable ($165.95), and Sales Revenue ($3,319.00). This is so because the amounts charged to customers, the Accounts Receivable figures, are partly for the purchase of merchandise (Sales Revenue) and partly for taxes charged on the sale. The check marks in the Posting Reference column show that individual amounts have been posted to the customer accounts. The absence of account numbers under the column totals shows that the total amounts have not yet been posted.

EXHIBIT 7-13 Special Journals Designed to Account for Sales Tax

Sales Journal Page 4

Date	Inv. No.	Account Debited	Post. Ref.	Accounts Receivable Dr.	Sales Tax Payable Cr.	GST Payable Cr.	Sales Revenue Cr.	Cost of Goods Sold Dr. Inventory Cr.
2010								
Nov. 2	422	Anne Fortin	✔	1,047.20	65.45	46.75	935.00	600.00
13	423	Brent Mooney	✔	777.28	48.58	34.70	694.00	380.00
18	424	Debby Levy	✔	1,015.84	63.49	45.35	907.00	550.00
27	425	Dan Girardi	✔	876.96	54.81	39.15	783.00	500.00
30		Totals		3,717.28	232.33	165.95	3,319.00	2,030.00

Cash Receipts Journal Page 5

	Debits			Credits			Other Accounts			Cost of Goods
Date	Cash	Sales Discounts	Accounts Receivable	Sales Revenue	PST Payable	GST Payable	Account Title	Post. Ref.	Amount	Sold Dr. Inventory Cr.
2010										
Nov. 6	560			500	35	25				290
12	1,000						Note payable to Scotiabank	222	1,000	
29	1,120			1,000	70	50				750
30	2,680			1,500	105	75			1,000	1,040

Purchases Journal Page 2

				Credits			Debits			
								Other Accounts		
Date	Account Credited	Terms	Post. Ref.	Accounts Payable	Inventory	GST Recoverable	Account Title	Post. Ref.	Amount	
2010										
Nov. 2	JVC Canada Inc. 210240	3/15, n/30	✔	735.00	700.00	35.00				
5	Electrohome Ltd. 210152	n/30	✔	315.00	300.00	15.00				
9	City Office Supply Co. 210079	2/10, n/30	✔	472.50		22.50	Fixtures	191	450.00	
30	Totals			1,522.50	1,000.00	72.50			450.00	

Cash Payments Journal Page 4

					Debits			Credits	
Date	Ch. No.	Payee	Accounts Debited	Post. Ref.	Other Accounts	Accounts Payable	GST Recoverable	Inventory	Cash
2010									
Nov. 3	101	R. Landis Ltd.	Inventory	131	1,200		60		1,260
8	102	Grand and Toy	Supplies	161	100		5		105
26	130	JVC Canada Inc.	JVC Canada Inc. 210240	✔		742		21	721
30					1,300	742	65	21	2,086

Most companies that use point-of-sale cash registers have them programmed to calculate separate totals, as sales are being scanned, of taxable items and nontaxable items; the register then calculates the relevant taxes—sales tax, if applicable, and GST—and computes the total owing. Provincial sales tax (PST) and the federal GST are not applicable to all items. (For example, prescription medicines are excluded from both; reading material is excluded from most sales taxes but not from GST, except textbooks.) Most businesses calculate sales tax and GST at the time of sale.

Sales tax and GST are also discussed in Chapter 11.

Blending Computers and Special Journals in an Accounting Information System

Computerizing special journals to create accounting modules requires no drastic change in the accounting system's design. Systems designers create a special screen for each accounting application (**module**)—credit sales, cash receipts, purchases on account, payroll, and cash payments. The special screen for credit sales would prompt the operator entering the data, for example, on a terminal or a cash register, to type in the following information:

- Date
- Customer number
- Customer name

- Invoice number
- Dollar amount of the sale
- Cost of the goods sold

These data can generate the sales journal and monthly statements for customers that show activity and ending balances.

DID YOU GET IT?

MyAccountingLab

To check your understanding of the material in this Learning Objective, complete this question. The solution appears on MyAccountingLab so you can check your progress.

12. At the time of printing, Nova Scotia, New Brunswick, and Newfoundland and Labrador had a harmonized sales tax (HST) rate of 13 percent, which combines the GST and PST rates into one rate. How would the special journals in Exhibit 7–13 change for a company operating in Nova Scotia?

OBJECTIVE ⑦

Assess the impact on accounting information systems of international financial reporting standards (IFRS)

Accounting-Cycle and Financial-Reporting Implications of IFRS

This chapter deals with the methods companies use to gather and record transactions. This part of the accounting cycle is not affected by international financial reporting standards (IFRS), except to the extent that companies reporting under IFRS may need to collect more information in order to properly prepare and present their financial information.

Perhaps the best example of the need to collect more or different information is that companies reporting under IFRS have to present a statement of comprehensive income, which could include some transactions that would not be reported under GAAP for private enterprises. Companies reporting under IFRS must ensure that their accounting system is able to properly record these transactions so that they can be included in the financial statements.

DID YOU GET IT?

To check your understanding of the material in this Learning Objective, complete this question. The solution appears on MyAccountingLab so you can check your progress.

13. A company has chosen to prepare its financial statements under IFRS beginning in 2011. Would this company be able to use the same special journals it was using in 2010 while reporting under GAAP for private enterprises?

As we conclude this chapter, we can reflect on our opening questions: What is an accounting information system, and why is it important? What are the differences between manual and computerized accounting systems? How can special journals be used to combine similar transactions and speed the accounting process? These questions were answered throughout this chapter. The Decision Guidelines end this chapter with a summary that provides guidelines for some of the major decisions accountants must make as they use an accounting information system.

DECISION GUIDELINES
Using Special Journals and Control Accounts

Decision	Guidelines
What is an accounting information system and why is it important?	An accounting information system is the combination of personnel, records, and procedures that a business uses to meet its needs for financial data. The system collects information, processes it, and produces reports that meet users' needs.
What are the main processing components of an accounting system?	Journals • General journal • Special journals Ledgers • General ledger • Subsidiary ledgers
What are the differences between manual and computerized accounting systems?	Computerized systems allow data to be entered or input into the accounting system using menus or modules, and they automatically post the data and, when directed, print reports. In a manual accounting system, every step in the accounting cycle must be completed manually, as illustrated in previous chapters.
Where do we record • Sales of merchandise on account? • Cash receipts? • Purchases on account? • Cash payments? • All other transactions?	Journals: Sales journal Cash receipts journal Purchases journal Cash payments journal General journal
How does the general ledger relate to the subsidiary ledgers?	**GENERAL LEDGER** **Accounts Receivable** **Accounts Payable** X,XXX XX **SUBSIDIARY LEDGERS** **ACCOUNTS RECEIVABLE FROM:** **ACCOUNTS PAYABLE TO:** **Arnold** **Barnes** **Agnew** **Black** XX XX X X
When do we post from the journals to • The general ledger? • Subsidiary ledgers?	—Monthly (or more often, if needed) —Daily
How do we achieve control over • Accounts receivable? • Accounts payable?	Balance the ledgers, as follows: **General Ledger** = **Subsidiary Ledger** Accounts receivable = Sum of individual *customer* accounts receivable Accounts payable = Sum of individual *supplier* accounts payable

Name: Taylor Company
Accounting Period: Month of March 2010
Key Fact: Merchandiser using perpetual inventory system

Taylor Company, a furniture supplier, completed the following selected transactions during March 2010:

Mar. 1 Sold $1,300 of lighting to Jen Zrilladich, terms n/30, invoice 310 (cost, $850).

3 Purchased inventory on credit terms of 1/10, n/60 from Lane Corp., $4,000.

4 Received $1,000 from a cash sale to a customer (cost $638).

6 Received $120 on account from Jim Bryant. The full invoice amount was $130, but Bryant paid within the discount period to earn the $10 discount.

9 Received $2,160 on a note receivable from Lesley Cliff. This amount includes the $2,000 note receivable plus $160 of interest revenue.

10 Purchased lighting from an artisan, $300, issuing cheque no. 401.

15 Sold $2,500 of outdoor seating to Pajo's Restaurant, terms n/30, invoice 311 (cost, $1,700).

15 Received $1,600 from a cash sale to a customer (cost $1,044).

24 Borrowed $4,400 by signing a note payable to Bank of Nova Scotia.

27 Received $2,400 on account from Lance Au. Payment was received after the discount period lapsed.

29 Paid Lane Corp. for the purchase made on May 3, cheque no. 402.

The general ledger showed the following balances at February 28, 2010: Cash, $2,234; Accounts Receivable, $5,580; Note Receivable—Lesley Cliff, $2,000; Inventory, $3,638; Jim Taylor, Capital, $13,452. The accounts receivable subsidiary ledger at February 28 contained debit balances as follows: Lance Au, $3,680; Melinda Fultz, $1,770; Jim Bryant, $130.

Required

1. Record the transactions in the cash receipts journal (page 7), cash payments journal (page 5), sales journal (page 8), and purchases journal (page 4). Taylor Company uses a perpetual inventory system. Disregard GST and PST in this question.

2. Compute column totals at March 31, 2010, in all the special journals. Show that total debits equal total credits in each of the special journals.

3. Post to the general ledger, the accounts receivable subsidiary ledger, and the accounts payable subsidiary ledger. Use complete posting references, including the following account numbers: Cash, 11; Accounts Receivable, 12; Note Receivable—Lesley Cliff, 13; Inventory, 14; Accounts Payable, 20; Note Payable—Bank of Nova Scotia, 22; Jim Taylor, Capital, 30; Sales Revenue, 41; Sales Discounts, 42; Interest Revenue, 46; and Cost of Goods Sold, 51. Insert Bal. in the Posting Reference column (Jrnl. Ref.) for each February 28 account balance.

4. Create a Schedule of Accounts Receivable to balance the accounts receivable subsidiary ledger with Accounts Receivable in the general ledger. Create a Schedule of Accounts Payable to balance the accounts payable subsidiary ledger with Accounts Payable in the general ledger.

SOLUTION

Requirements 1 and 2

Cash Receipts Journal

	Debits		Credits					Cost of Goods Sold Dr. Inventory Cr.
					Other Accounts			
Date	Cash	Sales Discounts	Accounts Receivable	Sales Revenue	Account Title	Post. Ref.	Amount	
2010								
Mar. 4	1,000			1,000				638
6	120	10	130		Jim Bryant	✔		
9	2,160				Note Receivable			
					Lesley Cliff	13	2,000	
					Interest Revenue	46	160	
15	1,600			1,600				1,044
24	4,400				Note Payable—			
					Bank of			
					Nova Scotia	22	4,400	
27	2,400		2,400		Lance Au	✔		
31	11,680	10	2,530	2,600	Total		6,560	1,682
	(11)	(42)	(12)	(41)			(✔)	(51/14)

Total Dr. = 11,690   Total Cr. = 11,690

Recall that Taylor Company uses the perpetual inventory system. As a result, record the cost of the goods sold and the inventory reduction for each sale transaction. Taylor's cash receipts journal has a column at the far right for this purpose.

Items recorded in the Other Accounts columns must be listed and posted individually.

For each transaction, make sure all amounts in the Debits columns equal all amounts in the Credits columns.

Selected transactions are explained more fully:

Mar. 4 and 15: For each of these sales transactions, the cost of goods sold and inventory reduction are also recorded.

Mar. 6: The debit columns include the $120 cash received (invoice amount less the discount) and the $10 discount. Accounts Receivable is credited for $130, and Jim Bryant is entered in the Other Accounts Account Title column so that his accounts receivable subsidiary ledger account balance is reduced by $130.

Mar. 9: This is an example of a compound entry with infrequently used accounts. Therefore, the Note Receivable—Lesley Cliff and Interest Revenue accounts are listed in the Other Accounts columns.

For Requirements 2 and 3:

In the Other Accounts columns above,
• the check mark in the Post. Ref. column indicates credits were individually posted to the accounts receivable subsidiary ledger
• the check mark under the Amount total indicates posting was completed for all items in the column

Note that the Inventory column under the Credits heading is used to record the reduction in inventory when cash discounts are taken. This is different from the March 10 purchase of inventory for cash, which is recorded in the Other Accounts column and posted separately.

Cash Payments Journal   Page 5

Date	Chq. No.	Accounts Debited	Post. Ref.	Debits — Other Accounts	Debits — Accounts Payable	Credits — Inventory	Cash
2010							
Mar. 10	401	Inventory	14	300			300
29	402	Lane Corp.	✔		4,000		4,000
31				300	4,000		4,300
				✔	(20)		(11)

Total Dr. = $4,300   Total Cr. = $4,300

Recall that Taylor Company uses the perpetual inventory system. As a result, record the cost of the goods sold and the inventory reduction for each sale transaction. Taylor's sales journal has a column at the far right for this purpose.

For each transaction, make sure all amounts in the Debits columns equal all amounts in the Credits columns.

Sales Journal   Page 8

Date	Invoice No.	Accounts Debited	Post. Ref.	Accounts Receivable Dr.	Sales Revenue Cr.	Cost of Goods Sold Dr. Inventory Cr.
2010						
Mar. 1	310	J. Zrilladich	✔	1,300	1,300	850
15	311	Pajo's Restaurant	✔	2,500	2,500	1,700
31				3,800	3,800	2,550
				(12)	(41)	(51/14)

Total Dr. = $3,800   Total Cr. = $3,800

Purchases Journal   Page 4

Date	Account Credited	Terms	Post. Ref.	Credits — Accounts Payable	Debits — Inventory	Debits — Other Accounts — Account Title	Debits — Other Accounts — Post. Ref.	Debits — Other Accounts — Amount
2010								
Mar. 3	Lane Corp.	$1/10, n/60$	✔	4,000	4,000			
31				4,000	4,000			
				(20)	(14)			

Total Cr. = $4,000   Total Dr. = $4,000

Requirement 3 **Accounts Receivable Subsidiary Ledger**

Lance Au

Date 2010	Item	Jrnl. Ref.	Debit	Credit	Balance
Feb. 28		Bal.			3,680
Mar. 27		CR. 7		2,400	1,280

Jim Bryant

Date 2010	Item	Jrnl. Ref.	Debit	Credit	Balance
Feb. 28		Bal.			130
Mar. 6		CR. 7		130	0

Melinda Fultz

Date 2010	Item	Jrnl. Ref.	Debit	Credit	Balance
Feb. 28		Bal.			1,770

Pajo's Restaurant

Date 2010	Item	Jrnl. Ref.	Debit	Credit	Balance
Mar. 15		S. 8	2,500		2,500

Jen Zrilladich

Date 2010	Item	Jrnl. Ref.	Debit	Credit	Balance
Mar. 1		S. 8	1,300		1,300

Accounts Payable Subsidiary Ledger

Lane Corp.

Date 2010	Item	Jrnl. Ref.	Debit	Credit	Credit Balance
Mar. 3		P. 4		4,000	4,000
Mar. 29		CP. 5	4,000		0

General Ledger

Cash No. 11

Date 2010	Item	Jrnl. Ref.	Debit	Credit	Debit Balance
Feb. 28		Bal.			2,234
Mar. 31		CR. 7	11,680		13,914
31		CP. 5		4,300	9,614

Accounts Receivable No. 12

Date 2010	Item	Jrnl. Ref.	Debit	Credit	Debit Balance
Feb. 28		Bal.			5,580
Mar. 31		CR. 7		2,530	3,050
31		S. 8	3,800		6,850

Note Receivable—Lesley Cliff No. 13

Date 2010	Item	Jrnl. Ref.	Debit	Credit	Debit Balance
Feb. 28		Bal.			2,000
Mar. 9		CR. 7		2,000	0

Inventory No. 14

Date 2010	Item	Jrnl. Ref.	Debit	Credit	Debit Balance
Feb. 28		Bal.			3,638
Mar. 10		CP. 5	300		3,938
31		CR. 7		1,682	2,256
31		S. 8		2,550	(294)
31		P. 4	4,000		3,706

Accounts Payable No. 20

Date 2010	Item	Jrnl. Ref.	Debit	Credit	Credit Balance
Mar. 31		P. 4		4,000	4,000
31		CP. 5	4,000		0

Note Payable—Bank of Nova Scotia No. 22

Date 2010	Item	Jrnl. Ref.	Debit	Credit	Credit Balance
Mar. 24		CR. 7		4,400	4,400

Jim Taylor, Capital No. 30

Date 2010	Item	Jrnl. Ref.	Debit	Credit	Credit Balance
Feb. 28		Bal.			13,452

Sales Revenue No. 41

Date 2010	Item	Jrnl. Ref.	Debit	Credit	Credit Balance
Mar. 31		CR. 7		2,600	2,600
31		S. 8		3,800	6,400

Sales Discounts No. 42

Date 2010	Item	Jrnl. Ref.	Debit	Credit	Debit Balance
Mar. 31		CR. 7	10		10

Interest Revenue No. 46

Date 2010	Item	Jrnl. Ref.	Debit	Credit	Credit Balance
Mar. 9		CR. 7		160	160

Cost of Goods Sold No. 51

Date 2010	Item	Jrnl. Ref.	Debit	Credit	Debit Balance
Mar. 31		CR. 7	1,682		1,682
31		S. 8	2,550		4,232

Recall that subsidiary ledger postings occur on the date of the transaction. General ledger postings occur at the end of the month. Both types of posting use CR.7, for example, to indicate the cash receipts journal as the source of the entry.

Requirement 4

From the general ledger:

Accounts Receivable $6,850

From the accounts receivable subsidiary ledger:

TAYLOR COMPANY
Schedule of Accounts Receivable
March 31, 2010

Lance Au..	$1,280
Melinda Fultz..	1,770
Pajo's Restaurant	2,500
Jen Zrilladich...	1,300
Total accounts receivable	$6,850

Note: If Taylor Company had used the periodic inventory system, account No. 51, Cost of Goods Sold, would not exist, so there would be no Cost of Goods Sold column in the cash receipts journal. As well, there would be no $1,682 credit posting to Inventory originating from the cash receipts journal. The same is true for the Cost of Goods Sold and Inventory columns in the sales journal.

At month end, customer account balances from the accounts receivable subsidiary ledger are listed and compared to the general ledger control account.

At March 31, 2010, the Accounts Payable balance in the general ledger is nil. All accounts in the accounts payable subsidiary ledger are nil, so both the control account and subsidiary ledger are in balance.

Summary

1. **Describe an effective accounting information system.** An effective *accounting information system* captures and summarizes transactions to provide timely, accurate information to users and decision makers. The five major aspects of a good accounting system are (1) control over operations, (2) compatibility with the particular features of the business, (3) flexibility in response to changes in the business, (4) reports that meet users' needs, and (5) a favourable cost/benefit relationship, with benefits outweighing costs.

2. **Understand the elements of computerized and manual accounting systems.** Computerized accounting systems process inputs faster than do manual systems and can generate more types of reports. The key components of a computerized accounting system are hardware, software, and company personnel. Account numbers play a bigger role in the operation of computerized systems than they do in manual systems, because computers classify accounts by account numbers. Both computerized and manual accounting systems require transactions to be classified by type.

   Computerized systems use a *menu* structure to organize accounting functions. The system can be designed so that data are entered and the computer does the rest. Posting, trial balances, financial statements, and closing procedures are easily completed in a computerized accounting system. Computerized accounting systems are integrated so that the different *modules* of the system are updated automatically. While computers cannot fix data entry errors, programs can reduce the chance of data errors by highlighting unbalanced or unusual journal entries.

3. **Journalize and post transactions using the sales journal, the cash receipts journal, and the accounts receivable subsidiary ledger.** Many accounting systems use *special journals* to record transactions by category. Credit sales are recorded in a *sales journal*, and cash receipts in a *cash receipts journal*. Posting from these journals is both to the *general ledger* and to the *accounts receivable subsidiary ledger*, which lists each customer and the amount receivable from that customer. The accounts receivable subsidiary ledger is the main device for ensuring that the company collects from customers.

4. **Journalize and post transactions using the purchases journal, the cash payments journal, and the accounts payable subsidiary ledger.** Credit purchases are recorded in a *purchases journal*, and cash payments in a *cash payments journal*. Posting from these journals is to the *general ledger* and to the *accounts payable subsidiary ledger*. The accounts payable subsidiary ledger helps the company stay current in payments to suppliers and take advantage of purchase discounts.

5. **Balance the ledgers.** At the end of the period, general ledger account balances are summarized on a trial balance to ensure total debits equal total credits. Accounts receivable subsidiary ledger customer account balances are totalled and compared to the Accounts Receivable control account in the general ledger. The same comparison is done for the accounts payable subsidiary ledger supplier account balances and the Accounts Payable control account in the general ledger. Balancing the ledgers helps to ensure the accounting records are accurate.

6. **Use special journals to record and post transactions with sales taxes.** In those provinces with provincial sales taxes, sellers must add and collect sales tax on the goods they sell to consumers and remit the tax to the provincial government. Sellers throughout Canada must do the same for the Goods and Services Tax (GST). Sellers must also pay GST on the goods and services they purchase but can recover this tax from the federal government. Special journals can include columns for PST Payable, GST Payable, and GST Recoverable, as applicable, to streamline accounting for these amounts.

7. **Assess the impact on accounting information systems of international financial reporting standards (IFRS).** Accounting information systems are not affected by IFRS, except to the extent that companies reporting under IFRS may need to collect more accounting information to properly prepare and present their financial information.

SELF-STUDY QUESTIONS

Test your understanding of the chapter by marking the correct answer for each of the following questions:

1. Why does a jewellery store need an accounting system that is different from what a physician uses? (*pp. 343–344*)
   a. They have different kinds of employees.
   b. They have different kinds of journals and ledgers.
   c. They have different kinds of business transactions.
   d. They work different hours.

2. Which feature of an effective information system is most concerned with safeguarding assets? (*p. 343*)
   a. Control
   c. Flexibility
   b. Compatibility
   d. Reports that meet users' needs
   e. Favourable cost/benefit relationship

3. The account number 211031 most likely refers to (*p. 347*)
   a. Liabilities
   c. Accounts Payable
   b. Current liabilities
   d. An individual supplier

4. A company uses a sales journal, a purchases journal, a cash receipts journal, a cash payments journal, and a general journal. A sales return for credit would be recorded in the (*p. 363*)
   a. Sales journal
   b. General journal
   c. Sales return and allowances journal
   d. Cash payments journal
   e. Accounts payable subsidiary ledger

5. Special journals help most by (*p. 351*)
   a. Limiting the number of transactions that have to be recorded
   b. Reducing the cost of operating the accounting system
   c. Improving accuracy in posting to subsidiary ledgers
   d. Easing the preparation of the financial statements

6. Centex Sound Systems purchased inventory costing $8,000 from Sony on account. Where should Centex record this transaction, and what account is credited? (*p. 358*)
   a. Cash payments journal; credit Cash
   b. Sales journal; credit Sales Revenue
   c. Purchases journal; credit Accounts Payable
   d. General journal; credit Inventory

7. Every transaction recorded in the cash receipts journal includes a (*p. 354*)
   a. Credit to Cash
   b. Debit to Accounts Receivable
   c. Debit to Sales Discounts
   d. Debit to Cash

8. Entries in the purchases journal are posted to the (*p. 360*)
   a. General ledger only
   b. General ledger and the accounts payable subsidiary ledger
   c. General ledger and the accounts receivable subsidiary ledger
   d. Accounts receivable subsidiary ledger and the accounts payable subsidiary ledger

9. Every transaction recorded in the cash payments journal includes a (*p. 360*)
   a. Debit to Accounts Payable
   b. Debit to an Other Account
   c. Credit to Inventory
   d. Credit to Cash

10. The individual accounts in the accounts receivable subsidiary ledger identify (*p. 353*)
    a. Payees
    b. Debtors
    c. Amounts to be paid
    d. Suppliers

Answers to Self-Study Questions

1.c 3.d 5.b 7.d 9.d
2.a 4.b 6.c 8.b 10.b

ACCOUNTING VOCABULARY

Accounting information system (*p. 343*)
Batch processing (*p. 348*)
Cash payments journal (*p. 360*)
Cash receipts journal (*p. 354*)
Control account (*p. 354*)
Credit memo (*p. 363*)
Database (*p. 344*)

Debit memo (*p. 364*)
Enterprise resource planning (ERP) (*p. 348*)
General journal (*p. 351*)
General ledger (*p. 353*)
Hardware (*p. 344*)
Menu (*p. 348*)
Module (*p. 348*)

Network   (p. 344)
Online processing   (p. 348)
Purchases journal   (p. 358)
Real-time processing   (p. 348)
Sales journal   (p. 351)

Server   (p. 344)
Software   (p. 344)
Special journal   (p. 351)
Subsidiary ledger   (p. 353)

SIMILAR ACCOUNTING TERMS

Accounts payable subsidiary ledger	Accounts payable ledger, accounts payable subledger
Accounts receivable subsidiary ledger	Accounts receivable ledger, accounts receivable subledger
Balancing the ledgers	Proving the ledgers, reconciling the ledgers, reconciling receivables and payables
Cash payments journal	Cash disbursements journal, cheque register
Credit memo	Credit memorandum
Database	Management information system
Debit memo	Debit memorandum
Online processing	Real-time processing

Assignment Material

QUESTIONS

1. Describe the five criteria of an effective accounting system.

2. Distinguish batch computer processing from online computer processing.

3. What accounting categories correspond to the account numbers 1, 2, 3, 4, and 5 in the chart of accounts in a typical computerized accounting system?

4. Why might the number 112 be assigned to Accounts Receivable and the number 1120708 to Carl Erickson, a customer?

5. Describe the function of menus in a computerized accounting system.

6. Name four special journals used in accounting systems. For what type of transaction is each designed?

7. Describe the two advantages that special journals have over recording all transactions in the general journal.

8. What is a control account, and how is it related to a subsidiary ledger? Name two common control accounts.

9. Graff Company's sales journal has one amount column headed Accounts Receivable Dr and Sales Revenue Cr. In this journal, 86 transactions are recorded. How many posting references or (✓) appear in the journal? State what each posting reference represents.

10. The accountant for Bannister Co. posted all amounts correctly from the cash receipts journal to the general ledger. However, she failed to post three credits to customer accounts in the accounts receivable subsidiary ledger. How would this error be detected?

11. At what two times is posting done from a special journal? What items are posted at each time?

12. Describe how to use the sales journal to account for sales tax collected from customers.

13. What is the purpose of balancing, or reconciling, the ledgers?

14. Posting from the journals of McKedrick Realty is complete. But the total of the individual balances in the accounts payable subsidiary ledger does not equal the balance in the Accounts Payable control account in the general ledger. Does this necessarily indicate that the trial balance is out of balance? Explain.

15. Assume that posting is completed. The trial balance shows no errors, but the sum of the individual accounts payable does not equal the Accounts Payable control balance in the general ledger. What two errors could cause this problem?

STARTERS

MyAccountingLab | All questions in this section appear in MyAccountingLab.

Features of an effective information system

Starter 7–1   Suppose you have invested your life savings in a company that prints rubberized logos on T-shirts. The business is growing fast, and you need a better accounting information system. Consider the features of an effective system, as discussed on pages 343–344. Which do you regard as most important? Why? Which feature must you consider if your financial resources are limited?

Starter 7–2 Identify each of the following items as an element of a computerized accounting system (c), a manual accounting system (m), or both (b).

Identifying the elements of computerized and manual accounting systems

1. The trial balance transferred to or entered on the work sheet.
2. Automatic posting to the general ledger.
3. The use of UPC codes for inventory.
4. Printing financial statements.
5. Closing the accounts by debiting Income Summary and crediting expenses.
6. Starting the cycle with account balances in the general ledger.

Starter 7–3 Complete the crossword puzzle.

Accounting system vocabulary
① ②

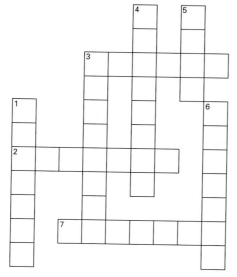

Across:
2. Electronic linkage that allows different computers to share the same information
3. Main computer in a networked system
7. Cost/_____ relationship must be favourable

Down:
1. Managers need _____ over operations in order to authorize transactions and safeguard assets
3. Programs that drive a computer
4. Electronic computer equipment
5. A _____ ible information system accommodates changes as the organization evolves
6. The opposite of debits

Starter 7–4 Assign account numbers (from the list that follows) to the accounts of LP Gas Co. Identify the headings, which are *not* accounts and would not be assigned an account number.

Assigning account numbers
②

Assets	LP, Capital
Current Assets	LP, Withdrawals
Inventory	Revenues
Accounts Payable	Selling Expenses

Numbers from which to choose:

151	301
191	311
201	411
281	531

Starter 7–5 Use the following abbreviations to indicate the journal in which you would record transactions a through n.

Using the journals
③ ④

G = General journal   P = Purchases journal
S = Sales journal   CP = Cash payments journal
CR = Cash receipts journal

Transactions:

a. _____ Cash sale of inventory
b. _____ Payment of rent
c. _____ Amortization of computer equipment
d. _____ Purchases of inventory on account
e. _____ Collection of accounts receivable
f. _____ Expiration of prepaid insurance
g. _____ Sale on account
h. _____ Payment on account
i. _____ Cash purchase of inventory
j. _____ Collection of dividend revenue earned on an investment
k. _____ Prepayment of insurance

l. _____ Borrowing money on a long-term note payable

m. _____ Purchase of equipment on account

n. _____ Cost of goods sold along with a credit sale

o. _____ Return of merchandise

Using the sales journal and the related ledgers

③

Starter 7–6 Use the sales journal and the related ledger accounts in Exhibit 7–7, page 352, to answer these questions about Austin Sound Centre.

1. How much inventory did Austin Sound have on hand at the end of November? Where can you get this information?

2. What amount did Austin Sound post to the Sales Revenue account? When did Austin Sound post to the Sales Revenue account? Assume a manual accounting system.

3. After these transactions, how much does Susan Levy owe Austin Sound? Where did you obtain this information? Be specific.

4. If there were no discounts, how much would Austin Sound hope to collect from all its customers? Where is this amount stored in a single figure?

Using accounts receivable records and balancing the ledgers

③ ⑤

Starter 7–7
1. A business that sells on account must have good accounts receivable records to ensure collection from customers. What is the name of the detailed record of amounts collectible from individual customers?

2. Where does the total amount receivable from all the customers appear? Be specific.

3. A key control feature of Austin Sound Centre's accounting system lies in the agreement between the detailed customer receivable records and the summary total in the general ledger. Use the data in Exhibit 7–7, page 352, to reconcile Austin Sound's accounts receivable records at November 30, 2010.

Using cash receipts data

③

Starter 7–8 The cash receipts journal of Austin Sound Centre appears in Exhibit 7–8, page 355, along with the company's various ledger accounts. Use the data in Exhibit 7–8 to answer the following questions raised by Steve Austin, owner of the business.

1. How much were total cash receipts during November?

2. How much cash did Austin Sound collect on account from customers? How much in total discounts did customers earn by paying quickly? How much did Austin Sound's accounts receivable decrease because of collections from customers during November?

3. How much were cash sales during November?

4. How much did Austin Sound borrow during November? Where else could you look to determine whether Austin Sound has paid off part of the loan?

Using the purchases journal

④

Starter 7–9 Use Austin Sound's purchases journal (Exhibit 7–9, page 359) to address these questions that Steve Austin, the owner of the business, is faced with.

1. How much were Austin Sound's total purchases of inventory during November?

2. Suppose it is December 1 and Austin wishes to pay the full amount that Austin Sound owes on account. Examine only the purchases journal. Then make a general journal entry to record payment of the correct amount on December 1. Include an explanation. What other entry would have to be made to keep the ledgers in balance?

Using the purchases journal and the cash payments journal

④

1. Increase in Accounts Payable $2,876

Starter 7–10 Refer to Austin Sound Centre's purchases journal (Exhibit 7–9, page 359) and cash payments journal (Exhibit 7–10, page 361). Steve Austin, the owner, has raised the following questions about the business.

1. How much did total credit purchases of inventory, supplies, equipment, and furniture increase Austin Sound's accounts payable during November?

2. How much of the accounts payable balance did Austin Sound pay off during November?

3. At November 30, after all purchases and all cash payments, how much does Austin Sound owe JVC Canada Inc.? How much in total does Austin Sound owe on account?

Starter 7–11 Answer the following questions about the November transactions of Austin Sound Centre. You will need to refer to Exhibits 7–7 through 7–10, which begin on page 352.

1. How much cash does Austin Sound have on hand at November 30?

2. Determine Austin Sound's gross sales revenue and net sales revenue for November.

3. How did Austin Sound purchase furniture—for cash or on account? Indicate the basis for your answer.

4. From whom did Austin Sound purchase supplies on account? How much in total does Austin Sound owe this company on November 30?

Using all the journals

2. Net sales revenue $7,456

Starter 7–12 Answer the following questions about Austin Sound Centre's special journals.

1. Refer to Austin Sound Centre's sales journal in Exhibit 7–7 on page 352. How would it look different if Austin Sound used the periodic inventory system and all credit sales transactions were subject to PST and GST? Give the headings for all new columns.

2. Refer to Austin Sound Centre's cash receipts journal in Exhibit 7–8 on page 355. How would it look different if Austin Sound used the periodic inventory system and all cash sales transactions were subject to PST and GST? Give the headings for all new columns.

3. Refer to Austin Sound Centre's purchases journal in Exhibit 7–9 on page 359. How would it look different if Austin Sound used the periodic inventory system and all purchases on account were subject to GST? Give the headings for all new columns.

4. Refer to Austin Sound Centre's cash payments journal in Exhibit 7–10 on page 361. How would it look different if Austin Sound used the periodic inventory system and most cash payments were subject to GST? Give the headings for all new columns.

Effects of taxes and the periodic inventory system on special journals

EXERCISES

MyAccountingLab | All questions in this section appear in MyAccountingLab.

Exercise 7–1

The head office of Worldwide Circuits wants to "go green" and reduce paper use and unnecessary reports. Which features of an effective accounting information system will allow for this initiative? Discuss.

Features of an effective accounting information system

Exercise 7–2

It is very important to set up a properly numbered chart of accounts, especially in a computerized accounting system. Use account numbers 101 through 106, 201, 221, 301, 321, 401, 501, and 521 to correspond to the following selected accounts from the general ledger of Casteel Map Company. List the accounts and their account numbers in proper order, starting with the most liquid current asset.

Setting up a chart of accounts

Randy Casteel, Capital	Amortization Expense—Computer Equipment
Accounts Receivable	Cost of Goods Sold
Cash	Note Payable, Long-Term
Accounts Payable	Randy Casteel, Withdrawals
Computer Equipment	Inventory
Supplies	Sales Revenue
Accumulated Amortization—Computer Equipment	

Exercise 7–3

Refer to Exhibit 7–5 on page 349. Which steps are automatic in a computerized accounting system as compared to a manual accounting system?

Elements of computerized and manual accounting systems

Exercise 7–4

Using a trial balance

②

Total assets $114,000

The following accounts and sums of accounts in the computerized accounting system of Zinn Supplies show some of the company's adjusted balances before closing:

Total assets	?
Current assets	33,600
Long-term assets	80,400
Total liabilities	?
Sam Zinn, Capital	81,600
Sam Zinn, Withdrawals	30,000
Total revenues	108,000
Total expenses	66,000

Compute the missing amounts.

Exercise 7–5

Using the sales and cash receipts journals (perpetual inventory system)

③

Total debits to Cash $1,060

The sales and cash receipts journals of Northern Electronics include the following entries:

Sales Journal

Date	Invoice No.	Account Debited	Post. Ref.	Accounts Receivable Dr. Sales Revenue Cr.	Cost of Goods Sold Dr. Inventory Cr.
May. 7	671	I. Pax	✔	220	72
10	672	W. Singh	✔	120	58
10	673	F. Zehr	✔	120	50
12	674	J. Legg	✔	240	120
31		Total		700	300

Cash Receipts Journal

	Debits		Credits		Other Accounts			
Date	Cash	Sales Discounts	Accounts Receivable	Sales Revenue	Account Title	Post. Ref.	Amount	Cost of Goods Sold Dr. Inventory Cr.
May. 16					I. Pax	✔		
19					F. Zehr	✔		
24	600			600				380
30					W. Singh	✔		

Complete the cash receipts journal for those transactions indicated. There are no sales discounts. Also, total the journal and show that total debits equal total credits.

Exercise 7–6

Classifying postings from the cash receipts journal

③

The cash receipts journal of Faubert Sports follows:

Cash Receipts Journal   Page 7

	Debits		Credits		Other Accounts		
Date	Cash	Sales Discounts	Accounts Receivable	Sales Revenue	Account Title	Post. Ref.	Amount
Jan. 2	790	40	830		Magna Corp.	(a)	
9	490		490		Big Fish Inc.	(b)	
19	4,480				Note Receivable	(c)	4,000
					Interest Revenue	(d)	480
30	310	20	330		J. T. Richards	(e)	
31	4,230			4,230			
31	10,300	60	1,650	4,230	Totals		4,480
	(f)	(g)	(h)	(i)			(j)

Faubert Sports' chart of accounts (general ledger) includes the following selected accounts, along with their account numbers:

Number	Account	Number	Account
110	Cash	510	Sales Revenue
120	Accounts Receivable	512	Sales Discounts
125	Note Receivable	515	Sales Returns
140	Land	520	Interest Revenue

Required Indicate whether each posting reference (a) through (j) should be

- A check mark (✓) for a posting to a customer account in the accounts receivable subsidiary ledger.
- An account number for a posting to an account in the general ledger. If so, give the account number.
- A letter (X) for an amount not posted.

Exercise 7–7

A customer account in the accounts receivable subsidiary ledger of Kettle Office Supplies follows:

Identifying transactions from postings to the accounts receivable subsidiary ledger

Beaver Valley Lumber Inc.   112590

Date		Jrnl. Ref.	Dr.	Cr.	Debit Balance
Nov. 1	....				800
9	....	S.5	2,360		3,160
18	....	J.8		380	2,780
30	....	CR.9		1,400	1,380

Required Describe the three posted transactions.

Exercise 7–8

During April, LV Company completed the following credit purchase transactions:

Apr.	5	Purchased supplies, $800, from Central Co.
	11	Purchased inventory, $2,400, from McDonald Ltd. LV Company uses a perpetual inventory system.
	19	Purchased equipment, $8,600, from Baker Corp.
	22	Purchased inventory, $4,420, from Khalil Inc.

Record these transactions first in the general journal—with explanations—and then in the purchases journal. Omit credit terms and posting references. After setting up the purchases journal form, which procedure for recording transactions is quicker? Why?

Recording purchase transactions in the general journal and purchases journal

Purchases journal: Total credit to Accounts Payable $16,220

Exercise 7–9

The purchases journal of Lightning Snowboards follows:

Posting from the purchases journal, balancing the ledgers

3. Total Accounts Payable $2,990

Purchases Journal   Page 7

Date	Account Credited	Terms	Post. Ref.	Accounts Payable Cr.	Inventory Dr.	Supplies Dr.	Other Accounts Dr. Acct. Title	Other Accounts Dr. Post. Ref.	Other Accounts Dr. Amt. Dr.
Sept. 2	Brotherton Inc.	n/30		800	800				
5	Rolf Office Supply	n/30		340		340			
13	Brotherton Inc.	2/10, n/30		1,400	1,400				
26	Marks Equipment Company	n/30		450			Equipment		450
30	Totals			2,990	2,200	340			450

Required

1. Open three-column general ledger accounts for Inventory (account #131), Supplies (account #141), Equipment (account #171), and Accounts Payable (account #210). Post to these accounts from the purchases journal. Use dates and posting references in the ledger accounts.

2. Open accounts in the accounts payable subsidiary ledger for Brotherton Inc., Rolf Office Supply, and Marks Equipment Company. Post from the purchases journal. Use dates and journal references in the ledger accounts.

3. Balance the Accounts Payable control account in the general ledger with the total of the balances in the accounts payable subsidiary ledger.

4. Does Lightning Snowboards use a perpetual or a periodic inventory system?

Exercise 7–10

Using the cash payments journal

④

3. Total credit to Cash $18,895

During February, Dean Products had the following transactions:

Feb.   3   Paid $245 on account to Marquis Corp. net of a $5 discount for an earlier purchase of inventory.
6   Purchased inventory for cash, $1,900.
11   Paid $150 for supplies.
15   Purchased inventory on account from Monroe Corporation, $774.
16   Paid $12,050 on account to LaGrange Ltd.; there was no discount.
21   Purchased furniture for cash, $1,400.
26   Paid $1,950 on account to Graff Software Ltd. for an earlier $2,000 purchase of inventory. The purchase discount was $50.
28   Made a semiannual interest payment of $1,200 on a long-term note payable. The entire payment was for interest. (Assume none of the interest had been accrued previously.)

Required

1. Prepare a cash payments journal similar to the one illustrated in this chapter. Omit the payee column.

2. Record the transactions in the cash payments journal. Which transaction should not be recorded in the cash payments journal? In what journal does it belong?

3. Total the amount columns of the cash payments journal. Determine that the total debits equal the total credits.

Using business documents to record purchases, sales, and returns

④

Eddie's: Credit Cash for $1,835

Exercise 7–11

The following documents describe two business transactions:

Invoice		
Date: March 14, 2010		
Sold to: Eddie's Bicycle Shop		
Sold by: Schwinn Company		
Terms: 2/10, n/30		
Items Purchased Bicycles		
Quantity	**Price**	**Total**
8	$152	$1,216
2	112	224
10	96	960
Total $2,400		

Debit Memo		
Date: March 20, 2010		
Issued to: Schwinn Company		
Issued by: Eddie's Bicycle Shop		
Items Returneed Bicycles		
Quantity	**Price**	**Total**
2	$152	$304
2	112	224
Total $528		
Reason: Damaged in shipment		

Required

1. Use the general journal to record these transactions and Eddie's Bicycle Shop's cash payment on March 21. Record the transactions first on the books of Eddie's Bicycle Shop and then on the books of Schwinn Company, which makes and sells bicycles. Both Eddie's Bicycle Shop and Schwinn Company use a perpetual inventory system as illustrated in Chapter 5. Schwinn Company's cost of the bicycles sold to Eddie's Bicycle Shop was $1,280. Schwinn Company's cost of the returned merchandise was $256. Round to the nearest dollar. Explanations are not required. Using the perpetual system of inventory, set up your answer in the following format:

Date	Eddie's Bicycle Shop Journal Entries	Schwinn Journal Entries

2. How would your answer be different if both of these companies used the periodic inventory system?

Exercise 7–12

Bright's Patio Shop sells garden and patio furniture. All its sales and purchases are subject to 5 percent GST, and its sales are also subject to 7 percent PST. Record the following transactions in the appropriate special journals, using the special journal formats shown in Exhibit 7–13 on page 367. Total each special journal at May 31.

Special journals using PST and GST (perpetual inventory system)

Total debit to Cash from cash receipts journal $4,480

May	1	Sold $1,300 of patio furniture to Jen Williams, terms n/30, invoice 310 (cost, $850).
	3	Purchased inventory on credit terms of 1/10, n/60 from Sisco Corp., $4,000.
	5	Sold inventory for cash, $200 (cost, $110).
	10	Purchased patio lanterns from an artisan, $300, issuing cheque no. 401.
	15	Sold $2,500 of outdoor seating to Pat's Restaurant, terms n/30, invoice 311 (cost, $1,700)
	22	Received payment from Jen Williams (May 1).
	26	Received payment from Pat's Restaurant (May 15).
	29	Paid Sisco Corp. for the purchase made on May 3, cheque no. 402.

SERIAL EXERCISE

This exercise continues the Haupt Consulting situation from Exercise 6–20 of Chapter 6. If you did not complete Exercise 6–20, you can still complete Exercise 7–13 as it is presented.

Exercise 7–13

Haupt Consulting had the following postclosing trial balance at December 31, 2010. Also shown are the account numbers for each account, including the revenue and expense accounts.

Accounting for both merchandising and service transactions under the perpetual inventory system using special journals

2. Jan. 31, 2011, balance of Accounts Receivable from the sales journal $4,000

HAUPT CONSULTING
Postclosing Trial Balance
December 31, 2010

101	Cash	$ 7,200	
102	Accounts receivable	1,500	
103	Software inventory	0	
104	Supplies	100	
105	Prepaid rent	0	
110	Equipment	2,000	
115	Accumulated amortization—equipment		$ 33
120	Furniture	3,600	
125	Accumulated amortization—furniture		60
201	Accounts payable		3,600
202	Salary payable		500
205	Unearned service revenue		600
301	Carl Haupt, capital		9,607
	Total	$14,400	$14,400

302	Carl Haupt, withdrawals
401	Service revenue
402	Sales revenue
501	Cost of goods sold
511	Rent expense
513	Utilities expense
515	Salary expense
521	Amortization expense—equipment
522	Amortization expense—furniture
530	Supplies expense

Consider the January 2011 transactions for Haupt Consulting Company that were presented in Chapter 6. Cost of goods sold, which was calculated using the moving-weighted-average-cost method in a perpetual inventory system, is shown in brackets after each sale.

Jan. 2 Completed a consulting engagement and received cash of $7,200.
2 Prepaid three months' office rent, $3,000.
7 Purchased 100 units of software inventory on account, $1,900, plus freight in, $100.
16 Paid employee salary, $1,400 (note $500 accrued in previous month).
18 Sold 70 software units on account, $3,100 (cost, $1,400).
19 Consulted with a client for a fee of $900 on account.
21 Paid on account, $2,000. (January 7 purchase)
22 Purchased 200 units of software inventory on account, $4,600.
24 Paid utilities, $300.
28 Sold 100 units of software for cash, $4,000 (cost, $2,261).
31 Recorded the following adjusting entries:
   Accrued salary expense, $1,400.
   Prepaid rent expired, $1,000.
   Amortization of office furniture, $60, and of equipment, $33.
   Physical count of inventory, 120 units (cost, $22.61 per unit).

Required

1. Open three-column ledger accounts for all the accounts listed in the December 31, 2010, postclosing trial balance, and for the withdrawals, revenue, and expense accounts listed below it. Use the account numbers shown. Insert the December 31, 2010, balances as the opening balances for January 1, 2011.

2. Journalize the January 2011 transactions in the following special journals: cash receipts journal (page 1), cash payments journal (page 1), sales journal (page 1), purchases journal (page 1), and general journal (page 6). Total each special journal at January 31, 2010.

3. Post the special journals totals to the three-column ledger accounts using the special journal posting references used in this chapter.

4. Prepare a trial balance in the Trial Balance columns of a work sheet. Record the January 31, 2010, adjusting entries on the work sheet, then complete the Adjusted Trial Balance columns of the work sheet for the month ended January 31, 2011.

5. Journalize and post the adjusting entries. Explanations are not required.

CHALLENGE EXERCISE

Exercise 7–14

Using the special journals

③ ④

1. Gross margin $3,935

1. Austin Sound Centre's special journals in Exhibits 7–7 through 7–10 (pp. 352–361) provide the manager with much of the data needed for preparation of the financial statements. Austin Sound uses the *perpetual* inventory system, so the amount of cost of goods sold is simply the ending balance in that account. The manager needs to know the business's gross margin for November. Compute the gross margin.

2. Suppose Austin Sound used the *periodic* inventory system. In that case, the business must compute cost of goods sold by the following formula:

Cost of goods sold:

Beginning inventory......................................	$ 3,885
+ Net purchases...	XXX
= Cost of goods available for sale....................	X,XXX
− Ending inventory..	(4,249)
= Cost of goods sold	$ XX

Perform this calculation of cost of goods sold for Austin Sound. Does this computation of cost of goods sold agree with your answer to Requirement 1?

BEYOND THE NUMBERS

Beyond the Numbers 7–1

Queen Technology Associates creates and sells cutting-edge network software. Queen's quality control officer estimates that 20 percent of the company's sales and purchases of inventory are returned for additional debugging. Queen needs special journals for

Designing a special journal ③ ④

- Sales returns and allowances
- Purchase returns and allowances

Required

1. Design on paper or on a computer the two special journals. For each journal, include a column for the appropriate business document.
2. Enter one transaction in each journal, using the Austin Sound transaction data illustrated on pages 363 and 364. Show all posting references, including those for column totals. In the purchase returns and allowances journal, assume debit memo number 14.

ETHICAL ISSUE

On a recent trip to Brazil, Carlo Degas, sales manager of Cyber Systems, took his wife along for a vacation and included her airfare and meals on his expense report, which he submitted for reimbursement. Chelsea Brindley, vice-president of sales and Degas's boss, thought his total travel and entertainment expenses seemed excessive. However, Brindley approved the reimbursement because she owed Degas a favour. Brindley, well aware that the company president routinely reviews all expenses recorded in the cash payments journal, had the accountant record the expenses of Degas's wife in the general journal as follows:

Sales Promotion Expense	9,000	
Cash...		9,000

Required

1. Does recording the transaction in the general journal rather than in the cash payments journal affect the amounts of cash and total expenses reported in the financial statements?
2. Why did Brindley want this transaction recorded in the general journal?
3. What is the ethical issue in this situation? What role does accounting play in the ethical issue?

PROBLEMS (GROUP A)

MyAccountingLab All questions in this section appear in MyAccountingLab.

Problem 7–1A

McMillan Distributors, which uses the perpetual inventory system and makes all credit sales on terms of 2/10, n/30, completed the following transactions during July. McMillan records all sales returns and all purchase returns in the general journal.

Using all the journals, the accounts receivable subsidiary, ledger and the accounts payable subsidiary ledger

③ ④

Jul.	2	Issued invoice no. 913 for sale on account to Teranishi Inc., $24,600. McMillan's cost of this inventory was $10,800.
	3	Purchased inventory on credit terms of 3/10, n/60 from Chicosky Corp., $14,802.

Jul.	5	Sold inventory for cash, $6,462 (cost, $2,880).
	5	Issued cheque no. 532 to purchase furniture for cash, $13,110.
	8	Collected interest revenue of $6,650.
	9	Issued invoice no. 914 for sale on account to Bell Ltd., $33,300 (cost, $13,860).
	10	Purchased inventory for cash, $6,858, issuing cheque no. 533.
	12	Received cash from Teranishi Inc. in full settlement of its account receivable from the sale on July 2.
	13	Issued cheque no. 534 to pay Chicosky Corp. the net amount owed from July 3.
	13	Purchased supplies on account from Manley Inc., $8,646. Terms were net end of month.
	15	Sold inventory on account to M. O. Brown, issuing invoice no. 915 for $3,990 (cost, $1,440).
	17	Issued credit memo to M. O. Brown for $3,990 for merchandise sent in error and returned by Brown. Also accounted for receipt of the inventory.
	18	Issued invoice no. 916 for credit sale to Teranishi Inc., $2,142 (cost, $762).
	19	Received $32,634 from Bell Ltd. in full settlement of its account receivable from July 9.
	20	Purchased inventory on credit terms of net 30 from Burgess Distributing Ltd., $12,282.
	22	Purchased furniture on credit terms of 3/10, n/60 from Chicosky Corp., $3,870.
	22	Issued cheque no. 535 to pay for insurance coverage, debiting Prepaid Insurance for $6,000.
	24	Sold supplies to an employee for cash of $324, which was the cost of the supplies.
	25	Issued cheque no. 536 to pay utilities, $6,718.
	28	Purchased inventory on credit terms of 2/10, n/30 from Manley Inc., $8,050.
	29	Returned damaged inventory to Manley Inc., issuing a debit memo for $4,050.
	29	Sold goods on account to Bell Ltd., issuing invoice no. 917 for $2,976 (cost, $1,320).
	30	Issued cheque no. 537 to pay Manley Inc. $2,646.
	31	Received cash in full on account from Teranishi Inc.
	31	Issued cheque no. 538 to pay monthly salaries of $14,082.

Required Use the following abbreviations to indicate the journal in which you would record each of the July transactions. Key each transaction by date. Also indicate whether the transaction would be recorded in the accounts receivable subsidiary ledger or the accounts payable subsidiary ledger.

G	=	General journal	P	=	Purchases journal
S	=	Sales journal	CP	=	Cash payments journal
CR	=	Cash receipts journal			

Problem 7–2A

Using the sales, cash receipts, and general journals (with the perpetual inventory system)

③

1. Cash receipts journal: Total debit to Cash $71,436

The general ledger of Cannin Distributors includes the following selected accounts, along with their account numbers:

Cash	11	Land		18
Accounts Receivable	12	Sales Revenue		41
Inventory	13	Sales Discounts		42
Notes Receivable	15	Sales Returns and Allowances		43
Supplies	16	Cost of Goods Sold		51

All credit sales are on the company's standard terms of 2/10, n/30. Transactions in July that affected sales and cash receipts were as follows:

Jul.	2	Sold inventory on credit to Fortin Inc., $1,400. Cannin's cost of these goods was $800.
	4	As a favour to a competitor, sold supplies at cost, $1,700, receiving cash.
	7	Cash sales of merchandise for the week totalled $3,780 (cost, $3,280).

Jul.	9	Sold merchandise on account to A. L. Price, $14,640 (cost, $10,220).
	10	Sold land that cost $25,000 for cash of $25,000.
	11	Sold goods on account to Sloan Forge Ltd., $10,208 (cost, $7,040).
	12	Received cash from Fortin Inc. in full settlement of its account receivable from July 2.
	14	Cash sales of merchandise for the week were $4,212 (cost, $3,060).
	15	Sold inventory on credit to the partnership of Wilkie & Blinn, $7,300 (cost, $4,520).
	18	Received inventory sold on July 9 to A. L. Price for $1,200. The goods shipped were the wrong size. These goods cost Cannin $880.
	20	Sold merchandise on account to Sloan Forge Ltd., $1,258 (cost, $900).
	21	Cash sales of merchandise for the week were $1,980 (cost, $1,380).
	22	Received $4,000 cash from A. L. Price in partial settlement of his account receivable.
	25	Received cash from Wilkie & Blinn for its account receivable from July 15.
	25	Sold goods on account to Olsen Inc., $3,040 (cost, $2,100).
	27	Collected $5,250 on a note receivable.
	28	Cash sales of merchandise for the week were $7,548 (cost, $4,920).
	29	Sold inventory on account to R. O. Bankston Inc., $484 (cost, $340).
	30	Received goods sold on July 25 to Olsen Inc. for $80. The wrong items were shipped. The cost of the goods was $50.
	31	Received $9,440 cash on account from A. L. Price.

Required

1. Use the appropriate journal to record the above transactions: a sales journal (omit the Invoice No. column), a cash receipts journal, or a general journal. Cannin Distributors records sales returns and allowances in the general journal.

2. Total each column of the sales journal and the cash receipts journal. Show that the total debits equal the total credits.

3. Show how postings would be made from the journals by writing the account numbers and check marks in the appropriate places in the journals.

Problem 7–3A

The cash receipts journal shown below contains five entries. All five entries are for legitimate cash receipt transactions, but the journal contains some errors in recording the transactions. In fact, only one entry is correct, and each of the other four entries contains one error.

Correcting errors in the cash receipts journal (perpetual inventory system)

(3)

Corrected cash receipts journal: Total debit to Cash $83,000

Cash Receipts Journal

Page 22

	Debits			Credits					
						Other Accounts			
Date	Cash	Sales Discounts	Accounts Receivable	Sales Revenue	Account Title	Post. Ref.	Amount	Cost of Goods Sold Dr. Inventory Cr.
Jan. 4		4,200		4,200				2,030
7	6,000	220			Debbie Hughes	✔	6,220	
13	57,400				Note Receivable	13	53,900	
					Interest Revenue	45	3,500	
20				4,620				2,100
30	15,400		10,780					
31	78,800	4,420	10,780	8,820	Totals		63,620	4,130
	(11)	(42)	(12)	(41)			(✔)	(51/13)

Total Dr. = $83,220   Total Cr. = $83,220

Required

1. Identify the correct entry in the cash receipts journal above.
2. Identify the error in each of the other four entries.
3. Using the following format, prepare a corrected cash receipts journal. All column totals are correct in the cash receipts journal that follows.

Cash Receipts Journal

	Debits		Credits					
					Other Accounts			
Date	Cash	Sales Discounts	Accounts Receivable	Sales Revenue	Account Title	Post. Ref.	Amount	Cost of Goods Sold Dr. Inventory Cr.
Jan. 4 7 13 20 30					Debbie Hughes Note Receivable Interest Revenue	✔ 13 45		
31	83,000	220	17,000	8,820	Totals		57,400	4,130
	(11)	(42)	(12)	(41)			(✔)	(51/13)

Total Dr. = $83,220   Total Cr. = $83,220

Problem 7–4A

Using the purchases, cash payments, and general journals

(4)

1. Cash payments journal: Total credit to Cash $39,962

The general ledger of Katie's Supplies includes the following accounts:

Cash	111	Furniture	187
Inventory	131	Accounts Payable	211
Prepaid Insurance	161	Rent Expense	564
Supplies	171	Utilities Expense	583

Transactions in August that affected purchases and cash payments were as follows:

Aug. 1 Purchased inventory on credit from Worth Corp., $13,800. Terms were 2/10, n/30.

1 Paid monthly rent, debiting Rent Expense for $4,000.

5 Purchased supplies on credit terms of 2/10, n/30 from Ross Supply Ltd., $900.

8 Paid electricity bill, $1,200.

9 Purchased furniture on account from Rite Office Supply, $18,200. Payment terms were net 30.

10 Returned the furniture to Rite Office Supply. It was the wrong colour.

11 Paid Worth Corp. the amount owed on the purchase of August 1.

12 Purchased inventory on account from Wynne Inc., $8,800. Terms were 3/10, n/30.

13 Purchased inventory for cash, $1,300.

14 Paid a semiannual insurance premium, debiting Prepaid Insurance, $2,400.

15 Paid the account payable to Ross Supply Ltd., from August 5.

18 Paid gas and water bills, $200.

21 Purchased inventory on credit terms of 1/10, n/45 from Cyber Software Ltd., $10,400.

21 Paid account payable to Wynne Inc., from August 12.

22 Purchased supplies on account from Favron Sales, $5,480. Terms were net 30.

25 Returned $2,400 of the inventory purchased on August 21 to Cyber Software Ltd.

31 Paid Cyber Software Ltd. the net amount owed from August 21.

Required

1. Katie's Supplies records purchase returns in the general journal. Use the appropriate journal to record the above transactions: a purchases journal, a cash payments journal (omit the Cheque No. column), or a general journal.

2. Total each column of the special journals. Show that the total debits equal the total credits in each special journal.

3. Show how postings would be made from the journals by writing the account numbers and check marks in the appropriate places in the journals.

Problem 7–5A

Foxey Distributors had the following transactions for the month of April 2010:

<table>
<tr><td>Apr.</td><td>1</td><td>Sold $1,500 of merchandise to James Moss, terms n/30. Inventory had a cost of $670. The sale was subject to 7 percent PST and 5 percent GST.</td></tr>
<tr><td></td><td>3</td><td>Purchased $14,250 of merchandise from MNO Suppliers Ltd., terms net 30, subject to 5 percent GST.</td></tr>
<tr><td></td><td>6</td><td>Paid for the purchase of April 3 (MNO Suppliers Ltd.), cheque no. 12.</td></tr>
<tr><td></td><td>7</td><td>Paid $3,250 wages to employee, cheque no. 13.</td></tr>
<tr><td></td><td>9</td><td>Owner withdrew $7,500 for personal use, cheque no. 14.</td></tr>
<tr><td></td><td>11</td><td>Collected the amount owed by James Moss (April 1).</td></tr>
<tr><td></td><td>13</td><td>Purchased equipment from MB Machinery Ltd., $14,250 plus 5 percent GST, terms n/30.</td></tr>
<tr><td></td><td>14</td><td>Issued a debit memo to MB Machinery Ltd. (April 13) for $750 plus 5 percent GST of equipment returned as defective.</td></tr>
<tr><td></td><td>15</td><td>Sold $2,000 of merchandise to St. Boniface School for cash. Inventory cost was $1,250. The sale was subject to 7 percent PST and 5 percent GST.</td></tr>
<tr><td></td><td>16</td><td>Paid the account owing to MB Machinery Ltd., cheque no. 15.</td></tr>
<tr><td></td><td>17</td><td>Purchased $18,750 plus 5 percent GST of equipment from Dearing Equipment Inc., terms net 60.</td></tr>
<tr><td></td><td>22</td><td>Paid a $4,500 note due to Commercial Bank, plus interest of $450, cheque no. 16.</td></tr>
<tr><td></td><td>24</td><td>Sold $1,100 of merchandise for cash; inventory cost was $750. The sale was subject to 7 percent PST and 5 percent GST.</td></tr>
<tr><td></td><td>25</td><td>Paid $750 to Canada Revenue Agency for income taxes owing from December 31, 2006, cheque no. 17.</td></tr>
<tr><td></td><td>26</td><td>Returned $4,250 plus 5 percent GST of the merchandise purchased from MNO Suppliers Ltd.</td></tr>
<tr><td></td><td>28</td><td>Purchased inventory for $3,000 plus 5 percent GST from Artois Ltd., promising to pay in 30 days.</td></tr>
<tr><td></td><td>30</td><td>Recorded the adjusting journal entries for the month of April.</td></tr>
</table>

Required

1. For each date, indicate which journal would be used to record the transaction assuming Foxey Distributors uses a general journal, a sales journal, a cash receipts journal, a purchases journal, and a cash payments journal.

2. Record the appropriate transactions in the cash receipts journal and the cash payments journal, using the special journal formats shown in Exhibit 7–13 on page 367.

Problem 7–6A

McMillan Distributors, which uses the perpetual inventory system and makes all credit sales on terms of 2/10, n/30, completed the following transactions during July:

<table>
<tr><td>Jul.</td><td>2</td><td>Issued invoice no. 913 for sale on account to Teranishi Inc., $24,600. McMillan's cost of this inventory was $10,800.</td></tr>
<tr><td></td><td>3</td><td>Purchased inventory on credit terms of 3/10, n/60 from Chicosky Corp., $14,802.</td></tr>
<tr><td></td><td>5</td><td>Sold inventory for cash, $6,462 (cost, $2,880).</td></tr>
<tr><td></td><td>5</td><td>Issued cheque no. 532 to purchase furniture for cash, $13,110.</td></tr>
<tr><td></td><td>8</td><td>Collected interest revenue of $6,650.</td></tr>
<tr><td></td><td>9</td><td>Issued invoice no. 914 for sale on account to Bell Ltd., $33,300 (cost, $13,860).</td></tr>
</table>

Understanding how manual accounting systems are used, using the cash receipts journal and the cash payments journal with GST and PST (perpetual inventory system)

2. Cash receipts journal: Total debit to Cash $5,152

Using all the journals, posting, balancing the ledgers

6. Total Accounts Receivable $2,976; total Accounts Payable $26,152

Jul.	10	Purchased inventory for cash, $6,858, issuing cheque no. 533.
	12	Received cash from Teranishi Inc. in full settlement of its account receivable from the sale on July 2.
	13	Issued cheque no. 534 to pay Chicosky Corp. the net amount owed from July 3. (Round to the nearest dollar.)
	13	Purchased supplies on account from Manley Inc., $8,646. Terms were net end of month.
	15	Sold inventory on account to M. O. Brown, issuing invoice no. 915 for $3,990 (cost, $1,440).
	17	Issued credit memo to M. O. Brown for $3,990 for merchandise sent in error and returned by Brown. Also accounted for receipt of the inventory.
	18	Issued invoice no. 916 for credit sale to Teranishi Inc., $2,142 (cost, $762).
	19	Received $32,634 from Bell Ltd. in full settlement of its account receivable from July 9.
	20	Purchased inventory on credit terms of net 30 from Burgess Distributing Ltd., $12,282.
	22	Purchased furniture on credit terms of 3/10, n/60 from Chicosky Corp., $3,870.
	22	Issued cheque no. 535 to pay for insurance coverage, debiting Prepaid Insurance for $6,000.
	24	Sold supplies to an employee for cash of $324, which was the cost of the supplies.
	25	Issued cheque no. 536 to pay utilities, $6,718.
	28	Purchased inventory on credit terms of 2/10, n/30 from Manley Inc., $8,050.
	29	Returned damaged inventory to Manley Inc., issuing a debit memo for $4,050.
	29	Sold goods on account to Bell Ltd., issuing invoice no. 917 for $2,976 (cost, $1,320).
	30	Issued cheque no. 537 to pay Manley Inc. $2,646.
	31	Received cash in full on account from Teranishi Inc.
	31	Issued cheque no. 538 to pay monthly salaries of $14,082.

Required

1. Open the following three-column general ledger accounts using the account numbers given:

Cash...................................	111	Sales Revenue.............................	411
Accounts Receivable...................	112	Sales Discounts............................	412
Supplies.......................................	116	Sales Returns and Allowances..	413
Prepaid Insurance.......................	117	Interest Revenue..........................	419
Inventory.....................................	118	Cost of Goods Sold.....................	511
Furniture......................................	151	Salaries Expense..........................	531
Accounts Payable.......................	211	Utilities Expense..........................	541

2. Open these accounts in the subsidiary ledgers: Accounts receivable subsidiary ledger—Bell Ltd., M. O. Brown, and Teranishi Inc.; accounts payable subsidiary ledger—Chicosky Corp., Manley Inc., and Burgess Distributing Ltd.

3. Enter the transactions in a sales journal (page 7), a cash receipts journal (page 5), a purchases journal (page 10), a cash payments journal (page 8), and a general journal (page 6), as appropriate.

4. Post daily to the accounts receivable subsidiary ledger and to the accounts payable subsidiary ledger. On July 31, post to the general ledger.

5 Total each column of the special journals. Show that the total debits equal the total credits in each special journal.

6. Balance the total of the customer account balances in the accounts receivable subsidiary ledger against Accounts Receivable in the general ledger. Do the same for the accounts payable subsidiary ledger and Accounts Payable in the general ledger.

MyAccountingLab | All questions in this section appear in MyAccountingLab.

Problem 7–1B

Crosby Sales Company, which uses the perpetual inventory system and makes all credit sales with terms 2/10, n/30, had the following transactions during January. Crosby records all sales returns and all purchase returns in the general journal.

Using all the journals, and the accounts receivable and accounts payable subsidiary ledgers

Jan.	2	Issued invoice no. 191 for sale on account to Wooten Design Ltd., $9,400. Crosby's cost of this inventory was $5,560.
	3	Purchased inventory on credit terms of 3/10, n/60 from Delwood Co., $23,600.
	4	Sold inventory for cash, $3,232 (cost, $2,040).
	5	Issued cheque no. 473 to purchase furniture for cash, $14,348.
	8	Collected interest revenue of $10,760.
	9	Issued invoice no. 192 for sale on account to Vachon Inc., $25,000 (cost, $13,200).
	10	Purchased inventory for cash, $3,104, issuing cheque no. 474.
	12	Received $9,212 cash from Wooten Design Ltd. in full settlement of its account receivable.
	13	Issued cheque no. 475 to pay Delwood Co. net amount owed from January 3.
	13	Purchased supplies on account from Lehigh Corp., $5,756. Terms were net end of month.
	15	Sold inventory on account to Franklin Ltd., issuing invoice no. 193 for $2,972 (cost, $1,640).
	17	Issued credit memo to Franklin Ltd. for $2,972 for merchandise sent in error and returned to Crosby by Franklin. Also accounted for receipt of the inventory.
	18	Issued invoice no. 194 for credit sale to Wooten Design Ltd., $7,300 (cost, $3,880).
	19	Received $24,500 from Vachon Inc. in full settlement of its account receivable from January 9.
	20	Purchased inventory on credit terms of net 30 from Jasper Sales Ltd., $5,600.
	22	Purchased furniture on credit terms of 3/10, n/60 from Delwood Co., $13,100.
	22	Issued cheque no. 476 to pay for insurance coverage, debiting Prepaid Insurance for $5,380.
	24	Sold an old computer to an employee for cash of $1,344, which was the value of the computer.
	25	Issued cheque no. 477 to pay utilities, $4,552.
	28	Purchased inventory on credit terms of 2/10, n/30 from Lehigh Corp., $1,684.
	29	Returned damaged inventory to Lehigh Corp., issuing a debit memo for $1,684.
	29	Sold goods on account to Vachon Inc., issuing invoice no. 195 for $5,268 (cost, $3,256).
	30	Issued cheque no. 478 to pay Lehigh Corp. on account from January 13.
	31	Received cash in full on account from Wooten Design Ltd. for credit sale of January 18. There was no discount.
	31	Issued cheque no. 479 to pay monthly salaries of $17,400.

Required Use the following abbreviations to indicate the journal in which you would record each of the January transactions. Key each transaction by date. Also indicate whether the transaction would be recorded in the accounts receivable subsidiary ledger or the accounts payable subsidiary ledger.

G =	General journal	P =	Purchases journal
S =	Sales journal	CP =	Cash payments journal
CR =	Cash receipts journal		

Problem 7–2B

Using the sales, cash receipts, and general journals (with the perpetual inventory system)

2. Cash receipts journal: Total debit to Cash $148,986

The general ledger of Beauchamp Supply includes the following accounts:

Cash...	111	Land	142
Accounts Receivable...................	112	Sales Revenue	411
Notes Receivable........................	115	Sales Discounts............................	412
Inventory.....................................	131	Sales Returns and Allowances..	413
Equipment...................................	141	Cost of Goods Sold	511

All credit sales are on the company's standard terms of 2/10, n/30. Transactions in November that affected sales and cash receipts were as follows:

Nov.		
	1	Sold inventory on credit to Ijiri Ltd., $4,000. Beauchamp Supply's cost of these goods was $2,228.
	5	As a favour to another company, sold new equipment for its cost of $23,080, receiving cash in this amount.
	6	Cash sales of merchandise for the week totalled $8,400 (cost, $5,400).
	8	Sold merchandise on account to McNair Ltd., $14,320 (cost, $11,854).
	9	Sold land that cost $64,000 for cash of $64,000.
	11	Sold goods on account to Nickerson Builders Inc., $12,198 (cost, $7,706).
	11	Received cash from Ijiri Ltd. in full settlement of its account receivable from November 1.
	13	Cash sales of merchandise for the week were $7,980 (cost, $5,144).
	15	Sold inventory on credit to Rapp and Howe, a partnership, $3,200 (cost, $2,068).
	18	Received inventory sold on November 8 to McNair Ltd. for $480. The goods shipped were the wrong colour. These goods cost Beauchamp Supply $292.
	19	Sold merchandise on account to Nickerson Builders, $14,400 (cost, $11,854).
	20	Cash sales of merchandise for the week were $9,320 (cost, $6,296).
	21	Received $6,400 cash from McNair Ltd. in partial settlement of its account receivable. There was no discount.
	22	Received payment in full from Rapp and Howe for its account receivable from November 15.
	22	Sold goods on account to Diamond Inc., $8,088 (cost, $5,300).
	25	Collected $6,400 on a note receivable.
	27	Cash sales of merchandise for the week totalled $8,910 (cost, $5,808).
	27	Sold inventory on account to Littleton Corporation, $7,580 (cost, $5,868).
	28	Received goods sold on November 22 to Diamond Inc. for $2,720. The goods were shipped in error, so were returned to inventory. The cost of these goods was $1,920.
	28	Received $7,440 cash on account from McNair Ltd.

Required

1. Use the appropriate journal to record the above transactions: a sales journal (omit the Invoice No. column), a cash receipts journal, and a general journal. Beauchamp Supply records sales returns and allowances in the general journal.

2. Total each column of the sales journal and the cash receipts journal. Determine that the total debits equal the total credits.

3. Show how postings would be made from the journals by writing the account numbers and check marks in the appropriate places in the journals.

Problem 7–3B

Correcting errors in the cash receipts journal (perpetual inventory system)

3. Corrected cash receipts journal: Total debit to Cash $131,900

The cash receipts journal on the next page contains five entries. All five entries are for legitimate cash receipt transactions, but the journal contains some errors in recording the transactions. In fact, only one entry is correct, and each of the other four entries contains one error.

Cash Receipts Journal

| Date | Debits | | Credits | | | | | Cost of Goods |
| | Cash | Sales Discounts | Accounts Receivable | Sales Revenue | Other Accounts | | | Sold Dr. |
					Account Title	Post. Ref.	Amount	Inventory Cr.
May. 3	7,110	340	7,450		Alcon Labs Ltd.	✔		
9			3,460	3,460	Carl Ryther	✔		
10	110,000			110,000	Land	19		
19	730							440
30	10,600			11,330				6,310
31	128,440	340	10,910	124,790	Totals			6,750
	(11)	(42)	(12)	(41)			(✔)	(51/13)

Total Dr. = $128,780   Total Cr. = $135,700

Required

1. Identify the correct entry in the cash receipts journal above.
2. Identify the error in each of the other four entries.
3. Using the following format, prepare a corrected cash receipts journal. All column totals are correct in the cash receipts journal that follows.

Cash Receipts Journal

| Date | Debits | | Credits | | | | | Cost of Goods |
| | Cash | Sales Discounts | Accounts Receivable | Sales Revenue | Other Accounts | | | Sold Dr. |
					Account Title	Post. Ref.	Amount	Inventory Cr.
May. 3					Alcon Labs Ltd.	✔		
9					Carl Ryther	✔		
10					Land	19		
19								
30								
31	131,900	340	10,910	11,330	Totals		110,000	6,750
	(11)	(42)	(12)	(41)			(✔)	(51/13)

Total Dr. = $132,240   Total Cr. = $132,240

Problem 7–4B

The general ledger of Argyle Supply Company includes the following accounts:

Cash	111	Equipment	189	
Inventory	131	Accounts Payable	211	
Prepaid Insurance	161	Rent Expense	562	
Supplies	171	Utilities Expense	565	

Using the purchases, cash payments, and general journals

④

1. Cash payments journal: Total credit to Cash $40,333

Transactions in November that affected purchases and cash payments were as follows:

Nov. 1 Paid monthly rent, debiting Rent Expense for $8,500.
      3 Purchased inventory on credit from Sylvania Ltd., $2,000. Terms were 2/15, n/45.

Nov.	4	Purchased supplies on credit terms of 2/10, n/30 from Harmon Sales Ltd., $800.
	7	Paid utility bills, $906.
	10	Purchased equipment on account from Epee Corp., $6,100. Payment terms were 2/10, n/30.
	11	Returned the equipment to Epee Corp. It was defective.
	12	Paid Sylvania Ltd. the amount owed on the purchase of November 3.
	12	Purchased inventory on account from Epee Corp., $21,000. Terms were 2/10, n/30.
	14	Purchased inventory for cash, $1,600.
	15	Paid an insurance premium, debiting Prepaid Insurance, $2,416.
	16	Paid the account payable to Harmon Sales Ltd. from November 4.
	17	Paid electricity bill, $700.
	20	Paid the November 12 account payable to Epee Corp., less the purchase discount.
	21	Purchased supplies on account from Master Supply Ltd., $7,540, terms net 30.
	22	Purchased inventory on credit terms of 1/10, n/30 from Linz Brothers Inc., $3,400.
	26	Returned $500 of inventory purchased on November 22 to Linz Brothers Inc.
	30	Paid Linz Brothers Inc. the net amount owed.

Required

1. Use the appropriate journal to record the above transactions: a purchases journal, a cash payments journal (do not use the Cheque No. column), or a general journal. Argyle Supply Company records purchase returns in the general journal.

2. Total each column of the special journals. Show that the total debits equal the total credits in each special journal.

3. Show how postings would be made from the journals by writing the account numbers and check marks in the appropriate places in the journals.

Problem 7–5B

Understanding how manual accounting systems are used, using the cash receipts and cash payments journals with GST and PST (perpetual inventory system)

②③④⑥

2. Cash receipts journal: Total debit to Cash $9,352

Lively Home Products had the following transactions for the month of June 2010:

Jun.	1	Sold $2,000 of merchandise to Thomas Chase, terms n/30. Inventory had a cost of $1,124. The sale was subject to 7 percent PST and 5 percent GST.
	3	Purchased $4,500 of merchandise from STU Suppliers Inc., terms net 30, subject to 5 percent GST.
	6	Paid for the purchase of June 3 (STU Suppliers Inc.), cheque no. 12.
	7	Paid $4,250 wages to employee, cheque no. 13.
	9	Owner withdrew $11,250 for personal use, cheque no. 14.
	11	Collected the amount owed by Thomas Chase (June 1).
	13	Purchased equipment from DE Machinery Inc. for $12,500 plus 5 percent GST, terms n/30.
	14	Issued a debit memo to DE Machinery Inc. (June 13) for $1,500 plus 5 percent GST of equipment returned as defective.
	15	Sold $3,750 plus 7 percent PST and 5 percent GST of merchandise to DePloy Construction Ltd. for cash. Inventory had a cost of $2,250.
	16	Paid the account owing to DE Machinery Inc. (June 13, 14), cheque no. 15.
	17	Purchased $10,500 plus 5 percent GST of equipment from Alfreds Equipment Inc., terms net 60.
	22	Paid a $7,500 note due to Commercial Bank, plus interest of $750, cheque no. 16.
	24	Sold $2,600 of merchandise for cash; inventory cost was $1,500. The sale was subject to 7 percent PST and 5 percent GST.
	25	Paid $1,125 to Canada Revenue Agency for income taxes owing for the year 2009, cheque no. 17.
	26	Returned $750 plus 5 percent GST of the merchandise purchased from STU Suppliers Inc.
	28	Purchased inventory for $4,500 plus 5 percent GST from Damon Ltd., promising to pay in 30 days.
	30	Recorded the adjusting journal entries for the month of June.

Required

1. For each date, indicate which journal would be used to record the transaction assuming Lively Home Products uses a general journal, a sales journal, a cash receipts journal, a purchases journal, and a cash payments journal.

2. Record the appropriate transactions in the cash receipts journal and the cash payments journal, using the special journal formats shown in Exhibit 7–13 on page 367.

Problem 7–6B

Crosby Sales Company, which uses the perpetual inventory system and makes all credit sales with terms 2/10, n/30, had these transactions during January:

Using all the journals, posting, balancing the ledgers (perpetual inventory system)

6. Total Accounts Receivable $5,268; total Accounts Payable $18,700

Jan. 2   Issued invoice no. 191 for sale on account to Wooten Design Ltd., $9,400. Crosby's cost of this inventory was $5,560.

3   Purchased inventory on credit terms of 3/10, n/60 from Delwood Co., $23,600.

4   Sold inventory for cash, $3,232 (cost, $2,040).

5   Issued cheque no. 473 to purchase furniture for cash, $4,348.

8   Collected interest revenue of $10,760.

9   Issued invoice no. 192 for sale on account to Vachon Inc., $25,000 (cost, $13,200).

10   Purchased inventory for cash, $3,104, issuing cheque no. 474.

12   Received $9,212 cash from Wooten Design Ltd. in full settlement of its account receivable.

13   Issued cheque no. 475 to pay Delwood Co. net amount owed from January 3.

13   Purchased supplies on account from Lehigh Corp., $5,756. Terms were net end of month.

15   Sold inventory on account to Franklin Ltd., issuing invoice no. 193 for $2,972 (cost, $1,640).

17   Issued credit memo to Franklin Ltd. for $2,972 for merchandise sent in error and returned to Crosby by Franklin. Also accounted for receipt of the inventory.

18   Issued invoice no. 194 for credit sale to Wooten Design Ltd., $7,300 (cost, $3,880).

19   Received $24,500 from Vachon Inc. in full settlement of its account receivable from January 9.

20   Purchased inventory on credit terms of net 30 from Jasper Sales Ltd., $5,600.

22   Purchased furniture on credit terms of 3/10, n/60 from Delwood Co., $13,100.

22   Issued cheque no. 476 to pay for insurance coverage, debiting Prepaid Insurance for $5,380.

24   Sold supplies to an employee for cash of $1,344, which was the value of the supplies.

25   Issued cheque no. 477 to pay utilities, $4,552.

28   Purchased inventory on credit terms of 2/10, n/30 from Lehigh Corp., $1,684.

29   Returned damaged inventory to Lehigh Corp., issuing a debit memo for $1,684.

29   Sold goods on account to Vachon Inc., issuing invoice no. 195 for $5,268 (cost, $3,256).

30   Issued cheque no. 478 to pay Lehigh Corp. on account from January 13.

31   Received cash in full on account from Wooten Design Ltd. for credit sale of January 18. There was no discount.

31   Issued cheque no. 479 to pay monthly salaries of $7,400.

Required

1. For Crosby Sales Company, open the following three-column general ledger accounts using the account numbers given:

Cash	111	Sales Revenue	411
Accounts Receivable	112	Sales Discounts	412
Supplies	116	Sales Returns and Allowances	413
Prepaid Insurance	117	Interest Revenue	419
Inventory	118	Cost of Goods Sold	511
Furniture	151	Salaries Expense	531
Accounts Payable	211	Utilities Expense	541

2. Open these accounts in the subsidiary ledgers: Accounts receivable subsidiary ledger—Vachon Inc., Franklin Ltd., and Wooten Design Ltd.; accounts payable subsidiary ledger—Delwood Co., Lehigh Corp., and Jasper Sales Ltd.

3. Enter the transactions in a sales journal (page 8), a cash receipts journal (page 3), a purchases journal (page 6), a cash payments journal (page 9), and a general journal (page 4), as appropriate. Disregard PST and GST in this question.

4. Post daily to the accounts receivable subsidiary ledger and to the accounts payable subsidiary ledger. On January 31, post to the general ledger.

5. Total each column of the special journals. Show that the total debits equal the total credits in each special journal.

6. Balance the total of the customer account balances in the accounts receivable subsidiary ledger against Accounts Receivable in the general ledger. Do the same for the accounts payable subsidiary ledger and Accounts Payable in the general ledger.

CHALLENGE PROBLEMS

Problem 7–1C

Advantage of an effective accounting system

An accounting information system that provides timely, accurate information to management is an important asset of any organization. This is especially true as organizations become larger and move into different parts of the world. The integration of computers into many organizations' information systems has enhanced their usefulness to the organization.

Required Assume your older sister is a pharmacist. She regards an information system as simply an accounting system that keeps track of her company's revenues and expenses. Explain to her how an effective accounting information system can make her a more effective pharmacist.

Problem 7–2C

Providing advice about a computerized accounting system

Information technology is increasingly sophisticated and everyone wants the latest technology. Your brother has asked you about installing this "wonderful" computer system in his car dealership and auto repair business. The salesperson has promised your brother that the system "will do everything you want and then some." Your brother has come to you for advice about acquiring this new computerized accounting information system. At present he uses a manual accounting system.

Required Provide the advice your brother wants, focusing on the costs of the new computerized accounting information system; your brother has been told all the positive aspects of purchasing the system.

Extending Your Knowledge

DECISION PROBLEMS

Reconstructing transactions from amounts posted to the accounts receivable subsidiary ledger

*Cash receipts journal:
Total debit to Cash $31,632*

Decision Problem 1

A fire destroyed some accounting records of Red Valley Company. The owner, Jennifer Chu, asks for your help in reconstructing the records. *She needs to know the beginning and ending balances of Accounts Receivable and the credit sales and cash receipts on account from customers during March.* All Red Valley Company sales are on credit, with payment terms of 2/10, n/30. All cash receipts on account reached Red Valley Company within the 10-day discount period, except as noted. The only accounting record preserved from the fire is the accounts receivable subsidiary ledger, which follows:

Adam Chi

Date		Jrnl. Ref.	Debit	Credit	Balance
Mar. 1	Balance				0
8		S.6	15,000		15,000
16		S.6	3,000		18,000
18		CR.8		15,000	3,000
19		J.5		600	2,400
27		CR.8		2,400	0

Anna Fowler

Date		Jrnl. Ref.	Debit	Credit	Balance
Mar. 1	Balance				3,300
5		CR.8		3,300	0
11		S.6	1,200		1,200
21		CR.8		1,200	0
24		S.6	12,000		12,000

Norris Associates Ltd.

Date		Jrnl. Ref.	Debit	Credit	Balance
Mar. 1	Balance				9,000
15		S.6	9,000		18,000
29		CR.8		8,700*	9,300

*Cash receipt did not occur within the discount period.

Robertson Inc.

Date		Jrnl. Ref.	Debit	Credit	Balance
Mar. 1	Balance				1,500
3		CR.8		1,500	0
25		S.6	12,000		12,000
29		S.6	3,600		15,600

Decision Problem 2

The external auditor must ensure that the amounts shown on the balance sheet for Accounts Receivable represent actual amounts that customers owe the company. Each customer account in the accounts receivable subsidiary ledger must represent an actual credit sale to the person or company indicated, and the customer's balance must not have been collected. This auditing concept is called *validity,* or *validating* the existence of the accounts receivable.

Understanding an accounting system

The auditor must also ensure that all amounts that the company owes are included in Accounts Payable and other liability accounts. For example, all credit purchases of inventory made by the company (and not yet paid) should be included in the balance of the Accounts Payable account. This auditing concept is called *completeness.*

Required Suggest how an auditor might test a customer's Account Receivable balance for validity. Indicate how the auditor might test the balance of the Accounts Payable account for completeness.

Comprehensive Problem for Part 1

1. COMPLETING A MERCHANDISER'S ACCOUNTING CYCLE

3. Net income $29,400
Total assets $278,610

The end-of-month trial balance of Skelly Building Materials at January 31, 2010, is shown below.

SKELLY BUILDING MATERIALS
Trial Balance
January 31, 2010

Account Number	Account	Balance Debit	Balance Credit
110	Cash	$ 16,430	
120	Accounts receivable	19,090	
130	Inventory	60,400	
140	Supplies	2,700	
150	Building	188,170	
151	Accumulated amortization—building		$ 36,000
160	Fixtures	45,600	
161	Accumulated amortization—fixtures		5,800
200	Accounts payable		23,300
205	Salary payable		0
210	Interest payable		0
240	Unearned sales revenue		6,560
250	Note payable, long-term		82,000
300	S. Skelly, capital		144,980
311	S. Skelly, withdrawals	9,200	
400	Sales revenue		187,970
402	Sales discounts	4,800	
430	Sales returns and allowances	5,640	
500	Cost of goods sold	103,000	
600	Selling expense	21,520	
700	General expense	10,060	
705	Interest expense	0	
	Total	$486,610	$486,610

a. Supplies consumed during the month, $1,500. One-half is selling expense, and the other half is general expense.

b. Amortization for the month: building, $4,000; fixtures, $4,800. One-fourth of amortization is selling expense, and three-fourths is general expense.

c. Unearned sales revenue still unearned, $1,200.

d. Accrued salaries, a general expense, $3,650.

e. Accrued interest expense, $3,280.

f. Inventory on hand, $58,720. Skelly Building Materials uses the perpetual inventory system.

Required

1. Using three-column ledger accounts, open the accounts listed on the trial balance, inserting their unadjusted balances. Also open account number 312, Income Summary. Date the balances of the following accounts January 1:

Supplies; Building; Accumulated Amortization—Building; Fixtures; Accumulated Amortization—Fixtures; Unearned Sales Revenue; and S. Skelly, Capital. Date the balance of S. Skelly, Withdrawals, January 31.

2. Enter the trial balance on a work sheet, and complete the work sheet for the month ended January 31, 2010. Skelly Building Materials groups all operating expenses under two accounts, Selling Expense and General Expense. Leave two blank lines under Selling Expense and three blank lines under General Expense.

3. Prepare the company's multi-step income statement and statement of owner's equity for the month ended January 31, 2010. Also prepare the balance sheet at that date in report form.

4. Journalize the adjusting and closing entries at January 31, 2010, using page 3 of the general journal.

5. Post the adjusting and closing entries, using dates and posting references.

6. Compute Skelly Building Materials' current ratio and debt ratio at January 31, 2010, and compare these values with the industry averages of 1.9 for the current ratio and 0.57 for the debt ratio. Compute the gross margin percentage and the rate of inventory turnover for the month (the inventory balance at the end of December 2009 was $66,500) and compare these ratio values with the industry averages of 0.36 for the gross margin ratio and 1.7 times for inventory turnover. Does Skelly Building Materials appear to be stronger or weaker than the average company in the building materials industry?

2. COMPLETING THE ACCOUNTING CYCLE FOR A MERCHANDISING ENTITY

Note: This problem can be solved with or without special journals. See Requirement 2. Dalhani Distributors closes its books and prepares financial statements at the end of each month. Dalhani uses the perpetual inventory system. The company completed the following transactions during August 2010.

5. Net loss $2,114
Total assets $118,586

Aug.	1	Issued cheque no. 682 for August office rent $2,000. (Debit Rent Expense.)
	2	Issued cheque no. 683 to pay salaries of $3,240, which includes salary payable of $930 from July 31. Dalhani does *not* use reversing entries.
	2*	Issued invoice no. 503 for sale on account to R. T. Loeb, $600. Dalhani's cost of this merchandise was $190.
	3	Purchased inventory on credit terms of 1/15, n/60 from Grant Ltd., $1,400.
	4	Received net amount of cash on account from Fullam Corp., $4,116, within the discount period.
	4	Sold inventory for cash, $2,330 (cost, $1,104).
	5	Received from Park-Hee Inc. merchandise that had been sold earlier for $550 (cost, $174). The wrong merchandise had been sent.
	5	Issued cheque no. 684 to purchase supplies for cash, $780.
	6	Collected interest revenue of $1,100.
	7	Issued invoice no. 504 for sale on account to K. D. Skipper Inc., $2,400 (cost, $760).
	8	Issued cheque no. 685 to pay Fayda Corp. $2,600 of the amount owed at July 31. This payment occurred after the end of the discount period.
	11	Issued cheque no. 686 to pay Grant Ltd. the net amount owed from August 3.
	12*	Received cash from R. T. Loeb in full settlement of her account from August 2. R. T. Loeb notified Dalhani that only one-quarter of the goods ordered had been received, but agreed to pay now if Dalhani held the remaining goods in his warehouse until September.

---

*Dalhani Distributors sold inventory on account to R. T. Loeb on August 2 and collected in full on August 12. Loeb indicated that the shipment was incomplete and arranged with Dalhani that he would ship the goods to Loeb in September. At August 31, $450 of unearned sales revenue needs to be recorded and the cost of this merchandise ($142) needs to be removed from Cost of Goods Sold and returned to Inventory.

Aug. 16   Issued cheque no. 687 to pay salary expense of $1,240.

      19   Purchased inventory for cash, $850, issuing cheque no. 688.

      22   Purchased furniture on credit terms of 3/15, n/60 from Beaver Corporation, $510.

      23   Sold inventory on account to Fullam Corp., issuing invoice no. 505 for $9,966 (cost, $3,152).

      24   Received half the July 31 amount receivable from K. D. Skipper Inc.— after the end of the discount period.

      25   Issued cheque no. 689 to pay utilities, $2,432.

      26   Purchased supplies on credit terms of 2/10, n/30 from Fayda Corp., $180.

      30   Returned damaged inventory to company from whom Dalhani made the cash purchase on August 19, receiving cash of $850.

      30   Granted a sales allowance of $176 to K. D. Skipper Inc.

      31   Purchased inventory on credit terms of 1/10, n/30 from Suncrest Supply Ltd., $10,330.

      31   Issued cheque no. 690 to Jack West, owner of Dalhani, for $1,700.

Required

1. Open the following three-column ledger accounts with their account numbers and July 31 balances in the ledgers indicated.

   General Ledger:

101	Cash	$ 4,490
102	Accounts Receivable	24,560
104	Interest Receivable	0
105	Inventory	41,800
109	Supplies	1,340
117	Prepaid Insurance	2,200
140	Note Receivable, Long-Term	11,000
160	Furniture	37,270
161	Accumulated Amortization—Furniture	10,550
201	Accounts Payable	10,600
204	Salary Payable	930
207	Interest Payable	4,320
208	Unearned Sales Revenue	0
220	Note Payable, Long-term	42,000
301	Jack West, Capital	54,260
303	Jack West, Withdrawals	0
400	Income Summary	0
401	Sales Revenue	0
402	Sales Discounts	0
403	Sales Returns and Allowances	0
410	Interest Revenue	0
501	Cost of Goods Sold	0
510	Salary Expense	0
513	Rent Expense	0
514	Amortization Expense—Furniture	0
516	Insurance Expense	0
517	Utilities Expense	0
519	Supplies Expense	0
523	Interest Expense	0

   Accounts receivable subsidiary ledger: Fullam Corp., $4,200; R. T. Loeb; Park-Hee Inc., $11,590; K. D. Skipper Inc., $8,770.

   Accounts payable subsidiary ledger: Beaver Corporation; Fayda Corp., $10,600; Grant Ltd.; Suncrest Supply Ltd.

2. Ask your professor for directions. Journalize the August transactions either in the general journal (page 9; explanations not required) or, as illustrated in Chapter 7, in a series of special journals: a sales journal (page 4), a cash receipts journal (page 11), a purchases journal (page 8), a cash payments journal (page 5), and a general journal (page 9). Dalhani makes all credit sales on terms of 2/10, n/30.

3. Post daily to the accounts receivable subsidiary ledger and the accounts payable subsidiary ledger. On August 31, 2010, post to the general ledger.

4. Prepare a trial balance in the Trial Balance columns of a work sheet, and use the following information to complete the work sheet for the month ended August 31, 2010.

   a. Accrued interest revenue, $1,000.
   b. Supplies on hand, $990.
   c. Prepaid insurance expired, $550.
   d. Amortization expense, $230.
   e. Accrued salary expense, $1,030.
   f. Accrued interest expense, $1,320.
   g. Unearned sales revenue, $450 (refers to August 2 transaction).
   h. Inventory on hand, $47,700.

5. Prepare Dalhani's multi-step income statement and statement of owner's equity for August 2010. Prepare the balance sheet at August 31, 2010.

6. Journalize and post the adjusting and closing entries.

7. Prepare a postclosing trial balance at August 31, 2010. Also, balance the total of the customer accounts in the accounts receivable subsidiary ledger against the Accounts Receivable balance in the general ledger. Do the same for the accounts payable subsidiary ledger and Accounts Payable in the general ledger.

What are internal controls, and why are they important?
What is the *Sarbanes–Oxley Act* and why is it important to some Canadian companies? How can companies use bank accounts to control cash?

Is there an approach to use when facing an ethical issue?

These questions and others will be answered throughout this chapter. The Decision Guidelines at the end of this chapter will provide a framework for making ethical judgments.

LEARNING OBJECTIVES

1. Define internal control

2. List and describe the components of internal control and control procedures

3. Prepare a bank reconciliation and the related journal entries

4. Apply internal controls to cash receipts

5. Apply internal controls to cash payments

6. Make ethical business judgments

7. Assess the impact on cash of international financial reporting standards (IFRS)

Mary Logan* worked for about four years at a branch of the Royal Canadian Legion in British Columbia. Logan was the Abbotsford Legion's bookkeeper and office manager and, in addition, managed the books at the Mission Legion. Irregularities came to light at the Abbotsford branch, criminal fraud was discovered, and Logan was eventually charged. In May 2007, at age 41, Logan was sentenced to serve 18 months in prison. She was also sued in a civil case by the Legion branch.

During the civil case, Logan said she had inflated her paycheques by $1,000 a total of 58 times. According to the Legion's lawyer, "There was some evidence that when the Legion was in financial difficulty, [Logan] would make a deposit, get her [pay] cheque certified, and let other cheques bounce." The amount of the fraud totalled $200,000, causing the Abbotsford branch of the Legion to struggle financially, and it was forced to downsize.

"She ruined an 80-year community service organization. Stealing that money put us in a destitute situation," said the Legion president at the time.

Logan also has to serve a three-year probation that ends in 2011 and includes the following conditions: she is banned from working in any financial jobs, such as bookkeeping or accounting, for anyone except herself, and she is to have no cheque-signing authority on any accounts other than personal accounts. She must keep her probation officer informed of her whereabouts, activities, and employment. She must go to counselling, and she is barred from any branch of the Royal Canadian Legion.

In July 2009, Logan applied to have her probation cancelled and, along with it, the conditions of her probation. The outcome is pending.

---

* The name has been changed.

Source: Christina Toth, "Former Legion Bookkeeper Wants Her Probation Erased," *The Abbotsford Times,* July 24, 2009.

Every company, especially an expanding company, faces
similar challenges:

- How will the company safeguard its assets?
- How will the company make sure its managers and employees follow policies
  that are best for the company?

This chapter discusses *internal control*—the organizational plan that companies
use to protect their assets and records. The chapter applies internal control techniques mainly to cash, because cash is the most liquid asset. The chapter also
provides a framework for making ethical judgments in business. The material
covered in this chapter is some of the most important in all of business. Unfortunately, it is sometimes overlooked, as in the actual case of the bookkeeper in the
chapter-opening story.

Cash

Cash—including cash on hand in funds such as *petty cash*, cash on deposit in
banks and trust companies, and cash equivalents, such as Treasury Bills—is the
most liquid asset an organization has. Accordingly, it is usually the first item
under the heading "Current Assets" on the balance sheet.

Cash's liquidity is a virtue because it is easily exchangeable for other assets.
However, cash's liquidity is also a disadvantage because it is the most easily
stolen asset. The next section will explain how organizations strive to protect their
cash by using internal controls.

Internal Control

One of a business owner's key responsibilities is to control operations. The owners set goals, they hire managers to lead the way, and employees carry out the
plan.

OBJECTIVE ①
Define internal control

Both in Canada—in the *CICA Handbook*—and internationally, **internal control**
consists of the process designed and put in place by management to provide
reasonable assurance that the organization will achieve its objectives of reliable
financial reporting, effective and efficient operations, and compliance with applicable laws and regulations. You may see examples of these controls when you are
processing transactions at a bank or a retail store. The teller at a bank may need a
supervisor to authorize a transaction. Internal control is designed and put in place
to address risks that threaten the achievement of any of the organization's objectives. Key internal control objectives are:

1. **Encouraging operational efficiency**. A company must optimize the use of
   resources, minimize expenses, and ensure management's business policies
   are implemented and followed.

2. **Preventing and detecting error and fraud**. Companies must prevent and detect error and fraud, which lead to a waste of company resources.

3. **Safeguarding assets and records**. A company must protect its assets so that company resources are not wasted needlessly. Safeguarding records ensures they are accurate and complete when needed for decision making.

4. **Providing accurate, reliable information**. A company must provide accurate, reliable information, including accounting records. This is essential for decision making.

REAL WORLD EXAMPLE

One of the auditor's first steps in auditing a business is to understand and evaluate its internal controls. If a company has good controls, then misstatements are minimized and are usually corrected before the financial statements are prepared. If the control system is weak, then misstatements can go undetected. The auditor increases the tests of the accounting records or performs other audit procedures if the company's internal control system is weak.

Companies cannot afford to waste resources. In the chapter-opening story, the bookkeeper took money from her employer and hid the theft. She stole a not-for-profit organization's resources. A company must safeguard its assets, or it could experience the type of fraud illustrated in this story and waste its resources.

Accurate, reliable records are essential. Without reliable records, a manager cannot tell what investments to make or how much to charge for products, and banks cannot determine whether to make a loan.

How critical are internal controls? They are so important that the United States Congress passed a law that requires public companies—those that sell their shares of stock to the public—to maintain a system of internal controls.

The *Sarbanes–Oxley Act*

In the early 2000s, the Enron and WorldCom accounting scandals rocked the United States. Enron overstated profits and went out of business almost overnight. WorldCom (now MCI) reported expenses as assets, and overstated both profits and assets. The company is just now emerging from bankruptcy. The same accounting firm, Arthur Andersen, had audited both companies' financial statements. Arthur Andersen then closed its doors.

As the scandals unfolded, many people asked, "How can these things happen? Where were the auditors?" To address public concern, Congress passed the *Sarbanes–Oxley Act of 2002* (SOX). SOX revamped corporate governance in the United States and affected the accounting profession. Here are some of the SOX provisions:

1. Public companies must issue an internal control report, and the outside auditor must evaluate the client's internal controls.

2. A new body, the Public Company Accounting Oversight Board, oversees the work of auditors of public companies.

3. Accounting firms may not both audit a public client and provide certain consulting services for the same client.

4. Stiff penalties await violators—25 years in prison for securities fraud; 20 years for an executive making false sworn statements.

In 2005, the former chief executive officer of WorldCom, Edmonton-born Bernie Ebbers, was convicted of securities fraud and sentenced to 25 years in prison. Kenneth Lay, CEO of Enron, was also convicted but died of natural causes prior to sentencing. You can see that the lack of internal controls and related matters can have serious consequences.

SOX is having an impact on Canadian companies in two ways:

1. Canadian companies, such as Bank of Montreal and EnCana Corporation, are listed on the New York Stock Exchange and, therefore, must abide by SOX. This is true for any Canadian company listed on a U.S. stock exchange.

2. Canadian regulators, such as the Ontario Securities Commission, are implementing some of the requirements of SOX.

SOX ensures that managers give careful attention to internal controls in their companies.

Exhibit 8–1 shows the shield that internal controls provide for an organization. Internal controls enable people to do business securely and effectively. How does a business achieve good internal control? The next section identifies the components of internal control.

EXHIBIT 8–1 The Shield of Internal Control

DID YOU GET IT?

To check your understanding of the material in this Learning Objective, complete this question. The solutions appear on MyAccountingLab so you can check your progress.

1. Internal controls do not only apply to "big business." We do things every day that mirror the four internal control measures described in this Learning Objective. Consider your car, for example. Suppose you always lock the doors, and you buy gas at the station with the lowest price per litre. How do these personal acts relate to an internal control plan?

The Components of Internal Control

A business can achieve its internal control objectives by applying five components:

- Control environment
- Risk assessment
- Control procedures
- Monitoring of controls
- Information system

> **OBJECTIVE 2**
> List and describe the components of internal control and control procedures

Control Environment   The control environment is the "tone at the top" of the business. It starts with the owner and the top managers. They must behave honourably to set a good example for company employees. The owner must demonstrate the importance of internal controls if he or she expects the employees to take the controls seriously.

Risk Assessment   A company must identify its risks. For example, a food producer faces the risk that its food products may harm people. An airline faces the risk of bad weather that could cause accidents, and all companies face the risk of bankruptcy. Companies facing difficulties are tempted to falsify the financial statements to make themselves look better than they really are.

Control Procedures   These are the procedures designed to ensure that the business's goals are achieved. Examples include assigning responsibilities, separating duties, and using security devices to protect assets. The next section discusses internal control procedures.

Monitoring of Controls   Companies hire auditors to monitor their controls. Internal auditors monitor company controls to safeguard assets, and external auditors monitor the controls to provide reasonable assurance that the accounting records are accurate.

Information System   As we have seen, the information system is critical. The owner of a business needs accurate information to keep track of assets, and measure profits and losses.

Exhibit 8–2 diagrams the components of internal control.

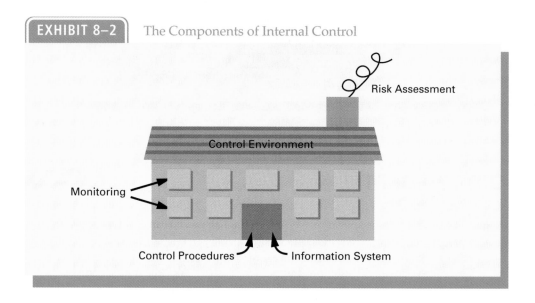

EXHIBIT 8–2   The Components of Internal Control

Internal control is a management priority, not merely a part of the accounting system. Thus it is a responsibility not only of accountants but also of managers in all the functional areas throughout the organization. Internal controls are most effective when employees at all levels and in all areas adopt the organization's goals and ethical standards.

In Sun-Rype Products Ltd.'s 2008 Annual Report (in Appendix B), Sun-Rype's top managers take responsibility for the financial statements and the related system of internal control. The report states, "Management is responsible for establishing and maintaining adequate internal control over financial reporting to provide reasonable assurance regarding the reliability of financial reporting and the preparation of financial statements for external purposes in accordance with GAAP."

Let's examine in detail how businesses create an effective system of internal control.

Internal Control Procedures

REAL WORLD EXAMPLE

Most banks and retail businesses assign each cashier a money tray and hold the cashier responsible if that fund is short at the end of the shift. This internal control device clearly assigns responsibility to each employee. Shortages or discrepancies can be traced to the person responsible.

Whether the business is Sun-Rype Products Ltd. or a local department store, an effective system of internal controls has these characteristics.

Competent, Reliable, and Ethical Personnel   Employees should be *competent*, *reliable*, and *ethical*. Paying good salaries will attract high-quality employees. Companies must also train employees to do their job and must supervise their work. This will help to build a competent staff.

Assignment of Responsibilities   In a business with good internal controls, no important duty is overlooked. Each employee has certain responsibilities. For example, two important duties are writing cheques and doing the accounting. In a large company, the **treasurer** is responsible for cash management. The **controller** is the chief accounting officer. The controller approves invoices (bills) for payment and the treasurer signs the cheques. With clearly assigned responsibilities, all duties are carried out.

Proper Authorization An organization generally has written rules that outline approved procedures. Any deviation from policy requires *proper authorization*. For example, managers or assistant managers of retail stores must approve customer cheques for amounts above the store's usual limit. Likewise, deans or heads of departments of colleges and universities must give the authorization for a first-year or second-year student to enrol in courses that are restricted to upper-year or upper-level students.

Separation of Duties Smart management divides the responsibilities for transactions between two or more people or departments. *Separation of duties* (also called segregation of duties) limits the chances for fraud and promotes the accuracy of accounting records by dividing up the three tasks of authorization, recording, and custody. Separation of duties can be divided into three parts:

1. *Separate operations from accounting*. Accounting should be completely separate from operating departments, such as production and sales. What would happen if sales personnel recorded the company's revenue transactions? Sales figures could be inflated, and top managers wouldn't know how much the company actually sold. This is why companies should separate accounting and sales duties.

2. *Separate the custody of assets from accounting*. Accountants must not handle cash, and cashiers must not have access to the accounting records. If one employee had both cash-handling and accounting duties, that person could steal cash and conceal the theft by making a fictitious entry in the general ledger. In the same way, the treasurer of a company handles cash and the controller accounts for cash. Neither person has both responsibilities.

   Only warehouse employees with no accounting duties should have custody of inventory. If they were allowed to account for the inventory, they could steal it and write it off as obsolete by debiting Loss on Inventory Obsolescence and crediting Inventory. A *write-off* is an entry that credits an asset account.

3. *Separation of the authorization of transactions from the custody of related assets*. Persons who authorize transactions should not handle the related asset. For example, the same individual should not authorize the payment of a supplier's invoice and also sign the cheque to pay the invoice.

   Even small businesses should have internal controls and some separation of duties. For example, if the bookkeeper writes all cheques and keeps the general ledger records, the owner should sign all cheques and reconcile the monthly bank statement.

Internal and External Audits To demonstrate to users and to satisfy management that the financial statements fairly present the financial position of an organization and the results of its operations, most companies have an audit. An **audit** is an examination of the organization's financial statements and the accounting systems, controls, and records that produced them. To evaluate the company's accounting system, auditors examine the system of internal controls.

Audits can be internal or external. *Internal auditors* are employees of the organization. They ensure that employees are following company policies and that operations are running efficiently. Internal auditors also determine whether the company is following legal requirements.

External auditors are completely independent of the organization. They are hired to determine that the organization's financial statements are prepared in accordance with generally accepted accounting principles. Both internal and external auditors

REAL WORLD EXAMPLE

In some audits, procedures and even the audit itself may occur as a surprise to the employees so that they cannot cover up fraud and/or weaknesses in the system.

should be independent of the operations they examine, and both should suggest improvements that can help the business run efficiently.

Documents and Records   Business *documents and records* provide the details of business transactions. Such documents include sales invoices and purchase orders, and records include journals and ledgers. Documents should be pre-numbered because a gap in the numbered sequence draws attention to a possible missing document.

In a bowling alley, for example, a key document is the score sheet. The manager can check on cashiers by comparing the number of games scored with the amount of cash received. By multiplying the number of games by the price per game to estimate the revenue and comparing this amount with each day's cash receipts, the manager can see whether the business is collecting all its revenues.

Electronic Devices and Computer Controls   Businesses use electronic devices to protect assets. For example, retailers such as Winners control their inventories by attaching an *electronic sensor* to merchandise. The cashier removes the sensor at checkout. If a customer tries to remove from the store an item with the sensor attached, an alarm sounds. According to Checkpoint Systems, which manufactures electronic sensors, these devices reduce loss due to theft by as much as 50 percent.

Other Controls   Businesses of all types keep cash and important documents in *fireproof vaults*. *Burglar alarms* protect buildings and *security cameras* protect other property. *Loss-prevention specialists* train employees to spot suspicious activity.

Retailers receive most of their cash from customers on the spot. To safeguard cash, they use *point-of-sale terminals* that serve as a cash register and also record each transaction. Several times each day a supervisor removes the cash for deposit in the bank.

Employees who handle cash are in a tempting position. Many businesses purchase *fidelity bonds* on cashiers. The bond is an insurance policy that reimburses the company for any losses due to the employee's theft. Before issuing a fidelity bond, the insurance company investigates the employee's record.

Mandatory vacations and *job rotation* improve internal controls. General Electric Canada, for example, moves employees from job to job. This improves morale by giving employees a broad view of the business. Also, knowing that someone else will be doing that job next month keeps an employee honest.

Internal Controls for E-Commerce

E-commerce creates its own unique types of risks. Hackers may gain access to confidential information, such as account numbers and passwords that would normally be unavailable in face-to-face transactions. Confidentiality is a significant challenge for companies doing business online. To convince people to buy online, companies must ensure security of customer data.

Pitfalls   E-commerce pitfalls include:

• Stolen credit-card numbers

• Computer viruses and Trojans

• Phishing expeditions and identity theft

Stolen credit-card numbers. Suppose you buy several CDs online from Future Shop. To make the purchase, your credit-card number must travel through cyberspace, potentially exposing it and other personal data to people who will steal this information and use it themselves or sell it to others to use.

Wireless networks (Wi-Fi) are creating new security hazards. In the U.S., amateur hacker Carlos Salgado Jr. used his home computer to steal 100,000 credit-card numbers from an Internet service provider. The cards represented a combined

REAL WORLD EXAMPLE

If a clerk in a retail store makes a mistake on the sales receipt, the receipt is not destroyed but is marked VOID. Most businesses use pre-numbered sales receipts, so a missing receipt would be noted.

credit limit exceeding $1 billion. Salgado was caught when he tried to sell the credit-card numbers to an undercover FBI agent. There have been other cases of companies potentially exposing their customers' financial data to outsiders due to a breach in their Internet security systems.

Computer viruses and Trojans. A **computer virus** is a malicious program that (a) enters program code without consent, and (b) performs destructive actions. A **Trojan** hides inside a legitimate program and works like a virus. Viruses can destroy or alter data, make bogus calculations, and infect files. Most firms have found a virus somewhere in their organization.

Suppose that an individual plants a virus into your school's computer that changes all the grades for students for a semester. This type of virus or Trojan could undermine not only a grade, but a school's reputation as well.

Phishing expeditions. Thieves phish by creating bogus websites, such as AOL4Free.com. This neat-sounding website attracts lots of visitors and the thieves obtain account numbers and passwords from unsuspecting visitors. They use the data for illicit purposes.

Identity theft. Identity theft occurs when thieves obtain and control your personal data to steal your assets, make purchases, or obtain loans in your name without your knowledge or permission. This can often have a devastating effect on a person's finances, by leaving them with no assets, by leaving them with debts, or by ruining their credit record. Identity theft is a growing problem, which is why you should never give private information or PINs to companies or people you don't know, especially over the Internet.

Security Measures   To address the risks posed by e-commerce, companies have devised a number of security measures, including

- Encryption
- Firewalls

Encryption. The server holding confidential information may not be secure. One technique for protecting customer data is encryption. **Encryption** rearranges messages by a mathematical process. The encrypted message cannot be read by anyone who does not know the process. An accounting example uses check-sum digits for account numbers. Each account number has its last digit equal to the sum of the previous digits, for example, Customer Number 2237, where $2 + 2 + 3 = 7$. Any account number that fails this test triggers an error message.

Firewalls. **Firewalls** limit access to a local network. Network members can access the network but nonmembers cannot. Usually several firewalls are built into the system. Think of a fortress with multiple walls protecting the queen's chamber at the centre. At the point of entry, passwords, personal identification numbers (PINs), and signatures are used to restrict entry. More sophisticated firewalls are used deeper in the network. You start with Firewall 3 and work toward the centre.

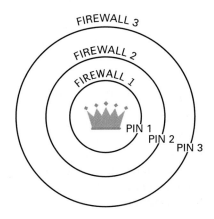

The Limitations of Internal Control—Costs and Benefits

Unfortunately, most internal controls can be circumvented or overcome. Collusion—where two or more people work as a team—can beat internal controls. Consider the Classic Theatre. Geoff and Lana can design a scheme in which Geoff sells the tickets and pockets the cash from 10 customers. Lana, the ticket taker, admits 10 customers without tickets. Geoff and Lana then split the cash. To prevent this situation, the manager must take additional steps, such as counting the people in the theatre and matching that figure against the number of ticket stubs retained. But that takes time away from other duties.

The stricter the internal control system, the more it costs. A complex system of internal control may strangle the business with red tape. How tight should the controls be? Internal controls must be judged in the light of the costs and benefits. An example of a good cost/benefit relationship: a security guard at a store costs about $28,000 a year. On average, each guard prevents about $50,000 of theft. The net benefit to the store is $22,000.

Sun-Rype Products Ltd. management acknowledges the limitations of internal controls in the 2008 Annual Report by stating:

> While management believes that the current disclosure controls and procedures and internal controls over financial reporting provide a reasonable level of assurance of achieving their objectives, it cannot be expected that existing disclosure controls and procedures or internal financial controls will prevent all human error and circumvention or overriding of the controls and procedures. A control system, no matter how well conceived or operated, can provide only reasonable, not absolute, assurance that the objectives of the control system are met.

The Bank Account as a Control Device

Cash is the most liquid asset because it is the medium of exchange. Increasingly, cash consists of electronic impulses in a bank's accounting system with no paper cheques or deposit slips. Cash is easy to conceal, easy to move, and relatively easy to steal. As a result, most businesses create specific controls for cash.

Keeping cash in a *bank account* helps because banks have established practices for safeguarding customers' money. Banks also provide customers with detailed records of their transactions. To take full advantage of these control features, a business should deposit all cash receipts in the bank and make all cash payments through the bank. An exception is a petty cash transaction, which we look at later.

The documents used to control a bank account include

- Signature cards
- Deposit slips
- Cheques
- Bank statements
- Bank reconciliations

Signature Card Banks require each person authorized to transact business through an account to sign a *signature card*. The signature card shows each authorized person's signature. This helps protect against forgery. The teller sees an electronic copy of this card when processing a transaction on the account.

Deposit Slip Banks supply standard forms such as *deposit slips* or *deposit tickets*. The customer fills in the dollar amount of each deposit. As proof of the transaction, the customer keeps a deposit receipt.

Cheque   To pay cash from an account, the depositor writes a **cheque**, which is the document that tells the bank to pay the designated party a specified amount of money. There are three parties to a cheque:

- The *maker*, who signs the cheque
- The *payee*, to whom the cheque is paid
- The *bank* on which the cheque is drawn

Exhibit 8–3 shows a cheque drawn on the bank account of Business Research Inc., the maker. The cheque has two parts: the cheque itself and the *remittance advice*, an optional attachment that tells the payee the reason for payment.

EXHIBIT 8–3   Cheque with Remittance Advice

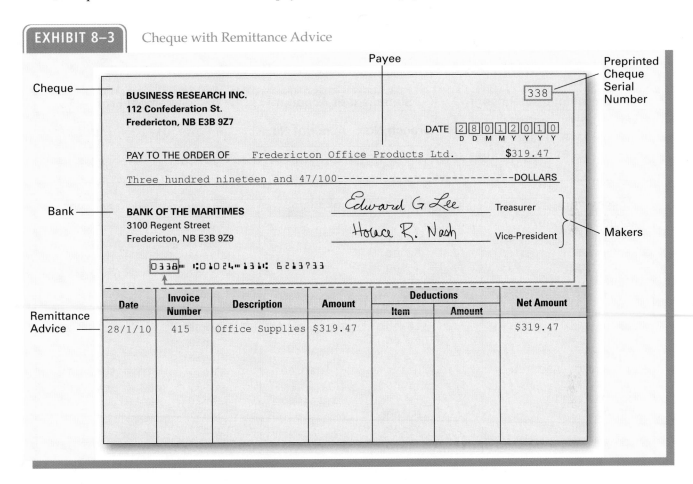

Bank Statement   Banks often send monthly statements to their customers. A **bank statement** reports what the bank did with the customer's cash. The statement shows the account's beginning and ending balances for the period, and lists cash receipts and payments transacted through the bank. Included with the statement are either the maker's *cancelled cheques* that have been cashed by the payee, or copies of these cheques. The statement also lists deposits and other changes in the account. Exhibit 8–4 is the bank statement of Business Research Inc. for the month ended January 31, 2010. The total deposits and total withdrawals are shown at the bottom of the bank statement. Details of the transactions appear in the body of the statement.

Electronic funds transfer (EFT) moves cash by electronic communications rather than by paper documents. It is much cheaper for a company to pay employees by EFT (direct deposit) than by issuing hundreds of payroll cheques. Also, many people make mortgage, rent, insurance, credit-card, and other payments either by prior arrangement with their bank or by means of electronic banking; they never write cheques for those payments. The bank statement lists EFT deposits and payments.

EXHIBIT 8–4 Bank Statement

BUSINESS ACCOUNT

Bank of the Maritimes
3100 REGENT STREET
FREDERICTON, NEW BRUNSWICK
E3B 9Z9

1024/   0/   5

BUSINESS RESEARCH INC.
112 CONFEDERATION ST.
FREDERICTON, NB

E3B 9Z7

For Current Interest Rates:
CALL OUR INFOLINE
1-800-386-2093
QUEBEC 1-800-386-1600
TORONTO 416-987-7735

Statement of Account	
Branch No.	Account No.
1024	1316213733

Statement From – To	
JAN 01/10 JAN 31/10	
Page 1 **of** 1	

DESCRIPTION	WITHDRAWALS	DEPOSITS	DATE	BALANCE
BALANCE FORWARD			Jan01	6,556.12
DEPOSIT		1,112.00	Jan04	
NSF CHEQUE	52.00		Jan04	
NSF CHARGE	25.00		Jan04	7,591.12
CHQ#00256	100.00		Jan06	
CHQ#00334	100.00		Jan06	7,391.12
DEPOSIT		194.60	Jan08	7,585.72
CHQ#00335	100.00		Jan08	7,485.72
CHQ#00332	3,000.00		Jan12	
CHQ#00333	150.00		Jan12	4,335.72
EFT RENT COLLECTION		900.00	Jan17	5,235.72
EFT INSURANCE	361.00		Jan20	4,874.72
BANK COLLECTION		2,114.00	Jan26	6,988.72
CHQ#00336	1,100.00		Jan31	
SERVICE CHARGES	14.25		Jan31	
INTEREST CREDIT		28.01	Jan31	5,902.48
	5,002.25	4,348.61		

One method of transferring funds electronically is through the use of a *debit card*. When you make a purchase from a store and pay with a debit card, you authorize your bank to immediately withdraw the money for the purchase from your bank account and deposit it into the store's bank account. You will see the amount of the withdrawal on your monthly bank statement or passbook, and the store will see the amount of the deposit on its monthly bank statement. Debit cards and bank cards will be discussed more fully in Chapter 9.

DID YOU GET IT?

MyAccountingLab

To check your understanding of the material in this Learning Objective, complete these questions. The solutions appear on MyAccountingLab so you can check your progress.

2. Geoff works the late movie shift at Classic Theatre. Occasionally, Geoff must sell tickets *and* take the tickets as customers enter the theatre. Standard procedure requires that Geoff tear the tickets, give one-half to the customer, and keep the other half. To control cash receipts, the manager compares each night's cash receipts with the number of ticket stubs on hand.

   (a) How could Geoff take money from the theatre's cash receipts and hide the theft? What additional steps should the manager take to strengthen the internal control over cash receipts?

   (b) What is the internal control weakness in this situation? Explain the weakness.

   (c) What electronic device is often used at concerts and events to ensure legitimate tickets are presented by the patrons?

3. What problems can result when a sales clerk can also grant credit approval and record the sales in addition to handling the cash?

4. Match each of these terms with its description.

Computer virus	Collecting passwords and personal data using bogus websites
Encryption	Using passwords and personal identification numbers to limit access to a local network
Trojan	Rearranging messages and data so they cannot be read during transmission over the Internet
Firewall	Malicious and destructive program that enters program code without consent
Phishing	A malicious program that hides inside a legitimate program to corrupt data

The Bank Reconciliation

> OBJECTIVE 3
> Prepare a bank reconciliation and the related journal entries

There are two records of the business's cash:

1. The Cash account in the company's general ledger. Exhibit 8–5 shows that Business Research Inc.'s ending cash balance is $3,294.21.

2. The bank statement, which shows the cash receipts and payments transacted through the bank. In Exhibit 8–4, the bank shows an ending balance of $5,902.48 for Business Research Inc.

The books and the bank statement usually show different cash balances. Differences arise because of a time lag in recording transactions, called a **timing difference**. Three examples of timing differences follow:

- When you write a cheque, you immediately deduct the amount of the cheque from the balance in your cheque book. But the bank does not subtract this amount from your account until the bank pays it. That may take days, even weeks, if the payee waits to cash the cheque.

- Likewise, you immediately add the amount of the cash receipt for each deposit you make to your account. But it may take a day or more for the bank to add deposits to your balance.

- Any EFT payments and cash receipts are recorded by the bank before you learn of them.

To ensure accurate cash records, you need to update your chequebook—either online or after you receive your bank statement. All businesses do the same. As part of this updating process, a document called the **bank reconciliation** is prepared by

In this introductory accounting course, you have learned that

- Debit means the **left** side of an account
- Credit means the **right** side of an account

In banking,

- Debits are bad (for you)
- Credits are good (for you)

The key is to remember that all the information you receive from the bank, such as statement amounts and credit memos, is *always* from the bank's point of view.

- To the bank, your deposit account is a liability (a credit-balance account). The bank owes your money to you because you can withdraw it or write cheques on it at any time. The bank thus has a Deposit Payable, a liability, for your cash on deposit, which is a credit and good for you.
- The opposite is true for a bank loan, which to a bank is a receivable (a debit-balance account). The bank thus has a Loan Receivable, an asset, for the money you owe the bank, which is a debit and bad for you.

LEARNING TIPS

These are the journal entries for NSF cheques. This journal entry was made by EeZee Transit when J. Doe paid his account by cheque:

Cash   XX
   Accounts Rec.—J. Doe   XX

The entry to record the receipt of cash is made when the cheque is received, even though the bank will soon add the cash to EeZee Transit's account. However, J. Doe did not have enough cash in his chequing account to cover the cheque, so the bank removed the cash from EeZee Transit's account. EeZee Transit must reverse the original entry as follows:

Accounts Rec. —J. Doe   XX
   Cash   XX

Since very few cheques received will be NSF, it is much more efficient to record the cash when the cheque is received than to wait until the cheque clears the maker's bank.

the company (not the bank). The bank reconciliation explains the differences between the company's cash records and the bank balance. It ensures that all cash transactions have been accounted for, and it establishes that bank and book records of cash are correct. The person who prepares the bank reconciliation should have no other cash duties. Otherwise, he or she could steal cash and manipulate the bank reconciliation to hide the theft.

EXHIBIT 8–5 Cash Records of Business Research Inc.

General Ledger:

ACCOUNT Cash   No. 1100

Date	Item	Jrn. Ref.	Debit	Credit	Balance
2010					
Jan. 1	Balance	✔			6,556.12 Dr
2	Cash receipt	CR. 9	1,112.00		7,668.12 Dr
7	Cash receipt	CR. 9	194.60		7,862.72 Dr
31	Cash payments	CP. 17		6,160.14	1,702.58 Dr
31	Cash receipt	CR. 10	1,591.63		3,294.21 Dr

Cash Payments:

Cheque No.	Amount
332	$3,000.00
333	510.00
334	100.00
335	100.00
336	1,100.00
337	286.00
338	319.47
339	83.00
340	203.14
341	458.53
Total	$6,160.14

Items on the Bank Reconciliation Here are the items that appear on a bank reconciliation. They all cause differences between the bank balance and the book balance. (We refer to the company's cash records as the "Book" records.)

1. Items to show on the *Bank* side of the bank reconciliation. The bank side contains items not yet recorded by the bank or errors made by the bank. These items include the following:

   a. **Deposits in transit** (outstanding deposits). The company has recorded (posted) these deposits, but the bank has not. *Add* deposits in transit.

   b. **Outstanding cheques.** These cheques have been issued by the company and recorded on its books but the bank has not yet paid/processed them. *Subtract* outstanding cheques.

   c. **Bank errors.** Correct all bank errors on the Bank side of the reconciliation.

2. Items recorded on the *book* side of the bank reconciliation. The book side contains items not yet recorded by the company in its accounting records, but recorded by the bank. Items to show on the book side include the following:

   a. **Bank collections.** Bank collections are cash receipts. Many businesses have their customers pay directly to the company bank account. If a company receives high-dollar-value payments, it might use a *lock-box system* to reduce theft and circulate cash faster than if the cash had to be collected and deposited by company personnel. An example of a bank collection is a bank's collecting a note receivable for the company. *Add* bank collections.

b. **Electronic funds transfers (EFTs)**. The bank may receive or pay cash on behalf of the depositor. An EFT may be a cash receipt or a cash payment.

c. **Service charge**. This cash payment is the bank's fee for processing the depositor's transactions. *Subtract* services charges.

d. **Interest revenue on chequing account**. Depositors earn interest if they keep a specified amount of cash in their accounts. This is sometimes true of business chequing accounts. The bank statement identifies this cash receipt. *Add* interest revenue.

e. **Nonsufficient funds cheques (NSF)**. These are cash receipts that turn out to be worthless. NSF cheques (sometimes called *bounced cheques, rubber cheques,* or *hot cheques*) are cash payments on a bank reconciliation. *Subtract* NSF cheques.

f. **The cost of printed cheques**. This cash payment is handled like a service charge. *Subtract* this cost.

g. **Book errors**. Correct all book errors on the book side of the reconciliation.

Preparing the Bank Reconciliation

The steps in preparing the bank reconciliation are as follows:

1. Start with two figures, the balance in the business's Cash account in the general ledger (*balance per books*) and the balance shown on the bank statement (*balance per bank*) on the same date. These two amounts will probably disagree because of the timing differences discussed earlier.

2. Add to, or subtract from, the *bank* balance those items that appear correctly on the books but not on the bank statement.

   a. Add *deposits in transit* to the bank balance. Deposits in transit are identified by comparing the deposits listed on the bank statement to the business's list of cash receipts. They appear as cash receipts on the books but not as deposits on the bank statement.

   b. Subtract *outstanding cheques* from the bank balance. Outstanding cheques are identified by comparing the cancelled cheques returned with the bank statement to the business's list of cheques written for cash payment. Outstanding cheques appear as cash payments on the books but not as paid cheques on the bank statement. If cheques were outstanding on the bank reconciliation for the preceding month and have still not been cashed, add them to the list of outstanding cheques on this month's bank reconciliation. Outstanding cheques are usually the most numerous item on a bank reconciliation.

3. Add to, or subtract from, the *book* balance those items that appear on the bank statement but not on the company books.

   a. Add to the book balance (1) *bank collections,* (2) *EFT cash receipts,* and (3) *interest revenue* earned on the money in the bank. These items are identified by comparing the deposits listed on the bank statement with the business's list of cash receipts. They show up as cash receipts on the bank statement but not on the books.

   b. Subtract from the book balance (1) *EFT cash payments,* (2) *service charges,* (3) *the cost of printed cheques,* and (4) *other bank charges* (for example, charges for NSF or stale-dated cheques). These items are identified by comparing the other charges listed on the bank statement to the cash payments recorded on the business's books. They appear as subtractions on the bank statement but not as cash payments on the books.

KEY POINT

Errors can be made by the bank or on the books. The balance that is adjusted for the error depends on where the error occurred. If the bank makes the error, the bank statement balance is adjusted. If the error is on the books, the book balance is adjusted.

4. Compute the *adjusted bank balance* and *adjusted book balance*. The two adjusted balances should be equal.

5. Journalize each item in step 3, that is, each item listed on the book portion of the bank reconciliation. These items must be recorded on the business's books because they affect cash.

6. Correct all book errors, and notify the bank of any errors it has made.

Bank Reconciliation Illustrated The bank statement in Exhibit 8–4 (page 412) indicates that the January 31, 2010, bank balance of Business Research Inc. is $5,902.48. However, the company's Cash account has a balance of $3,294.21, as shown in Exhibit 8–5. This situation calls for a bank reconciliation. Exhibit 8–6,

---

| EXHIBIT 8–6 | Bank Reconciliation |

PANEL A: Reconciling Items

1. Deposit in transit, $1,591.63.
2. Bank error: The bank deducted $100 for a cheque written by another company. Add $100 to bank balance.
3. Outstanding cheques: no. 337, $286.00; no. 338, $319.47; no. 339, $83.00; no. 340, $203.14; no. 341, $458.53.
4. EFT receipt of rent revenue, $900.00.

5. Bank collection of note receivable, $2,114.00, including interest revenue of $114.00.
6. Interest earned on bank balance, $28.01.
7. Book error: cheque no. 333 for $150.00 paid to Brown Corp. on account was recorded as $510.00.
8. Bank service charges, $39.25 ($25.00 + $14.25).
9. NSF cheque from L. Ross, $52.00.
10. EFT payment of insurance expense, $361.00.

PANEL B: Bank Reconciliation

BUSINESS RESEARCH INC.
Bank Reconciliation
January 31, 2010

Bank			Books		
Bank Balance, January 31, 2010		$5,902.48	Books Balance, January 31, 2010		$3,294.21
Add:			Add:		
1. Deposit of January 31 in transit		1,591.63	4. EFT receipt of rent revenue		900.00
2. Correction of bank error			5. Bank collection of note receivable,		
—Business Research Associates			including interest revenue of $114.00		2,114.00
cheque erroneously charged			6. Interest revenue earned on		
against company account..................		100.00	bank balance		28.01
		$7,594.11	7. Correction of book error—Overstated		
			amount of cheque no. 333...............		360.00
3. Less: outstanding cheques					6,696.22
No. 337............................	$286.00		Less:		
338............................	319.47		8. Service charges $39.25		
339............................	83.00		9. NSF cheque 52.00		
340............................	203.14		10. EFT payment of insurance		
341............................	458.53	(1,350.14)	expense 361.00		(452.25)
Adjusted bank balance		**$6,243.97**	**Adjusted book balance**		**$6,243.97**

↑ ——————— | Amounts should agree | ——————— ↑

Each reconciling item is treated in the same way in every situation. Here is a summary of how to treat the various reconciling items:

BANK BALANCE—ALWAYS
- *Add* deposits in transit.
- *Subtract* outstanding cheques.
- *Add* or *subtract* corrections of bank errors.

BOOK BALANCE—ALWAYS
- *Add* bank collections, interest revenue, and EFT receipts.
- *Subtract* service charges, NSF cheques, and EFT payments.
- *Add* or *subtract* corrections of book errors.

Panel A lists the reconciling items for your easy reference and Panel B shows the completed reconciliation.

Journalizing Transactions from the Reconciliation The bank reconciliation is an accountant's tool that is separate from the company's journals and ledgers. It explains the effects of all cash receipts and all cash payments through the bank. But it does *not* account for transactions in the journals. To ensure that the transactions are entered into the accounts, we must make journal entries and post to the ledger. Each item on the Book side of the bank reconciliation requires a journal entry and affects the Cash account.

The bank reconciliation in Exhibit 8–6 requires Business Research Inc. to make the journal entries shown in Exhibit 8–7, dated January 31, 2010, to bring the Cash account up to date. The numbers in parentheses correspond to the reconciling items listed in Exhibit 8–6, Panel A.

EXHIBIT 8–7 Business Research Inc. Journal Entries Resulting from the Bank Reconciliation

General Journal				Page 11
Date 2010	Accounts	Post Ref.	Debit	Credit
(4) Jan. 31	Cash...		900.00	
	Rent Revenue...			900.00
	Receipt of monthly rent.			
(5) Jan. 31	Cash...		2,114.00	
	Notes Receivable..................................			2,000.00
	Interest Revenue...................................			114.00
	Note Receivable collected by bank.			
(6) Jan. 31	Cash...		28.01	
	Interest Revenue...................................			28.01
	Interest earned on bank balance.			
(7) Jan. 31	Cash...		360.00	
	Accounts Payable—Brown Corp...............			360.00
	Correction of cheque no. 333.			
(8) Jan. 31	Bank Charges Expense.....................................		39.25	
	Cash...			39.25
	Bank service charges ($25.00 NSF + $14.25).			
(9) Jan. 31	Accounts Receivable—L. Ross.......................		52.00	
	Cash...			52.00
	NSF cheque returned by bank.			
(10) Jan. 31	Insurance Expense		361.00	
	Cash...			361.00
	Payment of monthly insurance.			

The journal entries in Exhibit 8–7 update the company's books.

The entry for the NSF cheque (entry 9) needs explanation. Upon learning that L. Ross's $52 cheque to Business Research Inc. was not good, Business Research Inc. credits Cash to update the Cash account. Since Business Research Inc. still has a receivable from L. Ross, it must debit Accounts Receivable—L. Ross to reinstate the receivable from L. Ross and pursue collection from him.

Online and Telephone Banking Canadian banks now permit online and telephone banking, where customers use their computers or telephones to effect transactions such as paying bills, transferring money from one account to another, and arranging a loan. With online banking, customers use a computer and an Internet connection to effect transactions. The bank supplies a confirmation number on the customer's computer screen to show the transaction has occurred, and the transaction is confirmed by its appearance in the passbook or on a subsequent bank statement. There is no other "paper trail" as evidence of the transaction.

Since bank statements are usually received monthly, a bank reconciliation is often performed only once a month. However, with online access to bank account information, you are able to print your bank account history at any time. The account history—like a bank statement—lists deposits, cheques, EFT receipts and payments, automated teller machine (ATM) deposits and withdrawals, and interest earned on the bank balance. The account history looks very similar to the bank statement. Thus, companies and individuals could prepare bank reconciliations more frequently than once a month.

How Owners and Managers Use the Bank Reconciliation

The bank reconciliation can be a powerful control device, as the following example illustrates.

Randy Vaughn is a CA in Regina, Saskatchewan. Vaughn owns several apartment complexes that are managed by his cousin Alexis Vaughn. His accounting practice keeps him busy, so he has little time to devote to the properties. Vaughn's cousin approves tenants, collects the monthly rent cheques, arranges custodial and maintenance work, hires and fires employees, writes the cheques, and performs the bank reconciliation. This concentration of duties in one person is terrible from an internal control standpoint. Vaughn's cousin could be stealing from him. As a CA, he is aware of this possibility, so Vaughn exercises some internal controls over his cousin's activities:

1. Periodically, he drops by his properties to see whether the apartments are in good condition.
2. To control cash, Vaughn uses a bank reconciliation. On an irregular basis, he examines the bank reconciliations as prepared by his cousin. He matches every cheque that cleared the bank to the journal entry on the books. Vaughn would know immediately if his cousin were writing cheques to herself. Vaughn sometimes prepares his own bank reconciliation to see whether it agrees with his cousin's work.
3. To keep his cousin on her toes, Vaughn lets her know that he periodically checks her work.
4. Vaughn has a simple method for controlling cash receipts. He knows the occupancy level of his apartments. He also knows the monthly rent he charges. He multiplies the number of apartments—say 100—by the monthly rent (which averages $500 per unit) to arrive at an expected monthly rent revenue of $50,000. By tracing the $50,000 revenue to the bank statement, Vaughn can tell that his rent money went into his bank account.

Control activities such as these (often referred to as "executive controls") are critical in small businesses. With only a few employees, a separation of duties may not be feasible. The owner must oversee and, if possible, become involved in the operations of the business, or the assets may disappear.

To check your understanding of the material in this Learning Objective, complete these questions. The solutions appear on MyAccountingLab so you can check your progress.

5. List the three items that can appear on the bank side of a bank reconciliation. Why does the company *not* need to record the reconciling items that appear on the bank side of the bank reconciliation?

6. Jonas Company's July 31, 2010, bank statement balance is $9,000 and shows a service charge of $30, interest earned of $10, and an NSF cheque for $600. Deposits in transit total $2,400 and outstanding cheques are $1,150. The bookkeeper incorrectly recorded as $152 a cheque of $125 in payment of an account payable. The company's book balance at July 31, 2010, was $10,843.

   (a) Prepare the bank reconciliation for Jonas Company at July 31, 2010. Calculate the adjusted bank balance first, then calculate the adjusted book balance below it. Draw an arrow to show that both adjusted balances agree.

   (b) Prepare the journal entries needed to update the company's books.

Internal Control over Cash Receipts

Internal control over cash receipts (the term includes cash, cheques, credit card charges, and debit card payments) ensures that all cash receipts are deposited quickly for safekeeping in the bank. Companies receive cash over the counter and through the mail. Each source of cash has its own security measures.

OBJECTIVE 4
Apply internal controls to cash receipts

Cash Receipts over the Counter Exhibit 8–8 illustrates a cash receipt made over the counter in a department store. The point-of-sale terminal (cash register) provides control over cash receipts. Consider a Canadian Tire store. The terminal is positioned so that customers can see the amounts the cashier scans into the terminal. No person willingly pays more than the marked price for an item, so the customer helps prevent the sales clerk from overcharging. For each transaction, Canadian Tire issues a receipt to ensure that each sale is recorded.

The cash drawer opens only when the clerk enters a transaction and the machine records it. At the end of the day, a manager proves the cash by comparing the cash in the drawer against the machine's record of sales. This step helps prevent theft by the clerk.

At the end of the day—or several times a day if business is brisk—the cashier or other employee with cash-handling duties deposits the cash in the bank. The machine tape then goes to the accounting department as the basis for the journal entry to record sales revenue. These security measures, coupled with oversight by a manager, discourage theft.

It is important to deposit all cash receipts *intact* at least daily. Neither managers nor employees should use cash received to make purchases or other cash payments. In some rare circumstances where records are destroyed or missing, the bank statement can be used to reconstruct transactions.

Cash Receipts by Mail Many companies receive payments (cheques and credit card authorizations) by mail. Exhibit 8–9 shows how companies control payments received by mail. All incoming mail is opened by a mailroom employee.

The mailroom then sends all customer payments to the treasurer, who has the cashier deposit the money in the bank. The remittance advices, or records of payment, go to the accounting department for the journal entries to Cash and customers' accounts. As a final step, the controller compares the records of the day's cash receipts:

1. Bank deposit amount from the treasurer
2. Debit to Cash from the accounting department

EXHIBIT 8–8

Cash Receipts over the Counter

EXHIBIT 8–9 Cash Receipts by Mail

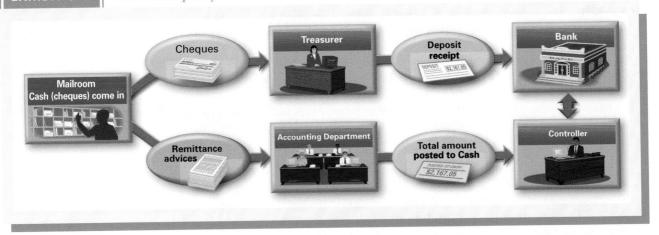

The debit to Cash should equal the amount deposited in the bank. All cash receipts are safe in the bank, and the company books are up to date.

Many companies use a lock-box system. Customers send their cheques to a post office box belonging to the bank; the bank deposits the cheques directly to the company's bank account. Internal control is tight because company personnel never touch incoming cash.

Cash Short and Over   A difference may exist between actual cash receipts and the day's record of cash received. Usually, the difference is small and results from honest errors. When the recorded cash balance exceeds cash on hand, we have a *cash short* situation. When the actual cash exceeds the recorded cash balance, we have a *cash over* situation. Suppose the tapes from a cash register at Little Short Stop convenience store indicated sales revenue of $15,000, but the cash received was $14,980. To record the day's sales for that register, the store would make this entry:

Cash	14,980	
Cash Short and Over	20	
Sales Revenue...		15,000
Daily cash sales.		

As the entry shows, Cash Short and Over, an expense account, is debited when sales revenue exceeds cash receipts. This account is credited when cash receipts exceed sales. A debit balance in Cash Short and Over typically appears on the income statement as a part of Miscellaneous Expense; a credit balance typically appears as part of Other Revenue.

The Cash Short and Over account's balance should be small. The debits and credits for cash shorts and overs collected over an accounting period tend to cancel each other out. A large balance signals the accountant to investigate. For example, too large a debit balance may mean an employee is stealing. Cash Short and Over, then, acts as an internal control device.

Exhibit 8–10 summarizes the internal controls over cash receipts.

DID YOU GET IT?

MyAccountingLab

To check your understanding of the material in this Learning Objective, complete these questions. The solutions appear on MyAccountingLab so you can check your progress.

7. When cash is received by mail, what keeps the mailroom employee from pocketing a customer cheque and destroying the remittance advice?

8. Suppose the tapes from the cash registers at a Burger King restaurant indicated sales revenue of $7,252, but the cash received was $7,262. Journalize the day's sales.

EXHIBIT 8–10   Internal Controls over Cash Receipts

Element of Internal Control	Internal Controls over Cash Receipts
Competent, reliable, ethical personnel	Companies carefully screen employees for undesirable personality traits. They commit time and effort to training programs.
Assignment of responsibilities	Specific employees are designated as cashiers, supervisors of cashiers, or accountants for cash receipts.
Proper authorization	Only designated employees, such as department managers, can grant exceptions for customers, approve cheque receipts above a certain amount, allow customers to purchase on credit, and void sales.
Separation of duties	Cashiers and mailroom employees who handle cash do not have access to the accounting records. Accountants who record cash receipts have no opportunity to handle cash.
Internal and external audits	Internal auditors examine company transactions for agreement with management policies. External auditors examine the internal controls over cash receipts to determine whether the accounting system produces accurate amounts for revenues, receivables, and other items related to cash receipts.
Documents and records	Customers receive receipts as transaction records. Bank statements list cash receipts for deposit. Customers who pay by mail include a remittance advice showing the amount of cash they sent to the company.
Electronic devices and computer control	Cash registers serve as transaction records. Each day's receipts are matched with customer remittance advices and with the day's deposit slip with the bank.
Other controls	Cashiers are bonded. Cash is stored in vaults and banks. Employees are rotated among jobs and are required to take vacations.

Internal Control over Cash Payments

Cash payments are as important as cash receipts. It is therefore critical to control cash payments. Companies make most payments by cheque. They also pay small amounts from a petty cash fund. Let's begin with cash payments by cheque.

> OBJECTIVE (5)
> Apply internal controls to cash payments

Controls over Payments by Cheque

As we have seen, companies need a good separation of duties between operations and writing cheques for cash payments.

Payment by cheque is an important internal control.

- The cheque provides a record of the payment.
- The cheque must be signed by an authorized official.
- Before signing the cheque, the official should study the evidence supporting the payment.

Controls over Purchase and Payment   To illustrate the internal control over cash payments, let's suppose the business is paying for merchandise inventory. The purchasing and payment process follows these steps, as outlined in Exhibit 8–11:

1. The company sends a *purchase order* to the supplier.
2. The supplier ships the merchandise and mails the *invoice*, or bill. (We introduced the invoice in Chapters 2 and 5.)
3. The company receives the goods. The receiving department checks the goods for damage and prepares a list of the goods received on a *receiving report*.

EXHIBIT 8–11 Cash Payments by Cheque

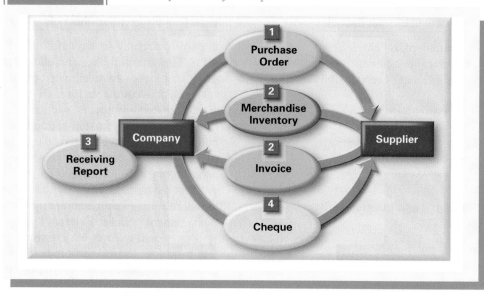

4. After the accounting department checks and confirms all the foregoing documents, the company sends a *cheque* to the supplier.

For good internal control, the purchasing agent should neither receive the goods nor approve the payment. If these duties are not separated, a purchasing agent could buy goods and have them shipped to his home. Or the purchasing agent could increase the price of purchases, approve the payment, and then split the price increase with the supplier.

Exhibit 8–12 shows the company's payment packet of documents. Before signing the cheque for payment, the controller or the treasurer should examine the packet to prove that all the documents agree. Only then does the company know that:

1. It received the goods ordered—proved by the receiving report.
2. It is paying only for the goods received—proved by the purchase order and receiving report.

After payment, the cheque signer should punch a hole through the payment packet or otherwise mark the packet and its contents. These actions alert the company that it has paid the bill. Dishonest employees have been known to present a bill for cash payment two or more times.

Some companies include a voucher in their payment packet. This document summarizes the payment details and has spaces for the signatures of officials who can approve the payment. Other companies may stamp the invoice and fill in the blanks with this same information.

EXHIBIT 8–12

Payment Packet

Streamlined Procedures   Technology is streamlining payment procedures. **Evaluated Receipts Settlement (ERS)** compresses the approval process into a single step: comparing the receiving report with the purchase order. If the two documents match, that proves that the company received the merchandise it ordered. Then the company pays the supplier.

An even more streamlined process bypasses people and documents altogether. In Electronic Data Interchange (EDI), Canadian Tire's computers can communicate directly with the computers of suppliers like General Tire, Rubbermaid, and Procter & Gamble. When Canadian Tire's inventory of automobile tires reaches a certain (low) level, the computer sends a purchase order to General Tire. General Tire ships the tires and invoices Canadian Tire electronically. Then an EFT sends the payment from Canadian Tire to General Tire.

Exhibit 8–13 summarizes the internal controls over cash payments.

EXHIBIT 8–13 | Internal Controls over Cash Payments

Element of Internal Control	Internal Controls over Cash Payments
Competent, reliable, ethical personnel	Cash payments are entrusted to high-level employees, with larger amounts paid by the treasurer or assistant treasurer.
Assignment of responsibility	Specific employees approve purchase documents for payment. Executives examine approvals, then co-sign cheques.
Proper authorization	Large expenditures must be authorized by the company owner or board of directors to ensure agreement with organizational goals.
Separation of duties	Computer operators and other employees who handle cheques have no access to the accounting records. Accountants who record cash payments have no opportunity to handle cash.
Internal and external audits	Internal auditors examine company transactions for agreement with management policies. External auditors examine the internal controls over cash payments to determine whether the accounting system produces accurate amounts for expenses, assets, and other items related to cash payments.
Documents and records	Suppliers issue invoices that document the need to pay cash. Bank statements list cash payments (cheques and EFT payments) for reconciliation with company records. Cheques are pre-numbered and used in sequence to account for payments.
Electronic devices, computer controls, and other controls	Evaluated Receipts Settlement (ERS) streamlines the cheque approval process. Machines stamp the amount on a cheque in indelible ink. Paid invoices are punched or otherwise mutilated to avoid duplicate payment.

Controlling Petty Cash Payments

It is wasteful to write a cheque for an employee's taxi fare (while on company business), or the delivery of a package across town. To meet these needs, companies keep cash on hand to pay small amounts. This fund is called **petty cash**.

Even though petty cash payments are small, the business needs internal controls, such as the following:

1. Designate a custodian of the petty cash fund.
2. Keep a specific amount of cash on hand in a secure location.
3. Support all fund payments for expenses with a petty cash ticket or voucher.

Creating the Petty Cash Fund   The petty cash fund is opened when a cheque is written for the designated amount. The cheque is made payable to the petty cash custodian. Assume that on February 28 the business creates a petty cash fund of $400. The custodian cashes a $400 cheque and places the money in the fund. Starting the fund is recorded as follows:

Feb. 28	Petty Cash	400	
	Cash		400
	To open the petty cash fund.		

For each petty cash payment, the custodian prepares a *petty cash ticket* or *petty cash voucher* like the one illustrated in Exhibit 8–14.

Signatures (or initials) identify the recipient of the cash (Lewis Wright) and the fund custodian (MAR). Requiring both signatures reduces fraudulent payments. The custodian keeps all the pre-numbered petty cash tickets in the fund. The sum of the cash plus the total of the ticket amounts should equal the opening balance ($400) at all times. Also, the Petty Cash account keeps its $400 balance at all times. As the use of company debit cards increases, the use of petty cash accounts is decreasing.

No journal entries are made for petty cash payments until the fund is replenished. At that time, all petty cash payments will be recorded in a summary

EXHIBIT 8–14 Petty Cash Ticket

PETTY CASH TICKET

Date __Mar. 25, 2010__   No. __45__

Amount ___$34.00___

For __Payment for delivery of contract.___

Debit___Delivery Expense, Acct. No. 545___

Received by ___*Lewis Wright*___   Fund Custodian __*MAR*__

---

entry. This procedure avoids the need to journalize many payments for small amounts.

Maintaining the Petty Cash account at its designated balance is the nature of an **imprest system**. This system clearly identifies the amount of cash for which the fund custodian is responsible and is the system's main internal control feature. Imprest systems are also used for branch-office funds, not just petty cash. Payments reduce the cash in the fund, so periodically the fund must be replenished.

Replenishing the Petty Cash Fund   On March 31, the petty cash fund holds

- $230 in petty cash
- $164 in petty cash tickets

We can see that $6 is missing:

Fund balance	$400
Cash on hand	$230
Petty cash tickets	164
Total accounted for	$394
Amount of cash missing	$ 6

To replenish the petty cash fund, we need to bring the cash on hand up to $400. The company writes a cheque, payable to Petty Cash, for $170 ($400 – $230). The fund custodian cashes this cheque and puts $170 back in the fund. Now the fund holds $400 cash, as it should.

The petty cash tickets identify the accounts to debit, as shown in the entry to replenish the fund (items assumed for this illustration):

Mar. 31	Office Supplies	46	
	Delivery Expense	34	
	Cash Short and Over	6	
	Selling Expense	84	
	Cash		170
	To replenish the petty cash fund.		

KEY POINT

Attached to the petty cash ticket is a cash register receipt, invoice, or other documentation to support the payment.

The cash payments appear to have exceeded the sum of the tickets, since the fund was short $6, so Cash Short and Over was debited for the missing amount ($6). If the sum of the tickets exceeds the payment, Cash Short and Over is credited. Replenishing the fund does *not* affect the Petty Cash account. Petty Cash keeps its $400 balance at all times.

The petty cash fund *must* be replenished on the balance sheet date. Otherwise, the income statement will understate the expenses listed on the tickets.

The Petty Cash account in the general ledger is debited only when the fund is started (see the February 28 entry) or when its amount is changed. In our illustration, suppose the business decides to raise the fund amount from $400 to $500 because of increased demand for petty cash. This step would require a $100 debit to the Petty Cash account and a $100 credit to the Cash account.

Reporting Cash on the Balance Sheet

Cash is the first asset listed on the balance sheet because it is the most liquid asset. Businesses often have several bank accounts and several petty cash funds, but they combine all cash amounts into a single total called "Cash and Cash Equivalents" for reporting on the balance sheet.

Cash equivalents include liquid assets such as term deposits and certificates of deposit. These interest-bearing accounts can be withdrawn with no penalty after a short period of time. These assets are sufficiently similar to be reported along with cash.

Cash that is restricted and unavailable for immediate use should not be reported as a current asset if the company does not expect to spend the cash within a year or within the company's operating cycle, if longer than a year. For example, some banks require their depositors to maintain a *compensating balance* on deposit in the bank in order to borrow from the bank. The compensating balance is not included in the cash amount on the balance sheet because it is not available for immediate use.

DID YOU GET IT?

MyAccountingLab

To check your understanding of the material in this Learning Objective, complete these questions. The solutions appear on MyAccountingLab so you can check your progress.

9. Two officers' signatures are required for cheques over $1,000. One officer is going on vacation and pre-signs several cheques. The cheques are locked in the vault. What is the internal control feature in this scenario, and is it effective?

10. Leitch Design Studios established a $300 petty cash fund. James C. Brown (JCB) is the fund custodian. At the end of the first week, the petty cash fund contains the following:

    1. Cash: $163
    2. Petty cash tickets:

No.	Amount	Issued to	Signed by	Account Debited
1	$14	B. Jarvis	B. Jarvis and JCB	Office Supplies
2	39	S. Bell	S. Bell	Delivery Expense
4	43	R. Tate	R. Tate and JCB	—
5	33	G. Blair	G. Blair and JCB	Travel Expense

   (a) Identify three internal control weaknesses revealed in the given data.
   (b) Prepare the general journal entries to record
       i. Establishment of the petty cash fund.
       ii. Replenishment of the fund. Assume petty cash ticket no. 4 was issued for the purchase of office supplies.
   (c) What is the balance in the Petty Cash account immediately before replenishment? Immediately after replenishment?

Ethics and Accounting

Robert Schad, President and CEO of Husky Injection Molding Systems Ltd. in Bolton, Ontario, said, "Ethical practice is, quite simply, good business." Schad has been in business long enough to see the danger in unethical behaviour. Sooner or later unethical conduct comes to light, as was true in our chapter-opening story on page 402. Moreover, ethical behaviour wins out in the end because it is the right thing to do.

OBJECTIVE 6
Make ethical business judgments

Corporate and Professional Codes of Ethics

Most companies have a code of ethics to encourage employees to behave ethically. But codes of ethics are not enough by themselves. Owners and managers must set a high ethical tone. They must make it clear that the company will not tolerate unethical conduct.

Accountants have additional incentives to behave ethically. As professionals, they are expected to maintain higher standards than society in general. Their ability to attract business depends entirely on their reputation.

REAL WORLD EXAMPLE

In a survey, 81 percent of companies had a corporate code of conduct. Another 7 percent planned to establish such a code.

As you learned in Chapter 1, there are three professional accounting designations in Canada: the Chartered Accountants, the Certified General Accountants, and the Certified Management Accountants. Members of each of the professional bodies must adhere to the rules of professional conduct of their respective organizations. These documents set minimum standards of conduct for members. Unacceptable actions can result in expulsion from the organization, which makes it impossible for the person to remain a professional accountant.

Ethical Issues in Accounting

In many situations the ethical choice is easy. For example, stealing cash, as in the chapter-opening story, is illegal and unethical. In other cases, the choices are more difficult. But, in every instance, ethical judgments are a personal decision. What should I do in a given situation? Let's consider an ethical issue in accounting.

Sonja Kleberg is preparing the income tax return of a client who earned more income than expected. On January 2, the client pays for advertising to run in late January and asks Sonja to backdate the expense to the preceding year. Backdating would decrease taxable income of the earlier year and postpone a few dollars in tax payments. After all, there is a difference of only two days between January 2 and December 31. This client is important to Kleberg. What should she do?

She should refuse the request because the transaction took place in January of the new year.

What internal control device could prove that Kleberg behaved unethically if she backdated the transaction in the accounting records? A Canada Revenue Agency audit could prove that the expense occurred in January rather than in December. Falsifying tax returns is both illegal and unethical.

Weighing tough ethical judgments requires a decision framework. A framework is shown in the Decision Guidelines box. Consider the six questions shown there as general guidelines; they will guide you through answering tough ethical questions.

DECISION GUIDELINES — Framework for Making Ethical Judgments

Decision	Guidelines
1. What are the facts?	1. *Determine the facts.*
2. What is the ethical issue, if any?	2. *Identify the ethical issues.* The root word of ethical is *ethics*, which *Canadian Oxford Dictionary* defines as "the science of morals in human conduct; moral philosophy; moral principles in human conduct; moral correctness."
3. What are the alternatives?	3. *Specify the alternatives.* "Do nothing" is always an alternative.
4. Who is involved in the situation?	4. *Identify the stakeholders, the people involved.*
5. What are the possible consequences of each alternative in question 3?	5. *Assess the possible outcomes of each alternative.*
6. What should be done?	6. *Make a decision.*

DID YOU GET IT?

MyAccountingLab

To check your understanding of the material in this Learning Objective, complete this question. The solution appears on MyAccountingLab so you can check your progress.

11. Suppose, David Duncan, the lead external auditor for Enron Corporation, thinks Enron may be understating the liabilities on its balance sheet. Enron's transactions are very complex, and outsiders may never figure this out. Duncan asks his firm's Standards Committee how he should handle the situation. They reply, "Require Enron to report all its liabilities." Enron is Duncan's most important client, and Enron is pressuring Duncan to certify the liabilities. Duncan tries to rationalize that Enron's reported amounts are okay. What should Duncan do? To make his decision, Duncan could follow the framework outlined in the Decision Guidelines feature. Apply those guidelines to David Duncan's situation.

The Effects of IFRS on Cash

Cash is the lifeblood for companies, and they must generate more cash from their operating activities than they spend in order to be successful in the long term. Because of its liquidity, there is little that is different in the way cash is valued under GAAP for private enterprises, as shown in this chapter, and under international financial reporting standards (IFRS). A goal of IFRS is to present balance-sheet information as close to fair value as possible. Almost always, the Cash balance is at its fair value. The principles for accounting for and reporting cash have been converged; that is, the treatment is the same under both set of principles and standards. In Chapter 17, we discuss the cash flow statement, and we will discuss cash and IFRS in more detail then.

OBJECTIVE 7

Assess the impact on cash of international financial reporting standards (IFRS)

The presentation of cash on the balance sheet, however, can be different under IFRS. In Chapter 4, we showed some different possibilities for presenting information on the balance sheet. We saw, for example, that British Airways presents cash at the end of the asset side of the balance sheet in its IFRS-based financial statements. As shown in this chapter, cash is typically listed first on the balance sheet of a company reporting under GAAP for private enterprises. Canadian companies reporting under IFRS can choose how to present their financial information—both ways of presenting cash are acceptable.

DID YOU GET IT?

MyAccountingLab

To check your understanding of the material in this Learning Objective, complete this question. The solution appears on MyAccountingLab so you can check your progress.

12. Why is the valuation of cash under IFRS the same as it is under GAAP for private enterprises?

As we conclude this chapter, we return to our opening questions: What are internal controls, and why are they important? What is the *Sarbanes–Oxley Act of 2002* and why is it important to some Canadian companies? How can companies use bank accounts to control cash? Is there an approach to use when facing an ethical issue? These questions were answered throughout this chapter.

Summary Problem for Your Review

The Cash account of Cambridge Dental Associates at February 28, 2010, follows:

Cash

Feb.	1	Bal.	7,990	Feb.	3		800
	6		1,600		12		6,200
	15		3,600		19		2,200
	23		2,200		25		1,000
	28		4,800		27		1,800
	28	Bal.	8,190				

Cambridge Dental Associates receives the February 2010 bank statement data in the first week of March 2010 (negative amounts appear in parentheses):

Bank Statement for February 2010

Description	Withdrawals	Deposits	Date	Balance
Balance Forward			Feb01	$ 7,990
Deposits		1,600	Feb07	9,590
Chqs total for day	800		Feb08	8,790
Deposits		3,600	Feb15	12,390
Chqs total for day	6,200		Feb16	6,190
Chqs total for day	2,200		Feb23	3,990
Deposits		2,200	Feb24	6,190
NSF cheque, M. E. Crown	1,400		Feb24	4,790
Bank collection of note receivable		2,000*	Feb26	6,790
EFT rent expense	660		Feb28	6,130
Service Charge	20		Feb28	6,110
Interest		5	Feb28	6,115
	11,280	9,405		

*Includes principal of $1,762 plus interest of $238.

Additional data: Cambridge Dental Associates deposits all cash receipts in the bank and makes all cash payments by cheque.

Required

1. Prepare the bank reconciliation of Cambridge Dental Associates at February 28, 2010.

2. Journalize the entries based on the bank reconciliation.

SOLUTION

Requirement 1

CAMBRIDGE DENTAL ASSOCIATES
Bank Reconciliation
February 28, 2010

Bank
Bank Balance, February 28, 2010... $ 6,115
Add: Deposit of February 28 in transit 4,800
10,915
Less: Outstanding cheques issued on Feb. 25 ($1,000)
and Feb. 27 ($1,800).. (2,800)
Adjusted bank balance, February 28, 2010 .... $8,115 ◄

Books
Book Balance, February 28, 2010... $8,190
Add: Bank collection of note receivable,
including interest of $238 2,000
Add: Interest earned on bank balance 5
10,195
Less: Service charge .... $ 20
NSF cheque.. 1,400
EFT—Rent expense 660 (2,080)
Adjusted book balance, February 28, 2010 .... $8,115 ◄

Name: Cambridge Dental Associates
Accounting Period: Month of February 2010
Key Fact: Existing, ongoing business

Before creating the bank reconciliation, compare the Cash account and the bank statement. Cross out all items that appear in both places. The items that remain are the reconciling items.

Begin with the ending balance on the bank statement.

- Add deposits (debits) from the Cash account not on the bank statement.
- Deduct cheques (credits) from the Cash account not on the bank statement.

Begin with the ending balance in the Cash general ledger account.

- Add money received by the bank on behalf of the company (increases to the bank statement balance).
- Deduct bank charges, NSF cheques, or pre-authorized payments (decreases to the bank statement balance).

Requirement 2

Feb. 28	Cash..	2,000		
	Note Receivable...		1,762	
	Interest Revenue..		238	
	Note receivable collected by bank ($2,000 – $238).			
28	Cash..	5		
	Interest Revenue..		5	
	Interest earned on bank balance.			
28	Bank Charges Expense	20		
	Cash..		20	
	Bank service charge.			
28	Accounts Receivable—M. E. Crown	1,400		
	Cash..		1,400	
	NSF cheque returned by bank.			
28	Rent Expense...	660		
	Cash..		660	
	Monthly rent expense.			

Prepare journal entries for all reconciling items from the "books" section of the bank reconciliation.

Summary

1. **Define internal control.** *Internal control* is the organizational plan and all related measures adopted by an entity to meet management's objectives of operational efficiency, implementing and following management's business policies, prevention and detection of fraud and error, safeguarding of assets, reliability of accounting records, and timely preparation of reliable financial information.

2. **List and describe the components of internal control and control procedures.** An effective internal control system includes these features: *competent, reliable, and ethical personnel; clear assignment of responsibilities; proper authorization; separation of duties; internal and external audits; documents and records;* and *electronic devices and computer controls.* Many companies also make use of fireproof vaults, point-of-sale terminals, fidelity bonds, mandatory vacations, and job rotation. Effective computerized internal control systems must meet the same basic standards as good manual systems must meet.

3. **Prepare a bank reconciliation and the related journal entries.** The *bank account* helps to control and safeguard cash. Businesses use the *bank statement* and the *bank reconciliation* to account for banking transactions.

4. **Apply internal controls to cash receipts.** To control cash receipts over the counter, companies use point-of-sale terminals that customers can see, and require that cashiers provide customers with receipts. A duplicate tape inside the machine or a link to a central computer records each sale and cash transaction. To control cash receipts by mail, a mailroom employee should be assigned the responsibility for opening the mail. This is an essential separation of duties—the accounting department should not open the mail. At the end of the day, the controller compares the two records of the day's cash receipts: the bank deposit amount from the cashier and the debit to Cash from the accounting department.

5. **Apply internal controls to cash payments.** To control payments by cheque, cheques should be issued and signed only when a *payment packet* including the purchase order, invoice (bill), and receiving report (all with appropriate signatures) has been prepared. To control petty cash payments, the custodian of the fund should require a completed petty cash ticket for all payments.

6. **Make ethical business judgments.** To make ethical decisions, people should proceed in six steps: (1) Determine the facts. (2) Identify the ethical issues. (3) Specify the alternatives. (4) Identify the stakeholders, the people involved. (5) Assess the possible outcomes of each alternative. (6) Make the decision.

7. **Assess the impact on cash of international financial reporting standards (IFRS).** The principles for accounting for and reporting cash have been converged; that is, the treatment is the same under both GAAP for private enterprises and IFRS. However, cash often appears as the last item on an IFRS balance sheet, rather than as the first item on a GAAP-for-private-enterprises balance sheet. Both methods are acceptable for Canadian companies reporting under IFRS.

SELF-STUDY QUESTIONS

Test your understanding of the chapter by marking the correct answer for each of the following questions:

1. Which of the following is an objective of internal control? (pp. 403–404)
   a. Safeguarding assets
   b. Providing information for decision making while maintaining reliable records and control systems
   c. Encouraging operating efficiency and optimizing the use of resources
   d. Preventing and detecting fraud and error
   e. All the above are objectives of internal control.

2. Janice Gould receives cash from customers. Her other assigned job is to post the collections to customer accounts receivable. Her company has weak (pp. 406–408)
   a. Ethics
   b. Assignment of responsibilities
   c. Computer controls
   d. Separation of duties

3. What internal control function is performed by auditors? (p. 407)
   a. Objective opinion on the fair presentation of the financial statements
   b. Assurance that all transactions are accounted for correctly
   c. Communication of the results of the audit to regulatory agencies
   d. Guarantee that company employees have behaved ethically

4. Encryption (p. 409)
   a. Creates firewalls to protect data
   b. Cannot be broken by hackers
   c. Avoids the need for separation of duties
   d. Rearranges messages by a special process

5. The bank account serves as a control device over (p. 410)
   a. Cash receipts   c. Both of the above
   b. Cash payments   d. None of the above

6. Which of the following items appears on the Bank side of a bank reconciliation? (p. 414)
   a. Book error
   b. Outstanding cheque
   c. NSF cheque
   d. Interest revenue earned on bank balance

7. Which of the following items appears on the book side of a bank reconciliation? (pp. 414–415)
   a. Outstanding cheques   c. Both a and b
   b. Deposits in transit   d. None of the above

8. Which of the following reconciling items requires a journal entry on the books of the company? (p. 417)
   a. Book error
   b. Outstanding cheque
   c. NSF cheque
   d. Interest revenue earned on bank balance
   e. All of the above, except (b)
   f. None of the above

9. The internal control feature that is specific to petty cash is (p. 424)
   a. Separation of duties
   b. Assignment of responsibility
   c. Proper authorization
   d. The imprest system

10. Ethical judgments in accounting and business (p. 426)
    a. Require employees to break laws to get ahead
    b. Force decision makers to think about what is good and bad
    c. Always hurt someone
    d. Are affected by internal controls but not by external controls

Answers to Self-Study Questions
1. e   3. a   5. c   9. d
2. d   4. d   6. b   8. e   10. b
                      7. d

ACCOUNTING VOCABULARY

Audit   (p. 407)
Bank collection   (p. 414)
Bank reconciliation   (p. 413)
Bank statement   (p. 411)
Cheque   (p. 411)
Computer virus   (p. 409)
Controller   (p. 407)
Deposit in transit   (p. 414)
Electronic funds transfer (EFT)   (p. 411)
Encryption   (p. 409)

Evaluated Receipts Settlement   (p. 422)
Firewall   (p. 409)
Imprest system   (p. 424)
Internal control   (p. 403)
Nonsufficient funds (NSF) cheque   (p. 415)
Outstanding cheque   (p. 414)
Petty cash   (p. 423)
Timing difference   (p. 413)
Treasurer   (p. 407)
Trojan   (p. 409)

SIMILAR ACCOUNTING TERMS

Cash receipts	Cash, cheques, and other negotiable instruments received
Separation of duties	Segregation of duties, division of duties
Invoice	Bill

Assignment Material

QUESTIONS

1. Which of the features of effective internal control is the most fundamental? Why?

2. Which company employees bear primary responsibility for a company's financial statements and for maintaining the company's system of internal control? How do these persons carry out this responsibility?

3. Identify at least seven features of an effective system of internal control.

4. Separation of duties may be divided into three parts. What are they?

5. What is an audit? Identify the two types of audit and the differences between them.

6. Why are documents and records a feature of internal control systems?

7. How has an accounting system's reliance on electronic devices altered internal control?

8. Why should the same employee not write the computer programs for cash payments, sign cheques, and mail the cheques to payees?

9. Briefly state how each of the following serves as an internal control measure over cash: bank account, signature card, deposit slip, and bank statement.

10. Are internal control systems designed to be foolproof and perfect? What is a fundamental constraint in planning and maintaining systems?

11. How can internal control systems be circumvented?

12. Each of the items in the following list must be accounted for in the bank reconciliation. Next to each item, enter the appropriate letter from the following possible treatments: (a) bank side of reconciliation—add the item; (b) bank side of reconciliation—subtract the item; (c) book side of reconciliation—add the item; and (d) book side of reconciliation—subtract the item.

    _____ Outstanding cheque

    _____ NSF cheque

    _____ Bank service charge

    _____ Cost of printed cheques

    _____ EFT receipt

    _____ Bank error that decreased bank balance

    _____ Deposit in transit

    _____ Bank collection

    _____ EFT payment

    _____ Customer's cheque returned because of unauthorized signature

    _____ Book error that increased balance of Cash account

13. What purpose does a bank reconciliation serve?

14. What role does a cash register play in an internal control system?

15. Describe internal control procedures for cash received by mail.

16. What documents make up the payment packet? Describe three procedures that use the payment packet to ensure that each payment is appropriate.

17. What balance does the Petty Cash account have at all times? Does this balance always equal the amount of cash in the fund? When are the two amounts equal? When are they unequal?

18. Suppose a company has six bank accounts, two petty cash funds, and three certificates of deposit that can be withdrawn on demand. How many cash amounts would this company likely report separately on its balance sheet?

19. Why should accountants adhere to a higher standard of ethical conduct than many other members of society do?

20. "Our managers know that they are expected to meet budgeted profit figures. We don't want excuses. We want results." Discuss the ethical implications of this policy.

Definition of internal control
①

Starter 8-1 Internal controls are designed to safeguard assets; encourage employees to follow company policies; promote operational efficiency; provide accurate, reliable information; and ensure accurate records. Which objective must the internal controls accomplish for the business to survive? Give your reason.

Applying the definition of internal controls
①

Starter 8-2 How does the *Sarbanes–Oxley Act of 2002* relate to internal controls? Be specific.

Applying the definition of internal controls
①

Starter 8-3 Explain in your own words why separation of duties is often described as the cornerstone of internal control for safeguarding assets. Describe what can happen if the same person has custody of an asset and also accounts for the asset.

Characteristics of an effective system of internal control
②

Starter 8-4 How do external auditors differ from internal auditors? How does an external audit differ from an internal audit? How are the two types of audits similar?

Aspects of a bank reconciliation
③

Starter 8-5 Answer the following questions about the bank reconciliation:

1. Is the bank reconciliation a journal, a ledger, an account, or a financial statement? If none of these, what is it?

2. What is the difference between a bank statement and a bank reconciliation?

Preparing a bank reconciliation
③

Adjusted balance $6,200

Starter 8-6 The Cash account of Ranger Security Systems reported a balance of $4,960 at May 31, 2010. There were outstanding cheques totalling $1,800 and a May 31 deposit in transit of $400. The bank statement, which came from Royal Bank, listed a May 31 balance of $7,600. Included in the bank balance was a collection of $1,260 on account from Kelly Brooks, a Ranger customer who pays the bank directly. The bank statement also shows a $40 service charge and $20 of interest revenue that Ranger earned on its bank balance. Prepare Ranger's bank reconciliation at May 31, 2010.

Recording transactions from a bank reconciliation
③

Starter 8-7 After preparing Ranger Security Systems' bank reconciliation in Starter 8-6, journalize the company's transactions that arise from the bank reconciliation. Date each transaction May 31, 2010, and include an explanation with each entry.

Control over cash receipts
④

Starter 8-8 Deirdre Chevis sells furniture for DuBois Furniture Company. Chevis is having financial problems and takes $500 that she received from a customer. She recorded the sale through the cash register. What will alert Betsy DuBois, the owner, that something is wrong?

Control over cash receipts by mail
④

Starter 8-9 Review the internal controls over cash receipts by mail. Exactly what is accomplished by the final step in the process, performed by the controller?

Internal control over payments by cheque
⑤

Starter 8-10 A purchasing agent for Westgate Wireless receives the goods that he purchases and also approves payment for the goods. How could this purchasing agent cheat his company? How could Westgate avoid this internal control weakness?

Petty cash
⑤

April 30 Credit Cash Short and Over for $12

Starter 8-11 Record the following petty cash transactions of Lexite Laminated Surfaces in general journal form (explanations are not required):

Apr.	1	Established a petty cash fund with a $400 balance.
	30	The petty cash fund has $38 in cash and $374 in petty cash tickets that were issued to pay for Office Supplies ($234) and Entertainment Expense ($140). Replenished the fund with $362 of cash and recorded the expenses.

Making an ethical judgment
⑥

Starter 8-12 Gwen O'Malley, an accountant for Ireland Limited, discovers that her supervisor, Barney Stone, made several errors last year. Overall, the errors overstated the company's net income by 20 percent. It is not clear whether the errors were deliberate or accidental. What should O'Malley do?

EXERCISES

MyAccountingLab | All questions in this section appear in MyAccountingLab.

Exercise 8–1

Lane & Goble Bookstore has a liberal return policy. A customer can return any product for a full refund within 30 days of purchase. When a customer returns merchandise, Lane & Goble policy specifies:

Identifying and correcting an internal control weakness

- Store clerk issues a pre-numbered return slip, refunds cash from the cash register, and keeps a copy of the return slip for review by the manager.
- Store clerk places the returned goods back on the shelf as soon as possible.

   Lane & Goble uses a periodic inventory system.

1. How can a dishonest store clerk steal from Lane & Goble? What part of company policy enables the store clerk to steal without getting caught?

2. How can Lane & Goble improve its internal controls to prevent this theft?

Exercise 8–2

U.K. Trader Nick Leeson worked for Baring Securities (Singapore) Limited (BSS) as the general manager and head trader. Due to his experience in operations, he also acted as head of the "back office" that does the record keeping and tracks who owes what to whom. Leeson appeared to be making huge profits by speculating on Japan's Nikkei stock market—until he fled Singapore, leaving behind a loss of £827,000,000 hidden in an unused error account on the Barings balance sheet. As a result of this situation, Barings Bank collapsed.

Correcting an internal control weakness

   What internal control weaknesses at BSS allowed this loss to grow so large? How could Barings have avoided and/or limited the size of the loss?

Exercise 8–3

The following situations suggest either a strength or a weakness in internal control. Identify each as a *strength* or a *weakness* and give your reason for each answer.

Identifying internal control strengths and weaknesses

a. Top managers delegate all internal control procedures to the accounting department.

b. The accounting department orders merchandise and approves invoices for payment.

c. Cash received over the counter is controlled by the clerk, who rings up the sale and places the cash in the register. The clerk matches the total recorded by the register to each day's cash sales.

d. The vice-president, who signs cheques, assumes the accounting department has matched the invoice with other supporting documents and therefore does not examine the payment packet.

Exercise 8–4

Identify the missing internal control procedure in the following situations:

Identifying internal controls

a. In the course of auditing the records of a company, you find that the same employee orders merchandise and approves invoices for payment.

b. Business is slow at the Ridge Theatre on Tuesday, Wednesday, and Thursday nights. To reduce expenses, the owner decides not to use a ticket taker on those nights. The ticket seller (cashier) is told to keep the tickets as a record of the number sold.

c. The same trusted employee has served as cashier for 10 years.

d. When business is brisk, One-Stop Convenience Store deposits cash in the bank several times during the day. The manager at the convenience store wants to reduce the time employees spend delivering cash to the bank, so he starts a new policy. Cash will build up over weekends, and the total will be deposited on Monday.

e. Grocery stores such as No Frills and Wal-Mart purchase large quantities of their merchandise from a few suppliers. At one grocery store, the manager decides to reduce paperwork. He eliminates the requirement that a receiving department employee prepare a receiving report, which lists the quantities of items received from the supplier.

Exercise 8–5

The following questions pertain to internal control. Consider each situation separately.

Explaining the role of internal control

1. Wong Company requires that all documents supporting a cheque be cancelled (stamped Paid) by the person who signs the cheque. Why do you think this practice is required? What might happen if it were not?

2. Separation of duties is an important consideration if a system of internal control is to be effective. Why is this so?

3. Cash may be a relatively small item on the financial statements. Nevertheless, internal control over cash is very important. Why is this true?

4. Many managers think that safeguarding assets is the most important objective of internal control systems, while auditors emphasize internal control's role in ensuring reliable accounting data. Explain why managers are more concerned about safeguarding assets and auditors are more concerned about the quality of the accounting records.

Exercise 8–6

Classifying bank reconciliation items
③

The following items could appear on a bank reconciliation:

a. Outstanding cheques
b. Deposits in transit
c. NSF cheque
d. Bank collection of a note receivable on our behalf
e. Interest earned on bank balance
f. Service charge
g. Book error: We credited Cash for $100. The correct credit was $1,000
h. Bank error: The bank decreased our account for a cheque written by another customer

Classify each item as (1) an addition to the book balance, (2) a subtraction from the book balance, (3) an addition to the bank balance, or (4) a subtraction from the bank balance.

Exercise 8–7

Preparing a bank reconciliation
③

Adjusted balance $32,280

Adams Enterprises began operations on January 2, 2010, depositing $20,000 in the bank. During this first month of business, the following transactions occurred that affected the Cash account in the general ledger:

Date	Description	Dr	Cr
Jan. 2	Deposit	$20,000	
5	Payment, cheque 001		$ 6,000
8	Payment, cheque 002		8,000
9	Cash sales	8,000	
15	Payment, cheque 003		5,000
18	Cash sales	6,000	
20	Bank loan	50,000	
26	Equipment purchase, cheque 004		37,000
30	Payment on account, cheque 005		8,500
31	Cash sales	12,800	

Shortly after the end of January, the company received its first bank statement:

Description	Withdrawals	Deposits	Date	Balance
Balance Forward			Jan01	0
Deposit		20,000	Jan02	20,000
Chq#001	6,000		Jan07	14,000
Deposit		8,000	Jan09	22,000
Chq#002	8,000		Jan13	14,000
Deposit		6,000	Jan18	20,000
Bank Loan		50,000	Jan20	70,000
Chq#004	37,000		Jan28	33,000
Deposit		1,000	Jan29	34,000
Service Charge	24		Jan31	33,976
Interest		4	Jan31	33,980
	51,024	85,004		

In preparing to do the bank reconciliation, Adams Enterprises noticed that the $1,000 deposit on January 29 was a bank error and informed the bank. The bank will correct the error on the next bank statement.

Required Prepare Adams Enterprises' bank reconciliation at January 31, 2010.

Exercise 8–8

Marshland Travel's general ledger Cash account showed the following transactions during October 2010:

Preparing a bank reconciliation
③
Adjusted balance $19,334

Date	Description	Dr	Cr	Balance
Oct. 1	Opening balance			$ 12,800
2	Deposit	$10,000		22,800
5	Payment, cheque 233		$6,000	16,800
8	Payment, cheque 234		8,000	8,800
9	Deposit	8,000		16,800
15	Payment, cheque 235		5,000	11,800
18	Deposit	5,200		17,000
26	Payment, cheque 236		3,300	13,700
30	Payment, cheque 237		4,750	8,950
31	Deposit	10,500		19,450

The bank statement for the month ending October 31, 2010, is shown below:

Description	Withdrawals	Deposits	Date	Balance
Balance Forward			Oct01	12,800
Deposit		10,000	Oct02	22,800
Chq#00233	6,000		Oct07	16,800
Deposit		8,000	Oct09	24,800
Chq#00234	8,000		Oct10	16,800
Deposit		5,200	Oct18	22,000
Chq#00235	5,000		Oct18	17,000
Service Charge	120		Oct31	16,880
Service Charge	120		Oct31	16,760
Interest		4	Oct31	16,764
	19,240	23,204		

Marshland Travel informed its bank that the bank charged a service charge two times. The bank has agreed to reverse one of the bank charges on the next month's bank statement.

Required   Prepare Marshland Travel's bank reconciliation at October 31, 2010.

Exercise 8–9

Robbie Daechsel's chequebook lists the entries shown here:

Preparing a bank reconciliation
③
Adjusted balance $8,678

Date	Cheque No.	Item	Cheque	Deposit	Balance
Jul. 1					$ 1,934
4	622	West Coast Sports	$ 104		1,830
9		Dividends received		$ 200	2,030
13	623	TELUS	152		1,878
14	624	Esso	138		1,740
18	625	Cash	134		1,606
26	626	Canadian Cancer Society	66		1,540
28	627	Park Lane Apartments	1,466		74
31		Paycheque		8,666	8,740

Daechsel's July bank statement is shown below:

Balance		$1,934
Add: Deposits		200
Deduct cheques: No.	Amount	
622	$104	
623	152	
624	158*	
625	134	(548)
Other charges:		
Printed cheques.................................	$26	
Service charge...................................	16	(42)
Balance..		$1,544

*This is the correct amount of cheque number 624

> **Required** Prepare Robbie Daechsel's bank reconciliation at July 31, 2010. How much cash does Daechsel actually have on July 31?

Exercise 8–10

Preparing a bank reconciliation

Adjusted balance $30,784

Bob Nichols operates two gas stations. He has just received the monthly bank statement at May 31 from Royal Bank, and the statement shows an ending balance of $23,440. Listed on the statement are an EFT rent collection of $1,600, a service charge of $60, two NSF cheques totalling $380, and a $100 charge for printed cheques. In reviewing his cash records, Nichols identifies outstanding cheques totalling $1,716 and a May 31 deposit in transit of $9,060. During May, he recorded a $1,440 cheque for the salary of a part-time employee by debiting Salary Expense and crediting Cash for $144. Nichols' Cash account shows a May 31 balance of $31,020. Prepare the bank reconciliation at May 31, 2010.

Exercise 8–11

Making journal entries from a bank reconciliation

Using the data from Exercise 8–10, record the entries that Nichols should make in the general journal on May 31, 2010. Include an explanation for each of the entries.

Exercise 8–12

Applying internal controls to the bank reconciliation

A jury convicted the treasurer of GTX Company of stealing cash from the company. Over a three-year period, the treasurer allegedly took almost $100,000 and attempted to cover the theft by manipulating the bank reconciliation.

> **Required** What is a likely way that a person would manipulate a bank reconciliation to cover a theft? Be specific. What internal control arrangement could have avoided this theft?

Exercise 8–13

Evaluating internal control over cash receipts

When you pay for goods at Luigi's Discount Store, the cash register displays the amount of the sale, the cash received, and any change returned to you. Suppose the register also produces a customer receipt but keeps no record of the sales transactions. At the end of the day, the clerk counts the cash in the register and gives it to the cashier for deposit in the company bank account.

> **Required** Write a memo to Luigi Verone, the owner. Identify the internal control weakness over cash receipts, and explain how the weakness gives an employee the opportunity to steal cash. State how to prevent such a theft.

Exercise 8–14

Petty cash, cash short and over

Record the following selected transactions of Kelly's Fine Foods in general journal format (explanations are not required):

2010
Jun.   1   Established a petty cash fund with an $800 balance.
        2   Journalized the day's cash sales. Cash register tapes show a $9,750 total, but the cash in the register is $9,770.
        10   The petty cash fund has $313 in cash and $468 in petty cash tickets issued to pay for Office Supplies ($242), Delivery Expense ($139), and Entertainment Expense ($87). Replenished the fund.

Exercise 8–15

1. Explain how an *imprest* petty cash system works.

2. Atlantic Press maintains an imprest petty cash fund of $200, which is under the control of Brenda Montague. At November 30, the fund holds $40 cash and petty cash tickets for office supplies, $120, and delivery expense, $50.

    Journalize (a) establishment of the petty cash fund on November 1 and (b) replenishment of the fund on November 30.

3. Prepare a T-account for Petty Cash, and post to the account. What is Petty Cash's balance at all times?

Control over petty cash

3. Petty Cash balance $200

Exercise 8–16

Maritime Distributors created a $400 imprest petty cash fund. During the first month of use, the fund custodian authorized and signed petty cash tickets as shown below.

Accounting for petty cash
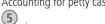

Ticket No.	Item	Account Debited	Amount
1	Delivery of flyers to customers	Delivery Expense	$128.80
2	Stamp purchase	Postage Expense	105.98
3	Newsletter	Supplies Expense	40.40
4	Key to closet	Miscellaneous Expense	9.52
5	Staples	Supplies Expense	14.72

Required Make general journal entries to (a) create the petty cash fund and (b) record its replenishment. Cash in the fund totals $97.58, so $3.00 is missing. Include explanations.

Exercise 8–17

Refer to the Maritime Distributors petty cash fund data in Exercise 8–16. Suppose, one month later, the company decided to increase the petty cash fund by $100 to reduce the number of times the fund has to be replenished. Journalize the increase in the petty cash fund.

Accounting for petty cash
 .

Exercise 8–18

You have a part-time job in a local delicatessen, which is part of a chain of delicatessens. You received the job through your parent's friendship with Samantha Stevens, the deli manager. The job is going well, but you are puzzled by the actions of Samantha and her husband, Fred. Each day, one or both of them fills takeout orders and takes them to Samantha's office. Later you notice Fred and Samantha enjoying the takeout orders, sometimes with friends. You know the orders were not rung through the checkout counter. When you ask a co-worker about the practice, you are told that Samantha is the boss and can do as she wishes, and besides, many employees help themselves to meals.

Evaluating the ethics of conduct by a manager
6

Required You have been given the assignment in a business ethics course to comment on the issue. Apply the decision guidelines for ethical judgments outlined in the Decision Guidelines feature on page 426 to decide whether a manager of a deli should help herself or himself to meals on a regular basis and not pay for what he or she takes.

SERIAL EXERCISE

This exercise continues the Haupt Consulting situation from Exercise 7–13 of Chapter 7. If you did not complete Exercise 7–13, you can still complete Exercise 8–19 as it is presented.

Exercise 8–19

Preparing a bank reconciliation

1. Adjusted balance $17,452

Haupt Consulting Company performs systems consulting. Haupt's February Cash from its general ledger appears below:

Cash

Jan.	31	Bal. 10,000	chq. 207	4,000	Feb. 1
Feb.	6	2,500	chq. 208	795	Feb. 14
Feb.	13	3,000	chq. 209	1,415	Feb. 14
Feb.	20	4,800	chq. 210	190	Feb. 28
Feb.	27	3,600	chq. 211	400	Feb. 28
Feb.	28 Unadj. Bal.	17,100			

Haupt Consulting's bank statement dated February 28, 2011, follows:

Description	Withdrawals	Deposits	Date	Balance
Balance Forward			Jan31	$10,500
Deposit		750*	Feb01	11,250
EFT to Cheap Cheques	17		Feb02	11,233
Chq 206	1,250*		Feb02	9,983
Deposit		2,500	Feb08	12,483
Deposit		3,000	Feb14	15,483
Chq 207	4,000		Feb17	11,483
Chq 209	1,415		Feb18	10,068
EFT Hot Houses				
(a customer)		500	Feb20	10,568
Deposit		4,800	Feb22	15,368
EFT to Internet Service	125		Feb28	15,243
Chq 208	795		Feb28	14,448
Bank Service Charge	13		Feb28	14,435
Interest Credit		7	Feb28	14,442
	7,615	11,557		

*This was a reconciling item on the January 2011 bank reconciliation.

Required

1. Prepare the February 2011 bank reconciliation.

2. Journalize and post any transactions required from the bank reconciliation. Key all items by date. Compute each account balance, and denote the balance as *Bal.*

BEYOND THE NUMBERS

Beyond the Numbers 8–1

Correcting an internal control weakness

This case is based on a situation experienced by one of the authors. Alpha Construction Company, headquartered in Chattanooga, Tennessee, built a Roadway Inn Motel in Cleveland, 35 kilometres east of Chattanooga. The construction foreman, whose name was Slim, moved into Cleveland in March to hire the 40 workers needed to complete the project. Slim hired the construction workers, had them fill out the necessary tax forms, and sent the employment documents to the home office, which opened a payroll file for each employee.

Work on the motel began on April 1 and ended September 1. Each Thursday evening, Slim filled out a time card that listed the hours worked by each employee during the five-day workweek that ended at 5 p.m. on Thursday. Slim faxed the time sheets to the home office, which prepared the payroll cheques on Friday morning. Slim drove to the home office after lunch on Friday, picked up the payroll cheques, and returned to the construction site. At 5 p.m. on Friday, Slim distributed the payroll cheques to the workers.

a. Describe in detail the internal control weakness in this situation. Specify what negative result(s) could occur because of the internal control weakness.

b. Describe what you would do to correct the internal control weakness.

ETHICAL ISSUE

John Sullivan owns apartment buildings in Nova Scotia, New Brunswick, and Quebec. Each property has a manager who collects rent, arranges for repairs, and runs advertisements in the local newspaper. The property managers transfer cash to Sullivan monthly and prepare their own bank reconciliations.

The manager in New Brunswick has been stealing large sums of money. To cover the theft, she understates the amount of outstanding cheques on the monthly bank reconciliation. As a result, each monthly bank reconciliation appears to balance. However, the balance sheet reports more cash than Sullivan actually has in the bank. In negotiating the sale of the New Brunswick property, Sullivan is showing the balance sheet to prospective investors.

Required

1. Identify two parties other than Sullivan who can be harmed by this theft. In what ways can they be harmed?

2. Discuss the role accounting plays in this situation.

PROBLEMS (GROUP A)

 All questions in this section appear in MyAccountingLab.

Problem 8–1A

An employee of Bonneville Marketing recently stole thousands of dollars of the company's cash. The company has decided to install a new system of internal controls.

Identifying the characteristics of an effective internal control system

Required As controller of Bonneville Marketing, write a memo to the owner, Elizabeth Bonneville, explaining how a separation of duties helps to safeguard assets.

Problem 8–2A

Each of the following situations has an internal control weakness:

Identifying internal control weaknesses

a. Waterloo Software Associates sells accounting software. Recently, the development of a new software program stopped while the programmers redesigned Waterloo Software Associates' accounting system. Waterloo Software Associates' own accountants could have performed this task.

b. Judy Sloan has been your trusted employee for 30 years. She performs all cash handling and accounting duties. She has just purchased a new Lexus and a new home in an expensive suburb. As the owner of the company, you wonder how she can afford these luxuries because you pay her $35,000 per year and she has no sources of outside income.

c. Sanchez Hardwoods Ltd., a private corporation, falsified sales and inventory figures to get a large loan. The company prepared its own financial statements. The company received the loan but later went bankrupt and couldn't repay the loan.

d. The office supply company from which The Family Shoe Store purchases sales receipts recently notified Family that the last shipped receipts were not pre-numbered. Louise Bourseault, the owner of Family, replied that she never uses the receipt numbers, so the omission is not important.

e. Discount stores such as Wal-Mart make most of their sales for cash, with the remainder in debit-card and credit-card sales. To reduce expenses, one store manager ceases purchasing fidelity bonds on the cashiers.

Required

1. Identify the missing internal control characteristic in each situation.
2. Identify the business's possible problem caused by each control weakness.
3. Propose a solution to each internal-control problem.

Problem 8–3A

Excel Spreadsheet Template

Using the bank reconciliation as a control device

1. Adjusted balance $33,920

The cash receipts and the cash payments of River Estates Development for November 2010 are as follows:

Cash Receipts (Posting reference is CR)		Cash Payments (Posting reference is CP)	
Date	**Cash Debit**	**Cheque No.**	**Cash Credit**
Nov. 5	$ 6,872	1221	$ 3,638
7	940	1222	2,288
13	3,446	1223	858
15	2,130	1224	222
19	882	1225	1,632
24	1,750	1226	218
30	5,196	1227	8,936
Total	$21,216	1228	1,996
		1229	660
		1230	5,448
		Total	$25,896

The Cash account of River Estates shows a balance of $31,766 on November 30, 2010. On December 3, 2010, River Estates received this bank statement:

Bank Statement for November 2010

Description	Withdrawals	Deposits	Date	Balance
Balance Forward			Nov01	36,446
EFT Rent Collection		1,760	Nov01	38,206
Deposit		6,872	Nov06	45,078
NSF Cheque	866		Nov08	44,212
Chq#001221	3,638		Nov09	40,574
Deposit		940	Nov10	41,514
Chq#001222	2,288		Nov13	39,226
Chq#001223	858		Nov14	38,368
Deposit		3,446	Nov14	41,814
Chq#001224	222		Nov15	41,592
Deposit		2,130	Nov15	43,722
EFT Insurance	550		Nov19	43,172
Deposit		882	Nov20	44,054
Chq#001225	1,632		Nov22	42,422
Deposit		1,750	Nov25	44,172
Chq#001226	218		Nov29	43,954
Chq#001227	9,936		Nov30	34,018
Bank Collection		2,860	Nov30	36,878
Service Charge	50		Nov30	36,828
	20,258	20,640		

Explanations: EFT—electronic funds transfer, NSF—nonsufficient funds

Additional data for the bank reconciliation:

a. The EFT deposit was a receipt of monthly rent. The EFT debit was payment of monthly insurance.

b. The NSF cheque was received late in October from a customer.

c. The $2,860 bank collection of a note receivable on November 30 included $200 interest revenue.

d. The correct amount of cheque number 1227, a payment on account, is $9,936. (The River Estates Development accountant mistakenly recorded the cheque for $8,936.)

Required

1. Prepare the bank reconciliation of River Estates Development at November 30, 2010.

2. Describe how a bank account and the bank reconciliation help River Estates managers control the business's cash.

Problem 8–4A

The October 31, 2010, bank statement of RCI Distributors has just arrived. To prepare RCI Distributors' bank reconciliation, you gather the following data:

a. The October 31 bank balance is $38,212.

b. The bank statement includes two charges for NSF cheques from customers. One was for $138 and the other was for $370.

c. The following RCI Distributors cheques are outstanding at October 31:

Cheque No.	Amount
712	$1,098
922	86
934	114
939	1,112
940	416
941	894

Excel Spreadsheet Template

Preparing a bank reconciliation and related journal entries

1. Adjusted balance $36,242

d. A few customers pay their accounts by EFT. The October bank statement lists a $12,732 deposit against customer accounts.

e. The bank statement includes two special deposits: $1,796, which is the amount of dividend revenue the bank collected on behalf of RCI Distributors, and $30, the interest revenue RCI earned on its bank balance during October.

f. The bank statement lists a $62 subtraction for the bank service charge.

g. On October 31, the company deposited $932, but this deposit does not appear on the bank statement.

h. The bank statement includes an $818 deduction for a cheque drawn by RCI Communications. RCI promptly notified the bank of its error.

i. RCI's Cash account shows a balance of $22,254 on October 31.

Required

1. Prepare the bank reconciliation for RCI Distributors at October 31, 2010.

2. Record in general journal form the entries necessary to bring the book balance of Cash into agreement with the adjusted book balance on the reconciliation. Include an explanation for each entry.

Problem 8–5A

Calibre Interiors makes all sales on credit. Cash receipts arrive by mail, usually within 30 days of sale. Sarah Romano opens envelopes and separates the cheques from the accompanying remittance advices. Romano forwards the cheques to another employee, who makes the daily bank deposit but has no access to the accounting records. Romano sends the remittance advices, which show the amount of cash received, to the accounting department for entry in the accounts. Her only other duty is to grant sales allowances to customers. (Recall that a *sales allowance* decreases the amount that the customer must pay.) When she receives a customer cheque for less than the full amount of the invoice, she records the sales allowance and forwards the document to the accounting department.

Identifying internal control weakness in cash receipts

Required You are a new management employee of Calibre Interiors. Write a memo to the company president, Mary Briscall, identifying the internal control weakness in this situation. State how to correct the weakness.

Problem 8–6A

A-1 Machines is located in Saskatoon, Saskatchewan, with a sales territory covering the province.

The company has established a large petty cash fund to handle small cash payments and cash advances to the salespeople to cover frequent sales trips.

Applying internal controls to cash payments, including petty cash transactions

The controller, Margaret Hamm, has decided that two people (Anne Bloom and Tom Hurry) should be in charge of the fund as money is often needed when one person may be out for coffee or lunch. Hamm also feels this will increase internal control, as the work of one person will serve as a check on that of the other.

Regular small cash payments are handled by either Bloom or Hurry, who make the payment and have the person receiving the money sign a sheet of paper listing the date and reason for the payment. Whenever a salesperson requires an advance for a trip, he or she simply signs a receipt for the money received. The salespeople later submit receipts for the cost of the trip to either Bloom or Hurry to offset the cash advance.

Hamm is puzzled that the fund is almost always out of balance and either over or short.

Required Comment on the internal control procedures of A-1 Machines. Suggest changes that you think would improve the system.

Problem 8–7A

Accounting for petty cash transactions

2. Fund should hold $23.50.

Suppose that, on June 1, Devine Design creates a petty cash fund with an imprest balance of $400. During June, Lucie Ducharme, the fund custodian, signs the following petty cash tickets:

Ticket No.	Item	Amount
101	Office supplies	$ 26.64
102	Cab fare for executive	60.00
103	Delivery of package across town	29.33
104	Dinner money for sales manager entertaining a customer	133.33
105	Office supplies	127.20

On June 30, prior to replenishment, the fund contains these tickets plus $34.39. The accounts affected by petty cash payments are Office Supplies Expense, Travel Expense, Delivery Expense, and Entertainment Expense.

Required

1. Explain the characteristics and internal control features of an imprest fund.
2. On June 30, how much cash should the petty cash fund hold before it is replenished?
3. Make general journal entries to (a) create the fund and (b) replenish it. Include explanations.
4. Make the July 1 entry to increase the fund balance to $500. Include an explanation, and briefly describe what the custodian does in this case.

Problem 8–8A

Preparing a bank reconciliation and related journal entries
③
1. Adjusted balance $7,664.00

Truro Electronics had a computer failure on March 1, 2010, which resulted in the loss of data, including the balance of its Cash account and its bank reconciliation from February 28, 2010. The accountant, Matt Vincent, has been able to obtain the following information from the records of the company and its bank:

a. An examination showed that two cheques (#244 for $345.00 and #266 for $632.50) had not been cashed as of March 1. Vincent recalled that there was only one deposit in transit on the February 28 bank reconciliation, but was unable to recall the amount.

b. The cash receipts and cash payments journals contained the following entries for March 2010:

Cash Receipts: Amounts	Cash Payments: Cheque #	Amount
$ 908.50	275	$ 310.50
1,748.00	276	448.50
3,726.00	277	466.90
1,955.00	278	811.90
736.00	279	577.30
$9,073.50	280	3,916.90
	281	void
	282	448.50
	283	1,058.00
		$8,038.50

c. The company's bank provided the following statement as of March 31, 2010:

Date		Cheques and Other Debits	Deposits and Other Credits		Balance
Mar. 1	#276	448.50		2,346.00	6,520.50
2	#266	632.50			5,888.00
5	#277	466.90			5,421.10
8				908.50	6,329.60
14	#275	310.50		1,196.00	7,215.10
17	EFT	529.00			6,686.10
19			EFT	414.00	7,100.10
22	#279	577.30		1,748.00	8,270.80
22	#280	3,976.90	EFT	1,196.00	5,489.90
24			EFT	471.50	5,961.40
27	NSF	805.00		3,726.00	8,882.40
28	SC	50.00			8,832.40
31	#283	1,058.00		1,955.00	9,729.40

d. The deposit made on March 14 was for the collection of a note receivable ($1,100.00) plus interest.

e. The electronic funds transfers (EFTs) had not yet been recorded by Truro Electronics as the bank statement was the first notification of them.

   • The March 17 EFT was for the monthly payment on an insurance policy for Truro Electronics.

   • The March 19 and 24 EFTs were collections on accounts receivable.

   • The March 22 EFT was in error—the transfer should have been to Truro Auto Parts.

f. The NSF cheque on March 27 was received from a customer as payment for electronics purchased for $805.00.

g. Cheque no. 280 was correctly written for $3,976.90 for the purchase of office supplies, but incorrectly recorded by the cash payments clerk.

Required

1. Prepare a bank reconciliation as of March 31, 2010, including the calculation of the book balance of March 31, 2010.

2. Prepare all journal entries that would be required by the bank reconciliation.

Problem 8–9A

North Venture Capital in Sudbury, Ontario, has received a request for investment funds from Different View Products. The funds are for the production of a new product that will dramatically enhance communications on mining sites. Stewart Donolo, an account manager at North Venture, is assigned to research the application.

Making an ethical judgement
6

With unlimited access to Different View's records, Donolo learns that one of the potential major customers for this product is Goldore, a local mining company. North Venture Capital has invested in Goldore. Donolo has access to the confidential information that Goldore's operations will be on hold pending further investigation of identified deposits. The future of Goldore will be strong, but in the short term, Goldore will not be making large operational purchases.

Donolo believes there will be a market for the Different Views product. He has a strong motivation to have Different Views succeed and North Venture Capital to share in this success.

Required Apply the ethical judgment framework outlined in the Decision Guidelines feature on page 426 to help Stewart Donolo plan his next action.

PROBLEMS (GROUP B)

  All questions in this section appear in MyAccountingLab.

Problem 8–1B

White Falls Real Estate prospered during the past 10 years. Business was so good that the company bothered with few internal controls. The recent decline in the local real estate market, however, has caused White Falls to experience a shortage of cash. Carol Stuart, the company owner, is looking for ways to save money.

Identifying the characteristics of an effective internal control system
1 2

Required As controller of the company, write a memorandum to convince Carol Stuart of the company's need for a system of internal control. Be specific in telling her how an internal control system could possibly lead to saving money. Include the definition of internal control, and briefly discuss each characteristic, beginning with competent, reliable, and ethical personnel.

Problem 8–2B

Identifying internal control weaknesses
② ④ ⑤

Each of the following situations has an internal control weakness:

a. Public accounting firms, law firms, and other professional organizations use paraprofessional employees to do some of their routine tasks. For example, a draftsman might prepare drawings to assist an architect. In the architecture firm of Bradshaw and Bos, Nancy Bos, the senior partner, turns over some of her high-level design work to less-qualified draftsmen.

b. Mike Strickland owns a firm that performs interior design services. His staff consists of 12 professional designers, and he manages the office. Often his work requires him to travel to meet with clients. During the past six months, he has observed that when he returns from a business trip, the design jobs in the office have not progressed satisfactorily. He learns that when he is away several of his senior employees take over office management and neglect their design duties. One employee could manage the office.

c. Alison Wong has been an employee of Your Kitchen Store for many years. Because the business is relatively small, Wong performs all accounting duties, including opening the mail, preparing the bank deposit, and preparing the bank reconciliation.

d. Most large companies have internal audit staffs that continuously evaluate the business's internal control. Part of the internal auditor's job is to evaluate how efficiently the company is running. For example, is the company purchasing inventory from the least expensive wholesaler? After a particularly bad year, Eagle Distributors eliminates its internal audit department to reduce expenses.

e. In evaluating the internal control over cash payments, an auditor learns that the purchasing agent is responsible for purchasing materials for use in the company's manufacturing process, approving the invoices for payment, and signing the cheques. No supervisor reviews the purchasing agent's work.

Required

1. Identify the missing internal control characteristic in each situation.
2. Identify the problem that could be caused by each control weakness.
3. Propose a solution to each internal control problem.

Excel Spreadsheet Template

Preparing and using the bank reconciliation as a control device
③

Problem 8–3B

The cash receipts and the cash payments of Campbell Hardware for January 2010 are as follows:

Cash Receipts (Posting reference is CR)		Cash Payments (Posting reference is CP)	
Date	Cash Debit	Cheque No.	Cash Credit
Jan. 3	$20,988	311	$ 3,672
8	1,480	312	1,668
10	1,980	313	12,562
16	7,488	314	2,584
22	20,736	315	8,588
29	2,404	316	3,600
31	1,728	317	1,304
Total	$56,804	318	6,268
		319	800
		320	12,964
		Total	$54,010

The Cash account of Campbell Hardware shows a balance of $39,478 at January 31, 2010.

Campbell Hardware received the bank statement shown below on January 31, 2010.

Bank Statement for January 2010

Description	Withdrawals	Deposits	Date	Balance
Balance Forward			Jan01	36,684
EFT Rent Collection		1,052	Jan01	37,736
Deposit		20,988	Jan04	58,724
Chq#00311	3,672		Jan07	55,052
Deposit		1,480	Jan09	56,532
Deposit		1,980	Jan12	58,512
Chq#00313	12,436		Jan13	46,076
NSF Cheque	3,356		Jan14	42,720
Chq#00312	1,668		Jan15	41,052
Deposit		7,488	Jan17	48,540
Chq#00314	2,584		Jan18	45,956
EFT Insurance	1,316		Jan21	44,640
Bank Collection		12,744	Jan22	57,384
Deposit		20,736	Jan23	78,120
Chq#00315	8,588		Jan26	69,532
Chq#00316	3,600		Jan30	65,932
Service Charge	140		Jan31	65,792
	37,360	66,468		

Additional data for the bank reconciliation:

a. The EFT deposit was a receipt of monthly rent. The EFT debit was payment of monthly insurance.

b. The NSF cheque was received from B. Crawford.

c. The $12,744 bank collection of a note receivable on January 22 included $500 interest revenue.

d. The correct amount of cheque no. 313, a payment on account, is $12,436. (Campbell Hardware's accountant mistakenly recorded the cheque for $12,562.)

Required

1. Prepare the Campbell Hardware bank reconciliation at January 31, 2010.

2. Describe how a bank account and the bank reconciliation help Campbell Hardware's owner control the business's cash.

Problem 8–4B

The July 31, 2010, bank statement of Red Star Shoes has just arrived from the Royal Bank. To prepare the Red Star Shoes bank reconciliation, you gather the following data:

Excel Spreadsheet Template

Preparing a bank reconciliation and the related journal entries

③

a. The Red Star Shoes Cash account shows a balance of $39,518 on July 31.

b. The bank statement includes two charges for returned cheques from customers. One is a $3,558 cheque received from St. Mary's Collegiate and deposited on July 20, returned by St. Mary's Collegiate's bank with the imprint "Unauthorized Signature." The other is an NSF cheque in the amount of $988 received from Mavis Jones. This cheque had been deposited on July 17.

c. Red Star Shoes pays rent ($5,850) and insurance ($1,920) each month by EFT.

d. The following Red Star Shoes cheques are outstanding at July 31:

Cheque No.	Amount
291	$ 306
322	1,074
327	4,712
329	82
330	3,096
331	32
332	1,860

e. The bank statement includes a deposit of $11,466, collected by the bank on behalf of Red Star Shoes. Of the total, $11,008 is collection of a note receivable, and the remainder is interest revenue.

f. The bank statement shows that Red Star Shoes earned $26 in interest on its bank balance during July. This amount was added to the Red Star Shoes account by the bank.

g. The bank statement lists a $144 subtraction for the bank service charge.

h. On July 31, the Red Star Shoes accountant deposited $3,378, but this deposit does not appear on the bank statement.

i. The bank statement includes a $4,200 deposit that Red Star Shoes did not make. The bank had erroneously credited the Red Star Shoes account for another bank customer's deposit.

j. The July 31 bank balance is $50,534.

Required

1. Prepare the bank reconciliation for Red Star Shoes at July 31, 2010.

2. Record in general journal form the entries that bring the book balance of Cash into agreement with the adjusted book balance on the reconciliation. Include an explanation for each entry.

Problem 8–5B

Identifying internal control weaknesses in cash receipts
④

Belmont Bakery makes all sales of its bread to retailers on account. Cash receipts arrive by mail, usually within 30 days of the sale. Gary Donell opens envelopes and separates the cheques from the accompanying remittance advices. Donell forwards the cheques to another employee, who makes the daily bank deposit but has no access to the accounting records. Donell sends the remittance advices, which show the amount of cash received, to the accounting department for entry in the accounts. Donell's only other duty is to grant sales allowances to customers. (Recall that a *sales allowance* decreases the amount that the customer must pay.) When he receives a customer cheque for less than the full amount of the invoice, he records the sales allowance and forwards the document to the accounting department.

Required You are the new controller of Belmont Bakery. Write a memo to the company president, John Senick, identifying the internal control weakness in this situation. State how to correct the weakness.

Problem 8–6B

Applying internal controls to cash payments, including petty cash transactions
⑤

MEI Distributors is located in Moncton, New Brunswick, with a sales territory covering the Maritime provinces and Newfoundland. Employees live in New Brunswick and all report to work at the company's offices in Moncton.

The company has established a large petty cash fund to handle cash payments and cash advances to its salespeople to cover trips to and from New Brunswick on sales calls.

The controller, Shelly Frum, has decided that two people (Sarah Wong and Martha Davis) should be in charge of the petty cash fund, since money is often needed when one person is out of the office. Frum also feels this will increase internal control, because the work of one person will serve as a check on that of the other.

Regular small cash payments are handled by either Wong or Davis, who make the payment and have the person receiving the money sign a sheet of paper giving the date and reason for the payment. Whenever a salesperson requires an advance for a sales trip, that person simply signs a receipt for the money received. The salesperson later submits receipts covering the costs incurred to either Wong or Davis to offset the cash advance.

Frum, a family friend as well as the controller, doesn't think the system is working and, knowing you are studying accounting, has asked for your advice.

Required Write a memo to Frum commenting on the internal control procedures of MEI. Suggest changes that you think would improve the system.

Problem 8–7B

Accounting for petty cash transactions
③

Suppose that on September 1, Twain Motors opens a new showroom in Timmins, Ontario, and creates a petty cash fund with an imprest balance of $500. During September, Lisa Manfield, the fund custodian, signs the petty cash tickets shown on the next page.

Ticket No.	Item	Amount
1	Courier for package received	$ 19.67
2	Refreshments for showroom opening	141.00
3	Computer disks	48.07
4	Office supplies	37.50
5	Dinner money for sales manager entertaining a customer	87.50

On September 30, prior to replenishment, the fund contains these tickets plus $161.34. The accounts affected by petty cash payments are Office Supplies Expense, Entertainment Expense, and Delivery Expense.

Required

1. Explain the characteristics and the internal control features of an imprest fund.
2. On September 30, how much cash should this petty cash fund hold before it is replenished?
3. Make the general journal entries to (a) create the fund, and (b) replenish it. Include explanations.
4. Make the entry on October 1 to increase the fund balance to $600. Include an explanation and briefly describe what the custodian does.

Problem 8–8B

Excel Communications had a computer failure on February 1, 2010, which resulted in the loss of data, including the balance of its Cash account and its bank reconciliation from January 31, 2010. The accountant, Brad Eyers, has been able to obtain the following information from the records of the company and its bank:

Preparing a bank reconciliation and related journal entries

a. An examination showed that two cheques (#461 for $345.00 and #492 for $525.00) had not been cashed as of February 1. Barker recalled that there was only one deposit in transit on the January 31 bank reconciliation, but was unable to recall the amount.

b. The cash receipts and cash payments journal contained the following entries for February 2010:

Cash Receipts: Amounts	Cash Payments: Cheque #	Amount
$ 876.00	499	$ 678.00
1,230.00	500	651.00
1,245.00	501	2,278.50
912.00	502	846.00
2,460.00	503	327.00
$6,723.00	504	820.00
	505	void
	506	314.00
	507	843.00
		$6,757.50

c. The bank provided the following statement as of February 28, 2010:

Date	Cheques and Other Debits		Deposits and Other Credits	Balance
Feb. 1	#500	651.00	660.00	3,579.00
3	#492	525.00		3,054.00
5	#501	2,278.50		775.50
8			876.00	1,651.50
16	#499	678.00	585.00	1,558.50
17	EFT	442.50		1,116.00
19			EFT 720.00	1,836.00
21	#503	327.00	1,230.00	2,739.00
22	#504	860.00	EFT 336.50	2,215.50
24			EFT 471.00	2,686.50
26	NSF	1,492.50	1,245.00	2,439.00
27	SC	37.50		2,401.50
27	#507	843.00	912.00	2,470.50

d. The deposit made on February 16 was for the collection of a note receivable ($560.00) plus interest.

e. The EFTs had not yet been recorded by Excel Communications since the bank statement was the first notification of them.

  • The February 17 EFT was for the monthly payment on an insurance policy for Excel Communications.

  • The February 19 and 24 EFTs were collections on accounts receivable.

  • The February 22 EFT was in error—the transfer should have been to Accel Communications.

f. The NSF cheque on February 26 was received from a customer as payment of $1,492.50 for installation of a satellite purchased from Excel.

g. Cheque #504 was correctly written for $860.00 for the purchase of office supplies, but incorrectly recorded by the cash payments clerk.

Required

1. Prepare a bank reconciliation as of February 28, 2010, including the calculation of the book balance of February 28, 2010.

2. Prepare all journal entries that would be required by the bank reconciliation.

Problem 8–9B

Making an ethical judgment

Hans Skinner is a vice-president of the Laurentian Bank in Markham, Ontario. Active in community affairs, Skinner serves on the board of directors of Orson Tool & Dye. Orson is expanding rapidly and is considering relocating its factory. At a recent meeting, board members decided to try to buy 20 hectares of land on the edge of town. The owner of the property is Sherri Alkiore, a customer of the Laurentian Bank. Alkiore is a recent widow. Skinner knows that Alkiore is eager to sell her local property. In view of Alkiore's anguished condition, Skinner believes she would accept almost any offer for the land. Realtors have appraised the property at $4 million.

Required Apply the ethical judgment framework outlined in the Decision Guidelines feature on page 426 to help Skinner decide what his role should be in Orson's attempt to buy the land from Alkiore.

CHALLENGE PROBLEMS

Problem 8–1C

Management's role in internal control

"Effective internal control must begin with top management." "The 'tone at the top' is a necessary condition if an organization is to have an effective system of internal control."

Statements such as these are becoming a more important part of internal control literature and thought.

The chapter lists a number of characteristics that are important for an effective system of internal control. Many of these characteristics have been part of the internal control literature for years.

Required Explain why you think a commitment to good internal control by top management is fundamental to an effective system of internal control.

Problem 8–2C

Applying internal controls to cash transactions

Many companies require some person other than the person preparing the bank reconciliation to review the reconciliation. Organizations routinely require cheques over a certain amount to be signed by two signing officers. The purchasing department orders goods but the receiving department receives the goods.

Required All of the above situations have a common thread. What is that common thread and why is it important?

Extending Your Knowledge

DECISION PROBLEMS

Surrey Tech Solutions has poor internal control over cash. Recently Shikha Ghandi, the owner, has suspected the cashier of stealing. Details of the business's cash position at April 30, 2010, follow:

Using the bank reconciliation to detect a theft

Adjusted bank balance $12,200

a. The Cash account in the ledger shows a balance of $12,900.
b. The April 30 bank statement shows a balance of $8,600. The bank statement lists a $400 credit for a bank collection, a $20 debit for the service charge, and an $80 debit for an NSF cheque. C. J. Ellis, the Surrey Tech Solutions accountant, has not recorded any of these items on the books.
c. At April 30 the following cheques are outstanding:

Cheque No.	Amount	Cheque No.	Amount
402	$200	531	1,200
527	600	561	400

d. There is a $6,000 deposit in transit at April 30, 2010.
e. Arlo Bing, the cashier, handles all incoming cash and makes bank deposits. He also writes cheques and reconciles the monthly bank statement.

Ghandi asks you to determine whether Bing has stolen cash from the business and, if so, how much. Perform a bank reconciliation, using the format illustrated in Exhibit 8–6 on page 416. There are no bank or book errors. Ghandi also asks you to evaluate the internal controls and recommend any changes needed to improve them.

FINANCIAL STATEMENT CASES

Financial Statement Case 1

Study Management's Report and the auditors' report on Canadian Western Bank's (CWB's) 2008 financial statements, given in Appendix A. Answer the following questions about CWB's internal controls and cash position:

Audit opinion, management responsibility, internal controls and cash

5. $13,553,000 increase

1. What is the name of CWB's outside auditing firm? What office of this firm signed the auditor's report? How long after CWB's year end did the auditors issue their opinion?
2. Who bears primary responsibility for the financial statements? How can you tell?
3. Which of the two reports indicates who bears primary responsibility for internal controls?
4. What standard of auditing did the outside auditors use in examining CWB's financial statements? By what accounting standards were the statements evaluated?
5. By how much did CWB's cash position change during fiscal 2008?
6. The cash flow statement (discussed in detail in Chapter 17) tells why the change in cash position occurred. Which type of activity—operating, investing, or financing—contributed most to this change?

Financial Statement Case 2

For Sun-Rype Products Ltd., study the auditor's report that is given in Appendix B and the Management's Discussion & Analysis given on MyAccountingLab. Answer the following questions about Sun-Rype's internal controls and cash position:

Audit opinion, management responsibility, internal controls and cash

5. $2,178 thousand decrease

1. What is the name of Sun-Rype's outside auditing firm? What office of this firm signed the auditor's report? How long after Sun-Rype's year end did the auditors issue their opinion?
2. Who bears responsibility for the financial statements? How can you tell?
3. Where in the annual report does it indicate who bears primary responsibility for internal controls?
4. What standard of auditing did the outside auditors use in examining Sun-Rype's financial statements? By what accounting standards were the statements evaluated?
5. By how much did Sun-Rype's cash position change during 2008?
6. The cash flow statement, discussed in detail in Chapter 17, tells why the change in cash position occurred. Which type of activity—operating, investing, or financing—contributed most to this change?

9 Receivables

What are accounts receivable, and why are they important?
What are notes receivable, and how is interest computed on them?
How are receivables reported on the balance sheet?
Which ratios use receivables to evaluate a company's financial position?

These questions and others will be answered throughout this chapter. The Decision Guidelines at the beginning and end of this chapter will provide the answers in a useful summary.

LEARNING OBJECTIVES

1 Define common types of receivables, and design internal controls for receivables

2 Use the allowance method to account for uncollectibles, and estimate uncollectibles by the percent-of-sales, aging-of-accounts-receivable, and the percent-of-accounts-receivable methods

3 Explain the direct write-off method to account for uncollectibles

4 Account for credit-card and debit-card sales

5 Account for notes receivable

6 Report receivables on the balance sheet

7 Use the acid-test ratio and days' sales in receivables to evaluate a company

8 Understand the impact on accounts receivable of international financial reporting standards (IFRS)

CHAPTER 9 APPENDIX

A1 Discount a note receivable

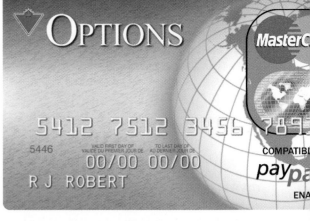

Canadian Tire Corporation, Limited, is a successful Canadian retailer. In 2008, its gross operating revenue was over $9.1 billion and its net earnings were approximately $374 million. As a major retailer intent on increasing its market share, Canadian Tire is providing services customers may not expect. The company provides a Canadian Tire Options MasterCard for customers and is entering into other personal financial service segments including personal loans, mortgages, and other banking services!

Issuing credit cards to customers increases sales immediately as customers use their credit cards to make purchases. It also provides an additional source of income from the interest charged monthly on outstanding credit-card balances. Although Canadian Tire has to manage a credit department, it avoids the fees charged by other credit-card companies for processing the transactions. The interest revenue Canadian Tire earns on mortgages offsets the interest it pays on the savings accounts and guaranteed investment certificates it offers.

Has the policy been successful for Canadian Tire? "Gross average loans receivable were $3.9 billion at the end of the year, reflecting a 7.1 per cent increase in the average account balance and a 0.1 per cent increase in the number of accounts carrying a balance."[1]

The retail banking initiative has been in pilot since October 2006, testing high-interest savings accounts, guaranteed investment certificates, and residential mortgages. "Financial Services had accumulated more than $166 million in high-interest savings accounts, approximately $973 million in total GIC deposits, and approximately $139 million in outstanding mortgage balances as at the end of 2008."[1]

---

[1] Canadian Tire Corporation, Limited, *2008 Annual Report*, pages 29 and 30.

As Canadian Tire's financial services business grows, so do its revenues and receivables. This chapter shows how to account for receivables. The chapter also covers notes receivable, a more formal type of receivable that includes a written promise to pay and a stated interest rate.

A *receivable* arises when a business (or person) sells goods or services to another party on credit. The receivable is the seller's claim for the amount of the transaction. A receivable also arises when one person lends money to another. Each credit transaction involves two parties:

- The **creditor**, who sells something and obtains a receivable, which is an asset.
- The **debtor**, who makes the purchase and has a payable, which is a liability.

A receivable is an asset, just as cash is. But the receivable is slightly different: It's very close to cash, but it's not cash yet. The major advantage of selling on credit is more sales, because it is easier for customers to buy, and therefore net income will be higher. The major disadvantages of selling on credit are that some customers will pay late or not at all; also, credit sales are more costly because the company must maintain a credit department and a billing department.

This chapter focuses on accounting for receivables by the seller (the creditor).

OBJECTIVE 1
Define common types of receivables, and design internal controls for receivables

Receivables: An Introduction

Types of Receivables

Receivables are monetary claims against others. The three major types of receivables are

- Accounts receivable
- Notes receivable
- Other receivables

Accounts receivable, also called *trade receivables,* are amounts to be collected from customers. Accounts receivable are *current assets*. The Accounts Receivable account in the general ledger serves as a *control account* because it summarizes the total of the receivables from all customers. As we saw in Chapter 7, companies also keep a *subsidiary ledger* of the receivable from each customer. This is illustrated as follows:

KEY POINT

Trade Accounts Receivable does not include amounts due from employees or officers (these are called Receivables from Employees or from Officers). Trade Accounts Receivable arise from selling goods or services to customers.

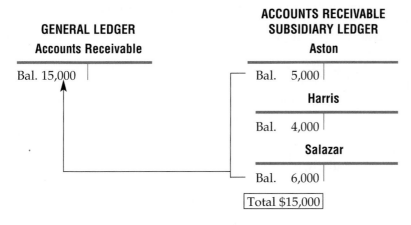

GENERAL LEDGER
Accounts Receivable

Bal. 15,000

ACCOUNTS RECEIVABLE
SUBSIDIARY LEDGER

Aston
Bal. 5,000

Harris
Bal. 4,000

Salazar
Bal. 6,000

Total $15,000

Notes receivable are more formal than accounts receivable. The debtor promises in writing to pay the creditor a definite sum at a definite future date—the *maturity* date. A written document known as a *promissory note* serves as the evidence of the receivable. Notes receivable due within one year, or one operating cycle if longer than one year, are current assets. Notes due beyond one year are *long-term.*

Other receivables is a miscellaneous category that may include loans to employees. Usually these are long-term receivables, but they are current assets if receivable within one year or less. Receivables can be reported as shown in Exhibit 9–1, where they are highlighted for emphasis (amounts assumed).

EXHIBIT 9–1	Receivables on the Balance Sheet

EXAMPLE COMPANY
Partial Balance Sheet—Assets Section
Date

Assets		
Current assets:		
Cash..		$ 1,000
Accounts receivable..	**$20,000**	
Less: Allowance for doubtful accounts	(1,500)	18,500
Notes receivable, short-term*.................................		**5,000**
Inventories		7,000
Prepaid expenses...		1,500
Total current assets...		33,000
Investments and long-term receivables:		
Available-for-sale investments	6,000	
Notes receivable, long-term	**16,000**	
Other receivables	**4,000**	
Total noncurrent assets		26,000
Property, plant, and equipment		
(net of amortization)..		15,000
Total assets..		$74,000

*This balance could also include the short-term portion of long-term receivables.

Establishing Internal Control over the Collection of Receivables

Businesses that sell on credit receive most cash receipts by mail or electronically. Therefore, internal control over collections is very important. A critical element of internal control (introduced in Chapter 8) is the separation of cash-handling and cash-accounting duties. Consider the following case:

> Mathers Supply Co. is family-owned and has loyal workers. Most company employees have been with Mathers for at least five years. The company makes 90 percent of its sales on account.
> The office staff consists of a bookkeeper and a supervisor. The bookkeeper maintains the general ledger and the accounts receivable subsidiary ledger. He also makes the daily bank deposit. The supervisor manages the office.

Can you identify the internal control weakness here? The bookkeeper has access to the general ledger and the accounts receivable subsidiary ledger, and also handles the cash. The bookkeeper could steal a customer's cheque and write off the customer's account as uncollectible.[2] Unless someone reviews the bookkeeper's work regularly, the theft may go undetected.

_____
[2] The bookkeeper would need to forge the endorsements of the cheques and deposit them in a bank account that he controls.

How can Mathers Supply correct this control weakness? *The bookkeeper should not be allowed to handle cash.* The supervisor should open the mail, list the amounts received, and have the owner make all bank deposits.

Using a bank lock box can achieve the same result. Customers send their payments directly to Mathers Supply Co.'s bank, which deposits the customer's payment into the company's bank account. We examined the lock-box system in Chapter 8, page 420.

Many companies and individuals now make payments via their bank using the online account payment system. The bank offers a list of companies and government departments to whom you can link and make online payments directly. One example is the direct payment online of a credit-card bill; another is the direct payment online of property taxes in many parts of Canada.

Managing the Collection of Receivables: The Credit Department

Most companies have a credit department to evaluate customers. The extension of credit requires a balancing act. The company does not want to lose sales to good customers, but it also wants to avoid uncollectible receivables.

For good internal control over cash collections of receivables, the credit department should have no access to cash. For example, if a credit employee handles cash, he or she could pocket the money received from a customer. He or she could also then label the customer's account as uncollectible, and the company would write off the account receivable as discussed in the next section. The company would stop billing that customer, and the employee would have covered up the theft. For this reason, a sharp separation of duties is important.

The Decision Guidelines feature below identifies the main issues in controlling and managing receivables. These guidelines serve as a framework for the remainder of the chapter.

DECISION GUIDELINES Controlling, Managing, and Accounting for Receivables

The main issues in *controlling* and *managing* the collection of receivables, plus a plan of action, are as follows:

Issue	Action
Extend credit only to customers most likely to pay.	Run a credit check on prospective customers.
Separate cash-handling (custody), credit (authorization), and accounting (recording) duties to keep employees from stealing cash collected from customers.	Design the internal control system to separate the duties of custody, authorization, and recording.
Pursue collection from customers to maximize cash flow.	Keep a close eye on collections from customers.

The main issues in *accounting* for receivables, and the related plans of action, are as follows:

Issue	Action
Report receivables at their *net realizable value,* which is the amount we expect to collect.	Estimate the amount of uncollectible receivables.
	The *balance sheet* reports receivables at net realizable value (accounts receivable — allowance for uncollectible accounts).
Report the expense associated with failure to collect receivables. This is called *Uncollectible-Account Expense.*	The *income statement* reports the expense of failing to collect from customers.

Accounting for Uncollectible Accounts (Bad Debts)

Selling on credit (on account) creates an account receivable. The revenue—service revenue for a service company or sales revenue for a merchandiser—is recorded as follows (amounts assumed):

Accounts Receivable......................................	6,000	
Service Revenue..		6,000
Performed service on account.		
Accounts Receivable......................................	10,000	
Sales Revenue...		10,000
Sold goods on account.		

The business collects cash for most accounts receivable and makes this entry, which is the same for both service and merchandising companies (amount assumed):

Cash	10,000	
Accounts Receivable..................................		10,000
Collected cash on account.		

Selling on credit provides both a benefit and a cost to the selling company.

- *The benefit:* The business increases sales revenues and profits by making sales to a wide range of customers. Customers can buy now but pay later.
- *The cost:* The company will be unable to collect from some customers, and that creates an expense. The expense is called **bad-debt expense**, **uncollectible-account expense**, or **doubtful-account expense**.

Bad-debt expense varies from company to company. The older the receivable, the less valuable it is because of the decreasing likelihood of collection. At Alma Ladder Ltd., a $25 million construction-equipment and supply firm, 85 percent of company sales are on account. Each $1.00 of accounts receivable is worth $0.98 because of bad debts. Bad-debt expense is an operating expense, in the same way as salary expense and amortization expense are.

How do companies account for these uncollectible accounts? They use the allowance method or, in certain limited cases, the direct write-off method. We begin the next section with the allowance method because it represents GAAP.

DID YOU GET IT?

To check your understanding of the material in this Learning Objective, complete this question. The solution appears on MyAccountingLab so you can check your progress.

1. A local furniture store's information system logs the details of a credit sale to a customer when the sale is made. However, the accounting system doesn't record the credit sale as revenue until the order has been shipped. After shipment or delivery, the invoice is generated, the revenue recorded, and the receivable created.

Jack Gordon is a salesman at the store. He earns commission on his sales, which are mostly on account, and December has been a great month for sales. January is typically a slow sales month. Jack would like to move credit sales from December to January to smooth out his earnings and defer personal income taxes. What internal controls would prevent Jack from improperly recording a credit sale in January if the goods were delivered in December?

The Allowance Method

Most companies use the **allowance method** to measure bad debts. The key concept is to record bad-debt expense in the same period as the sales revenue, which is an application of the *matching objective*. The business doesn't wait to see which customers will not pay. Instead, it records bad-debt expense on the basis of estimates developed from past experience. Sometimes estimated items appear on the financial statements because we may have to estimate the amount of an expense to match it with its related revenue. (Amortization is another example of such an estimate.)

The business records Bad-Debt Expense for the estimated amount, and sets up **Allowance for Doubtful Accounts** (or **Allowance for Uncollectible Accounts**), a contra account to Accounts Receivable. The allowance is the amount of receivables that the business expects *not* to collect. Subtracting the allowance from Accounts Receivable yields the net amount that the company does expect to collect, as shown in the following partial balance sheet (using assumed numbers):

OBJECTIVE ②
Use the allowance method to account for uncollectibles, and estimate uncollectibles by the percent-of-sales, aging-of-accounts-receivable, and the percent-of-accounts-receivable methods

KEY POINT

The longer an account is outstanding, the less chance there is of collection. But even if a past-due account is collected in full, there is a cost associated with collecting an account late. Also, when an account is past due, the seller is essentially giving an interest-free loan to the buyer because the seller does not have the cash to use in the business. This increases the seller's cost of doing business.

Accounts receivable.....................................	$10,000
Less: Allowance for doubtful accounts	900
Accounts receivable, net	$ 9,100

Customers owe this company $10,000, of which the business expects to collect $9,100. The company estimates that it will not collect $900 of its accounts receivable. In this example, $9,100 is the net realizable value (NRV) of the accounts receivable.

Many Canadian companies do not provide information on their gross receivables and allowance for doubtful accounts, but rather simply report the net receivable. They sometimes report the details in the notes to the financial statements. For example, Sun-Rype Products Ltd., in its annual report for the year ended December 31, 2008, reported the following information about trade receivables in its Note 18, Financial Risk Management, (b) Credit Risk:

(in thousands of dollars)	
Trade receivables	$11,438

Of the trade receivables outstanding at December 31, 2008, 97% are not due, and 3% are between 30 and 90 days overdue. Outstanding amounts totalling less than $0.1 million are considered impaired in that there is doubt about ultimate collection of the amounts due to the length of time the amounts have been outstanding. An allowance has been made to fully provide for the possible noncollection of these amounts.

KEY POINT

The amount of bad-debt expense depends on the volume of credit sales, the effectiveness of the credit department, and the diligence of the collection department.

Bad-Debt Expense is included in Sun-Rype's Selling, General, and Administrative Expenses total of $29,053 on its income statement.

In the sections that follow, we show how to arrive at these amounts.

Estimating Uncollectibles

How are bad debts estimated? Companies base estimates on their past experience. There are three ways to estimate uncollectibles:

- *Percent-of-sales method (income-statement approach)*
- *Aging-of-accounts-receivable method (balance-sheet approach)*
- *Percent-of-accounts-receivable method (balance-sheet approach)*

The three approaches work under the allowance method, and all normally require an adjusting entry at the end of the period.

Percent-of-Sales Method The **percent-of-sales method** computes bad-debt expense as a percent of net credit sales. This method is also called the **income-statement**

KEY POINT

The percent-of-sales approach is often referred to as the income-statement approach to estimating bad-debt expense because the entry is based on credit sales for the period (an income-statement figure).

approach because it focuses on the amount of expense. Assume it is December 31, 2010, and the accounts have these balances *before the year-end adjustments:*

Accounts Receivable	Allowance for Doubtful Accounts
100,000	1,000

Accounts Receivable reports the amount that customers owe the company. If it were to collect from all customers, the company would receive $100,000. Allowance for Doubtful Accounts should report the amount of the receivables that the company expects *not* to collect.

Suppose it becomes clear to the company that it will *fail to collect* more than $1,000 of the receivables. The allowance is too low, so the company needs to bring it up to a more realistic credit balance. That requires an adjusting entry at the end of the period.

How the Percent-of-Sales Method Works   Based on prior experience, the company's bad-debt expense is 2 percent of net credit sales, which were $500,000 in 2010. The adjusting entry to record bad-debt expense for 2010 and to update the allowance is:

2010
Dec. 31   Bad-Debt Expense 10,000
                Allowance for Doubtful Accounts   10,000
                To record bad-debt expense for the year ($500,000 × 0.02).

After posting, the accounts are ready for reporting on the 2010 balance sheet.

Accounts Receivable	Allowance for Doubtful Accounts
100,000	1,000
	Adj. 10,000
	11,000

Net accounts receivable, $89,000

Now the allowance for doubtful accounts is realistic. The balance sheet will report accounts receivable at the net amount of $89,000 ($100,000 − $11,000). The income statement will report the estimated bad-debt expense of $10,000, along with other operating expenses for the period.

Aging-of-Accounts-Receivable Method   Another method for estimating uncollectible accounts is the **aging-of-accounts-receivable method**. This method is also called the **balance-sheet approach** because it focuses on accounts receivable. Assume it is December 31, 2010, and the accounts have these balances *before the year-end adjustment:*

Accounts Receivable	Allowance for Doubtful Accounts
100,000	1,000

Again, the allowance balance is too low. In the aging-of-accounts-receivable method, the company groups each customer account (Baring Tools Co., etc.) according to how long amounts due have been outstanding. The computer can sort customer accounts by age. Exhibit 9–2 shows how the company groups its accounts receivable. This is called an aging schedule.

Customers owe the company $100,000, but the company expects *not* to collect $10,100 of this amount. These amounts appear in the lower-right corner of the aging schedule. Notice that the percentage uncollectible increases as a customer account gets older.

KEY POINT

The aging-of-accounts-receivable method is often referred to as the balance-sheet approach to estimating bad debts because the computation focuses on Accounts Receivable (a balance-sheet figure).

Aging Schedule

Age of Account

Customer Name	1–30 Days	31–60 Days	61–90 Days	Over 90 Days	Total Balance
Baring Tools Co.	$20,000				$ 20,000
Calgary Pneumatic Parts Ltd.	10,000				10,000
Red Deer Pipe Corp.		$3,000	$ 5,000		8,000
Seal Coatings Inc.			9,000	$1,000	10,000
Other accounts*	30,000	2,000	12,000	8,000	52,000
Totals..............................	$60,000	$5,000	$26,000	$9,000	$100,000
Estimated percent uncollectible...............	× 1%	× 2%	× 5%	× 90%	
Allowance for Doubtful Accounts....	$ 600	$ 100	$ 1,300	$8,100	$ 10,100

*Each of the "Other accounts" would appear individually.

How the Aging-of-Accounts-Receivable Method Works The aging-of-accounts-receivable method tells the company what the credit balance of the allowance account needs to be—$10,100 in this case. The aging-of-accounts-receivable method works like this:

Allowance for Doubtful Accounts:

Credit balance needed	$10,100
Unadjusted balance already in the allowance....	1,000
Adjusting entry for this amount	$ 9,100

To adjust the allowance, the company makes this adjusting entry at the end of the period:

```
2010
Dec. 31   Bad-Debt Expense .........................................................   9,100
               Allowance for Doubtful Accounts............................          9,100
          To record expense for the year ($10,100 − $1,000).
```

This method requires an extra step—remember to first take into account the balance in Allowance for Doubtful Accounts before calculating the amount to be recorded.

After posting, the accounts are ready for reporting on the balance sheet.

Accounts Receivable		Allowance for Doubtful Accounts	
100,000			1,000
		Adj.	9,100
		Bal.	10,100

Net accounts receivable, $89,900

As with the percent-of-sales method, the income statement reports the bad-debt expense.

Report accounts receivable at net realizable value ($89,900) because that is the amount the company expects to realize, or collect in cash.

KEY POINT

It is a common mistake to forget to include the unadjusted balance in the Allowance account when computing bad-debt expense under the aging approach. The unadjusted balance of the Allowance account represents current accounts receivable that have previously been expensed as uncollectible accounts but have not yet been written off. These doubtful accounts should *not* be included in the bad-debt expense for the current period.

Percent-of-Accounts-Receivable Method Another balance-sheet-based method of determining the allowance for doubtful accounts is the **percent-of-accounts-receivable method**. This method is similar to the aging-of-accounts-receivable method; companies can determine what the credit balance of the allowance account needs to be by calculating it as a percent of the Accounts Receivable balance. For example, assume Accounts Receivable are $100,000 and Allowance for Doubtful Accounts has a credit balance of $1,000 at December 31, 2010, *before the year-end adjustment*. Based on experience, the company determines that the allowance should be 5 percent of Accounts Receivable, or $5,000. The adjusting entry is calculated as follows:

Allowance for Doubtful Accounts:	
Credit balance needed	$5,000
Unadjusted balance already in the allowance ...	1,000
Adjusting entry for this amount	$4,000

To adjust the allowance, the company makes this adjusting entry at the end of the period:

2010			
Dec. 31	Bad-Debt Expense	4,000	
	Allowance for Doubtful Accounts		4,000
	To record bad-debt expense for the year ($5,000 − $1,000).		

Using the Allowance Methods Together In practice, many companies use the percent-of-sales and the aging-of-accounts-receivable or the percent-of-accounts-receivable methods together.

- For *interim statements* (monthly or quarterly), companies use the percent-of-sales method because it is easier to apply. The percent-of-sales method focuses on the amount of bad-debt *expense*, calculated by multiplying sales by a chosen percent. The adjusting entry is for the amount generated *by* the percent-of-sales method.

- At the end of the year, these companies use the aging-of-accounts-receivable method or the percent-of-accounts-receivable method to ensure that Accounts Receivable is reported at *expected net realizable value*. These two methods focus on the amount of the receivables—the *asset*—that is uncollectible. The adjusting entry is for the amount required to bring the Allowance for Doubtful Accounts *to* the amount generated by the aging-of-accounts-receivable or the percent-of-accounts-receivable method.

- Using the methods together provides good measures of both the expense and the asset. Exhibit 9–3 summarizes and compares the three methods.

EXHIBIT 9–3 Comparing the Percent-of-Sales, the Aging-of-Accounts-Receivable, and the Percent-of-Accounts-Receivable Methods for Estimating Uncollectibles

Writing Off Uncollectible Accounts

During early 2010, the company collects on most of its $100,000 of accounts receivable and records the cash receipts as follows:

2010
Jan.–Mar. Cash 80,000
            Accounts Receivable 80,000
        To record collections on account.

Suppose that, after repeated attempts to collect, the company's credit department determines that it cannot collect a total of $1,200 from customers Auger ($900) and Kirsh ($300). The company then writes off the receivables of these customers:

2010
Mar. 31 Allowance for Doubtful Accounts 1,200
            Accounts Receivable—Auger 900
            Accounts Receivable—Kirsh....................................... 300
        To write off uncollectible accounts.

Since Allowance for Doubtful Accounts is a contra-asset account, the write-off of uncollectible accounts has no effect on total assets, liabilities, or equity.

Assets	=	Liabilities	+	Owner's Equity
+1,200	=	0	+	0
−1,200				

Although a write-off of uncollectible accounts affects neither an expense account nor the net amount of receivables, these accounts must be eliminated from the accounts receivable records because the company does not want to waste time and money pursuing collections from these customers. However, a record of these customers will still be retained in the system or by the credit department for future reference and possible future credit applications.

DID YOU GET IT?

MyAccountingLab

To check your understanding of the material in this Learning Objective, complete these questions. The solutions appear on MyAccountingLab so you can check your progress.

2. Suppose a company records a credit sale to a new customer in 2009. In 2010, the company discovers the customer is bankrupt; the company will be unable to collect its receivable from the customer. The bad-debt expense for this customer is recorded in 2010. What are the accounting problems with this situation? Is recording the bad-debt expense in 2010 incorrect?

3. Acadia Building Supplies is a chain of hardware and building supply stores concentrated in the Maritimes. The company's year-end balance sheet for 2009 reported:

Accounts receivable $4,000,000
Allowance for doubtful accounts.. (175,000)

(a) How much of the December 31, 2009, balance of Accounts Receivable did Acadia Building Supplies expect to collect? Stated differently, what was the expected net realizable value of these receivables?

(b) Journalize, without explanations, year 2010 entries for Acadia Building Supplies:

   i. Estimated bad-debt expense was $140,000 for the first three quarters of the year, based on the percent-of-sales method.

   ii. Write-offs of Accounts Receivable totalled $160,000.

   iii. December 31, 2010, aging of receivables indicates, using estimated amounts, that $192,000 of total receivables is uncollectible.

Prepare a T-account for Allowance for Doubtful Accounts, as follows:

Allowance for Doubtful Accounts

2010 Write-offs	Dec. 31, 2009 Bal.	175,000
	2010 Expense	
	Bal. before Adj.	
	Dec. 31, 2010 Adj	
	Dec. 31, 2010 Bal.	192,000

Post all three transactions to the Allowance for Doubtful Accounts T-account.

(c) Report Acadia Building Supplies' receivables and related allowance on the December 31, 2010, balance sheet. Accounts Receivable totals $4,155,000.

(d) What is the expected net realizable value of receivables at December 31, 2010? How much is bad-debt expense for 2010?

The Direct Write-Off Method

OBJECTIVE ③
Explain the direct write-off method to account for uncollectibles

As previously mentioned, there is another way to account for uncollectible receivables that is not appropriate for most companies, called the **direct write-off method.** Under the direct write-off method, the company waits until it decides that a customer's account receivable is uncollectible. Then the company writes off the customer's account receivable by debiting Bad-Debt Expense and crediting the customer's Account Receivable, as follows (using assumed data):

2010			
Jan. 2	Bad-Debt Expense	2,000	
	Accounts Receivable—Sterling..................................		2,000
	Wrote off an uncollectible account.		

The direct write-off method is defective for two reasons:

1. It does not set up an allowance for doubtful accounts. As a result, the direct write-off method always reports the receivables at their full amount. Assets are then overstated on the balance sheet, since the business likely does not expect to collect the full amount of accounts receivable.

2. It does not match the bad-debt expense against revenue very well. In this example, the company made the sale to Sterling in 2009 and should have estimated and recorded the bad-debt expense during 2009, matching the bad-debt expense to its related sales revenue. That is the only way to measure net income properly. By recording the bad-debt expense in 2010, the company overstates net income in 2009 and understates net income in 2010. Both years' net income amounts are incorrect.

The direct write-off method is easier to use than an allowance method, but it fails to match expenses and revenues properly. It is acceptable only if uncollectibles are immaterial (very low) in amount or if the difference between using an allowance method and the direct write-off method is immaterial. It works for retailers such as small neighbourhood stores or bakeries, because those companies carry almost no receivables.

Recovery of Accounts Previously Written Off

When an account receivable is written off as uncollectible, the customer still owes the money. However, the company may stop pursuing collection and write off the account as uncollectible.

Some companies turn delinquent receivables over to a lawyer or a collection agency to help recover some of the cash. This is called *recovery of a bad account*. Let's see how to record the recovery of an account that we wrote off earlier. Recall that on March 31, 2010, the company wrote off the $900 receivable from customer Auger (see page 459). Suppose it is now October 4, 2010, and the company unexpectedly receives $900 from Auger. To account for this recovery, the company makes two journal entries to (1) reverse the earlier write-off and (2) record the cash collection, as follows:

2010
(1) Oct. 4	Accounts Receivable—Auger..		900	
	Allowance for Doubtful Accounts.............................			900
	Reinstated Auger's account receivable.			

2010
(2) Oct. 4	Cash..		900	
	Accounts Receivable—Auger.....................................			900
	Collected on account.			

Follow through the entries to Auger's subsidiary ledger account, shown in the T-account below: first the credit sale, then the write-off, then the reversal of the write-off, and finally the credit to the account when Auger pays in full. The customer's subsidiary account shows the complete credit history—an important feature of the subsidiary ledger system.

Accounts Receivable—Auger

Sale	900	900	Write-off	
Reinstate	900	900	Collection	

DID YOU GET IT?

To check your understanding of the material in this Learning Objective, complete these questions. The solutions appear on MyAccountingLab so you can check your progress.

4. (a) How accurately does the direct write-off method measure income?

   (b) How accurately does the direct write-off method value accounts receivable?

5. Refer to Did You Get It? Question 3 on page 459. Complete that question again, but this time assume Acadia Building Supplies uses the direct write-off method to account for uncollectible receivables. This means that no allowance for doubtful accounts is estimated or recorded, so disregard those aspects of the question.

6. In 2009, Jenning Restaurant Supplies wrote off the $800 receivable from Lou's Rib House after learning the restaurant was bankrupt. On July 5, 2010, Jenning received $300 of this amount from the courts, with a report that the rest will never be recovered. Make the journal entries to account for this recovery. Jenning uses the allowance method to account for bad debts.

Credit-Card and Debit-Card Sales

Credit-Card Sales

Credit-card sales are common in both traditional and online retailing. American Express, VISA, and MasterCard are popular. The customer presents the credit card to pay for purchases. The credit-card company pays the seller and then bills the customer, who pays the credit-card company.

Credit cards offer the convenience of buying without having to pay the cash immediately. A VISA customer receives a monthly statement from VISA, detailing each of the customer's credit-card transactions. The customer can write one cheque to cover the total of these credit-card purchases.

Retailers accept credit cards from customers to increase revenue. Not only are credit cards more convenient for the customer, but research shows that customers purchase more with credit cards than with cash only. After a credit-card sale is made, the retailer receives the amount of the sale less a fee from the credit-card company. This transaction is essentially a sale of the receivable to the credit-card

OBJECTIVE 4
Account for credit-card and debit-card sales

KEY POINT

Credit-card companies conduct extensive research on credit risks. They research an applicant's job history, credit history, salary, home rental or ownership, length of time at current address, and other credit transactions.

company. The credit-card company previously performed the credit check and now assumes the risk of uncollectible accounts. Hence, retailers do not have to keep accounts receivable records, and they do not have to collect cash from customers.

These benefits to the seller do not come free. The seller pays a fee to the credit-card company and, therefore, receives less than the full amount of the sale. The credit-card company takes a fee of 1 to 5 percent[3] on the sale. Accounting for credit-card sales differs for bank credit cards and for non-bank credit cards.

Bank Credit Cards   VISA and MasterCard are known as *bank credit cards*. With bank credit cards, the seller deposits the VISA or MasterCard receipt at the bank and receives cash for the sale immediately, less the credit-card company's fee. Suppose you and your family have lunch at The Keg restaurant. You pay the bill—$100—with a VISA card. The Keg's entry to record the $100 VISA card sale, subject to the credit-card company's (assumed) 2 percent discount, which is an *expense* to The Keg for a credit-card transaction, is as follows:

2010			
Mar. 2	Cash	98	
	Credit-Card Discount Expense......................................	2	
	Sales Revenue..		100
	Recorded VISA credit-card sale less a 2 percent		
	credit-card discount expense.		

Non-bank Credit Cards   Credit cards other than VISA and MasterCard are known as *non-bank credit cards*. With non-bank credit cards, the seller mails the credit-card receipts to the credit-card company and awaits payment, less the credit-card company's fee. Suppose that in the example above, you pay the bill at the Keg—$100—with an American Express card, a non-bank credit card. The Keg's entry to record the $100 non-bank credit-card sale, subject to the credit-card company's (assumed) 2 percent discount, which is an *expense* to The Keg for a credit-card transaction, is as follows:

2010			
Mar. 2	Accounts Receivable—American Express	98	
	Credit-Card Discount Expense......................................	2	
	Sales Revenue..		100
	Recorded American Express credit-card sale		
	less 2 percent credit-card discount expense.		

On collection of the cash, The Keg records the following:

2010			
Mar. 15	Cash	98	
	Accounts Receivable—American Express		98
	Collected from American Express.		

In both the bank credit card and the non-bank credit card examples, the customer pays either VISA or American Express the $100 after later receiving the monthly statement from the credit-card company, The Keg receives $98 from the credit-card company, and the credit-card company keeps $2 for this transaction.

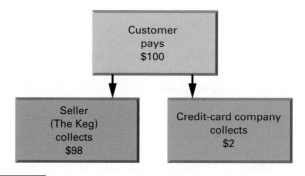

---

[3] The rate varies among companies and over time.

Debit-Card Sales

Debit cards are fundamentally different from credit cards. Using a *debit card* is like paying with cash, except that you don't have to carry cash or write a cheque. All banks issue debit cards. When a business makes a sale, the customer "swipes" her debit card through an Interac card reader and enters her personal identification number (PIN). The bank deducts the cost of the purchase from the customer's account immediately and transfers the purchase amount, less a debit-card service fee for allowing the transaction, into the business's account. The journal entry for the business is the same as the journal entry for a bank-credit-card sale. For example, suppose you buy groceries at a grocery store for a total cost of $56.35. You swipe your debit card, enter your PIN, and the grocery store records the sale as follows:

Cash	55.85	
Debit Card Service Fee	0.50	
Sales Revenue		56.35
To record a debit-card sale.		

Credit-Card and Debit-Card Risk Both credit cards and debit cards bear a risk for the cardholder, the issuer, and the business accepting the card. The cards can be lost, and stolen cards can be used to make purchases for which the card-issuer will not receive payment. All parties should recognize this risk when they use, issue, and accept credit and debit cards.

Credit Balances in Accounts Receivable

Occasionally, customers overpay their accounts or return merchandise for which they have already paid. The result is a credit balance in the customer's account receivable. For example, Leather and Stuff's subsidiary ledger contains 213 accounts, with balances as shown:

210	accounts with *debit* balances totalling	$ 185,000
3	accounts with *credit* balances totalling	(2,800)
	Net total of all balances	$ 182,200

Leather and Stuff should not report the asset Accounts Receivable at the net amount—$182,200. Why not? The credit balance—$2,800—is a liability, even though most customers will apply an overpayment to their next purchase. Like any other liability, customer credit balances are debts of the business. A balance sheet that did not indicate this liability would be misleading. Therefore, Leather and Stuff would report on its balance sheet as follows:

Assets		**Liabilities**	
Current:		Current:	
Accounts receivable	$185,000	Credit balances in	
		customer accounts	$2,800

Many companies would include this $2,800 with Other Accounts Payable.

DID YOU GET IT?

To check your understanding of the material in this Learning Objective, complete this question. The solution appears on MyAccountingLab so you can check your progress.

7. Restaurants do a large volume of business by customer credit cards and debit cards. Suppose a Swiss Chalet restaurant had these transactions on a Thursday in September:

MasterCard credit-card sales	$15,000
Non-bank credit-card sales	3,000
Debit-card sales	5,000

Suppose MasterCard charges merchants 2 percent, the non-bank credit-card companies charge 3 percent, and the debit-card transactions charge 2.5 percent. Record these sale transactions for this Swiss Chalet restaurant.

Notes Receivable: An Overview

OBJECTIVE 5
Account for notes receivable

Notes receivable are more formal than accounts receivable. The debtor signs a promissory note accepting the conditions of borrowing. The note also serves as evidence of the transaction. Let's define the special terms used for notes receivable:

- **Promissory note.** A written promise to pay a specified sum of money at a particular future date.
- **Maker** of the note (**debtor**). The entity that signs the note and promises to pay the required amount; the maker of the note is the *debtor*.
- **Payee** of the note (**creditor**). The entity to whom the maker promises future payment; the payee of the note is the *creditor*.
- **Principal.** The amount lent by the payee and borrowed by the maker of the note.
- **Interest.** The revenue to the payee for lending money; interest is an expense to the debtor.
- **Interest period.** The period of time during which interest is to be computed, extending from the original date of the note to the maturity date; also called the **note term,** or simply the **time period.**
- **Interest rate.** The percentage rate of interest specified by the note, always stated for a period of one year; therefore, a 6 percent note means that the amount of interest for *one year* is 6 percent of the note's principal amount.
- **Maturity date** (also called **due date**). The date on which final payment of the note is due.
- **Maturity value.** The sum of the principal plus interest due at maturity.

Exhibit 9–4 illustrates a promissory note. Many of the special terms just defined are highlighted on it.

KEY POINT

You need to know the following—September, April, June, and November have 30 days. All the rest have 31, except February, which has 28 and one day more every four years.

Identifying the Maturity Date of a Note

Some notes specify the maturity date, as shown in Exhibit 9–4. Other notes state the period of the note, in days or months. When the period is given in months, the note matures on the same day of the month as the date the note was issued. A six-month note dated February 16 matures on August 16.

EXHIBIT 9–4   A Promissory Note

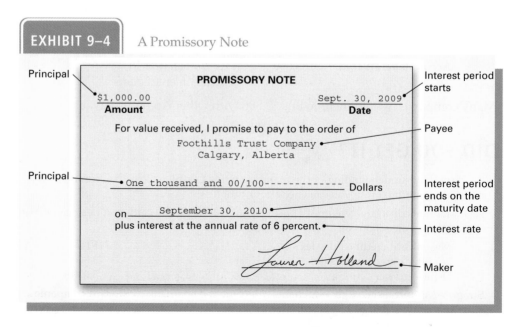

A 120-day note dated September 14, 2009, matures on January 12, 2010, as shown below:

Month		Number of Days	Cumulative Total
Sept.	2009	16*	16
Oct.	2009	31	47
Nov.	2009	30	77
Dec.	2009	31	108
Jan.	2010	12	120

*$30 - 14 = 16$

When the period is given in days, the maturity date is determined by counting the days from date of issue. The 120-day note dated September 14, 2009, would have to be *repaid* by January 12, 2010. In counting the days remaining for a note, remember to

- Count the maturity date
- Omit the date the note was issued

Computing Interest on a Note

KEY POINT

Time means interest period.

The formula for computing interest is:

Amount of interest = Principal × Interest rate × Time

Using the data in Exhibit 9–4, Foothills Trust Company computes its interest revenue for one year on its note receivable as:

Amount of interest		Principal	Interest rate		Time
$60	=	$1,000	×	0.06	× 1 (year)

The maturity value of the note is $1,060 ($1,000 principal + $60 interest). The time element is one (1) because the note's term is one year.

When the term of a note is stated in months, we compute the interest based on the 12-month year. Interest on a $2,000 note at 10 percent for three months is computed as:

Amount of interest		Principal	Interest rate		Time
$50	=	$2,000	×	0.10	× $3/12$

When the interest period of a note is stated in days, we usually compute interest based on a 365-day year. The interest on a $5,000 note at 12 percent for 60 days is computed as:

Amount of interest		Principal	Interest rate		Time
$98.63	=	$5,000	×	0.12	× $60/365$

> *Keep in mind that interest rates are stated as an annual rate.* Therefore, the time in the interest formula should also be expressed in terms of a year.

Accounting for Notes Receivable

Recording Notes Receivable

Consider the loan agreement shown in Exhibit 9–4. After Lauren Holland signs the note and presents it to Foothills Trust Company, the trust company, gives her $1,000 cash. At maturity date, Holland pays the trust company $1,060

($1,000 principal + $60 interest). The trust company's entries (assuming it has a September 30 year end) are as follows:

2009
Sept. 30   Note Receivable—L. Holland 1,000
                Cash   1,000
            Lent money at 6% for 1 year.

2010
Sept. 30   Cash 1,060
                Note Receivable—L. Holland   1,000
                Interest Revenue   60
            Collected note at maturity.
            (Interest revenue = $1,000 × 0.06 × 1)

Some companies sell merchandise in exchange for notes receivable. This arrangement often occurs when the payment term extends beyond the customary accounts receivable period, which generally ranges from 30 to 60 days as indicated by the company's credit terms of 2/10, net 30 or net 60.

Suppose that, on October 20, 2010, Midland Distributors sells plumbing supplies for $15,000 to Western Builders. Western signs a 90-day promissory note at 10 percent interest. Midland's entries to record the sale and collection from Western (Midland's year end is June 30) are

2010
Oct. 20   Note Receivable—Western Builders 15,000.00
                Sales Revenue 15,000.00
            To record sale. Note at 10% for 90 days.

2011
Jan. 18   Cash 15,369.86
                Note Receivable—Western Builders ...   15,000.00
                Interest Revenue 369.86
            To record collection at maturity.
            (Interest revenue = $15,000 × 0.10 × $^{90}/_{365}$)

A company may accept a note receivable from a trade customer who fails to pay an account receivable on time. The customer signs a promissory note and gives it to the creditor.

Suppose Clifford Sales sees that it will not be able to pay off its account payable to Fridoris Supply, which is due in 15 days. Fridoris Supply may accept a 12-month, $6,000 note receivable, with 9 percent interest, from Clifford Sales on October 1, 2010. Fridoris Supply's entry is

2010
Oct. 1   Note Receivable—Clifford Sales 6,000
                Accounts Receivable—Clifford Sales ..   6,000
            Received a note at 9% for 12 months.

Accruing Interest Revenue

A note receivable may be outstanding at the end of the accounting period. The interest revenue earned on the note up to the year end is part of that year's earnings. Recall that interest revenue is earned over time, not just when cash is received. We saw in Chapter 3, on page 121, that accrued revenue creates an asset for the amount that has been earned but not received.

Let's continue with the Fridoris Supply note receivable from Clifford Sales. Fridoris Supply's accounting period ends December 31.

• How much of the total interest revenue does Fridoris Supply earn in 2010 (for October, November, and December)?

$$\$6,000 × 0.09 × {}^{3}/_{12} = \$135$$

Fridoris Supply makes this adjusting entry to accrue interest revenue at December 31, 2010:

2010			
Dec. 31	Interest Receivable.....................................	135	
	Interest Revenue		135
	To accrue interest revenue earned in 2010		
	but not yet received ($6,000 \times 0.09 \times {}^3/_{12}$).		

- How much interest revenue does Fridoris Supply earn in 2011 (for January through September)?

$$\$6,000 \times 0.09 \times {}^9/_{12} = \$405$$

On the note's maturity date, Fridoris Supply makes this entry:

2011			
Sept. 30	Cash	6,540	
	Note Receivable—Clifford Sales		6,000
	Interest Receivable...............................		135
	Interest Revenue		405
	To collect a note receivable on which interest		
	has been accrued previously. Interest receivable		
	is $135 ($6,000 \times 0.09 \times {}^3/_{12}$) and interest revenue		
	is $405 ($6,000 \times 0.09 \times {}^9/_{12}$).		

The entries for accrued interest at December 31, 2010, and for collection in 2011 assign the correct amount of interest to each year.

A company holding a note may need cash before the note matures. A procedure for selling the note, called discounting a note receivable, appears in the Chapter 9 Appendix beginning on page 474.

Dishonoured Notes Receivable

If the maker of a note does not pay a note receivable at maturity, the maker **dishonours** or **defaults on the note**. Because the note has expired, it is no longer in force. But the debtor still owes the payee. The payee must transfer the note receivable amount to Accounts Receivable since Notes Receivable contains only notes that have not yet matured.

Suppose Whitehorse Hardware has a six-month, 10 percent note receivable for $5,000 from Northern Cabinets. On the February 3 maturity date, Northern Cabinets defaults. Whitehorse Hardware would record the default as follows:

Feb. 3	Accounts Receivable—Northern Cabinets	5,250	
	Note Receivable—Northern Cabinets		5,000
	Interest Revenue		250
	To record the default on a note receivable.		
	Accounts receivable is $5,250		
	[$5,000 + ($5,000 \times 0.10 \times {}^6/_{12}$)] and interest		
	revenue is $250 ($5,000 \times 0.10 \times {}^6/_{12}$).		

Whitehorse Hardware would pursue collection from Northern Cabinets for this account receivable and would account for the receivable in the normal way. Further accrual of interest from this point until payment is received could only be recorded if collection is likely, according to the revenue-recognition criterion.

DID YOU GET IT?

To check your understanding of the material in this Learning Objective, complete these questions. The solutions appear on MyAccountingLab so you can check your progress.

8. On April 1, 2009, Mediterranean Importers loaned $20,000 cash to Bud Shriver on a one-year, 7 percent note. Record the loan transaction and any year-end transactions for Mediterranean.
9. Refer to the previous question. The loan was repaid on April 1, 2010, with its related interest. Record the repayment for Mediterranean, assuming no reversing entries were used.
10. Refer to question 8. Suppose Shriver defaulted on the note at maturity instead of repaying it. How would Mediterranean Importers record the default?

Reporting Receivables on the Balance Sheet: Actual Company Reports

OBJECTIVE 6
Report receivables on the balance sheet

Let's look at how some companies report their receivables on the balance sheet. Terminology and set-up vary.

Canadian GAAP for private enterprises indicate that it is not necessary to present the allowance for doubtful accounts in the financial statements because it is assumed that an adequate allowance for doubtful accounts has been made if no statement has been made to the contrary. *Financial Reporting in Canada*, published by the CICA, indicates that only 36 of the 200 companies surveyed, or 18 percent, made reference on the balance sheet or in the notes to the allowance in 2007.[4]

One Canadian company that did provide information was Canadian National Railway Company (CN). In its 2008 annual report, CN reported the following (amounts in millions):

	December 31	
	2008	2007
Current assets		
Accounts receivable (note 4)	$913	$370
Notes to the Consolidated Financial Statements		
4. Accounts receivable	939	397
Provision for doubtful accounts	(26)	(27)
	$913	$370

While some companies, like CN, provide information about the allowance for doubtful accounts, as was suggested above, many companies in Canada, such as Enbridge Inc., the Calgary-based energy company, and Sobey's, the food retailer, tend to show only net accounts receivable. They do not show the allowance.

DID YOU GET IT?

To check your understanding of the material in this Learning Objective, complete this question. The solution appears on MyAccountingLab so you can check your progress.

11. Refer to the December 31, 2008, CN data given above.
    (a) How much did customers owe CN at December 31, 2008?
    (b) How much did CN expect to collect at December 31, 2008?
    (c) How much did CN expect not to collect at December 31, 2008?

---

[4] Byrd, C., I. Chen, and J. Smith, *Financial Reporting in Canada 2007* (Toronto: Canadian Institute of Chartered Accountants, 2007), online edition, Chapter 23—Accounts and Notes Receivable.

Using Accounting Information for Decision Making

The balance sheet lists assets in their order of relative liquidity (closeness to cash):

OBJECTIVE 7
Use the acid-test ratio and days' sales in receivables to evaluate a company

- Cash comes first because it *is* the most liquid asset.

- Short-term investments (covered in a later chapter) come next because they are almost as liquid as cash. They can be sold for cash whenever the owner wishes.

- Current receivables are less liquid than short-term investments because the company must collect the receivables.

- Merchandise inventory is less liquid than receivables because the goods must first be sold.

A partial balance sheet of Winpak Ltd., the packaging company whose head office is in Winnipeg, provides an example in Exhibit 9–5.

EXHIBIT 9–5 Winpak Ltd.'s Partial Balance Sheet

WINPAK LTD.
Partial Consolidated Balance Sheet (adapted)
As at December 31, 2008, and December 31, 2007

(thousands of U.S. dollars)	2008	2007
Current Assets		
Cash and cash equivalents	$ 19,796	$ —
Accounts receivable	63,175	57,308
Income taxes receivable	—	6,292
Inventories	68,117	74,742
Prepaid expenses	2,060	1,945
Future income taxes	3,363	2,702
	$156,511	$142,989
Current Liabilities		
Bank indebtedness (unsecured)	$ —	$ 5,037
Accounts payable and accrued liabilities	33,298	38,061
Income taxes payable	2,017	—
	$ 35,315	$ 43,098

Balance-sheet data become more useful when the relationships among assets, liabilities, and revenues are calculated. Let's examine two important ratios.

Acid-Test (or Quick) Ratio

Owners and managers use ratios for decision making. In Chapter 4, for example, we discussed the current ratio, which indicates the ability to pay current liabilities with current assets. A more stringent measure of the ability to pay current liabilities is the **acid-test** (or **quick**) **ratio**. The acid-test ratio tells whether the entity could pay all its current liabilities if they came due immediately.

KEY POINT

The average acid-test ratio in the computer industry is 1.20. For auto dealers, the average is 0.20, and for restaurants, 0.40.

For Winpak Ltd. (Exhibit 9–5)

$$\text{Acid-test ratio} = \frac{\text{Cash + Short-term investments + Net current receivables}}{\text{Total current liabilities}}$$

$$= \frac{\$19,796 + \$0 + \$63,175}{\$35,315}$$

$$= 2.35$$

The higher the acid-test ratio, the better able the business is to pay its current liabilities. Winpak's ratio is 2.35, showing excellent liquidity.

What is an acceptable acid-test ratio value? In general, an acid-test ratio of 1.00 is considered safe. However, the answer depends on the industry. Automobile dealers can operate smoothly with an acid-test ratio of 0.20. Several things make this possible: In particular, car dealers have almost no current receivables. The acid-test ratio for most department stores clusters about 0.80, while travel agencies average 1.10.

Days' Sales in Receivables

After a business makes a credit sale, the next critical event in the business cycle is collection of the receivable. Several financial ratios centre on receivables. **Days' sales in receivables**, also called *days sales uncollected* or the **collection period**, indicates how many days it takes to collect the average level of receivables. The shorter the collection period, the more quickly the organization has cash to use for operations. The longer the collection period, the less cash is available to pay bills and expand. Days' sales in receivables can be computed in two steps, as follows:

1. $$\text{One day's sales} = \frac{\text{Net sales}}{365 \text{ days}}$$

2. $$\begin{array}{l}\text{Days' sales in} \\ \text{average accounts} \\ \text{receivable}\end{array} = \frac{\text{Average net accounts receivable}}{\text{One day's sales}} = \frac{\text{(Beginning net receivables + Ending net receivables)/2}}{\text{One day's sales}}$$

For Winpak Ltd. (Exhibit 9–5) (Dollar amounts in thousands):

1. $$\text{One day's sales} = \frac{\$512,037^*}{365} = \$1,403 \text{ per day}$$

2. $$\begin{array}{l}\text{Days' sales in} \\ \text{average net accounts} \\ \text{receivable}\end{array} = \frac{(\$63,175 + \$57,308)/2}{\$1,403} = 42.9 \text{ days}$$

---

*Taken from Winpak's 2007 income statement, not reproduced here.

On average, it takes Winpak Ltd. about 43 days to collect its accounts receivable. The length of the collection period depends on the credit terms of the sale. For example, sales on net 30 terms should be collected within approximately 30 days. When there is a discount, such as 2/10, net 30, the collection period may be shorter. Terms of net 45 result in a longer collection period.

A company should watch its collection period closely. Whenever the collection period lengthens, the business must find other sources of financing, such as borrowing. During recessions, customers pay more slowly, and a longer collection period may be unavoidable.

Investors and creditors do not evaluate a company on the basis of one or two ratios. Instead they analyze all the information available. They then stand back and ask, "What is our overall impression of this company?"

To check your understanding of the material in this Learning Objective, complete these questions. The solutions appear on MyAccountingLab so you can check your progress.

12. Use the data in Exhibit 9–5 to compute Winpak Ltd.'s current ratio at December 31, 2008. Then compare Winpak Ltd.'s current ratio and acid-test ratio. Why is the current ratio higher?

13. Can days' sales in receivables be computed in one step instead of two?

Understanding the Impact of IFRS on Accounts Receivable

One of the factors in Canada deciding to require IFRS for publicly accountable enterprises in Canada was to make the financial statements more *relevant* for users of an enterprise's financial information. One key aspect to increased relevance is to have more accounts reported at fair value, as opposed to historical cost.

> **OBJECTIVE 8**
> Understand the impact on accounts receivable of international financial reporting standards (IFRS)

The standard setters in Canada, the Accounting Standards Board, had already been moving toward this goal long before the implementation of IFRS. Assets categorized as current, including accounts receivable, are essentially reported at their fair values. How do we know this? We subtract the allowance for doubtful accounts from the gross receivables and show the anticipated amount that a company will be able to collect. Because of this deduction, we are really presenting the account at its estimated collectible amount, or its fair value.

Where the Canadian standard is already substantially the same as the international standard, we say that the standards are converged. This is the case with respect to accounts receivable. There is one presentation difference, which is that the international standard reports the account as "Trade Receivables." In Canada, however, companies will be able to choose whether they wish to use that terminology or stay with the current terminology.

DID YOU GET IT?

MyAccountingLab

To check your understanding of the material in this Learning Objective, complete this question. The solution appears on MyAccountingLab so you can check your progress.

14. In determining how accounts should be presented, accountants are concerned about the values being both relevant and reliable. We discussed "relevance" above. "Reliable" refers to the concept that the value presented can be relied upon to be accurate. Is the accounts receivable value presented on the balance sheet both relevant and reliable under IFRS?

As we conclude this chapter, we return to our opening questions: What are accounts receivable, and why are they important? What are notes receivable, and how is interest computed on notes receivable? How are receivables reported on the balance sheet? Which ratios use receivables to evaluate a company's financial position? These questions were answered throughout this chapter and the Decision Guidelines end this chapter with a summary that shows that accounting for receivables is the same for your own start-up business as it is for Winpak and Canadian Tire.

Decision	Guidelines

Accounts Receivable

How much of our receivables will we collect?

Less than the full amount of the receivables because we cannot collect from some customers.

How do we report receivables at their net realizable value?

1. Use the *allowance method* to account for uncollectible receivables. Set up the Allowance for Doubtful Accounts.
2. Estimate uncollectibles by the
   a. *Percent-of-sales method* (income-statement approach) (page 455)
   b. *Aging-of-accounts-receivable method* (balance-sheet approach) (page 456)
   c. *Percent-of-accounts-receivable method* (balance-sheet approach) (page 458)
3. Write off uncollectible receivables as they prove uncollectible.
4. $\dfrac{\text{Net accounts}}{\text{receivable}} = \dfrac{\text{Accounts}}{\text{Receivable}} - \dfrac{\text{Allowance for}}{\text{Doubtful Accounts}}$

Is there a simple way to account for uncollectible receivables?

Yes, but it is unacceptable for most companies.
The *direct write-off method* uses no Allowance for Doubtful Accounts and thus reports receivables at their full amount. Under this method, simply debit Bad-Debt Expense and credit the customer's account. This method is acceptable only when uncollectibles are insignificant.

Notes Receivable

What two other accounts are related to notes receivable?

Notes receivable are related to:
- *Interest Revenue*
- *Interest Receivable* (interest revenue earned but not collected)

How do we compute the interest on a note receivable?

Amount of interest = Principal × Interest rate × Time

Receivables in General

How can we use receivables to evaluate a company's financial position?

- Acid-test ratio $= \dfrac{\text{Cash} + \text{Short-term investments} + \text{Net current receivables}}{\text{Total current liabilities}}$

- $\dfrac{\text{Days' sales in average}}{\text{accounts receivable}} = \dfrac{\text{Average net accounts receivable}}{\text{One day's sales}}$

How do we report receivables on the balance sheet?

Accounts receivable	$XXX
Less: Allowance for doubtful accounts	(X)
Accounts receivable, net	$ XX
Notes receivable	XXX
Other receivables	XXX

Any long-term receivables are listed with the non-current assets.

Summary Problem for Your Review

Suppose Belker Distributors engaged in the following transactions:

2009

Apr. 1 Lent $20,000 to Blatchford Agencies. Received a six-month, 10 percent note.

Oct. 1 Collected the Blatchford Agencies' note at maturity.

Nov. 30 Lent $15,000 to Fane Industries on a three-month, 12 percent note.

Dec. 31 Accrued interest revenue on the Fane Industries note.

2010

Feb. 28 Collected the Fane Industries note at maturity.

Belker Distributors' accounting period ends on December 31.

Required

Explanations are not needed.

1. Record the 2009 transactions on April 1, October 1, and November 30 on Belker Distributors' books.
2. Make the adjusting entry needed on December 31, 2009.
3. Record the February 28, 2010, collection of the Fane Industries note.

Name: Belker Distributors
Industry: Retailer
Accounting Period: Years ended December 31, 2009 and 2010

SOLUTION

Requirement 1

2009

Apr. 1	Note Receivable—Blatchford Agencies........	20,000	
	Cash..		20,000
Oct. 1	Cash...	21,000	
	Note Receivable—Blatchford Agencies....		20,000
	Interest Revenue ($20,000 × 0.10 × $^{6}/_{12}$)....		1,000
Nov. 30	Note Receivable—Fane Industries	15,000	
	Cash..		15,000

The Blatchford Agencies' note receivable is for six *months*, so calculate interest based on 12 months in a year (not 365 days in a year).

Requirement 2

Adjusting Entry

2009

Dec. 31	Interest Receivable	150	
	Interest Revenue...		150

Interest receivable is $150 ($15,000 × 0.12 × $^{1}/_{12}$).

The Fane Industries' note receivable is for three *months*, so calculate accrued interest on December 31, 2009 based on 12 months in a year.

Requirement 3

2010

Feb. 28	Cash..	15,450	
	Note Receivable—Fane Industries		15,000
	Interest Receivable		150
	Interest Revenue...		300

Interest revenue is $300 ($15,000 × 0.12 × $^{2}/_{12}$).
Cash is $15,450 [$15,000 + ($15,000 × 0.12 × $^{3}/_{12}$)].

Calculate interest based on 12 *months* in a year (not 365 days in a year).

CHAPTER 9 APPENDIX

Discounting (Selling) a Note Receivable

A payee of a note receivable may need cash before the maturity date of the note. When this occurs, the payee may sell the note, a practice called **discounting a note receivable.** The price to be received for the note is determined by present-value concepts. We discuss these concepts in detail in Chapter 15. But the transaction between the seller and the buyer of the note can take any form agreeable to the two parties. Here we illustrate one procedure used for discounting short-term notes receivable. To receive cash immediately, the seller is willing to accept a lower price than the note's maturity value.

To illustrate, suppose EMCO Ltd. lent $15,000 to Dartmouth Builders on October 20, 2009. The maturity date of the 90-day, 10 percent Dartmouth note is January 18, 2010. Suppose EMCO discounts the Dartmouth Builders note at the National Bank on December 9, 2009, when the note is 50 days old. The bank applies a 12 percent annual interest rate in computing the discounted value of the note.

The bank will use a discount rate that is higher than the interest rate on the note in order to earn some interest on the transaction. EMCO may be willing to accept this higher rate in order to get cash quickly. The discounted value, called the *proceeds,* is the amount EMCO receives from the bank. The proceeds can be computed in five steps, as shown in Exhibit 9–1A. At maturity the bank collects $15,370 from the maker of the note and earns $202 interest revenue from holding the note.

EXHIBIT 9–1A   Discounting (Selling) a Note Receivable: EMCO Ltd. Discounts the Dartmouth Builders Note

Step	Computation	
1. Compute the original amount of interest of the note receivable.	$15,000 × 0.10 × 90/365	= $ 370
2. Maturity value of note = Principal + Interest	$15,000 + $370	= $15,370
3. Determine the period (number of days, months, or years) the bank will hold the note (the discount period).	Dec. 9, 2009, to Jan. 18, 2010	= 40 days
4. Compute the bank's discount on the note. This is the bank's interest revenue from holding the note.	$15,370 × 0.12 × 40/365	= $ 202
5. Seller's proceeds from discounting the note receivable* = Maturity value of note – Bank's discount on the note	$15,370 – $202	= $15,168

*(Buyer's cost of purchasing)
The authors thank Doug Hamilton for suggesting this exhibit.

KEY POINT

Just as a company can sell a note receivable, a company can also sell accounts receivable for less than full value to receive cash right away. Also, accounts receivable can be pledged as security for a loan, and this fact must be disclosed in the financial statements.

EMCO Ltd.'s entry to record discounting (selling) the note on December 9, 2009, based on the calculations in Exhibit 9–1A, is

2009			
Dec. 9	Cash...	15,168	
	Note Receivable—Dartmouth Builders		15,000
	Interest Revenue		168
	To record discounting a note receivable.		

When the proceeds from discounting a note receivable are less than the principal amount of the note, the payee records a debit to Interest Expense for the amount of the difference. For example, EMCO could discount the note receivable for cash proceeds of $14,980. The entry to record this transaction would be

2009			
Dec. 9	Cash..	14,980	
	Interest Expense	20	
	Note Receivable—Dartmouth Builders		15,000

In the discounting of the note receivable just described, interest revenue accrued from the original date of the note (October 20, 2009) to the date of discounting (December 9, 2009). Since the amount is not material, we will recognize this fact but disregard the interest revenue here.

DID YOU GET IT?

MyAccountingLab

To check your understanding of the material in this Learning Objective, complete this question. The solution appears on MyAccountingLab so you can check your progress.

15. If a 60-day note dated April 16 is discounted on May 2, what is the discount period?

Summary

1. **Define common types of receivables, and design internal controls for receivables.** A *receivable* arises when a business (or person) sells goods or services to another party on credit. The receivable is the seller's claim for the amount of the transaction. A receivable also arises when one person lends money to another. Each credit transaction involves two parties: the *creditor*, who sells something and obtains a receivable, which is an asset, and the *debtor*, who makes the purchase and has a payable, which is a liability. Companies that sell on credit receive most customer collections in the mail. Good *internal control* over mailed-in cash receipts means separating cash-handling duties from cash-accounting duties.

2. **Use the allowance method to account for uncollectibles, and estimate uncollectibles by the percent-of-sales, aging-of-accounts-receivable, and the percent-of-accounts-receivable methods.** Uncollectible receivables are accounted for by the allowance method or the direct write-off method. The *allowance method* matches expenses to sales revenue and also results in a more realistic measure of net accounts receivable. The *percent-of-sales method*, the *aging-of-accounts-receivable method*, and the *percent-of-accounts-receivable method* are the main approaches to estimating bad debts under the allowance method.

3. **Explain the direct write-off method to account for uncollectibles.** The *direct write-off method* is easy to apply, but it fails to match the bad-debt expense to the corresponding sales revenue. Also, Accounts Receivable are reported at their full amount, which is misleading because it suggests that the company expects to collect all its accounts receivable.

4. **Account for credit-card and debit-card sales.** When customers pay for their purchases using a *credit card*, the credit-card company pays the vendor and collects from the customer. Bank credit cards, such as VISA and MasterCard, reimburse a vendor as soon as receipts are deposited in the bank. Non-bank credit cards, such as American Express, reimburse vendors at a later date, creating a receivable for the vendor until payment is received from the credit-card company. When a customer pays with a *debit card*, the issuer (usually a financial institution) removes the amount of the purchase from the customer's bank account and puts it into the vendor's account. As with bank credit cards, there is no receivable for the vendor when a customer uses a debit card to pay for purchases.

5. **Account for notes receivable.** *Notes receivable* are formal credit agreements. Interest earned by the creditor is computed by multiplying the note's principal amount by the interest rate times the length of the interest period.

6. **Report receivables on the balance sheet.** All accounts receivable, notes receivable, and allowance accounts appear in the balance sheet. However, companies use various formats and terms to report these assets.

7. **Use the acid-test ratio and days' sales in receivables to evaluate a company.** The *acid-test ratio* measures the ability to pay current liabilities from the most liquid current assets. *Days' sales in receivables* indicates how long it takes to collect the average level of receivables.

8. **Understand the impact on accounts receivable of international financial reporting standards (IFRS).** For accounts receivable, Canadian GAAP for private enterprises are substantially the same as IFRS. There is one presentation difference—IFRS report Accounts Receivable as "Trade Receivables." However, Canadian companies can choose to use either term.

A1. **Discount a note receivable.** The payee of a note receivable will sometimes discount, or sell, the note to a bank or other third party before the maturity date of the note. One method of calculating the proceeds appears in Exhibit 9–1A on page 474.

SELF-STUDY QUESTIONS

Test your understanding of the chapter by marking the correct answer for each of the following questions:

1. The party that holds a receivable is called the (*p. 451*)
   a. Creditor
   b. Debtor
   c. Maker
   d. Security holder

2. A critical element of internal control over cash receipts is (*p. 452*)
   a. Assigning an honest employee the responsibility for handling cash
   b. Separating the cash-handling and cash-accounting duties
   c. Ensuring that cash is deposited in the bank daily
   d. Centralizing the opening of incoming mail in a single location

3. The function of the credit department is to (*p. 453*)
   a. Collect accounts receivable from customers
   b. Report bad credit risks to other companies
   c. Evaluate customers who apply for credit
   d. Write off uncollectible accounts receivable

4. Keady Marina made the following general journal entry related to uncollectibles:

   Bad-Debt Expense 700
       Allowance for Doubtful Accounts....   700

   The purpose of this entry is to (*pp. 455–458*)
   a. Write off uncollectibles
   b. Close the expense account
   c. Age the accounts receivable
   d. Record bad-debt expense

5. The credit balance in Allowance for Doubtful Accounts is $12,600 prior to the adjusting entries at the end of the period. The aging of the accounts indicates that an allowance of $81,200 is needed. The amount of expense to record is (*pp. 455–458*)
   a. $12,600
   b. $68,600
   c. $81,200
   d. $93,800

6. Keady Marina also made this general journal entry:

   Allowance for Doubtful Accounts......... 1,800
       Accounts Receivable (detailed).........   1,800

   The purpose of this entry is to (*p. 459*)
   a. Write off uncollectibles
   b. Close the expense account
   c. Age the accounts receivable
   d. Record bad-debt expense

7. Keady Marina also made this general journal entry:

   Accounts Receivable (detailed)..............   640
       Allowance for Doubtful Accounts.....   640

   The purpose of this entry is to (*p. 460–461*)
   a. Write off uncollectibles
   b. Close the expense account
   c. Reverse the write-off of receivables
   d. Record bad-debt expense

8. A six-month, $40,000 note specifies interest of 8 percent. The full amount of interest on this note will be (*p. 465*)
   a. $400
   b. $800
   c. $1,600
   d. $3,200

9. The note in Self-Study Question 8 was issued on August 31, and the company's accounting year ends on December 31. The year-end balance sheet will report interest receivable of (*pp. 466–467*)
   a. $533
   b. $1,067
   c. $1,600
   d. $3,200

10. The best acid-test ratio among the following is (*p. 470*)
    a. 0.10
    b. 0.80
    c. 1.0
    d. 1.2

Answers to Self-Study Questions

1. a   5. b ($81,200 − $12,600 = $68,600)
2. b   6. a
3. c   7. c
4. d

8. c ($40,000 × 0.08 × $^6/_{12}$ = $1,600)
9. b ($40,000 × 0.08 × $^4/_{12}$ = $1,067)
10. d

ACCOUNTING VOCABULARY

Acid-test ratio   *(p. 469)*
Aging-of-accounts-receivable method   *(p. 456)*
Allowance for Doubtful Accounts   *(p. 455)*
Allowance for Uncollectible Accounts   *(p. 455)*
Allowance method   *(p. 455)*
Bad-debt expense   *(p. 454)*
Balance-sheet approach   *(p. 456)*
Collection period   *(p. 470)*
Creditor   *(pp. 451, 464)*
Days' sales in receivables   *(p. 470)*
Debtor   *(pp. 451, 464)*
Default on a note   *(p. 467)*
Direct write-off method   *(p. 460)*
Discounting a note receivable   *(p. 474)*
Dishonour a note   *(p. 467)*
Doubtful-account expense   *(p. 454)*
Due date   *(p. 464)*

Income-statement approach   *(p. 455)*
Interest   *(p. 464)*
Interest period   *(p. 464)*
Interest rate   *(p. 464)*
Maker of a note   *(p. 464)*
Maturity date   *(p. 464)*
Maturity value   *(p. 464)*
Note term   *(p. 464)*
Payee of a note   *(p. 464)*
Percent-of-accounts-receivable method   *(p. 458)*
Percent-of-sales method   *(p. 455)*
Principal   *(p. 464)*
Promissory note   *(p. 464)*
Quick ratio   *(p. 469)*
Receivable   *(p. 451)*
Time period   *(p. 464)*
Uncollectible-account expense   *(p. 454)*

SIMILAR ACCOUNTING TERMS

Acid-test ratio	Quick ratio
Aging-of-accounts-receivable method (of estimating uncollectibles)	Balance-sheet approach (of estimating uncollectibles)
Allowance for Doubtful Accounts	Allowance for Uncollectible Accounts; Allowance for Bad Debts
Bad-debt expense	Uncollectible-account expense; Doubtful-account expense
Days' sales in receivables	Collection period
Dishonour a note	Default on a note
Interest period	Note period; Note term; Time
Maturity date	Due date
Percent-of-Accounts-Receivable Method (of estimating uncollectibles)	Balance-sheet approach (of estimating uncollectibles)
Percent-of-Sales Method (of estimating uncollectibles)	Income-statement approach (of estimating uncollectibles)

Assignment Material

QUESTIONS

1. Name the two parties to a receivable/payable transaction. Which party has the receivable? Which has the payable? The asset? The liability?

2. List three categories of receivables. State how each category is classified for reporting on the balance sheet.

3. Many businesses receive most of their cash on credit sales through the mail. Suppose you own a business so large that you must hire employees to handle cash receipts and perform the related accounting duties. What internal control feature should you use to ensure that cash received from customers is not taken by a dishonest employee?

4. What duty must be withheld from a company's credit department in order to safeguard cash? If the credit department does this job, what can a dishonest credit department employee do?

5. Name the two methods of accounting for uncollectible receivables. Which method is easier to apply? Which method is consistent with GAAP?

6. Which of the two methods of accounting for uncollectible accounts—the allowance method or the direct write-off method—is preferable? Why?

7. Identify the accounts debited and credited to account for uncollectibles under (a) the allowance method, and (b) the direct write-off method.

8. What is another name for Allowance for Doubtful Accounts? What are two other names for Bad-Debt Expense?

9. Which entry decreases net income under the allowance method of accounting for uncollectibles: the entry to record bad-debt expense, or the entry to write off an uncollectible account receivable?

10. Identify and briefly describe the three ways to estimate bad-debt expense and uncollectible accounts.

11. Briefly describe how a company may use both the percent-of-sales method and aging-of-accounts-receivable method (or the percent-of-accounts-receivable method) to account for uncollectibles.

12. How does a credit balance arise in a customer's account receivable? How does the company report this credit balance on its balance sheet?

13. Show three ways to report Accounts Receivable of $100,000 and Allowance for Doubtful Accounts of $2,800 on the balance sheet or in the related notes.

14. What are the benefits of credit-card sales to a retailer? What is the cost to the retailer? How is the cost of a credit-card sale recorded?

15. Use the terms *maker, payee, principal, maturity date, promissory note,* and *interest* in an appropriate sentence or two describing a note receivable.

16. Name three situations in which a company might receive a note receivable. For each situation, show the account debited and the account credited to record receipt of the note.

17. For each of the following notes receivable, compute the amount of interest revenue earned during 2009:

	Principal	Interest rate	Interest period	Maturity date
a. Note #1	$ 10,000	3%	60 days	Nov. 30, 2009
b. Note #2	50,000	7	3 months	Sept. 30, 2009
c. Note #3	100,000	5	½ year	Dec. 31, 2009
d. Note #4	15,000	9	90 days	Jan. 15, 2010

18. When the maker of a note dishonours the note at maturity, what accounts does the payee debit and credit?

19. Why does the payee of a note receivable usually need to make adjusting entries for interest at the end of the accounting period?

20. Whitehorse Hardware has a policy of charging 2 percent interest on overdue (past 60 days) accounts receivable. Northern Cabinets has declared bankruptcy, and it is unlikely that full payment on this account will be collected. Should Whitehorse charge additional interest on the Northern Cabinets account receivable?

21. Why is the acid-test ratio a more stringent measure of the ability to pay current liabilities than is the current ratio?

22. Which measure of days' sales in receivables is preferable, 30 or 40? Give your reason.

*23. Why would a payee sell a note receivable before its maturity date?

STARTERS

MyAccountingLab | All questions in this section appear in MyAccountingLab.

Applying the allowance method (percent-of-sales) to account for uncollectibles

2. Accounts Receivable, net $66,000

Starter 9–1 During its first year of operations, Spring Break Travel earned revenue of $700,000 on account. Industry experience suggests that Spring Break's bad debts will amount to 2 percent of revenues. At December 31, 2009, accounts receivable total $80,000. The company uses the allowance method to account for uncollectibles.

1. Journalize Spring Break Travel's bad-debt expense using the percent-of-sales method.

2. Show how Spring Break should report accounts receivable on its balance sheet at December 31, 2009.

Applying the allowance method (percent-of-sales) to account for uncollectibles

(2)

4. Bad-Debt Expense $16,000

Starter 9–2 This exercise continues the situation of Starter 9–1, in which Spring Break Travel ended 2009 with Accounts Receivable at $80,000 and Allowance for Doubtful Accounts at $14,000.

During 2010, Spring Break Travel completed these transactions:

1. Service revenue on account, $800,000 (assume no cost of goods sold).

2. Collections on account, $840,000.

3. Write-offs of uncollectibles, $12,000.

4. Bad-debt expense, 2 percent of service revenue.

Journalize Spring Break Travel's 2010 transactions.

---

* This Question covers Chapter 9 Appendix topics.

Starter 9–3 Granite Importers Inc. had the following balances at December 31, 2010, before the year-end adjustments:

Applying the allowance method (aging-of-accounts and percent-of-accounts-receivable) to account for uncollectibles

1. Bad-Debt Expense $400

Accounts Receivable	Allowance for Doubtful Accounts
148,000	4,000

The aging of accounts receivable yields these data:

	Age of Accounts Receivable		
	0–60 Days	Over 60 Days	Total Receivables
Accounts receivable	$140,000	$8,000	$148,000
Percent uncollectible	× 2%	× 20%	

1. Journalize Granite Importers Inc.'s entry to adjust the allowance account to its correct balance at December 31, 2010.
2. Prepare the T-account for Allowance for Doubtful Accounts.
3. Repeat question 1 assuming that, instead of aging the accounts, the allowance is calculated as 3 percent of the accounts-receivable balance.

Starter 9–4 Diane Libbey is a lawyer in Vancouver. She uses the direct write-off method to account for uncollectible receivables.

Applying the direct write-off method to account for uncollectibles

1. Bad-Debt Expense $4,000

At May 31, Libbey's accounts receivable totalled $28,000. During June, she earned revenue of $40,000 on account and collected $38,000 on account. She also wrote off uncollectible receivables of $4,000.

1. Use the direct write-off method to journalize Libbey's write-off of the uncollectible receivables.
2. What is Libbey's balance of Accounts Receivable at June 30? Does she expect to collect the full amount? Explain.

Starter 9–5 University Cycle Shop had trouble collecting its account receivable from Matt Wilson. On January 19, University finally wrote off Wilson's $1,200 account receivable. University turned the account over to a lawyer, who pursued Wilson for payment for the rest of the year. On December 31, Wilson sent a $1,200 cheque to University Cycle Shop with a note that said, "Here's your money. Please call off your bloodhound!"

Collecting a receivable previously written off

Journalize for University Cycle Shop:

Jan. 19 Write-off of Wilson's account against Allowance for Doubtful Accounts.
Dec. 31 Reinstatement of Wilson's account.
   31 Collection of cash from Wilson.

Starter 9–6 Gas stations do a large volume of business by customer credit cards and debit cards. Suppose a Petro-Canada station had these transactions on a Saturday in July:

Recording credit-card and debit-card sales

Debit cards, Cash $15,760

VISA credit-card sales	$20,000
Non-bank credit-card sales	5,000
Debit-card sales	16,000

Suppose VISA charges merchants 2 percent, non-bank credit-card companies charge 3.5 percent, and the bank charges 1.5 percent for debit card transactions. Record these sale transactions for the Petro-Canada station.

Starter 9–7 For each of the following notes receivable, compute the amount of interest revenue earned during 2010. Use a 365-day year where applicable, and round to the nearest dollar.

Computing interest amounts on notes receivable

Note #1 $8,000

	Principal	Interest Rate	Interest Period During 2010
Note 1	$200,000	8%	6 months
Note 2	30,000	12	75 days
Note 3	20,000	9	60 days
Note 4	100,000	10	3 months

Accounting for a note receivable

b. Debit Cash $203,945

Starter 9–8 Royal Bank lent $200,000 to Johann Schroeder on a 90-day, 8 percent note. Record the following transactions for Royal Bank, rounding to the nearest dollar (explanations are not required):

a. Lending the money on May 6.

b. Collecting the principal and interest at maturity. Specify the date. For the computation of interest, use a 365-day year.

Using the acid-test ratio and days' sales in receivables to evaluate a company

a. 1.01

Starter 9–9 Vision Electronics, which makes DVD players, reported the following items at February 28, 2010 (amounts in thousands, with last year's—2009— amounts also given as needed):

Accounts Payable.................... $ 898	Accounts Receivable, net:	
Cash... 430	February 28, 2010 .... $ 440	
Inventories:		
February 28, 2009 300		
February 28, 2010 380	Cost of Goods Sold 2,400	
February 28, 2009................. 320	Short-term investments........... 330	
Net sales revenue.................... 3,860	Other current assets............... 180	
Long-term assets 820	Other current liabilities.......... 290	
Long-term liabilities 20		

Compute Vision Electronics' (a) acid-test ratio, and (b) days' sales in average receivables for 2010. Evaluate each ratio value as strong or weak. Assume Vision Electronics sells on terms of net 30.

Computing key ratios for a company

a. 1.48

Starter 9–10 Use the data in Starter 9–9 to compute the following 2010 ratios for Vision Electronics:

a. Current ratio

b. Debt ratio

c. Gross margin percentage

d. Rate of inventory turnover

EXERCISES

MyAccountingLab All questions in this section appear in MyAccountingLab.

Exercise 9–1

Identifying and correcting an internal control weakness

Suppose McCain Foods, the Canadian food products company, is opening a district office in Fredericton, New Brunswick. Sylvester Heath, the office manager, is designing the internal control system for the office. Heath proposes the following procedures for credit checks on new customers, sales on account, cash collections, and write-offs of uncollectible receivables:

• The credit department will run a credit check on all customers who apply for credit.

• Sales on account are the responsibility of McCain's salespersons. Credit sales above $50,000 (which is a reasonable limit) require the approval of the sales manager.

• Cash receipts come into the credit department, which separates the cash received from the customer remittance slips. The credit department lists all cash receipts by the name of the customer and the amount of cash received. The cash goes to the treasurer for deposit in the bank. The remittance slips go to the accounting department for posting to individual customer accounts in the accounts receivable subsidiary ledger. Each day's listing of cash receipts goes to the controller for her end-of-day comparison with the daily deposit slip and the day's listing of the total dollar amount posted to customer accounts from the accounting department. The three amounts must agree.

• The credit department reviews customer accounts receivable monthly. Late-paying customers are notified that their accounts are past due. After 90 days, the credit department turns over past-due accounts to a lawyer or collection agency for collection. After 180 days, the credit department writes off a customer account as uncollectible.

Identify the internal control weakness in this situation, and propose a way to strengthen the controls.

Exercise 9–2

Using the allowance (percent-of sales) method for bad debts

On February 28, Big Mountain Ski Equipment had a $25,500 debit balance in Accounts Receivable. During March, the company had sales of $65,500, which included $58,000 in credit sales. March collections were $53,000, and write-offs of uncollectible receivables totalled $1,250. Other data include:

a. February 28 credit balance in Allowance for Doubtful Accounts is $1,300.

b. Bad-debt expense is estimated as 2 percent of credit sales.

Required

1. Prepare journal entries to record sales, collections, write-offs of uncollectibles during March, and bad-debt expense by the allowance method (using the percent-of-sales method).

2. Prepare T-accounts to show the ending balances in Accounts Receivable and Allowance for Doubtful Accounts. Compute *net* Accounts Receivable at March 31. How much does Big Mountain expect to collect?

2. Accounts Receivable,
net $28,040

Exercise 9–3

At December 31, 2010, the Accounts Receivable balance of Stenner's Electronics is $600,000. The allowance for doubtful accounts has a $17,800 credit balance. Accountants for Stenner's Electronics prepare the following aging schedule for its accounts receivable:

Excel Spreadsheet Template

Using the aging approach to estimate bad debts and reporting receivables on the balance sheet

2. Accounts Receivable,
net $577,000

Accounts Receivable	Age of Accounts			
	1–30 Days	31–60 Days	61–90 Days	Over 90 Days
$600,000	$280,000	$160,000	$140,000	$20,000
Estimated percent uncollectible	0.5%	2.0%	6.0%	50.0%

Required

1. Journalize the adjusting entry for doubtful accounts based on the aging schedule. Show the T-account for the allowance at December 31, 2010.

2. Show how Stenner's Electronics will report Accounts Receivable on its December 31, 2010, balance sheet.

3. Suppose all the facts of this situation are the same except that Allowance for Doubtful Accounts has a $1,800 debit balance. Calculate the amount of the adjusting entry.

Exercise 9–4

Alliksaar Landscaping Services started the year 2010 with an Accounts Receivable balance of $38,500 and an Allowance for Doubtful Accounts balance of $2,310. During the year, $4,290 of accounts receivable were identified as uncollectible. Sales Revenue for 2010 was $429,000, including credit sales of $422,400. Cash collections on account were $413,600 during the year.
The aging of accounts receivable yields these data:

Using the allowance method to account for uncollectibles

5. Accounts receivable,
net $40,260

	Age of Accounts				
	0–30 Days	31–60 Days	61–90 Days	Over 90 Days	Total Receivables
Amount of receivable	$26,400	$6,600	$5,500	$4,510	$43,010
Percent uncollectible	× 1%	× 1%	× 3%	× 50%	

You're the accountant preparing the December 31, 2010, year-end entries.

Required

1. Journalize Alliksaar's (a) credit sales, (b) cash collections on account, (c) write-off of the accounts receivable identified as uncollectible, and (d) bad-debt expense based on 1 percent of credit sales.

2. Prepare a T-account for the Accounts Receivable and Allowance for Doubtful Accounts accounts.

3. Calculate the balance in the Allowance for Doubtful Accounts based on the aging-of-accounts-receivable method.

4. Make any adjustment required to the Allowance for Doubtful Accounts based on your calculation in Requirement 3.

5. Show how Alliksaar Landscaping Services should report Accounts Receivable on the balance sheet.

Exercise 9–5

Sales, write-offs, and
bad-debt recovery

High Performance Cell Phones sold $40,000 of merchandise to Brodie Trucking Company on account. Brodie paid only $28,000 of the account receivable. After repeated attempts to collect, High Performance finally wrote off its accounts receivable from Brodie. Six months later, High Performance received Brodie's cheque for $12,000 with a note apologizing for the late payment.

Journalize the following for High Performance Cell Phones:

a. Sale on account, $40,000 (ignore cost of goods sold).

b. Collection of $28,000 on account.

c. Write-off of the remaining portion of the Brodie account receivable. High Performance uses the allowance method for uncollectibles.

d. Reinstatement of Brodie's account receivable.

e. Collection in full from Brodie, $12,000.

Exercise 9–6

Using the direct write-off
method for bad debts

2. Accounts Receivable,
ending bal. $29,250

Refer to the situation of Exercise 9–2.

Required

1. Record bad-debt expense for February by the direct write-off method.

2. What amount of net Accounts Receivable would Big Mountain Ski Equipment report on its February 28 balance sheet under the direct write-off method? Does Big Mountain Ski Equipment expect to collect this much of the receivable? Give your reason.

Exercise 9–7

Contrasting the allowance
method and the direct
write-off method to
account for uncollectibles

a. Bad-Debt Expense $6,000

Return to the example of accounting for uncollectibles that begins under the heading "Writing Off Uncollectible Accounts" on page 459. Suppose past experience indicates that the company will fail to collect 2 percent of net credit sales, which totalled $300,000 during the three-month period January through March of 2010.

Record bad-debt expense for the three-month period January through March under

a. The allowance method.

b. The direct write-off method (You need not identify individual customer accounts. Use the data given for Auger and Kirsh on page 461.)

Which method of accounting for uncollectibles is better? What makes this preferred method better? Mention accounting principles in your answer.

Exercise 9–8

Recording notes receivable and
accruing interest revenue

Nov. 30 Interest
Revenue $159.70

Record the following transactions in the journal of Seaview Properties, which ends its accounting year on November 30:

Oct.	1	Lent $44,000 cash to Joe Lazarus on a one-year, 2 percent note.
Nov.	3	Sold goods to Highwater Inc., receiving a 100-day, 4 percent note for $3,162.50.
	16	Received a $2,200, six-month, 4 percent note on account from STM Inc.
	30	Accrued interest revenue on all notes receivable.

Exercise 9–9

Accounting for debit-card sales
and notes receivables

Apr. 1, 2010 Cash $11,440

Record the following transactions in the general journal of Joe's Plumbing Store. Assume Scotiabank charges merchants $0.50 per debit-card transaction and MasterCard charges 3 percent of sales as service fees.

2009

Mar.	31	Recorded Scotiabank debit-card sales of $22,000, consisting of 1,500 transactions.
	31	Recorded MasterCard credit-card sales of $33,000.
Apr.	1	Lent $11,000 to Sam Brown on a one-year, 4 percent note.
Dec.	31	Accrued interest revenue on the Brown note.

2010

| Apr. | 1 | Received the maturity value of the note from Brown. |

Exercise 9–10

Franklin Ltd., a gift store, reported the following amounts in its 2010 financial statements. The 2009 figures are given for comparison.

Evaluating ratio data
⑦
1. 2010, 0.76

	2010		2009	
Current assets:				
Cash...		$ 6,000		$ 20,000
Short-term investments		46,000		22,000
Accounts receivable	$120,000		$148,000	
Less:				
Allowance for uncollectibles ..	14,000	106,000	12,000	136,000
Inventory		384,000		378,000
Prepaid insurance.........................		4,000		4,000
Total current assets		$ 546,000		$ 560,000
Total current liabilities....................		$ 208,000		$ 214,000
Net sales...		$1,460,000		$1,464,000

Required

1. Determine whether Franklin Ltd.'s acid-test ratio improved or deteriorated from 2009 to 2010. How does Franklin Ltd.'s acid-test ratio compare with the industry average of 0.90?

2. Compare the days' sales in receivables measure for 2010 with the company's credit terms of net 30. What action, if any, should Franklin Ltd. take?

Exercise 9–11

Swift Media Sign Company sells on account. Recently, Swift reported these figures:

Collection period for receivables
⑦
1. 25 days

	2010	2009
Net sales	$1,200,120	$1,140,000
Receivables at year end	85,600	76,400

Required

1. Compute Swift Media Sign Company's days' sales in average receivables for 2010.

2. Suppose Swift's normal credit terms for a sale on account are "2/10, net 30." How well does Swift's collection period compare to the company's credit terms? Is this good or bad for Swift? Explain.

*Exercise 9–12

Major Corporation installs switching systems and receives its pay in the form of notes receivable. It installed a system for the city of Brandon, Manitoba, receiving a nine-month, 10 percent, $400,000 note receivable on May 31, 2010. To obtain cash quickly, Major discounted the note with HSBC on June 30, 2010. The bank charged a discount rate of 11 percent.

Discounting a note receivable

Cash proceeds $398,467

Compute Major Corporation's cash proceeds from discounting the note. Follow the five-step procedure outlined in Exhibit 9–1A. Round to the nearest dollar.

*Exercise 9–13

Use your answers to Exercise 9–12 to journalize Major Corporation's transactions as follows (round to the nearest dollar):

Accounting for notes receivable, including a discounted note

Jun. 30 debit to Cash $398,467

May 31   Sold a telecommunications system, receiving a 9-month, 10 percent, $400,000 note from the city of Brandon. Major Corporation's cost of the system was $262,500.

Jun. 30   Received cash for interest revenue for one month.

      30   Discounted the note to HSBC at a discount rate of 11 percent.

---

*These Exercises cover Chapter 9 Appendix topics.

Accounting for notes receivable, including a discounted note

5 A1

Sept. 1 debit to Cash $3,720

Gander Outdoors Store sells on account. When a customer account becomes three months old, Gander Outdoors Store converts the account to a note receivable and immediately discounts the note to a bank. During 2010, Gander Outdoors Store completed these transactions:

May	29	Sold goods on account to Raj Sivak, $4,800.
Sept.	1	Received a $4,000, 60-day, 8 percent note and cash of $800 from Raj Sivak in satisfaction of his past-due account receivable.
	1	Sold the Sivak note by discounting it to a bank for proceeds of $3,720.

Required Record the transactions in Gander Outdoors Store's journal.

SERIAL EXERCISE

This exercise continues the Haupt Consulting situation from Exercise 8–19 of Chapter 8. If you did not complete Exercise 8–19, you can still complete Exercise 9–15 as it is presented.

Exercise 9–15

Applying the allowance (percent-of-sales) method to account for uncollectibles

Feb. 1 Bad Debt Expense $120

It is February 1, 2011. Carl Haupt, owner of Haupt Consulting, has reviewed the receivables list from the January transactions (from Chapter 6, page 328). He has identified that Gene was not going to pay his receivable from January 19. Haupt Consulting uses the allowance method for receivables, estimating uncollectibles to be 3 percent of credit sales.

Required

1. Journalize the entry to record and establish the allowance for doubtful accounts using the percent-of-sales method for January 2011 credit sales.
2. Journalize the entry to record the identification of Gene's bad debt.

CHALLENGE EXERCISE

Exercise 9–16

Evaluating debit-card sales for profitability

Net income with debit cards, $409,250

Current Fashions provides store credit and manages its own receivables. Average experience for the past three years has been as follows:

	Cash	Credit	Total
Sales	$1,040,000	$700,000	$1,740,000
Cost of Goods Sold	624,000	420,000	1,044,000
Bad-Debt Expense	—	38,000	38,000
Other Expenses	145,600	126,000	271,600

Helen Tran, the owner, is considering whether to accept bank credit cards and discontinue providing store credit. Typically, the availability of bank credit cards increases credit sales by 15 percent. But the bank credit-card companies charge approximately 3 percent of credit-card sales. If Tran switches to bank credit cards, she can save $5,000 on accounting and other expenses, and will eliminate bad-debt expense. She figures that cash customers will continue buying in the same volume regardless of the type of credit the store offers.

Required Should Current Fashions start offering bank credit-card service and discontinue providing store credit? Show the computations of net income under the present plan and under the bank credit-card plan.

*This Exercise covers Chapter 9 Appendix topics.

BEYOND THE NUMBERS

Beyond the Numbers 9–1

Beacon Communications' cash flow statement reported the following *cash* receipts and *cash* payments (the amount in brackets) for the year ended August 31, 2010:

Reporting receivables on the balance sheet

Aug. 31, 2010, Accounts Receivable $252,500

BEACON COMMUNICATIONS
Cash Flow Statement
For the Year Ended August 31, 2010

Cash flows from operating activities:	
Cash receipts from customers...	$1,655,000
Interest received..	4,600
Cash flows from investing activities:	
Loans made on notes receivable	(27,500)
Collection of loans on notes receivable...	55,000

Beacon's balance sheet one year earlier—at August 31, 2009—reported Accounts Receivable of $187,500 and Notes Receivable of $41,500. Credit sales for the year ended August 31, 2010, totalled $1,720,000, and the company collects all of its accounts receivable because uncollectibles rarely occur.

Beacon Communications needs a loan, and the manager is preparing the company's balance sheet at August 31, 2010. To complete the balance sheet, the owner needs to know the balances of Accounts Receivable and Notes Receivable at August 31, 2010. Supply the needed information; T-accounts are helpful.

ETHICAL ISSUES

Fast Ed's auto showroom sells cars. Fast Ed's bank requires the company to submit quarterly financial statements in order to keep its line of credit. Notes Receivable and Accounts Receivable are 50 percent of current assets. Therefore, Bad-Debt Expense and Allowance for Doubtful Accounts are important accounts.

Fast Ed's president, Ed Edwards, likes net income to increase in a smooth pattern rather than to increase in some periods and decrease in other periods. To report smoothly increasing net income, Edwards underestimates bad-debt expense in some accounting periods. In other accounting periods, Edwards overestimates the expense. He reasons that the income overstatements roughly offset the income understatements over time.

Required   Is Fast Ed's practice of smoothing income ethical? Give your reasons, mentioning any accounting principles that might be violated.

PROBLEMS (GROUP A)

MyAccountingLab All questions in this section appear in MyAccountingLab.

Problem 9–1A

Lincoln Hockey distributes merchandise to sporting goods stores and hockey shops. All sales are on credit, so virtually all cash receipts arrive in the mail. Business has tripled in the last year, and the owner, Frank Lincoln, has hired an accountant to manage the financial aspect of the business. Lincoln has requested that strong internal controls over cash receipts and receivables be the first priority.

Designing internal controls for receivables

Required   Assume you are Corbin Tao, the new accountant. Write a memo to Frank Lincoln outlining the internal controls you intend to establish for Lincoln Hockey. Assume also that you have two employees in the accounting department and a receptionist who report to you. Use this format for your memo:

Date:	_____
To:	Frank Lincoln
From:	Corbin Tao, Accountant
Re:	Proposed internal controls over cash receipts and receivables

Problem 9–2A

Accounting for uncollectibles by the direct write-off and allowance methods

4. Net Accounts Receivable, allowance method $180,650

On March 31, 2010, Summitt Manufacturing had a $145,000 debit balance in Accounts Receivable. During April, the business had sales revenue of $525,000, which included $495,000 in credit sales. Other data for April include

a. Collections on accounts receivable, $455,000.

b. Write-offs of uncollectible receivables, $2,250.

Required

1. Record bad-debt expense for April by the direct write-off method. Use T-accounts to show all April activity in Accounts Receivable and Bad-Debt Expense.

2. Record bad-debt expense and write-offs of customer accounts for April by the allowance method. Use T-accounts to show all April activity in Accounts Receivable, Allowance for Doubtful Accounts, and Bad-Debt Expense. The March 31 unadjusted balance in Allowance for Doubtful Accounts was $600 (debit). Bad-debt expense was estimated at 1 percent of credit sales.

3. What amount of bad-debt expense would Summitt report on its April income statement under the two methods? Which amount better matches expense with revenue? Give your reason.

4. What amount of *net* accounts receivable would Summitt report on its April 30 balance sheet under the two methods? Which amount is more realistic? Give your reason.

Problem 9–3A

Use the percent-of-sales, aging-of-accounts-receivable, and percent-of-accounts-receivable methods for uncollectibles

3. Accounts Receivable, net in 2010, $317,661

The September 30, 2010, balance sheet of Kaslo Products reports the following:

Accounts Receivable	$310,000
Allowance for Doubtful Accounts (credit balance).................................	9,000

During the last quarter of 2010, Kaslo Products completed the following selected transactions:

Dec. 30   Wrote off the following accounts receivable as uncollectible: Bert Almond, $2,500; Blocked Inc., $2,200; and Small Mall, $1,100.

      31   Recorded bad-debt expense based on the aging of accounts receivable, as follows:

	Age of Accounts			
Accounts Receivable	**1–30 Days**	**31–60 Days**	**61–90 Days**	**Over 90 Days**
Total = $328,500	$179,000	$95,000	$37,500	$17,000
Estimated percent uncollectible	0.1%	0.3%	5.0%	50.0%

Required

1. Record the transactions in the general journal.

2. Open the Allowance for Doubtful Accounts three-column ledger account, and post entries affecting that account. Keep a running balance.

3. Most companies report two-year comparative financial statements. If Kaslo Products' Accounts Receivable balance was $310,000 and the Allowance for Doubtful Accounts stood at $10,000 at December 31, 2009, show how the company will report its accounts receivable in a comparative balance sheet for 2010 and 2009.

4. Suppose, on December 31, the bad-debt expense was based on an estimate of 3 percent of the accounts receivable balance, rather than on the aging of accounts receivable. Record the December 31, 2010, entry for bad-debt expense in the general journal.

Problem 9–4A

Using the percent-of-sales and aging-of-accounts-receivable approaches for uncollectibles

3. Net Accounts Receivable $138,032.50

Rosehill Co. completed the following transactions during 2009 and 2010:

2009

Dec. 31   Estimated that bad-debt expense for the year was 2 percent of credit sales of $385,000 and recorded that amount as expense.

      31   Made the closing entry for bad-debt expense.

2010

Mar.	26	Sold inventory to Mabel Arnold, $6,187.50, on credit terms of 2/10, n/30. Ignore cost of goods sold.
Sept.	15	Wrote off Mabel Arnold's account as uncollectible after repeated efforts to collect from her.
Nov.	10	Received $1,650 from Arnold, along with a letter stating her intention to pay her debt in full within 30 days. Reinstated her account in full.
Dec.	5	Received the balance due from Arnold.
	31	Made a compound entry to write off the following accounts as uncollectible: Curt Major, $2,200; Bernadette Lalonde, $962.50; Ellen Smart, $1,470.
	31	Estimated that bad-debt expense for the year was 1 percent of credit sales of $490,000 and recorded the expense.
	31	Made the closing entry for Bad-Debt Expense.

Required

1. Open three-column general ledger accounts for Allowance for Doubtful Accounts and Bad-Debt Expense. Keep running balances.
2. Record the transactions in the general journal and post to the two ledger accounts.
3. The December 31, 2010, balance of Accounts Receivable is $146,000. Show how Accounts Receivable would be reported at that date.
4. Assume that Rosehill Co. begins aging accounts receivable on December 31, 2010. The balance in Accounts Receivable is $146,000, the credit balance in Allowance for Doubtful Accounts is $7,967.50 (use your calculations from Requirement 3), and the company estimates that $9,900 of its accounts receivable will prove uncollectible.

   a. Make the adjusting entry for uncollectibles.
   b. Show how Accounts Receivable will be reported on the December 31, 2010, balance sheet after this adjusting entry.

Problem 9–5A

A company received the following notes during 2009:

Accounting for notes receivable, including accruing interest revenue

(5)

1. Note (a) $9,090.00

Note	Date	Principal Amount	Interest Rate	Term
(a)	Sept. 30	$ 9,000	4%	3 months
(b)	Nov. 19	12,000	3	60 days
(c)	Dec. 1	15,000	5	1 year
(d)	Dec. 15	20,000	6	2 years

Required

1. Determine the due date and maturity value of each note. Compute the interest for each note. Round all interest amounts to the nearest cent.
2. Journalize a single adjusting entry at December 31, 2009, to record accrued interest revenue on the notes. An explanation is not required.
3. Journalize the collection of principal and interest on note (b). Explanations are not required.
4. Show how these notes will be reported on December 31, 2009.

Problem 9–6A

Record the following selected transactions in the general journal of Fraser Paper Products. Explanations are not required.

Accounting for credit-card sales, notes receivable, dishonoured notes, and accrued interest revenue

(4)(5)

Jan. 20, 2010, debit Cash $18,118.36

2009

Nov.	21	Received an $18,000, 60-day, 4 percent note from Mary Fisher on account.
	30	Recorded VISA credit card sales of $26,000. VISA charges 2.5 percent of sales.
Dec.	31	Made an adjusting entry to accrue interest on the Fisher note.
	31	Made an adjusting entry to record bad-debt expense based on 2 percent of credit sales of $1,950,000.
	31	Made a compound closing entry for Interest Revenue and Bad-Debt Expense (ignore credit-card sales and charges).

2010

Jan.   20   Collected the maturity value of the Fisher note.

Mar.   14   Lent $10,000 cash to Morgan Supplies, receiving a six-month, 5 percent note.

         30   Received a $5,600, 30-day, 10 percent note from Marv Leech on his past-due account receivable.

May   29   Leech dishonoured (failed to pay) his note at maturity; after attempting to collect his note for one month, wrote off the account as uncollectible.

Sept.   14   Collected the maturity value of the Morgan Supplies note.

         30   Wrote off as uncollectible the accounts receivable of Sue Parsons, $3,250 and Mac Gally, $5,200.

Problem 9–7A

Journalizing uncollectible notes receivable and accrued interest revenue

Dec. 31, 2009, debit Bad-Debt Expense $4,350

Assume that Ponoka Tire, a large tire distributor, completed the following selected transactions:

2009

Dec.   1   Sold tires to Select Movers Inc., receiving a $20,000, six-month, 5 percent note. Ignore cost of goods sold.

      31   Made an adjusting entry to accrue interest on the Select Movers note.

      31   Made an adjusting entry to record bad-debt expense based on an aging of accounts receivable. The aging analysis indicates that $28,100 of accounts receivable will not be collected. Prior to this adjustment, the credit balance in Allowance for Doubtful Accounts is $23,750.

2010

Jun.   1   Collected the maturity value of the Select Movers note.

      30   Sold tires for $8,000 on MasterCard. MasterCard charges 1.75 percent.

Jul.   21   Sold merchandise to Marco Donolo, receiving a 45-day, 3 percent note for $5,600. Ignore cost of goods sold.

Sept.   4   Donolo dishonoured (failed to pay) its note at maturity; converted the maturity value of the note to an account receivable.

Nov.   11   Sold merchandise to Solomon Tractor for $4,800, receiving a 120-day 5 percent note. Ignore cost of goods sold.

Dec.   2   Collected in full from Donolo.

      31   Accrued the interest on the Solomon Tractor note.

Required   Record the transactions in the general journal. Explanations are not required. Round interest amounts to the nearest cent.

Problem 9–8A

Excel Spreadsheet Template

Using ratio data to evaluate a company's financial position

⑦

For 2010: a. 1.52

The comparative financial statements of Crane River Company for 2010, 2009, and 2008 included the following selected data:

	2010	2009	2008
		(In thousands)	
Balance Sheet			
Current assets:			
Cash	$ 40	$ 40	$ 20
Short-term investments	140	200	120
Receivables, net	380	300	240
Inventories	840	760	680
Prepaid expenses	60	60	40
Total current assets	$1,460	$1,360	$1,100
Total current liabilities	$ 960	$ 820	$ 760
Income Statement			
Sales revenue	$5,200	$5,000	$3,800

Required

1. Compute these ratios for 2010 and 2009:
   a. Current ratio
   b. Acid-test ratio
   c. Days' sales in receivables

2. Write a memo explaining to Tony Crane, owner of Crane River Company, which ratio values showed improvement from 2009 to 2010 and which ratio values deteriorated. Discuss whether this trend is favourable or unfavourable for the company.

Problem 9–9A

Temporary Personnel started business on January 1, 2009. The company produced monthly financial statements and had total sales of $500,000 (of which $400,000 was on credit) during the first four months.

On April 30, Accounts Receivable had a balance of $236,400 (no accounts have been written off to date), which was made up of the following accounts aged according to the date of the sale:

Using the allowance method of accounting for uncollectibles, estimating uncollectibles using the aging-of-accounts method, reporting receivables on the balance sheet

2. a. Accounts Receivable, net May 31, $259,875

| Customer | | Month of Sale | | |
	January	February	March	April
Target Distributors	$ 3,600	$ 1,000	$ 2,000	$ 1,800
PG Courier	1,000	1,200	3,400	2,400
Parsons Transport	5,000	14,000	8,000	4,000
Nixon & Nixon	2,000	7,400	8,120	28,400
Other Accounts Receivable	23,760	16,360	53,480	49,480
	$35,360	$39,960	$75,000	$86,080

The following accounts receivable transactions took place in May 2009:

May 12 Decided the PG Courier account was uncollectible and wrote it off.
15 Collected $6,600 from Target Distributors for sales made in the first three months.
21 Decided the Parsons Transport account was uncollectible and wrote it off.
24 Collected $2,000 from Nixon & Nixon for sales made in the month of January.
26 Received a cheque from Parsons Transport for $18,200 plus four cheques of $3,200 each, post-dated to June 26, July 26, August 26, and September 26.
31 Total sales in the month were $380,000; 90 percent of these were on credit, and 75 percent of the credit sales were collected in the month.

Required

1. Temporary Personnel has heard that other companies in the industry use the allowance method of accounting for uncollectibles, with many of these estimating the uncollectibles through an aging of accounts receivable.
   a. Journalize the adjustments that would have to be made on April 30 (for the months of January through April), assuming the following estimates of uncollectibles:

Age of Accounts Receivable	Percent Estimated Uncollectible
From current month	3%
From prior month	5
From two months prior	7
From three months prior	20
From four months prior	45

(Round your total estimate to the nearest whole dollar.)

   b. Journalize the transactions of May 2009.
   c. Journalize the month-end adjustment, using the table that appears in requirement 1a.

2. For the method of accounting for the uncollectibles used above, show
   a. The balance sheet presentation of the accounts receivable.
   b. The overall effect of the uncollectibles on the income statement for the months of April and May 2009.

Problem 9–10A

Eastern Supply uses the allowance method in accounting for uncollectible accounts with the estimate based on the aging-of-accounts-receivable method. The company had the following account balances on August 31, 2010:

Accounts Receivable	$1,374,000
Allowance for Doubtful Accounts (credit balance)	145,200

Using the allowance method of accounting for uncollectibles, estimating uncollectibles by the percent-of-sales and the aging-of-accounts-receivable methods, accounting for notes receivable

2. Bad-Debt Expense, debit $97,920

The following transactions took place during September 2010:

Sept.	2	Elbow Inc., which owes $96,000, is unable to pay on time and has given a 25-day, 8 percent note in settlement of the account.
	6	Determined the account receivable from Irma Good ($25,200) was uncollectible and wrote it off.
	9	Received notice that a customer (Tony Goad) has filed for bankruptcy. Goad owes $38,400. The courts will confirm the amount recoverable at a later date.
	11	Determined the account receivable from Kay Walsh ($18,240) was uncollectible and wrote it off.
	15	Irma Good, whose account was written off on September 6, has paid $18,000 on the account and promises to pay the balance in 30 days.
	18	Received a cheque from the courts in the amount of $30,000 as final settlement of Goad's account.
	27	Elbow Inc. paid the note received on September 2.
	27	Determined the account receivable for Dave Campbell ($10,080) was uncollectible and wrote it off.
	30	Sales for the month totalled $1,440,000 (of which 85 percent were on credit) and collections on account totalled $1,202,400.
	30	Eastern Supply did an aging of accounts receivable that indicated that $150,000 is expected to be uncollectible. The company recorded the appropriate adjustment.

Required

1. Record the above transactions in the general journal.

2. What would be the adjusting entry required on September 30 if the company used the percent-of-sales method with an estimate of uncollectibles equal to 8 percent of credit sales?

3. Which of the two methods of estimating uncollectible accounts would normally be more accurate? Why?

*Problem 9–11A

Discounting notes receivable

2. Proceeds from discounting: Note (a) $10,031.58

A company received the following notes during 2010. The notes were discounted on the dates and at the rates indicated.

Note	Date	Principal Amount	Interest Rate	Term	Date Discounted	Discount Rate
(a)	Jun. 15	$10,000	8%	60 days	July 15	12%
(b)	Aug. 1	4,500	10	90 days	Aug. 27	12
(c)	Nov. 21	6,000	15	90 days	Dec. 4	15

Required

Identify each note by letter, compute interest using a 365-day year for all notes, round all interest amounts to the nearest cent, and present entries in general journal form. Explanations are not required.

1. Determine the due date and maturity value of each note.

2. Determine the discount and proceeds from the sale (discounting) of each note.

3. Journalize the discounting of notes (a) and (b).

PROBLEMS (GROUP B)

All questions in this section appear in MyAccountingLab.

Problem 9–1B

Controlling accounts receivable

North York Laboratories provides laboratory testing for samples that veterinarians send in. All work is performed on account, with regular monthly billing to participating veterinarians. Pete Wilson, accountant for North York Laboratories, receives and opens the mail. Company procedure requires him to separate customer cheques from the remittance slips, which list

---

*This Problem covers Chapter 9 Appendix topics.

the amounts he posts as credits to customer accounts receivable in the subsidiary ledger. Wilson deposits the cheques in the bank. He computes each day's total amount posted to customer accounts and makes sure that this total agrees with the bank deposit slip. This is intended to ensure that all receipts are deposited in the bank. Wilson does all customer credit checks, authorizes customer credit limits, and deals with all customer inquiries.

Required   As the auditor of North York Laboratories, write a memo to the owners evaluating the company's internal controls over accounts receivable. If the system is effective, identify its strong features. If the system has flaws, propose a way to strengthen the controls.

Problem 9–2B

On June 30, 2010, Alberta Wireless had a $1,013,100 debit balance in Accounts Receivable. During July, the company had sales revenue of $1,430,000, which included $1,415,700 in credit sales. Other data for July include:

Accounting for uncollectibles by the direct write-off and allowance methods

a. Collections of accounts receivable, $1,099,945.

b. Write-offs of uncollectible receivables, $47,630.

Required

1. Record bad-debt expense for July by the direct write-off method. Use T-accounts to show all July activity in Accounts Receivable and Bad-Debt Expense.

2. Record bad-debt expense and write-offs of customer accounts for July by the allowance method. Use T-accounts to show all July activity in Accounts Receivable, Allowance for Doubtful Accounts, and Bad-Debt Expense. The June 30 unadjusted balance in Allowance for Doubtful Accounts was $25,950 (credit). Bad-debt expense was estimated at 2 percent of credit sales.

3. What amount of bad-debt expense would Alberta Wireless report on its July income statement under the two methods? Which amount better matches expense with revenue? Give your reason.

4. What amount of *net* accounts receivable would Alberta Wireless report on its July 31 balance sheet under the two methods? Which amount is more realistic? Give your reason.

Problem 9–3B

The November 30, 2010, balance sheet of Sage Company reports the following:

Using the percent-of-sales, aging-of-accounts-receivable, and percent-of-accounts-receivable methods for uncollectibles

Accounts Receivable	$358,000
Allowance for Doubtful Accounts (credit balance).................................	7,700

At the end of each quarter, Sage estimates bad-debt expense to be 3 percent of credit sales. At the end of the year, the company ages its accounts receivable and adjusts the balance in Allowance for Doubtful Accounts to correspond to the aging schedule. During the last month of 2010, Sage completes the following selected transactions:

Dec.	9	Made a compound entry to write off the following uncollectible accounts: M. Yang, $710; Tory Ltd., $315; and S. Roberts, $1,050.
	18	Wrote off as uncollectible the $1,360 account receivable from Acme Ltd. and the $790 account receivable from Data Services.
	31	Recorded bad-debt expense based on credit sales of $420,000.
	31	Recorded bad-debt expense based on the following summary of the aging of accounts receivable.

	Age of Accounts			
Accounts Receivable	1–30 Days	31–60 Days	61–90 Days	Over 90 Days
Total = $341,900	$188,400	$78,500	$40,500	$34,500
Estimated percent uncollectible	0.15%	0.5%	5.0%	35.0%

Required

1. Record the transactions in the general journal.

2. Open the Allowance for Doubtful Accounts three-column ledger account, and post entries affecting that account. Keep a running balance.

3. Most companies report two-year comparative financial statements. If Sage Company's Accounts Receivable balance was $299,500 and the Allowance for Doubtful Accounts stood at $9,975 on December 31, 2009, show how the company will report its accounts receivable on a comparative balance sheet for 2010 and 2009.

4. Suppose, on December 31, the bad-debt expense was based on an estimate of 4 percent of the accounts receivable balance, rather than on the aging of accounts receivable. Record the December 31, 2010, entry for bad-debt expense in the general journal.

Problem 9–4B

Using the percent-of-sales and aging-of-accounts methods for uncollectibles

Select Clothing completed the following selected transactions during 2009 and 2010:

2009

Dec.	31	Estimated that bad-debt expense for the year was 2 percent of credit sales of $748,000 and recorded that amount as expense.
	31	Made the closing entry for bad-debt expense.

2010

Feb.	17	Sold inventory to Bruce Jones, $1,412, on credit terms of 2/10, n/30. Ignore the cost of goods sold.
Jul.	29	Wrote off Jones' account as uncollectible after repeated efforts to collect from the customer.
Sept.	6	Received $1,150 from Jones, along with a letter stating his intention to pay his debt in full within 45 days. Reinstated the account in full.
Oct.	21	Received the balance due from Jones.
Dec.	31	Made a compound entry to write off the following accounts as uncollectible: Sean Rooney, $1,610; Sargent Ltd., $3,075; and Linda Lod, $11,580.
	31	Estimated that bad-debt expense for the year was 2 percent of credit sales of $860,000 and recorded the expense.
	31	Made the closing entry for Bad-Debt Expense.

Required

1. Open three-column general ledger accounts for Allowance for Doubtful Accounts and Bad-Debt Expense. Keep running balances.

2. Record the transactions in the general journal and post to the two ledger accounts.

3. The December 31, 2010, balance of Accounts Receivable is $501,000. Show how Accounts Receivable would be reported at that date.

4. Assume that Select Clothing begins aging its accounts on December 31, 2010. The balance in Accounts Receivable is $501,000, the credit balance in Allowance for Doubtful Accounts is $15,895, and the company estimates that $16,100 of its accounts receivable will prove uncollectible.

   a. Make the adjusting entry for uncollectibles.

   b. Show how Accounts Receivable will be reported on the December 31, 2010, balance sheet.

Problem 9–5B

Accounting for notes receivable, including accruing interest revenue

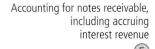

Instaloan issued the following notes during 2009.

Note	Date	Principal Amount	Interest Rate	Term
(a)	Oct. 31	$33,000	6%	6 months
(b)	Nov. 10	12,000	5	60 days
(c)	Dec. 1	30,000	7	1 year

Required

1. Determine the due date and maturity value of each note. Compute the interest for each note. Round all interest amounts to the nearest cent.

2. Journalize a single adjusting entry at December 31, 2009, to record accrued interest revenue on all three notes. An explanation is not required.

3. Journalize the collection of principal and interest on note (b). Explanations are not required.

4. Show how these notes will be reported on December 31, 2009.

Problem 9–6B

Record the following selected transactions in the general journal of Quick Couriers. Explanations are not required.

Accounting for debit-card sales, notes receivable, dishonoured notes, and accrued interest revenue

2009
Dec. 12   Received a $5,775, 120-day, 8 percent note from Jacques Alard to settle his $5,775 account receivable balance.
     31   Made an adjusting entry to accrue interest on the Alard note.
     31   Made an adjusting entry to record bad-debt expense in the amount of 5 percent of credit sales of $288,200.
     31   Recorded $88,000 of debit-card sales. Royal Bank's debit-card service fee is 1.75 percent.
     31   Made a compound closing entry for sales revenue, interest revenue, bad-debt expense, and debit-card service fees.

2010
Apr. 11   Collected the maturity value of the Alard note.
Jun. 1   Lent $16,500 cash to Mercury Inc., receiving a six-month, 7 percent note.
Oct. 31   Received a $3,025, 60-day, 8 percent note from Jim Keller on his past-due account receivable.
Dec. 1   Collected the maturity value of the Mercury Inc. note.
     30   Jim Keller dishonoured (failed to pay) his note at maturity; wrote off the receivable as uncollectible, debiting Allowance for Doubtful Accounts.
     31   Wrote off as uncollectible the account receivable of Art Pierce, $853, and of John Grey, $623.

Problem 9–7B

Mercury Food Products completed the following selected transactions:

Journalizing credit-card sales, uncollectibles, notes receivable, and accrued interest revenue

2009
Nov. 1   Sold goods to Buy Low Foods, receiving a $300,000, six-month, 5 percent note. Ignore cost of goods sold.
Dec. 5   Recorded VISA credit-card sale of $30,000. VISA charges a 2.5 percent fee.
     31   Made an adjusting entry to accrue interest on the Buy Low note.
     31   Made an adjusting entry to record bad-debt expense based on an aging of accounts receivable. The aging analysis indicates that $174,000 of accounts receivable will not be collected. Prior to this adjustment, the credit balance in Allowance for Doubtful Accounts is $140,000.

2008
May   1   Collected the maturity value of the Buy Low note.
     15   Received a 60-day, 8 percent, $7,200 note from Sherwood Market on account.
Jun. 23   Sold merchandise to Delta Foods, receiving a 30-day, 6 percent note for $18,000. Ignore cost of goods sold.
Jul. 14   Collected the maturity value of the Sherwood Market note.
     23   Delta Foods dishonoured (failed to pay) its note at maturity; converted the maturity value of the note to an account receivable.
Nov. 16   Lent $15,600 cash to Urban Provisions, receiving a 120-day, 8 percent note.
Dec. 5   Collected in full from Delta Foods.
     31   Accrued the interest on the Urban Provisions note.

Required   Record the transactions in the general journal. Explanations are not required.

Excel Spreadsheet Template

Using ratio data to evaluate a company's financial position

Problem 9–8B

The comparative financial statements of West Heights for 2010, 2009, and 2008 included the selected data shown below.

	2010	2009	2008
	(In millions)		
Balance Sheet			
Current assets:			
Cash	$ 180	$ 160	$ 120
Short-term investments	280	340	252
Receivables, net	560	520	488
Inventories	720	680	600
Prepaid expenses	100	40	80
Total current assets	$ 1,840	$ 1,740	$1,540
Total current liabilities	$ 1,160	$ 1,200	$1,320
Income Statement			
Sales revenue	$11,680	$10,220	$8,400

Required

1. Compute these ratios for 2010 and 2009:
   a. Current ratio
   b. Acid-test ratio
   c. Days' sales in receivables

2. Write a memo explaining to Jack Dodds, owner of West Heights, which ratio values showed improvement from 2009 to 2010, and which ratio values showed deterioration. Discuss whether this factor conveys a favourable or an unfavourable impression about the company.

Problem 9–9B

Using the allowance method of accounting for uncollectibles, estimating uncollectibles using the aging-of-accounts-receivable method, reporting receivables on the balance sheet

Airdrie Services Inc. started business on March 1, 2009. The company produces monthly financial statements and had total sales of $600,000 (of which $570,000 were on credit) during the first four months.

On June 30, the Accounts Receivable account had a balance of $210,000 (no accounts have been written off to date), which was made up of the following accounts aged according to the date of the provision of services:

	Month of Service			
Customer	**March**	**April**	**May**	**June**
Torrance Trucks	$ 2,520	$ 1,200	$ 1,800	$ 1,440
Milloy Ltd.	1,500	1,140	1,632	4,344
Cody Craven	6,876	4,464	9,168	7,908
Mort Black	6,408	3,468	12,624	15,912
Other Accounts Receivable	14,760	23,916	31,380	57,540
	$32,064	$34,188	$56,604	$87,144

The following accounts receivable transactions took place in July 2009:

Jul. 12   Determined the account of Milloy Ltd. was uncollectible and wrote it off.
15   Collected $4,200 from Torrance Trucks for services in the first three months.
21   Decided the account of Cody Craven was uncollectible and wrote it off.
24   Collected $6,408 from Mort Black for services in the month of March.
26   Received a cheque from Wayne for $9,600 plus two cheques, of $9,408 each, post-dated to September 10 and November 10.
31   Total sales of service in the month were $162,000; 90 percent of these were on credit and 60 percent of the credit sales were collected in the month.

Required

1. Airdrie Services Inc. has heard that other companies in the industry use the allowance method of accounting for uncollectibles, with many of these estimating the uncollectibles through an aging of accounts receivable.

   a. Journalize the adjustments that would have to be made on June 30 (for the months of March through June), assuming the following estimates of uncollectibles:

Age of Accounts Receivable	Estimated Percent Uncollectible
From current month	1%
From prior month	3
From two months prior..	6
From three months prior..	20
From four months prior..	35

   (Round your total estimate to the nearest whole dollar.)

   b. Journalize the transactions of July 2009.
   c. Journalize the month-end adjustment, using the table that appears in requirement 1a.

2. For the method of accounting for the uncollectibles used above, show

   a. The balance-sheet presentation of the accounts receivable.
   b. The overall effect of the uncollectibles on the income statement for the months of June and July 2009.

Problem 9–10B

Barrie Supplies uses the allowance method for accounting for uncollectible accounts with the estimate based on an aging of accounts receivable. The company had the following account balances on September 30, 2010:

Accounts Receivable	$498,000
Allowance for Doubtful Accounts (credit balance)..................................	56,000

Using the allowance method of accounting for uncollectibles, estimating uncollectibles by the percent-of-sales and the aging-of-accounts-receivable methods, accounting for notes receivable

The following transactions took place during the month of October 2010:

Oct.   2   Albert Morrison, who owes $51,000, is unable to pay on time and has given a 20-day, 8 percent note in settlement of the account.

       6   Determined the account receivable for Donald Timble ($15,000) was uncollectible and wrote it off.

       9   Received notice that a customer (Will Wong) has filed for bankruptcy. Wong owes $35,000. The courts will confirm the amount recoverable at a later date.

     11   Determined the account receivable for Susan Knight ($7,200) was uncollectible and wrote it off.

     15   Timble, whose account was written off on October 6, paid $11,000 on his account and promises to pay the balance in 60 days.

     18   Received a cheque from the courts in the amount of $23,000 as final settlement of Wong's account.

     22   Morrison paid the note received on October 2.

     25   Determined the account receivable for Donald Purcell ($8,200) was uncollectible and wrote it off.

     31   Sales for the month totalled $743,000 (of which 95 percent were on credit) and collections on account totalled $520,000.

     31   Barrie Supplies did an aging of accounts receivable that indicated that $60,000 is expected to be uncollectible. The company recorded the appropriate adjustment.

Required

1. Record the above transactions in the general journal.

2. What would be the adjusting entry required on October 31 if the company used the percent-of-sales method with an estimate of uncollectibles equal to 3 percent of credit sales?

3. Which of the two methods of estimating uncollectible accounts would normally be more accurate? Why?

*Problem 9–11B

A company received the following notes during 2010. The notes were discounted on the dates and at the rates indicated.

Note	Date	Principal Amount	Interest Rate	Term	Date Discounted	Discount Rate
(a)	Aug. 18	$10,000	11%	6 months	Nov. 18	13%
(b)	Jul. 15	9,000	9	90 days	Jul. 26	12
(c)	Sept. 1	8,000	10	180 days	Nov. 2	13

Required

Identify each note by letter, compute interest for each note, round all interest amounts to the nearest cent, and present entries in general journal form. Explanations are not required.

1. Determine the due date and maturity value of each note.

2. Determine the discount and proceeds from the sale (discounting) of each note.

3. Journalize the discounting of notes (a) and (b).

CHALLENGE PROBLEMS

Problem 9–1C

Kitchener Builders Supply is a six-store chain of retail stores selling home renovation materials and supplies mainly on credit; the company has its own credit card and does not accept other cards. Kitchener Builders Supply had a tendency to institute policies that conflicted with each other. Management rarely became aware of these conflicts until they became serious.

Recently, the owner, Angela Kim, who has been reading all the latest management texts, has instituted a new bonus plan. All managers are to be paid bonuses based on the success of their department. For example, the bonus for George Tatulis, the sales manager, is based on how much he can increase sales. The bonus for Sonia Petrov, the credit manager, is based on reducing the bad-debt expense.

Required Describe the conflict that the bonus plan has created for the sales manager and the credit manager. How might the conflict be resolved?

Problem 9–2C

Days' sales in receivables is a good measure of a company's ability to collect the amounts owing to it. You have owned shares in Locking Office Equipment Ltd. for some years and follow the company's progress by reading the annual report. You noticed the most recent report indicated that the days' sales in receivables had increased over the previous year, and you are concerned.

Required Suggest reasons that may have resulted in the increase in the number of days' sales in receivables.

---

*This Problem covers Chapter 9 Appendix topics.

Extending Your Knowledge

DECISION PROBLEMS

Decision Problem 1

Otto Jacina Advertising has always used the direct write-off method to account for uncollectibles. The company's revenues, bad-debt write-offs, and year-end receivables for the most recent year follow.

Comparing allowance and direct write-off methods for uncollectibles

2. $38,390

Year	Revenues	Write-Offs	Receivables at Year End
2010	$187,000	$3,300	$44,000

Otto Jacina is applying for a bank loan, and the loan officer requires figures based on the allowance method of accounting for bad debts. Jacina estimates that bad debts run about 3 percent of revenues each year.

Required

Jacina must give the banker the following information:

1. How much more or less would net income be for 2010 if Jacina were to use the allowance method for bad debts?

2. How much of the receivables balance at the end of 2010 does Jacina expect to collect?

Compute these amounts, and then explain for Jacina why net income is more or less for 2010 using the allowance method versus the direct write-off method for uncollectibles.

Decision Problem 2

Garneau Camping Products sells its products either for cash or on notes receivable that earn interest. The business uses the direct write-off method to account for uncollectible accounts. Paul Garneau, the owner, has prepared Garneau Camping Products' financial statements. The most recent comparative income statements, for 2010 and 2009, are as follows:

Uncollectible accounts and evaluating a business

1. 2010 net income $238,704

	2010	2009
Total revenue	$528,000	$468,000
Total expenses	282,600	252,000
Net income	$245,400	$216,000

Based on the increase in net income, Garneau seeks to expand his operations. He asks you to invest $60,000 in the business. You and Garneau have several meetings, at which you learn that notes receivable from customers were $120,000 at the end of 2009 and $540,000 at the end of 2010. Also, total revenues for 2010 and 2009 include interest at 12 percent on the year's ending notes receivable balance. Total expenses include bad-debt expense of $7,200 each year, based on the direct write-off basis. Garneau estimates that bad-debt expense would be 3 percent of sales revenue if the allowance method were used.

Required

1. Prepare for Garneau Camping Products a comparative single-step income statement that identifies sales revenue, interest revenue, bad-debt expense, and other expenses, all computed in accordance with GAAP.

2. Is Garneau Camping Products' future as promising as Garneau's income statement makes it appear? Give the reason for your answer.

FINANCIAL STATEMENT CASES

Financial Statement Case 1

Loans receivable and
related uncollectibles

Canadian Western Bank (CWB)—like all other businesses—makes adjusting entries prior to year end to measure assets, liabilities, revenues, and expenses properly.

Examine CWB's balance sheet in Appendix A at the back of this book. A bank lends money and collects interest as its main revenue source. However, like accounts receivable, not all the loans will be repaid and provisions must be made to expense losses. Find the section entitled Loans in the asset section of the balance sheet and also refer to Note 6 to answer the questions below.

Required

1. What are impaired loans and how (by what criteria) are loans determined to be impaired?

2. What is the total of net impaired loans before the allowance for October 31, 2008?

3. Refer to the total in Requirement 2. How much of the impaired loans are real estate? What would CWB do to ensure that it collects the amount owing?

4. What was the value of foreclosed real estate held for sale in 2008? 2007? Why do you think this difference existed?

Financial Statement Case 2

Accounts receivable and related
uncollectibles

2. 2008, 27.98 days

Answer the following questions using the financial statements for Sun-Rype Products Ltd. in Appendix B at the end of this book.

1. Analyze the Accounts Receivable accounts at December 31, 2008. What is the total receivable? What was the total receivable at December 31, 2007?

2. How many days' sales are in Accounts Receivable at December 31, 2008? How does this compare to the number of days' sales of the previous year? You will need the 2006 Receivables amount, which is $12,676,000. Show all calculations.

3. How does this compare to the previous year? What factors would cause a change in the numbers of days' sales or collections that you calculated in Question 2?

10 Property, Plant, and Equipment; Goodwill; and Intangible Assets

What do we mean by property, plant, and equipment, and why are they important?

Should you capitalize or expense costs associated with a new asset and with an existing asset?

What is amortization, and how can amortization expense be calculated?

How is amortization reported on the income statement and the balance sheet?

Can a company use different amortization methods for accounting and income tax purposes?

These questions and others will be answered throughout this chapter. The Decision Guidelines at the end of the chapter will provide the answers in a useful summary.

LEARNING OBJECTIVES

1. Measure the cost of property, plant, and equipment

2. Calculate and account for amortization

3. Account for other issues: Amortization for income tax purposes, partial years, and revised assumptions

4. Account for the disposal of property, plant, and equipment

5. Account for natural resources

6. Account for goodwill and intangible assets

7. Understand the impact on property, plant, and equipment of international financial reporting standards (IFRS)

8. Understand the impact on intangible assets of international financial reporting standards (IFRS)

CHAPTER 10 APPENDIX

A1. Explain capital cost allowance and amortization for income tax purposes

Have you ever taken a flight on a commercial airline—Air Canada, WestJet, or CanJet? These companies have some of the most interesting assets in the world—airplanes.

How long can a commercial airplane keep flying safely and efficiently? Some airlines like to use a Boeing 737 for a long time, sometimes 20 years, because that delays spending cash to buy new planes. WestJet's fleet of Next-Generation aircraft have an average age of 4.3 years, "one of the youngest fleets of any large North American commercial airline,"[1] and are 30 percent more fuel efficient than its previous 200-series aircraft.[2] Top managers of the airlines try to strike a balance between getting the most use from a plane and using one that consumes less fuel.

How do the airlines account for the use of an airplane? They record amortization over the plane's useful life. Managers also have to consider how much they can sell a plane for when it's taken out of service. The airlines don't amortize this residual value because they get it back when they sell a plane.

This chapter covers these and other matters about property, plant, and equipment. *Property, plant, and equipment* include the long-term tangible assets that a business uses to operate, such as airplanes for WestJet, copy equipment for FedEx Kinko's, and automobiles for Discount Car and Truck Rentals. Capital assets also include *intangibles*—those assets with no physical form, such as trademarks and copyrights. The chapter also shows how to account for natural resources such as oil and timber.

---

[1] WestJet, August 6, 2009, "Management's Discussion and Analysis of Financial Results for the Three and Six Months Ended June 30, 2009," filed online at SEDAR.com, accessed August 10, 2009.

[2] WestJet, April 27, 2006, press release filed online at SEDAR.com, accessed August 10, 2009.

Property, plant, and equipment are identifiable tangible assets. These assets have some special characteristics. For example, you hold them for uses in the business—not to sell as inventory. Also,

- Property, plant, and equipment assets are relatively expensive, and their cost can be a challenge to determine.
- Property, plant, and equipment assets last a long time—usually for several years. If property, plant, and equipment assets wear out or become obsolete, you need to amortize them.
- Property, plant, and equipment assets may be sold or traded in. Accounting for the disposal of property, plant, and equipment is more complicated than selling inventory.

Property, plant, and equipment assets pose some accounting challenges. This chapter addresses these issues and shows how to account for

1. Property, plant, and equipment assets, which are useful because of their physical characteristics; and
2. Goodwill and other intangible assets, which have no physical form.

Chapter 10 concludes our coverage of assets, except for long-term investments. After completing this chapter, you should understand the various assets of a business and how to account for them.

Property, plant, and equipment and intangible assets have their own terminology. Exhibit 10–1 shows which expense or loss applies to each category of property, plant, and equipment and intangible assets.

Measuring the Cost of Property, Plant, and Equipment

OBJECTIVE ①
Measure the cost of property, plant, and equipment

The *cost principle of measurement* directs a business to carry an asset on the balance sheet at its cost—the amount paid for the asset, or the market value if the asset is transferred into the business. The general rule for measuring cost (repeated from Chapter 5) is

$$\text{The cost of an asset} = \begin{array}{l}\textbf{The sum of all the costs incurred to bring the}\\\textbf{asset to its intended purpose, net of all discounts}\end{array}$$

KEY POINT

Property, plant, and equipment are sometimes referred to as long-lived assets or long-term assets.

The *cost* of *property, plant, and equipment* is the purchase price plus taxes plus other acquisition costs including commissions, and all other *necessary* costs incurred to ready the asset for its intended use. In Chapter 5, we applied this principle to determine the cost of inventory. These costs vary, so we discuss each asset individually.

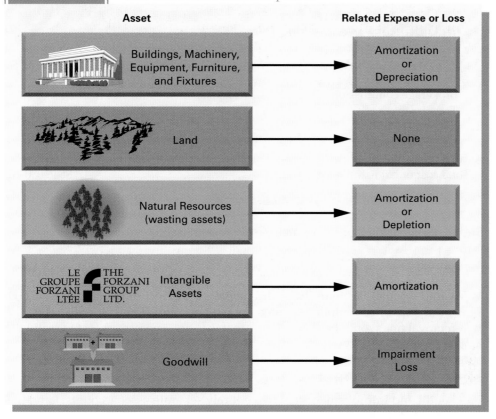

Asset	Related Expense or Loss
Buildings, Machinery, Equipment, Furniture, and Fixtures	Amortization or Depreciation
Land	None
Natural Resources (wasting assets)	Amortization or Depletion
Intangible Assets	Amortization
Goodwill	Impairment Loss

Property

Generally speaking, the property portion of long-lived tangible assets refers to land and land improvements. We will review each category separately.

Land

The cost of land includes the following costs paid by the purchaser:

- the purchase price
- the brokerage commission
- the survey and legal fees
- any property taxes in arrears
- the cost for grading and clearing the land, and for demolishing or removing any unwanted buildings

The cost of land is not amortized and does *not* include the cost of

- fencing
- paving
- sprinkler systems
- lighting

These separate capital assets—called *land improvements*—are subject to amortization.

Suppose Sleeman Breweries pays $500,000 to purchase 100 hectares of land. The company also pays $30,000 in brokerage commission, $10,000 in transfer taxes, $5,000 for removal of an old building, a tree-removal fine of $200, and a $1,000

KEY POINT

Land is not amortized because it does not wear out as do buildings and equipment.

LEARNING TIPS

The cost of an asset includes all costs *necessary* to ready the asset for its intended use; "cost" will even include amounts not yet paid in cash, such as a note payable on the asset.

survey fee. What is the cost of this land? Exhibit 10–2 shows that all the *necessary* costs incurred to bring the land to its intended use are part of the land's cost.

EXHIBIT 10–2	Measuring the Cost of Land		
Purchase price of land..			$500,000
Add related costs:			
Brokerage commission..	$30,000		
Transfer taxes	10,000		
Removal of building..	5,000		
Survey fee...	1,000		
Total incidental costs...			46,000
Total cost of land...			$546,000

Sleeman's entry to record the purchase of the land is:

Land..	546,000	
Cash		546,000

We would say that Sleeman Breweries *capitalized* the cost of the land at $546,000. This means that the company debited an asset account (Land) for $546,000. The tree-removal fine would be expensed since it was not a necessary cost to ready the land for use.

Land Improvements

Land and Land Improvements are two entirely separate asset accounts. Land improvements include

- lighting
- signs
- fences
- paving
- sprinkler systems
- landscaping

These costs are debited to the Land Improvements account and then amortized over their useful lives. It could be argued that decorative items such as trees and shrubs should be classified as land, since they would not decline in value. The accountant would need to use professional judgment to determine the proper classification.

Suppose Sleeman Breweries spent $35,000 for the construction of fences around the land it had purchased above. The entry to record the expenditure is:

Land Improvements..	35,000	
Cash		35,000

The fences are a land improvement, and their cost will be amortized over the useful life of the fences.

Plant (Buildings)

Plant refers to buildings a company owns. These buildings may include manufacturing facilities and offices.

The cost of constructing a building includes

- architectural fees
- building permits
- contractors' charges
- payments for materials, labour, and overhead

The time to complete a new building can be many months, even years, and the separate expenditures can be numerous. If the company constructs its own assets, the cost of the building may include the cost of interest on money borrowed to finance the construction.

When an existing building is purchased, its cost includes all the usual items (but not GST), plus all the costs to repair and renovate the building for its intended use.

Equipment (and Machinery)

The equipment category includes the productive assets a company builds or acquires to produce the products it sells, or the trucks to distribute products.

The cost of machinery and equipment includes

- purchase price (less any discounts)
- transportation charges
- insurance while in transit
- provincial sales tax (PST)
- purchase commission
- installation costs
- cost of testing the asset before it is used

After the asset is set up, we cease capitalizing these costs to the Machinery and Equipment account. Thereafter, insurance, taxes, and maintenance costs are recorded as expenses.

There are many different types of equipment. WestJet has baggage-handling equipment and planes, FedEx Kinko's has copy equipment, and Purolator has delivery trucks.

The goods and services tax (GST) paid on the purchase of an asset is recoverable if the acquired asset is used to earn income. Therefore, it would not be part of the capitalized cost of the asset. For example, equipment purchased for $50,000 in Manitoba would incur PST of 7 percent ($3,500) and GST of 5 percent ($2,500) for a total cost of $56,000. Assuming the equipment was to be used to earn revenue, the cost of the asset would be $53,500, not $56,000, since the GST would be recovered from Canada Revenue Agency (CRA).

Furniture and Fixtures

Another category of equipment is commonly referred to as *furniture and fixtures*. This category includes desks, chairs, filing cabinets, and display racks. The cost of furniture and fixtures includes the basic cost of the asset (less any discounts), plus all other necessary costs to ready the asset for use. As was indicated above for machinery and equipment, GST is recoverable from CRA. All companies have furniture and fixtures, but they are most important to service organizations and retail businesses.

Leasehold Improvements

Leasehold improvements are similar to land improvements. *Leasehold improvements* are alterations to assets the company is leasing. For example, suppose TELUS Communications Inc., the telephone company, leases some of its vehicles. The company also customizes some of these vehicles to meet its special needs. For example, TELUS may paint its logo on a rental truck and install special racks on the truck. These improvements are assets of TELUS even though the company does not own the truck. The cost of improvements to leased assets appears on the company's balance sheet as *leasehold improvements*. The cost of leasehold improvements should be amortized over the term of the lease including the renewal option or the useful life of the leased asset, whichever is shorter.

Construction in Progress and Capital Leases

Construction in Progress *Construction in progress* is an asset, such as a warehouse, that the company is constructing for its own use. Suppose that, on the balance sheet date, the construction is incomplete and the building is not ready for use. The construction costs would still be shown as assets because the company expects the building, when completed, to render future benefits for the company.

Capital Leases A *capital lease* is an arrangement where a capital asset is acquired by making regular periodic payments that are required by the lease contract. Companies report assets leased through capital leases on the balance sheet in the same way as purchased assets. Why? Because their lease payments secure the use of the asset over the term of the lease. For example, WestJet has assets under capital leases with a gross value of $2,482 million included in its 2008 balance sheet.

A capital lease is different from an operating lease, which is an ordinary rental agreement, such as an apartment lease or the rental of a Budget automobile or a photocopier. The lessee (the renter) records operating lease payments as Rent Expense or Lease Expense.

A Lump-Sum (or Basket) Purchase of Assets

A company may pay a single price for several assets purchased as a group—a "basket purchase." For example, suppose a company pays one price for land and an office building. For accounting purposes, the company must identify the cost of each asset as shown in the diagram at left. The total cost (100 percent) is divided among the assets according to their relative fair values. This allocation technique is called the *relative-fair-value method*.

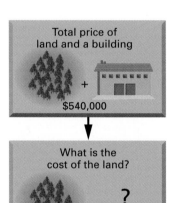

Total price of land and a building

+

$540,000

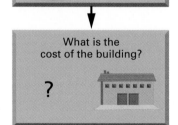

What is the cost of the land?

?

What is the cost of the building?

?

Suppose High Liner Foods Incorporated, a seafood and pasta company located in Nova Scotia, purchases land and a building in Lunenberg to be used as a warehouse. The combined purchase price of the land and building is $540,000. An appraisal indicates that the land's market (sales) value is $200,000 and the building's market (sales) value is $400,000.

First, calculate the ratio of each asset's market value to the total market value of both assets combined. Total appraised value is $200,000 + $400,000 = $600,000. Thus, the land, valued at $200,000, is $1/3$, or 33.33 percent, of the total market value. The building's appraised value is $2/3$, or 66.67 percent, of the total. The cost of each asset is determined as follows:

Asset	Market (Sales) Value	Fraction of Total Value		Total Purchase Price		Cost of Each Asset
Land	$200,000	$200,000 ÷ $600,000 = $1/3$	×	$540,000	=	$180,000
Building	$400,000	$400,000 ÷ $600,000 = $2/3$	×	$540,000	=	$360,000
Total	$600,000					$540,000

Suppose High Liner pays cash. The entry to record the purchase of the land and building is

Land	180,000	
Building	360,000	
Cash		540,000

KEY POINT

It does not matter what the seller claims each asset is worth or what the book value is on the seller's books. The market (fair) value is determined by appraisal or some other objective method.

Without the relative-fair-value method of allocating costs for tax purposes, the tendency would be to record higher estimates of the cost of equipment (which is amortized the fastest) and lower estimates of the cost of land (which is not amortized), resulting in the greatest amortization expense and the lowest income taxes early in the life of the assets. Just the opposite reasoning might apply for financial reporting purposes.

Betterments versus Repairs

When a company spends money on a capital asset it already owns, it must decide whether to debit an asset account for *betterments* or an expense account for *repairs*. Examples of these expenditures range from replacing the windshield on an

Airways Limousine automobile in Toronto to adding an extension to a building at Big Rock Brewery in Alberta.

Betterments are debited to an asset account because they

A capital expenditure causes the asset's cost to increase, which necessitates a revision of amortization.

- increase the capacity or efficiency of the asset, or

- extend its useful life.

For example, the cost of a major overhaul that extends an Airways Limousine automobile's useful life is a betterment. The amount of the expenditure, said to be *capitalized*, is a debit to the asset account Automobile.

Repairs, such as maintenance expenses and truck-repair expenses, do not extend the asset's capacity or efficiency but merely maintain the asset in working order. These expenses are matched against revenue. Examples include the following costs incurred after a period of use: repainting a Big Rock Brewery truck, repairing a dented fender, and replacing tires. These costs are debited to Repair Expense.

The distinction between betterments and repairs requires judgment. Does the cost extend the life of the asset (a betterment), or does it only maintain the asset in good order (a repair)? The other factor to consider is the materiality constraint. Most companies have a minimum dollar limit for betterments. For example, a $400 betterment to a truck would be expensed if the company had a $500 minimum dollar limit for betterments.

Exhibit 10–3 illustrates the distinction between betterments (capital expenditures) and repairs (expenses) for several delivery truck expenditures.

EXHIBIT 10–3 Delivery Truck Expenditures—Betterment or Repair?

Betterment: Debit an Asset Account	Repair: Debit Repair and Maintenance Expense
Betterments	**Repairs**
Major engine overhaul	Repair of transmission or other mechanism
Modification of truck for new use	Oil change, lubrication, and so on
Addition to storage capacity of truck	Replacement tires or windshield
	Paint job

Treating a betterment as a repair, or vice versa, creates an accounting error. Suppose a company incurs the cost of a betterment to enhance the service potential of equipment and expenses this cost. This is an accounting error because the cost should have been debited to an asset. On the income statement, this error

- overstates expenses, and
- understates net income.

On the balance sheet, this error causes the Equipment account to be understated.

Capitalizing an expense creates the opposite error. Expenses are understated and net income is overstated. The balance sheet overstates assets.

DID YOU GET IT?

MyAccountingLab

To check your understanding of the material in this Learning Objective, complete these questions. The solutions appear on MyAccountingLab so you can check your progress.

1. Which of the following would you include in the cost of machinery?

   (a) Installation charges

   (b) Testing of the machine

   (c) Repair to machinery necessitated by installer's error

   (d) First-year maintenance cost

2. How would Tim Hortons divide a $600,000 lump-sum purchase price for land, building, and equipment with estimated market values of $108,000, $432,000, and $180,000, respectively? Round to two decimal places.

3. Classify each of the following as a betterment or a repair.

    (a) Installing new tires on a cement truck

    (b) Painting the company logo on a new delivery truck

    (c) Repainting a delivery truck that was damaged in an accident

    (d) Replacing the motor in a delivery truck

    (e) Installing an elevating device in a delivery truck

    (f) Safety test on a delivery truck when the licence is renewed

    (g) Installing carrying racks on the roof of the delivery truck

Measuring Amortization

OBJECTIVE ②
Calculate and account for amortization

As we have seen previously, **amortization**, defined in Section 3061 of the *CICA Handbook*, is the allocation of the cost of property, plant, and equipment (except for land) less salvage value or residual value to expense over its useful life. Another term used in the United States to describe the allocation of the cost when referring to property, plant, and equipment is *depreciation*. Amortization matches the asset's cost (expense) against the revenue earned by the asset (see Chapter 3, page 112, for a discussion of the matching objective). Exhibit 10–4 shows this process for the purchase of a jet by Air Canada. The primary purpose of amortization accounting is to measure income. Of less importance is the need to account for the asset's decline in usefulness.

EXHIBIT 10–4   Amortization and the Matching of Expense to Revenue

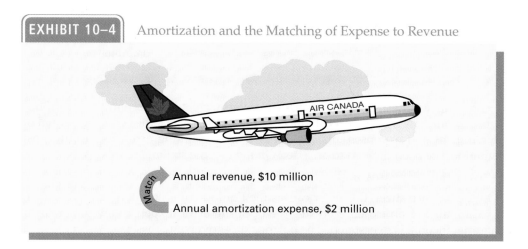

Annual revenue, $10 million

Annual amortization expense, $2 million

    Suppose Air Canada buys a Boeing 777 jet. Air Canada believes it will get 20 years' service from the plane. Using the straight-line amortization method, Air Canada expenses 1/20th of the asset's cost in each of its 20 years' use.

    Let's contrast what amortization *is* with what it *is not*.

1. *Amortization is not a process of valuation.* Businesses do not record amortization based on the market (fair) value of their property, plant, and equipment; they use their actual cost.

2. *Amortization does not mean that the business sets aside cash to replace assets as they become fully amortized.* Amortization has nothing to do with establishing a cash fund for the replacement of assets.

Causes of Amortization

All assets except land wear out. For some tangible assets, physical *wear and tear* creates the need to amortize their value. For example, physical factors wear out the jets that Air Canada and WestJet fly. The same is true of Zellers' store fixtures.

Assets such as computers and software or jet aircraft may become *obsolete* before they wear out. An asset is obsolete when another asset can do the job more efficiently. Thus an asset's useful life may be shorter than its physical life. Accountants usually amortize computers over a short period of time—perhaps two to four years—even though they know the computers can be used much longer. In all cases, the asset's cost is amortized over its expected useful life.

Measuring Amortization

Amortization for a capital asset is based on three factors about the asset:

1. Cost
2. Estimated useful life
3. Estimated residual value

The asset's cost is known. The other two factors must be estimated.

Estimated useful life is the length of the service period expected from the asset. Useful life may be expressed in years, units of output, kilometres, or other measures. For example, a building's useful life is stated in years, a bookbinding machine's in the number of books the machine can bind, and a delivery truck's in kilometres.

Estimated residual value—also called **salvage value**—is the asset's expected cash value at the end of its useful life. **Scrap value** is the asset's value at the end of its physical life. For example, a business may believe that a machine's useful life (and physical life) will be seven years. After that time, the company expects to sell the machine as scrap metal. The expected cash receipt is the machine's residual value. Estimated residual value is *not* amortized, because the business expects to receive this amount when the machine is sold. If there is no residual value, then the company amortizes the full cost of the asset. Cost minus residual value is called **amortizable cost**.

Of the factors entering the computation of amortization, only one factor is known—cost. The other two factors—useful life and residual value—must be estimated. Amortization, then, is an estimated amount.

Amortization Methods

Three methods are used widely in Canada for computing amortization:

- straight-line
- units-of-production
- declining-balance

The declining-balance method is one of two *accelerated* amortization methods, so called because they expense greater amounts of amortization near the start of an asset's life and lesser amounts toward the end. The other accelerated method is sum-of-the-year's-digits, which is little used (if at all) in Canada and will not be discussed in this text. The three methods listed allocate different amounts of amortization expense to each period, but they all result in the same total amortization over the life of the asset. Exhibit 10–5 presents the data we will use to illustrate amortization for a RONA store delivery truck. We cover the three most widely used methods.

KEY POINT

While the exact cost of the asset is known, the useful life and residual value must be estimated. It is important that these estimates be as accurate as possible, because they have an impact on the amount of net income in each period that the asset is used.

KEY POINT

Note that the residual value is the portion of the asset's cost that will *not* be consumed or used; therefore, it should *not* be amortized.

KEY POINT

The total amount of amortization recorded for an asset cannot exceed its amortizable cost. An asset can be used after it is fully amortized.

KEY POINT

It is impossible to quantify the exact amount of the useful life of an asset that has been used up during the period, but there is no doubt that a portion of the asset has been consumed. An estimate of the amount must be made using one of the amortization methods. Without this expense, there would be no *matching* of the cost of the asset with the revenues generated during the time the asset is used.

EXHIBIT 10–5 Data for Recording Amortization for a RONA Truck

Data Item	Amount
Cost of truck	$65,000
Estimated residual value	5,000
Amortizable cost	$60,000
Estimated useful life	
Years	5 years
Units of production	400,000 units (kilometres)

LEARNING TIPS

The formula for the straight-line rate is: 1/Useful life. If an asset has a five-year useful life, then 1/5 of the asset is amortized each year. The straight-line rate is 1/5, or 20 percent.

Straight-Line Method The **straight-line method** allocates an equal amount of amortization to each year of asset use. Amortizable cost is divided by useful life in years to determine annual amortization. The equation for straight-line amortization, applied to the RONA delivery truck data from Exhibit 10–5, is

$$\text{Straight-line amortization} = \frac{\text{Cost} - \text{Residual value}}{\text{Useful life in years}}$$

$$= \frac{\$65,000 - \$5,000}{5}$$

$$= \$12,000 \text{ per year}$$

The entry to record each year's amortization is

Amortization Expense—Delivery Truck	12,000	
Accumulated Amortization—Delivery Truck		12,000

Assume that this truck was purchased on January 1, 2010, and the business's fiscal year ends on December 31. A *straight-line amortization schedule* is presented in Exhibit 10–6. The final column of Exhibit 10–6 shows the asset's *book value* (also referred to as the *carrying value*), which is cost less accumulated amortization. We introduced book value in Chapter 3.

EXHIBIT 10–6 Straight-Line Amortization for a Truck

Date	Asset Cost	Amortization for the Year			Accumulated Amortization	Asset Book Value
		Amortization Rate	Amortizable Cost	Amortization Amount		
01-01-2010	$65,000					$65,000
31-12-2010		1/5 ×	$60,000 =	$12,000	$12,000	53,000
31-12-2011		1/5 ×	60,000 =	12,000	24,000	41,000
31-12-2012		1/5 ×	60,000 =	12,000	36,000	29,000
31-12-2013		1/5 ×	60,000 =	12,000	48,000	17,000
31-12-2014		1/5 ×	60,000 =	12,000	60,000	5,000

As an asset is used, accumulated amortization increases and the asset's book value decreases. See the Accumulated Amortization and the Asset Book Value columns in Exhibit 10–6. An asset's final book value is its *residual value* ($5,000 in Exhibit 10–6). At the end of its useful life, the asset is said to be *fully amortized*.

Units-of-Production Method   The **units-of-production (UOP) method** allocates a fixed amount of amortization to each unit of output produced by the asset. The equation for the UOP method, applied to the Exhibit 10–5 data, is

$$\text{Units-of-production amortization per unit of output} = \frac{\text{Cost} - \text{Residual Value}}{\text{Useful life in units of production}}$$

$$= \frac{\$65{,}000 - \$5{,}000}{400{,}000 \text{ kilometres}}$$

$$= \$0.15 \text{ per kilometre}$$

This truck was driven 90,000 kilometres in the first year, 120,000 in the second, 100,000 in the third, 60,000 in the fourth, and 30,000 in the fifth. The amount of UOP amortization per period varies with the number of units the asset produces. Exhibit 10–7 shows the UOP amortization schedule for this asset.

EXHIBIT 10–7   Units-of-Production Amortization for a Truck

Date	Asset Cost	Amortization for the Year			Amortization Amount	Accumulated Amortization	Asset Book Value
		Amortization Per Kilometre		Number of Kilometres			
01-01-2010	$65,000						$65,000
31-12-2010		$ 0.15	×	90,000	= $ 13,500	$13,500	51,500
31-12-2011		0.15	×	120,000	= 18,000	31,500	33,500
31-12-2012		0.15	×	100,000	= 15,000	46,500	18,500
31-12-2013		0.15	×	60,000	= 9,000	55,500	9,500
31-12-2014		0.15	×	30,000	= 4,500	60,000	5,000

Double-Declining-Balance Method   The **double-declining-balance (DDB) method** involves computing annual amortization by multiplying the asset's book value by a constant percentage, which is two times (double) the straight-line amortization rate. DDB rates are computed as follows:

1. Compute the straight-line amortization rate per year, for example, for the truck: (100% ÷ 5 years = 20% per year).

2. Multiply the straight-line rate by 2. For the truck example, the DDB rate is 20% × 2 = 40%. To do the calculation in one step, compute 2 ÷ Useful life in years. Express the result as a fraction or a percent, then multiply by the book value at the beginning of the period.

3. Compute the year's DDB amortization. Multiply the asset's book value (cost less accumulated amortization) at the beginning of the year by the DDB rate. Ignore residual value except for the last year. The first year's amortization for the truck in Exhibit 10–5 is:

$$\text{DDB amortization for first year} = \begin{array}{c}\text{Asset book value} \\ \text{at the beginning} \\ \text{of the period}\end{array} \times \text{DDB rate}$$

$$= \$65{,}000 \times 0.40$$

$$= \$26{,}000$$

The same approach is used to compute DDB amortization for all later years, except for the final year.

The final year's amortization is the amount needed to reduce the asset's book value to its residual value. In the DDB amortization schedule in Exhibit 10–8, the fifth and final year's amortization is $3,424—the $8,424 book value less the $5,000 residual value.

KEY POINT

With declining-balance amortization, the asset's book value will rarely equal its residual value in the final year. Amortization expense in the final year is a "plug" figure, the amount that will reduce the asset's book value to the residual value.

The DDB method differs from the other methods in two ways:

1. Residual value is ignored initially. In the first year, amortization is calculated on the asset's full cost.
2. Final-year amortization is the amount needed to bring the asset's book value to the residual value. It is a "plug" figure.

EXHIBIT 10–8 Double-Declining-Balance Amortization for a Truck

			Amortization for the Year					
Date	Asset Cost	DDB Rate		Asset Book Value		Amortization Amount	Accumulated Amortization	Asset Book Value
01-01-2010	$65,000							$65,000
31-12-2010		0.40	×	$65,000	=	$26,000	$26,000	39,000
31-12-2011		0.40	×	39,000	=	15,600	41,600	23,400
31-12-2012		0.40	×	23,400	=	9,360	50,960	14,040
31-12-2013		0.40	×	14,040	=	5,616	56,576	8,424
31-12-2014						3,424*	60,000	5,000

*Amortization in 2014 is the amount needed to reduce the asset's book value to the residual value of $5,000 ($8,424 − $5,000 = $3,424).

Comparing Amortization Methods

LEARNING TIPS

Students sometimes confuse the DDB formula with other methods. Rather than use amortizable cost (as other methods do), the formula for DDB is *book value* × DDB rate. (The book value in the first year is its original cost.)

Let's compare the three methods we have just discussed. Annual amounts vary by method but the total is $60,000 for all methods.

	Amount of Amortization per Year		
Year	Straight-Line	Units-of-Production	Double-Declining-Balance
2010	$12,000	$13,500	$26,000
2011	12,000	18,000	15,600
2012	12,000	15,000	9,360
2013	12,000	9,000	5,616
2014	12,000	4,500	3,424
Total	$60,000	$60,000	$60,000

Which method is best? That depends on the asset. A business should match an asset's expense against the revenue that the asset produces.

Straight-Line Method For an amortizable asset that generates revenue fairly evenly over time, such as office furniture, the straight-line method follows the matching objective. During each period the asset is used, an equal amount of amortization is recorded.

KEY POINT

The DDB method is an accelerated amortization method. An accelerated method expenses more asset cost in the early years of an asset's life than in the later years. This method assumes that an asset is more useful (productive) in its early years and therefore should be amortized more then.

Units-of-Production Method The UOP method best fits an asset that wears out because of physical use, rather than obsolescence. Amortization can be variable over time and is recorded only when the asset is used. More use leads to greater amortization. An example is a commercial airplane.

DDB Method The DDB, or accelerated, method works best for assets that produce more revenue in their early years, such as computerized equipment. The greater expense recorded in the early periods matches best against those periods' greater revenue.

Comparisons Exhibit 10–9 graphs the relationship between annual amortization amounts for the three methods.

EXHIBIT 10–9 Amortization Patterns for the Various Methods

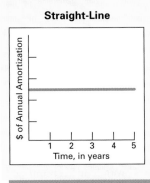

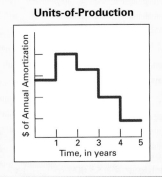

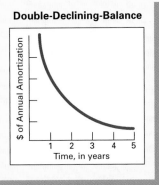

- The graph of straight-line amortization is flat because annual amortization is the same amount in each period.
- UOP amortization follows no particular pattern because annual amortization varies depending on the amount of use of the asset.
- DDB amortization is greatest in the first year and less in the later years.

A recent survey indicated that for companies using a single amortization method, 92 percent use straight-line amortization. For companies using more than one method, the most popular combination was the straight-line and UOP methods, used by 52 percent of companies.[3] For example, ATCO Ltd., the conglomerate based in Calgary, uses straight-line, while WestJet uses straight-line amortization for most capital assets and UOP amortization for its aircraft.

DID YOU GET IT?

MyAccountingLab

To check your understanding of the material in this Learning Objective, complete these questions. The solutions appear on MyAccountingLab so you can check your progress.

4. Sonoma Industrial Products purchased equipment on January 2, 2010, for $176,000. The expected life of the equipment is 10 years or 100,000 units of production, and its residual value is $16,000. Using three amortization methods, the annual amortization expense and total accumulated amortization at the end of 2010 and 2011 are:

	Method A		Method B		Method C	
Year	Annual Amortization Expense	Accumulated Amortization	Annual Amortization Expense	Accumulated Amortization	Annual Amortization Expense	Accumulated Amortization
2010	$16,000	$16,000	$35,200	$35,200	$ 4,800	$ 4,800
2011	16,000	32,000	28,160	63,360	22,400	27,200

(a) Identify the amortization method used in each instance, and show the equation and computation for each. (Round off to the nearest dollar.)

(b) Assume continued use of the same method through the year 2012. Determine the annual amortization expense, accumulated amortization, and book value of the equipment for 2010 through 2012 under each method, assuming 12,000 units of production in 2012.

---

[3] Lavigne, A., D. Paul and J. Tang, Chapter 8 Property, Plant and Equipment—Analysis and Discussion, in *Financial Reporting in Canada, 2008*, thirty-third edition. Toronto: Canadian Institute of Chartered Accountants, 2009, online edition.

5. Give the amortization method that is described by the following statements:
   a. Amortization expense declines over the life of the asset.
   b. Book value declines over the life of the asset.
   c. Amortization expense fluctuates with use.
   d. Amortization expense is the same each period.
   e. This method best fits an asset that amortizes because of physical use.
   f. This method best fits an asset that generates revenue evenly each period.
   g. This method is the most common.
   h. This method records the most amortization over the life of the asset.

6. On January 1, 2010, Kaplan Marketing Co. purchased, for $75,000, equipment that had an expected four-year life and a $3,000 residual value. Through an accounting error, Armstrong expensed the entire cost of the equipment at the time of purchase. What is the effect (overstated, understated, or correctly stated) on (1) total assets and (2) net income in 2010 to 2013?

Other Issues in Accounting for Property, Plant, and Equipment

OBJECTIVE 3

Account for other issues: Amortization for income tax purposes, partial years, and revised assumptions

Amortization for accounting and income tax purposes differs (discussed briefly below). At certain times, amortization must be calculated for partial years; it also happens that amortization assumptions have to be revised. This section covers these topics.

The Relationship between Amortization and Income Taxes

Most companies use the straight-line method for reporting capital asset values and amortization expense to their owners and creditors on their financial statements. But businesses must often keep a separate set of records for calculating the amortization expense they claim on their tax returns because Canada Revenue Agency (CRA) specifies the maximum amortization taxpayers can deduct for income tax purposes. This amount is often different from amortization expense reported on the income statement. Amortization for income tax purposes is discussed in more detail in the Chapter 10 Appendix beginning on page 528.

Amortization for Partial Years

Companies purchase property, plant, and equipment whenever they need them—for example, on February 8 or August 17. They do not wait until the beginning of a year or a month. Therefore, companies develop policies to compute amortization for partial years. Suppose a company purchases a building as a maintenance shop on April 1, 2010, for $600,000. The building's estimated life is 18 years and its estimated residual value is $60,000. The company's fiscal year ends on December 31. How does the company compute amortization for the year ended December 31, 2010?

Many companies compute partial-year amortization by first calculating a full year's amortization. They then multiply full-year amortization by the fraction of the year during which they used the asset. In this case, the company needs to record nine months' amortization, for April to December. Assuming the straight-line method, the 2010 amortization for the maintenance shop is $22,500, computed as follows:

$$\textbf{Full-year amortization:} \quad \frac{\$600,000 - \$60,000}{18 \text{ years}} = \$30,000$$

$$\textbf{Partial-year amortization: } \$30,000 \times 9/12 = \$22,500$$

Another policy

- Records a full month's amortization on an asset bought on or before the 15th of the month.
- Records no amortization on assets purchased after the 15th of the month.

If the company purchased the building above on August 17, then it would record no amortization for August. In this case, the year's amortization for four months (September to December) would be $10,000 ($30,000 × $^4/_{12}$).

Partial-year amortization is computed under the DDB amortization method in the same way—by applying the appropriate percentage of the year during which the asset is used.

For the UOP amortization method, partial-year and full-year amortization are calculated the same way because amortization is based on the number of units produced. Amortization for the UOP method is *not* a function of time, so partial-year amortization is not an issue as it is for the other amortization methods.

Most companies use computerized systems to account for property, plant, and equipment, which will automatically calculate the amortization expense for each period.

Change in the Useful Life of an Amortizable Asset

Estimating the useful life of property, plant, and equipment assets subject to amortization poses an accounting challenge. As previously discussed, a business must estimate the useful life of these assets to compute amortization. This prediction is the most difficult part of accounting for amortization. As the asset is used, the business may change the asset's estimated useful life, based on experience and new information. Such a change is called a change in accounting estimate. Gennum Corporation, the company that creates the technology and intellectual property for broadcasting and communication, included the following note in its November 30, 2008, financial statements:

> **Note 1. Summary of Significant**
> **Accounting Policies, Capital Assets**
> … Equipment and furniture are depreciated using the straight-line method over estimated useful lives ranging from five to seven years. Computer software and hardware are amortized using the straight-line method over the estimated useful life of three years. Capitalized expenditures related to operating systems are amortized using the straight-line method over their estimated useful life of ten years. Leasehold improvements are amortized using the straight-line method over the term of the lease, including one renewal period.
>
> In 2007, the company re-evaluated the estimated useful lives of its buildings and determined that the estimated useful lives should be increased to thirty years from twenty years. The impact of this change was applied on a prospective basis commencing with the first quarter of 2007. The impact of this change of accounting estimate resulted in a decrease in depreciation expense of $503 in 2007.

The majority of the Company's buildings were sold in 2008; therefore, the change in estimate had a minimal impact in the year.

Accounting changes like these are very rare despite the fact that no business has perfect foresight. To *record* a change in accounting estimate, the asset's remaining amortizable book value is spread over its adjusted, or new, remaining useful life. The change is accounted for prospectively.

Assume that a machine owned by Big Rock Brewery Income Trust cost $400,000, and the company originally believed the asset had a 16-year useful life with no residual value. Using the straight-line method, the company would record $25,000 of amortization each year ($400,000 ÷ 16 years = $25,000). Suppose Big Rock Brewery used the asset for four years. Accumulated amortization reached $100,000 ($25,000 × 4 years = $100,000), leaving a book value of $300,000 ($400,000 − $100,000). From its experience with the asset during the first four years, management believes the asset will remain useful for the next 20 years. At the start of Year 5, the company would compute a revised annual amortization amount and record it as follows:

Asset's Remaining Amortizable Book Value	÷	(New) Estimated Useful Life Remaining	=	(New) Annual Amortization Amount
$300,000	÷	20 years	=	$15,000

The yearly amortization entry based on the new estimated useful life is

Amortization Expense—Machine	15,000	
Accumulated Amortization—Machine		15,000

The equation for revised straight-line amortization is

$$\text{Revised Straight-line amortization} = \frac{\text{Cost} - \text{Accumulated amortization} - \text{New residual value}}{\text{Estimated remaining useful life in years}}$$

"Cost" in the equation is the original cost recorded in the general ledger plus any additions to the asset's cost, such as building an addition to add more space to an existing warehouse.

Companies use this equation when changes in the useful life of an asset are made partway through the year. Suppose, in our Big Rock Brewery example, the company used the machine for four-and-a-half years and then realized the machine will remain useful for 24 years in total. The revised straight-line amortization per year for the next 19.5 years (24 years – 4.5 years) is calculated as

$$\text{Revised straight-line amortization} = \frac{\$400,000 - (4.5 \times \$25,000) - \$0}{19.5 \text{ years}}$$

$$= \frac{\$287,500}{19.5}$$

$$= \$14,744$$

Since amortization is an estimate, always round amortization calculations to the nearest whole dollar.

Using Fully Amortized Assets

A *fully amortized asset* is one that has reached the end of its *estimated* useful life. No more amortization is recorded for the asset. If the asset is no longer useful, it is disposed of. But the asset may still be useful, and the company may continue using it. The asset account and its accumulated amortization remain on the books, but no additional amortization is recorded.

To check your understanding of the material in this Learning Objective, complete these questions. The solutions appear on MyAccountingLab so you can check your progress.

7. On April 17, 2010, Logan Services purchased a used crane for $65,000. The company expects the crane to remain useful for 4 years (600 hours of use) and to have a residual value of $5,000. The company expects the crane to be used for 130 hours until December 31, 2010, the year end. Compute the amortization for 2010 using the following amortization methods: (a) straight-line, (b) UOP, and (c) DDB.

8. On January 10, 1990, ABC Co. purchased for $800,000 a building that had an estimated residual value of $50,000 and a useful life of 40 years. On January 13, 2010, a $200,000 addition to the building increased its residual value by $50,000. Calculate straight-line amortization expense for 2010.

9. (a) A fully amortized asset has a cost of $100,000 and zero residual value. What is the asset's accumulated amortization? What is its carrying value?

   (b) The asset cost $100,000. Now suppose its residual value is $10,000. How much is its accumulated amortization if it is fully amortized?

Disposing of Property, Plant, and Equipment

Eventually, an amortizable asset no longer serves its purpose. The asset may be worn out, obsolete, or no longer useful to the business for some other reason. The owner may sell the asset or exchange it. If the asset cannot be sold or exchanged, then it is junked. In all cases, the business should bring amortization up to date and then remove the asset from the books.

OBJECTIVE (4)
Account for the disposal of property, plant, and equipment

To record the disposal of property, plant, and equipment:

- Debit the asset's accumulated amortization account.
- Credit the asset account.

Suppose a business is disposing of a machine and the final year's amortization expense has just been recorded. The cost was $60,000, and there is no residual value. The machine's accumulated amortization thus totals $60,000. Assume this asset cannot be sold or exchanged, so it is junked. The entry to record its disposal is

Accumulated Amortization—Machinery........................	60,000	
Machinery		60,000
To dispose of a fully amortized machine.		

Now both accounts have zero balances, as shown in the T-accounts below:

Machinery		Accumulated Amortization—Machinery	
60,000	60,000	60,000	60,000

If assets are junked before being fully amortized, the company records a loss equal to the asset's book value. Suppose Zellers' store fixtures that cost $40,000 are junked at a loss. Accumulated amortization is $30,000 and book value is therefore $10,000. Disposal of these store fixtures generates a loss, as follows:

Accumulated Amortization—Store Fixtures	30,000	
Loss on Disposal of Property, Plant, and Equipment	10,000	
Store Fixtures...		40,000
To dispose of store fixtures.		

All losses, including this Loss on Disposal of Property, Plant, and Equipment, decrease net income. Along with expenses, losses are reported on the income statement.

When an asset is junked partway through the year, a partial year's amortization must be recorded to update accumulated amortization. Then record the loss on disposal, and remove the asset from the books.

Selling Property, Plant, and Equipment

Suppose Goldcorp Inc., the gold-mining company, sells surplus office furniture on September 30, 2010, for $50,000 cash. The furniture cost $100,000 when purchased on January 1, 2007, and has been amortized on a straight-line basis with a 10-year useful life and no residual value. Prior to recording the sale of the furniture, Goldcorp accountants must update its amortization. Since Goldcorp uses the calendar year as its accounting period, partial amortization must be recorded for nine months from January 1, 2010, to the sale date of September 30. The straight-line amortization entry at September 30, 2010, is

Sept. 30	Amortization Expense—Furniture...................	7,500	
	Accumulated Amortization—Furniture.......		7,500
	To update amortization ($100,000 ÷ 10 years × $\frac{9}{12}$).		

Now, after this entry is posted, the Furniture and the Accumulated Amortization—Furniture accounts appear as follows:

Furniture	**Accumulated Amortization—Furniture**
Jan. 1, 2007 100,000	Dec. 31, 2007 10,000
	Dec. 31, 2008 10,000
	Dec. 31, 2009 10,000
	Sept. 30, 2010 7,500
	Balance 37,500

Book value = $62,500

Suppose Goldcorp sells the office furniture for $50,000 cash. The loss on the sale is $12,500, computed as follows:

Cash received from selling the asset.....................................		$50,000
Book value of asset sold:		
Cost...	$100,000	
Accumulated amortization up to date of sale................	37,500	62,500
Gain (loss) on sale of the asset...		($12,500)

Goldcorp's entry to record the sale of the furniture for $50,000 cash is

Sept. 30	Cash	50,000	
	Loss on Disposal of Property, Plant,		
	and Equipment...	12,500	
	Accumulated Amortization—Furniture...........	37,500	
	Furniture..		100,000
	To dispose of furniture.		

When recording the sale of property, plant, and equipment, companies must

- Record a partial year's amortization to update accumulated amortization if the sale is made partway through the year.
- Remove the balances in the asset account (Furniture, in this case) and its related accumulated amortization account.
- Record a gain or a loss if the cash received differs from the asset's book value.

In our example, cash of $50,000 is less than the book value of $62,500. The result is a loss of $12,500.

LEARNING TIPS

When an asset is sold, a gain or loss on the sale is determined by comparing the proceeds from the sale to the asset's book value:

- Proceeds > Book value = Gain
- Proceeds < Book value = Loss

If the sale price had been $70,000, Goldcorp would have had a gain of $7,500 (Cash, $70,000 – Asset book value, $62,500). The entry to record this gain would be as follows:

Sept. 30	Cash		70,000	
	Accumulated Amortization—Furniture		37,500	
	Furniture			100,000
	Gain on Disposal of Property, Plant, and Equipment			7,500
	To dispose of furniture.			

A gain is recorded when an asset is sold for more than book value. A loss is recorded when the sale price is less than book value. Gains increase net income and losses decrease net income. All gains and losses are reported on the income statement in the "other gains and losses" section.

Exchanging Property, Plant, and Equipment

Businesses often exchange old tangible assets (property, plant and equipment) for newer, more efficient assets. The most common exchange transaction is a trade-in.

Section 3831 of the *CICA Handbook*, "Non-monetary Transactions," guides the accounting treatment of tangible asset exchanges because property, plant, and equipment are defined as non-monetary assets. The first thing to determine in any exchange transaction is whether the transaction has commercial substance. **Commercial substance** exists when the entity's future cash flows from the new asset received will differ in risk, timing, or amount from the cash flows from the old asset given up in the exchange. In other words, if the economic conditions of the company receiving the new asset change, the exchange transaction has commercial substance.

If an exchange transaction has commercial substance, then the new asset is recorded at its fair market value. The old asset is valued at its net book value plus any cash paid as part of the trade-in. A gain or loss is recorded for the old asset in the same way as when an asset is sold for cash.

KEY POINT

Why is the trade-in allowance usually different from the book value? The book value depends on the asset's historical cost and on the amortization method used. The trade-in allowance is based on the market value of the asset being traded in (or may be an adjustment to the selling price of the new asset).

Suppose Horton Hardware owns a delivery truck that it purchased for $42,000 on January 2, 2006. The old truck was expected to last seven years and was amortized on a straight-line basis. On January 2, 2011, Horton Hardware exchanged this truck for a newer truck that had a fair market value of $53,000. Horton Hardware received a trade-in allowance of $8,000 for the old truck and paid the seller $45,000 cash. Horton Hardware will receive better gas mileage with the new truck and will be able to save delivery expenses by delivering more bulky items with the new truck. Therefore, *this exchange of assets has commercial substance.* The entry to record this exchange would be as follows:

New Truck	53,000	
Loss on Exchange of Assets	4,000	
Accumulated Amortization—Old Truck (5 × $6,000)	30,000	
Cash		45,000
Old Truck		42,000
To record exchange of the old truck and cash for a new truck.		

If an exchange transaction does not have commercial substance, then the new asset is recorded at the book value of the old asset. No gain or loss is reported for the old asset. Since most entities agree to an exchange of non-monetary assets only if it creates an economic improvement and, thus, has commercial substance, an exchange of non-monetary assets without commercial substance is expected to be rare, and will be discussed no further.

Exhibit 10–10 summarizes the accounting treatment of non-monetary-asset exchange transactions.

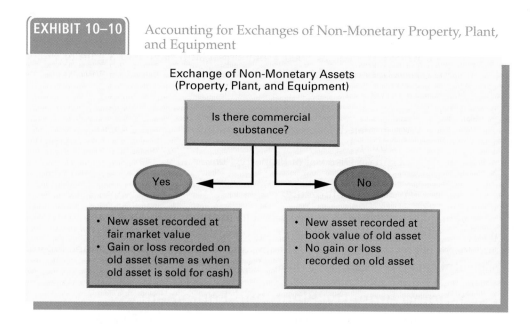

Internal Control of Property, Plant, and Equipment

Internal control of property, plant, and equipment includes safeguarding them and having an adequate accounting system. Recall from Chapter 8 the importance of a strong system of internal controls within a business. To see the need for controlling capital assets, consider the following situation. The home office and top managers of Petrol Mfg. Ltd. are in Calgary. The company manufactures gas pumps in Michigan, then sells them in Europe. Top managers and owners of the company rarely see the manufacturing facility and therefore cannot control their capital assets by on-the-spot management. What features does their internal control system need?

Safeguarding property, plant, and equipment includes:

1. Assigning responsibility for custody of the assets.
2. Separating custody of assets from accounting for the assets (separation of duties being a cornerstone of internal control in almost every area).
3. Setting up security measures—for instance, guards and restricted access to property, plant, and equipment—to prevent theft.
4. Protecting property, plant, and equipment from the elements (rain, snow, and so on).
5. Having adequate insurance against fire, storm, and other casualty losses.
6. Training operating personnel in the proper use of the assets.
7. Checking property, plant, and equipment regularly for existence and condition.
8. Keeping a regular maintenance schedule.

DID YOU GET IT? MyAccountingLab

To check your understanding of the material in this Learning Objective, complete these questions. The solutions appear on MyAccountingLab so you can check your progress.

10. ABC Catering Service purchased equipment on January 8, 2007, for $58,500. ABC expected the equipment to last six years and to have a residual value of $4,500.

    (a) Suppose ABC sold the equipment for $43,000 on December 29, 2009. Journalize the sale of the equipment, assuming straight-line amortization is used.

(b) Suppose ABC sold the equipment for $23,000 on December 29, 2009. Journalize the sale of the equipment, assuming straight-line amortization is used.

11. Suppose Quik Trip Stores' comparative income statement for two years included these items:

	2010	2009
	($ thousands)	
Net sales...	$7,200	$6,800
Income from operations	49	65
Gain on sale of store facilities.................................	28	—
Income before income taxes....................................	$ 77	$ 65

Which was the better year for Quik Trip: 2010 or 2009? Explain.

12. In 2008, Luk's Catering purchased a portable food heater for $3,100 cash. The journal entry to record the purchase included a debit to Catering Equipment. During 2008 and 2009, Luk's Catering recorded total amortization of $2,200 on the heater. On January 2, 2010, Luk's Catering traded in the old food heater for a new one that is more efficient, paying $2,900 cash. This exchange transaction has commercial substance. Journalize Luk's Catering's exchange of equipment.

Accounting for Natural Resources (Wasting Assets)

Natural resources are tangible capital assets that are often called *wasting assets* because they are used up in the process of production. Examples include iron ore, coal, oil, gas, and timber. Natural resources are like inventories in the ground (coal) or on top of the ground (timber). Natural resources are expensed through amortization. Some companies use the word **depletion** to describe amortization of natural resources. Amortization expense, or *depletion*, is that portion of the cost of natural resources that is used up in a particular period. Amortization expense for natural resources is computed by the *UOP* formula:

OBJECTIVE 5
Account for natural resources

$$\frac{\text{Amortization}}{\text{expense}} = \frac{(\text{Cost} - \text{Residual value})}{\text{Estimated total units of natural resource}} \times \frac{\text{Number of}}{\text{units removed}}$$

An oil well may cost $300,000 and contain an estimated 10,000 barrels of oil. (Natural resources usually have no residual value.) The amortization rate would be $30 per barrel ($300,000 ÷ 10,000 barrels). If 3,000 barrels are extracted during the first year, amortization expense is $90,000 (3,000 barrels × $30 per barrel). The amortization entry for the year is

Amortization Expense—Oil	90,000	
Accumulated Amortization—Oil		90,000

If 4,500 barrels are removed the next year, amortization is $135,000 (4,500 barrels × $30 per barrel).

Accumulated Amortization for natural resources is a contra account similar to Accumulated Amortization for property, plant, and equipment. Natural resource assets can be reported on the balance sheet as is shown for oil in the following example.

Property, plant, and equipment:		
Land		$120,000
Buildings...	$800,000	
Equipment..	160,000	
	960,000	
Less: Accumulated amortization	410,000	
		550,000
Oil and gas properties:		
Oil..	**340,000**	
Less: Accumulated amortization.............................	**75,000**	
Net oil and gas properties		265,000
Property, plant, and equipment, net		$935,000

Future Removal and Site Restoration Costs

There is increasing concern on the part of individuals and governments about the environment. Often, in the past, a company exploiting natural resources, such as a mining company, would simply abandon the site once the ore body was mined completely. Now, there is legislation in most jurisdictions requiring a natural resource company to remove buildings, equipment, and waste, and to restore the site once a location is to be dismantled and abandoned.

The *CICA Handbook* refers to future removal and site restoration costs as an "asset retirement obligation," which is estimated at the time the asset is acquired or the obligation becomes known. The liability (a credit) for the asset retirement obligation is measured at the end of each period at the best estimate of the future expenditures required to settle the present obligation. This estimate is determined by the judgment of management, supplemented by experience of similar transactions and perhaps reports from independent experts. The same amount is recorded as an asset retirement cost (a debit) and added to the carrying amount of its related asset (such as a factory). The asset retirement cost must then be expensed using a systematic and rational method over the asset's useful life. Asset retirement obligations are reviewed at each balance sheet date and adjusted to reflect the current best estimate. Companies must give a general description of the asset retirement obligations and the associated long-lived assets; the amount of the asset retirement obligation at the end of the year; the total amount paid toward the liability during the year; and, if readily determinable, the fair value of assets that are legally restricted for purposes of settling asset retirement obligations.

DID YOU GET IT?

MyAccountingLab

To check your understanding of the material in this Learning Objective, complete these questions. The solutions appear on MyAccountingLab so you can check your progress.

13. Suppose West Fraser Timber Co. Ltd. purchases, for $600,000, land that contains an estimated 400,000 fbm (foot-board measures) of timber. The land can be sold for $100,000 after the timber has been cut. If West Fraser harvests 200,000 fbm in the year of purchase, how much amortization should be recorded?

14. Suppose your company is in mining. It has acquired a piece of property with good assay results and its geologists believe the mine will be productive for 20 years. The provincial government has approved the project as long as your company agrees to restore the land to its original condition at the end of the mine's useful life. According to GAAP, your company must estimate the cost of this restoration and record an asset retirement obligation (a liability) and the related asset retirement cost (a debit) on its balance sheet each year. What is the purpose of this disclosure?

Accounting for Goodwill and Intangible Assets

As we saw earlier in this chapter, **intangible assets** have no physical form. Instead, these assets convey special rights from ownership of patents, copyrights, trademarks, franchises, leaseholds, and goodwill.

OBJECTIVE 6
Account for goodwill and intangible assets

In our technology-driven economy, intangibles are very important. Consider the online auctioneer eBay. The company has no physical products or equipment, but it helps people buy and sell everything from toys to bathroom tiles. Each month eBay serves millions of customers. In a sense, eBay is a company of intangibles.

The intellectual capital of eBay, Research In Motion, or Open Text is difficult to measure, but when one company buys another, we get a glimpse of the value of the acquired intellectual capital. Intangibles can account for most of a company's market value, so companies must value their intangibles just as they do their physical and financial assets.

Intangibles are expensed as they expire through amortization. Amortization applies to intangibles in the same way as it applies to property, plant, and equipment, and natural resources.

Amortization is computed over the lesser of the asset's legal life or estimated useful life. Obsolescence often shortens an intangible asset's useful life. Amortization expense for intangibles can be written off directly against the intangible asset account with *no accumulated amortization account*. The residual value of most intangibles is zero.

Some intangibles have indefinite lives. For these intangibles, the company records no systematic amortization in each period. Instead, it accounts for any decrease in the value of the intangible, as we shall see for goodwill.

Specific Intangibles

Patents **Patents** are federal government grants conveying an exclusive right for 20 years to produce and sell an invention. The invention may be a product or a process. Patented products include Bombardier Ski-Doos® and the Research In Motion BlackBerry®. Like any other asset, a patent may be purchased. Suppose Research in Motion pays $2,000,000 to acquire a patent, and it believes the expected useful life of the patent is five years. Amortization expense is $400,000 per year ($2,000,000 ÷ 5 years). The company's acquisition and amortization entries for this patent are as follows:

Jan.	1	Patent.. 2,000,000	
		Cash	2,000,000
		To acquire a patent.	
Dec.	31	Amortization Expense—Patent 400,000	
		Patent...	400,000
		To amortize the cost of a patent ($2,000,000 ÷ 5).	

At the end of the first year, Research in Motion would report the patent at $1,600,000 ($2,000,000 minus the first year's amortization of $400,000).

Copyrights **Copyrights** are exclusive rights to reproduce and sell software, a book, a musical composition, a film, or some other work of art. Issued by the federal government, copyrights extend 50 years beyond the end of the author's life. A company may pay a large sum to purchase an existing copyright from the owner. For example, the publisher McClelland & Stewart Ltd. may pay the author of a popular novel tens of thousands of dollars or more for the book's copyright. The useful life of a copyright for a popular book may be two or three years; on the other hand, some copyrights, especially of musical compositions, such as works by the Beatles, seem to remain valuable over several decades.

Trademarks and Brand Names   **Trademarks** and **brand names** (or **trade names**) are distinctive identifications of products or services. For example, The Sports Network has its distinctive logo of the white letters *tsn* on a red background, and the Edmonton Oilers and Toronto Blue Jays have insignia that identify their respective teams. Molson Canadian, Swiss Chalet chicken, WestJet, and Roots are everyday trade names. Advertising slogans such as Speedy Muffler's "At Speedy you're a somebody" are also legally protected. The cost of a trademark or trade name is amortized over its useful life.

Franchises and Licences   **Franchises** and **licences** are privileges granted by a private business or a government to sell a product or service in accordance with specified conditions. The Edmonton Oilers hockey organization is a franchise granted to its owners by the National Hockey League. Subway and Re/Max Ltd. are other well-known franchises. The acquisition cost of a franchise or licence is amortized over its useful life.

Leaseholds   A **leasehold** is a right arising from a prepayment that a lessee (renter) makes to secure the use of an asset from a lessor (landlord). For example, most malls lease the space to the mall stores and shops that you visit. Often, leases require the lessee to make this prepayment in addition to monthly rental payments. The prepayment is a debit to an intangible asset account entitled Leaseholds. This amount is amortized over the life of the lease by debiting Rent Expense and crediting Leaseholds.

Sometimes lessees modify or improve the leased asset. For example, a lessee may construct a fence on leased land. The lessee debits the cost of the fence to a separate intangible asset account, Leasehold Improvements, and amortizes its cost over the lesser of the term of the lease and of its useful life.

Goodwill   Goodwill is truly a unique asset. *Goodwill* in accounting is a more limited term than in everyday use, as in "goodwill among men." In accounting, **goodwill** is the excess of the cost to purchase a company over the market value of its net assets (assets minus liabilities). Why might an acquiring company pay an amount greater than the market value of net assets acquired when purchasing a going business? The business being acquired might have good customer relations, a good location, efficient operations, a monopoly in the marketplace, strong sources of financing, and other factors that make it more valuable than just the net assets being acquired.

Suppose Purolator acquires Regional Express Ltd. at a cost of $10 million. The market value of Regional Express's assets is $9 million, and its liabilities total $1 million. In this case, Purolator paid $2 million for goodwill, computed as follows:

Purchase price paid for Regional Express Ltd.		$10 million
Sum of the market value of Regional Express's assets	$9 million	
Less: Regional Express's liabilities	1 million	
Market value of Regional Express's net assets		8 million
Excess is called *goodwill*		$ 2 million

Purolator's entry to record the acquisition of Regional Express Ltd., including its goodwill, would be

Assets (Cash; Receivables; Inventories;		
Property, Plant, and Equipment; all at market value)	9,000,000	
Goodwill	2,000,000	
Liabilities		1,000,000
Cash		10,000,000
Purchased Regional Express Ltd.		

Goodwill has the following special features:

1. Goodwill is recorded, at its cost, only by the company that purchases another company. A company's favourable location, superior product, or outstanding reputation may create goodwill for a company, but it is never recorded by that entity. Instead, goodwill is recorded *only* by the acquiring entity when it buys another company. A purchase transaction provides objective evidence of the value of the goodwill.

2. Goodwill has an indefinite life, so it is not amortized like other intangibles. According to GAAP, the purchaser must assess the goodwill every year and, if its value is impaired (if the fair value falls below the carrying value in the accounting records), the goodwill must be written down to reflect the impairment. The write-down amount is accounted for as a loss in the year of the write-down. For example, suppose Purolator's goodwill—purchased above—is worth only $1,500,000 at the end of the first year. In that case, Purolator would make this entry:

Loss on Goodwill	500,000	
Goodwill..		500,000
Recorded loss on goodwill ($2,000,000 − $1,500,000).		

Purolator would then report this goodwill at its current value of $1,500,000.

Accounting for Research and Development Costs Accounting for research and development (R&D) costs is one of the most difficult issues the accounting profession has faced. R&D is the lifeblood of companies such as Bombardier, Research in Motion, and Open Text because it is vital to the development of new products and processes. The cost of R&D activities is one of these companies' most valuable (intangible) assets.

Canada requires *development costs* meeting certain criteria to be capitalized, while other countries require such costs to be expensed in the year incurred. Canada and most other countries require *research costs* to be expensed as incurred.

Some critics argue that R&D costs represent future benefits and should be capitalized, others agree with the present accounting standards, and still others think all R&D costs should be expensed.

Ethical Issues: Property, Plant, and Equipment, and Intangible Assets

The main ethical issue in accounting for property, plant, and equipment and for intangible assets is whether to capitalize or expense a particular cost. In this area, companies have split personalities. On the one hand, they want to save on taxes. This motivates companies to expense as many costs as possible to decrease taxable income. But they also want their financial statements to look as good as possible, with high net income and high reported amounts for assets.

In most cases, whether a cost is capitalized or expensed for tax purposes, it must be treated the same way for accounting purposes in the financial statements. What, then, is the ethical path? Accountants should follow the general guidelines for capitalizing a cost:

Capitalize all costs that provide a future benefit for the business, and expense all other costs.

Many companies have gotten into trouble by capitalizing costs that really should have been expensed. They made their financial statements look better than the facts warranted. WorldCom committed this type of accounting fraud, and its former top executives are now in prison as a result. There are few cases of companies getting into trouble by following the general guidelines, or even by erring on the side of expensing questionable costs. This is another example of accounting conservatism. We discussed accounting conservatism in Chapter 6, page 310.

DID YOU GET IT?

To check your understanding of the material in this Learning Objective, complete these questions. The solutions appear on MyAccountingLab so you can check your progress.

15. Suppose a company paid $650,000 on January 5, 2009, to acquire a patent that it believes will have a five-year useful life. The company's year end is December 31.

   (a) Journalize the purchase of the patent and the amortization entry at year end.

   (b) Suppose this same patent was acquired on May 13, 2009. Journalize the purchase of the patent and the amortization entry at year end.

16. Suppose Research In Motion acquires Novel Networks, a small computer company that produces specialized computer programs, for $2,000,000. Novel Networks' assets have a book value of $500,000 and a market value of $400,000. Its liabilities have a market value of $300,000. Record the acquisition of Novel Networks by Research In Motion.

17. (a) Suppose Mega Stores was having a bad year—net income below expectations and lower than last year's income. For amortization purposes, Mega Stores decided to extend the estimated useful lives of its amortizable assets. This decision was *not* based on any belief that the actual useful life was longer than originally thought. How would this accounting change affect Mega Stores' (a) amortization expense, (b) net income, and (c) owner's equity? Is this decision ethical?

   (b) Suppose that the Mega Stores' change in accounting estimate turned a loss year into a profitable year. Without the change, the company would have reported a net loss for the year. But the change enabled the company to report positive net income. Under GAAP, Mega Stores' annual report must disclose the change in accounting estimate. Would users of the financial statements, such as the bank, evaluate Mega Stores as better or worse in response to this disclosure?

Understand the Impact on Property, Plant, and Equipment of IFRS

OBJECTIVE 7

Understand the impact on property, plant, and equipment of international financial reporting standards (IFRS)

One of the more complex differences between GAAP for private enterprises and IFRS is in the area of property, plant, and equipment, and a discussion of many of the differences is beyond the scope of this textbook. However, a brief review of IFRS for property, plant, and equipment will introduce some of these differences.

IFRS follow the general principle of capitalizing an asset when the asset will provide future economic benefit. However, after an asset has been capitalized, IFRS call for companies to capitalize replacement parts and to derecognize the parts that are replaced. In other words, each part of an item of property, plant, and equipment that is significant relative to the total cost of the asset must be amortized separately. For example, if a company purchases a building, it would have to amortize the significant components of the building separately. The roof may be amortized over a different period of time than the heating and air conditioning system, for example. This change will add considerable complexity to the accounting for property, plant, and equipment.

Measuring the cost of the asset at acquisition follows the same principle as was shown in this chapter for private enterprises. However, in the years following acquisition, the basis of measurement may differ under IFRS. Companies have the option to use the method described in this chapter or they can follow a revaluation model. Under the revaluation approach, the carrying amount of the property, plant, and equipment is its fair value at the date of revaluation (which could be annually, but not necessarily). The accounting under this method is quite complex and beyond the scope of introductory accounting.

DID YOU GET IT?

To check your understanding of the material in this Learning Objective, complete this question. The solution appears on MyAccountingLab so you can check your progress.

18. Under IFRS, companies will need to calculate amortization separately for the major components of an amortizable asset. Would this provide better information for the users of financial information?

Understand the Impact on Intangible Assets of IFRS

Under IFRS, an intangible asset is defined as "an identifiable non-monetary asset without physical substance," a definition that is very nearly the same as the definition under Canadian GAAP for private enterprises. The word "identifiable" allows for the separation of intangible assets from goodwill under IFRS. Goodwill is not considered an intangible asset under IFRS because it is not separately identifiable.

OBJECTIVE 8

Understand the impact on intangible assets of international financial reporting standards (IFRS)

Accounting for intangible assets under IFRS is more complex than under Canadian GAAP for private enterprises. Intangible assets that have been purchased or acquired from other parties are accounted for in a manner similar to the acquisition of property, plant, and equipment described in this chapter. Internally generated intangible assets must be analyzed to determine whether they will provide a future benefit to the company. If they will, they can be capitalized and amortized; if not, they will be expensed in the current period.

As with property, plant, and equipment, companies have the option of using a cost model to determine the carrying amount of the intangible asset. This method is similar to the method allowed under Canadian GAAP for private enterprises. Companies may also follow a revaluation model, and carry the intangible asset at its fair value on the balance sheet. The accounting for the revaluation method is quite complex and beyond the scope of introductory accounting.

DID YOU GET IT?

To check your understanding of the material in this Learning Objective, complete this question. The solution appears on MyAccountingLab so you can check your progress.

19. Suppose your publicly traded company has developed a process that will make the manufacture of a product more efficient and will streamline costs. The only costs associated with this internally generated patent are the legal costs associated with registering the patent. Your company immediately sells the patent to another publicly traded company for about 100 times the cost of the patent. How would your company value the patent before it is sold? How will the acquiring company record the acquisition of the patent?

As we conclude this chapter, we return to our opening questions: What do we mean by property, plant, and equipment, and why are they important? Should you capitalize or expense costs associated with a new asset and with an existing asset? What is amortization, and how can amortization expense be calculated? How is amortization reported on the income statement and the balance sheet? Can a company use different amortization methods for accounting and income tax purposes? These questions were answered throughout this chapter. The Decision Guidelines end this chapter by applying the answers to decisions a franchise owner must make.

Suppose you buy an Extreme Fitness Club franchise and invest in fitness equipment. You have some decisions to make about how to account for the franchise and the equipment. The Decision Guidelines will help you maximize your cash flow and do the accounting properly. Remember that there can be exceptions to these guidelines if amounts are immaterial.

Decision	Guidelines
Should you capitalize or expense a cost?	General rule: Capitalize all costs that provide *future benefit*. Expense all costs that provide *no future benefit*.
Should you capitalize or expense • Cost associated with a new asset? • Cost associated with an existing asset?	Capitalize all costs that bring the asset to its intended use. Capitalize only those costs that add to the asset's usefulness or its useful life. Expense all other costs as maintenance or repairs.
Which amortization method should you use: • For financial reporting? • For income tax?	Use the method that best matches amortization expense against the revenues produced by the asset. Use the maximum CCA rates allowed by CRA to produce the greatest deductions from taxable income (see Chapter 10 Appendix). A company can use different amortization methods for financial reporting and for income tax purposes. In Canada, this practice is considered both legal and ethical.

Summary Problems for Your Review

Problem 1

Name: Sonoma Industrial Products
Industry: Industrial products producer
Accounting Period: Asset sale on July 2, 2012

Sonoma Industrial Products purchased equipment on January 2, 2010, for $176,000. The expected life of the equipment is 10 years or 100,000 units of production, and its residual value is $16,000. Management has amortized the equipment using the DDB method. On July 2, 2012, Sonoma sold the equipment for $100,000 cash.

Required Record Sonoma Industrial Products' amortization for 2012 using the DDB method, and the sale of the equipment on July 2, 2012.

Problem 2

Name: Meben Logistics
Industry: Not stated
Accounting Period: Revised amortization in 2010

Meben Logistics purchased a building at a cost of $500,000 on January 2, 2006. Meben has amortized the building by using the straight-line method, a 35-year life, and a residual value of $150,000. On January 2, 2010, the business changed the useful life of the building from 35 years to 25 years. The fiscal year of Meben Logistics ends on December 31.

Required Record amortization for 2010 assuming no change in the building's residual value.

SOLUTION

Problem 1

Double-Declining-Balance

Year	Annual Amortization Expense	Accumulated Amortization	Book Value
Start			$176,000
2010	$35,200	$ 35,200	140,800
2011	28,160	63,360	112,640
2012	22,528	85,888	90,112

2012

Jul. 2   Amortization Expense—Equipment 11,264
      Accumulated Amortization—Equipment   11,264
      To record amortization expense for the period
      Jan. 1, 2012, to Jun. 30, 2012. ($112,460 × 0.20 × ½)

Amortization expense must first be recorded for the portion of the year that the asset was used before it was sold. Since the asset was sold during 2012, use 2012's book value in the amortization-expense calculation.

Jul. 2   Cash... 100,000
      Accumulated Amortization—Equipment* 74,624
      Loss on Sale of Equipment 1,376
      Equipment..   176,000
      To record sale of equipment.

If Cash > Book value, then record a gain on disposal.

If Cash < Book value, then record a loss on disposal.

*$35,200 + $28,160 + $11,264 = $74,624.

Problem 2

The equation for revised straight-line amortization is

$$\text{Revised Straight-line Amortization} = \frac{\text{Cost} - \text{Accumulated Amortization} - \text{New Residual Value}}{\text{Estimated Remaining Useful Life in Years}}$$

where

Cost = $500,000 (given)
Accumulated Amortization = [($500,000 − $150,000) ÷ 35 years] × 4 years
                    = $40,000
New Residual Value = $150,000 (the same as old residual value)
Estimated Remaining Useful Life in Years = 25 − 4 = 21 years

Calculating the estimated remaining useful life in years can cause confusion. In this case, the expected useful life changed from 35 years to 25 years. Since amortization has already been expensed for the first 4 years, 21 years remain in the building's new 25-year useful life.

Therefore,

$$\text{Revised Straight-line Amortization} = \frac{\$500,000 - \$40,000 - \$150,000}{21 \text{ years}} = \$14,762 \text{ per year, rounded}$$

2010

Dec. 31   Amortization Expense—Building................... 14,762
      Accumulated Amortization—Building......   14,762
      To record annual amortization for 2010.

CHAPTER 10 APPENDIX

Capital Cost Allowance

OBJECTIVE A1

Explain capital cost allowance
and amortization for income
tax purposes

Canada Revenue Agency (CRA) allows corporations as well as individuals with business or professional income to compute deductions from income to recognize the consumption or use of capital assets. The deductions are called **capital cost allowance (CCA)**, the term CRA uses to describe amortization for tax purposes. CRA specifies the *maximum* rates allowed for each asset class, called *CCA rates*. A taxpayer may claim from zero to the maximum CCA allowed in a year. Most taxpayers claim the maximum CCA since this provides the largest deduction from taxable income as quickly as possible. Claiming the maximum CCA reduces taxable income and thus tax payable, leaving more cash available for investment or other business uses.

Some typical CRA rates and classes are as follows:

	Rate	Class
Automobiles	30%	10
Most buildings bought after 1987	4%	1
Computer software	100%	12
Office furniture and fixtures	20%	8
Computers	45%	45

CRA allows the taxpayer to claim only 50 percent of the normal CCA rate in the year of acquisition. However, there are some exceptions and Class 12 is one of them. Class 12 assets have a full 100 percent CCA rate in the year of acquisition.

The CCA rate is applied to the balance in the asset class at the end of the year (cost minus accumulated CCA claimed to date) in the same manner as with the DDB method discussed on pages 509 to 511.

To illustrate, during the year beginning January 2, 2010, Doug Copely, an entrepreneur, bought a computer and an accounting software package to help him account for his business income. The computer cost $2,500 and the software cost $300. Doug decided to amortize the computer and the software on a straight-line basis over five years, and expects the computer and software to have no value at the end of five years. These assumptions led to an amortization expense of $500.00 per year ($2,500 ÷ 5 years) for the computer and an amortization expense of $60.00 per year ($300 ÷ 5 years) for the software.

For income tax purposes, the computer is considered to be a Class 45 asset. The CCA rate for Class 45 assets is 45 percent. The software is considered to be a Class 12 asset. The CCA rate for Class 12 assets is 100 percent. Remember that for most asset classes, a taxpayer can claim only 50 percent of normal CCA in the year of acquisition, which in Doug's case is the year 2010. In 2010, Doug could claim up to the maximum CCA of $562.50 ([$2,500 × 45%] × 50%) for the computer. However, he can claim up to the maximum CCA of $300.00 for the software in 2010. These are the only capital assets in these classes.

In 2011, Doug would apply the Class 45 rate of 45 percent to the cost of the computer remaining after the 2010 CCA is deducted. In 2011, he could claim up to the maximum CCA of $871.87 ([$2,500.00 – $562.50] × 45%) for the computer. Following the same process in 2012, Doug could claim up to the maximum CCA of $479.53 ([$2,500.00 – $562.50 – $871.87] × 45%) for the computer. The table below shows the maximum CCA that Doug could deduct from his business income for the first six years:

	2010	2011	2012	2013	2014	2015
Computer	$562.50	$871.87	$479.53	$263.74	$145.06	$79.78
Software	$300.00	0	0	0	0	0

Notice that in 2015, the sixth year that Doug owned the computer, he is able to deduct CCA for income tax purposes. However, for accounting purposes, the computer would be fully amortized at the end of 2014, the fifth year, since Doug decided to amortize the computer on a straight-line basis over five years. This example shows that amortization expense deducted from income on the income statement often differs from the CCA claimed by a taxpayer on the tax return.

CRA will allow a company to use any amortization method it chooses as long as the amount of CCA claimed for tax purposes does not exceed the maximum amount allowed by CRA. For tax purposes, most companies select the maximum amount allowed by CRA, which results in accelerated amortization of an item. Accelerated amortization minimizes taxable income and income tax payments in the early years of the asset's life, thereby maximizing the business's cash at the earliest possible time. Straight-line amortization spreads amortization evenly over the life of the asset, which would *not* minimize income tax in the same way. CCA and amortization issues are quite complicated. These issues are studied more fully in advanced accounting courses and tax courses.

Summary

1. **Measure the cost of property, plant, and equipment.** Property, plant, and equipment are tangible, long-lived assets that the business uses in its operations. The cost of a tangible asset is the purchase price plus applicable taxes (but not GST), purchase commissions, and all other necessary amounts incurred to acquire the asset and to prepare it for its intended use.

2. **Calculate and account for amortization.** The process of allocating a property, plant, and equipment asset's cost to expense over the period the asset is used is called *amortization*. Three common methods businesses use to account for the amortization of property, plant, and equipment are *straight-line*, units-of-production (*UOP*), and *double-declining-balance (DDB)*. All these methods require accountants to estimate the asset's useful life and residual value.

3. **Account for other issues: Amortization for income tax purposes, partial years, and revised assumptions.** Amortization for financial statement purposes and income tax purposes often differs. This is both legal and ethical. When assets are purchased or sold during the year, calculate partial-year amortization. When significant changes occur to an asset's cost, residual value, or useful life, annual amortization expense must be revised for all future years to reflect the changes.

4. **Account for the disposal of property, plant, and equipment.** Before disposing of, selling, or trading in a property, plant, and equipment asset, the business updates the asset's amortization. Disposal is then recorded by removing the book balances from both the asset account and its related accumulated amortization account. Sales often result in a gain or a loss, which is reported on the income statement. Disposal may or may not result in a reported gain or loss, depending on the circumstances.

5. **Account for natural resources.** The cost of natural resources (wasting assets), a special category of long-lived assets, is expensed through amortization (depletion). Amortization of natural resources is computed on a UOP basis.

6. **Account for goodwill and intangible assets.** *Intangible assets* are assets that have no physical form. They give their owners a special right to current and expected future benefits. The major types of intangible assets are patents, copyrights, trademarks, franchises and licences, leaseholds, and goodwill. Amortization of these intangibles is computed on a straight-line basis over the lesser of the legal life and useful life. Goodwill is not amortized, but its carrying value is assessed annually and written down if its market value is less than its carrying value.

7. **Understand the impact on property, plant, and equipment of international financial reporting standards (IFRS).** Canadian GAAP for private enterprises and IFRS are converged in many aspects of accounting for property, plant, and equipment. However, under IFRS, each part of an item of property, plant, and equipment that is significant relative to the total cost of the asset must be amortized separately. IFRS also allow companies to value property, plant, and equipment at fair market value at each balance-sheet date subsequent to acquisition if they so choose.

8. **Understand the impact on intangible assets of international financial reporting standards (IFRS).** Under IFRS, intangible assets that have been purchased or acquired from other parties are accounted for like

property, plant, and equipment. Internally generated intangible assets must be analyzed: if they will provide a future benefit to the company, they can be capitalized and amortized; if not, they will be expensed in the current period. IFRS allow companies the option to use a revaluation model and measure the intangible assets at their fair market value at the end of each fiscal year, or to use the cost model.

A1. **Explain capital cost allowance and amortization for income tax purposes.** CRA allows companies and individuals to claim capital cost allowance (CCA) (amortization) against taxable income but sets maximum rates that may be claimed for each class of amortizable assets. Many companies use the maximum rates allowed for tax purposes but lower rates (for example, straight-line) for income-statement purposes.

SELF-STUDY QUESTIONS

Test your understanding of the chapter by marking the correct answer for each of the following questions:

1. Which of the following payments is not included in the cost of land? (*p. 501*)
   a. Removal of old building
   b. Legal fees
   c. Property taxes in arrears paid at acquisition
   d. Cost of fencing and lighting

2. Roche Products paid $150,000 for two machines valued at $120,000 and $60,000. Roche will record these machines at costs of (*p. 504*)
   a. $120,000 and $60,000
   b. $75,000 each
   c. $100,000 and $50,000
   d. $90,000 and $60,000

3. Which of the following items is a repair? (*p. 505*)
   a. New brakes for delivery truck
   b. Paving of a company parking lot
   c. Cost of a new engine for a truck
   d. Building permit paid to construct an addition to an existing building

4. Which of the following definitions fits amortization? (*p. 506*)
   a. Allocation of the asset's market value to expense over its useful life
   b. Allocation of the asset's cost to expense over its useful life
   c. Decreases in the asset's market value over its useful life
   d. Increases in the fund set aside to replace the asset when it is worn out

5. Which amortization method's amounts are not computed based on time? (*p. 509*)
   a. Straight-line
   b. Units-of-production (UOP)
   c. DDB
   d. All are based on time

6. Which amortization method gives the greatest amount of expense in the early years of using the asset? (*pp. 510–511*)
   a. Straight-line
   b. UOP
   c. DDB
   d. All are equal

7. A company paid $900,000 for a building and was amortizing it by the straight-line method over a 40-year life, with estimated residual value of $60,000. After 10 years, it became evident that the building's *remaining* useful life would be 40 years with a residual value of $50,000. Amortization for the 11th year is (*p. 514*)
   a. $16,000
   b. $17,250
   c. $21,000
   d. $28,000

8. Labrador Stores scrapped an automobile that cost $28,000 and had a book value of $2,500. The entry to record this disposal is (*p. 515*)

   a. Loss on Disposal of Automobile   2,500
        Automobile   2,500
   b. Accumulated Amortization   28,000
        Automobile   28,000
   c. Accumulated Amortization   25,500
        Automobile   25,500
   d. Accumulated Amortization...........   25,500
        Loss on Disposal of Automobile...   2,500
        Automobile   28,000

9. Amortization of a natural resource is computed in the same manner as which amortization method? (*p. 519*)
   a. Straight-line
   b. UOP
   c. Declining-balance

10. Lacy Company paid $1,100,000 to acquire Gentech Systems. Gentech's assets had a market value of $1,800,000 and its liabilities were $800,000. In recording the acquisition, Lacy will record goodwill of (*pp. 522–523*)
   a. $100,000
   b. $1,000,000
   c. $1,100,000
   d. $0

Answers to Self-Study Questions

1. d   **2.** c [($120,000 ÷ ($120,000 + $60,000)) × $150,000 = $100,000;
($60,000 ÷ ($120,000 + $60,000)) × $150,000 = $50,000]   **3.** a   **4.** b   **5.** b   **6.** c

7. a Amortizable cost = $900,000 − $60,000 = $840,000
$840,000 ÷ 40 years = $21,000 per year
$900,000 − ($21,000 × 10 years) = $690,000
($690,000 − 50,000) ÷ 40 years = $16,000 per year

8. d   **9.** b   **10.** a [$1,100,000 − ($1,800,000 − $800,000) = $100,000]

530   **Part 2** Accounting for Assets and Liabilities

ACCOUNTING VOCABULARY

Amortizable cost   (p. 507)
Amortization   (p. 506)
Betterment   (p. 505)
Brand name   (p. 522)
Capital cost allowance (CCA)   (p. 528)
Commercial substance   (p. 517)
Copyright   (p. 521)
Depletion   (p. 519)
Double-declining-balance (DDB) method   (p. 509)
Estimated residual value   (p. 507)
Estimated useful life   (p. 507)
Franchise   (p. 522)

Goodwill   (p. 522)
Intangible asset   (pp. 499, 521)
Leasehold   (p. 522)
Licence   (p. 522)
Patent   (p. 521)
Repair   (p. 505)
Salvage value   (p. 507)
Scrap value   (p. 507)
Straight-line method   (p. 508)
Trademark   (p. 522)
Trade name   (p. 522)
Units-of-production (UOP) method   (p. 509)

SIMILAR ACCOUNTING TERMS

Amortization	Depreciation (for assets such as property, plant, and equipment); Depletion (for natural resources)
Natural resources	Wasting assets
Property, plant, and equipment	Long-lived assets; Long-term assets; Capital assets
Trade name	Brand name
Residual value	Salvage value; Scrap value

Assignment Material

QUESTIONS

1. Describe how to measure the cost of property, plant, and equipment. Would an ordinary cost of repairing the asset after it is placed in service be included in the asset's cost?

2. Suppose land with a building on it is purchased for $1,050,000. How do you account for the $75,000 cost of removing this unwanted building?

3. When assets are purchased as a group for a single price and no individual asset cost is given, how is each asset's cost determined?

4. Distinguish a betterment from a repair. Why are they treated differently for accounting purposes?

5. Define amortization. What are common misconceptions about amortization?

6. To what types of property, plant, and equipment assets does amortization expense apply?

7. Which amortization method does each of the graphs at the bottom of the page characterize: straight-line, UOP, or DDB?

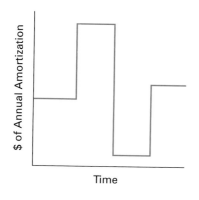

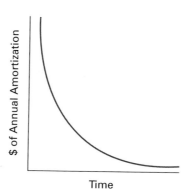

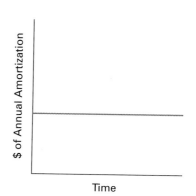

8. Explain the concept of accelerated amortization. Which of the three amortization methods results in the most amortization in the first year of the asset's life?

9. The level of business activity fluctuates widely for Milton Schoolbus Co., reaching its slowest time in June through August each year. At other times, business is brisk. What amortization method is most appropriate for the company's fleet of school buses? Why?

10. Felix Data Centre uses the most advanced computers available to keep a competitive edge over other data service centres. To maintain this advantage, the company usually replaces its computers before they are worn out. Describe the major factors affecting the useful life of a property, plant, and equipment asset, and indicate which seems more relevant to this company's computers.

11. Which amortization method does not consider estimated residual value in computing amortization during the early years of the asset's life?

12. Describe how to compute amortization for less than a full year, and how to account for amortization for less than a full month.

13. Hudson Company paid $25,000 for office furniture. The company expected it to remain in service for six years and to have a $1,000 residual value. After two years' use, company accountants believe the furniture will last for the next seven years. How much amortization will Hudson record for each of these last seven years, assuming straight-line amortization and no change in the estimated residual value? (Round your answer to the nearest dollar.)

14. When a company sells property, plant, and equipment before the year's end, what must it record before accounting for the sale?

15. Describe how to determine whether a company experiences a gain or a loss when an existing piece of equipment is exchanged for a new piece of equipment.

16. What expense applies to natural resources? By which amortization method is this expense computed?

17. How do intangible assets differ from most other assets? Why are they assets at all? What expense applies to intangible assets?

18. Why is the cost of patents and other intangible assets often expensed over a shorter period than the legal life of the asset?

19. Your company has just purchased another company for $1,000,000. The market value of the other company's net assets is $700,000. What is the $300,000 excess called? What type of asset is it? How is this asset amortized under GAAP?

20. Bombardier Inc. is recognized as a world leader in the manufacture and sale of transportation systems and industrial products. The company's success has created vast amounts of business goodwill. Would you expect to see this goodwill reported on Bombardier Inc. financial statements? Why, or why not?

*21. What is capital cost allowance (CCA)?

*22. Does amortization affect income taxes? How does amortization affect cash provided by operations?

STARTERS

MyAccountingLab | All questions in this section appear in MyAccountingLab.

Measuring the cost of property, plant, and equipment

Starter 10–1 This chapter lists the costs included for the acquisition of land. First is the purchase price of the land, which is obviously included in the cost of the land. The reasons for including the other costs are not so obvious. For example, the removal of a building looks more like an expense. State why the costs listed are included as part of the cost of the land. After the land is ready for use, will these costs be capitalized or expensed?

Lump-sum purchase of assets
(1)
Land $219,780

Starter 10–2 Suppose you make a lump-sum purchase of land, building, and equipment. At the time of your purchase, the land has a current market value of $240,000, the building's market value is $300,000, and the equipment's market value is $180,000. Journalize the lump-sum purchase of the three assets for a total cost of $660,000. You sign a note payable for this amount.

Capitalizing versus expensing amortizable-asset costs
(1)

Starter 10–3 JetQuick Airways repaired one of its Boeing 767 aircraft at a cost of $600,000, which JetQuick paid in cash. JetQuick erroneously capitalized this cost as part of the cost of the plane. How will this accounting error affect JetQuick's net income? Ignore amortization.

Computing amortization by three methods—first year only
(2)
2. Book value $32,800,000

Starter 10–4 At the beginning of 2010, JetQuick Airways purchased a used Boeing jet at a cost of $40,000,000. JetQuick expects the plane to remain useful for five years (6,000,000 miles) and to have a residual value of $4,000,000. JetQuick expects the plane to be flown 750,000 miles the first year. (Note: "Miles" is the unit of measure used in the airline industry.)

1. Compute JetQuick's first-year amortization on the jet using the following methods:

   a. Straight-line   b. UOP   c. DDB

2. Show the jet's book value at the end of the first year under the straight-line method.

---

*These Questions cover Chapter 10 Appendix topics.

Starter 10–5 At the beginning of 2010, JetQuick Airways purchased a used Boeing aircraft at a cost of $40,000,000. JetQuick expects the plane to remain useful for five years (6,000,000 miles) and to have a residual value of $4,000,000. JetQuick expects the plane to be flown 750,000 miles the first year and 500,000 miles the second year. Compute second-year amortization on the plane using the following methods:

a. Straight-line

b. UOP

c. DDB

Computing amortization by three methods—second year

c. $9,600,000

Starter 10–6 On March 31, 2010, JetQuick Airways purchased a used Boeing jet at a cost of $40,000,000. JetQuick expects to fly the plane for five years and expects it to have a residual value of $4,000,000. Compute JetQuick's amortization on the plane for the year ended December 31, 2010, using the straight-line method.

Partial-year amortization

Starter 10–7 Assume the Goldeyes Baseball Club paid $60,000 for a hot dog stand with a 10-year useful life and no residual value. After using the hot dog stand for four years, the club determines that the asset will remain useful for only two more years. Record amortization on the hot dog stand for year 5. The company uses the straight-line method for amortizing assets.

Computing and recording amortization after a change in useful life

Starter 10–8 Return to the RONA delivery truck example in Exhibit 10–6 on page 508. Suppose RONA sold the truck on December 31, 2012, for $30,000 cash, after using the truck for three full years. Amortization for 2012 has already been recorded. Make the journal entry to record RONA's sale of the truck under straight-line amortization.

Recording a gain or loss on disposal

Gain on sale $1,000

Starter 10–9 In 2008, Global Travel purchased a computer for $4,000, debiting Computer Equipment. During 2008 and 2009, Global recorded total amortization of $2,000 on the computer. In January 2010, Global traded in the computer for a new one with a fair market value of $4,200, paying $2,500 cash. This exchange transaction has commercial substance. Journalize Global Travel's exchange of computers.

Exchanging property, plant, and equipment assets

Loss on exchange $300

Starter 10–10 EnCana, the giant oil company, holds huge reserves of oil and gas assets. Assume that at the end of 2010, EnCana's cost of oil and gas assets totalled approximately $18 billion, representing 2.4 billion barrels of oil and gas reserves in the ground.

1. Which amortization method does EnCana use to compute its annual amortization expense for the oil and gas removed from the ground?

2. Suppose EnCana removed 0.8 billion barrels of oil during 2010. Record EnCana's amortization expense for 2010.

Accounting for the amortization of natural resources

2. Amortization Expense
$6.0 billion

Starter 10–11 Media-related companies have little in the way of property, plant, and equipment. Instead, their main asset is goodwill. When one media company buys another, goodwill is often the most costly asset acquired. Assume that Media Watch paid $800,000 to acquire *The Thrifty Nickel*, a weekly advertising paper. At the time of the acquisition, *The Thrifty Nickel's* balance sheet reported total assets of $1,300,000 and liabilities of $700,000. The fair market value of *The Thrifty Nickel's* assets was $1,200,000.

1. How much goodwill did Media Watch purchase as part of the acquisition of *The Thrifty Nickel*?

2. Journalize Media Watch's acquisition of *The Thrifty Nickel*.

Accounting for goodwill

Goodwill $300,000

Starter 10–12 This exercise summarizes the accounting for patents and research costs.

InnoTech Applications paid $1,600,000 in research costs for a new software program. InnoTech also paid $1,000,000 to acquire a patent on other software. After readying the software for production, InnoTech's sales revenue for the first year totalled $3,400,000. Cost of goods sold was $400,000, and selling expenses were $800,000. All these transactions occurred during 2010. InnoTech expects the patent to have a useful life of five years. Prepare InnoTech Applications' income statement for the year ended December 31, 2010, complete with a heading.

Accounting for patents and for research and development cost

Net income $400,000

*Starter 10–13 This exercise uses the JetQuick Airways data from Starter 10–4. JetQuick is comparing the CCA method used for income tax purposes with the straight-line amortization method.

1. Calculate the amount of CCA, at a rate of 25%, that JetQuick will be able to take in its first year.

2. Why does the Government of Canada, through the CCA, regulate the amount of amortization that a company can take for income tax purposes?

EXERCISES

MyAccountingLab | All questions in this section appear in MyAccountingLab.

Exercise 10–1

The accounting firm of Pratt & Taylor purchased land, paying $150,000 cash as a down payment and signing a $310,000 note payable for the balance. In addition, the company paid property tax in arrears of $3,000, a legal fee of $1,500, and a $20,500 charge for levelling the land and removing an unwanted building. The company constructed an office building on the land at a cost of $1,200,000. It also paid $30,000 for a fence around the boundary of the property, $8,500 for the company sign near the entrance to the property, and $11,500 for special lighting of the grounds. During installation of the fence, $2,000 of damage to the fence was incurred. Determine the cost of the company's land, land improvements, and building.

Exercise 10–2

Allocating cost to assets
acquired in a lump-sum
purchase

Truck 1: $21,600

Mirobel Trucking bought three used trucks for $60,000. An independent appraisal of the trucks produced the following figures:

Truck No.	Appraised Value
1	$24,000
2	22,000
3	20,000

Mirobel Trucking paid 25 percent in cash and signed a note for the remainder. Record the purchase in the general journal, identifying each truck's individual cost in a separate Truck account.

Exercise 10–3

Measuring the cost of an
asset, distinguishing
betterments from repairs

Classify each of the following expenditures as (1) a cost/betterment, (2) a repair (expense) related to a machine used to earn revenue, or (3) other: (a) purchase price; (b) sales tax paid on the purchase price; (c) transportation and insurance while the machine is in transport from seller to buyer; (d) installation; (e) training of personnel for initial operation of the machine; (f) special reinforcement to the machine platform; (g) income tax paid on income earned from the sale of products manufactured by the machine; (h) major overhaul to extend useful life by three years; (i) ordinary recurring repairs to keep the machine in good working order; (j) lubrication before the machine is placed in service; (k) periodic lubrication after the machine is placed in service; and (l) GST on the purchase price.

Exercise 10–4

Firestone Shoes is a family-owned retail shoe operation with two stores. Assume that early in year 1, Firestone Shoes purchased computerized point-of-sale and operating systems costing $150,000. Bob Firestone expects this equipment will support the inventory and accounting requirements for four years. Because of technology obsolescence, no residual value is anticipated. Through error, Firestone Shoes accidentally expensed the entire cost of the equipment at the time of the purchase. Firestone Shoes' accounting policy for equipment amortization is the straight-line amortization method. The company is operated as a sole proprietorship, so it pays no corporate income tax.

---

*This Starter covers Chapter 10 Appendix topics.

Required

Compute the overstatement or understatement in these items immediately after purchasing the equipment.

1. Equipment
2. Net income

Exercise 10–5

Ron Alexander has just slept through the class in which Professor Larston explained the concept of amortization. Because the next test is scheduled for Wednesday, Alexander texts Nancy Wu to ask for her notes from the lecture. Wu texts back: "Amortization—sounds like Greek 2 me." Alexander next tries Sally Nadeau, who responds that she thinks amortization is what happens when an asset wears out. Barry Orwell is confident that amortization is the process of building up a cash fund to replace an asset at the end of its useful life. Explain the concept of amortization to Alexander. Evaluate the explanations of Nadeau and Orwell. Be specific.

Explaining the concept of amortization

Exercise 10–6

Zhang Machine & Dye bought a machine on January 2, 2010, for $460,000. The machine was expected to remain in service for three years and produce 2,000,000 parts. At the end of its useful life, company officials estimated that due to technological changes, the machine's residual value would only be $10,000. The machine produced 700,000 parts in the first year, 660,000 in the second year, and 650,000 in the third year.

Required

1. Prepare a schedule of *amortization expense* per year for the machine using the straight-line, UOP, and DDB amortization methods.
2. Which method tracks the wear and tear on the machine most closely? Why?
3. After one year under the DDB method, the company switched to the straight-line method. Prepare a schedule of amortization expense for this situation, showing all calculations.

Excel Spreadsheet Template

Determining amortization amounts by three methods

1. Amortization expense in 2010: Straight-line $150,000; UOP $157,500; DDB $306,667

Exercise 10–7

Massicote Marketing Services purchased land and a building for $1,200,000. The land had a fair value of $300,000 and the building $900,000. The building was amortized on a straight-line basis over a 50-year period. The estimated residual value was $50,000. After using the building for 20 years, the company realized that wear and tear on the building would force the company to replace it before 50 years. Starting with the 21st year, the company began amortizing the building over a revised *total* life of 35 years with zero residual value. Record amortization expense on the building for years 20 and 21.

Changing the useful life of property, plant, and equipment

Amortization for Year 21 $37,333

Exercise 10–8

On January 13, 2009, Sinclair Gifts purchased store fixtures for $65,000 cash, expecting the fixtures to remain in service for 10 years. Sinclair Gifts has amortized the fixtures on a DDB basis with an estimated residual value of $5,000. On September 30, 2010, Sinclair Gifts sold the fixtures for $17,000 cash because they were not "green" technology. Record both the amortization expense on the fixtures for the years ended December 31, 2009 and 2010, and the sale of the fixtures on September 30, 2010. Round all calculations to the nearest dollar.

Analyzing the effect of a sale of property, plant, and equipment; DDB amortization

Loss on sale $27,200

Exercise 10–9

Timmins Distribution is a large warehousing and distribution company that operates throughout Eastern Canada. Timmins Distribution uses the UOP method to amortize its trucks because its managers believe UOP amortization best measures the wear and tear on the trucks. Timmins Distribution trades in used trucks often to keep driver morale high and to maximize fuel efficiency. Consider these facts about one Mack truck in the company's fleet:

When acquired in 2006, the tractor/trailer rig cost $585,000 and was expected to remain in service for eight years, or 1,500,000 kilometres. Estimated residual value was $60,000.

Measuring the cost of property, plant, and equipment, using UOP amortization; trading in a used asset

Gain on exchange of trucks $113,000

The truck was driven 150,000 kilometres in 2007, 195,000 kilometres in 2008, and 235,000 kilometres in 2009. After 100,000 kilometres in 2010, the company traded in the Mack truck for a Freightliner rig with a fair market value of $500,000. Timmins Distribution paid cash of $40,000. This trade-in will bring in significantly more income to Timmins by reducing operating cost. Determine Timmins Distribution's cost of the new truck. Prepare the journal entry to record the trade-in.

Exercise 10–10

Recording natural resources
and amortization

(3) Amortization
Expense $212,550

Clear Lake Mining Ltd. paid $900,000 for the right to extract ore from a 300,000-tonne mineral deposit. In addition to the purchase price, the company also paid a $1,000 filing fee, a $5,000 licence fee to the province of Quebec, and $75,000 for a geological survey. Because Clear Lake Mining Ltd. purchased the rights to the minerals only, the company expected the asset to have zero residual value when fully depleted. During the first year of production, the company removed 65,000 tonnes of ore. Make general journal entries to record (1) purchase of the mineral rights (debit Mineral Asset), (2) payment of fees and other costs, and (3) amortization for first-year production.

Exercise 10–11

Recording intangibles,
amortization, and a change
in the asset's useful life

2. Amortization for
Year 3 $315,000

1. Worman Company manufactures flat screen monitors for the graphics industry and has recently purchased for $525,000 a patent for the design of a new monitor. Although it gives legal protection for 20 years, the patent is expected to provide Worman Company with a competitive advantage for only five years. Assuming the straight-line method of amortization, use general journal entries to record (1) the purchase of the patent, and (2) amortization for year 1.
2. After using the patent for two years, Worman Company learns at an industry trade show that another company is designing a more effective monitor. Based on this new information, Worman Company decides to amortize the remaining cost of the patent over the current year, giving the patent a total useful life of three years. Record amortization for year 3.

Exercise 10–12

Measuring goodwill

2. Goodwill $10 million

Bolton Industries acquired companies with assets with a market value of $45 million and liabilities of $30 million. Thompson paid $25 million for these acquisitions during the year ended December 31, 2010.

Required

1. How would a value be assigned to the net assets acquired?
2. What value would be assigned to goodwill?
3. Will the goodwill be amortized? If so, by how much?

Exercise 10–13

Accounting for goodwill

1. Goodwill $48,900

The financial statements of Dane Transportation for the year ended December 31, 2009, reported the following details of acquisitions (adapted):

Assets:	In thousands
Cash	$ 3,400
Noncash Current Assets	8,400
Property, Plant, and Equipment	72,000
Intangibles	700
	$84,500
Liabilities:	
Long-term debt	$16,400

Dane Transportation paid $117,000 cash for the acquisitions. Assume that the book value of the assets is equal to their fair value.

Required

1. How much goodwill did Dane Transportation purchase as part of the 2009 acquisitions?
2. Prepare the Dane Transportation Inc. summary journal entry to record the acquisition for 2009.

3. Assume that, in 2010, the annual review of goodwill identified a 15-percent impairment of the goodwill acquired in 2009. Prepare the journal entry required to record this impairment.

Exercise 10–14

In 2010, Camden Electronics purchased Raytheon Electronics, paying $2.0 million in a note payable. The market value of Raytheon Electronics' assets was $3.1 million, and Raytheon Electronics had liabilities of $1.8 million.

Computing and recording goodwill

1. Goodwill $700,000

Required

1. Compute the cost of the goodwill purchased by Camden Electronics.

2. Record the purchase by Camden Electronics.

3. At 2010 year end, the annual review of goodwill value indicated no impairment of goodwill. Record the entry Camden will make for goodwill for 2010.

4. At 2011 year end, the annual review of goodwill value indicated a 40-percent impairment of the Raytheon Electronics goodwill. Record the entry for the goodwill impairment for 2011.

*Exercise 10–15

In 2009, Maxwell Inc. paid $625,000 for equipment that is expected to have a five-year life. In this industry, the residual value is estimated to be 5 percent of the asset's cost. Maxwell Inc. plans to use straight-line amortization for accounting purposes. For income tax purposes, Maxwell chooses to use the maximum CCA rate of 20 percent and is subject to the half-year rule in 2009.

Selecting the amortization method for income tax purposes

Required

1. Calculate the amortization expense in 2009 and 2010 for accounting and tax purposes.

2. Why does the federal government regulate the amount of amortization a company can deduct when calculating income for income tax purposes?

SERIAL EXERCISE

This exercise continues the Haupt Consulting situation from Exercise 9–15 of Chapter 9. If you did not complete Exercise 9–15, you can still complete Exercise 10–16 as it is presented.

Exercise 10–16

In Chapter 2, on page 92, we learned that Haupt Consulting had paid $2,000 cash for a Dell computer on December 3, 2010. The computer is expected to remain in service for five years. We also learned that on December 4, Haupt Consulting purchased office furniture on account for $3,600. The furniture is expected to last for five years.

Computing and journalizing amortization

1. Dec. 2010 Amortization Expense—Equipment $67

Required

1. Calculate the amount of amortization for each asset for the year ended December 31, 2010, assuming Haupt Consulting uses DDB amortization for both assets.

2. Journalize the entry to record the amortization expense to December 31, 2010. Date the entry December 31, 2010.

---

*This Exercise covers Chapter 10 Appendix topics.

CHALLENGE EXERCISE

Exercise 10–17

Reconstructing transactions from the financial statements

② ④

1. $118 thousand

Great Lake Furniture Limited's 2010 financial statements reported these amounts (in thousands of dollars):

| | December 31 | | | |
| | 2010 | | 2009 | |
Properties	Cost	Accumulated Amortization	Cost	Accumulated Amortization
Land	$ 41,378	—	$ 35,073	—
Buildings	116,832	$ 51,566	105,325	$ 46,981
Equipment..	17,940	11,712	16,575	10,678
Vehicles...	13,994	11,533	13,513	10,680
Computer hardware and software...	6,869	4,335	5,885	3,614
Leasehold improvements..................	26,178	7,461	21,081	6,220
	$223,191	$ 86,607	$197,452	$ 78,173
Net book value		$136,584		$119,279

In the 2010 annual report, Great Lake Furniture Limited reported amortization expense of $8,552,000. In addition, the company reported it had disposed of certain property, plant, and equipment assets and acquired others. The gain on disposal of property, plant, and equipment was $56,000.

Required

1. What was the accumulated amortization of the assets disposed of during 2010?

2. Assume that Great Lake Furniture Limited acquired assets costing $27,681,000 during 2010. What was the cost price of the assets sold during the year?

3. Write the journal entry to record the disposal of the property, plant, and equipment during the year.

BEYOND THE NUMBERS

Beyond the Numbers 10–1

The following questions are unrelated except that they apply to property, plant, and equipment:

1. Charlotte Quick, the owner of Quick Secretarial Services, regularly debits the cost of repairs and maintenance of amortizable assets to Property, Plant, and Equipment. Why would she do that, since she knows she is violating GAAP?

2. It has been suggested that, since many intangible assets have no value except to the company that owns them, they should be valued at $1 or zero on the balance sheet. Many accountants disagree with this view. Which view do you support? Why?

3. Marv Brown, the owner of Lakeshore Motors, regularly buys property, plant, and equipment and debits the cost to Repairs and Maintenance Expense. Why would he do that, since he knows this action violates GAAP?

ETHICAL ISSUES

Canam Group Developers purchased land and a building for a lump sum of $8.0 million. To get the maximum tax deduction, Canam's owner allocated 85 percent of the purchase price to the building and only 15 percent to the land. A more realistic allocation would have been 75 percent to the building and 25 percent to the land.

Required

1. Explain the tax advantage of allocating too much to the building and too little to the land.

2. Was Canam Group Developers' allocation ethical? If so, state why. If not, why not? Identify who was harmed.

PROBLEMS (GROUP A)

MyAccountingLab All questions in this section appear in MyAccountingLab.

Problem 10–1A

Bennett Distributors incurred the following costs in acquiring land and a building, making land improvements, and constructing and furnishing an office building for its own use.

Identifying the elements of property, plant, and equipment's cost

2. Amortization Expense: Land Improvements $5,479; Office Building $28,771

a. Purchase price of 2 hectares of land, including an old building that will be used for storage of maintenance equipment (land appraised market value is $1,300,000; building appraised market value is $300,000)	$1,150,000
b. Real estate taxes in arrears on the land to be paid by Bennett Distributors	6,000
c. Additional dirt and earth moving	6,000
d. Legal fees on the land acquisition	4,500
e. Fence around the boundary of the land	70,000
f. Building permit for the office building	1,000
g. Architect fee for the design of the office building	40,000
h. Company signs near front and rear approaches to the company property	14,000
i. Renovation of the storage building	160,000
j. Concrete, wood, steel girders, and other materials used in the construction of the office building	700,000
k. Masonry, carpentry, roofing, and other labour to construct the office building	550,000
l. Parking lots and concrete walks on the property	31,500
m. Lights for the parking lot, walkways, and company signs	12,500
n. Supervisory salary of construction supervisor (90 percent to office building and 10 percent to storage building)	100,000
o. Office furniture for the office building	135,000
p. Transportation of furniture from seller to the office building	2,000
q. Flowers and plants	3,500

Bennett Distributors amortizes buildings over 40 years, land improvements over 20 years, and furniture over 6 years, all on a straight-line basis with zero residual value.

Required

1. Set up columns for Land, Land Improvements, Office Building, Storage Building, and Furniture. Show how to account for each of Bennett's costs by listing the cost under the correct account. Determine the total cost of each asset.

2. Assuming that all construction was complete and the assets were placed in service on February 25, record amortization for the year ended December 31. Round figures to the nearest dollar.

Problem 10–2A

Accurate Research surveys Canadian opinions. The company's balance sheet reports the following assets under Property, Plant, and Equipment: Land, Buildings, Office Furniture, Communication Equipment, and Video Equipment. The company has a separate Accumulated Amortization account for each of these assets except land. Assume that the company completed the following transactions during 2010:

Recording property, plant, and equipment transactions; exchanges; changes in useful life

Dec. 31, 2010, Amortization Expense—Buildings $700,000

Feb. 2 Traded in communication equipment with a book value of $26,000 (cost of $202,000) for similar new equipment with a fair market value of $196,000. The seller gave Accurate a trade-in allowance of $36,000 on the old equipment, and the company paid the remainder in cash. This transaction meets the criteria for commercial substance.

<table>
<tr><td>Jul.</td><td>19</td><td>Sold a building that had cost $1,050,000 and had accumulated amortization of $740,000 through December 31, 2009. Amortization is computed on a straight-line basis. The building has a 30-year useful life and a residual value of $90,000. Accurate received $150,000 cash and a $1,300,000 note receivable.</td></tr>
<tr><td>Oct.</td><td>21</td><td>Purchased used communication and video equipment from the A.C. Neilsen Company of Canada Ltd. Total cost was $200,000 paid in cash. An independent appraisal valued the communication equipment at $170,000 and the video equipment at $80,000.</td></tr>
<tr><td>Dec.</td><td>31</td><td>Recorded amortization as follows:</td></tr>
</table>

Equipment is amortized by the DDB method over a six-year life. Record amortization on the equipment purchased on February 2 and on October 21 separately.

Amortization on buildings is computed by the straight-line method. The company had assigned buildings an estimated useful life of 30 years and a residual value that is 30 percent of cost. After using the buildings for 10 years, the company has come to believe that their *total* useful life will be 20 years. Residual value remains unchanged. The buildings cost $15,000,000.

Required Record the transactions in the journal of Accurate Research.

Problem 10–3A

Explaining the concept of amortization

The board of directors of Little People Nursery School is having its regular quarterly meeting. Accounting policies are on the agenda, and amortization is being discussed. Marcia Goodwin, a new board member, has some strong opinions about two aspects of amortization policy. She argues that amortization must be coupled with a fund to replace company assets. Otherwise, she argues, there is no substance to amortization. Goodwin also challenges the five-year estimated life over which Little People Nursery School is amortizing the centre's computers. She notes that the computers will last much longer and should be amortized over at least 10 years.

Required Write a paragraph or two to explain the concept of amortization to Goodwin and to answer her arguments.

Problem 10–4A

Excel Spreadsheet Template

Computing amortization by three methods

1. Book value, Dec. 31, 2012: Straight-line $113,675; UOP $109,100; DDB $42,000

On January 5, 2010, Keitly Construction purchased a used crane at a total cost of $300,000. Before placing the crane in service, the company spent $12,500 painting it, $4,800 replacing tires, and $11,400 overhauling the engine. Karen Keitly, the owner, estimates that the crane will remain in service for four years and have a residual value of $42,000. The crane's annual usage is expected to be 2,400 hours in each of the first three years and 2,200 hours in the fourth year. In trying to decide which amortization method to use, Mary Blundon, the accountant, requests an amortization schedule for each of the following generally accepted amortization methods: straight-line, UOP, and DDB.

Required

1. Assuming Keitly Construction amortizes this crane individually, prepare an amortization schedule for each of the three amortization methods listed, showing asset cost, amortization expense, accumulated amortization, and asset book value. Assume a December 31 year end.
2. Keitly Construction prepares financial statements for its bankers using the amortization method that maximizes reported income in the early years of asset use. Identify the amortization method that meets the company's objective.

Problem 10–5A

Journalizing property, plant, and equipment transactions; asset exchanges; betterments versus repairs

Dec. 31, 2010, Amortization Expense $3,600

Assume that Rees Warehousing completed the following transactions:

2009
<table>
<tr><td>Mar.</td><td>3</td><td>Paid $8,000 cash for a used forklift.</td></tr>
<tr><td></td><td>5</td><td>Paid $1,500 to have the forklift engine overhauled.</td></tr>
<tr><td></td><td>7</td><td>Paid $1,000 to have the forklift modified for specialized moving of auto parts.</td></tr>
</table>

| Nov. | 3 | Paid $550 for an oil change and regular maintenance. |
| Dec. | 31 | Used the DDB method to record amortization on the forklift. (Assume a three-year life and no residual value.) |

2010

Feb.	13	Replaced the forklift's broken fork for $400 cash, the deductible on Rees Warehousing's insurance. The new fork will not increase the useful life of the forklift.
Jul.	10	Traded in the forklift for a new forklift costing $18,000. The dealer granted a $3,000 allowance on the old forklift, and Rees Warehousing paid the balance in cash. Recorded 2010 amortization for the year to date and then recorded the exchange of forklifts. This transaction has commercial substance.
Dec.	31	Used the DDB method to record amortization on the new forklift. (Assume a five-year life.)

Rees Warehousing's amortization policy indicates that the company will take a full month's amortization on purchases occurring before the 15th day of the month and will not take any amortization for the month if the transaction occurs after the 15th day of the month.

Required   Record the transactions in the general journal, indicating whether each transaction amount should be capitalized as an asset or expensed. Round all calculations to the nearest dollar.

Problem 10–6A

Part 1 Oilco Canada Limited sells refined petroleum products. The company's balance sheet includes reserves of oil assets.

Suppose Oilco paid $15 million cash for an oil lease that contained an estimated reserve of 1,990,000 barrels of oil. Assume that the company paid $550,000 for additional geological tests of the property and $170,000 to prepare the surface for drilling. Prior to production, the company signed a $120,000 note payable to have a building constructed on the property. Because the building provides on-site headquarters for the drilling effort and will be abandoned when the oil is depleted, its cost is debited to the Oil Properties account and included in amortization charges. During the first year of production, Oilco removed 125,000 barrels of oil, which it sold on credit for $75 per barrel.

Required   Make general journal entries to record all transactions related to the oil and gas property, including amortization and sale of the first-year production.

Part 2 CTS Canada provides telephone service to most of Canada. Assume that CTS Canada purchased another company, which carried these figures:

Book value of assets	$1,536,000
Market value of assets	1,800,000
Liabilities	540,000

Required

1. Make the general journal entry to record CTS Canada's purchase of the other company for $1,620,000 cash.

2. How should CTS Canada account for goodwill at year end and in the future? Explain in detail.

Part 3 Suppose Research in Motion Limited (RIM) purchased a patent for $1,400,000. Before using the patent, RIM incurred an additional cost of $250,000 for a lawsuit to defend the company's right to purchase it. Even though the patent gives RIM legal protection for 20 years, company management has decided to amortize its cost over an 8-year period because of the industry's fast-changing technologies.

Required   Make general journal entries to record the patent transactions, including straight-line amortization for one year.

Accounting for natural resources, intangibles, and the related expenses

Part 1 Amortization Expense $994,975

Problem 10–7A

Identifying the elements of property, plant, and equipment's cost; accounting for amortization by two methods; accounting for disposal of property, plant, and equipment; distinguishing betterments from repairs

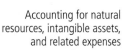

2. Total Property, Plant, and Equipment $590,727

Dueck Toy Co. has a fiscal year ending August 31. The company completed the following selected transactions:

2009

Mar. 2 Paid $640,000 plus $20,000 in legal fees (pertaining to all assets purchased) to purchase the following assets from a competitor that was going out of business:

Asset	Appraised Value	Estimated Useful Life	Estimated Residual Value
Land	$360,000	—	—
Buildings	240,000	8 years	$20,000
Equipment................	120,000	3 years	2,000

Dueck Toy Co. plans to use the straight-line amortization method for the building and for the equipment.

Jun. 2 Purchased a delivery truck with a list price of $39,000 for $36,000 cash. The truck is expected to be used for three years and driven a total of 280,000 kilometres; it is then expected to be sold for $4,000. It will be amortized using the UOP method.

3 Paid $3,000 to paint the truck with the company's colours and logo.

Aug. 31 Recorded amortization on the assets. The truck had been driven 20,000 kilometres since it was purchased.

2010

Jan. 4 Dueck Toy Co. paid $11,000 to Gill Services Ltd. for work done on the equipment. The job consisted of annual maintenance ($1,200) and the addition of automatic controls ($9,800), which will increase the expected useful life of the equipment to a total of five years and increase its expected residual value by $1,000.

Aug. 25 Sold the truck for $23,600. The truck had an odometer reading of 140,000 kilometres.

31 Recorded amortization on the assets.

Required

1. Record the above transactions of Dueck Toy Co. Round all amounts to the nearest dollar.

2. Show the balance sheet presentation of the assets at August 31, 2010.

Problem 10–8A

Accounting for natural resources, intangible assets, and related expenses

On October 2, 2009, Jaffar Mines Inc. acquired Bassett Exploration Ltd. for $11,000,000. At the time of the acquisition, Bassett's balance sheet contained the following items, which were transferred to Jaffar Mines Inc.:

- Mining Equipment: original cost of $22,000,000 and a present market value of $1,500,000. The equipment is expected to last another 10 years and have a residual value of $30,000 at that time.
- Mineral Rights: the rights to mine property by Grise Fiord. The mineral rights originally cost Bassett $3,000,000 but now have an appraised market value of $8,400,000. The mine is expected to produce 75,000,000 tonnes of ore over the next 10 years.
- Mortgage Payable: a $1,400,000 mortgage is outstanding on the mining equipment with interest at current rates.

Required

1. Journalize the purchase of Bassett Exploration Ltd. by Jaffar Mines Inc.

2. Journalize the adjusting entries required for the year ending September 30, 2010, to amortize the cost of the assets, assuming 3,500,000 tonnes of ore were taken out of the mine. Use the most appropriate methods and time frames from the data given.

3. Show how the assets would appear on Jaffar Mines Inc.'s balance sheet as of September 30, 2010.

Problem 10–1B

The owner of Big Boy Movers incurred the following costs in acquiring land, making land improvements, and constructing and furnishing the company's office building in the year ended December 31, 2010.

Identifying the elements of property, plant, and equipment's cost

a. Purchase price of 4 hectares of land, including an old building that will be used for a garage (land appraised market value is $450,000; building appraised market value is $50,000)	$ 400,000
b. Additional dirt and earth moving	15,000
c. Fence around the boundary of the land	25,000
d. Legal fee for title search on the land	2,000
e. Real estate taxes in arrears on the land to be paid by Big Boy Movers	4,800
f. Company signs at front of the company property	4,000
g. Building permit for the office building	1,000
h. Architect fee for the design of the office building	75,000
i. Masonry, carpentry, roofing, and other labour to construct office building	850,000
j. Concrete, wood, steel girders, and other materials used in the construction of the office building	650,000
k. Renovation of the garage	35,000
l. Flowers and plants	15,000
m. Parking lot and concrete walks on the property	48,500
n. Lights for the parking lot, walkways, and company signs	14,500
o. Supervisory salary of construction supervisor (95 percent to office building and 5 percent to garage renovation)	100,000
p. Office furniture for the office building	160,000
q. Transportation and installation of office furniture	2,500

Big Boy Movers amortizes buildings over 35 years, land improvements over 15 years, and furniture over 5 years, all on a straight-line basis with zero residual value.

Required

1. Set up columns for Land, Land Improvements, Office Building, Garage Building, and Furniture. Show how to account for each of Big Boy Movers' costs by listing the cost under the correct account. Determine the total cost of each asset.

2. Assuming that all construction was complete and the assets were placed in service on June 30, record amortization for the year ending December 31, 2010. Round figures to the nearest dollar.

Problem 10–2B

Belkin Freight provides general freight service in Canada. The business's balance sheet includes the following assets under Property, Plant, and Equipment: Land, Buildings, and Motor Carrier Equipment. Belkin Freight has a separate accumulated amortization account for each of these assets except land.

Recording property, plant, and equipment transactions; exchanges; changes in useful life

Assume that Belkin Freight completed the following transactions during 2010:

Feb. 6 Traded in motor-carrier equipment with a book value of $86,000 (cost of $280,000) for similar new equipment with a fair market value of $330,000. Belkin Freight received a trade-in allowance of $120,000 on the old equipment and paid the remainder in cash. This transaction met the criteria for commercial substance.

Jun. 3 Sold a building that had cost $1,250,000 and had accumulated amortization of $577,500 through December 31, 2009. Amortization is computed on a straight-line basis. The building has a 40-year useful life and a residual value of $150,000. Belkin Freight received $300,000 cash and a $1,000,000 note receivable.

Sept. 25   Purchased land and a building for cash for a single price of $790,000. An independent appraisal valued the land at $250,000 and the building at $375,000.

Dec. 31   Recorded amortization as follows:

Motor-carrier equipment has an expected useful life of four years and an estimated residual value of 6 percent of cost. Amortization is computed using the DDB method.

     Amortization on buildings is computed by the straight-line method. The company had assigned to its older buildings, which cost $3,900,000, an estimated useful life of 30 years with a residual value equal to 30 percent of the asset cost. However, the owner of Belkin Freight has come to believe that the buildings will remain useful for a total of 35 years. Residual value remains unchanged. The company has used all its buildings, except for the one purchased on September 25, for 10 years. The new building carries a 35-year useful life and a residual value equal to 30 percent of its cost. Make separate entries for amortization on the building acquired on September 25 and the other buildings purchased in earlier years.

Required   Record the transactions in Belkin Freight's general journal.

Problem 10–3B

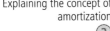
Explaining the concept of amortization

The board of directors of Mauger Properties Ltd. is reviewing the 2010 annual report. A new board member, a dermatologist with little business experience, questions the company accountant about the amortization amounts. The dermatologist wonders why amortization expense has decreased from $250,000 in 2008, to $230,000 in 2009, and to $215,000 in 2010. He states that he could understand the decreasing annual amounts if the company had been disposing of properties each year, but that has not occurred. Further, he notes that growth in the city is increasing the values of company properties. Why is the company recording amortization when the property values are increasing?

Required   Write a short response to explain the concept of amortization to the dermatologist and to answer his questions.

Problem 10–4B

Excel Spreadsheet Template

Computing amortization by three methods

On January 5, 2010, Steele Inc. paid $438,000 for equipment used in manufacturing computer equipment. In addition to the basic purchase price, the business paid $2,200 transportation charges, $600 insurance for the goods in transit, $35,200 provincial sales tax, and $20,000 for a special platform on which to place the equipment in the plant. Steele Inc.'s owner estimates that the equipment will remain in service for four years and have a residual value of $20,000. The equipment will produce 75,000 units in the first year, with annual production decreasing by 10,000 units during each of the next three years (that is, 65,000 units in year 2, 55,000 units in year 3, and so on). In trying to decide which amortization method to use, owner Jay Steele has requested an amortization schedule for each of three generally accepted amortization methods: straight-line, UOP, and DDB.

Required

1. For each of the generally accepted amortization methods listed above, prepare an amortization schedule showing asset cost, amortization expense, accumulated amortization, and asset book value. Assume a December 31 year end.

2. Steele Inc. prepares financial statements for its creditors using the amortization method that maximizes reported income in the early years of asset use. Identify the amortization method that meets the business's objective.

Problem 10–5B

Journalizing property, plant, and equipment transactions; betterments versus repairs

Assume that Luxury Limousines completed the following transactions:

2009

Jan.   5   Paid $40,000 cash for a used limousine.
       6   Paid $4,000 to have the engine overhauled.
       9   Paid $1,500 to have the company logo put on the limousine.
Jun.   15   Paid $600 for a minor tune-up after limousine was put into use.
Dec.   31   Recorded amortization on the limousine by the DDB method. (Assume a five-year life.)

2010

Mar. 9   Traded in the limousine for a new limousine costing $75,000. The dealer granted a $25,000 allowance on the old limousine, and the company paid the balance in cash. Recorded year 2010 amortization for the year to date and then recorded the exchange of the limousines. This transaction has commercial substance.

Aug. 9   Repaired the new limousine's damaged fender for $2,500 cash.

Dec. 31   Recorded amortization on the new limousine by the DDB method. (Assume an eight-year life and a residual value of $20,000.)

Luxury Limousine's amortization policy states that the company will take a full month's amortization on purchases occurring before the 15th day of the month and will not take any amortization for the month if the purchase occurs after the 15th day of the month.

Required Record the transactions in the general journal, indicating whether each transaction amount should be capitalized as an asset or expensed. Round all calculations to the nearest dollar.

Problem 10–6B

Part 1 Kitkan Inc. is a global producer and marketer of rolled aluminum products.

Suppose Kitkan Inc. paid $4.4 million cash for a lease giving the firm the right to work a mine that contained an estimated 400,000 tonnes of bauxite. Assume that the company paid $30,000 to remove unwanted buildings from the land and $130,000 to prepare the surface for mining. Further assume that Kitkan Inc. signed a $140,000 note payable to a landscaping company to return the land surface to its original condition after the lease ends. During the first year, Kitkan Inc. removed 37,000 tonnes of bauxite, which it sold on account for $40 per tonne.

Accounting for natural resources, intangibles, and the related expenses

Required Make general journal entries to record all transactions related to the bauxite, including amortization and sale of the first year's production.

Part 2 The Roasted Bean Ltd. operates franchised coffee shops. Assume that The Roasted Bean Ltd. purchased another company, which carried these figures:

Book value of assets	$3.6 million
Market value of assets	4.4 million
Liabilities	2.2 million

Required

1. Make the general journal entry to record The Roasted Bean Ltd.'s purchase of the other company for $2.5 million cash.

2. How should The Roasted Bean Ltd. account for goodwill at year end and in the future? Explain in detail.

Part 3 Suppose Susan McMillan purchased a Roasted Bean franchise licence for $250,000. In addition to the basic purchase price, McMillan also paid a lawyer $8,000 for assistance with the negotiations. McMillan believes the appropriate amortization period for the cost of the franchise licence is 10 years.

Required Make general journal entries to record the franchise transactions, including straight-line amortization for one year.

Problem 10–7B

Cardston TV owns a televison station in the interior of British Columbia. Its year end is June 30. The company completed the following transactions:

2010

Apr. 1   Paid $2,175,000 plus $75,000 in legal fees (pertaining to all assets purchased) to purchase the following assets from a competitor that was going out of business:

Identifying the elements of property, plant, and equipment's cost; accounting for amortization by two methods; accounting for disposal of property, plant, and equipment; distinguishing betterments from repairs

Asset	Appraised Value	Estimated Useful Life	Estimated Residual Value
Land	$600,000	—	—
Buildings	960,000	30 years	$120,000
Equipment................	840,000	5 years	80,000

Cardston TV plans to use the straight-line amortization method for the building and for the equipment.

May 1   Purchased a mobile broadcast unit truck with a list price of $300,000 for $245,000 cash. It is expected that the truck will be used for seven years and driven a total of 300,000 kilometres; it is then expected to be sold for $55,000. It will be amortized using the UOP method.

3   Paid $10,000 to paint the truck with the station's colours and logo.

Jun. 30   Recorded amortization on the assets. The mobile unit had been driven 12,500 kilometres since it was purchased.

Dec. 30   Cardston TV paid $25,500 to Maxwell Maintenance for work done on the equipment. The job consisted of annual maintenance ($1,500) and the addition of automatic controls ($24,000), which will increase the expected useful life of the equipment by one year (making a total of six years) and increase its expected residual value by $10,000.

2011

Jun. 1   Sold the mobile unit truck for $200,000. The truck had an odometer reading of 82,000 kilometres.

30   Recorded amortization on the assets.

Required

1. Record the above transactions of Cardston TV. Round all amounts to the nearest dollar.
2. Show the balance sheet presentation of the assets at June 30, 2011.

Problem 10–8B

Accounting for property, plant and equipment, and amortization; accounting for natural resources and amortization; accounting for intangible assets and amortization

On January 4, 2010, Northern Mines Ltd. acquired Cambrian Mines Inc. for $3,750,000. At the time of the acquisition, Cambrian Mines Inc.'s balance sheet contained the following items, which were transferred to Northern Mines Ltd.:

- Mining Equipment: original cost of $1,500,000 and a present market value of $1,000,000. The equipment is expected to last another eight years and have a residual value of $40,000 at that time.

- Mineral Rights: the rights to mine property near Ste. Rose du Lac. The mineral rights originally cost Cambrian Mines Inc. $2,500,000 but now have an appraised market value of $3,250,000. The mine is expected to produce 30,000,000 tonnes of ore over the next 12 years.

- Leasehold: the rights to rent office space in a nearby town for $2,375 per month for the next eight years. The leasehold has a market value today of $12,500 because of high rental rates in the area.

- Mortgage Payable: a $750,000 mortgage is outstanding on the mining equipment with interest at current rates.

Required

1. Journalize the purchase of Cambrian Mines Inc. by Northern Mines Ltd.
2. Journalize the adjusting entries required for the year ending December 31, 2010, to amortize the cost of the assets—assuming 2,750,000 tonnes of ore were taken out of the mine. Use the most appropriate methods and time frames from the data given.
3. Show how the assets would appear on Northern Mines Ltd.'s balance sheet as of December 31, 2010.

CHALLENGE PROBLEMS

Problem 10–1C

The owner of newly formed Lake of the Woods Air Taxi, a friend of your family, knows you are taking an accounting course and asks for some advice. Mr. Linden tells you that he is pretty good at running the company but doesn't understand accounting. Specifically, he has two concerns:

Understanding amortization and betterments and repairs

1. The company has just paid $400,000 for two used float planes. His accountants tell him that he should use accelerated amortization for his financial statements but he understands that straight-line amortization will result in lower charges to expense in the early years. He wants to use straight-line amortization.

2. A friend told him that Lake of the Woods Air Taxi should capitalize all repairs to the planes and "spread the cost out over the life of the planes." He wonders if there is anything wrong with this advice.

Required Respond to Mr. Linden's questions using your understanding of amortization, and betterments and repairs.

Problem 10–2C

Courtnell Mining Corp. is a new company that has been formed to mine for nickel in Northern Ontario. The ore body is estimated to contain 100,000 metric tonnes of pure nickel for which the world price is $15,000 per metric tonne. The costs of mine development are estimated to be $80,000,000.

Accounting for natural resources

Required Calculate the costs that would be charged against the nickel production in the form of amortization on a per-metric-tonne basis. Estimate any costs you think should also be included. Do not include the costs to mine and refine the ore, or shipping and selling costs.

Extending Your Knowledge

DECISION PROBLEM

Suppose you are considering investing in two businesses, Zastre Associates and Chen Co. The two companies are virtually identical, and both began operations at the beginning of 2010. During the year, each company purchased inventory as follows:

Measuring profitability based on different inventory and amortization methods

1. Net income: Zastre Associates $116,000

Jan.	10	12,000	units at $ 7	=	$ 84,000
Mar.	11	5,000	units at 9	=	45,000
Jul.	9	10,000	units at 10	=	100,000
Oct.	12	12,000	units at 11	=	132,000
Totals		39,000			$361,000

During 2010, both companies sold 30,000 units of inventory.

In early January 2010, both companies purchased equipment costing $400,000 that had a five-year estimated useful life and a $40,000 residual value. Zastre Associates uses the first-in, first-out (FIFO) method for its inventory and straight-line amortization for its equipment. Chen Co. uses the weighted-average method for inventory and DDB amortization. Both companies' trial balances at December 31, 2010 included the following:

Sales revenue	$560,000
Operating expenses (excluding amortization expense).....	110,000

Required

1. Prepare both companies' income statements.

2. Write an investment newsletter to address the following questions for your clients: Which company appears to be more profitable? Which company will have more cash to invest in promising projects? Which company would you prefer to invest in? Why?

FINANCIAL STATEMENT CASES

Financial Statement Case 1

Property, plant, and equipment, and intangible assets

2. Depreciation expense for 2008: $6,370 thousand

Refer to the financial statements of Canadian Western Bank (CWB) in Appendix A and answer the following questions.

1. Which amortization method does CWB use for property, plant, and equipment for the purpose of reporting to shareholders and creditors in the financial statements? What rates are used? Where did you find your answer?

2. What was the total amount of depreciation and amortization expense for fiscal 2008? For fiscal 2007? (CWB uses the term *depreciation* instead of *amortization*.)

3. What types of intangible assets does CWB have listed on the 2008 financial statements? How does CWB define goodwill?

4. How are intangibles written down?

5. Explain the meaning of *fair value asset impairment tests*.

Financial Statement Case 2

Property, plant, and equipment, and intangible assets

2. Amortization expense $2,288 thousand

Refer to Sun-Rype Products Ltd.'s financial statements in Appendix B and answer the following questions.

1. With respect to manufacturing operations, which amortization method does Sun-Rype Products Ltd. use for the purpose of reporting to shareholders and creditors in the financial statements? What rates are used, and where did you find your answer?

2. What was the total amount of amortization expense for 2008 as shown on the income statement?

3. Sun-Rype Products Ltd. shows one amount for amortization on the income statement, yet the change in accumulated amortization from 2007 to 2008 in Note 5 of the notes to the financial statements is a larger amount. What is the amount of the difference, and what could be the reason(s) for this difference?

4. Note 1 (d), "Significant Accounting Policies" in the notes to the financial statements includes the subsection "Impairment of Long-Lived Assets." Explain the meaning of this subsection, and give an example of when it is used.

11 Current Liabilities and Payroll

What are current liabilities of known and unknown amount, and why are they important?

What is the ethical and legal challenge in accounting for current and potential liabilities?

What are the key elements of a payroll system, and how is payroll recorded and reported?

These questions and others will be answered throughout this chapter The Decision Guidelines at the midpoint and end of this chapter will provide the answers in a useful summary.

LEARNING OBJECTIVES

1. Account for current liabilities of known amount

2. Account for current liabilities that must be estimated

3. Compute payroll amounts

4. Record basic payroll transactions

5. Use a payroll system, implement internal controls, and report current liabilities on the balance sheet

6. Describe the impact on current liabilities of international financial reporting standards (IFRS)

Computers, cameras, and automobiles are guaranteed against defects, usually for a specified period of time. Many other new products are too. When you buy a new car, the manufacturer agrees to repair it if something goes wrong within a specified number of kilometres. Do you ever consider this guarantee when you buy a product? That may motivate you to select a Honda over a Chevrolet. If not, you should consider the product guarantee because it can vary from company to company and repairs can be expensive.

Product guarantees are called warranties, and warranties are an important liability of companies such as Bombardier Recreational Products Inc., General Motors, and Dell Computers. Warranties pose an accounting challenge because companies such as Bombardier Recreational Products don't know which vehicle might have to be repaired. If this type of information could be known in advance, companies such as Bombardier might question whether or not to sell these products. But it's almost certain that companies will have unforeseen problems with some of their new products, so companies like Bombardier and General Motors record a warranty liability based on estimates.

In this chapter we will see how companies account for their product warranties. We will also learn about the other current liabilities, such as accounts payable and payroll liabilities.

Current liabilities are obligations due within one year or within the company's operating cycle if it is longer than one year. Obligations due beyond that period of time are *long-term liabilities.* We discussed current liabilities and long-term liabilities in Chapter 4, pages 178 and 179.

Current Liabilities of Known Amount

OBJECTIVE ①
Account for current liabilities of known amount

The amounts of most current liabilities are known. A few current liabilities must be estimated. Let's begin with current liabilities of known amount.

Accounts Payable

Amounts owed for products or services that are purchased on account are *accounts payable.* We have seen many accounts payable examples in previous chapters. For example, most businesses purchase inventories and office supplies on account. Brick Brewing Co. Limited, Ontario's largest Canadian-owned and Canadian-based publicly held brewery, reported accounts payable and accrued liabilities of almost $5.5 million at January 31, 2009 (see Exhibit 11–1).

EXHIBIT 11–1 How Brick Brewing Co. Limited Reports Its Current Liabilities

BRICK BREWING CO. LIMITED
Balance Sheet (partial, adapted)
January 31, 2009

Current Liabilities	
Accounts payable and accrued liabilities	$3,846,187
Current portion of long-term debt	924,000
Current portion of obligations under capital lease	419,282
Deferred grants	270,758
	$5,460,227

One of Brick Brewing's common transactions is the credit purchase of its inventory. Brick Brewing's accounts payable and perpetual inventory systems are integrated. After the order is placed and the goods are received, clerks enter inventory and accounts payable data into the system. Brick Brewing Co. Limited records the purchase of inventory on account as follows (amount assumed):

Nov. 22	Inventory	600	
	Accounts Payable		600
	Purchase on account.		

The purchase increases both Inventory and Accounts Payable. Then, to pay the liability, Brick Brewing debits Accounts Payable and credits Cash, as follows:

Dec. 5	Accounts Payable...	600	
	Cash..		600
	Paid on account.		

Short-Term Notes Payable

Short-term notes payable are a common form of financing. For example, Home Supply Ltd. discloses in its December 31, 2009, annual report that it owes $24,744 in short-term borrowings. Short-term notes payable are promissory notes that must be paid within one year. The following entries are typical for a short-term note payable that Home Supply Ltd. might have issued in 2009 to purchase inventory:

KEY POINT

The interest on a note is separate from the principal. The accrued interest should be credited to Interest Payable—*not* to Note Payable.

2009			
Oct. 31	Inventory...	16,000	
	Note Payable, Short-Term.................................		16,000
	Purchase of inventory by issuing a one-year 10-percent note payable.		

At year end, it is necessary to accrue interest expense for two months.

2009			
Dec. 31	Interest Expense	267	
	Interest Payable		267
	Accrued interest expense at year end ($16,000 × 0.10 × $\frac{2}{12}$).		

The balance sheet at December 31, 2009, will report the note payable of $16,000 and the related interest payable of $267 as current liabilities. The income statement for 2009 will report interest expense of $267. The balance sheet and the income statement are as follows:

HOME SUPPLY LTD.
Balance Sheet
December 31, 2009

Assets		Liabilities	
		Current liabilities:	
Various..................................	$XXX	Note payable, short-term......	$16,000
		Interest payable.....................	267

HOME SUPPLY LTD.
Income Statement
For the Year Ended December 31, 2009

Revenue:.............................	$XXX
Expenses:	
Interest expense	$267

The following entry records payment of the note at maturity:

2010			
Oct. 31	Note Payable, Short-Term..	16,000	
	Interest Payable	267	
	Interest Expense	1,333	
	Cash..		17,600
	Paid a note payable and interest at maturity. Interest expense is $1,333 ($16,000 × 0.10 × $\frac{10}{12}$). Cash paid is $17,600 [$16,000 + ($16,000 × 0.10)].		

LEARNING TIPS

Interest Payable must have a zero balance after the October 31, 2010 note payment is recorded. After interest is paid, it is no longer a liability; the amount previously accrued must be eliminated with a debit to Interest Payable.

Interest expense of $267 was correctly allocated to the year ended December 31, 2009. Home Supply Ltd.'s interest expense for 2010 will be $1,333. At maturity, Home Supply Ltd. will pay a full year's interest, allocated as shown in this diagram.

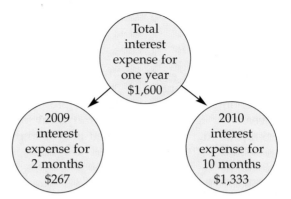

Short-Term Bank Loans and Operating Lines of Credit

Short-term bank loans are very similar to short-term notes payable. They are arranged with a bank or other financial institution, and are for a fixed time period at an interest rate negotiated between the bank and the borrower. If the bank loan is for less than one year or less than the company's operating cycle, it is considered short-term. Interest expense is recorded separately from the loan, and interest expense on a bank loan is accrued at the end of the year in the same way as for a note payable.

Many companies, and many people as well, arrange an operating **line of credit** with a financial institution to have cash available in case of a temporary cash shortfall. A line of credit is like a bank loan that is negotiated once, then drawn upon when needed. Interest is payable monthly only on the amount of the line of credit actually used—if the line of credit is not used, no interest is payable. Interest paid on a line of credit is recorded as interest expense. While most lines of credit are payable on demand (the bank can demand immediate repayment at any time), banks rarely demand repayment without warning. Typically, the amount of the principal to be repaid each month is flexible, with a minimum repayment required every month.

Many lines of credit are *secured*, meaning assets are pledged as security in case the borrower cannot repay the loan. Unsecured lines of credit do not have assets pledged as security. However, they often charge a higher rate of interest than secured lines of credit. Brick Brewing Co. Limited has a bank operating line of credit with interest at prime plus 0.25 percent. The line of credit is secured by a general security agreement over all assets, other than real property, and a collateral mortgage in the amount of $5,500,000 over real property.

Goods and Services Tax and Sales Tax Payable

There are two basic consumption taxes levied on purchases in Canada that are visible to the consumer: the goods and services tax (GST) levied by the federal government and the provincial sales taxes (PSTs) levied by all the provinces except Alberta; there are, at present, no sales taxes in the Yukon, Nunavut, or the Northwest Territories. The GST was introduced in Chapter 5, page 238. There are also excise or luxury taxes, which are a form of sales tax levied by the federal and provincial governments on products such as cigarettes, gasoline, jewellery, and alcoholic beverages; these taxes are hidden in that they are collected by the manufacturer.

The focus of discussion in this section will be on the consumption or visible taxes; the GST and PSTs will be discussed in turn below. In order to simplify the discussion, the material concerning calculation and payment of the GST will exclude the PST and the material concerning calculation and payment of the PST will generally exclude the GST. Nova Scotia, New Brunswick, and Newfoundland and Labrador have harmonized the GST with their PST. (At the time of printing,

Ontario and British Columbia were considering implementing harmonized sales taxes in the future.) The harmonized sales tax (HST) will be described below. Quebec's sales tax (QST) is charged on the price including GST, and Prince Edward Island's PST is charged on the price including GST.

Goods and Services Tax   In 1991, the federal government, through Canada Revenue Agency (CRA), implemented a GST that is collected from the ultimate consumer and includes most goods and services consumed in Canada. The tax and its application may be covered in an introductory tax course and is beyond the scope of this text; the ensuing discussion deals primarily with basic facts about the tax and how to account for it.

There are three categories of goods and services with respect to the GST:

1. Zero-rated supplies such as basic groceries, prescription drugs, goods and services exported from Canada to nonresidents, and medical devices;
2. Exempt supplies such as educational services, health care services, and financial services; and
3. Taxable supplies, which basically includes everything that is not zero-rated or exempt.

At the time of writing this text, the GST rate is 5 percent. The tax is collected by the individual or entity (called the *registrant*) supplying the taxable good or service (called *taxable supplies*) to the final consumer. The GST is remitted to the Receiver General. Suppliers of taxable goods and services have to pay tax on their purchases. However, they are able to deduct the amount of GST paid (called an *input tax credit*) from the GST they have collected from their sales of goods and services in calculating the amount due to the federal government. The GST Return and the net tax must be remitted to the Receiver General quarterly for most registrants and monthly for larger registrants.

For example, Mary Janicek, who lives in Whitehorse in the Yukon (no provincial tax), purchased a power lawn mower on July 2, 2009, with the intention of earning money by cutting grass during the summer.[1] The lawn mower cost $240; the GST was $12. Because Janicek is planning to use the mower exclusively to cut grass for a fee, she could recover the $12. However, assuming she were a registrant, she would have to charge all her customers the 5-percent GST on her lawn-mowing services and remit it to the government. During the three-month first quarter, Janicek earned revenue of $2,000 and related GST of $100, and thus collected $2,100. She spent $105—$100 plus GST of $5—on gasoline for the mower. Her input tax credit of $17 included the $12 GST on the lawn mower and $5 GST on gasoline for the mower. The entries to record these transactions would be as follows:

2009

Jul. 2	Equipment..	240	
	GST Recoverable	12	
	Cash..		252
	To record purchase of power mower.		
Jul.–Sept.	Supplies Expense	100	
	GST Recoverable	5	
	Cash..		105
	To record purchase of gasoline for power mower.		
Jul.–Sept.	Cash..	2,100	
	Lawn-Mowing Revenue		2,000
	GST Payable...		100
	To record revenue from mowing lawns.		

---

[1] If your business earns less than $30,000 per year, it does not have to be registered for GST purposes. In reality, Janicek's business would be below the minimum threshold of $30,000, so Mary is unlikely to be a registrant. The scenario is illustrative. A business is only required to become a GST registrant if taxable revenues exceed $30,000 for the last four consecutive quarters.

REAL WORLD EXAMPLE

This is how you calculate the GST recoverable when both GST and PST are included in the total cost of a product purchased: divide the total cost of the product by the sum of 1 + the PST rate + the GST rate; then, multiply the result by the GST rate. For example, suppose a company purchases an item in Ontario (where PST is 8 percent) with a total cost of $226, which includes PST and GST. What is the possible GST recoverable?

A: $226 ÷ (1 + 0.08 + 0.05) = $200
$200 × 0.05 = $10

The GST recoverable on this purchase is $10.

Janicek would be required to remit $83 ($100 − $12 − $5) as her first quarterly payment. Since Janicek would be recovering the GST paid on the purchase of the mower and gasoline of $17 ($12 + $5), she would credit the recovery to the GST Recoverable account, to bring its balance to zero. The entry would be as follows:

Oct. 31	GST Payable...	100	
	Cash		83
	GST Recoverable		17
	To record payment of GST payable net of		
	input tax credits to Receiver General.		

In the Mary Janicek example, we used two accounts—GST Recoverable (a receivable) and GST Payable—to illustrate input tax credits and GST collections to be remitted to the Receiver General. Some registrants use only one account—GST Payable—to record input tax credits *and* GST collections. When the GST Return is sent to the Receiver General, the final account balance in the GST Payable account is remitted if the balance is a credit, or a refund is requested if the balance is a debit. However, since CRA wants a report of both amounts, we will continue to use the two-account approach to illustrate input tax credits and GST collections.

Because they collect the GST for the federal government, the registrants owe the Receiver General the net tax collected; the account GST Payable is a current liability. Most companies include GST owing with Accounts Payable and Accrued Liabilities, and GST Recoverable as a current asset on their balance sheets. One can be netted against the other on the balance sheet.

Provincial Sales Tax All the provinces except Alberta (as well as the Yukon, Nunavut, and the Northwest Territories) levy a tax on sales to the final consumers of products; sales tax is not levied on sales to wholesalers or retailers (unless they are the final consumers of the product, such as office supplies). The final sellers charge their customers the PST in addition to the price of the item sold. The following PST rates were in effect at the time of writing:

British Columbia	7%	
Saskatchewan	5%	
Manitoba	7%	
Ontario	8%	
Quebec	7.5%	(QST based on price including GST)
Prince Edward Island	10%	(PST based on price including GST)
New Brunswick	13%	(blended with GST)
Nova Scotia	13%	(blended with GST)
Newfoundland and Labrador	13%	(blended with GST)

As this list shows, four provinces charge PST and GST separately on the purchase price of a taxable good or service. Two provinces charge PST on the sum of the purchase price and the GST. Three provinces charge a combined GST and PST rate of 13 percent on the purchase price. This 13-percent rate is known as *Harmonized Sales Tax* (*HST*). By harmonizing their PST with the GST, New Brunswick, Nova Scotia, and Newfoundland and Labrador have reduced the cost of collecting and administering consumption taxes. (Ontario and British Columbia are considering adopting the HST as early as July 1, 2010.)

Consider a taxable item that costs $100 before tax. Ontario charges PST and GST separately; a taxable sale of $100 would have GST of $5 (0.05 × $100) and PST of $8 (0.08 × $100). Prince Edward Island charges PST on GST; a taxable sale of $100 would have GST of $5 (0.05 × $100) and PST of $10.50 [0.10 × ($100 + $5)]. Nova Scotia has harmonized the PST and the GST; a taxable sale of $100 would have PST and GST of $13 (0.13 × $100).

Consider Super Stereo Products, an electronics superstore located in Ottawa. Super Stereo does not pay PST on its purchase of a TV set from Panasonic because it is inventory for resale, but you, as a consumer, would have to pay the province of Ontario's 8-percent PST to Super Stereo when you buy a Panasonic TV from the store. Super Stereo pays the PST it collected from you to the provincial government.

Panasonic, the manufacturer, would not have a sales tax liability at its year end, but Super Stereo probably would. (For purposes of the discussion of sales tax, we will ignore the GST.)

Suppose one Saturday's sales at the Super Stereo store totalled $20,000. The business would have collected an additional 8 percent in PST, which would equal $1,600 ($20,000 × 0.08). The business would record that day's sales as follows:

Cash	21,600	
Sales Revenue...		20,000
Sales Tax Payable		1,600
To record cash sales of $20,000 and the related PST of 8 percent.		

Because the retailers owe to the province the sales tax collected, the account Sales Tax Payable is a current liability. Most companies include Sales Tax Payable with Accounts Payable and Accrued Liabilities on their balance sheets.

Companies forward the collected sales tax to the taxing authority at regular intervals (typically monthly for large companies and quarterly for small companies), at which time they debit Sales Tax Payable and credit Cash. Observe that Sales Tax Payable does not correspond to any sales tax expense that the business is incurring. Nor does this liability arise from the purchase of any asset. Rather, it is the cash that the business is collecting on behalf of the government.

Current Portion of Long-Term Debt

Some long-term notes payable and bonds payable are paid in instalments, which means that portions of the principal are repaid at specific time intervals. The **current portion of long-term debt** is the amount of the principal that is payable within one year—a current liability. The remaining portion of the long-term debt is a long-term liability.

To illustrate, suppose Home Supply Ltd. borrowed $100,000 on January 1, 2009. This loan is to be repaid in instalments of $10,000 per year for 10 years on December 30 each year. On December 30, 2009, the first principal repayment of $10,000 is made (ignore interest), leaving a balance of $90,000. The December 31, 2009, balance sheet reports the $10,000 portion due to be repaid on December 30, 2010, as a current liability called "current portion of long-term debt" and reports the remaining $80,000 portion as long-term debt. On December 31, 2009, the company may make an adjusting entry to shift the current instalment of the long-term debt to a current liability amount as follows:

LEARNING TIPS

A current liability is due within one year, or within the company's operating cycle if it is longer than one year. The portion of a long-term debt payable within the year is classified as a current liability. The interest payable is classified separately from the principal.

2009			
Dec. 31	Long-Term Debt...	10,000	
	Current Portion of Long-Term Debt		10,000
	To transfer the portion of long-term debt due in 2010 to the current liability account.		

Brick Brewing Co. Limited's balance sheet (Exhibit 11–1, page 550) reports Current Portion of Long-Term Debt of $924,000 as a current liability. On its full balance sheet, Brick Brewing reports long-term debt ($2,067,900) immediately after total current liabilities. *Long-term debt* refers to loans payable that are due later than one year beyond the balance sheet date.

The liabilities for the current portion of long-term debt do *not* include any accrued interest payable. The account, Current Portion of Long-Term Debt, represents only the appropriate portion of the *principal amount owed.* Interest Payable is a separate account for a different liability—the interest that must be paid.

What would be the effect if Brick Brewing Co. Limited reported its full liability as long-term? Two ratios that would have been distorted by this accounting error are the current ratio and the acid-test ratio. Reporting a liability as long-term could mislead external users because it understates current liabilities overstating these two ratios and reporting an overly positive view of the company. This example shows that accounting includes both *recording* transactions and *reporting* the information, and highlights that reporting is every bit as important as recording.

Accrued Expenses (Accrued Liabilities)

Every accrued expense (liability) involves a debit to an *expense* and a credit to a *liability*.

An **accrued expense** is an expense that has not yet been paid. An accrued expense creates a liability, which explains why accrued expenses are also called **accrued liabilities.** Accrued expenses typically occur with the passage of time, such as interest payable on long-term debt. We introduced accrued expenses in Chapter 3, page 120.

Like most other companies, Brick Brewing Co. Limited has salaries payable, other payroll liabilities, interest payable, and property taxes payable. We illustrated the accounting for interest payable on pages 551 and 552. The next section, plus the second half of this chapter, covers accounting for payroll liabilities.

Payroll Liabilities

Payroll, also called **employee compensation,** is a major expense of many businesses. For service organizations—such as public accounting firms and real-estate brokers—payroll is *the* major expense. Payroll expense for salaries and wages usually causes an accrued liability at year end. We show how to account for payroll expense in the second half of this chapter.

Unearned Revenues

Unearned Revenue is a liability, *not* a revenue.

Unearned revenues are also called *deferred revenues* and *revenues collected in advance.* As we saw in Chapter 3, pages 121 and 122, an unearned revenue is a liability because it represents an obligation to provide a good or service. Each of these account titles indicates that the business has received cash from its customers before it has earned the revenue. The company has an obligation to provide goods or services to the customer. Let's consider an example.

Canadian Business may be purchased every two weeks or by means of a subscription. When subscribers pay in advance to have *Canadian Business* delivered to their home or business, Rogers Publishing incurs a liability to provide future service. The liability account is called Unearned Subscription Revenue (which could also be titled Unearned Subscription Income or Deferred Subscription Income).

Assume that Rogers Publishing charges $39.95 for Bob Baylor's one-year subscription to *Canadian Business.* Rogers Publishing's entries would be

2010
Jul. 2   Cash 39.95
             Unearned Subscription Revenue...................   39.95
             To record receipt of cash at the start of a
             one-year subscription.

After receiving the cash on July 2, 2010, Rogers Publishing owes its customer magazines that Rogers Publishing will provide over the next 12 months. Rogers Publishing's liability is:

Unearned Subscription Revenue

	39.95

During 2010, Rogers Publishing delivers one-half of the magazines and earns $19.98 ($39.95 × $\frac{1}{2}$) of the subscription revenue. At December 31, 2010, Rogers

Publishing makes the following adjusting entry to decrease (debit) the liability Unearned Subscription Revenue and increase (credit) Subscription Revenue:

2010

Dec. 31	Unearned Subscription Revenue......................	19.98	
	Subscription Revenue.....................................		19.98
	Earned revenue that was collected in advance ($39.95 × $\frac{1}{2}$).		

After posting, Rogers Publishing still owes the subscriber $19.97 for unearned revenue. Rogers Publishing has earned $19.98 of the revenue, as follows:

Unearned Subscription Revenue				Subscription Revenue	
Dec. 31	19.98	Jul. 2	39.95	Dec. 31	19.98
		Bal.	19.97		

Customer Deposits Payable

Some companies require cash deposits from customers as security on borrowed assets. These amounts are called Customer Deposits Payable because the company must refund the cash to the customer under certain conditions. For example, telephone companies may demand a cash deposit from a customer before installing a telephone. Utility companies and businesses that lend tools and appliances commonly demand a deposit as protection against damage and theft. Certain manufacturers of products sold through individual dealers, such as Avon or Mary Kay, require deposits from the dealers who sell their products; the deposit is usually equal to the cost of the sample kit provided to the dealer. Companies whose products are sold in returnable containers collect deposits on those containers. Because the deposit is returned to the customer, the amount collected represents a liability.

DID YOU GET IT?

To check your understanding of the material in this Learning Objective, complete these questions. The solutions appear on MyAccountingLab so you can check your progress.

1. Suppose a Harvey's restaurant in Charlottetown, Prince Edward Island, made cash sales of $4,000 subject to the 5-percent GST and 10-percent PST. Record the sales and the related consumption taxes (P.E.I. charges PST on GST). Also record payment of the PST to the provincial government and the GST to the Receiver General (assume input tax credits amount to $69).

2. Repeat the previous question, but assume the Harvey's restaurant is located in Manitoba. The input tax credits amount to $69.

3. At December 31, 2009, Snippy Hair Salons reported a 6-percent long-term debt payable as follows:

Current Liabilities (in part)

Portion of long-term debt due within one year	$10,000
Interest payable*	6,300

Long-Term Debt (in part)

Long-term debt..	$200,000

Snippy Hair Salons pays interest on June 30 each year. Show how Snippy Hair Salons would report its liabilities on the year-end balance sheet one year later—December 31, 2010. The current maturity of the long-term debt is $10,000 each year until the liability is paid off.

---

*Calculated as $210,000 × 0.06 3 $^{6}/_{12}$

Current Liabilities that Must Be Estimated

OBJECTIVE ②

Account for current liabilities that must be estimated

A business may know that a liability exists but not know the exact amount. It cannot simply ignore the liability. This liability must be reported on the balance sheet.

Estimated current liabilities vary among companies. A prime example is Estimated Warranty Payable, which is common for companies such as Bombardier Recreational Products Inc. and Dell Inc.

Estimated Warranty Payable

Many companies guarantee their products against defects under *warranty* agreements. Ninety-day warranties and one-year warranties are common.

The matching objective leads us to record the *warranty expense* in the same period we record the revenue. The expense occurs when you make a sale, not when you pay the warranty claim. (For a review of the matching objective, see Chapter 3, page 112). At the time of the sale, the company does not know the exact amount of warranty expense, but the business must estimate its warranty expense and the related liability.

Assume that Collico Fabricating Ltd. made sales in 2009 of $80 million that are subject to warranty. In Note 2, "Significant Accounting Policies," Collico indicates that the company provides warranty coverage for its products for one year from date of sale. Assume that, in the past, the warranty provision and actual warranty cost was 1 percent of fabricating sales. Further, assume the company believes that 0.9 percent of the value of products sold in 2009 is the appropriate estimate of the cost of warranty work to be performed in the future. The company would record the sales of $80 million and the warranty expense of $720,000 ($80,000,000 × 0.009) in the same period as follows:

2009			
Various	Accounts Receivable...	80,000,000	
dates	Sales Revenue (fabricating)............................		80,000,000
	Sales on account.		
Dec. 31	Warranty Expense...	720,000	
	Estimated Warranty Payable..........................		720,000
	To accrue warranty expense.		

Assume that the costs paid to repair defective merchandise total $700,000. If Collico repairs the defective products, Collico makes this journal entry:

2009–2010			
Various	Estimated Warranty Payable.............................	700,000	
dates	Cash		700,000
	To pay *repair* costs for defective products sold under warranty.		

If Collico replaces the defective products, rather than repairs them, Collico makes this journal entry:

2009–2010			
Various	Estimated Warranty Payable.............................	700,000	
dates	Inventory..		700,000
	To *replace* defective products sold under warranty.		

Collico Fabricating Ltd.'s expense on the income statement is the estimated amount of $720,000, not the $700,000 actually paid. After paying these warranty claims, Collico Fabricating Ltd.'s liability account would have a credit balance of $20,000.

LEARNING T I P S

A warrantied product may be sold in one year but repaired in another year. The dilemma in accounting is when the repair should be expensed—in the year the product is sold or in the year the product is repaired? The matching objective requires matching the warranty expense with the revenue from the sale in the year of the sale.

Estimated Warranty Payable

700,000	720,000
	Bal. 20,000

While warranty expense is often calculated as a percent of sales dollars, it can also be calculated as a percent of units of product sold. For example, suppose a tire company sells 50,000 tires in one year. It estimates, based on experience, that 0.5 percent of them, or 250 tires, will need to be replaced in the future. If the tires cost $50 each, the warranty expense is estimated to be $12,500 (250 × $50). The journal entry to record the warranty expense is the same as that shown above.

Estimated Vacation Pay Liability

All companies are required by law to grant paid vacations to their employees. The employees receive this benefit when they take their vacation, but they earn the compensation by working the other days of the year. The law requires most employers to provide a minimum number of weeks' holiday per year (usually two, but sometimes more, based on the number of years worked). To match expense with revenue properly, the company accrues the vacation pay expense and liability for each of the 50 work weeks of the year. Then, the company records payment during the two-week vacation period. Employee turnover, terminations, and ineligibility (for example, no vacation allowed until one full year has been worked) force companies to estimate the vacation pay liability and accrue vacation expense incurred.

Suppose a company's January payroll is $100,000 and vacation pay adds 4 percent, or $4,000 (with the 4 percent calculated as two weeks of annual vacation divided by 50 work weeks each year). Experience indicates that only 90 percent of the available vacations will be taken. Therefore, the January vacation pay estimate is $3,600 ($4,000 × 0.90). In January, the company records the vacation pay accrual as follows:

Jan. 31	Vacation Pay Expense...	3,600	
	Estimated Vacation Pay Liability.......................		3,600

Each month thereafter, the company makes a similar entry.

If an employee takes a two-week vacation in August, his or her $2,000 monthly salary is recorded as follows:

Aug. 31	Estimated Vacation Pay Liability...	2,000	
	Various Withholding Accounts and Wages Payable[2]		2,000

Income Tax Payable (for a Corporation)

Corporations pay income tax in the same way as individual taxpayers do. Corporations file their income tax returns with Canada Revenue Agency (CRA) and their provincial governments after the end of the fiscal year, so they must estimate their income tax payable for reporting on the balance sheet. During the year, corporations make monthly tax instalments (payments) to the government(s), based on their estimated tax for the year. A corporation with a December 31 year end would record the payment of $100,000 of income tax expense for September as follows:

Sept. 30	Income Tax Expense	100,000	
	Cash..		100,000
	To pay monthly income tax instalment.		

---
[2] The various payroll accounts are discussed later in the chapter.

Assume at December 31, the corporation calculates actual tax expense for the year to be $1,240,000. Accordingly, the corporation pays the last monthly instalment of $100,000 on December 30, and accrues the additional $40,000 at December 31. The entries are

Dec. 30	Income Tax Expense	100,000	
	Cash		100,000
	To pay monthly income tax.		
31	Income Tax Expense	40,000	
	Income Tax Payable		40,000
	To accrue income tax at year end.		

The corporation will pay off this tax liability during the next year when it files its tax returns with Canada Revenue Agency and its provincial government, so Income Tax Payable is a current liability.

Contingent Liabilities

A *contingent liability* is not an actual liability. Instead, it is a potential liability that depends on a *future* event arising out of past events. For example, Packenham town council may sue North Ontario Electric Supply Ltd., the company that installed new street lights in Packenham, claiming that the electrical wiring is faulty. The past transaction is the street-light installation. The future event is the court case that will decide the suit. North Ontario Electric Supply Ltd. thus faces a contingent liability, which may or may not become an actual obligation.

It would be misleading for North Ontario Electric Supply Ltd. to withhold knowledge of the lawsuit from its creditors or from anyone considering investing in the business. The *disclosure principle* of accounting (see Chapter 6, page 310) requires a company to report any information deemed relevant to outsiders of the business. The goal is to give people relevant, reliable information for decision making.

The *CICA Handbook* requires *contingent losses* generally to be accrued or disclosed in the financial statements but bars *contingent gains* from being recognized *until* they are realized. This approach follows the principle of conservatism. The accounting profession divides contingent liabilities into three categories. Each category indicates a likelihood that a contingency will cause a loss and become an actual liability. The three categories of contingent liabilities, along with how to report them, are shown in Exhibit 11–2.

EXHIBIT 11–2   Contingent Liabilities: Three Categories

Level of Uncertainty*	How to Report the Contingency
Likely	Amount can be reasonably estimated: Accrue an expense (loss) and report an actual liability. Amount cannot be reasonably estimated: Disclose in the notes.
Unlikely	If loss would be significant, note disclosure is suggested.
Not determinable	Note disclosure is required.

*Determined by management. Management also determines the appropriate disclosure.

Sometimes the contingent liability has a definite amount. Sometimes the amount that will have to be paid, if the contingent liability becomes an actual liability, is not known at the balance sheet date. For example, companies face lawsuits, which may cause possible future obligations of amounts to be determined by the courts. In another case, Canada Revenue Agency (CRA) may have indicated to the entity that a reassessment of its income and taxes has been made or is forthcoming but the company may not know the amount of its liability at the financial statement date.

Sun-Rype Products Ltd. reported the following in Note 16(b) in the Notes to the Financial Statements for the year ended December 31, 2008:

> (b) Under the terms of a processing and filling systems agreement expiring December 31, 2012, the Company is contingently liable for annual rental payments of $0.8 million should the Company's purchase of annual volumes of beverage packaging materials not meet certain minimum thresholds. Based on historical purchase levels these rental payments would only be payable in the event of a dramatic decline in market demand.

Since the Sun-Rype contingency is "not determinable," and based on possible future market conditions, disclosure was provided in Note 16(b) and no liability was recorded or reported on the balance sheet.

Ethical Issues in Accounting for Current and Contingent Liabilities

Accounting for current liabilities poses an ethical challenge. Businesses want to look as successful as possible. A company likes to report a high level of net income on the income statement because that makes the company look successful. High asset values and low liabilities make the company look safe to lenders and help the company borrow at lower interest rates.

Owners and managers may be tempted to overlook some expenses and liabilities at the end of the period. For example, a company can fail to accrue warranty expense or employee vacation pay. This will cause total expenses to be understated and net income to be overstated on the income statement.

Contingent liabilities also pose an ethical challenge. Because contingencies are not real liabilities, they are easy to overlook. But a contingent liability can be very important. A business with a contingent liability walks a tightrope between (1) disclosing enough information to enable outsiders to evaluate the company realistically, and (2) not giving away too much information, which could harm the company. Ethical business owners and managers do not play games with their accounting. Falsifying financial statements can ruin one's reputation in the business community and lead to criminal convictions.

DID YOU GET IT?

MyAccountingLab

To check your understanding of the material in this Learning Objective, complete these questions. The solutions appear on MyAccountingLab so you can check your progress.

4. Maxim Limited, a new company, made sales of $400,000. The company estimated warranty repairs at 5 percent of sales. Maxim's actual warranty payments were $19,000. Record sales, warranty expense, and warranty payments. How much is Maxim's estimated warranty payable at the end of the period?

5. Maxim Limited, a new company, made sales of 10,000 units at a cost of $40 per unit. The company offers a one-year warranty that replaces any defective units with a new one. The company estimated warranty replacements at 5 percent of units sold. Maxim's actual warranty replacements were 475 units. Record sales, warranty expense, and warranty payments. How much is Maxim's estimated warranty payable at the end of the period?

6. How does a contingent liability differ from an actual liability?

At this halfway point of the chapter, review what you have learned by studying the following Decision Guidelines.

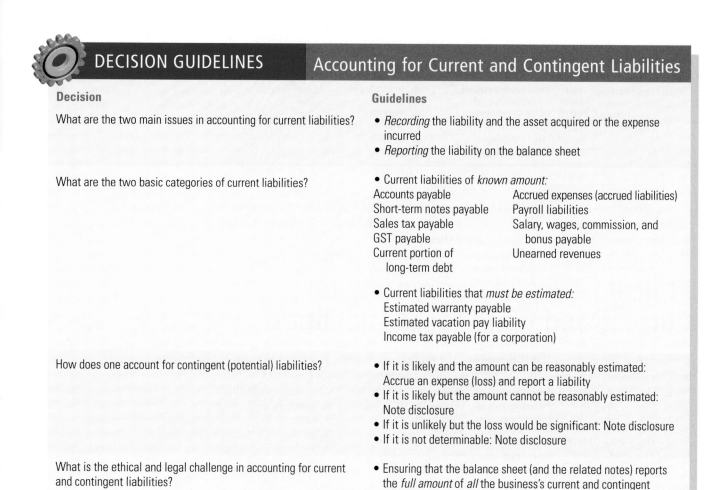

DECISION GUIDELINES | Accounting for Current and Contingent Liabilities

Decision	Guidelines
What are the two main issues in accounting for current liabilities?	• *Recording* the liability and the asset acquired or the expense incurred • *Reporting* the liability on the balance sheet
What are the two basic categories of current liabilities?	• Current liabilities of *known amount:* Accounts payable Accrued expenses (accrued liabilities) Short-term notes payable Payroll liabilities Sales tax payable Salary, wages, commission, and GST payable bonus payable Current portion of Unearned revenues long-term debt • Current liabilities that *must be estimated:* Estimated warranty payable Estimated vacation pay liability Income tax payable (for a corporation)
How does one account for contingent (potential) liabilities?	• If it is likely and the amount can be reasonably estimated: Accrue an expense (loss) and report a liability • If it is likely but the amount cannot be reasonably estimated: Note disclosure • If it is unlikely but the loss would be significant: Note disclosure • If it is not determinable: Note disclosure
What is the ethical and legal challenge in accounting for current and contingent liabilities?	• Ensuring that the balance sheet (and the related notes) reports the *full amount* of *all* the business's current and contingent liabilities

Accounting for Payroll

OBJECTIVE ③
Compute payroll amounts

Labour costs are so important that most businesses develop or purchase a special payroll system. This section covers the basics of accounting for payroll.

There are numerous ways to express an employee's gross pay:

- *Salary* is pay stated at an annual, monthly, or weekly rate, such as $48,000 per year, $4,000 per month, or $1,000 per week.
- *Wages* are pay amounts stated at an hourly rate, such as $20 per hour.
- *Commission* is pay stated as a percentage of a sale amount, such as a 5-percent commission on a sale. A realtor thus earns $5,000 on a $100,000 sale of real estate.
- *Piecework* is pay based on the number of pieces produced by the employee, such as number of trees planted or shirts sewn.
- *Bonus* is pay over and above base salary (wage or commission). A bonus is usually paid for exceptional performance—in a single amount after year end.
- *Benefits* are extra compensation items that aren't paid directly to the employee. Benefits could include health, life, and disability insurance. The employer pays

the insurance company, which then provides coverage for the employee. Another type of benefit, a pension, sets aside money for the employee for his or her retirement.

Businesses pay employees at a base rate for a set period—called *straight time*. For additional hours—called *overtime*—the employee may get a higher rate of pay.

Lucy Guild is an administrator and bookkeeper for MicroAge Electronics Inc. Lucy earns $700 per week for straight time (35 hours), so her hourly pay rate is $20 ($700 ÷ 35). The company pays *time and a half* for overtime. That rate is 150 percent (1.5 times) the straight-time rate. Thus Lucy earns $30 for each hour of overtime ($20 × 1.5 = $30). For working 37 hours during a week, she earns $760, computed as follows:

Straight-time pay for 35 hours	$700
Overtime pay for 2 overtime hours (2 × $30.00).........	60
Total pay	$760

Gross Pay and Net Pay

Two pay amounts are important for accounting purposes:

- **Gross pay** is the total amount of salary, wages, commission, piecework, and bonus earned by the employee during a pay period. Gross pay is the amount before income taxes or any other deductions. Gross pay is the employer's expense. In the preceding illustration, Lucy Guild's gross pay was $760.

- **Net pay**, also called *take-home pay*, is the amount the employee keeps. Net pay equals gross pay minus all deductions. The employer writes a paycheque to each employee or makes an electronic funds transfer (EFT) to each employee's bank account for his or her net pay.

The federal government and most provincial governments require by law that employers act as collection agents for employee's income taxes, which are deducted from employee paycheques. Insurance companies, labour unions, charitable organizations such as the United Way, and other organizations may also take portions of employees' pay. Amounts withheld from an employee's paycheque are called *deductions*. Exhibit 11–3 illustrates gross and net pay.

EXHIBIT 11–3	Gross Pay and Net Pay

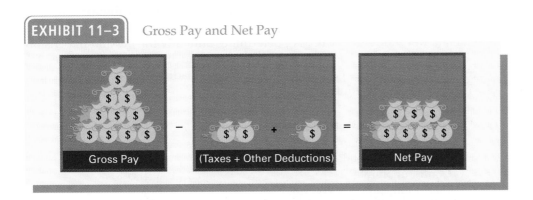

In addition to employee income taxes, CPP (or QPP) contributions, and EI premiums that employers must withhold from pay, employers themselves must pay some payroll expenses, such as the employer's share of Canada (or Quebec) Pension Plan and EI. Many companies also pay employee *fringe benefits,* such as medical and life insurance premiums and pension plan payments.

Payroll Deductions

Payroll deductions create the difference between gross pay and net pay. They are *withheld* from employees' pay and fall into two categories:

- *Required* (or *statutory*) *deductions,* which include employee income tax, EI, and Canada Pension Plan or Quebec Pension Plan deductions.

- *Optional deductions,* which include union dues (which may be automatic deductions for all unionized employees), insurance premiums, charitable contributions, and other amounts that are withheld at the employee's request.

After being withheld, payroll deductions become the liability of the employer, which assumes responsibility for paying the outside party. For example, the employer pays the government the employee income tax withheld and pays the union the employee union dues withheld.

Required Payroll Deductions

Employees' Withheld Income Tax Payable   The law requires employers to withhold income tax from their employees' salaries and wages. The amount of income tax deducted from gross pay is called **withheld income tax**. For most employees, this deduction is the largest. The amount withheld depends on the employee's gross pay and on the amount of nonrefundable tax credits the employee claims. Each employee files a Personal Tax Credits Return (Form TD1), which is used by employers to determine how much income tax to withhold from an employee's gross pay.

The employer sends its employees' withheld income tax to the government. The amount of the income tax withheld by the employer determines how often the employer submits tax payments. Most employers must remit the taxes to the government at least monthly; larger employers must remit two or four times a month, depending on the total amounts withheld. Every business must account for payroll taxes on a calendar-year basis regardless of its fiscal year.

The employer accumulates taxes withheld in the Employee Income Tax Payable account. The word *payable* indicates that the account is a liability of the employer, even though the employees are the people taxed. The payable is eliminated when the employer pays the withheld taxes to the government.

Employees' Withheld Canada (or Quebec) Pension Plan Contributions Payable   The **Canada (or Quebec) Pension Plan** (CPP or QPP) provides retirement, disability, and death benefits to employees who are covered by it. Employers are required to deduct premiums from each employee required to make a contribution (basically all employees between 18 and 70 years of age). The federal government, through the Canada Revenue Agency (CRA), determines annually the maximum pensionable earnings level, the basic annual exemption, and the contribution rate. The contribution rate changes each year and has been steadily increasing. At the time of writing, the following information was applicable:

Maximum pensionable earnings	$46,300
Basic annual exemption	3,500
Maximum contributory earnings	42,800
Contribution rate	4.95%
Maximum employee contribution	
($42,800 × 4.95%)	$2,118.60

CRA provides tables that the employer uses to calculate the amount to deduct from each employee's pay each pay period; the tables take into account the basic exemption of $3,500 of income but also assume that the employee will be working for 12 months. For example, if your total employment income was earned when you worked for two months during the summer and earned $2,500 per month, the withholding would be $109.31 each month, the normal deduction for an employee earning $2,500 per month. However, based on your total income of $5,000 (2 × $2,500) and the basic exemption of $3,500, CPP (QPP) is $74.25 [($5,000 − $3,500) × 0.0495], and your overpayment of $144.37 ($109.31 + $109.31 − $74.25) will be recovered when you file your income tax return.

KEY POINT

Divide the annual exemption of $3,500 by the number of pay periods in a year to ensure the correct amount of CPP exemption is calculated. For weekly pays, divide by 52; for two-week pay periods, divide by 26.

Once the employee reaches the maximum contribution of $2,118.60, the employer stops deducting for that year. Some employees may have had more than one employer in a year; for example, you may have had a job for the summer and now have a part-time job while you are back at school. CRA requires each employer to deduct CPP contributions (the Quebec government in the case of QPP); however, you recover the overpayment when you file your income tax return for the year. The employers do not recover any overpayment.

The employer must remit the CPP contributions withheld and the employer's share, discussed below, every month to CRA (or to the Quebec government, for the QPP). Larger employers must remit two or four times a month, depending on the amounts withheld.

Employees' Withheld Employment Insurance Premiums Payable The *Employment Insurance Act* requires employers to deduct **Employment Insurance (EI)** premiums from each employee each time that employee is paid. The purpose of the Employment Insurance Fund is to provide assistance to contributors to the fund who cannot work for a variety of reasons. The most common reason is that the employee has been laid off; another reason is maternity leave.

The federal government, through CRA, establishes annually the maximum annual insurable earnings level and the EI premium rate. The rate has been decreasing in recent years because the Employment Insurance Fund has a surplus. At the time of writing, the following information was applicable:

Maximum insurable earnings	$42,300
Premium rate	1.73%
Maximum employee contribution	
($42,300 × 1.73%)	$731.79

CRA provides tables that the employer uses to calculate the amount to deduct from each employee's gross pay each pay period. For example, if you earned $2,000 per month, $34.60 ($2,000 × 1.73%) per month would be deducted for EI.

As with the CPP, CRA requires every employer to deduct EI premiums from every eligible employee. Overpayments may be recovered when the employee files his or her income tax return.

The employer must remit the EI premiums withheld and the employer's share, discussed below, to CRA every month. Larger employers must remit two or four times a month depending on the amounts withheld.

Optional Payroll Deductions

As a convenience to their employees, many companies make payroll deductions and disburse cash according to employee instructions. Union dues (which may not be optional), insurance payments, registered pension plan or retirement savings plan payments, payroll savings plans, and donations to charities such as the United Way are examples. The account Employees' Union Dues Payable holds employee deductions for union membership.

Employer Payroll Costs

Employers bear expenses for at least three payroll costs: (1) CPP (or QPP) contributions, (2) Employment Insurance Plan premiums, and (3) Workers'

Compensation Plan premiums. Some provinces also levy a health tax on employers. Most employers must remit both employee and employer shares monthly. Larger employers must remit twice or four times monthly depending on the size of their payroll. Workers' Compensation payments are remitted quarterly.

Employer Canada (or Quebec) Pension Plan Contributions In addition to being responsible for deducting and remitting the employee contribution to the CPP (or QPP), the employer must also pay into the program. The employer must match exactly the employee's contribution. Every employer must do so whether or not the employee also contributes elsewhere. Unlike the employee, the employer may not obtain a refund for overpayment.

Employer Employment Insurance Premiums The employer calculates the employee's premium and remits it together with the employer's share, which is generally 1.4 times the employee's premium, to CRA. The maximum dollar amount of the employer's contribution would be 1.4 times the maximum employee's contribution of $731.79, which amounts to $1,024.51. Almost all employers and employees are covered by this program, unless someone is self-employed or is related to the employer.

Workers' Compensation Premiums Unlike the previous two programs, which are administered by the federal government (the Quebec government for the QPP), **Workers' Compensation** plans are administered provincially. The purpose of the programs is to provide financial support for workers injured on the job. The cost of the coverage is borne by the employer; the employee does not pay a premium to the fund.

In Manitoba, for example, almost all employees are covered by the program. There are over 70 different categories that the Workers' Compensation Board uses to determine the cost of coverage. The category a group of workers is assigned to is based on the risk of injury to workers in that group, which is based on that group's and similar groups' experience. The employer pays a premium equal to the rate assessed times the employer's gross payroll.

Provincial Payroll Taxes Certain provinces levy taxes on employers to pay for provincial health care while others levy a combined health care and post-secondary education tax to pay for provincial health care and post-secondary education.

Payroll Withholding Tables

We have discussed the tables that employers use in calculating the withholdings that must be made from employees' wages for income taxes, CPP (or QPP) contributions, and EI premiums. Exhibit 11–4 provides illustrations of all four tables for a resident of Saskatchewan for 2009. Suppose an employee, Lynne Graham, is paid a salary of $2,000 twice a month (semi-monthly). Graham is single so her TD1 form for both federal and provincial taxes indicates a claim code of 1. From Panel A of Exhibit 11–4, you can see that Graham will have $229.75 deducted for federal income taxes, and from Panel B, you can see that she will have $153.50 deducted for Saskatchewan income taxes. Panel C indicates that Graham would have $92.00 deducted from each pay for CPP, and Panel D shows that $34.60 would be deducted for EI. Graham's employer would keep track, as we will demonstrate later in the chapter, of Graham's CPP and EI deductions and, when they reached the maximums of $2,118.60 and $731.79, respectively, would stop deducting premiums from Graham's pay. The employer's share would be $92.00 for CPP (matches employee's share), while the employer's share for EI would be $48.44 (1.4 times employee share). In addition, at the assessed rate, the workers' compensation premium to be paid by the employer on Lynne Graham's salary would be $15.00.

EXHIBIT 11–4 | Payroll Withholding Tables

Panel A

Saskatchewan
Federal Tax Deductions
Effective April 1, 2009
Semi-Monthly: 24 Pay Periods Per Year

Pay	Federal claim codes										
	0	1	2	3	4	5	6	7	8	9	10
From Less than	Deduct from each pay										
1969 – 1987	290.65	225.80	219.65	207.30	195.00	182.65	170.35	158.00	145.70	133.35	121.05
1987 – 2005	294.60	229.75	223.60	211.30	198.95	186.65	174.30	162.00	149.65	137.35	125.00
2005 – 2023	298.55	233.75	227.55	215.25	202.90	190.60	178.25	165.95	153.60	141.30	128.95
2023 – 2041	302.55	237.70	231.55	219.20	206.90	194.55	182.25	169.90	157.60	145.25	132.95
2041 – 2059	306.50	241.65	235.50	223.15	210.85	198.50	186.20	173.85	161.55	149.20	136.90

Panel B

Saskatchewan
Provincial Tax Deductions
Effective April 1, 2009
Semi-Monthly: 24 Pay Periods Per Year

Pay	Federal claim codes										
	0	1	2	3	4	5	6	7	8	9	10
From Less than	Deduct from each pay										
1961 – 1979	209.60	148.80	144.60	136.20	127.80	119.40	111.00	102.55	94.15	85.75	77.35
1979 – 1997	211.95	151.15	146.95	138.55	130.15	121.70	113.30	104.90	96.50	88.10	79.70
1997 – 2015	214.30	153.50	149.30	140.85	132.45	124.05	115.65	107.25	98.85	90.45	82.05
2015 – 2033	216.65	155.80	151.60	143.20	134.80	126.40	118.00	109.60	101.20	92.80	84.35
2033 – 2051	219.00	158.15	153.95	145.55	137.15	128.75	120.35	111.95	103.50	95.10	86.70

Panel C

Canada Pension Plan Contributions

Semi-Monthly (24 pay periods per year)

Pay From To	CPP
1929.37 – 1939.36	88.53
1939.37 – 1949.36	89.03
1949.37 – 1959.36	89.52
1959.37 – 1969.36	90.02
1969.37 – 1979.36	90.51
1979.37 – 1989.36	91.01
1989.37 – 1999.36	91.50
1999.37 – 2009.36	92.00
2009.37 – 2019.36	92.49

Panel D

Employment Insurance Premiums

Semi-Monthly (24 pay periods per year)

Insurable Earnings From To	EI Premium
1997.95 – 1998.55	34.57
1998.56 – 1999.13	34.58
1999.14 – 1999.71	34.59
1999.72 – 2000.28	34.60
2000.29 – 2000.86	34.61
2000.87 – 2001.44	34.62
2001.45 – 2002.02	34.63
2002.03 – 2002.60	34.64
2002.61 – 2003.17	34.65

Exhibit 11–5 shows the disbursement of Graham's payroll costs by her Saskatchewan employer, assuming she pays $20 of union dues each pay period.

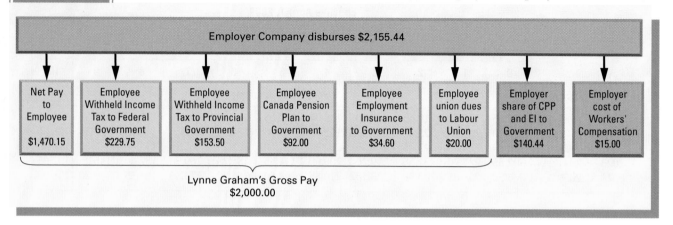

EXHIBIT 11–5 Disbursement of Lynne Graham's Payroll Costs by an Employer Company (Saskatchewan)

Employer Company disburses $2,155.44

| Net Pay to Employee $1,470.15 | Employee Withheld Income Tax to Federal Government $229.75 | Employee Withheld Income Tax to Provincial Government $153.50 | Employee Canada Pension Plan to Government $92.00 | Employee Employment Insurance to Government $34.60 | Employee union dues to Labour Union $20.00 | Employer share of CPP and EI to Government $140.44 | Employer cost of Workers' Compensation $15.00 |

Lynne Graham's Gross Pay $2,000.00

DID YOU GET IT?

MyAccountingLab

To check your understanding of the material in this Learning Objective, complete these questions. The solutions appear on MyAccountingLab so you can check your progress.

7. Use the tables in Exhibit 11–4 to determine federal tax, Saskatchewan provincial tax, CPP, and EI withholdings for the following employees, who are paid semi-monthly:
   (a) Agatha Cross is paid $2,002 each pay period, with a federal and provincial claim code of 4.
   (b) Peter Simpson is paid $1,998 each pay period, with a federal and provincial claim code of 2.
   (c) Lana Morris is paid $2,000 each pay period, with a federal and provincial claim code of 3.

8. Compute the annual net pay of an employee who earns an annual salary of $60,000. Total income tax deducted was $10,000, annual union dues were $1,500, and this employee was eligible for CPP and EI. (You can use Exhibit 11–5 as a guide.)

9. Refer to the previous question. What is the total cost to the employer for this employee, assuming the employer does not pay Workers' Compensation?

Payroll Entries

OBJECTIVE 4
Record basic payroll transactions

The journal entries in this section show an employer's entries to record a monthly payroll of $60,000 (all amounts are assumed for illustration only).

The first journal entry records the employer's salary expense, which is the gross salary of all employees ($60,000) for a month. The employer acts as a collection agent for CRA (income tax and Canada Pension), the provincial government (income tax), the Employment Insurance Commission, and the union, withholding the employees' contributions from their gross pay. The remaining amount is the employees' net (take-home) pay of $46,278.

KEY POINT

Payroll liabilities are accrued liabilities. These liabilities are to various entities.

Salary Expense (or Wages or Commission Expense)..................	60,000	
Employee (federal and provincial) Income Tax Payable		8,100
Canada Pension Plan Payable...		2,970
Employment Insurance Payable		1,120
Employee Union Dues Payable		1,532
Salaries Payable (net pay)...		46,278

To record salary expense and employee withholdings.

To the employee:	For net wages, salaries, and bonuses
To the government:	For income tax withheld, Employment Insurance, and Canada (or Quebec) Pension Plan
To outside providers of benefits:	For insurance premiums, union dues, payroll savings plans

The second journal entry represents the employer's share of CPP and EI. Remember, the employer's share is 1.0 times and 1.4 times the employee's share, respectively, for these two deductions.

Employee Benefits Expense	4,538	
Canada Pension Plan Payable		2,970
Employment Insurance Payable		1,568

To record employer's share of CPP (1.0 × $2,970)
and EI (1.4 × $1,120).

The third journal entry records employee benefits paid by the employer. This company has a dental benefits plan for its employees for which it pays the premiums.

Employee Dental Benefits Expense	1,092	
Employee Benefits Payable		1,092

To record employee benefits payable by employer.

In this example, the total payroll expense for the month is made up of base salary ($60,000) plus the employer's share of CPP and EI ($4,538) plus fringe benefits ($1,092) for a total of $65,630. There would also be Workers' Compensation, which, you will recall, is paid completely by the employer, and other costs depending on the province in which the company operates.

The final journal entries record the payment of the employee withholdings and the employer expenses to CRA and other parties that provide employee benefits. Each payment that requires a separate cheque also requires a separate journal entry. These entries are covered more fully in the next section.

Employee (federal and provincial) Income Tax Payable	8,100	
Canada Pension Plan Payable	2,970	
Employment Insurance Payable	1,120	
Canada Pension Plan Payable	2,970	
Employment Insurance Payable	1,568	
Cash		16,728

To record payment to Canada Revenue Agency (CRA)
for federal and provincial income tax withholdings,
CPP and EI withholdings (employee portions), and CPP
and EI expense (employer portions); Cheque #XX1.

Employee Union Dues Payable	1,532	
Cash		1,532

To record payment to Workers' Union for union dues
withheld from employees; Cheque #XX2.

Employee Benefits Payable	1,092	
Cash		1,092

To record payment to Mega Dental for employee
benefits; Cheque #XX3.

A company's payments to people who are not employees—outsiders called independent contractors—are *not* company payroll expenses. Consider two technical writers, Elena and Scott. Elena is the company's technical writer. Scott is a contractor hired to help Elena during the busy season. Elena is an employee of the company, and her compensation is a debit to Salary Expense. Scott, however, performs writing services for many clients, and the company debits Contract Labour when it pays him. Any payment for services performed by a person outside the company is a debit to an expense account other than payroll.

DID YOU GET IT?

To check your understanding of the material in this Learning Objective, complete this question. The solution appears on MyAccountingLab so you can check your progress.

10. Record the payroll, payroll deductions, and employer payroll costs, given the following information about an Ontario company:

Gross pay	$190,000
Employee withheld income tax	22,800
Employee withheld CPP	9,300
Employee withheld EI	3,500
Union dues	2,945

Employer cost for CPP = 1.0 × Employee amount
Employer cost for EI = 1.4 × Employee amount
Pension plan paid by employer only = 1.0 percent of gross pay

The Payroll System

OBJECTIVE 5
Use a payroll system, implement internal controls, and report current liabilities on the balance sheet

Good business requires paying employees accurately and on time. A payroll system accomplishes these goals. The components of the payroll system are:

- A payroll register
- Payroll cheques
- Employee earnings records

Payroll Register

Each pay period, the company organizes payroll data in a special journal called the *payroll register*. The payroll register is like a cash payments journal and serves as a cheque register for recording payroll cheques. We introduced the cash payments journal in Chapter 7, page 360.

Exhibit 11–6 is a payroll register for Leduc Petroleum. The payroll register has columns for each employee's gross pay, deductions, and net pay. This record gives the employer the information needed to record salary expense for the pay period as follows:

2009

Dec. 31	Office Salaries Expense	4,464.00	
	Sales Salaries Expense	9,190.00	
	Employee Income Tax Payable		2,358.19
	Canada Pension Plan Payable		402.70
	Employment Insurance Payable		235.12
	United Way Payable		155.00
	Salaries Payable		10,502.99
	To record payroll expenses for the week ended December 31, 2009.		
31	Employee Benefits Expense	731.87	
	Canada Pension Plan Payable		402.70
	Employment Insurance Payable ($235.12 × 1.4)		329.17
	To record the cost of employer's portion of payroll expenses for the week ended December 31, 2009.		

EXHIBIT 11–6 Payroll Register for Leduc Petroleum

Week ended December 31, 2009

| | | Gross Pay | | | Deductions | | | | | | Net Pay | | Account Debited | | |
| | | a | b | c | d | e | f | g | h | i | j | k | l | m |
Employee Name	Hours	Straight Time	Overtime	Total	Federal Income Tax	Prov. Inc. Tax (Alberta)	Canada Pension Plan	Employ-ment Insurance	United Way	Total	(o–h) Amount	Cheque No.	Office Salaries Expense	Sales Salaries Expense
Chen, W.L.*	40	500.00		500.00	37.25	14.85	21.42	8.65	2.00	84.17	415.83	1621	500.00	
Drumm, C.L.	46	400.00	90.00	490.00	36.15	13.70	20.92	8.48	2.00	81.25	408.75	1622		490.00
Elias, M.	41	560.00	21.00	581.00	48.75	20.45	25.43	10.05		104.68	476.32	1623	581.00	
Vokovich, E.A.**	40	1,360.00		1,360.00	201.25	97.95			15.00	314.20	1,045.80	1641		1,360.00
Total		12,940.00	714.00	13,654.00	1,686.15	672.04	402.70	235.12	155.00	3,151.01	10,502.99		4,464.00	9,190.00

*W.L. Chen earned gross pay of $500. His net pay was $415.83, paid with cheque number 1621. Chen is an office worker, so his salary is debited to Office Salaries Expense.

**E.A. Vokovich has exceeded maximum pensionable earnings of $46,300 and so has had the Canada Pension Plan maximum, $2,118.60, already deducted. Vokovich has also exceeded the maximum insurable Employment Insurance earnings of $42,300 and so has already had the maximum, $731.79, deducted.

Payroll Cheques

Most companies pay employees by cheque or by electronic funds transfer (EFT). A *payroll cheque* has an attachment, or stub, that details the employee's gross pay, payroll deductions, and net pay. These amounts come from the payroll register, like that in Exhibit 11–6. Exhibit 11–7 shows payroll cheque number 1622, issued to C.L. Drumm for net pay of $408.75 earned during the week ended December 31, 2009. To enhance your ability to use payroll data, trace all amounts on the cheque attachment to the payroll register in Exhibit 11–6.

EXHIBIT 11–7   Payroll Cheque

Leduc Petroleum										1622	

Leduc Petroleum
Payroll Account
Red Deer, Alberta

January 4, 2010

Pay to the
Order of _____ C.L. Drumm _____ $ 408.75

Four hundred and eight ------------------------ 75/100 ___ Dollars

The Bank of Nova Scotia
Red Deer
Alberta T4P 3L9

Anna Figaro
Treasurer

⑆111900031⑆ 0787⑈500004454⑈

Pay			Deductions						Net Pay	Cheque No.
Straight Time	Over-time	Gross	Federal Income Tax	Prov. Income Tax	C.P.P.	Employ-ment Ins.	United Way	Total		
400.00	90.00	490.00	36.15	13.70	20.92	8.48	2.00	81.25	408.75	1622

Increasingly, companies are paying employees by electronic funds transfer. The employee can authorize the company to make all deposits directly to her or his bank. With no cheque to write and deliver to the employee, the company saves time and money. As evidence of the deposit, most companies issue to employees either a paper or an electronic pay summary slip showing the data for that pay period (similar to the cheque-stub data above) plus year-to-date data.

Recording Cash Payments for Payroll

Most employers must record at least three cash payments: for payments of net pay to employees, for payments of payroll withholdings to the government, and for payments to third parties for employee fringe benefits.

Net Pay to Employees   When the employer pays employees, the company debits Salaries Payable and credits Cash. Using the data in Exhibit 11–6, the company would make the following entry to record the cash payment (column (j)) for the December 31, 2009, weekly payroll:

2010			
Jan. 4	Salaries Payable	10,502.99	
	Cash		10,502.99

Payroll Withholdings to the Government and Other Organizations The employer must send income taxes withheld from employees' pay and the employee deductions and employer's share of CPP (or QPP) contributions and EI premiums to Canada Revenue Agency (the Quebec government in the case of QPP). The payment for a given month is due on or before the 15th day of the following month. In addition, the employer has to remit any withholdings for union dues, charitable donations, etc.; the payment would probably be made in the following month.

Assume federal income tax of $6,972.80, Province of Alberta income tax of $2,567.40, CPP contributions of $1,645.02, EI premiums of $997.02, and United Way contributions of $465 were deducted in calculating the net pay for the employees of Leduc Petroleum for the four weeks ended December 3, 10, 17, and 24, 2009. Based on those amounts and columns (d) through (j) in Exhibit 11–6, the business would record payments to CRA and United Way for the month of December 2009 as follows:

```
2010
Jan. 10   Employee Income Tax Payable
              ($6,972.80 + $1,686.15 + $2,567.40 + $672.04)..............11,898.39
          Canada Pension Plan Payable
              ($1,645.02 + $402.70 + $1,645.02 + $402.70)...................  4,095.44
          Employment Insurance Payable
              [$997.02 + $235.12 + 1.4 × ($997.02 + $235.12)] ............  2,957.14
              Cash...........................................................................              18,950.97
          To record payment to CRA for December 2009 withholdings.
      10  United Way Payable..............................................................  620.00
              Cash...........................................................................                 620.00
          To record payment to United Way for
          December 2009 withholdings ($465.00 + $155.00).
```

Payments to Third Parties for Fringe Benefits The employer sometimes pays for employees' dental benefits coverage and for a company pension plan. Assuming the total cash payment for these benefits is $1,927.14 and the payment is made to one company, this entry would be

```
2010
Jan. 10   Employee Benefits Payable—Dental Plan........................  600.14
          Employee Benefits Payable—Pension Plan.....................  1,327.00
              Cash...........................................................................               1,927.14
          To record payment for employee dental benefits
          coverage and company pension plan.
```

Earnings Record

The employer must file Summary of Remuneration Paid returns with Canada Revenue Agency (CRA) and must provide the employee with a Statement of Remuneration Paid, Form T4, by February 28 of the following year. Therefore, employers maintain an earnings record for each employee. (These earnings records are also used for EI claims.) Exhibit 11–8 (p. 574) is a five-week excerpt from the earnings record of employee Jason C. Jenkins.

The employee earnings record is not a journal or a ledger, and it is not required by law. It is an accounting tool—like the work sheet—that the employer uses to prepare payroll withholdings reports. The information provided on the employee earnings record with respect to year-to-date earnings also indicates when an employee has earned $46,300, the point at which the employer can stop withholding CPP contributions. (Recall that, unlike the employee, the employer may not obtain a refund for overpayment of CPP.) The same is true for EI deductions: the employer stops withholding EI contributions after the employee has earned $42,300. There is no maximum income tax deduction.

EXHIBIT 11–8 Employee Earnings Record for 2009

Employee Name and Address:

Jenkins, Jason C.
1400 Camousen Crescent
Victoria, BC V5J 5K9

Social Insurance No.: 978-010-789
Marital Status: Married
Net Claims Code: 4
Pay Rate: $700 per week; overtime $26.25 per hour.
Job Title: Salesperson

| Week Ended | Gross Pay | | | | Deductions | | | | | | Net Pay | |
	Hours	Straight Time	Overtime	Total	To Date	Federal Income Tax	Province of BC Income Tax	Canada Pension Plan	Employment Insurance	United Way	Total	Amount	Cheque No.
Jan. 4	40	700.00		700.00	700.00	51.35	19.25	31.32	12.11	2.00	116.03	583.97	403
Dec. 3	40	700.00		700.00	35,437.50	51.35	19.25	31.32	12.11	2.00	116.03	583.97	1525
Dec. 10	40	700.00		700.00	36,137.50	51.35	19.25	31.32	12.11	2.00	116.03	583.97	1548
Dec. 17	44	700.00	105.00	805.00	36,942.50	66.70	26.90	36.52	13.93	2.00	146.05	658.95	1574
Dec. 24	48	700.00	210.00	910.00	37,852.50	88.90	34.70	41.49	15.74	2.00	182.83	727.17	1598
Dec. 31	46	700.00	157.50	857.50	38,710.00	78.60	31.05	39.11	14.84	2.00	165.60	691.90	1632
Total		36,400.00	2,310.00	38,710.00	38,710.00	2,839.66	1,064.53	1,742.90	669.68	104.00	6,420.77	32,289.23	

Exhibit 11–9 is the Statement of Remuneration Paid, Form T4, for employee Jason C. Jenkins. The employer prepares this form for each employee and a form called a T4 Summary—Summary of Remuneration Paid, which summarizes the information on all the T4s issued by the employer for that year. The employer sends the T4 Summary and one copy of each T4 to CRA by February 28 each year. CRA uses the documents to ensure that the employer has correctly paid to the government all amounts withheld on its behalf from employees, together with the employer's share. The employee gets two copies of the T4; one copy must be filed with the employee's income tax return, while the second copy is for the employee's records.

EXHIBIT 11–9 Employee Statement of Remuneration Paid (Form T4)

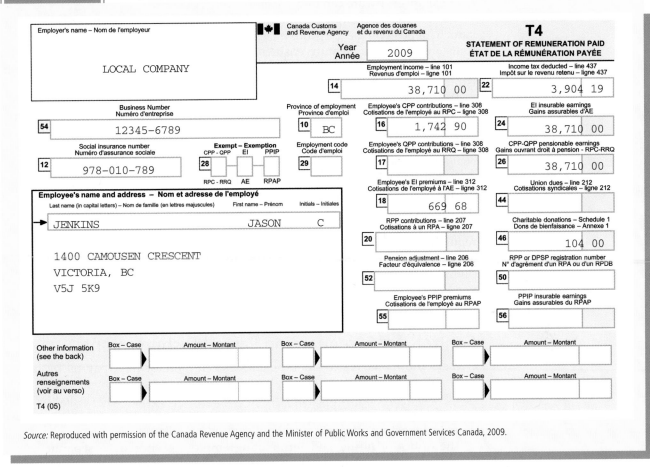

Source: Reproduced with permission of the Canada Revenue Agency and the Minister of Public Works and Government Services Canada, 2009.

CRA matches the income on the T4 filed by the employer against the income reported on the employee's income tax return, filed by the employee, to ensure that the employee properly reported his or her income from employment.

Employers and employees can use the Internet to file T4 information for reporting as well as to file tax information.

Internal Control over Payroll

The internal controls over cash payments discussed in Chapter 8 also apply to payroll. There are two main types of controls for payroll: controls for efficiency and controls for safeguarding payroll disbursements.

Controls for Efficiency

Payroll transactions are ideally suited for computer processing. Employee payroll data can be stored in a file. The computer performs the calculations, prints the payroll register and the paycheques, and updates the employee earnings records electronically.

Payroll Systems and Internal Control

Companies use the payroll module of their accounting software to perform the detailed payroll calculations. This software is updated regularly by the software manufacturer to ensure that the tax tables and rates reflect the changes implemented by any of the laws relating to payroll deductions. At the end of the calendar year, this software can prepare employees' T4 slips.

The payroll software also interfaces with the banking system to instruct the bank to deposit the net pay into the employees' bank accounts by electronic funds transfers (EFT). This feature ensures that the appropriate employee is paid and that the payroll cheques are not lost. Not issuing paycheques also reduces administrative costs to the company.

Reconciling the bank account can be time consuming because of the large number of paycheques. There may be a large number of outstanding cheques for the bank reconciliation. To limit the number of outstanding cheques, some companies use one bank account strictly for payroll purposes. This helps to keep the payroll charges and outstanding cheques separate from the company's day-to-day business charges and cheques, making each account's reconciliation easier and reducing the chance for errors.

Other payroll controls for efficiency include following established policies for hiring and terminating employees, and complying with government regulations. Hiring and termination policies provide guidelines for keeping a qualified, diligent workforce dedicated to achieving the business's goals. Complying with government regulations helps companies avoid paying fines and penalties.

Controls for Safeguarding Payroll Disbursements

Owners and managers of small businesses can monitor their payroll by having personal contact with employees. Large corporations cannot do so. A particular risk is that a paycheque may be written to a fictitious person and cashed by a dishonest employee. To guard against this and other possible crimes, large businesses adopt strict internal control policies for payrolls.

The duties of hiring and terminating employees should be separated from payroll accounting and from distributing paycheques. Issuing paycheques only to employees with a photo ID ensures that only actual employees receive pay. Comparing the current employee list to a list of former employees ensures that terminated employees are not continuing to receive paycheques. A formal time-keeping system helps ensure that employees actually worked the number of hours claimed. Employees may punch time cards at the start and end of the work day to prove their attendance.

As we saw in Chapter 8, the foundation for good internal control is separation of duties. This is why companies have separate departments for the following payroll functions:

- hiring and terminating employees—Human Resources department
- maintaining employee earnings records—Payroll or Accounting department

Reporting Payroll Expense and Liabilities

At the end of each period, a company reports all its current liabilities on the balance sheet. At December 31, 2008, Teck Cominco Limited had the current liabilities shown in Exhibit 11–10. Teck combines all payroll liabilities under a single heading, Accounts Payable and Accrued Liabilities (Note 10).

EXHIBIT 11–10 Teck Cominco Limited Partial Balance Sheet as at December 31, 2008

Current liabilities	(in $ millions)
Accounts payable and accrued liabilities (Note 10) ..	$1,506
Current portion of long-term debt (Note 11)..............	1,336
Short-term debt (Note 11)	6,436
	$9,278

Note 10. Accounts Payable and Accrued Liabilities	($ in millions)
Trade payables..	$ 670
Current derivative liabilities..	252
Payroll related liabilities..	176
Capital project accruals	82
Commercial and government royalties	78
Resource taxes payable...	69
Accrued interest..	68
Current portion of asset retirement obligations (Note 12(a))	16
Other	95
	$1,506

DID YOU GET IT?

MyAccountingLab

To check your understanding of the material in this Learning Objective, complete these questions. The solutions appear on MyAccountingLab so you can check your progress.

11. The payroll register for Quesnel Quarries showed the information below for the weekly pay period ending July 10, 2009. Use this information to record the payroll expenses for the week and the employer's portion of payroll expenses for the week.

Straight-time wages...	$21,840
Overtime wages	2,500
Deductions:	
Federal income tax...	1,850
Provincial income tax	980
Canada Pension Plan..	1,200
Employment Insurance...	470
Union Dues	420

12. Centurion Homes of Calgary, Alberta, builds houses and has four construction crews. The supervisors hire—and terminate—workers and keep their hourly records. Each Friday morning the supervisors telephone their workers' hours to the home office, where accountants prepare the weekly paycheques. Around noon the supervisors pick up the paycheques. They return to the construction site and

pay the workers at day's end. What is the internal control weakness in this situation? Propose a way to improve the internal controls.

13. From the following information, determine whether the accounts are current or long-term liabilities. Show how the current liabilities would be presented on the balance sheet at December 31, 2009, assuming a separate line on the balance sheet for each item. Perform any calculations that may be required.

    a. A one-year, 6-percent note payable for $3,000 was issued on November 3, 2009.

    b. A $10,000, 180-day, 5-percent bank loan was arranged and effective on September 17, 2009.

    c. A $10,000, two-year, 5-percent bank loan was arranged and effective on September 17, 2009. The loan must be repaid in full on September 17, 2011.

    d. A $10,000, two-year, 5-percent bank loan was arranged and effective on January 2, 2009. Half of the loan must be repaid on January 2, 2010, and the remainder repaid on January 2, 2011.

    e. Of the $5,000 unearned subscription revenue that was recorded during the year, $3,200 was earned by December 31.

    f. The company expects to pay future warranty costs of 2 percent of sales for the $350,000 of goods sold during 2009.

The Impact on Current Liabilities of International Financial Reporting Standards (IFRS)

OBJECTIVE ⑥

Describe the impact on current liabilities of international financial reporting standards (IFRS)

As was discussed in Chapter 9, one of the factors in Canada's decision to require international financial reporting standards (IFRS) for publicly accountable enterprises in Canada was to make the financial statements more *relevant* to users of an enterprise's financial information. Chapter 9 also highlighted that many current-asset accounts were already converged with international standards because they reflect fair values.

The same rationale holds true for current liabilities. These obligations to parties outside the company are typically carried at their fair value, and because of this fact, the Canadian standard and the international standard are fully converged. The way Canadian companies now determine the values of their current liabilities will not change as they move to IFRS.

As with accounts receivable, there is a potential change in terminology. Canadian companies typically refer to current liabilities as *accounts payable* and *accrued liabilities*. Under IFRS, the preferred terms are *trade payables* and *provisions*. These terms are optional for Canadian companies reporting under IFRS.

DID YOU GET IT?

MyAccountingLab

To check your understanding of the material in this Learning Objective, complete this question. The solution appears on MyAccountingLab so you can check your progress.

14. Delow Corporation employs 10 people. At year end, these employees are entitled to 10 weeks of vacation they have not yet taken. Delow decides to set up a Vacation Payable account and estimates that it owes the employees $20,000. The amount was determined by multiplying the number of weeks of vacation owed by the average weekly salary for the employees (10 employees × $2,000 owed per employee). Delow is publicly accountable and is following IFRS. Do you agree with the accounting treatment for this account? Is the determined value relevant and reliable?

As we conclude this chapter, we return to our payroll-related opening questions: What are the key elements of a payroll system, and how is payroll recorded and reported? These questions were answered throughout this section of the chapter. The Decision Guidelines that follow provide the answers in a useful summary.

DECISION GUIDELINES — Accounting for Payroll

Decision	Guidelines
What are the key elements of a payroll accounting system?	• Personal Tax Credits Return, Form TD1(E) • Payroll register • Payroll bank account and payroll cheques (or payroll statements, in the case of EFT transfers) • Employee earnings record • Statement of Remuneration Paid, Form T4

What are the key terms in the payroll area?	*Gross pay* (Total amount earned by the employee)
	— *Payroll deductions:*
	  a. Withheld income tax
	  b. Withheld CPP (or QPP) deductions—equal amount paid by employer
	  c. Withheld EI deductions—employer pays 1.4 times employee deduction
	  d. Optional deductions (registered pension plan or retirement savings plan, charitable contributions)
	= *Net (take-home) pay*

What is the employer's total payroll expense?	*Gross pay*
	+ *Employer's payroll expenses*
	  a. CPP (or QPP) expense
	  b. EI expense—employer pays 1.4 times amount employee pays
	+ *Fringe benefits for employees*
	  a. Insurance (dental, drug plan, and disability)
	  b. Employer's share of registered pension plan or retirement savings plan (and other retirement benefits)
	  c. Workers' Compensation premiums
	  d. Club memberships and other benefits
	= *Employer's total payroll costs*

Where are payroll amounts reported?	• Payroll expenses on the income statement • Payroll liabilities on the balance sheet

Summary Problem for Your Review

Best Threads, a clothing store in Moose Jaw, Saskatchewan, employs one salesperson, Sheila Kingsley. Her straight-time pay is $420 per week. She earns time and a half for hours worked in excess of 35 per week. For Kingsley's wage rate and "net claim code" on her Personal Tax Credits Return (TD1), the federal income tax withholding rate is approximately 11.5 percent, and the provincial rate is 7.7 percent. CPP is 4.95 percent on income until the maximum total contribution of $2,118.60 is reached, while EI premiums are 1.73 percent until the maximum total contribution of $731.79 is reached. In addition, Best Threads pays Kingsley's Blue Cross supplemental health insurance premiums of $31.42 a month and dental insurance premiums of $18.50 a month.

During the week ended February 28, 2009, Kingsley worked 48 hours.

Required

1. Compute Kingsley's gross pay and net pay for the week.
2. Record the following payroll entries that Best Threads would make:

   a. Expense for Kingsley's wages including overtime pay (ignore the basic CPP exemption)

   b. Cost of employer's share of Kingsley's withholdings (ignore the basic CPP exemption)

   c. Expense for fringe benefits

   d. Payment of cash to Kingsley

   e. Payment Best Threads must make to Canada Revenue Agency (CRA)

   f. Payment of fringe benefits for the month

3. How much total payroll expense did Best Threads incur for the week? How much cash did the business spend on its payroll?
4. What payroll-related accounts and amounts would appear on the balance sheet at February 28, 2009, if all payments were made in March 2009?
5. To improve internal control, companies often use a separate payroll bank account for employee payments. Why?

Name: Best Threads
Industry: Clothing store in Saskatchewan
Accounting Period: Week ended February 28, 2009

SOLUTION

Requirement 1

To compute gross pay, first separate hours worked into straight-time and overtime hours. Then multiply each by the appropriate hourly pay rate.

Gross pay:		
Straight-time pay for 35 hours		$420.00
Overtime pay		
Rate per hour ($420 ÷ 35 × 1.5)	$18.00	
Hours (48 − 35)	× 13	234.00
Total gross pay		$654.00

Compute the amount of each withholding, either using the information given or by consulting tax, CPP, and EI tables.

Gross pay − Total withholdings = Net pay

Net pay:		
Gross pay		$654.00
Less: Withheld federal income tax ($654 × 0.115)	$ 75.21	
Withheld provincial income tax ($654 × 0.077)	50.36	
Withheld CPP ($654 × 0.0495)	32.37	
Withheld EI ($654 × 0.0173)	11.31	169.25
Net pay		$484.75

Requirement 2

a. Sales Salary Expense 654.00

    Employee Income Tax Payable ($75.21 + $50.36)............. 125.57

    Canada Pension Plan Payable 32.37

    Employment Insurance Payable... 11.31

    Wages Payable 484.75

    To record expense for S. Kingsley's wages.

> This journal entry uses the gross pay, withholdings, and net pay amounts calculated in Requirement 1. "Wages Payable" is the amount of net pay.

b. Employee Benefits Expense 48.20

    Canada Pension Plan Payable 32.37

    Employment Insurance Payable... 15.83

    To record cost of employer's portion of S. Kingsley's wages.

        CPP is $32.37 ($32.37 × 1).

        EI is $15.83 ($11.31 × 1.4).

> Remember that the employer's EI expense is 1.4 times the employee's EI withholding.

c. Medical and Dental Expense 49.92

    Employee Benefits Payable 49.92

    To record expense of fringe benefits ($31.42 + $18.50).

d. Wages Payable 484.75

    Cash 484.75

    To record payment of wages to S. Kingsley.

> This journal entry issues the paycheque or sends the funds by EFT to the employee's bank account.

e. Employee Income Tax Payable................................... 125.57

    Canada Pension Plan Payable ($32.37 + $32.37) 64.74

    Employment Insurance Payable ($11.31 + $15.83) 27.14

    Cash 217.45

    To record payment to CRA.

> Employers pay to CRA:
> - federal and provincial taxes withheld from the employee
> - EI premiums withheld from employee + paid by employer
> - CPP (or QPP) withholdings from employee + paid by employer

f. Employee Benefits Payable.. 49.92

    Cash 49.92

    To record payment of monthly fringe benefits.

Requirement 3

Best Threads incurred *total payroll expense* of $752.12 (gross salary of $654.00 + employer's cost of CPP of $32.37 + employer's cost of EI of $15.83 + fringe benefits of $49.92). See entries a to c.

    Best Threads paid cash of $752.12 on payroll (Kingsley's net pay of $484.75 + payment to CRA of $217.45 + fringe benefits of $49.92). See entries d to f.

> Total payroll expense = Gross salary + EI expense + CPP expense + Fringe benefits
>
> Total cash paid = Net pay + CRA payment + Fringe benefits payment (everyone who was sent a cheque)

Requirement 4

The accounts and amounts that would appear on the February 28, 2009, balance sheet are:

Employee Income Tax Payable...	$125.57
Canada Pension Plan Payable	64.74
Employment Insurance Payable..	27.14
Employee Benefits Payable	49.92
Wages Payable	484.75

Requirement 5

Companies use separate bank accounts for payroll to help in the timely reconciliation of all the bank accounts, especially if the company has a large number of employees. A separate payroll bank account allows a company to identify and focus on payroll issues when they arise. Questions may be raised about the status of employees if payroll cheques are not cashed within a normal time frame. For example, an employee may have moved and no longer work for the company, so the paycheques remain uncashed.

Summary

1. **Account for current liabilities of known amount.** *Current liabilities* may be divided into those of *known amount* and those that must be *estimated*. Trade accounts payable, short-term notes payable, interest payable, GST payable, employee benefits payable, and unearned revenues are current liabilities of known amount.

2. **Account for current liabilities that must be estimated.** Current liabilities that must be estimated include warranties payable, vacation pay, and the corporation's income tax payable.

   Contingent liabilities are not actual liabilities but potential liabilities that may arise in the future. Contingent liabilities, like current liabilities, may be of known amounts or indefinite amounts. A business that faces a lawsuit not yet decided in court has a contingent liability of indefinite amount.

3. **Compute payroll amounts.** *Payroll* accounting handles the expenses and liabilities arising from compensating employees. Employers must withhold federal and provincial income taxes, CPP (or QPP) contributions, and EI premiums from employees' pay and send these *withholdings* together with the employer's share of the latter two to the appropriate government. In addition, many employers allow their employees to pay for insurance and union dues and to make gifts to charities through payroll deductions. An employee's net pay is the gross pay less all withholdings and optional deductions.

4. **Record basic payroll transactions.** An *employer's* payroll expenses include the employer's share of CPP (or QPP) contributions and EI premiums; employers also pay provincial health and post-secondary education taxes in those provinces that levy them, as well as Workers' Compensation. Also, employers may provide their employees with fringe benefits, such as dental coverage and retirement pensions.

5. **Use a payroll system, implement internal controls, and report current liabilities on the balance sheet.** A basic *payroll system* consists of a payroll register, a payroll bank account, payroll cheques or EFTs, and an earnings record for each employee. Good *internal controls* over payroll help the business to achieve efficiency and to safeguard the company's cash. The cornerstone of internal control is the separation of duties.

   The company reports on the balance sheet all current liabilities that it owes: current liabilities of known amount, including payroll liabilities and current liabilities that must be estimated.

6. **Describe the impact on current liabilities of international financial reporting standards (IFRS).** Current liabilities are typically carried at their fair value, so the way Canadian companies now determine the values of their current liabilities will not change as they move to IFRS. Under IFRS, the preferred terms are *trade payables* and *provisions* for *accounts payable* and *accrued liabilities*, but these terms are optional for Canadian companies reporting under IFRS.

SELF-STUDY QUESTIONS

Test your understanding of the chapter by marking the correct answer for each of the following questions:

1. A $10,000, 9-percent, one-year note payable was issued on July 31. The balance sheet at December 31 will report interest payable of (*pp. 551–552*)
   a. $0 because the interest is not due yet
   b. $522.74
   c. $375
   d. $900

2. Which of the following liabilities creates no expense for the company? (*pp. 554–555*)
   a. Interest
   b. Sales tax
   c. Employment Insurance
   d. Warranty

3. Known liabilities of uncertain amounts should be (*p. 558*)
   a. Contingent liabilities
   b. Ignored. Record them when they are paid.
   c. Reported on the balance sheet
   d. Reported only in the notes to the financial statements

4. Suppose Canadian Tire estimates that warranty costs will equal 1 percent of tire sales. Assume that November tire sales totalled $900,000, and the company's outlay in replacement tires and cash to satisfy warranty claims was $7,400. How much warranty expense should the November income statement report? (*pp. 558–559*)
   a. $1,600
   b. $7,400
   c. $9,000
   d. $16,400

5. Nu Systems Company is a defendant in a lawsuit that claims damages of $55,000. On the balance sheet date, it appears unlikely that the court will render a judgment against the company. How should Nu Systems Company report this event in its financial statements? (*pp. 560–561*)
   a. Omit mention because no judgment has been rendered
   b. Disclose the contingent liability in a note
   c. Report the loss on the income statement and the liability on the balance sheet.
   d. Do both b and c

6. Emilie Frontenac's weekly pay for 40 hours is $400, plus time and a half for overtime. The federal tax rate, based on her income level and deductions, is 10.5 percent, the provincial rate is 8.8 percent, the QPP rate is 4.95 percent on her weekly earnings, and the EI rate is 1.73 percent on her weekly earnings. What is Emilie's take-home pay for a week in which she works 50 hours? *(pp. 564–566)*

   a. $426.34   c. $428.42
   b. $460.97   d. $407.10

7. Which of the following represents a cost to the employer? *(p. 576)*

   a. Withheld income tax
   b. Canada Pension Plan
   c. Employment Insurance
   d. Both b and c

8. The main reason for using a separate payroll bank account is to *(p. 576)*

   a. Safeguard cash by preventing the writing of payroll cheques to fictitious employees
   b. Safeguard cash by limiting paycheques to amounts based on time cards
   c. Increase efficiency by isolating payroll disbursements for analysis and control
   d. Do all of the above

9. The best step to ensure good internal controls in the payroll area is *(p. 576)*

   a. Using a payroll bank account
   b. Separating payroll duties
   c. Using a payroll register
   d. Using time cards

10. Which of the following items is reported as a current liability on the balance sheet? *(p. 561)*

   a. Short-term notes payable
   b. Estimated warranties
   c. Payroll withholdings
   d. All of the above

Answers to Self-Study Questions

1. c $10,000 × 0.09 × $^6/_{12}$ = $375   2. b   3. c   4. c $900,000 × 0.01 = $9,000   5. b

6. d Overtime pay: $400 ÷ 40 = $10; $10 × 1.5 = $15 per hour; $15 per hour × 10 hours = $150

Gross pay = $400 + $150 = $550

Deductions = ($550 × 0.105) + ($550 × 0.088) + ($550 × 0.0495) + ($550 × 0.0173) =

$57.75 + $48.40 + $27.23 + $9.52 = $142.90

Take-home pay = $550.00 − $142.90 = $407.10

7. d   8. c   9. b   10. d

ACCOUNTING VOCABULARY

Accrued expense *(p. 556)*
Accrued liability *(p. 556)*
Canada (or Quebec) Pension Plan *(p. 564)*
Current portion of long-term debt *(p. 555)*
Employee compensation *(p. 556)*
Employment Insurance (EI) *(p. 565)*
Gross pay *(p. 563)*

Line of credit *(p. 552)*
Net pay *(p. 563)*
Payroll *(p. 556)*
Short-term note payable *(p. 551)*
Withheld income tax *(p. 564)*
Workers' Compensation *(p. 566)*

SIMILAR ACCOUNTING TERMS

Current portion of long-term debt	Current maturity
Unearned revenues	Deferred revenues; Revenues collected in advance; Customer prepayments
Payroll register	Payroll journal; Payroll record

Assignment Material

QUESTIONS

1. What distinguishes a current liability from a long-term liability? What distinguishes a contingent liability from an actual liability?

2. A company purchases a machine by signing a $50,000, 4-percent, one-year note payable on June 30. Interest is to be paid at maturity. What two current liabilities related to this purchase does the company report on its December 31 balance sheet? What is the amount of each current liability?

3. Explain how GST that is paid by consumers is a liability of the store that sold the merchandise. To whom is GST paid?

4. What is meant by the term *current portion of long-term debt*, and how is this item reported in the financial statements?

5. Why is an accrued expense a liability?

6. Describe the similarities and differences between an account payable and a short-term note payable.

7. At the beginning of the school term, what type of account is the tuition that your college or university collects from students? What type of account is the tuition at the end of the school term?

8. Why is a customer deposit a liability? Give an example.

9. Murray Company warrants its products against defects for two years from date of sale. During the current year, the company made sales of $1,000,000. Management estimated warranty costs on those sales would total $30,000 over the two-year warranty period. Ultimately, the company paid $35,000 cash on warranties. What is the company's warranty expense for the year? What accounting principle or objective governs this answer?

10. Identify one contingent liability of a definite amount and one contingent liability of an indefinite amount.

11. What are the two basic categories of current liabilities? Give an example of each.

12. Why is payroll expense relatively more important to a service business such as a public accounting firm than it is to a merchandising company such as Zellers?

13. Two people are studying Beauregarde Company's manufacturing process. One person is Beauregarde Company's factory supervisor, and the other person is an outside consultant who is an expert in the industry. Which person's salary is the payroll expense of Beauregarde Company? Identify the expense account that Beauregarde Company would debit to record the pay of each person.

14. What are two elements of an employer's payroll expense in addition to salaries, wages, commissions, and overtime pay?

15. What determines the amount of income tax that is withheld from employee paycheques?

16. What is the Canada (or Quebec) Pension Plan? Who pays contributions toward it? What are the funds used for?

17. Identify three required deductions and two optional deductions from employee paycheques.

18. Identify the employee benefit expenses an employer pays.

19. Who pays EI premiums? What are these funds used for?

20. Briefly describe a basic payroll accounting system's components and their functions.

21. How much EI has been withheld from the pay of an employee who has earned $52,288 during the current year? What is the employer's EI expense for this employee?

22. Briefly describe the two principal types of internal controls over payroll.

23. Why do some companies use a special payroll bank account?

24. Identify three internal controls designed to safeguard payroll cash.

STARTERS

MyAccountingLab All questions in this section appear in MyAccountingLab.

Accounting for a note payable

(b) Credit Cash for $35,200

Starter 11–1 On June 30, 2009, Langley Corp. purchased $32,000 of inventory on a one-year, 10-percent note payable. Journalize the company's (a) accrual of interest expense on December 31, 2009, and (b) payment of the note plus interest on June 30, 2010.

Reporting a short-term note payable and the related interest

Interest Expense $1,600

Starter 11–2 Refer to the data in Starter 11–1. Show what Langley Corp. reports for the note payable and related interest payable on its balance sheet at December 31, 2009, and on its income statement for the year ended on that date.

Accounting for warranty expense and warranty payable

2. Estimated Warranty Payable bal. $4,000

Starter 11–3 Arctic Corporation guarantees its snowmobiles for three years. Company experience indicates that warranty costs will be 4 percent of sales.

Assume that an Arctic dealer made sales totalling $600,000 during 2009, its first year of operations. The company received cash for 30 percent of the sales and notes receivable for the remainder. Warranty payments totalled $20,000 during 2009.

1. Record the sales, warranty expense, and warranty payments for Arctic Corporation.
2. Post to the Estimated Warranty Payable T-account. At the end of 2009, what is the estimated warranty payable balance for Arctic Corporation?

Starter 11–4 Refer to the data given in Starter 11–3.

What amount of warranty expense will Arctic Corporation report during 2009? Does the warranty expense for the year equal the year's cash payments for warranties? Which accounting principle or objective addresses this situation?

Applying GAAP, reporting warranties in the financial statements

Starter 11–5 Harley-Davidson, Inc., the motorcycle manufacturer, used to include the following note (adapted) in its annual report:

Interpreting an actual company's contingent liabilities

Notes to Consolidated Financial Statements

7 (in Part): Commitments and Contingencies (Adapted)

The Company self-insures its product liability losses in the United States up to $3 million.

Catastrophic coverage is maintained for individual claims in excess of $3 million up to $25 million.

---

1. Why are these *contingent* (versus real) liabilities?
2. How can a contingent liability become a real liability for Harley-Davidson? What are the limits to the company's product liabilities in the United States?

Starter 11–6 begins a sequence of exercises that ends with Starter 11–8.

Starter 11–6 Fred Lind is paid $640 for a 40-hour work week and time-and-a-half for hours worked above 40.

Computing an employee's total pay

2. Net pay $733.22

1. Compute Lind's gross pay for working 50 hours during the first week of February.
2. Lind is single, and his income tax withholding is 10 percent of total pay. His only payroll deductions are taxes withheld, CPP of 4.95 percent and EI of 1.73 percent. Compute Lind's net pay for the week.

Starter 11–7 Return to the Fred Lind payroll situation in Starter 11–6. Lind's employer, Jones Golf Corp., pays all the standard payroll expenses plus benefits for employee pensions (5 percent of gross pay), BC health insurance ($60 per employee per month), and disability insurance ($8 per employee per month).

Compute Jones Golf Corp.'s total expense of employing Fred Lind for the 50 hours that he worked during the first week of February. Carry amounts to the nearest cent.

Computing the payroll expense of an employer

Total expense $1,005.87

Starter 11–8 After solving Starters 11–6 and 11–7, journalize for Jones Golf Corp. the following expenses related to the employment of Fred Lind:

a. Salary expense
b. Benefits
c. Employer payroll expenses

Round all amounts to the nearest cent.

Making payroll entries

a. Salary Payable $733.22

Starter 11–9 Suppose you work for an accounting firm all year and earn a monthly salary of $4,000. There is no overtime pay. Your withheld deductions consume 20 percent of gross pay. In addition to payroll deductions, you elect to contribute 4 percent monthly to your pension plan. Your employer also deducts $60 monthly for your payment of the health insurance premium.

Compute your net pay for November.

Computing payroll amounts

Net pay $2,980

Starter 11–10 Refer to the payroll information in Starters 11–6 and 11–7.

1. How much was the company's total salary expense for the week for Fred Lind?
2. How much cash did Fred Lind take home for his work?
3. How much did the *employee* pay this week for
   a. Income tax?
   b. CPP and EI?
4. How much expense did the *employer* have this week for
   a. CPP and EI?
   b. Benefits?

Starter 11–11 What are some of the important elements of good internal control to safe-guard payroll disbursements?

EXERCISES

 All questions in this section appear in MyAccountingLab.

Exercise 11–1

Record the following note payable transactions of Lambda Company in the company's general journal. Explanations are not required.

2009
Jun. 1   Purchased delivery truck costing $86,000 by issuing a one-year, 4-percent note payable.
Dec. 31 Accrued interest on the note payable.
2010
Jun. 1   Paid the note payable at maturity.

Exercise 11–2

Make general journal entries to record the following transactions of Mehta Products for a two-month period. Explanations are not required.

Jun. 30 Recorded cash sales of $115,000 for the month, plus PST of 8 percent collected on behalf of the province of Ontario and GST of 5 percent. Record the two taxes in separate accounts.
Jul. 6   Sent June PST and GST to the appropriate authorities (Minister of Finance for PST and Receiver General for GST). Assume no GST input tax credits.

Exercise 11–3

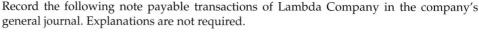
Suppose Jupitor Technologies borrowed $2,000,000 on December 31, 2006, by issuing 5-percent long-term debt that must be paid in four equal annual instalments plus interest each January 2, commencing in 2008.

Required   Insert the appropriate amounts in the following excerpts from the company's partial balance sheet to show how Jupitor Technologies should report its current and long-term liabilities for this debt.

| | **December 31,** | | | |
	2007	**2008**	**2009**	**2010**
Current liabilities:				
Current portion of long-term debt.......	$ _____	$ _____	$ _____	$ _____
Interest payable	$ _____	$ _____	$ _____	$ _____
Long-term liabilities:				
Long-term debt..	$ _____	$ _____	$ _____	$ _____

Exercise 11–4

Assume Vesper Electronics completed these selected transactions during December 2009:

1. Music For You Inc., a chain of music stores, ordered $105,000 worth of CD players. With its order, Music For You Inc. sent a cheque for $105,000. Vesper Electronics will ship the goods on January 3, 2010.

2. The December payroll of $600,000 is subject to employee withheld income tax of 16 percent, CPP expenses of 4.95 percent for the employee and 4.95 percent for the employer, EI deductions of 1.73 percent for the employee and 1.4 times the employee rate of 1.73 percent for the employer. On December 31, Vesper Electronics pays employees but accrues all tax amounts.

3. Sales of $30,000,000 are subject to estimated warranty cost of 2 percent. This was the first year the company provided a warranty, and no warranty claims have been recorded or paid.

4. On December 2, Vesper Electronics signed a $50,000 note payable that requires annual payments of $12,500 plus 4-percent interest on the unpaid balance each December 2. Vesper calculates interest on this note based on days, not months.

Required Report these items on Vesper Electronics' balance sheet at December 31, 2009.

Exercise 11–5

The management of Aero Marketing Services examines the following company accounting records at August 29, immediately before the end of the year, August 31:

Recording current liabilities

Total current assets	$ 325,000
Property, plant, and equipment	1,079,500
	$1,404,500
Total current liabilities	$ 192,500
Long-term liabilities	247,500
Owner's equity	964,500
	$1,404,500

Aero's banking agreement with Royal Bank requires the company to keep a current ratio of 2.25 or better. How much in current liabilities should Aero pay off within the next two days in order to comply with its borrowing agreements?

Exercise 11–6

The law firm Garner & Brown received from a large corporate client an annual retainer fee of $120,000 on January 2, 2010. The fee is based on anticipated monthly services of $10,000.

Accounting for unearned revenue

2. Services to be provided: $110,000

Required

1. Using the account title Retainer Fees for unearned revenue, journalize (1) Garner & Brown's receipt of retainer fees, and (2) the provision of services in the month of January 2010.

2. Post the journal entries in Requirement 1 to the unearned revenue account (Retainer Fees) T-account. What is the value of services to be provided to the client in the remaining 11 months?

Exercise 11–7

Assume *The Globe and Mail* completed the following transactions for one subscriber during 2009:

Accounting for unearned revenue

2. Unearned subscription revenue $75.00

Oct.	1	Sold a six-month subscription, collecting cash of $150 plus PST of 7 percent and GST of 5 percent.
Nov.	15	Remitted (paid) the PST to the Province of British Columbia and the GST to the Receiver General.
Dec.	31	Made the necessary adjustment at year end to record the amount of subscription revenue earned during the year.

Required

1. Using *The Globe and Mail* (assumed) account title Unearned Subscription Revenue, journalize the transactions above.

2. Post the entries to the Unearned Subscription Revenue T-account. How much does *The Globe and Mail* owe the subscriber at December 31, 2009?

Accounting for warranty expense
and the related liability

2. Estimated Warranty Payable
bal. $14,020

The accounting records of Harroy Industries included the following at January 1, 2010:

Estimated Warranty Payable

	Jan. 1, 2010 12,400

In the past, Harroy Industries' warranty expense has been 3 percent of sales. During 2010, Harroy Industries made sales of $519,000 and paid $13,950 to satisfy warranty claims.

Required

1. Record Harroy Industries' warranty expense and warranty payments during 2010. Explanations are not required.

2. What balance of Estimated Warranty Payable will Harroy Industries report on its balance sheet at December 31, 2010?

Exercise 11–9

Reporting a contingent liability

Teale Security Systems is a defendant in lawsuits brought against the monitoring service of its installed systems. Damages of $500,000 are claimed against Teale Security Systems but the company denies the charges and is vigorously defending itself. In a recent newspaper interview, the president of the company stated that he could not predict the outcome of the lawsuits. Nevertheless, he said management does not believe that any actual liabilities resulting from the lawsuits will significantly affect the company's financial position.

Required Describe what, if any, disclosure Teale Security Systems should provide of this contingent liability. Total liabilities are $2.0 million. If you believe note disclosure is required, write the note to describe the contingency.

Exercise 11–10

Accruing a contingency

Refer to the Teale Security Systems situation in the preceding exercise. Suppose that Teale Security Systems' lawyers advise that preliminary judgment of $150,000 has been rendered against the company. The company will appeal the decision.

Required Describe how to report this situation in the Teale Security Systems financial statements. Journalize any entry required under GAAP. Explanations are not required.

Exercise 11–11

Computing net pay

Net pay $3,901.24

Sylvia Chan is a clerk in the shoe department of The Bay in Winnipeg. She earns a base monthly salary of $1,875 plus a 7-percent commission on her sales. Through payroll deductions, Chan donates $15 per month to a charitable organization and pays dental insurance premiums of $39.15. Compute Chan's gross pay and net pay for December, assuming her sales for the month are $50,000. The income tax rate on her earnings is 20 percent, the CPP contribution is 4.95 percent (account for the $3,500 basic annual exemption), and the EI premium rate is 1.73 percent. Chan has not yet reached the CPP or EI maximum earning levels.

Exercise 11–12

 **Excel Spreadsheet
Template**

Computing and recording gross
pay and net pay

1. Net pay $328.02

Brad Jackson works for a Bob's Burgers takeout for straight-time earnings of $10.50 per hour, with time and a half for hours in excess of 35 per week. Jackson's payroll deductions include income tax of 20 percent, CPP of 4.95 percent on earnings (account for the $3,500 basic annual exemption), and EI of 1.73 percent on earnings. In addition, he contributes $2.50 per week to the United Way. Assume Jackson worked 40 hours during the week. He has not yet reached the CPP or EI maximum earning levels.

Required

1. Compute Jackson's gross pay and net pay for the week.

2. Make a general journal entry to record the restaurant's wage expense for Jackson's work, including his payroll deductions and the employer payroll costs. Round all amounts to the nearest cent. An explanation is not required.

Exercise 11–13

Greenlife Manufacturing incurred salary expense of $95,000 for September. The company's payroll expense includes CPP of 4.95 percent and EI of 1.4 times the employee payment, which is 1.73 percent of earnings. Also, the company provides the following fringe benefits for employees: dental insurance (cost to the company of $5,723.09), life insurance (cost to the company of $461.09), and pension benefits through a private plan (cost to the company of $1,945.60). Record Greenlife Manufacturing's payroll expenses for CPP, EI, and employee fringe benefits. Ignore the CPP basic exemption.

Recording a payroll

Total of CPP and EI Expense
$7,003.40

Exercise 11–14

Study the Employee Earnings Record for J.C. Jenkins in Exhibit 11–8, page 574. In addition to the amounts shown in the exhibit, the employer also paid all employee benefits plus (a) an amount equal to 5 percent of gross pay into Jenkins' pension retirement account, and (b) dental insurance for Jenkins at a cost of $35 per month. Compute the employer's total payroll expense for employee J.C. Jenkins during 2009. Carry all amounts to the nearest cent.

Using a payroll system to compute total payroll expense

Total payroll expense
$43,745.95

SERIAL EXERCISE

This exercise continues the Haupt Consulting situation from Exercise 10–16 of Chapter 10. If you did not complete Exercise 10–16, you can still complete Exercise 11–15 as it is presented.

Exercise 11–15

In Chapter 3, on page 148, we learned that Haupt Consulting had hired a part-time secretary to be paid $1,500 salary on the 20th day of each month. The following additional payroll information is available for the January 20, 2011, pay date:

Recording a payroll

1. Net pay $1,175.99

Federal income tax to be withheld..	$138.55
Provincial income tax to be withheld...	99.70

The employee is eligible for CPP and EI deductions. Use the 2009 rates given in this chapter and account for the CPP basic exemption in any calculations.

Required

1. Compute the secretary's gross pay and net pay for the week.

2. Make a general journal entry to record Haupt Consulting's salary expense for the secretary, including her payroll deductions and the employer payroll costs. Round all amounts to the nearest cent.

CHALLENGE EXERCISES

Exercise 11–16

Suppose the balance sheets of a corporation for two years reported these figures:

Accounting for and reporting current liabilities

1. Current ratios:
2010 1.24
2009 0.85

	Billions	
	2010	**2009**
Total current assets..	$ 14.50	$12.92
Property, plant, and equipment, net	44.74	40.96
	$59.24	$53.88
Total current liabilities	$11.66	$15.12
Long-term liabilities	29.92	23.32
Shareholders' equity..	17.66	15.44
	$59.24	$53.88

The notes to the 2010 financial statements report that during 2010, because of some refinancing arrangements, the corporation was able to reclassify $7.0 billion from current liabilities to long-term liabilities.

Required

1. Compute the corporation's current ratio at the end of each year. Describe the trend that you observe.

2. Suppose that the corporation had not refinanced and not been able to reclassify the $7.0 billion of current liabilities as long-term during 2010. Recompute the current ratio for 2010 to include the $7.0 billion. Why do you think the corporation decided to reclassify the liabilities as long-term?

Exercise 11–17

Analyzing current
liability accounts

1. Payment of notes
payable $55 mil.

Gamma Company recently reported notes payable and accrued payrolls and benefits as follows:

	December 31,	
	2010	2009
	(in millions of dollars)	
Current liabilities (partial):		
Notes payable	$ 26	$ 78
Accrued payrolls and benefits	270	298

Assume that during 2010, Gamma Company borrowed $3.0 million on notes payable. Also assume that Gamma paid $250 million for employee compensation and benefits during 2010.

Required

1. Compute Gamma Company's payment of notes payable during 2010.
2. Compute Gamma Company's employee compensation expense for 2010.

BEYOND THE NUMBERS

Beyond the Numbers 11–1

Suppose a large manufacturing company is the defendant in numerous lawsuits claiming unfair trade practices. The company has strong incentives not to disclose these contingent liabilities. However, GAAP require companies to report their contingent liabilities.

Required

1. Why would a company prefer not to disclose its contingent liabilities?
2. Describe how a bank could be harmed if a company seeking a loan did not disclose its contingent liabilities.
3. What is the ethical tightrope that companies must walk when they report their contingent liabilities?

Beyond the Numbers 11–2

The following questions are not related.

a. A warranty is like a contingent liability in that the amount to be paid is not known at year end. Why are warranties payable shown as a current liability, whereas contingent liabilities are reported in the notes to the financial statements?

b. A friend comments that he thought that liabilities represented amounts owed by a company. He asks why unearned revenues are shown as a current liability. How would you respond?

c. Auditors have procedures for determining whether they have discovered all of a company's contingent liabilities. These procedures differ from the procedures used for determining that accounts payable are stated correctly. How would an auditor identify a client's contingent liabilities?

ETHICAL ISSUE

Many companies, such as Campeau Corporation, borrowed heavily during the 1970s and 1980s to exploit the advantage of financing operations with debt. At first, the companies were able to earn operating income much higher than their interest expense and were therefore quite profitable. However, when the business cycle turned down, their debt burdens pushed the companies to the brink of bankruptcy. Operating income was less than interest expense.

Required   Is it unethical for managers to commit a company to a high level of debt? Or is it just risky? Who could be hurt by a company's taking on too much debt? Discuss.

PROBLEMS (GROUP A)

 All questions in this section appear in MyAccountingLab.

Problem 11–1A

The following selected transactions of Truestar Communications, a Saskatchewan company, occurred during 2009 and 2010. The company's year end is December 31.

Journalizing liability-related transactions

① ②

2009
Jan.	3	Purchased a machine at a cost of $350,000 plus 5-percent GST, signing a 3-percent, six-month note payable for that amount.
	29	Recorded the month's sales of $1,570,000 (excludes PST and GST), 80 percent on credit and 20 percent for cash. Sales amounts are subject to 7-percent PST plus 5-percent GST.
Feb.	5	Paid January's PST and GST to the appropriate authorities.
	28	Borrowed $3,000,000 on a 5-percent note payable that calls for annual instalment payments of $300,000 principal plus interest.
Jul.	3	Paid the six-month, 3-percent note at maturity.
Nov.	30	Purchased inventory for $150,000 plus GST, signing a six-month, 3-percent note payable.
Dec.	31	Accrued warranty expense, which is estimated at 1 percent of annual sales of $8,000,000.
	31	Accrued interest on all outstanding notes payable. Make a separate interest accrual entry for each note payable.

2010
Feb.	28	Paid the first instalment and interest for one year on the long-term note payable.
May	31	Paid off the 3-percent note plus interest at maturity.

Required   Record the transactions in the company's general journal. Use days in any interest calculations, not months. Round all amounts to the nearest whole dollar. Explanations are not required.

Problem 11–2A

Morgan Motors is the Morgan dealer located in Victoria, British Columbia, and the only dealer in Western Canada. The dealership repairs and restores Morgan vintage cars. Hal Irwin, the general manager, is considering changing insurance companies because of a disagreement with Len Legrew, agent for the Dominion of Canada Insurance Company. Dominion is doubling Morgan Motors' liability insurance cost for the next year. In discussing insurance coverage with you, a trusted business associate, Legrew brings up the subject of contingent liabilities.

Identifying contingent liabilities

②

Required   Write a memorandum to inform Morgan Motors of specific contingent liabilities arising from the business. In your discussion, define a contingent liability.

Problem 11–3A

Computing and recording
payroll amounts

(3) (4)

b. Total employee earnings
$51,084

The partial monthly records of Westwood Golf Shop show the following figures:

Employee Earnings

Regular employee earnings...	$39,894	
Overtime pay	a	
Total employee earnings	b	

Deductions and Net Pay

Withheld income tax	12,758
Canada Pension Plan..............	c

Employment Insurance..........	$	956
Medical insurance...................		1,082
Total deductions......................		15,894
Net pay		35,190

Accounts Debited

Salaries Expense......................	d
Wages Expense	13,876
Sales Commission Expense ...	3,362

Required

1. Determine missing amounts a, b, c, and d.

2. Prepare the general journal entry to record Westwood Golf Shop's payroll for the month. Credit Payroll Payable for net pay. No explanation is required.

Problem 11–4A

**Excel Spreadsheet
Template**

Computing and recording
payroll amounts

(3) (4)

1. Net pay $61,751.61

Assume that Raji Patel is a vice-president in Maple Capital's leasing operations. During 2009, she worked for the company all year at a $7,500 monthly salary. She also earned a year-end bonus equal to 10 percent of her salary.

Patel's federal income tax withheld during 2009 was $2,398 per month. Also, there was a one-time federal withholding tax of $4,512 on her bonus cheque. She paid $356.85 per month into the CPP until she had paid the maximum of $2,118.60. In addition, Patel paid $157.50 per month EI through her employer until the maximum of $731.79 had been reached. She had authorized Maple Capital to make the following payroll deductions: life insurance of $55 per month and United Way of $37.50 per month.

Maple Capital incurred CPP expense equal to the amount deducted from Patel's pay and EI equal to 1.4 times the amount Patel paid. In addition, Maple Capital paid dental and drug insurance of $38 per month and pension benefits of 7 percent of her base salary.

Required

1. Compute Patel's gross pay, payroll deductions, and net pay for the full year 2009. Round all amounts to the nearest cent.

2. Compute Maple Capital's total 2009 payroll expense for Patel.

3. Prepare Maple Capital's general journal entries (explanations are not required) to record its expense for

   a. Patel's total earnings for the year, her payroll deductions, and her net pay. Debit Salary Expense and Bonus Expense as appropriate for salary and employee benefit expense. Credit liability accounts for the payroll deductions and Cash for net pay.

   b. Employer payroll expenses for Patel. Credit the appropriate liability accounts.

   c. Fringe benefits provided to Patel. Credit Health Insurance Payable and Company Pension Payable.

Problem 11–5A

Journalizing, posting, and
reporting liabilities

(1) (2) (3) (4) (5)

3. Total liabilities $558,708

The general ledger of Shell Storage Units at June 30, 2010, the end of the company's fiscal year, includes the following account balances before adjusting entries.

Notes Payable, Short-Term	$ 20,000	Employee Insurance	
Accounts Payable...................	235,620	Benefits Payable.......................	_____
Current Portion of		Estimated Vacation	
Long-Term Debt Payable	_____	Pay Liability	$ 12,360
Interest Payable	_____	Sales Tax and GST Payable.....	5,972
Salaries Payable......................	_____	Unearned Rent Revenue	15,000
Employee Income Tax		Long-Term Debt Payable.........	250,000
Payable..................................	_____		
Employer Payroll Costs			
Payable.................................	_____		

The additional data needed to develop the adjusting entries at June 30 are as follows:

a. The $20,000 short-term note payable was issued on February 28. It matures six months from date of issuance and bears interest at 4.5 percent.

b. The long-term debt is payable in annual instalments of $50,000 with the next instalment due on August 31. On that date, Shell Storage Units will also pay one year's interest at 5 percent. Interest was last paid on August 31 of the preceding year.

c. Gross salaries for the last payroll of the fiscal year were $6,328. Of this amount, employee payroll withholdings payable were $1,365, and salary payable was $4,963.

d. Employer Payroll Costs Payable was $820, and Shell Storage's liability for employee health insurance was $991.

e. Shell Storage estimates that vacation pay expense is 4 percent of gross salaries of $147,500 after adjustment for the last payroll of the fiscal year.

f. On March 1, the company collected one year's rent of $15,000 in advance.

g. At June 30, Shell Storage is the defendant in a $137,500 lawsuit, which the company expects to win. However, the outcome is uncertain.

Required

1. Open T-accounts for the listed accounts, inserting their unadjusted June 30, 2010, balances.

2. Post the June 30, 2010, adjusting entries to the T-accounts opened. Round all amounts to the nearest whole dollar.

3. Prepare the liability section of Shell Storage Units' balance sheet at June 30, 2010.

Problem 11–6A

The payroll records of Scotia Video Productions Inc. provide the following information for the weekly pay period ended September 21.

Excel Spreadsheet Template

Using payroll register, recording a payroll
③ ④ ⑤
1. Total net pay $2,155.54

Employee	Hours Worked	Hourly Earnings Rate	Income Tax	Canada Pension Plan	Employ-ment Insurance	United Way	Year-to-Date Earnings at End of Previous Week
Molly Dodge	43	$30	$474.10	$ 0	$ 0	$25	$47,200
Tally Lafarge	40	13	67.60	22.41	9.00	2	19,760
George White	49	10	63.70	23.15	9.26	2	20,250
Luigi Pogge	42	20	352.00	39.24	0	5	43,050

Tally Lafarge and George White work in the office, and Molly Dodge and Luigi Pogge work in sales. All employees are paid time and a half for hours worked in excess of 40 hours per week. Show computations.

Required

1. Enter the appropriate information in a payroll register similar to Exhibit 11–6.

2. Record the payroll information in the general journal, crediting net pay to Cash.

3. The employer's payroll costs include matching each employee's CPP contribution (employee rate 4.95 percent; maximum $2,118.60) and paying 1.4 times the employee's EI premium (employee rate 1.73 percent; maximum $731.79). Record the employer's payroll costs in the general journal.

4. Why was there no deduction of CPP or EI for Dodge and no deduction of EI for Pogge?

Problem 11–7A

Following are five pertinent facts about events during the current year at Island Fisheries, a Prince Edward Island fisheries supply company:

Reporting current liabilities
⑤

a. Sales of $911,000 were covered by Island Fisheries' product warranty. At January 1, the estimated warranty payable was $14,600. During the year Island recorded warranty expense of 1 percent of sales and paid warranty claims of $15,600.

b. On August 31, Island Fisheries signed a six-month, 6-percent note payable to purchase supplies costing $45,000. The note requires payment of principal and interest at maturity.

c. On November 30, Island Fisheries received rent of $21,000 in advance from a sub-tenant in its building. This rent will be earned evenly over three months.

d. December sales totalled $80,000 and Island Fisheries collected GST of 5 percent plus PST of 10 percent on these sales. These taxes will be sent to the appropriate authorities early in January.*

e. Island Fisheries owes $150,000 on a long-term note payable. At December 31, $40,000 of this principal plus 5-percent accrued interest since September 30 are payable within one year.

*Note: Prince Edward Island bases PST on price including GST.

Required For each item, indicate the account and the related amount to be reported as a *current* liability on Island Fisheries' December 31 (year-end) balance sheet. Round all amounts to the nearest whole dollar.

Problem 11–8A

Accounting for current liabilities, making basic payroll entries, reporting current liabilities

2. Total current liabilities
$1,390,840.80

Seaward Marine of St. John's, Newfoundland operates a marine supply company with the following information available:

- 13 percent HST is applicable to all purchases and sales (assumed for this Problem).
- Payroll costs—the employer's shares of CPP and EI are 1.0 times and 1.4 times the employees' share, respectively. The company pays Workers' Compensation of 3 percent and estimates vacation pay at 4 percent of all earnings.

The company prepares quarterly financial statements and had the following transactions for April, May, and June of 2009:

Apr. 30   Recorded the month's purchases of inventory, $387,500 (not including HST). All purchases are on credit. The company uses the periodic inventory system.

30   Recorded the month's sales of $707,500 (not including HST), of which 80 percent were on credit.

30   Recorded and paid the payroll for the month. Gross earnings were $147,500, with deductions of
- Employee income taxes equal to 22 percent of gross earnings
- CPP deductions equal to 4.95 percent* of gross earnings (employees' share)
- EI deductions equal to 1.73 percent of gross earnings (employees' share)
- Union dues deduction equal to $2,625.

May 2   Borrowed $125,000 from the bank by signing a 6-percent, 30-day note payable with the principal and interest payable on the maturity date.

7   Paid the HST for the month of April.

15   Sent cheques for all payroll deductions and contributions, including the employer's share, to the appropriate authorities.

31   Recorded the month's purchases of inventory, $300,000 (not including HST). All purchases are on credit.

31   Recorded the month's sales of $725,000 (not including HST), of which 70 percent were on credit.

31   Recorded and paid the payroll for the month. Gross earnings were $157,500, with deductions of
- Employee income taxes equal to 22 percent of gross earnings
- CPP deductions equal to 4.95 percent* of gross earnings (employees' share)
- EI deductions equal to 1.73 percent of gross earnings (employees' share)
- Union dues deduction equal to $2,710.

Jun. 1   Paid the note payable from May 2.

7   Paid the HST for the month of May.

15   Sent cheques for all payroll deductions and contributions, including the employer's share, to the appropriate authorities.

30   Recorded the month's purchases of $425,000 (not including HST). All purchases are on credit.

30   Recorded the month's sales of $750,000 (not including HST), of which 85 percent were on credit.

Jun. 30   Recorded and paid the payroll for the month. Gross earnings were
           $177,500, with deductions of
           • Employee income taxes equal to 22 percent of gross earnings
           • CPP deductions equal to 4.95 percent* of gross earnings (employees'
             share)
           • EI deductions equal to 1.73 percent of gross earnings (employees' share)
           • Union dues deduction equal to $2,848.50.

           *For purposes of this calculation, ignore the basic exemption of $3,500.

Required

1. Journalize all the transactions and any adjustments that would be required on
   June 30, 2009 (the end of the first quarter). Use days, not months, to calculate interest
   amounts.
2. Show the current liability section of the balance sheet as of June 30, 2009. Assume there
   are nil balances in all accounts at April 1, 2009.

Problem 11–9A

Eastern Explorations produces and sells customized mining equipment in New
Brunswick. The company offers a 60-day, all parts and labour—and an extra 90-day,
parts-only—warranty on all of its products. The company had the following transactions
in 2010:

Accounting for current liabilities,
accounting for contingent
liabilities, reporting current
liabilities

2. Total current liabilities
$38,040

Jan. 31   Sales for the month totalled $80,000 (not including HST), of which 90 per-
           cent were on credit. The company collects 13-percent HST on all sales and
           estimates its warranty costs at 4 percent of sales.
      31   Based on last year's property tax assessment, estimated that the property
           taxes for the year would be $80,000 (4 percent of last year's $2,000,000 as-
           sessed value). Recorded the estimated property taxes for the month;
           credit Estimated Property Taxes Payable.
Feb. 4   Completed repair work for a customer. The parts ($500) and labour ($850)
           were all covered under the warranty.
      7   Sent a cheque for the appropriate HST for the month of January (the com-
           pany had paid $3,700 of HST on purchases in January).
      28   Recorded the estimated property taxes for the month of February.
      28   Sales for the month totalled $92,000 (not including HST), of which 85 per-
           cent were on credit. The company estimates its warranty costs at 4 percent
           of sales.
Mar. 7   Sent a cheque for the appropriate HST for the month of February (the
           company had paid $4,750 of HST on purchases in February).
      8   Eastern Explorations received notice that it was being sued by a customer
           for an accident resulting from the failure of its product. The company's
           lawyer was reluctant to estimate the likely outcome of the lawsuit, but
           another customer indicated that a similar case had resulted in a $250,000
           settlement.
      15   Completed repair work for a customer. The parts ($2,500) and labour
           ($1,200) were all covered under the warranty.
      21   Completed repair work for a customer. The parts ($750) were covered by
           the warranty, but the labour ($1,100) was not. Payment from the customer
           is due for the labour in 30 days.
      31   Sales for the month totalled $88,000 (not including HST), of which 90 per-
           cent was on credit. The company estimates its warranty costs at 4 percent
           of sales.
      31   Received the property tax assessment for 2010. It showed the assessed
           value of the property to be $2,200,000 and a tax rate of 4 percent of the as-
           sessed value. The company made the appropriate adjustment and used
           the Property Taxes Payable account.

Required

1. Journalize the above transactions.
2. Show the appropriate financial statement presentation for all liabilities at March 31, 2010.

Problem 11–1B

Journalizing liability-related transactions

The following transactions of Prairie Technology of Edmonton, Alberta, occurred during 2009 and 2010. The company's year end is December 31.

2009

Mar. 3   Purchased a machine for $66,000, signing a six-month, 4.5-percent note payable.

31   Recorded the month's sales of $134,500, one-quarter for cash, and three-quarters on credit. All sales amounts are subject to 5-percent GST, to be calculated on the sales of $134,500.

Apr. 7   Paid March's GST to the Receiver General.

May 31   Borrowed $75,000 with a 5-percent note payable that calls for annual instalment payments of $15,000 principal plus interest.

Sept. 3   Paid the six-month, 4.5-percent note at maturity.

30   Purchased inventory at a cost of $25,000, signing a 5-percent, six-month note payable for that amount.

Dec. 31   Accrued warranty expense, which is estimated at 1.5 percent of annual sales of $1,445,000.

31   Accrued interest on all outstanding notes payable. Make a separate interest accrual entry for each note payable.

2010

Mar. 31   Paid off the 5-percent inventory note, plus interest, at maturity.

May 31   Paid the first instalment and interest for one year on the long-term note payable.

Required   Record the transactions in the company's general journal. Explanations are not required. Use days in any interest calculations, not months. Round all amounts to the nearest whole dollar.

Problem 11–2B

Identifying contingent liabilities

Deborah Landers provides skating lessons for children ages 8 through 15. Most students are beginners. Landers rents ice time from the local arena. Because this is a new business venture, Landers wants to save money and does not want to purchase insurance. She seeks your advice about her business exposure to liabilities.

Required   Write a memorandum to inform Landers of specific contingent liabilities that could arise from the business. It will be necessary to define a contingent liability because she is a professional skater, not a businessperson. Propose a way for Landers to limit her exposure to these possible liabilities.

Problem 11–3B

Computing and reporting payroll amounts

The partial monthly records of Perfecto Products show the following figures:

Employee Earnings		Dental and	
Regular earnings	a	drug insurance.........................	$ 1,556
Overtime pay	$13,994	Total deductions	c
Total employee earnings........	b	Net pay	140,810

Deductions and Net Pay		**Accounts Debited**	
Withheld income tax	31,704	Salaries Expense	66,468
Canada Pension Plan..............	9,200	Wages Expense	d
Employment Insurance..........	3,492	Sales Commission Expense ...	59,356

Required

1. Determine missing amounts a, b, c, and d.

2. Prepare the general journal entry to record Perfecto Products' payroll for the month. Credit Payroll Payable for net pay. No explanation is required.

Problem 11–4B

Assume that Marcy Jones is a marketing director in Metro Mobility's head office in Toronto. During 2009, she worked for the company all year at a $6,500 monthly salary. She also earned a year-end bonus equal to 20 percent of her salary.

Jones' monthly income tax withholding for 2009 was $1,762.28. Also, she paid a one-time withholding tax of $4,095.11 on her bonus cheque. She paid $307.31 per month toward the CPP until the maximum ($2,118.60) had been withheld. In addition, Jones' employer deducted $136.50 per month for EI until the maximum ($731.79) had been withheld. Jones authorized the following deductions: 1.5 percent per month of her monthly pay to Metro's charitable donation fund and $68 per month for life insurance.

Metro Mobility incurred CPP expense equal to the amount deducted from Jones' pay. EI cost the company 1.4 times the amount deducted from Jones' pay. In addition, the company provided Jones with the following fringe benefits: dental and drug insurance at a cost of $65 per month, and pension benefits to be paid to Jones upon retirement. The pension contribution is based on her income and was $5,350 in 2009.

Excel Spreadsheet Template

Computing and recording payroll amounts

Required

1. Compute Jones' gross pay, payroll deductions, and net pay for the full year 2009. Round all amounts to the nearest cent.

2. Compute Metro Mobility's total 2009 payroll cost for Jones.

3. Prepare Metro Mobility's summary general journal entries (explanations are not required) to record its expense for

   a. Jones' total earnings for the year, her payroll deductions, and her net pay. Debit Salary Expense and Executive Bonus Compensation as appropriate for sales and employee benefit expense. Credit liability accounts for the payroll deductions and Cash for net pay.

   b. Employer payroll expenses for Jones. Credit the appropriate liability accounts.

   c. Fringe benefits provided to Jones. Credit Health Insurance Payable and Company Pension Payable.

Problem 11–5B

Grafton Hardware's general ledger at June 30, 2010, the end of the company's fiscal year, includes the following account balances before adjusting entries. Parentheses indicate a debit balance.

Journalizing, posting, and reporting liabilities

Note Payable, Short-Term	$ 74,000	Employee Insurance	
Accounts Payable	335,680	Benefits Payable	$_____
Current Portion of		Estimated Vacation Pay	
Long-Term Debt Payable	_____	Liability	7,896
Interest Payable	_____	GST Payable	4,900
Salaries Payable	_____	Property Tax Payable	7,284
Employee Withholdings Payable	_____	Unearned Service Revenue	18,000
Employer Payroll Costs Payable	_____	Long-Term Debt Payable	300,000

The additional data needed to develop the adjusting entries at June 30 are as follows:

a. The $74,000 short-term note payable was issued on July 31, 2009; matures one year from date of issuance; and bears interest at 5 percent.

b. The long-term debt is payable in annual instalments of $60,000, with the next instalment due February 28, 2011. On that date, Grafton Hardware will also pay one year's interest at 5.5 percent. Interest was last paid on February 28, 2010.

c. Gross salaries for the last payroll of the fiscal year were $21,446. Of this amount, employee withholdings were $4,756, and salaries payable were $16,690.

d. Employer payroll costs were $2,788, and Grafton Hardware's liability for employee life insurance was $300.

e. Grafton Hardware estimates that vacation pay is 4 percent of gross salaries of $240,000 after adjustment for the last payroll of the fiscal year.

f. On March 1, 2010, the company collected one year's service contract revenue of $18,000 in advance.

g. At June 30, 2010, Grafton Hardware is the defendant in a $50,000 lawsuit, which the store expects to win. However, the outcome is uncertain.

Required

1. Open T-accounts for the listed accounts, inserting their unadjusted June 30, 2010, balances.

2. Post the June 30, 2010, adjusting entries to the accounts opened. Round all amounts to the nearest whole dollar.

3. Prepare the liability section of Grafton Hardware's balance sheet at June 30, 2010. Show total current liabilities and total liabilities.

4. Is there a contingent liability? If yes, write the note to describe it and indicate where it should appear.

Problem 11–6B

Excel Spreadsheet Template

Using a payroll register, recording a payroll

  ③ ④ ⑤

Assume that payroll records of a branch of Indigo Books provided the following information for the weekly pay period ended December 18, 2009:

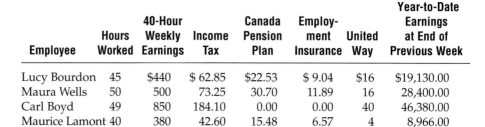

Employee	Hours Worked	40-Hour Weekly Earnings	Income Tax	Canada Pension Plan	Employment Insurance	United Way	Year-to-Date Earnings at End of Previous Week
Lucy Bourdon	45	$440	$ 62.85	$22.53	$ 9.04	$16	$19,130.00
Maura Wells	50	500	73.25	30.70	11.89	16	28,400.00
Carl Boyd	49	850	184.10	0.00	0.00	40	46,380.00
Maurice Lamont	40	380	42.60	15.48	6.57	4	8,966.00

Lucy Bourdon and Maurice Lamont work in the office, and Maura Wells and Carl Boyd are sales staff. All employees are paid time and a half for hours worked in excess of 40 hours per week. Show computations. Explanations are not required for journal entries.

Required

1. Enter the appropriate information in a payroll register similar to Exhibit 11–6.

2. Record the payroll information in the general journal, crediting net pay to Cash.

3. The employer's payroll costs are calculated by matching the employee's CPP contribution (employee rate 4.95 percent; maximum $2,118.60) and paying 1.4 times the employee's EI premium (employee rate 1.73 percent; maximum $731.79). Record the employer's payroll costs in the general journal.

4. Why is no CPP or EI deducted for Boyd?

Problem 11–7B

Reporting current liabilities

 ⑤

Following are six pertinent facts about events during the year at Manitoba Manufacturing, a farm-equipment company:

a. On June 30, Manitoba Manufacturing signed a nine-month, 5-percent note payable to purchase a machine costing $120,000. The note requires payment of principal and interest at maturity.

b. Sales of $2,103,000 were covered by Manitoba Manufacturing's product warranty. At January 1, estimated warranty payable was $29,300. During the year, Manitoba Manufacturing recorded warranty expense of 3 percent of sales and paid warranty claims of $55,700.

c. On November 15, Manitoba Manufacturing received $10,000 on deposit for a tractor. The tractor will be delivered in March of next year.

d. December sales totalled $323,000 and Manitoba Manufacturing collected GST of 5 percent on these sales. This amount will be sent to the appropriate authority early in January.

e. Manitoba Manufacturing owes $200,000 on a long-term note payable. At December 31, 4-percent interest for the year plus $40,000 of this principal are payable within one year.

Required

For each item, indicate the account and the related amount to be reported as a *current* liability on Manitoba Manufacturing's December 31 (year-end) balance sheet. Round all amounts to the nearest whole dollar.

Problem 11–8B

Mogul Mountain, an Alberta company, is a ski resort with the following information available:

Accounting for current liabilities, making basic payroll entries; reporting current liabilities

- Goods and Services Tax: 5-percent GST is applicable to all purchases and sales (assumed for this Problem).

- Employer Payroll Costs: the employer's shares of CPP and EI are 1.0 times and 1.4 times the employees' shares, respectively. The company pays Workers' Compensation of 4 percent and estimates vacation pay at 4 percent of all earnings.

The company prepares quarterly financial statements and had the following transactions for the first three months of 2010:

Jan. 31   Recorded the month's purchases, $312,000 (not including GST). All purchases were on credit.

31   Recorded the month's sales of $429,000 (not including GST), of which 85 percent were on credit.

31   Recorded and paid the payroll for the month. Gross earnings were $95,000, with deductions of
- Employee income taxes equal to 17 percent of gross earnings
- CPP deductions equal to 4.95 percent* of gross earnings (employees' share)
- EI deductions equal to 1.73 percent of gross earnings (employees' share)
- Union dues deduction equal to $1,560

Feb. 3   Borrowed $50,000 from the bank by signing a 3-percent, 30-day note payable with the principal and interest payable on the maturity date.

7   Paid the GST for the month of January.

15   Sent cheques for all payroll deductions and contributions, including the employer's share, to the appropriate authorities.

28   Recorded the month's purchases, $349,000 (not including GST). All purchases were on credit.

28   Recorded the month's sales of $550,000 (not including GST), of which 75 percent were on credit.

28   Recorded and paid the payroll for the month. Gross earnings were $115,000, with deductions of
- Employee income taxes equal to 17 percent of gross earnings
- CPP deductions equal to 4.95 percent* of gross earnings (employees' share)
- EI deductions equal to 1.73 percent of gross earnings (employees' share)
- Union dues deduction equal to $1,872

Mar. 5   Paid the note payable from February 3.

7   Paid the GST for the month of February.

15   Sent cheques for all payroll deductions and contributions, including the employer's share, to the appropriate authorities.

31   Recorded the month's purchases, $365,000 (not including GST). All purchases were on credit.

31   Recorded the month's sales of $625,000 (not including GST), of which 80 percent were on credit.

31   Recorded and paid the payroll for the month. Gross earnings were $145,000, with deductions of
- Employee income taxes equal to 17 percent of gross earnings
- CPP deductions equal to 4.95 percent* of gross earnings (employees' share)
- EI deductions equal to 1.73 percent of gross earnings (employees' share)
- Union dues deduction equal to $2,100

Required

1. Journalize all the transactions, and any adjustments that would be required on March 31, 2010 (the end of the first quarter). Round all amounts to the nearest whole dollar. Use days, not months, to calculate interest amounts.

2. Show the current liability section of the balance sheet as of March 31, 2010. Assume there are nil balances in all accounts at January 1, 2010.

---

* For purposes of this calculation, ignore the basic exemption of $3,500.

Problem 11–9B

Accounting for current liabilities, accounting for contingent liabilities, reporting current liabilities

Standard Technologies produces and sells customized network systems in Nova Scotia. The company offers a 60-day, all software and labour—and an extra 90-day, parts-only—warranty on all of its products. The company had the following transactions in 2010:

Jan. 31 Sales for the month totalled $350,000 (not including HST), of which 95 percent were on credit. The company collects 13-percent HST on all sales and estimates its warranty costs at 2 percent of sales.

31 Based on last year's property tax assessment, estimated that the property taxes for the year would be $57,000 (3 percent of last year's $1,900,000 assessed value). Recorded the estimated property taxes for the month; credit Estimated Property Taxes Payable.

Feb. 4 Completed repair work for a customer. The software ($3,000) and labour ($3,250) were all covered under the warranty.

7 Remitted the appropriate HST for the month of January (the company had paid $15,610 HST on purchases in January).

28 Recorded the estimated property taxes for the month of February.

28 Sales for the month totalled $325,000 (not including HST), of which 90 percent were on credit. The company estimates its warranty costs at 2 percent of sales.

Mar. 7 Remitted the appropriate HST for the month of February (the company had paid $18,648 HST on purchases in February).

8 Standard Technologies received notice that it was being sued by a customer for an error resulting from the failure of its product. The company's lawyer was reluctant to estimate the likely outcome of the lawsuit, but another customer indicated that a similar case had resulted in a $100,000 settlement.

15 Completed repair work for a customer. The software ($3,500) and labour ($2,750) were all covered under the warranty.

21 Completed repair work for a customer. The software ($1,500) was covered by the warranty, but the labour ($1,650) was not. Payment for the labour is due from the customer in 30 days.

31 Sales for the month totalled $315,000 (not including HST), of which 80 percent was on credit. The company estimates its warranty costs will increase to 4 percent of sales.

31 Received the property tax assessment for 2010. It showed the assessed value of the property to be $2,300,000 and a tax rate of 2.8 percent of the assessed value. The company made the appropriate adjustment and used the Property Taxes Payable account.

Required

1. Journalize the above transactions.
2. Show the appropriate financial statement presentation for all liabilities.

CHALLENGE PROBLEMS

Problem 11–1C

Verifying the completeness of liabilities

Public accounting firms acting as auditors of companies are very careful to ensure that all of the company's accounts payable are recorded in the proper period. In other words, they want to ensure that all payables relating to the year under review are recorded as a liability at year end.

Required Explain why you think auditors are so concerned that all payables owing at year end be properly recorded in the right accounting period.

Problem 11–2C

Accounting for estimated liabilities

There is no consensus on the proper amount for airlines to record with respect to frequent-flier expense. Two alternative scenarios are presented below:

a. The person claiming a ticket under the frequent-flier program would use a seat that otherwise would be empty.

b. The person claiming a ticket under the frequent-flier program would use a seat that otherwise would be used by a full-fare-paying passenger.

Required

1. Recommend to an airline how much it should record as a liability under each of the scenarios. Which amount would you suggest the airline record, given that it doesn't know which will occur?

2. Write a response to the person who states that, since it is not known if the frequent-flier miles will be used, the liability is contingent and need not be expensed until the passenger actually uses the frequent-flier miles. This person suggests that because the liability is contingent, not actual, it should be disclosed in the notes.

Extending Your Knowledge

DECISION PROBLEM

Maquinna Construction is a large road-building business in Ontario. The owner is Neil Maquinna, who oversees all company operations. He employs 15 work crews, each made up of 6 to 10 members. Construction supervisors, who report directly to Maquinna, lead the crews. Most supervisors are long-time employees, so Maquinna trusts them to a great degree. The company's office staff consists of an accountant and an office manager.

Because crew needs may vary in the construction industry, supervisors hire and terminate their own crew members. Supervisors notify the office of all personnel changes. Also, supervisors forward to the office the employee TD1 forms, which the crew members fill out to claim tax-withholding exemptions. Each Thursday the supervisors submit weekly time sheets for their crews, and the accountant prepares the payroll. At noon on Friday the supervisors come to the office to get paycheques for distribution to the workers at 5 p.m.

Maquinna Construction's accountant prepares the payroll, including the payroll cheques, which are written on a single payroll bank account. Neil Maquinna signs all payroll cheques after matching the employee name to the time sheets submitted by the supervisor. Often the construction workers wait several days to cash their paycheques. To verify that each construction worker is a bona fide employee, the accountant matches the employee's endorsement signature on the back of the cancelled payroll cheque with the signature on that employee's TD1 form. Delays occur in completing this task as well as in reconciling the payroll bank account.

Identifying internal control weaknesses and their solution

Required

1. List one *efficiency* weakness in Maquinna Construction's payroll accounting system. How can the business correct this weakness?

2. Identify one way that a supervisor can defraud Maquinna Construction under the present system.

3. Discuss a control feature Maquinna Construction can use to *safeguard* against the frauds you identified in Requirement 2.

FINANCIAL STATEMENT CASES

Financial Statement Case 1

Details about a company's current and contingent liabilities appear in a number of places in the annual report. Use the Canadian Western Bank (CWB) financial statements in Appendix A to answer the following questions.

Current and contingent liabilities ① ②

1. Give the breakdown of CWB's current liabilities at October 31, 2008.

2. Why are deposits classified as a liability for CWB?

3. How much was CWB's other indebtedness at October 31, 2008, and what is included in this balance?

4. Does CWB have any commitments and contingent liabilities outstanding? Describe the main types of commitments and contingencies, and discuss where you found this information.

5. Why are commitments not shown on the balance sheet as a liability?

Financial Statement Case 2

Current and contingent liabilities

Details about a company's current and contingent liabilities appear in a number of places in the annual report. Use the Sun-Rype Products Ltd. financial statements in Appendix B to answer the following questions.

1. Give the breakdown of Sun-Rype's current liabilities at December 31, 2008.

2. In general, how is the current portion of long-term debt calculated?

3. How much were Sun-Rype's long-term obligations and other indebtedness at December 31, 2008? What is the account Long-Term Obligations, and where did you find this information?

4. Does Sun-Rype have any commitments coming due in 2009? If so, where did you find information about them? Why are commitments not shown on the balance sheet as a liability?

5. Does Sun-Rype Products Ltd. have any contingent liabilities at December 31, 2008? How do you know?

Comprehensive Problem for Part 2

COMPARING TWO BUSINESSES

Suppose you are ready to invest in a small resort property. Two locations look promising: Nootka Resort in Victoria, British Columbia, and Critter Cove Resort in Nova Scotia. Each place has its appeal, but Nootka Resort wins out. The main allure is that the price is better. The property owners provide the following data:

	Nootka Resort	Critter Cove Resort
Cash	$ 18,250	$ 34,150
Accounts receivable	10,950	9,800
Inventory	39,700	36,600
Land	144,750	358,000
Buildings	960,000	1,048,600
Accumulated amortization—buildings	(63,772)	(440,100)
Furniture and fixtures	401,500	499,150
Accumulated amortization—furniture and fixtures	(120,500)	(286,400)
Total assets	$1,390,878	$1,259,800
Total liabilities	$ 601,500	$ 539,550
Owner's equity	789,378	720,250
Total liabilities and owner's equity	$1,390,878	$1,259,800

Income statements for the last three years report total net income of $284,100 for Nootka Resort and $151,400 for Critter Cove Resort.

Inventories Nootka Resort uses the FIFO inventory method, and Critter Cove Resort uses the weighted-average method. If Nootka Resort had used weighted-average, its reported inventory would have been $3,750 lower. If Critter Cove Resort had used FIFO, its reported inventory would have been $3,200 higher. Three years ago there was little difference between weighted-average and FIFO amounts for Nootka, and between weighted-average and FIFO amounts for Critter Cove.

Property, Plant, and Equipment Nootka Resort uses the straight-line amortization method and an estimated useful life of 35 years for buildings and 7 years for furniture and fixtures. Estimated residual values are $216,000 for buildings and $0 for furniture and fixtures. Nootka Resort's buildings and furniture and fixtures are three years old.

Critter Cove Resort uses the double-declining-balance method and amortizes buildings over 35 years with an estimated residual value of $245,000. The furniture and fixtures, now two years old, are being amortized over seven years with an estimated residual value of $45,450.

Accounts Receivable Nootka Resort uses the direct write-off method for uncollectibles. Critter Cove Resort uses the allowance method. The Nootka Resort owner estimates that $1,075 of the company's receivables are doubtful. Prior to the current year, uncollectibles were insignificant. Critter Cove Resort's receivables are already reported at net realizable value.

Required

1. To compare the two resorts, convert Nootka Resort's net income to the accounting methods and the estimated useful lives used by Critter Cove Resort.
2. Compare the two resorts' net income after you have revised Nootka Resort's figures. Which resort looked better at the outset? Which resort looks better when they are placed on equal footing?

WINNING THE

WEST

CWB | CANADIAN WESTERN BANK GROUP
BANK · TRUST · INSURANCE

2008 ANNUAL REPORT

FINANCIAL STATEMENTS

MANAGEMENT'S RESPONSIBILITY FOR FINANCIAL REPORTING

The consolidated financial statements of Canadian Western Bank and related financial information presented in this annual report have been prepared by management, who are responsible for the integrity and fair presentation of the information presented, which includes the consolidated financial statements, Management's Discussion and Analysis (MD&A) and other information. The consolidated financial statements were prepared in accordance with Canadian generally accepted accounting principles, including the requirements of the Bank Act and related rules and regulations issued by the Office of the Superintendent of Financial Institutions Canada. The MD&A has been prepared in accordance with the requirements of securities regulators, including National Instrument 51-102 of the Canadian Securities Administrators (CSA).

The consolidated financial statements, MD&A and related financial information reflect amounts which must, of necessity, be based on informed estimates and judgments of management with appropriate consideration to materiality. The financial information presented elsewhere in this annual report is fairly presented and consistent with that in the consolidated financial statements.

Management has designed the accounting system and related internal controls, and supporting procedures are maintained to provide reasonable assurance that financial records are complete and accurate, assets are safeguarded and the Bank is in compliance with all regulatory requirements. These supporting procedures include the careful selection and training of qualified staff, defined division of responsibilities and accountability for performance, and the written communication of policies and guidelines of business conduct and risk management throughout the Bank.

We, as the Bank's Chief Executive Officer and Chief Financial Officer, will certify Canadian Western Bank's annual filings with the CSA as required by Multilateral Instrument 52-109 (Certification of Disclosure in Issuers' Annual and Interim Filings).

The system of internal controls is also supported by the internal audit department, which carries out periodic inspections of all aspects of the Bank's operations. The Chief Internal Auditor has full and free access to the Audit Committee and to the external auditors.

The Audit Committee, appointed by the Board of Directors, is comprised entirely of independent directors who are not officers or employees of the Bank. The Committee is responsible for reviewing the financial statements and annual report, including management's discussion and analysis of operations and financial condition, and recommending them to the Board of Directors for approval. Other key responsibilities of the Audit Committee include meeting with management, the Chief Internal Auditor and the external auditors to discuss the effectiveness of certain internal controls over the financial reporting process and the planning and results of the external audit. The Committee also meets regularly with the Chief Internal Auditor and the external auditors without management present.

The Conduct Review Committee, appointed by the Board of Directors, is composed of directors who are not officers or employees of the Bank. Their responsibilities include reviewing related party transactions and reporting to the Board of Directors those transactions which may have a material impact on the Bank.

The Office of the Superintendent of Financial Institutions Canada, at least once a year, makes such examination and inquiry into the affairs of the Bank and its federally regulated subsidiaries as is deemed necessary or expedient to satisfy that the provisions of the relevant Acts, having reference to the safety of the depositors and policyholders, are being duly observed and that the Bank is in a sound financial condition.

KPMG LLP, the independent auditors appointed by the shareholders of the Bank, have performed an audit of the consolidated financial statements and their report follows. The external auditors have full and free access to, and meet periodically with, the Audit Committee to discuss their audit and matters arising therefrom.

Larry M. Pollock
President and Chief Executive Officer

November 24, 2008

Tracey C. Ball, FCA
Executive Vice President and Chief Financial Officer

AUDITORS' REPORT

TO THE SHAREHOLDERS OF CANADIAN WESTERN BANK

We have audited the Consolidated Balance Sheet of Canadian Western Bank as at October 31, 2008 and the Consolidated Statements of Income, Comprehensive Income, Changes in Shareholders' Equity and Cash Flow for the year then ended. These consolidated financial statements are the responsibility of the Bank's management. Our responsibility is to express an opinion on these consolidated financial statements based on our audit.

We conducted our audit in accordance with Canadian generally accepted auditing standards. Those standards require that we plan and perform an audit to obtain reasonable assurance whether the financial statements are free of material misstatement. An audit includes examining, on a test basis, evidence supporting the amounts and disclosures in the financial statements. An audit also includes assessing the accounting principles used and significant estimates made by management, as well as evaluating the overall financial statement presentation.

In our opinion, these consolidated financial statements present fairly, in all material respects, the financial position of the Bank as at October 31, 2008 and the results of its operations and its cash flow for the year then ended in accordance with Canadian generally accepted accounting principles.

The consolidated financial statements as at October 31, 2007 and for the year then ended were audited by other auditors, who expressed an opinion without reservation on these statements in their report dated November 30, 2007.

KPMG LLP

KPMG LLP
Chartered Accountants
Edmonton, Alberta

November 24, 2008

CONSOLIDATED BALANCE SHEETS

FOR THE YEAR ENDED OCTOBER 31

($ thousands)

		2008	2007
Assets			
Cash Resources			
Cash and non-interest bearing deposits with financial institutions		$ 8,988	$ 6,446
Deposits with regulated financial institutions	(Note 3)	464,193	405,122
Cheques and other items in transit		18,992	1,122
		492,173	412,690
Securities	(Note 4)		
Issued or guaranteed by Canada		347,777	630,396
Issued or guaranteed by a province or municipality		452,045	251,418
Other securities		429,142	459,812
		1,228,964	1,341,626
Securities Purchased Under Resale Agreements	(Note 5)	77,000	206,925
Loans	(Note 6)		
Residential mortgages		2,134,327	1,780,442
Other loans		6,565,280	5,688,160
		8,699,607	7,468,602
Allowance for credit losses	(Note 7)	(75,538)	(63,022)
		8,624,069	7,405,580
Other			
Land, buildings and equipment	(Note 8)	31,893	25,736
Goodwill	(Note 9)	6,933	6,933
Intangible assets	(Note 9)	2,155	2,681
Insurance related	(Note 10)	52,943	51,744
Derivative related	(Note 11)	9,980	1,496
Other assets	(Note 12)	74,622	69,629
		178,526	158,219
Total Assets		$ 10,600,732	$ 9,525,040
Liabilities and Shareholders' Equity			
Deposits	(Note 13)		
Payable on demand		$ 383,083	$ 376,488
Payable after notice		2,010,039	1,843,799
Payable on a fixed date		6,747,597	5,931,631
Deposit from Canadian Western Bank Capital Trust	(Note 14)	105,000	105,000
		9,245,719	8,256,918
Other			
Cheques and other items in transit		29,036	22,177
Insurance related	(Note 15)	134,769	124,480
Derivative related	(Note 11)	163	1,307
Other liabilities	(Note 16)	136,897	134,665
		300,865	282,629
Subordinated Debentures			
Conventional	(Note 17)	375,000	390,000
Shareholders' Equity			
Retained earnings		448,203	372,739
Accumulated other comprehensive income (loss)		(5,203)	(5,931)
Capital stock	(Note 18)	221,914	219,004
Contributed surplus		14,234	9,681
		679,148	595,493
Total Liabilities and Shareholders' Equity		$ 10,600,732	$ 9,525,040
Contingent Liabilities and Commitments	(Note 20)		

Jack C. Donald
Chairman

Larry M. Pollock
President and Chief Executive Officer

CONSOLIDATED STATEMENTS OF INCOME

($ thousands, except per share amounts)

		2008	2007
Interest Income			
Loans		$ 491,991	$ 439,668
Securities		52,929	45,590
Deposits with regulated financial institutions		17,847	13,677
		562,767	498,935
Interest Expense			
Deposits		317,554	275,840
Subordinated debentures		22,267	17,846
		339,821	293,686
Net Interest Income		222,946	205,249
Provision for Credit Losses	(Note 7)	12,000	10,200
Net Interest Income after Provision for Credit Losses		210,946	195,049
Other Income			
Credit related		26,998	22,426
Insurance, net	(Note 21)	15,866	15,263
Trust services		13,299	14,943
Retail services		7,689	7,290
Gains on sale of securities		4,725	438
Foreign exchange gains		1,225	2,159
Other		438	302
		70,240	62,821
Net Interest and Other Income		281,186	257,870
Non-Interest Expenses			
Salaries and employee benefits		87,660	76,506
Premises and equipment		22,360	20,239
Other expenses		23,145	22,780
Provincial capital taxes		2,001	2,409
		135,166	121,934
Net Income before Provision for Income Taxes		146,020	135,936
Provision for Income Taxes	(Note 24)	44,001	39,654
Net Income		$ 102,019	$ 96,282
Earnings Per Common Share	(Note 25)		
Basic		$ 1.61	$ 1.54
Diluted		1.58	1.50

CONSOLIDATED STATEMENTS OF CHANGES IN SHAREHOLDERS' EQUITY

FOR THE YEAR ENDED OCTOBER 31

($ thousands)

		2008	2007
Retained Earnings			
Balance at beginning of year		$ 372,739	$ 297,675
Net income		102,019	96,282
Dividends		(26,555)	(21,218)
Balance at end of year		448,203	372,739
Accumulated Other Comprehensive Income (Loss)			
Balance at beginning of year		(5,931)	(1,494)
Other comprehensive income (loss)		728	(4,437)
Balance at end of year		(5,203)	(5,931)
Total retained earnings and accumulated other comprehensive income		443,000	366,808
Capital Stock	(Note 18)		
Balance at beginning of year		219,004	215,349
Issued on exercise of employee stock options		1,646	2,464
Transferred from contributed surplus on the exercise or exchange of options		1,264	1,191
Balance at end of year		221,914	219,004
Contributed Surplus			
Balance at beginning of year		9,681	6,340
Amortization of fair value of employee stock options	(Note 19)	5,817	4,532
Transferred to contributed surplus on the exercise or exchange of options		(1,264)	(1,191)
Balance at end of year		14,234	9,681
Total Shareholders' Equity		$ 679,148	$ 595,493

CONSOLIDATED STATEMENTS OF COMPREHENSIVE INCOME

FOR THE YEAR ENDED OCTOBER 31

($ thousands)

	2008	2007
Net Income	$ 102,019	$ 96,282
Other Comprehensive Income (Loss), net of tax		
Available-for-sale securities		
Losses from change in fair value[1]	(2,631)	(5,544)
Reclassification to other income[2]	(3,271)	(295)
	(5,902)	(5,839)
Derivatives designated as cash flow hedges		
Gains (losses) from change in fair value[3]	9,341	(403)
Reclassification to net interest income[4]	(1,773)	1,805
Reclassification to other liabilities for derivatives terminated prior to maturity[5]	(938)	–
	6,630	1,402
	728	(4,437)
Comprehensive Income for the Year	$ 102,747	$ 91,845

(1) Net of income tax benefit of $1,170 (2007 – tax benefit of $2,720).
(2) Net of income tax benefit of $1,454 (2007 – tax benefit of $144).
(3) Net of income tax expense of $4,104 (2007 – tax benefit of $197).
(4) Net of income tax benefit of $775 (2007 – tax expense of $882).
(5) Net of income tax benefit of $429 (2007 – $nil).

CONSOLIDATED STATEMENTS OF CASH FLOW

FOR THE YEAR ENDED OCTOBER 31
($ thousands)

		2008		2007
Cash Flows from Operating Activities				
Net income		$ 102,019	$	96,282
Adjustments to determine net cash flows:				
Provision for credit losses		12,000		10,200
Depreciation and amortization		6,896		6,017
Future income taxes, net		276		1,387
Gain on sale of securities, net		(4,725)		(438)
Accrued interest receivable and payable, net		2,719		13,287
Current income taxes payable, net		(454)		(1,777)
Amortization of fair value of employee stock options		5,817		4,532
Other items, net		(5,164)		13,183
		119,384		142,673
Cash Flows from Financing Activities				
Deposits, net		988,801		1,965,953
Debentures issued	(Note 17)	50,000		195,000
Debentures redeemed	(Note 17)	(65,000)		(3,126)
Common shares issued	(Note 18)	1,646		2,464
Dividends		(26,555)		(21,218)
		948,892		2,139,073
Cash Flows from Investing Activities				
Interest bearing deposits with regulated financial institutions, net		(57,057)		(55,550)
Securities, purchased		(2,609,432)		(2,860,204)
Securities, sales proceeds		1,303,698		960,350
Securities, matured		1,421,159		1,437,710
Securities purchased under resale agreements, net		129,925		(197,925)
Loans, net		(1,230,489)		(1,633,943)
Land, buildings and equipment		(12,527)		(7,012)
		(1,054,723)		(2,356,574)
Change in Cash and Cash Equivalents		13,553		(74,828)
Cash and Cash Equivalents at Beginning of Year		(14,609)		60,219
Cash and Cash Equivalents at End of Year *		$ (1,056)	$	(14,609)
* Represented by:				
Cash and non-interest bearing deposits with financial institutions		$ 8,988	$	6,446
Cheques and other items in transit (included in Cash Resources)		18,992		1,122
Cheques and other items in transit (included in Other Liabilities)		(29,036)		(22,177)
Cash and Cash Equivalents at End of Year		$ (1,056)	$	(14,609)
Supplemental Disclosure of Cash Flow Information				
Amount of interest paid in the year		$ 336,106	$	267,963
Amount of income taxes paid in the year		44,179		40,044

NOTES TO CONSOLIDATED FINANCIAL STATEMENTS

OCTOBER 31, 2008

($ thousands, except per share amounts)

1. BASIS OF PRESENTATION

These consolidated financial statements of Canadian Western Bank (CWB or the Bank) have been prepared in accordance with subsection 308 (4) of the Bank Act, which states that, except as otherwise specified by the Office of the Superintendent of Financial Institutions Canada (OSFI), the financial statements are to be prepared in accordance with Canadian generally accepted accounting principles (GAAP). The significant accounting policies used in the preparation of these financial statements, including the accounting requirements of OSFI, are summarized below and in the following notes. These accounting policies conform, in all material respects, to Canadian GAAP.

The preparation of financial statements in conformity with Canadian GAAP requires management to make estimates and assumptions that affect the reported amounts of assets and liabilities and the disclosure of contingent assets and liabilities at the date of the financial statements as well as the reported amount of revenues and expenses during the year. Key areas of estimation where management has made subjective judgments, often as a result of matters that are inherently uncertain, include those relating to the allowance for credit losses, fair value of financial instruments, goodwill and intangible assets, provision for unpaid claims and adjustment expenses, future income tax asset and liability, other than temporary impairment of securities and fair value of employee stock options. Therefore, actual results could differ from these estimates.

a) Basis of Consolidation

The consolidated financial statements include the assets, liabilities and results of operations of the Bank and all of its subsidiaries, after the elimination of intercompany transactions and balances. Subsidiaries are defined as corporations whose operations are controlled by the Bank and are corporations in which the Bank is the beneficial owner. See Note 34 for details of the subsidiaries and affiliate.

b) Business Combinations

Business acquisitions are accounted for using the purchase method.

c) Translation of Foreign Currencies

Assets and liabilities denominated in foreign currencies are translated into Canadian dollars at rates prevailing at the balance sheet date. Revenues and expenses in foreign currencies are translated at the average exchange rates prevailing during the year. Realized and unrealized gains and losses on foreign currency positions are included in other income, except for unrealized foreign exchange gains and losses on available-for-sale securities that are included in other comprehensive income.

d) Specific Accounting Policies

To facilitate a better understanding of the Bank's consolidated financial statements, the significant accounting policies are disclosed in the notes, where applicable, with related financial disclosures by major caption:

Note	Topic
2	Financial instruments
3	Cash resources
4	Securities
5	Securities purchased under resale agreements and securities purchased under reverse resale agreements
6	Loans
7	Allowance for credit losses
8	Land, buildings and equipment
9	Goodwill and intangible assets
10	Insurance related other assets
11	Derivative financial instruments
12	Other assets
13	Deposits
14	Trust capital securities
15	Insurance related other liabilities
16	Other liabilities
17	Subordinated debentures
18	Capital stock
19	Share incentive plan
20	Contingent liabilities and commitments
21	Insurance operations
22	Disclosures on rate regulation
23	Employee future benefits
24	Income taxes

e) **Change in Accounting Policies**

Effective November 1, 2007, the Bank adopted new accounting standards issued by the Canadian Institute of Chartered Accountants (CICA): *Financial Instruments – Disclosure and Presentation* and *Capital Disclosures.* The new standards require additional disclosures regarding financial instruments and capital management practices. As a result of adopting these standards, new or enhanced disclosure is provided in Note 2 Financial Instruments, Note 6 Loans and Note 31 Capital Management.

In addition, as permitted by the CICA, certain of the required disclosure is provided in the Management's Discussion and Analysis (MD&A). The relevant MD&A sections are identified by shading and shaded areas form an integral part of these audited consolidated financial statements.

f) **Future Accounting Changes**

International Financial Reporting Standards

The CICA will transition Canadian GAAP for publicly accountable entities to International Financial Reporting Standards (IFRS). The Bank's consolidated financial statements will be prepared in accordance with IFRS for the fiscal year commencing November 1, 2011.

The Bank has embarked on a project to identify and evaluate the impact of the implementation of IFRS on the consolidated financial statements and to develop a plan to complete the transition. The impact of the transition to IFRS on the Bank's consolidated financial statements is not yet determinable. Additional information on the Bank's transition plan and the expected impact of the transition will be provided commencing in the quarterly reports for 2009, the third fiscal year prior to transition.

2. FINANCIAL INSTRUMENTS

As a financial institution, most of the Bank's balance sheet is comprised of financial instruments and the majority of net income results from gains, losses, income and expenses related to the same.

Financial instrument assets include cash resources, securities, securities purchased under resale agreements, loans and derivative financial instruments. Financial instrument liabilities include deposits, securities purchased under reverse resale agreements, derivative financial instruments and subordinated debentures.

The use of financial instruments exposes the Bank to credit, liquidity and market risks. A discussion of how these are managed can be found in the Risk Management section of the 2008 Annual Report beginning on page 54.

Income and expenses are classified as to source, either securities or loans for income, and deposits or subordinated debentures for expense. Gains on the sale of securities, net, are shown separately in other income.

3. CASH RESOURCES

Cash resources have been designated as available-for-sale and are reported on the balance sheet at fair value with changes in fair value reported in other comprehensive income, net of income taxes.

Included in deposits with regulated financial institutions are available-for-sale financial instruments reported on the consolidated balance sheets at the fair value of $459,875 (2007 – $362,849), which is $940 higher (2007 – $1,070 lower) than amortized cost.

4. SECURITIES

Securities have been designated as available-for-sale, are accounted for at settlement date and reported on the balance sheet at fair value with changes in fair value reported in other comprehensive income, net of income taxes.

Securities are purchased with the original intention to hold the securities to maturity or until market conditions render alternative investments more attractive. If an impairment in value is other than temporary, any write-down to net realizable value is reported in the consolidated statements of income. Gains and losses realized on disposal of securities and adjustments to record any other than temporary impairment in value are included in other income. Amortization of premiums and discounts are reported in interest income from securities in the consolidated statements of income.

Securities designated as held-for-trading, which are purchased for resale over a short period of time, are carried at fair value. Gains and losses realized on disposal and adjustments to fair value are reported in other income in the consolidated statements of income in the period during which they occur. There were no securities designated as held-for-trading at any time during 2007 and 2008.

The analysis of securities at carrying value, by type and maturity, is as follows:

| | Maturities | | | | 2008 Total Carrying Value | 2007 Total Carrying Value |
	Within 1 Year	Over 1 to 3 Years	Over 3 to 5 Years	Over 5 Years		
Securities issued or guaranteed by						
Canada	$ 246,395	$ 91,116	$ 10,266	$ –	$ 347,777	$ 630,396
A province or municipality	135,770	260,642	53,442	2,191	452,045	251,418
Other debt securities	59,745	62,471	35,464	11,027	168,707	236,255
Equity securities						
Preferred shares	43,352	49,023	137,684	26,173	256,232	221,878
Other equity	–	–	–	4,203[2]	4,203	1,679
Total[1]	$ 485,262	$ 463,252	$ 236,856	$ 43,594	$ 1,228,964	$ 1,341,626

(1) All securities have been designated as available-for-sale.
(2) Includes securities with no specific maturity.

The analysis of unrealized gains and losses on securities reflected on the balance sheet is as follows:

| | 2008 | | | | 2007 | | | |
	Amortized Cost	Unrealized Gains	Unrealized Losses	Fair Value	Amortized Cost	Unrealized Gains	Unrealized Losses	Fair Value
Securities issued or guaranteed by								
Canada	$ 346,360	$ 1,417	$ –	$ 347,777	$ 630,270	$ 415	$ 289	$ 630,396
A province or municipality	450,831	1,442	228	452,045	251,432	260	274	251,418
Other debt securities	170,665	686	2,644	168,707	237,958	160	1,863	236,255
Equity securities								
Preferred shares	274,061	–	17,829	256,232	227,331	34	5,487	221,878
Other equity	5,802	49	1,648	4,203	2,850	–	1,171	1,679
Total	$ 1,247,719	$ 3,594	$ 22,349	$ 1,228,964	$ 1,349,841	$ 869	$ 9,084	$ 1,341,626

The securities portfolio is primarily comprised of high quality debt instruments and preferred shares that are not held for trading purposes and are typically held until maturity. Fluctuations in value are generally attributed to changes in interest rates, market spreads and shifts in the interest rate curve. Unrealized losses at year-end are considered to be temporary in nature.

5. SECURITIES PURCHASED UNDER RESALE AGREEMENTS AND SECURITIES PURCHASED UNDER REVERSE RESALE AGREEMENTS

Securities purchased under resale agreements represent a purchase of Government of Canada securities by the Bank effected with a simultaneous agreement to sell them back at a specified price on a future date, which is generally short term. The difference between the cost of the purchase and the predetermined proceeds to be received on a resale agreement is recorded as securities interest income.

Securities purchased under reverse resale agreements represent a sale of Government of Canada securities by the Bank effected with a simultaneous agreement to buy them back at a specified price on a future date, which is generally short term. The difference between the proceeds of the sale and the predetermined cost to be paid on a resale agreement is recorded as deposit interest expense. There were no reverse resale agreements outstanding at year-end.

Securities purchased under resale agreements have been designated as available-for-sale and are reported on the consolidated balance sheets at fair value with changes in fair value reported in other comprehensive income, net of income taxes.

Interest earned or paid is recorded in interest income or expense as earned.

6. LOANS

Loans are recorded at amortized cost and are stated net of unearned income, unamortized premiums and an allowance for credit losses (Note 7).

Interest income is recorded using the effective interest method, except for loans classified as impaired. Loans are determined to be impaired when payments are contractually past due 90 days, or where the Bank has taken realization proceedings, or where the Bank is of the opinion that the loan should be regarded as impaired. An exception may be made where management determines that the loan is well secured and in the process of collection and the collection efforts are reasonably expected to result in either repayment of the loan or restoring it to a current status within 180 days from the date the payment went in arrears. All loans are classified as impaired when a payment is 180 days in arrears other than loans guaranteed or insured for both principal and interest by the Canadian government, the provinces or a Canadian government agency. These loans are classified as impaired when payment is 365 days in arrears.

Impairment is measured as the difference between the carrying value of the loan at the time it is classified as impaired and the present value of the expected cash flows (estimated realizable amount), using the interest rate inherent in the loan at the date the loan is classified as impaired. When the amounts and timing of future cash flows cannot be reliably estimated, either the fair value of the security underlying the loan, net of any expected realization costs, or the current market price for the loan may be used to measure the estimated realizable amount. At the time a loan is classified as impaired, interest income will cease to be recognized in accordance with the loan agreement, and any uncollected but accrued interest will be added to the carrying value of the loan, together with any unamortized premiums, discounts or loan fees. Subsequent payments received on an impaired loan are recorded as a reduction of the recorded investment in the loan. Impaired loans are returned to performing status when the timely collection of both principal and interest is reasonably assured and all delinquent principal and interest payments are brought current and all charges for loan impairment have been reversed.

Loan fees, net of directly related costs, are amortized to interest income over the expected term of the loan. Premiums paid on the acquisition of loan portfolios are amortized to interest income over the expected term of the loans.

Outstanding gross loans and impaired loans, net of allowances for credit losses, are as follows:

	2008				2007			
	Gross Amount	Gross Impaired Amount	Specific Allowance	Net Impaired Loans	Gross Amount	Gross Impaired Amount	Specific Allowance	Net Impaired Loans
Consumer and personal	$ 1,288,160	$ 11,462	$ 305	$ 11,157	$ 1,062,898	$ 2,878	$ 351	$ 2,527
Real estate[1][3]	3,673,158	51,909	2,948	48,961	2,887,822	1,098	896	202
Industrial	1,391,287	20,456	5,647	14,809	1,325,431	11,261	2,550	8,711
Commercial	2,347,002	7,809	6,111	1,698	2,192,451	5,867	3,617	2,250
Total	$ 8,699,607	$ 91,636	$ 15,011	76,625	$ 7,468,602	$ 21,104	$ 7,414	13,690
General allowance[2]				(60,527)				(55,608)
Net impaired loans after general allowance				$ 16,098				$ (41,918)

(1) Multi-family residential mortgages are presented as real estate loans in this table.
(2) The general allowance for credit risk is available for the total loan portfolio.
(3) Foreclosed real estate assets with a carrying value of $901 (2007 – $nil) are held for sale. Foreclosed real estate assets are generally liquidated quickly to repay the outstanding loan.

Outstanding impaired loans, net of allowance for credit losses, by provincial location of security, are as follows:

	2008			2007		
	Gross Impaired Amount	Specific Allowance	Net Impaired Loans	Gross Impaired Amount	Specific Allowance	Net Impaired Loans
Alberta	$ 48,436	$ 9,204	$ 39,232	$ 9,163	$ 3,927	$ 5,236
British Columbia	40,656	4,626	36,030	8,864	2,013	6,851
Saskatchewan	2,155	792	1,363	3,061	1,458	1,603
Manitoba	389	389	–	16	16	–
Total	$ 91,636	$ 15,011	76,625	$ 21,104	$ 7,414	13,690
General allowance[1]			(60,527)			(55,608)
Net impaired loans after general allowance			$ 16,098			$ (41,918)

(1) The general allowance for credit risk is not allocated by province.

During the year, interest recognized as income on impaired loans totaled $360 (2007 – $414).

Gross impaired loans exclude certain past due loans, which are loans where payment of interest or principal is contractually in arrears but which are not classified as impaired. Details of such past due loans that have not been included in the gross impaired amount are as follows:

As at October 31, 2008	1 – 30 days		31 – 60 days		61 – 90 days		More than 90 days		Total
Residential mortgages	$ 7,217	$	8,550	$	347	$	–	$	16,114
Other loans	11,732		4,010		342		–		16,084
	$ 18,949	$	12,560	$	689	$	–	$	32,198

Certain process changes were required to compile the above information and comparative figures are not available.

7. ALLOWANCE FOR CREDIT LOSSES

An allowance for credit losses is maintained which, in the Bank's opinion, is adequate to absorb credit related losses in its loan portfolio. The adequacy of the allowance for credit losses is reviewed at least quarterly. The allowance for credit losses is deducted from the outstanding loan balance.

The allowance for credit losses consists of specific provisions and the general allowance for credit risk. Specific provisions include all the accumulated provisions for losses on identified impaired loans required to reduce the carrying value of those loans to their estimated realizable amount. The general allowance for credit risk includes provisions for losses inherent in the portfolio that are not presently identifiable by management of the Bank on an account-by-account basis. The general allowance for credit risk is established by taking into consideration historical trends in the loss experience during economic cycles, the current portfolio profile, estimated losses for the current phase of the economic cycle and historical experience in the industry.

Actual write-offs, net of recoveries, are deducted from the allowance for credit losses. The provision for credit losses in the consolidated statements of income is charged with an amount sufficient to keep the balance in the allowance for credit losses adequate to absorb all credit related losses.

The following table shows the changes in the allowance for credit losses during the year:

	2008					2007				
	Specific Allowance		General Allowance for Credit Losses		Total		Specific Allowance		General Allowance for Credit Losses	Total
Balance at beginning of year	$ 7,414	$	55,608	$	63,022	$	5,484	$	48,037 $	53,521
Provision for credit losses	7,081		4,919		12,000		2,629		7,571	10,200
Write-offs	(2,577)		–		(2,577)		(786)		–	(786)
Recoveries	3,093		–		3,093		87		–	87
Balance at end of year	$ 15,011	$	60,527	$	75,538	$	7,414	$	55,608 $	63,022

8. LAND, BUILDINGS AND EQUIPMENT

Land is carried at cost. Buildings, equipment and furniture, and leasehold improvements are carried at cost less accumulated depreciation and amortization. Depreciation and amortization are calculated primarily using the straight-line method over the estimated useful life of the asset, as follows: buildings – 20 years, equipment and furniture – three to five years, and leasehold improvements – term of the lease. Gains and losses on disposal are recorded in other income in the year of disposal. Land, building and equipment, if no longer in use or considered impaired, are written down to the fair value.

Operating leases primarily comprise branch and office premises and are not capitalized. Total costs, including free rent periods and step-rent increases, are expensed on a straight-line basis over the lease term.

	Cost	Accumulated Depreciation and Amortization	2008 Net Book Value	2007 Net Book Value
Land	$ 2,783	$ –	$ 2,783	$ 2,783
Buildings	5,337	3,090	2,247	1,669
Computer equipment	25,490	19,897	5,593	5,688
Office equipment and furniture	15,776	10,450	5,326	4,521
Leasehold improvements	28,165	12,221	15,944	11,075
Total	$ 77,551	$ 45,658	$ 31,893	$ 25,736

Depreciation and amortization for the year amounted to $6,370 (2007 – $5,474).

9. GOODWILL AND INTANGIBLE ASSETS

Goodwill is the excess of the purchase price paid for the acquisition of a subsidiary over the fair value of the net assets acquired, including identifiable intangible assets. Goodwill and other intangibles with an indefinite life are not amortized, but are subject to a fair value impairment test at least annually. Other intangibles with a finite life are amortized to the statement of income over their expected lives not exceeding 10 years. These intangible assets are tested for impairment whenever circumstances indicate that the carrying amount may not be recoverable. Any impairment of goodwill or other intangible assets will be charged to the consolidated statement of income in the period of impairment.

	Cost	Accumulated Amortization	2008 Net Book Value	2007 Net Book Value
Goodwill	$ 6,933	$ –	$ 6,933	$ 6,933
Identifiable intangible assets				
Customer relationships	3,950	2,115	1,835	2,305
Trademark	300	–	300	300
Others	330	310	20	76
	4,580	2,425	2,155	2,681
Total	$ 11,513	$ 2,425	$ 9,088	$ 9,614

Amortization of customer relationships and other intangible assets for the year amounted to $526 (2007 – $543). The trademark has an indefinite life and is not subject to amortization. Goodwill includes $3,679 related to the banking and trust segment and $3,254 related to the insurance segment. There were no writedowns of goodwill or intangible assets due to impairment.

10. INSURANCE RELATED OTHER ASSETS

	2008	2007
Instalment premiums receivable	$ 24,333	$ 22,803
Reinsurers' share of unpaid claims and adjustment expenses	11,561	10,915
Deferred policy acquisition costs	8,924	8,626
Recoverable on unpaid claims	6,939	7,257
Due from reinsurers	1,186	2,143
Total	$ 52,943	$ 51,744

11. DERIVATIVE FINANCIAL INSTRUMENTS

Interest rate, foreign exchange and equity contracts such as futures, options, swaps, floors and rate locks are entered into for risk management purposes in accordance with the Bank's asset liability management policies. It is the Bank's policy not to utilize derivative financial instruments for trading or speculative purposes. Interest rate swaps and floors are primarily used to reduce the impact of fluctuating interest rates. Equity contracts are used to economically offset the return paid to depositors on certain deposit products that are linked to a stock index. Foreign exchange contracts are only used for the purposes of meeting needs of clients or day-to-day business.

The Bank designates certain derivative financial instruments as either a hedge of the fair value of recognized assets or liabilities or firm commitments (fair value hedges), or a hedge of highly probable future cash flows attributable to a recognized asset or liability or a forecasted transaction (cash flow hedges). The Bank has designated all interest rate swaps as cash flow hedges. On an ongoing basis, the Bank assesses whether the derivatives that are used in hedging transactions are effective in offsetting changes in fair values or cash flows of the hedged items.

Certain derivatives embedded in other financial instruments, such as the return on fixed term deposits that are linked to a stock index, are treated as separate derivatives when their economic characteristics and risks are not closely related to those of the host contract and the combined contract is not carried at fair value. Embedded derivatives identified in contracts entered into after November 1, 2002 have been separated from the host contract and are recorded at fair value.

Interest income received or interest expense paid on derivative financial instruments is accounted for on the accrual basis and recognized as interest income or expense, as appropriate, over the term of the hedge contract. Premiums on purchased contracts are amortized to interest expense over the term of the contract. Accrued interest receivable and payable and deferred gains and losses for these contracts are recorded in other assets or liabilities as appropriate. Realized and unrealized gains or losses associated with derivative instruments, which have been terminated or cease to be effective prior to maturity, are deferred under other assets or other liabilities, as appropriate, and amortized into income over the original hedged period. In the event a designated hedged item is terminated or eliminated prior to the termination of the related derivative instrument, any realized or unrealized gain or loss on such derivative instrument is recognized in other income.

Derivative financial instruments are recorded on the balance sheet at fair value as either other assets or other liabilities with changes in fair value related to the effective portion of cash flow interest rate hedges recorded in other comprehensive income, net of income taxes. Changes in fair value related to the ineffective portion of cash flow hedges and all other derivative financial instruments are reported in other income on the consolidated statement of income.

The Bank enters into derivative financial instruments for risk management purposes. Derivative financial instruments are financial contracts whose value is derived from an underlying interest rate, foreign exchange rate, equity or commodity instrument or index.

Derivative financial instruments primarily used by the Bank include:

· interest rate swaps, which are agreements where two counterparties exchange a series of payments based on different interest rates applied to a notional amount;

· equity swap contracts, which are agreements where one counterparty agrees to pay or receive from the other cash flows based on changes in the value of an equity index as well as a designated interest rate applied to a notional amount; and

· foreign exchange forwards and futures, which are contractual obligations to exchange one currency for another at a specified price for settlement at a predetermined future date.

Interest rate swaps and other instruments are used as hedging devices to control interest rate risk. The Bank enters into these interest rate derivative instruments only for its own account and does not act as an intermediary in this market. The credit risk is limited to the amount of any adverse change in interest rates applied on the notional contract amount should the counterparty default. Equity contracts are used to offset the return paid to depositors on certain deposit products where the return is linked to a stock index. The credit risk is limited to the average return on an equity index, applied on the notional contract amount should the counterparty default. The principal amounts are not exchanged and, hence, are not at risk. The Asset Liability Committee (ALCO) of the Bank establishes and monitors approved counterparties (including an assessment of credit worthiness) and maximum notional limits. Approved counterparties are limited to rated financial institutions or their associated parent/affiliate with a minimum rating of A high or equivalent.

Foreign exchange transactions are undertaken only for the purposes of meeting the needs of clients and of day-to-day business. Foreign exchange markets are not speculated in by taking a trading position in currencies. Maximum exposure limits are established and monitored by ALCO and are defined by allowable unhedged amounts. The position is managed within the allowable target range by spot and forward transactions or other hedging techniques. Exposure to foreign exchange risk is not material to the Bank's overall financial position.

The following table summarizes the derivative financial instrument portfolio and the related credit risk. Notional amounts represent the amount to which a rate or price is applied in order to calculate the exchange of cash flows. The notional amounts are not recorded on the consolidated balance sheets. They represent the volume of outstanding transactions and do not represent the potential gain or loss associated with the market risk or credit risk of such instruments. The replacement cost represents the cost of replacing, at current market rates, all contracts with a positive fair value. The future credit exposure represents the potential for future changes in value and is based on a formula prescribed by OSFI. The credit risk equivalent is the sum of the future credit exposure and the replacement cost. The risk-weighted balance represents the credit risk equivalent weighted according to the credit worthiness of the counterparty as prescribed by OSFI. Additional discussion of OSFI's capital adequacy requirements is provided on page 42 of Management's Discussion and Analysis.

| | 2008 | | | | | 2007 | | | | |
	Notional Amount	Replace-ment Cost	Future Credit Exposure	Credit Risk Equivalent	Risk-Weighted Balance	Notional Amount	Replace-ment Cost	Future Credit Exposure	Credit Risk Equivalent	Risk-Weighted Balance
Interest rate swaps	$ 593,000	$ 9,978	$ 1,825	$ 11,803	$ 2,361	$ 482,000	$ 946	$ 1,010	$ 1,956	$ 391
Equity contracts	4,400	–	304	304	61	6,000	515	480	995	199
Foreign exchange contracts	2,600	2	26	28	14	3,405	35	34	68	14
Total	$ 600,000	$ 9,980	$ 2,155	$ 12,135	$ 2,436	$ 491,405	$ 1,496	$ 1,524	$ 3,019	$ 604

The following table shows the derivative financial instruments split between those contracts that have a positive fair value (favourable contracts) and those that have a negative fair value (unfavourable contracts).

| | 2008 | | | | 2007 | | | |
| | Favourable Contracts | | Unfavourable Contracts | | Favourable Contracts | | Unfavourable Contracts | |
	Notional Amount	Fair Value	Notional Amount	Fair Value	Notional Amount	Fair Value	Notional Amount	Fair Value
Interest rate swaps	$ 593,000	$ 9,978	$ –	$ –	$ 273,000	$ 946	$ 209,000	$ (498)
Equity contracts	–	–	4,400	(139)	6,000	515	–	–
Foreign exchange contracts	1,300	2	1,300	(175)	2,594	35	811	(63)
Embedded derivatives in equity linked deposits	n/a	151	n/a	–	n/a	–	n/a	(746)
Other forecasted transactions	–	–	–	–	–	–	–	–
Total	$ 594,300	$ 10,131	$ 5,700	$ (314)	$ 281,594	$ 1,496	$ 209,811	$ (1,307)

The aggregate contractual or notional amount of the derivative financial instruments on hand, the extent to which instruments are favourable or unfavourable and, thus, the aggregate fair values of these financial assets and liabilities can fluctuate significantly from time to time. The average fair values of the derivative financial instruments on hand during the year are set out in the following table.

	2008	2007
Favourable derivative financial instruments (assets)	$ 4,094	$ 867
Unfavourable derivative financial instruments (liabilities)	$ 322	$ 1,124

The following table summarizes maturities of derivative financial instruments and weighted average interest rates paid and received on contracts.

| | 2008 Maturity | | | | 2007 Maturity | | | |
| | 1 Year or Less | | More than 1 Year | | 1 Year or Less | | More than 1 Year | |
	Notional Amount	Contractual Interest Rate	Notional Amount	Contractual Interest Rate	Notional Amount	Contractual Interest Rate	Notional Amount	Contractual Interest Rate
Interest Rate Contracts								
Interest rate swaps – receive fixed amounts[1]	$ 228,000	2.98%	$ 365,000	2.89%	$ 394,000	4.82%	$ 88,000	4.83%
Equity Contracts[2]	2,400		2,000		1,600		4,400	
Foreign Exchange Contracts[3]	2,600		–		3,405		–	
Total	$ 233,000		$ 367,000		$ 399,005		$ 92,400	

(1) The Bank pays floating interest amounts based on the one-month (30-day) Canadian Bankers' Acceptance rate. Interest rate swaps mature between December 2008 and January 2013.
(2) The Bank receives amounts based on the specified equity index and pays amounts based on the one-month (30-day) Canadian Bankers' Acceptance rate. Equity contracts mature between February 2009 and March 2011.
(3) The contractual interest rate is not meaningful for foreign exchange contracts. Foreign exchange contracts mature between January 2009 and May 2009.

During the year, a net unrealized after tax gain of $9,341 (2007 – $403 after tax loss) was recorded in other comprehensive income for changes in fair value of the effective portion of derivatives designated as cash flow hedges and $nil (2007 – $nil) was recorded in other income for changes in fair value of the ineffective portion of derivatives classified as cash flow hedges. Amounts accumulated in other comprehensive income are reclassified to net income in the same period that interest on certain floating rate loans (i.e. the hedged items) affect income. A net gain after tax of $1,773 (2007 – $1,805 net loss after tax) was reclassified to net income. During the year, $938 after tax (2007 – $nil) was reclassified to other liabilities for derivatives terminated prior to maturity and the deferred balance will be amortized into net income over the original hedged period. A net gain of $2,432 (2007 – $68 net loss) after tax recorded in accumulated other comprehensive income (loss) as at October 31 is expected to be reclassified to net income in the next 12 months and will offset variable cash flows from floating rate loans.

There were no forecasted transactions that failed to occur.

12. OTHER ASSETS

		2008	2007
Accrued interest receivable		$ 40,241	$ 39,245
Future income tax asset	(Note 24)	16,142	16,944
Financing costs[1]		4,636	4,667
Accounts receivable		6,004	3,550
Prepaid expenses		3,520	2,589
Taxes receivable		1,259	–
Other		2,820	2,634
Total		$ 74,622	$ 69,629

(1) Amortization for the year amounted to $1,037 (2007 – $839).

13. DEPOSITS

Deposits are accounted for on an amortized cost basis. Costs relating to the issuance of fixed term deposits are amortized over the expected life of the deposit using the effective interest method.

	Individuals	Business and Government	Financial Institutions	2008 Total
Payable on demand	$ 16,071	$ 367,012	$ –	$ 383,083
Payable after notice	732,630	1,277,409	–	2,010,039
Payable on a fixed date	4,601,439	2,136,158	10,000	6,747,597
Deposit from CWB Capital Trust[1]	–	105,000	–	105,000
Total	$ 5,350,140	$ 3,885,579	$ 10,000	$ 9,245,719

	Individuals	Business and Government	Financial Institutions	2007 Total
Payable on demand	$ 15,873	$ 360,615	$ –	$ 376,488
Payable after notice	788,199	1,055,600	–	1,843,799
Payable on a fixed date	3,909,616	2,012,015	10,000	5,931,631
Deposit from CWB Capital Trust[1]	–	105,000	–	105,000
Total	$ 4,713,688	$ 3,533,230	$ 10,000	$ 8,256,918

(1) The senior deposit note of $105 million from CWB Capital Trust is reflected as a Business and Government deposit payable on a fixed date. This senior deposit note bears interest at an annual rate of 6.199% until December 31, 2016 and, thereafter, at the CDOR 180-day Bankers' Acceptance rate plus 2.55%. This note is redeemable at the Bank's option, in whole or in part, on and after December 31, 2011, or earlier in certain specified circumstances, both subject to the approval of OSFI. Each one thousand dollars of WesTS principal is convertible at any time into 40 non-cumulative redeemable CWB First Preferred Shares Series 1 of the Bank at the option of CWB Capital Trust. CWB Capital Trust will exercise this conversion right in circumstances in which holders of CWB Capital Trust Capital Securities Series 1 (WesTS) exercise their holder exchange rights. See Note 14 for more information on WesTS and CWB Capital Trust.

14. TRUST CAPITAL SECURITIES

In 2006, the Bank arranged for the issuance of innovative capital instruments, CWB Capital Trust Capital Securities Series 1 (WesTS), through Canadian Western Bank Capital Trust (CWB Capital Trust), a special purpose entity. CWB Capital Trust, an open-end trust, issued non-voting WesTS and the proceeds were used to purchase a senior deposit note from CWB.

Canadian Institute of Chartered Accountants (CICA) Accounting Guideline (AcG-15) provides a framework for identifying Variable Interest Entities ("VIEs") and requires the consolidation of a VIE if the Bank is the primary beneficiary of the VIE. The only special purpose entity in which the Bank participates is CWB Capital Trust. Although CWB owns the unit holder's equity and voting control of CWB Capital Trust through Special Trust Securities, the Bank is not exposed to the majority of any CWB Capital Trust losses and is, therefore, not the primary beneficiary under AcG-15. Accordingly, CWB does not consolidate CWB Capital Trust and the WesTS issued by CWB Capital Trust are not reported on the consolidated balance sheets, but the senior deposit note is reported in deposits (see Note 13) and interest expense is recognized on the senior deposit note.

Holders of WesTS are eligible to receive semi-annual non-cumulative fixed cash distributions. No cash distributions will be payable by CWB Capital Trust on WesTS if CWB fails to declare regular dividends on its preferred shares or, if no preferred shares are outstanding, on its common shares. In this case, the net distributable funds of CWB Capital Trust will be distributed to the Bank as holder of the residual interest in CWB Capital Trust.

Should CWB Capital Trust fail to pay the semi-annual distributions in full, CWB has contractually agreed not to declare dividends of any kind on any of the preferred or common shares for a specified period of time.

The following information presents the outstanding WesTS:

Issuance date	August 31, 2006
Distribution dates	June 30, December 31
Annual yield	6.199%
Earliest date redeemable at the option of the issuer	December 31, 2011
Earliest date exchangeable at the option of the holder	Anytime
Trust capital securities outstanding	105,000
Principal amount	$105,000

The significant terms and conditions of the WesTS are

1) Subject to the approval of OSFI, CWB Capital Trust may, in whole (but not in part), on the redemption date specified above, and on any distribution date thereafter, redeem the WesTS without the consent of the holders.

2) Subject to the approval of OSFI, upon occurrence of a special event as defined, prior to the redemption date specified above, CWB Capital Trust may redeem all, but not part, of the WesTS without the consent of the holders.

3) The WesTS may be redeemed for cash equivalent to (i) the early redemption price if the redemption occurs prior to December 31, 2016 or (ii) the redemption price if the redemption occurs on or after December 31, 2016. Redemption price refers to an amount equal to one thousand dollars plus the unpaid distributions to the redemption date. Early redemption price refers to an amount equal to the greater of (i) the redemption price and (ii) the price calculated to provide an annual yield, equal to the yield on a Government of Canada bond issued on the redemption date with a maturity date of December 31, 2016, plus 0.50%.

4) Holders of WesTS may, at any time, exchange each one thousand dollars of principal for 40 First Preferred Shares Series 1 of the Bank. CWB's First Preferred Shares Series 1 pay semi-annual non-cumulative cash dividends with an annual yield of 4.00% and will be redeemable at the option of the Bank, with OSFI approval, on or after December 31, 2011, but not at the option of the holders. This exchange right will be effected through the conversion by CWB Capital Trust of the corresponding amount of the deposit note of the Bank. The WesTS exchanged for the Bank's First Preferred Shares Series 1 will be cancelled by CWB Capital Trust.

5) Each WesTS will be exchanged automatically without the consent of the holders for 40 non-cumulative redeemable CWB First Preferred Shares Series 2 upon occurrence of any one of the following events: (i) proceedings are commenced for the winding up of the Bank, (ii) OSFI takes control of the Bank, (iii) the Bank has a Tier 1 capital ratio of less than 5% or Total capital ratio of less than 8%, or (iv) OSFI has directed the Bank to increase its capital or provide additional liquidity and the Bank elects such automatic exchange or the Bank fails to comply with such direction. Following the occurrence of an automatic exchange, the Bank would hold all of the Special Trust Securities and all of the WesTS, and the primary asset of CWB Capital Trust would continue to be the senior deposit note. The Bank's First Preferred Shares Series 2 pay semi-annual non-cumulative cash dividends with an annual yield of 5.25% and will be redeemable at the option of the Bank, with OSFI approval, on or after December 31, 2011, but not at the option of the holders.

6) For regulatory capital purposes, WesTS are included in Tier 1 capital to a maximum of 15% of net Tier 1 capital with the remainder included in Tier 2 capital. All of the outstanding WesTS amount are currently included in Tier 1 capital.

7) The non-cumulative cash distribution on the WesTS will be 6.199% paid semi-annually until December 31, 2016 and, thereafter, at CDOR 180-day Bankers' Acceptance rate plus 2.55%.

15. INSURANCE RELATED OTHER LIABILITIES

	2008	2007
Unpaid claims and adjustment expenses	$ 76,176	$ 68,561
Unearned premiums	56,799	54,537
Due to insurance companies and policyholders	987	558
Unearned reinsurance commissions	807	824
Total	$ 134,769	$ 124,480

16. OTHER LIABILITIES

		2008	2007
Accrued interest payable		$ 101,584	$ 97,869
Accounts payable		24,895	26,265
Taxes payable		5,260	4,455
Deferred revenue		2,485	2,570
Leasehold inducements		1,373	1,588
Future income tax liability	(Note 24)	1,300	1,550
Other		–	368
Total		$ 136,897	$ 134,665

17. SUBORDINATED DEBENTURES

Financing costs relating to the issuance of subordinated debentures are amortized over the expected life of the related subordinated debenture using the effective interest method.

Each of the following qualifies as a bank debenture under the Bank Act and is subordinate in right of payment to all deposit liabilities. All redemptions are subject to the approval of OSFI.

Interest Rate	Maturity Date	Earliest Date Redeemable by CWB at Par	2008	2007
5.550%[1]	November 19, 2014	November 20, 2009	$ 60,000	$ 60,000
5.426%[2]	November 21, 2015	November 22, 2010	70,000	70,000
5.070%[3]	March 21, 2017	March 22, 2012	120,000	120,000
5.571%[4]	March 21, 2022	March 22, 2017	75,000	75,000
5.950%[5]	June 27, 2018	June 27, 2013	50,000	–
5.660%[6]	July 7, 2013	July 8, 2008	–	30,000
5.960%[6]	October 24, 2013	October 25, 2008	–	35,000
			$ 375,000	$ 390,000

(1) These conventional debentures have a 10-year term with a fixed interest rate for the first five years. Thereafter, the interest rate will be reset quarterly at the Canadian dollar CDOR 90-day Bankers' Acceptance rate plus 160 basis points.

(2) These conventional debentures have a 10-year term with a fixed interest rate for the first five years. Thereafter, the interest rate will be reset quarterly at the Canadian dollar CDOR 90-day Bankers' Acceptance rate plus 180 basis points.

(3) These conventional debentures have a 10-year term with a fixed interest rate for the first five years. Thereafter, the interest rate will be reset quarterly at the Canadian dollar CDOR 90-day Bankers' Acceptance rate plus 155 basis points. Of the $125,000 debentures issued, $5,000 were acquired by Canadian Direct Insurance Incorporated, a wholly owned subsidiary, and have been eliminated on consolidation.

(4) These conventional debentures have a 15-year term with a fixed interest rate for the first 10 years. Thereafter, the interest rate will be reset quarterly at the Canadian dollar CDOR 90-day Bankers' Acceptance rate plus 180 basis points.

(5) These conventional debentures have a 10-year term with a fixed interest rate for the first five years. Thereafter, the interest rate will be reset quarterly at the Canadian dollar CDOR 90-day Bankers' Acceptance rate plus 302 basis points.

(6) These conventional debentures had a 10-year term with a fixed interest rate for the first five years and were redeemed by the Bank at face value on July 8 and October 25, 2008, respectively.

18. CAPITAL STOCK

Authorized:

An unlimited number of common shares without nominal or par value;

33,964,324 class A shares without nominal or par value; and

25,000,000 first preferred shares without nominal or par value, issuable in series, of which 4,200,000 first preferred shares Series 1 and 4,200,000 first preferred shares Series 2 have been reserved (see Note 14).

Issued and fully paid:

	2008		2007	
	Number of Shares	Amount	Number of Shares	Amount
Common Shares				
Outstanding at beginning of year	62,836,189 $	219,004	61,936,260 $	215,349
Issued on exercise or exchange of options	620,953	1,646	899,929	2,464
Transferred from contributed surplus on exercise or exchange of options	–	1,264	–	1,191
Outstanding at end of year	63,457,142 $	221,914	62,836,189 $	219,004

The Bank is prohibited by the Bank Act from declaring any dividends on common shares when the Bank is or would be placed, as a result of the declaration, in contravention of the capital adequacy and liquidity regulations or any regulatory directives issued under the Act. In addition, should CWB Capital Trust fail to pay the semi-annual distributions in full on the CWB Capital Trust Securities Series 1 (see Note 14), the Bank has contractually agreed to not declare dividends on any of its common and preferred shares for a specified period of time. These limitations do not restrict the current level of dividends.

19. SHARE INCENTIVE PLAN

The fair value based method has been adopted to account for stock options granted to employees on or after November 1, 2002. The estimated fair value is recognized over the applicable vesting period as an increase to both salary expense and contributed surplus. In accordance with GAAP, no expense is recognized for options granted prior to November 1, 2002. When options are exercised, the proceeds received and the applicable amount, if any, in contributed surplus are credited to capital stock.

The Bank has authorized 5,505,404 common shares (2007 – 5,176,357) for issuance under the share incentive plan. Of the amount authorized, options exercisable into 5,204,882 shares (2007 – 4,911,277) are issued and outstanding. The options generally vest within three years and are exercisable at a fixed price equal to the average of the market price on the day of and the four days preceding the grant date. All options expire within eight years of date of grant. Outstanding options expire on dates ranging from December 2008 to September 2013.

The details of, and changes in, the issued and outstanding options follow:

	2008		2007	
	Number	Weighted Average Exercise	Number	Weighted Average Exercise
Options	of Options	Price	of Options	Price
Balance at beginning of year	4,911,277 $	16.96	5,030,040 $	13.07
Granted	1,249,032	28.39	1,118,000	25.49
Exercised or exchanged	(838,177)	8.98	(1,122,863)	7.61
Forfeited	(117,250)	24.26	(113,900)	20.98
Balance at end of year	5,204,882 $	20.83	4,911,277 $	16.96
Exercisable at end of year	1,870,500 $	13.10	1,656,077 $	9.30

Further details relating to stock options outstanding and exercisable follow:

	Options Outstanding			Options Exercisable	
Range of Exercise Prices	Number of Options	Weighted Average Remaining Contractual Life (years)	Weighted Average Exercise Price	Number of Options	Weighted Average Exercise Price
$10.00 to $10.84	863,800	0.7	$ 10.08	863,800	$ 10.08
$11.18 to $17.58	1,052,700	1.8	15.77	1,006,700	15.69
$19.16 to $21.46	1,068,290	3.1	21.45	–	–
$22.29 to $26.38	1,640,500	3.8	25.68	–	–
$28.11 to $31.18	579,592	4.1	31.15	–	–
Total	5,204,882	2.8	$ 20.83	1,870,500	$ 13.10

The terms of the share incentive plan allow the holders of vested options a cashless settlement alternative whereby the option holder can either (a) elect to receive shares by delivering cash to the Bank in the amount of the option exercise price or (b) elect to receive the number of shares equivalent to the excess of the market value of the shares under option, determined at the exercise date, over the exercise price. Of the 838,177 (2007 – 1,122,863) options exercised or exchanged, option holders exchanged the rights to 651,727 (2007 – 796,213) options and received 434,503 (2007 – 572,777) shares in return under the cashless settlement alternative.

Salary expense of $5,817 (2007 – $4,532) was recognized relating to the estimated fair value of options granted since November 1, 2002. The fair value of options granted was estimated using a binomial option pricing model with the following variables and assumptions: (i) risk-free interest rate of 3.8% (2007 – 4.2%), (ii) expected option life of 4.0 (2007 – 4.0) years, (iii) expected volatility of 23% (2007 – 19%), and (iv) expected dividends of 1.49% (2007 – 1.31%). The weighted average fair value of options granted was estimated at $5.84 (2007 – $4.94) per share.

During the year, $1,264 (2007 – $1,191) was transferred from contributed surplus to share capital, representing the estimated fair value recognized for 804,177 (2007 – 795,863) options granted after November 1, 2002 and exercised during the year.

20. CONTINGENT LIABILITIES AND COMMITMENTS

a) Credit Instruments

In the normal course of business, the Bank enters into various commitments and has contingent liabilities which are not reflected in the consolidated balance sheets. These items are reported below and are expressed in terms of the contractual amount of the related commitment.

	2008	2007
Credit Instruments		
Guarantees and standby letters of credit	$ 232,649	$ 202,194
Commitments to extend credit	3,190,420	2,367,215
Total	$ 3,423,069	$ 2,569,409

Guarantees and standby letters of credit represent the Bank's obligation to make payments to third parties when a customer is unable to make required payments or meet other contractual obligations. These instruments carry the same credit risk, recourse and collateral security requirements as loans extended to customers and generally have a term that does not exceed one year. Losses, if any, resulting from these transactions are not expected to be material.

Commitments to extend credit to customers also arise in the normal course of business and include undrawn availability under lines of credit and commercial operating loans of $931,957 (2007 – $800,301) and recently authorized but unfunded loan commitments of $2,258,463 (2007 – $1,566,915). In the majority of instances, availability of undrawn commercial commitments is subject to the borrower meeting specified financial tests or other covenants regarding completion or satisfaction of certain conditions precedent. It is also usual practice to include the right to review and withhold funding in the event of a material adverse change in the financial condition of the borrower. From a liquidity perspective, undrawn credit authorizations will be funded over time, with draws in many cases extending over a period of months. In some instances, authorizations are never advanced or may be reduced because of changing requirements. Revolving credit authorizations are subject to repayment which, on a pooled basis, also decreases liquidity risk.

b) Lease Commitments

The Bank has obligations under long-term non-cancellable operating leases for the rental of premises. Minimum future lease commitments for each of the five succeeding years and thereafter are as follows:

2009	$	8,036
2010		7,931
2011		7,678
2012		7,355
2013		7,334
2014 and thereafter		28,873
Total	$	67,207

c) Guarantees

A guarantee is defined as a contract that contingently requires the guarantor to make payments to a third party based on i) changes in an underlying economic characteristic that is related to an asset, liability or equity security of the guaranteed party, ii) failure of another party to perform under an obligating agreement, or iii) failure of another third party to pay indebtedness when due.

Significant guarantees provided to third parties include guarantees and standby letters of credit as discussed above.

In the ordinary course of business, the Bank enters into contractual arrangements under which the Bank may agree to indemnify the other party. Under these agreements, the Bank may be required to compensate counterparties for costs incurred as a result of various contingencies, such as changes in laws and regulations and litigation claims. A maximum potential liability cannot be identified as the terms of these arrangements vary and generally no predetermined amounts or limits are identified. The likelihood of occurrence of contingent events that would trigger payment under these arrangements is either remote or difficult to predict and, in the past, payments under these arrangements have been insignificant.

The Bank issues personal and business credit cards through an agreement with a third party card issuer. The Bank has indemnified the card issuer from loss if there is a default on the issuer's collection of the business credit card balances. The Bank has provided no indemnification relating to the personal or reward credit card balances. The issuance of business credit cards and establishment of business credit card limits are approved by the Bank and subject to the same credit assessment, approval and monitoring as the extension of direct loans. At year-end, the total approved business credit card limit was $11,503 (2007 – $9,728), and the balance outstanding was $2,778 (2007 – $2,238).

No amounts are reflected in the consolidated financial statements related to these guarantees and indemnifications.

d) Legal Proceedings

In the ordinary course of business, the Bank and its subsidiaries are party to legal proceedings. Based on current knowledge, the Bank does not expect the outcome of any of these proceedings to have a material effect on the consolidated financial position or results of operations.

21. INSURANCE OPERATIONS

Premiums Earned and Deferred Policy Acquisition Costs
Insurance premiums are included in other income on a daily pro rata basis over the terms of the underlying insurance policies. Unearned premiums represent the portion of premiums written that relate to the unexpired term of the policies in force and are included in other liabilities.

Policy acquisition costs are those expenses incurred in the acquisition of insurance business. Acquisition costs comprise advertising and marketing expenses, insurance advisor salaries and benefits, premium taxes and other expenses directly attributable to the production of business. Policy acquisition costs related to unearned premiums are only deferred, and included in other assets, to the extent that they are expected to be recovered from unearned premiums and are amortized to income over the periods in which the premiums are earned. If the unearned premiums are not sufficient to pay expected claims and expenses (including policy maintenance expenses and unamortized policy acquisition costs), a premium deficiency is said to exist. Anticipated investment income is considered in determining whether a premium deficiency exists. Premium deficiencies are recognized by writing down the deferred policy acquisition cost asset.

Unpaid Claims and Adjustment Expenses
The provision for unpaid claims represents the amounts needed to provide for the estimated ultimate expected cost of settling claims related to insured events (both reported and unreported) that have occurred on or before each balance sheet date. The provision for adjustment expenses represents the estimated ultimate expected costs of investigating, resolving and processing these claims. These provisions are included in other liabilities and their computation takes into account the time value of money using discount rates based on projected investment income from the assets supporting the provisions.

All provisions are periodically reviewed and evaluated in light of emerging claims experience and changing circumstances. The resulting changes in estimates of the ultimate liability are recorded as incurred claims in the current period.

Reinsurance Ceded

Earned premiums and claims expenses are recorded net of amounts ceded to, and recoverable from, reinsurers. Estimates of amounts recoverable from reinsurers on unpaid claims and adjustment expenses are recorded in other assets and are estimated in a manner consistent with the liabilities associated with the reinsured policies.

a) **Insurance Revenues, Net**

Insurance revenues, net reported in other income on the consolidated statements of income is presented net of claims, adjustment expenses and policy acquisition costs.

	2008	2007
Net earned premiums	$ 97,943	$ 94,914
Commissions and processing fees	2,876	2,751
Net claims and adjustment expenses	(64,380)	(62,391)
Policy acquisition costs	(20,573)	(20,011)
Insurance revenues, net	$ 15,866	$ 15,263

b) **Unpaid Claims and Adjustment Expenses**

(i) Nature of Unpaid Claims

The establishment of the provision for unpaid claims and adjustment expenses and the related reinsurers' share is based on known facts and interpretation of circumstances and is, therefore, a complex and dynamic process influenced by a large variety of factors. These factors include experience with similar cases and historical trends involving claim payment patterns, loss payments, pending levels of unpaid claims, product mix or concentration, claims severity, and claims frequency patterns.

Other factors include the continually evolving and changing regulatory and legal environment, actuarial studies, professional experience and expertise of the claims department personnel and independent adjusters retained to handle individual claims, quality of the data used for projection purposes, existing claims management practices, including claims handling and settlement practices, effect of inflationary trends on future claims settlement costs, investment rates of return, court decisions, economic conditions and public attitudes. In addition, time can be a critical part of the provision determination since, the longer the span between the incidence of a loss and the payment or settlement of the claim, the more variable the ultimate settlement amount can be. Accordingly, short-tailed claims, such as property claims, tend to be more reasonably predictable than long-tailed claims, such as liability claims.

Consequently, the establishment of the provision for unpaid claims and adjustment expenses relies on the judgment and opinions of a large number of individuals, on historical precedent and trends, on prevailing legal, economic, social and regulatory trends and on expectations as to future developments. The process of determining the provisions necessarily involves risks that the actual results will deviate, perhaps substantially, from the best estimates made.

(ii) Provision for Unpaid Claims and Adjustment Expenses

An annual evaluation of the adequacy of unpaid claims is completed at the end of each financial year. This evaluation includes a re-estimation of the liability for unpaid claims relating to each preceding financial year compared to the liability that was originally established. The results of this comparison and the changes in the provision for unpaid claims and adjustment expenses follow:

	2008	2007
Unpaid claims and adjustment expenses, net, beginning of year	$ 50,389	$ 40,561
Claims incurred		
In the current year	67,457	62,406
In prior periods	(3,077)	(15)
Claims paid during the year	(57,093)	(52,563)
Unpaid claims and adjustment expenses, net, end of year	57,676	50,389
Reinsurers' share of unpaid claims and adjustment expenses	11,561	10,915
Recoverable on unpaid claims	6,939	7,257
Unpaid claims and adjustment expenses, net, end of year	$ 76,176	$ 68,561

The provision for unpaid claims and adjustment expenses and related reinsurance recoveries are discounted using rates based on the projected investment income from the assets supporting the provisions, and reflecting the estimated timing of payments and recoveries. The investment rate of return used for all cash flow periods and all lines of business was 4.1% (2007 – 4.3%). However, that rate was reduced by a 1% (2007 – 1%) provision for adverse deviation in discounting the provision for unpaid claims and adjustment expenses and related reinsurance recoveries. The impact of this provision for adverse deviation results in an increase of $850 (2007 – $821) in unpaid claims and adjustment expenses and related reinsurance recoveries.

Policy balances, included in insurance related other assets and other liabilities, analyzed by major lines of business are as follows:

	2008		2007	
	Automobile	Home	Automobile	Home
Unpaid claims and adjustment expenses	$ 64,181	$ 11,995	$ 59,379	$ 9,182
Reinsurers' share of unpaid claims and adjustment expenses	11,561	–	10,904	11
Unearned premiums	40,886	15,913	40,741	13,796

c) **Underwriting Policy and Reinsurance Ceded**

Reinsurance contracts with coverage up to maximum policy limits are entered into to protect against losses in excess of certain amounts that may arise from automobile, personal property and liability claims.

Reinsurance with a limit of $180,000 (2007 – $180,000) is obtained to protect against certain catastrophic losses. Retention on catastrophic events and property and liability risks is generally $1,000 (2007 – $1,000). Retentions are further reduced by quota share reinsurance and, for the British Columbia automobile insurance product, by the underlying mandatory coverage provided by the provincially governed Crown corporation. Due to the geographic concentration of the business, management believes earthquakes and windstorms are its most significant exposure to catastrophic losses. Utilizing sophisticated computer modelling techniques developed by independent consultants to quantify the estimated exposure to such losses, management believes there is sufficient catastrophe reinsurance protection.

There was no quota share agreement in effect for the past two years. The previous quota share agreement, ceding 10% of gross retention, expired October 31, 2006.

At October 31, 2008, $11,561 (2007 – $10,915) of unpaid claims and adjustment expenses were recorded as recoverable from reinsurers. Failure of a reinsurer to honour its obligation could result in losses. The financial condition of reinsurers is regularly evaluated to minimize the exposure to significant losses from reinsurer insolvency.

The amounts shown in other income are net of the following amounts relating to reinsurance ceded to other insurance companies:

	2008	2007
Premiums earned reduced by	$ 6,849	$ 7,057
Claims incurred reduced by	2,987	1,466

22. DISCLOSURES ON RATE REGULATION

Canadian Direct Insurance Incorporated (Canadian Direct), a wholly owned subsidiary, is licensed under insurance legislation in the provinces in which it conducts business. Automobile insurance is a compulsory product and is subject to different regulations across the provinces in Canada, including those with respect to rate setting. Rate setting mechanisms vary across the provinces, but they generally fall under three categories: "use and file", "file and use" and "file and approve". Under "use and file", rates are filed following use. Under "file and use", insurers file their rates with the relevant authorities and wait for a prescribed period of time and then implement the proposed rates. Under "file and approve", insurers must wait for specific approval of filed rates before they may be used.

The authorities that regulate automobile insurance rates, in the provinces in which Canadian Direct is writing that business, are listed below. Automobile direct written premiums in these provinces totaled $71,300 in 2008 (2007 – $71,700) and represented 100% (2007 – 100%) of direct automobile premiums written.

Province	Rate Filing	Regulatory Authority
Alberta	File and approve or File and use	Alberta Automobile Insurance Rate Board
British Columbia	File and use	British Columbia Utilities Commission

Relevant regulatory authorities may, in some circumstances, require retroactive rate adjustments, which could result in a regulatory asset or liability. At October 31, 2008, there was no regulatory asset or liability.

23. EMPLOYEE FUTURE BENEFITS

All employee future benefits are accounted for on an accrual basis. The Bank's contributions to the group retirement savings plan and employee share purchase plan totaled $6,183 (2007 – $4,876).

24. INCOME TAXES

The Bank follows the asset and liability method of accounting for income taxes whereby current income taxes are recognized for the estimated income taxes payable for the current year. Future tax assets and liabilities represent the cumulative amount of tax applicable to temporary differences between the carrying amount of the assets and liabilities, and their values for tax purposes. Future tax assets and liabilities are measured using enacted or substantively enacted tax rates expected to apply to taxable income in the years in which those temporary differences are expected to be recovered or settled. Changes in future income taxes related to a change in tax rates are recognized in income in the period of the tax rate change. All future income tax assets are expected to be realized in the normal course of operations.

The provision for income taxes consists of the following:

	2008	2007
Consolidated statements of income		
Current	$ 43,725	$ 38,267
Future	276	1,387
	44,001	39,654
Shareholders' equity		
Future income tax expense related to:		
Unrealized losses on available-for-sale securities	(2,624)	(2,864)
Gains on derivatives designated as cash flow hedges	2,900	685
	276	(2,179)
Total	$ 44,277	$ 37,475

A reconciliation of the statutory tax rates and income tax that would be payable at these rates to the effective income tax rates and provision for income taxes that is reported in the consolidated statements of income follows:

	2008		2007	
Combined Canadian federal and provincial income taxes				
and statutory tax rate	$ 44,536	30.5%	$ 44,832	33.0%
Increase (decrease) arising from:				
Tax-exempt income	(3,579)	(2.5)	(4,124)	(3.0)
Stock-based compensation	1,774	1.2	1,486	1.1
Future federal and provincial tax rate reductions[1]	999	0.7	–	–
Income tax recovery	–	–	(3,495)	(2.6)
Other	271	0.2	955	0.7
Provision for income taxes and effective tax rate	$ 44,001	30.1%	$ 39,654	29.2%

(1) Future federal and provincial tax rate reductions represent the revaluation of future income tax assets to reflect corporate income tax rate reductions enacted for accounting purposes.

Future income tax balances are comprised of the following:

	2008	2007
Net future income tax assets		
Allowance for credit losses	$ 16,103	$ 16,235
Other temporary differences	39	709
	$ 16,142	$ 16,944
Net future income tax liabilities		
Intangible assets	$ 742	$ 923
Allowance for credit losses	(845)	(729)
Other temporary differences	1,403	1,356
	$ 1,300	$ 1,550

The Bank has approximately $11,140 (2007 – $11,140) of capital losses that are available to apply against future capital gains and have no expiry date. The tax benefit of these losses has not been recognized in the consolidated financial statements.

25. EARNINGS PER COMMON SHARE

Basic earnings per common share is calculated based on the average number of common shares outstanding during the year. Diluted earnings per share is calculated based on the treasury stock method, which assumes that any proceeds from the exercise of in-the-money stock options would be used to purchase the Bank's common shares at the average market price during the year.

The calculation of earnings per common share follows:

	2008	2007
Numerator		
Net income - basic and diluted	$ 102,019	$ 96,282
Denominator		
Weighted average of common shares outstanding - basic	63,214,117	62,354,101
Dilutive instruments:		
Employee stock options[1]	1,227,017	1,897,449
Weighted average number of common shares outstanding - diluted	64,441,134	64,251,550
Earnings per Common Share		
Basic	$ 1.61	$ 1.54
Diluted	1.58	1.50

(1) At October 31, the denominator excludes 3,334,382 (2007 – 365,000) employee stock options with an average adjusted exercise price of $27.45 (2007 – $31.38) where the exercise price, adjusted for unrecognized stock-based compensation, is greater than the average market price.

26. TRUST ASSETS UNDER ADMINISTRATION

Trust assets under administration of $4,347,723 (2007 – $4,283,900) represent the fair value of assets held for personal and corporate clients, administered by subsidiaries, and are kept separate from the subsidiaries' own assets. Trust assets under administration are not reflected in the consolidated balance sheets and relate to the banking and trust segment.

27. RELATED PARTY TRANSACTIONS

The Bank makes loans, primarily residential mortgages, to its officers and employees at various preferred rates and terms. The total amount outstanding for these types of loans is $64,836 (2007 – $56,045). The Bank offers deposits, primarily fixed term deposits to its officers, employees and their immediate family at preferred rates. The total amount outstanding for these types of deposits is $127,219 (2007 – $102,776).

28. INTEREST RATE SENSITIVITY

The Bank is exposed to interest rate risk as a result of a difference, or gap, between the maturity or repricing behaviour of interest sensitive assets and liabilities. The interest rate gap is managed by forecasting core balance trends. The repricing profile of these assets and liabilities has been incorporated in the table following showing the gap position at October 31 for select time intervals. Figures in brackets represent an excess of liabilities over assets or a negative gap position.

October 31, 2008	Floating Rate and Within 1 Month	1 to 3 Months	3 Months to 1 Year	Total Within 1 Year	1 Year to 5 Years	More than 5 Years	Non-Interest Sensitive	Total
Assets								
Cash resources and securities	$ 176	$ 220	$ 339	$ 735	$ 921	$ 46	$ 18	$ 1,720
Loans	4,964	484	774	6,222	2,461	95	(77)	8,701
Other assets	–	–	–	–	–	–	179	179
Derivative financial instruments[1]	–	80	150	230	367	–	–	597
Total	5,140	784	1,263	7,187	3,749	141	120	11,197
Liabilities and Equity								
Deposits	3,472	883	1,967	6,322	2,832	105	(14)	9,245
Other liabilities	3	6	25	34	33	9	225	301
Debentures	–	–	–	–	300	75	–	375
Shareholders' equity	–	–	–	–	–	–	679	679
Derivative financial instruments[1]	597	–	–	597	–	–	–	597
Total	4,072	889	1,992	6,953	3,165	189	890	11,197
Interest Rate Sensitive Gap	$ 1,068	$ (105)	$ (729)	$ 234	$ 584	$ (48)	$ (770)	$ –
Cumulative Gap	$ 1,068	$ 963	$ 234	$ 234	$ 818	$ 770	$ –	$ –
Cumulative Gap as a Percentage of Total Assets	9.5%	8.6%	2.1%	2.1%	7.3%	6.9%	–	–
October 31, 2007								
Total assets	$ 4,377	$ 552	$ 1,868	$ 6,797	$ 2,921	$ 195	$ 100	$ 10,013
Total liabilities and equity	4,013	692	1,666	6,371	2,638	194	810	10,013
Interest Rate Sensitive Gap	$ 364	$ (140)	$ 202	$ 426	$ 283	$ 1	$ (710)	$ –
Cumulative Gap	$ 364	$ 224	$ 426	$ 426	$ 709	$ 710	$ –	$ –
Cumulative Gap as a Percentage of Total Assets	3.6%	2.2%	4.3%	4.3%	7.1%	7.1%	–	–

(1) Derivative financial instruments are included in this table at the notional amount.
(2) Accrued interest is excluded in calculating interest sensitive assets and liabilities.
(3) Potential prepayments of fixed rate loans and early redemption of redeemable fixed term deposits have not been estimated. Redemptions of fixed term deposits where depositors have this option are not expected to be material. The majority of fixed rate loans, mortgages and leases are either closed or carry prepayment penalties.

The effective, weighted average interest rates for each class of financial asset and liability are shown below.

(%)

October 31, 2008	Floating Rate and Within 1 Month	1 to 3 Months	3 Months to 1 Year	Total Within 1 Year	1 Year to 5 Years	More than 5 Years	Total
Assets							
Cash resources and securities	2.7%	3.0%	3.2%	3.0%	4.4%	5.8%	3.8%
Loans	4.8	4.7	6.2	5.0	6.1	5.9	5.3
Derivative financial instruments	–	4.1	3.7	3.8	3.5	–	3.6
Total	4.7	4.2	5.1	4.8	5.4	5.8	5.0
Liabilities							
Deposits	2.1	3.6	4.0	2.9	4.2	6.4	3.3
Debentures	–	–	–	–	5.4	5.6	5.4
Derivative financial instruments	2.9	–	–	2.9	–	–	2.9
Total	2.2	3.6	4.0	2.9	4.2	5.7	3.4
Interest Rate Sensitive Gap	2.5%	0.6%	1.1%	1.9%	1.2%	0.1%	1.6%
October 31, 2007							
Total assets	6.6%	5.2%	5.2%	6.1%	5.9%	5.7%	6.0%
Total liabilities	3.9	4.4	4.3	4.1	4.2	5.6	4.1
Interest Rate Sensitive Gap	2.7%	0.8%	0.9%	2.0%	1.7%	0.1%	1.9%

Based on the current interest rate gap position, it is estimated that a one-percentage point increase in all interest rates would increase net interest income by approximately 4.8% (2007 – 2.5%) and decrease other comprehensive income by $19,982, net of tax. A one-percentage point decrease in all interest rates would decrease net interest income and increase other comprehensive income by a similar amount. Information on the estimated change in other comprehensive income at October 2007 is not readily available.

29. FAIR VALUE OF FINANCIAL INSTRUMENTS

The fair value of a financial instrument on initial recognition is the value of the consideration given or received. Subsequent to initial recognition, financial instruments measured at fair value that are quoted in active markets are based on bid prices for financial assets and offer prices for financial liabilities. For certain securities and derivative financial instruments where an active market does not exist, fair values are determined using valuation techniques that refer to observable market data, including discounted cash flow analysis, option pricing models and other valuation techniques commonly used by market participants. The fair value of financial assets recorded on the consolidated balance sheets at fair value (cash, securities, securities purchased under resale agreements and derivatives) was determined using published market prices quoted in active markets for 92% (2007 – 87%) of the portfolio and estimated using a valuation technique based on observable market data for 8% (2007 – 13%) of the portfolio. The fair value of liabilities recorded on the consolidated balance sheets at fair value (derivatives) was determined using a valuation technique based on observable market data.

Fair value represents the estimated consideration that would be agreed upon in a current transaction between knowledgeable, willing parties who are under no compulsion to act. The fair value of a financial instrument on initial recognition is normally the transaction price (i.e. the value of the consideration given or received). Subsequent to initial recognition, financial instruments measured at fair value on the consolidated balance sheets that are quoted in active markets are based on bid prices for financial assets and offer prices for financial liabilities. For certain securities and derivative financial instruments where an active market does not exist, fair values are determined using valuation techniques that refer to observable market data, including discounted cash flow analysis, option pricing models and other valuation techniques commonly used by market participants.

Several of the Bank's significant financial instruments, such as loans and deposits, lack an available trading market as they are not typically exchanged. Therefore, these instruments have been valued assuming they will not be sold, using present value or other suitable techniques and are not necessarily representative of the amounts realizable in an immediate settlement of the instrument.

Changes in interest rates are the main cause of changes in the fair value of the Bank's financial instruments. The carrying value of loans, deposits and subordinated debentures are not adjusted to reflect increases or decreases in fair value due to interest rate changes as the Bank's intention is to realize their value over time by holding them to maturity.

The table below sets out the fair values of financial instruments (including certain derivatives) using the valuation methods and assumptions referred to below the table. The table does not include assets and liabilities that are not considered financial instruments.

		2008			2007		
		Book Value	Fair Value	Fair Value Over (Under) Book Value	Book Value	Fair Value	Fair Value Over (Under) Book Value
Assets							
Cash resources	(Note 3)	$ 492,173	$ 492,173	$ –	$ 412,690	$ 412,690	$ –
Securities	(Note 4)	1,228,964	1,228,964	–	1,341,626	1,341,626	–
Securities purchased under				–			
resale agreements		77,000	77,000	–	206,925	206,925	–
Loans[1]		8,700,672	8,635,811	(64,861)	7,406,733	7,325,340	(81,393)
Other assets[2]		82,782	82,782	–	77,573	77,573	–
Derivative related		9,980	9,980	–	1,496	1,496	–
Liabilities							
Deposits[1]		9,258,776	9,247,017	(11,759)	8,256,918	8,219,463	(37,455)
Other liabilities[3]		232,678	232,678	–	215,798	215,798	–
Subordinated debentures		375,000	387,774	12,774	390,000	386,690	(3,310)
Derivative related		163	163	–	1,307	1,307	–

(1) Loans and deposits exclude deferred premiums and deferred revenue, which are not financial instruments.
(2) Other assets exclude land, buildings and equipment, goodwill and other intangible assets, reinsurers' share of unpaid claims and adjustment expenses, future income tax asset, prepaid and deferred expenses, financing costs and other items that are not financial instruments.
(3) Other liabilities exclude future income tax liability, deferred revenue, unearned insurance premiums and other items that are not financial instruments.
(4) For further information on interest rates associated with financial assets and liabilities, including derivative instruments, refer to Note 28.

The methods and assumptions used to estimate the fair values of financial instruments are as follows:

· cash resources and securities are reported on the consolidated balance sheets at the fair value disclosed in Notes 3 and 4. These values are based on quoted market prices, if available. Where a quoted market price is not readily available, other valuation techniques are based on observable market rates used to estimate fair value;

· loans reflect changes in the general level of interest rates that have occurred since the loans were originated and are net of the allowance for credit losses. For floating rate loans, fair value is assumed to be equal to book value as the interest rates on these loans automatically reprice to market. For all other loans, fair value is estimated by discounting the expected future cash flows of these loans at current market rates for loans with similar terms and risks;

· other assets and other liabilities, with the exception of derivative financial instruments, are assumed to approximate their carrying value, due to their short-term nature;

· for derivative financial instruments where an active market does not exist, fair values are determined using valuation techniques that refer to observable market data, including discounted cash flow analysis, option pricing models and other valuation techniques commonly used by market participants;

· deposits with no stated maturity are assumed to be equal to their carrying values. The estimated fair values of fixed rate deposits are determined by discounting the contractual cash flows at current market rates for deposits of similar terms; and

· the fair values of subordinated debentures are determined by reference to current market prices for debt with similar terms and risks.

Fair values are based on management's best estimates based on market conditions and pricing policies at a certain point in time. The estimates are subjective and involve particular assumptions and matters of judgment and, as such, may not be reflective of future fair values.

30. RISK MANAGEMENT

As part of the Bank's risk management practices, the risks that are significant to the business are identified, monitored and controlled. The most significant risks include credit risk, liquidity risk, market risk, insurance risk, operational risk and litigation risk. The nature of these risks and how they are managed is provided in the commentary on pages 54 to 57 of the MD&A.

As permitted by the CICA, certain of the risk management disclosure related to risks inherent with financial instruments is in the Management Discussion & Analysis (MD&A). The relevant MD&A sections are identified by shading and the shaded areas form an integral part of these audited consolidated financial statements.

Information on specific measures of risk, including the allowance for credit losses, derivative financial instruments, interest rate sensitivity, fair value of financial instruments and liability for unpaid claims are included elsewhere in these notes to the consolidated financial statements.

31. CAPITAL MANAGEMENT

OSFI requires banks to measure capital adequacy in accordance with instructions for determining risk-adjusted capital and risk-weighted assets, including off-balance sheet commitments. Based on the deemed credit risk of each type of asset, a weighting of 0% to 150% is assigned. As an example, a loan that is fully insured by the Canada Mortgage and Housing Corporation (CMHC) is applied a risk weighting of 0% as the Bank's risk of loss is nil, while uninsured commercial loans are assigned a risk weighting of 100% to reflect the higher level of risk associated with this type of asset. The ratio of regulatory capital to risk-weighted assets is calculated and compared to OSFI's standards for Canadian financial institutions. Off-balance sheet assets, such as the notional amount of derivatives and some credit commitments, are included in the calculation of risk-weighted assets and both the credit risk equivalent and the risk-weight calculations are prescribed by OSFI. As Canadian Direct is subject to separate OSFI capital requirements specific to insurance companies, the Bank's investment in CDI is deducted from total capital and CDI's assets are excluded from the calculation of risk-weighted assets.

Current regulatory guidelines require banks to maintain a minimum ratio of capital to risk-weighted assets and off-balance sheet items of 8%, of which 4% must be core capital (Tier 1) and the remainder supplementary capital (Tier 2). However, OSFI has established that Canadian banks need to maintain a minimum total capital adequacy ratio of 10% with a Tier 1 ratio of not less than 7%. CWB's Tier 1 capital is comprised of common shareholders' equity and innovative capital (to a regulatory maximum of 15% of net Tier 1 capital), while Tier 2 capital includes subordinated debentures (to the regulatory maximum amount of 50% of net Tier 1 capital), the inclusion of the general allowance for credit losses (to the regulatory maximum) and any innovative capital not included in Tier 1.

Capital funds are managed in accordance with policies and plans that are regularly reviewed and approved by the Board of Directors and take into account forecasted capital needs and markets. The goal is to maintain adequate regulatory capital to be considered well capitalized, protect customer deposits and provide capacity for internally generated growth and strategic opportunities that do not otherwise require accessing the public capital markets, all while providing a satisfactory return for shareholders.

The Bank has a share incentive plan that is provided to officers and employees who are in a position to materially impact the longer term financial success of the Bank as measured by share price appreciation and dividend yield. Note 19 to the consolidated financial statements details the number of shares under options outstanding, the weighted average exercise price and the amounts exercisable at year-end.

Basel II Capital Adequacy Accord

Effective November 1, 2007, the Office of the Superintendent of Financial Institutions (OSFI) required Canadian financial institutions to manage and report regulatory capital in accordance with a new capital management framework, commonly called Basel II. Basel II introduced several significant changes to the risk-weighting of assets and the calculation of regulatory capital. The Bank has implemented the standardized approach to calculating risk-weighted assets for both credit and operational risk. Changes for CWB under Basel II include a reclassification into lower risk-weight categories for residential mortgages and loans to small- to medium-sized enterprises, as well as a new capital requirement related to operational risk.

Basel II had a modest positive impact on the overall required level of regulatory capital for CWB. New procedures and system enhancements were developed to conform to the new framework, including the formalization of internal capital adequacy assessment processes.

During the year, the Bank complied with all internal and external capital requirements.

CAPITAL STRUCTURE AND REGULATORY RATIOS AT YEAR-END

($ thousands)

	2008[1]	2007
Tier 1 Capital		
Retained earnings	$ 448,203	$ 372,739
Accumulated other comprehensive income, net of tax[2]	(6,973)	(1,741)
Capital stock	221,914	219,004
Contributed surplus	14,234	9,681
Innovative capital instrument[3]	105,000	105,000
Less goodwill of subsidiaries[7]	(6,933)	(3,679)
Total	775,445	701,004
Tier 2 Capital		
General allowance for credit losses (Tier A)[4]	60,527	55,627
Subordinated debentures (Tier B)[5]	380,000	350,502
Total	440,527	406,129
Less investment in insurance subsidiary	(47,700)	(47,864)
Total Regulatory Capital	$ 1,168,272	$ 1,059,269
Regulatory Capital to Risk-Weighted Assets		
Tier 1 capital	8.9%	9.1%
Tier 2 capital	5.1%	5.3%
Less investment in insurance subsidiary	(0.5)%	(0.7)%
Total Regulatory Capital Adequacy Ratio	13.5%	13.7%
Assets to Regulatory Capital Multiple[6]	9.2	9.1

(1) Regulatory capital and capital ratios are calculated in accordance with the requirements of the Office of the Superintendent of Financial Institutions. Beginning in 2008, capital is managed and reported in accordance with the requirements of the Basel II Capital Adequacy Accord (Basel II). Prior year ratios have been calculated using the previous framework.

(2) Accumulated other comprehensive income related to unrealized losses on certain available-for-sale equity securities, net of tax, reduces Tier 1 capital.

(3) Innovative capital may be included in Tier 1 capital to a maximum of 15% of net Tier 1 capital. Any excess innovative capital outstanding is included in Tier 2B capital.

(4) Banks are allowed to include their general allowance for credit losses up to a prescribed percentage of risk-weighted assets in Tier 2A capital. At October 31, 2008, the Bank's general allowance represented 0.70% (2007 – 0.72%) of risk-weighted assets.

(5) Tier 2B capital may be included in Tier 2 capital to a maximum of 50% of net Tier 1 capital. Any excess Tier 2B capital is included in capital as net Tier 1 capital increases. At October 31, 2008, $nil (2007 – $44,498) of subordinated debentures exceed the Tier 2B threshold and are available for inclusion in the future.

(6) Total assets plus off-balance sheet credit instruments, such as letters of credit and guarantees, less goodwill divided by regulatory capital.

(7) Beginning in 2008 with Basel II, goodwill related to the Bank's trust and insurance subsidiaries is deducted from Tier 1 capital. Prior to 2008, goodwill related to the insurance subsidiary was deducted from total capital.

32. SEGMENTED INFORMATION

The Bank operates principally in two industry segments – banking and trust, and insurance. These two segments differ in products and services but are both within the same geographic region.

The banking and trust segment provides services to personal clients and small- to medium-sized commercial business clients primarily in Western Canada. The insurance segment provides home and automobile insurance to individuals in Alberta and British Columbia.

	Banking and Trust		Insurance		Total	
	2008	2007	2008	2007	2008	2007
Net interest income (teb)[1]	$ 222,837	$ 205,867	$ 5,780	$ 4,792	$ 228,617	$ 210,659
Less teb adjustment	5,191	5,023	480	387	5,671	5,410
Net interest income per financial statements	217,646	200,844	5,300	4,405	222,946	205,249
Other income[2]	54,338	47,506	15,902	15,315	70,240	62,821
Total revenues	271,984	248,350	21,202	19,720	293,186	268,070
Provision for credit losses	12,000	10,200	–	–	12,000	10,200
Non-interest expenses[3]	125,748	113,456	9,418	8,478	135,166	121,934
Provision for income taxes	40,589	36,185	3,412	3,469	44,001	39,654
Net Income[5]	$ 93,647	$ 88,509	$ 8,372	$ 7,773	$ 102,019	$ 96,282
Total Average Assets ($ millions)[4]	$ 9,747	$ 8,014	$ 184	$ 164	$ 9,931	$ 8,178

(1) Taxable Equivalent Basis (teb) - Most banks analyze revenue on a taxable equivalent basis to permit uniform measurement and comparison of net interest income. Net interest income (as presented in the consolidated statements of income) includes tax-exempt income on certain securities. Since this income is not taxable, the rate of interest or dividends received is significantly lower than would apply to a loan or security of the same amount. The adjustment to taxable equivalent basis increases interest income and the provision for income taxes to what they would have been had the tax-exempt securities been taxed at the statutory rate. The taxable equivalent basis does not have a standardized meaning prescribed by GAAP and, therefore, may not be comparable to similar measures presented by other banks.

(2) Other income for the insurance segment is presented net of claims, adjustment costs and policy acquisition costs (see Note 21) and also includes the gain on the sale of securities.

(3) Amortization of intangible assets of $276 (2007 – $293) is included in the banking and trust segment and $250 (2007 – $250) in the insurance segment. Amortization of land, buildings and equipment total $5,040 (2007 – $4,365) for the banking and trust segment and $1,330 (2007 – $1,109) for the insurance segment while additions amounted to $10,552 (2007 – $6,010) for the banking and trust segment and $1,975 (2007 – $1,002) for the insurance segment. Goodwill of $3,679 (2007 – $3,679) is allocated to the banking and trust segment and $3,254 (2007 – $3,254) to the insurance segment.

(4) Assets are disclosed on an average daily balance basis as this measure is most relevant to a financial institution and is the measure reviewed by management.

(5) Transactions between the segments are reported at the exchange amount, which approximates fair market value.

33. SUBSEQUENT EVENT

On December 1, 2008, the Bank acquired 72.5% ownership of Adroit Investment Management Ltd. with an effective date of November 1, 2008. Adroit Investment Management Ltd. is an Edmonton, Alberta based firm specializing in wealth management for individuals, corporations and institutional clients.

34. SUBSIDIARIES AND AFFILIATE

CANADIAN WESTERN BANK SUBSIDIARIES[1]
(annexed in accordance with subsection 308(3) of the Bank Act)
OCTOBER 31, 2008

	Address of Head Office	Carrying Value of Voting Shares Owned by the Bank[2]
Canadian Direct Insurance Incorporated	Suite 600, 750 Cambie Street Vancouver, British Columbia	$ 50,820
Canadian Western Trust Company	Suite 2300, 10303 Jasper Avenue Edmonton, Alberta	45,879
Valiant Trust Company	Suite 310, 606 4th St. S.W. Calgary, Alberta	13,982
Canadian Western Financial Ltd.	Suite 2300, 10303 Jasper Avenue Edmonton, Alberta	1,334
Canadian Western Bank Capital Trust[3]	Suite 2300, 10303 Jasper Avenue Edmonton, Alberta	1,000

(1) The Bank owns 100% of the voting shares of each entity.
(2) The carrying value of voting shares is stated at the Bank's equity in the subsidiaries.
(3) In accordance with accounting standards, this entity is not consolidated as the Bank is not the primary beneficiary.

ANNUAL REPORT
For the Year Ended December 31, 2008

Auditors' Report

To the Shareholders of Sun-Rype Products Ltd.

We have audited the balance sheets of Sun-Rype Products Ltd. as at December 31, 2008 and 2007 and the statements of operations, comprehensive income, retained earnings and cash flows for the years then ended. These financial statements are the responsibility of the Company's management. Our responsibility is to express an opinion on these financial statements based on our audits.

We conducted our audits in accordance with Canadian generally accepted auditing standards. Those standards require that we plan and perform an audit to obtain reasonable assurance whether the financial statements are free of material misstatement. An audit includes examining, on a test basis, evidence supporting the amounts and disclosures in the financial statements. An audit also includes assessing the accounting principles used and significant estimates made by management, as well as evaluating the overall financial statement presentation.

In our opinion, these financial statements present fairly, in all material respects, the financial position of the Company as at December 31, 2008 and 2007 and the results of its operations and its cash flows for the years then ended in accordance with Canadian generally accepted accounting principles.

Deloitte & Touche LLP

Chartered Accountants
Vancouver, British Columbia
February 23, 2009

Sun-Rype Products Ltd.
Balance Sheets
As at December 31
(in thousands of dollars)

	2008	2007
Assets		
Current		
Cash	$ 625	$ 2,687
Accounts receivable	11,830	7,392
Unrealized foreign exchange gain on derivatives	718	-
Income taxes recoverable	6,987	818
Inventories (note 3)	27,778	17,304
Prepaid expenses	554	381
Future income taxes (note 4)	-	435
	48,492	29,017
Property, plant and equipment (note 5)	25,130	27,867
	$ 73,622	$ 56,884
Liabilities and Shareholders' Equity		
Current		
Bank operating loan (note 6)	$ 12,554	$ -
Promissory note payable (note 7)	400	500
Accounts payable and accrued liabilities	15,229	12,688
Unrealized foreign exchange loss on derivatives	-	460
Future income taxes (note 4)	11	-
Current portion, obligation under capital leases (note 8)	97	-
Current portion, long-term obligations (note 9)	220	321
Current portion, long-term debt (note 10)	1,500	-
	30,011	13,969
Obligation under capital leases (note 8)	395	-
Long-term obligations (note 9)	145	744
Long-term debt (note 10)	12,750	-
Future income taxes (note 4)	1,343	1,148
	44,644	15,861
Shareholders' equity		
Share capital and contributed surplus (note 11)	18,698	18,698
Retained earnings	10,280	22,325
	28,978	41,023
	$ 73,622	$ 56,884

Commitments, guarantees and contingencies   (note 16)

Approved by the Board of Directors

_____
D. Selman, Director

_____
D. Souter, Director

See accompanying notes to financial statements

Sun-Rype Products Ltd.
Statements of Operations and Comprehensive Income
For the years ended December 31
(in thousands of dollars, except per share amounts)

	2008	2007
Net sales (note 12)	$ 125,368	$ 135,134
Cost of sales (note 13)	111,277	93,298
Gross profit	14,091	41,836
Expenses		
Selling, general, and administrative	29,053	28,538
Amortization	2,288	4,186
Interest	879	148
Loss on disposal of property, plant and equipment	-	213
Foreign exchange loss	-	1,977
	32,220	35,062
Earnings (loss) before income taxes	(18,129)	6,774
Income taxes (note 4)	(6,456)	2,138
Net earnings (loss) and comprehensive income (loss)	$ (11,673)	$ 4,636
Earnings (loss) per share		
Basic and diluted	$ (1.08)	$ 0.43

See accompanying notes to financial statements

Sun-Rype Products Ltd.
Statements of Retained Earnings
For the years ended December 31
(in thousands of dollars)

	2008	2007
Retained earnings, beginning of year, as previously reported	$ 22,325	$ 19,310
Adoption of new accounting standards (note 2)	61	-
Retained earnings, beginning of year, as restated	22,386	19,310
Net earnings (loss)	(11,673)	4,636
Dividends paid	(433)	(1,621)
Retained earnings, end of year	$ 10,280	$ 22,325

See accompanying notes to financial statements

Sun-Rype Products Ltd.
Statements of Cash Flows
For the years ended December 31
(in thousands of dollars)

	2008	2007
Cash provided by (used in):		
Operating activities		
Net earnings (loss)	$ (11,673)	$ 4,636
Non-cash items:		
Deferred compensation (recovery)	(241)	168
Amortization	4,470	4,186
Loss on disposal of property, plant and equipment	-	213
Unrealized foreign exchange loss (gain)	(1,294)	784
Future income taxes	609	(310)
	(8,129)	9,677
Changes in non-cash working capital items (note 15)	(18,690)	913
	(26,819)	10,590
Financing activities		
Bank operating loan advances	27,554	-
Repayment of long-term debt	(750)	-
Reduction of obligation under capital leases	(79)	-
Reduction of long-term obligations	(459)	(232)
Dividends paid	(433)	(1,621)
	25,833	(1,853)
Investing activities		
Proceeds on disposal of property, plant and equipment	39	98
Payments for property, plant and equipment	(1,231)	(7,358)
	(1,192)	(7,260)
Effect of exchange rate changes on cash position	116	(324)
Increase (decrease) in cash position	(2,178)	1,153
Cash, beginning of year	2,687	1,534
Cash, end of year	$ 625	$ 2,687

Supplemental cash flow information   (note 15)

See accompanying notes to financial statements

1. SIGNIFICANT ACCOUNTING POLICIES

Basis of presentation

The financial statements of Sun-Rype Products Ltd. (the "Company") have been prepared in accordance with Canadian generally accepted accounting principles ("Canadian GAAP") and reflect the following significant accounting policies:

(a) Measurement uncertainty

The presentation of financial statements in conformity with Canadian GAAP requires management to make estimates and assumptions that affect the reported amounts of assets and liabilities at the date of the financial statements and the reported amounts of revenues and expenses disclosed during reporting periods. Significant areas that involve estimates include provisions for uncollectible accounts receivable, the amortization rate and estimated useful life of property, plant and equipment, provisions for sales returns and allowances, provisions for obsolete inventory, and impairment of long-lived assets. The actual amounts could differ from those estimates.

(b) Inventories

Raw materials and supplies are recorded at the lower of cost, determined on a weighted average basis, and net realizable value, being the estimated selling price of finished goods less the estimated costs of completion of the finished goods. Minor parts and supplies are included in inventory at the lower of cost, determined on a weighted average basis, and replacement cost.

Finished goods are recorded at the lower of cost and net realizable value. Finished goods include the cost of direct labour, direct materials and variable and fixed overhead related to production, including amortization, applied at a standard rate, which approximates actual costs.

(c) Property, plant and equipment

Property, plant and equipment, including major spares, are recorded at cost, net of investment tax credits. The Company uses the straight-line method of recording amortization over the estimated useful lives of the property, plant and equipment as follows:

Buildings	10 - 20 years
Equipment - Processing	5 - 10 years
- Other	3 - 5 years

(d) Impairment of long-lived assets

The Company regularly compares the carrying value of long-lived assets to the estimated undiscounted future cash flows that may be generated from future use and eventual disposition of those assets. The Company records an impairment loss in the period when it is determined that the carrying amount of the asset exceeds the undiscounted estimate of future cash flows from the asset. The impairment loss is measured as the difference between the carrying amount and estimated fair value of the asset.

1. SIGNIFICANT ACCOUNTING POLICIES (continued)

    (e) Asset retirement obligations

The Company recognizes legal obligations associated with the retirement of property, plant and equipment that result from its acquisition, construction or normal operations. These obligations are recorded at fair value and subsequently adjusted for the accretion of discount and any changes in the underlying cash flows. The asset retirement cost is capitalized as part of the cost of the related asset, and amortized to earnings over the remaining life of the asset. Other than as described in Note 16, the Company has determined that it has no material asset retirement obligations at December 31, 2008.

    (f) Revenue recognition

Sales are recognized upon the transfer of risk and title to finished goods to customers, which typically occurs upon shipment and when collectibility of proceeds is reasonably assured. The Company deducts from gross sales all payments to customers related to pricing discounts, returns and allowances, certain sales and marketing discounts, promotion funds, co-operative advertising, coupons and product listing fees.

    (g) Marketing and product launch costs

The Company expenses new product marketing and launch costs as incurred.

    (h) Long-term incentive plan

The Company maintains a long-term incentive plan ("LTIP") that is more fully described in Note 9. A portion of the LTIP liability will vary with the market price of the Company's common shares.

The Company recognizes the LTIP compensation expense when earned and throughout the deferral period to the extent that the fair value of the performance units earned has changed. Should any amounts be forfeited due to future circumstances, these amounts will be accounted for in the period in which the forfeiture is confirmed.

    (i) Research and development

The Company incurs costs for activities that relate to research and development of new products. Research costs are expensed as they are incurred. Development costs are also expensed as incurred unless they meet all the criteria for deferral under Canadian GAAP and their recovery is reasonably assured. To date no amounts have been capitalized. Investment tax credits arising from research and development activities are deducted from the related costs and are accordingly included in the determination of earnings when there is reasonable assurance that the credits will be realized.

    (j) Income taxes

The Company uses the liability method of accounting for income taxes. Under this method, temporary differences arising from the tax basis of an asset or liability and the corresponding carrying amount on the balance sheet are used to calculate future income tax assets or liabilities. Future income tax assets or liabilities are calculated using tax rates anticipated to be in effect in the periods that the temporary differences are expected to reverse. The effect of a change in income tax rates on future income tax assets and liabilities is recognized in income in the period the change is substantively enacted.

1. SIGNIFICANT ACCOUNTING POLICIES (continued)

(k) Financial instruments

The Company's financial instruments are classified into one of the following categories: held for trading, held-to-maturity investments, loans and receivables, available-for-sale financial assets, and other financial liabilities. The classification determines the accounting treatment of the instrument. The classification is determined by the Company when the financial instrument is initially recorded, based on the underlying purpose of the instrument.

The Company's financial assets and financial liabilities are classified and measured as follows:

Financial Instrument	Category	Measurement
Cash	Held for trading	Fair value
Accounts receivable	Loans and receivables	Amortized cost
Currency contracts	Held for trading	Fair value
Bank operating loan	Held for trading	Fair value
Promissory note payable	Other financial liabilities	Amortized cost
Accounts payable	Other financial liabilities	Amortized cost
Long-term obligations	Other financial liabilities	Amortized cost
Long-term debt	Other financial liabilities	Amortized cost

(l) Foreign currency translation

Transactions denominated in foreign currencies are translated into Canadian dollars at the exchange rate prevailing at the time of each transaction. At the balance sheet date, monetary assets and liabilities denominated in a foreign currency are translated at the period end rate of exchange. Exchange gains and losses arising on translation or settlement of foreign currency-denominated items are included in the determination of net income for the current period.

(m) Foreign exchange forward contracts

The Company periodically enters into foreign exchange forward contracts to manage foreign exchange risk associated with anticipated future purchases denominated in foreign currencies. Realized and unrealized gains and losses resulting from changes in the market value of these contracts are recorded as foreign exhange gain or loss each period unless they meet specified criteria to qualify as hedging instruments under Canadian GAAP. If these contracts meet the criteria for hedging instruments, any unrealized gains or losses are deferred and recognized in earnings when the related hedged transaction is recognized in earnings.

(n) Earnings per share

Basic earnings per share is calculated by dividing the net earnings available to common shareholders by the weighted average number of common shares outstanding during the year. Diluted earnings per share is calculated using the treasury stock method, which assumes that any outstanding stock option grants are exercised, if dilutive, and the assumed proceeds are used to purchase the Company's common shares at the average market price during the year.

2.   ADOPTION OF NEW ACCOUNTING STANDARDS

(a) Inventories

Effective January 1, 2008, the Company adopted CICA Handbook Section 3031 "Inventories" without restatement of the results of operations of prior periods. As a result of the adoption of this Section, the Company's inventory accounting policy has been changed as follows:

Raw materials and supplies are recorded at the lower of cost, determined on a weighted average basis, and net realizable value, being the estimated selling price of finished goods less the estimated costs of completion of the finished goods. Under the previous policy raw materials and supplies were recorded at the lower of cost, determined on a weighted average basis, and replacement cost.

Finished goods are recorded at the lower of cost and net realizable value. Finished goods include the cost of direct labour, direct materials and variable and fixed overhead related to production, including amortization, applied at a standard rate, which approximates actual costs. Under the previous policy, fixed overhead costs related to production were considered a period cost and, as such, were not included as a component of inventory but were expensed in the period they were incurred.

As a result of the requirement for adoption of this Section, management undertook a review of its accounting for parts and supplies included in inventories for financial statement purposes. From this review management determined that major equipment spares were more appropriately classified as property, plant and equipment, and amortized in accordance with the Company's accounting policy for property, plant and equipment. As a result, the Company's inventory accounting policy has been changed as follows:

Minor parts and supplies are included in inventory at the lower of cost, determined on a weighted average basis, and replacement cost. Major replacement parts and spares are included in property, plant and equipment. Under the previous policy all parts and supplies were included in inventory and recorded at the lower of cost, determined on a weighted average basis, and replacement cost.

As a result of these changes in accounting policy, the following adjustments have been made at January 1, 2008:

(in thousands of dollars)		
Inventories decreased by	$	(228)
Property, plant and equipment increased by		321
Future income tax asset reduced by		(32)
Retained earnings increased by		61

2. ADOPTION OF NEW ACCOUNTING STANDARDS (continued)

   (b) Capital disclosures and financial instruments – disclosures and presentation

   Effective January 1, 2008, the Company adopted CICA Handbook Section 1535 "Capital Disclosures"; Section 3862 "Financial Instruments – Disclosures"; and Section 3863 "Financial Instruments – Presentation".

   (i) Section 1535 establishes guidelines for the disclosure of information on the Company's capital and how it is managed. This enhanced disclosure enables users to evaluate the Company's objectives, policies and processes for managing capital. See Note 17.

   (ii) Sections 3862 and 3863 replaced the existing Section 3861 "Financial Instruments – Disclosure and Presentation." Section 3862 requires enhanced disclosure on the nature and extent of financial instrument risks and how the Company manages those risks. Section 3863 carries forward the existing presentation requirements and provides additional guidance for the classification of financial instruments. See Note 18.

   Future accounting and reporting changes

   Goodwill and Intangible Assets

   In February 2008, the Canadian Institute of Chartered Accountants issued Section 3064, "Goodwill And Intangible Assets", replacing Section 3062, "Goodwill And Other Intangible Assets", and Section 3450, "Research and Development Costs". This Section establishes standards for the recognition, measurement, presentation and disclosure of goodwill subsequent to its initial recognition and for intangible assets. The new Section will be applicable to financial statements for fiscal years beginning on or after October 1, 2008. Accordingly, the Company will adopt the new standards for its fiscal year beginning January 1, 2009. The adoption of this Section is not expected to have a material impact on the Company's financial statements.

3. INVENTORIES

(in thousands of dollars)	2008	2007
Raw materials and supplies	$ 16,633	$ 13,412
Finished goods	11,145	3,892
	$ 27,778	$ 17,304

Sun-Rype Products Ltd.
Notes to Financial Statements
For the years ended December 31, 2008 and 2007

4. INCOME TAXES

The income tax provision differs from the amount that would be computed by applying the combined federal and provincial statutory income tax rates as a result of the following:

(in thousands of dollars)	2008	2007
Statutory income tax rates	30.4%	33.8%
Income tax expense (recovery) at statutory rates	$ (5,511)	$ 2,292
Effect on income taxes of:		
Non-deductible expenses	24	28
Tax rate changes, including differences in rates applying to tax loss carry-back	(896)	(118)
Other	(73)	(64)
Effective income tax expense (recovery)	$ (6,456)	$ 2,138

The income tax expense (recovery) consists of the following:

(in thousands of dollars)	2008	2007
Current income tax expense (recovery)	$ (7,065)	$ 2,448
Future income tax expense (recovery)	609	(310)
	$ (6,456)	$ 2,138

The future income tax balances are recorded as follows:

(in thousands of dollars)	2008	2007
Future income tax assets – current	$ -	$ 435
Future income tax liabilities – current	(11)	-
Future income tax liabilities – long-term	(1,343)	(1,148)
Net future income tax liability	$ (1,354)	$ (713)

Significant components of future income tax assets and liabilities include:

(in thousands of dollars)	2008	2007
Accrued liabilities	$ 158	$ 711
Obligations under capital leases	135	-
Losses and other deductions	90	14
Future income tax assets	383	725
Property, plant and equipment	(1,535)	(1,360)
Other	(202)	(78)
Future income tax liabilities	(1,737)	(1,438)
Net future income tax liability	$ (1,354)	$ (713)

5. PROPERTY, PLANT AND EQUIPMENT

(in thousands of dollars)

	2008		
	Cost	Accumulated Amortization	Net Book Value
Land	$ 170	$ -	$ 170
Buildings	16,643	13,293	3,350
Processing equipment	51,860	32,229	19,631
Other equipment	8,522	6,543	1,979
	$ 77,195	$ 52,065	$ 25,130

	2007		
	Cost	Accumulated Amortization	Net Book Value
Land	$ 170	$ -	$ 170
Buildings	16,624	12,572	4,052
Processing equipment	50,384	28,560	21,824
Other equipment	7,775	5,954	1,821
	$ 74,953	$ 47,086	$ 27,867

Included in processing equipment at December 31, 2008, is construction in progress with a cost of $0.1 million that has not been amortized (December 31, 2007 - $0.7 million).

6. BANK OPERATING LOAN

The Company maintains a $20.0 million standby operating line of credit with a Canadian bank, which bears interest at the bank's prime lending rate plus 1% (December 31, 2008 – 4.5%). This facility is secured as described in note 10.

7. PROMISSORY NOTE PAYABLE

The promissory note payable is due on demand, is secured by a letter of credit and bears interest at the bank prime rate plus 0.25% (December 31, 2008 – 3.75%). Subsequent to December 31, 2008, the promissory note was repaid.

8. OBLIGATION UNDER CAPITAL LEASES

The Company has acquired equipment through capital leases that bear interest at a weighted average rate of 4.64% and require payments to the lease expiry dates as follows:

(in thousands of dollars)	2008
Years ending December 31:	
2009	$ 118
2010	118
2011	118
2012	118
2013	76
Total minimum lease payments	548
Less amount representing interest	56
Balance of the obligation	492
Current portion	97
Long-term portion	$ 395

Included in property, plant and equipment at December 31, 2008, are leased assets with a cost of $0.6 million (December 31, 2007 - nil) and accumulated amortization of $0.1 million (December 31, 2007 - nil). Interest on capital leases of $18,500 is included in interest expense in 2008 (2007 - nil).

9. LONG-TERM OBLIGATIONS

(in thousands of dollars)	2008	2007
Deferred management compensation	$ 148	$ 298
Long-term incentive plan	217	767
Total	365	1,065
Current portion	220	321
Long-term portion	$ 145	$ 744

Deferred management compensation

Under the terms of employment agreements with certain senior officers, the Company has provided for compensation to be paid to the individuals at the date they cease their employment. No compensation expense relating to these employment agreements was recorded in 2008 or 2007. Subsequent to December 31, 2008, the remaining deferred management compensation was paid.

9. LONG-TERM OBLIGATIONS (continued)

Long-term Incentive Plan ("LTIP")

In 2005 the Company's board of directors adopted an LTIP for its senior officers that entitles these officers to earn awards that will be confirmed during the two-year period following the year in which the awards are earned. The LTIP awards are comprised of a combination of cash and performance units. A performance unit is a notional unit, equivalent in value to the average trading price of the Company's common shares for the previous 20 trading days. At the termination of employment, the performance units are settled in cash.

No compensation expense was recorded in 2008 as performance units were not awarded (2007 – $0.2). Revaluation of the performance units resulted in an expense recovery of $0.2 million in 2008 (2007 – $0.1 million). As at December 31, 2008, 37,428 performance units have been granted under the plan. Subsequent to December 31, 2008, 12,067 performance units were settled in cash as a result of terminations of employment.

10. LONG-TERM DEBT

(in thousands of dollars)	2008
Bank loan repayable at $125,000 per month plus interest at the bank's prime lending rate plus 1% (December 31, 2008 – 4.5%)	$ 14,250
Current portion	1,500
Long-term portion	$ 12,750

The Company has a further $5.0 million committed revolving financing facility bearing interest at the bank's prime lending rate plus 1% available for future capital expenditures.

These facilities and the bank operating loan (note 6) are secured by a general assignment of accounts receivable, inventories and demand debentures creating a fixed and floating charge over all Company assets.

Principal repayments due for the remaining term of the long-term debt are as follows:

Year	Amount (in thousands of dollars)
2009	$ 1,500
2010	1,500
2011	1,500
2012	1,500
2013	1,500
2014 and thereafter	6,750
	$ 14,250

Sun-Rype Products Ltd.
Notes to Financial Statements
For the years ended December 31, 2008 and 2007

11. SHARE CAPITAL AND CONTRIBUTED SURPLUS

Authorized

100,000,000 common shares fully participating and without par value

Issued and fully paid capital

(in thousands of dollars)	2008	2007
10,827,600 Common shares	$ 17,756	$ 17,756
Contributed surplus	942	942
	$ 18,698	$ 18,698

Earnings per share

The weighted average number of common shares outstanding in 2008 and 2007, on a basic and diluted basis, was 10,827,600.

Employee share purchase plan

The Company has an employee share purchase plan ("ESPP") enabling eligible employees to acquire publicly traded Company common shares through payroll deductions with financial assistance provided by the Company. Eligible employees may contribute a monthly amount not to exceed 7% of salary, and the Company contributes a further 35% of the employee contribution. All funds and equity shares held by the administrator pursuant to the ESPP are held for the account of the individual employee. The Company's 2008 contributions of $0.2 million to the ESPP are included in selling, general and administrative expense (2007 - $0.2 million).

12. CUSTOMER CONCENTRATION

The Company's customers consist mainly of Canadian grocery stores, mass merchandisers and club stores. Net sales to three customers, individually representing more than 10% of net sales, are as follows:

(in thousands of dollars)	2008	2007
Net sales	$ 68,079	$ 71,237
Percentage of total net sales	54.3%	52.7%

13. COST OF SALES

(in thousands of dollars)	2008	2007
Cost of inventories expensed	$ 107,442	$ 93,298
Write-down of inventories	1,653	-
Amortization	2,182	-
	$ 111,277	$ 93,298

14. POST-EMPLOYMENT BENEFITS

The Company maintains a defined contribution (money purchase) pension plan for substantially all of its salaried employees. The Company's 2008 contributions of $0.3 million to the plan are included in selling, general and administrative expense (2007 - $0.3 million).

15. SUPPLEMENTAL CASH FLOW INFORMATION

(in thousands of dollars)	2008	2007
Changes in non-cash working capital items:		
Accounts receivable	$ (4,439)	$ 5,284
Inventories	(10,350)	1,404
Prepaid expenses	(173)	-
Promissory note payable	(100)	(100)
Accounts payable and accrued liabilities	2,541	(4,623)
Income taxes	(6,169)	(1,052)
	$ (18,690)	$ 913
Cash flows during the year resulting from:		
Payment of interest	$ 879	$ 148
Payment (recovery) of income taxes	$ (896)	$ 3,503

Non-cash transactions:

During 2008, the Company repaid $15.0 million of bank operating loan advances with proceeds from the issuance of long-term debt (2007 – nil).

During 2008, the Company acquired property, plant and equipment for $0.6 million directly financed through capital leases (2007 – nil).

At December 31, 2008, accounts payable and accrued liabilities includes nil for unpaid property, plant and equipment purchases (2007 - $0.1 million).

16. COMMITMENTS, GUARANTEES AND CONTINGENCIES

(a) The Company has entered into operating lease and rental commitments for equipment and office space for the next five years as follows:

Year	Amount (in thousands of dollars)
2009	$ 144
2010	131
2011	80
2012	63
2013	3

(b) Under the terms of a processing and filling systems agreement expiring December 31, 2012, the Company is contingently liable for annual rental payments of $0.8 million should the Company's purchase of annual volumes of beverage packaging materials not meet certain minimum thresholds. Based on historical purchase levels these rental payments would only be payable in the event of a dramatic decline in market demand.

16. COMMITMENTS, GUARANTEES AND CONTINGENCIES (continued)

(c) In the normal course of business, the Company enters into commitments to purchase certain minimum quantities of raw materials, primarily in US dollars. At December 31, 2008, the Company has commitments to purchase approximately $4.0 million of these materials in 2009 and $0.2 million in 2010.

(d) The Company periodically enters into foreign exchange forward purchase contracts to manage foreign exchange risk associated with anticipated future purchases and contractual commitments denominated in foreign currencies. At December 31, 2008, the Company had currency contracts outstanding that allow the Company to purchase USD$5 million at an average exchange rate of 1.0743 should the spot rate be above the rates on the individual contracts, while requiring the Company to purchase US dollars at an average exchange rate of 1.0383 should the spot rate be below the rates on the individual contracts. At December 31, 2008, the Company has recorded an unrealized foreign exchange gain of $0.7 million to reflect the fair value of these currency contracts.

(e) The Company is subject to regulations that require the handling and disposal of asbestos that is contained in a certain property in a special manner if the property undergoes major renovations or demolition. Otherwise, the Company is not required to remove the asbestos from the property. The Company has determined that there is an indeterminate settlement date for this asset retirement obligation because the range of time over which the Company may settle the obligation cannot be estimated. Therefore, the Company cannot reasonably estimate the fair value of the liability. The Company will recognize a liability in the period in which sufficient information is available to reasonably estimate its fair value.

17. CAPITAL MANAGEMENT

The Company's objectives when managing capital are:

(i) To safeguard the Company's ability to continue as a going concern, so that it can continue to provide returns for shareholders and benefits for other stakeholders, and

(ii) To maintain a flexible capital structure which optimizes the cost of capital at acceptable risk.

The Company includes shareholders' equity, lease financing, and bank financing in the definition of capital. The Company sets the amount of its capital structure in proportion to risk. The Company manages the capital structure and makes adjustments to it in light of changes in economic conditions and the risk characteristics of the underlying assets. In order to maintain or adjust the capital structure, the Company may adjust the amount of dividends paid to shareholders, purchase shares for cancellation pursuant to normal course issuer bids, issue new shares, issue new debt, or issue new debt to replace existing debt with different characteristics.

17. CAPITAL MANAGEMENT (continued)

During 2008, the Company's capital strategy was changed from prior periods such that certain investments in property, plant and equipment, and other assets will be considered for financing with long-term capital. Previously all investments in property, plant and equipment, and other assets were financed with working capital, using temporary bank overdraft financing as needed. During 2008, the Company acquired equipment using capital lease financing (note 8).

The Company's credit facilities are reviewed annually in order to make sure that sufficient funds are available to meet its financial needs. During 2008, the Company revised its financing and replaced temporary bank financing with long-term debt (note 10).

The Company uses temporary bank financing during the year as cash flows are required by its cyclical production schedule (note 6).

Under its bank credit facilities (notes 6 and 10), the Company is required to comply with certain financial covenants regarding current ratio and total liabilities to tangible net worth ratio. At December 31, 2008, the Company is in compliance with these financial covenants.

18. FINANCIAL RISK MANAGEMENT

The Company's financial instruments are exposed to certain financial risks, including currency risk, credit risk, liquidity risk, and interest rate risk.

(a) Currency risk

The Company is exposed to the financial risk related to the fluctuations of foreign exchange rates. The Company has customers in Canada and the United States and a significant portion of its purchases are incurred in US dollars. A significant change in the currency exchange rate of the Canadian dollar relative to the US dollar could have a material effect on the Company's results of operations, financial position and cash flows. Foreign currency risk is managed in accordance with the Company's treasury policy, the objective of which is to mitigate the impact of foreign exchange rate fluctuations on the Company's results of operations, financial position and cash flows. Under this policy the Company enters into foreign exchange forward purchase contracts to manage foreign exchange risk associated with anticipated future purchases. The policy prohibits speculative foreign exchange transactions.

The fair value of foreign exchange forward purchase contracts is determined using exchange rates available on the balance sheet date.

At December 31, 2008, the Company is exposed to currency risk through the following assets and liabilities denominated in US dollars:

(in thousands of dollars)	2008	2007
Cash	$ 625	$ 1,846
Accounts receivable	1,296	276
US dollar currency contracts asset (liability)	718	(460)
Accounts payable and accrued liabilities	(3,544)	(1,681)
Net exposure	$ (905)	$ (19)

18. FINANCIAL RISK MANAGEMENT (continued)

(a) Currency risk (continued)

Based on the above net exposure at December 31, 2008, and assuming all other variables remain constant, a 10% depreciation or appreciation of the Canadian dollar against the US dollar would result in a decrease or increase of $0.1 million in the Company's net earnings.

(b) Credit risk

Credit risk is the risk of an unexpected loss if a customer or a third party to a financial instrument fails to meet its contractual obligations.

The Company's cash equivalents are held through large Canadian financial institutions.

As at December 31, 2008, the Company is exposed to credit risk through the following assets:

(in thousands of dollars)	2008	2007
Trade receivables	$ 11,438	$ 6,876
Other receivables	392	516
Net credit risk	$ 11,830	$ 7,392

The Company maintains credit policies that include a review of a counter party's financial condition, measurement of credit exposure and monitoring of concentration of exposure to any one customer or counter party. At December 31, 2008, 81% of trade receivables are due from ten customers (2007 - 81%).

Of the trade receivables outstanding at December 31, 2008, 97% are not due, and 3% are between 30 and 90 days overdue. Outstanding amounts totalling less than $0.1 million are considered impaired in that there is doubt about ultimate collection of the amounts due to the length of time the amounts have been outstanding. An allowance has been made to fully provide for the possible non-collection of these amounts.

The Company's other receivables include GST and investment tax credits due from the Federal Government of Canada.

(c) Liquidity risk

Liquidity risk is the risk that the Company will not be able to meet its financial obligations as they fall due. The Company manages liquidity risk by maintaining financial forecasts as well as long-term operating and strategic plans. Managing liquidity requires monitoring of projected cash inflows and outflows using forecasts of the Company's financial position to ensure adequate and efficient use of cash resources. The appropriate liquidity level is established based on historical volatility and seasonal requirements, as well as planned investments and the debt maturity requirements.

The Company's bank operating loan and promissory note payable are due on demand.

Accounts payable and accrued liabilities are generally due within 60 days. The current portions of employee future benefits, obligation under capital leases and bank loans are due within 12 months.

18. FINANCIAL RISK MANAGEMENT (continued)

(d) Interest rate risk

Interest rate risk is the risk that the fair value or future cash flows of a financial instrument will fluctuate because of changes in market interest rates.

As at December 31, 2008, the Company is exposed to interest rate risk through the following liabilities:

(in thousands of dollars)	2008	2007
Bank operating loan	$ 12,554	$ -
Promissory note payable	400	500
Long-term debt	14,250	-
	$ 27,204	$ 500

The Company's bank operating loan, promissory note payable, and long-term debt bear interest based on the bank's prime borrowing rate. Based on the above exposure at December 31, 2008, and assuming all other variables remain constant, a one hundred basis point increase or decrease of the bank prime borrowing rate would result in an decrease or increase of $0.2 million in the Company's net earnings.

19. SEGMENTED INFORMATION

The Company has one reportable operating segment, the processing, packaging and marketing of food products. The Company's assets are located in Canada and substantially all of the Company's net sales are in Canada.

20. RELATED PARTY TRANSACTIONS

The Company has entered into the following transactions with companies that are controlled by a director and shareholder of the Company who controls 48.5% of the Company's outstanding common shares:

(a) In the normal course of business, the Company sells products to a related company that is a major food retailer in western Canada. Sales to this retailer are less than 10% of the Company's net sales. These transactions are recorded at the exchange amounts, which are the amounts agreed upon between the related parties, and are consistent with transactions with non-related customers.

(b) In February 2009, the Company entered into a management agreement with a related company under which the Company will receive administrative, advisory and executive services for a period of three years beginning January 1, 2009, for an annual fee of $0.6 million. Included in selling, general and administrative expense for 2008 is $0.1 million for services provided prior to commencement of the term of the agreement. These transactions are recorded at the exchange amounts, which are the amounts agreed upon between the related parties.

21. COMPARATIVE FIGURES

Certain items in the comparative figures have been reclassified in the financial statements.

Appendix C

Standard Setting in Canada

How are accounting standards developed and monitored? In Canada, there are two bodies that have been given regulatory control over standard setting.

The Accounting Standards Oversight Council (ACSOC) is an independent volunteer body that, among other duties, oversees and provides input on the activities of the Accounting Standards Board. ACSOC consists of up to 25 business, government, and academic leaders. The Council assists the Accounting Standards Board in setting high-quality accounting standards for all Canadian enterprises.

The Accounting Standards Board (AcSB) is the body that develops and establishes standards and guidance governing financial accounting and reporting in the private sector in Canada. As the standard-setter for the private sector in Canada, the AcSB determines the format and content of financial statements, and strives to ensure that the information within them is relevant, reliable, understandable, and comparable.

Beginning in 2011, publicly accountable companies in Canada will follow international financial reporting standards (IFRS). These financial reporting standards have been developed and approved by the International Accounting Standards Board (IASB), of which Canada is a member.

The accounting standards established by the AcSB are the primary source of generally accepted accounting principles (GAAP) in Canada. The *CICA Handbook— Accounting* produced by the Canadian Institute of Chartered Accountants (CICA) contains accounting standards that apply to all types of profit-oriented enterprises and not-for-profit organizations in Canada.

The Objective of Financial Reporting

The basic objective of financial reporting is to provide information that is useful in making investment and lending decisions. Accounting information can be useful in decision making only if it is *understandable, relevant, reliable* and *comparable*.

Accounting information must be *understandable* to users if they are to be able to use it. *Relevant* information is useful in making predictions and for evaluating past performance—that is, the information has feedback value. For example, Canadian Tire Corporation, Limited's disclosure of the profitability of each of its lines of business is relevant for investor evaluations of the company. To be relevant, information must be timely. *Reliable* information is free from significant error—that is, it has validity. Also, it is free from the bias of a particular viewpoint—that is, it is verifiable and neutral. *Comparable* information can be compared from period to period to help investors and creditors assess the entity's progress through time. These characteristics combine to shape the assumptions and principles that comprise GAAP. Exhibit C-1 on the next page summarizes the assumptions, principles and constraints that accounting has developed to provide useful information for decision making.

Assumptions, Principles, and Financial Statements	Quick Summary	Text Reference
Assumptions		
Economic-entity assumption	Accounting draws a boundary around each organization to be accounted for.	Chapter 1
Going-concern assumption	Accountants assume the business will continue operating for the foreseeable future.	Chapter 1
Stable-monetary-unit assumption	Accounting information is expressed primarily in monetary terms.	Chapter 1
Time period assumption	Ensures that accounting information is reported at regular intervals.	Chapter 3
Cost/benefit constraint	The benefits of the information produced should exceed the costs of producing the information.	Chapter 1
Materiality constraint	Accountants consider the materiality of an amount when making disclosure decisions.	Chapters 1 and 6
Principles, Criteria, and Characteristics		
Reliability (objectivity) characteristic	Accounting records and statements are based on the most reliable data available	Chapter 1
Consistency (comparability) characteristic	Businesses should use the same accounting methods from period to period.	Chapter 6
Recognition criteria: For Revenues	Tell accountants when to record revenue (only after it has been earned) and the amount of revenue to record (the cash value of what has been received).	Chapter 3
For Expenses (includes the matching objective)	Direct accountants to (1) identify all expenses incurred during the period, (2) measure the expenses, and (3) match the expenses against the revenues earned during the period. The goal is to measure net income.	Chapter 3
Measurement: Cost Basis	Assets and services, revenues and expenses are recorded at their actual historical cost.	Chapter 1
Other Bases (used in limited circumstances		
Disclosure principle	A company's financial statements should report enough information for outsiders to make informed decisions about the company.	Chapter 6
Financial Statements		
Balance sheet	Assets = Liabilities + Owners' Equity at a point in time (for proprietorships and partnerships). Assets = Liabilities + Shareholders' Equity at a point in time (for corporations).	Chapters 1 and 13
Income statement	Revenues and gains − Expenses and losses = Net income or net loss for the period	Chapters 1 and 14
Cash flow statement	Cash receipts − Cash payments = Increase or decrease in cash during the period, grouped under operating, investing, and financing activities	Chapters 1 and 17
Statement of owner's equity	Beginning owner's equity + Net income (or − Net loss) − Withdrawals = Ending owner's equity	Chapter 1
Statement of retained earnings	Beginning retained earnings + Net income (or − Net loss) − Dividends = Ending retained earnings	Chapter 14

Appendix D

Typical Charts of Accounts for Different Types of Businesses (For Businesses Discussed in Chapters 1–12).

SERVICE PROPRIETORSHIP

ASSETS

Cash
Accounts Receivable
Allowance for
   Doubtful Accounts
Notes Receivable,
   Short-Term
Goods and Services Tax
   Recoverable
Interest Receivable
Supplies
Prepaid Rent
Prepaid Insurance
Notes Receivable,
   Long-Term
Land
Furniture
Accumulated
   Amortization—
   Furniture
Equipment
Accumulated
   Amortization—
   Equipment
Building
Accumulated
   Amortization—
   Building

LIABILITIES

Accounts Payable
Notes Payable, Short-Term
Salaries Payable
Wages Payable
Goods and Services Tax
   Payable
Employee Income Tax
   Payable
Employment Insurance
   Payable
Canada Pension Plan
   Payable
Quebec Pension Plan
   Payable
Employee Benefits Payable
Interest Payable
Unearned Service Revenue
Notes Payable, Long-
   Term

OWNER'S EQUITY

Owner, Capital
Owner, Withdrawals

Revenues and Gains

Service Revenue
Interest Revenue
Gain on Sale of Land
   (or Furniture,
   Equipment, or
   Building)

Expenses and Losses

Salaries Expense
Wages Expense
Employee Benefits
   Expense
Insurance Expense for
   Employees
Rent Expense
Insurance Expense
Supplies Expense
Bad-Debt Expense
Amortization Expense—
   Furniture
Amortization Expense—
   Equipment
Amortization Expense—
   Building
Property Tax Expense
Interest Expense
Miscellaneous Expense
Loss on Sale (or Exchange)
   of Land (Furniture,
   Equipment, or Buildings)

SERVICE PARTNERSHIP

Same as Service Proprietorship, except for Owners' Equity:

OWNERS' EQUITY

Partner 1, Capital
Partner 2, Capital
Partner N, Capital
Partner 1, Withdrawals
Partner 2, Withdrawals
Partner N, Withdrawals

MERCHANDISING CORPORATION

ASSETS	LIABILITIES	SHAREHOLDERS' EQUITY	

ASSETS

Cash
Short-Term Investments
Fair-Value Valuation
   Allowance
Allowance for Doubtful
   Accounts
Notes Receivable,
   Short-Term
Goods and Services Tax
   Recoverable
Interest Receivable
Inventory
Supplies
Prepaid Rent
Prepaid Insurance
Notes Receivable,
   Long-Term
Investment Subject to
   Significant Influence
Long-Term Investments
Other Receivables,
   Long-Term
Land
Land Improvements
Accumulated
   Amortization—Land
   Improvements
Furniture and Fixtures
Accumulated
   Amortization—
   Furniture and Fixtures
Equipment
Accumulated
   Amortization—
   Equipment
Buildings
Accumulated
   Amortization—Buildings
Organization Cost
Franchises
Patents
Leaseholds
Goodwill

LIABILITIES

Accounts Payable
Notes Payable, Short-
   Term
Current Portion of
   Bonds Payable
Salaries Payable
Wages Payable
Goods and Services Tax
   Payable
Employee Income Tax
   Payable
Employment Insurance
   Payable
Canada Pension Plan
   Payable
Quebec Pension Plan
   Payable
Employee Benefits
   Payable
Interest Payable
Income Tax Payable
Unearned Service
   Revenue
Notes Payable, Long-Term
Bonds Payable
Lease Liability

Non-Controlling Interest

SHAREHOLDERS' EQUITY

Common Shares
Retained Earnings
Dividends

Revenues and Gains

Sales Revenue
Interest Revenue
Dividend Revenue
Equity-Method
   Investment Revenue
Gain on Sale of
   Investments
Unrealized Gain on Short-
   Term Investments
Gain on Sale of Land
   (Furniture and Fixtures,
   Equipment, or Building)
Discontinued
   Operations—Gain

Expenses and Losses

Cost of Goods Sold
Salaries Expense
Wages Expense
Commission Expense
Payroll Benefits Expense
Insurance Expense for
   Employees
Rent Expense
Insurance Expense
Supplies Expense
Bad-Debt Expense
Amortization Expense—
   Land Improvements
Amortization Expense—
   Furniture and Fixtures
Amortization Expense—
   Equipment
Amortization Expense—
   Buildings
Incorporation Expense
Amortization Expense—
   Franchises
Amortization Expense—
   Leaseholds
Income Tax Expense
Loss on Writedown of
   Goodwill
Loss on Sale of
   Investments
Unrealized Loss on Short-
   Term Investments
Loss on Sale (or
   Exchange) of Land (or
   Furniture and Fixtures,
   Equipment, or
   Buildings)
Discontinued
   Operations—Loss

MANUFACTURING CORPORATION

Same as Merchandising Corporation, except for Assets and Certain Expenses:

ASSETS	EXPENSES (CONTRA EXPENSES IF CREDIT BALANCE)
Inventories:	Overhead Production Volume Variance
Materials Inventory	Direct Materials Price Variance
Work in Progress Inventory	Direct Materials Efficiency Variance
Finished Goods Inventory	Direct Labour Price Variance
Factory Wages	Direct Labour Efficiency Variance
Factory Overhead	Overhead Flexible Budget Variance

Glossary

Account The detailed record of the changes that have occurred in a particular asset, liability, or item of owner's equity during a period (p. 52).

Account payable A liability that is backed by the general reputation and credit standing of the debtor (p. 16).

Account receivable An asset, a promise to receive cash from customers to whom the business has sold goods or services (p. 16).

Accounting The system that measures business activities, processes that information into reports and financial statements, and communicates the findings to decision makers (p. 2).

Accounting cycle Process by which accountants produce an entity's financial statements for a specific period (p. 165).

Accounting equation The most basic tool of accounting: Assets = Liabilities + Owner's Equity (proprietorship) or Assets = Liabilities + Shareholders' Equity (corporation) (p. 13).

Accounting information system The combination of personnel, records, and procedures that a business uses to meet its need for financial data (p. 343).

Accrual-basis accounting Accounting that recognizes (records) the impact of a business event as it occurs, regardless of whether the transaction affected cash (p. 109).

Accrued expense An expense that has been incurred but not yet paid in cash (pp. 120, 556).

Accrued liability Another name for an accrued expense (p. 556).

Accrued revenue A revenue that has been earned but not yet received in cash (p. 121).

Accumulated amortization The cumulative sum of all amortization expense from the date of acquiring a capital asset (p. 118).

Acid-test ratio Ratio of the sum of cash plus short-term investments plus net current receivables to current liabilities. Tells whether the entity could pay all its current liabilities if they came due immediately. Also called the quick ratio (p. 469).

Adjusted trial balance A list of all the ledger accounts with their adjusted balances (p. 125).

Adjusting entry Entry made at the end of the period to assign revenues to the period in which they are earned and expenses to the period in which they are incurred. Adjusting entries help measure the period's income and bring the related asset and liability accounts to correct balances for the financial statements (p. 114).

Aging-of-accounts-receivable method A way to estimate bad debts by analyzing individual accounts receivable according to the length of time they have been due (p. 456).

Allowance for Doubtful Accounts A contra account, related to accounts receivable, that holds the estimated amount of collection losses. Also called allowance for uncollectible accounts (p. 455).

Allowance for Uncollectible Accounts Another name for allowance for doubtful accounts (p. 455).

Allowance method A method of recording collection losses based on estimates made prior to determining that the business will not collect from specific customers (p. 455).

Amortizable cost The asset's cost minus its estimated residual value (p. 507).

Amortization The term the *CICA Handbook* uses to describe the systematic charging of the cost of a capital asset; it is often called depletion when applied to natural resources. The term is also used to describe the writing off to expense of capital assets (pp. 117, 506).

Asset An economic resource a business owns that is expected to be of benefit in the future (p. 5).

Audit The examination of financial statements by outside accountants, the most significant service that public accountants perform. The conclusion of an audit is the accountant's professional opinion about the financial statements (pp. 5, 407).

Bad-debt expense Cost to the seller of extending credit. Arises from the failure to collect from credit customers. Also called doubtful-account expense or uncollectible account expense (p. 454).

Balance sheet List of an entity's assets, liabilities and owner equity (proprietorship) or shareholder equity (corporation) as of a specific date. Also called the statement of financial position (p. 20).

Balance-sheet approach Another name for the aging-of-accounts-receivable method of estimating uncollectibles (p. 456).

Bank collection Collection of money by the bank on behalf of a depositor (p. 414).

Bank reconciliation Process of explaining the reasons for the difference between a depositor's records and the bank's records about the depositor's bank account (p. 413).

Bank statement Document for a particular bank account showing its beginning and ending balances and listing the month's transactions that affected the account (p. 411).

Batch processing Computerized accounting for similar transactions in a group or batch (p. 348).

Betterment Expenditure that increases the capacity or efficiency of an asset or extends its useful life. Capital expenditures are debited to an asset account (p. 505).

Brand name Distinctive identification of a product or service (p. 522).

Canada (or Quebec) Pension Plan All employees and self-employed persons in Canada (except in Quebec where the pension plan is the Quebec Pension Plan) between 18 and 70 years of age are required to contribute to the Canada Pension Plan administered by the Government of Canada (p. 564).

Capital Another name for the owner's equity of a business (p. 13).

Capital cost allowance Amortization allowed for income tax purposes by Canada Revenue Agency; the rates allowed are called capital cost allowance rates (p. 528).

Carrying value (of property, plant, and equipment) The asset's cost less accumulated amortization (p. 119).

Cash-basis accounting Accounting that records only transactions in which cash is received or paid (p. 109).

Cash flow statement Reports cash receipts and cash payments classified according to the entity's major activities: operating, investing, and financing (p. 21).

Cash payments journal Special journal used to record cash payments by cheque (p. 360).

Cash receipts journal Special journal used to record cash receipts (p. 354).

Chart of accounts List of all the accounts and their account numbers in the ledger (p. 55).

Cheque Document that instructs the bank to pay the designated person or business the specified amount of money (p. 411).

Closing entries Entries that transfer the revenue, expense, and owner withdrawal balances from these respective accounts to the capital account (p. 172).

Closing the accounts Step in the accounting cycle at the end of the period that prepares the accounts for recording the transactions of the next period. Closing the accounts consists of journalizing and posting the closing entries to set the balances of the revenue, expense, and owner withdrawal accounts to zero (p. 172).

Collection period Another name for the days' sales in receivables (p. 470).

Commercial substance In an exchange of tangible capital assets, commercial substance exists when an entity's future cash flows from the new asset received will differ in risk, timing, or amount from the cash flows from the old asset given up. With commercial substance, the new asset is recorded at its fair market value, and a gain or loss on the exchange is recorded if applicable (p. 517).

Computer virus A malicious computer program that reproduces itself, gets included in program code without consent, and destroys program code (p. 409).

Conservatism Concept by which the least favourable figures are presented in the financial statements (p. 310).

Consistency A business must use the same accounting methods and procedures from period to period or disclose a change in method (p. 310).

Contra account An account that always has a companion account and whose normal balance is opposite that of the companion account (p. 118).

Control account An account whose balance equals the sum of the balances in a group of related accounts in a subsidiary ledger (p. 354).

Controller The chief accounting officer of a company (p. 407).

Copyright Exclusive right to reproduce and sell a book, musical composition, film, or other work of art. Issued by the federal government, copyrights extend 50 years beyond the author's life (p. 521).

Corporation A business owned by shareholders that begins when the federal government or provincial government approves its articles of incorporation. A corporation is a legal entity, an "artificial person," in the eyes of the law (p. 8).

Cost of goods sold The cost of the inventory that the business has sold to customers, the largest single expense of most merchandising businesses. Also called cost of sales (pp. 226, 256).

Cost of sales Another name for cost of goods sold (pp. 226, 256).

Cost principle of measurement States that assets and services are recorded at their purchase cost and that the accounting record of the asset continues to be based on cost rather than current market value (p. 12).

Credit The right side of an account (p. 58).

Credit memo The document issued by a seller for a credit to a customer's Account Receivable (p. 363).

Creditor The party to a credit transaction who sells a service or merchandise and obtains a receivable (pp. 451, 464).

Current asset An asset that is expected to be converted to cash, sold, or consumed during the next 12 months, or within the business's normal operating cycle if longer than a year (p. 178).

Current liability A debt due to be paid within one year or one of the entity's operating cycles if the cycle is longer than a year (p. 178).

Current portion of long-term debt Amount of the principal that is payable within one year (p. 555).

Current ratio Current assets divided by current liabilities. Measures the ability to pay current liabilities from current assets (p. 182).

Database Computerized storehouse of information that can be systematically assessed in a variety of report forms (p. 344).

Days' sales in receivables Ratio of average net accounts receivable to one day's sales. Indicates how many days' sales remain in Accounts Receivable awaiting collection (p. 470).

Debit The left side of an account (p. 58).

Debit memo The document issued by a buyer to reduce the buyer's Account Payable to a seller (p. 364).

Debt ratio Ratio of total liabilities to total assets. Gives the proportion of a company's assets that it has financed with debt (p. 183).

Debtor The party to a credit transaction who makes a purchase and creates a payable (pp. 451, 464).

Default on a note Failure of the maker of a note to pay at maturity. Also called dishonour of a note (p. 467).

Deferred revenue Another name for unearned revenue (p. 121).

Depletion Another word to describe the amortization of natural resources or wasting assets (p. 519).

Deposit in transit A deposit recorded by the company but not yet by its bank (p. 414).

Direct write-off method A method of accounting for bad debts by which the company waits until the credit department decides that a customer's account receivable is uncollectible and then debits Bad-Debt Expense and credits the customer's Account Receivable (p. 460).

Disclosure principle A business's financial statements must report enough information for outsiders to make knowledgeable decisions about the business (p. 310).

Discounting a note receivable Selling a note receivable before its maturity date (p. 474).

Dishonour a note Failure of the maker of a note to pay a note receivable at maturity. Also called default on a note (p. 467).

Double-declining-balance (DDB) method A type of amortization method that expenses a relatively larger amount of an asset's cost nearer the start of its useful life than does the straight-line method (p. 509).

Doubtful-account expense Another name for bad-debt expense (p. 454).

Due date The date on which the final payment of a note is due. Also called the maturity date (p. 464).

Electronic funds transfer (EFT) System that transfers cash by digital communication rather than paper documents (p. 411).

Employee compensation Payroll, a major expense of many businesses (p. 556).

Employment Insurance All employees and employers in Canada must contribute to the Employment Insurance Fund, which provides assistance to unemployed workers (p. 565).

Encryption The process of rearranging plain-text messages by some mathematical formula to achieve confidentiality (p. 409).

Enterprise resource planning (ERP) Integrates all company data into a single data warehouse (p. 348).

Entity An organization or a section of an organization that, for accounting purposes, stands apart from other organizations and individuals as a separate economic unit. This is the most basic concept in accounting (p. 11).

Estimated residual value Expected cash value of an asset at the end of its useful life. Also called residual value, scrap value, and salvage value (p. 507).

Estimated useful life Length of the service that a business expects to get from an asset; may be expressed in years, units of output, kilometres, or other measures (p. 507).

Evaluated Receipts Settlement A streamlined payment procedure that compresses the approval process into a single step: comparing the receiving report with the purchase order (p. 422).

Expense Decrease in owner's equity (proprietorship) or shareholders' equity (corporation) that occurs in the course of delivering goods or services to customers or clients (p. 14).

Financial accounting The branch of accounting that provides information to people outside the business (p. 4).

Financial statements Business documents that report financial information about an entity to persons and organizations outside the business (p. 2).

Firewall Barriers used to prevent entry into a computer network or a part of a network. Examples include passwords, personal identification numbers (PINs), and fingerprints (p. 409).

First-in, first-out (FIFO) method Inventory costing method by which the first costs into inventory are the first costs out to cost of goods sold. Ending inventory is based on the costs of the most recent purchases (p. 304).

Franchise Privileges granted by a private business or a government to sell a product or service in accordance with specified conditions (p. 522).

General journal Journal used to record all transactions that do not fit one of the special journals (p. 351).

General ledger Ledger of accounts that are reported in the financial statements (p. 353).

Generally accepted accounting principles (GAAP) Accounting guidelines, formulated by the CICA's Accounting Standards Committee, that govern how businesses report their results in financial statements to the public (p. 9).

Going-concern assumption Accountants' assumption that the business will continue operating in the forseeable future (p. 12).

Goodwill Excess of the cost of an acquired company over the sum of the market values of its net assets (assets minus liabilities) (p. 522).

Gross margin Excess of sales revenue over cost of goods sold. Also called gross profit (p. 226).

Gross margin method A way to estimate inventory based on a rearrangement of the cost of goods sold model: Beginning inventory + Net purchases = Cost of goods available for sale. Cost of goods available for sale − Cost of goods sold = Ending inventory. Also called the gross profit method (p. 315).

Gross margin percentage Gross margin divided by net sales revenue. A measure of profitability (p. 247).

Gross pay Total amount of salary, wages, commissions, or any other employee compensation before taxes and other deductions are taken out (p. 563).

Gross profit Another name for gross margin (p. 226).

Gross profit method Another name for the gross margin method (p. 315).

Hardware Electronic equipment that includes computers, disk drives, monitors, printers, and the network that connects them (p. 344).

Imprest system A way to account for petty cash by maintaining a constant balance in the petty cash account, supported by the fund (cash plus disbursement tickets) totalling the same amount (p. 424).

Income from operations Another name for operating income (pp. 242, 262).

Income statement List of an entity's revenues, expenses, and net income or net loss for a specific period. Also called the statement of earnings or statement of operations (p. 20).

Income-statement approach Another name for the percent-of-sales method of estimating uncollectibles (p. 455).

Income Summary A temporary "holding tank" account into which the revenues and expenses are transferred prior to their final transfer to the Capital account (p. 173).

Intangible asset An asset with no physical form, a special right to current and expected future benefits (pp. 499, 521).

Interest The revenue to the payee for loaning out the principal, and the expense to the maker for borrowing the principal (p. 464).

Interest period The period of time during which interest is to be computed, extending from the original date of the note to the maturity date (p. 464).

Interest rate The percentage rate that is multiplied by the principal amount to compute the amount of interest on a note (p. 464).

Internal control Organizational plan and all the related measures adopted by an entity to meet management's objectives of discharging statutory responsibilities, profitability, prevention and detection of fraud and error, safeguarding of assets, reliability of accounting records, and timely preparation of reliable financial information (p. 403).

Inventory All goods that a company owns and expects to sell in the normal course of operation (p. 225).

Inventory turnover Ratio of cost of goods sold to average inventory. Measures the number of times a company sells its average level of inventory during a year (p. 248).

Invoice A seller's request for cash from the purchaser (p. 230).

Journal The chronological accounting record of an entity's transactions (p. 52).

Leasehold Prepayment that a lessee (renter) makes to secure the use of an asset from a lessor (landlord) (p. 522).

Ledger The book of accounts (p. 52).

Liability An economic obligation (a debt) payable to an individual or an organization outside the business (p. 13).

Licence Privileges granted by a private business or a government to sell a product or service in accordance with special conditions (p. 522).

Limited-liability company (LLC) A form of proprietorship in which the company and not the proprietor is liable for the company's debts (p. 9).

Limited-liability partnership (LLP) A form of partnership in which each partner's personal liability for the business's debts is limited to a certain amount (p. 8).

Line of credit Similar to a bank loan, it is negotiated once, then drawn upon when needed. Interest is paid monthly only on the amount of the line of credit actually used (p. 552).

Liquidity Measure of how quickly an item may be converted to cash (p. 178).

Long-term asset An asset other than a current asset (p. 178).

Long-term liability A liability other than a current liability (p. 179).

Lower-of-cost-and-net-realizable-value (LCNRV) rule Requires that an asset be reported in the financial statements at the lower of its historical cost or its market value (current replacement cost for inventory) (p. 311).

Maker of a note The person or business that signs the note and promises to pay the amount required by the note agreement. The maker is the debtor (p. 464).

Management accounting The branch of accounting that generates information for internal decision makers of a business, such as top executives (p. 4).

Matching objective The basis for recording expenses. Directs accountants to identify all expenses incurred during the period, measure the expenses, and match them against the revenues earned during that same span of time (p. 112).

Materiality concept A company must perform strictly proper accounting only for items and transactions that are significant to the business's financial statements (p. 310).

Maturity date The date on which the final payment of a note is due. Also called the due date (p. 464).

Maturity value The sum of the principal and interest due at the maturity date of a note (p. 464).

Measurement The process of determining the amount at which an item is recognized in the financial statements. (p. 12)

Menu A list of options for choosing computer functions (p. 348).

Module Separate compatible units of an accounting package that are integrated to function together (p. 348).

Moving-weighted-average-cost method A weighted-average cost method where unit cost is changed to reflect each new purchase of inventory (p. 305).

Multi-step income statement Format that contains subtotals to highlight significant relationships. In addition to net income, it also presents gross margin and income from operations (p. 245).

Net earnings Another name for net income or net profit (p. 20).

Net income Excess of total revenues over total expenses. Also called net earnings or net profit (p. 20).

Net loss Excess of total expenses over total revenues (p. 20).

Net pay Gross pay minus all deductions; the amount of employee compensation that the employee actually takes home (p. 563).

Net profit Another name for net income or net earnings (p. 20).

Net purchases Purchases less purchase discounts and purchase returns and allowances (p. 255).

Net sales Sales revenue less sales discounts and sales returns and allowances (p. 225).

Network The system of electronic linkages that allow different computers to share the same information (p. 344).

Nominal account Another name for a temporary account (p. 172).

Nonsufficient funds (NSF) cheque A "bounced" cheque, one for which the maker's

bank account has insufficient money to pay the cheque (p. 415).

Normal balance The balance that appears on the side of an account—debit or credit—where we record increases (p. 61).

Note payable A liability evidenced by a written promise to make a future payment (p. 16).

Note receivable An asset evidenced by another party's written promise that entitles you to receive cash in the future (p. 53).

Note term Another name for the interest period of a note (p. 464).

Online processing Computerized processing of related functions, such as the recording and posting of transactions, on a continuous basis (p. 348).

Operating cycle The time span during which cash is paid for goods and services that are sold to customers who then pay the business in cash (p. 178).

Operating expense Expense, other than cost of goods sold, that is incurred in the entity's major line of business: rent, amortization, salaries, wages, utilities, property tax, and supplies expense (pp. 242, 260).

Operating income Gross margin minus operating expenses plus any other operating revenues. Also called income from operations (pp. 242, 262).

Other expense Expense that is outside the main operations of a business, such as a loss on the sale of capital assets (pp. 242, 262).

Other revenue Revenue that is outside the main operations of a business, such as a gain on the sale of capital assets (pp. 242, 262).

Outstanding cheque A cheque issued by the company and recorded on its books but not yet paid by its bank (p. 414).

Owner's equity In a proprietorship, the claim of an owner of a business to the assets of the business. Also called capital (p. 13).

Owner withdrawals Amounts removed from the business by an owner (p. 14).

Partnership An unincorporated business with two or more owners (p. 7).

Patent A federal government grant giving the holder the exclusive right for 20 years to produce and sell an invention (p. 521).

Payee of a note The person or business to whom the maker of a note promises future payment. The payee is the creditor (p. 464).

Payroll Employee compensation, a major expense of many businesses (p. 556).

Percent-of-accounts-receivable method Another balance-sheet-based method of determining the allowance for doubtful accounts (p. 458).

Percent-of-sales method A method of estimating uncollectible receivables as a percent of the net credit sales (or net sales) (p. 455).

Periodic inventory system Type of inventory accounting system in which the business does not keep a continuous record of the inventory on hand. Instead, at the end of the period the business makes a physical count of the on-hand inventory and applies the appropriate unit costs to determine the cost of the ending inventory (p. 228).

Permanent account Another name for a real account—asset, liability, or owner's equity—that is not closed at the end of the period (p. 172).

Perpetual inventory system Type of accounting inventory system in which the business keeps a continuous record for each inventory item to show the inventory on hand at all times (p. 228).

Petty cash Fund containing a small amount of cash that is used to pay minor expenditures (p. 423).

Postclosing trial balance List of the ledger accounts and their balances at the end of the period after the journalizing and posting of the closing entries. The last step of the accounting cycle, the postclosing trial balance ensures that the ledger is in balance for the start of the next accounting period (p. 176).

Posting Transferring of amounts from the journal to the ledger (p. 64).

Prepaid expense A category of miscellaneous assets that typically expire or get used up in the near future. Examples include prepaid rent, prepaid insurance, and supplies (p. 115).

Principal The amount loaned out by the payee and borrowed by the maker of a note (p. 464).

Promissory note A written promise to pay a specified amount of money at a particular future date (p. 464).

Property, plant, and equipment Long-lived tangible capital assets, such as land, buildings, and equipment, used to operate a business (p. 117, 195).

Proprietorship An unincorporated business with a single owner (p. 7).

Purchases journal Special journal used to record all purchases of inventory, supplies and other assets on account (p. 358).

Quick ratio Another name for the acid-test ratio (p. 469).

Real account Another name for a permanent account (p. 172).

Real-time processing Computerized processing of related functions, such as the recording and posting of transactions, on a continuous basis. Also called online processing (p. 348).

Receivable A monetary claim against a business or an individual, acquired mainly by selling goods and services and by lending money (p. 451).

Recognition criteria for revenues The basis for recording revenues; tells accountants when to record revenue and the amount of revenue to record (p. 111).

Reliability characteristic Requires that accounting information be dependable (free from error and bias) (p. 11).

Repair Expenditure that merely maintains an asset in its existing condition or restores the asset to good working order. Repairs are expensed (matched against revenue) (p. 505).

Retail method A method of estimating ending inventory based on the total cost and total selling price of opening inventory and net purchases (p. 316).

Revenue Increase in owner's equity (proprietorship) or shareholders' equity (corporation) that is earned by delivering goods or services to customers or clients (p. 14).

Reversing entry An entry that switches the debit and the credit of a previous adjusting entry. The reversing entry is dated the first day of the period following the adjusting entry (p. 191).

Sales Another name for sales revenue (p. 225).

Sales discount Reduction in the amount receivable from a customer, offered by the seller as an incentive for the customer to pay promptly. A contra account to sales revenue (p. 236).

Sales journal Special journal used to record credit sales (p. 351).

Sales returns and allowances Decrease in the seller's receivable from a customer's return of merchandise or from granting the customer an allowance from the amount the customer owes the seller. A contra account to sales revenue (p. 236).

Sales revenue Amount that a merchandiser earns from selling inventory before subtracting expenses. Also called sales (p. 225).

Salvage value Another name for estimated residual value (p. 507).

Scrap value Another name for estimated residual value (p. 507).

Server The main computer in a network, where the program and data are stored (p. 344).

Shareholder A person who owns shares of stock in a corporation (p. 8).

Short-term note payable Note payable due within one year, a common form of financing (p. 551).

Single-step income statement Format that groups all revenues together and then lists and deducts all expenses together without drawing any subtotals (p. 246).

Software Set of programs or instructions that cause the computer to perform the work desired (p. 344).

Special journal An accounting journal designed to record one specific type of transaction (p. 351).

Specific identification method Another name for the specific-unit-cost method (p. 303).

Specific-unit-cost method Inventory cost method based on the specific cost of particular units of inventory (p. 303).

Stable-monetary-unit assumption Accountants' basis for ignoring the effect of inflation and making no adjustments for the changing value of the dollar (p. 12).

Statement of earnings Another name for the income statement (p. 20).

Statement of financial position Another name for the balance sheet (p. 20).

Statement of operations Another name for the income statement. Also called the statement of earnings (p. 20).

Statement of owner's equity Summary of the changes in an entity's owner's equity during a specific period (p. 20).

Straight-line method Amortization method in which an equal amount of amortization expense is assigned to each year (or period) of asset use (p. 508).

Subsidiary ledger Book of accounts that provides supporting details on individual balances, the total of which appears in a general ledger account (p. 353).

Temporary account Another name for a nominal account. The revenue and expense accounts that relate to a particular accounting period and are closed at the end of the period are temporary accounts. For a proprietorship, the owner withdrawal account is also temporary (p. 172).

Time period Another name for the interest period (p. 464).

Time–period assumption Ensures that accounting information is reported at regular intervals (p. 113).

Timing difference A time lag in recording transactions (p. 413).

Trademarks and trade names Distinctive identifications of a product or service (p. 522).

Transaction An event that affects the financial position of a particular entity and may be reliably recorded (p. 14).

Treasurer The person in a company responsible for cash management (p. 407).

Trial balance A list of all the ledger accounts with their balances (p. 53).

Trojan A computer virus that does not reproduce but gets included into program code without consent and performs actions that can be destructive (p. 409).

Uncollectible-account expense Another name for bad-debt expense (p. 454).

Unearned revenue A liability created when a business collects cash from customers in advance of doing work for the customer. The obligation is to provide a product or a service in the future. Also called deferred revenue (p. 121).

Units-of-production (UOP) method Amortization method by which a fixed amount of amortization is assigned to each unit of output produced by the capital asset (p. 509).

Weighted-average-cost method Inventory costing method based on the weighted-average cost of inventory during the period. Weighted-average cost is determined by dividing the cost of goods available for sale by the number of units available. Also called the average cost method (p. 309).

Withheld income tax Income tax deducted from employees' gross pay (p. 564).

Work sheet A columnar document designed to help move data from the trial balance to the financial statements (p. 166a).

Workers' Compensation A provincially administered plan that is funded by contributions by employers and that provides financial support for workers injured on the job (p. 566).

Index

Electronic Data Interchange (EDI), 422
electronic devices, 408
electronic funds transfer (EFT), 411, 415
electronic sensors, 408
employee compensation. *See* payroll
employees, as users of accounting information, 4
employer payroll costs, 565–566
Employment Insurance (EI), 565, 566
encryption, 409
ending inventory, 315–316
Enron Corporation, 5–6
enterprise resource planning (ERP), 348–350
equation format, 181
equipment, 54
equipment (and machinery), 503
equity. *See* owners' equity
errors
   see also correction
   bank errors, 414
   bank reconciliation, 414–415
   internal control and, 404
   inventory errors, 312–314, 313f, 314f
   trial balance errors, 76–77
estimated residual value, 507
estimated useful life, 507
estimated vacation pay liability, 559
estimated warranty payable, 558–559
estimates
   current liabilities, 558–560
   ending inventory, 315–316
   estimated vacation pay liability, 559
   estimated warranty payable, 558–559
   gross margin method, 315–316, 315f
   retail method, 316, 316f
   uncollectibles, 455–458
ethics
   and accounting, 5–7, 425–426
   accounting scandals, 5
   accrual accounting, 129–130
   in business, 5–7
   cash-basis accounting, 129–130
   codes of ethics, 425–426
   contingent liabilities, 561–562
   corporate codes of ethics, 425–426
   current liabilities, 561–562
   decision guidelines, 426
   intangible assets, 523
   inventory, 314
   personnel, and control procedures, 406
   professional codes of ethics, 425–426
   property, plant, and equipment, 523–524
   Sarbanes-Oxley Act of 2002, 6
Evaluated Receipts Settlement (ERS), 422
exchange transactions, 517
executive controls, 418
exempt supplies, 553
expected net realizable value, 458
expenses
   see also specific expenses
   and accounting equation, 60f
   accounts, 55
   accrued expenses. *See* accrued expenses
   closing a net income, 173
   defined, 14, 60
   general expenses, 242, 260
   matching objective, 112, 112f, 506f
   operating expenses, 242, 260
   other revenue and expense, 242, 262
   payment of, 16–17
   payroll expenses, 577
   prepaid expenses. *See* prepaid expenses
   recognition criteria, 112, 112f
   rules of debit and credit, 60
external auditors, 407

F

fidelity bonds, 408
financial accounting, 4, 4f
financial ratios. *See* ratios
financial statements
   see also specific financial statements
   balance sheet, 20
   cash flow statement, 21
   defined, 2
   headings, 21
   hierarchy of financial-statement concepts, 10f
   income statement, 20
   International Financial Reporting Standards
      (IFRS), 184
   merchandisers, 226f, 242–247, 243f, 260–262
   preparation, to complete accounting cycle, 170

preparation from adjusted trial balance, 127
relationships among, 21–24, 22f, 128–129
service companies, 226f
standard elements, 11
statement of owner's equity, 20
use of, 2
fireproof vaults, 408
firewalls, 409
first-in, first-out (FIFO), 304–305, 304f, 307–308,
   307f, 309
fixed assets. *See* property, plant, and equipment
fixtures, 54, 503
flexible systems, 344
flow of accounting data, 65–73, 65f
FOB destination terms, 233
FOB shipping point, 233
formats
   account format, 181
   balance sheet, 181–182, 181f
   equation format, 181
   income statement, 245–246
Forzani Group Ltd., 300–301, 301f
franchises, 522
free on board (FOB), 233–234, 233f
freight in, 234
freight or freight in, 227
freight out, 234
fringe benefits, 573
Frito-Lay Canada, 51
full price. *See* list price
fully amortized asset, 514–515
furniture, 54, 503
future removal costs, 520

G

GAAP. *See* generally accepted accounting
   principles (GAAP)
General Electric Canada, 408
general expenses, 242, 260
general journal
   see also journal and journalizing
   balancing the ledgers, 366
   role of, 362–366
   vs. special journals, 351
general ledger, 353, 356, 366
generally accepted accounting principles (GAAP), 9
   see also CICA Handbook
going-concern assumption, 12
Goods and Services Tax (GST)
   see also sales taxes
   as current liability, 552–554
   exempt supplies, 553
   input tax credit, 553
   perpetual inventory system, 238–239
   recoverability of, 503, 554
   registrant, 553
   taxable supplies, 553
   zero-rated supplies, 553
goodwill, 501f, 522–523
government regulatory agencies, 3
gross margin, 226
gross margin method, 315–316, 315f
gross margin percentage, 247–248, 248f
gross pay, 563, 563f
gross profit. *See* gross margin
gross profit method. *See* gross margin method
GST, 238–239

H

hardware, 344
historical cost. *See* actual cost

I

identity theft, 409
imprest system, 424
income
   net income, 20, 173–175
   operating income, 242, 262
income from operations, 242, 262
income statement
   described, 20
   formats, 245–246
   headings, 21
   merchandising business, 225, 242
   multi-step income statement, 245
   operating expenses, 242
   relationships with other financial statements, 21–24,
      22f, 128–129, 128f
   single-step format, 246, 246f

income-statement approach, 455–456
Income Summary, 173
income tax payable, 559–560
income taxes
   and amortization, 512
   capital cost allowance, 528–529
   CCA rates, 528
inflation, 12
information systems. *See* accounting
   information system
input tax credit, 553
inputs, 346
intangible assets
   amortization, 117
   brand names, 522
   copyrights, 521
   decision guidelines, 525–526
   defined, 499, 521
   ethics, 523–524
   franchises, 522
   goodwill, 522–523
   IFRS, impact of, 525
   importance of, 521
   leaseholds, 522
   licences, 522
   no accumulated amortization account, 521
   patents, 521
   related expenses, 501f
   research and development costs, 523
   trademarks, 522
interest on note, 464, 465
interest period, 464
interest rate, 464
interest revenue, 415, 466–467
interim statements, 458
internal auditors, 407
internal control
   bank account, 410–419
   cash payments, 421–424
   cash receipts, 419–421
   components of, 405–406, 406f
   control environment, 405
   control procedures, 405–408
   costs and benefits, 410
   defined, 403
   described, 343
   e-commerce, 408–409
   information system, 406
   key objectives, 403–404
   limitations, 410
   monitoring of controls, 406
   payroll, 575–576
   property, plant, and equipment, 518
   receivables, collection of, 452–453
   risk assessment, 405
   shield of internal control, 405f
International Accounting Standards Board, 24
International Financial Reporting
   Standards (IFRS)
   accounting-cycle implications, 130–131
   accounts receivable, 471
   adoption of, 24
   Canada's adoption of, 6, 24
   cash, 427
   collection of information, 368
   current liabilities, 578
   described, 24
   financial-reporting implications, 130–131
   financial statement presentation, 184
   intangible assets, 525
   internal control, 403
   inventory costing methods, 317
   matching principle, 249
   merchandising businesses, 249
   property, plant, and equipment, 524
   revenue recognition, 249
Intrawest Corporation, 54
inventory
   and accounting principles, 309–310
   adjustment, based on physical count, 240
   cash sale, 235
   conservatism, 310
   consistency, 310
   cost of inventory, 226–227
   costing methods. *See* inventory costing methods
   decision guidelines, 318
   defined, 225
   disclosure principle, 310
   ending inventory, estimate of, 315–316
   ethical issues, 314
   gross margin method, 315–316, 315f
   gross margin percentage, 247–248, 248f